ADVANCED TEXTS IN ECONOMETRICS

General Editors

C. W. J. Granger G. E. Mizon

DYNAMIC ECONOMETRICS

DAVID F. HENDRY

OXFORD UNIVERSITY PRESS
1995

Oxford University Press, Walton Street, Oxford OX2 6DP
Oxford New York
Athens Auckland Bangkok Bombay
Calcutta Cape Town Dar es Salaam Delhi
Florence Hong Kong Istanbul Karachi
Kuala Lumpur Madras Madrid Melbourne
Mexico City Nairobi Paris Singapore
Taipei Tokyo Toronto
and associated companies in
Berlin Ibadan

Published in the United States
by Oxford University Press Inc., New York

British Library Cataloguing in Publication Data
Data available

Library of Congress Cataloging in Publication Data
Data available

ISBN 0–19–828317–2
ISBN 0–19–828316–4 (Pbk)

1 3 5 7 9 10 8 6 4 2

Printed in Great Britain
on acid-free paper by
Biddles Ltd.,
Guildford & King's Lynn

To Evelyn and Vivien

'The only way to a position in which our science might give positive advice on a large scale to politicians and business men, leads through quantitative work. For as long as we are unable to put our arguments into figures, the voice of our science, although occasionally it may help to dispel gross errors, will never be heard by practical men. They are, by instinct, econometricians all of them, in their distrust of anything not amenable to exact proof.'

From Joseph A. Schumpeter: 'The Common Sense of Econometrics', *Econometrica*, 1 (1933), p.12.

Contents

Figures

Tables

Preface

This book reports in a systematic and integrated framework the outcome of a twenty-five year research programme into econometric modelling. It is the fourth major revision of a work not previously published in English. The delays are mainly due to my earlier dissatisfaction with the treatment of many issues of methodology and technique. Each attempt to write a comprehensive analysis revealed the need for considerable research to resolve problems central to the book's objective of explaining how to practice econometrics. Even after more than two decades the task is incomplete, but the material now permits a coherent analysis of econometric modelling of economic time series.

The structure of the book departs in important respects from conventional treatments of econometrics, even though the objectives are the same: it is perhaps closest to Spanos (1986) in approach. Many econometrics texts focus on analysing the properties of econometric techniques when the model coincides with the process which generated the observed data. In practice, the generating process is unknown and evolutionary, necessitating iterative data modelling, and this book confronts the resulting problems. Topics arise in relation to empirical issues and are resolved in that context, so theory and evidence are blended throughout.

The presentation is organized in terms of four levels of knowledge, corresponding to probability, estimation, modelling, and forecasting. Probability theory assumes the data-generating process is known, and derives the properties of the observed outcomes. This aspect is developed in Part I and comprises about 40 per cent of the book. The necessary concepts, models, and processes are discussed. Then estimation and inference are studied in Part II, assuming the form of the data-generation process is known, but its parameters are unknown. Practical problems, modelling, and applications comprise Part III, in the relevant setting where even the form of the data-generation process is unknown to the investigator. The fourth level, where the future is unknown, is the subject of the separate book *A Theory of Economic Forecasting* with Michael P. Clements. Instead, Part IV describes the technical background to the main text, doing triple duty to assist readers commencing the book with gaps in any of the necessary topics, making the book more nearly self-contained, and clarifying its foundations. This material is placed in appendices, despite being logically prior, partly because much of it will be known by economists undertaking empirical research, and partly to avoid a technical start to what aims to be an operational approach.[1]

[1] This organization reflects the Oxford M.Phil. economics course, where the technology is taught in separate courses prior to, or in parallel with, the methodology and practice of econometrics.

As a consequence, the book is complementary to most extant econometrics texts. Part I centres on the theory of reduction, which explains both the origin of empirical models and the design of congruent data representations. The main concepts of econometrics are analysed, including autocorrelation, causality, collinearity, common factors, conditioning, constancy, exogeneity, heteroscedasticity, identification, innovation, invariance, marginalizing, measurement, simultaneity, stationarity, trends, unit roots, and white noise. Particular expositional aids include an information taxonomy and model typologies. Monte Carlo methods, and the recent literature on Wiener processes, cointegration, and equilibrium correction are discussed (also the subject of the separate book *Cointegration, Error Correction and the Econometric Analysis of Non-Stationary Data* with Anindya Banerjee, Juan J. Dolado, and John W. Galbraith).

Part II focuses on maximum likelihood and related methods for a range of processes of interest in economics. Estimator generating equations summarize the proliferation of existing econometric estimators, and the non-central chi-square distribution is used to explain testing.

The practical problems considered in Part III include the issues of model discovery, evaluation, data mining, model mis-specification, an exposition of encompassing and its application to testing between conditional and expectational models, and an empirical study of the demand for money in the UK.

The appendix chapters record some widely-used results in matrix algebra, then trace the development of probability ideas from stochastic events through to random variables and their distributions, deriving regression as a conditional expectation. Sampling and likelihood follow naturally, as do estimation and inference, with a more detailed analysis of the multiple regression model and its properties. The underlying assumptions are weakened to stationary stochastic processes in a chapter on asymptotic distribution theory. Numerical optimization methods are then described. The final appendix chapter describes macro-econometric models, and methods of predicting from them, for the benefit of non-economists who might read this book.

The material is intended for three distinct, but overlapping, audiences. First, the book is designed for economists investigating empirical phenomena. Because of this objective, the text weaves together theory and evidence at every stage: almost 150 figures illustrate the analyses, usually in blocks of four related graphs. Empirical researchers concerned with practical and methodological aspects of econometrics should not find the mathematical level of the main text daunting, beyond the few sections marked with an asterisk, which suffer more from a lack of familiarity than intrinsic difficulty. Technical results appear in the solved examples, appendices and exercises. A better understanding of econometrics is certainly gained by knowing this material, but many empirical-modelling problems can be tackled without a mastery of all the foundations. Where a conflict occurred between conveying an idea simply, and expressing it in a technically correct but more complicated form, the former was chosen. For example, the notation does not reflect that conditioning is on σ-fields, rather than on the associated outcomes; and the assumptions postulated for most theorems are unnecessarily strong. In particular, the analysis is mainly for linear models, or linear conditional expectations, and usually assumes joint normality after sequential conditioning.

Secondly, the book discusses ideas, concepts, and tools relevant for advanced undergraduate and graduate econometrics students. Although the primary focus is on modelling economic time-series data, many topics conventionally discussed in econometrics textbooks are also analysed, albeit from a different perspective, and often entailing different conclusions. Instructors will see that commencing with the appendices creates an appropriate order for teaching intermediate and advanced econometrics. The solved examples and exercises are included to facilitate its use in teaching; a workbook of answers is in preparation. An important feature of classroom teaching of econometrics in Oxford is the live presentation of computer information to the audience: almost all the graphs recorded below have been presented on-screen during lectures, as have many of the regression estimates, Monte Carlo simulations, and numerical optimization illustrations. The econometric modelling software system PcGive (see Doornik and Hendry, 1994b, 1994a) was developed to sustain both the econometric approach and this style of teaching, as was the Monte Carlo program PcNaive (see Hendry, Neale and Ericsson, 1991). My experience is that regular exposure of students to live illustrations, which can be designed *ad lib* for the needs of the moment, or re-run with minor alterations to answer a student's query, greatly assists mathematically-weaker participants, especially those who wish to master econometrics as potential tool users and critics, rather than as prospective tool makers.

Finally, the book is relevant to statisticians involved in the analysis of social science time series. Many of the modelling difficulties discussed in the text are faced by all disciplines that empirically investigate human behaviour in the aggregate, including the issues of interdependence, dynamics, serial correlation, non-constancy, non-stationarity, conditioning, marginalizing, data inaccuracy, and dimensionality. It has been a constant source of encouragement to see the adoption of the approach described herein in cognate social sciences.

The first draft of my book on dynamic specification was prepared for a set of lectures that I presented jointly with Pravin K. Trivedi to IRI in the early 1970s. The second (incomplete) draft was written around the time of Davidson, Hendry, Srba and Yeo (1978), using a 'detective story' approach which relied heavily on the ingenuity of the investigator to discover useful econometric models. At that stage, Jean-François Richard joined me as a co-author, and we initiated the research programme reported in my recent book *Econometrics: Alchemy or Science?* The effort of merging the 'LSE' and 'CORE' approaches has added almost fifteen years, but provided a major stimulus to our research over this period. In total, more than fifty published articles were written to solve problems highlighted by earlier versions of the book, about a dozen of these as potential chapters. Once the preliminary formalization was complete, Bob Marshall also joined our team, and we worked on rewriting the late 1970s draft. Unfortunately, the pressures of other commitments, and the difficulty of progressing when we were separated by 3,000 miles, slowed writing to a snail's pace.

The present incarnation is based around my lectures on econometric methodology at Oxford University during 1989. The lectures were initially tape recorded and transcribed by Duo Qin, who also carried out the first round of editing and commented extensively on the text. Without having this text in hand (entitled *Lectures on Econometric*

Methodology, and scheduled to be published in 1990, but now defunct) the book may never have been completed — I am greatly indebted to Duo for her continual help and prompting to finish the book. The exercises were originally prepared as examination questions for the M.Phil. degree in Economics at Oxford, and the 'model' answers were first developed by Carlo Favero and myself. The final version of the book also draws on related courses which I delivered at Duke University, the University of California at San Diego, and at Oxford, together with some recent research findings to complete the treatment. It proved difficult to translate into book form the lectures initially recorded by Duo, and rewriting that original text lost some of the flavour and freshness of the live approach. I tried to retain the spirit of my lectures where that would help other teachers adapt the material to their own requirements should they so desire.

Given the long gestation period of the book, I have accumulated a vast debt to many colleagues, which it gives me great pleasure to acknowledge. Without extensive intellectual, moral, financial, and physical support it would have been impossible to complete the task; and the kindness and generosity with which this has been proffered presents a nobler face of humanity than that which confronts us all too miserably in daily newspapers. The general debt which econometricians owe to our pioneers is clear from the references, and is documented in my recent book *The Foundations of Econometric Analysis* with Mary S. Morgan (Hendry and Morgan, 1995). In *Alchemy* (Hendry, 1993a), I recorded my gratitude to the many teachers who initiated me into the subject, but acknowledgement of that debt merits repetition: my thanks to Meghnad Desai, Jim Durbin, Peter Fisk, Derek Peare, Bill Phillips, Bert Shaw, and especially Denis Sargan. Three institutions also deserve credit: Aberdeen University which risked accepting me as an undergraduate; the London School of Economics, which financed my graduate studies through a scholarship from Guinness plc (an honour enhanced by knowing that 'Student' had worked for them), and employed me for twelve years; and the University of Oxford and Nuffield College, which together have employed me since 1982.

I record with intellectual and social pleasure the roles of my many co-authors in advancing the research frontier, as well as their essential advice and encouragement when writing the book. In particular, my grateful thanks go to Gordon Anderson, Yoshi Baba, Anindya Banerjee, Julia Campos, Yock Chong, Michael Clements, Steven Cook, James Davidson, Juan Dolado, Jurgen Doornik, Robert Engle, Neil Ericsson, Carlo Favero, Jean-Pierre Florens, John Galbraith, Bernadette Govaerts, Robin Harrison, Robert Marshall, Grayham Mizon, Mary Morgan, John Muellbauer, Anthony Murphy, Adrian Neale, Adrian Pagan, Duo Qin, Jean-François Richard, Denis Sargan, Gregor Smith, Aris Spanos, Frank Srba, Ross Starr, Andrew Tremayne, Hong-Anh Tran, Pravin Trivedi, David Trumbull, Thomas von Ungern-Sternberg, Stephen Yeo, and Kenneth Wallis, on all of whose work I have drawn heavily.

As noted above, I owe Duo Qin a bouquet of thanks for producing the draft lectures text, and for her energy in driving me to complete a version on the grounds that there could always be a second edition! Julia Campos, Neil Ericsson, Tony Hall, and Søren Johansen thoroughly criticized the many obscurities, infelicities, and downright errors of that version and prompted a greatly improved — if further delayed — final product. I listened to their advice; I acknowledged the merits of their case; and even if they may not feel that the final product embodies all their good ideas, I am delighted to express my gratitude for their tremendous input of time and effort.

I am also indebted to Hughes Dauphin, Luigi Ermini, Oliver Linton, Claudio Lupi, Pekke Pere, and Neil Shephard for their helpful comments on earlier drafts, as well as to several of those already acknowledged. In particular, Julia Campos kindly checked much of the final typescript and helped remove many mistakes, and Ian Preston checked drafts of most of the solved examples.

Over the years, many kind and insightful colleagues have commented constructively and helpfully on my work, and in addition to those already acknowledged, grateful thanks go to Chris Allsopp, Gunnar Bårdsen, Peter Boswijk, Tony Courakis, David Cox, Angus Deaton, Ian Domowitz, Andreas Fischer, John Flemming, Chris Gilbert, Terence Gorman, Clive Granger, Josef Gruber, Andrew Harvey, Svend Hylleberg, Eilev Jansen, Katarina Juselius, Jan Kiviet, Teun Kloek, Knud Munk, Michel Mouchart, Steve Nickell, Denise Osborn, Gary Phillips, Robin Rowley, Mark Salmon, Peter Sinclair, Timo Teräsvirta, Tom Rothenberg, Honor Stamler, and Hal White.

Throughout my career, I have been ably supported by a sequence of superb research officers, who greatly increased my productivity: in temporal order, I am indebted to Robin Harrison, Andy Tremayne, Frank Srba, Yock Chong, Neil Ericsson, John Parker, Jon Faust, Adrian Neale, Yoshi Baba, Steven Cook, Mike Clements, and Jurgen Doornik. I have also been fortunate to have had a sequence of excellent secretaries including Luba Mumford, Raija Thomson, Christine Wills, Jean Brotherhood, and Maureen Baker, all of whom are offered my heartfelt thanks for their many contributions.

Writing, documenting, indexing, and preparing the camera-ready copy for the book was close to a nightmare, and I am very grateful to Jurgen Doornik for his immense help in organising the typesetting. The project could well have aborted without his wonderful help, his programs T3TEXTEX and PSP, and his unique ability to quickly develop powerful macros for such tasks as indexing or changing styles. The excellent copy editing of Virginia Williams noticeably improved the layout, and Andrew Schuller kindly steered the book to a final conclusion.

Twenty generations of students and seminar participants have helped clarify, and at times redirect, my approach with constructively-critical comments and ideas: they are far too numerous to thank individually, although my gratitude extends to them all. Individuals who made particularly large impacts include Karim Abadir, John Aldrich, Ted Anderson, Manuel Arellano, Alok Bhargava, Larry Boland, Jeremy Bray, Trevor Breusch, Georgio Calzolari Nancy Cartwright, Manfred Deistler, Kevin Hoover, George Judge, Ed Leamer, Essi Maasoumi, James MacKinnon, Edmund Malinvaud, Paul Newbold, Charles Nelson, Mark Nerlove, Hashem Pesaran, Peter Phillips, Gene Savin, Peter Schmidt, Chris Sims, and Mike Wickens. My apologies to all colleagues whose work I have inadvertently failed to acknowledge, or whose contributions are not fully documented in the text.

It is a pleasure to thank the many institutions which sustained my research while writing the book, particularly the UK Economic and Social Research Council for twenty years of research finance. Shorter spells of invaluable support were provided by Yale University, the University of California at Berkeley, the Australian National University, the Centre for Operations Research and Econometrics at the University of Louvain-la-Neuve, Duke University, and on a larger scale by the University of California at San Diego during many enjoyable and productive visits.

Finally, I owe a great debt to Evelyn and Vivien for their patience, support, and encouragement while I was doing the research for, and writing, the book. Evelyn thought *Dynamic Econometrics* would end up as my own Festschrift, but I am sure she is the first to be pleased that her prediction proved incorrect.

Two data-sets are extensively analysed in the text (especially in Ch.16). The first is a computer generated data-set that is distributed for tutorials with PcGive (the book of which reveals the underlying data-generation process, simulated to represent quarterly data over 1953(1)–1992(3)); the second set comprises quarterly time series over 1960(1)–1989(2) for UK monetary and related variables, as investigated by Hendry and Ericsson (1991b).

These data can be downloaded through anonymous ftp from *hicks.nuff.ox.ac.uk*. The files are stored in the directory called *pub\dynects* in both ASCII and PcGive format. Please read the 'readme' file in this directory before proceeding. The ASCII files are human-readable when listed on a computer screen, and each is for a single variable, named, for example, CONS.DAT, INC.DAT etc. for the artificial data; and M1.UKM, TFE.UKM etc. for the Hendry and Ericsson data. Readers possessing PcGive will find it more convenient to use the files called DATA.IN7 and DATA.BN7; and UKM1.IN7 and UKM1.BN7. The .BN7 files are binary and have to be downloaded as such.

The graphs in the text are PcGive screen captures in either 600 × 480 or 800 × 640 mode. Their drawbacks are apparent to the practised eye; the advantages are more obvious to the pocket, not to mention the greatly increased speed and accuracy of production. The text was produced from camera-ready copy prepared by the Scientific Word™ TeX-processing program in combination with emTeX and DVIPS. The bibliography was compiled by BIBTeX.

DFH
September, 1994

Part I

Concepts, Models, and Processes in Econometrics

1

Introduction

We first consider the main problem in econometric modelling of economic time series, namely how to discover sustainable and interpretable relationships between observed economic variables. After stating the aims of the book, critical and constructive aspects of data modelling are distinguished, and the difficulties attendant on the latter are emphasized. The roles of theories, instruments, and evidence are discussed. Four levels of knowledge are distinguished as they play an important role in the book. Some economic time series are examined graphically. A simple statistical mechanism which could generate data with many of the salient features of the observed series is conjectured and its properties analysed. An inconsistency between the implications of the conjectured mechanism and the model fitted to the observed data highlights the ease of critical evaluation as against the difficulty of constructive progress, setting the scene for studying econometric modelling in the rest of the book. The final section introduces the concept of an empirical model.

1.1 Empirical econometric modelling

This book concerns econometric modelling of economic time series. Econometrics involves the 'mutual penetration of quantitative economic theory and statistical observation' (Frisch, 1933), so we will examine the concepts, models, procedures and tools of econometrics and investigate the systematic application of econometric methods to the analysis of economic time-series data. Modelling denotes matching theory and data in a formal quantitative framework, so we will consider the roles of economic theory and empirical evidence and their links. This will involve a careful consideration of econometric methodology, where methodology denotes the study of methods: in the sense of Boland (1989), methodology has a small 'm' here, and concerns all decisions taken during the process of relating ideas to evidence. Time-series data exhibit many specific properties, so these too will be subject to scrutiny.

A key problem in empirical econometrics concerns matching economic theories with observed data features to develop quantitative, empirically-relevant models. All models are not born equal, and we seek those which are useful in practice for understanding economic behaviour, for testing economic theories, for forecasting the future, and for analysing economic policy. Achieving these four objectives requires discovering sustainable relationships between observed economic magnitudes. To find such relationships entails rejecting models which lack desirable characteristics, so we must be able to critically evaluate empirical models and test their associated theories against the available evidence. This group of activities constitutes econometric modelling.

Empirical econometric models are systems of quantitative relationships linking observed data series. They have four main roles in economics. First, they are data summaries: there exist too many variables of potential interest in economics for us to investigate them all, so summarization is essential, and econometric models are one way of doing so. Secondly, econometric models allow us to interpret empirical evidence: facts rarely speak for themselves, and a well-defined framework, such as an econometric model, will prove invaluable. Thirdly, there are often several competing theoretical explanations for economic phenomena: econometric models play an important role in evaluating the relative explanatory powers of these theories. Finally, econometric models are the primary vehicle for the accumulation and consolidation of empirical knowledge about how economies function. In the long run, this may be their main *raison d'être*. Since econometrics is essentially empirical in nature, it offers a potentially scientific approach to understanding human conduct, and is the major source of systematic empirical information about economic behaviour.

At this stage, how well econometric models succeed in achieving any or all of their ostensible objectives is an open issue. From the outset, however, it must be stressed that the economy is too large and complicated for us to develop 'true' models of it. Rather, empirical models are invariably simplifications and, in that sense, inevitably false, although as we will see, there is also a sense in which they can be true but unhelpful. Consequently, we must develop other criteria than truth to judge empirical models and select between them, and do so in a way which does not introduce contradictions due to the falsity of the models.

Given a new insight from economic analysis, a new source of data, or a previously unanticipated phenomenon, how should one develop an econometric model thereof? It would be convenient if principles of econometric modelling could be enunciated, whose systematic application to empirical evidence ensured a model with desirable properties. Reading that sentence probably provokes a host of questions including:

What defines 'desirable properties'?

How could one establish that such desirable properties were achieved in practice?

Need a unique model-choice always result from applying modelling principles?

If the principles work for one time, place and problem, what could ensure that they would work in another?

Since we cannot know in advance what exists to be discovered, how can principles be formulated for modelling new phenomena?

If the resulting models are claimed to be 'true', does this entail all three attributes, namely the truth, the whole truth and nothing but the truth?

What criteria exist for ascertaining the truth status of empirical models?

These questions all raise methodological issues, some much deeper than others. The book analyses these and many other practical issues arising in dynamic econometrics.

To clarify the basis of the book's approach, consider the sufficient conditions for successful empirical econometric research proposed in Hendry (1987) as the four 'golden prescriptions' of econometrics:

(i) think brilliantly: if you think of the right answer before modelling, then the empirical results will be optimal and, of course, confirm your brilliance. Many conventional textbooks simply assume that the model is correct — we will not do so below, although the methods proposed deliver the right results if this case happens to apply.
(ii) be infinitely creative: if you do not think of the correct model before commencing, the next best is to think of it as you proceed. While no valid constructive method can be proposed, data evidence can help guide model development in a systematic manner.
(iii) be outstandingly lucky: if you do not think of the 'true model' before starting nor discover it *en route*, then luckily stumbling over it before completing the study is the final sufficient condition. This may be the most practical of these suggestions. Failing this last prescription:
(iv) stick to doing theory.

These sufficient conditions are tantamount to the assumption of omniscience of the modeller and we cannot rely on their sustaining a viable methodology. Fortunately, these prescriptions are not necessary. The book argues that no realistic sufficient conditions can be established which ensure the discovery of a 'good' empirical model, nor are any required for empirical econometrics to progress. However, there are a number of necessary conditions which can rule out many poor models, allowing us to focus on the best remaining candidates.

1.2 The problems of econometrics

The problems of econometrics are many and varied. The economy is a complicated, dynamic, non-linear, high-dimensional, and evolving entity, so studying it will be difficult. Society and its social system both alter over time, laws change and technological innovations occur, so establishing invariants of the system will not be easy. Time-series data samples are short, highly aggregated, heterogeneous, non-stationary, time dependent, and interdependent, so we have little empirical information from which to learn. Economic magnitudes are inaccurately measured, are subject to considerable later revision, and important variables are often not measured or are unobservable, so all our inferences will be both imprecise and tentative. Economic theories change over time, and rival explanations co-exist, so no firm theoretical basis exists for models. And econometricians themselves appear to be in disarray about how their subject should be practised. It is unsurprising that the subject has many critics: Hendry (1980) records earlier criticisms, and more recent complaints include Sims (1980) (incredible restrictions), Leamer (1983) (let's take the con out of econometrics) and Summers (1991) (no value added), as well as an annual spate of sceptical remarks about 'data mining', 'inaccurate forecasting', and 'garbage in, garbage out': Granger (1990) provides a useful compendium of critiques.

Most of the issues just raised will be analysed at some stage in this book. Few will be completely resolved, although many should be clearer after we have formalized the problems and critically evaluated the procedures commonly adopted for empirical research. 'Theory-driven' approaches, in which a model is derived from a priori theory and calibrated from data evidence, lie at one extreme. These suffer from theory dependence in that their credibility depends on the credibility of the theory from which they arose — when that theory is discarded, so is the associated evidence. All too often 'golden prescription' (i) is needed to justify the results obtained. 'Data-driven' approaches, where models are developed to closely describe the data, lie at the other extreme. These suffer from sample dependence in that accidental and transient data features are embodied as tightly in the model as permanent aspects, so that extensions of the data set often reveal predictive failure. An interactive blend of theory and evidence naturally suggests itself. To make progress in developing a viable approach, we first need a formal analysis within a well-defined framework — a task to which we turn.

1.3 The aims of this book

The primary aims of the book are to develop an operational econometric methodology which sustains empirical modelling of economic time series, and to clarify the status of empirical econometric models however they were developed. The former is a constructive aim whereas the latter involves critical evaluation. The ingredients of the analysis include:

the structure of economic data processes and the properties of the resulting data;
concepts of model construction;
the formulation of relevant model classes;
the derivation of empirical models by reductions of data processes;
the interpretation of empirical evidence in the light of subject-matter theory;
techniques for estimation and inference;
numerical optimization and Monte Carlo methods;
methods of empirical model building and model evaluation;
relevant computer software.

Many conventional econometrics concepts will be discussed, often from a different perspective, including: aggregation, autocorrelation, causality, collinearity, diagnostic testing, exogeneity, heteroscedasticity, identification, measurement errors, parameters, regression, simultaneity, stationarity, stochastic processes, and trends. However, some less familiar concepts will also occur, namely: cointegration, common factors, conditioning, congruence, constancy, encompassing, equilibrium correction, estimator generation, information taxonomy, innovations, invariance, marginalizing, model typologies, progressive research strategies, reduction, search procedures, symptomatologies, unit roots, and white noise. Throughout, concepts are illustrated by examples based on economic time series and artificial (computer-generated) data; PcGive and PcFiml are used for empirical modelling (Doornik and Hendry, 1994b, 1994a), and PcNaive for Monte Carlo (Hendry, Neale and Ericsson, 1991).

To implement these aims, ideas will be developed in the following sequence. First, we consider the situation where we know the complete structure of the process which generates economic data and the values of all its parameters. This is the equivalent of a probability theory course, but involves economic theory and econometric concepts, and is referred to as level A. Part I of the book comprises the bulk of this material. The main tools to be developed concern time-series data processes, empirical models, model typologies, and the many concepts germane to the theory of reduction and its associated information taxonomy. Probability and distribution theory in the abstract (as opposed to their application in econometrics) are treated in Chapter A2.

Given that background, we consider a known economic structure with unknown values of the parameters. This material, denoted level B, is developed in Part II and is equivalent to an estimation and inference course in statistics, but focusing on econometrically relevant aspects. The main tools are likelihood functions, associated estimator-generating equations, numerical optimization, and model-evaluation statistics. Chapter A1 records a number of useful results from matrix algebra, and Chapters A3–A5 provide an introduction to statistical theory, estimation and inference; asymptotic distribution theory; and numerical optimization methods respectively.

In Part III, we examine the empirically relevant situation where neither the form of the data-generation process nor its parameter values are known. This part, denoted level C, is equivalent to a model-building course, and involves the issues of model discovery, evaluation, data mining, model-search procedures, and the whole gamut of methodological considerations which are currently under debate in econometrics. Major tools include recursive methods, encompassing, super exogeneity, and invariance tests, building upon the methods considered in Parts I and II: for example, the approach of simplifying initially general models is the empirical counterpart of the theory of reduction in Part I. Chapter A6 offers a background sketch of macro-econometric models.

The fourth level of knowledge, denoted level D, relates to forecasting the future when the data outcomes are unknown. The associated material is treated in a separate book (Clements and Hendry, 1995) although aspects arise throughout the present volume. The four main levels of knowledge A–D are tightly integrated, and the resolution of many of the conundrums at level C depends on the framework developed at level A. Section 1.8 discusses these four knowledge levels in greater detail.

1.4 Constructive and destructive approaches

Stated more precisely, the minimal objective of the book is to provide a structured set of tools for the critical appraisal of empirical evidence in time-series econometrics. Its most ambitious aim is to develop an organized approach to econometrics which will enable the reader to undertake applied econometrics research and establish a credible evidential basis for the results. That second aim is much higher than the first because the critical application of econometric tools for model evaluation is much easier than the constructive application of tools for empirical model discovery.

The dichotomy between construction and destruction is an old one in the philosophy of science, and is an important aspect of the approach adopted here: Herschel (1830) distinguished between the context of discovery and the context of evaluation, and the book by Popper (1963) is entitled *Conjectures and Refutations*. Although critically evaluating empirical evidence is a destructive use of econometrics, the tools needed to understand and criticize empirical evidence are a minimum essential item in every economist's tool kit. We will establish a legitimate basis for evaluating empirical models, even though its rigorous application is partly open to a charge of nihilism and may not win us many friends. The second, or constructive role, which would offset nihilism, is unfortunately far removed from the first. It aims to provide methods which, in an economic theory context and given previous empirical evidence, will help in the development of new empirical models, which have at least the status that the first set of tools will not show those models to be invalid. We will not be able to establish an unimpeachable constructive methodology, but we will learn much about how to proceed, and how not to proceed, for efficient research.

The importance of the destruction–construction dichotomy can be seen by considering a rudimentary statistical experiment — rolling dice. Imagine the following scenario: a cubical die has six faces numbered 1 through 6, each number occurs exactly once and the die is perfectly symmetrical on every axis. On rolling the die, forty consecutive sixes are observed. A first reaction is to conclude that at least one of the previous assertions must have been false; either the die was not perfectly symmetrical; or it was not cubical; or it did not show precisely the six different numbers $\{1, 2, 3, 4, 5, 6\}$. A second thought might be that there was some way of interfering with the die when it was rolled, an implicit assumption being that the rolls were independent. Whatever the explanation, from the observed outcome one can refute the hypothesis that the experiment involved 'a symmetric, balanced cubical die with faces showing the six different numbers $\{1, 2, 3, 4, 5, 6\}$, rolled without interference'. Moreover, that hypothesis can be rejected without knowing much about statistics or probability theory, and without knowing why the hypothesis is invalid.

Now consider the constructive aspect of the same problem. The outcome of forty consecutive sixes could have arisen for many reasons. The die might have only sixes on it, so that a six always results; there might exist a mechanism for attracting the face opposite to the only six; or some other mechanism, about which we have not thought, could guarantee that the only six must end face up no matter how the die is rolled. Perhaps there is a bias in the way the die is picked up and rolled along a set of four faces which ensures that a six ends up at the top. Or the outcome may be due to extraordinary chance interacting with a bias in the rolling mechanism. There is a further possibility: while we may believe that the same die is rolled each time, the die itself might have been changed (say to a triangular pyramid with four faces instead of six) and therefore the experiment was altered during its execution. A constructive modelling exercise requires that the 'solution' be discovered — somehow.

It should not be surprising that we cannot enunciate a mechanistic approach to the discovery of new knowledge; we do not know what undiscovered entities exist and hence cannot know in advance how best to discover them. An iterative process of obtaining evidence, checking creative conjectures, revising the framework, and reinterpreting the evidence will be essential at the constructive stage. Consequently, the best tools are those that foster scientific discovery in general, namely, systematic study, knowledge accumulation and consolidation, clever ideas, creative insights, and good luck: but we do not assume omniscience since, given any conjectures, we will usually be able to test their validity. In practice, observed outcomes will not be as clear cut as 40 consecutive sixes — perhaps four sixes out of eight throws would be a better analogy — so that issues of statistical inference from small data samples complicate the analysis. As background to their application in econometrics, the next two sections discuss scientific method and the interacting roles of measurement instruments, empirical evidence, and theories.

1.5 A brief discourse on scientific method

Science is a public approach to the measurement and analysis of observable phenomena. Its essential aspects are that it is a systematic study of empirical evidence, with accumulated evidence consolidated and unified in theories, which are evaluated in turn against further observation statements. Theory creation can arise in a multitude of ways, but much of science is deductive, contingent on the pre-existing framework. Empirical evidence needs to be replicable, and explaining the ever increasing body of substantiated empirical evidence is the final arbitrator of the validity of theories. Objectivity of approach, potential falsifiability of claims, and progressivity of knowledge and understanding are all key elements. Criticism is therefore the life-blood of science: claims and predictions are hazarded to potential rejection, with the survivors retained for future rounds. In practice, since science is a human endeavour — with human capital, reputation, and ego involved — progress is not a steady trend towards greater understanding but rather 'higgledy-piggledy growth' (see Little, 1962, and Mirowski, 1988). Theories are rarely rejected but rather decay into disuse; evidence can be inaccurate, rationalized, or even amended to ensure that theories 'fit the facts'; instruments may prove to be faulty; and deliberate attempts to falsify results occur (see Kohn, 1987). Science has proved to be an instrument of great generality and power, which facilitates systematic research and the consolidation of accumulating empirical evidence, and has an impressive, albeit imperfect, track record: see e.g. Mason (1962) or Messadié (1991).[1]

[1] The philosophy of scientific method has evolved over the centuries from Aristotle, through Bacon, Galileo, and Descartes to Herschel (1830) and Poincaré (1905), and includes contributions from many philosophers such as (*inter alia*) Popper (1959, 1963), Nagel (1961), Kuhn (1962), Hempel (1966), Lakatos (1974), Feyerabend (1975), and Cartwright (1983, 1989). Chalmers (1982) and Harré (1985) provide useful overviews. References closely related to the histories of the sciences are Marks (1967), Losee (1980), and Harré (1981). Applications of such analyses to economics, as well as internal discussions, exist in abundance, including Mill (1865), Keynes (1891), Robbins (1932), Friedman (1953), von Mises (1978), Blaug (1980), Caldwell (1982), Boland (1982, 1989), Hausman (1984) and Mirowski (1988). Neither set of references is

Since the validity of any outcome is intrinsic to the product, not to its method of discovery or construction, methodology can at best reveal the benefits and drawbacks of alternative research strategies in certain states of nature. Naturally, important differences exist between social and other sciences, partly because the behaviour of animate beings rather than inanimate substances is under study, partly because the investigator is a participant, and partly because of the evolutionary nature of economic behaviour. These attributes differentiate economics from the physical, biological, and psychological sciences in turn. However, various commonalties exist in all sciences, which is why science can be construed as an instrument for studying empirical phenomena. There is no unique model of how science proceeds, nor even of why it has proved such a successful instrument for progress, but my own view is that the fundamental ingredients are systematic study, an empirical basis, and knowledge accumulation.

Given this succinct description of the salient characteristics of scientific method, four issues merit comment. First, experimentation may be useful as part of that method, and is a powerful tool for discovery and evaluation, but it is not essential to either science or progressivity (see Gould, 1989, for a related analysis in palaeontology, and Medawar, 1969, for the converse view of the key role of experimentation). That is fortunate for economics, since although both social and laboratory experiments are feasible, the former are expensive and by their nature must fail to control potentially important factors, whereas the latter are artificial and not yet sufficiently advanced to provide a substantive empirical base.[2] Most economic data is non-experimental and Hicks (1979) correctly stressed that time-series econometrics has much in common with history, in that contingency plays a key role. Such difficulties significantly affect the structure of econometrics, but do not preclude a scientific approach.

Second, beyond omniscience, there do not appear to be sufficient conditions for the truth of claims about empirical phenomena: in particular, there is no criterion for knowing when empirical truth has been established. This issue has special force in statistical subjects, where apparently contradictory statements may be 'true' simultaneously. For example, that one variable y is a linear function of a second variable z with an independent normally-distributed, constant-variance error, is consistent with the claim that y is a linear function of another variable x, unrelated to z, again with an independent normally-distributed, constant-variance error, in that we can construct worlds in which both statements are true, albeit neither is the whole truth. We develop weaker, but operational, criteria below.

Third, methodical study and knowledge accumulation can highlight gaps and act as prompts for discovery, but cannot specify how best to discover what we do not know. Consequently, much methodology concerns issues of research efficiency rather than principles of discovery. However, the absence of a best, or dominant, strategy does not entail

complete, but each serves to establish the wealth of insights in the literature. Cartwright (1989) argues that econometrics provides a model for how science can uncover structures in nature.

[2] Examples of social experiments include time of day usage of electric power (see Aigner, 1984) and the New Jersey negative income tax trials (see Hausman and Wise, 1985); examples of laboratory experiments are provided in Smith (1982), and overviewed by Roth (1988).

that 'anything goes', since many strategies may be dominated even if none is optimal: try driving a car with your eyes closed. In practice, almost every conceivable means of discovery has operated in some instance: systematic analysis (Lavoisier establishing the combustion properties of oxygen); luck (perhaps Fleming noticing the effects of penicillin); serendipity (Penzias and Wilson uncovering the background cosmic radiation); brilliant intuition (Faraday's dynamo); trial and error (Crick and Watson modelling DNA); false theories (Kepler's attempts to characterize planetary orbits); superb theories (Eddington's test of relativity by gravitational effects on photons); careful observation (Harvey's model of the circulation of blood); new instruments (Galileo's discovery of the moons of Jupiter by a telescope is one of thousands of possible examples); and so on. These examples may be challenged in detail, and doubtless other methods abound, but both points merely emphasize that there is no unique discovery path.

Finally, despite their distinction being fuzzy at the boundaries, discovery and justification are distinct contexts, as argued in §1.4. The dichotomy will prove invaluable in econometrics, but operating in a negative manner: models developed on one data set need outside information to claim any evaluation content. The view that scientific progress is dependent on individual contributions (which is questioned by Bernal, 1971) suggests letting 'a thousand flowers bloom' in the context of discovery: however, weeds must be removed in the context of evaluation, so whimsy has no place there (see Hendry and Mizon, 1990). As we show below, empirical econometric models are designed to satisfy various criteria, and by doing so acquire no excess corroborated content. Conversely, by performing as anticipated against new data, new rival models, or new tests, they can acquire objective credibility.

It is difficult to know what the alternative mode of analysis might be if a scientific one is not adopted. Historical method is not precluded, and few would deem the methodologies of alchemy or astrology to be acceptable. In practice, the claim by McCloskey (1983) that 'rhetoric' dominates reflects only a small segment of discourse; the debates on econometric methodology surveyed in Pagan (1987) are all within an ostensible scientific framework, and primarily concern methods of inference rather than methodology. Theories must be internally consistent to avoid contradictions; empirical evidence must enter to determine relevance; knowledge accumulation is essential if progress is to occur; systematic study is vital to avoid inefficiency; checking is needed to preclude false claims; replication is necessary to ensure that hypotheses concern the real world and not just the data under analysis (see Backhouse, 1992); and so on. There do not seem to be viable alternatives to a scientific approach, albeit that the subject matter, tools, and models of economics are different from other disciplines, and that there are many problems such as regime shifts and poor data.

1.6 Theories, instruments, and evidence

Scientific progress results from a three-way interaction between theories, instruments (i.e. tools), and empirical evidence. At any existing state of theoretical analysis, measurement tools, and empirical knowledge, new contributions can arrive in any arena and potentially influence any aspect of earlier findings. This does not entail abandoning previous findings *en bloc*, and iterative revisions of views, tools, and theories occur. While the scientific process operates in a similar way in economics to physical and biological sciences, there are important differences due to the nature of the subject matter under study, just as there are between the other sciences noted.

Empirical evidence comprises sensory data and observations derived from sensory data using instruments or measurement tools. The latter may be highly indirect and may take a long time to be accepted as empirical evidence (as has happened in natural sciences with telescopes and microscopes: see e.g. Drake, 1980). Instruments require their own theoretical analyses and empirical practices, and naturally these are different across subjects (e.g. optical theory for telescopes; atomic theory for X-ray machines etc.). Since econometrics is the major empirical tool in economics it needs analysis along such lines. Much econometric theory concerns determining the 'operating characteristics' of methods of estimation, inference, and forecasting in different states of nature. A major contrast with physical sciences is that rather little is known about the relevance to the actual economy of the postulated states, and hence an additional iterative sequence is induced as discussed in §1.10. This is one consequence of the non-experimental nature of economic time-series data. For example, an econometric theory based on a stationary stochastic environment will not perform as anticipated if the real world generates non-stationary data. Thus, the instrument itself needs careful calibration, which has induced a large literature on econometric theory that proceeds in rough synchrony with growth in our understanding of the properties of economic data.

Theories can be distinguished in terms of levels, where low-level theories or measurement systems are well established and widely accepted (e.g. the optical theory underpinning telescopes), whereas high-level theories assume the validity of lower levels and are subject to doubt (perhaps considerable doubt, as in theories about how solar systems form, or whether economic agents hold rational expectations). Facts can then be defined as items of empirical information which depend only on low-level theories and measurement systems, and can be reliably replicated. Low-level theories, evidence, or instruments may be rejected as unsound at a later stage, jeopardizing previous analyses, but that is an inevitable risk in scientific research, independent of whether the subject is physical or social science. High-level empirical evidence is construed to be that which depends on high-level theories and measurements.

Consequently, all empirical evidence is theory laden to some degree, but generally the theories in question are low-level ones which are part of the background knowledge base and are not subject to scrutiny in the current analysis. Measurements of gross national product (GNP) are certainly far from exact, but are given to economics by an outside agency; a series of expectations created to be rational by construction would involve much higher levels of theory. A theory-based econometric relationship would represent high-level empirical evidence.

Whether theoretical advances lead or follow empirical discoveries depends in part on the pre-eminence accorded to theory, and both instances occur in practice. In economics, data analysis is difficult, but since contributions can and do affect any existing findings in an empirical science, no aspect (theory, evidence, or instruments) can claim precedence. Dramatic criticisms or substantive reconstructions can overturn the existing edifice either as a 'revolution' or by an incommensurate 'paradigm shift'. However, granted an insistence on progression, empirical evidence or new theories alone will not overturn the *status quo*. The former creates anomalies (evidence that is apparently inconsistent with the existing knowledge state), the reactions to which may be diverse but frequently will prompt new theories and further empirical research. The latter may lead to questioning the status of previous evidence, and often induces a search for new findings, but 'isolation' strategies also exist, so haphazard progress or even degeneration can result.

1.7 Economic analysis and statistical theory

The first internal methodological problems concern the respective roles of economic analysis and statistical theory in econometrics. Since economic theories are highly abstract, many of the points from §1.6 are relevant to the relation of economic theory to empirical evidence. The latter concerns whether or not probability concepts are applicable to economic data. The analysis must be rather superficial at this stage but several important issues can be discussed.

In economics, examples of current low-level theories include national income accounting (though some of its concepts, such as income, or depreciation, remain open to revision), supply–demand analyses, and the foundations of theories in constrained optimization (again subject to debate about what is optimized and what the relevant constraints comprise). High-level theories include such notions as permanent income, rational expectations and related idealizations, and most theories of investment behaviour.

The theory-laden nature of observations entails that 'measurement without theory' is impossible, and could only relate to the level of the theories used. However, most empirical evidence depends on low-level theories, so a data-based approach to studying the economy is feasible. Since 'theory without measurement' is common, the crucial issue for research efficiency is the appropriate blend of theory and empirical evidence. No methodological principle seems to be at stake, because the outcome depends on the relative usefulness of the existing high-level theories as against the accuracy of the available data compiled with present instruments. When theories are really useful (albeit something that can only be known after the fact), research may be best undertaken closely in line with theoretical predictions; but when extant high-level theories are of little value (as when phlogiston was the best theory of combustion before Lavoisier), empirical research will contribute most when it relies mainly on low levels of theory (this seems to be the thrust of the rejoinder by Vining, 1949 to Koopmans, 1947: see Hendry, 1993b, and Quah, 1993, who cites Edwin Hubble's discovery of the expanding universe from observation alone).

A related difficulty concerns how to proceed if the empirical and theoretical models are inconsistent (viz., the empirical model contains variables precluded by the theory, or the coefficients have signs which are not interpretable within the theoretical framework etc.). If the model is rejected, the issue remains as to why the theory cannot explain the results of the model. If the model is not rejected, then the theory must be altered to avoid maintaining two contradictory propositions. In practice, either or both of the model or the theory may be revised till apparent consistency is achieved. This aspect of model design will be investigated below.

The assessment of empirical evidence raises complicated and evolving issues, irrespective of whether it is predominantly theory based or data based, or a mixture. Much of the book is devoted to developing an appropriate framework for the appraisal of econometric evidence, but a few preliminary remarks are feasible. First, econometrics is a young discipline, so later developments can overturn what were once regarded as well-established facts, by showing that the low-level theories of previous researchers were incorrect. Since earlier evidence may be an artefact of invalid low-level assumptions, both theories and evidence only merit tentative acceptance. Conversely, evidence is not self-explanatory, so some subject-matter theory is essential in order to interpret any empirical claim, whether it concerns the parameters of structural models, regression findings, stylized facts, or graphs. Empirical models which are not quantitative facsimiles of theory models are sometimes dismissed as the outcome of data mining, connoting a prejudiced search for corroborative evidence (see Leamer, 1978, and Hendry, Leamer and Poirier, 1990). Certainly, a model-search process which deliberately ignores, or camouflages, conflicting results is unscientific, but the approach remains open to analysis by seeing how well the resulting model accounts for the findings of rival studies, called encompassing (see e.g. Mizon and Richard, 1986, Gilbert, 1986, and Ch.14). When a modelling approach relies on corroboration of prior theory, it is potentially subject to paradoxes of corroboration (see e.g. Caldwell, 1982, and Ericsson and Hendry, 1989), although some of these can be resolved by encompassing. The approach investigated below seeks to characterize data in a parsimonious way within a general theoretical framework, as well as providing a statistical baseline against which other models can be evaluated. It will be argued that the drawbacks of data mining and theory calibration do not apply to such an approach.

Many empirical models are accompanied by test statistics which claim to assess their adequacy. However, investigators can iteratively revise models in the light of adverse data evidence, so we must distinguish between tests which are used implicitly as model design criteria (indices which reflect the exploitation of data evidence) and genuine tests in the Neyman–Pearson sense (which use previously unavailable evidence). The former tell us about the adequacy of the design of the model, the latter about the adequacy of the model: Chapter 13 discusses this issue.

The interpretation of data evidence, the status of empirical models, modelling strategies, and the role of test statistics in model evaluation are among the more controversial topics in applied econometrics. They are interdependent in that (for example) some of the worries about 'data mining' arise because tests can be made insignificant by revising models in the light of misfits. For the moment we just claim that such issues can be analysed, and partially resolved, using the approach described in later chapters.

We turn now to the role of statistical theory in econometrics. Its role has been another long-standing debate in economics due to the non-experimental, heterogeneous and interdependent nature of its observations (see Morgan, 1987, 1989 for an analysis of the probability revolution following Haavelmo, 1944, and Qin, 1993, for the subsequent history). Since many of the relevant concepts will be introduced later, we must temporarily proceed as if economic data can bear a probabilistic interpretation and merely suggest an illustration which supports that claim. In most countries, growth in real GNP of 200–300 per cent per annum is essentially impossible; 20–50 per cent p.a. is extremely unlikely; 4–6 per cent p.a. is imaginable if somewhat high, 2–4 per cent p.a. is quite likely and so on. Moreover, there are few occasions over the last century when statements wildly different from those just made would have been credible; similar considerations apply to many other real economic variables.

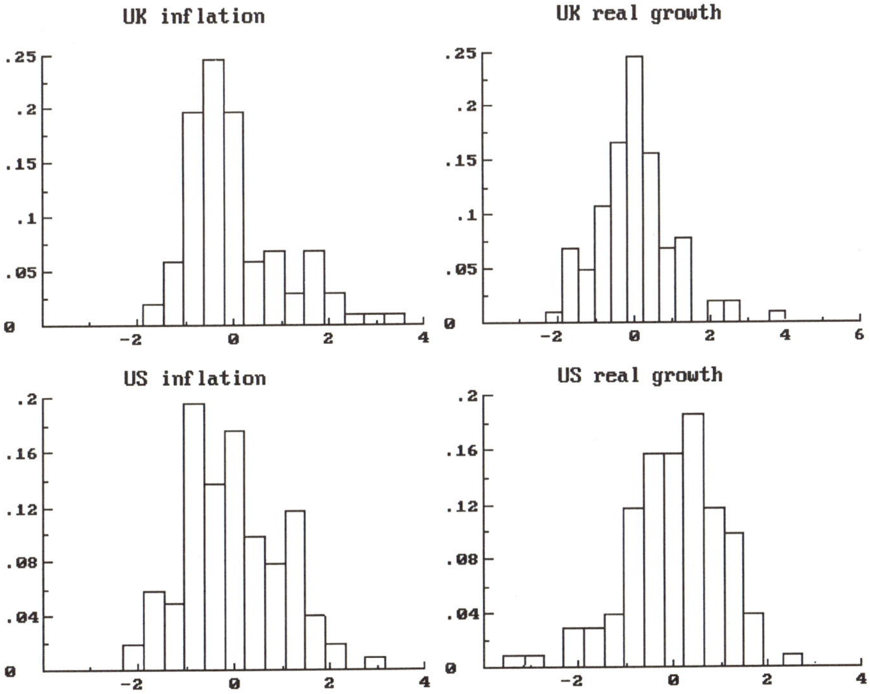

Fig. 1.1 Histograms of economic time series

To illustrate this discussion, histograms of the quarterly growth rate of real output and inflation in the UK and the USA over 1960(1)–1988(2) are shown in Fig. 1.1, standardized to have a zero sample mean and a unit variance.[3] Blocks of four graphs are implicitly labelled a, b, d, and c reading clockwise from the top left. The four figures describe empirical distributions which appear to be amenable to analysis: later we will consider the constancy over time of such distributions.

[3] Most histograms presented in the book are standardized in this way, the main exceptions being for the densities of correlation coefficients which have a bounded range.

Meanwhile, we will analyse economic behaviour as if it can be characterized in terms of random variables, assuming that the corresponding density functions are continuous. We will review the legitimacy of applying that framework once the relevant concepts have been developed. Chapter A2 introduces many of the concepts and techniques from probability theory and statistics that underlie the present treatment.

1.8 Four levels of knowledge

Consider econometric modelling in the light of the dice-rolling example above. We distinguish four different levels of knowledge potentially available to an investigator.

1.8.1 Probability theory

At level A, we assume that the probability structure of all the events involved is known. In the dice-rolling example, the theory postulated an experiment with a perfect (symmetric and balanced) cubical die where the six faces each bear a different number from the set $\{1, 2, 3, 4, 5, 6\}$, and the outcome on each roll is independent of the outcomes on earlier rolls. This experiment defines the data-generation process for observed outcomes. The probability p of the outcome being $\{6\}$ equals one sixth, denoted by $\mathsf{p} = \mathsf{P}(\{6\}) = 1/6$, which is a mathematical proposition within probability theory, given the assumptions.

In econometric terms, level A requires complete knowledge of the probability structure of all relevant economic behaviour. That is a hypothetical situation entailing an unrealistic level of knowledge, but in order to study the properties of statistical methods, much of the book focuses on the case where we pretend to know the data-generation process in every detail. Such an assumption can be misleading as a guide to reality, since in practice we know rather little about the structure of most economic mechanisms. Thus, while understanding the probability structure of hypothetical cases is an essential tool, it is only the first of many necessary but insufficient tools for the econometric analysis of empirical evidence.

1.8.2 Estimation theory

At level B, assume that a particular die has six faces labelled 1 through 6, and we want to estimate the probability p of observing the outcome $\{6\}$ from independent rolls. We can only learn the answer empirically in this state of nature, and cannot deduce the probability from the available information alone, because we do not know how perfect the die is. We estimate the probability by observing the die being rolled a large number of times, recording how frequently $\{6\}$ occurs and then appealing to a theory based on level A analysis. Such a theory might describe the limits of empirical frequencies of independent outcomes in a world of fixed population probabilities. This aspect corresponds to an estimation problem in econometrics, and so concerns good ways of determining the numerical values of unknown features of a model. Estimation methods or estimators are a second important set of tools in our tool kit and, like the first, are necessary but not sufficient for solving the model discovery problem. For example, the generating mechanism assumed at level A to justify the estimation method may not coincide with the actual data-generation process, so that the supposedly optimal estimator transpires to be poor in practice. Nevertheless, given any econometric issue, such as modelling the investment behaviour of firms, we need a method for estimating the unknown parameters in the model, and level B will be concerned with that problem. Unfortunately, this case is still unrealistic: the assertion that the die is known to remain the same throughout time and has six faces each with different numbers corresponds to a level of knowledge well beyond what we can hope to achieve in economics. Applied econometric problems correspond more closely to the next level.

1.8.3 Modelling theory

Here we know that there is a die with some numbers on it, and from a set of observed outcomes, we are asked to find the probability p of observing a $\{6\}$. This is a difficult problem to solve, because we do not know how many faces the die has, how often the number 6 occurs on the faces of that die, whether it is biased, whether successive rolls are independent or are even conducted in the same way each time, and so on. The only strategy is to record all the numbers that appear when the die is rolled; build and estimate a model of the behaviour of the die from that string of information; and compute the probability of observing $\{6\}$ from the model. This is a modelling problem, and is analogous to the practical problems confronted in empirical econometrics. We do not know if an investment function exists, nor what it should look like, although we can draw on earlier research by economists who formulated theories of investment, and econometricians who built empirical models of investment behaviour. If an assumption of rationality on the part of economic agents is approximately valid, we can reduce the range of possibilities to be examined. However, due to technical difficulties, there is a dearth of realistic stochastic, dynamic theoretical models, and so the empirical modelling problem is hard.

Most empirical econometric evidence falls under level C. It is difficult to build useful models of unknown data-generating mechanisms but this already slightly hopeless situation does not reflect all the troubles with model building. Generally, we want econometric models in order to predict what will happen in situations beyond the data under analysis, including future situations (forecasting), and potential changes in policy (counterfactual analysis). That leads us to the fourth level.

1.8.4 Forecasting theory

If the die still exists, what is the probability of getting $\{6\}$ on the next roll? The die might have changed shape from when the probabilities were estimated in the pre-prediction period, or the numbers on the faces may have switched, as may have the probabilities of observing each face. Since the probability process is not known, we cannot know that we are predicting the same entity as was modelled earlier. Nevertheless, models that capture the actual invariants of economic decisions, perhaps by modelling the process of change *en route*, will sustain prediction and are discussed in Chapter 14 (forecasting is considered in Clements and Hendry, 1994). Chapter 16 illustrates this situation with a model of money demand under financial innovation.

1.8.5 The origins of the methodological crisis

There was almost a consensus about econometric modelling methodology in the 1950s and 1960s. First, an economic theory would be formulated, based on optimization by the relevant economic agents, given their assumed constraints and information sets. The economic theory would involve variables with names like consumption, income, inflation, and so on, and a mathematical model of that theory would be developed. An error term was then added to the model to reflect the inexactness of the theory. A research assistant or investigator would collect data series with the same names as the theory variables and calculate a few (or a few hundred!) regressions. Finally, from the small number of regressions presented by the research assistant, or sifted by the investigator, the one which seemed to best suit the prior intuition of the principal investigator was selected and published as, say, the consumption function. Systems of such equations comprised 'structural models', which purported to characterize the structure of agents' decision taking.

A structural model is most useful when the world changes, since extrapolation is adequate when the world is constant. When the oil crisis occurred in 1973(4), many econometric models 'broke down' in that they failed to forecast accurately for a wide range of economic variables. We are not concerned with whether the oil crisis itself could be forecasted, but with the failure of models to correctly track the data after the occurrence became an historical fact. Because the earlier paradigm did not seem to work when it was most needed, that episode of predictive failure led to a rethinking of econometric methodology.

In retrospect, the consensus operated only at levels A and B. At level A, economists formulated an economic probability model of (say) consumers' behaviour. That delivered a number of unknown parameters, equivalent in our analogy to the probability p of obtaining $\{6\}$. Next, they scanned econometrics textbooks, such as Johnston (1963), Goldberger (1964), or Theil (1971) to find the recipe that applied to their probability problem. Then they input the data to the relevant algorithm and estimated the unknown parameters (level B). The results were compared to the initial theory and the analysis was terminated if the estimates corroborated the theory, or the model was revised otherwise.

Unfortunately, large shocks can alter the relationship between a model and the pre-existing probability structure of the economic mechanism, and may affect the existence of some of the entities in econometric models. Only those models which embodied aspects of the economy which were invariant to the changes induced by the oil crisis could have forecasted accurately. We will discuss prediction under changed states of nature in Part III (level C). To discover the invariants necessary to sustain such prediction, we must first analyse model building and its underlying concepts: developing that aspect comprises most of Part I (level A). As an intermediate step, to build empirical models we also need to estimate any unknown parameters and test conjectures about their values: that topic is covered in Part II (level B). Many textbooks focus 60–70 per cent on level B, 10–20 per cent on level A, and reserve only a little space for levels C and D: moreover, they mainly analyse mathematical-statistical problems, not empirical-discovery problems. In this book, about 40 per cent will be devoted to level A, and about 30 per cent to each of levels B and C, focusing on econometric modelling. As noted above, level D is analysed in a separate book.

However, to understand modelling, estimation, or inference, we must begin by assuming a probability structure and so must first conjecture the data-generation process in economics. This is a crucial difficulty which prevents our following the logical order A $\rightarrow$ B $\rightarrow$ C $\rightarrow$ D: the relevant probability theory is unclear given that the economic mechanism is unknown. There is a circularity problem, in that until we solve modelling problems and discover the processes that generate economic data, we cannot derive the probabilities of events, and hence cannot know how to appropriately estimate the unknown parameters in any given model. Consequently, we must proceed iteratively, stopping at every stage to ascertain what was learnt from each empirical model about the mechanism, and hence whether the original probability model was adequate to explain the evidence. We will now loop round once on the basis of a few representative economic time series, noting the concepts needed to describe their behaviour, and sketching the approach which embodies the ingredients to be developed in later chapters.

1.9 Some economic time series

While almost any conceivable graph of a variable over time is possible in economics, many economic time series have similar characteristics, a feature we will exploit to guide the first formulation of a data-generating mechanism. Some of the data are from published statistical sources about actual economies, while others are computer-generated data, having nothing to do with any existing economy. This is intended to illustrate the ability of present formulations to generate data series that resemble economic time series in many respects.

The notation is as follows: L denotes log (logarithm to base e); Δ denotes difference; P denotes price; M denotes money, and so LM is log(money). Letting lower-case letters denote logs, $\Delta LM = \log M_t - \log M_{t-1} = \Delta m_t$. Also, Δp_t is equivalent to $\Delta_1 p_t$, and $\Delta_4 p_t = p_t - p_{t-4}$, which is annual inflation when the base frequency is quarterly. A useful property of the log-transform (matching the result that $\partial \log X / \partial X = 1/X$) is that $100\Delta m_t$ is the percentage change in M_t to a local approximation because:

$$\Delta \log M_t = \log \left(M_t/M_{t-1}\right) = \log \left(1 + \Delta M_t/M_{t-1}\right) \simeq \Delta M_t/M_{t-1}.$$

Since the change in the log is inversely proportional to the level, a hundred times small differences in the vertical axis units in graphs of the logs of economic variables are interpretable in terms of percentage changes.

Figures 1.2a–d respectively show the graphs of $\{LM,\ LP\}$; $\{\Delta LM,\ \Delta LP\}$; C cross-plotted against Y (the first is artificial data generated on a computer, whereas the second is UK real income); and the annual rates of inflation in the US and from artificial data (can you tell which is which?). Each time-series graph is matched to have the same means to highlight the relationships between the series.

Four general features of many economic time series can be seen from these graphs:

(i) many economic time series are smooth when graphed in levels;
(ii) but look somewhat erratic when graphed in changes;
(iii) there is often an apparent linear trend in the level;
(iv) whereas the changes are less trending, if at all.

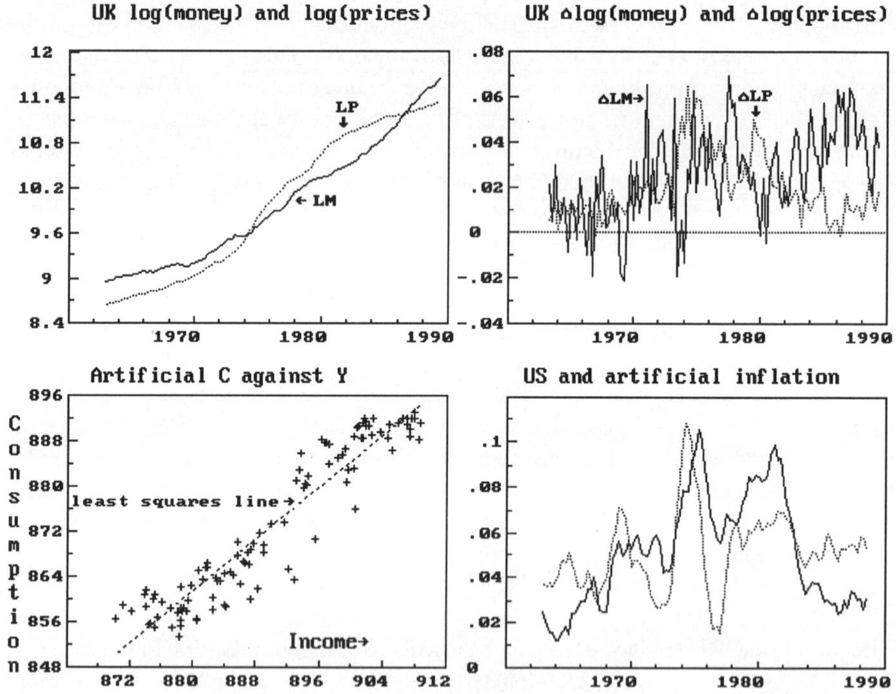

Fig. 1.2 UK, US and artificial time series

Smooth and trending variables tend to have high sample correlations, whether or not they are connected causally. For example, Fig. 1.2c shows the cross-plot of two unconnected series, namely an artificial series mimicking consumption and the actual UK aggregate income series. Nevertheless, these two variables have a high sample correlation. As a second example, Fig. 1.2d records US quarterly inflation at an annual rate (i.e. a variable of the form $\Delta_4 p_t$), together with an artificial series representing a four-period difference. Again, the two series have similar cyclical shapes, and knowledge of US economic history is required to ascertain which series characterized what happened (the solid line shows $\Delta_4 p_t$ for the US). These data series suggest a fifth general feature:

(v) economic time series tend to have high sample correlations with each other.

A further aspect of the graph of $\Delta_4 p_t$ for the UK is shown in Fig. 1.3b: it is neither as erratic as the first difference Δp_t (shown in Fig. 1.3c), nor as smooth as the level p_t in

Fig. 1.3a. If we difference Δp_t again to get the change in the quarterly rate of inflation, namely $\Delta\Delta p_t$ or $\Delta^2 p_t$, we obtain the erratic series shown in Fig. 1.3d, which has no apparent trend. This pattern suggests the two final features of economic time series:

(vi) they are less smooth for single-period than multi-period differencing;
(vii) they are more erratic and less systematic the more times they are differenced.

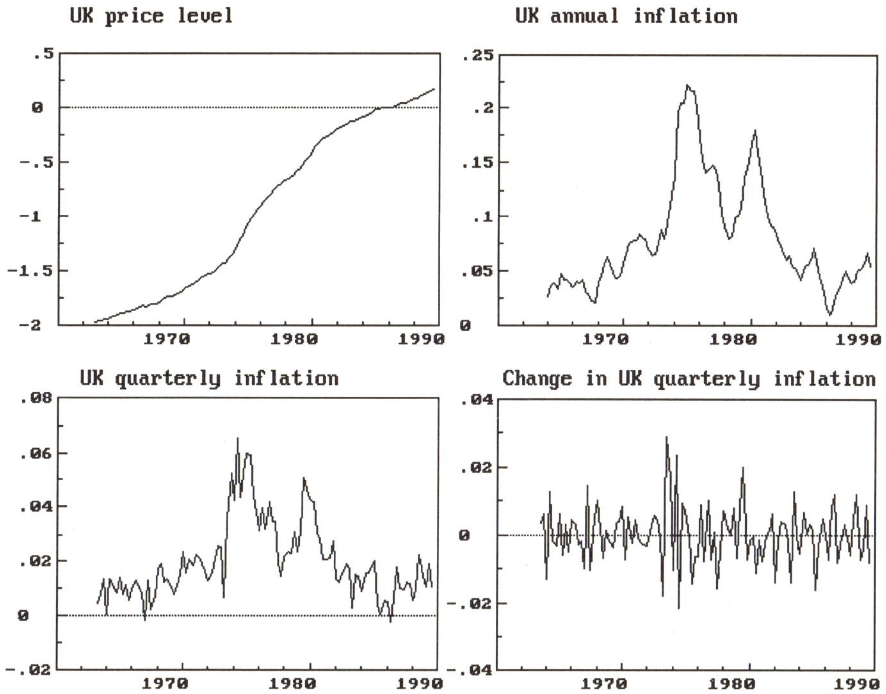

Fig. 1.3 Time series of the UK price level and its differences

While (i)–(vii) are not independent characteristics of economic time series, any putative theory of how such data were generated must be able to replicate these features.

1.10 A first data-generation process

From the above evidence based on a few observed economic time series (at level C) and computer-generated data (at level A so far as the author is concerned), we return to the question: 'What class of data-generation processes should provide the starting point for our theoretical econometric analysis?' Since empirical research must proceed in an iterative cycle, we first conjecture a potentially relevant probability process as the mechanism that generated the data. Given that probability process, we derive estimators for any unknown parameters in models of the process, then estimate some models using the resulting methods. These models may suggest that we began from the wrong generating mechanism, in which case we return to revise our ideas about that conjectured process; or the results may be consistent with our initial mechanism, in which case we continue. Empirical modelling keeps cycling through such a process until it achieves internal consistency, such that the probability model delivers an inference method, which, when applied to a modelling problem, delivers empirical models at level C which resemble the mechanism initially assumed at level A. Convergence is not assured, and even if it occurs, does not guarantee that the resulting framework is correct in any sense, although an internally inconsistent approach is even less appetizing.

We start with a simple equation for our first data-generation process (abbreviated to its acronym DGP below), known as a random walk with drift:

$$\Delta y_t = \alpha + \epsilon_t \quad \text{where} \quad \epsilon_t \sim \mathsf{IN}\left[0, \sigma_\epsilon^2\right] \quad \text{for} \quad t = 1, \ldots, T. \tag{1.1}$$

In (1.1), α is a constant and $\epsilon_t \sim \mathsf{IN}\left[0, \sigma_\epsilon^2\right]$ denotes that $\{\epsilon_t\}$ is an independently sampled, normally distributed random variable with mean zero and variance σ_ϵ^2, so that:

$$\mathsf{E}\left[\epsilon_t\right] = 0, \ \mathsf{E}\left[\epsilon_t^2\right] = \sigma_\epsilon^2 \quad \text{and} \quad \mathsf{E}\left[\epsilon_t \epsilon_s\right] = 0 \ \forall t \neq s, \tag{1.2}$$

where $\mathsf{E}\left[\cdot\right]$ denotes an expectation. An $\mathsf{IN}\left[0, \sigma_\epsilon^2\right]$ process is also white noise (by analogy with the interference which can mask radio reception), defined more precisely in Chapter 2. For a given value of α, (1.1) generates Δy_t by randomly sampling ϵ_t from $\mathsf{IN}\left[0, \sigma_\epsilon^2\right]$.

To interpret (1.1), let y_t denote $\log Y_t$ so that α is the average growth rate of Y_t, and $100\sigma_\epsilon$ is the percentage standard deviation of Y around Y_{t-1}. When $\alpha = 0$, $\{\Delta y_t\}$ is white noise and hence erratic, comparable to the first-difference inflation measure; when $\alpha \neq 0$, $\{\Delta y_t\}$ varies randomly around α, and does not trend. Thus, (1.1) satisfies two of the four general features noted in §1.9, namely (ii) and (iv).

To investigate the properties of the level of y_t from (1.1), first undo the difference:

$$y_t = y_{t-1} + \alpha + \epsilon_t. \tag{1.3}$$

When $\alpha = 0$, the level of y_t moves randomly from its preceding value in either direction depending on ϵ_t, in units determined by σ_ϵ; if $\alpha \neq 0$, y_t also drifts in one direction or the other depending on the sign of α (hence the name of the process). By solving backwards in time by repeated substitution, until the initial time period (denoted zero), we have:

$$\begin{aligned} y_t &= y_{t-2} + 2\alpha + \epsilon_t + \epsilon_{t-1} \\ &= y_{t-3} + 3\alpha + \epsilon_t + \epsilon_{t-1} + \epsilon_{t-2} \\ &= \cdots \\ &= y_0 + \alpha t + \sum_{j=1}^{t} \epsilon_j. \end{aligned} \tag{1.4}$$

The present level y_t is equal to the initial condition y_0, plus a linear deterministic trend with coefficient α, plus the sum of all past errors. Cumulating the errors will make them smooth, so y_t will be smooth also, and will trend when $\alpha \neq 0$. Thus, (1.1) satisfies

§1.9 (i), (iii), and consequently (v). Accumulating pure random numbers over time, as in (1.4), smooths them and induces properties like those of economic variables, including §1.9 (v), so it will be difficult to determine from casual inspection of data evidence which series are genuinely connected, and which merely have similar time patterns (see Hendry, 1980, for an example using cumulative rainfall and the price level). By way of terminology, when a time series has a representation like (1.4), it is said to be integrated of first order, denoted $\mathsf{I}(1)$. The first difference Δy_t in (1.1) is integrated of order zero denoted $\mathsf{I}(0)$ (see Ch.2).

Extending the second line of (1.4) by one further lag:

$$\Delta_4 y_t = \sum_{i=0}^{3} \Delta y_{t-i} = 4\alpha + \epsilon_t + \epsilon_{t-1} + \epsilon_{t-2} + \epsilon_{t-3},$$

and hence $\Delta_4 y_t$ will be a rather smooth time series, like the fourth difference measure of inflation above, so (1.1) also satisfies §1.9 (vi). Finally, $\Delta^2 y_t = \Delta\epsilon_t$ will be very erratic, in the sense that it will alternate rapidly between positive and negative values, so §1.9 (vii) could be characterized as well by (1.1). Since the mechanism in (1.1) could generate data with the seven general features §1.9 (i)–(vii), it provides a potentially viable DGP despite its simplicity, and hence will constitute our initial level-A process. We first assume that economic data are characterized by the mechanism in (1.1), investigate their probability structure given that (1.1) is the level-A mechanism, then examine the properties of procedures applied to such time series. While the results contradict the assumed DGP, (1.1) provides a good start.

First, we derive the statistical properties of $\{\Delta y_t\}$ given (1.1):

$$\mathsf{E}[\Delta y_t] = \alpha, \tag{1.5}$$

and hence:

$$\mathsf{E}\left[(\Delta y_t - \alpha)^2\right] = \mathsf{E}\left[\epsilon_t^2\right] = \sigma_\epsilon^2 = \mathsf{V}[\Delta y_t], \tag{1.6}$$

where $\mathsf{V}[\cdot]$ denotes the variance. Further, there is no temporal dependence in $\{\Delta y_t\}$ since the autocovariances are defined by:

$$\mathsf{C}[\Delta y_t, \Delta y_{t-s}] = \mathsf{E}[(\Delta y_t - \alpha)(\Delta y_s - \alpha)] = \mathsf{E}[\epsilon_t \epsilon_s] = 0 \quad \text{for} \quad t \neq s. \tag{1.7}$$

Autocorrelations are defined by:

$$\mathsf{r}_s = \mathsf{corr}(\Delta y_t, \Delta y_{t-s}) = \frac{\mathsf{C}[\Delta y_t, \Delta y_{t-s}]}{\sqrt{\mathsf{V}[\Delta y_t]\,\mathsf{V}[\Delta y_{t-s}]}} \tag{1.8}$$

so from (1.6) and (1.7), these are all zero as well. Since $\Delta y_t - \alpha = \epsilon_t \sim \mathsf{IN}\left[0, \sigma_\epsilon^2\right]$, we deduce that $\Delta y_t \sim \mathsf{IN}\left[\alpha, \sigma_\epsilon^2\right]$.

Next, from the representation in levels in (1.4), taking y_0 as a fixed number:

$$\mathsf{E}[y_t] = y_0 + \alpha t, \tag{1.9}$$

and hence $\mathsf{V}[y_t] = \mathsf{E}\left[(y_t - y_0 - \alpha t)^2\right]$ is given by:

$$\mathsf{V}[y_t] = \mathsf{E}\left[\left(\sum_{j=1}^{t} \epsilon_j\right)^2\right] = \mathsf{E}\left[\sum_{i=1}^{t}\sum_{j=1}^{t} \epsilon_i \epsilon_j\right] = \sum_{i=1}^{t}\sum_{j=1}^{t} \mathsf{E}[\epsilon_i \epsilon_j] = \sum_{j=1}^{t} \mathsf{E}\left[\epsilon_j^2\right] = \sigma_\epsilon^2 t. \tag{1.10}$$

Also, the covariance $\mathsf{C}[y_t, y_s] = \mathsf{E}[(y_t - y_0 - \alpha t)(y_s - y_0 - \alpha s)]$ is:

$$\mathsf{C}[y_t, y_s] = \mathsf{E}\left[\sum_{i=1}^{t}\sum_{j=1}^{s} \epsilon_i \epsilon_j\right] = \sum_{j=1}^{s} \mathsf{E}\left[\epsilon_j^2\right] = \sigma_\epsilon^2 s \; \forall t > s. \tag{1.11}$$

Finally:

$$\mathsf{corr}^2(y_t, y_{t-1}) = \frac{\{\mathsf{C}[y_t, y_{t-1}]\}^2}{\mathsf{V}[y_t]\,\mathsf{V}[y_{t-1}]} = \frac{\{\sigma_\epsilon^2 (t-1)\}^2}{\sigma_\epsilon^2 t \sigma_\epsilon^2 (t-1)} = 1 - \frac{1}{t}. \tag{1.12}$$

Similarly, $\mathsf{corr}^2(y_t, y_{t-k})$ has a numerator of $\sigma_\epsilon^2(t-k)^2$ and a denominator of $\sigma_\epsilon^2 t(t-k)$ and hence equals $1 - (k/t)$. When $k < 0$, let $s = t - k$ so $t = s + k$, and $r = -k > 0$, in which case:

$$\mathsf{corr}^2(y_t, y_{t-k}) = \mathsf{corr}^2(y_{s+k}, y_s) = \mathsf{corr}^2(y_s, y_{s-r}) = 1 - \frac{r}{s} = 1 + \frac{k}{(t-k)}. \tag{1.13}$$

To summarize, both the mean and the variance of y_t trend over time, and successive y_t are highly interdependent, with autocovariances of a similar magnitude to the variance. Finally, because $\{y_t\}$ is the sum of a large number of errors, even if these were non-normal, $\{y_t - y_0 - \alpha t\}$ would be approximately normally distributed, despite being $\mathsf{I}(1)$ from (1.4). Overall, $\{y_t\}$ has a complicated probability structure despite the simplicity of the initially postulated DGP in (1.1).

Before developing statistical procedures based on treating (1.1) as the DGP (at level A), we must critically appraise the empirical relevance of (1.1) viewed as a model for data at level C. The first issue is the role of the initial conditions and their treatment as fixed at y_0. Second, (1.4) entails that shocks to the level of y never die out, whatever their source and whenever they occurred, which need not be realistic. Third, α is assumed constant over time but empiricall may not be. Fourth, the assumption that ϵ_t is $\mathsf{IN}[\cdot]$, and that the parameters of that distribution are constant over time, must be viewed sceptically. Last, when y_t is the actual value Y_t of an economic variable, rather than the logarithm of Y_t, then σ_ϵ is in the same absolute units as Y. From (1.10), the ratio of σ_ϵ^2 to the variance of Y_t would tend to zero over time, so the process would eventually have a negligibly small percentage standard error. Under the interpretation that $y_t = \log Y_t$, however, σ_ϵ could remain constant over time, yet the process in (1.1) would still be stochastic. Since many economic variables are inherently positive, we often interpret data and DGPs in terms of logs of the original variables. We will analyse each of these five issues in more detail in due course, though not in the order just noted.

As an illustration of investigating the validity of the assumptions in (1.1) when applied at level C, consider the third issue: is α constant? This example also highlights the dichotomy with which we began. If α is non-constant, the assumed DGP will not be a useful starting point for investigating the probability structure of data-generation processes, since we would have the wrong mechanism from which to deduce probabilities. Let us inspect quarterly UK money growth (Δm_t) to see the extent to which its α is constant. When α is constant and (1.1) actually generated Δy_t, then the equation for regressing Δy_t on a constant, which calculates the mean of Δy_t over the selected sample period, should be the same for every sub-sample. For the whole sample, from (1.1):

$$\hat{\alpha} = T^{-1} \sum_{t=1}^{T} \Delta y_t = \alpha + T^{-1} \sum_{t=1}^{T} \epsilon_t \tag{1.14}$$

so that $\hat{\alpha} \sim \mathsf{N}\left[\alpha, T^{-1}\sigma_\epsilon^2\right]$. Using the full sample of $T = 105$ observations from 1963(2)–1989(2) to calculate the parameters of the normal distribution in (1.14) and letting $\underset{e}{\sim}$ denote an estimated distribution, for UK Δm_t we obtain:

$$\hat{\alpha} \underset{e}{\sim} \mathsf{N}\left[0.026, (0.0020)^2\right]. \tag{1.15}$$

We have assumed that ordinary least-squares estimation is a legitimate technique to apply to series like (1.1), and this is easily proved under the hypothesis that (1.1) is the DGP. Next, divide the full sample into n non-overlapping sub-samples where we take $n = 8$; each sub-sample has $T = 13$ (in the last sub-sample $T = 14$) from which to separately estimate α. From the full-sample distribution, the best estimates of $(\alpha, \sigma_\epsilon)$ are (0.026, 0.021) with a 95 per cent confidence interval for α of (0.022, 0.030). Given the theoretical distribution in (1.14) and the estimates in (1.15) applied to $T = 13$, we anticipate that in the ith sub-sample:

$$\hat{\alpha}_i \underset{e}{\sim} \mathsf{N}\left[0.026, (0.00568)^2\right]. \tag{1.16}$$

Thus, 95 per cent of the $\hat{\alpha}_i$ values should lie in the range (0.014, 0.038). The eight sub-sample estimates are shown in Table 1.1. The range is (0.006, 0.045), which covers more than plus or minus three standard deviations based on (1.16), and hence is an unlikely outcome if (1.1) is the DGP. Perhaps more worrying is the evident upward trend in the growth rate of m.

By generalizing this model of the $\{\Delta m_t\}$ data based on that last comment, a graphical analysis is possible. If (1.1) generates Δy_t, then the coefficients from regressing Δy_t on a constant and a trend should be the same for every sub-sample, and the latter should be zero:

$$\Delta y_t = \alpha + \beta t + \epsilon_t \text{ where } \beta = 0. \tag{1.17}$$

The reason for adding the parameter β in (1.17) is to allow cross-plots of Δy_t against t (see Fig. 1.4 below). Later, we will develop more formal tests for coefficients being constant (which also reject the hypothesis that α is constant) but, for the present, the

Table 1.1 Sub-sample estimates

Sample	$\hat{\alpha}$	$100(\hat{\sigma}_\epsilon/\sqrt{T})$
1	0.010	0.34
2	0.006	0.47
3	0.028	0.48
4	0.025	0.72
5	0.035	0.48
6	0.019	0.36
7	0.036	0.37
8	0.045	0.39

graphical illustration suffices. When the trend is included in (1.17), then regression theory implies that for $T = 13$:

$$\tilde{\alpha} \sim \mathsf{N}\left[\alpha,\ \frac{2\,(2T+1)}{T\,(T-1)}\ \sigma_\epsilon^2\right] \underset{e}{\sim} \mathsf{N}\left[0.026, (0.0124)^2\right], \tag{1.18}$$

since $\sum_{t=1}^{T} t = ½T(T+1)$ and $\sum_{t=1}^{T} t^2 = ⅙T(T+1)(2T+1)$, when (1.1) is the DGP (so $\beta = 0$). The numerical estimates use (1.15) for α and σ_ϵ^2, so that the anticipated 95 per cent range for estimated α_i is $(0.001, 0.051)$. Figure 1.4 shows the full-sample cross-plot of Δm_t against a trend and reveals an apparently statistically significant upward trend:

$$\widehat{\Delta m_t} = \underset{(0.0035)}{0.0070} + \underset{(0.00006)}{0.00035}t \tag{1.19}$$

where estimated standard errors are shown in parentheses below coefficients. The new 95 per cent confidence interval for α is $(0.000, 0.014)$, which barely intersects that based on (1.15).

When nine sub-sample regressions are estimated as shown in Fig. 1.4c, there are periods with negative trend coefficients (the downward sloping lines on the graph) and periods with positive trend coefficients (the upward sloping lines). Certainly, some variation due to sampling is anticipated, as determined by (1.18), but Figs. 1.4b–d seem to reveal more than random variation: the range of the estimated α_i is $(-0.093, 0.226)$, which again suggests that the claimed DGP in (1.1) is not an adequate mechanism for this time series.

It is essential to be clear about what has, and has not, been established by demonstrating that the empirical outcome is inconsistent with the DGP assumptions. We have not shown that $\alpha = \mathsf{E}[\Delta y_t]$ is in fact non-constant, since there are many potential explanations for the apparent non-constancy of the estimated intercept in the above regressions. Equally, we have not established the existence of a trend in the $\{\Delta m_t\}$ process, since (1.19) itself may be an invalid model of the DGP (for example, the residuals are autocorrelated, so the quoted standard errors are incorrect). Those implications highlight a difficulty for any constructive methodology: a contradiction between a model and the postulated mechanism may arise for many reasons, some of which might never be discovered.

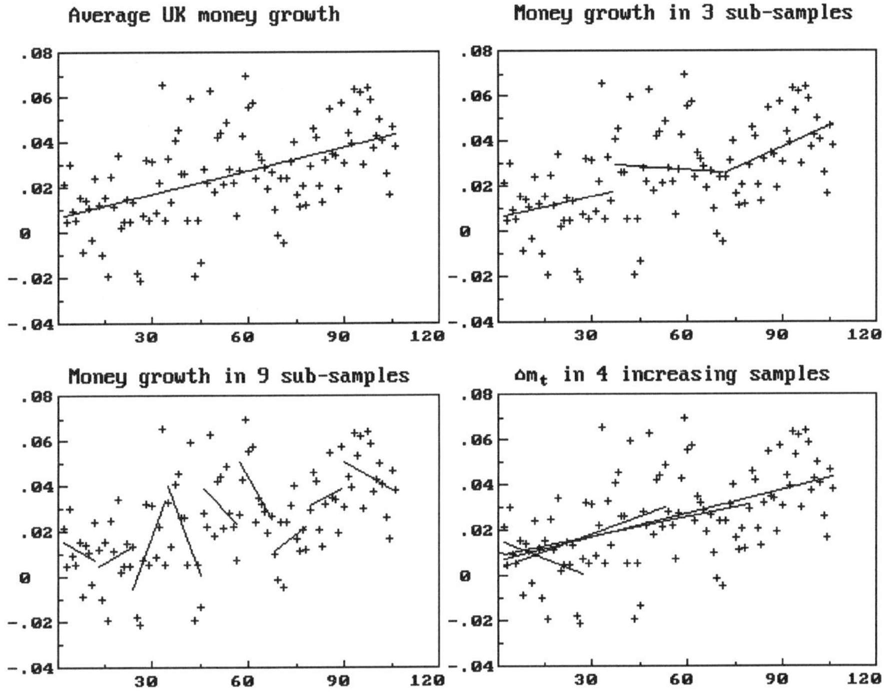

Fig. 1.4 UK money growth in different sub-samples

Conversely, by demonstrating a contradiction between the assumed constancy of α in (1.1) and the excessive variation in estimates of α across sub-samples, we have shown that (1.1) is not fully adequate as a DGP, thereby illustrating the validity of a destructive methodology. Either way, in order to progress we must generalize the DGP to allow for whatever phenomena induced the above contradiction, which will require a creative contribution and constitutes our value added as researchers.

1.11 Empirical models as derived entities

Econometrics is sometimes viewed as the economics equivalent of experimental control. In such a framework, it is argued that although economists primarily obtain non-experimental data, the impact of uncontrolled variables can be removed after the event by partialling out their effects using techniques like multiple regression and its many sophisticated derivatives (see Wold, 1969). In a laboratory experiment, controlling an effect *ex ante* or recording its values and then removing its influence *ex post* by an appropriate analysis can produce nearly equivalent outcomes. However, that approach to econometrics requires that all relevant uncontrolled effects are measured and removed: since a major objective of econometric analyses is to determine what factors are relevant, there seems little hope of attaining that requirement. Indeed, econometrics textbooks often devote much space to investigating the consequences of various mis-specifications, without much positive advice except 'think of the correct model at the outset'. So long as doubt persists over the relevance of variables, any given effect which might matter in reality can be removed by adding enough other variables which proxy the correct influences, or made to seem central even if irrelevant (see Ch.15).

Imagine that you are a physicist, conducting an experiment with a cyclotron to find out whether quarks remain linked despite impacts from high energy particles. Collide some massive particles with target particles and observe an image of what occurs. In such a situation, what the image records is determined by the properties of the experiment conducted. The output is caused by the inputs, and the experimental process can be treated as if it is a mechanism in that the data are generated by the experiment conducted. We can express that last statement in the form:

$$\underset{\text{output}}{y_t} = \underset{\text{input}}{f(z_t)} + \underset{\text{perturbation}}{\nu_t} \tag{1.20}$$

where y_t is the observed outcome of the experiment when z_t is the experimental input, $f(\cdot)$ is the mapping from input to output, and ν_t is a small, random perturbation which varies between experiments conducted at the same values of z. This equation holds in the sense that given the same inputs $\{z_t\}$, repeating the experiment will generate essentially the same outputs: otherwise the experimental outcome could not be replicated. The important point is that the causation is going from the right-hand side to the left-hand side in (1.20).

Econometric models in which the outputs are generated by the inputs can be constructed at either level A or level B, but if (1.20) is invoked at level C, then the model is being claimed to be the data-generation process. To apply the logic used by physicists (say) to the empirical analysis of data in econometrics requires the omniscient assumption that the model is the mechanism which generated the data. In economics, we do not know how the data were actually generated, and we do not control the economy in the way that a physical scientist can control an experiment. Indeed, we will probably never know how economic data are generated. Consequently, although econometric equations might look identical to (1.20), there must be a fundamental difference since the model could not be the DGP. Rather, in the econometric model:

$$\underset{\text{observed}}{y_t} = \underset{\text{explanation}}{g(z_t)} + \underset{\text{remainder}}{\epsilon_t} \tag{1.21}$$

so the left-hand side is determining the right, rather than the other way round. Essentially, (1.21) shows that y_t can be decomposed into two components, namely $g(z_t)$ (the part which we can explain) and ϵ_t (the part which we cannot explain). Such a separation is feasible even when y_t does not in fact depend on $g(z_t)$, but instead depends on completely different factors $h(x_t)$, say. In econometrics, we should write:

$$\epsilon_t = y_t - g(z_t) \tag{1.22}$$

to describe the way models function at level C, since we do not know how y_t is generated and hence cannot know that $g(z_t)$ actually generated y_t. We interpret (1.22) as follows: whatever we do on the right-hand side of the equation by way of changing the specification of $g(z_t)$ or the measurement of y_t, the left-hand side ϵ_t is derived as a result. In contrast to the process $\{\nu_t\}$ in (1.20), $\{\epsilon_t\}$ in (1.21) does not arise as a random drawing from nature: it is merely what is left over from y_t after extracting $g(z_t)$. To base econometric modelling on the 'input causes output' formulation in (1.20) is to apply a result which is valid at level A (where the mechanism is known) to data at level C (where the mechanism is unknown). That can be an egregious mistake in empirical econometrics, where the structure of the DGP is probably much more complicated than the model.

The theory of reduction developed in Part I explains how to analyse data in a non-experimental world where ϵ_t is derived, and hence reflects everything omitted from the model, including all the mistakes in formulating $g(\cdot)$ or selecting z. Nevertheless, we can still construct a coherent and useful theory of econometrics and this book develops the relevant concepts and structures. The conventional tools of regression analysis, testing procedures, and so on are still needed, but they play different roles and will be given different explanations, derived from the theory of reduction.

Before exploring that route, however, we must consider a number of concepts which are prerequisites to the econometric analysis; more complete explanations of many of these will be presented in later chapters, but preliminary formulations are presented in Chapter 2 to advance the discussion.

1.12 Exercises

1.1 Load the data in the DATA files. Graph the four variables *CONS*, *INC*, *INFLAT*, and *OUTPUT* (these were generated on a computer).

(a) Calculate the means, standard deviations, and the inter-correlations of the four variables. Knowing that each of the variables (x_t say) is $100 \log X_t$ when X_t is the generated variable: (i) interpret the standard deviations; (ii) discuss the inter-correlations between the variables.

(b) What aspect of the graph of each time series does the numerical value of the data standard deviation reflect (i.e. trend, variation about the mean, etc.)?

(c) Calculate $\Delta x_t = x_t - x_{t-1}$ (the percentage growth rate) for each variable and repeat (a). Contrast the various results with those for the levels. Are the Δx_t results easier to interpret? If so, explain why? If not, why are the levels easier?

(d) Repeat (a), (b), (c) for the two sub-periods: (i) up to 1973(4); and (ii) from 1974(1) onwards. Reinterpret the earlier results.

1.2 Repeat exercise 1.1 for the data-set in the computer file UKM1 which comprises quarterly, seasonally adjusted data on the four variables M_t, Y_t, P_t, and R_t for the UK over 1960(1)–1988(2), where these relate to nominal measures of the transactions money stock, total final expenditure, the implicit deflator of *TFE*, and the opportunity cost of holding M1.

1.3 Is it useful to distinguish model construction from destruction? Provide one example in favour of such a dichotomy and one example against. Would the distinction be useful if (1.20) characterized econometric modelling?

1.4 Equations (1.7) and (1.11) define the autocovariances of the processes $\{\Delta y_t\}$ and $\{y_t\}$ respectively. Explain why these differ so markedly. For one of the money stock series, calculate the autcorrelation $\mathsf{corr}(y_t, y_{t-1})$. Next, calculate the residuals y_t^* from regressing your choice of variable on t and calculate $\mathsf{corr}(y_t^*, y_{t-1}^*)$. How similar are these (auto)correlations? How do they compare to that for $\mathsf{corr}(\Delta y_t, \Delta y_{t-1})$? What do you deduce about the impact of 'detrending'?

1.5 The data listed below are a subset of the whole period of UKM1. One forecast for 1972(2) is retained (see (d) below). The data are for the logarithm (to base e) of holdings of narrow money M1 (the log of M1 is denoted by m) and income (y) in the UK over the sample period 1969(4)–1972(1) in constant prices (i.e. deflated by the implicit deflator P for income):

year	qtr	$m-p$	y
1969	4	10.564	10.756
1970	1	10.547	10.744
1970	2	10.562	10.765
1970	3	10.546	10.772
1970	4	10.550	10.783
1971	1	10.588	10.763
1971	2	10.574	10.788
1971	3	10.577	10.806
1971	4	10.613	10.809
1972	1	10.636	10.796
Mean		10.576	10.778
Variance		0.000876	0.000475
Covariance $[(m-p), y]$		0.000391	

(a) Plot the data and calculate the regression of $(m-p)$ on y and a constant using only the summary statistics on means, variances and the covariance (i.e. do it by hand!).

(b) Explain how to test the hypothesis that the log of the velocity of circulation (i.e., $p+y-m$) does not depend on income.

(c) Critically evaluate the assumptions underlying both the estimates and the test in (b), explaining how you would assess the validity of at least four of the necessary assumptions.

(d) The data for 1972(2) are $(m-p) = 10.663$, $y = 10.813$. Comment on your results in the light of this information.

(Adapted from Oxford M.Phil. Qualifying Examination)

1.6 By using the fact that $\boldsymbol{A}^{-1}\boldsymbol{A} = \boldsymbol{I}$, prove the claim that:

$$\begin{pmatrix} T & \frac{1}{2}T(T+1) \\ \frac{1}{2}T(T+1) & \frac{1}{6}T(T+1)(2T+1) \end{pmatrix}^{-1} = \begin{pmatrix} \frac{2(2T+1)}{T(T-1)} & -\frac{6}{T(T-1)} \\ -\frac{6}{T(T-1)} & \frac{12}{T(T+1)(T-1)} \end{pmatrix}.$$

Hence derive the distribution in (1.18).

2

Econometric Concepts

This chapter introduces a number of the main concepts needed to understand empirical modelling of economic time series: parameter and parameter space; constancy; structure; distributional shape; identification and observational equivalence; interdependence; stochastic process; conditioning; white noise; autocorrelation; stationarity; integratedness; trend; heteroscedasticity; dimensionality; aggregation; and marginalization. Given these concepts, a general formulation of a data-generation process for economics is presented, illustrated by a static solved example. Next, models, mechanisms, and processes are distinguished. A sequential factorization of the joint data density induces an innovation-error representation of the DGP, and introduces martingale difference sequences. These concepts help explain how empirical models arise. Autocorrelated generating processes are investigated, and a sequential factorization is shown to implement an important reduction. The strands of analysis are linked to the notion of model design, and illustrated by a dynamic solved example.

2.1 Parameter

A parameter (or parameter vector) is a numerical entity which indexes a process or a density function, and does not alter across realizations of the random variables being studied. We denote parameters by Greek letters $(\alpha, \beta, \mu, \theta, \psi, \ldots)$, and use bold face to denote a vector, so that λ is a scalar whereas $\boldsymbol{\gamma}' = (\gamma_1 \ldots \gamma_n)$ is a $1 \times n$ row vector.

The term coefficient also refers to a numerical entity which remains constant across realizations of random variables, but may vary over time. A coefficient is usually a conjectured parameter in a model, again denoted by a Greek symbol.

A parameter is a point in a parameter space, which delineates the set of admissible values that the parameter can assume. Thus, when the parameter is θ, the parameter space is denoted by Θ, and we write $\theta \in \Theta$ where $\Theta = \{\theta; \forall \text{ admissible } \theta\}$. For example, let $\mathbb{R}$ denote the real line $(-\infty, \infty)$ and $\mathbb{R}_+$ the positive real line $(0, \infty)$, then any value of $\alpha \in \mathbb{R}$ together with any value of $\sigma^2 \in \mathbb{R}_+$ is written as $(\alpha, \sigma^2) \in \mathbb{R} \times \mathbb{R}_+$, where $\times$ denotes the Cartesian product of the two spaces. In many cases, Θ will be a restricted space (e.g. when $|\alpha| < 1$). The point θ_p in Θ that generated the data is called the population parameter.

A process may depend on many scalar parameters, only some of which will be of interest to an investigator. Parameters are of interest if they are uniquely defined (identifiable: see §2.5), constant over historically relevant time periods and across regimes (see §2.2), and interpretable in the light of subject matter theory.

2.2 Constancy

A coefficient α is constant over the time period $\mathcal{T} = \{\ldots, -2, -1, 0, 1, 2, \ldots\}$ if α has the same value for all $t \in \mathcal{T}$. By definition, a parameter must remain constant across realizations of the stochastic process, but we will require that the parameters of an analysis are constant over time as well. This is a fundamental requirement for empirical modelling, and its implications need to be understood. Models which have no set of constancies will be useless for forecasting the future, analysing economic policy, or testing economic theories, since they lack entities on which to base those activities.

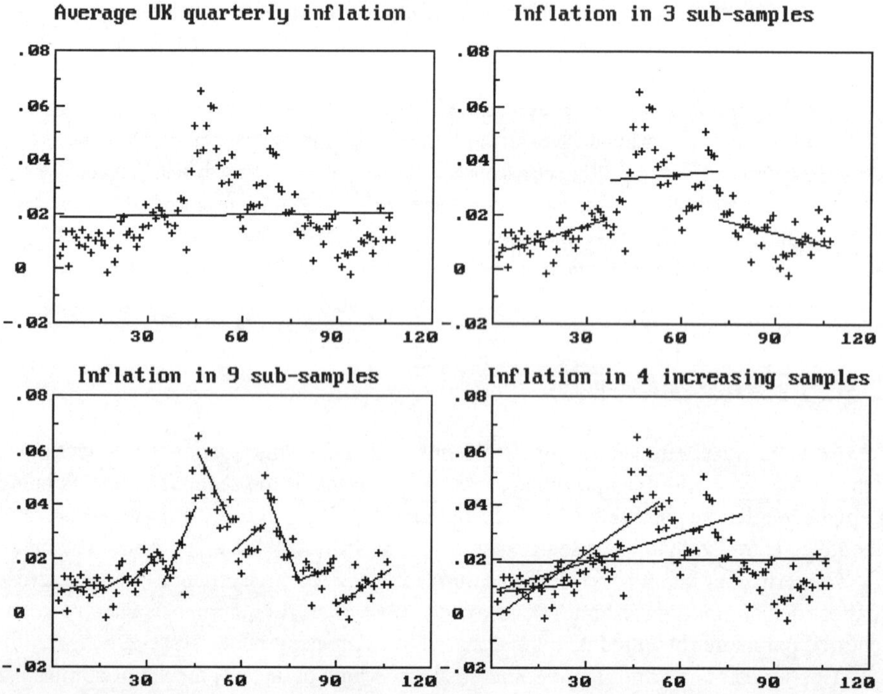

Fig. 2.1 UK inflation

The graph of Δm_t against t in Fig. 1.4 suggested that the equivalent parameter to α in (2.1) was not constant over time. The similar plots for Δp_t shown in Fig. 2.1 for a regression of Δp_t on an intercept and trend reveal that the full-sample trend coefficient is close to zero, but that sub-sample coefficients are not.

When analysing data at level C, we can assert the form of the DGP, but without careful specification of parameters and accounting for previous evidence, a contradiction can ensue between the claimed mechanism and the observable data properties. As an analogy, if it was asserted that a particular die (rolled behind a screen) had six faces and probabilities were calculated using such a model, a seventh number would be a considerable surprise. Although the probability mechanism may have been the same as in earlier rolls, a different model must be used thereafter, refuting model constancy. At least we learn that a crucial aspect of the problem had been omitted.

Models with 'varying coefficients' still have an underlying set of constant parameters which characterize the probability mechanism. For example, when the data are defined for a sample space Ω, let:

$$\alpha_t = \alpha_{t-1} + \nu_t \quad \text{where} \quad \nu_t \sim \mathsf{IN}\left[0, \sigma_\nu^2\right] \quad \text{and} \quad \{\nu_t\} \quad \text{does not depend on } \Omega.$$

This is a random coefficients model, but it has many constant parameters including the constant unit root in the α process, the unchanging functional form, constant zero mean and fixed variance of the distribution of $\{\nu_t\}$, and the constant absence of serial dependence in $\{\nu_t\}$.

2.3 Structure

Structure has many meanings in econometrics. The notion began in Frisch (1934) as (a) the set of exact economic relations which held when data were perfectly measured. Then the concept evolved (b) to describe a system of invariant equations which characterized the behaviour of economic agents (Haavelmo, 1944, and Wold and Juréen, 1953). Later, it came (c) to describe an entity called a structural model which was to be contrasted with a system having derived parameters, called a reduced form, where the former was intended to be interpretable in the light of economic theory. Occasionally, (d) it has been used as a synonym for the population parameter value $\boldsymbol{\theta}_p \in \boldsymbol{\Theta}$ (see Hendry, 1993b for a history; and for recent discussions, see Bårdsen and Fisher, 1993, and Juselius, 1993). Another usage (e) connotes 'being derived from inter-temporal optimization by economic agents', and such a notion of structure often claims to embody the 'deep parameters' of the theory. As an example, consider the equation $\mathsf{E}[y_t] = \beta \mathsf{E}[z_t]$ for $\beta \in \mathbb{R}$. This satisfies sense (a); could satisfy (b), (c) and (e) depending on how agents behave; and when $\beta = \beta_p$, satisfies (d) as well. Conversely, the same equation would fail on (b)–(e) when β is not constant across changes in the process generating z_t, the equation is not the decision function of agents, and $\beta \neq \beta_p$.

A parameter is defined to be invariant to a change in the DGP if it remains constant despite the intervention. A system (or equation) all of whose parameters are invariant is said to be autonomous. We construe structure as the set of basic, permanent features of the economic mechanism. Thus, $\boldsymbol{\theta} \in \boldsymbol{\Theta}$ defines a structure if it is invariant and directly characterizes the relations of the economy under analysis (i.e. is not derived from more basic parameters). The parameters of an economic structure may include those of agents' decision rules, but no presumption is made that these rules are derived by intertemporal optimization. Structure need not be identifiable and entails a correspondence between a model and reality that is not open to independent testing. A number of necessary conditions follow as consequences of this definition — a parameter can be structural only if it is:

(i) constant and so is invariant to an extension of the sample period;
(ii) unaltered by changes elsewhere in the economy and so is invariant to regime shifts; and
(iii) remains the same for extensions of the information set and so is invariant to adding more variables to an analysis.

All of these aspects are open to scrutiny empirically so necessary attributes of structure are testable, even if sufficient ones are not. However, a parameter need not be structural even when it is invariant to all three extensions of information, since it could be derived from the more basic structural parameters. Structural change is said to occur when any element(s) of $\boldsymbol{\theta}$ alter.

One of the aims of econometrics is to discover the autonomous relations which determine economic behaviour although it remains an important and unresolved issue as to whether structure exists. We return to that issue in Part III.

2.4 Distributional shape

Let $\mathsf{D}_{\mathsf{x}}(x_t|\theta)$ denote the distribution of a random variable X_t which depends on the parameter $\theta \in \Theta$, where x_t is an observation on X_t. An important aspect of the consistency of model and mechanism concerns the shape of a random variable's statistical distribution function, and hence the form of the underlying data density. At level A, the functional form of $\mathsf{D}_{\mathsf{x}}(x_t|\theta)$ and the value of the parameter $\theta \in \Theta$ together determine the shape, location, and spread of the distribution. For example, the bell-shaped univariate normal density, denoted above by $\mathsf{N}\left[\mu_x, \sigma_x^2\right]$, is defined by:

$$\mathsf{D}_{\mathsf{x}}\left(x \mid \mu_x, \sigma_x^2\right) = \left(2\pi\sigma_x^2\right)^{-\frac{1}{2}} \exp\left(-\frac{\left[x-\mu_x\right]^2}{2\sigma_x^2}\right),$$

where $\mathsf{E}[X] = \mu_x$ and $\mathsf{V}[X] = \sigma_x^2$.

At level C, such aspects must be postulated in the model specification and checked against the data evidence. The graphs in Fig. 2.2 show the (standardized) histograms of $\{p_t\}$, $\{\Delta_4 p_t\}$, $\{\Delta p_t\}$, and $\{\Delta^2 p_t\}$ each together with an interpolated density function (how the interpolant is calculated is not relevant here: see §A3.6 for details). Both representations reveal a somewhat uniform but perhaps bimodal density for $\{p_t\}$. However, the distribution of the difference $\{\Delta p_t\}$ in Fig. 2.2c is unimodal, nearly symmetric and approximately normal, and $\left\{\Delta^2 p_t\right\}$ comes closest to normality. Thus, normality might be a reasonable characterization of the innovation error driving the time series.

In passing, we see that the same variable can be non-normal in levels yet nearly normal in differences. When $\epsilon_t \sim \mathsf{IN}\left[0, \sigma_\epsilon^2\right]$, the two models:[1]

$$\Delta y_t = \alpha + \epsilon_t \tag{2.1}$$

$$y_t = y_{t-1} + \alpha + \epsilon_t \tag{2.2}$$

are isomorphic in that their parameters are related by a one–one transformation and they have the same error process. Consequently, some other effect must account for non-normal levels. In Δy_t, the effect of y_{t-1} is extracted from y_t, revealing that this period's y deviates from last period's y by an error which is nearly normally distributed. The observed bimodality in y_t can arise when α changes from a lower to a higher value during the sample period, but remains small relative to σ_ϵ. Thus, Δy_t will remain approximately normal, whereas y_t becomes the sum of a normally distributed component $(\sum \epsilon_t)$ and a uniformly distributed component (αt), which is small (large) when α is small (large), so will exhibit bimodality.

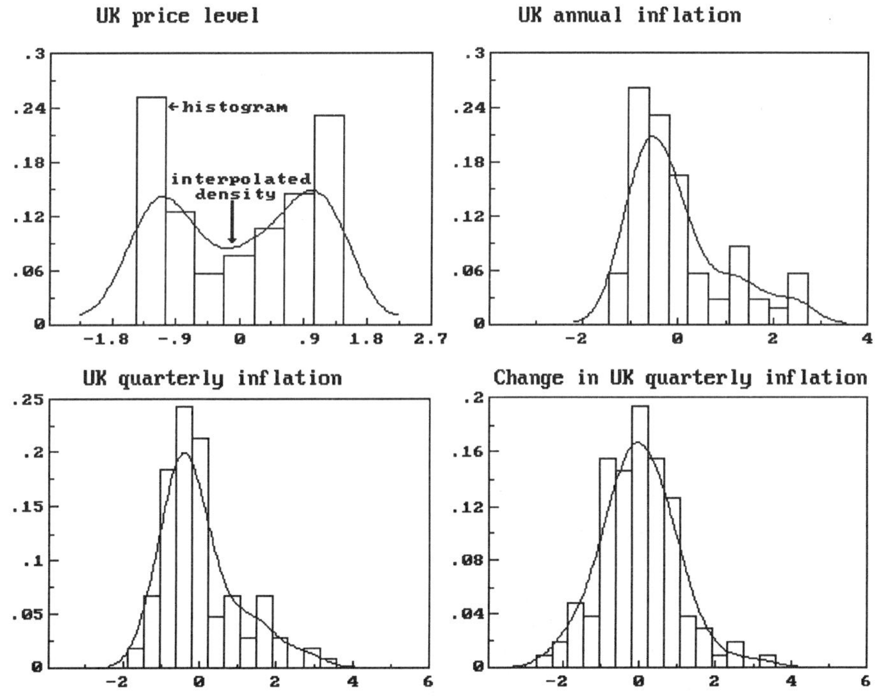

Fig. 2.2 Histograms and densities for aggregate price data

[1] For notational simplicity henceforth, random variables and outcomes will not be explicitly distinguished unless a clear confusion would result.

This explanation can be checked using artificial data. Figure 2.3 shows the histograms and interpolated densities for $\{y_t\}$ and $\{\Delta y_t\}$ generated as in (2.1), but doubling α from 0.05 to 0.10 at the sample mid-point in Figs. 2.3a,b; whereas Figs. 2.3c,d show the corresponding graphs for constant α, with an error which is autocorrelated so that clusters of changes with the same sign occur together. The bimodality of the first graph is pronounced.

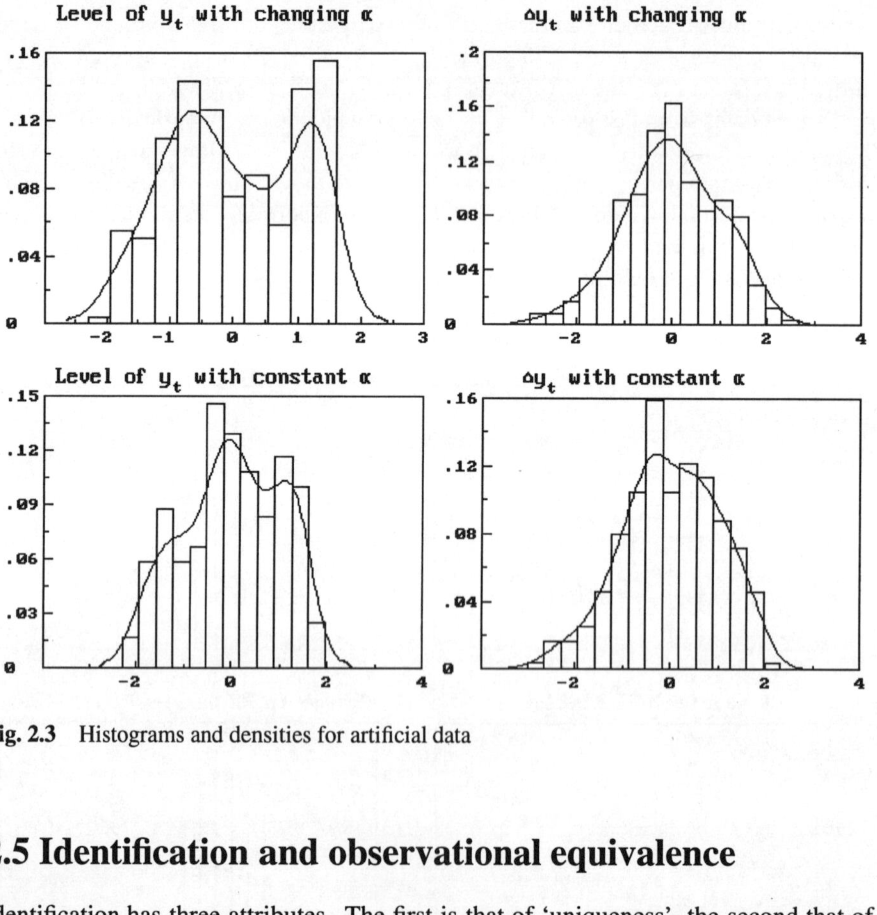

Fig. 2.3 Histograms and densities for artificial data

2.5 Identification and observational equivalence

Identification has three attributes. The first is that of 'uniqueness', the second that of 'correspondence to the desired entity', and the third that of 'satisfying the assumed interpretation (usually of a theory model)'. As an analogy, a regression of quantity on price delivers a unique function of the data second moments, but need not correspond to any underlying demand behaviour, and may be incorrectly interpreted as a supply schedule due to a positive sign on price. The first sense of identification was used in Koopmans (1950a) and is often the sense intended in econometrics. Conditions for the correct interpretation of parameters in the light of a theory model and for the correspondence of parameters between models and DGPs are not easily specified, as they depend on subject matter considerations. In practice, the meaning of 'identified' can be ambiguous as in 'Have you identified the parameters of the money demand function?', so it is important to clarify which attributes are at issue.

At level A, the distribution $\mathsf{D}_{\mathsf{x}}(x_t|\theta)$ must be well defined for clarity of analysis. At level B, to learn about θ from the data requires a mapping from the data to θ. Consequently, both levels require θ to be unique. Let $\theta_1 \in \Theta$ and $\theta_2 \in \Theta$ be two distinct values of the parameter. First, we require there to exist observations x_t for which $\mathsf{D}_{\mathsf{x}}(x_t|\theta_1) \neq \mathsf{D}_{\mathsf{x}}(x_t|\theta_2)$ implies that $\theta_1 \neq \theta_2$. Thus, if a distributional form generates a given x_t with different probabilities, it must be because $\mathsf{D}_{\mathsf{x}}(\cdot)$ has different values of the parameter. In that case, θ is called a sufficient parameter (see Madansky, 1976).

Secondly, if $\theta_1 \neq \theta_2$ (different numerical values of the same parameter) implies that there are observations x_t for which $\mathsf{D}_{\mathsf{x}}(x_t|\theta_1) \neq \mathsf{D}_{\mathsf{x}}(x_t|\theta_2)$, then θ is (uniquely) identifiable. Thus, it is possible to identify which parameter value generated the data when different parameters lead to different event probabilities. Uniqueness is a fundamental requirement of a parameter. For example, α in (2.1) is identified (increasing α increases Δy_t). By way of contrast, if ϵ_t also had a non-zero mean of β, then neither α nor β could be uniquely disentangled from the data alone (however large the sample), so both would be unidentifiable, although their sum would be identified. The concept of (unique) identification applies separately to the DGP and to models thereof: the parameters of the former could be identified yet those of a model of it could be non-unique (e.g. the DGP has $\mathsf{E}[\Delta y_t] = \mu$ but the model involves $\alpha + \beta$). Conversely, the model may have a unique parameterization but the potential parameters of interest from the DGP may be unobtainable. We develop more operational conditions for identification later.

A related but distinct concept is that of observational equivalence. If two models always generate identical outcomes, they are said to be observationally equivalent and data alone cannot distinguish between them. A sufficient condition is that all of their parameters are unidentifiable, but this is not necessary and identified models can be observationally equivalent. For example, since $\mathsf{D}_{\mathsf{x}}(x_t|\theta)$ is unchanged under one–one transformations of the parameter θ to $\psi = f(\theta)$ then $\mathsf{D}_{\mathsf{x}}(x_t|\theta)$ for $\theta \in \Theta$ and $\mathsf{D}_{\mathsf{x}}(x_t|\psi)$ for $\psi \in \Psi$ are observationally equivalent.

2.6 Interdependence

Much of the force of economic analysis is about inter-relationships between variables, e.g. explaining consumption behaviour in terms of income, or inflation by the pressure of demand. To generalize the preceding framework to allow for interconnections requires vectors, where all the relevant variables like Δy_t are stacked, so we could reinterpret (2.1) with Δy_t, α, and ϵ_t as vectors. Just stacking all the variables in a column, but treating them essentially as single variables, is inadequate, however, since the economy is interdependent. The Walrasian view is that all economic quantities are interrelated, and in practice, some of the worst mistakes in applied economics arise from forgetting about other inter-correlated, relevant factors since their untreated influences can seriously contaminate the effects that are included. More generally, we must abandon the idea of analysing each variable (or group of variables) in isolation, and formulate the joint density function of all the variables relevant to the problem under study to capture interdependencies.

Formally, the use of vector and matrix algebra does not greatly alter the analysis. Denote a column vector of n random variables by the bold-face symbol $\boldsymbol{x}_t$, written in row vector (transposed) form as $\boldsymbol{x}_t' = (x_{1t} \dots x_{nt})$. Then the joint density function of all the observable variables $\boldsymbol{x}_t$ at time t is $\mathsf{D_x}(\boldsymbol{x}_t|\boldsymbol{\theta})$ for the parameter vector $\boldsymbol{\theta} \in \Theta$. Denote the n-dimensional multivariate normal density of $\boldsymbol{x}_t$ by $\mathsf{N}_n[\boldsymbol{\mu}, \boldsymbol{\Sigma}]$ where $\mathsf{E}[\boldsymbol{x}_t] = \boldsymbol{\mu}$ is the vector of means and $\mathsf{E}\left[(\boldsymbol{x}_t - \boldsymbol{\mu})(\boldsymbol{x}_t - \boldsymbol{\mu})'\right] = \boldsymbol{\Sigma}$ is the variance matrix of rank n then:

$$\mathsf{D_x}(\boldsymbol{x}_t \mid \boldsymbol{\mu}, \boldsymbol{\Sigma}) = (2\pi)^{-\frac{n}{2}} |\boldsymbol{\Sigma}|^{-\frac{1}{2}} \exp\left\{-\tfrac{1}{2}(\boldsymbol{x}_t - \boldsymbol{\mu})' \boldsymbol{\Sigma}^{-1} (\boldsymbol{x}_t - \boldsymbol{\mu})\right\}, \tag{2.3}$$

where $|\boldsymbol{\Sigma}| \neq 0$ is the determinant of $\boldsymbol{\Sigma}$. Unfortunately, the practical problems are radically changed by allowing $n > 1$, especially at level C where the contents of $\boldsymbol{x}_t$ are not known (see §2.16).

2.7 Stochastic process

A discrete-time stochastic process is a collection of random variables $\{X_t(\omega)\}$ where $t \in \mathcal{T}$ denotes time, and $\omega \in \Omega$ denotes an elementary event or outcome when Ω is the relevant sample space. The stochastic process is defined relative to a probability space $(\Omega, \mathcal{F}, \mathsf{P})$, where $\mathcal{F}$ is the event space and $\mathsf{P}(\cdot)$ is an appropriate probability measure such that $\mathsf{P}(\mathcal{A})$ is defined for all events $\mathcal{A} \in \mathcal{F}$ (Ch.A2 reviews probability spaces and random variables). For a fixed value t_0 of t, $X_{t_0}(\omega)$ is a random variable for $\omega \in \Omega$, whereas for a fixed value ω_0 of ω, $X_t(\omega_0)$ is a realization of the stochastic process for $t \in \mathcal{T}$. Different values of ω induce different realizations. This dual characteristic of time-dated random variables was implicit in our notation $\{y_t\}$ for the process $\{y_t(\omega)\}$ in (2.2). The dependence of y_t on ω at each t was not made explicit, and we follow that convention below.

An obvious example of a stochastic process for students is their exam mark history and prospect. At each exam, a different outcome was conceivable (had they worked more or less, slept better, listened carefully to more lectures etc.), so the mark achieved on any given occasion is a random variable; the mark sequence recorded in their *vita* is one realization from the possible histories ('if only I had read Hendry's book'). Two stochastic processes were used above, namely (2.1) and (2.2) relating respectively to an $\mathsf{IN}\left[\alpha, \sigma_\epsilon^2\right]$ process and a random walk with drift. A third generalizes the first to an independent, identically distributed variate denoted $\mathsf{IID}\left[\alpha, \sigma^2\right]$, with higher moments constant but otherwise unspecified. Much of this book concerns stochastic processes of relevance to the analysis of economic data, and an overall formulation is offered in section §2.19. The notation does not distinguish explicitly between random variables and their realizations: the generic variable is denoted by X with outcome x (which could also denote $\log X$, and will be distinguished when necessary). Where statistical operators are used (such as expectations) it is to be understood that they apply to the random variables with the same symbol. Thus, $\mathsf{E}[x_t] = \mu$ entails that the (log of the) random variable denoted in general by X has a population mean of μ.

2.8 Conditioning

On the assumption that the past is immutable, it is legitimate to condition what is observed today on what happened last period, and only seek to explain the deviation from what happened last period. Successive levels of economic time series are highly intercorrelated, but changes will be less interdependent than the original series (and may be closer to normality than the levels, as noted in §2.4). If shocks like $\{\epsilon_t\}$ in (2.1) clustered in sign, that would invalidate (2.1) as the DGP, but we might imagine extending conditioning to include earlier events. Since the deviation from the past, conditional on the entire history of the process, must be an entity that does not depend on the past (which has been taken into account), it will be close to an unsystematic term. This argument will be formalized in §2.27. Denote the history by $\mathbf{X}_{t-1} = \left(\mathbf{X}_0 : \mathbf{X}_{t-1}^1\right)$ where $\mathbf{X}_0$ is the set of (pre-sample) initial conditions and $\mathbf{X}_{t-1}^1 = (\mathbf{x}_1 \ldots \mathbf{x}_{t-1})$. The joint density of $\mathbf{X}_T^1 = (\mathbf{x}_1 \ldots \mathbf{x}_T)$ given $\mathbf{X}_0$ is denoted by $\mathsf{D_X}\left(\mathbf{X}_T^1|\mathbf{X}_0, \boldsymbol{\theta}\right)$ where $\boldsymbol{\theta} \in \boldsymbol{\Theta}$.

Two aspects of conditioning need to be noted. First, conditioning is on events, not on outcomes (see Ch.A2). In principle, therefore, conditioning on the past is on past events, which are sets in $\mathcal{F}$, not on the realizations of $\mathbf{X}_{t-j}$. This could be denoted by the sigma field $\sigma(\mathbf{X}_{t-1})$. We leave the dependence on the event space implicit (unless misunderstandings would result) and hence write a conditional density for a single observation as (e.g.) $\mathsf{D_X}(\mathbf{x}_t|\mathbf{X}_{t-1}, \boldsymbol{\theta})$, where | separates the outcome from the conditioning set. Secondly, there is a crucial distinction between conditioning on contemporaneous and lagged xs and on the complete sample. In regression analysis, the conditioning set is often written as $\mathbf{X} = \mathbf{X}_T^1$. We will often make statements of the form $\mathsf{E}[Y_t|X_t]$ (the conditional mean of random variable Y_t for the event set associated with X_t) or $\mathsf{E}\left[y_t|\mathbf{X}_{t-1}^1\right]$, but almost never make claims about $\mathsf{E}[\mathbf{y}|\mathbf{X}]$. This is because in time-series econometrics, elements in $\mathbf{X}$ often depend on past ys, in which case conditioning on future xs will be invalid: Chapters 4 and 5 discuss this issue in detail.

2.9 White noise

A mean-zero stochastic process is white noise if its elements are mutually uncorrelated. Let $\{u_t\}$ denote a zero-mean, finite-variance stochastic process, so $\mathsf{E}[u_t] = 0$ and $\mathsf{E}[u_t^2] < \infty$. Then:

$$\{u_t\} \text{ is (weak) white noise if } \mathsf{E}[u_t u_s] = 0 \; \forall t \neq s.$$

The parenthetical comment is sometimes omitted. The condition that $\mathsf{E}\left[u_t^2\right] = \sigma_u^2$ (a constant) is called homoscedasticity; its converse of non-constant variance is called heteroscedasticity and is considered in §2.15. Then:

$$\{u_t\} \text{ is strong white noise if } \mathsf{E}[u_t u_s] = 0 \; \forall t \neq s \text{ and } \mathsf{E}\left[u_t^2\right] = \sigma_u^2.$$

An IID $[0, \sigma_\epsilon^2]$ process is an example of strong white noise and is sometimes called strict white noise since independence is much stronger than $\mathsf{E}[u_t u_s] = 0$. Let $\boldsymbol{U}_{t-1} = (\boldsymbol{U}_0, u_1, \ldots, u_{t-1})$ denote the history of the process up to time t, where $\boldsymbol{U}_0$ are the initial conditions, then white noise is the second-moment property defined by u_t being uncorrelated with $\boldsymbol{U}_{t-1}$: i.e. $\mathsf{E}[u_t \boldsymbol{U}_{t-1}] = \mathbf{0}$. We show below that white noise can be predictable and can have considerable structure.

2.10 Autocorrelation

If $\mathsf{E}[u_t \boldsymbol{U}_{t-1}] \neq \mathbf{0}$, then the series $\{u_t\}$ is said to be autocorrelated or serially correlated (i.e. correlated with its own lagged values). Thus, autocorrelation induces time dependence in a process, such that from the history $\boldsymbol{U}_{t-1}$, a better prediction of the next realization than zero is possible: (2.2) is one example of an autocorrelated process $\{y_t\}$. Many models have been proposed to account for the phenomenon of autocorrelation. One of the earliest was the autoregressive process due to Yule (1927):

$$y_t = \alpha_0 + \alpha_1 y_{t-1} + \epsilon_t \text{ with } \epsilon_t \sim \mathsf{IN}\left[0, \sigma_\epsilon^2\right], \tag{2.4}$$

where normality is convenient but not essential (whereas ϵ_t being white noise is part of the definition). The first-order autoregressive process is denoted AR(1) and the general case of an AR(r) is:

$$y_t = \alpha_0 + \alpha_1 y_{t-1} + \alpha_2 y_{t-2} + \cdots + \alpha_r y_{t-r} + \epsilon_t. \tag{2.5}$$

A second major class of stochastic-dynamic processes, called moving averages (MA), is due to Slutsky (1937). MA processes are close to the 'inverses' of autoregressions but can be more tedious to estimate. An MA(s) takes the form:

$$y_t = \gamma_0 + \epsilon_t + \gamma_1 \epsilon_{t-1} + \gamma_2 \epsilon_{t-2} + \cdots + \gamma_s \epsilon_{t-s} \text{ with } \epsilon_t \sim \mathsf{IN}\left[0, \sigma_\epsilon^2\right]. \tag{2.6}$$

A further generalization to the class of autoregressive-moving average (ARMA) models originates from Wold (1938), was formalized by Quenouille (1957) and popularized by Box and Jenkins (1976). The general ARMA(r, s) process is:

$$y_t = \alpha_0 + \alpha_1 y_{t-1} + \alpha_2 y_{t-2} + \cdots + \alpha_r y_{t-r} + \epsilon_t + \gamma_1 \epsilon_{t-1} + \cdots + \gamma_s \epsilon_{t-s}, \tag{2.7}$$

where $\{\epsilon_t\}$ remains white noise. When $y_t = \Delta x_t$ say, then (2.7) is an integrated ARMA, denoted ARIMA(r, s). However, (2.4) will suffice for expository purposes.

A convenient summary of the autocorrelation properties of a variable is its correlogram, namely the sequence of correlations of the form: $\{\mathsf{r}_1, \mathsf{r}_2, \mathsf{r}_3, \ldots, \mathsf{r}_n\}$ where $\mathsf{r}_j = \mathsf{corr}(y_t, y_{t-j})$. From the definition of a white-noise process, its correlogram is null (or flat), since $\mathsf{r}_j = 0$ for $j \geq 1$. Conversely, the correlogram of an autocorrelated process is not everywhere null. Empirical serial correlations are often reported in terms of graphs of estimated correlograms, which plot the sample correlation coefficient $\hat{\mathsf{r}}_j$ on one axis and j on the other. One formula for calculating the sample estimates of the $\{\mathsf{r}_j\}$ is:

$$\hat{\mathsf{r}}_j = \sum_{t=j+1}^{T} (y_t - \bar{y}_0)(y_{t-j} - \bar{y}_j) \left[\sum_{t=j+1}^{T} (y_t - \bar{y}_0)^2 \sum_{t=j+1}^{T} (y_{t-j} - \bar{y}_j)^2 \right]^{-\frac{1}{2}} \tag{2.8}$$

where:

$$\bar{y}_0 = (T-j)^{-1} \sum_{t=j+1}^{T} y_t \text{ and } \bar{y}_j = (T-j)^{-1} \sum_{t=j+1}^{T} y_{t-j} \text{ for } j = 1, \ldots, n.$$

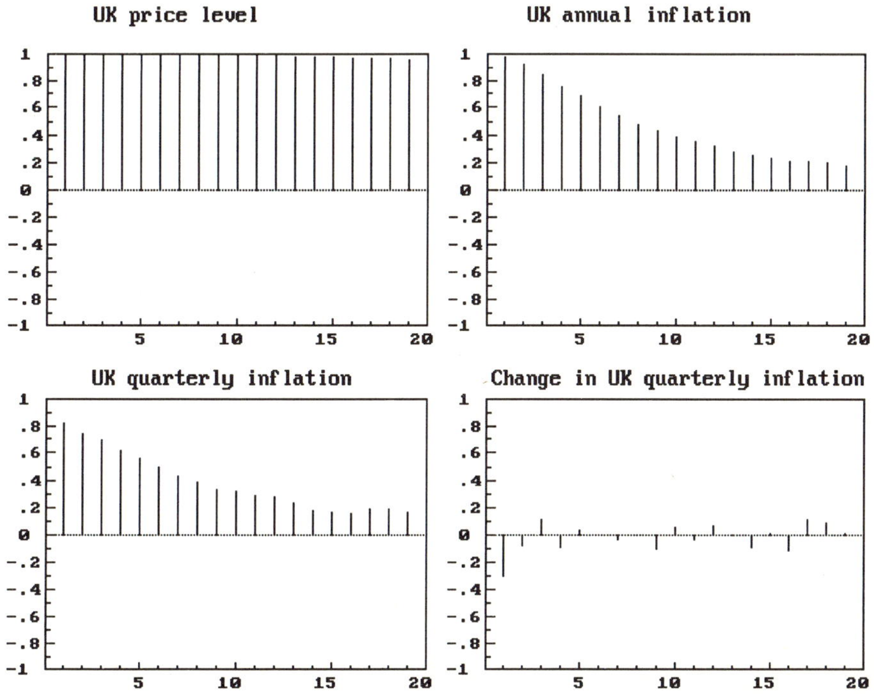

Fig. 2.4 Empirical correlograms

An important property of most autocorrelated processes is that they can be transformed to white noise, and the illustration in §1.10 showed a transformation of the random variable y_t that was white noise, namely $\{\Delta y_t\}$ as in (2.1): this aspect is analysed in Chapter 4. Here, we demonstrate the result empirically by transforming the autocorrelated time series $\{p_t\}$ (the price level in the UK) to near white noise, showing the correlograms graphically. Figures 2.4a–d plot the four correlograms for the level, the annual difference $\Delta_4 p_t$, the first difference Δp_t, and the change in the first difference, $\Delta^2 p_t$. The level is so highly positively autocorrelated that $\hat{\mathsf{r}}_{20}$ in Fig. 2.4a is still almost unity;

Fig. 2.4b shows that annual inflation is much less autocorrelated as its correlogram 'dies out' although it is positive for twenty lags; quarterly inflation is less autocorrelated; and the change in inflation in Fig. 2.4d has a flat, nearly null, correlogram after the first term of -0.3. The next two concepts help explain some of these outcomes.

2.11 Stationarity

Let $\{y_t(\omega), t \in \mathcal{T}, \omega \in \Omega\}$ be a stochastic process. Then $\{y_t\}$ is said to be weakly stationary when the moments of the $\{y_t\}$ process are such that $\forall t \in \mathcal{T}$, $\mathsf{E}[y_t(\omega)] = \mu$ where $|\mu| < \infty$, $\mathsf{E}[(y_t(\omega)-\mu)^2] = \sigma_y^2 < \infty$, and $\mathsf{E}[(y_t(\omega)-\mu)(y_{t-s}(\omega)-\mu)] = \gamma(s)$ is finite and independent of t for all s. That the first two unconditional moments are finite and independent of t is necessary for weak stationarity. Denote the distribution function of $\{y_t\}$ by $\mathsf{D_Y}(\cdot)$ where for a time period $(t_1 \ldots t_k)$:

$$\mathsf{D_Y}\left(y_{t_1}, \ldots, y_{t_k}\right) = \mathsf{D_Y}\left(y_{t_1+h}, \ldots, y_{t_k+h}\right) \; \forall h, k, \tag{2.9}$$

so that the joint distribution of all collections $\{y_{t_1}, \ldots, y_{t_k}\}$ is unaltered by 'translation' h-periods along the time axis, then $\{y_t\}$ is called strictly stationary. Neither concept implies the other since strictly stationary processes need not have finite second moments, and weak stationarity is not enough to ensure that the distribution of $\{y_{t_1}, \ldots, y_{t_k}\}$ is constant over time. In many situations, the moments or the distribution depend on the initial conditions of the process, so the process only becomes stationary asymptotically (see e.g. Spanos, 1986). Usually, we require weak (asymptotic) stationarity of a transformation of the process under analysis. From §2.9, strong white noise is weakly stationary and strict white noise is strictly stationary; a weakly stationary normal process is strictly stationary.

The model in (2.6) when $s = 1$ provides a useful illustration. Take expectations of both sides:

$$\mathsf{E}\left[y_t\right] = \gamma_0 + \mathsf{E}\left[\epsilon_t\right] + \gamma_1 \mathsf{E}\left[\epsilon_{t-1}\right] = \gamma_0 \tag{2.10}$$

since $\mathsf{E}\left[\epsilon_t\right] = 0 \; \forall t$. Then, as $\mathsf{E}\left[\epsilon_t \epsilon_{t-1}\right] = 0$:

$$\mathsf{V}\left[y_t\right] = \mathsf{V}\left[\epsilon_t\right] + \gamma_1^2 \mathsf{V}\left[\epsilon_{t-1}\right] = \left(1 + \gamma_1^2\right) \sigma_\epsilon^2 \tag{2.11}$$

Thus, the first two unconditional moments are constant. Finally, from (2.6):

$$\mathsf{E}\left[\left(y_t - \gamma_0\right)\left(y_{t-1} - \gamma_0\right)\right] = \gamma_1 \mathsf{E}\left[\epsilon_{t-1}^2\right] = \gamma_1 \sigma_\epsilon^2 \tag{2.12}$$

and $\mathsf{E}\left[\left(y_t - \gamma_0\right)\left(y_{t-j} - \gamma_0\right)\right] = 0 \; \forall j > 1$. Consequently, the autocorrelations, which die out rapidly, are independent of t, so the MA(1) process is weakly stationary. The AR(1) process needs restrictions to be stationary, even asymptotically and is considered in Chapter 4.

2.12 Integratedness

An integrated stochastic process is one like (2.2) where past errors accumulate, so that integratedness entails that the current observation behaves as the cumulation of all past perturbations. A finite (non-zero) variance stochastic process which does not accumulate past errors is said to be integrated of order zero, denoted I(0), and satisfies §1.4 (ii) and (iv), whereas an I(1) process satisfies §1.4 (i) and (iii), and its first difference is I(0). A stationary process is therefore I(0). When the level $\{y_t\}$ is I(n), the first difference $\{\Delta y_t\}$ is I($n-1$), the second difference $\{\Delta^2 y_t\}$ is I($n-2$) and so on (see Box and Jenkins, 1976). Figure 1.3 illustrated various degrees of integratedness in terms of the time-series graphs generated by differencing the UK price level zero, one, and two times, assuming that the level is I(2). The I(0) process was erratic and non-systematic (although I(0) processes need not be white noise); the I(1) process was more systematic and cyclical, but trend free (as $\alpha \simeq 0$ in terms of (2.1)); but the I(2) process was smooth and trending. We explain that last finding by the level integrating an already integrated error, such that when $\Delta^2 p_t = \epsilon_t$ with $p_0 = p_{-1} = 0$, the error on p_t is given by:

$$\sum_{j=1}^{t}\left(\sum_{k=1}^{j}\epsilon_k\right) = \sum_{j=1}^{t}(t-j+1)\,\epsilon_j .$$

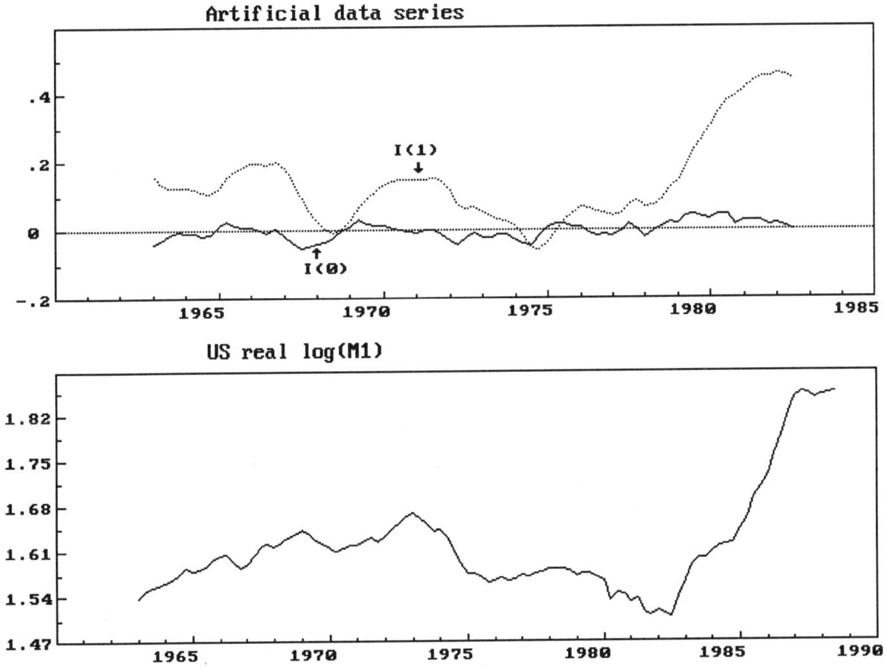

Fig. 2.5 Artificial and economic time series

Correlograms can reveal information about integratedness, as in Fig. 2.4. In practice, economic time series tend not be precisely integrated of any given order, but to behave approximately as $\mathsf{I}(n)$, where $n = 1$ or 2 for real and nominal magnitudes respectively: see Fig. 1.2 for example. Initially, we will treat real and nominal variables as if they were exactly integrated of the appropriate order. To illustrate that notion, Fig. 2.5a plots two artificial time series that are precisely I(0) and I(1) respectively; clear differences in their behaviour can be seen, especially the widely wandering nature of the I(1) series and its considerable positive autocorrelation (when the variable is 'high', the next observation is high as well). For comparison, Fig. 2.5b plots $\log(M1/P)$ in the US, which is remarkably similar to the artificial I(1) series in Fig. 2.5a.

2.13 Cointegration

Linear combinations of $\mathsf{I}(1)$ processes are usually $\mathsf{I}(1)$ as well. However, it may happen that the integration cancels between series to yield an $\mathsf{I}(0)$ outcome: this is called cointegration. As a possible example, consumption and income could be $\mathsf{I}(1)$ but saving (given by their difference $s_t = i_t - c_t$) could be $\mathsf{I}(0)$. Cointegrated processes define a 'long-run equilibrium trajectory' for the economy, departures from which induce 'equilibrium corrections' which move the economy back towards its path.[2]

Continuing with the bivariate example, consider:

$$\begin{array}{rcl} \Delta c_t & = & \alpha_0 + \alpha_1 s_{t-1} + \epsilon_t \\ \Delta i_t & = & \beta_0 + \beta_1 s_{t-1} + \nu_t \end{array} \quad \text{where} \quad \begin{pmatrix} \epsilon_t \\ \nu_t \end{pmatrix} \sim \mathsf{IN}\left[\mathbf{0}, \boldsymbol{\Sigma}\right]. \qquad (2.13)$$

A key relation between cointegration and integration is that the process in (2.13) must be $\mathsf{I}(1)$. Form the linear combination:

$$\beta_1 \Delta c_t - \alpha_1 \Delta i_t = (\beta_1 \alpha_0 - \alpha_1 \beta_0) + \beta_1 \epsilon_t - \alpha_1 \nu_t$$

where $(\beta_1 \epsilon_t - \alpha_1 \nu_t) \sim \mathsf{IN}\left[\mathbf{0}, \omega^2\right]$, so the first differences are $\mathsf{I}(0)$ as claimed. This result suggests an economic rationale for integrated data due to agents using equilibrium corrections in several relations (see Engle and Granger, 1987, Banerjee, Dolado, Galbraith and Hendry, 1993). We return to cointegration analysis in later chapters.

2.14 Trend

Any non-constant function of time will increase (or decrease) over time and is said to impart a deterministic trend to a time series. A vast variety of trend factors occurs in empirical research. Standard examples include polynomials in t of order greater than zero ($\sum_{j=1}^{n} \gamma_j t^j$), $\log t$, $\sqrt{t}$ etc. as well as split or segmented trends ($\gamma_1 t$ till time t_0 then $\gamma_2 t$ thereafter). For example, adding βt to $\{y_t\}$ will impart a linear trend to that

[2] Davidson, Hendry, Srba and Yeo (1978) refer to these as error corrections: see Ch.6.

time series when $\beta \neq 0$. Differencing reduces the order of a polynomial in t by unity, so the first difference of (2.2) removes both the unit root and the linear deterministic trend.

Integrated processes induce deterministic trends in variance as shown in the derivation of (2.2) from (2.1), and such series are said to have stochastic trends. In addition, an I(1) process with drift in its difference specification, such as (2.1), will induce a linear deterministic trend in its levels representation. As seen above, however, differenced variables can also exhibit apparent linear trends.

A class of models which can impart trends to time series is discussed by Harvey (1981b).[3] They have the form:

$$\begin{aligned} y_t &= \mu_t + \epsilon_t \\ \mu_t &= \mu_{t-1} + \gamma + \nu_t \end{aligned}$$

where $\{\epsilon_t\}$ and $\{\nu_t\}$ are IID, mutually independent processes. Differencing y_t yields $\Delta y_t = \Delta\epsilon_t + \gamma + \nu_t$, so the generated series has a stochastic trend and a negative moving-average error, and exhibits a linear deterministic trend when $\gamma \neq 0$.

2.15 Heteroscedasticity

Heteroscedasticity arises when the error variance σ^2 changes across the sample, perhaps as a result of economic behaviour. However,there are many statistical ways of generating heteroscedasticity: incorrect data transformations or choice of functional form; changes in the distributions of shocks etc. Non-constant error variances are denoted by σ_t^2, which may depend on other variables (e.g. $\sigma_t^2 = f(x_t)$ for dependence on x_t), past information, or time.

A popular model of second moments in time series is the class of autoregressive, conditional heteroscedastic (ARCH) processes introduced by Engle (1982a). Consider a stationary data process $\{x_t\}$ when $\mathsf{E}[x_t|x_{t-1}] = 0$ but $\mathsf{E}[x_t^2|x_{t-1}] = \lambda_0 + \lambda_1 x_{t-1}^2$, so that the conditional variance follows an autoregressive scheme, with $0 < \lambda_0$ and $0 \leq \lambda_1 < 1$ to ensure positive variances. Unconditionally, when $|\lambda_1| < 1$ such a process is homoscedastic:

$$\mathsf{E}[x_t^2] = \lambda_0 + \lambda_1 \mathsf{E}[x_{t-1}^2] = \frac{\lambda_0}{1-\lambda_1} = \omega^2 \text{ (say)}.$$

When sequential densities $\mathsf{D}_{\mathsf{x}}(x_t|\boldsymbol{X}_{t-1}, \boldsymbol{\theta})$ are given by $x_t|\boldsymbol{X}_{t-1} \sim \mathsf{N}[0, \lambda_0 + \lambda_1 x_{t-1}^2]$, successive x_t cannot be independent and the joint density $\mathsf{D}_{\mathsf{X}}(x_1 \ldots x_T|\boldsymbol{X}_0, \boldsymbol{\theta})$ must be non-normal.

Variants of time-dependent heteroscedasticity are often used to model error processes $\{\epsilon_t\}$, and include a multitude of acronyms such as generalized ARCH (GARCH) where

[3] He calls these structural time-series models, but we refer to them as structured since 'structural' is an over-used word, defined more precisely above.

$h_t = \mathsf{E}\left[\epsilon_t^2|\mathcal{I}_{t-1}\right]$ depends on its own previous value h_{t-1} with coefficient ϕ_1; integrated GARCH (IGARCH), where $\lambda_1 + \phi_1 = 1$; and so on. For example, GARCH(1, 1) has the form:

$$h_t = \lambda_0 + \lambda_1 \epsilon_{t-1}^2 + \phi_1 h_{t-1}.$$

Alternatively, h_t might enter the conditional mean of an $\{x_t\}$ process leading to GARCH in mean (GARCH-M). See Bollerslev, Chou and Kroner (1992) for a survey.

Variance changes may or may not violate stationarity: if they are genuine changes in unconditional variances, then they do so by definition, but apparent changes in variances may arise from mixtures of distributions (such as a rare drawing from a constant Poisson process impinging on a constant normal distribution).

2.16 Dimensionality

A dimensionality problem arises from the extremely large number of variables potentially present in any analysis which seeks to characterize the complete joint density for an economic problem: generally, n is too large to analyse $\boldsymbol{x}_t$ in economics. A crude estimate of n is somewhere between 10^{15} and 10^{30} elementary transactions per annum in an economy like the UK (where nominal GNP is of the order of \$$10^{12}$ p.a. in 1993). Despite the enormous range covered by this estimate of n, it serves its purpose: it is impossible to count a number as large as 10^{15} in a lifetime, even proceeding at one number per second. We must first filter the data, to reduce the number of variables to a subset of manageable proportions. Thus, a theory of reduction is an essential component linking level C to level A, and this theory is one of the central pillars of the book. It was initially developed to explain what is obtained when, as in empirical research, a vast number of variables is reduced to (say) the few that are analysed (as in the figures above). The next two sections on aggregation and marginalization concern issues in the theory of reduction, and a complete treatment is presented in Chapter 9.

2.17 Aggregation

A first step in data reduction is aggregation and the associated issue in economics is the theory of index numbers to sustain meaningful discussion of aggregates like prices and quantities. We cannot discuss index number theory in detail here (see e.g. Diewert, 1988), but macroeconomic data are invariably based on calculations involving many millions of items which are not directly comparable (like oranges, tractors, haircuts and life insurance) but which we make comparable via nominal values, deflated by price indices. If X denotes the nominal value of a variable with price index P and real (or constant price) value Y, then $Y = X/P$. A linear relation holds in logs: $\log Y = \log X - \log P$ although linear identities may no longer hold. Indices cannot be exact but are essential to render the data-analysis task manageable in economics (the issue of measurement errors is considered in Ch.12). Our data are inevitably highly aggregated and there is no real hope of handling detailed disaggregated time-series data on all major variables in a subject like economics. The crucial issues concern the extent of aggregation and its consequences, not whether we should aggregate.

Consider a cross-section sample $(x_1, \ldots, x_N)$ of size N on a scalar random variable x_i where the time index is suppressed for the present. The sample mean is:

$$\bar{x} = N^{-1} \sum_{j=1}^{N} x_j = N^{-1} x^* \tag{2.14}$$

where x^* is the total of the $\{x_j\}$. The mean is one aggregate data summary. A second aggregate is the sample variance:

$$V[x] = (N-1)^{-1} \sum_{j=1}^{N} (x_j - \bar{x})^2 . \tag{2.15}$$

Consider a one-to-one mapping of the original data-set on to the transformed data-set:

$$(x_1, \ldots, x_N) \leftrightarrow (\bar{x}, x_2, \ldots, x_N) . \tag{2.16}$$

There is no loss of information involved in this operation, although there is aggregation, since we can recover x_1 from the transformed set. Aggregating further:

$$(x_1, \ldots, x_N) \mapsto (\bar{x}, V[x], x_3, \ldots, x_N) , \tag{2.17}$$

there is a slight loss of information since x_1 and x_2 can still be retrieved, but not their order in the sample. Whether that loss of information matters or not depends on the objectives of the study so aggregation *per se* may or may not lose information.

Extend the example so that $x_i \sim \mathsf{IN}[\mu_x, \sigma_x^2]$ (independently across the N individuals) with the restriction that the mean $\mathsf{E}[x_i] = \mu_x$, and variance $\mathsf{E}[(x_i - \mu_x)^2] = \sigma_x^2$ are the same for all individuals. Then the aggregate x^* and the associated sample mean are distributed as:

$$x^* = \sum_{j=1}^{N} x_j \sim \mathsf{N}\left[N\mu_x, N\sigma_x^2\right] \text{ and } \bar{x} \sim \mathsf{N}\left[\mu_x, \frac{\sigma_x^2}{N}\right].$$

Since we generally analyse aggregate, rather than average, data in time-series economics, the preceding results suggest that variances of aggregates should be large when N is large. In practice, aggregates usually have small variances and three factors account for this. First, the relative standard deviation is the same for the mean and the aggregate, and when $\mu_x \neq 0$ is given by $\sigma_x / (\mu_x \sqrt{N})$. This unit-free measure is often cited in judging data variability. Secondly, individual behaviour is interdependent, and offsetting reactions reduce aggregate variance. Thirdly, many econometric studies of time series use logs of variables, rather than the original levels, as a legitimate data transformation for those economic variables which are inherently positive (such as prices, incomes, employment, etc.). An important feature of the log transformation is its effect on the variance of aggregate data as follows.

A random variable $z > 0$ has a log-normal distribution $\mathsf{LN}\left[\theta, \tau^2\right]$ if $\log z$ is normally distributed. The density function $\mathsf{D_z}\left(z|\theta, \tau^2\right)$ is (see Johnson and Kotz, 1970b Ch.14):

$$\mathsf{D_z}\left(z \mid \theta, \tau^2\right) = \left(z\tau\sqrt{2\pi}\right)^{-1} \exp\left(-\frac{\left[\log z - \theta\right]^2}{2\tau^2}\right),$$

where $z > 0$ with:

$$\mathsf{E}\left[z\right] = \exp\left(\theta + \frac{\tau^2}{2}\right) = \mu,$$

and:

$$\mathsf{V}\left[z\right] = \exp\left(\tau^2\right)\left(\exp\left(\tau^2\right) - 1\right)\exp\left(2\theta\right) = \mu^2\left(e^{\tau^2} - 1\right).$$

The median of z is $\exp(\theta)$ where $\theta = \log\mu - \frac{1}{2}\tau^2$ and 100τ is a percentage standard deviation. Since $\partial \log z / \partial z = 1/z$:

$$\mathsf{D_{logz}}\left(\log z \mid \theta, \tau^2\right) = \left(\tau^2 2\pi\right)^{-\frac{1}{2}} \exp\left(-\frac{\left[\log z - \theta\right]^2}{2\tau^2}\right),$$

so $\log z \sim \mathsf{N}\left[\theta, \tau^2\right]$, which is what determined the choice of parameters of $\mathsf{LN}\left[\cdot\right]$.

Consider a log transformation of a log-normally distributed average $\bar{x} \sim \mathsf{LN}[\theta_x, \tau_x^2]$ where $\mathsf{E}[\bar{x}] = \mu_x$ and $\mathsf{V}[\bar{x}] = \mu_x^2(e^{\tau_x^2} - 1) = N^{-1}\sigma_x^2$. Using $\exp(a) \simeq 1 + a$ for small a, then $\tau_x^2 \simeq N^{-1}(\sigma_x/\mu_x)^2$ and so:

$$\log \bar{x} \underset{app}{\sim} \mathsf{N}\left[\theta_x, N^{-1}\left(\frac{\sigma_x}{\mu_x}\right)^2\right]$$

where $\underset{app}{\sim}$ denotes 'approximately distributed as'. Since $\log x^* = \log\bar{x} + \log N$ where $\log N$ is fixed and $\theta_x = \log\mu_x + O\left(N^{-1}\right)$:

$$\log x^* \underset{app}{\sim} \mathsf{N}\left[\log N\mu_x, N^{-1}\left(\frac{\sigma_x}{\mu_x}\right)^2\right],$$

neglecting $\frac{1}{2}\left(\sigma_x/\mu_x\right)^2$ as trivial compared to $\log N\mu_x$. Thus, despite using aggregates rather than averages, the percentage standard deviation falls when analysing log models of aggregate data, the reduction factor being $\sqrt{N}$ relative to the individual data.

2.18 Marginalization

The second step in data reduction is marginalization, or the elimination of information deemed unnecessary for the purposes of the statistical analysis. For example, in (2.16) if only the sample mean were wanted, we could eliminate $(x_2, \ldots, x_n)$, or in technical terms, marginalize $(\bar{x}, x_2, \ldots, x_n)$ with respect to $(x_2, \ldots, x_n)$. There is almost always a loss of information in marginalizing, but that loss may be small or large. A key question in the theory of reduction concerns how to measure any loss of information. The theory of sufficient statistics deals with this issue in part (see §A3.1). For example, there is no loss of information in reducing data from a normal distribution to their mean and variance. However, after reduction to mean and variance alone, it is impossible to test whether the data came from a normal distribution. Therefore, any measure of loss of information is dependent upon the objectives of the study. When we are certain that the distribution is normal, we need only retain the mean and variance, so to marginalize with respect to $(x_3, \ldots, x_n)$ in (2.17) involves no loss of information. But if we needed to test conjectures about the shape of the distribution, there is a loss of information from discarding $(x_3, \ldots, x_n)$ since normality cannot be checked from the first two sample moments alone. Marginalization is generally carried out with respect to what is apparently unwanted information: the actual irrelevance of that information at level C must always be open to doubt, but is also open to evaluation.

Extend the model in (2.16) such that at each t:

$$x_{it} \sim \mathsf{IN}\left[\mu_i, \sigma_i^2\right] \text{ with } \bar{x}_t = N^{-1} \sum_{j=1}^{N} x_{jt}.$$

When $\bar{\mu} = N^{-1} \sum \mu_i$ is the parameter of interest (e.g. the aggregate propensity to spend if x_{it} is the consumption–income ratio), then conditional on retaining $\bar{x}_t$, the remaining xs will be an order of magnitude less informative about $\bar{\mu}$ than is $\bar{x}_t$, even if the $\{\mu_i\}$ are different across the N individuals. Conversely, if the $\{\mu_i\}$ could be modelled as a simple function of other observables (e.g. $\mu_i = \pi_1$ for $z_{it} \leq 0$ and $\mu_i = \pi_2$ for $z_{it} > 0$, for some z_{it}) a more informative analysis would result from partial disaggregation. For example, in studies of consumers' behaviour, the average propensity to consume may be different for distinct income sources — earnings versus rents — or for young and old versus middle aged, so that retaining information at the less aggregated level could yield considerable insight.

2.19 A general formulation

We have considered many of the basic concepts in the theory of reduction in §2.1 to §2.18. That theory concerns how to analyse data in a non-experimental world where the error process $\{\epsilon_t\}$ of the model contains both the unpredictable shocks from nature and everything omitted from the model, including all the mistakes in formulating the model, selecting the explanatory variables etc.[4] Nevertheless, a coherent and useful theory of econometrics can be constructed, and this book develops the relevant concepts and structures. The conventional tools of regression analysis, testing procedures, and so on, are still needed, but they play different roles and have different explanations, derived from the theory of reduction. We now synthesize the previous discussion in terms of a more

[4] See Florens, Mouchart and Rolin (1990) for a general treatment from a Bayesian perspective.

general DGP which incorporates the necessary ingredients for characterizing economic data, and relate that to the linear econometric equation represented in Chapter 1.

Let $\{x_t\}$ denote a stochastic process where x_t is a vector of n random variables, and consider the sample $X_T^1 = (x_1 \ldots x_T)$, where $X_{t-1}^1 = (x_1 \ldots x_{t-1})$. Denote the initial conditions by $X_0 = (\ldots x_{-r} \ldots x_{-1}\ x_0)$, leaving open their starting point, and let $X_{t-1} = (X_0 : X_{t-1}^1)$. The density function of X_T^1 conditional on X_0 is given by $\mathsf{D}_X(X_T^1|X_0, \theta)$ where $\mathsf{D}_X(\cdot)$ is represented parametrically by a k-dimensional vector of parameters $\theta = (\theta_1 \ldots \theta_k)'$ with parameter space $\Theta \subseteq \mathbb{R}^k$. All elements of θ need not be the same at each t, and some of the $\{\theta_i\}$ may reflect transient effects or regime shifts. Thus, the DGP of $\{x_t\}$ is written as:

$$\mathsf{D}_X\left(X_T^1 \mid X_0, \theta\right) \text{ for } \theta \in \Theta. \tag{2.18}$$

Read (2.18) as saying that the complete sample $\{x_t, t = 1, \ldots, T\}$ is generated from a joint density function $\mathsf{D}_X(\cdot)$ characterized by a parameter vector $\theta \in \Theta$, given initial conditions X_0. The population parameter is θ_p.

A density function is invariant under one–one transformations of its parameters, in that the probability structure is unaffected. Thus, we refer to any one–one transformation of θ as the DGP. As stressed in §2.5, however, different values of θ alter probabilities in identified, sufficient parameterizations.

Denote models of the DGP by M_i, then two models M_1 and M_2 are isomorphic if their parameters are one–one transformations of each other, in which case they are the same model in different parameterizations. This is written as $\mathsf{M}_1 \doteq \mathsf{M}_2$. Isomorphic models have the same number of parameters. Let the k_i coefficients of model M_i be:

$$\alpha_i \in \mathcal{A}_i \subseteq \mathbb{R}^{k_i}. \tag{2.19}$$

Then a model M_1 is nested in M_2, denoted by $\mathsf{M}_1 \subseteq \mathsf{M}_2$, if there exist one–one transformations of the form $\tau_i : \mathcal{A}_i \mapsto \mathcal{B}_i$ where $\beta_i = \tau_i(\alpha_i)$ with $\beta_i \in \mathcal{B}_i$ such that $\mathcal{B}_1 \subseteq \mathcal{B}_2$.[5] Thus, the model number is a shorthand for its parameter space. Nesting needs to be decided at the level of the joint density, and occurs when one model can be derived from another, so that its parameter space is *de facto* a subspace. Ostensible non-nesting means that there is no simplification of either model as stated which produces the other model except at a null point.

Models like (2.1) are extremely special cases of (2.18), so all of the relevant features of the earlier analysis in §1.10 are captured in (2.18) allowing us to analyse integrated processes, interdependent, heteroscedastic data, non-constant coefficients and so on. However, (2.18) is too general to offer any specific guidance for analysing economic data, so much of the remainder of the book will be concerned with adding flesh to this first skeleton.

In particular, when the generic econometric equation is of the form $y_t = f(z_t) + \epsilon_t$, the mapping by which (2.18) is reduced to that form will involve aggregation, marginalization, conditioning and several other steps to be discussed below. Reductions involve

[5] For other characterizations of nesting, see Pesaran (1987) and Gourieroux and Monfort (1991).

transformations of the parameters from the $\boldsymbol{\theta}$ which determines the stochastic features of the data to the coefficients $\boldsymbol{\beta}$ of the empirical model. The quality of the resulting model (in terms of its coefficients being identified, invariant, and of interest) depends on the reductions needed to derive the model from the DGP. If these do violence to the data structure, we should not expect useful models to result: such aspects will be the subject of model evaluation. Moreover, by determining how empirical models are derived from DGPs we might hope to obtain guidelines for empirical modelling.

2.20 A static solved example

The following example raises many of the issues that recur throughout the book, albeit in simplified form.[6] Consider the DGP in (2.20), where $\boldsymbol{f}_t \sim \mathsf{IN}_3[\boldsymbol{\mu}, \boldsymbol{\Omega}]$ denotes an independently distributed, normal random vector of the three variables $\boldsymbol{f}_t = (y_t : z_t : x_t)'$, with $\mathsf{E}[\boldsymbol{f}_t] = \boldsymbol{\mu}$ and $\mathsf{E}\left[(\boldsymbol{f}_t - \boldsymbol{\mu})(\boldsymbol{f}_t - \boldsymbol{\mu})'\right] = \boldsymbol{\Omega}$:

$$\begin{pmatrix} y_t \\ z_t \\ x_t \end{pmatrix} \sim \mathsf{IN}_3\left[\begin{pmatrix} \mu_1 \\ \mu_2 \\ \mu_3 \end{pmatrix}, \begin{pmatrix} \omega_{11} & \omega_{12} & \omega_{13} \\ \omega_{21} & \omega_{22} & \omega_{23} \\ \omega_{31} & \omega_{32} & \omega_{33} \end{pmatrix}\right]. \tag{2.20}$$

(a) What is the exact form of the density of y_t (i.e. calculate the mean, variance and the type of the distribution $\mathsf{D}_\mathsf{y}(y_t)$)?
(b) Derive the conditional density $\mathsf{D}_{\mathsf{y}|\mathsf{z}}(y_t|z_t)$ of y_t given z_t.
(c) What is the density of $\boldsymbol{w}_t|x_t$ where $\boldsymbol{w}_t = (y_t : z_t)'$?
(d) Derive the density $\mathsf{D}_{\mathsf{y}|\mathsf{z,x}}(y_t|z_t, x_t)$ of $y_t|z_t$,x_t. Obtain $\mathsf{D}_{\mathsf{y}|\mathsf{z}}(y_t|z_t)$ by marginalizing $\mathsf{D}_{\mathsf{y}|\mathsf{z,x}}(y_t|z_t, x_t)$ with respect to x_t and check that the same parameters as (b) result.
(e) Since $\mathsf{D}_{\mathsf{x,y,z}}(x_t, y_t, z_t)= \mathsf{D}_{\mathsf{x}|\mathsf{y,z}}(x_t|y_t, z_t)\,\mathsf{D}_{\mathsf{y}|\mathsf{z}}(y_t|z_t)\,\mathsf{D}_\mathsf{z}(z_t)$, is the presence of x_t in the DGP irrelevant to $\mathsf{D}_{\mathsf{y}|\mathsf{z}}(y_t|z_t)$? Does this result hold generally?
(f) Discuss the senses in which $\mathsf{D}_{\mathsf{y}|\mathsf{z}}(y_t|z_t)$ might be a legitimate model.
(g) In each of the following three cases, describe how (if at all) the results or their interpretation are affected by learning that in the relevant economy, agents form plans according to: (i) $\mathsf{E}[y_t] = \beta\mathsf{E}[z_t]$; or (ii) $\mathsf{E}[y_t|z_t] = \gamma z_t$; or (iii) $\mathsf{E}[y_t|x_t] = \delta\mathsf{E}[z_t|x_t]$. In particular, how are the interpretations of the parameters of the conditional densities in (b) and (d) affected in each of the three cases (i)–(iii)?
(h) Is there any contradiction between the models in (d), (f), and (g)? Do the values of the ω_{ij} affect the answer? Does it matter which, if any, of (i)–(iii) holds?

Solution

(a) $\mathsf{D}_\mathsf{y}(y_t)$ follows directly from the DGP: as that is a normal distribution, the marginal distribution is $y_t \sim \mathsf{IN}[\mu_1, \omega_{11}]$, so $\mathsf{E}[y_t] = \mu_1$ and $\mathsf{E}[(y_t - \mu_1)^2] = \omega_{11}$.

[6] Adapted from Oxford M.Phil. Examination 1983.

(b) $\mathsf{D}_{\mathsf{y}|\mathsf{z}}(y_t|z_t)$ follows from conditioning in a bivariate normal density (see Ch.A2):

$$\mathsf{E}[y_t \mid z_t] = \mu_1 + \left(\omega_{12}\omega_{22}^{-1}\right)(z_t - \mu_2) = (\mu_1 - \gamma_1\mu_2) + \gamma_1 z_t,$$

on setting $\gamma_1 = \omega_{12}\omega_{22}^{-1}$. Letting $\gamma_0 = \mu_1 - \gamma_1\mu_2$ this can be written as the model:

$$y_t = \gamma_0 + \gamma_1 z_t + \epsilon_t, \tag{2.21}$$

where ϵ_t is a linear function of jointly normally distributed variables and so is also normal. Next:

$$\mathsf{V}[y_t \mid z_t] = \mathsf{E}\left[(y_t - \mathsf{E}[y_t|z_t])^2 \mid z_t\right] = \mathsf{E}\left[\epsilon_t^2\right] = \omega_{11} - \omega_{12}^2\omega_{22}^{-1} = \sigma^2 < \omega_{11}.$$

Thus:

$$y_t \mid z_t \sim \mathsf{N}\left[\gamma_0 + \gamma_1 z_t, \sigma^2\right].$$

(c) As in (b):

$$\mathsf{E}[\boldsymbol{w}_t \mid x_t] = \begin{pmatrix} \mu_1 \\ \mu_2 \end{pmatrix} + \begin{pmatrix} \omega_{13} \\ \omega_{23} \end{pmatrix} \omega_{33}^{-1}(x_t - \mu_3) = \boldsymbol{\lambda}_0 + \boldsymbol{\lambda}_1 x_t, \tag{2.22}$$

and:

$$\begin{aligned} \mathsf{V}[\boldsymbol{w}_t \mid x_t] &= \begin{pmatrix} \omega_{11} & \omega_{12} \\ \omega_{12} & \omega_{22} \end{pmatrix} - \begin{pmatrix} \omega_{13} \\ \omega_{23} \end{pmatrix} (\omega_{13} \quad \omega_{23})\, \omega_{33}^{-1} \\ &= \begin{pmatrix} \omega_{11} - \omega_{13}^2\omega_{33}^{-1} & \omega_{12} - \omega_{23}\omega_{13}\omega_{33}^{-1} \\ \omega_{12} - \omega_{23}\omega_{13}\omega_{33}^{-1} & \omega_{22} - \omega_{23}^2\omega_{33}^{-1} \end{pmatrix}. \end{aligned} \tag{2.23}$$

Denoting this last matrix by $\boldsymbol{\Psi}$:

$$\boldsymbol{w}_t \mid x_t \sim \mathsf{N}[\boldsymbol{\lambda}_0 + \boldsymbol{\lambda}_1 x_t, \boldsymbol{\Psi}].$$

(d) Similarly:

$$\begin{aligned} \mathsf{E}[y_t \mid z_t, x_t] &= \mu_1 + (\omega_{12} \quad \omega_{13}) \begin{pmatrix} \omega_{22} & \omega_{23} \\ \omega_{32} & \omega_{33} \end{pmatrix}^{-1} \begin{pmatrix} z_t - \mu_2 \\ x_t - \mu_3 \end{pmatrix} \\ &= \rho_0 + \rho_1 z_t + \rho_2 x_t, \end{aligned} \tag{2.24}$$

where $\rho_0 = \mu_1 - \rho_1\mu_2 - \rho_2\mu_3$, and:

$$\begin{pmatrix} \rho_1 \\ \rho_2 \end{pmatrix} = \begin{pmatrix} \omega_{22} & \omega_{23} \\ \omega_{32} & \omega_{33} \end{pmatrix}^{-1} \begin{pmatrix} \omega_{21} \\ \omega_{31} \end{pmatrix}. \tag{2.25}$$

Consequently, for example, $\rho_1 = \left(\omega_{22} - \omega_{23}\omega_{33}^{-1}\omega_{32}\right)^{-1}\left(\omega_{21} - \omega_{23}\omega_{33}^{-1}\omega_{31}\right)$. Also:

$$\begin{aligned} \mathsf{V}[y_t \mid z_t, x_t] &= \omega_{11} - (\omega_{12} \quad \omega_{13}) \begin{pmatrix} \omega_{22} & \omega_{23} \\ \omega_{32} & \omega_{33} \end{pmatrix}^{-1} \begin{pmatrix} \omega_{21} \\ \omega_{31} \end{pmatrix} \\ &= \tau^2 = \mathsf{V}[u_t], \end{aligned} \tag{2.26}$$

where $u_t = y_t - \mathsf{E}[y_t|z_t, x_t]$. Finally:

$$y_t \mid z_t, x_t \sim \mathsf{N}\left[\rho_0 + \rho_1 z_t + \rho_2 x_t, \tau^2\right].$$

Marginalizing this conditional density with respect to x_t involves substituting for the density of x_t conditional on z_t, namely $x_t|z_t \sim \mathsf{N}\left[(\mu_3 - \varphi\mu_2) + \varphi z_t, \psi^2\right]$ where $\varphi = \omega_{32}\omega_{22}^{-1}$ and $\psi^2 = \omega_{33} - \omega_{23}^2\omega_{22}^{-1}$. In model form, $x_t = (\mu_3 - \varphi\mu_2) + \varphi z_t + \xi_t$, so from (2.24):

$$\begin{aligned} y_t &= \rho_0 + \rho_1 z_t + \rho_2 x_t + u_t \\ &= \{\rho_0 + \rho_2(\mu_3 - \varphi\mu_2)\} + (\rho_1 + \rho_2\varphi) z_t + u_t + \rho_2\xi_t \\ &= \mu_1 - \rho_1\mu_2 - \rho_2\mu_3 + \rho_2(\mu_3 - \varphi\mu_2) + (\rho_1 + \rho_2\varphi) z_t + (u_t + \rho_2\xi_t) \\ &= \mu_1 + (\rho_1 + \rho_2\varphi)(z_t - \mu_2) + \eta_t \end{aligned} \tag{2.27}$$

where $\eta_t = u_t + \rho_2\xi_t$ is orthogonal to z_t by construction. However:

$$(\rho_1 + \rho_2\varphi) = \frac{\left(\omega_{21} - \omega_{23}\omega_{33}^{-1}\omega_{31}\right)}{\left(\omega_{22} - \omega_{23}\omega_{33}^{-1}\omega_{32}\right)} + \frac{\left(\omega_{31} - \omega_{32}\omega_{22}^{-1}\omega_{21}\right)}{\left(\omega_{33} - \omega_{32}\omega_{22}^{-1}\omega_{23}\right)}\omega_{22}^{-1}\omega_{23}$$

which must equal γ_1 in (2.21) (i.e. $\omega_{12}\omega_{22}^{-1}$). It not difficult, using matrix algebra, to check from (2.27) that $\rho_1 + \rho_2\varphi = (\rho_1 \quad \rho_2)(1 \quad \varphi)' = \gamma_1$ since:

$$\begin{aligned} (\rho_1 \quad \rho_2)\begin{pmatrix}1\\ \varphi\end{pmatrix} &= (\omega_{21} \quad \omega_{31})\begin{pmatrix}\omega_{22} & \omega_{23}\\ \omega_{32} & \omega_{33}\end{pmatrix}^{-1}\begin{pmatrix}\omega_{22}^{-1}\omega_{22}\\ \omega_{22}^{-1}\omega_{32}\end{pmatrix} \\ &= \omega_{22}^{-1}(\omega_{21} \quad \omega_{31})\begin{pmatrix}\omega_{22} & \omega_{23}\\ \omega_{32} & \omega_{33}\end{pmatrix}^{-1}\begin{pmatrix}\omega_{22} & \omega_{23}\\ \omega_{32} & \omega_{33}\end{pmatrix}\begin{pmatrix}1\\ 0\end{pmatrix} \\ &= \omega_{22}^{-1}(\omega_{21} \quad \omega_{31})\begin{pmatrix}1\\ 0\end{pmatrix} \\ &= \omega_{22}^{-1}\omega_{21} = \gamma_1. \end{aligned} \tag{2.28}$$

(e) Any joint density can be factorized as:

$$\mathsf{D}_{\mathsf{x,y,z}}(x_t, y_t, z_t) = \mathsf{D}_{\mathsf{x|y,z}}(x_t \mid y_t, z_t)\mathsf{D}_{\mathsf{y|z}}(y_t \mid z_t)\mathsf{D}_{\mathsf{z}}(z_t)$$

and $\mathsf{D}_{\mathsf{y|z}}(y_t|z_t)$ is $\mathsf{D}_{\mathsf{y|x,z}}(y_t|x_t, z_t)$ marginalized with respect to x_t (from (d)). The crucial point is that the parameterization is altered from that of the DGP by marginalizing unless x_t is irrelevant (i.e. ρ_2 above is zero), mapping from $(\rho_0, \rho_1, \rho_2, \tau^2)$ to $(\gamma_0, \gamma_1, \sigma^2)$. Thus, whether or not x_t is irrelevant depends on which parameters are of interest. It is unclear how $(\gamma_0, \gamma_1, \sigma^2)$ could be interesting if $\rho_2 \neq 0$, since the $\{\rho_i\}$ are confounded in the $\{\gamma_i\}$. If $\omega_{13} = \omega_{23} = 0$, then $\rho_0 = \gamma_0$, $\rho_1 = \gamma_1$, $\rho_2 = 0$, $\tau^2 = \sigma^2$, and x_t is irrelevant.

(f) Despite the preceding analysis, $\mathsf{D}_{\mathsf{y|z}}(y_t|z_t)$ is a legitimate model since, given the DGP, it is true that $y_t|z_t \sim \mathsf{N}[\gamma_0 + \gamma_1 z_t, \sigma^2]$. The error ϵ_t in (2.21) is a homoscedastic, white-noise process which is independent of both z_t and $\boldsymbol{W}_{t-1}^1 =$

$(\mathbf{w}_1 \ldots \mathbf{w}_{t-1})$. Nevertheless, $\mathsf{D}_{y|z}(y_t|z_t)$ is a reduction of $\mathsf{D}_{y|x,z}(y_t|x_t, z_t)$, so a loss of information results unless x_t is irrelevant as analysed in (e). For example, $\tau^2 \leq \sigma^2$ if x_t matters in $\mathsf{D}_{y|x,z}(y_t|x_t, z_t)$, and so poorer fits and forecasts will be obtained from $\mathsf{D}_{y|z}(y_t|z_t)$. More importantly, if a regime shift occurs in the economy and affects the parameters of the marginal distribution of x_t only, then $\mathsf{D}_{y|z}(y_t|z_t)$ may change even when $\mathsf{D}_{y|x,z}(y_t|x_t, z_t)$ does not. Thus, less understanding and poorer policy may ensue from the more reduced model.

(g) All three possible states affect the implications above.

$$\text{(i):}\quad \mathsf{E}\left[y_t\right] = \beta \mathsf{E}\left[z_t\right] \text{ implies } \mu_1 = \beta\mu_2.$$

Plans of type (i) link the unconditional means and cover such cases as permanent consumption depending on permanent income. In terms of (b) above, $\gamma_0 = (\beta - \gamma_1)\,\mu_2$, so unless $\beta = \gamma_1$, least-squares estimation of (2.21) will not deliver β as the coefficient of z_t, and to learn β from γ_0 will involve learning μ_2 from the marginal distribution of z_t. A serious misinterpretation of the evidence could result if the regression coefficient γ_1 is assumed to be the parameter of interest β.

$$\text{(ii):}\quad \mathsf{E}\left[y_t \mid z_t\right] = \gamma z_t \text{ implies } \mu_1 = \gamma\mu_2 \text{ and } \gamma_1 = \gamma \text{ in (2.21).}$$

Thus, valid inferences will result since the intercept will be zero and regression analysis will deliver the parameter of interest γ. Plans of type (ii) are contingent in that the decision about y_t depends on the outcome for z_t.

$$\text{(iii):}\quad \mathsf{E}\left[y_t \mid x_t\right] = \delta \mathsf{E}\left[z_t \mid x_t\right].$$

Plans of type (iii) link the conditional means, and correspond to agents forming expectations about z_t given information on x_t, and planning y_t accordingly. As in (b):

$$\mathsf{D}_{y|x}\left(y_t \mid x_t\right) = \mathsf{N}\left[\theta_0 + \theta_1 x_t, \rho^2\right]$$

and:

$$\mathsf{D}_{z|x}\left(z_t \mid x_t\right) = \mathsf{N}\left[\phi_0 + \phi_1 x_t, \zeta^2\right]$$

are well defined given (2.20), where the derived parameters are $\theta_0 = \mu_1 - \theta_1\mu_3$, $\theta_1 = \omega_{13}\omega_{33}^{-1}$, $\phi_0 = \mu_2 - \phi_1\mu_3$, and $\phi_1 = \omega_{23}\omega_{33}^{-1}$. Thus, (iii) entails the restriction that $\theta_0 = \delta\phi_0$ and $\theta_1 = \delta\phi_1$, and hence by substitution, that $\mu_1 = \delta\mu_2$ and $\omega_{13} = \delta\omega_{23}$. These two restrictions have different implications as follows. Taking them in the reverse order, $\omega_{13} = \delta\omega_{23}$ translates into $\mathsf{C}[y_t, x_t] = \delta\mathsf{C}[z_t, x_t]$ where $\mathsf{C}[\cdot]$ denotes covariance. This is similar to the conventional regression formula where e.g. $\mathsf{C}[y_t, z_t] = \gamma\mathsf{C}[z_t, z_t]$, except that a second (instrumental) variable is used in the last term. Just as an estimator of γ can be obtained corresponding to regression (called ordinary least squares, OLS), so can another estimator based on $\mathsf{C}[y_t, x_t] = \delta\mathsf{C}[z_t, x_t]$ and it is called an instrumental variables estimator (IVE).

The restriction that $\mu_1 = \delta\mu_2$ is reminiscent of (i), and a similar analysis applies. When $\omega_{12} = \delta\omega_{22}$, then regression is valid, but otherwise the parameters of the marginal distribution of z_t enter the conditional distribution of $y_t|z_t$.

(h) Since all the models are reductions of (2.20), there are no contradictions, but there may be information losses. The values of ω_{ij} clearly matter, as does which of (i)–(iii) holds.

2.21 Models, mechanisms, and DGPs

Chapter 1 treated the DGP as distinct from a model thereof, and we now clarify that distinction. There is an economic mechanism which operates in reality: this comprises the transacting, producing, transporting (etc.) behaviour of economic agents at some time and place. The data-generation process superimposes a measurement system on that mechanism, which usually records only part of the information economists require, and may do so with substantial error. At level A, the DGP characterizes the actual stochastic structure of the observables. For example, when (2.1) is how $\{y_t\}$ is generated, then it is the DGP, and an analysis of the properties of samples $\{y_1, \dots, y_T\}$ from that process will match their anticipated behaviour. In a Monte Carlo study, where a numerical mimic of a DGP is simulated on a computer, (2.1) can be a DGP, and not merely a model of the DGP.

A theoretical (economic) model is a conjectured representation of the DGP. Such a model is a cognitive entity, usually derived from subject-matter theory. It may or may not be stochastic, and generally is contingent on many (usually implicit) restrictions and assumptions about 'everything else held constant'. Often it is unclear precisely what state of nature is envisaged in a theory model as too many factors are unspecified.

A statistical generating mechanism (SGM) is close to an operational counterpart of a conjectured model. It has two components namely (i) a probability mechanism; and (ii) a sampling mechanism (see Spanos, 1986). The former denotes the family of probability distributions such as $\mathsf{D_x}(\boldsymbol{x}_t|\boldsymbol{\theta})$ for $\boldsymbol{\theta} \in \Theta$, and characterizes the probability process for a single observation. The normal distribution $\boldsymbol{x}_t \sim \mathsf{N}_n[\boldsymbol{\mu}, \boldsymbol{\Sigma}]$ is often used as an example. Thus, (i) concerns the distributional shape and the parameterization. Similarly, (ii) determines how the data sample is drawn. There are many possible sampling mechanisms, a commonly assumed one being IID. Combining the two examples leads to the SGM: $\boldsymbol{x}_t \sim \mathsf{IN}_n[\boldsymbol{\mu}, \boldsymbol{\Sigma}]$, namely independent sampling from $\mathsf{N}_n[\boldsymbol{\mu}, \boldsymbol{\Sigma}]$. This is not a reasonable SGM for economic data, but is used below for scalar error processes like $\{\epsilon_t\}$ in (2.1) with $\boldsymbol{\mu} = 0$ and $\boldsymbol{\Sigma} = \sigma_\epsilon^2$. One could imagine such an SGM operating naturally; at each point in time, behaviour is perturbed by an independent error term ϵ_t drawn from a normal distribution centred on zero with variance σ_ϵ^2. Thus, an SGM is a conjectured DGP, perhaps conditional on some specified set of events. However, like a theoretical model, an SGM may not represent the relevant DGP adequately. At level C, where applied research occurs, an SGM could only be a model of the complicated, evolving, and high-dimensional DGP which seems to characterize economics. We now consider the relation of the postulated SGM to the actual DGP given the observed data.

Language induces a confusion in referring to a 'statistical model' unless the assumed level of knowledge is clear. We need different terms for the mechanism and models thereof, and will use the term DGP only for the actual process which generated the data.

Model denotes any conjectured representation of the DGP, with the possibility that the model coincides with the DGP. It is also useful to distinguish an economic model (which could be non-stochastic) from a statistical model, and the term 'model' in isolation will usually denote an economic model, even when that model is stochastic.

An empirical model bridges the gap between a theoretical model or SGM and the DGP. It is specified by coefficients which depend on the parameters of the DGP and are sometimes called pseudo-true values. As an illustration, consider a stationary bivariate DGP defined by:

$$\begin{aligned} y_t &= \beta_1 z_t + \beta_2 y_{t-1} + \epsilon_{1t} \\ z_t &= \lambda_1 z_{t-1} + \epsilon_{2t} \end{aligned} \quad \text{where } \epsilon_t \sim \mathsf{IN}_2\left[\mathbf{0}, \boldsymbol{\Sigma}\right], \tag{2.29}$$

when an investigator modelling the long-run dependence of y_t on z_t is unaware of the lagged dependent variable or the error inter-correlation and estimates a regression of y_t on z_t. The population coefficients of that regression will depend on all the parameters of (2.29), and we derive some of the analytical formulae in §2.29. Further, as in Chapter 1, the 'errors' on that empirical model are derived functions of those of the DGP. In practice, therefore, an estimated model (any model specified with estimated coefficients) must be an estimated empirical model.

At level A, we know $\mathsf{D_X}(\cdot)$ and the value of $\boldsymbol{\theta}$, so the SGM is completely specified, and we can investigate probability statements about the data it generates. At level C, however, we know neither $\mathsf{D_X}(\cdot)$ nor $\boldsymbol{\theta}$, so how can we progress? The solution lies in an iterative approach: first conjecture the SGM, deduce what ought to be observed, contrast that with what is observed, and revise the framework in the light of any mis-match. The SGM also occurs at level C as a model of the DGP. This dual role of the SGM is inevitable, and to clarify what status it has, when it is not claimed to be the DGP, we call the sample joint data density $\mathsf{D_X}\left(\mathbf{X}_T^1|\mathbf{X}_0, \boldsymbol{\theta}\right)$ the Haavelmo distribution (see Spanos, 1989b).

That finesse leaves two major problems, alluded to in Chapter 1. First, we cannot assume in general that successive $\mathbf{x}_t$ are independently sampled in time-series economics. However, the DGP in (2.1) showed how to generate interdependent data from an SGM which had an independent error process $\{\epsilon_t\}$. That route offers a general solution provided such an SGM is reasonable for the error process. Because of its central role at levels B and C, we consider the independence assumption for $\{\epsilon_t\}$ in more detail in the next two sections. In particular, we must develop a general procedure for data analysis when the sampling mechanism is unknown, as this will be the usual case in time-series econometrics. The second major problem is the meaning to attach to parameters in an SGM when it is an empirical model and not the DGP. That issue is examined in §2.24.

2.22 Factorizations

The following discussion is intentionally at a heuristic and non-technical level; hopefully this will not induce technical mistakes. For more rigorous justifications see *inter alia* Grimmett and Stirzaker (1982) and White (1984); the appendix offers an introductory discussion.

Let $(\Omega, \mathcal{F}, \mathsf{P}(\cdot))$ be the probability space where $\mathsf{P}(\mathcal{A})$ represents the probability measure for events $\mathcal{A} \in \mathcal{F}$ and Ω is the sample space. Consider two events $\mathcal{A} \in \mathcal{F}$ and $\mathcal{B} \in \mathcal{F}$ such that $\mathsf{P}(\mathcal{A}) > 0$ and $\mathsf{P}(\mathcal{B}) > 0$. A necessary and sufficient condition for $\mathcal{A}$ and $\mathcal{B}$ to be independent is that:

$$\mathsf{P}(\mathcal{A} \cap \mathcal{B}) = \mathsf{P}(\mathcal{A})\,\mathsf{P}(\mathcal{B}). \tag{2.30}$$

There is an intermediate stage in deriving the condition in (2.30). To convey the same information as $\mathsf{P}(\mathcal{A} \cap \mathcal{B})$, we could report the probability of observing $\mathcal{A}$ given what $\mathcal{B}$ was observed to be, together with the probability of observing $\mathcal{B}$. Thus, a more general decomposition is to factorize $\mathsf{P}(\mathcal{A} \cap \mathcal{B})$ into a conditional probability $\mathsf{P}(\mathcal{A}|\mathcal{B})$ and a marginal probability $\mathsf{P}(\mathcal{B})$:

$$\mathsf{P}(\mathcal{A} \cap \mathcal{B}) = \mathsf{P}(\mathcal{A} \mid \mathcal{B})\,\mathsf{P}(\mathcal{B}). \tag{2.31}$$

Comparing (2.31) with (2.30), the condition for independence is $\mathsf{P}(\mathcal{A}|\mathcal{B}) = \mathsf{P}(\mathcal{A})$: the probability of observing any given event $\mathcal{A}$ does not depend upon the outcome of the event $\mathcal{B}$. Under independence, there is a strong separation between the occurrence of the two events $\mathcal{A}$ and $\mathcal{B}$. When independence does not hold, we might imagine writing heuristically:

$$\mathsf{P}(\{\mathcal{A} \mid \mathcal{B}\} \cap \mathcal{B}) = \mathsf{P}(\mathcal{A}|\mathcal{B})\,\mathsf{P}(\mathcal{B}),$$

so by analogy with (2.30), the events $\{\mathcal{A}|\mathcal{B}\}$ and $\mathcal{B}$ are independent: in the factorization of the joint probability in (2.31), the conditional and marginal components behave as if their arguments were independent.

In elementary treatments of statistics, a condition ensuring independence between successive observations on random variables often appears to be essential: many examples show that estimation and inference can go awry if (an unknown) dependence exists between outcomes. Since the data $\{y_t\}$ from (2.1) are not independent even if $\epsilon_t \sim \mathsf{IN}\left[0, \sigma_\epsilon^2\right]$, how can we analyse (2.1)?

The resolution of this apparent difficulty lies in factorizing joint probabilities as in (2.31). The essential ingredient in (2.30) is that $\mathsf{P}(\mathcal{A} \cap \mathcal{B})$ is a product of two factors: it is not essential that the product only involves the marginal probabilities $\mathsf{P}(\mathcal{A})$ and $\mathsf{P}(\mathcal{B})$. A product which involves conditional and marginal probabilities can also sustain inference. To utilize this result in practice, we need two more steps. First, the factorization in (2.31) could be written as $\mathsf{P}(\mathcal{B}|\mathcal{A})\,\mathsf{P}(\mathcal{A})$; which direction of conditioning should be selected? This question cannot be answered in any generality until Chapter 5, except in an important special case, which is precisely the relevant one here, namely when $\mathcal{A}$ follows $\mathcal{B}$ in time. Since the past is immutable, conditioning on past events is usually valid. Secondly, we need to switch from events to random variables and factorize the joint density via sequential conditioning where $\mathcal{A}$ is $\sigma(\boldsymbol{x}_t)$ and $\mathcal{B}$ is $\sigma(\boldsymbol{X}_{t-1})$. This step follows by analogy from the usual mapping of events to random variables (see Ch.A2). We consider factorizations in terms of the random variables $\{\boldsymbol{x}_t\}$ and so for

$\boldsymbol{X}_T^1 = \left(\boldsymbol{x}_T : \boldsymbol{X}_{T-1}^1\right)$ write:

$$\mathsf{D_X}\left(\boldsymbol{X}_T^1 \mid \boldsymbol{X}_0, \boldsymbol{\theta}\right) = \mathsf{D_x}\left(\boldsymbol{x}_T \mid \boldsymbol{X}_{T-1}^1, \boldsymbol{X}_0, \boldsymbol{\theta}\right) \mathsf{D_X}\left(\boldsymbol{X}_{T-1}^1 \mid \boldsymbol{X}_0, \boldsymbol{\theta}\right).$$

Continuing for $t = T-1, \ldots, 1$:

$$\mathsf{D_X}\left(\boldsymbol{X}_T^1 \mid \boldsymbol{X}_0, \boldsymbol{\theta}\right) = \prod_{t=1}^{T} \mathsf{D_x}\left(\boldsymbol{x}_t \mid \boldsymbol{X}_{t-1}, \boldsymbol{\theta}\right). \tag{2.32}$$

Sections 2.23 and 2.27 demonstrate that (2.32) side-steps both the need for independence in, and knowledge of, the sampling mechanism. Unsurprisingly, such a feature plays an important role in moving from level A to level C.

Already we can partly resolve the doubts held in the 1930s by many economists about the validity of applying probability-based analyses to economic data. The main reason for their doubts was not that the generating mechanism was unknowable: rather, they believed that economic data were too heterogeneous and interdependent to support statistical procedures (as an example of such an argument, see Keynes, 1939). Were independence in the sampling mechanism essential to sustain statistical inference, probability theory would be inapplicable in economics. Fortunately, the necessary condition concerns the sampling mechanism of the $\{\epsilon_t\}$ and not that of the $\{y_t\}$, and is a weaker condition than independence in the sense that (2.31) is weaker than (2.30). This development was introduced to economics by Haavelmo (1944) (see Morgan, 1987, and Spanos, 1989b). We weaken the requirements below by allowing $\{\epsilon_t\}$ to be a derived process.

Conditional on what happened last period, consider the new component of information perturbing the economy. This new component is literally the news in the economy, and is exactly what could not be predicted from last period about this period's outcome. In (2.1) for example, that component is $\{\epsilon_t\}$ with:

$$\mathsf{E}\left[\Delta y_t\right] = \alpha \;\; \text{so that } \mathsf{E}\left[y_t \mid y_{t-1}\right] = y_{t-1} + \alpha.$$

Consequently:

$$y_t = \mathsf{E}\left[y_t \mid y_{t-1}\right] + \epsilon_t, \tag{2.33}$$

so that given y_{t-1}, the distribution of $y_t|y_{t-1}$ around its conditional mean $(y_{t-1} + \alpha)$ depends on the distribution of ϵ_t alone. Once the predictable (i.e. $\mathsf{E}\left[y_t|y_{t-1}\right]$) is removed, only unpredictable components remain (namely ϵ_t). A similar point holds for the joint density in (2.32). The decomposition in (2.33) can be reversed to construct ϵ_t as the news or innovation given by $\epsilon_t = y_t - \mathsf{E}\left[y_t|y_{t-1}\right]$, and this concept is the subject of the next section.

2.23 Innovation processes

Although independence initially seemed an essential requirement for statistical inference, many central limit theorems depend on what is known as a martingale difference property (see Hall and Heyde, 1980 or White, 1984). Knowing that two random variables U and V are independent allows us to factorize their joint probability distribution: $\mathsf{D}_{\mathsf{u,v}}(u,v) = \mathsf{D}_{\mathsf{u}}(u)\,\mathsf{D}_{\mathsf{v}}(v)$. A weaker requirement involves just factorizing expectations: $\mathsf{E}[UV] = \mathsf{E}[U]\,\mathsf{E}[V]$; this underlaid the construct of white noise. Independence is sufficient for that, but not necessary (for an excellent discussion, see Whittle, 1970). The martingale property is also an intermediate stage. For a stochastic process $\{x_t,\ t = 1,\ldots,T\}$ where $\boldsymbol{X}_{t-1} = (\boldsymbol{X}_0, x_1, \ldots, x_{t-2}, x_{t-1})$ and $|\mu| < \infty$:[7]

x_t is a martingale relative to $\boldsymbol{X}_{t-1}$ if $\mathsf{E}[x_t] = \mu$ and $\mathsf{E}[x_t|\boldsymbol{X}_{t-1}] = x_{t-1}$.

In other words, the best prediction of x_t is the previous outcome x_{t-1}. Possible examples of martingales in economics are interest rates and equity prices. If x_t is a martingale, then its process can be written as $x_t = x_{t-1} + \nu_t$ where $\mathsf{E}[\nu_t|\boldsymbol{X}_{t-1}] = 0$. Further, $\nu_t = x_t - x_{t-1} = \Delta x_t$ is a martingale difference sequence (MDS).

Generally, any stochastic process $\{x_t\}$ is made up of the two components: (a) what can be predicted once the history of the process $\boldsymbol{X}_{t-1}$ is known; and (b) what cannot. For the mean:

$$x_t = \mathsf{E}[x_t \mid \boldsymbol{X}_{t-1}] + \nu_t \tag{2.34}$$

where $\{\nu_t\}$ denotes the unpredictable news (which is why such errors are called 'nus'). To investigate the properties of a martingale, take conditional expectations in (2.34):

$$\mathsf{E}[x_t \mid \boldsymbol{X}_{t-1}] = \mathsf{E}[x_t \mid \boldsymbol{X}_{t-1}] + \mathsf{E}[\nu_t \mid \boldsymbol{X}_{t-1}]. \tag{2.35}$$

In (2.35), $\mathsf{E}[\nu_t \mid \boldsymbol{X}_{t-1}]$ must be zero by construction. When $\mathsf{E}[\nu_t] = 0$ and $\mathsf{E}[\nu_t^2] = \sigma_\nu^2 < \infty$, and the information set available at time t is $\boldsymbol{X}_{t-1}$ then we have the following definition:

ν_t is a mean-innovation process with respect to $\boldsymbol{X}_{t-1}$ if $\mathsf{E}[\nu_t|\boldsymbol{X}_{t-1}] = 0\ \forall t$.

A mean-innovation process is denoted by MIP. Further:

ν_t is an innovation process with respect to $\boldsymbol{X}_{t-1}$ if $\mathsf{D}_\nu(\nu_t|\boldsymbol{X}_{t-1}) = \mathsf{D}_\nu(\nu_t)\ \forall t$.

A random variable x_t is said to be unpredictable in mean from an information set $\mathcal{I}_{t-1}$ if $\mathsf{E}[x_t|\mathcal{I}_{t-1}]$ does not depend on $\mathcal{I}_{t-1}$. Since $x_t = \mathsf{E}[x_t|\boldsymbol{X}_{t-1}] + \nu_t$ implies $\mathsf{E}[\nu_t|\boldsymbol{X}_{t-1}] = 0\ \forall t$, then ν_t is unpredictable in mean from the history $\boldsymbol{X}_{t-1}$ of x and hence is an innovation by construction. In (2.35), ν_t is unpredictable in mean with respect to the whole available information set, and so cannot be predicted from a subset of $\boldsymbol{X}_{t-1}$. But ν_t is a function of $\boldsymbol{X}_t$ (namely $x_t - \mathsf{E}[x_t|\boldsymbol{X}_{t-1}]$), and hence it cannot be predicted from its own past. Thus, the MIP $\{\nu_t\}$ is also an MDS, despite (2.35) involving conditioning on $\boldsymbol{X}_{t-1}$ rather than on the history of ν_t.

To establish that a MIP is an MDS, let $w_t = \sum_{s=1}^{t} \nu_s$ and introduce $\boldsymbol{W}_{t-1} = (\boldsymbol{W}_0, w_1, \ldots, w_{t-1})$. Then $\mathsf{E}[\nu_t|\boldsymbol{W}_t] = \nu_t$ (since $v_t + \sum_{s=1}^{t-1} \nu_s = w_t \in \boldsymbol{W}_t$) and

[7] The conditioning argument should be interpreted as an event relative to the σ-field , not the outcome of a random variable: see Ch.A2.

$\mathsf{E}[\nu_t | \boldsymbol{W}_{t-1}] = 0$ (because ν_t is unpredictable from its own past). Take the conditional expectation of w_t with respect to $\boldsymbol{W}_{t-1}$:

$$\mathsf{E}[w_t \mid \boldsymbol{W}_{t-1}] = \mathsf{E}\left[\sum_{s=1}^{t} \nu_s \mid \boldsymbol{W}_{t-1}\right] = \sum_{s=1}^{t-1} \nu_s = w_{t-1}.$$

Thus, $\{w_t\}$ is a martingale, and since $\nu_t = w_t - w_{t-1} = \Delta w_t$, then $\{\nu_t\}$ is an MDS.

We now demonstrate that these results can be implemented in practice. Consider the level of an autocorrelated random variable, taking as an example real M1 in the UK, denoted by $\{m_t - p_t\}$. Figure 2.6 plots its correlogram, and the correlograms for the residuals from regressing $(m_t - p_t)$ on one lag, on two lags, and on eight lags of itself respectively. As can be seen, the degree of autocorrelation dies out as more of the history is partialled out, leading in Fig. 2.6d to a correlogram like that of an unpredictable series.

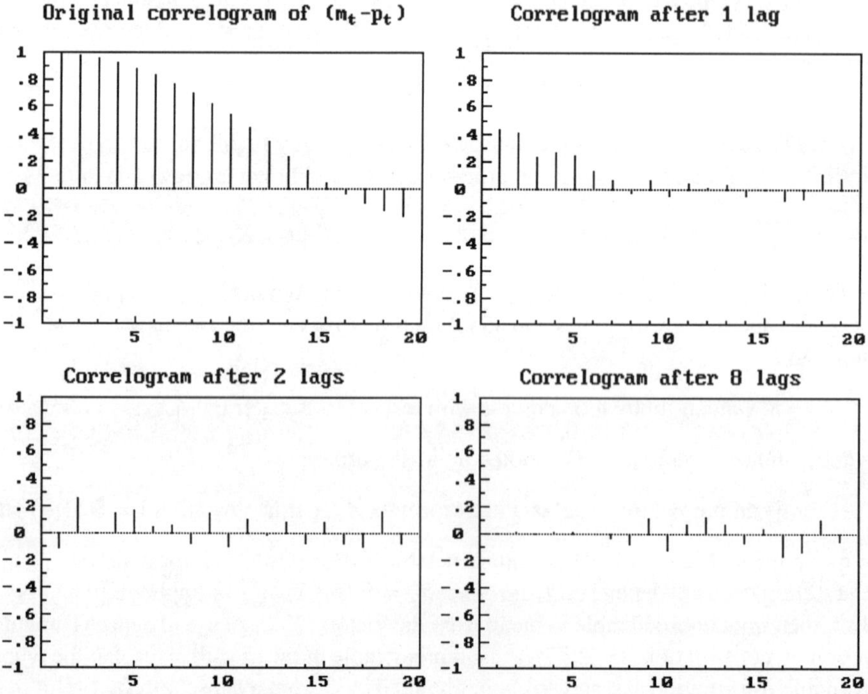

Fig. 2.6 Correlograms after removing lagged information

2.24 Empirical models

The condition 'with respect to the available information set' is crucial in defining an innovation because an innovation might be partly predictable from a different information set. A computer random-number generator provides an example. Such random numbers, denoted $(r_i, i = 1, \ldots, n)$, have the property that starting from a fixed seed r_0 and using a fixed formula, a given computer always generates the same stream $\{r_1, \ldots, r_n\}$. The random numbers are replicable in spite of their apparent randomness but are random in the sense that, without knowledge of the generating formula, the next random number is unpredictable however many have been drawn: r_{n+1} is an innovation relative to the past random numbers $\boldsymbol{R}_n$.[8] But since the computer can reliably reproduce this random number at the $(n+1)^{st}$ stage, r_{n+1} is also perfectly predictable from knowledge of the generating mechanism and ceases to be an innovation. Thus, r_{n+1} is unpredictable on one information set (the history of the process) but is perfectly predictable on another (the seed plus the formula that generates the series). Although an innovation is unique given the information set, it is not unique in general since its status depends upon the information set.

At level A, the complete information structure is known, so that the relevant innovation processes are well-specified and unique. If we denote the DGP innovation process with respect to the entire history $\boldsymbol{X}_{t-1}$ by $\{\nu_t\}$, then ν_t is also an innovation against any subset of the history. As such, $\{\nu_t\}$ is an autonomous process, unaffected by our choice of models or modelling procedures.

At level B, the structure of $\mathsf{D}_X(\cdot)$ is known, and the only unknown is the numerical value of the parameter $\boldsymbol{\theta}$, so the innovation process $\{\nu_t\}$ is again unique and autonomous.

However, at level C, the appropriate information structure is unknown since we do not know $\mathsf{D}_X(\cdot)$. Thus, what constitutes an innovation process (denoted by $\{\epsilon_t\}$) in one model of the DGP may not be an innovation in a different model. Since the status of $\{\epsilon_t\}$ is relative to the information available, it cannot be treated as an autonomous process. This raises the methodological problem of establishing the truth of empirical models, and we are in a position to understand this issue, if not to resolve it.

The claim that a set of random numbers $\{r_i\}$ is generated from a given seed and formula is only one of many possible ways of generating those random numbers. If there are several generators in the computer, and we sample from them using a replicable mechanism, the resulting $\{r_i\}$ remain random and replicable. A postulated formula may match the random numbers generated by the computer for a period then fail, but in the final resort the computer program can be checked for the truth of any claim. In the real world (level C), there are no criteria for empirical truth comparable to looking at the computer program: we cannot have irrefutable knowledge of what underlies human (economic) behaviour.

As a consequence, data analysis is analogous to peeling an onion with an indefinite number of layers, taking off one layer to find another layer below. Creating innovations as in (2.34) is akin to that unpeeling process, since the resulting innovation depends on the information used in the conditioning set and its variance falls as information expands. At level C, we cannot know where to stop without a criterion for the truth of explanations

[8] At least until the generator starts to cycle.

of empirical phenomena, and hence cannot usefully talk about 'true' empirical models. This is the primary reason why a constructive methodology cannot have a rigorous and sound basis. Nevertheless, when the information set of one model demonstrates that the innovation process of a second model is predictable, we can reject that second model as an incomplete explanation relative to the first. Thus, destructive methodologies remain applicable.

The concept of an innovation process helps clarify the earlier assertion that empirical models in economics are derived and not autonomous. At level A, the DGP is autonomous because it is the generating mechanism. At level C, models are defined by their information sets $\boldsymbol{X}_T^1$ and (mean) innovations can be constructed from the observed data by extracting the component $\mathsf{E}[x_t|\boldsymbol{X}_{t-1}]$ from x_t which leaves the (mean) innovation ϵ_t. However, $\{\epsilon_t\}$ is only unpredictable against the information set $\boldsymbol{X}_{t-1}$ and may be predictable from other information. As shown above, $\{\epsilon_t\}$ is a martingale difference sequence constructed by:

$$\epsilon_t = x_t - \mathsf{E}[x_t \mid \boldsymbol{X}_{t-1}]. \tag{2.36}$$

The sequence $\{\epsilon_t\}$ behaves like a set of independent drawings from a probability distribution although a different $\{\epsilon_t\}$ process and a different entailed empirical model result for different $\boldsymbol{X}_{t-1}$. Let U denote the universe of relevant variables. Changes in the empirical model, its parameters $\boldsymbol{\alpha}$ and its associated innovation process $\{\epsilon_t\}$ as the choice of $\boldsymbol{X}_{t-1}$ alters depend on the properties of $\mathsf{D}_{\mathsf{U}}(\cdot|\boldsymbol{\theta})$ and the mapping from U to X. The parameters $\boldsymbol{\alpha}$ of the empirical model are functions of the parameters $\boldsymbol{\theta}$ of the DGP, denoted by $\boldsymbol{\alpha} = \boldsymbol{g}(\boldsymbol{\theta})$, and alter as $\boldsymbol{\theta}$ changes. Hence models are derived from DGPs and we must interpret $\boldsymbol{\alpha}$ accordingly even though once the complete SGM is specified, $\boldsymbol{\alpha}$ appears to be well defined in its own right. Formally, the empirical model is the population manifestation of the postulated model given the DGP.

An economic model might be specified as an equation (or system of equations) with theoretically defined parameters $\boldsymbol{\beta}$ plus an error term with certain assumed properties (such as $u_t \sim \mathsf{IN}[0, \sigma_u^2]$). In such a case, the status of $\boldsymbol{\beta}$ may be unclear until the conditions needed to estimate the postulated model are specified. For example, in the model:

$$y_t = z_t\beta + u_t \text{ where } u_t \sim \mathsf{IN}\left[0, \sigma_u^2\right],$$

until the relationship between z_t and u_t is specified, the meaning of β is uncertain since $\mathsf{E}[z_t u_t]$ could be either zero or non-zero on the information provided. Using least squares as the estimator implicitly imposes $\mathsf{E}[z_t u_t] = 0$, or else an inconsistent formulation results. This indirect route to model specification occurs in practice, so we allow for it in the framework, although our own approach would proceed from the joint density of $\{(y_t, z_t), t = 1, \ldots, T\}$ (see Ch.6).

It can (and does) happen that the error process of an empirical model in economics is not an innovation with respect to its own information set. Models without innovation errors against their own conditioning information are incomplete explanations. This can happen at level C because of restrictive SGM assumptions relative to the actual but unknown DGP, as occurred with (2.1) when we sought to explain the inflation data. To understand this issue more fully, we reconsider white-noise processes.

2.25 White noise and innovations

White noise was defined in §2.9 for a zero-mean, finite-variance stochastic process $\{u_t\}$ with $\mathsf{E}[u_t] = 0$ and $\mathsf{E}[u_t^2] = \sigma_u^2 < \infty$ by $\mathsf{E}[u_t \boldsymbol{U}_{t-1}] = \mathbf{0}$ where $\boldsymbol{U}_{t-1} = \{\boldsymbol{U}_0, u_1, \ldots, u_{t-1}\}$. Define an empirical model to be data coherent if its error process is white noise (see Davidson *et al.*, 1978), then we have the following theorem:

a MIP $\{\epsilon_t\}$ must be white noise, but a white-noise process $\{u_t\}$ need not be a MIP.

We established the first part of this result in §2.23, by demonstrating that a MIP is an MDS and so is not predictable in expectation from its own past, since $\mathsf{E}[\epsilon_t | \boldsymbol{E}_{t-1}] = 0$ implies that $\mathsf{E}[\epsilon_t \boldsymbol{E}_{t-1}] = \mathbf{0}$ when $\boldsymbol{E}_{t-1} = (\boldsymbol{E}_0, \epsilon_1, \ldots, \epsilon_{t-1})$. A counter-example shows that the converse is false, namely, a white-noise process need not be a MIP. Let $\{u_t\}$ be a white-noise process which depends on two mutually independent, strong white-noise processes $\{\eta_t\}$ and $\{v_t\}$ where $u_t = \eta_{t-1} + v_t$. Then:

$$\begin{aligned} \mathsf{E}[u_t u_{t-1}] &= \mathsf{E}[(\eta_{t-1} + v_t)(\eta_{t-2} + v_{t-1})] \\ &= \mathsf{E}[\eta_{t-1}\eta_{t-2}] + \mathsf{E}[\eta_{t-1} v_{t-1}] + \mathsf{E}[v_t \eta_{t-2}] + \mathsf{E}[v_t v_{t-1}] \end{aligned} \tag{2.37}$$

all of which are zero since $\{\eta_t\}$ and $\{v_t\}$ are white noise and independent of each other. Further, $\mathsf{E}[u_t u_{t-k}] = 0 \; \forall k > 1$. Hence $\{u_t\}$ is white noise. However:

$$\mathsf{E}[u_t \eta_{t-1}] = \mathsf{E}[\eta_{t-1}\eta_{t-1}] + \mathsf{E}[v_t \eta_{t-1}] = \mathsf{V}[\eta_{t-1}] \neq 0 \tag{2.38}$$

so $\{u_t\}$ is not an innovation against the lagged information η_{t-1}. Consequently, data coherence is a weak property of an empirical model. We will return to the methodological implications of this result for the theory of reduction and the properties of models with assumed autoregressive errors.

There are three important implications of these results concerning choices between models, information sets, and predictor functions respectively. First, consider two distinct empirical models denoted M_1 and M_2 with MIPs $\{\nu_t\}$ and $\{\epsilon_t\}$ relative to their own information sets, where ν_t and ϵ_t have constant, finite variances σ_ν^2 and σ_ϵ^2 respectively. Then M_1 variance-dominates M_2 if $\sigma_\nu^2 < \sigma_\epsilon^2$, denoted by $\mathsf{M}_1 \succ \mathsf{M}_2$. Variance-dominance is transitive since if $\mathsf{M}_1 \succ \mathsf{M}_2$ and $\mathsf{M}_2 \succ \mathsf{M}_3$ then $\mathsf{M}_1 \succ \mathsf{M}_3$, and anti-symmetric since if $\mathsf{M}_1 \succ \mathsf{M}_2$ then it cannot be true that $\mathsf{M}_2 \succ \mathsf{M}_1$. It follows from §2.23 that a model without a MIP error can be variance-dominated by a model with a MIP on a common data-set.

Second, a DGP with finite variance cannot be variance-dominated in the population by any models thereof (see e.g. Theil, 1971, p543). Let $\boldsymbol{U}_{t-1}$ denote the universe of information for the DGP and let $\boldsymbol{X}_{t-1}$ be a subset, with associated innovation sequences $\{\nu_{u,t}\}$ and $\{\nu_{x,t}\}$. Then as $\{\boldsymbol{X}_{t-1}\} \subseteq \{\boldsymbol{U}_{t-1}\}$, $\mathsf{E}[\nu_{u,t} | \boldsymbol{X}_{t-1}] = 0$, whereas $\mathsf{E}[\nu_{x,t} | \boldsymbol{U}_{t-1}]$ need not be zero. Equally, a model with an innovation error cannot be variance-dominated by a model which uses only a subset of the same information. In finite samples, randomness and degrees-of-freedom corrections could lead to estimated models violating such conditions.

Third, if $\epsilon_t = x_t - \mathsf{E}[x_t|\boldsymbol{X}_{t-1}]$, then σ_ϵ^2 is no larger than the variance of any other empirical model error defined by $\xi_t = x_t - G[x_t|\boldsymbol{X}_{t-1}]$ whatever the choice of $G[\cdot]$. This result is just an application of the conditional expectation being the minimum mean-square error predictor and is proved as follows. Let σ_ξ^2 denote $\mathsf{E}[\xi_t^2]$ where $\mathsf{E}[\xi_t^2] = \mathsf{E}[(x_t - G[x_t|\boldsymbol{X}_{t-1}])^2]$, then:

$$\sigma_\xi^2 = \mathsf{E}\left[\left(\{x_t - \mathsf{E}\left[x_t \mid \boldsymbol{X}_{t-1}\right]\} - \{G\left[x_t \mid \boldsymbol{X}_{t-1}\right] - \mathsf{E}\left[x_t \mid \boldsymbol{X}_{t-1}\right]\}\right)^2\right].$$

The first term on the right is ϵ_t and the second is a function $H\left[x_t|\boldsymbol{X}_{t-1}\right]$, say. Since ϵ_t is a MIP against $\boldsymbol{X}_{t-1}$, then $\mathsf{E}\left[\epsilon_t H\left[x_t|\boldsymbol{X}_{t-1}\right]\right] = 0$, and hence:

$$\sigma_\xi^2 = \mathsf{E}\left[\left(\epsilon_t - H\left[x_t \mid \boldsymbol{X}_{t-1}\right]\right)^2\right] = \sigma_\epsilon^2 + \mathsf{E}\left[H\left[x_t \mid \boldsymbol{X}_{t-1}\right]\right]^2 \geq \sigma_\epsilon^2.$$

The converse of this result is false: the model with the smallest error variance in a class need be neither the conditional expectation nor the DGP.

These implications favour general rather than simple empirical models, given any choice of information set, and suggest first modelling the conditional expectation, then higher moments. A model which nests all contending explanations as special cases must variance-dominate in its class, but need not have a useful interpretation (perhaps having non-constant parameters). To offset a tendency to build monster empirical models, we introduce a parsimony condition. Let model M_j be characterized by a parameter vector with κ_j elements, then (see Hendry and Richard, 1982):

> M_1 is parsimoniously undominated in the class $\{\mathsf{M}_i\}$ if $\forall i$, $\kappa_1 \leq \kappa_i$ and no $\mathsf{M}_i \succ \mathsf{M}_1$.

Model-selection procedures (such as AIC or the Schwarz criterion: see Judge, Griffiths, Hill, Lütkepohl and Lee, 1985) seek parsimoniously undominated models using different penalties for lack of parsimony. These criteria for model choice hold as population constructs and are necessary but not sufficient. Since no sufficient criteria exist in an empirical science, other model selection criteria, suggested by the theory of reduction, will be added to the list of necessary conditions in due course. Some of these are sufficient for other necessary conditions and hence provide stronger requirements.

2.26 Autocorrelated shocks

The analysis in §2.25 helps clarify two problems in econometrics. Sometimes equations are defined with autocorrelated error processes as in:

$$y_t = z_t\beta + u_t \ \text{ where } \ u_t = \rho u_{t-1} + \epsilon_t \ \text{ and } \ \epsilon_t \sim \mathsf{IN}\left[0, \sigma_\epsilon^2\right].$$

Because white-noise errors can be constructed (via a mean innovation), models can be rewritten by sequential conditioning as in (2.34) to yield a mechanism which has a mean-innovation error: this includes the representation of the DGP.[9] So even if the economic world has autocorrelated shocks, that is essentially a metaphor since an isomorphic construction allows us to rewrite the DGP with an innovation process. Models with autoregressive errors must be a restriction on a parameterization, rather than a necessary ingredient of generating mechanisms and Chapter 7 will investigate that issue in detail.

Second, since an innovation is relative to the available information, there are no definitive criteria for terminating empirical modelling at level C. Achieving a white-noise error does not ensure that an extension of the information set will not produce a better model.[10] Econometric textbooks often assume the DGP is known, so the issue of extending the information set does not arise, and a truth criterion (namely, matching the DGP) is available. If the lack of a truth criterion is not to pose insuperable difficulties at level C, we require alternative criteria which play an equivalent role. Such criteria must specify when to terminate a modelling exercise in practice and how to select between empirical models, yet do so in a way that produces acceptable models. Since none of the models coincides with the DGP, we must take care to avoid contradictions. Moreover, should the DGP transpire to be one of the models considered, the criteria should select it even if we could not be sure that such a model was the truth. These considerations point towards a methodology for analysing empirical observations which will unfold as we proceed.

2.27 Sequential factorization

Reconsider sequential factorization in a slight generalization of the first statistical generating mechanism written in the form:

$$y_t = \alpha + \beta y_{t-1} + \epsilon_t \text{ for } t = 1, \ldots, T, \tag{2.39}$$

but assuming that $|\beta| < 1$, with initial condition $y_0 = 0$ and $\epsilon_t \sim \mathsf{IN}\left[0, \sigma^2\right]$. The concepts developed above apply directly to (2.39). When (2.39) is the DGP, for $t > 1$:

$$\mathsf{E}\left[y_t \mid y_{t-1}\right] = \alpha + \beta y_{t-1} \text{ and hence } y_t - \mathsf{E}\left[y_t \mid y_{t-1}\right] = \epsilon_t. \tag{2.40}$$

When it is not known that (2.39) is the DGP, we use an SGM with the less restrictive conditioning set $\mathbf{Y}_{t-1}$ to ensure a mean innovation error process. Let $\nu_t = y_t - \mathsf{E}\left[y_t | \mathbf{Y}_{t-1}\right]$, then since $\mathsf{E}\left[y_t | \mathbf{Y}_{t-1}\right] = \mathsf{E}\left[y_t | y_{t-1}\right]$, given (2.39), $\nu_t = y_t - \alpha - \beta y_{t-1} = \epsilon_t$. Thus, when the empirical model includes the DGP as a special case, the model's innovation coincides with the error that generated the data: the methodology works when we stumble over the truth.

[9] Moving-average errors may provide a more parsimonious representation. These can usually be mapped to an invertible form providing over-differencing has not occurred. Also, by suitable scaling transformations, any non-constant variances can be removed in principle; in practice, it is not easy to construct homoscedastic MIPs.

[10] Since white-noise processes need not be MIPs, a better model may exist on the same information.

When $\beta \neq 0$, the ys can be highly interdependent: depending upon the value of β, the correlation of y_t with y_{t-1} can exceed 0.99. This highlights one aspect of why 1930s econometricians were worried about serial correlation in time series since it is not obvious how much net information is acquired from observing $\{y_t\}$ in such a situation. Consider the joint probability distribution of the whole sample $\mathbf{Y}_T^1 = (y_1, \ldots, y_T) = \left(\mathbf{Y}_{T-1}^1 : y_T\right)$ from (2.39), given the parameters $\boldsymbol{\theta}' = \left(\alpha, \beta, \sigma^2\right) \in \Theta \subset \mathbb{R}^2 \times \mathbb{R}_+$ and the initial conditions $\mathbf{Y}_0$:

$$\mathsf{D_Y}\left(\mathbf{Y}_T^1 \mid \mathbf{Y}_0, \boldsymbol{\theta}\right) = \mathsf{D_Y}\left(y_1, \ldots, y_T \mid \mathbf{Y}_0, \boldsymbol{\theta}\right) = \mathsf{D_Y}\left(\mathbf{Y}_{T-1}^1 : y_T \mid \mathbf{Y}_0, \boldsymbol{\theta}\right). \quad (2.41)$$

To analyse interdependent data like that generated by (2.39), repeatedly factorize the joint distribution into its sequence of conditional densities as in (2.32):

$$\begin{aligned} \mathsf{D_Y}\left(\mathbf{Y}_{T-1}^1 : y_T \mid \mathbf{Y}_0, \boldsymbol{\theta}\right) &= \mathsf{D_y}\left(y_T \mid \mathbf{Y}_{T-1}, \boldsymbol{\theta}\right) \mathsf{D_Y}\left(\mathbf{Y}_{T-1}^1 \mid \mathbf{Y}_0, \boldsymbol{\theta}\right) \\ &= \cdots \\ &= \prod_{t=1}^{T} \mathsf{D_y}\left(y_t \mid \mathbf{Y}_{t-1}, \boldsymbol{\theta}\right). \end{aligned} \quad (2.42)$$

The final term in (2.42) reveals that the interdependent joint distribution of $\{y_t\}$ has been factorized into the product of T conditionally independent components $\mathsf{D_y}\left(y_t | \mathbf{Y}_{t-1}, \boldsymbol{\theta}\right)$. The means of each of these conditional distributions are given by (2.40), and the variability in y_t around its conditional mean determines $\mathsf{D_y}(\cdot)$ given $\mathbf{Y}_{t-1}$. Thus, from (2.42), since $\nu_t = y_t - \mathsf{E}\left[y_t | \mathbf{Y}_{t-1}\right]$:[11]

$$\prod_{t=1}^{T} \mathsf{D_y}\left(y_t \mid \mathbf{Y}_{t-1}, \boldsymbol{\theta}\right) = \prod_{t=1}^{T} \mathsf{D_y}\left(\nu_t \mid \mathbf{Y}_{t-1}, \boldsymbol{\theta}\right). \quad (2.43)$$

As it happens, $\{\nu_t | \mathbf{Y}_{t-1}\} = \{\epsilon_t\}$ in this problem, but more generally, $\{\nu_t | \mathbf{Y}_{t-1}\}$ will be a constructed mean-innovation process. Unsurprisingly, the joint density of the ys collapses to the product of the densities of the generating errors. However, (2.42) is more general than that, since it reveals the first main factorization theorem:

> the joint density for any set $\mathbf{Y}_T^1$ can be written as a product of the densities of the mean innovations constructed on the sequential information set.

Chapter 4 extends this analysis. Such a factorization is important because:

(a) a complicated intercorrelated data process is reduced to one expressed in terms of mean-innovation errors; and
(b) it is generic and involves no loss of information, in that from the νs and the sequential conditional means, we can recover the original data, precisely because the νs are constructed from that data.

[11] The Jacobian for transforming from $\{y_t\}$ to $\{\nu_t\}$ is unity.

In general, however, $\{\nu_t\}$ in these derivations is neither an autonomous process impinging on an otherwise non-stochastic model nor is it sequentially independent: at level C, the error term is constructed by the specification of the empirical model. Thus, the error terms have a different status in empirical research from that assumed at level A, unless we invoke an assumption which transforms level C into level A. Leamer (1978) calls this assumption the 'axiom of correct specification', and we call it the 'assumption of omniscience'. At level A, econometrics asserts omniscience by postulating that the DGP is known. Such an assumption is essential for theoretical derivations, is manifestly sufficient (when true) to sustain empirical research, but it is not one on which to base a practical methodology for analysing data. It is more than just inconvenient to work from an assumption which is always falsified in practice. However, an important aspect of the approach here is that the assumption of omniscience is not necessary for empirical modelling. Precisely because the error term is constructed by the specification of the model (via the data history), the error and the model can be designed to satisfy certain desirable properties by suitable choice of the information set, an issue to which we now turn.

2.28 Model design

Because the error process is constructed at level C, it is not autonomous in general. The corresponding empirical model is not autonomous either, but is designed jointly with the error. Since empirical models are human artefacts, they are designed either explicitly or implicitly to have certain properties. Crudely, in the 1950s, the design criteria were that the signs of coefficients were 'correct' (i.e. matched theoretically-based preconceptions); in the 1960s, white-noise errors were usually required; in the 1970s more sophisticated questions were asked about models, including whether they had constant parameters, satisfied valid exogeneity conditions, and so on. Chapter 9 presents design criteria in detail.

Since empirical models are designed and we lack omniscience, then without an external criterion, we cannot tell of a given mean-innovation process whether it is that of the DGP or merely constructed as a model's MIP. Nevertheless, we can tell when it is not a MIP, such as when errors are autocorrelated. Similarly, non-constant coefficients reveal that parameters are not invariant. More generally, we need to formulate operational criteria for model design. Such criteria cannot be postulated arbitrarily, no matter how plausible they seem: to make the methodology viable, the relevant criteria must also be delivered by the theory.

Given any formalized DGP, there exists a set of analytical rules such that any model entailed by that mechanism can be derived mathematically. The theory of reduction seeks to explain how to get from the DGP to each empirical model; i.e. what reductions are entailed by each model. In the process of reduction from the DGP, some information will be lost. Models will be better representations of the DGP the less information they lose and the more they retain. This insight resolves the problem of selecting design criteria in terms of how much information is lost at each step of the reduction sequence: design criteria correspond to selecting models which minimize the information lost by reduction. Hence we do not need auxiliary conditions of model adequacy postulated from outside. However, we do need to investigate the range of possible reductions and measures of potential information losses. Most existing model-building criteria transpire to measure losses involved in reductions, so the approach achieves an important synthesis as well.

Before further analysis, we discriminate between explicit design and covert design. In the former, modelling aims to achieve certain pre-assigned criteria. In the latter, the model-design criteria are hidden and so the meaning of reported results may be unclear; investigators sometimes act as if they are unaware that they are designing their models. As an analogy, we generally drive across bridges without worrying about the soundness of their construction because we are reasonably sure that someone rigorously checked their engineering principles and practice. Economists must do likewise with models or else attach the warning 'not responsible if attempted use leads to collapse'. Stretching the analogy, one would be very worried by an engineering approach in which, when bridges showed cracks, thick wallpaper was pasted on top to hide the cracks. Covert design, where a sequence of econometrics problems is patched seriatim, looks all too like wallpapering over cracks and may help explain why empirical econometric evidence has low esteem in economics.

To summarize: at level C, the data-generation process is unknown, but determines the form and parameters of empirical models, which arise as reductions of that DGP directed by a conjectured SGM. A taxonomy of reduction stages is developed in Chapter 9. Each reduction induces a design criterion corresponding to no information loss from that reduction. An empirical model is well designed if there is no loss of information at each stage of reduction and will thereby satisfy all of the design criteria. We cannot know whether any given model corresponds to the truth, but models can be tested against available information sets to evaluate the adequacy of their construction. Models which do not satisfy the design criteria can be rejected. Models which satisfy all of the design criteria (called congruent since they match the available evidence in all measured respects) are retained. Chapters 4–7 prepare the ground, but already we have the criteria of mean innovation errors, with variance dominance, and structural, and hence constant, parameters.

2.29 A dynamic solved example

Consider the process:

$$y_t = \alpha z_t + \beta y_{t-1} + \epsilon_{1t} \text{ where } |\beta| < 1 \tag{2.44}$$

when

$$z_t = \lambda z_{t-1} + \epsilon_{2t} \text{ where } |\lambda| < 1 \tag{2.45}$$

and

$$\epsilon_t = \begin{pmatrix} \epsilon_{1t} \\ \epsilon_{2t} \end{pmatrix} \sim \mathsf{IN}_2 \left[\begin{pmatrix} 0 \\ 0 \end{pmatrix}, \begin{pmatrix} \sigma_{11} & \sigma_{12} \\ \sigma_{12} & \sigma_{22} \end{pmatrix} \right]. \tag{2.46}$$

(a) Derive $\mathsf{E}[\boldsymbol{x}_t|\boldsymbol{x}_{t-1}]$, $\mathsf{V}[\boldsymbol{x}_t|\boldsymbol{x}_{t-1}]$ and hence $\mathsf{D}_\mathsf{x}(\boldsymbol{x}_t|\boldsymbol{x}_{t-1},\boldsymbol{\theta})$ where $\boldsymbol{x}'_t = (y_t\ z_t)$ and $\mathsf{D}_\mathsf{x}(\cdot)$ denotes a density function.

(b) To what uses might $\mathsf{D}_\mathsf{x}(\boldsymbol{x}_t|\boldsymbol{x}_{t-1},\boldsymbol{\theta})$ be put in: (i) economics; (ii) econometrics?

(c) Derive $\mathsf{E}[\boldsymbol{x}_t]$ and $\mathsf{V}[\boldsymbol{x}_t]$. Show that $\mathsf{V}[\boldsymbol{x}_t|\boldsymbol{x}_{t-1}]$ is never larger than $\mathsf{V}[\boldsymbol{x}_t]$ in the sense that $\mathsf{V}[\boldsymbol{x}_t] - \mathsf{V}[\boldsymbol{x}_t|\boldsymbol{x}_{t-1}]$ is positive semi-definite. What are: (i) the economic; and (ii) the econometric implications of this result?

(d) Derive $\mathsf{E}[y_t|z_t,y_{t-1}]$ from (a) (or otherwise) and discuss your result in relation to equation (2.44). Why is the conditional expectation not the same as equation (2.44) in general? What conditions ensure that they coincide? Can these conditions be interpreted: (i) economically; (ii) statistically?

(e) Derive $\mathsf{D}_\mathsf{z}(z_t|z_{t-1},\boldsymbol{\psi})$. What does the result tell you about the use of information on the past of y when predicting future z? Is the absence of y_{t-1} in (2.45) of any importance in economics? Is the past of z useful in predicting y? Always (given (2.44)+(2.45))?

(f) Derive $\mathsf{D}_\mathsf{y}(y_t|\,\boldsymbol{Y}_{t-1},\boldsymbol{\mu})$. What does the result tell you about the loss of information in the reduction from eliminating current and past values of z from (2.44)?

Solution

(a) By direct substitution from (2.44) and (2.45):

$$\boldsymbol{x}_t \mid \boldsymbol{x}_{t-1} \sim \mathsf{N}_2\left[\begin{pmatrix}\beta & \alpha\lambda\\ 0 & \lambda\end{pmatrix}\begin{pmatrix}y_{t-1}\\ z_{t-1}\end{pmatrix}, \begin{pmatrix}\sigma_{11}+2\alpha\sigma_{12}+\alpha^2\sigma_{22} & \sigma_{12}+\alpha\sigma_{22}\\ \sigma_{12}+\alpha\sigma_{22} & \sigma_{22}\end{pmatrix}\right]. \tag{2.47}$$

Thus, $\boldsymbol{x}_t|\boldsymbol{x}_{t-1} \sim \mathsf{N}_2[\boldsymbol{\pi}\boldsymbol{x}_{t-1},\boldsymbol{\Omega}]$ so that $\mathsf{D}_\mathsf{x}(\boldsymbol{x}_t|\boldsymbol{x}_{t-1},\boldsymbol{\theta})$ is normal, with $\mathsf{E}[\boldsymbol{x}_t|\boldsymbol{x}_{t-1}] = \boldsymbol{\pi}\boldsymbol{x}_{t-1}$ and $\mathsf{V}[\boldsymbol{x}_t|\boldsymbol{x}_{t-1}] = \boldsymbol{\Omega} = \{\omega_{ij}\}$.

(b) This question is probing the reverse of the solved example in §2.20: given the behavioural equations, what is the joint density of the observables? Since $\mathsf{E}[\boldsymbol{x}_t|\boldsymbol{x}_{t-1}] = \boldsymbol{\pi}\boldsymbol{x}_{t-1}$, the conditional mean is non-constant over time, whereas $\boldsymbol{\Omega}$ remains constant. In both economics and econometrics, the sequential joint density is the statistical generating mechanism (e.g. how the data would be generated in a Monte Carlo study), even when (2.44) and (2.45) capture the structure of the agents' behaviour. One role of (2.47) in economics is as the baseline against which any claimed structural model can be tested: (2.44) and (2.45) restrict $\boldsymbol{\pi}$ to have one zero coefficient (corresponding to no effect from past y to z: see Ch.5), and that hypothesis can be tested against an unrestricted estimate of $\boldsymbol{\pi}$. A second role of (2.47) in econometrics is for forecasting future outcomes of $\boldsymbol{x}_t$ given data on $\boldsymbol{x}_{t-1}$, and it is also central to estimation via the likelihood function (see Ch.10).

(c) Since the bivariate process is stationary (because $|\beta| < 1, |\lambda| < 1$: see Ch.A4) we have $\mathsf{E}[z_t] = (1-\lambda)^{-1}\mathsf{E}[\epsilon_{2t}] = 0$; and $\mathsf{E}[y_t] = (1-\beta)^{-1}(\alpha\mathsf{E}[z_t] + \mathsf{E}[\epsilon_{1t}]) = 0$. As $\mathsf{V}[z_t] = \mathsf{E}[z_t^2]$ $(= \sigma_z^2 = \sigma_{22}(1-\lambda^2)^{-1})$, $\mathsf{C}[y_t,z_t] = \mathsf{E}[z_t y_t]$ $(= \sigma_{yz})$, and $\mathsf{V}[y_t] = \mathsf{E}[y_t^2]$ $(= \sigma_y^2)$ then:

$$\begin{aligned}\mathsf{V}[z_t] &= \mathsf{E}\left[(\lambda z_{t-1}+\epsilon_{2t})^2\right] = \lambda^2\sigma_z^2+\sigma_{22} = \omega_{22}+\lambda^2\sigma_z^2;\\ \mathsf{C}[y_t,z_t] &= \mathsf{E}\left[(\beta y_{t-1}+\alpha\lambda z_{t-1}+\epsilon_{1t}+\alpha\epsilon_{2t})(\lambda z_{t-1}+\epsilon_{2t})\right]\\ &= \left(\alpha\lambda^2\sigma_z^2+\sigma_{12}+\alpha\sigma_{22}\right)(1-\beta\lambda)^{-1}\\ &= \omega_{12}+\left(\alpha\lambda^2\sigma_z^2+\beta\lambda\omega_{12}\right)(1-\beta\lambda)^{-1};\end{aligned}$$

and:

$$\begin{aligned}\mathsf{V}[y_t] &= \mathsf{E}\left[(\beta y_{t-1}+\alpha\lambda z_{t-1}+\epsilon_{1t}+\alpha\epsilon_{2t})^2\right]\\ &= \left[(\alpha\lambda)^2\sigma_z^2+\sigma_{11}+\alpha^2\sigma_{22}+2\alpha\sigma_{12}+2\alpha\beta\lambda\sigma_{yz}\right](1-\beta^2)^{-1}\\ &= \omega_{11}+\left(\alpha^2\lambda^2\sigma_z^2+2\alpha\beta\lambda\sigma_{yz}+\beta^2\omega_{11}\right)(1-\beta^2)^{-1}.\end{aligned}$$

Thus, the unconditional distribution of $\boldsymbol{x}_t$ is $\mathsf{N}_2[\mathbf{0}, \boldsymbol{V}]$ where:

$$\boldsymbol{V}=\begin{pmatrix}\sigma_y^2 & \sigma_{yz}\\ \sigma_{yz} & \sigma_z^2\end{pmatrix}.$$

In each case, the result has been written as a deviation from the conditional (co)variance, so the matrix we require to check for being positive semi-definite is:

$$\begin{pmatrix}\left[\alpha^2\lambda^2\sigma_z^2+2\alpha\beta\lambda\sigma_{yz}+\beta^2\omega_{11}\right](1-\beta^2)^{-1} & \left[\alpha\lambda^2\sigma_z^2+\beta\lambda\omega_{12}\right](1-\beta\lambda)^{-1}\\ \left[\alpha\lambda^2\sigma_z^2+\beta\lambda\omega_{12}\right](1-\beta\lambda)^{-1} & \lambda^2\sigma_z^2\end{pmatrix}. \tag{2.48}$$

Deriving and checking this result as above is both tedious and restricted to the particular parameters in the DGP. A general solution is, in fact, easier. Write (2.47) as the model:

$$\boldsymbol{x}_t=\boldsymbol{\pi}\boldsymbol{x}_{t-1}+\boldsymbol{\nu}_t, \tag{2.49}$$

where $\boldsymbol{\nu}_t \sim \mathsf{IN}_2[\mathbf{0},\boldsymbol{\Omega}]$ and $\boldsymbol{\Omega}=\mathsf{V}[\boldsymbol{x}_t|\boldsymbol{x}_{t-1}]$, so that given weak stationarity, $\mathsf{E}[\boldsymbol{x}_t]=\mathbf{0}$ and $\mathsf{V}[\boldsymbol{x}_t]=\boldsymbol{V}=\boldsymbol{\pi}\boldsymbol{V}\boldsymbol{\pi}'+\boldsymbol{\Omega}$. Thus, $\boldsymbol{V}-\boldsymbol{\Omega}=\boldsymbol{\pi}\boldsymbol{V}\boldsymbol{\pi}'$ which is positive semi-definite. It can be checked by direct multiplication that $\boldsymbol{\pi}\boldsymbol{V}\boldsymbol{\pi}'$ is equal to the matrix in (2.48).

The implications of this result are that: (i) if (say) a policy agency controls the z process and changes the values of its parameters (λ,ω_{22}), then both the equations in $\mathsf{D_x}(\boldsymbol{x}_t|\boldsymbol{x}_{t-1},\boldsymbol{\theta})$ in (2.47) will change, whereas (2.44) will not change if $(\alpha,\beta,\sigma_{11})$ are invariant parameters. Thus, the policy agency can alter $\mathsf{V}[\boldsymbol{x}_t]$ by altering (λ,ω_{22}); (ii) dynamics amplify variance, or conversely conditioning reduces variance, with clear implications for modelling.

(d) Using the properties of the multivariate normal, for $\gamma=\sigma_{12}\sigma_{22}^{-1}$:

$$\begin{aligned}\mathsf{E}[y_t \mid z_t, y_{t-1}] &= \beta y_{t-1}+\alpha\lambda z_{t-1}+(\sigma_{12}+\alpha\sigma_{22})\,\sigma_{22}^{-1}(z_t-\lambda z_{t-1})\\ &= (\gamma+\alpha)\,z_t+\beta y_{t-1}-\gamma\lambda z_{t-1}.\end{aligned} \tag{2.50}$$

This equation differs from (2.44) (the structural representation) if $\sigma_{12} \neq 0$, since in that case there are two influences from z_t onto y_t, namely through α and σ_{12}. If $\sigma_{12} = 0$:

$$\mathsf{E}\left[y_t \mid z_t, y_{t-1}\right] = \beta y_{t-1} + \alpha z_t,$$

so that $\sigma_{12} = 0$ is the condition needed to ensure that (2.44) coincides with the conditional regression. Moreover, that extra condition is testable in this model. The economic interpretation is that the agents' plan in (2.44) need not be a contingent one, but is if $\sigma_{12} = 0$. The statistical interpretation is that the form of the DGP intimately links the conditional model of y_t given z_t and $\boldsymbol{x}_{t-1}$ with the marginal model of z_t. This notion will reappear in the context of exogeneity below. If $\sigma_{12} \neq 0$, the regression will not capture the parameters of interest, and its coefficients will be susceptible to change as (λ, ω_{22}) changes.

(e) $\mathsf{D}_z\left(z_t|z_{t-1}, \psi\right)$ is the marginal process of (2.47) and hence is $\mathsf{N}\left[\lambda z_{t-1}, \omega_{22}\right]$. The past of y is irrelevant to predicting future z and this can be important for predicting future y conditional on future z. Note that the economy in (2.44)+(2.45) is decomposable and is a causal chain from z to y. Conversely, if $\alpha\lambda \neq 0$, the past of z matters for predicting y.

(f) This part is more difficult to solve, since we must marginalize the joint density with respect to $\boldsymbol{Z}_T^1$, which includes all values of z. Write the first equation in (2.47) as:

$$y_t = \beta y_{t-1} + \alpha\lambda z_{t-1} + \nu_{1t}. \tag{2.51}$$

Lag (2.51) by one period, multiply by λ and subtract the result from (2.51) to create the term $(z_{t-1} - \lambda z_{t-2})$ which will reduce to ν_{2t-1} by (2.45) and (2.47):

$$\begin{aligned} y_t - \lambda y_{t-1} &= \beta\left(y_{t-1} - \lambda y_{t-2}\right) + \alpha\lambda\left(z_{t-1} - \lambda z_{t-2}\right) + \left(\nu_{1t} - \lambda\nu_{1t-1}\right) \\ &= \beta\left(y_{t-1} - \lambda y_{t-2}\right) + \left(\alpha\lambda\nu_{2t-1} + \nu_{1t} - \lambda\nu_{1t-1}\right). \end{aligned} \tag{2.52}$$

More efficient techniques for solving this kind of problem are developed below. The next step is to derive the conditional expectation of y_t given $\boldsymbol{Y}_{t-1}$. Again this is not easy, since we must express every term in (2.52) as a function of the conditioning information. First, $\nu_{2t} = \omega_{12}\omega_{11}^{-1}\nu_{1t} + \eta_t$ where η_t is independent of ν_{1t} and past values thereof due to normality. Thus:

$$\begin{aligned} y_t &= (\lambda + \beta)\, y_{t-1} - \beta\lambda y_{t-2} + \nu_{1t} - \lambda\left(1 - \alpha\omega_{12}\omega_{11}^{-1}\right)\nu_{1t-1} + \alpha\lambda\eta_{t-1} \\ &= \gamma_1 y_{t-1} + \gamma_2 y_{t-2} + \nu_{1t} + \gamma_3\nu_{1t-1} + \alpha\lambda\eta_{t-1}. \end{aligned} \tag{2.53}$$

From (2.48), $|\gamma_3| < 1$ since $|\lambda| < 1$ and:

$$\alpha\omega_{12} = \alpha\sigma_{12} + \alpha^2\sigma_{22} < \omega_{11} = \sigma_{11} + 2\alpha\sigma_{12} + \alpha^2\sigma_{22}.$$

The error on (2.53) is an invertible first-order MA, which can be rewritten as $u_t + \phi u_{t-1}$, where ϕ is determined by matching moments $\mathsf{E}[u_t u_{t-1}] = \phi\mathsf{E}[u_{t-1}^2] = \phi\sigma_u^2$ with $\mathsf{E}[(\nu_{1t} + \gamma_3\nu_{1t-1} + \alpha\lambda\eta_{t-1})^2] = (1 + \gamma_3^2)\omega_{11} + \alpha^2\lambda^2\sigma_\eta^2$ and:

$$\mathsf{E}\left[\left(\nu_{1t} + \gamma_3\nu_{1t-1} + \alpha\lambda\eta_{t-1}\right)\left(\nu_{1t-1} + \gamma_3\nu_{1t-2} + \alpha\lambda\eta_{t-2}\right)\right] = \gamma_3\omega_{11}.$$

Then $\{u_t + \phi u_{t-1}\}$ can be eliminated by repeatedly substituting backwards in time from lagged versions of (2.53):

$$u_{t-1} = y_{t-1} - \gamma_1 y_{t-2} - \gamma_2 y_{t-3} - \phi u_{t-2}. \tag{2.54}$$

Terms in longer lags of u_{t-i} are multiplied by increasing powers of ϕ and hence decrease in importance. The outcome is that $\mathsf{E}\left[y_t | \, Y_{t-1}\right]$ depends (with decreasing weights) on all the lags $(y_{t-1}, y_{t-2}, y_{t-3}, \ldots)$. When $\phi \simeq 0$ however:

$$\mathsf{E}\left[y_t \mid Y_{t-1}\right] \simeq (\lambda + \beta)\, y_{t-1} - \beta\lambda y_{t-2}, \tag{2.55}$$

and there is little loss from this approximation, although still a loss of information relative to (2.47) from eliminating Z_T^1 when $\alpha \neq 0$, since e.g. the error variance of $y_t - \mathsf{E}\left[y_t | \, Y_{t-1}\right]$ using (2.55) exceeds ω_{11}. Also note that the $\{\gamma_i\}$ confound the parameters of (2.44) and (2.45), so that information on α is lost.

2.30 Exercises

2.1 Load the data set DATA.

(a) Calculate the correlograms for *CONS*, *INC*, *INFLAT* and *OUTPUT* (i.e. the plot of $\mathsf{corr}(x_t, x_{t-j})$ for $j = 1, \ldots, 20$ for each x_t). How alike are these correlograms across the variables? What economic meaning could such autocorrelations have? How do the correlograms alter for the first difference of each variable?

(b) Regress $CONS_t$ on INC_t and INC_{t-1}; and $\Delta CONS_t$ on ΔINC_t and ΔINC_{t-1} over the whole sample. The DGP is actually consistent with the implication of the Permanent Income/Life-Cycle Hypothesis (PI/LCH) of a long-run unit income elasticity for consumption, so how do you explain your results? Would they refute or be consistent with the PI/LCH if the data were genuine?

(c) Did you look at the data on *CONS* and *INC* carefully? Did you cross plot the levels (and the differences) of the putative consumption function?

2.2 Repeat exercise 2.1 for the data-set in UKM1. Modify 2.1(b) to $\log{(M/P)}_t$ on $\log Y_t$, or R_t on Δp_t. Take account of the ideas discussed in the solved example and any that arose from doing exercise 1.1.

2.3 Consider the data-generation process of $\boldsymbol{x}_t' = (y_t \; z_t)$:

$$y_t = \alpha z_t + \beta z_{t-1} + \epsilon_{1t}, \tag{2.56}$$

when

$$z_t = \lambda z_{t-1} + \epsilon_{2t} \text{ where } |\lambda| < 1, \tag{2.57}$$

and:

$$\epsilon_t = \begin{pmatrix} \epsilon_{1t} \\ \epsilon_{2t} \end{pmatrix} \sim \mathsf{IN}_2 \left[\begin{pmatrix} 0 \\ 0 \end{pmatrix}, \begin{pmatrix} \sigma_{11} & \sigma_{12} \\ \sigma_{12} & \sigma_{22} \end{pmatrix} \right]. \tag{2.58}$$

(a) An investigator postulates the model:

$$\mathsf{E}\left[y_t \mid z_t\right] = \gamma z_t. \tag{2.59}$$

What is the relation that will actually be obtained given (2.56)+(2.57)? (i.e. derive $\mathsf{E}\left[y_t|z_t\right]$, and discuss your result in relation to these equations).

(b) Why is the conditional expectation of y_t given ($\boldsymbol{Z}_t$, $\boldsymbol{Y}_{t-1}$) not the same as equation (2.56) in general? What are: (i) the economic; and (ii) the econometric implications of this result?

(c) Realizing that z_{t-1} has been omitted from (2.59), the investigator now postulates:

$$\mathsf{E}\left[y_t \mid \boldsymbol{Z}_t\right] = \gamma z_t + \delta z_{t-1}. \tag{2.60}$$

What is the relation of the resulting empirical model to the DGP. Under what conditions will the correct parameters be obtained from (2.60)?

2.4 For the stationary process $\{x_t, t = 1, \ldots, T\}$ with history $\boldsymbol{X}_{t-1}^1 = (x_1, \ldots, x_{t-1})$, it happens that $\mathsf{E}\left[x_t|\boldsymbol{X}_{t-1}^1\right] = \pi x_{t-1}$.

(a) Let $\epsilon_t = x_t - \mathsf{E}\left[x_t|\boldsymbol{X}_{t-1}^1\right]$. Show that: (i) $\mathsf{E}\left[\epsilon_t\right] = 0$; (ii) $\mathsf{E}\left[\epsilon_t x_{t-1}|\boldsymbol{X}_{t-1}^1\right] = 0$; (iii) $\mathsf{E}\left[\epsilon_t\epsilon_{t-1}|\boldsymbol{X}_{t-1}^1\right] = 0$. Do (ii) and (iii) generalize to longer lags (i.e. is $\mathsf{E}\left[\epsilon_t\epsilon_{t-2}|\boldsymbol{X}_{t-1}^1\right] = 0$)? What are the implications of (i)–(iii) for model formulation?

(b) Let $v_t = x_t - G\left[x_t|\boldsymbol{X}_{t-1}^1\right]$ where $G\left[\cdot\right]$ is any other predictor of x_t. Show that conditional on using $\boldsymbol{X}_{t-1}^1$, $\mathsf{E}\left[\epsilon_t^2\right] \leq \mathsf{E}\left[v_t^2\right]$. What are the implications of this result for fitting models?

2.5 Consider the model:

$$\begin{aligned} y_t &= \beta z_{t-1} + u_{1t} \text{ where } u_{1t} \sim \mathsf{IN}\left[0, \sigma_{11}\right] \\ z_t &= \lambda z_{t-1} + u_{2t} \text{ where } u_{2t} \sim \mathsf{IN}\left[0, \sigma_{22}\right] \end{aligned}$$

and it is known that $\mathsf{E}\left[u_{1t}u_{2t}\right] = 0$. Given only the above information:

(a) Is u_{1t} white noise? Is $\mathsf{E}\left[u_{1t}z_{t-1}\right] = 0$?

(b) You now discover that actually $u_{1t} = \alpha u_{2t-1} + \epsilon_{1t}$ where $\mathsf{E}\left[\epsilon_{1t}u_{2s}\right] = 0\ \forall t, s$. How does that affect your answers to (a) and (b)?

2.6 Load the variables in DATA.

(a) Formulate a model of $CONS_t$ on a constant, estimated by least squares and look at the residual correlogram. What does it show?

(b) Now add $CONS_{t-1}$ as a regressor, re-estimate and examine the residual correlogram. Describe the changes from (a).

(c) Continue by adding $CONS_{t-2}, \ldots, CONS_{t-4}$. What happens to the residual correlogram? Does this match the theoretical analysis above?

2.7 Repeat exercise 2.6 using the UK data series for $\log M_t$, $\log\left(M/P\right)_t$ and $\log P_t$.

2.8 Describe the relationships between the concepts of the economic mechanism, a data-generation process, a theory model, a statistical model, an empirical model, and an estimated model. Carefully explain the concept of an empirical model in econometrics. Why are all five concepts required? Discuss how their inter-connections pose problems for empirical modelling. Why is a separate concept of an empirical model required in addition to the postulated model? Does the problem arise because the DGP is unknown and is such a difficulty unique to the social sciences?

2.9 When $\epsilon_t \sim \mathsf{IN}\left[0, \sigma_\epsilon^2\right]$ and $s = 1$, prove that $\{y_t\}$ in (2.6) is strictly stationary.

(a) Derive the conditions for stationarity of the $\{y_t\}$ process over $t = 1, \ldots, T$ when:

$$y_t = \alpha y_{t-1} + u_t \text{ where } u_t \sim \mathsf{IN}\left[0, \sigma_u^2\right].$$

Pay special attention to the treatment of the initial condition y_0.

2.10 Show that the following $\{y_t\}$ process over $t = 1, \ldots, T$ is non-stationary when:

$$y_t = y_{t-1} + u_t \text{ where } u_t \sim \mathsf{IN}\left[0, \sigma_u^2\right] \text{ and } y_0 = 0.$$

2.11 Consider the process $\{u_t\}$ when:

$$u_t = \sum_{j=0}^{\infty} \gamma_j \epsilon_{j,t-j}$$

and $\epsilon_{j,t} \sim \mathsf{IN}\left[0, \sigma_j^2\right]$ with $\mathsf{E}\left[\epsilon_{j,t}\epsilon_{k,s}\right] = 0 \; \forall j, k, t, s$ except when $j = k$ and $t = s$. Prove that $\{u_t\}$ is white noise, but not an innovation. Hence derive conditions on the distribution of $\{v_{1,t}, v_{2,t}\}$ under which the infinite moving average:

$$u_t = \sum_{j=0}^{\infty} \rho^j v_{1,t-j} + v_{2,t}$$

is white noise. Comment on the implications for econometric modelling strategies (taken from Davidson and Hendry, 1981).

2.12 The series $\{x_t\}$ is generated by the process:

$$x_t + \alpha x_{t-1} = \epsilon_t + \beta \epsilon_{t-1} \text{ where } -1 < \alpha, \beta < 1.$$

(a) Show that stationarity holds under appropriate initial conditions.

(b) Letting $\mathsf{V}\left[x_t\right]$ denote the variance of x_t, establish that under stationarity:

$$\mathsf{V}\left[x_t\right] = \sigma^2 \frac{\left(1 - 2\alpha\beta + \beta^2\right)}{\left(1 - \alpha^2\right)};$$

and:

$$\rho_1 = \frac{(\beta - \alpha)(1 - \alpha\beta)}{\left(1 - 2\alpha\beta + \beta^2\right)} \text{ with } \rho_r = \alpha\rho_{r-1} \text{ for } r = 2, 3, \ldots,$$

where $\rho_r = \mathsf{E}\left[x_t x_{t-r}\right] / \mathsf{E}\left[x_t^2\right]$.

(c) Derive the values of α and β from knowledge of ρ_r for $r = 2, 3, \ldots$ etc.

(Oxford M.Phil., 1992)

3

Econometric Tools and Techniques

To develop an empirically viable econometric methodology, a number of tools are required. First, since the DGP is unknown in practice, methods for estimating the values of any unknown parameters are essential. The theory of least squares estimation as a recursive estimator is reviewed. Secondly, techniques for evaluating the validity of claimed empirical models will also be needed, and the logic of testing in empirical modelling is discussed. In both cases, the analysis relies on conventional statistical methods, which entails the need for methods to investigate the properties of statistical tools applied to economic data. Thus, techniques for analysing tools are considered, specifically large sample distribution theory and Monte Carlo simulation techniques. More detailed discussions of estimation and inference are provided in Part II and the appendix; here we provide the minimum background for the remainder of Part I. The chapter concludes with discussions of ergodicity and non-stationarity due to unit roots.

3.1 Review

In Chapters 1 and 2, the data-generation process was represented as the joint data density function $\mathsf{D_X}(\cdot)$:

$$\mathsf{D_X}\left(\boldsymbol{X}_T^1 \mid \boldsymbol{X}_0, \boldsymbol{\theta}_p\right) \text{ with } \boldsymbol{\theta}_p \in \Theta \subseteq \mathbb{R}^k, \tag{3.1}$$

where $\boldsymbol{X}_T^1$ denotes the observed data $(\boldsymbol{x}_1, \ldots, \boldsymbol{x}_T)$, $\boldsymbol{\theta}_p$ is the $k \times 1$ population parameter vector lying in the parameter space Θ, and $\boldsymbol{X}_0$ denotes the initial conditions. We distinguished four levels of knowledge about $\mathsf{D_X}(\cdot)$ and $\boldsymbol{\theta}_p$ when $\boldsymbol{X}_T^1$ is observed:

A: $\mathsf{D_X}(\cdot)$ and $\boldsymbol{\theta}_p$ are known: this concerns the probability structure of the process.
B: $\mathsf{D_X}(\cdot)$ is known, but $\boldsymbol{\theta}_p$ is unknown: this concerns estimation theory.
C: Neither $\mathsf{D_X}(\cdot)$ nor $\boldsymbol{\theta}_p$ are known: this necessitates data modelling.
D: $\mathsf{D_X}(\cdot)$ and $\boldsymbol{\theta}_p$ are unknown: we seek to predict future $(\boldsymbol{x}_{T+1}, \ldots, \boldsymbol{x}_{T+h})$.

At levels A and B, (3.1) is the DGP. At levels C and D, (3.1) is the Haavelmo distribution, following Haavelmo (1944) who used the joint data density as the basis for econometric analysis (see Spanos, 1989b). From the empirical data series examined earlier, we formulated the simple mechanism:

$$y_t = y_{t-1} + \alpha + \epsilon_t \text{ where } \epsilon_t \sim \mathsf{IID}\left[0, \sigma_\epsilon^2\right], \tag{3.2}$$

as a description of a single series $\{y_t\}$ from the set of xs, where the $\{\epsilon_t\}$ process was assumed to be white noise. This equation is a special case of the structural process (3.1). For the data series examined, (3.2) was not adequate as it stood, although it captured several salient data features. We discussed conditions for reducing data via aggregation, marginalization, and conditioning. An empirical model was introduced as a relationship between observed data, with an error process which was derived from the data properties, and so was not an autonomous entity. The roles of economic analysis and statistical theory, and the dichotomy of constructive and destructive approaches, were discussed. We continue the analysis for the first three levels of knowledge noted above.

3.2 Estimating unknown parameters

A knowledge of regression analysis, as discussed in Chapter A3, will prove adequate for Part I, despite the subject matter being time series: in Part II, we consider likelihood and related techniques (also reviewed in Ch.A3). This section begins with an applied example in §3.2.1, develops recursive estimation techniques in §3.2.2 and concludes with a solved theoretical example in §3.2.3.

3.2.1 An empirical example

To provide some flesh for the econometric theory skeleton developed in Chapter A3, consider an illustration based on the artificial data-set involving *CONS*, *INC* and *INFLAT* (denoted by c, i and Δp noting that all the variables are of the form 100 log). The example departs from the assumptions underlying the multiple regression model in that $(c-i)_{t-1}$ is used as a regressor, but the large-sample validity of that departure is established in Chapter A4. Here, the numerical estimates and their interpretation are the focus of interest. The DGP equation for c, with population values shown below, is:

$$\begin{array}{lcccccccc} \Delta c_t & = - & \beta_0 & + & \beta_1 \, \Delta i_t & - & \beta_2 \, (c-i)_{t-1} & - & \beta_3 \, \Delta p_t + u_t, \\ \boldsymbol{\theta}_p & & 0.90 & & 0.40 & & 0.15 & & 0.90 \end{array} \tag{3.3}$$

where $u_t \sim \mathsf{IN}[0,1]$, and $\Delta c_t = c_t - c_{t-1}$ etc. (no claim is made as to the validity of conditioning). Full-sample OLS estimation over 1953(2) to 1992(3) yields:

$$\begin{array}{lcccccccc} \widehat{\Delta c_t} & = & -\underset{(0.30)}{0.95} & + & \underset{(0.03)}{0.49}\, \Delta i_t & - & \underset{(0.02)}{0.16}\, (c-i)_{t-1} & - & \underset{(0.08)}{0.95}\, \Delta p_t \\ \text{(SE)} & & & & & & & & \\ \{\mathsf{r}^2_{xy.z}\} & & \{-\} & & \{0.68\} & & \{0.26\} & & \{0.45\} \\ \multicolumn{9}{l}{\mathsf{R}^2 = 0.76 \;\; \hat{\sigma}_u = 1.09\% \;\; F(3,154) = 162.3 \;\; DW = 1.96} \end{array} \tag{3.4}$$

Assuming Δi_t and Δp_t can be taken as given, a one-point increase in Δi_t induces a 0.49-point increase in Δc_t, with a feedback effect later from the fact that c_{t-1} will be higher next period (dynamics are considered in Chs. 4 and 6). The overall R^2 entails that 76 per cent of the variance in Δc_t is accounted for by the regression, which has an estimated standard error of 1.09% (see §1.9). The estimated coefficients have relatively small standard errors (shown in parentheses below estimated coefficients) and correspondingly high squared partial correlations (denoted $r^2_{xy.z}$), especially for Δi_t. The F-test rejects the null hypothesis that all three regression coefficients are zero, and the individual t-tests do so for each coefficient in turn: however, the joint null that $\boldsymbol{\beta} = \mathbf{0}$ is usually unreasonable for time series because it implies that the dependent variable must be IID under the null. Individual coefficients are well determined even after allowing for other influences on Δc_t; this is because the regressor variables have low intercorrelations in the formulation adopted, especially in relation to their correlations with the dependent variable, as shown in Table 3.1. The partial correlations are all larger in absolute value than the corresponding simple correlation, and that for $(c-i)_{t-1}$ has changed sign.

Table 3.1 Correlation structure

	Δi_t	$(c-i)_{t-1}$	Δp_t
Δc_t	0.74	0.13	−0.48
Δi_t	–	0.24	−0.19
$(c-i)_{t-1}$	–	–	−0.59

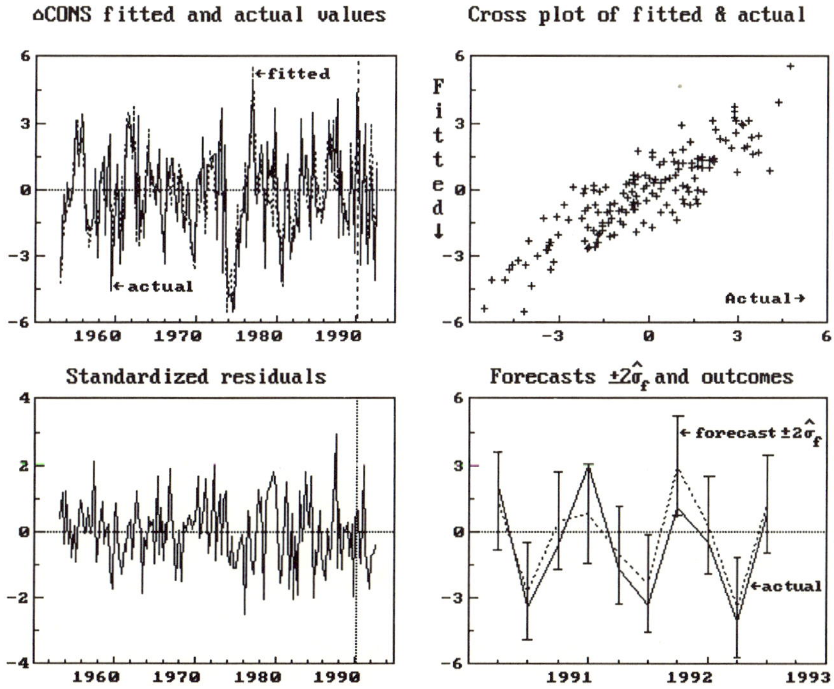

Fig. 3.1 Graphical regression statistics

Figure 3.1 shows the four most relevant graphs associated with (3.4), namely the time series of the actual and fitted values in 3.1a; their cross-plot in 3.1b; the time series of the residuals in 3.1c; and the forecasts and outcomes for the last ten available observations in 3.1d, plotted with $\pm 2\hat{\sigma}_f$ centred on the forecast values (where $\hat{\sigma}_f$ is the estimated forecast standard error): the vertical line in Figs. 3.1a and 3.1c denotes the end of the estimation sample. The goodness of fit is clear, the residuals are close to white noise matching the value of the DW statistic, and the forecasts lie well inside the 95 per cent confidence intervals.

Since the model specification coincides with the DGP equation in this illustration, the outcomes are reasonably close to the population values. In general, at level C, such knowledge is not available, and much of the remainder of the book is concerned with establishing the status of empirical estimates when the model cannot be asserted to be the DGP. The first step down that route is to extend least squares estimation theory to sub-samples of the data-set.

3.2.2 Recursive estimation

When analysing economic time series, we are interested in how parameter estimates change as the sample size changes, both as an issue of theory and of practice. Concerning theory, convergence in probability, almost-sure convergence and central limit theorems analyse how estimators behave as the sample size increases for constant parameters. This aspect is the subject of Chapter A4. Concerning practice, regime shifts in an economy may change the convergence point of estimators of coefficients in models at level C. These considerations suggest computing sequences of estimates instead of just the full-sample values discussed above, and recursive estimation allows this to be done efficiently. Relative to standard regression notation, we add an explicit notation for time, and rewrite the multiple regression model at intermediate sample sizes as:

$$\boldsymbol{y}_t^1 = \boldsymbol{Z}_t^1 \boldsymbol{\beta} + \boldsymbol{u}_t^1 \quad \text{for } t = T_0, \ldots, T. \tag{3.5}$$

In (3.5), $\boldsymbol{y}_t^1$ is a $t \times 1$ vector of observations on the dependent variable, $\boldsymbol{Z}_t^1$ is a $t \times k$ matrix of observations on the regressors, $\boldsymbol{\beta}$ is a $k \times 1$ vector of unknown coefficients, and $\boldsymbol{u}_t^1$ is a $t \times 1$ vector of disturbances, asserted to satisfy $\mathsf{E}[\boldsymbol{Z}_t^{1\prime}\boldsymbol{u}_t^1] = \boldsymbol{0}\ \forall t$. Consider the sequence of $T - T_0 + 1$ estimates of $\boldsymbol{\beta}$:

$$\hat{\boldsymbol{\beta}}_t = \left(\boldsymbol{Z}_t^{1\prime}\boldsymbol{Z}_t^1\right)^{-1} \boldsymbol{Z}_t^{1\prime}\boldsymbol{y}_t^1 \quad \text{for} \quad t = T_0, \ldots, T. \tag{3.6}$$

It is expensive to invert large matrices (although the most expensive calculation in regression is forming the matrix of second moments $(\boldsymbol{Z}_T^{1\prime}\boldsymbol{Z}_T^1)$), but we can exploit the recursive structure of $\boldsymbol{Z}_{t+1}^{1\prime}\boldsymbol{Z}_{t+1}^1$ since:

$$\boldsymbol{Z}_{t+1}^{1\prime}\boldsymbol{Z}_{t+1}^1 = \boldsymbol{Z}_t^{1\prime}\boldsymbol{Z}_t^1 + \boldsymbol{z}_{t+1}\boldsymbol{z}_{t+1}^\prime. \tag{3.7}$$

Updating the second-moment matrix in a sequence as in (3.7) costs no more than computing the whole-sample matrix once. A similar result holds for $\boldsymbol{Z}_{t+1}^{1\prime}\boldsymbol{y}_{t+1}^1$.

Next, partitioned inversion as in Chapter A1 avoids the sequence of matrix inversions by treating $(Z_{t+1}^{1\prime} Z_{t+1}^{1})^{-1}$ in (3.7) as a special case:

$$A = \left(Z_t^{1\prime} Z_t^1\right), \; B = C' = z_{t+1}, \text{ and } D = -1.$$

From (A1.A1.12):

$$\begin{aligned} \left(Z_{t+1}^{1\prime} Z_{t+1}^{1}\right)^{-1} &= \left(Z_t^{1\prime} Z_t^1 + z_{t+1} z_{t+1}'\right)^{-1} \\ &= \left(Z_t^{1\prime} Z_t^1\right)^{-1} - \lambda_{t+1} \lambda_{t+1}' \left(1 + z_{t+1}' \lambda_{t+1}\right)^{-1}, \end{aligned} \tag{3.8}$$

where $\lambda_{t+1} = \left(Z_t^{1\prime} Z_t^1\right)^{-1} z_{t+1}$ and:

$$\left(1 + z_{t+1}' \lambda_{t+1}\right) = \left(1 + z_{t+1}' \left(Z_t^{1\prime} Z_t^1\right)^{-1} z_{t+1}\right),$$

which is a scalar. Once $(Z_t^{1\prime} Z_t^1)^{-1}$ has been computed, it is easy to calculate next period's $(Z_{t+1}^{1\prime} Z_{t+1}^{1})^{-1}$ by (3.8), and hence every inverse from sample sizes T_0 to T, given $(Z_{T_0}^{1\prime} Z_{T_0}^{1})^{-1}$ initially. The cost of a sequence of regressions from T_0 to T, when T_0 is small and T is large, is roughly 50 per cent more than the cost of the one regression at T only, but provides a great deal of extra information (see Teräsvirta, 1970, Brown, Durbin and Evans, 1975, and Hendry and Neale, 1987). Using (3.8) in the usual OLS formula yields:

$$\hat{\beta}_{t+1} = \left(Z_{t+1}^{1\prime} Z_{t+1}^{1}\right)^{-1} Z_{t+1}^{1\prime} y_{t+1}^{1} = \hat{\beta}_t + \lambda_{t+1} \nu_{t+1} \left(1 + z_{t+1}' \lambda_{t+1}\right)^{-1}, \tag{3.9}$$

where $\nu_{t+1} = y_{t+1} - \hat{\beta}_t' z_{t+1}$ is the 1-step ahead forecast error, with variance $\sigma_\nu^2(t+1) = \sigma_u^2(1 + z_{t+1}' \lambda_{t+1})$. These, and related results on recursively updating the residual sum of squares (RSS), are easily proved: try doing so before reading the solved example.

The above calculations assume that β is constant, and the only non-constancy is in the sampling fluctuations of the estimates due to the increasing sample size. Once all the sub-sample RSS values are known, Chow (1960) test statistics can be calculated as follows. Under the null that β and σ_u^2 are constant over the whole sample, $RSS = y' M_Z y$ where $M_Z = I_T - Z_T^1 (Z_T^{1\prime} Z_T^1)^{-1} Z_T^{1\prime}$. If β changes from β_1 to β_2 at time T^*, but σ_u^2 remains constant, then the linear model can be written as (using the subscripts 1 and 2 to denote the samples pre and post T^*):

$$\begin{pmatrix} y_1 \\ y_2 \end{pmatrix} = \begin{pmatrix} Z_1 & \mathbf{0} \\ \mathbf{0} & Z_2 \end{pmatrix} \begin{pmatrix} \beta_1 \\ \beta_2 \end{pmatrix} + \begin{pmatrix} u_1 \\ u_2 \end{pmatrix} = Z^* \beta^* + u. \tag{3.10}$$

The residual sum of squares from (3.10), denoted RSS^*, can never be greater than that from (3.5) (why?), and the difference $(RSS - RSS^*)$ will be distributed independently of RSS^* since it represents the increase in the residual sum of squares from imposing the constraint that $\beta_1 = \beta_2$. An F-statistic can be constructed from this information under the null hypothesis that $\beta_1 = \beta_2$, given the maintained hypothesis that σ_u^2 stays constant.

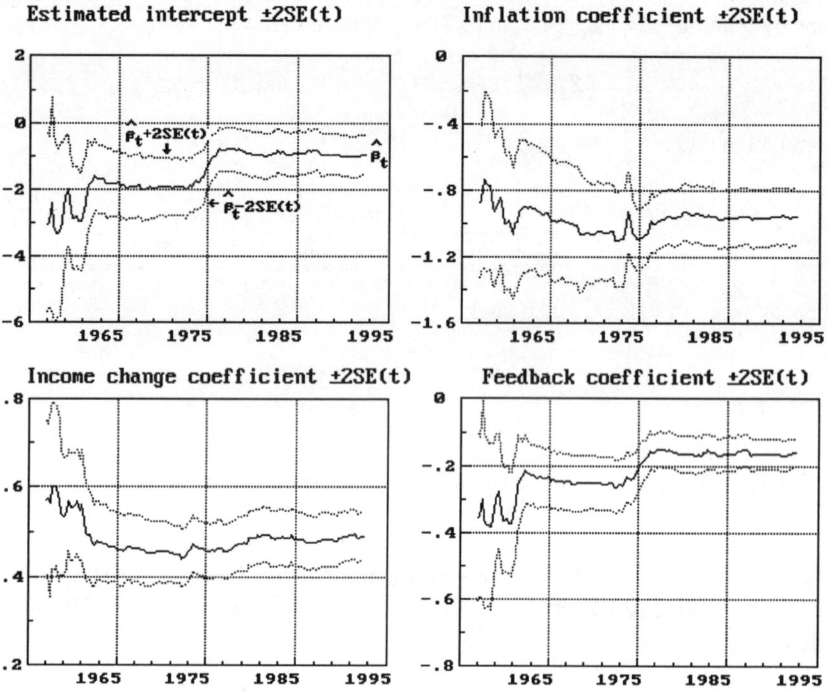

Fig. 3.2 Graphical recursive statistics

The special feature of the test suggested by Chow (1960) is that it allows for the possibility that $r(Z_2) < k$, when there are insufficient observations to estimate β_2. In that case, RSS is compared with the residual sum of squares from the first sub-sample up to T^* denoted RSS^0. The change in the residual sum of squares $RSS - RSS^0$ can be interpreted as due to adding a set of $(0, 1)$ dummy variables $\mathcal{D} = \{\boldsymbol{d}_j, j = T^*+1, \ldots, T\}$ with coefficient vector γ, where $\boldsymbol{d}_j$ is a zero vector except for element j which is unity (see Salkever, 1976). A conventional F-test of the hypothesis $\gamma = \mathbf{0}$ then delivers the relevant Chow test. This test can be calculated at every breakpoint T^* between T_0 and T from the recursive formulae, but care is required in making inferences from such a sequence if it is desired to control the rejection frequency when the null of constant β is true.

A practical problem with computing estimates recursively is the large number of items to be reported. One solution is to summarize the outcomes graphically. For a bivariate model, the recursive estimates of the regression line can be shown for increasing sample size on a cross-plot (i.e. T_0, $T_0 + \tau$, up to T) as in Fig. 2.3. Alternatively, and essential when the number of variables exceeds two, the recursive estimates of the individual coefficients and a measure of their uncertainty can be plotted. Figure 3.2 reports the coefficient estimates for equation (3.4), for every sample size from $T_0, T_0 + 1,$

$T_0 + 2, \ldots, T$. The three lines in each of Figs. 3.2a–d respectively relate to:$\{\hat{\beta}_{it}\}$ (in the centre), with $\pm 2\mathsf{SE}(\hat{\beta}_{it})$ (the estimated coefficient standard error at time t), where $\mathsf{SE}(\hat{\beta}_{it})$ is denoted by $\mathsf{SE}(t)$ on the graph. The partial slopes of the regression lines for each coefficient change somewhat as the sample size increases, and some later estimates lie outside earlier 95 per cent confidence intervals.

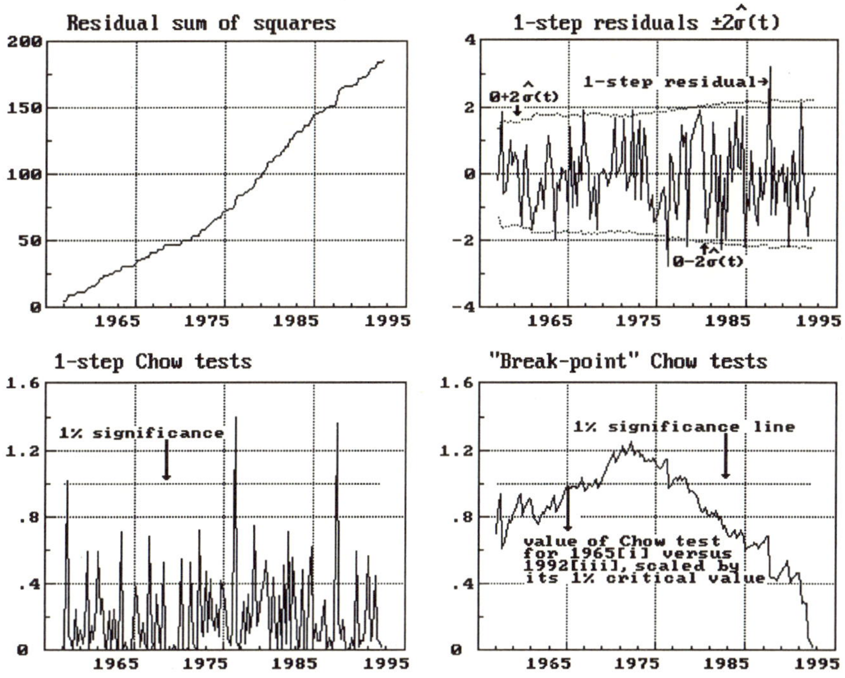

Fig. 3.3 Graphical recursive evaluation statistics

Next, four summary statistics are reported in Figs. 3.3a–d, namely the RSS, the $\{\nu_t\}$ from (3.9) together with $\pm 2\sigma_\nu(t)$ shown, in Fig. 3.3b, on either side of the origin (denoted by $\hat{\sigma}(t)$ on the graph, as a generic symbol for equation standard error), 1-step and 'breakpoint' Chow tests. The test statistics are scaled by their 1 per cent significance values at each possible breakpoint, so values above the straight lines at unity are significant on a one-off test. The small increase in $\sigma_\nu(t)$ over time reveals a relatively constant equation, matching the sequence of Chow tests of the hypothesis that β is constant over the sample (graphed in Figs. 3.3c–d): it is invalid to condition on Δi_t in (3.4), and the shock to the system in 1973(4) induces apparent parameter change. Despite the caveats noted above, some form of sub-sample investigation is necessary to discover such failures in a model and we return to this issue below. A solved example completes the analysis of recursive estimates.

3.2.3 A solved recursive example

Consider a linear equation with k linearly independent variables in z_t:

$$y_t = \beta' z_t + \epsilon_t \text{ where } \epsilon_t \sim \mathsf{IN}\left[0, \sigma_\epsilon^2\right] \text{ for } t = 1, \ldots, T. \tag{3.11}$$

The vector β is to be estimated at the sequence of sample sizes $J = M > k, \ldots, T$.

(a) Describe an algorithm which sequentially updates $(Z_J' Z_J)^{-1}$ commencing from $(Z_M' Z_M)^{-1}$ (when $Z_J' = (z_1 \ldots z_J)$). Using that result, obtain recursive estimation rules for β, its variance, and σ_ϵ^2 at each J.

(b) Derive the 1-step ahead residuals and their variances. Show from the estimation algorithm for β at each J, that the sequence $\{\hat{\beta}_M, \hat{\beta}_{M+1}, \ldots, \hat{\beta}_T\}$ is a heteroscedastic random walk.

(c) Explain how to use these results to test the hypothesis that β is constant against the alternative that it is not. Comment on the likely properties of such a test.

(Oxford M.Phil., 1987)

Solution to (a)

Using the explicit notation for time introduced in (3.5):

$$y_t^1 = Z_t^1 \beta + \epsilon_t^1 \quad t = 1, \ldots, T. \tag{3.12}$$

The sequence of $T - M + 1$ estimates of β is given in (3.6) and the recursive updating structure of $\left(Z_{t+1}^{1\prime} Z_{t+1}^1\right)$ in (3.7). Partitioned inversion avoids a sequence of matrix inversions as shown in (3.8) where $\lambda_{t+1} = \left(Z_t^{1\prime} Z_t^1\right)^{-1} z_{t+1}$ as before and we let:

$$z_{t+1}' \lambda_{t+1} = \kappa_{t+1} = \omega_{t+1} - 1 \tag{3.13}$$

Once $(Z_t^{1\prime} Z_t^1)^{-1}$ is computed, $(Z_{t+1}^{1\prime} Z_{t+1}^1)^{-1}$ is calculated by the rank-one update in (3.8), as is every inverse from sample sizes M to T, given $(Z_M^{1\prime} Z_M^1)^{-1}$. From (3.8) and (3.6) at time $t + 1$, using (3.13):

$$\begin{aligned}
\hat{\beta}_{t+1} &= \left[\left(Z_t^{1\prime} Z_t^1\right)^{-1} - \lambda_{t+1} \lambda_{t+1}' \omega_{t+1}^{-1}\right] \left[Z_t^{1\prime} y_t^1 + z_{t+1} y_{t+1}\right] \\
&= \hat{\beta}_t + \left(Z_t^{1\prime} Z_t^1\right)^{-1} z_{t+1} y_{t+1} \\
&\quad - \left(\lambda_{t+1} \lambda_{t+1}' Z_t^{1\prime} y_t^1 + \lambda_{t+1} \lambda_{t+1}' z_{t+1} y_{t+1}\right) \omega_{t+1}^{-1} \\
&= \hat{\beta}_t + \lambda_{t+1} y_{t+1} - \lambda_{t+1} \left(z_{t+1}' \hat{\beta}_t + \kappa_{t+1} y_{t+1}\right) \omega_{t+1}^{-1} \\
&= \hat{\beta}_t + \lambda_{t+1} \left(y_{t+1} - z_{t+1}' \hat{\beta}_t\right) \omega_{t+1}^{-1} \\
&= \hat{\beta}_t + \lambda_{t+1} \nu_{t+1} \omega_{t+1}^{-1}
\end{aligned} \tag{3.14}$$

where $\nu_{t+1} = y_{t+1} - z_{t+1}' \hat{\beta}_t$ as above. This establishes (3.9). The variance of ν_{t+1} is $\sigma_\epsilon^2 \omega_{t+1}$ (derived in (b) below). Note the difference between the 1-step ahead forecast error:

$$\nu_{t+1} = y_{t+1} - z_{t+1}' \hat{\beta}_t = \epsilon_{t+1} + \left(\beta - \hat{\beta}_t\right)' z_{t+1}, \tag{3.15}$$

and the recursive residual:

$$\begin{aligned}\hat{\epsilon}_{t+1} &= y_{t+1} - \hat{\boldsymbol{\beta}}'_{t+1} z_{t+1} &&= \nu_{t+1} - \left(\hat{\boldsymbol{\beta}}_{t+1} - \hat{\boldsymbol{\beta}}_t\right)' z_{t+1} \\ &= \nu_{t+1} - \boldsymbol{\lambda}'_{t+1} z_{t+1} \nu_{t+1} \omega_{t+1}^{-1} &&= \nu_{t+1} \omega_{t+1}^{-1}.\end{aligned} \tag{3.16}$$

The last expression on the first row of (3.16) will prove useful later.

Next, from (3.6):

$$\mathsf{V}\left[\hat{\boldsymbol{\beta}}_{t+1}\right] = \sigma_\epsilon^2 \left(\mathbf{Z}_{t+1}^{1\prime} \mathbf{Z}_{t+1}^1\right)^{-1} = \mathsf{V}\left[\hat{\boldsymbol{\beta}}_t\right] \left(\boldsymbol{I} - z_{t+1} \boldsymbol{\lambda}'_{t+1} \omega_{t+1}^{-1}\right) \tag{3.17}$$

so we need a rule for updating the estimated residual variance σ_ϵ^2 at $t+1$, denoted by:

$$\hat{\sigma}_\epsilon^2 (t+1) = \frac{RSS_{t+1}}{(t+1-k)}. \tag{3.18}$$

This follows from an updating formula for RSS_{t+1} where at time t:

$$RSS_t = \sum_{j=1}^{t} \tilde{\epsilon}_j^2 \text{ when } \tilde{\epsilon}_j = y_j - \hat{\boldsymbol{\beta}}'_t \boldsymbol{z}_j \text{ and } \sum_{j=1}^{t} \boldsymbol{z}_j \tilde{\epsilon}_j = \mathbf{0}.$$

At time $t+1$:

$$RSS_{t+1} = \sum_{j=1}^{t+1} \hat{\epsilon}_j^2 \text{ where } \hat{\epsilon}_j = y_j - \hat{\boldsymbol{\beta}}'_{t+1} \boldsymbol{z}_j,$$

and from (3.14) for $j = 1, \ldots, t$:

$$\hat{\epsilon}_j = y_j - \hat{\boldsymbol{\beta}}'_{t+1} \boldsymbol{z}_j = y_j - \hat{\boldsymbol{\beta}}'_t \boldsymbol{z}_j - \boldsymbol{\lambda}'_{t+1} \boldsymbol{z}_j \nu_{t+1} \omega_{t+1}^{-1} = \tilde{\epsilon}_j - \boldsymbol{\lambda}'_{t+1} \boldsymbol{z}_j \nu_{t+1} \omega_{t+1}^{-1}.$$

Thus, using (3.16):

$$\begin{aligned}RSS_{t+1} &= \sum_{j=1}^{t+1} \left(y_j - \hat{\boldsymbol{\beta}}'_{t+1} \boldsymbol{z}_j\right)^2 \\ &= \nu_{t+1}^2 \omega_{t+1}^{-2} + \sum_{j=1}^{t} \left(\tilde{\epsilon}_j - \boldsymbol{\lambda}'_{t+1} \boldsymbol{z}_j \nu_{t+1} \omega_{t+1}^{-1}\right)^2 \\ &= \nu_{t+1}^2 \omega_{t+1}^{-2} + \sum_{j=1}^{t} \tilde{\epsilon}_j^2 + \boldsymbol{\lambda}'_{t+1} \left(\sum_{j=1}^{t} \boldsymbol{z}_j \boldsymbol{z}'_j\right) \boldsymbol{\lambda}_{t+1} \nu_{t+1}^2 \omega_{t+1}^{-2} \\ &= \nu_{t+1}^2 \omega_{t+1}^{-2} + RSS_t + \kappa_{t+1} \nu_{t+1}^2 \omega_{t+1}^{-2} \\ &= RSS_t + \nu_{t+1}^2 \omega_{t+1}^{-1},\end{aligned} \tag{3.19}$$

where $\nu_{t+1} / \sqrt{\omega_{t+1}}$ is the standardized innovation, since:

$$\boldsymbol{\lambda}'_{t+1} \left(\sum_{j=1}^{t} \boldsymbol{z}_j \boldsymbol{z}'_j\right) \boldsymbol{\lambda}_{t+1} = z'_{t+1} \left(\mathbf{Z}_t^{1\prime} \mathbf{Z}_t^1\right)^{-1} \left(\mathbf{Z}_t^{1\prime} \mathbf{Z}_t^1\right) \boldsymbol{\lambda}_{t+1} = z'_{t+1} \boldsymbol{\lambda}_{t+1} = \kappa_{t+1}.$$

From (3.19), $\hat{\sigma}_\epsilon^2 (t+1)$ is easily obtained using (3.18).

Solution to (b)

We have solved most of this part already. From (3.15):

$$\begin{aligned}
\mathsf{E}\left[\nu_{t+1}^2\right] &= \mathsf{E}\left[\left(\epsilon_{t+1} + \left(\beta - \hat{\beta}_t\right)' z_{t+1}\right)^2\right] \\
&= \mathsf{E}\left[\epsilon_{t+1}^2\right] + \mathsf{E}\left[z_{t+1}'\left(\beta - \hat{\beta}_t\right)\left(\beta - \hat{\beta}_t\right)' z_{t+1}\right] \qquad (3.20) \\
&= \sigma_\epsilon^2 + z_{t+1}'\mathsf{V}\left[\hat{\beta}_t\right] z_{t+1} \\
&= \sigma_\epsilon^2\left(1 + \lambda_{t+1}' z_{t+1}\right) = \sigma_\epsilon^2 \omega_{t+1}.
\end{aligned}$$

From (3.14), $\hat{\beta}_{t+1} = \hat{\beta}_t + \lambda_{t+1}\nu_{t+1}\omega_{t+1}^{-1}$, so the update has a unit coefficient on the previous value, with an error $u_{t+1} = \lambda_{t+1}\nu_{t+1}\omega_{t+1}^{-1}$. Since $\mathsf{E}\left[\nu_{t+1}^2\right] = \sigma_\epsilon^2\omega_{t+1}$, then:

$$\mathsf{E}\left[u_{t+1}u_{t+1}'\right] = \mathsf{E}\left[\lambda_{t+1}\nu_{t+1}^2\lambda_{t+1}'\right]\omega_{t+1}^{-1} = \sigma_\epsilon^2\lambda_{t+1}\lambda_{t+1}'\omega_{t+1}^{-1}, \qquad (3.21)$$

which is not constant over t. Hence $\{u_{t+1}\}$ is heteroscedastic. In (c), we will show that the $\{\nu_t\}$ are independent when the $\{\epsilon_t\}$ are $\mathsf{IN}\left[0, \sigma_\epsilon^2\right]$.

Solution to (c)

The sequence of Chow tests discussed in §3.2.2 is easily calculated from the update formula in (3.19). Alternatively, under the null that β is constant, the 1-step ahead residual process $\{\nu_t\}$ has a mean of zero, a variance of $\sigma_\epsilon^2\omega_t$, and is a linear function of normal variables, so $\nu_t/\sqrt{\omega_t} \sim \mathsf{N}\left[0, \sigma_\epsilon^2\right]$. However, we need to show that the $\{\nu_t\}$ are independent and the following proof spells out the necessary steps. Although it is intuitively clear that the $\{\nu_t\}$ are independent for strongly exogenous z, since they are unpredictable given past information, that is hard to prove in view of their empirical construction. Using (3.15):

$$\begin{aligned}
\mathsf{E}\left[\nu_{t+1}\nu_t\right] &= \mathsf{E}\left[\left(\epsilon_{t+1} + \left(\beta - \hat{\beta}_t\right)' z_{t+1}\right)\left(\epsilon_t + \left(\beta - \hat{\beta}_{t-1}\right)' z_t\right)\right] \\
&= \mathsf{E}\left[\left(z_{t+1}'\left(\beta - \hat{\beta}_t\right)\left(\beta - \hat{\beta}_{t-1}\right)' z_t\right) + \left(z_{t+1}'\left(\beta - \hat{\beta}_t\right)\epsilon_t\right)\right].
\end{aligned}$$

From (3.14) and (3.16):

$$\begin{aligned}
\left(\beta - \hat{\beta}_t\right) &= \left(\beta - \hat{\beta}_{t-1}\right) - \lambda_t\left(\epsilon_t + \left(\beta - \hat{\beta}_{t-1}\right)' z_t\right)\omega_t^{-1} \\
&= \left(I - \omega_t^{-1}\lambda_t z_t'\right)\left(\beta - \hat{\beta}_{t-1}\right) - \epsilon_t\omega_t^{-1},
\end{aligned}$$

and since:

$$z_{t+1}'\left(\hat{\beta}_t - \beta\right) = z_{t+1}'\left(Z_t^{1\prime}Z_t^1\right)^{-1}Z_t^{1\prime}\epsilon_t^1 = \lambda_{t+1}'Z_t^{1\prime}\epsilon_t^1,$$

then as $\mathsf{E}\left[\left(\beta - \hat{\beta}_{t-1}\right)\epsilon_t\right] = \mathbf{0}$, using (3.17) for time t:

$$\begin{aligned}
\mathsf{E}\left[\nu_{t+1}\nu_t\right] &= z'_{t+1}\left(\boldsymbol{I} - \omega_t^{-1}\boldsymbol{\lambda}_t z'_t\right)\mathsf{V}\left[\hat{\beta}_{t-1}\right]z_t - \boldsymbol{\lambda}'_{t+1}Z_t^{1\prime}\mathsf{E}\left[\epsilon_t^1\epsilon_t\right] \\
&= z'_{t+1}\mathsf{V}\left[\hat{\beta}_t\right]z_t - \sigma_\epsilon^2\boldsymbol{\lambda}'_{t+1}z_t \\
&= \sigma_\epsilon^2\boldsymbol{\lambda}'_{t+1}z_t - \sigma_\epsilon^2\boldsymbol{\lambda}'_{t+1}z_t = 0.
\end{aligned}$$

Thus, constancy tests such as Chow, CUSUM (cumulative sum of residuals) and CUSUM^2 statistics can be based on $\nu_t/\sqrt{\omega_t} \sim \mathsf{IN}\left[0, \sigma_\epsilon^2\right]$ (see e.g. Brown *et al.*, 1975). The main problem with the 'one-off' Chow test is that it requires knowledge of the time at which the possible parameter change occurred, and this is unlikely at level C. Considering all possible tests at that critical value will not yield the correct size (see Ch.13 for a discussion). The converse problem with the complete sequence of tests based on functions of $\{\nu_t/\sqrt{\omega_t}\}$ is that the correct overall critical value of the test sequence is both difficult to calculate and likely to induce low power.

3.3 Methods for evaluating models

The theory of statistical inference provides a natural starting point for model-evaluation methods and several examples were presented above. Neyman and Pearson (1928) formulated a theory of hypothesis testing applicable to a class of situations equivalent to quality control. Imagine a manufacturing process for gadgets which must satisfy certain quality criteria to maintain the producer's reputation. If the equipment operates normally, a small percentage δ of the gadgets will be defective on average; if the equipment malfunctions, a larger percentage $\lambda(m)$ of defective units will result, dependent on the type of malfunction m. A sample of gadgets is examined, involving their destruction, to test for equipment malfunction. The null hypothesis is that the equipment is functional, the alternative is that it is malfunctioning although the state m is unknown. A sample reveals that γ per cent of the gadgets examined are defective and the key issue is the validity of the null hypothesis in the light of that sample evidence. There are costs attached to the number of gadgets tested, to incorrectly rejecting the null (which implies destroying an acceptable batch of gadgets) and to incorrectly accepting it (loss of reputation due to low quality output).

Given an appropriate statistical model which determines the probability of a defective gadget under the null, a critical number ψ of defectives in a sample of size n can be computed such that there is a small probability of observing more than ψ defectives when the null is correct: conventionally, that probability is set at 5 per cent or 1 per cent, but it should be set at the cost-minimizing value α per cent. Such quality control testing seems to work well in practice.

However, consider the following scenario. A zealous employee removes all obviously defective gadgets before the sample is drawn. Now how well will the test procedure detect an equipment malfunction? Possibly not at all, depending on the ease with which defective gadgets can be spotted prior to the formal quality control test. Unfortunately, this last example may be a good analogy for much of econometric testing, a view supported by the regularity with which empirical economic models seem to have passed such tests: the sample of reported results is biased in so far as failed models remain unpublished. In general, there are two classes of tests, corresponding to the distinct contexts discussed in §1.4:

(i) genuine tests of the Neyman–Pearson type for model evaluation as in quality control; and:
(ii) selection tests for model discovery, where the test outcomes are used as design criteria in the sense discussed in Chapter 2.

When a 'test' statistic is cited, you must ask 'Was that a selection criterion statistic or a genuine test statistic?' If a model is selected precisely because some criterion is satisfactory, then the value of that criterion cannot also be a test of the model's validity: by construction, models satisfy statistical tests which are used as the grounds for their selection. In so far as tests are used as one-off quality control checks in sense (i), Chapter A3 discusses the basic principles of statistical inference and Chapters A4 and 13 develop an econometrically relevant theory. For the remainder of Part I, t, F, and χ^2 tests will be treated as conventional tests, not selection criteria.

3.4 Statistical theory

This is the main body of technique developed for data analysis. Chapter A3 covers the elements of statistical theory necessary for understanding the material in the rest of the book. A major difficulty in statistics is that deriving statistical distributions can be tedious, for reasons which are well exemplified by the simplest example of an independent sample on a random variable $\{X_t\}$ drawn from a normal distribution:

$$X_t \sim \mathsf{IN}\left[\mu, \sigma^2\right] \text{ where } |\mu| < \infty \text{ and } 0 < \sigma^2 < \infty \text{ for } t = 1, \ldots, T. \tag{3.22}$$

We use t as an index here, since a notion of time is standard below.

The distributions of the sample mean $\bar{X}$ and sample variance s, viewed as estimators of μ and σ^2 respectively, are unproblematical to obtain, but that of $\bar{X} / \sqrt{s}$ is far from trivial and was only solved by Gosset in 1908 (under a pseudonym: see Student, 1908). When the $\{X_t\}$ are from dynamic or non-linear processes, or we need to calculate derived functions such as:

$$g\left(h_1\left\{X_1, \ldots, X_T\right\}, \ldots, h_k\left\{X_1, \ldots, X_T\right\}\right), \tag{3.23}$$

then exact distributions often become mathematically intractable. There are three ways of obtaining distributions in such cases, namely, using approximations (briefly discussed in Ch.A4), large-sample or asymptotic distribution theory (also discussed in Ch.A4), and Monte Carlo or numerical simulation. The last two are the subjects of reviews in §3.5 and §3.6 respectively.

3.5 Asymptotic distribution theory

Asymptotic, rather than exact, distributions assume that the sample size T can increase indefinitely, so we eventually collect an infinite amount of information. Often, as T tends to infinity, the distribution of $g\left(\left[h\left\{\cdot\right\}\right]\right)$ in (3.23) becomes sufficiently simple to derive analytically. One reason for that result is linearity, since in essence the large-sample outcome is so close to the population value that a linear approximation is adequate. A second (related) reason is that laws of large numbers and central limit theorems apply to functions of stochastic quantities, letting us prove that they converge to well-known distributions such as the normal.

Chapter A4 develops the necessary background results on the orders of magnitude of sequences of random variables; the convergence of random variables as the sample size tends to infinity; laws of large numbers; central limit theorems for stationary processes; and discusses two examples of these in detail. It also analyses dynamic processes and instrumental variables, again with examples. A number of the results will not be used until Part II, which also analyses large-sample theory for maximum likelihood estimation. Processes with unit roots are discussed in section 3.8 below. For more general treatments of asymptotic distribution theory, see Spanos (1986), Sargan (1988), White (1984), McCabe and Tremayne (1993) and Davidson (1994).

3.6 Monte Carlo

An important practical technique for studying the distributions of derived statistics is Monte Carlo experimentation. Monte Carlo is a method for solving deterministic (i.e. mathematical) problems by solving a stochastic problem which delivers the same result. At first encounter, that idea seems odd and raises two questions: 'why adopt such a circuitous route ?' and 'how do we know the exact and stochastic problems have the same answer?' An illustration will help clarify the answers. Consider calculating:

$$\int_a^b x^e e^{-\frac{1}{2}x^2} \mathrm{d}x,$$

when $a \geq 0$. This integral is difficult to evaluate analytically. However, the integral also corresponds to the expected value over the interval $[a, b]$ of the eth power of a random variable X distributed as $\surd(2\pi)$ times the standard normal. When random numbers from $\mathsf{IN}[0, 1]$ can be created on a computer, their mean over $[a, b]$ can be calculated numerically, solving the integration problem (on scaling by $\surd(2\pi)$).

We must prove in advance that the stochastic problem has the same solution as the analytical one, which is often straightforward to do. Further, the route is not completely indirect, in that the analytical problem should be solved as far as feasible, then the intractable remainder obtained numerically. We consider a pure simulation approach in §3.6.1; more sophisticated Monte Carlo techniques in §3.6.2; methods for analysing experimental results in §3.6.4; invariance arguments in §3.6.5; and conclude with a recursive Monte Carlo technique in §3.6.6. More detailed analyses relevant to econometrics are provided in Hendry (1984b), Hendry, Neale and Ericsson (1991) and Davidson and MacKinnon (1993).

3.6.1 Distribution sampling

In econometrics, a Monte Carlo experiment usually involves directly mimicking the desired DGP on a computer (although experiments were conducted manually before computers were invented). The artificial DGP should reflect all relevant aspects of the economy, in order to produce data that are applicable to the real world econometric problem under study. Random samples of size T are then drawn from that DGP, and the modelling methods or statistics of interest are calculated from the resulting samples of artificial data. This process is repeated M times to create a sufficiently large Monte Carlo sample on the behaviour of the relevant statistics. The empirical distributions of these statistics based on the artificial data then simulate the actual, but unknown, distributions we seek to derive. This particular approach is termed distribution sampling, and was used e.g. by Student (1908) to check his hypothesized distribution for the t-statistic.

A basic statistical theorem underlies Monte Carlo when the sample size M is sufficiently large. Let:

$$W_i \sim \mathsf{IID}\left[\mu, \sigma^2\right] \text{ where } |\mu| < \infty \text{ and } 0 < \sigma^2 < \infty \text{ for } i = 1, \ldots, M, \tag{3.24}$$

when μ, σ^2 and the form of the distribution are all unknown. Let $\mathbb{E}$ denote an expectation with respect to the random variables in the Monte Carlo (to distinguish from E in the econometric model; similarly for $\mathcal{V}[\cdot]$). Let:

$$\widetilde{W} = M^{-1} \sum_{j=1}^{M} W_j, \tag{3.25}$$

then:

$$\mathbb{E}\left[\widetilde{W}\right] = \mu, \ \mathbb{E}\left[\left(\widetilde{W} - \mu\right)^2\right] = \frac{\sigma^2}{M} \text{ and } \widetilde{W} \sim \mathsf{N}\left[\mu, \frac{\sigma^2}{M}\right]. \tag{3.26}$$

The last result in (3.26) is only approximate for finite M. Further, if:

$$\tilde{\sigma}^2 = (M-1)^{-1} \sum_{j=1}^{M} \left(W_j - \widetilde{W}\right)^2, \tag{3.27}$$

then:

$$\mathbb{E}\left[\tilde{\sigma}^2\right] = \sigma^2 \text{ and } \mathcal{V}\left[\widetilde{W}\right] = \mathbb{E}\left[\frac{\tilde{\sigma}^2}{M}\right] = \frac{\sigma^2}{M}. \tag{3.28}$$

From (3.26), the Monte Carlo sample mean $\widetilde{W}$ of a set of IID drawings is an unbiased estimator of the population mean μ, with a variance of σ^2/M, and is normally distributed around μ when M is large. From (3.28), the sample variance is an unbiased estimator of the unknown population variance, and when divided by the sample size delivers an unbiased estimator of the variance of the sample mean around μ, so we can calculate measures of the uncertainty due to the experiment. $\tilde{\sigma}$ is called the Monte Carlo Standard Deviation (MCSD) and $\tilde{\sigma}/M$ is the Monte Carlo Standard Error (MCSE). Histograms and estimated density functions help describe the distributional shape (see Ch.A3).

To apply these results to estimate the theoretical moments of any desired distribution from the moments of artificial samples, we must generate $\{W_i\}$ with the requisite properties despite the fact that $\mathsf{D}(\cdot)$, μ, and σ^2 are unknown. The trick in Monte Carlo is to design experiments such that the $\{W_i\}$ are the derived functions $g(h_1\{\cdot\},\ldots,h_k\{\cdot\})$ in (3.23) whose properties we wish to ascertain, such as the moments of regression coefficients or their standard errors. Generate the $\{W_i\}$ from more basic random variables $\{X_t\}$, whose distribution is known, and calculate $W_i = g(\cdot)$. The Monte Carlo DGP for the $\{X_t\}$ must mimic that for the econometric problem to ensure that (e.g.):

$$\mathbb{E}[W_i] = \mu = \mathsf{E}[g(h_1\{X_1,\ldots,X_T\},\ldots,h_k\{X_1,\ldots,X_T\})].$$

The $\{W_i\}$ are the random variables with the unknown distribution in (3.24), but we estimate the parameters of their distribution from samples based on large numbers of sets of $\{X_1,\ldots,X_T\}$ thereby simulating the properties of $g(\cdot)$.

To illustrate the use of Monte Carlo methods to solve distributional problems, consider determining the properties of the mean $\bar{Y}$ of a stationary autoregressive process as an estimator of the unknown expectation $\mathsf{E}[Y_t] = \mu$, from a sample $(Y_1,\ldots,Y_T)$:

$$\bar{Y} = T^{-1}\sum_{t=1}^{T} Y_t. \tag{3.29}$$

In (3.29), $\bar{Y}$ is the estimator of interest. To simulate the DGP, let:

$$Y_t = \rho Y_{t-1} + \phi + \epsilon_t \text{ with } \epsilon_t \sim \mathsf{IN}[0,1] \text{ where } |\rho| < 1 \text{ and } \phi \in (-\infty,\infty). \tag{3.30}$$

Also, $Y_0 \sim \mathsf{N}[\mu,(1-\rho^2)^{-1}]$, and $t = 1,\ldots,T$. Then (3.30) defines the DGP, which is a function of ϕ and ρ, where $\mu = \phi/(1-\rho)$. The 'experimenter' must know the value of the parameters (ρ,ϕ) to generate data, but the 'econometrician' only observes the sample of Ys. This schizophrenia mimics level C where 'nature' is the experimenter (and knows the DGP) and a human is the econometrician.

Choose particular values for the parameters (ρ,ϕ), say $\rho = 0.5$ and $\phi = 3$, and for the sample size T, such as $T = 50$. Then $\mu = 6$. The triplet $(\rho,\phi,T) = (0.5,3,50)$ defines an experiment. If only one experiment is conducted, the results are specific to the parameter values chosen, but experiments can be conducted at a range of parameter values. General results can often be established via invariance arguments which prove that the outcome for one experiment will be replicated at all other values of the relevant parameter in the admissible parameter space: we return to that issue in §3.6.5.

Next, generate a set of $\{Y_t\}$ from (3.30), using random numbers to simulate the random variables $\{\epsilon_t\}$, and draw a sample of size fifty, denoted by $(Y_1,\ldots,Y_{50})$. Calculate the sample mean $\bar{Y}$ and denote the outcome on the first replication by $W_1 = \bar{Y}$, which is a function of $(Y_1,\ldots,Y_{50})$ and hence of $(\epsilon_1,\ldots,\epsilon_{50})$, so $W_1 = W_1(\epsilon_1,\ldots,\epsilon_{50})$. Independently repeat this whole process M times (1000 say), to generate a random sample of

Ws each of which is based on the mean of fifty Ys: $(W_1, \ldots, W_{1000})$. This collection at one point in the parameter space provides M trials of the experiment. For the DGP (3.30), the results in Chapter A4 show that the distribution of $\{W_i\}$ should be $\mathsf{N}[6, 4/50]$, but in general we only know that the properties of $\{W_i\}$ derive from those of $\{Y_t\}$ via the functions $g(\cdot)$. In the present example $\mathbb{E}[W_j] = \mathsf{E}[\bar{Y}] = \mu$ by construction. Let:

$$\widetilde{W} = \sum_{j=1}^{1000} \frac{W_j}{1000},$$

then:

$$\widetilde{W} \sim \mathsf{N}\left[\mu, \frac{4}{TM}\right] \underset{e}{\sim} \mathsf{N}\left[6, \frac{1}{12500}\right].$$

The MCSE of $\widetilde{W}$ will decrease as the Monte Carlo replication sample size M increases. We can check that anticipated outcome against the sample result to analyse $\widetilde{W}$ as an estimator of μ, using the computer program PcNaive (an acronym from *Numerical Analysis of Instrumental Variables Estimators*: Hendry *et al.*, 1991).

An experiment of $M = 1000$ at $(\rho, \phi) = (0.5, 3)$ with $\mu = 6$ and $T = 50$ yields $\widetilde{W} = 6.001\ (0.009)$ where the number in parentheses is the MCSE of $\widetilde{W}$ (namely $\tilde{\sigma}/\sqrt{M} \simeq 2/\sqrt{(TM)}$). The feasible range for $\mathbb{E}[\widetilde{W}] = \mu$ is small given the value of the estimated standard error so the Monte Carlo is precise. From (3.26), an approximate 95 per cent confidence interval for μ is given by $[5.982, 6.018]$.

3.6.2 Antithetic variates

Despite the precision of the outcome in §3.6.1, it is useful to highlight the distinction between distribution sampling and Monte Carlo. The above approach is naive in that an efficient Monte Carlo would use methods of variance reduction. Here we consider two possibilities.

The first method is called antithetic variates and will be explained in the context of a substantive problem (see Hendry and Trivedi, 1972). The essence of the method is to exploit the fact that the random numbers are known to the investigator, and so can be reused. By careful choice of how they are reused, the uncertainty in the Monte Carlo can be reduced. Since the reused original random numbers would have arisen anyway at some point in a sufficiently large experiment, there is no loss of randomness by their reuse. Thus, we design the experiment to minimize the uncertainty by selecting sets of random numbers which offset each other's variability, which is the source of the name antithetic.

Consider antithetic variates for a statistic with an unknown mean μ linearly dependent on standardized errors $\nu_t \sim \mathsf{N}[0, 1]$, for $t = 1, \ldots, T$. The SGM is $y_t = \gamma + \nu_t$ and the relevant statistic is:

$$\hat{\gamma} = T^{-1} \sum_{t=1}^{T} y_t = \gamma + T^{-1} \sum_{t=1}^{T} \nu_t, \tag{3.31}$$

where $\mathsf{E}[\hat{\gamma}] = \mu$, but the value of μ is unknown. Its Monte Carlo estimator is denoted W. Generate the errors using random numbers $\epsilon_t \sim \mathsf{N}[0,1]$ to obtain the vector $(\epsilon_1, \ldots, \epsilon_T)$. First compute the value $W_1(\epsilon_1, \ldots, \epsilon_T) = \hat{\gamma}_1$ which is an unbiased estimator of μ. Since the $\{\epsilon_t\}$ are random so are $\{-\epsilon_t\}$ and $\mathsf{P}(\epsilon_t \le r) = \mathsf{P}(-\epsilon_t \ge -r)\ \forall r$ by symmetry, so $W_1^*(-\epsilon_1, \ldots, -\epsilon_T) = \hat{\gamma}_1^*$ is as likely as $W_1(\epsilon_1, \ldots, \epsilon_T)$. Since each of W_1 and W_1^* is an unbiased estimator of μ from (3.31), so is their average $\widetilde{W} = \frac{1}{2}(W_1 + W_1^*)$. Since:

$$W_1 = \mu + T^{-1}\sum_{t=1}^{T}\epsilon_t \text{ and } W_1^* = \mu - T^{-1}\sum_{t=1}^{T}\epsilon_t,$$

then $\widetilde{W} \equiv \mu$. But this must occur in every trial of matched pairs, so $\mathcal{V}[\widetilde{W}] \equiv 0$. Thus, we have proved in two replications that the sample mean is an unbiased estimator of the population mean for all possible values of μ.

Sometimes, antithetic variates can be used to establish the unbiasedness of estimators which are too complex to analyse algebraically, and are an important member of the class of variance reduction techniques (see e.g. Hendry, 1984b). A powerful illustration is the following extension of the regression model in (3.5) for a sample size of T when the $T \times k$ matrix $\boldsymbol{Z}$ is fixed in repeated samples:

$$\boldsymbol{y} = \boldsymbol{Z}\boldsymbol{\beta} + \boldsymbol{u} \quad \text{where } \boldsymbol{u} \sim \mathsf{N}_T[\boldsymbol{0}, \boldsymbol{\Omega}(\boldsymbol{\theta})], \tag{3.32}$$

and $\boldsymbol{\Omega}(\boldsymbol{\theta})$ is a positive-definite, symmetric covariance matrix, dependent on a vector of unknown parameters $\boldsymbol{\theta}$. We wish to study the bias in the least-squares estimator of $\boldsymbol{\beta}$ in a three-step approach where $\boldsymbol{\beta}$ is first estimated by OLS, then $\boldsymbol{\theta}$ is estimated from the residuals to yield $\boldsymbol{\Omega}(\hat{\boldsymbol{\theta}})$ and finally, $\boldsymbol{\beta}$ is re-estimated from the generalized least-squares (GLS) formula:

$$\tilde{\boldsymbol{\beta}} = \left(\boldsymbol{Z}'\boldsymbol{\Omega}(\hat{\boldsymbol{\theta}})^{-1}\boldsymbol{Z}\right)^{-1}\boldsymbol{Z}'\boldsymbol{\Omega}(\hat{\boldsymbol{\theta}})^{-1}\boldsymbol{y}. \tag{3.33}$$

We are not concerned with the optimality of $\tilde{\boldsymbol{\beta}}$ as an estimator of $\boldsymbol{\beta}$; ($\tilde{\boldsymbol{\beta}}$ is essentially fully efficient under the present assumptions), merely with the bias $\mathsf{E}[\tilde{\boldsymbol{\beta}} - \boldsymbol{\beta}]$, if any. Technically, $\mathsf{E}[\tilde{\boldsymbol{\beta}} - \boldsymbol{\beta}]$ involves calculating a high-dimensional integral of the right-hand side of (3.33); even if $\hat{\boldsymbol{\theta}}$ is unbiased for $\boldsymbol{\theta}$, and $\boldsymbol{\Omega}(\hat{\boldsymbol{\theta}})$ for $\boldsymbol{\Omega}(\boldsymbol{\theta})$, it would not follow that $\boldsymbol{\Omega}(\hat{\boldsymbol{\theta}})^{-1}$ was unbiased for $\boldsymbol{\Omega}(\boldsymbol{\theta})^{-1}$. Conventional Monte Carlo could be applied as in §3.6.1, and for sufficiently large M would produce precise answers for any given parameter values.

The double benefits of antithetic variates are that an exact answer is provided, and it holds for all relevant values of $\boldsymbol{\beta}$ and $\boldsymbol{\theta}$. From (3.33):

$$\tilde{\boldsymbol{\beta}} - \boldsymbol{\beta} = \left(\boldsymbol{Z}'\boldsymbol{\Omega}(\hat{\boldsymbol{\theta}})^{-1}\boldsymbol{Z}\right)^{-1}\boldsymbol{Z}'\boldsymbol{\Omega}(\hat{\boldsymbol{\theta}})^{-1}\boldsymbol{u}. \tag{3.34}$$

Generate the matrix $\boldsymbol{Z}$ once, and select values for $\boldsymbol{\beta}$ and $\boldsymbol{\theta}$. Next, generate $\boldsymbol{u}$ from $\mathsf{N}_T[\boldsymbol{0}, \boldsymbol{\Omega}(\boldsymbol{\theta})]$, store its value, and create $\boldsymbol{y}$ from (3.32). First compute $\hat{\boldsymbol{\beta}}$ from OLS, derive the residuals:

$$\hat{\boldsymbol{u}} = \boldsymbol{y} - \boldsymbol{Z}\hat{\boldsymbol{\beta}} = \left(\boldsymbol{I}_T - \boldsymbol{Z}(\boldsymbol{Z}'\boldsymbol{Z})^{-1}\boldsymbol{Z}'\right)\boldsymbol{u}, \tag{3.35}$$

and hence calculate $\hat{\boldsymbol{\theta}}$ and $\boldsymbol{\Omega}(\hat{\boldsymbol{\theta}})$. Finally, compute (3.34) to get the first replication value of $\tilde{\boldsymbol{\beta}}$, which we denote by $\tilde{\boldsymbol{\beta}}(\boldsymbol{u})$.

Since $\boldsymbol{\Omega} = \mathsf{E}[\boldsymbol{u}\boldsymbol{u}']$ is a positive function of $\boldsymbol{u}$, we take $\hat{\boldsymbol{\theta}}$ to be quadratic in the elements of $\hat{\boldsymbol{u}}$, so $\boldsymbol{\Omega}(\hat{\boldsymbol{\theta}})$ takes the same value for $\hat{\boldsymbol{u}}$ and $-\hat{\boldsymbol{u}}$:

$$\boldsymbol{\Omega}(\hat{\boldsymbol{\theta}}\{\hat{\boldsymbol{u}}\}) \equiv \boldsymbol{\Omega}(\hat{\boldsymbol{\theta}}\{-\hat{\boldsymbol{u}}\}).$$

But from (3.35) since $\boldsymbol{Z}$ is fixed, changing the sign of $\boldsymbol{u}$ merely entails changing the sign of $\hat{\boldsymbol{u}}$. The pair $\boldsymbol{u}, -\boldsymbol{u}$ offset each other's variability perfectly (their average is identically zero, and their correlation is -1), and will be our antithetic pair here. Thus, repeat the first replication using $-\boldsymbol{u}$ in place of $\boldsymbol{u}$ to calculate $\tilde{\boldsymbol{\beta}}(-\boldsymbol{u})$. Naturally, we are concerned with the induced variability in the Monte Carlo estimates of $\mathsf{E}[\tilde{\boldsymbol{\beta}} - \boldsymbol{\beta}]$, so let us calculate the variability in our estimator of that bias after this one trial of the antithetic pair. The mean of the trial is $\bar{\boldsymbol{\beta}} = \frac{1}{2}[\tilde{\boldsymbol{\beta}}(\boldsymbol{u}) + \tilde{\boldsymbol{\beta}}(-\boldsymbol{u})]$ which from (3.34) is:

$$\begin{aligned}
&\tfrac{1}{2}\left[\left\{\boldsymbol{\beta}+\left(\boldsymbol{Z}'\boldsymbol{\Omega}(\hat{\boldsymbol{\theta}})^{-1}\boldsymbol{Z}\right)^{-1}\boldsymbol{Z}'\boldsymbol{\Omega}(\hat{\boldsymbol{\theta}})^{-1}\boldsymbol{u}\right\}\right.\\
&\quad\left.+\left\{\boldsymbol{\beta}+\left(\boldsymbol{Z}'\boldsymbol{\Omega}(\hat{\boldsymbol{\theta}})^{-1}\boldsymbol{Z}\right)^{-1}\boldsymbol{Z}'\boldsymbol{\Omega}(\hat{\boldsymbol{\theta}})^{-1}(-\boldsymbol{u})\right\}\right]\\
&=\tfrac{1}{2}\left[2\boldsymbol{\beta}+\left(\boldsymbol{Z}'\boldsymbol{\Omega}(\hat{\boldsymbol{\theta}})^{-1}\boldsymbol{Z}\right)^{-1}\boldsymbol{Z}'\boldsymbol{\Omega}(\hat{\boldsymbol{\theta}})^{-1}\boldsymbol{u}-\left(\boldsymbol{Z}'\boldsymbol{\Omega}(\hat{\boldsymbol{\theta}})^{-1}\boldsymbol{Z}\right)^{-1}\boldsymbol{Z}'\boldsymbol{\Omega}(\hat{\boldsymbol{\theta}})^{-1}\boldsymbol{u}\right]\\
&\equiv\boldsymbol{\beta}.
\end{aligned} \tag{3.36}$$

Since that outcome happens on every trial, $\bar{\boldsymbol{\beta}}$ always equals $\boldsymbol{\beta}$ with zero Monte Carlo variance. In other words, $\tilde{\boldsymbol{\beta}}$ is everywhere unbiased for $\boldsymbol{\beta}$, and here simulation analysis is as good as a mathematical proof — and indeed has been accomplished without actually doing the Monte Carlo at all (compare Kakwani, 1967).

However, antithetic variates of the $\{u_t\}, \{-u_t\}$ variety do not always work well. For example, when the DGP is a zero-mean, first-order autoregressive process (lower case denotes a random variable):

$$y_t = \alpha y_{t-1} + \epsilon_t \text{ where } |\alpha| < 1 \text{ and } y_0 = 0 \text{ with } \epsilon_t \sim \mathsf{IN}\left[0, \sigma_\epsilon^2\right], \tag{3.37}$$

for $t = 1, \ldots, T$, then switching the sign of $\{\epsilon_t\}$ switches the sign of $\{y_t\}$. Further:

$$\hat{\alpha} = \left(\sum_{t=1}^{T} y_{t-1}^2\right)^{-1} \sum_{t=1}^{T} y_t y_{t-1} = \alpha + \left(T^{-1}\sum_{t=1}^{T} y_{t-1}^2\right)^{-1} T^{-1}\sum_{t=1}^{T} y_{t-1}\epsilon_t = W_1, \tag{3.38}$$

so the sign of $\hat{\alpha}$ is unaffected by changing the sign of all the $\{\epsilon_t\}$ and hence:

$$W_1(\epsilon_1, \ldots, \epsilon_T) \equiv W_1^*(-\epsilon_1, \ldots, -\epsilon_T).$$

Thus, the repeated trial is wasted.

3.6.3 Control variables

A second approach to variance reduction is provided by the method of control variables. The reason for using Monte Carlo to study the distribution of $\hat{\alpha}$ in (3.38) is its mathematical intractability, due to dependence between the numerator and denominator. That problem does not entail that all aspects of the problem are intractable. We can calculate the moments of the $\{y_t\}$ in (3.37) as in Chapter 1:

$$\mathsf{E}[y_t] = 0,\ \mathsf{E}\left[y_t^2\right] \simeq \frac{\sigma_\epsilon^2}{(1-\alpha^2)} \text{ and } \mathsf{E}[y_t y_{t-1}] \simeq \frac{\alpha\sigma_\epsilon^2}{(1-\alpha^2)}.$$

The approximations are due to having assumed that $y_0 = 0$ (see Ch.4 for more detail). Thus:

$$\mathsf{E}\left[T^{-1}\sum_{t=1}^{T} y_t y_{t-1}\right] \simeq \frac{\alpha\sigma_\epsilon^2}{(1-\alpha^2)} \text{ and } \mathsf{E}\left[T^{-1}\sum_{t=1}^{T} y_{t-1}^2\right] \simeq \frac{\sigma_\epsilon^2}{(1-\alpha^2)}.$$

Although we know the expectations of the numerator and denominator of $\hat{\alpha}$ separately:

$$\mathsf{E}[\hat{\alpha}] \neq \left(\mathsf{E}\left[T^{-1}\sum_{t=1}^{T} y_{t-1}^2\right]\right)^{-1} \mathsf{E}\left[T^{-1}\sum_{t=1}^{T} y_t y_{t-1}\right].$$

Finally, the distribution of $\hat{\alpha}$ in large samples is (see Ch.A4):

$$\sqrt{T}(\hat{\alpha}-\alpha) \sim \mathsf{N}\left[0, (1-\alpha^2)\right] \text{ with } \mathsf{V}[\hat{\alpha}] = \sigma_\epsilon^2 \left(\sum_{t=1}^{T} y_{t-1}^2\right)^{-1}.$$

Also:

$$\widehat{\mathsf{V}[\hat{\alpha}]} = \hat{\sigma}_\epsilon^2 \left(\sum_{t=1}^{T} y_{t-1}^2\right)^{-1} \text{ where } \hat{\sigma}_\epsilon^2 = T^{-1}\sum_{t=1}^{T} (y_t - \hat{\alpha} y_{t-1})^2,$$

and both of these are statistics with unknown means to be estimated in the Monte Carlo. The quantity $\widehat{\mathsf{V}[\hat{\alpha}]}^{\frac{1}{2}}$ is the estimated standard error (ESE) and is estimated in the Monte Carlo by $M^{-1}\sum_{i=1}^{M} \widehat{\mathsf{V}[\hat{\alpha}_i]}^{\frac{1}{2}}$.

Invent a new 'estimator' $\tilde{\alpha}$, which will be the control variable:

$$\tilde{\alpha} = \alpha + T^{-1}\left(\sum_{t=1}^{T} y_{t-1}\epsilon_t\right) / \left[\sigma_\epsilon^2 \left(1-\alpha^2\right)^{-1}\right]. \quad (3.39)$$

We can calculate $\tilde{\alpha}$ in a Monte Carlo (since we generate all of its components) but not in a level C econometric analysis where (α, σ^2) are unknown. The construction of $\tilde{\alpha}$ in

(3.39) is based on $\hat{\alpha}$ but replaces the denominator of the latter by its population value, since:

$$\operatorname*{plim}_{T\to\infty} T^{-1}\sum_{t=1}^{T} y_{t-1}^2 = \sigma_\epsilon^2\left(1-\alpha^2\right)^{-1}.$$

Two important consequences follow. First, from (3.39):

$$\mathbb{E}\left[\tilde{\alpha}\right] = \alpha + T^{-1}\mathbb{E}\left(\sum_{t=1}^{T} y_{t-1}\epsilon_t\right) / \left[\sigma_\epsilon^2\left(1-\alpha^2\right)^{-1}\right] = \alpha.$$

Thus, in the Monte Carlo, $\tilde{\alpha}$ is an unbiased estimator of α and with some algebra it can be shown that $\mathcal{V}\left[\tilde{\alpha}\right] = T^{-1}\left(1-\alpha^2\right)$. Secondly, from Cramér's theorem (see Ch.A4), $\sqrt{T}\left(\tilde{\alpha}-\alpha\right)$ has the same limiting distribution as $\sqrt{T}\left(\hat{\alpha}-\alpha\right)$ and so in the identity:

$$\hat{\alpha} \equiv \tilde{\alpha} + \left(\hat{\alpha}-\tilde{\alpha}\right), \tag{3.40}$$

the first term has a known expectation, and the second is $O_p\left(T^{-1}\right)$. Thus, a more precise outcome can be obtained by calculating $\hat{\alpha}$ and $\tilde{\alpha}$ in every replication, recording their difference and at the completion of the replications adding back the known value of $\mathbb{E}\left[\tilde{\alpha}\right]$.

An alternative interpretation of the role of control variables is to note that (3.40) defines a function of the $\{\epsilon_t\}$ which can help control for variation in the Monte Carlo due to the particular random numbers generated. That notion is similar to the role of antithetic variates above, and, continuing that reasoning, we see that:

$$\mathsf{V}\left(\hat{\alpha}-\tilde{\alpha}\right) = \mathsf{V}\left(\hat{\alpha}\right) + \mathsf{V}\left(\tilde{\alpha}\right) - 2\mathsf{C}\left(\hat{\alpha},\tilde{\alpha}\right) \leq \mathsf{V}\left(\hat{\alpha}\right) \text{ if } \mathsf{V}\left(\tilde{\alpha}\right) \leq 2\mathsf{C}\left(\hat{\alpha},\tilde{\alpha}\right). \tag{3.41}$$

The variance of the controlled experiment will be less than that of the uncontrolled if the correlation between $\hat{\alpha}$ and $\tilde{\alpha}$ is sufficiently high, which it must be for large T from Cramér's theorem. Thus, there is a close link between control variates and asymptotic distribution theory. Other functions of the $\{\epsilon_t\}$ than those based on Cramér's theorem may help to control the experimental variation (for regression methods, see Ripley, 1987, and Davidson and MacKinnon, 1993).

3.6.4 Response surfaces

We return to the pure distribution sampling approach in §3.6.1 to investigate the apparent limitation that the experiment is specific to the one value of the parameters, including the implicit value of $\sigma_\epsilon^2 = 1$, and the one sample size $T = 50$ considered. The first approach we consider to resolving that difficulty is to repeat experiments for a range of relevant values of $\left\{\rho, \phi, \sigma_\epsilon^2\right\}$, and T. That raises the problem of summarizing the mass of results generated. Tabulation is possible but both hard to remember and not conducive to general findings, so instead, we consider a more general technique known as response surfaces.

The usual objective in a Monte Carlo study is not simply to calculate the properties of a distribution at a few points in the parameter space, but to solve the analogue of the corresponding mathematical analysis, which would be applicable to the admissible parameter space. The DGP is the joint density of the observables given the parameters, and for different parameter values, different samples of observables result. In turn, the distributions of statistics of interest depend on the parameters of the DGP. For example, $\mathsf{E}[\hat{\alpha}]$ from (3.38) depends on α and T, which we can write as the conditional expectation:

$$\mathsf{E}[\hat{\alpha} \mid \alpha, T] = \psi(\alpha, T).$$

In principle, σ_ϵ also might matter, but does not do so here. Thus, we re-state the objective of the Monte Carlo as numerically establishing functions like $\psi(\alpha, T)$. A single experiment determines one point on the function, and could be viewed as a pilot study, whereas a set of experiments would enable the conditional expectation $\psi(\alpha, T)$ to be estimated by regression from the given parameter values. We will not investigate that avenue further here, however, as our main use of Monte Carlo will be to illustrate analytical results. The reader interested in greater detail is referred to Hendry (1984b).

3.6.5 Invariance

Next, we investigate the extent to which specificity can be reduced by invariance arguments, which would also help offset the expense in time and energy of undertaking many experiments. Consider the simple example $y_t = \mu + \epsilon_t$: since $y_t - \mu = \epsilon_t$, we need only analyse the $\{\epsilon_t\}$ in the experiments, calculate $\bar{\epsilon}$, $\mathsf{V}[\bar{\epsilon}]$ etc., and at the end recover the relevant function of $\bar{y}$ from $\bar{y} \equiv \mu + \bar{\epsilon}$. What is true for $\bar{\epsilon}$ holds for all $(\bar{y} - \mu)$ and so results are not specific to any value of μ. Repeating the experiment for a different μ but the same seed for the random numbers would generate identical outcomes. Alternatively, repeating that experiment for the same μ and a different seed would produce another sample of $\{W_i\}$ from the population of all possible experiments. Similar arguments should convince you that σ^2 is also irrelevant above to the behaviour of $\widetilde{W}$ as an estimator of μ, beyond being a scaling factor. The transform: $(y_t - \mu) / \sigma_\epsilon^2 \sim \mathsf{IN}[0, 1]$ defines a canonical experiment in this context, from which the outcomes for all other values of μ and $\sigma_\epsilon > 0$ can be obtained by multiplication (for σ_ϵ) or addition (for μ). In more complicated DGPs, invariance arguments can be used for many estimators of interest. For example, in (3.38), $\hat{\alpha}$ is also independent of σ_ϵ, as can be demonstrated numerically by using the same random numbers at two values of σ_ϵ, and showing that $\hat{\alpha}$ is unaltered (see Breusch, 1986).

Figure 3.4 shows the histogram (standardized to have a mean of zero and a variance of unity) of the $(W_i, i = 1, \ldots, M)$ when estimating the autoregressive coefficient α in (3.37) for $(\alpha, \sigma_\epsilon^2, T) = (0.5, 1, 25)$ using $M = 10\,000$. The non-parametrically estimated density function is also shown, where both are approximating the unknown $\mathsf{D_w}(w|\alpha, \sigma_\epsilon^2)$. The shape of the estimated density is close to normality although the location, scale and shape depend on α and T (but not on σ_ϵ^2). Figure 3.5 reports 10 000 drawings from an $\mathsf{N}[0, 1]$ distribution for comparison.

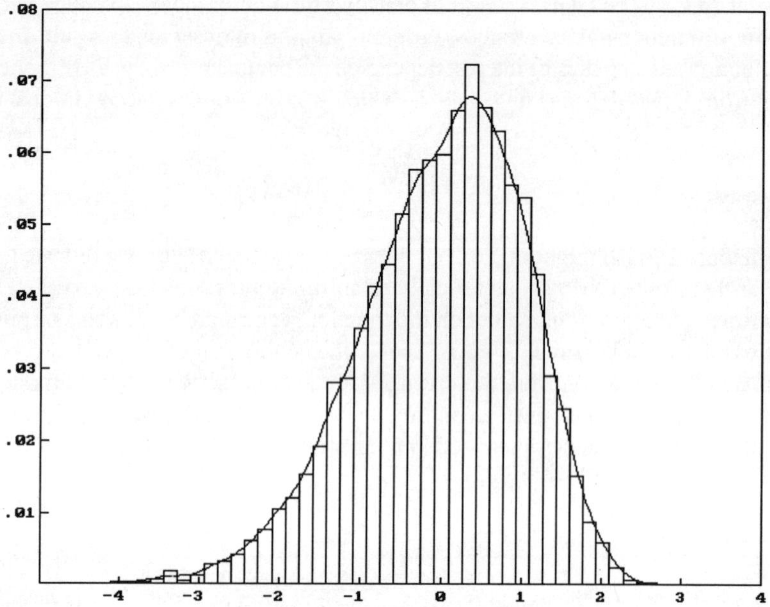

Fig. 3.4 Histogram and density for the autoregressive coefficient, $\alpha = 0.5$

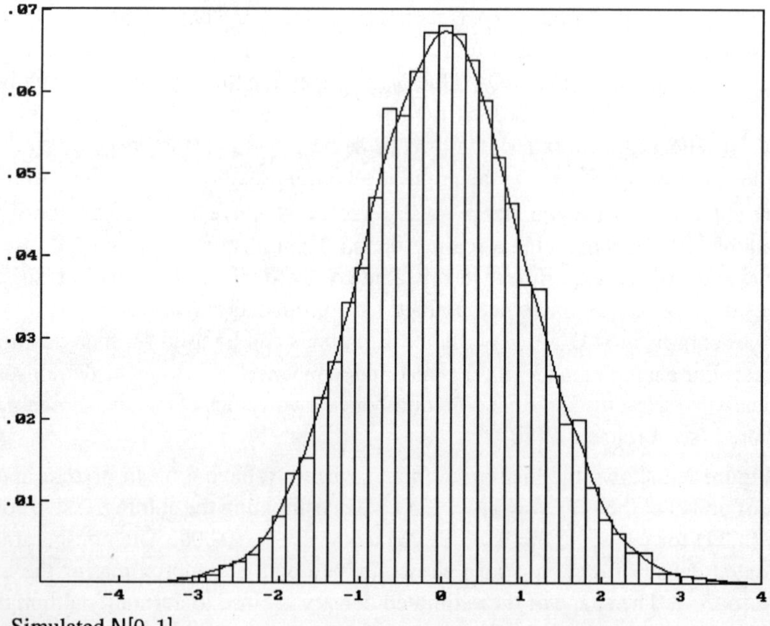

Fig. 3.5 Simulated $\mathsf{N}[0, 1]$

3.6.6 Recursive Monte Carlo

The second important specificity of the experiments so far is analysing only one sample size T. This limitation can be overcome by recursive Monte Carlo (see Hendry and Neale, 1987). Instead of simply calculating the Monte Carlo at the largest sample size T, compute all the relevant statistics recursively as the sample is generated, from T_0 (the smallest feasible sample size of interest) to T. For estimating the sample mean, the formulae are straightforward special cases of those developed for recursive least-squares estimation in §3.2.2 above.

To illustrate these claims for the sample mean, let $\bar{y}_\tau$ be the mean for a sample of size τ then for $\tau = T_0, \ldots, T$:

$$\bar{y}_\tau = \tau^{-1} \sum_{t=1}^{\tau} y_t = \tau^{-1} y_\tau + (\tau - 1)\tau^{-1} \bar{y}_{\tau-1} = \tau^{-1} y_\tau + (1 - \tau^{-1}) \bar{y}_{\tau-1}. \quad (3.42)$$

Once $\bar{y}_{t-1}$ is known at any t, the next $\bar{y}_t$ is trivial to calculate as a weighted average of the new y_t and the previous mean. The $\widetilde{W}_\tau$ at each τ is updated in a similar way at every replication. Here is a nearly 'free lunch', namely $(T - T_0 + 1)$ values of $\{\bar{y}_t\}$, rather than just the full sample mean $\bar{y}_T$, for little extra computational cost. Similar recursive formulae can be obtained for calculating variances and so on.

However, the output is massive: $(T - T_0 + 1) \times M$ values for every statistic investigated. Fortunately, we can analyse the behaviour of statistics across sample sizes by graphical methods, e.g. by reporting the mean across replications and plus or minus twice its standard error at each sample size, as in Fig. 3.6. The figure shows the outcome of a Monte Carlo study of the mean for the DGP in §3.6.5. The mean $\widetilde{W}_\tau - \mu$ at each $\tau \in [T_0, T]$ is close to zero and the Monte Carlo estimate of the expected value of $\bar{y}$ has a small 95 per cent confidence interval at every sample size. From Chapter A4:

$$\bar{y}_T \xrightarrow{P} \mu \text{ as } T \to \infty,$$

and since $\widetilde{W}_\tau = M^{-1} \sum_{i=1}^{M} W_{\tau,i}$ where each W_τ is a value of $\bar{y}_\tau$:

$$\widetilde{W}_T \xrightarrow{P} \mu \text{ as } T \to \infty.$$

Thus, the uncertainty decreases as T increases, at the rate $1/\sqrt{T}$. The confidence intervals for $(\mathsf{E}[\widetilde{W}_\tau] - \mu)$ include zero and range from $(-0.006, 0.010)$ at $T_0 = 15$ to $(-0.003, 0.006)$ at $T = 50$, a reduction of $\sqrt{(10/3)}$ as anticipated from statistical theory. Despite the small size of the uncertainty measures, $\tilde{W}_\tau$ wanders rather erratically as τ changes, given that it is the average across 10000 independent samples. The explanation for that phenomenon follows from the analysis of martingales in Chapter A4. Let $S_\tau = \sum_{t=1}^{\tau} (y_t - \mu)$, then $S_\tau = S_{\tau-1} + (y_\tau - \mu)$ and hence $\mathsf{E}[S_\tau | S_{\tau-1}] = S_{\tau-1}$. Consequently $(\bar{y}_\tau - \mu) = \tau^{-1} S_\tau$ is a 'scaled' martingale and it derives its behaviour from that of the martingale, as does $\widetilde{W}_\tau$. In later chapters, we will use Monte Carlo in both its modes: across replications at a given T to study bias and distributional shape; and across τ for all replications to consider convergence issues.

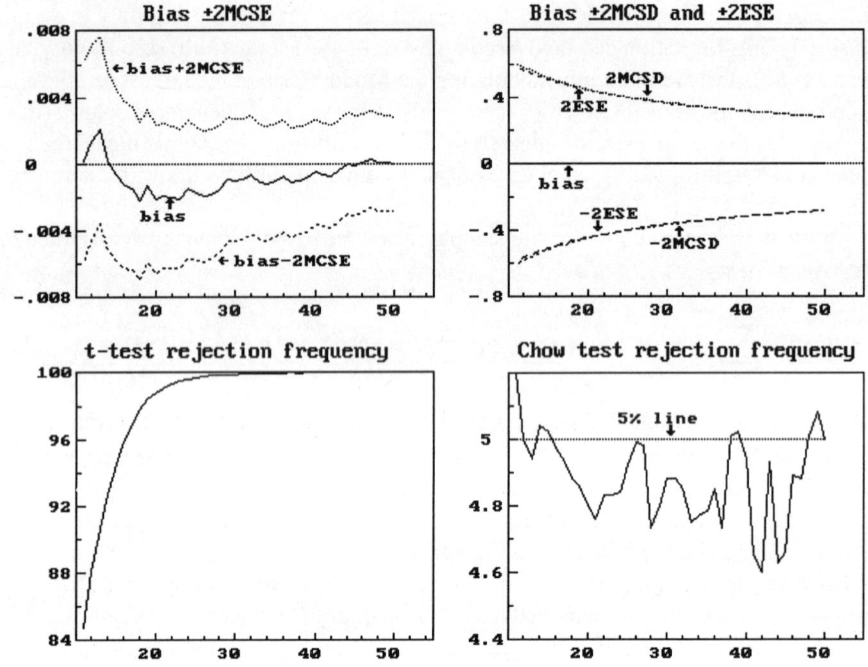

Fig. 3.6 Recursive Monte Carlo statistics

3.7 Ergodicity

We now apply that last dichotomy to reconsider actual economic data, using UK GNP as an example (see Fig. 3.7). The time-series reported is based on the recorded data: assume there are no observational errors. Even so, the recorded sequence is not the only path that GNP might have taken. At each point in time, we can imagine a distribution of possible outcomes, only one of which materializes. Implicit in the graph is a series of such distributions around the observed values, although the actual outcomes may not be the centres of those distributions. The figure sketches a few of these distributions.

As in Chapter 2, we treat economic data as a stochastic process having a time component and a stochastic component. For the present, leave aside the possibility that the stochastic distributions might differ at different points in time, and assume that the data series is strictly stationary. The statistical ergodic theorem concerns what information can be gleaned from an average over time (such as $\bar{y}$ above) about the common average at each point in time (i.e. $\mathsf{E}[y_t]$). The former is all that can be calculated from one historical realization of a given random variable, so strong assumptions are required to infer expectations from time averages. The following discusses one set of sufficient conditions and illustrates the type of restrictions needed on a stochastic process to obtain ergodicity.

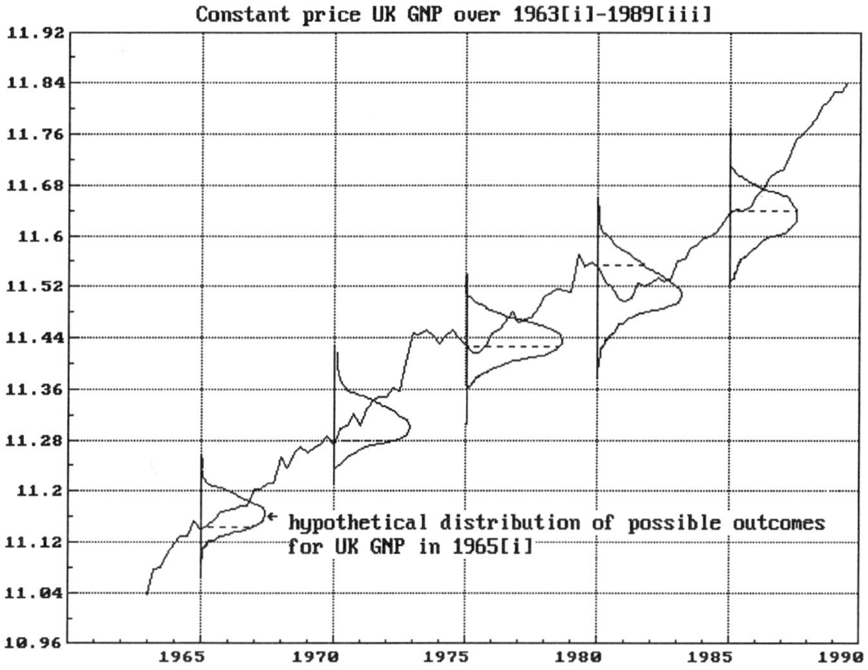

Fig. 3.7 Hypothetical distributions for UK GNP

Let $\{y_t(\omega), t \in \mathcal{T}, \omega \in \Omega\}$ be a stationary stochastic process, such that $\mathsf{E}[y_t(\omega)] = \mu < \infty$ and $\mathsf{E}\left[(y_t(\omega) - \mu)^2\right] = \sigma_y^2 < \infty \; \forall t \in \mathcal{T}$, and let $\bar{y}$ be the time average. Then:

$$\mathsf{E}[\bar{y}] = T^{-1} \sum_{t=1}^{T} \mathsf{E}[y_t] = \mu.$$

Thus, $\bar{y}$ is unbiased for μ. To establish consistency, it is sufficient that $\mathsf{V}[\bar{y}] \to 0$ as $T \to \infty$. Letting $c_{ts} = \mathsf{E}[(y_t - \mu)(y_s - \mu)]$:

$$\mathsf{V}[\bar{y}] = \mathsf{E}\left[(\bar{y} - \mu)^2\right] = T^{-2} \sum_{t=1}^{T} \sum_{s=1}^{T} \mathsf{E}[(y_t - \mu)(y_s - \mu)] = T^{-2} \sum_{t=1}^{T} \sum_{s=1}^{T} c_{ts}. \quad (3.43)$$

When $t = s$, $c_{tt} = \sigma_y^2$; and under stationarity for $t \neq s$, $c_{ts} = \gamma(t - s)$ (say) which only depends on the time difference between t and s, not on their absolute values. Further,

$\gamma(t-s) = \gamma(s-t)$, and hence from (3.43), letting $\rho(t) = \gamma(t)/\sigma_y^2$ so $|\rho(t)| < 1$:

$$\mathsf{V}[\bar{y}] = T^{-1}\sigma_y^2 + 2T^{-2}\sum_{t=1}^{T}(T-t)\gamma(t) = T^{-1}\sigma_y^2\left[1 + 2\sum_{t=1}^{T}\left(1 - \frac{t}{T}\right)\rho(t)\right] \tag{3.44}$$

A necessary condition for the term $[\cdot]$ to converge to a finite quantity (and hence for $\mathsf{V}[\bar{y}] \rightarrow 0$) is that $\rho(t) \rightarrow 0$ as $t \rightarrow \infty$; and a sufficient condition is that it does so fast enough (e.g. geometrically). To be ergodic, the memory of a stochastic process should fade in the sense that the covariance between increasingly distant observations converges to zero sufficiently rapidly: elements of the time series should be asymptotically uncorrelated. Chapter A4 provides a more extensive discussion.

In the simple Monte Carlo, each random sample $\{y_{1_j}, \ldots, y_{t_j}\}$ for $j = 1, \ldots, M$ is generated as a time series. The average over time in each replication converges to μ, which is the expected value. As Fig. 3.6 showed for an IID sample, in practice that time average is close to the stochastic average μ, providing one example of ergodicity where $\mathsf{E}[y_t] = \mu$ can be successfully inferred from a time sample mean $\bar{y}$.

Whether economic reality is an ergodic process after suitable transforms is a deep issue which we cannot analyse rigorously in this book. Chapter 2 revealed that the expected value of an integrated process is not constant over time, so the question arises as to whether the statistical ergodic theorem is applicable to such a process. First, note that the differenced series did have constant moments, so the theorem may be applicable to such time series. Historically, growth rates of real variables have not varied wildly, and a number of ratios (such as consumption/income, capital/output etc.) also have fluctuated within relatively narrow bands. Thus, ergodicity is not precluded for such functions of the original time series. At level A, we will assume ergodicity for all of the I(0) series considered, and will only analyse DGPs where time averages of suitably transformed variables sustain inferences about parameters of interest. At level C, in Part III, we will be concerned with regime shifts and other factors that might induce structural change in the economy, and which in practice make ergodicity untenable without careful formulation of the stochastic variables for which it is claimed. For example, a mixture of distributions may be needed, including one component which generates large shocks with a low probability. The regularity of predictive failure in empirical econometrics suggests that the problem is a serious one.

3.8 Non-stationarity*

The final step is to generalize the analysis to I(1) time series using the martingales and MDS established in Chapter 2: see Chapter A4 for more detail. Let $\{x_t\}$ be a standardized, normally distributed, zero-mean, unit-variance MDS so that $x_t \sim \mathsf{IN}[0,1]$ (and so stationary and ergodic), and let $S_t = \sum_{t=1}^{T} x_t$ where $S_0 = 0$. Then for $0 \leq \kappa < \tau < T$,

$\mathsf{E}[S_T - S_\kappa] = 0$, so that:

$$\mathsf{E}\left[(S_T - S_\kappa)^2\right] = \mathsf{E}\left[\left(\sum_{t=\kappa+1}^{T} x_t\right)^2\right] = (T - \kappa),$$

and $\mathsf{E}[(S_T - S_\tau)(S_{\tau-1} - S_\kappa)] = 0$. Thus, $S_T \sim \mathsf{N}[0, T]$ is a random walk with independent increments, and $S_T/\sqrt{T} \sim \mathsf{N}[0,1]$. Generally, when the distribution of $\{x_t\}$ is well behaved, if we suitably standardize S_T, its limiting distribution will also be well behaved. The analysis involves the notions of limit theorems in function spaces, known as functional limit theorems, and invariance principles, so-called because the same form of limiting distribution results for a wide range of processes $\{x_t\}$, with different degrees of heterogeneity and memory.

Figure 3.8a illustrates a sample realization of a random walk S_T for $T = 10$. We will describe the various stages of analysis in terms of this example, mapping the original random walk into a form which is more suitable for analysis. The discussion draws on a range of recent publications including Dickey and Fuller (1979, 1981), Hall and Heyde (1980), Stock (1987), Phillips (1986, 1987a, 1987b, 1988b), Park and Phillips (1988, 1989), Phillips and Perron (1988), Chan and Wei (1988), Banerjee and Hendry (1992) and Banerjee, Dolado, Galbraith and Hendry (1993).

Detailed study of functional limit theorems is beyond the scope of this book, but we consider the convergence of a transformation of $S_T/\sqrt{T}$ to a continuous Wiener process, denoted by $W(j)$ for $j \in [0,1]$. A Wiener process is like a continuous random walk defined on the interval $[0,1]$ (regard this as the horizontal axis), but with unbounded variation despite being continuous, so it can be imagined as jumping around erratically (i.e. vertically). In any sub-interval $[a,b] \subset [0,1]$, $W(j)$ for $j \in [a,b]$ remains erratic. There are few convenient analytical expressions for the distribution of $W(j)$, but for fixed j, $W(j) \sim \mathsf{N}[0,j]$. Some functionals of $W(j)$ are related to the normal as shown below, and other functions have been tabulated. The distribution of $W(j)$ plays an important role in processes with unit roots, and illustrates limiting distributions with direct relevance to economic time series. The formulation shows how to get from S_T to a Wiener process, and notes a general theorem which explains why the resulting theory is in some respects remarkably simple.

First, map the increasing interval from 0 to T into the fixed interval $[0,1]$ so that results do not depend on the actual value of T, by dividing $[0,1]$ into $T+1$ parts at $0, \frac{1}{T}, \frac{2}{T}, \ldots, 1$. Let $[jT]$ denote the integer part of jT for $j \in [0,1]$. For example, if $T = 100$ and $j = 0.1163$, then $[jT] = [11.63] = 11$. From S_T, construct a new random function denoted by $R_T(j)$:

$$R_T(j) = \frac{S_{[jT]}}{\sqrt{T}} = \frac{1}{\sqrt{T}} \sum_{t=1}^{[jT]} x_t \quad \text{for } j \in [0,1]. \tag{3.45}$$

For example, $R_{100}(0.1163) = S_{11}/10 = 0.1\sum_{t=1}^{10} x_t$ whereas $R_{100}(0.12) = S_{12}/10$. Then, $R_T(j)$ is a random variable defined over $[0,1]$, and is a (right) continuous, but non-differentiable, step function, equal to the same value of $S_{[jT]}/\sqrt{T}$ within steps, and jumping to the next value whenever j becomes sufficiently large that $[jT]$ jumps to the next integer: e.g. when $j = 0.12$, then $[jT] = 12$ in the example. Figure 3.8b shows this second stage mapping, leading to the step function graph of $R_T(j)$ in Fig. 3.8c. Thus, (3.45) is the algebraic relation corresponding to the mapping between Fig. 3.8a and Fig. 3.8c, other than the scaling to ensure a non-degenerate limiting distribution.

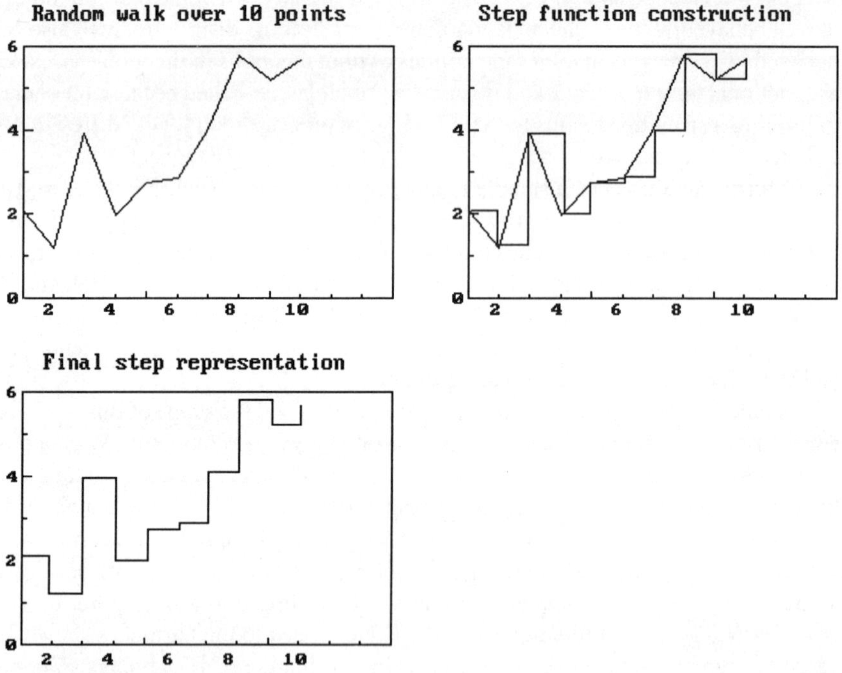

Fig. 3.8 Constructing the step function

As $T \to \infty$, $R_T(j)$ becomes increasingly dense on the unit interval and varies continuously, but erratically. Figs. 3.9a–d show the increasingly-wide wandering of a random walk for $T = 10,\ 100,\ 1000$, and 2000 respectively. The horizontal axis length is fixed, so the vertical axis variability increases as T grows.

Let $\Rightarrow$ denote weak convergence in the sense that the probability measures converge: this is the analog for function spaces of convergence in distribution for random variables (see Hall and Heyde, 1980). Then, under weak assumptions about $\{x_t\}$ (e.g. stationarity and mixing), we have the following convergence result:

$$R_T(j) \Rightarrow W(j) \quad \text{for } j \in [0,1] \quad \text{as } T \to \infty. \tag{3.46}$$

This formulation establishes how $W(j)$ arises, and the way in which the limiting distribution of S_T leads to a Wiener process. As noted, although our explanation used an

IID process for $\{x_t\}$, the convergence holds under much weaker conditions (see, e.g., Phillips, 1988b).

Next, if $f(\cdot)$ is a continuous functional on $[0,1]$, then:

$$f\left(R_T\left(j\right)\right) \Rightarrow f\left(W\left(j\right)\right). \tag{3.47}$$

Once we have established the mapping from S_T through $R_T\left(\cdot\right)$ to $W\left(\cdot\right)$, the corresponding distributions of $f(R_T(\cdot))$ can be derived directly. This is like an analog of Slutsky's theorem for plims in I(0) processes, applied to scaled distributions. Together, these last two results provide a general approach to distributions in integrated processes.

An important feature of distributions involving I(1) variables is that functionals of Wiener processes arise widely, whereas conventional methods of obtaining limiting distributions tend to be specific to the particular assumptions made about the data or error process (e.g. moments often are dependent on an IID assumption). Many of the statistics regularly used in empirical research involving I(1) time series have different distributions from those characterizing I(0) data. In particular, many statistics do not converge to constants but to random variables and different critical values may be required for tests. The solved example extends the analysis, and Chapter 4 applies it to an analysis of the nonsense regressions problem.

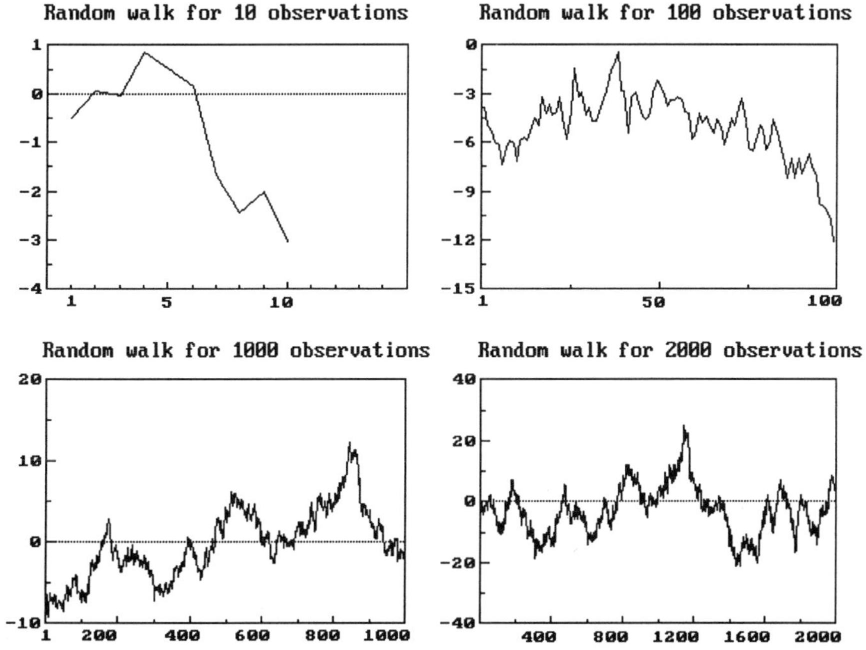

Fig. 3.9 Random walks over increasing sample sizes

3.9 A solved example*

Consider the following generation process for a random variable y_t:

$$y_t = \beta y_{t-1} + e_t \text{ where } e_t \sim \mathsf{IN}[0,1], \; \beta = 1, \text{ and } y_0 = 0. \tag{3.48}$$

(a) Derive (i) $\mathsf{E}[T^{-1}\sum_{t=2}^{T} y_{t-1}e_t]$; (ii) $\mathsf{E}[T^{-1}\sum_{t=1}^{T} y_t^2]$; (iii) $\mathsf{E}[T^{-1}\sum_{t=2}^{T} y_t y_{t-1}]$; and (iv) $\mathsf{V}[T^{-1}\sum_{t=1}^{T} y_t^2]$.
(b) Derive the limiting distribution of the sample mean.
(c) Obtain the limiting distribution of the least-squares estimator of β.

(Adapted from Oxford M.Phil., 1987)

Solution to (a): Moments of a random walk

Since $y_0 = 0$, we have that (i) $\mathsf{E}[T^{-1}\sum_{t=2}^{T} y_{t-1}e_t] = 0$ and as $\mathsf{E}[y_t^2] = t$, then (see Fuller, 1976):

$$\begin{aligned}
\text{(ii) } \mathsf{E}\left[T^{-1}\sum_{t=1}^{T} y_t^2\right] &= T^{-1}\sum_{t=1}^{T} t &&= \tfrac{1}{2}T^{-1}T(T+1) = \tfrac{1}{2}(T+1). \\
\text{(iii) } \mathsf{E}\left[T^{-1}\sum_{t=2}^{T} y_t y_{t-1}\right] &= T^{-1}\sum_{t=2}^{T}(t-1) &&= \tfrac{1}{2}T^{-1}T(T-1) = \tfrac{1}{2}(T-1). \\
\text{(iv) } \mathsf{V}\left[T^{-1}\sum_{t=2}^{T} y_t^2\right] &= \mathsf{E}\left[\left(T^{-1}\sum_{t=1}^{T} y_t^2 - \tfrac{1}{2}(T+1)\right)^2\right] \\
&= T^{-2}\sum_{t=1}^{T}\sum_{s=1}^{T}\mathsf{E}\left[y_t^2 y_s^2\right] - \tfrac{1}{4}(T+1)^2 \\
&= T^{-2}\left[3\sum_{t=1}^{T} t^2 + 2\sum_{t=1}^{T}\sum_{s=1}^{t-1}\left(ts + 2s^2\right)\right] - \tfrac{1}{4}(T+1)^2 \\
&\simeq (T+1)^2/3.
\end{aligned}$$

The last equality uses $\sum_{t=1}^{T} t^2 = T(T+1)(2T+1)/6$ and $\sum_{t=1}^{T} t^3 = \left[\tfrac{1}{2}T(T+1)\right]^2$. More generally, it can be shown that $\sum_{t=1}^{T} t^n / T^{n+1} \to (n+1)^{-1}$ as $T \to \infty$.

Solution to (b): Distribution of the mean of a random walk

To illustrate the type of analysis arising in unit-root processes, we derive the distribution of the sample mean:

$$\bar{y} = T^{-1}\sum_{t=1}^{T} y_t. \tag{3.49}$$

The difficulty in the derivation of the limiting distribution of $\bar{y}$ is due to $\{y_t\}$ being a random walk and so the mean converges to a functional of a Wiener process. Let:

$$R_T(j) = \frac{y_{[jT]}}{\sqrt{T}} = \frac{y_{i-1}}{\sqrt{T}} \text{ for } \frac{i-1}{T} \leq j < \frac{i}{T} \quad (i = 1, \ldots, T); \tag{3.50}$$

and:

$$R_T(1) = \frac{y_T}{\sqrt{T}}. \tag{3.51}$$

Then $R_T(j)$ is a step function with steps at i/T, for $i = 1, \ldots, T$, and is constant between steps as in Fig. 3.8c. Consequently:

$$\begin{aligned} \int_0^1 R_T(s)\,\mathrm{d}s &= \sum_{i=1}^{T} \int_{(i-1)/T}^{i/T} R_T(s)\,\mathrm{d}s \\ &= \sum_{i=1}^{T} T^{-1} R_T(j) \\ &= T^{-1} \sum_{i=1}^{T} y_{i-1}/\sqrt{T} \\ &= \bar{y}_{(-1)}/\sqrt{T} \end{aligned} \tag{3.52}$$

where $\bar{y}_{(-1)}$ denotes the lagged sample mean. The first equality in (3.52) holds by construction. The second equality follows from noting that $R_T(\cdot)$ is $R_T(j)$ between $T^{-1}(i-1)$ and $T^{-1}i$, and so is constant. It also uses the result that for any constant c:

$$\int_{(i-1)/T}^{i/T} c\mathrm{d}r = cr\rfloor_{(i-1)/T}^{i/T} = \frac{ic}{T} - \frac{(i-1)\,c}{T} = T^{-1}c. \tag{3.53}$$

The third equality in (3.52) follows from the definition of $R_T(j)$ in (3.50).

Next, from (A4.81) and (A4.83):

$$\int_0^1 R_T(s)\,\mathrm{d}s \Rightarrow \int_0^1 W(r)\,\mathrm{d}r \tag{3.54}$$

and hence from (3.52) and (3.54):

$$\frac{\bar{y}_{(-1)}}{\sqrt{T}} \Rightarrow \int_0^1 W(r)\,\mathrm{d}r. \tag{3.55}$$

The unlagged sample mean $\bar{y}$ has the same limiting distribution, but it is easiest to use $\bar{y}_{(-1)}$.

An interesting aspect of this result combined with the Lindeberg–Feller central limit theorem in §A4.5 (also see e.g. Spanos, 1986) is to establish that:

$$\int_0^1 W(r)\,\mathrm{d}r \sim \mathsf{N}\left[0, \tfrac{1}{3}\right]. \tag{3.56}$$

To apply the central limit theorem, we need to construct a random variable:

$$X_t \sim \mathsf{ID}\left[\mu_t, \sigma_t^2\right] \tag{3.57}$$

where $|\mu_t| < \infty$, $0 < \sigma_t^2 < \infty$ and $B_T^2 = \sum_{t=1}^T \sigma_t^2$, such that:

$$\sqrt{T}\left(\bar{X}_T - \bar{\mu}_T\right) / \left(B_T/\sqrt{T}\right) \xrightarrow{D} \mathsf{N}\left[0, \tfrac{1}{3}\right]. \tag{3.58}$$

First, consider:

$$\bar{y}_{(-1)} = T^{-1}\sum_{t=1}^{T}\sum_{j=1}^{t-1} e_{t-j} = e_1 + \frac{T-1}{T}e_2 + \frac{T-2}{T}e_3 + \cdots + \frac{1}{T}e_T = \sum_{t=1}^{T} X_t, \tag{3.59}$$

where $X_t = \left(\frac{T-t+1}{T}\right)e_t$. Then, $\mathsf{E}\left[X_t\right] = \left(\frac{T-t+1}{T}\right)\mathsf{E}\left[e_t\right] = \mu_t = 0$ and:

$$\mathsf{V}\left[X_t\right] = \left(\frac{T-t+1}{T}\right)^2 \mathsf{E}\left[e_t^2\right] = \left(\frac{T-t+1}{T}\right)^2 = \sigma_t^2 < \infty. \tag{3.60}$$

Further:

$$\mathsf{E}\left[X_t X_s\right] = \left(\frac{T-t+1}{T}\right)\left(\frac{T-s+1}{T}\right)\mathsf{E}\left[e_t e_s\right] = 0 \ \forall t \neq s. \tag{3.61}$$

Thus:

$$X_t \sim \mathsf{IN}\left[0, \sigma_t^2\right], \tag{3.62}$$

as required. Note that $\mathsf{E}\left[X_t^3\right] = 0$ by normality, and $\bar{X}_T = T^{-1}\bar{y}_{(-1)}$. Finally:

$$\begin{aligned}
B_T^2 &= \sum_{t=1}^{T}\left(\tfrac{T-t+1}{T}\right)^2 \\
&= T^{-2}\sum_{t=1}^{T}\left(T^2 - 2T\left(t-1\right) + t^2 - 2t + 1\right) \\
&= T^{-1}\left(T^2 - 2\left[\tfrac{1}{2}T\left(T-1\right)\right] + \left(T+1\right)\left(2T+1\right)/6 - \left(T+1\right) + 1\right) \\
&\simeq \tfrac{T}{3} + \tfrac{1}{2}.
\end{aligned}$$

Thus:

$$\sqrt{T}\left(\bar{X}_T - \bar{\mu}_T\right) / \left(B_T/\sqrt{T}\right) = \frac{\bar{y}_{(-1)}}{\sqrt{3T}} \xrightarrow{D} \mathsf{N}\left[0, 1\right]. \tag{3.63}$$

Since:

$$\frac{\bar{y}_{(-1)}}{\sqrt{T}} \Rightarrow \int_0^1 W\left(r\right)\mathrm{d}r \ \text{ then } \int_0^1 W\left(r\right)\mathrm{d}r \sim \mathsf{N}\left[0, \tfrac{1}{3}\right]. \tag{3.64}$$

Many of the functionals to which sample moments of $\mathsf{I}(1)$ processes converge can be expressed in terms of normal densities by similar derivations. Table 3.2 provides a set of distributional results for the process $S_t = S_{t-1} + w_t$ where $w_t \sim \mathsf{IN}[0,1]$ associated with $W(r)$:

$$R_T(r) = \frac{1}{\sqrt{T}} \sum_{t=1}^{[rT]} w_t \Rightarrow W(r)$$

and $u_t \sim \mathsf{IN}[0,1]$, a second process independent of e_t with $Q_t = Q_{t-1} + u_t$ inducing $U(r)$. The results are proved by showing that the sample moment in question converges to both the functional and the density as in (3.55)–(3.64), implying that the functional has the density shown.

Table 3.2 Convergence results for normalized sample moments

	Sample	Moment	Functional	Density
1.	$T^{-\frac{3}{2}} \sum_{t=1}^{T} S_{t-1}$	$T^{-1} \sum_{t=1}^{T} S_{t-1}/\sqrt{T}$	$\int_0^1 W(r)\mathrm{d}r$	$\mathsf{N}[0, \frac{1}{3}]$
2.	$T^{-\frac{1}{2}} \sum_{t=1}^{T} w_t$	$T^{-1} \sum_{t=1}^{T} \sqrt{T} w_t$	$\int_0^1 \mathrm{d}W(r) = W(1)$	$\mathsf{N}[0, 1]$
3.	$T^{-\frac{3}{2}} \sum_{t=1}^{T} t w_t$	$T^{-1} \sum_{t=1}^{T} T^{-1} t \sqrt{T} w_t$	$\int_0^1 r\mathrm{d}W(r)$	$\mathsf{N}[0, \frac{1}{3}]$
4.	$T^{-1} \sum_{t=1}^{T} S_{t-1} w_t$	$T^{-1} \sum_{t=1}^{T} T^{-\frac{1}{2}} S_{t-1} \sqrt{T} w_t$	$\int_0^1 W(r)\mathrm{d}W(r)$	$\frac{1}{2}(\chi^2(1) - 1)$
5.	$T^{-\frac{5}{2}} \sum_{t=1}^{T} t S_t$	$T^{-1} \sum_{t=1}^{T} T^{-1} t T^{-\frac{1}{2}} S_{t-1}$	$\int_0^1 rW(r)\mathrm{d}r$	$\mathsf{N}[0, \frac{2}{15}]$
6.	$T^{-1} \sum_{t=1}^{T} S_{t-1} u_t$	$T^{-1} \sum_{t=1}^{T} T^{-\frac{1}{2}} S_{t-1} \sqrt{T} u_t$	$\int_0^1 W(r)\mathrm{d}U(r)$	$\mathsf{N}[0, \int_0^1 W(r)^2 \mathrm{d}r]$
7.	$T^{-2} \sum_{t=1}^{T} S_t Q_t$	$T^{-1} \sum_{t=1}^{T} T^{-\frac{1}{2}} S_t T^{-\frac{1}{2}} Q_t$	$\int_0^1 W(r)U(r)\mathrm{d}r$	—

We have just proved the result in 1.; those in 2. and 3. are well known from stationary analyses; 4. is demonstrated below; and 5.–7. follow as above. The table shows that, despite their initially unfamiliar appearance, Wiener-based asymptotics involve familiar functions of normal distributions. Generalizations hold for unit-root processes with non-zero means and/or trends. The density given in 6. is conditional on S_{t-1} and conditioning is valid here since $W(r)$ and $U(r)$ are independent Wiener processes; more usefully, it follows that, unconditionally:

$$\begin{aligned} &\left[T^{-2} \textstyle\sum_{t=1}^{T} S_{t-1}^2\right]^{-\frac{1}{2}} T^{-1} \textstyle\sum_{t=1}^{T} S_{t-1} u_t \\ &\Rightarrow \left[\textstyle\int_0^1 W(r)^2 \mathrm{d}r\right]^{-\frac{1}{2}} \textstyle\int_0^1 W(r)\,\mathrm{d}U(r) \sim \mathsf{N}[0,1]. \end{aligned}$$

Case 7. also applies when $S_t = Q_t$. Since the limits of integration are always the same and are for a common form of argument, both are often omitted, so that the outcomes are written simply as $\int W$, $\int W \mathrm{d}U$ etc.

Solution to (c): Distribution of the autoregressive coefficient

Since $y_0 = 0$ in the autoregressive model (3.48):

$$\hat{\beta} - \beta = \frac{T^{-1}\sum_{t=1}^{T} y_{t-1}e_t}{T^{-1}\sum_{t=1}^{T} y_{t-1}^2} \approx \begin{cases} O_p(1/T) & \text{for } \beta = 1 \\ O_p\left(1/\sqrt{T}\right) & \text{for } |\beta| < 1 \end{cases} \tag{3.65}$$

The orders of magnitude claimed in (3.65) will be established below. To obtain a non-degenerate limiting distribution, different scaling factors are needed in (3.65), namely T and $\sqrt{T}$ for I(1) and I(0) respectively. Even after appropriate scaling, the form of the limiting distribution is different from that holding under stationarity as will be shown.

When $\beta = 1$ the distribution of the least squares estimator in (3.65) is a functional of a Wiener process, and we can use extensions of the tools in the illustration of the distribution of the sample mean in (b) to derive its distribution (see e.g. Stock, 1987, and Phillips, 1987a). First:

$$T\left(\hat{\beta} - \beta\right) = \left(T^{-1}\sum_{t=1}^{T} y_{t-1}e_t\right) / \left(T^{-2}\sum_{t=1}^{T} y_{t-1}^2\right). \tag{3.66}$$

The expected value of the numerator is zero, and of the denominator is $\frac{1}{2}(T+1)/T \simeq \frac{1}{2}$ from (a) above. Let $u_t = y_{t-1}e_t$, then $\mathsf{E}[u_t] = 0,\ \mathsf{E}[u_t^2] = (t-1) = \sigma_u^2(t)$ and $\mathsf{E}[u_t u_{t-s}] = 0$. Thus:

$$u_t \sim \mathsf{ID}[0, (t-1)]. \tag{3.67}$$

To apply the second weak law of large numbers to $\bar{u} = T^{-1}\sum_{t=1}^{T} u_t$, we would need that:

$$\lim_{T\to\infty} T^{-2}\sum_{t=1}^{T} \sigma_u^2(t) = \lim_{T\to\infty} T^{-2}\sum_{t=1}^{T}(t-1) = \lim_{T\to\infty} T^{-2}\left[\tfrac{1}{2}T(T-1)\right] = \tfrac{1}{2} \tag{3.68}$$

converged to zero rather than $\frac{1}{2}$. Consequently, the numerator does not behave according to previously established results. Indeed, by direct derivation:

$$\mathsf{E}\left[\left(T^{-1}\sum_{t=1}^{T} y_{t-1}e_t\right)^2\right] = T^{-2}\sum_{t=1}^{T}\sum_{s=1}^{T}\mathsf{E}[u_t u_s] = \tfrac{1}{2}T^{-1}(T-1) = O(1). \tag{3.69}$$

The numerator in (3.66) is $O_p(1)$ and converges to a random variable. From Table 3.2:

$$T^{-1}\sum_{t=1}^{T} y_{t-1}e_t \Rightarrow \int_0^1 W(r)\,\mathrm{d}W(r). \tag{3.70}$$

To interpret this outcome heuristically, the averaging corresponds to integrating (analogous to taking expectations, noting the mapping onto $[0,1]$); from $y_{t-1}/\sqrt{T}$ we construct the analogue of $R_T(r)$ which converges weakly to a Wiener process $W(r)$; and

$e_t\sqrt{T} = \Delta y_t\sqrt{T}$ is the innovation over which averaging occurs and corresponds to $\mathsf{d}W(r)$. However from 4. in Table 3.2:

$$\int_0^1 W(r)\,\mathsf{d}W(r) = \tfrac{1}{2}\left(W(1)^2 - 1\right). \tag{3.71}$$

This is a stochastic integral, not a standard Riemann–Stieltjes one. For fixed r, since $W(r) \sim \mathsf{N}[0, r]$, then $W(1) \sim \mathsf{N}[0, 1]$ and hence $W(1)^2 \sim \chi^2(1)$, so that (3.71) is half of the deviation of a chi-square with one degree of freedom from its expected value. This result can be established directly as follows (see Fuller, 1976):

$$\begin{aligned} T^{-1}\sum_{t=1}^{T} y_{t-1}e_t &= T^{-1}\sum_{t=1}^{T}\sum_{j=1}^{t-1} e_j e_t = \tfrac{1}{2}T^{-1}\left[\left(\sum_{t=1}^{T} e_t\right)^2 - \sum_{t=1}^{T} e_t^2\right] \\ &= \tfrac{1}{2}\left(T^{-1}y_T^2 - T^{-1}\sum_{t=1}^{T} e_t^2\right) \Rightarrow \tfrac{1}{2}\left(\chi^2(1) - 1\right), \end{aligned} \tag{3.72}$$

since $y_T \sim \mathsf{N}[0, T]$ and $\mathsf{E}\left[e_t^2\right] = 1$, so that $T^{-1}y_T^2 \sim \chi^2(1)$.

We have already established in (a)(ii) and (a)(iv) that the expectation and asymptotic variance of the denominator in (3.66) are ½ and ⅓, so it converges to a random variable and not to a constant as in the I(0) case. Because $\sum y_{t-1}^2$ is scaled by T^{-2}, a well-defined limiting distribution results from convergence to a functional of a Wiener process:

$$T^{-2}\sum_{t=1}^{T} y_{t-1}^2 \Rightarrow \int_0^1 W(r)^2\,\mathsf{d}r. \tag{3.73}$$

Again, averaging induces integration; $T^{-1}y_{t-1}^2$ converges weakly to $W(r)^2$ for $r \in [0, 1]$; and we integrate over the range of r. The scaling by T^{-2} is needed to have a factor of T^{-1} for the average and two factors of $1/\sqrt{T}$ for the mappings of each y_{t-1} to a continuous Wiener process. While expressions such as (3.70) and (3.73) are less familiar as limiting forms, they are intuitively reasonable given the basic result in (3.52). The primary tool for calculating such integrals in practice is Monte Carlo simulation of the corresponding left-hand side. The relation of (3.73) to the normal is the major missing entry in Table 3.2, but Abadir (1994) presents an expression for the distribution of $\int_0^1 W(r)^2 \mathsf{d}r$ which can be used for accurate computations.

On the basis of (A4.83), from (3.70) and (3.73), the limiting distribution in (3.66) is:

$$T\left(\hat{\beta} - \beta\right) \Rightarrow \int_0^1 W(r)\,\mathsf{d}W(r) \Big/ \int_0^1 W(r)^2\,\mathsf{d}r. \tag{3.74}$$

This is the ratio of the convergence outcomes, analogous to that obtained using Slutsky's or Cramér's theorems in conventional situations. If we only scaled $(\hat{\beta} - \beta)$ by the usual factor of $\sqrt{T}$, then the ratio would converge to zero, establishing super convergence:

$$\sqrt{T}\left(\hat{\beta} - \beta\right) = \frac{1}{\sqrt{T}}\left(T^{-1}\sum_{t=1}^{T} y_{t-1}e_t\right) \Big/ \left(T^{-2}\sum_{t=1}^{T} y_{t-1}^2\right) \Rightarrow 0.$$

A similar expression holds for the t-statistic testing $\mathsf{H}_0\colon \beta = 1$:

$$\mathsf{t}_{\beta=1} \Rightarrow \tfrac{1}{2}\left(W(1)^2 - 1\right) / \left(\int_0^1 W(r)^2\, dr\right)^{\frac{1}{2}}. \tag{3.75}$$

The test in (3.75) is often called the Dickey–Fuller test after Dickey and Fuller (1979). The importance of the finding in (3.75) is that the distribution is not the standard t-distribution, and hence conventional critical values are not valid. The numerator is skewed to the right, being a $\chi^2(1)$ minus its expectation: since $\mathsf{P}\left(\chi^2(1) \leq 1\right) \simeq 0.70$, the majority of statistic outcomes will be negative. Figure 3.10 plots $\chi^2(1)$. The critical values are usually different from -2.0, even for large sample sizes, and using conventional critical values can lead to considerable over-rejection of the null of a unit root when it is true.

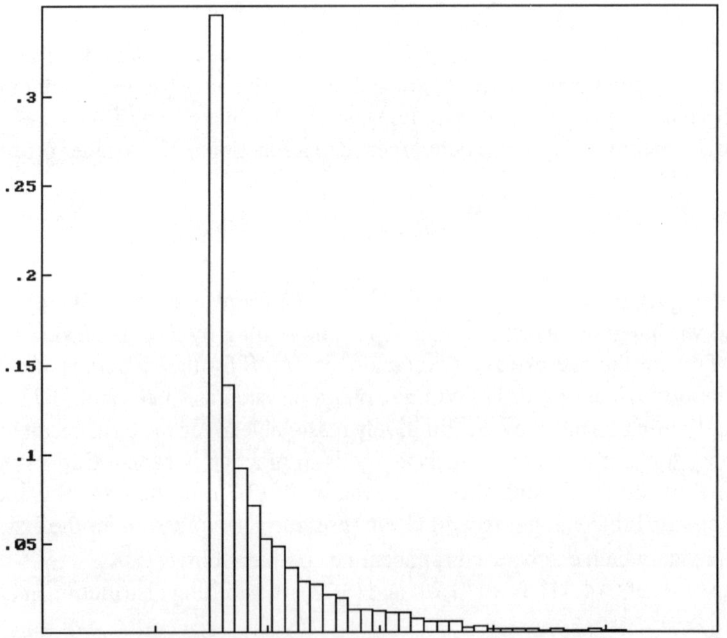

Fig. 3.10 Histogram of $\chi^2(1)$

However, the limiting distributions are altered by the presence of either an intercept in the estimated equation or a non-zero mean in the generating mechanism (or a trend term in either, etc.). Different critical values are required as the model or DGP alters. Most of the required critical values have been tabulated using Monte Carlo simulations by Dickey and Fuller (1979, 1981). MacKinnon (1991) estimated response functions for the critical values (denoted CV) by Monte Carlo, and for a random walk with no drift reports that:

$$CV\,(5\%) = -1.94 - 0.4T^{-1}. \tag{3.76}$$

Here, the result does not differ radically from the conventional value of -2.0. When a constant but no trend is included in the estimated equation, MacKinnon records:

$$CV\,(5\%) = -2.86 - 2.74T^{-1} - 8.36T^{-2}. \tag{3.77}$$

This is very different from -2.0 even for large sample sizes, so using the conventional critical value would lead to considerable over-rejection of the null of a unit root. Such response surfaces automatically provide critical values for tests in e.g. PcGive.

3.10 Vector Brownian motion*

Consider a general n-dimensional $\mathsf{I}(1)$ process:

$$\boldsymbol{p}_t = \boldsymbol{p}_{t-1} + \boldsymbol{v}_t \text{ where } \boldsymbol{p}_0 = \boldsymbol{0}, \tag{3.78}$$

and $\boldsymbol{v}_t$ is a well-behaved weakly stationary stochastic process with unconditional covariance $\mathsf{E}\left[\boldsymbol{v}_t\boldsymbol{v}_t'\right] = \boldsymbol{\Phi}_v$ and non-singular long-run covariance $\boldsymbol{\Omega}_v$. Sufficient conditions on $\{\boldsymbol{v}_t\}$ are that it is a stationary, linear, mixing process with finite integer moments of up to fourth order. The analysis in this section draws on Phillips and Durlauf (1986), Phillips (1986, 1987a, 1988b, 1991), and Park and Phillips (1988, 1989): see Banerjee *et al.* (1993) for an extensive discussion.

First we obtain the two covariance matrices $\boldsymbol{\Phi}_v$ and $\boldsymbol{\Omega}_v$ for a mean-zero, weakly-stationary, stochastic process $\{\boldsymbol{v}_t\}$. The long-run covariance matrix $\boldsymbol{\Omega}_v$ is given by:

$$\boldsymbol{\Omega}_v = \lim_{T\to\infty} \mathsf{E}\left[T^{-1}\left(\sum_{t=1}^{T}\boldsymbol{v}_t\right)\left(\sum_{s=1}^{T}\boldsymbol{v}_s'\right)\right] \tag{3.79}$$

which is the vector expression analogous to $\lim \mathsf{E}[T^{-1}(\sum_{t=1}^{T} v_t)^2]$ in the scalar case, so that $\boldsymbol{\Omega}_v$ is the variance matrix of the limiting distribution of the mean of $\{\boldsymbol{v}_t\}$.

To illustrate the analysis, we derive $\boldsymbol{\Phi}_v$ and $\boldsymbol{\Omega}_v$ for the special case of a stationary first-order vector autoregressive process:

$$\boldsymbol{v}_t = \boldsymbol{R}\boldsymbol{v}_{t-1} + \boldsymbol{\epsilon}_t \text{ where } \boldsymbol{\epsilon}_t \sim \mathsf{IN}_n\left[\boldsymbol{0}, \boldsymbol{\Sigma}\right] \tag{3.80}$$

where all the latent roots $\{\lambda_i\}$ of $\boldsymbol{R}$ lie inside the unit circle. The unconditional covariance matrix $\boldsymbol{\Phi}_v$ of $\{\boldsymbol{v}_t\}$ is:

$$\begin{aligned}\mathsf{E}\left[\boldsymbol{v}_t\boldsymbol{v}_t'\right] = \boldsymbol{\Phi}_v &= \mathsf{E}\left[\left(\boldsymbol{R}\boldsymbol{v}_{t-1} + \boldsymbol{\epsilon}_t\right)\left(\boldsymbol{v}_{t-1}'\boldsymbol{R}' + \boldsymbol{\epsilon}_t'\right)\right] \\ &= \boldsymbol{R}\mathsf{E}\left[\boldsymbol{v}_{t-1}\boldsymbol{v}_{t-1}'\right]\boldsymbol{R}' + \mathsf{E}\left[\boldsymbol{\epsilon}_t\boldsymbol{\epsilon}_t'\right] \\ &= \boldsymbol{R}\boldsymbol{\Phi}_v\boldsymbol{R}' + \boldsymbol{\Sigma}\end{aligned} \tag{3.81}$$

using stationarity. Then, vectorizing by stacking columns (see Ch.A1), $\boldsymbol{\Phi}_v$ is:

$$(\boldsymbol{\Phi}_v)^v = (\boldsymbol{R}\boldsymbol{\Phi}_v\boldsymbol{R}' + \boldsymbol{\Sigma})^v = (\boldsymbol{R} \otimes \boldsymbol{R})(\boldsymbol{\Phi}_v)^v + (\boldsymbol{\Sigma})^v \tag{3.82}$$

where $\otimes$ denotes a Kronecker product, so:

$$(\boldsymbol{\Phi}_v)^v = [\boldsymbol{I} - (\boldsymbol{R} \otimes \boldsymbol{R})]^{-1} (\boldsymbol{\Sigma})^v. \tag{3.83}$$

The inverse always exists since $|\lambda_i| < 1$. Alternatively, expanding (3.80):

$$\boldsymbol{v}_t = \sum_{i=0}^{\infty} \boldsymbol{R}^i \boldsymbol{\epsilon}_{t-i}$$

so that:

$$\mathsf{E}[\boldsymbol{v}_t \boldsymbol{v}_t'] = \mathsf{E}\left[\left(\sum_{i=0}^{\infty} \boldsymbol{R}^i \boldsymbol{\epsilon}_{t-i}\right)\left(\sum_{j=0}^{\infty} \boldsymbol{\epsilon}_{t-j}' \boldsymbol{R}^{j\prime}\right)\right] = \sum_{i=0}^{\infty} \boldsymbol{R}^i \boldsymbol{\Sigma} \boldsymbol{R}^{i\prime}.$$

Next, the long-run covariance matrix is:

$$\begin{aligned}
\boldsymbol{\Omega}_v &= \lim_{T\to\infty} \mathsf{E}\left[T^{-1}\left(\sum_{t=1}^{T} \boldsymbol{v}_t\right)\left(\sum_{s=1}^{T} \boldsymbol{v}_s'\right)\right] \\
&= \lim_{T\to\infty} T^{-1}\mathsf{E}\left[\left(\sum_{t=1}^{T} \boldsymbol{v}_t \boldsymbol{v}_t'\right) + \left(\sum_{t=s+1}^{T} \boldsymbol{v}_t \boldsymbol{v}_s'\right) + \left(\sum_{s=t+1}^{T} \boldsymbol{v}_t \boldsymbol{v}_s'\right)\right] \\
&= \boldsymbol{\Phi}_v + \boldsymbol{\Upsilon}_v' + \boldsymbol{\Upsilon}_v
\end{aligned}$$

say. However, since:

$$\mathsf{E}\left[\sum_{t=s+1}^{T} \boldsymbol{v}_t \boldsymbol{v}_s'\right] = \mathsf{E}\left[(\boldsymbol{v}_{s+1}\boldsymbol{v}_s') + (\boldsymbol{v}_{s+2}\boldsymbol{v}_s') + \cdots\right],$$

where $\mathsf{E}[\boldsymbol{v}_{s+j}\boldsymbol{v}_s'] = \boldsymbol{R}^j \boldsymbol{\Phi}_v$ then:

$$\boldsymbol{\Upsilon}_v' = \boldsymbol{R}\boldsymbol{\Phi}_v + \boldsymbol{R}^2 \boldsymbol{\Phi}_v + \cdots = \boldsymbol{R}(\boldsymbol{I} - \boldsymbol{R})^{-1} \boldsymbol{\Phi}_v \tag{3.84}$$

and hence:

$$\begin{aligned}
\boldsymbol{\Phi}_v + \boldsymbol{\Upsilon}_v' + \boldsymbol{\Upsilon}_v &= \boldsymbol{\Phi}_v + \boldsymbol{R}(\boldsymbol{I} - \boldsymbol{R})^{-1} \boldsymbol{\Phi}_v + \boldsymbol{\Phi}_v (\boldsymbol{I} - \boldsymbol{R}')^{-1} \boldsymbol{R}' \\
&= (\boldsymbol{I} - \boldsymbol{R})^{-1} \boldsymbol{\Phi}_v + \boldsymbol{\Phi}_v (\boldsymbol{I} - \boldsymbol{R}')^{-1} - \boldsymbol{\Phi}_v \\
&= (\boldsymbol{I} - \boldsymbol{R})^{-1} \boldsymbol{\Sigma} (\boldsymbol{I} - \boldsymbol{R}')^{-1},
\end{aligned}$$

where the second line uses the identity $\boldsymbol{\Phi}_v \equiv (\boldsymbol{I} - \boldsymbol{R})(\boldsymbol{I} - \boldsymbol{R})^{-1} \boldsymbol{\Phi}_v$ and the last uses (3.81).

For a second-order process:

$$\zeta_t = \boldsymbol{R}_1 \zeta_{t-1} + \boldsymbol{R}_2 \zeta_{t-2} + \epsilon_t \tag{3.85}$$

where $\epsilon_t \sim \mathsf{IN}_n\left[\mathbf{0}, \boldsymbol{\Sigma}\right]$:

$$\boldsymbol{\Omega}_\zeta = (\boldsymbol{I} - \boldsymbol{R}_1 - \boldsymbol{R}_2)^{-1} \boldsymbol{\Sigma} (\boldsymbol{I} - \boldsymbol{R}_1 - \boldsymbol{R}_2)^{-1\prime}, \tag{3.86}$$

and so on.

Consider a general non-singular long-run covariance $\boldsymbol{\Omega}_v = \boldsymbol{\Phi}_v + \boldsymbol{\Upsilon}_v + \boldsymbol{\Upsilon}_v'$ and standardize the process in (3.78) using $\boldsymbol{\Omega}_v^{-1} = \boldsymbol{K}_v \boldsymbol{K}_v'$ so that $\boldsymbol{K}_v' \boldsymbol{\Omega}_v \boldsymbol{K}_v = \boldsymbol{I}$ and hence:

$$\boldsymbol{m}_t = \boldsymbol{K}_v' \boldsymbol{p}_t = \boldsymbol{K}_v' \boldsymbol{p}_{t-1} + \boldsymbol{K}_v' \boldsymbol{v}_t \text{ where } \boldsymbol{K}_v' \boldsymbol{v}_t = \boldsymbol{e}_t. \tag{3.87}$$

For a general block-symmetric matrix $\boldsymbol{\Omega}$:

$$\boldsymbol{\Omega} = \begin{pmatrix} \boldsymbol{\Omega}_{11} & \boldsymbol{\Omega}_{12} \\ \boldsymbol{\Omega}_{21} & \boldsymbol{\Omega}_{22} \end{pmatrix},$$

then

$$\boldsymbol{K}' = \begin{pmatrix} \boldsymbol{\Omega}_{11.2}^{-\frac{1}{2}} & -\boldsymbol{\Omega}_{11.2}^{-\frac{1}{2}} \boldsymbol{\Omega}_{12} \boldsymbol{\Omega}_{22}^{-1} \\ \mathbf{0} & \boldsymbol{\Omega}_{22}^{-\frac{1}{2}} \end{pmatrix} = \begin{pmatrix} \boldsymbol{H} & -\boldsymbol{HC} \\ \mathbf{0} & \boldsymbol{\Omega}_{22}^{-\frac{1}{2}} \end{pmatrix}, \tag{3.88}$$

where $\boldsymbol{\Omega}_{11\cdot 2} = (\boldsymbol{\Omega}_{11} - \boldsymbol{\Omega}_{12} \boldsymbol{\Omega}_{22}^{-1} \boldsymbol{\Omega}_{21}) = \boldsymbol{H}^{-2}$, and $\boldsymbol{C} = \boldsymbol{\Omega}_{12} \boldsymbol{\Omega}_{22}^{-1}$. Then $\boldsymbol{m}_T/\sqrt{T}$ converges weakly to a standardized vector Brownian motion denoted $BM(\boldsymbol{I})$, or more generally:

$$T^{-\frac{1}{2}} \sum_{t=1}^{[Tr]} \boldsymbol{e}_t \Rightarrow \boldsymbol{B}(r) \text{ for } r \in [0,1] \text{ as } T \to \infty, \tag{3.89}$$

where $[Tr]$ is the integer part of Tr. In the bivariate case, $\boldsymbol{B}(r) = (B_1(r) : B_2(r))'$ when the $B_i(r)$ are the independent standardized Wiener processes associated with accumulating the $\{e_{it}\}$.

Consider the case when $\boldsymbol{e}_t \sim \mathsf{IN}_n[\mathbf{0}, \boldsymbol{I}]$: then using a component by component analysis of the standardized m_{it}, in the present bivariate case (see e.g. Banerjee and Hendry, 1992, for an exposition):

$$T^{-2} \sum_{t=1}^{T} \boldsymbol{m}_t \boldsymbol{m}_t' \Rightarrow \int_0^1 \boldsymbol{B}(r) \boldsymbol{B}(r)' \mathrm{d}r = \begin{pmatrix} \int_0^1 B_1(r)^2 \mathrm{d}r & \int_0^1 B_1(r) B_2(r) \mathrm{d}r \\ \int_0^1 B_1(r) B_2(r) \mathrm{d}r & \int_0^1 B_2(r)^2 \mathrm{d}r \end{pmatrix} \tag{3.90}$$

and:

$$T^{-1} \sum_{t=1}^{T} \boldsymbol{m}_{t-1} \boldsymbol{e}_t' \Rightarrow \int_0^1 \boldsymbol{B}(r) \mathrm{d}\boldsymbol{B}(r)' = \begin{pmatrix} \int_0^1 B_1(r) \mathrm{d}B_1(r) & \int_0^1 B_1(r) \mathrm{d}B_2(r) \\ \int_0^1 B_2(r) \mathrm{d}B_1(r) & \int_0^1 B_2(r) \mathrm{d}B_2(r) \end{pmatrix}. \tag{3.91}$$

Next, consider an expression of the form:

$$T^{-1}\sum_{t=1}^{T} \boldsymbol{m}_t \boldsymbol{e}_t' = T^{-1}\sum_{t=1}^{T} \boldsymbol{m}_{t-1} \boldsymbol{e}_t' + T^{-1}\sum_{t=1}^{T} \boldsymbol{e}_t \boldsymbol{e}_t' \Rightarrow \int_0^1 \boldsymbol{B}(r)\mathrm{d}\boldsymbol{B}(r)' + \boldsymbol{I}_n. \quad (3.92)$$

Thus, the error covariance matrix is added on if the cross-product under analysis is a contemporaneous rather than a lagged one.

Returning to the unstandardized and potentially autocorrelated process $\{\boldsymbol{v}_t\}$, then $\boldsymbol{p}_T/\sqrt{T}$ converges weakly to the vector Brownian motion $BM(\boldsymbol{\Omega})$, or more generally:

$$T^{-\frac{1}{2}}\sum_{t=1}^{[Tr]} \boldsymbol{v}_t \Rightarrow \boldsymbol{V}(r) \text{ for } r \in [0,1] \text{ as } T \to \infty. \quad (3.93)$$

Let $\boldsymbol{V}(r) = (V_1(r) : V_2(r))'$ in the bivariate case, where $V_1(r)$ and $V_2(r)$ are not independent in general. Corresponding to (3.90)–(3.92) (see Park and Phillips, 1988, 1989):

$$T^{-2}\sum_{t=1}^{T} \boldsymbol{p}_t \boldsymbol{p}_t' \Rightarrow \int_0^1 \boldsymbol{V}(r)\boldsymbol{V}(r)'\mathrm{d}r; \quad (3.94)$$

$$T^{-1}\sum_{t=1}^{T} \boldsymbol{p}_{t-1} \boldsymbol{v}_t' \Rightarrow \int_0^1 \boldsymbol{V}(r)\mathrm{d}\boldsymbol{V}(r)' + \boldsymbol{\Upsilon}_v, \quad (3.95)$$

where $\boldsymbol{\Upsilon}_v$ is non-zero when $\{\boldsymbol{v}_t\}$ is autocorrelated; and noting that $\mathsf{E}[\boldsymbol{v}_t \boldsymbol{v}_t'] = \boldsymbol{\Phi}_v$:

$$T^{-1}\sum_{t=1}^{T} \boldsymbol{p}_t \boldsymbol{v}_t' \Rightarrow \int_0^1 \boldsymbol{V}(r)\mathrm{d}\boldsymbol{V}(r)' + \boldsymbol{\Upsilon}_v + \boldsymbol{\Phi}_v. \quad (3.96)$$

The vector Brownian motion could be standardized using $\boldsymbol{B}(r) = \boldsymbol{K}_v'\boldsymbol{V}(r)$, such that $\boldsymbol{B}(r)$ is $BM(\boldsymbol{I})$. Multiplying out $\boldsymbol{K}_v'\boldsymbol{V}(r)$ using (3.78):

$$\boldsymbol{K}_v'\boldsymbol{V}(r) = \begin{pmatrix} \boldsymbol{H} & -\boldsymbol{HC} \\ \boldsymbol{0} & \boldsymbol{\Omega}_{22}^{-\frac{1}{2}} \end{pmatrix} \begin{pmatrix} V_1(r) \\ V_2(r) \end{pmatrix} = \begin{pmatrix} \boldsymbol{H}\boldsymbol{V}_1(r) - \boldsymbol{H}\boldsymbol{C}\boldsymbol{V}_2(r) \\ \boldsymbol{\Omega}_{22}^{-\frac{1}{2}} V_2(r) \end{pmatrix} = \begin{pmatrix} B_1(r) \\ B_2(r) \end{pmatrix} \quad (3.97)$$

Thus, in the bivariate case:

$$B_1(r) = h\left(V_1(r) - cV_2(r)\right) \text{ and } B_2(r) = \sigma_2^{-1/2}V_2(r). \quad (3.98)$$

Since the standardized vector Brownian motion $\boldsymbol{B}(r)$ has independent components, then $V_2(r)$ and $(\boldsymbol{V}_1(r) - \boldsymbol{\Omega}_{12}\boldsymbol{\Omega}_{22}^{-1}\boldsymbol{V}_2(r))$ are independent also.

3.11 A Monte Carlo study

Consider the following generation process for a random variable y_t:

$$y_t = \beta y_{t-1} + e_t \text{ where } e_t \sim \mathsf{IN}[0,1] \text{ and } y_0 = 0. \tag{3.99}$$

We investigate the three parameter values (i) $\beta = 1.0$, (ii) $\beta = 0.9$, and (iii) $\beta = 0.5$ using $M = 10\,000$ independent replications, computing the outcomes recursively for $T = 10, 11, \ldots, 100$. The data are generated as in (3.99), with the estimates calculated by OLS, so for $\beta = 1$ the results illustrate the behaviour of Wiener processes. The simulation results at $T = 100$ are shown in Table 3.3. MCSE, MCSD, and ESE are defined as before and ASE denotes the numerical value of the theoretical asymptotic standard error after scaling by $\sqrt{T}$.

Table 3.3 Monte Carlo outcomes

	$\beta = 1.0$	$\beta = 0.9$	$\beta = 0.5$
Mean $(\hat{\beta} - \beta)$	-0.018	-0.017	-0.009
MCSE	(0.0003)	(0.0005)	(0.001)
MCSD	0.031	0.049	0.087
ASE	–	0.044	0.084
ESE	0.021	0.046	0.088
R^2	0.937	0.883	0.488

The mean biases in estimating β are small as a proportion of β, and are close to the formula $-2\beta/T$ (see Ch.A4). However, for $\beta \geq 0.9$, the biases are large relative to the MCSD. The MCSD, ASE and ESE are all reasonably close within each experiment. There is little difference between the finite-sample outcomes at the two largest values of β, given the apparently large differences between the theoretical limiting distributions above. For β close to unity, it would be surprising if a Wiener-based result did not apply quite accurately in finite samples.

The results for the three parameter values are:

(i) $\beta = 1$. Figure 3.11a reports the recursively calculated sequence of mean biases, together with 2MCSD and 2ESE shown on either side. The standard errors decrease rapidly, and have similar paths as T increases, although the ESE is always smaller than the MCSD. The changing mean bias is noticeable, but Fig. 3.11d plots these separately to highlight the scale, the rate of change as T increases and the contrast as β alters.
Figure 3.12 records the standardized histogram and interpolated density at $T = 100$, and reveals a skewed distribution so that estimates of β less than unity are much more likely than estimates larger than unity even though $\beta = 1$. Naturally, this will make it difficult to discriminate between unit roots and stationary values near unity, since both will have a preponderance of outcomes less than unity.

(ii) Figure 3.13 reports the histogram and density for $\beta = 0.9$, and reveals similar behaviour, although the distribution is somewhat less skewed. Figure 3.11b shows that the ESE and MCSD are closer, but the bias as a function of T in Fig. 3.11d (the unlabelled line) is almost identical to that when $\beta = 1$.

(iii) When $\beta = 0.5$, the distribution is nearly symmetrical and close to normal at $T = 100$ as seen in Fig. 3.14. The ESE and MCSD are so close as to be indistinguishable in Fig. 3.11c, and the plot of the bias with T^{-1} in Fig. 3.11d shows a close match.

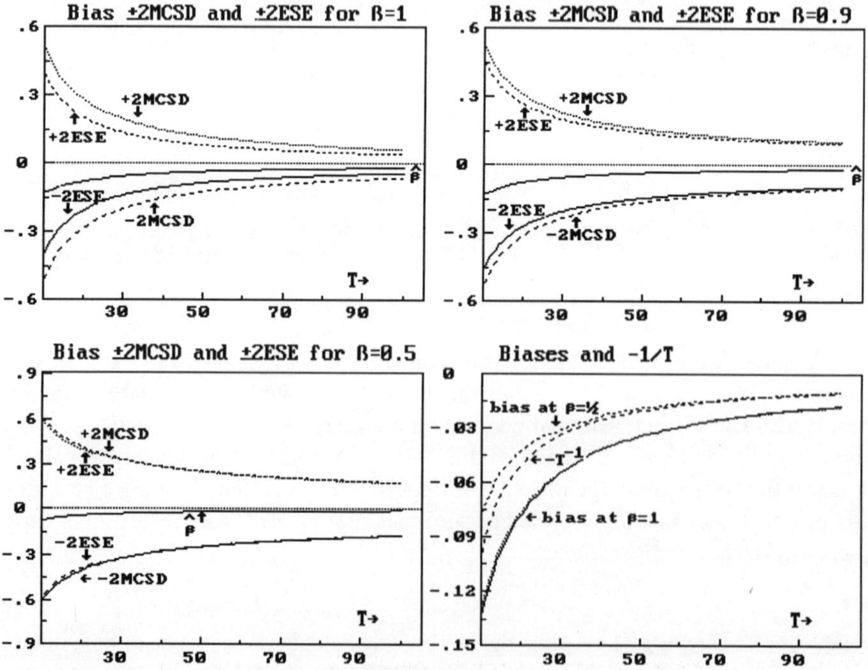

Fig. 3.11 Recursive Monte Carlo outcomes

To highlight the accuracy of stationary asymptotic theory, Fig. 3.15 plots ESE against ASE (rescaled by $\sqrt{T}$), so that both are viewed as estimators of $\sqrt{\left(\left(1-\beta^2\right)/T\right)}$. In this metric, ESE is an accurate estimator of ASE so stationary asymptotic theory appears to be a good guide at the sample sizes considered here when $\beta = 0.9$ or 0.5.

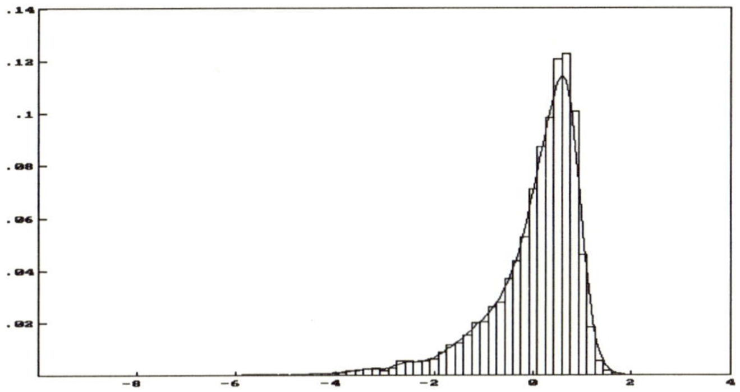

Fig. 3.12 Histogram and density of $\hat{\beta}$ when $\beta = 1$

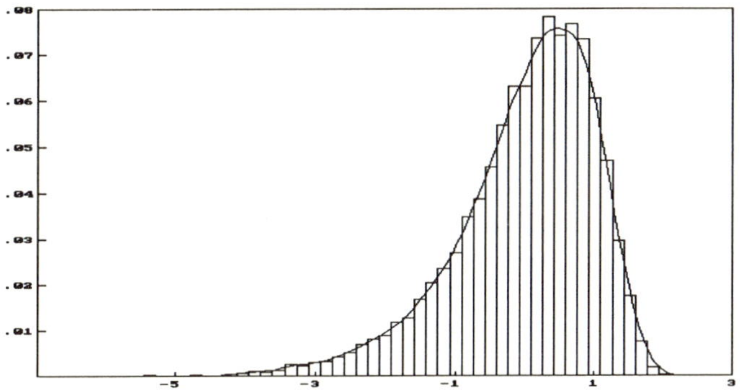

Fig. 3.13 Histogram and density of $\hat{\beta}$ when $\beta = 0.9$

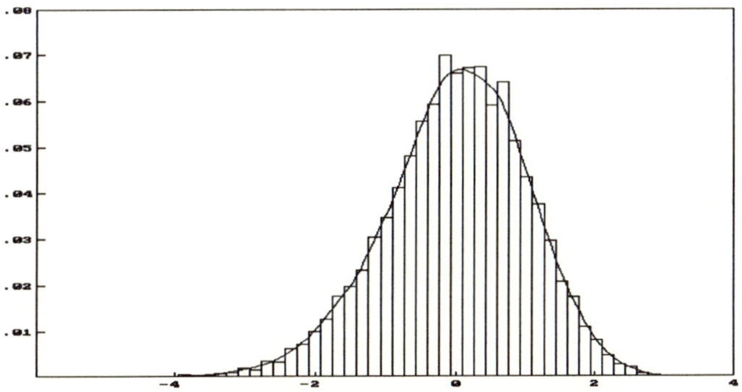

Fig. 3.14 Histogram and density of $\hat{\beta}$ when $\beta = 0.5$

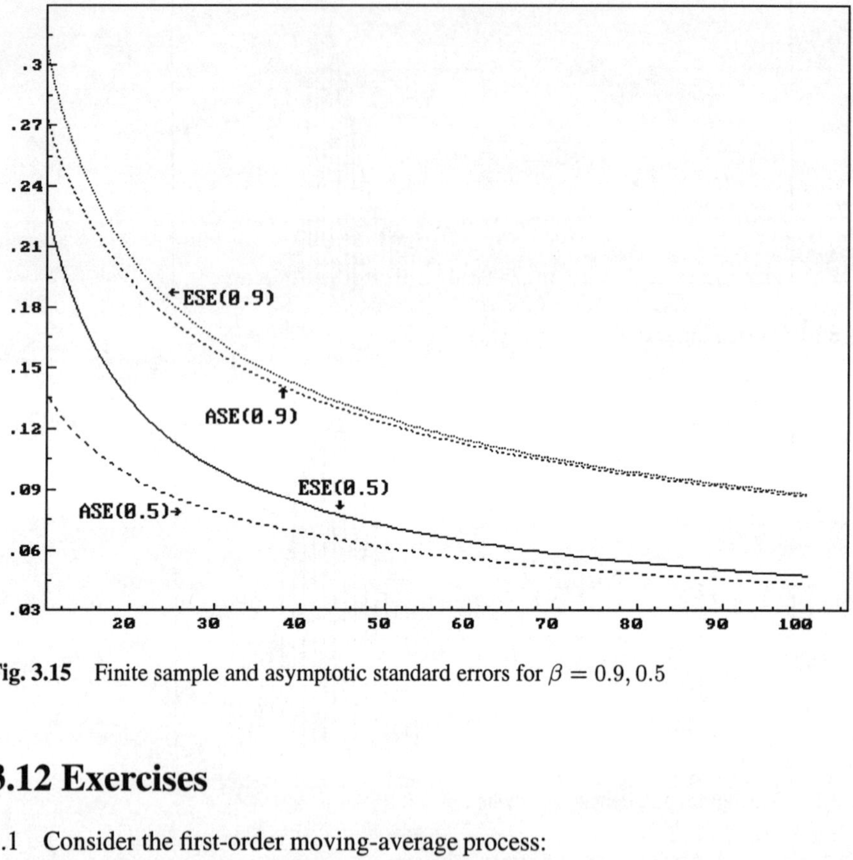

Fig. 3.15 Finite sample and asymptotic standard errors for $\beta = 0.9, 0.5$

3.12 Exercises

3.1 Consider the first-order moving-average process:

$$y_t = \mu_0 + \epsilon_t + \mu_1 \epsilon_{t-1} \text{ where } \epsilon_t \sim \mathsf{IN}\left[0, \sigma_\epsilon^2\right]. \tag{3.100}$$

(a) Derive the mean of y_t: are any stationarity conditions required on μ_1 for $\{y_t\}$ to have a constant mean?

(b) Derive $\mathsf{V}[y_t]$ — when is it constant over time?

(c) Derive: $\mathsf{r}_1 = \mathsf{corr}(y_t, y_{t-1})$, $\mathsf{r}_2 = \mathsf{corr}(y_t, y_{t-2})$, and hence $\mathsf{r}_j = \mathsf{corr}(y_t, y_{t-j})$. Can r_j take any value?

(d) Is $\{y_t\}$ in (3.100) generally stationary? If so, are all μ_1 values admissible? If not, what range of μ_1 is allowed? Let $\mu_1^* = 1/\mu_1$: what is $\mathsf{r}_j(\mu_1^*)$ in comparison to $\mathsf{r}_j(\mu_1)$?

(e) Apply the same techniques to the ARMA process:

$$y_t = \rho y_{t-1} + \epsilon_t + \mu \epsilon_{t-1} \text{ where } \epsilon_t \sim \mathsf{IN}\left[0, \sigma_\epsilon^2\right], \ |\mu| < 1 \text{ and } |\rho| < 1. \tag{3.101}$$

Obtain the first two moments and the correlogram $\{\mathsf{r}_j\}$.

3.2 Consider the model:

$$\begin{aligned} y_t &= \beta x_t + \epsilon_t \\ x_t &= \pi z_t + w_t \end{aligned} \tag{3.102}$$

where

$$\begin{pmatrix} \epsilon_t \\ w_t \\ z_t \end{pmatrix} \sim \mathsf{IN}_3 \left[\begin{pmatrix} 0 \\ 0 \\ 0 \end{pmatrix}, \begin{pmatrix} \sigma_\epsilon^2 & \alpha & 0 \\ \alpha & \sigma_w^2 & 0 \\ 0 & 0 & \sigma_z^2 \end{pmatrix} \right].$$

(a) Derive the limiting distributions of the instrumental-variables estimator $\tilde{\beta}$ of β and of the least-squares estimator $\hat{\beta}$ of β.

(b) Explain how would you undertake a Monte Carlo study of the behaviour of $\tilde{\beta}$ and $\hat{\beta}$ in finite samples. Obtain and use control variates for $\tilde{\beta}$ and $\hat{\beta}$ based on (a).

(c) On what criteria would you base a choice between $\tilde{\beta}$ and $\hat{\beta}$ as the 'least worst' estimator of β when: (i) $T = 10$; (ii) $T = 100$; (iii) $T = 2000$?

(d) Why might the behaviour of $\tilde{\beta}$ be erratic at any sample size T when $\sigma_z \pi / \sigma_w$ is small?

(Oxford M.Phil., 1986)

3.3 Design a Monte Carlo study to investigate estimation and inference about β in the model:

$$\begin{aligned} y_t &= \beta x_t + \epsilon_{1t} \\ x_t &= \alpha x_{t-1} + \epsilon_{2t} \end{aligned} \tag{3.103}$$

where

$$\begin{pmatrix} \epsilon_{1t} \\ \epsilon_{2t} \end{pmatrix} \sim \mathsf{IN}_2 \left[\begin{pmatrix} 0 \\ 0 \end{pmatrix}, \begin{pmatrix} \sigma_{11}^2 & 0 \\ 0 & \sigma_{22}^2 \end{pmatrix} \right].$$

Would different results ensue if $\{x_t\}$ were generated as in (3.103) but held fixed across replications?

3.4 Consider the conditional stationary process:

$$y_t \mid \boldsymbol{Z}_t, \boldsymbol{Y}_{t-1} \sim \mathsf{N}\left[\boldsymbol{\beta}' \boldsymbol{x}_t, \sigma^2\right] \quad \text{for } t = 1, \ldots, T, \tag{3.104}$$

where $\boldsymbol{\beta}$ is 2×1, $\boldsymbol{x}_t' = (z_t : y_{t-1})$, $\mathsf{E}[\boldsymbol{x}_t \boldsymbol{x}_t'] = \boldsymbol{M}$ $\forall t$ and $\boldsymbol{M}$ is positive definite.

(a) Derive the limiting distribution of the OLS estimator $\hat{\boldsymbol{\beta}}$ of $\boldsymbol{\beta}$.

(b) Obtain a control variate $\tilde{\boldsymbol{\beta}}$ for $\hat{\boldsymbol{\beta}}$ such that $\mathsf{E}[\tilde{\boldsymbol{\beta}}] = \boldsymbol{\beta}$ and $\mathsf{V}[\tilde{\boldsymbol{\beta}}] = \sigma^2 \boldsymbol{M}$ $\forall t$. Prove that $\tilde{\boldsymbol{\beta}}$ has the same limiting distribution as $\hat{\boldsymbol{\beta}}$.

(c) Explain the role of $\tilde{\boldsymbol{\beta}}$ in Monte Carlo studies of the first two moments of $\hat{\boldsymbol{\beta}}$, briefly describing how to design a study to test the hypothesis H_0: $\mathsf{E}[\hat{\boldsymbol{\beta}}] = \boldsymbol{\beta}$.

(Oxford M.Phil., 1983)

3.5 Consider conducting a Monte Carlo experiment to investigate the effects of structural breaks on regression estimators in the process:

$$y_t = \boldsymbol{\beta}' \boldsymbol{z}_t + \delta_t + \epsilon_t \quad \text{for } t = 1, \ldots, T, \tag{3.105}$$

where $\epsilon_t \sim \mathsf{IN}\left[0, \sigma_\epsilon^2\right]$, and $\{\boldsymbol{z}_t\}$ is fixed in repeated samples. The variable $\delta_t = 0$ till a break point S, $1 < S < T$, and $\delta_t = 1$ from S onwards.

(a) Describe how to formulate an experiment which highlights the relative importance of such factors as the effective size of the break δ, the time S of the break, the goodness-of-fit of (3.105), and the sample size T.
(b) Discuss any one method of improving the efficiency of your experiment over naïve Monte Carlo estimates.
(c) Explain how to examine the properties of a test which is claimed to be able to detect structural breaks.

(Oxford M.Phil., 1989)

3.6 Consider a linear system of $k > 1$ endogenous and $n > k$ conditioning, jointly stationary variables $\{\boldsymbol{y}_t, \boldsymbol{z}_t\}$ where $\boldsymbol{\pi}$ is $k \times n$:

$$\boldsymbol{y}_t = \boldsymbol{\pi} \boldsymbol{z}_t + \boldsymbol{\epsilon}_t \text{ where } \boldsymbol{\epsilon}_t \sim \mathsf{IN}_k\left[\mathbf{0}, \boldsymbol{\Omega}\right] \text{ for } t = 1, \ldots, T. \tag{3.106}$$

(a) Derive the (multivariate) least squares estimators $(\widehat{\boldsymbol{\pi}}, \widehat{\boldsymbol{\Omega}})$ of $(\boldsymbol{\pi}, \boldsymbol{\Omega})$ for T observations and obtain the limiting distribution of $\widehat{\boldsymbol{\pi}}$ as $T \to \infty$, carefully stating any necessary assumptions and any theorems used.
(b) Explain how to compute $\widehat{\boldsymbol{\pi}}$ recursively (without repeated inversion) over $t = M, \ldots, T$ where $M > k + n$.
(c) Explain how to recursively update the estimate of the ith diagonal element $\hat{\omega}_{ii}$ in $\widehat{\boldsymbol{\Omega}}$ and hence how to compute a sequence of F-tests for the constancy of the coefficients in the ith equation.

(Oxford M.Phil., 1988)

3.7 Consider the data-generation process:

$$\begin{aligned} y_t &= y_{t-1} + \epsilon_t \\ z_t &= z_{t-1} + \omega_t \end{aligned} \quad \text{where} \quad \begin{pmatrix} \epsilon_t \\ \omega_t \end{pmatrix} \sim \mathsf{IN}_2\left[\begin{pmatrix} 0 \\ 0 \end{pmatrix}, \begin{pmatrix} 1 & 0 \\ 0 & 1 \end{pmatrix}\right]. \tag{3.107}$$

Let $\boldsymbol{x}_t = (y_t : z_t)'$ where $\boldsymbol{x}_0 = \mathbf{0}$. Defining $\boldsymbol{v}_t = (v_{1t} : v_{2t})'$ such that $v_{1t} \equiv \epsilon_t$ and $v_{2t} \equiv \omega_t$, write the system as $\boldsymbol{x}_t = \boldsymbol{x}_{t-1} + \boldsymbol{v}_t$ with $\boldsymbol{v}_t \sim \mathsf{IN}_2[\mathbf{0}, \boldsymbol{I}]$. Let $\boldsymbol{B}(r) = (B_1(r) : B_2(r))'$ where the $B_i(r)$ are the independent standardized Wiener processes on $[0, 1]$ associated with accumulating the $\{v_{it}\}$. You may use without proof the following results for $\boldsymbol{x}_t$ where $\Rightarrow$ denotes weak convergence and $[Tr]$ is the integer part of Tr:

$$\frac{1}{\sqrt{T}} \sum_{t=1}^{[Tr]} \boldsymbol{v}_t \Rightarrow \begin{pmatrix} B_1(r) \\ B_2(r) \end{pmatrix}, \tag{3.108}$$

$$T^{-2} \sum_{t=1}^{T} \boldsymbol{x}_t \boldsymbol{x}_t' \Rightarrow \begin{pmatrix} \int_0^1 B_1(r)^2 \mathrm{d}r & \int_0^1 B_1(r) B_2(r) \mathrm{d}r \\ \int_0^1 B_1(r) B_2(r) \mathrm{d}r & \int_0^1 B_2(r)^2 \mathrm{d}r \end{pmatrix} \tag{3.109}$$

and:

$$T^{-1} \sum_{t=1}^{T} \boldsymbol{x}_{t-1} \boldsymbol{v}_t' \Rightarrow \begin{pmatrix} \int_0^1 B_1(r) \mathrm{d}B_1(r) & \int_0^1 B_1(r) \mathrm{d}B_2(r) \\ \int_0^1 B_2(r) \mathrm{d}B_1(r) & \int_0^1 B_2(r) \mathrm{d}B_2(r) \end{pmatrix}. \tag{3.110}$$

Note that:

$$\int_0^1 B_1(r)\mathrm{d}B_1(r) = \tfrac{1}{2}\left[\chi^2(1) - 1\right],$$

and:

$$\left(\int_0^1 B_2(r)^2\mathrm{d}r\right)^{-\frac{1}{2}} \int_0^1 B_1(r)\mathrm{d}B_2(r) \sim \mathsf{N}\left[0,1\right].$$

(a) When the data-generation process (DGP) is given by (3.107), show that $u_t = y_t - z_t$ is a random walk. Denote its standardized limiting distribution by $U(r)$ for $r \in [0,1]$, and using the fact that $u_t = (1 : -1)\boldsymbol{x}_t$ show that:

$$\int_0^1 U(r)\mathrm{d}B_1(r) = \int_0^1 B_1(r)\mathrm{d}B_1(r) - \int_0^1 B_2(r)\mathrm{d}B_1(r). \qquad (3.111)$$

(b) Derive the limiting distributions of $T^{-2}\sum_{t=1}^{T} u_t^2$ and $T^{-1}\sum_{t=1}^{T} u_{t-1}\epsilon_t$ as functions of the results in (3.108) to (3.110).

(c) Consider the model:

$$\Delta y_t = \phi\,(y - z)_{t-1} + e_t \qquad (3.112)$$

Show that the limiting distribution of the OLS estimator $\hat{\phi}$ of ϕ from (3.112) is given by:

$$T\left(\hat{\phi} - \phi\right) \Rightarrow \left(\int_0^1 U(r)^2 dr\right)^{-1} \int_0^1 U(r)\mathrm{d}B_1(r). \qquad (3.113)$$

(d) Derive the limiting distribution of the t-test, $\mathsf{t}_{\phi=0} = \hat{\phi}/\mathsf{SE}(\hat{\phi})$ of H_0: $\phi = 0$, and relate it to the Dickey–Fuller and normal distributions.

(Oxford M.Phil., 1993)

4

Dynamics and Interdependence

An awkward interaction between dynamics and interdependence is reviewed. When two time series y and z are $\mathsf{I}(1)$ and not causally related, testing the hypothesis of no relationship from a regression of y on z produces an excess number of rejections, namely 60 per cent to 80 per cent rather than the anticipated 5 per cent. This nonsense regressions phenomenon is illustrated by Monte Carlo along the lines first proposed by Yule (1926), re-emphasized by Granger and Newbold (1974) and analysed by Phillips (1986). The distribution of the sample correlation coefficient is shown to depart markedly from that conventionally assumed under the null for $\mathsf{I}(0)$ processes. Detrending does not solve the problem. Regressions between $\mathsf{I}(1)$ variables which are connected leads to the notion of cointegration discussed by Engle and Granger (1987). Such findings enforce a reconsideration of dynamics and interdependence, and hence both sequential and conditional factorizations of data density functions. The chapter concludes with an analysis of a bivariate dynamic process.

4.1 Nonsense regressions

We now consider the two important issues of dynamics and interdependence in empirical economics, focusing on their interaction when the data series under analysis are $\mathsf{I}(1)$. We commence from the tentative DGP for $\{y_t\}$ postulated in Chapter 1:

$$\Delta y_t = \alpha + \epsilon_t \text{ where } \epsilon_t \sim \mathsf{IID}\left[0, \sigma_\epsilon^2\right]. \tag{4.1}$$

Economics typically involves relationships between variables, so we will consider what would be observed when there is another $\mathsf{I}(1)$ variable z_t with the same type of behaviour as y_t in (4.1), generated by the DGP:

$$\Delta z_t = \gamma + \nu_t \text{ where } \nu_t \sim \mathsf{IID}\left[0, \sigma_\nu^2\right]. \tag{4.2}$$

To simplify the analysis, assume that the two shocks ϵ_t and ν_t are independent at all points in time, which implies that:

$$\mathsf{E}\left[\epsilon_t \nu_s\right] = 0 \; \forall t, s. \tag{4.3}$$

Also assume that y_0 and z_0 are zero and that $\alpha = \gamma = 0$, so that both variables are simple random walks. Other than stating a specific form for the error distributions, here taken to be normal, this completes the formulation of the statistical generating mechanism. From Chapter 1, y_t and z_t are the sums of all their respective past shocks.

We next specify the economic hypothesis. As an example, let y be the price level or the murder rate and z be the money stock or population. An economist may wish to describe the relationship between y and z in terms of the (log-linear) economic equation:

$$y_t = \beta_0 + \beta_1 z_t + u_t \tag{4.4}$$

where β_1 is interpreted as the derivative of y_t with respect to z_t: $\partial y_t/\partial z_t = \beta_1$. Conventionally, equations like (4.4) are estimated by OLS, assuming $\{u_t\}$ to be an IID process independent of z_t. From such regressions, economists often calculate t-statistics based on dividing estimated coefficients by their standard errors, and reject null hypotheses of the form H_0: $\beta = 0$ when the absolute value of the corresponding t-statistic exceeds 2.0. Since y_t and z_t are causally unrelated by construction in (4.1) and (4.2), the population value of β_1, interpreted as the derivative of y_t with respect to z_t, is zero. Our concern is to examine the properties of conventional estimation procedures applied to (4.4) when the SGM is as specified in (4.1) to (4.3). Although the SGM is known here because the analysis is at level A, the importance of the result is its relevance to level C where models like (4.4) may be postulated and fitted but the SGM is unknown.

From regression theory for fixed regressors, as exposited in §A3.7, if $\beta_1 = 0$ and $\mathsf{E}[z_t u_t] = 0$ then the investigator might believe that (where $^-$ denotes sample mean):

$$\mathsf{E}\left[\widehat{\beta}_1\right] = \mathsf{E}\left[\left(\sum_{t=1}^{T}(z_t - \bar{z})^2\right)^{-1} \sum_{t=1}^{T}(z_t - \bar{z})(u_t - \bar{u})\right] = 0. \tag{4.5}$$

Moreover, under H_0: $\beta_1 = 0$, the conventional probability p of the t-test of H_0 being significant might be thought to be:

$$\mathsf{p} = \mathsf{P}\left(|\mathsf{t}_{\beta_1=0}| \geq 2.0 \mid \mathsf{H}_0\right) = 0.05. \tag{4.6}$$

Such an analysis does not work well here as there is a balance problem in (4.4) when H_0 is assumed to be true. From its DGP (4.1), $\{y_t\}$ is I(1) and $\{u_t\}$ is assumed to be I(0), so equation (4.4) could be well-defined for non-zero values of β_1 since z_t is also I(1). But when $\beta_1 = 0$, the error term $\{u_t\}$ must be I(1) and there is a violation of the assumptions of (4.4) under the null hypothesis. With economic data, there may be internal inconsistencies in conducting hypothesis testing since it may be logically impossible to believe simultaneously that β_1 is zero and that the error term is I(0), given the actual behaviour of $\{y_t\}$.

What happens when such an inconsistency occurs? Because $\{y_t\}$ and $\{z_t\}$ are non-stationary, we first use Monte Carlo (see §3.6) to illustrate the issues involved: an asymptotic theoretical statistical analysis based on §3.8 is presented in §4.2. Generate y_t by its DGP (4.1), using $T = 100$, $\alpha = 0$, $y_0 = 0$, and $\epsilon_t \sim \mathsf{IN}[0, 1]$ so $\sigma_\epsilon = 1$. Similarly, for

z_t use $\gamma = 0$, $z_0 = 0$ and $\nu_t \sim \mathsf{IN}[0,1]$ so $\sigma_\nu = 1$ in (4.2). Then $\{y_t\}$ and $\{z_t\}$ are independently generated, consistent with (4.3). Finally, estimate the regression in (4.4). At each replication, record the estimated coefficients $\{\hat{\beta}_{1i},\ i = 1, \ldots, M\}$, their estimated standard errors based on the conventional regression formula (ESE_i), the frequency of rejection of the null hypothesis $\beta_1 = 0$, the value of the sample correlation between y and z, and the value of the Durbin–Watson (DW) statistic for residual serial correlation (see Durbin and Watson, 1950), using $M = 10\,000$ replications.

At $T = 100$, the Monte Carlo estimate of the mean value of β_1 in the experiment is $\bar{\beta}_1 = \widehat{\mathsf{E}[\hat{\beta}_1]} = 0.001\ (0.006)$ where the figure in parentheses is the MCSE. The hypothesis that $\mathsf{E}[\hat{\beta}_1] = 0$ cannot be rejected at $T = 100$, despite the MCSE being relatively small. The frequency distribution of $\tilde{\beta}_{1i} = (\hat{\beta}_{1i} - \mathsf{E}[\hat{\beta}_1])/\mathsf{MCSD}(\hat{\beta}_1)$ is shown in Fig. 4.1 (i.e. $\hat{\beta}_1$ standardized to have a zero mean and unit variance). $\mathsf{MCSD}(\hat{\beta}_1) = 0.63$, so values outside the $\pm 2\mathsf{MCSD}$ interval correspond to $|\hat{\beta}_1| \geq 1.26$. The shape of the distribution is reasonably normal, but the size of the sampling standard deviation reveals that some of the estimates are large in absolute value.

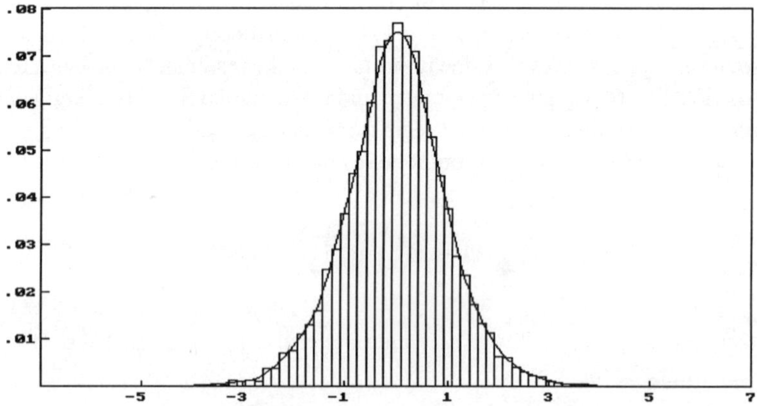

Fig. 4.1 Frequency distribution of $\hat{\beta}_1$

Turning to an analysis of the frequency of rejection of H_0, the probability p of a rejection in (4.6) is 0.76, which is far from the anticipated value of 0.05. We are more likely than not to reject the null hypothesis when it is true, and so make the wrong decision most of the time. Figure 4.2 reveals that the shape of the standardized 't'-distribution is not at fault. The problem is that the statistic calculated in each replication (mimicking empirical practice) does not have a mean-zero, unit-variance distribution. Instead $\bar{\mathsf{t}} = 0.02(0.07)$ and $\mathsf{MCSD}(\mathsf{t}) = 7.4$. Values of $|\mathsf{t}| > 2$ are very likely, and the empirical critical values in this experiment which ensure that:

$$\mathsf{P}\left(\{\text{Reject } \mathsf{H}_0\text{: } \beta_1 = 0\} \mid \mathsf{H}_0\right) = 0.05,$$

are ±14.8 rather than ±2.0. Thus, at $T = 100$:

$$\mathsf{P}\left(|\mathsf{t}_{\beta_1=0}| \geq 14.8 \mid \mathsf{H}_0\right) \simeq 0.05.$$

However, such critical values are no help at other sample sizes, as we will see shortly.

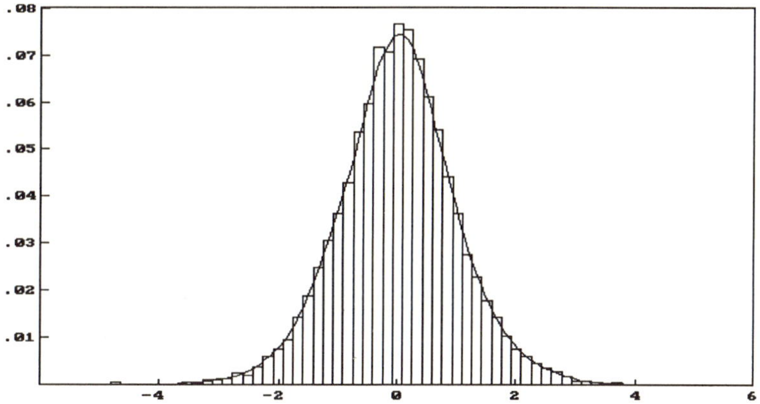

Fig. 4.2 Frequency distribution of the t-test of H_0: $\beta_1 = 0$

The nonsense regressions phenomenon is not specific to $T = 100$, and changing the sample size does not make the problem disappear. Figure 4.3a shows the graph of $\widetilde{\mathsf{E}[\hat{\beta}_1]}$ with $\widetilde{\mathsf{E}[\hat{\beta}_1]} \pm 2\mathsf{MCSE}$ for $T = 20, 21, \ldots, 100$ (see §3.6).[1] The bias is significantly different from zero only at small sample sizes but given the axis scale, it does not change greatly with T. Further, the value of MCSE does not fall much as T increases, which differs from what would be anticipated from conventional asymptotic distribution theory when regression estimators are consistent (see Ch.A4). Figure 4.3b, which records the mean value of the regression coefficient together with ±2MCSD and ±2ESE, is revealing: there is a radical difference between the two measures of uncertainty. ESE is what the economist would calculate on average in any one regression of the form of (4.4) given the model in (4.1)-(4.3); MCSD is what the Monte Carlo reveals the correct value of the sampling standard deviation to be. As the figure shows, a severe underestimate of the uncertainty in the estimate of β_1 would be reported.

The mean value of the t-statistic shown in Fig. 4.3c changes little as T increases from 20 to 100, but the standard deviation of t increases rapidly. Thus, the problem becomes worse as T increases, in that rejection becomes more likely despite the plausible intuition that when the series really are unrelated, then eventually that feature should dominate as $T \to \infty$. Figure 4.3d records the rejection frequencies $\hat{\mathsf{p}}$ at every sample size: $\hat{\mathsf{p}} \simeq 0.30$ at $T = 20$, but the rejection frequency steadily increases with T rising to $\hat{\mathsf{p}} = 0.76$.

[1] As $M = 10\,000$, $\mathsf{MCSE} = \mathsf{MCSD}(\hat{\beta}_1)/100$ determines the accuracy of the Monte Carlo estimates of $\mathsf{E}[\hat{\beta}_1]$.

The outcomes reveal the dangers of applying statistics justified in one context (e.g. IID processes) to data generated by a different probability mechanism.

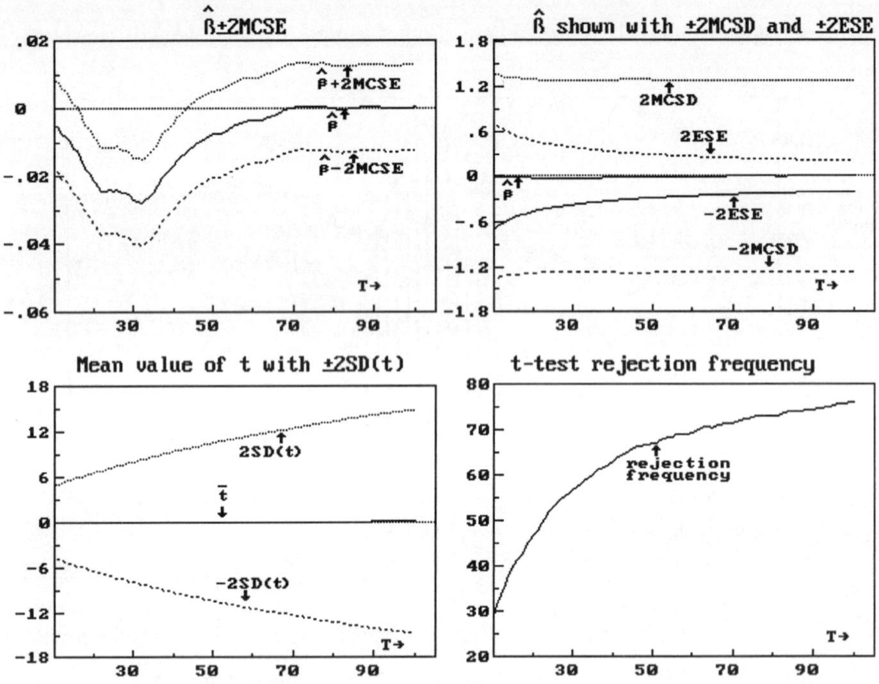

Fig. 4.3 Recursive outcomes for the nonsense regression simulation

A heuristic analysis is helpful. From (4.5):

$$\hat{\beta}_1 = \left[T^{-2} \sum_{t=1}^{T} (z_t - \bar{z})^2 \right]^{-1} T^{-2} \sum_{t=1}^{T} (z_t - \bar{z})(y_t - \bar{y}).$$

Based on the analysis in Chapter 3, we show below that the numerator and denominator of $\hat{\beta}_1$ both converge weakly to functionals of Wiener processes and hence $\hat{\beta}_1$ does not converge to zero, but to a random variable. The t-statistic is calculated in any sample by $\hat{\beta}_1/\mathsf{ESE}(\hat{\beta}_1)$ where:

$$\mathsf{ESE}\left(\hat{\beta}_1\right) = \hat{\sigma}_u \left(\sum_{t=1}^{T} (z_t - \bar{z})^2 \right)^{-\frac{1}{2}},$$

and:

$$\hat{\sigma}_u^2 = \frac{1}{T-2} \sum_{t=1}^{T} \left(y_t - \hat{\beta}_0 - \hat{\beta}_1 z_t \right)^2.$$

As z_t is I(1), its sample variance, namely $(T-1)^{-1}\sum_{t=1}^{T}(z_t - \bar{z})^2 = V_z[T]$, and $\hat{\sigma}_u^2$ both increase with T. Since $\hat{\beta}_0$ and $\hat{\beta}_1$ are selected by least squares to minimize $\hat{\sigma}_u^2$:

$$\hat{\sigma}_u^2 < \frac{1}{T-1}\sum_{t=1}^{T}(y_t - \bar{y})^2 = V_y[T],$$

so that

$$\mathsf{ESE}(\hat{\beta}_1) \leq (T-1)^{-\frac{1}{2}}(V_y[T]/V_z[T])^{\frac{1}{2}} \simeq 1/\sqrt{TS},$$

where $S = V_z[T]/V_y[T] \simeq 1$ (here) is the sample variance ratio. Thus, $\mathsf{t} \simeq \sqrt{(TS)}\hat{\beta}_1$ is centred on zero but with variance $O_p(TS)$, which diverges as $T \to \infty$ (the t statistic is a functional of Wiener processes).

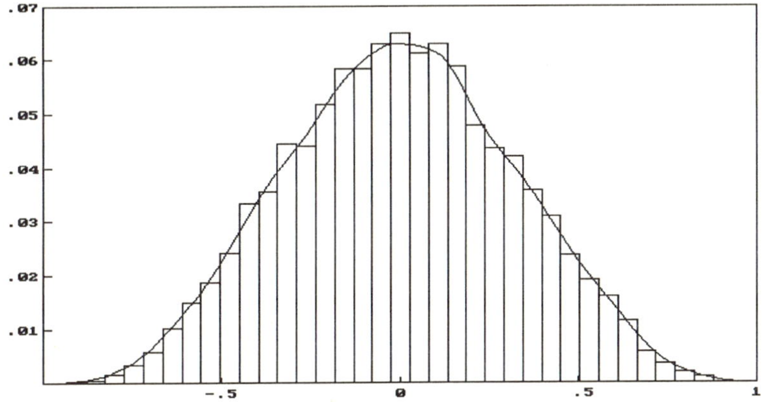

Fig. 4.4 Frequency distribution of R for two unrelated I(0) time series

With the DGP in (4.1)-(4.3), the problem of discriminating between genuine interdependence and nonsense regressions is difficult to solve because under both null and alternative, y_t and z_t have a high sample correlation (denoted R) so H_0: $\beta_1 = 0$ is almost always rejected in large samples. An early analysis is due to Yule (1926), who also used Monte Carlo. What Yule discovered about the distribution of R remains worth recording. We first consider three different situations where the time series $\{y_t\}$ and $\{z_t\}$ are both respectively: (a) $\mathsf{IN}[0,1]$; (b) $\mathsf{IN}[0,1]$ integrated once; and (c) $\mathsf{IN}[0,1]$ integrated twice. The figures are for $M = 10\,000$ replications of R with $T = 100$ for estimates of equation (4.4) when $\beta_0 = \beta_1 = 0$. The density $\mathsf{f_r}(\cdot)$ of R is shown on the graphs. We find the following:

(a) When both variables are $\mathsf{I}(0) \sim \mathsf{IN}[0,1]$, as Fig. 4.4 shows, R is well behaved and has a symmetric, near normal distribution centred on zero, despite being bounded by ± 1.

(b) When both variables are I(1), and the first differences are $\mathsf{IN}[0,1]$, $\mathsf{f_r}(r)$ is like a semi-ellipse with excess frequency at both ends of the distribution: see Fig. 4.5. Consequently, values of R well away from zero are far more likely than in case (a).

(c) When both variables are I(2), the first differences are I(1) and the second differences are IN[0, 1] then (see Fig. 4.6), $\mathsf{f_r}(r)$ becomes U-shaped and the most likely correlations between unrelated series are ± 1, precisely what would occur if the series were genuinely related.

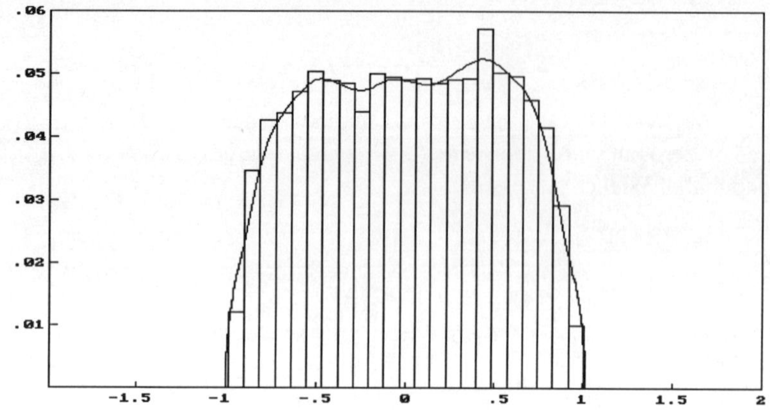

Fig. 4.5 Frequency distribution of R for two unrelated I(1) time series

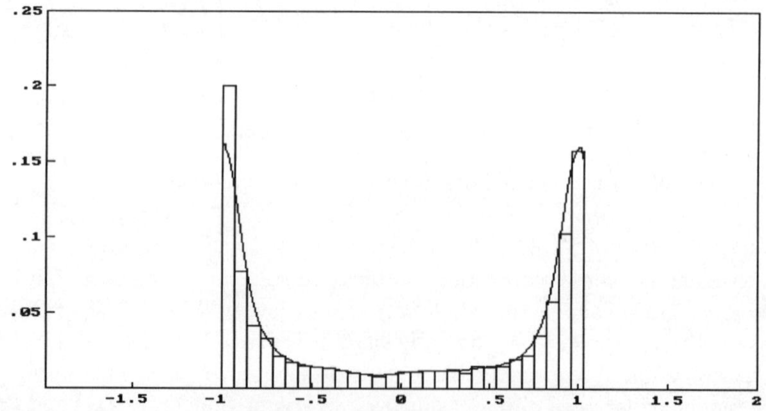

Fig. 4.6 Frequency distribution of R for two unrelated I(2) time series

If a test statistic based on R assumes the distribution to be case (a) when in fact the distribution is case (b), the rejection frequency will greatly exceed its claimed value. Case (c) is even worse: about the least likely outcome is the truth. There is almost no probability of finding $\mathsf{R} \simeq 0$ (which is the population value anticipated under the null) and the most likely value is $\mathsf{R} \simeq \pm 1$.[2] At level C, where the degree of integration of

[2] The figures pose problems for the density interpolation routine by the excess weight at the $-1, +1$ boundaries. They have been retouched to show more plausible densities.

data series is not known (and sometimes not investigated) mixtures of cases (a)–(c) are possible and for $T = 100$, Table 4.1 summarizes the outcomes.

Table 4.1 Monte Carlo outcomes for nonsense regressions

Case	Type	$\bar{\mathsf{R}}$	MCSD(R)	$\bar{\beta}_1$	ESE	MCSD	$\mathsf{P}(\lvert \mathsf{t}_{\beta_1=0}\rvert \geq 2)$
(a)	I(0) on I(0)	0.0004	0.101	0.0004	0.101	0.102	4.93%
(b)	I(1) on I(1)	−0.006	0.490	−0.009	0.102	0.631	75.70%
(c)	I(2) on I(2)	0.004	0.818	0.015	0.103	1.974	94.06%
(d)	I(0) on I(1)	0.0004	0.099	−0.0001	0.031	0.033	4.58%
(e)	I(1) on I(0)	0.0008	0.101	0.003	0.384	0.417	4.86%
(f)	I(2) on I(1)	−0.023	0.613	−1.84	3.84	33.52	85.30%
(g)	I(1) on I(2)	−0.013	0.610	−0.0005	0.005	0.036	84.44%

Denote the degree of integration of the two series by n_1 and n_2 respectively, and let $n = \max\{n_1, n_2\}$. The mean of R is close to zero in every case but its standard deviation increases with $n_1 + n_2$. The mean estimate of β_1 is small compared to the MCSD, especially when $n_1 = n_2$. The mean ESE reported by OLS is virtually unaffected by n when $n_1 = n_2$, but varies greatly when $n_1 \neq n_2$. The MCSD explodes as $n_1 + n_2$ increases, and the ESE underestimates the MCSD by a factor of ten to twenty fold for $n = 2$. The probability of falsely rejecting the null that $\beta_1 = 0$ rises to over 94 per cent for I(2) on I(2). Thus, the earlier analysis is not restricted to generating nonsense by regressing series of the same order on each other as cases (f) and (g) reveal for an I(2) on an I(1), and conversely; however, less serious problems seem to result for I(1) on I(0) or vice versa. The distribution of R for an I(1) on an I(2) is U-shaped as with two I(2) series and this also occurs for an I(2) on an I(1). Also, the distribution of the least squares coefficient estimate for an I(2) on an I(1) is long-tailed, peaked and distinctly non-normal. The t-rejection frequencies are similar in these two cases and intermediate between cases (b) and (c) above. The distribution of R when either series is I(0) is similar to when both are. Overall, potential nonsense emerges once both time series are integrated of higher order than zero.

Consider applying this analysis to a regression of prices on money. From Chapter 1, money and prices (being nominal variables) tend to be approximately I(2). Regressing one I(2) on another I(2) can be expected to produce an R^2 close to unity, but since such an outcome occurs independently of whether or not money causes prices or vice versa, the evidence tells us little about the mechanisms of the underlying economy. We have to forego the idea of basing inference on R^2, t-values and standard errors until the above problem does not affect the analysis.

In an important contribution to understanding the nonsense regressions problem, Phillips (1986) demonstrates that the DW statistic, calculated from the residuals of (4.4), converges to zero as the sample size tends to infinity. Figure 4.7 shows the frequency distribution of DW in the Monte Carlo. When two series are genuinely related, DW

converges to a non-zero value, so at least one statistic behaves differently between nonsense and genuine relationships to potentially allow discrimination. We turn next to the analysis underlying these claims.

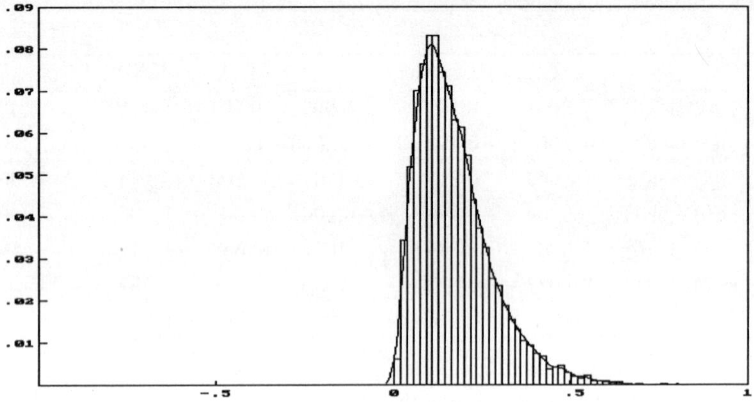

Fig. 4.7 Frequency distribution of DW for two unrelated I(1) time series

4.2 Analysing nonsense regressions*

Phillips's theoretical analysis of the outcome when testing two unrelated I(1) series for a relationship using a static least-squares fit is based on functionals of Wiener processes as in Chapter 3. The analysis here is a special case of that in Phillips (1986): the DGP is the same as (4.1)-(4.3), but the conjectured model is:

$$y_t = \beta z_t + u_t \text{ with } u_t \underset{c}{\sim} \mathsf{IN}\left[0, \sigma_u^2\right] \tag{4.7}$$

where $\underset{c}{\sim}$ denotes a conjectured distribution. A sample of size T is available on $\{y_t\}$ and $\{z_t\}$ which are independent random walks, so (4.7) is a nonsense regression linking two independent I(1) variables.

First:

$$\hat{\beta} = \sum_{t=1}^{T} y_t z_t / \sum_{t=1}^{T} z_t^2. \tag{4.8}$$

When both variables are I(1) but unrelated causally, the sums of squares and cross-products in regression estimation are functionals of independent Wiener processes. As in Chapter 3, let $W(r)$ and $V(r)$ denote independent Wiener processes for $r \in [0,1]$ associated with the partial sums:

$$\frac{1}{\sqrt{T\sigma_\epsilon^2}} \sum_{t=1}^{[Tr]} \epsilon_t \Rightarrow W(r) \text{ and } \frac{1}{\sqrt{T\sigma_\nu^2}} \sum_{t=1}^{[Tr]} \nu_t \Rightarrow V(r),$$

then from Table 3.2:

$$\begin{aligned} T^{-2}\textstyle\sum_{t=1}^{T} y_t^2 &\Rightarrow \sigma_\epsilon^2 \int_0^1 W(r)^2 \mathrm{d}r, \\ T^{-2}\textstyle\sum_{t=1}^{T} z_t^2 &\Rightarrow \sigma_\nu^2 \int_0^1 V(r)^2 \mathrm{d}r, \\ T^{-2}\textstyle\sum_{t=1}^{T} y_t z_t &\Rightarrow \sigma_\epsilon \sigma_\nu \int_0^1 W(r)V(r) \mathrm{d}r. \end{aligned} \tag{4.9}$$

From these expressions, the distributions of $\hat{\beta}$ and $\mathrm{t}_{\beta=0}$ can be obtained. Thus:

$$\hat{\beta} \Rightarrow \sigma_\epsilon \int_0^1 W(r)V(r)\mathrm{d}r \Big/ \left(\sigma_\nu \int_0^1 V(r)^2 \mathrm{d}r \right). \tag{4.10}$$

This shows that the non-normalized coefficient estimate has a well-defined limiting distribution, and does not converge in probability to zero as in the stationary case. Since $W(r)$ and $V(r)$ are independent, $\hat{\beta}$ will be near zero, matching the Monte Carlo outcome. Next, let:

$$\hat{u}_t = y_t - \hat{\beta} z_t \text{ so that } \hat{\sigma}_u^2 = \sum_{t=1}^{T} \hat{u}_t^2 / (T-1)$$

then from (4.9):

$$\begin{aligned} T^{-1}\hat{\sigma}_u^2 &= \left[\sum_{t=1}^{T} y_t^2 - \hat{\beta}^2 \sum_{t=1}^{T} z_t^2 \right] / T(T-1) \\ &= [T(T-1)]^{-1} \left[\sum_{t=1}^{T} y_t^2 - \left(\sum_{t=1}^{T} y_t z_t \right)^2 / \left(\sum_{t=1}^{T} z_t^2 \right) \right] \\ &\simeq \left[T^{-2} \sum_{t=1}^{T} y_t^2 - \left(T^{-2} \sum_{t=1}^{T} y_t z_t \right)^2 / \left(T^{-2} \sum_{t=1}^{T} z_t^2 \right) \right] \\ &\Rightarrow \sigma_\epsilon^2 \left\{ \int_0^1 W(r)^2 \mathrm{d}r - \left[\int_0^1 W(r)V(r)\mathrm{d}r \right]^2 / \int_0^1 V(r)^2 \mathrm{d}r \right\}, \end{aligned} \tag{4.11}$$

and hence $\hat{\sigma}_u^2$ diverges instead of converging to the claimed (but non-existent) σ_u^2. In terms of the recursive estimation procedures described in Chapter 3, the rapid increase in the residual standard deviation as the sample size increased would signal a problem with the model formulation, although it would not explain why that phenomenon occurred.

Further, $\mathrm{t}_{\beta=0} = \hat{\beta}(\sum_{t=1}^{T} z_t^2)^{1/2} / \hat{\sigma}_u$ equals:

$$\begin{aligned} &\left(\sum_{t=1}^{T} y_t z_t \Big/ \sum_{t=1}^{T} z_t^2 \right) \left[(T-1) \sum_{t=1}^{T} z_t^2 \right]^{\frac{1}{2}} \left(\sum_{t=1}^{T} y_t^2 - \left(\sum_{t=1}^{T} y_t z_t \right)^2 \Big/ \sum_{t=1}^{T} z_t^2 \right)^{-\frac{1}{2}} \\ &= \sqrt{T-1} \left[T^{-2} \sum_{t=1}^{T} y_t z_t \right] \left(\left[T^{-2} \sum_{t=1}^{T} y_t^2 \right] \left[T^{-2} \sum_{t=1}^{T} z_t^2 \right] - \left[T^{-2} \sum_{t=1}^{T} y_t z_t \right]^2 \right)^{-\frac{1}{2}} \end{aligned} \tag{4.12}$$

Consequently, $T^{-\frac{1}{2}}\mathrm{t}_{\beta=0}$ tends weakly to:

$$\left(\int_0^1 W(r)V(r)\mathrm{d}r\right)\left[\left(\int_0^1 W(r)^2\mathrm{d}r\right)\left(\int_0^1 V(r)^2\mathrm{d}r\right)-\left(\int_0^1 W(r)V(r)\mathrm{d}r\right)^2\right]^{-\frac{1}{2}}. \tag{4.13}$$

The importance of the formula in (4.13) is twofold:

(i) Although $\beta = 0$, $\mathrm{t}_{\beta=0}$ diverges, and requires to be standardized by $1/\sqrt{T}$ to yield a well-behaved limiting distribution; the rate of divergence of $\sqrt{T}$ matches that observed above.

(ii) The asymptotic distribution is non-standard, so that conventionally calculated critical values will not be correct, even for the standardized distribution of $\mathrm{t}_{\beta=0}/\sqrt{T}$. However, appropriate critical values of $\mathrm{t}_{\beta=0}/\sqrt{T}$ could be calculated by simulation.

If valid inference is to result, tests for the presence of genuine links between variables must take account of the outcome when there are no links. To distinguish between nonsense and genuine relations, the autocorrelation properties of the residuals must be investigated. On H_0: $\beta = 0$, $y_t = u_t$, and so u_t will be I(1) rather than I(0) as usually assumed: this logical inconsistency under the null lies at the heart of the problem. Thus, consider the DW statistic when H_0: $\beta = 0$ is true, ignoring the absence of an intercept for simplicity:

$$\begin{aligned} DW &= \sum_{t=2}^{T}(\hat{u}_t - \hat{u}_{t-1})^2 \,/ \sum_{t=2}^{T}\hat{u}_t^2 \\ &= T^{-1}\left(T^{-1}\sum_{t=2}^{T}\left[y_t - y_{t-1} - \hat{\beta}(z_t - z_{t-1})\right]^2 /T^{-1}\hat{\sigma}_u^2\right) \qquad (4.14) \\ &= T^{-1}\left(\left\{T^{-1}\sum_{t=2}^{T}\left[\epsilon_t - \hat{\beta}\nu_t\right]^2\right\}/T^{-1}\hat{\sigma}_u^2\right), \end{aligned}$$

since y_t and z_t are both random walks. Although the numerator depends on $\hat{\beta}$, from (4.10) it has a well-behaved limiting distribution and hence the term in $\{\cdot\}$ is $O_p(1)$. From (4.11), the denominator is also $O_p(1)$, and so DW is $O_p\left(T^{-1}\right)$ and tends in probability to zero as $T \to \infty$.

To ensure that a nonsense regression has not been estimated, it is natural to test that the residuals are a stationary process. There are a number of approaches to doing so. For example, DW could be used as a test for a unit root in the residuals and from (4.14), should detect nonsense regressions with probability one in large enough samples (see Sargan and Bhargava, 1983). Alternatively, the Dickey–Fuller test (denoted DF), which was discussed in Chapter 3, could be applied to the residuals using:

$$\Delta\hat{u}_t = \rho\hat{u}_{t-1} + \omega_t,$$

perhaps augmented by lagged differences of residuals to whiten the error term (called ADF), or using non-parametric corrections (see Phillips and Perron, 1988). The null hypothesis H_0: $\rho = 0$ corresponds to a unit root in the residuals. The critical values of tests on the residuals are more negative than those of the DF test for observed data due to estimating β. When an intercept is included in the estimated equation, MacKinnon (1991) reports the following response function for the 5 per cent critical value of the t-test of H_0: $\rho = 0$ from a bivariate regression:

$$CV\,(5\%) = -3.34 - \frac{5.97}{T} - \frac{8.98}{T^2}.$$

To reject H_0 in favour of stationarity now requires a large negative t-value. While they are intuitively reasonable, we have not shown that the tests discussed above are optimal (see Bhargava, 1986, for an analysis of the DW-based test).

4.3 Spurious detrending*

Because $\mathsf{I}(1)$ processes appear empirically to manifest trends, it may be thought that detrending the data prior to analysis could alleviate the nonsense regression problem. As shown by Nelson and Plosser (1982), Said and Dickey (1984), Durlauf and Phillips (1986) and Schwert (1989), this is not the case. First, using partitioned inversion it is easily proved that adding a linear deterministic trend to a regression and using deviations of regressors from trend yield identical results (this is the famous Frisch and Waugh, 1933 theorem). Thus, a small extension of the previous analysis can be used to show that adding a trend to (4.7) will not remove the nonsense regression phenomenon.

Consider the augmented equation:

$$y_t = \beta z_t + \gamma t + u_t \text{ with } u_t \underset{c}{\sim} \mathsf{IN}\left[0, \sigma_u^2\right] \tag{4.15}$$

where the DGP remains two independent random walks. Then, by suitable scaling:

$$\begin{pmatrix} \widehat{\beta} \\ \sqrt{T}\widehat{\gamma} \end{pmatrix} = \begin{pmatrix} T^{-2}\sum_{t=2}^{T} z_t^2 & T^{-\frac{5}{2}}\sum_{t=2}^{T} t z_t \\ T^{-\frac{5}{2}}\sum_{t=2}^{T} t z_t & T^{-3}\sum_{t=2}^{T} t^2 \end{pmatrix}^{-1} \begin{pmatrix} T^{-1}\sum_{t=2}^{T} z_t y_t \\ T^{-\frac{3}{2}}\sum_{t=2}^{T} t y_t \end{pmatrix}$$

$$\Rightarrow \begin{pmatrix} \sigma_\nu \int_0^1 V(r)^2 \mathrm{d}r & \int_0^1 rV(r)\mathrm{d}r \\ \int_0^1 rV(r)\mathrm{d}r & (3\sigma_\nu)^{-1} \end{pmatrix}^{-1} \begin{pmatrix} \sigma_\epsilon \int_0^1 W(r)V(r)\mathrm{d}r \\ (\sigma_\epsilon/\sigma_\nu)\int_0^1 rW(r)\mathrm{d}r \end{pmatrix}. \tag{4.16}$$

Thus, $\widehat{\beta}$ still converges in distribution without normalization, and $\sqrt{T}\widehat{\gamma}$ is also well behaved asymptotically, both as functionals of the Wiener processes in (4.16). Hence, as in (4.11), $T^{-1}\widehat{\sigma}_u^2$ converges, and ESE requires normalization by $T^{-\frac{1}{2}}$, so that $T^{-\frac{1}{2}}\mathsf{t}_{\beta=0}$ converges to a non-degenerate limiting distribution.

The nonsense regression and spurious detrending results emphasize the dangers of attempting inference when the errors are not a stationary process. The example in Hendry (1980) illustrates the misleading inferences that can result from such a practice applied to a manifestly nonsense equation. To progress, we need to analyse the properties of (4.1) in detail, so the next step is to focus on dynamics. Having made some headway with dynamics (i.e. the properties of a one-equation DGP), we return to investigate interdependence between variables, but in a case we already understand, which is when the variables are IID. After completing those analyses, the two aspects are merged for DGPs that are both interdependent and dynamic to achieve a partial understanding of how to analyse economic data. This will introduce the concept of cointegration and lead on to exogeneity.

4.4 First-order autoregressive dynamics

Generalize (4.1) so the analysis of dynamics is applicable to a slightly wider range of cases:

$$y_t = \alpha_0 + \alpha_1 y_{t-1} + \epsilon_t \text{ where } \epsilon_t \sim \mathsf{IN}\left[0, \sigma_\epsilon^2\right], \tag{4.17}$$

where normality is convenient but not essential, whereas IID is part of the definition. When analysing dynamic processes, it is useful to introduce a lag operator L with the property of shifting variables back a period in time so that $L^k x_t = x_{t-k}\ \forall k$. The main advantage of using a lag operator is that L can be separated from the variables on which it originally operated so that lag transformations become easier. Using L, write equation (4.17) in lag operator form as:

$$y_t = \alpha_0 + (\alpha_1 L)\, y_t + \epsilon_t \text{ or } (1 - \alpha_1 L)\, y_t = \alpha_0 + \epsilon_t,$$

where $(1 - \alpha_1 L)$ is a first-order polynomial in L. From elementary algebra, a polynomial in Z such as $(1 - \alpha Z)$ has a zero of $1/\alpha$; or a root of $1/\alpha$ when the polynomial is equated to zero as in $(1 - \alpha Z) = 0$. In matrix algebra, however, it is easier to discuss roots in terms of latent (or eigen) roots of a matrix $\boldsymbol{\alpha}$, obtained by solving $|\lambda \boldsymbol{I} - \boldsymbol{\alpha}| = 0$ where $\boldsymbol{I}$ is a unit matrix (or for a scalar α, a 1×1 matrix equal to unity). This is equivalent to solving $(Z - \alpha) = 0$ in the present instance, and we will call α (instead of $1/\alpha$) the (latent) root even in scalar cases for consistency with later matrix extensions. Generalizing lag length and using operators:

$$\left(1 - \alpha_1 L - \alpha_2 L^2 - \cdots - \alpha_r L^r\right) y_t = \alpha_0 + \left(1 + \gamma_1 L + \cdots + \gamma_s L^s\right) \epsilon_t, \tag{4.18}$$

or $\alpha(L)\, y_t = \alpha_0 + \gamma(L)\, \epsilon_t$. Here the roots $\{\lambda_j\}$ of $\alpha\left(Z^{-1}\right)$ are of concern. Lag operators are developed in more detail in Chapter 6.

Returning to the analysis of (4.17), solve that equation backwards in time by repeated substitution for the longest lag in y:

$$\begin{array}{ccccccc} y_t & = & \alpha_0\left(1 + \alpha_1 + \cdots + \alpha_1^{t-1}\right) & + & \left(\epsilon_t + \alpha_1 \epsilon_{t-1} + \cdots + \alpha_1^{t-1} \epsilon_1\right) & + & \alpha_1^t y_0 \\ & = & a_t & + & b_t & + & c_t \end{array} \tag{4.19}$$

where the three terms on the right-hand side are denoted by a_t, b_t, and c_t respectively. Since the error terms in b_t are IID with mean zero, $\mathsf{E}[b_t] = 0\ \forall \alpha_1$ so long as t is finite. Therefore, the role of b_t is through its variance component:

$$\mathsf{V}[b_t] = \sigma_\epsilon^2 \sum_{j=0}^{t-1} \alpha_1^{2i} = \begin{cases} \sigma_\epsilon^2 \left(1-\alpha_1^{2t}\right)\left(1-\alpha_1^2\right)^{-1} & \text{when } |\alpha_1| < 1 \\ \sigma_\epsilon^2 t & \text{when } \alpha_1 = 1 \end{cases} \quad \forall t < \infty. \tag{4.20}$$

Consider each of the three terms in (4.19) under the following three different states of nature, classified in terms of the latent root α_1 of (4.17): (a) explosive root $|\alpha_1| > 1$; (b) unit root $\alpha_1 = 1$; (c) stable root $|\alpha_1| < 1$.

(a) Explosive root $|\alpha_1| > 1$

The term a_t diverges if $\alpha_0 \neq 0$, so the series is explosive: $a_t \to \pm\infty$. The variance of b_t from (4.20) will also explode for large enough t. Consequently, we can exclude this state of the world as transient, whatever value the term c_t has: $|\alpha_1| > 1$ can happen only for short periods.

(b) Unit root $\alpha_1 = 1$

The results for unit-root processes were established in Chapter 3. As an economic example, the theory of efficient markets specifies that the change from today's to tomorrow's exchange rate $\Delta y_{t+1} = (y_{t+1} - y_t)$ is unpredictable conditional on today's exchange rate y_t, so that $\mathsf{E}[\Delta y_{t+1}|y_t] = 0$ or $\mathsf{E}[y_{t+1}|y_t] = y_t$. Given such a theory, prices in efficient markets would follow a martingale, and as such correspond to a unit-root process.[3] We restrict attention to the positive unit root, so that $a_t = \alpha_0 t$ in (4.19):

$$y_t = \alpha_0 t + \sum_{j=0}^{t-1} \epsilon_{t-j} + y_0. \tag{4.21}$$

Thus, there is a trend in the mean if $\alpha_0 \neq 0$ (noting $\mathsf{E}[b_t] = 0$). Moreover, since $\mathsf{V}[b_t] = \sigma_\epsilon^2 t$ from (4.20), the variance also trends, and hence the first two moments diverge. The term c_t is equal to the initial condition y_0, the simplest case being $y_0 = 0$. When $\alpha_1 = 1$, (4.17) becomes $\Delta y_t = \alpha_0 + \epsilon_t$ and to recover the level of y_t one must 'integrate' this difference equation. Thus, there is the analogous problem to a constant of integration arising from a differential equation when it is integrated; even if (4.21) contained a separate intercept, the same differenced representation would result. However, we assume $y_0 = 0$ henceforth. For j-period-apart observations:

$$\rho_j = \mathsf{corr}(y_t, y_{t-j}) = \sqrt{1 - \frac{j}{t}}. \tag{4.22}$$

[3] The issue is more complicated than presented here due to interest costs, transactions charges, etc., but $\{\Delta y_t\}$ adjusted for these factors should be a martingale difference sequence.

When t is very large, $jt^{-1} \simeq 0$, so the size of j will have no perceptible impact on the correlations in (4.22), and these correlations will be almost unity everywhere for a unit-root process, so I(1) processes have a correlogram that dies out slowly. This brings us to the third state of nature.

(c) Stable root $|\alpha_1| < 1$

Here, the latent root is within the unit circle, so that the dependence between different points in the series is less than unity. This process was considered in §2.27 and we draw on that earlier analysis. From (4.19) with $y_0 = 0$:

$$\mathsf{E}\left[y_t\right] = a_t = \alpha_0 \sum_{i=0}^{t-1} \alpha_1^i = \frac{\alpha_0 \left(1 - \alpha_1^t\right)}{\left(1 - \alpha_1\right)}, \tag{4.23}$$

and so from (4.20):

$$\mathsf{V}\left[y_t\right] = \frac{\sigma_\epsilon^2 \left(1 - \alpha_1^{2t}\right)}{\left(1 - \alpha_1^2\right)}. \tag{4.24}$$

Since the mean and variance both change with time according to (4.23) and (4.24), $\{y_t\}$ is not a stationary process. To ease the analysis, we transform $\{y_t\}$ to a weakly stationary process whose mean and variance are independent of time. There are two ways to achieve this: either by assuming $t \to \infty$ (leading to asymptotic stationarity), or by making appropriate assumptions about c_t. To implement the latter, replace the assumption that $y_0 = 0$ by treating y_0 as a random drawing from the process:

$$y_0 \sim \mathsf{N}\left[\frac{\alpha_0}{\left(1 - \alpha_1\right)}, \frac{\sigma_\epsilon^2}{\left(1 - \alpha_1^2\right)}\right]. \tag{4.25}$$

This assumption is internally consistent with the model, in that the assumed distribution for y_0 in (4.25) has the same mean and variance as every other y_t $(t > 0)$, so the consequence of assuming the initial condition to have the distribution in (4.25) is that all observations have the same distribution:

$$\mathsf{E}\left[y_t\right] = \frac{\alpha_0}{\left(1 - \alpha_1\right)} \text{ and } \mathsf{V}\left[y_t\right] = \frac{\sigma_\epsilon^2}{\left(1 - \alpha_1^2\right)} \text{ for } t = 0, 1, \ldots, T. \tag{4.26}$$

Since (4.26) is true for all t, the first two moments of the process are independent of time, so that $\{y_t\}$ as defined in (4.17) and (4.25) is weakly stationary. The assumptions about y_0 in (4.25) are strong and few economic variables may satisfy them; if weak stationarity was generally true for the levels of economic variables, economics would be ahistorical in that any epoch would resemble any other, so the actual date of observation would be almost irrelevant.

Given the assumed normal distribution of $\{\epsilon_t\}$ and y_0:

$$y_t \sim \mathsf{N}\left[\frac{\alpha_0}{\left(1 - \alpha_1\right)}, \frac{\sigma_\epsilon^2}{\left(1 - \alpha_1^2\right)}\right] \ \forall t > 0. \tag{4.27}$$

The first important result entailed by (4.27) is that dynamics amplify variance. This claim can be illustrated in two different ways:

(i) If a process is dynamic in that (4.17) transforms $\{\epsilon_t\}$ to $\{y_t\}$, the variance of the observed output $\{y_t\}$ is an amplified version of the variance of the input $\{\epsilon_t\}$, where the amplification factor is $(1-\alpha_1^2)^{-1}$. If α_1 were close to unity, say 0.999, the variance of $\{y_t\}$ would be of the order of 500 times the variance of $\{\epsilon_t\}$. Many economic time series seem habit-dependent, in that their dynamics are close to the unit circle, so the variances of output series are large compared to those of input series (see Ch.7 for further analysis).

(ii) There is an alternative expression for this phenomenon. From the earlier analysis, $y_t = \mathsf{E}[y_t|y_{t-1}] + \epsilon_t$ and hence the conditional mean of y_t is not constant even though the unconditional mean of y_t is independent of time:

$$\mathsf{E}\left[y_t \mid y_{t-1}\right] = \alpha_0 + \alpha_1 y_{t-1} \tag{4.28}$$

and

$$\mathsf{V}\left[y_t \mid y_{t-1}\right] = \sigma_\epsilon^2.$$

Thus, (4.28) is dependent upon time, so that although the assumption in (4.25) is restrictive, it is not as strong as it might have looked at first sight: the day-to-day mean of y_t moves around, but is closely linked to the most recent realized value. However, the conditional variance is independent of time as shown in (4.28).[4] As the economy evolves, wandering widely because of its large unconditional variance, the region into which it strays at the next point in time is small in comparison. Since the conditional variance of $\{y_t\}$ is the (unconditional) variance of $\{\epsilon_t\}$, dynamics map conditional variances into unconditional variances. The same property is true of the mean: the original intercept of α_0 is scaled up by a factor of $(1-\alpha_1)^{-1}$. Consequently, negative dynamics (i.e. $\alpha_1 < 0$) dampen the mean, while positive dynamics (i.e. $0 < \alpha_1 < 1$) amplify it. In the limit, we return to case (b) and the variance diverges over time for $\{y_t\}$.

The next step is to obtain the correlogram $\{\rho_j\}$ between y_t and y_{t-j} for $j = 1, \ldots, T$ when $\{y_t\}$ is a stationary series and compare it with the correlogram of a unit-root process. Let:

$$\tilde{y}_t = y_t - \frac{\alpha_0}{(1-\alpha_1)} = \alpha_1 \tilde{y}_{t-1} + \epsilon_t, \tag{4.29}$$

which is a homogeneous difference equation in $\tilde{y}_t$. Then:

$$\mathsf{E}\left[\tilde{y}_t \tilde{y}_{t-1}\right] = \alpha_1 \mathsf{E}\left[\tilde{y}_{t-1}^2\right] = \alpha_1 \mathsf{V}\left[y_t\right], \tag{4.30}$$

which is independent of time. Thus, the first-order serial correlation ρ_1 for a stationary first-order autoregressive process like (4.17) is α_1. More generally, by repeated substitution from (4.29):

$$\rho_j = \mathsf{corr}\left(y_t, y_{t-j}\right) = \alpha_1^j. \tag{4.31}$$

Since $|\alpha_1| < 1$, the correlogram of a stationary series dies out exponentially. If the process is IID, so that $\alpha_1 = 0$, then $\rho_j = 0$ for $j \geq 1$.

[4] The next level of generalization would be to model the equation error variance in a similar way, and allow it to have a constant unconditional value but a changing conditional value. For example, $\mathsf{E}[\epsilon_t^2|\epsilon_{t-1}] = f(\epsilon_{t-1}^2)$ leads to the ARCH process noted in Ch.2 (see Engle, 1982a, and Spanos, 1994).

These results match the empirical correlograms shown in Chapter 2, given what might be anticipated for the level and difference of an I(1) process on the basis of (b) (i.e. $\rho_j \simeq 1\ \forall j > 0$) and (c) (i.e. $\rho_j = 0\ \forall j > 0$), taking account of the fact that the serial correlations are estimated. Thus, despite the simplicity of the initial DGP, the theory explains why the correlograms were as shown, given the validity of (4.17). This analysis of the three values for the latent root α_1 provides some guidance for investigating economic data despite the manifest over-simplification of only considering one lag and one variable. However, Chapter 7 shows that differencing is not necessarily the correct solution to non-stationarity once the multivariate nature of economics is taken into account.

4.5 Reduction and dynamics

The example of an AR(1) process also illustrates the exposition in Chapter 2 on interpreting empirical models. Formalize case (c) (stable root) as a normally-distributed sample $(y_0, y_1, \ldots, y_T)$ from the stochastic process $\{y_t\}$ which can be expressed for $|\alpha_1| < 1$ as:

$$\begin{pmatrix} y_0 \\ y_1 \\ y_2 \\ \vdots \\ y_{T-1} \\ y_T \end{pmatrix} \sim \mathsf{N}_{T+1}\left[\begin{pmatrix} \phi \\ \phi \\ \phi \\ \vdots \\ \phi \\ \phi \end{pmatrix}, \sigma_y^2 \begin{pmatrix} 1 & \alpha_1 & \alpha_1^2 & \cdots & \alpha_1^{T-1} & \alpha_1^T \\ \alpha_1 & 1 & \alpha_1 & \cdots & \alpha_1^{T-2} & \alpha_1^{T-1} \\ \alpha_1^2 & \alpha_1 & 1 & \cdots & \alpha_1^{T-3} & \alpha_1^{T-2} \\ \vdots & \vdots & \vdots & \ddots & \vdots & \vdots \\ \alpha_1^{T-1} & \alpha_1^{T-2} & \alpha_1^{T-3} & \cdots & 1 & \alpha_1 \\ \alpha_1^T & \alpha_1^{T-1} & \alpha_1^{T-2} & \cdots & \alpha_1 & 1 \end{pmatrix}\right] \tag{4.32}$$

where the sample comprises the whole data-set, including the initial conditions, with $\phi = \alpha_0(1-\alpha_1)^{-1}$ and $\sigma_y^2 = \sigma_\epsilon^2(1-\alpha_1^2)^{-1}$. Writing (4.32) in vector form:

$$\boldsymbol{Y}_T^0 \sim \mathsf{N}_{T+1}\left[\boldsymbol{\mu}, \sigma_y^2 \boldsymbol{\Omega}\right]. \tag{4.33}$$

The joint density function of the sample when $\boldsymbol{\theta}' = (\alpha_0 : \alpha_1 : \sigma_\epsilon^2)$ is:

$$\mathsf{D}_\mathsf{Y}\left(\boldsymbol{Y}_T^0 \mid \boldsymbol{\theta}\right) = \left(2\pi\sigma_y^2\right)^{-\frac{(T+1)}{2}} |\boldsymbol{\Omega}|^{-\frac{1}{2}} \exp\left[-\frac{1}{2\sigma_y^2}\left(\boldsymbol{Y}_T^0 - \boldsymbol{\mu}\right)' \boldsymbol{\Omega}^{-1}\left(\boldsymbol{Y}_T^0 - \boldsymbol{\mu}\right)\right]. \tag{4.34}$$

Considerable technical effort has been devoted to analytically calculating $|\boldsymbol{\Omega}|$ and $\boldsymbol{\Omega}^{-1}$ in (4.34) for AR and MA processes (see e.g. Wise, 1955) particularly for error, rather than data, autocorrelation. Because every term is correlated with every other, it is hard to make much sense of joint densities like (4.34), especially since it is hazardous to conduct inference when the sample is not random. However, the operation of $|\boldsymbol{\Omega}|$ and $\boldsymbol{\Omega}^{-1}$ on $(\boldsymbol{Y}_T^0 - \boldsymbol{\mu})$ in (4.34) in effect brings the sample back to 'independence' as established in §2.27 (also see §4.9). This can be shown by suitably factorizing $\boldsymbol{\Omega}^{-1} = \boldsymbol{L}\boldsymbol{L}'$ say, where $\boldsymbol{L}$ is upper triangular such that $\boldsymbol{L}'\boldsymbol{\Omega}\boldsymbol{L} = \boldsymbol{I}_{T+1}$ and hence $\boldsymbol{L}'\boldsymbol{Y}_T^0 \sim \mathsf{N}_{T+1}[\boldsymbol{L}'\boldsymbol{\mu}, \sigma_y^2\boldsymbol{I}]$.

While such an approach has its uses, especially for moving-average processes, we follow the same route as in §2.26.

Rewrite (4.34) using the sequential factorization:

$$\mathsf{D}_{\mathsf{Y}}\left(\boldsymbol{Y}_T^0 \mid \boldsymbol{\theta}\right) = \prod_{t=1}^{T} \mathsf{D}_{\mathsf{y}}\left(y_t \mid \boldsymbol{Y}_{t-1}^0, \boldsymbol{\theta}\right) \mathsf{D}_{\mathsf{y}}\left(y_0 \mid \boldsymbol{\theta}\right). \tag{4.35}$$

From §4.4, the distributions of the components $y_t| \boldsymbol{Y}_{t-1}^0$ are:

$$y_t \mid \boldsymbol{Y}_{t-1}^0 \sim \mathsf{N}\left[\left(\alpha_0 + \alpha_1 y_{t-1}\right), \sigma_\epsilon^2\right], \tag{4.36}$$

and from (4.25):

$$y_0 \sim \mathsf{N}\left[\frac{\alpha_0}{(1-\alpha_1)}, \frac{\sigma_\epsilon^2}{(1-\alpha_1^2)}\right].$$

Thus, given its history, each y_t $(t = 1, \ldots, T)$ is a drawing from a normal distribution with a different mean $(\alpha_0 + \alpha_1 y_{t-1})$ but the same variance σ_ϵ^2. Moreover, the history $\boldsymbol{Y}_{t-1}^0$ of the process up to time $t-1$ is fully captured by y_{t-1} alone. Using (4.36), the individual densities in (4.35) are:

$$\mathsf{D}_{\mathsf{y}}\left(y_t \mid \boldsymbol{Y}_{t-1}^0, \boldsymbol{\theta}\right) = \left(2\pi\sigma_\epsilon^2\right)^{-\frac{1}{2}} \exp\left[-\frac{1}{2\sigma_\epsilon^2}\left[y_t - \left(\alpha_0 + \alpha_1 y_{t-1}\right)\right]^2\right]. \tag{4.37}$$

Letting $y_t - (\alpha_0 + \alpha_1 y_{t-1}) = \epsilon_t$, $\mathsf{D}_{\mathsf{Y}}\left(\boldsymbol{Y}_T^0|\boldsymbol{\theta}\right)$ in (4.35) becomes:

$$\left(\frac{1}{2\pi\sigma_\epsilon^2}\right)^{\frac{T}{2}} \exp\left[-\frac{1}{2\sigma_\epsilon^2}\sum_{t=1}^{T}\epsilon_t^2\right]\left\{\left(\frac{1-\alpha_1^2}{2\pi\sigma_\epsilon^2}\right)^{\frac{1}{2}} \exp\left[-\frac{1-\alpha_1^2}{2\sigma_\epsilon^2}\left(y_0 - \frac{\alpha_0}{1-\alpha_1}\right)^2\right]\right\}. \tag{4.38}$$

Because the impact of the initial distribution $\mathsf{D}_{\mathsf{y}}(y_0|\boldsymbol{\theta})$ is one term relative to the T remaining terms, it is frequently neglected in both theory and practice. More importantly, however, the terms $\mathsf{D}_{\mathsf{y}}(y_t| \boldsymbol{Y}_{t-1}^0, \boldsymbol{\theta})$ from the sequential factorization in (4.35) correspond to $\mathsf{D}_{\mathsf{y}}(\epsilon_t|\boldsymbol{\theta})$ in (4.38), and hence are independent because of the normality assumption (but will be innovations in general).

As discussed in Chapter 2, sequential factorization reduces an interdependent density to a product of innovation densities whatever the underlying process; this particular case is just an example. When calculating the joint density (4.34) by inverting $\boldsymbol{\Omega}$ and deriving its determinant, all the cross-products cancel, leaving the same result as the sequential factorization in (4.38) (see §4.9 below). This property of sequential factorization is generic: sequential factorization by removing the conditional mean leaves a component that is a mean innovation relative to the history of the process, so the joint density becomes a product of the densities of the mean innovations. In the case of normal distributions, independence results and the log-density becomes proportional to the sum of squares of the errors, which is one justification for the use of least-squares estimators.

4.6 Interdependence

Next, we consider the issue of interdependence between variables. Then in §4.8, we will merge dynamics (from §4.5) with interdependence to develop a framework to distinguish nonsense regressions from genuine ones. We will discuss interdependence using the bivariate normal distribution; generalizations to matrix notation then follow easily. The main issue will be the interpretation of conditional factorizations and their relationships to regression analyses.

Consider the joint density function $\mathsf{D}_{\mathsf{y,z}}(y_t, z_t)$ of two random variables $\boldsymbol{x}_t' = (y_t : z_t)$ such that $\boldsymbol{x}_t \sim \mathsf{IN}_2[\boldsymbol{\mu}_t, \boldsymbol{\Sigma}]$ or:

$$\begin{pmatrix} y_t \\ z_t \end{pmatrix} \sim \mathsf{IN}_2\left[\begin{pmatrix} \mu_{1t} \\ \mu_{2t} \end{pmatrix}, \begin{pmatrix} \sigma_{11} & \sigma_{12} \\ \sigma_{12} & \sigma_{22} \end{pmatrix}\right]. \tag{4.39}$$

In (4.39), $\{\mu_t\}$ is assumed finite $\forall t$, and $\infty > |\boldsymbol{\Sigma}| > 0$. We take successive $\boldsymbol{x}_t$ to be independent because we know how to solve the problem when they are not: whatever the dynamics of the original process, the inference problem can be reduced to one involving mean innovations by sequential factorization. Therefore, we consider joint dependence in isolation from serial correlation in the data. However, the means of y_t and z_t are dependent on time (to mimic that aspect of sequential factorization). This feature is important in discriminating between models at level C, since data means usually vary over time, and the assumption of constant means does not deliver empirically applicable implications. The variances and covariances are assumed to be constant over time for simplicity, but this feature will be relaxed in Chapter 5.

The first results relate to the marginal distributions $\mathsf{D}_{\mathsf{y}}(y_t)$ and $\mathsf{D}_{\mathsf{z}}(z_t)$ of y_t and z_t respectively, using the concept of marginalizing from §2.17 and §A2.6. These marginal densities are obtained directly from (4.39) by eliminating (here, ignoring) the remaining variable:

$$\begin{aligned} y_t &\sim \mathsf{IN}\left[\mu_{1t}, \sigma_{11}\right], \\ z_t &\sim \mathsf{IN}\left[\mu_{2t}, \sigma_{22}\right]. \end{aligned} \tag{4.40}$$

Since the joint distribution is not constant over time because $\boldsymbol{\mu}_t$ changes, the marginal distributions cannot both be constant either. Also, we lose information about σ_{12} by reporting only the marginals unless the variables are known to be independent, so that σ_{12} is zero anyway. Nevertheless, (4.40) is 'true' if (4.39) is, although the two representations are not equally informative: and simultaneously, (4.41) below is also 'true'.

We turn next to the conditional distributions. The joint density is the product of one conditional with one marginal density:

$$\mathsf{D}_{\mathsf{y,z}}(y_t, z_t) = \begin{cases} \mathsf{D}_{\mathsf{y}|\mathsf{z}}(y_t \mid z_t)\, \mathsf{D}_{\mathsf{z}}(z_t) \\ \mathsf{D}_{\mathsf{z}|\mathsf{y}}(z_t \mid y_t)\, \mathsf{D}_{\mathsf{y}}(y_t) \end{cases}. \tag{4.41}$$

Because of normality, either conditional distribution can be obtained by calculating the conditional means and variances. For conditioning y_t on z_t:

$$\mathsf{E}\left[y_t \mid z_t\right] = \mu_{1t} + \sigma_{12}\sigma_{22}^{-1}\left(z_t - \mu_{2t}\right) = \gamma_{0t} + \gamma_1 z_t, \tag{4.42}$$

where $\gamma_{0t} = (\mu_{1t} - \gamma_1 \mu_{2t})$ and $\gamma_1 = \sigma_{12}\sigma_{22}^{-1}$; and:

$$\mathsf{V}[y_t \mid z_t] = \sigma_{11} - \sigma_{12}\sigma_{22}^{-1}\sigma_{21} = \omega_{11} \leq \sigma_{11}. \tag{4.43}$$

The conditional expectation in (4.42) is a regression (see §A2.8), although the conditional mean will not be constant in general. The conditional regression parameter γ_1 is constant purely because we assumed that the σ_{ij} were constant. Combining these results:

$$y_t \mid z_t \sim \mathsf{N}\left[\gamma_{0t} + \gamma_1 z_t, \omega_{11}\right]. \tag{4.44}$$

Similar results hold for the reverse conditioning:

$$\mathsf{E}[z_t \mid y_t] = \mu_{2t} + \sigma_{21}\sigma_{11}^{-1}(y_t - \mu_{1t}) = \delta_{0t} + \delta_1 y_t, \tag{4.45}$$

where $\delta_{0t} = (\mu_{2t} - \delta_1 \mu_{1t})$ and $\delta_1 = \sigma_{21}\sigma_{11}^{-1}$; and:

$$\mathsf{V}[z_t \mid y_t] = \sigma_{22} - \sigma_{21}\sigma_{11}^{-1}\sigma_{12} = \psi_{22} \leq \sigma_{22}. \tag{4.46}$$

Hence:

$$z_t \mid y_t \sim \mathsf{N}\left[\delta_{0t} + \delta_1 y_t, \psi_{22}\right]. \tag{4.47}$$

Each conditional distribution has three parameters, and the corresponding marginal has two, matching the five parameters of the joint density. As noted, the two marginals only have four parameters between them (so one is lost), whereas the two conditionals have six, so there is a redundant parameter (i.e. a connection between the parameters given by $\gamma_1\psi_{22} = \delta_1\omega_{11}$). Thus, neither of these last two factorizations conveys the same information as the joint density. However, either or both factorizations in (4.41) are fully informative about $\boldsymbol{\mu}_t$ and $\boldsymbol{\Sigma}$. For example, from $(\gamma_{0t}, \gamma_1, \omega_{11}, \mu_{2t}, \sigma_{22})$ and their relationships in (4.42) and (4.43) we can derive $(\mu_{1t}, \sigma_{11}, \sigma_{21}, \mu_{2t}, \sigma_{22})$. Nevertheless, there appears to be an arbitrary choice between which factorization to adopt when the two variables are interdependent and $\sigma_{21} \neq 0$.

To resolve that issue, introduce the economic model:

$$\mu_{1t} = \beta\mu_{2t}. \tag{4.48}$$

The most familiar example in economics of an equation resembling (4.48) is the permanent income hypothesis, where permanent consumption ($\mu_{1t} = \mathsf{E}[y_t]$) is asserted to be proportional to permanent income ($\mu_{2t} = \mathsf{E}[z_t]$) with the parameter of interest β. The permanent components are the means of their respective distributions, because they comprise everything except the transitory components, whereas the transitory components induce variations around the permanent components. Think of μ_{1t} as the plan made by an agent at time t about y_t, given that the mean value of y_t is under the control of that agent. The plan is to maintain a constant ratio β between y_t and the expectation μ_{2t} held by the agent about z_t, which is a variable the agent does not control. Remember that the entire analysis at this juncture is implicitly conditional on the past history of the process. Substitute the hypothesis (4.48) into the regression equation (4.42):

$$\mathsf{E}[y_t \mid z_t] = (\beta - \gamma_1)\mu_{2t} + \gamma_1 z_t. \tag{4.49}$$

A separate intercept in (4.48) would not complicate the problem. There are two different states of the world in (4.49): (i) $\beta = \gamma_1$; and (ii) $\beta \neq \gamma_1$.

(i) If $\beta = \gamma_1$, (4.49) reduces to:

$$\mathsf{E}\left[y_t \mid z_t\right] = \gamma_1 z_t = \beta z_t. \tag{4.50}$$

Thus, the term involving μ_{2t} disappears and the coefficient of z_t becomes the parameter of interest β, which is identifiable from the estimated regression coefficient alone. The regression delivers the parameter of interest in this state, and the parameters of (4.50) are constant if β is.

(ii) Next, consider $\beta \neq \gamma_1$. The regression remains (4.49) but the coefficient of z_t is not β, so we cannot derive the economic theory parameter of interest β from a regression of y_t on z_t, although we can learn about γ_1. Moreover, if $\mu_{2t} \neq 0$, then the intercept in (4.49) will not be constant. Even if $\mu_{2t} = 0$, we cannot learn β from the regression equation.

This is the second important aspect of the theory of reduction. If (i) holds, and so $\gamma_1 = \beta$, then the parameter of interest can be obtained from the conditional expectation of y_t given z_t in (4.50). Consequently, the marginal distribution of z_t can be neglected. In state (i), we do not need to study the complete joint density, but only the conditional density. This would be a useful reduction without loss of relevant information if there were only one y and many zs. Conditioning, i.e. analysing one variable conditional upon others, is an important reduction and potentially can be achieved in this framework.

To summarize the implications of the analysis, a joint density can be factorized arbitrarily, but without loss of information about its parameters, into the product of a conditional and a marginal density. Given an attempted reduction to analysing a conditional model only, we can still learn about the subject-matter parameters of interest if (i) holds and we calculate the regression. However, that does not hold in case (ii). Thus, we require a conceptual structure which clarifies when it is valid to condition, which is the topic of exogeneity investigated in Chapter 5. It will transpire that it is valid to calculate only the regression (4.50) when z_t is weakly exogenous for β. The necessary concept of exogeneity in this framework is a mapping between conditioning on contemporaneous variables (representing the interdependence between economic variables) and parameters of interest (arising from economic theory). Simply asserting that a variable z_t is exogenous may not deliver the appropriate information from an econometric analysis: it is important to state for which parameters z_t is exogenous.

Finally, in state (i), the choice of factorization ceases to be arbitrary. When (4.48) holds and $\gamma_1 = \beta$, consider (4.47): since $\boldsymbol{\Sigma}$ is non-singular when y_t and z_t are distinct random variables with non-zero variances, then $\sigma_{11}\sigma_{22} - \sigma_{12}\sigma_{21} \neq 0$, so that $\sigma_{11}\sigma_{22} \neq \sigma_{12}\sigma_{21}$. Thus, $\gamma_1\delta_1 = \sigma_{12}\sigma_{21}/\sigma_{11}\sigma_{22} \neq 1$, so that $\delta_1 \neq 1/\gamma_1 = 1/\beta$, and hence the reverse regression does not deliver the parameter of interest. Further:

$$\delta_{0t} = (\mu_{2t} - \delta_1\mu_{1t}) = (\mu_{2t} - \delta_1\beta\mu_{2t}) = (1 - \delta_1\beta)\,\mu_{2t} \neq 0.$$

In general, therefore, the reverse direction of regression will not have constant parameters even when the original direction has, except in the uninteresting case (for time series) that $\mu_{2t} = \mu_2 \; \forall t$, and all of the covariances are constant.

4.7 Cointegration

Regression methods may be applied in practice to models between I(1) variables which are in fact linked. Define a vector of n random variables $\{\boldsymbol{x}_t\}$ to be I(1) if the highest order of integration of any element is I(1). Linear combinations of $\boldsymbol{x}_t$ will usually be I(1), but as discussed in Chapter 2, some linear combinations, $\boldsymbol{\beta}'\boldsymbol{x}_t$ (say) where $\boldsymbol{\beta}$ is $n \times p$ for $p < n$, may be of reduced integrability and become I(0). Such combinations are cointegrated and $\boldsymbol{\beta}$ is the cointegration matrix (see Engle and Granger, 1987, and Banerjee, Dolado, Galbraith and Hendry, 1993). When $p = 1$, $\boldsymbol{\beta}$ is a vector and apart from normalization is unique; when $p > 1$, any $p \times p$ non-singular linear transform of $\boldsymbol{\beta}'$ will also induce cointegration, so only the cointegration space is uniquely defined.

A simple example is a bivariate regression when $n = 2$ and $\boldsymbol{x}_t = (y_t : z_t)'$ such that:

$$y_t = \beta_0 + \beta_1 z_t + \epsilon_t \text{ where } \epsilon_t \sim \mathsf{IN}\left[0, \sigma_\epsilon^2\right] \tag{4.51}$$

with:

$$z_t = z_{t-1} + \nu_t \text{ where } \nu_t \sim \mathsf{IN}\left[0, \sigma_\nu^2\right] \tag{4.52}$$

and $\mathsf{E}[\epsilon_t \nu_s] = 0 \quad \forall t, s$. From (4.52), $\{z_t\}$ is I(1), but as $\{\epsilon_t\}$ is $\mathsf{IN}[0, \sigma_\epsilon^2]$ then (4.51) differs fundamentally from a nonsense regression. By construction, $\{y_t - \beta_1 z_t\}$ is $\mathsf{IN}(\beta_0, \sigma_\epsilon^2)$ and hence constitutes an I(0) cointegrating linear combination of $\boldsymbol{x}_t$.

Considering the simplest case when $\beta_0 = 0$, estimation of (4.51) by OLS yields:

$$\begin{aligned} T\left(\hat{\beta}_1 - \beta_1\right) &= \left(T^{-2}\sum_{t=1}^{T} z_t^2\right)^{-1}\left(T^{-1}\sum_{t=1}^{T} z_t\epsilon_t\right) \\ &\Rightarrow \left(\int_0^1 V(r)^2 dr\right)^{-1}\int_0^1 V(r)\mathrm{d}W(r). \end{aligned} \tag{4.53}$$

Thus, the normalization is by T, as against unity for nonsense regressions and $\sqrt{T}$ for stationary processes, so such an estimator is said to be super-consistent (see Stock, 1987). From Table 3.2, conditional on $V(r)$ the limiting distribution is a linear mixture of normals and so is 'well behaved'. The key ingredients in this framework are that the regression induces cointegration (i.e. an I(0) error) and that there is a unit root in one of the processes (to make the vector I(1)): it is not essential that $\{\epsilon_t\}$ is IID and an extended analysis applies to higher degrees of integration. At level C, the vector process $\{\boldsymbol{x}_t\}$ is observed and the degrees of integration, the extent of cointegration (if any), and the form of models all have to be discovered from the evidence given the theory. We return to that issue in Parts II and III.

4.8 Bivariate dynamics

Prior to a formal analysis of exogeneity, we backtrack to apply the ideas developed in §4.5 and §4.6 to the nonsense regressions problem with which this chapter began. Let

$\boldsymbol{x}_t' = (y_t : z_t)$ denote the two variables under analysis, generated by (4.1)–(4.3). Let $\boldsymbol{X}_T^1 = (\boldsymbol{x}_1 \dots \boldsymbol{x}_T)$ be the complete data-set with density function $\mathsf{D_X}(\boldsymbol{X}_T^1|\boldsymbol{X}_0, \boldsymbol{\theta})$, where $\boldsymbol{X}_T^{1\prime} = (\boldsymbol{Y}_T^{1\prime} : \boldsymbol{Z}_T^{1\prime})$ and $\boldsymbol{\theta} \in \Theta$ is the vector of all relevant parameters, with parameter space Θ. As in (4.35), sequentially factorize the joint density conditional on $\boldsymbol{X}_0$ as:

$$\mathsf{D_X}\left(\boldsymbol{X}_T^1 \mid \boldsymbol{X}_0, \boldsymbol{\theta}\right) = \prod_{t=1}^{T} \mathsf{D_x}\left(\boldsymbol{x}_t \mid \boldsymbol{X}_{t-1}, \boldsymbol{\theta}\right). \tag{4.54}$$

Extending the analysis in §4.6 above, we next factorize each $\mathsf{D_x}(\boldsymbol{x}_t|\boldsymbol{X}_{t-1}, \boldsymbol{\theta})$ into a conditional distribution of y_t, given z_t and $\boldsymbol{X}_{t-1}$, and a marginal distribution for z_t given $\boldsymbol{X}_{t-1}$. Such a factorization will induce a transformation on the parameters from $\boldsymbol{\theta}$ to $\boldsymbol{\lambda} \in \Lambda$ (say) as in the examples in §4.6. For the tth observation where $\boldsymbol{\lambda}' = (\boldsymbol{\lambda}_1' : \boldsymbol{\lambda}_2')$:

$$\mathsf{D_x}\left(\boldsymbol{x}_t \mid \boldsymbol{X}_{t-1}, \boldsymbol{\theta}\right) = \mathsf{D_{y|z}}\left(y_t \mid z_t, \boldsymbol{X}_{t-1}, \boldsymbol{\lambda}_1\right) \mathsf{D_z}\left(z_t \mid \boldsymbol{X}_{t-1}, \boldsymbol{\lambda}_2\right). \tag{4.55}$$

Since $\{y_t\}$ and $\{z_t\}$ are independent by assumption from (4.3), the original joint density actually factorizes as:

$$\begin{aligned}\mathsf{D_X}\left(\boldsymbol{X}_T^1 \mid \boldsymbol{X}_0, \boldsymbol{\theta}\right) &= \mathsf{D_y}\left(\boldsymbol{Y}_T^1 \mid \boldsymbol{X}_0, \boldsymbol{\lambda}_1\right) \mathsf{D_z}\left(\boldsymbol{Z}_T^1 \mid \boldsymbol{X}_0, \boldsymbol{\lambda}_2\right) \\ &= \prod_{t=1}^{T} \mathsf{D_y}\left(y_t \mid \boldsymbol{Y}_{t-1}^1, \boldsymbol{X}_0, \boldsymbol{\lambda}_1\right) \prod_{t=1}^{T} \mathsf{D_z}\left(z_t \mid \boldsymbol{Z}_{t-1}^1, \boldsymbol{X}_0, \boldsymbol{\lambda}_2\right).\end{aligned} \tag{4.56}$$

Comparing the first terms in (4.55) and (4.56) reveals that z_t is irrelevant in the conditional distribution of y_t and that $\boldsymbol{X}_{t-1}$ in (4.55) can be simplified to $\left(\boldsymbol{Y}_{t-1}^1 : \boldsymbol{X}_0\right)$ so:

$$\mathsf{D_{y|z}}\left(y_t \mid z_t, \boldsymbol{X}_{t-1}, \boldsymbol{\lambda}_1\right) = \mathsf{D_{y|z}}\left(y_t \mid \boldsymbol{Y}_{t-1}^1, \boldsymbol{X}_0, \boldsymbol{\lambda}_1\right). \tag{4.57}$$

However, the economic model in (4.4) implicitly asserted the sequential conditional density:

$$\prod_{t=1}^{T} \mathsf{D_{y|z}}\left(y_t \mid z_t, \boldsymbol{X}_0, \beta\right). \tag{4.58}$$

In the context of (4.1)–(4.3), this is not a valid reduction. The invalid omission of $\boldsymbol{Y}_{t-1}^1$ helps explain why H_0: $\beta_1 = 0$ was rejected so frequently in the Monte Carlo study of regressing y_t on z_t. The irrelevance of z_t in (4.57) does not entail that $\beta_1 = 0$ in (4.58): this is a more formal statement of the 'balance problem' in §4.1.

Even without the additional complication of integrated processes, we might anticipate problems arising from the invalid elimination of $\boldsymbol{Y}_{t-1}^1$ in reducing the first conditional density in (4.57) to $\mathsf{D_{y|z}}(y_t|z_t, \boldsymbol{X}_0, \beta)$. Indeed, there is an analogous spurious regressions problem arising from mis-specified dynamics even in I(0) processes, albeit a less dramatic one, so long as:

$$\mathsf{D_{y|z}}\left(y_t \mid z_t, \boldsymbol{X}_{t-1}, \cdot\right) \neq \mathsf{D_{y|z}}\left(y_t \mid z_t, \cdot\right).$$

If the data are not independently sampled over time, no valid conditional factorization need exist when the history of the process is excluded from the conditioning information, yet sequential factorization is implicitly asserted as was the case in §4.1 due to the claim that $\{u_t\}$ was an IID process. Section 4.9 discusses the technical aspects in a single-variable model. This issue recurs in Chapter 7 where a detailed analysis of model types for dynamic processes will be presented.

There are other potential spurious regressions problems in econometrics, especially those deriving from different facets of interdependence. These will be the subject of later discussions in Chapters 6 and 7. First, however, a precise concept of exogeneity is essential for further progress, and that is the subject of the next chapter.

4.9 A solved example

Consider the data-generation process:

$$\boldsymbol{y} \mid \boldsymbol{Z} \sim \mathsf{N}_T\left[\boldsymbol{Z\beta}, \sigma_\epsilon^2 \boldsymbol{\Omega}\right], \tag{4.59}$$

where $\omega_{ij} = \alpha^{|i-j|}(1-\alpha^2)^{-1}$ with $|\alpha| < 1$, and it is valid to condition $\boldsymbol{y}' = (y_1 \dots y_T)$ on the $T \times k$ matrix of observations $\boldsymbol{Z}$.

(a) Let $\boldsymbol{\Omega}^{-1} = \boldsymbol{HH}'$ and show that :

$$\boldsymbol{H}' = \begin{pmatrix} \sqrt{1-\alpha^2} & 0 & 0 & 0 & \cdots & 0 \\ -\alpha & 1 & 0 & 0 & \cdots & 0 \\ 0 & -\alpha & 1 & 0 & \cdots & 0 \\ \vdots & \ddots & \ddots & \ddots & \ddots & \vdots \\ 0 & 0 & \ddots & -\alpha & 1 & 0 \\ 0 & 0 & \cdots & 0 & -\alpha & 1 \end{pmatrix}$$

where the patterns shown recur. Hence show that $\boldsymbol{H}'\boldsymbol{y}|\boldsymbol{H}'\boldsymbol{Z} \sim \mathsf{N}_T[\boldsymbol{H}'\boldsymbol{Z\beta}, \sigma_\epsilon^2 \boldsymbol{I}]$.

(b) When $k = 1$, and $\beta = 0$, but $\alpha \neq 0$, conduct a recursive Monte Carlo study of the rejection frequency of the t-test of the hypothesis that $\beta = 0$ in least squares estimation of the conjectured equation:

$$y_t = z_t\beta + u_t \quad \text{for } t = 1, \dots, T. \tag{4.60}$$

Investigate the values $\alpha = 0.0, 0.5, 0.7$ and 0.9, when $\{z_t\}$ is generated by:

$$z_t = \lambda z_{t-1} + \nu_t \quad \text{where} \quad \nu_t \sim \mathsf{IN}\left[0, \sigma_\nu^2\right], \tag{4.61}$$

and $\mathsf{E}\left[u_s\nu_t\right] = 0\ \forall t, s$, with $\sigma_\epsilon^2 = \sigma_\nu^2 = 1$ and $\lambda = 0.8$. Does the value of β matter?

Solution to (a)

If $\boldsymbol{\Omega}^{-1} = \boldsymbol{H}\boldsymbol{H}'$, then $\boldsymbol{I}_T = \boldsymbol{H}\boldsymbol{H}'\boldsymbol{\Omega}$ so that $\boldsymbol{H}^{-1} = \boldsymbol{H}'\boldsymbol{\Omega}$, and hence $\boldsymbol{I}_T = \boldsymbol{H}'\boldsymbol{\Omega}\boldsymbol{H}$. It is straightforward, if a little tedious, to verify either the second or the last equality by direct multiplication. Remember that the definition of the inverse of a non-singular matrix $\boldsymbol{D}$ is that $\boldsymbol{D}^{-1}\boldsymbol{D} = \boldsymbol{I}$. Next, write the process in (4.60) in model form as:

$$\boldsymbol{y} = \boldsymbol{Z}\beta + \boldsymbol{u} \text{ where } \boldsymbol{u} \sim \mathsf{N}_T\left[\boldsymbol{0}, \sigma_\epsilon^2\boldsymbol{\Omega}\right]. \tag{4.62}$$

Hence, $\boldsymbol{H}'\boldsymbol{u} \sim \mathsf{N}_T\left[\boldsymbol{0}, \sigma_\epsilon^2\boldsymbol{H}'\boldsymbol{\Omega}\boldsymbol{H}\right] = \mathsf{N}_T\left[\boldsymbol{0}, \sigma_\epsilon^2\boldsymbol{I}\right]$. Since:

$$\boldsymbol{H}'\boldsymbol{y} = \boldsymbol{H}'\boldsymbol{Z}\beta + \boldsymbol{H}'\boldsymbol{u} \text{ then } \boldsymbol{H}'\boldsymbol{y} \mid \boldsymbol{H}'\boldsymbol{Z} \sim \mathsf{N}_T\left[\boldsymbol{H}'\boldsymbol{Z}\beta, \sigma_\epsilon^2\boldsymbol{I}\right]. \tag{4.63}$$

Solution to (b)

The aim of this section of the example is to demonstrate the dangers of attempting to interpret tests in regression equations for stationary processes when the errors are not an innovation process. The DGP is fully specified parametrically and numerically by the information provided and takes the explicit form:

$$\begin{pmatrix} y_t \\ z_t \end{pmatrix} = \begin{pmatrix} \alpha & 0 \\ 0 & 0.8 \end{pmatrix} \begin{pmatrix} y_{t-1} \\ z_{t-1} \end{pmatrix} + \begin{pmatrix} \epsilon_t \\ \nu_t \end{pmatrix}, \tag{4.64}$$

where $\boldsymbol{w}_t = (\epsilon_t : \nu_t)' \sim \mathsf{IN}(\boldsymbol{0}, \boldsymbol{I})$. The equation to be estimated is (4.60), and the hypothesis of interest is denoted H_0: $\beta = 0$. H_0 is to be tested using the conventionally reported regression t-test $\mathsf{t}_{\beta=0} = \widehat{\beta}/\mathsf{ESE}(\widehat{\beta})$, and H_0 is to be rejected if $|\mathsf{t}_{\beta=0}| \geq 2$. The experiments are conducted using PcNaive as in Chapter 3, with $M = 10\,000$ replications.

Figure 4.8a shows the sequences of rejection frequencies of H_0 for $t = 10, \ldots, 100$ for the four values of α where it might be conventionally anticipated that the $\mathsf{t}_{\beta=0}$ test should reject 5 per cent of the time since the null is true. From Chapter A3, that claim implicitly assumes the validity of the untested assertion that $\{u_t\}$ in (4.60) is an innovation process. As can be seen, the rejection frequencies are close to 5 per cent when $\alpha = 0$ but depart markedly from 5 per cent for the two largest values of α. The extent of the excess rejection frequency is nearly independent of the sample size over the range investigated, unlike the nonsense regressions problem for I(1) data. The standard error of an estimated rejection frequency in an independent sample with rejection probability p is given by $\sqrt{(\mathsf{p}(1-\mathsf{p})/M)} \simeq 0.2$ per cent when $\mathsf{p} = 0.05$, so we can reject the claim that the rejection frequency of $\mathsf{t}_{\beta=0}$ is 5 per cent when $\alpha \neq 0$.

Figure 4.8b shows the mean estimated values of β, and reveals that the problem is not due to $\mathsf{E}[\widehat{\beta}] \neq 0$; Fig. 4.8c confirms that the culprit is not $\mathsf{E}[\mathsf{t}]$ either. However, Fig. 4.8d shows that the standard deviation of t deviates increasingly far from unity as α increases, and it is this phenomenon that leads to excess rejection of the correct hypothesis.

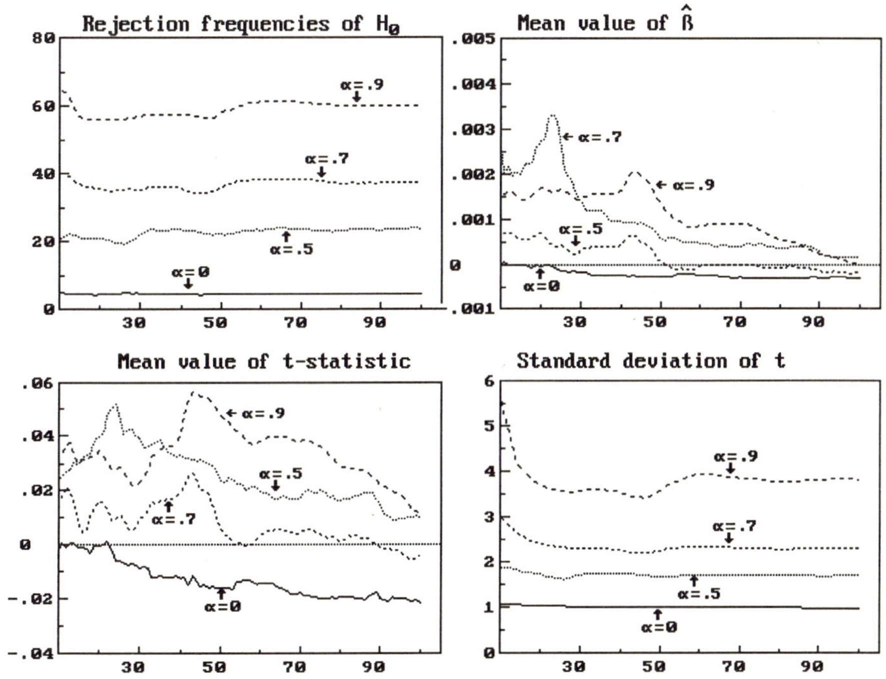

Fig. 4.8 Monte Carlo rejections for different values of α

As ever, an analysis pays dividends. Since it is valid to condition on Z, the following derivations exploit the relationship that $\mathsf{E}[X] = \mathsf{E}_Z(\mathsf{E}[X|Z])$. From (4.64), using the results in §4.5 and §A3.7, $\mathsf{E}[y_t] = \mathsf{E}[z_t] = 0$ so that:

$$\mathsf{E}\left[y_t y_s\right] = \alpha^{|t-s|}\left(1-\alpha^2\right)^{-1} \text{ and } \mathsf{E}\left[z_t z_s\right] = \lambda^{|t-s|}\left(1-\lambda^2\right)^{-1}. \tag{4.65}$$

Further:

$$\mathsf{E}\left[\hat{\beta}\right] = \mathsf{E}\left[\left(\sum_{t=1}^{T} z_t^2\right)^{-1} \sum_{t=1}^{T} y_t z_t\right] = \mathsf{E}_Z\left(\mathsf{E}\left[\left(\sum_{t=1}^{T} z_t^2\right)^{-1} \sum_{t=1}^{T} y_t z_t \mid Z\right]\right) = 0, \tag{4.66}$$

since $\mathsf{E}[y_t] = 0$.

Thus, $\mathsf{V}[\hat{\beta}] = \mathsf{E}[\hat{\beta}^2]$ and so:

$$
\begin{aligned}
\mathsf{V}\left[\hat{\beta}\right] &= \mathsf{E}_Z\left(\mathsf{E}\left[\left(\left(\sum_{t=1}^{T} z_t^2\right)^{-1}\sum_{t=1}^{T} y_t z_t\right)^2 \mid Z\right]\right) \\
&= \mathsf{E}_Z\left[\sum_{t=1}^{T}\sum_{s=1}^{T}\mathsf{E}\left[y_t z_t y_s z_s \mid Z\right]\left(\sum_{t=1}^{T} z_t^2\right)^{-2}\right] \\
&= \mathsf{E}_Z\left[\sum_{t=1}^{T}\sum_{s=1}^{T} z_t z_s \alpha^{|t-s|}\left(1-\alpha^2\right)^{-1}\left(\sum_{t=1}^{T} z_t^2\right)^{-2}\right] \\
&\simeq T^{-2}\left[\left(1-\lambda^2\right)\left(1-\alpha^2\right)^{-1}\right]\left[\sum_{t=1}^{T}\sum_{s=1}^{T}(\lambda\alpha)^{|t-s|}\right].
\end{aligned}
\tag{4.67}
$$

The last step uses the large-sample approximation $\mathsf{E}[(T^{-1}\sum_{t=1}^{T} z_t^2)^{-1}] \simeq (1-\lambda^2)$. Let $\psi = \alpha\lambda$, then the sum in (4.67) can be written as:

$$
\begin{aligned}
\sum_{t=1}^{T}\sum_{s=1}^{T}\psi^{|t-s|} &= T\left(1+2\left[\sum_{j=1}^{T-1}\left(1-T^{-1}[j-1]\right)\psi^j\right]\right) \\
&\simeq T\left(1+\left[2\psi(1-\psi)^{-1}\right]-2T^{-1}\sum_{j=1}^{T-1} j\psi^j\right).
\end{aligned}
\tag{4.68}
$$

Terms of $O(T^{-1})$ have been ignored. The sum in the last line of (4.68) is:

$$
\begin{aligned}
\sum_{j=1}^{T-1} j\psi^j &= \sum_{j=1}^{T-1}\psi^j + \sum_{j=2}^{T-1}(j-1)\psi^j \\
&\simeq \left[\psi(1-\psi)^{-1}\right] + \psi\left\{\sum_{j=1}^{T-1} j\psi^j\right\} - (T-1)\psi^T \\
&\simeq \psi(1-\psi)^{-2}
\end{aligned}
\tag{4.69}
$$

since $|\psi| < 1$. Thus, the last term in (4.68) is $O(T^{-1})$ relative to the other terms and can be neglected to the order of approximation of the present calculations. Collecting the remaining terms in (4.67):

$$
\begin{aligned}
\mathsf{V}\left[\hat{\beta}\right] &\simeq T^{-1}\left(1-\lambda^2\right)\left(1-\alpha\lambda+2\alpha\lambda\right)\left[\left(1-\alpha\lambda\right)\left(1-\alpha^2\right)\right]^{-1} \\
&= T^{-1}\left(1-\lambda^2\right)\left(1+\alpha\lambda\right)\left[\left(1-\alpha\lambda\right)\left(1-\alpha^2\right)\right]^{-1}.
\end{aligned}
\tag{4.70}
$$

This is the expression for the correct sampling variability of $\hat{\beta}$, and corresponds to what has been denoted by MCSD^2 in Chapter 3. However, what the econometrician conventionally calculates is the equivalent of ESE^2, which on average is given by:

$$
\begin{aligned}
\mathsf{E}\left[\hat{\sigma}_u^2\left(\sum_{t=1}^{T} z_t^2\right)^{-1}\right] &= \mathsf{E}_Z\left[\mathsf{E}\left[\hat{\sigma}_u^2\left(\sum_{t=1}^{T} z_t^2\right)^{-1} \mid Z\right]\right] \\
&\simeq T^{-1}\left(1-\lambda^2\right)\left(1-\alpha^2\right)^{-1},
\end{aligned}
\tag{4.71}
$$

from (4.64), since $\beta = 0$ implies that $u_t = \alpha u_{t-1} + \epsilon_t$ where $\epsilon_t \sim \mathsf{IN}[0, 1]$, so $\mathsf{E}[\hat{\sigma}_u^2] \simeq 1/(1-\alpha^2)$. Consequently, the ratio of the expected values of the correct MCSD^2 to the reported ESE^2 is:

$$\frac{\mathsf{E}\left[\mathsf{MCSD}^2\right]}{\mathsf{E}\left[\mathsf{ESE}^2\right]} = \frac{(1+\alpha\lambda)}{(1-\alpha\lambda)} > 1 \text{ when } \alpha\lambda > 0. \tag{4.72}$$

Further, the ratio diverges as $\alpha\lambda \to 1$.

Table 4.2 records the values of MCSD and ESE from the Monte Carlo at $T = 100$ together with their approximate expected values based on the square roots of (4.70) and (4.71).

Table 4.2 Monte Carlo MCSD and ESE

α	$\overline{\mathsf{ESE}}$	E[ESE]	$\overline{\mathsf{MCSD}}$	E[MCSD]
0.00	0.062	0.060	0.062	0.060
0.50	0.071	0.070	0.106	0.107
0.70	0.085	0.085	0.150	0.160
0.90	0.136	0.134	0.330	0.330

First, the asymptotic theory provides an excellent guide to the sampling outcomes at the largest sample size investigated and highlights the main determinants of the behaviour of the two measures of variance. Secondly, the MCSD and ESE indeed diverge as $\alpha\lambda$ increases. Since $\mathsf{t}_{\beta=0}$ uses the downwards biased measure ESE in its denominator instead of MCSD, it is unsurprising that an excessive number of rejections of the null hypothesis results. Figure 4.9 reports the four sets of recursive estimates of the mean bias together with ±2MCSD and ±2ESE shown on either side: MCSD and ESE move further apart the larger is α.

This spurious significance result is related to the nonsense regressions phenomenon discussed in §4.1, but is a milder form. Both emphasize the dangers of attempting inference when the errors are not an innovation process. Tests for the presence of residual serial correlation would reveal the problem, and in the Monte Carlo study, for example, the *DW* test detects the presence of residual serial correlation almost 100 per cent of the time for the non-zero values of α.

However, it is not valid to infer from rejecting the null hypothesis of white-noise errors that the alternative against which the test was constructed is true (e.g. a first-order autoregressive process based on the *DW* test outcome). Indeed, one cannot logically conclude that a null hypothesis is false for any specific reason, and the attempted constructive use of tests is examined in Chapter 7, where some serious defects emerge. This analysis and the Monte Carlo evidence both reinforce the conclusion that a structured approach to modelling economic time series is essential if viable empirical models are to be developed despite the complicated nature of the DGP. The next formalization is to investigate conditioning as a means of data reduction, and that involves an analysis of the concept of exogeneity.

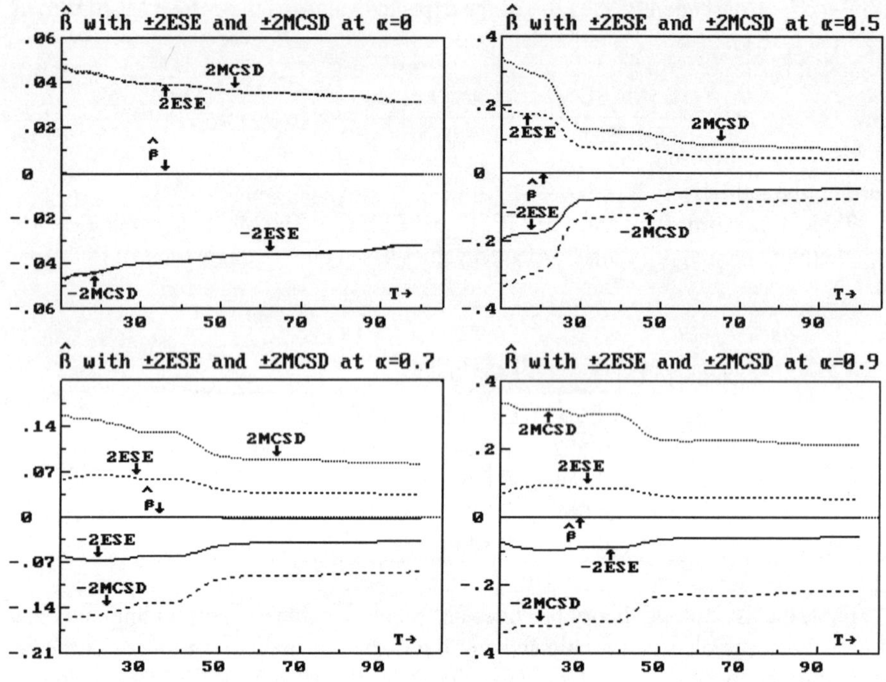

Fig. 4.9 Recursive bias estimates

4.10 Exercises

4.1 Using the data-set UKM1, cumulate R_t over time to create $G_t = \sum_{j=1}^{t} R_j$.
(a) Regress $\log M_t$ on $\log P_t$, and discuss the results.
(b) Regress $\log M_t$ on $\log G_t$. Discuss these results. What criteria, if any, would help to distinguish which of the preceding regressions was meaningful or nonsense?

4.2 Using the variable R_t from the data-set UKM1:
(a) Examine its correlogram, and compare the empirical results with what would be anticipated if R_t followed a first-order autoregressive process.
(b) Does the process seem to be stationary? If not, to what case does it conform?
(c) Fit a first-order autoregression to R_t and discuss the results. Are the residuals an innovation process? Are they approximately normally distributed?
(d) On the basis of all these results, how would you characterize R_t?
(e) Does it matter what sample period is selected? Is there any noticable change after 1984?
(f) Repeat the analysis in (a)–(c) using ΔR_t.

4.3 Consider the joint density of the three variables $\Delta \log M_t$, $\Delta \log P_t$, and $\Delta \log Y_t$ from the data-set UKM1.

(a) Estimate an autoregressive process for each variable, and discuss the results obtained. What order of lag length did you select and why? Are the results sensitive to the length chosen? Did you include an intercept? Does the sample period selected matter?

(b) To characterize the marginal distributions, regress each variable on two lagged values of itself and both other variables. Does the past of any variable help explain any other variable?

(c) Estimate a conditional model for $\Delta \log M_t$ given $\Delta \log P_t$ and $\Delta \log Y_t$, and one lagged value of each variation. Discuss your results, and interpret the evidence in light of the theoretical analysis in this chapter.

4.4 Using PcNaive, set up a Monte Carlo experiment to investigate the nonsense regressions problem when the following DGP holds:

$$\Delta y_t = \alpha + \epsilon_t \text{ where } \epsilon_t \sim \mathsf{IN}\left[0, \sigma_\epsilon^2\right] \text{ and } y_0 = 0; \tag{4.73}$$

$$\Delta z_t = \gamma + \nu_t \text{ where } \nu_t \sim \mathsf{IN}\left[0, \sigma_\nu^2\right] \text{ and } z_0 = 0;$$

when

$$\mathsf{E}\left[\epsilon_t \nu_s\right] = 0 \; \forall t, s. \tag{4.74}$$

In your experiment, consider $\left(\alpha, \gamma, \sigma_\epsilon^2, \sigma_\nu^2\right)$ in relation to the data being quarterly and in logs (α of 0.01 entails around 5 per cent p.a. growth, and $\sigma_\epsilon = 0.005$ is a 0.5 per cent equation standard error). The investigator postulates and estimates the equation:

$$y_t = \beta_0 + \beta_1 z_t + \beta_2 t + u_t \text{ where } u_t \underset{c}{\sim} \mathsf{IID}\left[0, \sigma_u^2\right], \tag{4.75}$$

and β_1 is interpreted as the derivative of y_t with respect to z_t.

(a) How often is the hypothesis H_0: $\beta_1 = 0$ rejected when the sample size is 40?

(b) Does the rejection frequency change much as the sample increases up to 100?

(c) How do changes in the parameters of the DGP affect the rejection frequency (e.g. does a difference between α and γ matter; is their absolute size important; or their relative magnitudes compared to σ_ϵ and σ_ν respectively; etc.)?

(d) How would you systematically investigate this parameter dependence?

(e) Could the problem of nonsense regressions be detected? If so, briefly describe the behaviour of the statistics that you would use in this task.

(f) List all the features of the experiment that could matter in determining the outcome you obtained (for example, normality, independent errors, etc.). How can this issue be studied systematically?

4.5 In the second-order autoregressive process defined by:

$$y_t = \phi_1 y_{t-1} + \phi_2 y_{t-2} + \epsilon_t \text{ where } \epsilon_t \sim \mathsf{IN}\left[0, \sigma_\epsilon^2\right], \tag{4.76}$$

derive the conditions on (ϕ_1, ϕ_2) under which (4.76) is stationary.

(a) Consider the following data-generation process for inflation:

$$\begin{aligned} i_t &= \rho + \mathsf{E}_t[\pi_{t+1}] + v_t \\ \pi_t &= \mu_0 + \mu_1 \pi_{t-1} + \mu_2 \pi_{t-2} + e_t, \end{aligned}$$

where i_t is the nominal interest rate, ρ is the real interest rate, π_t is the rate of inflation, $\mathsf{E}_t[\pi_{t+1}]$ is the conditional expectation of π_{t+1} given information available at time t, and v_t and e_t are mean-zero, independent white-noise processes, so that $\mathsf{E}[v_t e_s] = 0\ \forall t, s$. Under the assumptions of rational expectations and that the process generating inflation is stationary, by estimating the regression of i_t on a constant, π_{t-1} and π_{t-2}, is it possible to test the Fisher hypothesis that the long-run relationship between the nominal interest rate and inflation is H_0: $i^* = \rho + \pi^*$, where * denotes the unconditional expectation (steady-state value)?

(b) Show that a test of the sum of the inflation coefficients being unity in that regression is biased against finding evidence in favour of the Fisher hypothesis even though $\mathsf{E}[\pi_t v_s] = 0\ \forall t, s$.

(c) Given your answer to (b), and the stationarity of (4.76), will a relaxation of stationarity remove that bias? Comment on your findings, especially the causes and testability of the bias.

(d) Suggest an estimation procedure that allows a valid test.

(Oxford M.Phil., 1991)

4.6 Consider the data-generation process:

$$\begin{aligned} y_t &= y_{t-1} + \epsilon_t \\ z_t &= z_{t-1} + \nu_t \end{aligned} \tag{4.77}$$

where $\mathsf{E}[\epsilon_t \nu_s] = 0\ \forall t, s$. Let $W(r)$ and $V(r)$ be independent Wiener processes for $r \in [0, 1]$, and let $\Rightarrow$ denote weak convergence, then you may use without proof the following results:

$$T^{-2} \sum_{t=1}^{T} y_t^2 \Rightarrow \sigma_\epsilon^2 \int_0^1 W(r)^2 \mathrm{d}r;$$

$$T^{-2} \sum_{t=1}^{T} z_t^2 \Rightarrow \sigma_\nu^2 \int_0^1 V(r)^2 \mathrm{d}r;$$

$$T^{-2} \sum_{t=1}^{T} y_t z_t \Rightarrow \sigma_\epsilon \sigma_\nu \int_0^1 W(r) V(r) \mathrm{d}r.$$

(a) The model conjectured by an investigator is:

$$y_t = \beta z_t + \zeta_t \text{ with } \zeta_t \underset{c}{\sim} \mathsf{IN}\left[0, \sigma_\zeta^2\right], \tag{4.78}$$

where $\underset{c}{\sim}$ denotes 'is claimed to be distributed as'. A sample of size T is available on $\{y_t; z_t\}$. Derive the limiting distribution of the least-squares estimator of β:

$$\hat{\beta} = \left(\sum_{t=1}^{T} z_t^2\right)^{-1} \sum_{t=1}^{T} y_t z_t. \tag{4.79}$$

Explain any theorems used and discuss the implications of the result.

(b) Derive the limiting distribution of the t-test of H_0: $\beta = 0$ when (4.77) is true and:

$$\mathsf{t}_{\beta=0} = \hat{\beta}\left[\frac{\hat{\sigma}_\zeta^2}{\sum_{t=1}^{T} z_t^2}\right]^{-\frac{1}{2}},$$

where $\hat{\sigma}_\zeta^2$ is the residual variance from (4.78). Describe the implications of this result. What happens to the sample correlation coefficient of y with z as $T \to \infty$?

(c) Comment on the implications of the analysis for the problem of 'nonsense regressions' in time-series econometrics. Discuss how to extend these distributional findings to test for the existence of cointegration between y and z.

(Oxford M.Phil., 1992)

4.7 Let $\{y_t\}$ be generated for $t = 1, \ldots, T$ by the process:

$$y_t = \mu t + S_t \text{ where } S_t = \sum_{j=1}^{t} v_j \text{ and } v_t \sim \mathsf{IN}\left[0, \sigma_v^2\right] \text{ with } S_0 = 0.$$

Consider estimating by least squares the parameters of the model:

$$y_t = \mu + \rho y_{t-1} + v_t.$$

(a) Define the scaling matrix:

$$\mathbf{C}_T = \begin{pmatrix} T^{\frac{1}{2}} & 0 \\ 0 & T^{\frac{3}{2}} \end{pmatrix},$$

and show that:

$$\begin{aligned} \mathbf{C}_T\begin{pmatrix} \hat{\mu} - \mu \\ \hat{\rho} - 1 \end{pmatrix} &= \begin{pmatrix} 1 & T^{-2}\sum_{t=1}^{T} y_{t-1} \\ T^{-2}\sum_{t=1}^{T} y_{t-1} & T^{-3}\sum_{t=1}^{T} y_{t-1}^2 \end{pmatrix}^{-1} \begin{pmatrix} T^{-\frac{1}{2}}\sum_{t=1}^{T} v_t \\ T^{-\frac{3}{2}}\sum_{t=1}^{T} y_{t-1}v_t \end{pmatrix} \\ &= \mathbf{B}_T^{-1}\begin{pmatrix} T^{-\frac{1}{2}}\sum_{t=1}^{T} v_t \\ T^{-\frac{3}{2}}\sum_{t=1}^{T} y_{t-1}v_t \end{pmatrix}. \end{aligned}$$

(b) Given that

$$\begin{array}{ll} T^{-2}\sum_{t=1}^{T} S_t & \overset{P}{\to} 0, \\ T^{-5/2}\sum_{t=1}^{T} tS_t & \Rightarrow W_1, \\ T^{-3}\sum_{t=1}^{T} S_t^2 & \Rightarrow W_2, \\ T^{-3/2}\sum_{t=1}^{T} S_{t-1}v_t & \overset{P}{\to} 0, \end{array}$$

where W_1 and W_2 are non-degenerate distributions, $\overset{P}{\to}$ denotes convergence in probability and $\Rightarrow$ denotes weak convergence, show that:

$$\underset{T\to\infty}{\text{plim}}\ \boldsymbol{B}_T = \begin{pmatrix} 1 & \frac{1}{2}\mu \\ \frac{1}{2}\mu & \frac{1}{3}\mu^2 \end{pmatrix} = \boldsymbol{B}$$

and:

$$T^{-\frac{3}{2}}\sum_{t=1}^{T} y_{t-1}v_t \Rightarrow \mathsf{N}\left[0,\ \tfrac{1}{3}\,\sigma_v^2\mu^2\right].$$

(c) Since the asymptotic covariance between $T^{-1/2}\sum_{t=1}^{T} v_t$ and $T^{-3/2}\sum_{t=1}^{T} y_{t-1}v_t$ is $\frac{1}{2}\sigma^2\mu$, show that:

$$\begin{pmatrix} T^{-\frac{1}{2}}\sum_{t=1}^{T} v_t \\ T^{-\frac{3}{2}}\sum_{t=1}^{T} y_{t-1}v_t \end{pmatrix} \Rightarrow \mathsf{N}_2\left[\boldsymbol{0}, \sigma_v^2\boldsymbol{B}\right], \tag{4.80}$$

and hence:

$$\boldsymbol{C}_T\begin{pmatrix} \hat{\mu}-\mu \\ \hat{\rho}-1 \end{pmatrix} \Rightarrow \mathsf{N}_2\left[\boldsymbol{0}, \sigma_v^2\boldsymbol{B}^{-1}\right],$$

carefully stating any theorems and assumptions which you use.

(Oxford M.Phil., 1991)

Hints

Many of the functionals to which sample moments of I(1) processes converge are expressed in terms of normal densities in Table 3.2 for the process $y_t = \mu t + S_t$ where $S_t = S_{t-1} + v_t$ and $v_t \sim \mathsf{IN}[0,1]$. From 1. in Table 3.2:

$$T^{-1}\sum_{t=1}^{T} S_{t-1}/\sqrt{T} \Rightarrow \int_0^1 W(r)\mathrm{d}r \ \text{ so } T^{-1}\sum_{t=1}^{T}\left(S_{t-1}/\sqrt{T}\right)^2 \Rightarrow \int_0^1 W(r)^2\mathrm{d}r$$

and hence W_1 and W_2 can be made explicit. Since:

$$T^{-(n+1)}\sum_{t=1}^{T} t^n \to (n+1)^{-1} \text{ as } T\to\infty,$$

given $y_t = \mu t + S_t$, the only parts needed are 2. and 3. from Table 3.2, since:

$$T^{-1}\sum_{t=1}^{T} S_{t-1}v_t \Rightarrow \int_0^1 W(r)\mathrm{d}W(r) \text{ so that } T^{-\frac{3}{2}}\sum_{t=1}^{T} S_{t-1}v_t \xrightarrow{P} 0.$$

Thus, the other component converges to:

$$T^{-\frac{3}{2}}\sum_{t=1}^{T} y_{t-1}v_t = T^{-\frac{3}{2}}\sum_{t=1}^{T} \mu\,(t-1)\,v_t + T^{-\frac{3}{2}}\sum_{t=1}^{T} S_{t-1}v_t \Rightarrow \mu \int_0^1 r\mathrm{d}W(r),$$

which is a vector functional of Wiener processes. Alternatively by conventional methods:

$$\begin{pmatrix} T^{-\frac{1}{2}}\sum_{t=1}^{T} v_t \\ T^{-\frac{3}{2}}\sum_{t=1}^{T} y_{t-1}v_t \end{pmatrix} \xrightarrow{D} \begin{pmatrix} T^{-\frac{1}{2}}\sum_{t=1}^{T} v_t \\ \mu T^{-\frac{3}{2}}\sum_{t=1}^{T} t v_t \end{pmatrix} \xrightarrow{D} \mathsf{N}_2\left[\mathbf{0}, \sigma^2 \boldsymbol{B}\right].$$

5

Exogeneity and Causality

The concept of exogeneity as 'determined outside the system under analysis' is examined. Two counter-examples to intuitive formulations emphasize the requirement that a variable deemed to be exogenous should sustain valid inference when it is treated as given. The notion of weak exogeneity (see Engle, Hendry and Richard, 1983) is defined to fulfil that requirement and concerns conditional inference about parameters of interest without loss of information. A 'cobweb' model relates the concepts to economic notions. The counter-examples are re-examined to determine which aspect of weak exogeneity they violated, and this highlights an inherent ambiguity in definitions which depend on orthogonality between variables and unobserved errors. The concept of strong exogeneity is defined as weak exogeneity combined with Granger (1969) non-causality to provide a basis for conditional forecasting. Super exogeneity extends weak exogeneity to include the invariance of the parameters of the conditional model to interventions affecting the marginal model in order to sustain conditional policy analyses. Two concepts of causality are discussed. Finally, estimation and inference in conditional models of unit root processes are considered.

5.1 What are 'exogenous variables'?

Econometric problems frequently involve too many variables to be feasibly analysed together. Two main issues arise as a consequence of seeking appropriate reductions: causality and exogeneity. Causality issues arise when marginalizing with respect to variables and their lags. Exogeneity issues arise when seeking to analyse a subset of the variables given the behaviour of the remaining variables. The latter is the main focus of this chapter: we seek conditions which validate treating one subset of variables as given when analysing others. As presaged in Chapter 4, the requisite condition involves a relationship between contemporaneous variables and parameters of interest, and this leads to the concept of weak exogeneity (see Richard, 1980, and Engle *et al.*, 1983). Stronger conditions must be satisfied to justify conditional forecasting, leading to strong exogeneity which requires Granger (1969) non-causality as well as weak exogeneity; or conditional policy analysis, leading to super exogeneity which adds the requirement that parameters remain constant across policy changes to that of weak exogeneity. All three concepts are discussed below, together with a critical appraisal of other notions extant in the econometrics literature (see e.g. Sims, 1972).

The heuristic idea of exogeneity is: 'A variable is exogenous if it is determined outside the system under analysis' (see Koopmans, 1950b). As an illustration, a particular economic growth-theory model may assume that population growth is exogenous to the analysis. The purpose of such an exogeneity assumption must be clear, because in the long run, population almost certainly does depend on economic factors. Some aspects of the analysis may remain valid conditional on ignoring feedbacks from economic growth to population growth, whereas for other facets, treating population as given when it is not might generate misleading implications. Similar considerations affect econometric analyses. Merely asserting that a specific variable is 'exogenous' in a given model is not an adequate basis for inference. The discussion will focus on whether, for certain specific uses of an empirical model, a particular variable is determined outside the system under study.

It is important to distinguish between 'not caused' and 'exogenous' to ensure a clear discussion. Energy from the sun impinging on the earth may seem to be a natural exogenous variable in that it is determined by processes within the sun which are not affected by events on earth. However, even assuming that there was no mechanism for humanity to influence the amount of sunlight impinging on the earth, conditioning on sunlight in an econometric model may involve loss of relevant information. Although sunlight is not caused by human economic behaviour, that is neither necessary nor sufficient to justify its treatment as exogenous in any given econometric model. The first of two counter-examples in §5.2 illustrates that problem. Further, as the second counter-example demonstrates, knowing that a set of regressors is fixed in repeated samples is also neither necessary nor sufficient to justify their treatment as exogenous.

Section 5.3 discusses the concept of weak exogeneity, which is used in §5.5 to clarify why the counter-examples could be constructed. Section 5.4 relates weak exogeneity to economic models in the dynamic setting of the 'cobweb' model. Sections 5.6 and 5.7 examine aspects of exogeneity in greater detail. The more restrictive concepts of strong and super exogeneity are discussed in §5.8 and §5.9 respectively, and illustrated in §5.10. Section 5.11 investigates two notions of causality; and §5.12 solves two examples to highlight features of the definitions which are important in empirical research. Weak exogeneity when there are unit roots is considered in §5.13.

5.2 Two counter-examples

The issue of what constitute adequate grounds for assigning the status of exogenous to a variable is not as easily resolved as it might look at first sight. The purpose of the following two counter-examples is to demonstrate difficulties with cases that seem intuitively clear, thereby forcing a precise characterization of the conditions for exogeneity.

5.2.1 An expectations counter-example

The first counter-example involves a model of coffee prices, and introduces modelling issues relevant to many other econometric analyses. In the model, a coffee crop is freely traded in a market that is geographically distant from regions where coffee is grown. The quantity and price of coffee at each time t are denoted by Q_t and P_t respectively, where P_t is determined competitively. Commodity markets involve sophisticated arbitrage by agents who collect all the information they can about supply and demand conditions and then trade on the future price. To determine their best actions, they form an expectation of the price that will rule at the relevant future date. That expected price, relative to the current price, is a major determinant of the volume of the commodity that they currently demand. Denote the information set available to agents at the start of trading on day t by $\mathcal{I}_{t-1}$. The expected price formed for period t from $\mathcal{I}_{t-1}$ is denoted by P_t^e and is a determinant of the quantity demanded D_t. In turn, P_t^e depends on what agents think the volume of output and the demand for it will be on day t, and hence on how they form expectations about Q and D.

To make the analysis tractable, we consider a world in which the only additional variable determining the market's demand volume is the expected prevalence of frost in the supply region immediately prior to the market trading, denoted by F_t^e. We will shortly consider precisely how agents form their expectations and what information sets they use, but will simplify by assuming that F_t^e determines P_t^e.[1] The demand for coffee, in a linear equation form, is:

$$D_t = \alpha_0 + \alpha_1 F_t^e - \alpha_2 P_{t-1} + \alpha_3 Q_{t-1} + u_{1t}, \tag{5.1}$$

where $\alpha_i \geq 0$. The exogeneity problem arises from the supply of coffee S_t depending on the actual, and not on the expected, frost:

$$S_t = \gamma_0 + \gamma_1 P_t - \gamma_2 F_t + \gamma_3 P_{t-1} + u_{2t}, \tag{5.2}$$

where $\gamma_i \geq 0$. The price adjusts so rapidly that the market clears at $Q_t = D_t = S_t$. In (5.1)–(5.2), the $\{u_{it}\}$ are $\mathsf{IID}\left[0, \sigma_i^2\right]$ and mutually independent. We will reach incorrect conclusions when modelling the price of coffee if actual frost is treated as an 'exogenous' variable in this model even though frost is unaffected by coffee prices or output. This occurs precisely because price is influenced by both the expected frost and the actual frost, and the expected outcome usually differs from the realized value.

We formulate expectations as follows. Assume agents have an information set $\mathcal{I}_{t-1}$ on the basis of which they form rational plans about a variable y_t under their control, according to the expected value z_t^e held by them about a second variable z_t which they do not control (see Hendry and Richard, 1983):

$$y_t^p = \mathsf{E}\left[z_t \mid \mathcal{I}_{t-1}\right] \beta = z_t^e \beta, \tag{5.3}$$

[1] P_t^e involves expectations about an endogenous variable, which raises different issues from those presently under scrutiny, so it is eliminated from the analysis to focus on the role of F_t^e alone.

where y_t^p denotes the planned value. In (5.3), the coefficient β, which maps from the expectation about z_t onto the plan, is the parameter of interest. Taking expectations conditional on $\mathcal{I}_{t-1}$ in (5.3):

$$\mathsf{E}\left[y_t^p \mid \mathcal{I}_{t-1}\right] = \mathsf{E}\left[z_t^e \mid \mathcal{I}_{t-1}\right]\beta = z_t^e\beta = y_t^p. \tag{5.4}$$

Thus, the plan fully incorporates the available information.

When $z_t^e = \mathsf{E}\left[z_t|\mathcal{I}_{t-1}\right]$, the observed value of z_t will deviate by unanticipated news ν_t from the expected value given the information set available:

$$z_t = \mathsf{E}\left[z_t \mid \mathcal{I}_{t-1}\right] + \nu_t \text{ where } \mathsf{E}\left[\nu_t \mid \mathcal{I}_{t-1}\right] = 0. \tag{5.5}$$

Thus, ν_t is an innovation relative to $\mathcal{I}_{t-1}$. The assumption that $z_t^e = \mathsf{E}\left[z_t|\mathcal{I}_{t-1}\right]$ (rational expectations) is strong and is analysed in §6.2.

Next, let the outcome y_t deviate from the plan by another innovation ϵ_t, which is distributed independently of ν_t:

$$y_t = y_t^p + \epsilon_t. \tag{5.6}$$

The plan y_t^p is deemed to be rational if agents expect to implement it, namely if:

$$\mathsf{E}\left[y_t \mid \mathcal{I}_{t-1}\right] = y_t^p. \tag{5.7}$$

Taking conditional expectations in (5.6):

$$\mathsf{E}\left[y_t \mid \mathcal{I}_{t-1}\right] = \mathsf{E}\left[y_t^p \mid \mathcal{I}_{t-1}\right] + \mathsf{E}\left[\epsilon_t \mid \mathcal{I}_{t-1}\right] = y_t^p + \mathsf{E}\left[\epsilon_t \mid \mathcal{I}_{t-1}\right], \tag{5.8}$$

so that the plan is rational when $\mathsf{E}\left[\epsilon_t|\mathcal{I}_{t-1}\right] = 0$, and the perturbation ϵ_t is indeed an innovation against $\mathcal{I}_{t-1}$, and hence against any subset of $\mathcal{I}_{t-1}$. Consequently, ϵ_t is unpredictable from the plan:

$$\mathsf{E}\left[\epsilon_t \mid y_t^p\right] = 0 \text{ so that } \mathsf{E}\left[y_t \mid y_t^p\right] = y_t^p. \tag{5.9}$$

This formulation of agents' plans is general in that most of the models we consider will have a similar structure; however, the formulation of expectations here is not standard below, as discussed in §6.2. Equations (5.5)–(5.9) imply that agents can control the average rather than the actual outcome of their plans, and on average achieve their plans, but that agents cannot control variation around the average.

Express the model in terms of observable variables by substituting $(z_t - \nu_t)$ for $\mathsf{E}[z_t|\mathcal{I}_{t-1}]$ from (5.5) into (5.3) and the result of that operation into (5.6):

$$y_t = z_t\beta + (\epsilon_t - \beta\nu_t) = z_t\beta + \eta_t \text{ where } \eta_t = (\epsilon_t - \beta\nu_t). \tag{5.10}$$

If z_t were an exogenous variable 'determined outside the model', it would be valid to treat z_t in (5.10) as a conditioning variable and regress y_t on z_t to estimate β. However, since both η_t and z_t depend on ν_t from (5.10) and (5.5) respectively, z_t is correlated with the error term η_t. Indeed, $\mathsf{E}[z_t\eta_t]$ cannot be zero under the above specification since from (5.5) and (5.10):

$$\mathsf{E}[z_t\eta_t] = \mathsf{E}[(z_t^e + \nu_t)(\epsilon_t - \beta\nu_t)] = -\beta\sigma_v^2 \neq 0.$$

This outcome violates one of the basic conditions for a regression to be valid, namely $\mathsf{E}[z_t\eta_t] = 0$ and hence z_t is not exogenous for β in (5.10).

The problem can also be seen by considering the conditional expectation $\mathsf{E}[y_t|z_t]$:

$$\mathsf{E}[y_t \mid z_t] = z_t\beta + \mathsf{E}[\epsilon_t \mid z_t] - \beta\mathsf{E}[\nu_t \mid z_t]. \tag{5.11}$$

Since ϵ_t is independent of ν_t and $\mathsf{E}[\epsilon_t|\mathcal{I}_{t-1}] = 0$ then $\mathsf{E}[\epsilon_t|z_t] = 0$. However, $\mathsf{E}[\nu_t|z_t]$ cannot be zero since z_t depends on ν_t. To obtain a precise answer, assume that $\{y_t : z_t\}$ are jointly normal and stationary, and let:

$$\mathsf{E}[\nu_t \mid z_t] = \delta z_t \text{ where } \delta = \frac{\mathsf{E}[\nu_t z_t]}{\mathsf{E}[z_t^2]} = \frac{\sigma_v^2}{\mathsf{E}[z_t^2]}, \tag{5.12}$$

which is the population regression. From (5.11):

$$\mathsf{E}[y_t \mid z_t] = \beta(1-\delta)z_t = \gamma z_t \neq \beta z_t. \tag{5.13}$$

Consequently, incorrect inferences about β will result from taking z_t to be exogenous in (5.10), even though by assumption $\{z_t\}$ is unaffected by anything that happens in this model economy. The criterion of a variable to be exogenous based on being 'determined outside the system', in the simplistic sense that $\{z_t\}$ above is, will not correctly handle models involving expectations, or indeed any form of measurement errors. Most extant definitions of 'exogeneity' would deem z_t to fail their criterion when it is correlated with the equation error. However, from (5.13):

$$y_t = \gamma z_t + \zeta_t \text{ where } \mathsf{E}[z_t\zeta_t] = 0, \tag{5.14}$$

so that in the re-parameterized model, z_t is orthogonal to the error, leaving it unclear whether or not z_t is exogenous. We return to this ambiguity after analysing the dependence of the exogeneity status of z_t on the parameterization of the model.

In the coffee-price example, D_t is the plan for demand and F_t^e is the expectation on which it is based. Given market clearing, and letting $F_t = F_t^e + \omega_t$ solving for Q_t yields:

$$\begin{aligned} Q_t &= \alpha_0 + \alpha_1 F_t^e - \alpha_2 P_{t-1} + \alpha_3 Q_{t-1} + u_{1t} \\ &= \alpha_0 + \alpha_1 F_t - \alpha_2 P_{t-1} + \alpha_3 Q_{t-1} + (u_{1t} - \alpha_1\omega_t), \end{aligned} \tag{5.15}$$

so that F_t is correlated with the error. We conclude that in such models, variables cannot necessarily be treated as exogenous even when they are causally unaffected by the endogenous variables.

5.2.2 A fixed-regressor counter-example

A second condition that might seem adequate to determine the status of a variable as exogenous is when it is fixed across repeated samples. Surprisingly, such a condition by itself is not sufficient for exogeneity either. Generate y_t by:

$$y_t = \beta z_t + u_t \text{ where } u_t \sim \mathsf{IN}\left[0, \sigma_u^2\right], \tag{5.16}$$

where $\{z_t\}$ is fixed once and for all at time zero, prior to any y being generated: nothing affecting ys can affect any zs by construction. This condition alone is insufficient for $\{z_t\}$ to be exogenous, so fixity does not validate treating z_t as given when estimating β in (5.16) by regressing y_t on z_t given z_t. The reason is analogous to the first counter-example: as in Chapter 2, z_t can be partitioned into two components:

$$z_t = z_t^* + \nu_t \text{ where } z_t^* = \mathsf{E}\left[z_t \mid \mathcal{I}_{t-1}\right], \tag{5.17}$$

so that z_t^* is the systematic component (usually a function of past zs *inter alia*) and ν_t is the stochastic component, which is uncorrelated with z_t^*. A simple example of (5.17) is when z_t is generated by a stationary first-order autoregressive process where $z_t^* = \alpha z_{t-1}$ so that:

$$z_t = \alpha z_{t-1} + \nu_t \text{ where } \nu_t \sim \mathsf{IN}\left[0, \sigma_v^2\right], \tag{5.18}$$

and $|\alpha| < 1$ with $z_0 \sim \mathsf{N}\left[0, \sigma_v^2 / \left(1 - \alpha^2\right)\right]$. However, generating $\{z_t\}$ according to (5.18) prior to any y_t being generated and holding them fixed does not ensure that the νs do not affect the us in (5.16) since, for example, the assumptions do not preclude:

$$u_t = \phi \nu_{t-1} + \epsilon_t \text{ where } \epsilon_t \sim \mathsf{IN}\left[0, \sigma_\epsilon^2\right], \tag{5.19}$$

and $\mathsf{E}\left[\epsilon_t \nu_s\right] = 0 \ \forall t, s$. When (5.19) holds for $\phi \neq 0$, then $\mathsf{E}\left[z_t u_t\right] = \alpha \phi \sigma_v^2$ so z_t is correlated with u_t and hence is not exogenous. Therefore, the fixity of z_t in repeated samples is not sufficient for z_t to be exogenous: in repeated samples, $\{y_t\}$ is indeed generated by (5.16) from one set of $\{z_t\}$ only, but it is not valid to condition on z_t when (5.19) holds. The paradox arises because the joint distribution of $\{y_t : z_t\}$ has been incompletely specified.

Such examples force us to be precise about the conditions defining exogeneity, and hence clarify the meaning of the statement that 'an exogenous variable is determined outside the system under analysis'. In both counter-examples, z_t is not actually determined outside the relevant system as far as the models under analysis are concerned. In the first example, the expectation z_t^e of z_t, given the information set in (5.3), is exogenous, but the accuracy of the expectations is determined inside the system. Likewise in (5.16), it is irrelevant that z_t is fixed, since $\{z_t\}$ is correlated with the error, so it is as if $\{z_t\}$ were determined inside the system under analysis. An unambiguous concept of exogeneity, which applies irrespective of the type of model studied, is essential and is the objective of the next section.

5.3 Weak exogeneity

The required notion of exogeneity is met by the concept of weak exogeneity, proposed in Richard (1980) and analysed by Engle *et al.* (1983), building on the pioneering approach of Koopmans (1950b) and drawing on Barndorff-Nielsen (1978). The analyses of joint and conditional densities and sequential factorization in §2.22, §2.27 and §4.5 provide the basis for the discussion.

Consider the sequential joint density at time t of the two variables $\boldsymbol{x}_t = (y_t : z_t)'$ conditional on $\boldsymbol{X}_{t-1} = (\boldsymbol{X}_0, \boldsymbol{x}_1, \ldots, \boldsymbol{x}_{t-1})$:

$$\mathsf{D}_{\mathsf{x}}\left(y_t, z_t \mid \boldsymbol{X}_{t-1}, \boldsymbol{\theta}\right) \text{ where } \boldsymbol{\theta} = (\theta_1 \ldots \theta_n)' \in \Theta \subset \mathbb{R}^n. \tag{5.20}$$

Equation (5.20) is interpreted as the DGP. Generally, z_t is endogenous in the framework of the joint density function, but it may happen that the joint density can be factorized such that no analysis of how z_t is determined is necessary to learn how y_t is determined. Given that a joint density can always be factorized into a conditional density times a marginal density, we investigate the conditions under which only the former need be analysed to learn everything required about the parameters of interest in the system.

First, we take account of the existence of many one–one transformations from the original n parameters $\boldsymbol{\theta} \in \Theta$ to any new set of n parameters $\boldsymbol{\phi} \in \Phi$:

$$\boldsymbol{\phi} = \boldsymbol{f}(\boldsymbol{\theta}) \text{ where } \boldsymbol{\phi} \in \Phi \text{ and } \boldsymbol{\theta} \in \Theta. \tag{5.21}$$

In (5.21), $\boldsymbol{f}(\cdot)$ defines a one–one re-parameterization of θs into ϕs which belong to the admissible parameter space Φ. Choose the ϕs to be factorizable into two components $\boldsymbol{\phi}' = (\boldsymbol{\phi}_1' : \boldsymbol{\phi}_2')$, where $\boldsymbol{\phi}_i$ has n_i elements ($n_1 + n_2 = n$) corresponding to the factorization of the joint density (5.20) into a conditional density and a marginal density:

$$\mathsf{D}_{\mathsf{x}}\left(y_t, z_t \mid \boldsymbol{X}_{t-1}, \boldsymbol{\theta}\right) = \mathsf{D}_{\mathsf{y|z}}\left(y_t \mid z_t, \boldsymbol{X}_{t-1}, \boldsymbol{\phi}_1\right) \mathsf{D}_{\mathsf{z}}\left(z_t \mid \boldsymbol{X}_{t-1}, \boldsymbol{\phi}_2\right). \tag{5.22}$$

There are several important points to note about (5.22):

(a) The factorization can always be achieved if $\boldsymbol{\phi}_1$ and $\boldsymbol{\phi}_2$ are defined to support it;
(b) the number of parameters in the factorization is the same as in the original;
(c) the question 'Under what conditions is z_t exogenous?' translates into 'Under what conditions can the marginal density $\mathsf{D}_{\mathsf{z}}\left(z_t | \boldsymbol{X}_{t-1}, \boldsymbol{\phi}_2\right)$ in (5.22) be treated as determined outside the analysis of the conditional system $\mathsf{D}_{\mathsf{y|z}}\left(y_t | z_t, \boldsymbol{X}_{t-1}, \boldsymbol{\phi}_1\right)$?'

Let the joint density under analysis involve a subset $\boldsymbol{\psi}$ of the parameters $\boldsymbol{\theta}$, where $\boldsymbol{\psi}$ is a vector of $k \leq n_1$ parameters of interest. A necessary condition for z_t to be considered as determined outside the model of y_t is that $\boldsymbol{\psi}$ must not depend on $\boldsymbol{\phi}_2$. If $\boldsymbol{\psi}$ depended on $\boldsymbol{\phi}_2$, both factors in (5.22) must be analysed to learn $\boldsymbol{\psi}$, which involves the whole of $\boldsymbol{\phi}$ and hence the whole of $\boldsymbol{\theta}$, necessitating an analysis of the joint distribution.

To treat z_t as exogenous, we must be able to learn everything required about ψ uniquely from ϕ_1 alone. This consideration leads to the first requirement:

$$\text{(i)}\ \ \psi = g(\phi_1)\ \text{alone.}$$

The function $g(\phi_1)$ which determines ψ need not be one–one, and could be many–one, but it is essential that ϕ_1 by itself provides sufficient information from which to learn ψ, and that only ϕ_1 is informative about ψ. To justify taking z_t as given, and hence only analyse the conditional model, a second condition is needed to exclude the possibility that ϕ_1 depends on ϕ_2. Otherwise, more could be learnt about ϕ_1 from ϕ_2, indirectly yielding information about ψ. Thus, we add:

$$\text{(ii)}\ \ \phi_1\ \text{and}\ \phi_2\ \text{are variation free.}$$

Condition (ii) is a statement about the parameter spaces of ϕ_1 and ϕ_2, namely that ϕ_1 and ϕ_2 come from a product parameter space $(\phi_1, \phi_2) \in \Phi_1 \times \Phi_2$ where:

$$\Phi_1 \times \Phi_2 = \{(\phi_1, \phi_2) : \phi_1 \in \Phi_1 \text{ and } \phi_2 \in \Phi_2\}.$$

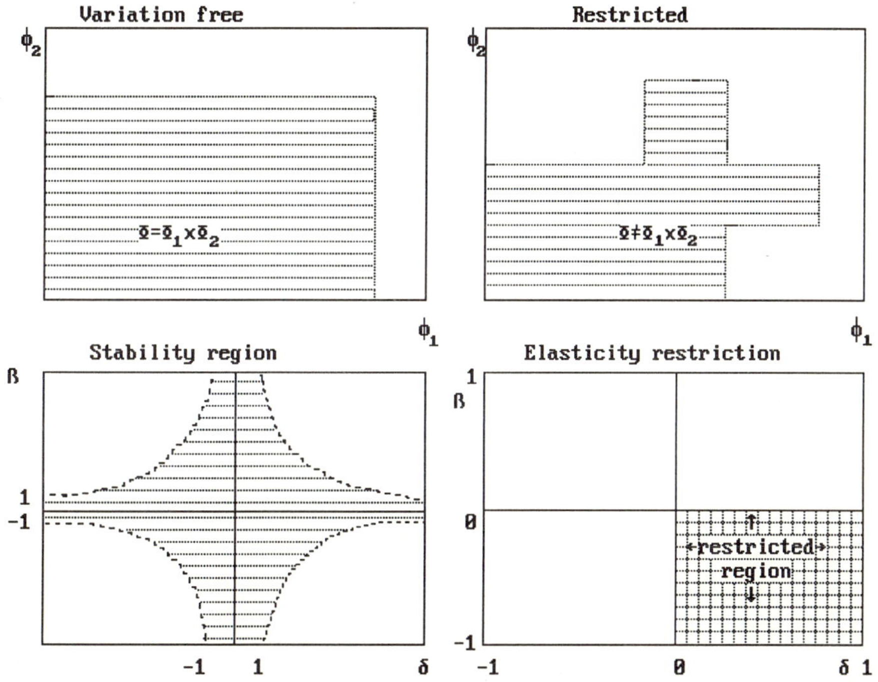

Fig. 5.1 Parameter space restrictions

Figure 5.1a illustrates a cross-product parameter space in which ϕ_1 and ϕ_2 are variation free, whereas Fig. 5.1b violates condition (ii). In Fig. 5.1a, any ϕ_2 from its parameter space Φ_2 can be matched with any ϕ_1 from Φ_1 and that outcome can be used to recover the parameters of the joint density without contradiction. In econometric terms, there are no cross-restrictions linking ϕ_1 and ϕ_2, so that knowledge of ϕ_2 is uninformative about ϕ_1. Figure 5.1b does not allow free choice, since some values of ϕ_2 constrain ϕ_1 more than others. Thus, we define weak exogeneity:

z_t is weakly exogenous for the parameters
of interest ψ if conditions (i) and (ii) hold.

The two conditions (i) and (ii) exclude the possibility that ψ depends on ϕ_2 either directly or indirectly, so nothing can be learnt about the parameters of interest from the marginal model and ψ can be obtained uniquely from the conditional model.

A variable can only be weakly exogenous with respect to a set of parameters of interest. It cannot be exogenous *per se*, which is where the earlier notions went wrong. Further, when z_t is weakly exogenous for ψ, the marginal model can be neglected so the conditional model is complete for purposes of statistical inference (see Koopmans, 1950b). To investigate the implications of this concept in more detail, we consider an economic model then apply its two components to the counter-examples in §5.2. This will highlight the inherent ambiguity in a condition sometimes used to characterize exogeneity, namely the orthogonality of a conditioning variable to an equation error, and also reveal an interesting example of a white-noise error that is not an innovation.

5.4 A cobweb model

Ericsson (1992a) illustrates the concepts of parameters of interest, variation free and weak exogeneity in an economic context using a cobweb model. The model characterizes a market with lags in the production process, and has been used to analyse the demand for and supply of agricultural commodities (see Lehfeldt, 1914, Moore, 1925, Tinbergen, 1930, and Suits, 1955, for early contributions, and Henderson and Quandt, 1971, pp. 142-145, for an exposition).

In the cobweb model, the endogenous and non-modelled variables are usually interpreted as the logs of price and quantity respectively, denoted by p_t and q_t. Using a linear representation, the model is:

$$p_t = \alpha + \beta q_t + \nu_{1t} \text{ where } \nu_{1t} \sim \mathsf{IN}\left[0, \sigma_\nu^2\right] \tag{5.23}$$

$$q_t = \gamma + \delta p_{t-1} + \epsilon_{2t} \text{ where } \epsilon_{2t} \sim \mathsf{IN}\left[0, \omega_{22}\right] \tag{5.24}$$

where $\mathsf{E}\left[\epsilon_{2t}\nu_{1s}\right] = 0 \ \forall t, s$, and δ is the parameter which captures the feedback from p_{t-1} to q_t: the parameter spaces are discussed below. The model in (5.23)–(5.24) has the following interpretation. Equation (5.23) is derived from a demand equation: the price p_t clears the market for a given quantity q_t supplied and the parameter β is the inverse price elasticity of demand. Equation (5.24) is a supply equation representing the quantities that farmers plan to produce in the present year q_t, given the price p_{t-1} of their output in the previous year and the parameter δ is the price elasticity of supply.

The stability of (5.23)–(5.24) as a system is determined by solving for p_t. Substituting (5.24) into (5.23) (see e.g. Christ, 1966):

$$p_t = \mu + \rho p_{t-1} + \epsilon_{1t} \text{ where } \epsilon_{1t} \sim \mathsf{IN}[0, \omega_{11}] \tag{5.25}$$

when $\rho = \beta\delta$ is the root of (5.25). If $|\rho| < 1$, the market is dynamically stable. If $|\rho| = 1$, the market generates prices which oscillate without dampening; and if $|\rho| > 1$, the market is dynamically unstable: see Chapter 4.

Consider how the parameters of interest (again denoted ψ) and the parameter spaces of (5.23)–(5.24) together determine whether or not the current value of q_t in (5.23) is weakly exogenous for ψ. Both conditions (i) and (ii) must be satisfied for weak exogeneity to hold. The parameters of the conditional model (5.23) are denoted by $\boldsymbol{\lambda}_1 = (\alpha : \beta : \sigma_v^2)'$, and those of the marginal model (5.24) by $\boldsymbol{\lambda}_2 = (\gamma : \delta : \omega_{22})'$.

Condition (i) requires that ψ be a function of the conditional model parameters $\boldsymbol{\lambda}_1$ only. When the parameter of interest is the demand elasticity $1/\beta$ alone, this condition is satisfied: β enters $\boldsymbol{\lambda}_1$, and $\boldsymbol{\lambda}_1$ only. Thus, q_t could be weakly exogenous for the elasticity $1/\beta$, depending upon whether or not condition (ii) is satisfied.

When the stability of the system is at issue, the parameter of interest is the root ρ. Then condition (i) is violated, since ρ requires knowledge of both $\beta \in \{\boldsymbol{\lambda}_1\}$ and $\delta \in \{\boldsymbol{\lambda}_2\}$, which necessitates analysing the full system. Thus, q_t is not weakly exogenous for the root ρ even though q_t does not even enter equation (5.25). Choosing the parameter of interest is not an innocuous decision.

Condition (ii) for weak exogeneity requires that the parameters $\boldsymbol{\lambda}_1$ of the conditional model and $\boldsymbol{\lambda}_2$ of the marginal model be variation free, so that $\Lambda = \Lambda_1 \times \Lambda_2$. Ericsson considers three situations where the parameters might or might not be variation free. Throughout, assume that $\sigma_v^2 \in \{\boldsymbol{\lambda}_1\}$ and $\omega_{22} \in \{\boldsymbol{\lambda}_2\}$ are variation free, and that the intercepts are irrelevant, to focus on the parameter space Λ of (β, δ) which is a subset of the plane $\mathbb{R}^2$. The parameter of interest is the demand elasticity $1/\beta$, since we have already established that q_t cannot be weakly exogenous for ρ.

First, suppose that β and δ are unrestricted real numbers. Their parameter space Λ is therefore $\mathbb{R}^2$, the whole real plane. For every value of δ, the parameter β can take any value in the interval $(-\infty, +\infty)$, which is Λ_1 here. The particular value taken by the marginal model parameter δ does not affect the range of the conditional model parameter β, and conversely. Hence, β and δ, and therefore $\boldsymbol{\lambda}_1$ and $\boldsymbol{\lambda}_2$, are variation free. The parameter space Λ is the product space of Λ_1 and Λ_2:

$$\Lambda = \Lambda_1 \times \Lambda_2 = (-\infty, +\infty) \times (-\infty, +\infty) = \mathbb{R}^2 \tag{5.26}$$

Thus, q_t is weakly exogenous for the elasticity $1/\beta$ in the first choice of parameter of interest.

Second, suppose that β and δ are restricted to ensure that the system (5.23)–(5.24) is dynamically stable, so that $|\beta\delta| < 1$. The parameter space Λ is shown in Fig. 5.1c, labelled 'stability region'. The value of δ affects the permissible range of β if stability is to be maintained. For example, when $\delta = 0.5$, then β must lie in the interval $(-2, +2)$, whereas when $\delta = 0.2$, β can lie in the interval $(-5, +5)$. Formally, Λ_1, (the parameter space of $\boldsymbol{\lambda}_1$), depends upon the values of the marginal process parameter δ (or $\boldsymbol{\lambda}_2$). Thus, $\boldsymbol{\lambda}_1$ and $\boldsymbol{\lambda}_2$ are not variation free: the parameter space Λ no longer equals $\Lambda_1 \times \Lambda_2$, the product of the spaces of β and δ. In such a setting, the value of δ is informative about β, even though δ does not determine the specific value of β. Inference using the conditional density (5.23) alone loses information about β from δ in the marginal density, so q_t is not weakly exogenous for the elasticity $1/\beta$.

Third, Ericsson supposes that economic theory could suggest the following restrictions: that the supply elasticity δ lies in the unit interval $[0, 1)$, and that the demand elasticity $1/\beta$ satisfies $-1 \leq \beta \leq 0$. The parameter space Λ appears in Fig. 5.1d as 'elasticity restrictions'. The parameter β must lie in the interval $[-1, 0]$, regardless of the value of δ; and δ must lie in the interval $[0, 1)$, regardless of the value of β. The parameters are variation free since the space in which (β, δ) lies is:

$$\Lambda = [-1, 0] \times [0, 1) = \Lambda_1 \times \Lambda_2.$$

Thus, under the 'elasticity restrictions', q_t is weakly exogenous for the elasticity $1/\beta$. As with parameters of interest, the choice of parameter space is important in determining a variable's status as exogenous or endogenous. These cases illustrate that the parameter space and the parameters of interest are crucial to the exogeneity status of a variable.

5.5 The counter-examples reconsidered

We return to the first counter-example to see what light the definition of weak exogeneity throws on why z_t was not exogenous earlier. The model in (5.3)–(5.9) is the DGP, β is the sole parameter of interest, and $\{z_t\}$ is generated by an equation of the same form as (5.18) so that we can derive an explicit expression for the expected value of z_t given the information set $\mathcal{I}_{t-1}$ in (5.3):

$$z_t^e = \mathsf{E}\left[z_t \mid \mathcal{I}_{t-1}\right] = \alpha z_{t-1}. \tag{5.27}$$

Since (5.27) defines z_t^e, we might try to obtain β by substituting (5.27) into (5.3) and then into (5.6) to obtain the marginal process:

$$y_t = \alpha\beta z_{t-1} + \epsilon_t. \tag{5.28}$$

This is an estimable equation with an innovation error which is independent of z_{t-1}. However, the coefficient of z_{t-1} is $\alpha\beta$. Thus, we need to know α in order to learn β from (5.28); and to learn α, we must model z_t. Hence we must investigate both marginal densities to obtain β, even following this route.

An analysis of the weak exogeneity status of z_t for β requires the conditional distribution of y_t given z_t and the history $\boldsymbol{X}_{t-1}$. Since (5.28) is the process that generates y_t, and by assumption ϵ_t is an innovation against $\boldsymbol{X}_{t-1}$ and is independent of ν_t, then ϵ_t is independent of z_t with $\mathsf{E}\left[\epsilon_t | z_t, \boldsymbol{X}_{t-1}\right] = 0$, and hence:

$$\mathsf{E}\left[y_t \mid z_t, \boldsymbol{X}_{t-1}\right] = \mathsf{E}\left[y_t \mid z_{t-1}\right] = \alpha\beta z_{t-1}. \tag{5.29}$$

Thus, the conditional model (5.29) coincides with the marginal model (5.28) and does not depend on z_t at all. But we could not learn β from (5.28) alone, so that z_t is not exogenous in this model. In terms of conditions (i) and (ii) in §5.3, ψ cannot be obtained from ϕ_1 alone.

The key to understanding exogeneity is commencing the analysis in terms of the joint density of all the observable variables, and not via equations which are incompletely specified statistically. For example, when the economic model is not the conditional expectation of y_t given z_t and $\boldsymbol{X}_{t-1}$ as in (5.29), but is specified as an equation like (5.10) so that:

$$\mathsf{E}\left[y_t \mid z_t\right] = \beta z_t + \mathsf{E}\left[\eta_t \mid z_t\right], \tag{5.30}$$

then by excluding the history $\boldsymbol{X}_{t-1}$, which is in fact what determines y_t, $\mathsf{E}\left[y_t|z_t\right]$ appears to depend on z_t. However, that dependence is indirect, and arises because z_t depends on the lagged zs. Hence, the conditional expectation $\mathsf{E}\left[y_t|z_t\right]$ is some function of z_t, but may not be informative about the parameters of interest and, here, the regression of y_t on z_t does not deliver the parameter of interest β.

From the definition of η_t in (5.10) and the independence between the errors ϵ_t and ν_t:

$$\mathsf{E}\left[\eta_t \mid z_t\right] = \mathsf{E}\left[\epsilon_t \mid z_t\right] - \beta\mathsf{E}\left[\nu_t \mid z_t\right] = -\beta\mathsf{E}\left[\nu_t \mid z_t\right]. \tag{5.31}$$

From (5.12), $\mathsf{E}\left[\nu_t|z_t\right] = \delta z_t$ where from (5.18), $\delta = \left(1-\alpha^2\right)$ so that $\mathsf{E}\left[\nu_t|z_t\right] = \left(1-\alpha^2\right) z_t$. Substitute this last expression into (5.31) then (5.30):

$$\mathsf{E}\left[y_t \mid z_t\right] = \beta z_t - \beta\left(1-\alpha^2\right) z_t = \alpha^2\beta z_t = \gamma z_t, \tag{5.32}$$

as in (5.13). Thus, regressing y_t on z_t estimates $\gamma = \alpha^2\beta$ instead of β.

In relation to the first substantive model, β cannot be obtained by regression of the observed coffee price on observed frost as we must learn α to learn β. Hence, z_t is not weakly exogenous for β. A similar analysis applies to the second counter-example, and it is left to the reader to ascertain which of (i) and/or (ii) of the conditions for weak exogeneity is violated.

5.6 An ambiguity in strict exogeneity

It is of methodological and substantive interest that in a stationary process, no problems need be discovered to suggest invalid conditioning for the regression (5.32) despite falsely assuming that z_t is exogenous. The reason is that the constructed error $\{\eta_t\}$ is orthogonal to z_t by virtue of estimating the regression model:

$$y_t = \alpha^2\beta z_t + \zeta_t = \gamma z_t + \zeta_t, \tag{5.33}$$

so $\mathsf{E}\left[z_t\zeta_t\right] = 0$ by construction. Therefore, there are two models (5.33): one from (5.32) where $\gamma = \alpha^2\beta$ and $\mathsf{E}\left[z_t\zeta_t\right] = 0$ by construction; and one from (5.10) where the coefficient is β but $\mathsf{E}\left[z_t\eta_t\right] \neq 0$. These two equations look alike, except for the vital difference that z_t is correlated with the error in one but not in the other. Is z_t exogenous or not, and does it matter which equation is consulted? One difficulty with an imprecise definition of exogeneity is this ambiguity: whether a variable is exogenous or not may depend on which equation is analysed. When we consider the structural equation (5.10), where z_t is correlated with η_t, then z_t is obviously not exogenous. But when we consult the regression equation (5.33), where z_t is not correlated with the error, z_t is exogenous on the definition that it is uncorrelated with the error. We conclude that it is not possible to define exogeneity in terms of whether a variable is, or is not, uncorrelated with an unobservable error.

The preceding example is one of an infinite class where in one parameterization, the variable is not exogenous, while in another parameterization it might be exogenous depending on the definition of exogeneity. Such problems will persist so long as exogeneity is defined to depend on the cross product between an observable variable intended to be exogenous, and an unobservable variable which can be changed by changing the interpretation of the model. Since the errors are unobservable, we can transform the equation to make the error correlated or uncorrelated with the regressor depending on the parameterization. Therefore, any definition which judges the exogeneity of a variable by its independence from the error, as in Sims (1972), is ambiguous. Conversely, weak exogeneity is the condition under which a reduction due to contemporaneous conditioning involves no loss of information about the parameters of interest and is the condition needed to sustain conditional inference about parameters of interest: Chapter 9 extends this aspect.

The analysis so far has deliberately abstracted from sequential factorization issues in order to focus on the contemporaneous dependence between jointly distributed variables. Consequently, we have not yet established conditions to sustain conditional forecasting or conditional policy and §5.8 and §5.9 will address such issues. Prior to developing additional exogeneity concepts, and linking these to reductions, we digress to investigate the properties of $\{\zeta_t\}$ in (5.33) as an issue of importance in its own right.

5.7 Can the model mis-specification be detected?

Continuing with the example in §5.5 and §5.6, we now examine the properties of ζ_t in (5.33), when the DGP is defined by (5.18) and (5.28):

$$\begin{pmatrix} y_t \\ z_t \end{pmatrix} \mid \boldsymbol{X}_{t-1} \sim \mathsf{N}_2 \left[\begin{pmatrix} 0 & \alpha\beta \\ 0 & \alpha \end{pmatrix} \begin{pmatrix} y_{t-1} \\ z_{t-1} \end{pmatrix}, \begin{pmatrix} \sigma_\epsilon^2 & 0 \\ 0 & \sigma_\nu^2 \end{pmatrix} \right], \tag{5.34}$$

where $|\alpha| < 1$. The parameters of the joint density are $\boldsymbol{\theta} = (\alpha : \beta : \sigma_\epsilon^2 : \sigma_\nu^2)'$ and as in (5.21), can be transformed to $\boldsymbol{\phi} = (\boldsymbol{\phi}_1' : \boldsymbol{\phi}_2')' = ([\alpha\beta : \sigma_\epsilon^2] : [\alpha : \sigma_\nu^2])'$, where $\boldsymbol{\phi}_1$ and $\boldsymbol{\phi}_2$ are the parameters of the conditional and marginal densities respectively, and are variation free despite the dependence of $\boldsymbol{\phi}_1$ on one of the parameters of $\boldsymbol{\phi}_2$. The parameter of interest is $\boldsymbol{\psi} = (\beta)$ and is not a function of $\boldsymbol{\phi}_1$ alone.

Conventionally, there is a different way of interpreting (5.33), namely in terms of omitting the variable z_{t-1}, so that it is a mis-specified equation for the DGP. Since z_t

is autoregressive from (5.34), one might expect to discover that (5.33) is a false model by finding its error ζ_t to be autocorrelated. Surprisingly, $\{\zeta_t\}$ is not autocorrelated, but is instead an example of an error that is white noise, namely is uncorrelated with itself lagged (see §2.25), although it is not an innovation process relative to the available information set $\boldsymbol{X}_{t-1}$, as we now demonstrate.

5.7.1 ζ_t is not an innovation relative to $\boldsymbol{X}_{t-1}$

To prove such a claim, we show that ζ_t depends on at least one observable element of $\boldsymbol{X}_{t-1}$. Since ζ_t is derived by construction from the regression (5.33):

$$\zeta_t = y_t - \gamma z_t \text{ where } \gamma = \alpha^2 \beta,$$

the conditional expectation is:

$$\begin{aligned} \mathsf{E}[\zeta_t \mid z_{t-1}] &= \mathsf{E}[y_t \mid z_{t-1}] - \alpha^2 \beta \mathsf{E}[z_t \mid z_{t-1}] \\ &= \alpha\beta z_{t-1} - \alpha^2 \beta \alpha z_{t-1} \\ &= \alpha\beta\left(1-\alpha^2\right) z_{t-1} \neq 0. \end{aligned} \tag{5.35}$$

Thus, ζ_t is predictable from z_{t-1} and so is not an innovation against $\mathcal{I}_{t-1} = \sigma\left(\boldsymbol{X}_{t-1}\right)$. In fact, from (5.33) and (5.34), since $\zeta_t = y_t - \alpha^2 \beta z_t$:

$$\begin{aligned} \zeta_t &= \alpha\beta z_{t-1} + \epsilon_t - \alpha^2\beta\left(\alpha z_{t-1} + \nu_t\right) \\ &= \alpha\beta\left(1-\alpha^2\right) z_{t-1} - \alpha^2\beta\nu_t + \epsilon_t, \end{aligned} \tag{5.36}$$

so (5.35) is a natural consequence. Although the random walk case $\alpha = 1$ appears to rescue the analysis, in so far as the expression in (5.35) would be zero, these are not germane to the present analysis: I(1) processes are considered in §5.13.

5.7.2 ζ_t is white noise

To prove this claim, first consider the covariance between ζ_t and ζ_{t-1} using (5.36), and noting that:

$$\mathsf{E}[\epsilon_t\epsilon_s] = \mathsf{E}[\nu_t\nu_s] = 0 \;\forall t \neq s;\; \mathsf{E}[\epsilon_t\nu_s] = 0 \;\forall t, s,$$

and

$$\mathsf{E}[\epsilon_t z_s] = \mathsf{E}[\nu_t z_s] = 0 \;\forall t > s.$$

Hence, from (5.36), $\mathsf{E}[\zeta_t\zeta_{t-1}]$ is given by:

$$\begin{aligned} &\mathsf{E}\left[\left\{\alpha\beta\left(1-\alpha^2\right) z_{t-1} + \epsilon_t - \alpha^2\beta\nu_t\right\}\left\{\alpha\beta\left(1-\alpha^2\right) z_{t-2} + \epsilon_{t-1} - \alpha^2\beta\nu_{t-1}\right\}\right] \\ &= \alpha^2\beta^2\left(1-\alpha^2\right)^2 \mathsf{E}[z_{t-1}z_{t-2}] - \alpha^3\beta^2\left(1-\alpha^2\right)\mathsf{E}[z_{t-1}\nu_{t-1}] \\ &= \alpha^3\beta^2\left(1-\alpha^2\right)^2 \sigma_\nu^2/\left(1-\alpha^2\right) - \alpha^3\beta^2\left(1-\alpha^2\right)\sigma_\nu^2 = 0, \end{aligned} \tag{5.37}$$

using (5.34) as all other cross-products vanish. Since $\mathsf{E}[\zeta_t\zeta_{t-1}] = 0$ and $(\zeta_1 \ldots \zeta_T) = \Xi_T^1$ is (jointly) normally distributed, the conditional expectation $\mathsf{E}[\zeta_t \mid \zeta_{t-1}] = 0$ as well. Similarly, $\mathsf{E}[\zeta_t \zeta_{t-2}]$ is:

$$\mathsf{E}\left[\left\{\alpha\beta\left(1-\alpha^2\right)z_{t-1}+\epsilon_t-\alpha^2\beta\nu_t\right\}\left\{\alpha\beta\left(1-\alpha^2\right)z_{t-3}+\epsilon_{t-2}-\alpha^2\beta\nu_{t-2}\right\}\right]$$
$$=\alpha^4\beta^2\left(1-\alpha^2\right)\sigma_\nu^2-\alpha^4\beta^2\left(1-\alpha^2\right)\sigma_\nu^2=0.$$

This result extends to $\mathsf{E}[\zeta_t \zeta_{t-k}]$ for all positive k, so that $\mathsf{E}[\zeta_t | \Xi_{t-1}] = 0$. Such an outcome is surprising given that: z_t is autoregressive; the model depends on the expected value of z_t; the DGP involves z_{t-1}; but we regress y_t on z_t omitting z_{t-1}. Nevertheless, z_t appears to be exogenous in (5.33) in the sense of being orthogonal to ζ_t and the errors are not serially correlated, but are not innovations: by including z_{t-1}, another investigator could develop a better model based on the same data. This is a worrying aspect of that model-building methodology, but is avoidable because it is a consequence of making arbitrary assumptions about exogeneity. As we will see in Chapter 9, an approach built on reducing joint densities circumvents such a problem, as well as resolving several of the other problems we will encounter in Chapters 6 and 7.

5.8 Strong exogeneity

Given the definition of weak exogeneity, we next consider the consequences of the potential dependence of z_t upon $\boldsymbol{Y}_{t-1}$. In (5.22), $\boldsymbol{X}_{t-1} = (\boldsymbol{Y}'_{t-1} : \boldsymbol{Z}'_{t-1})'$, so that the analysis in §5.3 did not preclude the possibility that the marginal density $\mathsf{D}_z(z_t|\boldsymbol{X}_{t-1}, \phi_2)$ depended on $\boldsymbol{Y}_{t-1}$. The definition of weak exogeneity was not concerned with whether or not a change in $\boldsymbol{Y}_{t-1}$ would alter z_t, since we sought conditions that would validate conditional inference despite treating z_t as if it were 'determined outside the model under analysis'. Weak exogeneity is not the only possible notion of exogeneity, but is specifically designed to clarify when a conditional model can be analysed without analysing the marginal model, yet not lose information about the parameters of interest. However, if z_t varies with $\boldsymbol{Y}_{t-1}$ then z_t is not exogenous in the sense of remaining unaltered if the sequence of ys is altered. Thus, weak exogeneity by itself would not be adequate for analyses which need z_t to be unaffected by past ys as, for example, in multi-period conditional forecasting.

Two other concepts of exogeneity can be developed: strong exogeneity and super exogeneity. These play analogous roles for conditional prediction and conditional economic policy respectively to that of weak exogeneity for conditional statistical inference. Weak exogeneity is the basis of all three. However, by itself, weak exogeneity is insufficient to sustain conditional predictions more than one period ahead because z_t may vary with $\boldsymbol{Y}_{t-1}$, nor can it sustain policy statements, where changes in z_t are asserted to induce certain conditional changes in y_t. Those are the senses in which it is weak. Conversely, since conditional predictions and conditional policy changes are activities of interest to economists, we must develop appropriate concepts to sustain them. Section 5.9 will concern super exogeneity; the remainder of this section focuses on strong exogeneity.

The definition of strong exogeneity is:

z_t is strongly exogenous for ψ if z_t is weakly exogenous for ψ and:
(iii) $\mathsf{D}_z(z_t \mid \boldsymbol{X}_{t-1}, \boldsymbol{\phi}_2) = \mathsf{D}_z\left(z_t \mid \boldsymbol{Z}_{t-1}^1, \boldsymbol{X}_0, \boldsymbol{\phi}_2\right)$.

When (iii) is satisfied, z_t does not depend upon $\boldsymbol{Y}_{t-1}$. Thus, strong exogeneity is close to the notion of fixed $\{z_t\}$, but retains the necessary components of the definition of weak exogeneity to avoid the earlier problems. The definition of strong exogeneity entails that we can learn everything we want to learn about ψ conditional on z_t, and that statements about future $\{y_{T+i}, i = 1, \ldots, H\}$ conditional on $\{z_{T+i}, i = 1, \ldots, H\}$ are not vitiated by intermediate y_{T+k} altering $\{z_{T+i}\}$.

The absence of feedback in (iii) is referred to as 'y does not Granger-cause z', following Granger (1969). Such a condition sustains marginalizing $\mathsf{D}_z(z_t|\boldsymbol{X}_{t-1}, \boldsymbol{\phi}_2)$ with respect to $\boldsymbol{Y}_{t-1}^1$, but does not concern conditioning. Consequently, Granger causality is neither necessary nor sufficient for weak exogeneity and cannot *per se* validate inference procedures. This is an important caveat: since $\boldsymbol{\phi}_2$ is unrestricted on both sides of condition (iii), ambiguities can result if Granger causality is used as a basis for testing or policy. For example, the concept of strict exogeneity is defined by Sims (1972) in terms of (iii) alone, and §5.2 and §5.5 above noted the resulting ambiguities. We return to the role of (iii) in §5.11.

Weak exogeneity was defined at a point in time and not with respect to the full sample, but when equation (5.22) holds $\forall t$:

$$\begin{aligned}\mathsf{D}_X\left(\boldsymbol{Y}_T^1, \boldsymbol{Z}_T^1 \mid \boldsymbol{X}_0, \boldsymbol{\theta}\right) &= \prod_{t=1}^{T} \mathsf{D}_x(y_t, z_t \mid \boldsymbol{X}_{t-1}, \boldsymbol{\theta}) \\ &= \prod_{t=1}^{T} \mathsf{D}_{y|z}(y_t \mid z_t, \boldsymbol{X}_{t-1}, \boldsymbol{\phi}_1) \prod_{t=1}^{T} \mathsf{D}_z(z_t \mid \boldsymbol{X}_{t-1}, \boldsymbol{\phi}_2).\end{aligned} \tag{5.38}$$

When z_t is strongly exogenous for ψ, then from (iii):

$$\prod_{t=1}^{T} \mathsf{D}_z(z_t \mid \boldsymbol{X}_{t-1}, \boldsymbol{\phi}_2) = \prod_{t=1}^{T} \mathsf{D}_z\left(z_t \mid \boldsymbol{Z}_{t-1}^1, \boldsymbol{X}_0, \boldsymbol{\phi}_2\right) = \mathsf{D}_Z\left(\boldsymbol{Z}_T^1 \mid \boldsymbol{X}_0, \boldsymbol{\phi}_2\right), \tag{5.39}$$

and hence from (5.38):

$$\mathsf{D}_X\left(\boldsymbol{Y}_T^1, \boldsymbol{Z}_T^1 \mid \boldsymbol{X}_0, \boldsymbol{\theta}\right) = \mathsf{D}_{Y|Z}\left(\boldsymbol{Y}_T^1 \mid \boldsymbol{Z}_T^1, \boldsymbol{X}_0, \boldsymbol{\phi}_1\right) \mathsf{D}_Z\left(\boldsymbol{Z}_T^1 \mid \boldsymbol{X}_0, \boldsymbol{\phi}_2\right). \tag{5.40}$$

The joint distribution factorizes into the product of distribution functions for $\boldsymbol{Y}_T^1|\boldsymbol{Z}_T^1$ and $\boldsymbol{Z}_T^1$, which is far stronger than the sequential factorizations used so far. Consequently, there are two ways to check on (iii): first, $\boldsymbol{Y}_{t-1}^1$ should not influence z_t in the marginal density (5.39); and secondly, future zs should not influence y_t in the conditional density in (5.40) which legitimizes conditioning each y_t on $\boldsymbol{Z}_T^1$ — maintaining the auxiliary belief that the arrow of time runs forwards only. Relating to Chapter A3, weak exogeneity sustains analysing $\mathsf{E}[y_t|z_t] = z_t\beta$, whereas strong exogeneity is needed to sustain the fixed-regressor form that $\mathsf{E}[\boldsymbol{y}|\boldsymbol{Z}] = \boldsymbol{Z}\boldsymbol{\beta}$.

5.9 Super exogeneity

As noted in §5.8, super exogeneity augments weak exogeneity with a condition concerning parameter invariance and hence is intimately related to the existence of structure and is the obverse of the so-called 'Lucas critique' of the use of estimated econometric models for policy analyses (see Lucas, 1976, and Ch.14 for an analysis, noting that Frisch, 1938, Haavelmo, 1944, and Marschak, 1953 all were concerned with that issue). Succinctly, a model cannot be used for policy if implementing the policy would change the model on which that policy was based, since then the policy outcome would not be what the model had predicted.

The property that the parameters of the y and z processes are variation free, which is the basis for weak exogeneity and is an issue within a model, does not rule out the possibility that ϕ_1 may change if ϕ_2 is changed, which is an issue outside the model as specified. This problem occurs because we have not formalized any relationship between ϕ_1 and ϕ_2 at what is sometimes called the level of deep parameters. In §5.7, ϕ_1 and ϕ_2 shared the parameter α, so ϕ_1 would change if $\alpha \in \phi_2$ altered, yet ϕ_1 and ϕ_2 were variation free. A clearer statement about the relationship between ϕ_1 and ϕ_2 is required to define super exogeneity.

An intervention at time t affecting the DGP $\mathsf{D_x}(\boldsymbol{x}_t|\boldsymbol{X}_{t-1},\boldsymbol{\theta})$ is defined as any action $\boldsymbol{\delta}_t \in \mathcal{A}_t$ by an agent from their available action set $\mathcal{A}_t$, which alters $\boldsymbol{\theta}$ from its current value to a different value $\boldsymbol{\theta}_t = \boldsymbol{g}(\boldsymbol{\theta},\boldsymbol{\delta}_t)$. Let $\mathcal{C}^{\delta}(t)$ denote a (possibly limited) class of interventions at time t on $\mathsf{D_x}(\boldsymbol{x}_t|\boldsymbol{X}_{t-1},\boldsymbol{\theta})$ which potentially affect $\boldsymbol{\theta}$, defined by:

$$\mathcal{C}^{\delta}(t) = \{\boldsymbol{\delta}_t : \boldsymbol{\theta}_t = \boldsymbol{g}(\boldsymbol{\theta},\boldsymbol{\delta}_t),\ \boldsymbol{\delta}_t \in \mathcal{A}_t\}.$$

Then, $\mathcal{C}^{\delta} = \{\mathcal{C}^{\delta}(t), t = 1,\dots,T\}$. Possible interventions include changes in monetary, fiscal and exchange rate policies, deregulation, nationalization, wars, inventions, and financial and technological innovations. Since the DGP is the observed economic mechanism, its parameterization can be affected by many forms of intervention. To define invariance of any subset of $\boldsymbol{\theta}$, or its transformation $\boldsymbol{\phi}$, over $\mathcal{C}^{\delta}$, we restrict the class of possible interventions under consideration by limiting the action sets $\{\mathcal{A}_t, t = 1,\dots,T\}$. Those of most relevance in the present setting describe changes in the marginal process brought about by a policy agency which controls ϕ_2. This approach leads to the following definition of invariance:

ϕ_1 is invariant to a class of interventions $\mathcal{C}^{\phi_2}$ if ϕ_1 is constant over $\mathcal{C}^{\phi_2}$.

Such invariant parameters satisfy one of the requirements for structure. The definition of super exogeneity follows:

z_t is super exogenous for ψ if z_t is weakly exogenous for ψ and:
(iv) ϕ_1 is invariant to $\mathcal{C}^{\phi_2}$.

Under super exogeneity, $\phi_2 \in \mathcal{C}^{\phi_2}$ can change without affecting ϕ_1. Since different elements $\phi_2 \in \mathcal{C}^{\phi_2}$ may occur at different points in time, the marginal distributions of the policy variables may be difficult to model, and hence valid conditioning will prove an invaluable asset in empirical modelling.

Super exogeneity requires weak exogeneity but not strong exogeneity. That is a vital weakening of the conditions relative to §5.8 if empirical models are to be useful for economic policy. Because governments monitor what happens in the economy and usually base their policies on the past outcomes of the variables they wish to influence, strong exogeneity is an unlikely condition for policy variables. Thus, we could rarely make valid economic policy statements if super-strong exogeneity was needed (i.e. their joint occurrence).

When all of the parameters of an econometric equation are invariant to the class $\mathcal{C}^{\phi_2}$, then the equation is autonomous, following Frisch (1938) and Haavelmo (1944) (see Aldrich, 1989, for a history of autonomy). A major objective of empirical modelling of economic time series is the discovery of autonomous relationships. At level C, it will prove difficult to ascertain the precise class $\mathcal{C}^{\phi_2}$ over which ϕ_1 is invariant, and Chapter 14 considers testing super exogeneity. The next section illustrates several facets of super exogeneity and both autonomous and non-autonomous equations.

5.10 An illustration of super exogeneity

Consider a generalization of the bivariate normal model introduced in Chapter 4:

$$\begin{pmatrix} y_t \\ z_t \end{pmatrix} \sim \mathsf{IN}_2 \left[\begin{pmatrix} \mu_{1t} \\ \mu_{2t} \end{pmatrix}, \begin{pmatrix} \sigma_{11t} & \sigma_{12t} \\ \sigma_{12t} & \sigma_{22t} \end{pmatrix} \right]. \tag{5.41}$$

The parameters of (5.41) are denoted by $\boldsymbol{\theta}_t \in \Theta_t$ where $\boldsymbol{\theta}_t = (\mu_{1t} : \mu_{2t} : \sigma_{11t} : \sigma_{12t} : \sigma_{22t})'$. To discuss conditions for the weak, strong, or super exogeneity of z_t, the parameters of interest must be specified, usually according to subject-matter theory. Suppose that the economic theory formulation entails:

$$\mu_{1t} = \beta \mu_{2t} \tag{5.42}$$

where β is the parameter of interest. From (5.41) and (5.42):

$$\begin{aligned} \mathsf{E}[y_t \mid z_t] &= \mu_{1t} + \sigma_{12t}\sigma_{22t}^{-1}(z_t - \mu_{2t}) \\ &= \left(\beta - \sigma_{12t}\sigma_{22t}^{-1}\right)\mu_{2t} + \sigma_{12t}\sigma_{22t}^{-1} z_t \\ &= \gamma_{1t} + \gamma_{2t} z_t, \end{aligned} \tag{5.43}$$

where $\gamma_{2t} = \sigma_{12t}\sigma_{22t}^{-1}$ and $\gamma_{1t} = (\beta - \gamma_{2t})\mu_{2t}$. The conditional variance is denoted by ω_t^2 where $\omega_t^2 = \sigma_{11t} - \sigma_{12t}\sigma_{22t}^{-1}\sigma_{21t}$. Thus, the parameters of the conditional and marginal densities respectively are:

$$\phi_{1t} = \left(\gamma_{1t} : \gamma_{2t} : \omega_t^2\right)' \text{ and } \phi_{2t} = (\mu_{2t} : \sigma_{22t})'.$$

When (5.43) is specified as the economic model:

$$y_t = \beta z_t + \epsilon_t \text{ where } \epsilon_t \underset{c}{\sim} \mathsf{IN}\left[0, \omega^2\right] \text{ for } t = 1, \ldots, T \tag{5.44}$$

then four conditions must be satisfied for z_t to be super exogenous for $\left(\beta, \omega^2\right)$:

(a) $\gamma_{2t} = \gamma_2$ is constant $\forall t$;
(b) $\omega_t^2 = \omega^2$ is constant $\forall t$;
(c) $\beta = \gamma_2$, so that z_t is weakly exogenous for β;
(d) ϕ_{1t} is invariant to C^{ϕ_2}.

Conditions (a) and (b) require that $\sigma_{12t}\sigma_{22t}^{-1}$ and $\sigma_{11t} - \sigma_{12t}\sigma_{22t}^{-1}\sigma_{21t}$ are constant over time, but that could occur simply because the σ_{ij} happened not to change. Condition (c) should in principle allow for the possibility that β is not constant even though weak exogeneity holds (see Engle and Hendry, 1993), but that additional complication has been omitted from the present formulation. Then (a)+(c) entail that $\gamma_{1t} = 0$ and hence the conditional expectation in (5.43) is independent of μ_{2t}, which is part of ϕ_{2t}. Condition (d) follows from the earlier discussion. We are not concerned with the existence of feedback from $\boldsymbol{Y}_{t-1}^1$ onto z_t, so the issue of the strong exogeneity of z_t for β does not arise, and remains as in §5.8.

Given that the four conditions (a)–(d) are satisfied, then:

$$\mathsf{E}\left[y_t \mid z_t\right] = \beta z_t, \tag{5.45}$$

in which case z_t is super exogenous for β in this model. There is only one way such an outcome could come about, namely if:

$$\sigma_{12t} = \beta\sigma_{22t} \ \forall t. \tag{5.46}$$

Nothing prevents this population covariance condition from holding, but likewise nothing forces it to hold. When it does occur, then z_t is super exogenous for β. The necessary condition (5.46) entails that the means in (5.42) are interrelated by the same parameter β as the covariances σ_{12t} are with the variances σ_{22t}. Indeed, assuming super exogeneity, the joint density takes the form:

$$\begin{pmatrix} y_t \\ z_t \end{pmatrix} \sim \mathsf{IN}_2\left[\begin{pmatrix} \beta\mu_{2t} \\ \mu_{2t} \end{pmatrix}, \begin{pmatrix} \omega^2 + \beta^2\sigma_{22t} & \beta\sigma_{22t} \\ \beta\sigma_{22t} & \sigma_{22t} \end{pmatrix}\right]. \tag{5.47}$$

Consequently, if z_t is super exogenous for β, then σ_{22t} and μ_{2t} can change without affecting (5.44) which thereby will deliver the correct policy conclusion. More precisely, under the condition of super exogeneity, the parameters (μ_{2t}, σ_{22t}) can change in the marginal model:

$$z_t \sim \mathsf{IN}\left[\mu_{2t}, \sigma_{22t}\right], \tag{5.48}$$

with the agents who determine y_t continuing to act exactly as they planned, and as we anticipated they would. Thus, the model in (5.44) will perform appropriately under super exogeneity for interventions characterized by C^{ϕ_2}: super exogeneity validates conditional policy in this setting.

Conversely, if z_t is not super exogenous for β, then policy scenario analyses may yield misleading conclusions. Super exogeneity may fail for any of three reasons:

(i) z_t is not weakly exogenous for β, in which case the coefficient in a regression of y_t on z_t will not generally coincide with β;

(ii) the regression coefficient is not constant;

(iii) β is not invariant to changes in $\mathcal{C}^{\phi_2}$.
In each case, the predicted changes in y_t may deviate systematically from the outcomes.

Since empirical models do not coincide one–one with the DGP, their parameters are more likely to be susceptible to change than this analysis suggests, and an important question concerns the 'size' of the class of interventions over which empirical model parameters are invariant. One approach to investigating this issue is to test models against a relevant range of historical interventions to establish whether or not invariance occurs. However, an empirical model may remain constant for some interventions yet fail for others and it is hard to tell whether a model is likely to be invariant to interventions that may eventuate. We return to this issue in Chapter 14 once the necessary inference tools have been developed.

A heuristic way to illustrate the difference between the necessary condition of invariance for super exogeneity and that of variation free which sustains weak exogeneity is as follows. In the former:

$$\frac{\partial \phi_{1t}}{\partial \phi_{2t}} = 0. \tag{5.49}$$

Under the variation-free condition, fixed values ϕ_{1t} and ϕ_{2t} are unlinked by cross restrictions, supporting weak exogeneity. For invariance, however, (5.49) highlights that for changing values, ϕ_{1t} and ϕ_{2t} remain unlinked. Thus, (5.49) is a much stronger condition than that of variation free. For example, because of (5.47) and the auxiliary assertion that β is determined in (5.42), then despite $\beta = \gamma_2 = \sigma_{12t}\sigma_{22t}^{-1}$:

$$\frac{\partial \beta}{\partial \sigma_{22t}} = 0. \tag{5.50}$$

This concludes the formal discussion of exogeneity in stationary processes and emphasizes the need for care when formulating equations like (5.44), a point reiterated in the solved examples in §5.12. First, we review the concept of causality, then the final section will focus on the role of weak exogeneity in integrated processes.

5.11 Causality

Two senses of causality will be discussed: §5.11.1 considers that associated with the presence/absence of feedback between variables (Granger, 1969); and §5.11.2 looks at a development of the concept of super exogeneity in terms of 'invariance under interventions' (Simon, 1953). The topic is an intellectual minefield, but some strands merit comment.

5.11.1 Granger non-causality

Let $(\Omega, \mathcal{F}, \mathsf{P}(\cdot))$ denote the probability space supporting the complete vector of variables $\boldsymbol{v}_t$ which characterizes an economy with sample space Ω. Let $\boldsymbol{V}_{t-1}^1 = (\boldsymbol{v}_1 \ldots \boldsymbol{v}_{t-1})$

denote the history of the stochastic process $\{\boldsymbol{v}_t\}$ up till time $t-1$, where $\mathcal{F}_{t-1}$ is the event space. Partition $\boldsymbol{v}_t$ into $(\boldsymbol{w}_t' : x_t')$, where x_t is a scalar, and $\boldsymbol{V}_{t-1}^1$ into $\left(\boldsymbol{W}_{t-1}^1 : \boldsymbol{X}_{t-1}^1\right)$. Consider the joint density:

$$\mathsf{D_v}\left(\boldsymbol{v}_t \mid \boldsymbol{V}_{t-1}, \cdot\right) = \mathsf{D_{x|w}}\left(x_t \mid \boldsymbol{w}_t, \boldsymbol{W}_{t-1}, \boldsymbol{X}_{t-1}, \cdot\right) \mathsf{D_w}\left(\boldsymbol{w}_t \mid \boldsymbol{W}_{t-1}, \boldsymbol{X}_{t-1}, \cdot\right). \quad (5.51)$$

When the marginal density $\mathsf{D_w}(\cdot)$ in (5.51) does not depend on $\boldsymbol{X}_{t-1}$, so that:

$$\mathsf{D_w}\left(\boldsymbol{w}_t \mid \boldsymbol{W}_{t-1}, \boldsymbol{X}_{t-1}, \cdot\right) = \mathsf{D_w}\left(\boldsymbol{w}_t \mid \boldsymbol{W}_{t-1}, \cdot\right), \quad (5.52)$$

then $\boldsymbol{X}_{t-1}$ does not Granger-cause $\boldsymbol{w}_t$. Thus, if, in the universe of information, deleting the history of one variable does not alter the joint distribution of any of the remaining variables, then the omitted variable was defined by Granger (1969) not to cause the remaining variables (here $\boldsymbol{w}_t$). In statistical terms, x is irrelevant to the behaviour of $\boldsymbol{w}_t$.

This definition has several drawbacks. First, and most fundamental, is the need to know the universe of information to ascertain the effect of deleting the history of any one variable. In practice, tests for Granger non-causality (GNC) have often been performed in limited information sets (sometimes bivariate) where the relevance or irrelevance of one of the variables cannot determine its actual relevance in $\mathsf{D_w}(\cdot)$. Further, most empirical tests have been conditional on a host of untested assumptions about other aspects of the model within which the tests were conducted, including parameter constancy, homoscedasticity, linearity in the associated data space, and fixed lag lengths. Other drawbacks to the concept are its dependence on a temporal ordering, so that 'contemporaneous causality' needs a separate construct, and the absence of parameters in the definition, as noted in §5.8 above. The last issue is important because if the conditional distribution of x contains information about the parameters of the marginal distribution in (5.51), and the latter determines the parameters of interest, then eliminating x could lead to a loss of information. Even so, GNC retains a role in the theory of reduction, as will be seen in Chapter 9, independently of any connotations of causality which the concept may have (see Zellner, 1979).

5.11.2 Invariance under interventions

Economic discourse often uses the term causality, in such phrases as 'money causes inflation'; or 'increased interest rates (r) will cause lower demand for durables (d).' Usually, such a notion of cause is based on a well-defined dependence in a theoretical model, such as $d = f(r)$ so that a change in r induces a corresponding change in d. The implication is then applied to the actual economy, however, and it is here that the logic is questionable. Economists are aware of the fallacy of inferring causes from correlations, so the inference process involves deducing from the theory model what observable connections should be present or absent in practice, and the theory model is then tested from the observed correlations. The issue of present concern is deciding when the empirical evidence is sufficiently strong to support claims that any predicted causality has been observed.

It should be clear from the previous chapter that merely corroborating a high correlation is not sufficient; nor is correctly finding the absence of a correlation. As a very contrived illustration related to instrument-validity tests, assume that pink elephants produce all the output in the USA. If so, human agents must be irrelevant, and hence there should be no correlation between changes in GNP and changes in the death rate of human beings. The empirical absence of that correlation hardly proves that pink elephants do produce all US output. Such *non sequiturs* are a trap for naïve corroboration strategies and for methodologies which focus purely on testing the implications of theories (for examples of other paradoxes of corroboration see Ericsson and Hendry, 1989, who draw on Hempel, 1965; Friedman, 1953, is one of the most forceful proponents of instrumentalism).

Granted that we need more powerful criteria, which will suffice? Simon (1953) suggests that the invariance of a relationship under interventions to an input variable provides an operational notion of cause (also see Hoover, 1990, and Cartwright, 1989, who discuss the general issues in an econometric context). Such a concept is close to that of super exogeneity as defined above, augmented by the requirement that a sufficient range of interventions has in fact occurred. Thus, if in the conditional model (5.15):

$$\mathsf{D}_{\mathsf{y}|\mathsf{z}}\left(y_t \mid z_t, \boldsymbol{X}_{t-1}, \phi_1\right),$$

there is a non-zero dependence of y_t on z_t, where z_t is super exogenous for $\psi = \boldsymbol{f}\left(\phi_1\right)$, and ϕ_2 has changed without affecting the conditional relationship between y_t and z_t, then z_t is deemed to cause the resultant changes in y_t. In effect, nature creates the experimental design. The power of any putative test to detect changes in ϕ_1 when ϕ_2 alters depends on the amount of change in the latter, and is a practical matter which does not raise any issue of principle: when changes in ϕ_2 are large and often without affecting $\mathsf{D}_{\mathsf{y}|\mathsf{z}}(\cdot)$, it seems reasonable to conclude that z_t causes y_t.

Given invariance under intervention of this form, the response of y_t to z_t is the same for different sequences $\{z_t\}$, and could sustain policy changes if z_t were under government control. Conversely, an absence of invariance could vitiate the proposed policy. As yet, we have not established whether economic models could have invariant parameters and return to this issue at level C in Chapter 14, when we discuss testing the Lucas (1976) critique. *En route*, we consider forms of econometric models which might meet the conditions required for super exogeneity. Both aspects of causality (constantly operating feedback and invariance under interventions) seem to operate in practice.

5.12 Two solved examples

Because weak exogeneity is such an important concept for empirical modelling, but its verification is not easy even at level A, two solved examples are provided, covering a number of facets of exogeneity and its implications.

Example A

Consider the DGP $\boldsymbol{x}_t|\boldsymbol{X}_{t-1} \sim \mathsf{N}_2\left[\boldsymbol{\pi}\boldsymbol{x}_{t-1}, \boldsymbol{\Omega}\right]$ of $\{\boldsymbol{x}_t : t = 1, \ldots, T\}$ where:

$$\boldsymbol{x}_t = \begin{pmatrix} y_t \\ z_t \end{pmatrix}, \ \boldsymbol{\pi} = \begin{pmatrix} \gamma + \beta\mu & \beta\lambda \\ \mu & \lambda \end{pmatrix}, \ \boldsymbol{\Omega} = \begin{pmatrix} \omega_{11} & \omega_{12} \\ \omega_{12} & \omega_{22} \end{pmatrix}. \tag{5.53}$$

The parameters $(\beta, \gamma, \lambda, \mu, \omega_{11}, \omega_{12}, \omega_{22})$ are variation free beyond ensuring $|\boldsymbol{\Omega}| \neq 0$.

(a) Derive $\mathsf{D_y}(y_t|\boldsymbol{x}_{t-1}, \boldsymbol{\theta}_1)$, $\mathsf{D_{y|z}}(y_t|z_t, \boldsymbol{x}_{t-1}, \boldsymbol{\phi}_1)$ and $\mathsf{D_z}(z_t|\boldsymbol{x}_{t-1}, \boldsymbol{\phi}_2)$. Show that the error variance of $\mathsf{D_{y|z}}(y_t|z_t, \boldsymbol{x}_{t-1}, \boldsymbol{\phi}_1)$ is never larger than ω_{11}. Establish conditions under which z_t is weakly exogenous for (γ, β). Briefly describe the properties of the resulting type of model.

(b) Establish when y does not Granger-cause z and describe how one might test that proposition. Can z_t be strongly exogenous for (γ, β) and how would that outcome affect the estimation or testing of the conditional model?

(c) If ω_{22} is not constant over time, under what conditions is z_t super exogenous for (γ, β)? If the specification of the marginal model for z_t is known (including the time at which ω_{22} changes), what would you investigate to check whether or not z_t is super exogenous for (γ, β)?

(d) Derive an equation in which z_t is predetermined (i.e. uncorrelated with current and future errors) even though z_t is not weakly exogenous for (γ, β). Are the errors in that equation: (i) white noise; or (ii) innovations against $\boldsymbol{x}_{t-1}$?

(Oxford M.Phil., 1987)

Solution

(a) From (5.53) the marginal distribution of y_t is:

$$\mathsf{D_y}(y_t \mid \boldsymbol{x}_{t-1}, \boldsymbol{\theta}_1) = \mathsf{N}\left[(\gamma + \beta\mu)\, y_{t-1} + \beta\lambda z_{t-1}, \omega_{11}\right],$$

so $\boldsymbol{\theta}_1 = (\gamma + \beta\mu : \beta\lambda : \omega_{11})'$. Similarly, the marginal distribution of z_t is:

$$\mathsf{D_z}(z_t \mid \boldsymbol{x}_{t-1}, \boldsymbol{\phi}_2) = \mathsf{N}\left[\mu y_{t-1} + \lambda z_{t-1}, \omega_{22}\right]$$

and hence $\boldsymbol{\phi}_2 = (\mu : \lambda : \omega_{22})'$. Note that $\mathsf{D_x}(\boldsymbol{x}_t|\boldsymbol{X}_{t-1}, \boldsymbol{\pi}, \boldsymbol{\Omega})$ has 7 parameters whereas $\boldsymbol{\theta}_1$ and $\boldsymbol{\phi}_2$ combined only have 6. To obtain $\mathsf{D_{y|z}}(y_t|z_t, \boldsymbol{x}_{t-1}, \boldsymbol{\phi}_1)$ we require:

$$\mathsf{E}\left[y_t \mid z_t, \boldsymbol{x}_{t-1}\right] = (\gamma + \beta\mu)\, y_{t-1} + \beta\lambda z_{t-1} + \omega_{12}\omega_{22}^{-1}\left(z_t - \mu y_{t-1} - \lambda z_{t-1}\right). \tag{5.54}$$

Setting $\omega_{12}\omega_{22}^{-1} = \delta$, and collecting terms:

$$\mathsf{E}\left[y_t \mid z_t, \boldsymbol{x}_{t-1}\right] = \left[\gamma + \mu(\beta - \delta)\right] y_{t-1} + \lambda(\beta - \delta)\, z_{t-1} + \delta z_t. \tag{5.55}$$

Next:

$$\mathsf{V}\left[y_t \mid z_t, \boldsymbol{x}_{t-1}\right] = \omega_{11} - \omega_{12}\omega_{22}^{-1}\omega_{21} = \omega_{11} - \delta^2\omega_{22} = \sigma^2 \leq \omega_{11} \tag{5.56}$$

since $\delta^2 \geq 0$ and $\omega_{22} \geq 0$. Since the conditional distribution is normal when the joint is:

$$\mathsf{D_{y|z}}(y_t \mid z_t, \boldsymbol{x}_{t-1}, \boldsymbol{\phi}_1) = \mathsf{N}\left[\delta z_t + (\gamma + \mu\left[\beta - \delta\right])\, y_{t-1} + \lambda(\beta - \delta)\, z_{t-1}, \sigma^2\right]. \tag{5.57}$$

Consequently $\boldsymbol{\phi}_1 = (\delta : \gamma + \mu(\beta - \delta) : \lambda(\beta - \delta) : \omega_{11} - \delta^2\omega_{22})'$; and $(\boldsymbol{\phi}_1 : \boldsymbol{\phi}_2)$ has 7 parameters.

The conditions under which z_t is weakly exogenous for (γ, β) are that:

(i) (γ, β) must only be a function of the parameters ϕ_1 of the conditional model;
(ii) the parameters ϕ_1 of the conditional model must be variation free from the parameters $\phi_2 = (\mu : \lambda : \omega_{22})'$ of the marginal model.

When $\delta = \beta$, then $\phi_1 = (\beta : \gamma : 0 : \sigma^2)'$ so both (i) and (ii) are satisfied. When $\delta \neq \beta$, the mean of the conditional distribution depends on (μ, λ) so to learn $(\beta : \gamma)$ in that case, we need to know (μ, λ). Thus, the condition for weak exogeneity to hold is $\omega_{12} = \beta\omega_{22}$. The resulting type of model is a partial adjustment, discussed in Chapter 7.

(b) To obtain strong exogeneity, Granger non-causality must be added to weak exogeneity; therefore, in addition to $\delta = \beta$, we need $\mu = 0$. If the series are individually stationary (so $|\gamma| < 1$ and $|\lambda| < 1$ when $\mu = 0$), then conventional tests for Granger causality can be implemented either by adding lagged ys to the marginal model for z or adding future zs to the conditional model for y. Section 5.13 considers tests when the series are non-stationary but cointegrated. If z is strongly exogenous for (γ, β), estimation and testing can be conducted conditional on $\boldsymbol{Z}_T^1 = (z_1 \ldots z_T)$ and not just on z_t, so conditional multi-step forecasts are potentially valid.

(c) If ω_{22t} is non-constant over time, super exogeneity of z_t for the parameters of interest requires $\omega_{12t} = \beta\omega_{22t}\ \forall t$. Super exogeneity can be checked using a Chow (1960) test pre and post the known breakpoint. Recursive stability tests on the estimates of γ and β could be tried, since if the estimates of γ and β remain stable when the marginal process for z_t changes, then z_t is super exogenous for β and γ. A test can also be implemented by specifying the alternative as (e.g.) $\beta = \beta_0 + \beta_1\omega_{22t}$ and testing if $\beta_1 = 0$ (see Engle and Hendry, 1993).

(d) If z_t is not weakly exogenous for (γ, β), then $\delta \neq \beta$ in $\mathsf{E}[y_t|z_t, \boldsymbol{x}_{t-1}]$. The corresponding stochastic equation can be written as:

$$y_t = [\gamma + \mu(\beta - \delta)]\, y_{t-1} + \lambda(\beta - \delta)\, z_{t-1} + \delta z_t + \epsilon_t. \tag{5.58}$$

By construction of a conditional expectation, ϵ_t must be orthogonal to (z_t, y_{t-1}, z_{t-1}). But by the DGP equation (5.53), $\boldsymbol{x}_{t-1}$ is the complete information set in the normal density, so $\{\epsilon_t\}$ must be a mean innovation and hence white noise. Consequently, $\mathsf{E}[\epsilon_{t+i}|z_t] = 0$. An equivalent result would not necessarily hold when the constructed equation in which z_t was predetermined took the form: $y_t = \tau y_{t-1} + \xi z_t + u_t$ (or the special case of that where $\tau = 0$), and generally $\{u_t\}$ would not be an innovation against past zs, violating a requirement for z_t to be predetermined.

Example B

The data-generation process in a certain economy is given by the following two-equation macro model:

$$y_t = \beta\mathsf{E}[z_t \mid \boldsymbol{X}_{t-1}] + \epsilon_{1t} \quad \text{(Private Sector Behaviour)} \tag{5.59}$$

$$z_t = \lambda y_{t-1} + \epsilon_{2t} \quad \text{(Policy Rule)} \tag{5.60}$$

$$\epsilon_t \sim \mathsf{IN}_2\left[\begin{pmatrix} 0 \\ 0 \end{pmatrix}, \begin{pmatrix} \sigma_{11t} & \sigma_{12t} \\ \sigma_{12t} & \sigma_{22t} \end{pmatrix}\right] = \mathsf{IN}_2\left[\mathbf{0}, \boldsymbol{\Sigma}_t\right], \tag{5.61}$$

where $\boldsymbol{X}_{t-1}$ is available information, and β is invariant to changes in the marginal distribution of $\{z_t\}$.

(a) When $\boldsymbol{\Sigma}_t$ is constant, obtain $\mathsf{E}\left[y_t|z_t, y_{t-1}\right]$ and establish the weak exogeneity status of z_t for β.
(b) When $\boldsymbol{\Sigma}_t$ is not constant, obtain $\mathsf{E}\left[y_t|z_t, y_{t-1}\right]$ and establish the super exogeneity status of z_t for β.
(c) If $\sigma_{12t} = 0$: (i) what is the parameter of $\mathsf{E}\left[y_t|z_t\right]$; (ii) is z_t weakly exogenous or predetermined; (iii) and is the parameter of $\mathsf{E}\left[y_t|z_t\right]$ invariant to changes in the parameters of the policy rule?

Solution

(a) Using the two equations (5.59) and (5.60) and the properties of a bivariate normal:

$$\mathsf{E}\left[y_t \mid z_t, y_{t-1}\right] = \beta\lambda y_{t-1} + \sigma_{12}\sigma_{22}^{-1}\left(z_t - \lambda y_{t-1}\right) = \phi z_t + \left(\beta - \phi\right)\lambda y_{t-1}. \tag{5.62}$$

Weak exogeneity requires that $\phi = \sigma_{12}\sigma_{22}^{-1} = \beta$ in which case $\mathsf{E}\left[y_t|z_t, y_{t-1}\right] = \beta z_t$. Otherwise, z_t is not weakly exogenous for β, since the conditional mean depends on λ.

(b) As in (a):

$$\mathsf{E}\left[y_t \mid z_t, y_{t-1}\right] = \beta\lambda y_{t-1} + \sigma_{12t}\sigma_{22t}^{-1}\left(z_t - \lambda y_{t-1}\right) = \phi_t z_t + \left(\beta - \phi_t\right)\lambda y_{t-1}, \tag{5.63}$$

where $\phi_t = \sigma_{12t}\sigma_{22t}^{-1}$. Then, $\phi_t = \beta\ \forall t$ ensures the super exogeneity of z_t for β, which thereby requires that $\sigma_{12t} = \sigma_{22t}\beta$, and hence that ϕ_t is constant over t.

(c) First, we repeat the analysis when $\sigma_{12t} \neq 0$, but from a different perspective. Using (5.60) in (5.59):

$$y_t = \beta\lambda y_{t-1} + \epsilon_{1t} = \beta z_t + \epsilon_{1t} - \beta\epsilon_{2t} = \beta z_t + u_t. \tag{5.64}$$

Now, $\mathsf{E}\left[y_t|z_t\right] = \beta z_t + \mathsf{E}\left[u_t|z_t\right] = \left(\beta + \gamma_t\right) z_t$ where:

$$\gamma_t = \frac{\mathsf{E}\left[u_t z_t\right]}{\mathsf{E}\left[z_t^2\right]} = \frac{\left(\sigma_{12t} - \beta\sigma_{22t}\right)}{\left(\lambda^2\sigma_{y_{t-1}}^2 + \sigma_{22t}\right)} \tag{5.65}$$

and $\sigma_{y_t}^2 = \mathsf{E}\left[y_t^2\right]$. As seen above, when $\sigma_{12t} = \sigma_{22t}\beta$ then $\gamma_t = 0$. However, when $\sigma_{12t} = 0$:

$$\gamma_t = -\frac{\beta\sigma_{22t}}{\left(\lambda^2\sigma_{y_{t-1}}^2 + \sigma_{22t}\right)} \neq 0.$$

unless $\beta = 0$ so:

$$\beta + \gamma_t = \frac{\beta\lambda^2\sigma^2_{y_{t-1}}}{\left(\lambda^2\sigma^2_{y_{t-1}} + \sigma_{22t}\right)},$$

and hence, in general, $\delta_t = (\beta + \gamma_t)$ is not invariant to any policy rule which allows changes in σ_{22}. Moreover:

$$\mathsf{E}\left[y_t \mid z_t, y_{t-1}\right] = \beta\lambda y_{t-1} \neq \mathsf{E}\left[y_t \mid z_t\right],$$

so that z_t is not weakly exogenous for β.
In the constructed equation:

$$y_t = \delta_t z_t + \nu_t,$$

even though $\mathsf{E}\left[\nu_t z_t\right] = 0$, $\{\nu_t\}$ is neither white noise, nor an innovation against available information, since from (5.60) and (5.64):

$$\mathsf{E}\left[\nu_t \mid \boldsymbol{X}_{t-1}\right] = \mathsf{E}\left[(\beta - \delta_t)\lambda y_{t-1} + \epsilon_{1t} - \delta_t\epsilon_{2t} \mid \boldsymbol{X}_{t-1}\right] = (\beta - \delta_t)\lambda y_{t-1} \neq 0,$$

and

$$\mathsf{E}\left[\nu_t\nu_{t-1}\right] = \lambda(\beta - \delta_t)\left[\beta\lambda^2(\beta - \delta_{t-1})\sigma^2_{y_{t-2}} + \sigma^2_{11,t-1} + \beta^2\sigma^2_{22,t-1}\right].$$

Consequently, it is not obvious what it means to ask if z_t is weakly exogenous for δ_t in that equation, especially as δ_t could hardly be deemed a parameter of interest. Finally, since ν_t is autocorrelated, z_t is not predetermined despite $\mathsf{E}\left[\nu_t z_t\right] = 0$ (from conditioning) as:

$$\begin{aligned}\mathsf{E}\left[\nu_{t+1}z_t\right] &= \lambda\mathsf{E}\left[\nu_{t+1}y_{t-1}\right] = \lambda^2(\beta - \delta_{t+1})\mathsf{E}\left[y_t y_{t-1}\right] \\ &= \beta\lambda^3(\beta - \delta_{t+1})\sigma^2_{y_{t-1}} \neq 0.\end{aligned}$$

5.13 Weak exogeneity and unit roots*

Estimation and inference in conditional models of unit-root processes also depend on the validity of the weak and/or strong exogeneity of contemporaneous regressors for the parameters of interest.[2] Following Engle and Granger (1987), many studies have estimated single equations between potentially cointegrated variables. Both static and dynamic models have been considered and a wide variety of outcomes has been found for the behaviour of alternative methods (see, *inter alia*, Stock, 1987, Phillips and Durlauf, 1986, Phillips and Loretan, 1991, Gonzalo, 1989, Banerjee, Dolado, Galbraith and Hendry, 1993, and Kiviet and Phillips, 1992). Formulations of weak exogeneity conditions and

[2] This section is based on Hendry (1994b).

tests for various parameters of interest in cointegrated systems have been discussed by Boswijk (1992), Dolado (1992), Hendry and Mizon (1993), Johansen (1992a, 1992c), Johansen and Juselius (1990) and Urbain (1992) among others. This section considers the effects of the presence and absence of both weak and strong exogeneity for the parameters of interest in cointegrating equations. Section 5.13.1 describes a DGP for two I(1) variables which captures the salient features of the problem. Section 5.13.2 delineates six cases to be investigated. Sections 5.13.3 and 5.13.4 obtain the asymptotic distributions of estimators and hypotheses tests for single-equation conditional linear relations and §5.13.5 notes a Monte Carlo study of their finite-sample behaviour to illustrate the role of weak exogeneity in sustaining valid single-equation inference in cointegrated processes.

5.13.1 A bivariate cointegrated system

Consider the following bivariate DGP for the I(1) vector $\boldsymbol{x}_t = (y_t : z_t)'$:

$$y_t = \beta z_t + w_{1t} \tag{5.66}$$

$$z_t = \lambda y_{t-1} + w_{2t} \tag{5.67}$$

where:

$$\begin{pmatrix} w_{1t} \\ w_{2t} \end{pmatrix} = \begin{pmatrix} 0 & 0 \\ \rho & 1 \end{pmatrix} \begin{pmatrix} w_{1t-1} \\ w_{2t-1} \end{pmatrix} + \begin{pmatrix} \epsilon_{1t} \\ \epsilon_{2t} \end{pmatrix} \tag{5.68}$$

and:

$$\begin{pmatrix} \epsilon_{1t} \\ \epsilon_{2t} \end{pmatrix} \sim \mathsf{IN}_2 \left[\begin{pmatrix} 0 \\ 0 \end{pmatrix}, \begin{pmatrix} \sigma_1^2 & \gamma\sigma_1\sigma_2 \\ \gamma\sigma_1\sigma_2 & \sigma_2^2 \end{pmatrix} \right] = \mathsf{IN}_2 \left[\mathbf{0}, \boldsymbol{\Sigma} \right]. \tag{5.69}$$

The DGP in (5.66)–(5.69) defines a cointegrated vector process in triangular form (see Phillips, 1991), which can be written in many ways, of which the following form is the most useful for our purposes:

$$\begin{aligned} y_t &= \beta z_t + \epsilon_{1t} \\ \Delta z_t &= \lambda \Delta y_{t-1} + \rho \left(y_{t-1} - \beta z_{t-1} \right) + \epsilon_{2t} \end{aligned} \tag{5.70}$$

where $\boldsymbol{\epsilon}_t = (\epsilon_{1t} : \epsilon_{2t})'$ is distributed as in (5.69).

The parameters in the DGP are $(\beta, \lambda, \rho, \gamma, \sigma_1, \sigma_2)$, where:

$\beta \neq 0$ determines cointegration between y_t and z_t;
$\lambda \neq 0$ determines Granger causality of Δy on Δz;
$\rho \neq 0$ determines a failure of weak exogeneity of z_t for (β, σ_1);
$\gamma \neq 0$ determines the presence of contemporaneity; and
σ_2 determines the signal-noise ratio for (5.66).

When $\beta \neq 0$, β and σ_1 can be normalized at unity without loss of generality, as is assumed henceforth, and we also set σ_2 to unity to focus on exogeneity. An investigator is interested in determining the parameter of interest β in (5.66) characterizing the long-run relationship between y_t and z_t.

Letting $\mathcal{I}_{t-1} = \sigma(\boldsymbol{X}_{t-1})$ denote available lagged information, from (5.69) and (5.70), the conditional expectation of y_t given $(z_t, \mathcal{I}_{t-1})$ is:

$$\mathsf{E}[y_t \mid z_t, \mathcal{I}_{t-1}] = \beta z_t + \gamma \Delta z_t - \gamma\rho(y_{t-1} - \beta z_{t-1}) - \gamma\lambda\Delta y_{t-1}. \tag{5.71}$$

For some parameter values in the DGP, the conditional expectation coincides with (5.66), whereas for other configurations, (5.66) and (5.71) differ markedly. In the latter case, it is unsurprising that estimation of (5.66) is not fully informative, and that weak exogeneity is violated. However, in cointegrated I(1) processes, a coincidence between the equation to be estimated and the conditional expectation of the dependent variable given all available information is not sufficient to justify least-squares estimation. This remains so even when the error is an innovation against the complete information set and highlights the role of weak exogeneity in justifying single-equation inference. The analysis illustrates the importance of weak exogeneity failures in this context, and stresses that no serious difficulties arise from either Granger causality alone, or contemporaneity by itself, provided weak exogeneity holds.

5.13.2 Six cases of interest

Six configurations of parameter values will be considered. In the first three, weak exogeneity holds and in the next three, weak exogeneity is violated.

(a) When $\lambda = \rho = \gamma = 0$, (5.66) is a valid regression equation between I(1) variables defined by the conditional expectation:

$$\mathsf{E}[y_t \mid z_t, \mathcal{I}_{t-1}] = \beta z_t. \tag{5.72}$$

Conditions (i)–(iii) in §5.3 and §5.8 are satisfied, so z_t is both weakly and strongly exogenous for the parameter of interest β.

(b) When $\lambda = \rho = 0$ but $\gamma \neq 0$, then (5.66) suffers from 'simultaneity bias' in that z_t and w_{1t} are correlated. A valid regression equation is given by the conditional expectation:

$$\mathsf{E}[y_t \mid z_t, \mathcal{I}_{t-1}] = \beta z_t + \gamma \Delta z_t. \tag{5.73}$$

In (5.73), z_t is both weakly and strongly exogenous for the parameters of interest (β, γ) or β as (i)–(iii) are satisfied. The addition of the impact variable Δz_t 'corrects' for the contemporaneous correlation between ϵ_{1t} and ϵ_{2t}, and restores valid single-equation inference.

(c) When $\rho = \gamma = 0$ but $\lambda \neq 0$, then y Granger-causes z. Now, z_t cannot be strongly exogenous for β, but could be weakly exogenous. The conditional expectation is:

$$\mathsf{E}[y_t \mid z_t, \mathcal{I}_{t-1}] = \beta z_t, \tag{5.74}$$

and the second equation is uninformative about β, allowing single equation inference without loss of information on the basis of (i)–(ii). Equation (5.66) is again correctly specified.

(d) When $\lambda = \gamma = 0$, but $\rho \neq 0$, there is a failure of weak exogeneity of z_t for β, even though the conditional expectation is:

$$\mathsf{E}\left[y_t \mid z_t, \mathcal{I}_{t-1}\right] = \beta z_t. \tag{5.75}$$

Nevertheless, z_t is not weakly exogenous for the parameter of interest β when $\rho \neq 0$ since:

$$\Delta z_t = \rho\left(y_{t-1} - \beta z_{t-1}\right) + \epsilon_{2t}, \tag{5.76}$$

so a more efficient analysis is feasible by jointly estimating (5.66) (or (5.75)) and (5.76). Here, (5.66) coincides with the conditional expectation, but weak exogeneity is violated by a failure of (ii). Below, we investigate the effects of that loss of information.

(e) When $\lambda = 0$ but $\rho \neq 0$ and $\gamma \neq 0$, weak exogeneity of z_t for β is violated, as the conditional expectation becomes:

$$\mathsf{E}\left[y_t \mid z_t, \mathcal{I}_{t-1}\right] = \beta z_t + \gamma\left[\Delta z_t - \rho\left(y_{t-1} - \beta z_{t-1}\right)\right]. \tag{5.77}$$

Condition (ii) is violated. Moreover, in such a situation, correcting for Δz_t as in (5.73) need not improve matters, since $(y_{t-1} - \beta z_{t-1})$ becomes an omitted regressor in place of w_{2t}, thereby replacing a white-noise variable by an autocorrelated one. When $\rho\gamma = -1$, there is a common factor of unity so the equilibrium correction vanishes from (5.77), which holds in first differences. Although y and z are cointegrated (through the marginal process), analysing only the conditional model would now lose all long-run information.

(f) When $\rho = 0$ but $\lambda \neq 0$ and $\gamma \neq 0$, the conditional expectation is:

$$\mathsf{E}\left[y_t \mid z_t, \mathcal{I}_{t-1}\right] = \beta z_t + \gamma\left[\Delta z_t - \lambda \Delta y_{t-1}\right]. \tag{5.78}$$

Condition (ii) is violated and consequently z_t is not weakly exogenous for (β, γ, λ). Nor are regressions of type (5.73) valid either, the omitted regressor now being Δy_{t-1}.

All of the conditional expectations are special cases of (5.71), but in many instances do not coincide with (5.66). Even when the model is the conditional expectation, the validity of weak exogeneity depends on a joint analysis of the system: in each of (d), (e), and (f) correct specification of the conditional expectation is insufficient to sustain single-equation analyses. Here, we only consider estimating cointegrating regressions in the form of (5.66).

5.13.3 Limiting distributions

We consider the special cases (a), (b), (d) and (e) in turn, then examine (c) and (f) (where $\lambda \neq 0$). When $\lambda = 0$ and $\rho \neq 0$, the DGP can be written as:

$$\begin{aligned} y_t &= \beta z_t + u_{1t} \\ \Delta z_t &= u_{2t} \end{aligned} \tag{5.79}$$

where the $\{u_t\}$ error process is first-order autoregressive with a non-singular long-run covariance matrix Ω_u as in §3.10. When $\rho = 0$ but $\lambda \neq 0$, the error process $\{\zeta_t\}$ becomes second-order autoregressive with non-singular long-run covariance matrix Ω_ζ say. Writing the process in differences as:

$$\begin{aligned} \Delta y_t &= v_{1t} \\ \Delta z_t &= v_{2t}, \end{aligned}$$

then because y_t and z_t are cointegrated, $\{v_t\}$ has a singular long-run covariance matrix.

5.13.3.1 OLS Estimation: $\lambda = 0$

(a) When $\lambda = \rho = \gamma = 0$, the OLS estimator of (5.66) is:

$$T\left(\hat{\beta} - \beta\right) = \left(T^{-2}\sum_{t=1}^{T} z_t^2\right)^{-1}\left(T^{-1}\sum_{t=1}^{T} z_t \epsilon_{1t}\right).$$

Using the results in Chapter 3 and Phillips (1986, 1987a):

$$T\left(\hat{\beta} - \beta\right) \Rightarrow \left(\int_0^1 B_2(r)^2 \mathrm{d}r\right)^{-1}\left(\int_0^1 B_2(r)\,\mathrm{d}B_1(r)\right). \qquad (5.80)$$

In (5.80), $B_1(r)$ and $B_2(r)$ are independent standardized Wiener processes derived from $\{u_t\}$ where the long-run variance of $\{u_{2t}\}$ is $\omega_{22} = 1$. Since the normalization of $(\hat{\beta} - \beta)$ is by T, OLS is super-consistent. From Chapter 3, conditional on $B_2(r)$:

$$T\left(\hat{\beta} - \beta\right) \sim \mathsf{N}\left[0, \left(\int_0^1 B_2(r)^2 dr\right)^{-1}\right]. \qquad (5.81)$$

Thus, the distribution of $T(\hat{\beta} - \beta)$ in (5.81) is a linear mixture of normals centred on zero and any finite-sample bias must be $o_p(1/T)$.

(b) When $\lambda = \rho = 0$ but $\gamma \neq 0$, then $\omega_{22} = 1$ and the limiting distribution of $T(\hat{\beta} - \beta)$ is:

$$\left(\int_0^1 B_2(r)^2 \mathrm{d}r\right)^{-1}\left[\left(1-\gamma^2\right)^{\frac{1}{2}}\int_0^1 B_2(r)\mathrm{d}B_1(r) + \gamma\left\{\int_0^1 B_2(r)\mathrm{d}B_2(r) + 1\right\}\right]. \qquad (5.82)$$

The term inside $\{\cdot\}$ in (5.82) is $\frac{1}{2}(\chi^2(1) + 1)$. The first term in $[\cdot]$ is a mixture of normals but scaled by $\surd(1-\gamma^2)$, so relative to (a), when $\gamma > 0$, the distribution is shifted rightwards and is non-normal. The conventional coefficient standard error based on:

$$\hat{\sigma}_1\left(\sum_{t=1}^{T} z_t^2\right)^{-\frac{1}{2}}$$

no longer correctly estimates the sampling standard deviation, and hypothesis tests could be distorted as shown below.

(d) When $\lambda = \gamma = 0$ but $\rho \neq 0$, then $\omega_{22} = 1 + \rho^2$, so the limiting distribution of $T(\hat{\beta} - \beta)$ becomes:

$$\left(\int_0^1 B_2(r)^2 \mathrm{d}r\right)^{-1} (1+\rho^2)^{-1} \left[\int_0^1 B_2(r)\mathrm{d}B_1(r) + \rho \int_0^1 B_2(r)\mathrm{d}B_2(r)\right]. \quad (5.83)$$

Note that:

$$DF_\alpha = \left(\int_0^1 B_2(r)^2 \mathrm{d}r\right)^{-1} \int_0^1 B_2(r)\mathrm{d}B_2(r) \quad (5.84)$$

is the Dickey and Fuller (1979, 1981) $T(\hat{\alpha} - 1)$ distribution for testing for a unit root ($\alpha = 1$) in the univariate marginal process for $\{z_t\}$. Thus, (5.83) is a mixture of the normal and Dickey–Fuller distributions, and for sufficiently large $\rho > 0$, the last term will impart a negative shift to the distribution (conversely for negative ρ). Again, inference is liable to be distorted.

(e) When $\lambda = 0$ but $\gamma \neq 0$ and $\rho \neq 0$, then $\omega_{22} = 1 + 2\gamma\rho + \rho^2$, so the limiting distribution of $T(\hat{\beta} - \beta)$ is:

$$\begin{aligned}&\left(\textstyle\int_0^1 B_2(r)^2 \mathrm{d}r\right)^{-1} \left[\left(\frac{(1-\gamma^2)^{\frac{1}{2}}}{\omega_{22}}\right) \textstyle\int_0^1 B_2(r)\mathrm{d}B_1(r)\right] \\ &+ \left(\textstyle\int_0^1 B_2(r)^2 \mathrm{d}r\right)^{-1} \left[\left(\frac{(\gamma+\rho)}{\omega_{22}}\right) \textstyle\int_0^1 B_2(r)\mathrm{d}B_2(r) + \frac{\gamma}{\omega_{22}}\right].\end{aligned} \quad (5.85)$$

The terms in $\omega_{22}^{-1}\left[\frac{1}{2}(\gamma+\rho)\left(\chi^2(1) - 1\right) + \gamma\right]$ will partially offset each other, so having both a failure of weak exogeneity and simultaneity may induce less distortion in practice than either alone. This matches the conclusions in (b) and (d) that the two cases ($\gamma \neq 0,\ \rho = 0$) and ($\gamma = 0,\ \rho \neq 0$) cause different directions of skewness to the limiting distribution.

When $\gamma = -\rho$, then $\gamma + \rho = 0$ which creates a diagonal long-run covariance matrix, but from (5.85) such a condition is not sufficient to sustain weak exogeneity, since at the point $\gamma = -\rho$:

$$T\left(\hat{\beta} - \beta\right) \Rightarrow \left(\int_0^1 B_2(r)^2 \mathrm{d}r\right)^{-1} \left[\left(\omega_{22}^{-1}\left(1-\gamma^2\right)^{\frac{1}{2}}\right) \int_0^1 B_2(r)\mathrm{d}B_1(r) + \frac{\gamma}{\omega_{22}}\right], \quad (5.86)$$

inducing limiting non-normality (compare Dolado, 1992). Also, correcting for 'simultaneity' by adding Δz_t as a regressor will be more or less successful depending on the parameters of the DGP. For example, in (a), the outcome is unaltered; in (b), a distinct improvement will occur relative to (5.82) because the distribution reverts to a mixture of normals, matching the weak exogeneity of z_t for the parameters of the conditional model (5.73); in (d), there is no change from the conclusions for (5.66); and in (e), the (left) skewness in the distribution could be exacerbated by correcting one of the two 'problems'.

5.13.3.2 OLS Estimation: $\rho = 0$

Now we turn to the cases (c) and (f) where $\rho = 0$ but $\lambda \neq 0$. A similar analysis to (5.85) applies.

(c) When $\rho = \gamma = 0$ but $\lambda \neq 0$, the limiting distribution of $T(\hat{\beta} - \beta)$ becomes:

$$T\left(\hat{\beta} - \beta\right) \Rightarrow (1 - \beta\lambda) \left(\int_0^1 B_2(r)^2 \mathrm{d}r\right)^{-1} \left(\int_0^1 B_2(r)\mathrm{d}B_1(r)\right). \quad (5.87)$$

Thus, despite the fact that y Granger-causes z, since $B_1(r)$ and $B_2(r)$ are independent Wiener processes, the distribution of the OLS estimator is a mixture of normals, centred on zero. The violation of strong exogeneity, when weak exogeneity is maintained, does not seriously affect inference in this unit-root model. Conditional on $B_2(r)$:

$$T\left(\hat{\beta} - \beta\right) \sim \mathsf{N}\left[0, (1 - \beta\lambda)^2 \left(\int_0^1 B_2(r)^2 \mathrm{d}r\right)^{-1}\right]. \quad (5.88)$$

(f) When $\rho = 0$ but $\lambda \neq 0$ and $\gamma \neq 0$, then weak exogeneity is violated and the limiting distribution of $T\left(\hat{\beta} - \beta\right)$ is:

$$\begin{aligned} &(1 - \beta\lambda) \left(\textstyle\int_0^1 B_2(r)^2 \mathrm{d}r\right)^{-1} \left[\left(1 - \gamma^2\right)^{\frac{1}{2}} \textstyle\int_0^1 B_2(r)\mathrm{d}B_1(r)\right] \\ &+\gamma (1 - \beta\lambda) \left(\textstyle\int_0^1 B_2(r)^2 \mathrm{d}r\right)^{-1} \left(\textstyle\int_0^1 B_2(r)\mathrm{d}B_2(r) + (1 - \beta\lambda)\right). \end{aligned} \quad (5.89)$$

Here, the $B_i(r)$ are associated with $\{\zeta_t\}$. As with (5.85), we find a mixture of a conditionally normal and a Dickey–Fuller distribution in (5.89), as well as a non-centrality effect when $\gamma \neq 0$, although the last two terms could partially offset each other. Inference could be seriously distorted, as investigated in §5.13.4.

5.13.4 Inference

We now consider tests of specification hypotheses of the form H_0: $\beta = \beta^*$ in the six cases.

5.13.4.1 Inference: $\lambda = 0$

(a) When $\lambda = \rho = \gamma = 0$, we can show that the error variance estimator is consistent:

$$\hat{\sigma}_1^2 = T^{-1} \sum_{t=1}^{T} \left(y_t - \hat{\beta} z_t\right)^2 = T^{-1} \sum_{t=1}^{T} \left(w_{1t} - T\left(\hat{\beta} - \beta\right) T^{-1} z_t\right)^2 \Rightarrow \sigma_1^2 \quad (5.90)$$

since the terms involving z_t are asymptotically negligible. This result is true independently of ρ and γ. Thus, from (5.81), the t-test of H_0: $\beta = \beta^*$ based on

$\mathsf{t}_{\beta=\beta*} = (\hat{\beta} - \beta^*)/\mathsf{SE}[\hat{\beta}]$ is:

$$\mathsf{t}_{\beta=\beta*} = \left(T^{-2}\sum_{t=1}^{T} z_t^2\right)^{-\frac{1}{2}} \left(\frac{T\left(\hat{\beta} - \beta^*\right)}{\hat{\sigma}_1}\right) \Rightarrow \mathsf{N}\left[0,1\right] \tag{5.91}$$

and so is asymptotically N[0, 1] when the null is true.

(b) When $\lambda = \rho = 0$ but $\gamma \neq 0$, the bias in the limiting distribution of $T(\hat{\beta} - \beta)$ in (5.82) is $O_p(T^{-1})$ and hence is negligible in large samples. However, the impact on inference does not vanish even asymptotically, since:

$$\mathsf{t}_{\beta=\beta*} \Rightarrow \left(1 - \gamma^2\right)^{\frac{1}{2}} \mathsf{N}\left[0,1\right] + \gamma DF_{\mathrm{t}} + \gamma \left(\int_0^1 B_2(r)^2 \mathrm{d}r\right)^{-\frac{1}{2}}. \tag{5.92}$$

Compared to (a), when $\gamma \neq 0$, the distribution in (5.92) is non-normal and conventional hypothesis tests will not have the correct size.

(d) When $\lambda = \gamma = 0$ but $\rho \neq 0$, the $\mathsf{t}_{\beta=\beta*}$ statistic will again not have an asymptotic normal distribution:

$$\mathsf{t}_{\beta=\beta*} \Rightarrow \left(1 + \rho^2\right)^{-1} \left(\mathsf{N}\left[0,1\right] + \rho DF_{\mathrm{t}}\right). \tag{5.93}$$

This is a weighted average of the normal and Dickey–Fuller 't' distribution:

$$DF_{\mathrm{t}} = \left(\int_0^1 B_2(r)^2 \mathrm{d}r\right)^{-\frac{1}{2}} \int_0^1 B_2(r) \mathrm{d}B_2(r). \tag{5.94}$$

(e) When $\lambda = 0$ but $\gamma \neq 0$ and $\rho \neq 0$, from (5.85), a result like (5.92) occurs with different weights for the three components.

5.13.4.2 Inference: $\rho = 0$

(c) When $\rho = \gamma = 0$ but $\lambda \neq 0$, from (5.88), t-tests of H_0 will be asymptotically $\mathsf{N}\left[0,1\right]$.

(f) When $\rho = 0$ but $\lambda \neq 0$ and $\gamma \neq 0$, as in (5.92) the same three terms recur from (5.89), but with new weights.

The Monte Carlo evidence in the next subsection reveals how badly distorted inference may be and well the asymptotic results describe finite-sample outcomes for both estimation and inference.

5.13.5 A Monte Carlo study

The Monte Carlo study used the DGP in (5.66)–(5.69), for specific values of the parameters (λ, ρ, γ) where $\beta = \sigma_1 = \sigma_2 = 1$. The study was undertaken recursively using PcNaive with 10 000 replications across sample sizes $T = 20, \ldots, 100$. Numerical values of the parameters were selected to illustrate the theoretical derivations and comprised combinations of λ, ρ, and γ from (0; 0.5) to cover the six cases (a)–(f).

(a) OLS is well behaved, being both mean and median unbiased, with about a 5 per cent rejection frequency of the hypothesis that $\beta = 1$.

(b) The cross-correlation between the errors in the DGP induces a noticeable positive bias in OLS, matching (5.84), with substantial skewness. This leads to considerable over-rejection of the correct null that $\beta = 1$. However, z_t is strongly exogenous for the parameters in (5.73), so single-equation inference need lose no relevant information when a properly specified model is used.

(d) The bias in OLS is negative and opposite to (b), matching (5.81). Again, there is considerable over-rejection of the correct null on β. Figure 5.2 records the standardized frequency distribution to illustrate the skewness. The model coincides with the conditional expectation, but z_t is not weakly exogenous for the parameters in (5.66) or (5.73). Thus, the information loss from ignoring the marginal model in (5.70) is marked and distorts several aspects of inference.

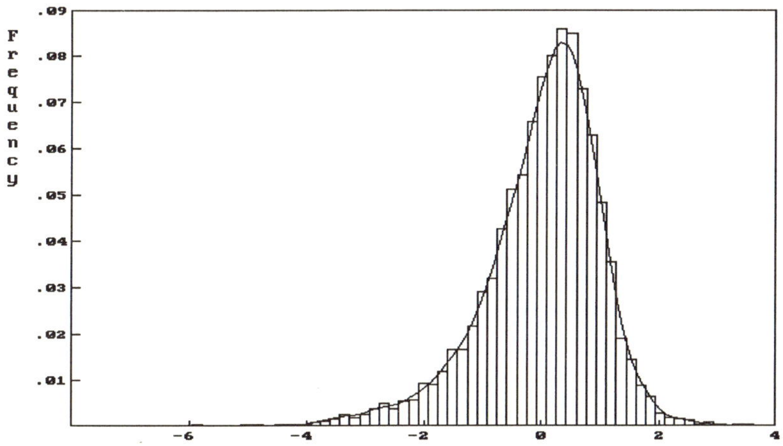

Fig. 5.2 Standardized frequency distribution of OLS biases in case (d)

(e) Now weak exogeneity is violated, yet OLS is nearly mean and median unbiased. Such an outcome is explained by the partial offset of the terms in (5.85) for the parameter values chosen. However, inference is distorted as the null rejection frequency of the 't'-test of $\beta^* = 1$ is very low.

We now consider the cases where $\rho = 0$ but $\lambda \neq 0$, so strong exogeneity cannot occur.

(c) When $\gamma = 0$, there is a slight mean bias in OLS, but inference is well behaved. Since weak exogeneity of z_t for β holds, and (5.87) shows that OLS is asymptotically a mixture of normals, the bias is analogous to that which occurs in finite sample when estimating stationary dynamic models.

(f) This is again an enigma at first sight as OLS is nearly mean and median unbiased, although the test size is low. The outcome matches the offset anticipated from (5.89) which attenuates the slight bias in (c) above.

Figures 5.3a,b record the biases in experiments (a), (b), (d), (e); and (c), (f) respectively. The substantial impact of the design variables on the biases is clear, as is the convergence of the biases to zero and the wide range of outcomes generated (positive biases have been plotted after a sign change to focus on absolute magnitudes). Since the estimated model is small, $T = 100$ is a 'large' sample, so the outcomes at the smaller sample sizes (e.g. 40–60) may be more representative of empirical behaviour.

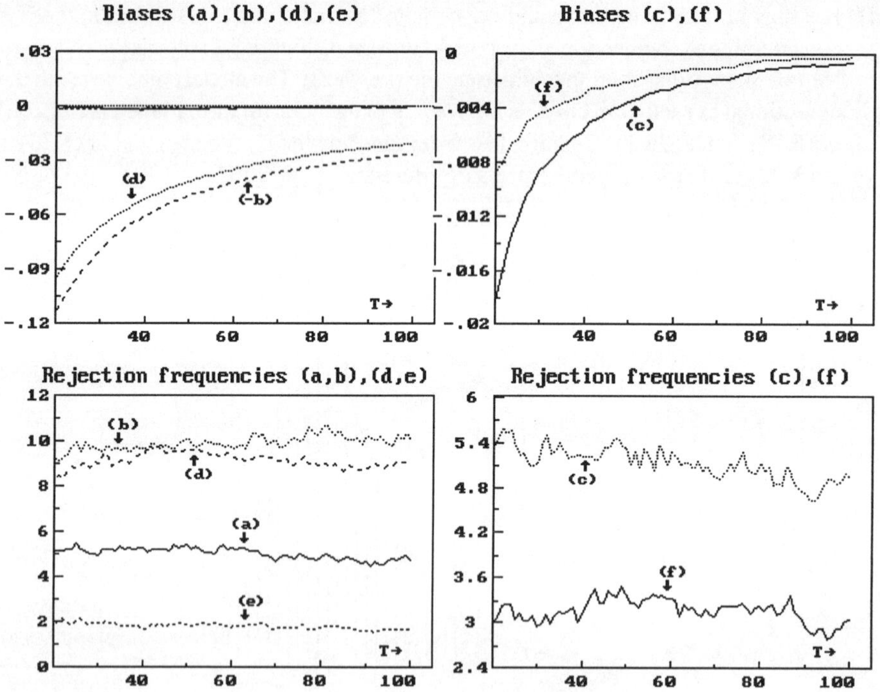

Fig. 5.3 Recursively computed biases and rejection frequencies

As both figures show, the biases are rather large at the smallest samples in cases (b) and (d). The unlabelled lines in 5.3a are for (a) and (d) where the biases are negligible throughout (under 2 per cent). The bias lines never cross, so conclusions about relative biases are relevant at all the sample sizes studied, and the differences between biases are significant. For $T \geq 50$ and the parameter values chosen, no biases exceed 10 per cent. However, the parameter points selected are not extreme and provide a relatively favourable state for methods which violate weak exogeneity: $\gamma\rho = -0.8$ in (5.71) would be more realistic, and would generate larger biases than those shown.

A less hopeful conclusion holds for inference when weak exogeneity fails. Although the non-centrality of the limiting distribution of the estimator only induces biases of $O_p\left(T^{-1}\right)$ which vanish quite rapidly in practice as Figs. 5.3a,b reveal, the biases are of the same order as the estimated standard errors and hence inference is liable to be distorted. This can be seen in Figs. 5.3c,d which plot the rejections of the correct null hypothesis of H_0: $\beta = 1$ using conventional t-tests at the 5 per cent significance level, in cases (a), (b), (d), (e); and (c) and (f) respectively. There is no tendency for the sizes of the tests to diverge from (converge on) 0.05 when weak exogeneity is present (absent). Despite the small bias in (e), the size is well below 5 per cent; whereas the biases in (b) and (d) induce over-rejection. Thus, inference can be distorted in practice when weak exogeneity fails to hold or the model is incorrectly specified in its I(0) components.

These results illustrate the impact of weak exogeneity failures in integrated data. Granger causality does not seriously impede inference when weak exogeneity holds, so strong exogeneity is not necessary to sustain inference. However, in cointegrated processes even when the model under analysis coincides with the conditional expectation, the absence of weak exogeneity can have adverse effects on estimation in small samples, and on inference both asymptotically and in small samples. Weak exogeneity seems to be at least as relevant in I(1) as in stationary processes as the basis for inference with no loss of relevant information.

5.14 Exercises

5.1 Consider the DGP $\boldsymbol{x}_t|\boldsymbol{x}_{t-1} \sim \mathsf{N}_2[\boldsymbol{\pi}\boldsymbol{x}_{t-1}, \boldsymbol{\Omega}]$ where:

$$\boldsymbol{x}_t = \begin{pmatrix} y_t \\ z_t \end{pmatrix}, \quad \boldsymbol{\pi} = \begin{pmatrix} \beta_1 & \beta_2\beta_3 \\ \beta_2 & 0 \end{pmatrix}, \quad \boldsymbol{\Omega} = \begin{pmatrix} \omega_{11} & \omega_{12} \\ \omega_{12} & \omega_{22} \end{pmatrix}. \tag{5.95}$$

(a) Derive a conditional model for y_t given z_t and $\boldsymbol{x}_{t-1}$, and establish that its error variance is never larger than ω_{11}. Under what conditions is z_t weakly exogenous for (β_1, β_3)?
(b) Under what conditions is z_t strongly exogenous for (β_1, β_3)?
(c) Derive an equation in which z_t is predetermined (i.e. uncorrelated with current and past errors) even though z_t is not weakly exogenous for (β_1, β_3). Are the errors in that equation: (i) white noise; or (ii) innovations against $\boldsymbol{x}_{t-1}$?

(Oxford M.Phil., 1982)

5.2 Consider the system:

$$\begin{aligned} y_t &= \beta z_t + u_t \\ u_t &= \rho u_{t-1} + \epsilon_{1t} \\ z_t &= \alpha y_{t-1} + \epsilon_{2t} \end{aligned} \tag{5.96}$$

where

$$\begin{pmatrix} \epsilon_{1t} \\ \epsilon_{2t} \end{pmatrix} \sim \mathsf{IN}_2\left[\begin{pmatrix} 0 \\ 0 \end{pmatrix}, \begin{pmatrix} \sigma_{11} & \sigma_{12} \\ \sigma_{12} & \sigma_{22} \end{pmatrix}\right], \tag{5.97}$$

with $|\rho| < 1$.
(a) Is z_t predetermined in (5.96)?
(b) Derive a form of equation in which z_t is predetermined.

(c) Is z_t weakly exogenous for β when $\rho \neq 0$? (Hint: can you derive β uniquely and unrestrictedly from $\mathsf{E}[y_t|z_t, y_{t-1}, z_{t-1}]$?).
(d) Under what conditions is z_t strongly exogenous for β?
(e) Under what conditions is z_t strictly exogenous in (5.96)?
(f) If z_t is predetermined in (5.96) when $\sigma_{12} \neq 0$, show that $\beta = \mathsf{E}[y_t z_t] / \mathsf{E}[z_t^2]$. What is the economic rationale for the resulting model? Hence (or otherwise) show that $\mathsf{E}[z_t u_{t-1}] \neq 0$, so that 'taking account' of the autocorrelation in (5.97) must now yield inconsistent estimates of β. (Hint: first show $\mathsf{E}[z_t \epsilon_{1t}] \neq 0$.)
(g) If $\rho = 0$, under what conditions is z_t weakly exogenous for β? Comment on this type of model, and its economic interpretation (See Engle *et al.*, 1983).
(h) Test for Granger causality between *CONS* and *INC*; and between *OUTPUT* and *INFLAT*. What do you conclude in each case? Does the length of lag used matter? Does the sample period selected matter? Would the unknown existence of other Granger-causality links alter the results in a substantive way (e.g. reverse your conclusions)? Did you test for any other cross-connections? In both directions?
(i) Repeat (h) for the UKM1 data-set, using M/P_t and Y_t; R_t and $\Delta \log P_t$.

(Oxford M.Phil., 1985, extended)

5.3 Consider the stationary process $\boldsymbol{x}_t|\boldsymbol{x}_{t-1} \sim \mathsf{N}_2[\boldsymbol{\pi}\boldsymbol{x}_{t-1}, \boldsymbol{\Omega}]$ where:

$$\boldsymbol{x}_t = \begin{pmatrix} y_t \\ z_t \end{pmatrix}, \quad \boldsymbol{\pi} = \begin{pmatrix} \lambda_1 & \lambda_3 + \lambda_2 - \lambda_1\lambda_2 \\ \lambda_3 & 1 - \lambda_3 \end{pmatrix}, \quad \boldsymbol{\Omega} = \begin{pmatrix} \omega_{11} & \omega_{12} \\ \omega_{12} & \omega_{22} \end{pmatrix}.$$

(a) What conditions are needed to ensure that $\{\boldsymbol{x}_t\}$ is stationary?
(b) What are $\mathsf{E}[\boldsymbol{x}_t\boldsymbol{x}_t']$ and $\mathsf{E}[\boldsymbol{x}_t\boldsymbol{x}_{t-1}']$ when $\{\boldsymbol{x}_t\}$ is stationary?
(c) Derive $\mathsf{E}[y_t|z_t, \boldsymbol{x}_{t-1}]$. What kind of model is this?
(d) Is z_t weakly exogenous for (λ_1, λ_2)? Is it strongly exogenous? Are there values of (λ_3, ω_{12}) for which z_t is strongly exogenous? If so, what is the resulting model form?

(Oxford M.Phil., 1983)

5.4 Consider the data generation process $\boldsymbol{x}_t|\boldsymbol{x}_{t-1} \sim \mathsf{N}_2[\boldsymbol{\pi}\boldsymbol{x}_{t-1}, \boldsymbol{\Omega}]$ where:

$$\boldsymbol{x}_t = \begin{pmatrix} y_t \\ z_t \end{pmatrix}, \boldsymbol{\pi} = \begin{pmatrix} 1-\gamma\lambda & \gamma \\ 1-\lambda & \lambda \end{pmatrix}, \boldsymbol{\Omega} = \begin{pmatrix} \sigma_{11} + 2\gamma\sigma_{12} + \gamma^2\sigma_{22} & \sigma_{12} + \gamma\sigma_{22} \\ \sigma_{12} + \gamma\sigma_{22} & \sigma_{22} \end{pmatrix}.$$

(a) Derive $\mathsf{E}[y_t|z_t, \boldsymbol{x}_{t-1}]$ and establish the conditions under which z_t is weakly exogenous for γ.
(b) What type of model results if: (i) z_t is weakly exogenous for γ; (ii) z_t is not weakly exogenous for γ?
(c) Establish when z_t is strongly exogenous for γ, and explain how to test that proposition. Would finding that z_t is strongly exogenous affect the statistical properties of estimators of γ?

(Oxford M.Phil., 1986)

5.5 In the data-generation process $\boldsymbol{x}_t|\boldsymbol{x}_{t-1} \sim \mathsf{N}_2[\boldsymbol{\pi}\boldsymbol{x}_{t-1}, \boldsymbol{\Omega}]$ where:

$$\boldsymbol{x}_t = \begin{pmatrix} y_t \\ z_t \end{pmatrix}, \ \boldsymbol{\pi} = \begin{pmatrix} 1-\gamma+\beta\mu & \gamma-\beta(1-\lambda) \\ \mu & \lambda \end{pmatrix}, \ \boldsymbol{\Omega} = \begin{pmatrix} \omega_{11} & \omega_{12} \\ \omega_{12} & \omega_{22} \end{pmatrix}.$$

(a) Derive $\mathsf{E}[y_t|z_t, x_{t-1}]$ and establish the conditions under which z_t is weakly exogenous for (γ, β).

(b) If $\Delta_1 y_t = y_t - y_{t-1}$, and it is asserted by an investigator that $\Delta_1 y_t = \alpha\Delta_1 z_t + \epsilon_t$ where $\mathsf{E}[\Delta_1 z_t \epsilon_t] = 0 \ \forall t$, what is $\mathrm{plim}_{T\to\infty}\tilde{\alpha}$ (where $\tilde{}$ denotes a least-squares estimator)? Under what conditions is $\tilde{\alpha}$ consistent for β (you may assume that the latent roots of $\boldsymbol{\pi}$ have modulus less than unity)?

(c) Comment on the formulation of the models in (a) and (b). Establish when z does not Granger-cause y and explain how you would test that proposition.

(Oxford M.Phil., 1984)

5.6 Consider the three-dimensional vector random variable $\boldsymbol{w}_t = (y_t, x_t, z_t)'$ with the joint distribution $\mathsf{D}_\mathsf{w}(\boldsymbol{w}_t|\boldsymbol{w}_{t-1}; \boldsymbol{\pi}, \boldsymbol{\Sigma})$ given by $\boldsymbol{w}_t|\boldsymbol{w}_{t-1} \sim \mathsf{N}_3[\boldsymbol{\pi}\boldsymbol{w}_{t-1}, \boldsymbol{\Sigma}]$ where:

$$\boldsymbol{\pi} = \begin{pmatrix} 0 & \alpha & \gamma \\ 0 & \delta & \theta \\ 0 & 0 & \mu \end{pmatrix} \text{ and } \boldsymbol{\Sigma} = \begin{pmatrix} \sigma_{11} & \sigma_{12} & \sigma_{13} \\ \sigma_{12} & \sigma_{22} & \sigma_{23} \\ \sigma_{13} & \sigma_{23} & \sigma_{33} \end{pmatrix}.$$

(a) Derive $\mathsf{E}[y_t|z_t, \boldsymbol{w}_{t-1}]$ and $\mathsf{E}[x_t|z_t, \boldsymbol{w}_{t-1}]$ as explicit functions of the parameters $(\boldsymbol{\pi}, \boldsymbol{\Sigma})$, where $\mathsf{E}[\cdot|\cdot]$ denotes a conditional expectation. Also derive the conditional distribution of $\boldsymbol{u}_t = (y_t, x_t)'$, given z_t and $\boldsymbol{w}_{t-1}$, denoted by $\mathsf{D}_{\mathsf{u}|\mathsf{z},\mathsf{w}}(\boldsymbol{u}_t|z_t, \boldsymbol{w}_{t-1}; \cdot)$.

(b) Define the concepts of weak and strong exogeneity. Consider the hypothesis that:

$$\mathsf{E}[y_t \mid z_t, \boldsymbol{w}_{t-1}] = \beta\mathsf{E}[x_t \mid z_t, \boldsymbol{w}_{t-1}] \tag{5.98}$$

What restrictions on the parameters of $\boldsymbol{\pi}$ are imposed by (5.98)? Under what conditions on $(\boldsymbol{\pi}, \boldsymbol{\Sigma})$ is z_t weakly exogenous for β in $\mathsf{D}_{\mathsf{u}|\mathsf{z},\mathsf{w}}(\boldsymbol{u}_t|z_t, \boldsymbol{w}_{t-1}; \cdot)$ when (5.98) is true?

(c) Derive $\mathsf{E}[y_t|x_t, \boldsymbol{w}_{t-1}]$ as a function of the parameters $(\boldsymbol{\pi}, \boldsymbol{\Sigma})$. Under what conditions, if any, on $(\boldsymbol{\pi}, \boldsymbol{\Sigma})$ is x_t weakly exogenous for β when (5.98) is true? Comment on how reasonable such conditions might be when (5.98) correctly describes agent behaviour.

(d) Is z_t strongly exogenous for β? Are there conditions under which x_t is strongly exogenous for β?

(Oxford M.Phil., 1991)

5.7 Consider the following DGP where $\boldsymbol{x}_t = (y_t : z_t)'$:[3]

$$\boldsymbol{x}_t \mid \boldsymbol{x}_{t-1} \sim \mathsf{N}_2[\boldsymbol{\pi}\boldsymbol{x}_{t-1}, \boldsymbol{\Omega}_t] \tag{5.99}$$

[3] This is a variant on the first solved example.

where

$$\pi = \begin{pmatrix} \gamma + \beta\mu & \beta(\lambda - \gamma) \\ \mu & \lambda \end{pmatrix} \text{ and } \boldsymbol{\Omega}_t = \begin{pmatrix} \omega_{11t} & \omega_{12t} \\ \omega_{21t} & \omega_{22t} \end{pmatrix}.$$

(a) When $\boldsymbol{\Omega}_t = \boldsymbol{\Omega}$ is constant over time in (5.99), obtain $\mathsf{E}[y_t|z_t, \mathbf{x}_{t-1}]$. Derive the conditional density $\mathsf{D}_{\mathsf{y}|\mathsf{z}}(y_t|z_t, \mathbf{x}_{t-1})$. Show that its error variance σ^2 is never larger than ω_{11}.

(b) Keeping $\boldsymbol{\Omega}$ constant and assuming that the parameters $(\beta, \gamma, \lambda, \mu, \omega_{11}, \omega_{12}, \omega_{22})$ are all variation free beyond $\boldsymbol{\Omega}$ being positive definite, establish conditions under which z_t is weakly exogenous for β. What type of model results if z_t is weakly exogenous for β? Which parameters determine the short-run and which the long-run response of y_t to z_t?

(c) When $\boldsymbol{\Omega}_t$ is not constant, derive $\mathsf{E}[y_t|z_t, \mathbf{x}_{t-1}]$. Is β invariant to changes in the marginal distribution of $\{z_t\}$? Establish conditions under which z_t is super exogenous for (β, σ^2).

(d) When $\omega_{12t} = 0$: (i) is z_t predetermined in $\mathsf{E}[y_t|z_t, \mathbf{x}_{t-1}]$; (ii) can z_t be super exogenous for the parameter $\boldsymbol{\delta}$ of $\mathsf{E}[y_t|z_t, \mathbf{x}_{t-1}]$ for changes in the parameters of the marginal distribution?

(Oxford M.Phil., 1992)

5.8 Consider the following bivariate DGP for the $\mathsf{I}(1)$ vector $\mathbf{x}_t = (y_t : z_t)'$:

$$\begin{aligned} y_t &= \beta z_t + \epsilon_{1t} \\ \Delta z_t &= \lambda \Delta y_{t-1} + \rho (y_{t-1} - \beta z_{t-1}) + \epsilon_{2t} \end{aligned} \tag{5.100}$$

where $\epsilon_t = (\epsilon_{1t} : \epsilon_{2t})'$ is distributed as in (5.101):

$$\begin{pmatrix} \epsilon_{1t} \\ \epsilon_{2t} \end{pmatrix} \sim \mathsf{IN}_2 \left[\begin{pmatrix} 0 \\ 0 \end{pmatrix}, \begin{pmatrix} \sigma_1^2 & \gamma\sigma_1\sigma_2 \\ \gamma\sigma_1\sigma_2 & \sigma_2^2 \end{pmatrix} \right] = \mathsf{IN}_2 [\mathbf{0}, \boldsymbol{\Sigma}]. \tag{5.101}$$

The parameters $(\beta, \sigma_1; \lambda, \rho, \gamma, \sigma_2)$ in (5.100) and (5.101) are all variation free beyond the requirement that $\boldsymbol{\Sigma}$ is positive definite; the parameter of interest is β.

(a) Derive the conditional expectation $\mathsf{E}[y_t|z_t, \mathbf{x}_{t-1}]$ of y_t given $(z_t, \mathbf{x}_{t-1})$ and the sequential density $\mathsf{D}_{\mathsf{y}|\mathsf{z}}(y_t|z_t, \mathbf{x}_{t-1})$. Under what conditions is z_t weakly exogenous for β?

(b) Explain the role of γ in this system, and what relation, if any, it has to the weak exogeneity of z_t for β. Briefly describe how to test the weak exogeneity of z_t for β.

(c) Under what conditions is z_t strongly exogenous for β? When z_t is weakly exogenous for β, explain how to test for Granger causality of Δy on Δz. What problems arise in testing for Granger causality of y on z when z_t is not weakly exogenous for β.

(Oxford M.Phil., 1993)

6

Interpreting Linear Models

Four interpretations of linear equations are distinguished, namely, a regression, a linear least-squares approximation, a contingent plan, or a behavioural model. Without further information, a linear equation may sustain any one of these interpretations, but the meaning and status of its parameters will differ according to which type is valid given the DGP. The properties of the four underlying types are discussed. Models of expectations formation are analysed and rational, consistent, unbiased, and economically-rational expectations are distinguished, the last highlighting the instrumental role of expectations in achieving plans. The dangers of 'autocorrelation corrections' are illustrated using one of the model types. A simple dynamic model called an autoregressive-distributed lag equation is introduced and its lag structure is investigated. A Monte Carlo study of its properties, an empirical illustration of UK money demand, and a solved example end the chapter.

6.1 Four interpretations of $y_t = \beta' z_t + \epsilon_t$

To proceed, we must clarify the meaning of the equation:

$$y_t = \beta' z_t + \epsilon_t. \tag{6.1}$$

The relationship in (6.1) is assumed to have arisen in the course of an economic analysis, and an investigator wishes to fit an analogue to the data-set $\{(y_t, z_t)\,; t = 1, \ldots, T\}$, where β is $k \times 1$. There are four distinct interpretations of (6.1), two based on statistical considerations and two on economic (see Wold, 1959, Richard, 1980, and Hendry, Pagan and Sargan, 1984). Without further information, a linear equation may sustain any one of these four interpretations, but the meaning and status of its parameters will differ according to which interpretation is valid.

In some DGPs, the four interpretations described below will coincide in the sense that they will not entail different observable implications. Conversely, across different states of nature, the four interpretations can be distinguished. Thus, at level C, it will be essential for testing economic theories, forecasting or conducting policy simulations to ascertain which statistical interpretation of any given economic model is valid. The first step in the analysis is to define the four types of model, determine their properties, and delineate worlds in which they differ. It should be clear from the previous five chapters that the joint distribution of $\{y_t, z_t\}$ matters; in particular, the exogeneity status of z_t for $\boldsymbol{\beta}$ is bound to be a crucial aspect of interpreting economic models. Equation (6.1) only specifies a part of the joint distribution, and the precise mechanism determining z_t will be introduced as we proceed, as will the properties of $\{\epsilon_t\}$. The complete specification of the joint distribution uniquely determines the model type. For simplicity, we only consider the bivariate case of a scalar variable z_t and an intercept, but no important aspects are lost by this simplification.

6.1.1 Regression

On the basis of §A2.8, the first interpretation of (6.1) is as a regression equation, namely the conditional expectation of one variable y_t given a second set of variables z_t, which in the scalar case becomes:

$$\mathsf{E}[y_t \mid z_t] = \beta_0 + \beta_1 z_t. \tag{6.2}$$

From (6.1) and (6.2), $y_t = \mathsf{E}[y_t|z_t] + \epsilon_t$. Regression is a generic construct and the regression function $\mathsf{E}[y_t|z_t] = g(z_t)$ will only yield a linear equation as in (6.2) for certain joint distributions of $\{y_t, z_t\}$. Consequently, the model in (6.1) will be a regression only if the joint distribution of y_t and z_t is a member of a class of distributions for which the conditional distribution of y_t given z_t is a linear function of z_t.

The best-known member of the class leading to linear regression is the normal distribution, so (6.1) could be a regression from a bivariate normal distribution, in which case $\boldsymbol{\beta}$ is the regression coefficient. Further, (6.1) will be a 'correct' specification of the conditional expectation, but $\boldsymbol{\beta}$ need not be a parameter of interest. Let the joint density function $\mathsf{D}_{\mathsf{y,z}}(y_t, z_t \mid \cdot)$ of the two random variables (y_t, z_t) be:

$$\begin{pmatrix} y_t \\ z_t \end{pmatrix} \sim \mathsf{IN}_2\left[\begin{pmatrix} \mu_{1t} \\ \mu_{2t} \end{pmatrix}, \begin{pmatrix} \sigma_{11} & \sigma_{12} \\ \sigma_{12} & \sigma_{22} \end{pmatrix}\right]. \tag{6.3}$$

Then, as established in §4.6:

$$\mathsf{E}[y_t \mid z_t] = \mu_{1t} + \sigma_{12}\sigma_{22}^{-1}(z_t - \mu_{2t}) = \gamma_0 + \gamma_1 z_t, \tag{6.4}$$

where $\gamma_1 = \sigma_{12}\sigma_{22}^{-1}$ and $\gamma_0 = (\mu_{1t} - \gamma_1\mu_{2t})$, providing that γ_0 is in fact constant over t. If so, then $\mathsf{E}[z_t\epsilon_t] = 0$ in (6.1) by construction, since from (6.1) and (6.4):

$$\mathsf{E}[y_t \mid z_t] = \gamma_0 + \gamma_1 z_t + \mathsf{E}[\epsilon_t \mid z_t] = \gamma_0 + \gamma_1 z_t.$$

Thus, the stronger condition that $\mathsf{E}[\epsilon_t|z_t] = 0$ is satisfied. Further, $\mathsf{E}[y_t|z_t]$ is the minimum-variance unbiased predictor of y_t as a function of z_t with error variance $\sigma_\epsilon^2 = \sigma_{11} - \sigma_{12}^2\sigma_{22}^{-1}$ (see §A2.7), so no other equation fits better on the given information set. When the parameters of (6.3) are variation free, then $(\gamma_0 : \gamma_1 : \sigma_\epsilon^2)$ and $(\mu_{2t} : \sigma_{22})$ are also, so z_t is weakly exogenous for γ_1. Nevertheless, because (6.1) is an incomplete specification of $\mathsf{D}_{\mathsf{y,z}}(y_t, z_t \mid \cdot)$, then γ_1 need not coincide with β_1 (as interpretation §6.1.4 will illustrate), in which case (6.4) may not provide a valid basis for using the empirical model.

Conversely, there are many joint distributions for which regressions (i.e. conditional expectations) are not linear, so (6.1) interpreted as a linear economic model need not correspond to the regression equation entailed by the DGP. An example which may occur relatively frequently in economics is when $\mathsf{D}_{\mathsf{y,z}}(y_t, z_t \mid \cdot)$ is a log-normal density, in which case $\log y_t$ and $\log z_t$ would be linearly related, although y_t and z_t would not.

6.1.2 Linear least-squares approximation

The next interpretation is that (6.1) is a linear least-squares approximation to:

$$y_t = f(z_t) + u_t. \tag{6.5}$$

The linear approximation to $f(z_t)$ here is given by:

$$f(z_t) = \delta_0 + \delta_1 z_t. \tag{6.6}$$

The coefficients $\boldsymbol{\delta} = (\delta_0 : \delta_1)'$ are selected by the least-squares criterion to be:

$$\underset{\boldsymbol{\delta}}{\operatorname{argmin}}\ h(\boldsymbol{\delta}) \quad \text{where}\ h(\boldsymbol{\delta}) = \sum_{t=1}^{T} v_t(\boldsymbol{\delta})^2 \quad \text{and}\ v_t(\boldsymbol{\delta}) = y_t - \delta_0 - \delta_1 z_t. \tag{6.7}$$

First, from differentiating $h(\boldsymbol{\delta})$ in (6.7):

$$\frac{\partial h(\boldsymbol{\delta})}{\partial \boldsymbol{\delta}} = \mathbf{0} \ \text{implies that} \sum_{t=1}^{T} v_t = 0 \ \text{and} \sum_{t=1}^{T} v_t z_t = 0.$$

Both of these properties hold for §6.1.1, but here they define the values of δ_0 and δ_1 in (6.6).

Secondly, (6.6) is not a linear Taylor-series approximation to a non-linear function $f(\cdot)$. The Taylor series approximation at a point is the tangent at that point and does not minimize the sum of squares of the residuals. Figure 6.1a illustrates this issue for the function $f(z_t) = \log(1 + z_t)$. As can be seen in the figure, a tangent at any point would lie wholly outside such a function and hence could not minimize $h(\boldsymbol{\delta})$ (see e.g. White, 1980c). By way of contrast, Fig. 6.1b shows the non-linear relation fitted to the data.

Thirdly, unless $f(\cdot)$ is linear, the linear least-squares approximation coefficient $\boldsymbol{\delta}$ will change as the sample size T changes. Figures 6.1c–d illustrate using linear least-squares approximations fitted to four increasing sub-samples of (i) $0.25T$; (ii) $0.5T$; (iii) $0.75T$; and (iv) T (the case in Fig. 6.1a) and in Fig. 6.1d for eight non-overlapping successive sub-samples. As the estimation sample size alters, the slope of the regression line changes markedly corresponding to changing values of $\boldsymbol{\delta}$. Interpretation §6.1.2 emphasizes the need for a concept like super exogeneity. For example, if $f(\cdot)$ in (6.6) is a non-linear function of z_t, then $\boldsymbol{\delta}$ will not be invariant to the value of z_t, and so z_t will not be super exogenous for $\boldsymbol{\delta}$ in the linear equation:

$$y_t = \delta_0 + \delta_1 z_t + v_t.$$

Fourthly, in all the figures it is apparent that the $\{v_t\}$ are autocorrelated: we return to that issue in §6.3 below.

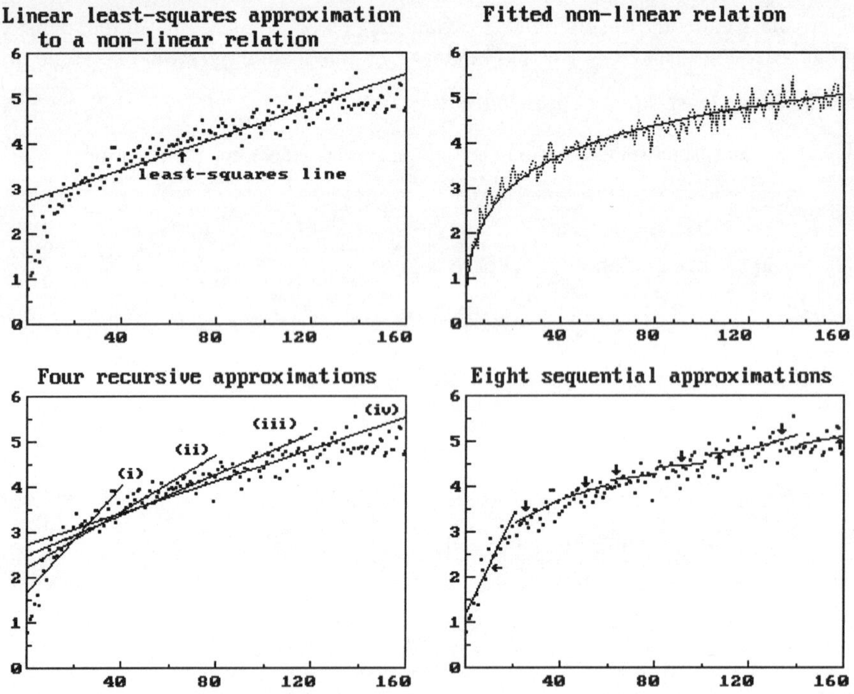

Fig. 6.1 Linear approximations to a non-linear relation

Finally, it is awkward terminology to describe (6.1) as a 'linear least-squares regression', since that phrase conflates two distinct concepts. Moreover, a regression coefficient could in principle be invariant to a class of interventions affecting the marginal distribution of $\{z_t\}$ (see §5.10), whereas a least-squares approximation to a non-linear function generally will not be invariant even over the fitted sample values. In that sense, if (6.1) does correspond to interpretation §6.1.2, then it would not be a useful model for most purposes. Conversely, interpretations §6.1.1 and §6.1.2 coincide for a bivariate normal distribution, which is a regular example at level A, but not necessarily the relevant DGP for level C.

6.1.3 Contingent plan

A contingent plan is one that is implemented only after observing the outcomes of any relevant conditioning variables. For example, a husband may arrange to collect the shopping if his spouse does not telephone before 4 p.m., and the spouse collects the shopping otherwise. Their actions are contingent on the telephone outcome by 4 p.m. However, neither needs to know the probability distribution of the event that the call might be made in order to formulate the plan *ex ante*, or execute it *ex post*. The third interpretation of (6.1) is as a contingent-plan model given the outcome of z_t:

$$y_t^p = \alpha_0 + \alpha_1 z_t \tag{6.8}$$

where the superscript ^{p} denotes an agent's plan. Contingent planning is a theme that will recur, since economic agents' plans often seem to take the form of contingent rules rather than the expectations formulations delivered by inter-temporal optimization in §6.1.4. The model in (6.8) assumes that the agent does not control z_t, but tries to control y_t as a linear function of z_t. A possible example is each individual's money holdings, given their income.

Since agents usually make their own plans, it is natural to require that they are rational in doing so, and hence that outcomes do not deviate systematically from what was planned. Thus, as in §5.2.1:

$$\mathsf{E}\left[y_t \mid y_t^p\right] = y_t^p. \tag{6.9}$$

At one extreme, (6.9) allows the possibility that $y_t \equiv y_t^p$. However, it seems unlikely that agents could guarantee to implement all plans precisely, so we allow the observed outcome to deviate from the plan by an innovation relative to the available information. For example, a minor accident (such as mis-dialling) might perturb the contingent shopping plan. Denote the innovation by e_t, then:

$$y_t = y_t^p + e_t \text{ where } e_t \sim \mathsf{IN}\left[0, \sigma_e^2\right]. \tag{6.10}$$

From (6.9) and (6.10), it follows that $\mathsf{E}\left[e_t | y_t^p\right] = 0$, so (6.9) is not an innocuous assumption but implicitly entails that the probability distribution of $\{e_t\}$ is unaffected by the outcome of the contingent variables.

If the plan involves a linear response to z_t, as in (6.8), then combined with (6.10), the resulting model coincides formally with the regression model (6.2):

$$\mathsf{E}\left[y_t \mid z_t\right] = \alpha_0 + \alpha_1 z_t. \tag{6.11}$$

In (6.11), z_t is weakly exogenous for the parameter of interest α, assuming that, since z_t is not controlled by the agent, α does not enter the marginal distribution of z_t. However, while z_t was weakly exogenous for the regression coefficient γ in (6.4) an explicit assumption was required for γ to coincide with the parameter of interest. Generally, z_t will not be weakly exogenous for the approximation coefficient in (6.7). In this respect, (6.8)–(6.10) entail stronger assumptions than (6.2) but deliver more useful models.

Conversely, a regression is linear only for a restricted class of joint distributions, whereas the contingent plan could in principle be linear whatever the marginal distribution of z_t. The major difference between interpretations 1 and 3 is that the former is purely statistical whereas the latter tries to ground the distribution of one of the variables in the actions of economic agents. It should not be assumed that the latter is thereby correct or superior to the former, or to §6.1.2. For example, if the assumed contingent plan model is linear but the underlying behaviour is non-linear, §6.1.3 may perform worse empirically than a non-linear regression. However, we will take $\{y_t : z_t\}$ to be jointly normal for most of the book so that contingent plan parameters coincide with regression coefficients and a contingent plan can be estimated using regression methods.

The conditions for the weak exogeneity of z_t for β in (6.1) highlight one situation in which a contingent plan will not be an appropriate model in economics. That is when an agent's reaction y_t to z_t, when the outcome of z_t is learned, does not coincide with the *ex ante* planning rule formulated contingently on z_t. The shopping example assumed that the husband would indeed implement the plan and do the collection if his spouse phoned. In practice, if the event of a call were realized, the individual might choose to decline to answer the telephone, so that the model would not adequately characterize his behaviour, and would correctly predict y_t only for the case in which the telephone call did not materialize. Indeed, the agent may even have had a second contingent plan to ignore any telephone calls that day, so that the model is mis-specified. Nevertheless, no aspect of the environment precluded the originally specified plan from being rational, and the plan could in principle remain unaltered even if the individual were certain that their spouse would call. However, a contingent plan cannot be the correct model if behaviour would not correspond to the planning rule once the contingent value is observed. This issue leads to the fourth interpretation.

6.1.4 Behavioural model

The final interpretation is that (6.1) is a behavioural model derived from:

$$y_t^p = \phi_0 + \phi_1 z_t^e. \tag{6.12}$$

The plan formed for time t depends on the value z_t^e which z_t is expected to take at the time the plan will be implemented. While agents try to control y_t, it is assumed that they do not control z_t. In economics, it is conventional to make rationality assumptions about expectations formation for uncontrolled variables, but care is required in defining 'rational' when forming an expectation. That is the topic of section 6.2. For the present discussion, the main point is that forming the expectation is merely an instrument in implementing the plan and is not an end in itself, whereas by definition the plan seeks to achieve the end product.

We continue to assume rationality of the plan in (6.12) as in (6.10), and in this subsection, merely assert that there is an information set $\mathcal{I}_{t-1}$ costlessly available to the agent upon which the expectation of z_t is conditioned:

$$z_t^e = \mathsf{E}\left[z_t \mid \mathcal{I}_{t-1}\right]. \tag{6.13}$$

The precise nature of the mapping of z_t onto $\mathcal{I}_{t-1}$ in (6.13), and the contents of $\mathcal{I}_{t-1}$ are not essential to this discussion. From (6.13):

$$z_t = z_t^e + \nu_t \tag{6.14}$$

where ν_t is an innovation relative to $\mathcal{I}_{t-1}$ given (6.13), assumed to be $\mathsf{IN}[0, \sigma_\nu^2]$. Substituting (6.12) and (6.14) into (6.10):

$$y_t = \phi_0 + \phi_1 z_t + (e_t - \phi_1 \nu_t) \tag{6.15}$$

which by defining $(e_t - \phi_1 \nu_t) = \epsilon_t$ appears at first sight to be the same as (6.1).

However, there is an irremovable difference: whereas z_t could be weakly exogenous for β in (6.1) for some DGPs, the conditional expectation of y_t given z_t is not $\phi_0 + \phi_1 z_t$ in this model unless $\sigma_\nu^2 = 0$. It is impossible to learn ϕ from regression in (6.15) because z_t is correlated with the error. Nevertheless, as demonstrated in Chapter 5, z_t can be orthogonalized with respect to the error by a new choice of parameters, rewriting the model as:

$$y_t = \pi_0 + \pi_1 z_t + \zeta_t \text{ where } \mathsf{E}[z_t \zeta_t] = 0. \tag{6.16}$$

Even if z_t is weakly exogenous for the regression parameter $\boldsymbol{\pi}$ in this transformed equation, $\boldsymbol{\pi}$ is not the parameter of interest. Instead, $\boldsymbol{\pi}$ is a function not only of the parameter of interest $\boldsymbol{\phi}$ but also of the parameters of the process generating z_t, denoted by $\boldsymbol{\lambda} : \boldsymbol{\pi} = \boldsymbol{f}(\boldsymbol{\phi}, \boldsymbol{\lambda})$. For example, when:

$$z_t = \lambda_0 + \lambda_1 z_{t-1} + \nu_t \text{ where } \nu_t \sim \mathsf{IN}\left[0, \sigma_v^2\right] \text{ and } |\lambda_1| < 1, \tag{6.17}$$

for $z_{t-1} \in \mathcal{I}_{t-1}$, then:

$$\mathsf{E}[z_t \mid z_{t-1}] = z_t^e = \lambda_0 + \lambda_1 z_{t-1}. \tag{6.18}$$

When the error on the plan is independent of the expectations error:

$$\mathsf{E}[y_t \mid z_t] = \phi_0 + \phi_1 z_t - \phi_1 \mathsf{E}[\nu_t \mid z_t] \tag{6.19}$$

where:

$$\mathsf{E}[\nu_t \mid z_t] = \mu_0 + \mu_1 z_t \tag{6.20}$$

and $(\mu_0 : \mu_1)$ are functions of $\left(\lambda_0 : \lambda_1 : \sigma_v^2\right)$ (using the technique in §5.5 extended for an intercept). Thus:

$$\mathsf{E}[y_t \mid z_t] = [\phi_0 - \phi_1 \mu_0] + \phi_1 [1 - \mu_1] z_t = \pi_0 + \pi_1 z_t. \tag{6.21}$$

From (6.21), the parameter of interest $\boldsymbol{\phi}$ cannot be obtained directly from the regression coefficient $\boldsymbol{\pi}$.

We can turn this problem into an advantage to discriminate between interpretations §6.1.3 and §6.1.4. Consider a scenario where there is a regime shift in how the government controls the interest rate z_t. Suppose for simplicity that the amount of money y_t that agents plan to hold depends only on z_t, but, due to events outside the private sector's control, the government's control rule for the interest rate shifts between two periods:

$$\begin{aligned} z_t &= \lambda_{0a} + \lambda_{1a} z_{t-1} + \nu_{at} \quad \text{for } t = 1, \ldots, T_n \\ z_t &= \lambda_{0b} + \lambda_{1b} z_{t-1} + \nu_{bt} \quad \text{for } t = T_{n+1}, \ldots, T. \end{aligned}$$

Then it is possible to tell whether or not z_t is a contingent-plan variable. If agents base their decisions on a behavioural plan as in (6.12), with expectations about z_t determined as in (6.18), then the regression coefficient π should change when the parameters of the control rule alter, since from (6.21):

$$\pi_{0a} + \pi_{1a} z_t = [\phi_0 - \phi_1 \mu_{0a}] + \phi_1 (1 - \mu_{1a}) z_t \quad \text{for } t = 1, \ldots, T_n;$$

$$\pi_{0b} + \pi_{1b} z_t = [\phi_0 - \phi_1 \mu_{0b}] + \phi_1 (1 - \mu_{1b}) z_t \quad \text{for } t = T_{n+1}, \ldots, T,$$

where $(\mu_{0j} : \mu_{1j})$ are functions of $(\lambda_{0j} : \lambda_{1j} : \sigma^2_{vj})$.

This is an example of the Lucas critique noted in §5.9. When an econometric model does not distinguish between the effects due to planning and the effects due to expectations, but expectations matter, then the econometric model should mis-predict when expectations processes alter. That is a testable hypothesis since if λ changes, π ought to change as well. Notice the converse: when the process generating z_t changes, but the parameters of the econometric model do not change, then agents could not have based their decisions on expected values of z_t. They must have been acting contingently, or at least not using model-based expectations. We apply this result in Chapter 14 to make the Lucas critique testable since there appear to be examples where π does not change despite regime shifts in determining variables (see e.g. Hendry, 1988). In equations with such a property, that finding suggests a different role for expectations formation by agents when forming their plans.

6.2 Expectations formation

6.2.1 Rational expectations

Economists have long been concerned with the role of expectations in decision taking (see e.g. Tinbergen, 1933). Muth (1961) defined expectations to be rational if they were formed according to the economic model underlying the behaviour. For example, if an economist postulates that z_t is generated by a first-order autoregression as in (6.17), then the agent is supposed to act as if that model were the DGP. Consequently, the rational expectation corresponds to the mathematical expectation taken assuming (6.17) holds as in (6.18).

An abuse of language has crept into professional discourse, since it might be irrational to form a 'rational' expectation. For example, (6.18) assumes that the expectation given the model is the mathematical expectation. That involves the sleight-of-hand that the model coincides one-to-one with the generating mechanism, which in general it will not. Even assuming that the model was the mechanism, it would be irrational to form a rational expectation if doing so required investing heavily to discover the DGP and then calculating the mathematical expectation of the variable given all the determinants in that DGP: agents need to know the DGP to form the rational expectation and hence know all relevant information. However, the cost of learning everything about the DGP is essentially infinite while the benefits from forming the expectation are finite. Imagine the cost of obtaining measurement-error free values of every relevant variable. Thus, such expectations are unlikely to describe how human beings form their beliefs about the future, and an 'as if' assumption is insufficient to justify expectations being rational in the sense of Muth.

We will call a Muthian expectation either just that or else a consistent expectation, since it generates internal consistency in model building: given an equation in which the plan depends on the expected value of z_t and given a model for z_t, then the expected value of z_t is the expectation delivered by that model. Such expectations help avoid internal contradictions in theories. Model-consistent expectations can be expressed heuristically as:

$$z_t^e = \mathsf{E}_{\mathrm{model}}\left[z_t \mid \text{model of } z_t\right].$$

Such expectations are sometimes used in large macro models: if an expectation of output two periods forward (say) is needed in the model to determine employment today, then the natural expectation of future output to use is the prediction from the model of the outcome two periods hence. That prediction is not the mathematical expectation of output given today's state of nature unless the model mimics reality in every aspect relevant to predicting the future.

The issue of expectations is important in the search for invariant structures in econometrics. We define rational expectations in relation to agents who optimize when making their plans. If the resulting plan requires a view about the future, agents should optimize in terms of the role the expectations play in the plan, and that may not involve optimizing with respect to the expectations. In particular, the required expectations need not be the mathematical expectations. As a contrived example, imagine planning to travel from Oxford to London by train, where past experience suggests the Oxford train leaves five minutes late. Probably you form a general expectation once, and arrive at the station just before the announced departure time of the train; if the train happens to be late, you wait. However, if you form the mathematical expectation of the departure time, in the sense of the mean of the probability distribution, you would on average arrive at the station after the actual departure times of many of the trains. In part, the contrivance here is due to the specific nature of scheduled transport departures, in part it reflects asymmetric costs of late versus early arrival, but in part it exploits a misconstruction of why agents form expectations. Most agents do not care directly about z_t except in so far as it is an instrument in achieving their plans. They usually do not intend as an independent objective to become famous as accurate forecasters of z_t.

Agents seem more likely to form economically-rational expectations (see Feige and Pearce, 1976). Given the loss function that agents seek to optimize, the costs and benefits of mistakes in predicting z_t are related to the discrepancy $z_t - z_t^e$. The loss can be reduced by improving the accuracy of predicting z_t but at a cost. An economically-rational expectation is one based on investing in information about z_t to form that expectation which minimizes the cost of the original problem of achieving the plan. In general, Muthian expectations are economically-rational expectations only if there are no costs to discovering the DGP, or collecting and processing information: in other words, only if econometrics is not needed. Agents must determine what information exists, ascertain its utility for their objectives, and decide how much to collect. Galbraith (1987) offers a perceptive discussion.

6.2.2 Unbiased expectations

In the train-catching example, the 'sensible' expectation was biased. Consider what might be achieved if agents form z_t^e as an unbiased predictor of z_t, so $\mathsf{E}[(z_t - z_t^e)|\mathcal{I}_{t-1}] = 0$ when $\mathcal{I}_{t-1}$ again denotes available information.

The first illustrative result is that any fitted autoregression can yield an unbiased predictor of z_t, if z_t is generated by a zero-mean, finite-order, stationary autoregressive process with a symmetrically distributed error. This claim holds even if an incorrect autoregressive model is used for z_t. Assume the DGP of $\{z_t\}$ is the nth-order stationary autoregressive process:

$$\rho(L) z_t = \nu_t \text{ where } \nu_t \sim \mathsf{IN}\left[0, \sigma_v^2\right] \text{ with } |\lambda_i| < 1 \text{ for } i = 1, \ldots, n, \tag{6.22}$$

when the λ_i are the latent roots of $\rho(L) = 0$. Despite not knowing the order n of $\rho(L)$, an unbiased prediction of z_{t+1} is provided by the first-order autoregression:

$$z_t = \rho z_{t-1} + u_t \tag{6.23}$$

where ρ is estimated from a sample of size T by:

$$\hat{\rho} = \sum_{t=2}^{T} z_t z_{t-1} / \sum_{t=2}^{T} z_{t-1}^2 \tag{6.24}$$

and the prediction of z_{T+1} uses:

$$\hat{z}_{T+1} = \hat{\rho} z_T \text{ with prediction error } e_{T+1} = z_{T+1} - \hat{z}_{T+1}. \tag{6.25}$$

We now show that $\mathsf{E}\left[e_{T+1}\right] = 0$. To prove that claim, we derive the prediction of z_{t+1} $\forall t$ from the predictor (6.25) and use antithetic variates to show that the prediction errors cancel between $\{\nu_t\}$ and $\{-\nu_t\}$ if ρ is estimated as in (6.24). For $t = 1, \ldots, T$, let:

$$z_t = \rho^*(L) z_{t-1} + \nu_t \text{ where } z_0 = \ldots = z_{-n+1} = 0, \tag{6.26}$$

and $\rho(L) = 1 - \rho^*(L)$. In a Monte Carlo experiment, generate the first replication of $(\nu_1, \ldots, \nu_{T+1})$ from which $(z_1, \ldots, z_{T+1})$ is derived using (6.26). The fitted autoregression is (6.22). Repeat the Monte Carlo using $(-\nu_1, \ldots, -\nu_{T+1})$ to generate $(-z_1, \ldots, -z_{T+1})$. From (6.26), the signs of $\{z_t\}$ are switched by using $\{-\nu_t\}$, so using (6.24):

$$\hat{\rho}(\{-\nu_t\}) = \sum_{t=2}^{T} (-z_t)(-z_{t-1}) / \sum_{t=2}^{T} (-z_{t-1})^2 = \hat{\rho}(\{\nu_t\}). \tag{6.27}$$

Thus, $\hat{\rho}$ is an even function of $\{\nu_t\}$ and is unaltered by the sign change in $\{\nu_t\}$, leading to the forecast error $-e_{T+1}$.[1] Thus, the average forecast error is $(e_{T+1} - e_{T+1})$ which is zero for all possible realizations of the stochastic process $\{\nu_t\}$, so that $\mathsf{E}\left[e_{T+1}\right] = 0$ despite the model mis-specification.

[1] As noted in Ch.3, antithetic variates are a useless technique for simulating the distribution of $\hat{\rho}$.

To summarize:

(i) a predictor can be unbiased for all values of the DGP even when it is wrong as a model of the DGP, so discovering that predictions are unbiased tells us little about the validity of the model;
(ii) conversely, unbiased predictions may be sub-optimal either because the mean is not a good representation of the central tendency of a (skewed) distribution, or the decision cost function is asymmetric.

These examples question any insistence on rational, unbiased, or consistent expectations being an essential component of model formulation. As elsewhere in any empirical science, judge the value of the approach by the results it delivers, not the principles it espouses.

Many economic models involve inter-temporal optimization by rational agents, and for agents to implement their plans over time, the whole of the future appears to be relevant. Agents are usually assumed to form rational, or at least unbiased, expectations about the entire trajectories of all uncontrolled variables. The above simple counter-examples suggest that more may be going on, in that agents may not find it worthwhile to collect the relevant information to solve their primary problem. There are implicit assumptions in the formulation of the inter-temporal optimization plans about the cost and the availability of information, corresponding to free information and zero-cost processing, omniscient knowledge of the structure of the DGP, and ignoring the problem of accuracy of the observed data. If all such costs were included, a different intertemporal optimization plan would result than the class of models which places great emphasis on expectations in their formulation: the essential econometric problem of discovering the DGP is inconsistent with the assumption that all agents already know it, or even act as if they knew it.

Generally, in derivations of inter-temporal theory, expectations processes are assumed constant. If expectations processes were to alter, the model would behave in a more complex way involving learning and adaptation, and raising the issue of invariance. However, if the DGP is not known to the agents, but they do know that it is susceptible to regime shifts that occur intermittently, many expectations models begin to look econometrically doubtful. Despite the above caveats, the behavioural model analysed in §6.1.4 is an important model class and we return to investigate the empirical role of expectations in Chapter 14.

6.2.3 Data-based expectations

The final class of expectations processes which will be analysed here are those based directly on data properties without the intervention of a formal parametric model with unknown parameters and error variances needing estimation by agents or econometricians. The relevant data functions are a class of univariate predictors which might be selected by agents due to costs of information collection and processing. Consider an integrated process $\{z_t\}$ which is $\mathsf{I}(d)$, such that $\{\Delta^d z_t\}$ is stationary, though not necessarily mean zero or an innovation. To forecast future zs, we investigate an agent who solves $\Delta^{d+1}\hat{z}_{t+1} = 0$ to obtain $\hat{z}_{t+1}$. The extra degree of differencing removes any mean from the stationary process. For example, when $d = 2$, then $\Delta^3 \hat{z}_{t+1} = 0$ implies that $\Delta^2 \hat{z}_{t+1} = \Delta^2 z_t$ so that $\hat{z}_{t+1} = z_t + \Delta z_t + \Delta^2 z_t$. There are a number of useful properties of predictors based on solving $\Delta^{d+1} \hat{z}_{t+1} = 0$.

(i) The predictor is unbiased if $\Delta^d z_t$ is a finite autoregressive process with a symmetric error: this follows from §6.2.2 above.

(ii) The predictor has no parameters other than the order of integration d, unlike (6.17).

(iii) The forecast error $(z_{t+1} - \hat{z}_{t+1})$ does not enter the conditional model when $\Delta^d z_t$ is a regressor, unlike (6.15).

(iv) $\Delta^{d+1} z_{t+1} = 0$ implies that $\Delta^{d+2} z_{t+1} = 0$, and hence if the level of d chosen by the econometrician is $d^* \geq d + 1$, and d alters but remains less than d^*, then the econometrician's model is 'correct' both before and after d changes although outliers may be apparent at the time that d changes.

(v) However, the converse is false, in that if d^* is too small, the resulting econometric model may fail when d alters because of the changed behaviour of the omitted higher-order differences.

(vi) If the order of integration of z_t increases but agents maintain the same d, then they may suffer predictive failure due to systematic under- or over-prediction, suggesting the need for them to revise their value of d.

(viii) The synthesis of rational and adaptive expectations for inflation into a 'change of gear' model in Flemming (1976, 62 ff.) provides an example of this class of model.

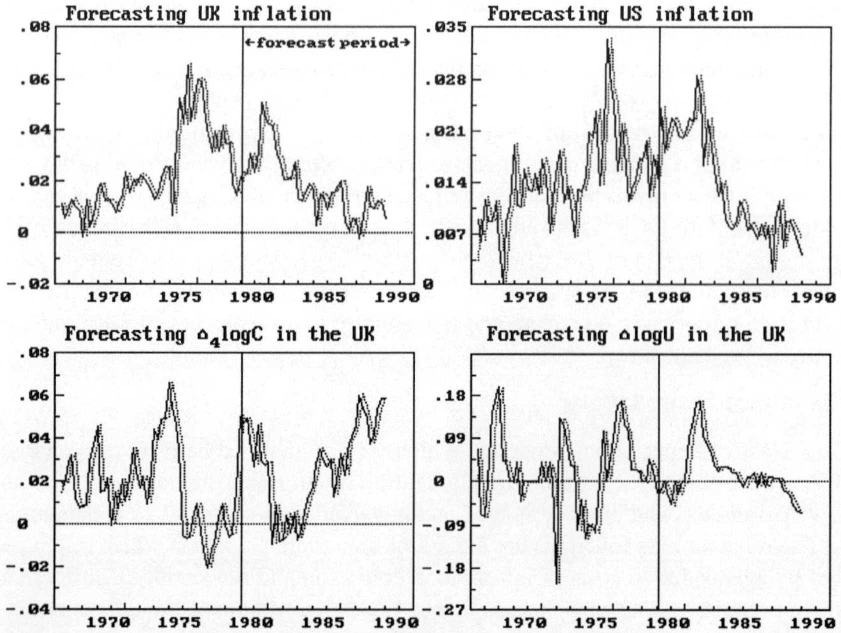

Fig. 6.2 Predictors based on data differences

As an illustration, Figs. 6.2a–d show Δp_t in the UK and the USA and $\Delta_4 c_t$ and Δu_t in the UK, where p_t is the GNP deflator, c_t is real consumers' expenditure (not seasonally adjusted) and u_t is unemployment (all in logs) as predictors for Δp_{t+1}, $\Delta_4 c_{t+1}$, and Δu_{t+1} respectively, implicitly obtained from mechanisms of the form $\Delta^2 \hat{z}_{t+1} = 0$. They all forecast reasonably well 1-step ahead, with residual standard errors of 0.8 per cent, 0.4 per cent, 1.2 per cent and 5.8 per cent, which are constant between the two halves of the sample. Other examples of predictors in this class are discussed by Campos and Ericsson (1988), Favero and Hendry (1992), and Hendry and Ericsson (1991a, 1991b).

6.3 Autocorrelation corrections

A feature of many published empirical econometric equations is the presence of an autocorrelation correction, usually for a first-order autoregressive error. In this subsection, we present an example of such a correction which induces an unsatisfactory outcome, as a prelude to a more detailed analysis in the next chapter.

At first sight, it may seem unlikely that the errors in empirical econometric models should be white noise, since the error is a composite of many small factors, some of which might manifest persistence over time. Nevertheless, as established in Chapter 2, by appropriate sequential factorization of the joint data density function, derived models can be written with an error that is an innovation against the available information, and hence is white noise if the history of the process is included in that information. From such a perspective, therefore, residual autocorrelation is a symptom of model mis-specification, and it is not obvious that 'correcting' mis-specifications need lead to an improved model, although there may exist criteria that would judge such a change to be an improvement. We also saw in Chapter 4 that inference in models with autocorrelated residuals can be misleading, so the issue is an important one in practice. The example is artificial, but at level C the DGP is unknown so that while the mistakes which the example exemplifies may be a caricature they are not unreasonable.

The example seeks to highlight the following issues:

(a) Mis-specified models may fail several diagnostic tests. Consequently, it is hazardous to interpret the outcome of any single test constructively, that is, to implement the alternative hypothesis when the test rejects. Autocorrelation corrections are an example of attempted constructive use of tests.
(b) It follows from (a) that generalizing an initially simple model on the basis of a sequence of test rejections can lead to an inappropriate model selection. Whether it does so or not depends in part on the order in which corrections to diagnostic test rejections happen to be calculated.
(c) Since the data in the example have no autoregressive component, the autocorrelation correction can only be treating a symptom of a problem and not the cause.
(d) Despite (c), it is possible by mechanistic autocorrelation corrections to generate a white-noise error in an invalid specification. Hence, reporting the absence of

residual autocorrelation after such corrections conveys no useful information about a model's validity.

Reconsider the linear approximation in §6.1.2 above, when in fact:

$$y_t = \log(1 + z_t) + u_t \text{ where } u_t \sim \mathsf{IN}[0, 0.04]. \tag{6.28}$$

Letting $\underset{c}{\sim}$ denote 'is claimed to be distributed as', then the postulated equation is:

$$y_t = \delta_0 + \delta_1 z_t + v_t \text{ where } v_t \underset{c}{\sim} \mathsf{IN}\left[0, \sigma_v^2\right]. \tag{6.29}$$

Figure 6.1 revealed the non-linear nature of the problem, but investigators do not always cross-plot time-series data, especially when there are many possible explanatory variables. Rather, a graph over time may be considered, which need not exhibit sufficient curvature to make it obvious that a non-linear function of z_t is required.

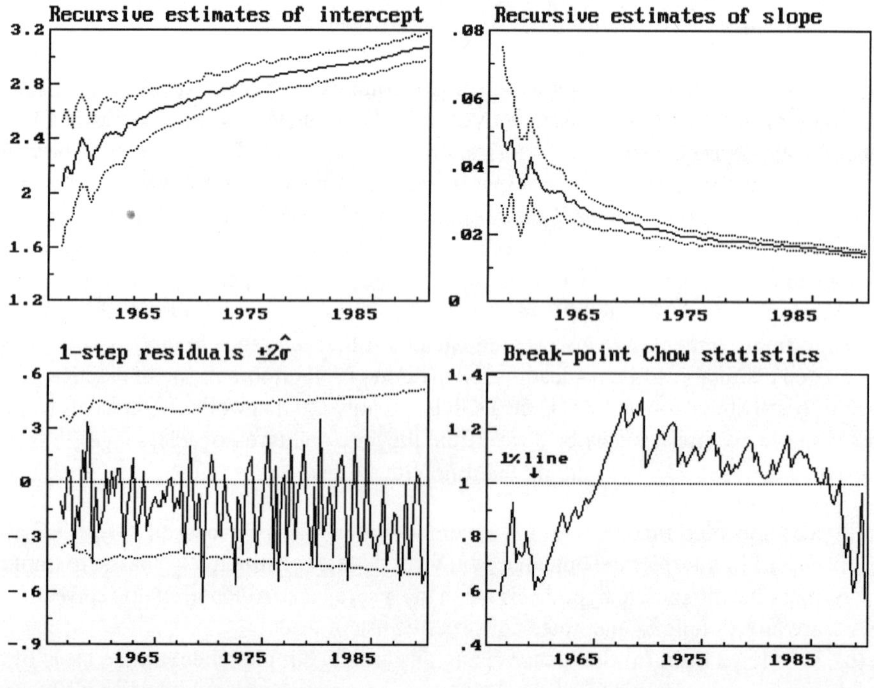

Fig. 6.3 Recursive estimation statistics

Figures 6.3a,b show the recursive sequences of estimates of δ_0 and δ_1 together with $\pm 2\mathsf{SE}_t$ (see §3.2.2): the estimated coefficient of z_t trends over the sample, with the 95 per cent confidence interval of the final estimate lying outside equivalent intervals earlier in the sample (e.g. before 1970). Figures 6.3c,d confirm the non-constancy in the fitted model using the 1-step residuals with $\pm 2\hat{\sigma}_v^2(t)$, and a sequence of breakpoint Chow tests scaled by their 1 per cent critical values; the outcomes reject the null of constant parameters in (6.29). Attempting to allow for changing or trending parameters would be one constructive use of such test information.

The full sample estimates for 1953(1)–1989(4) are:

$$y_t = \underset{(0.0005)}{0.014}\, z_t + \underset{(0.048)}{3.078}$$
$$\mathsf{R}^2 = 0.853 \quad \hat{\sigma} = 0.257 \quad DW = 1.34. \tag{6.30}$$

The value of the Durbin–Watson statistic signals the possibility of residual autocorrelation. Note, therefore, that all the inferences about parameter non-constancy are invalidated since they were predicated on the assumption that the errors were white noise, and conversely. This is point (a) above. Figures 6.4a,b show the residual correlogram from (6.30) and from the $\{u_t\}$ process, whereas Figs. 6.4c, d record the corresponding histograms with interpolated densities. The first reveals marked residual autocorrelation whereas the second shows none; the third reveals non-normality although the errors are normally distributed as shown in the last quadrant.

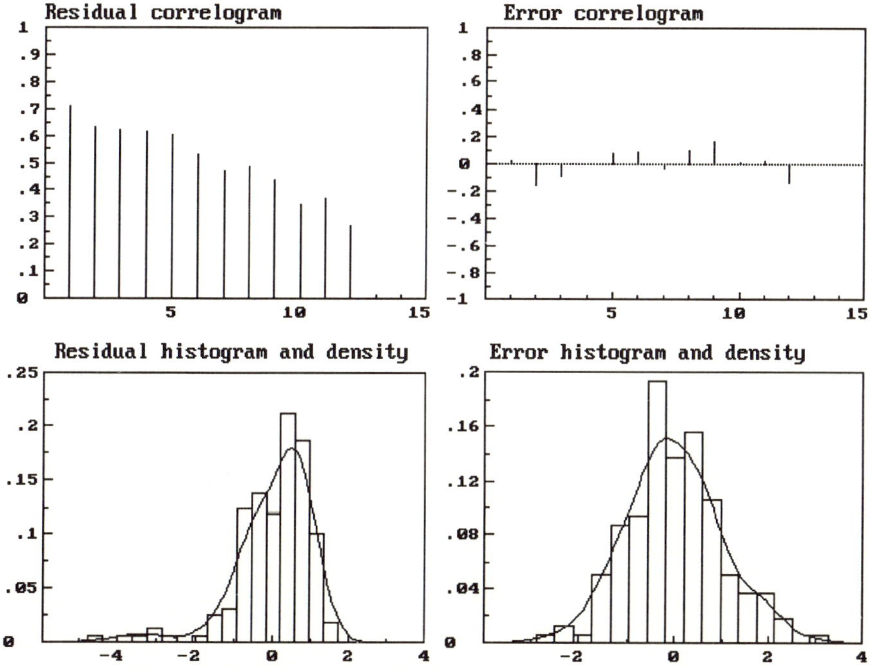

Fig. 6.4 Disturbance correlograms and densities

Now suppose an investigator calculated (6.30), but not the recursive tests. The usual route followed under such circumstances is to estimate an autoregressive error, supported by a reference to Cochrane and Orcutt (1949) , who do not in fact recommend such a procedure, but favour differencing (see Gilbert, 1989). However, this is the example alluded to in (b). The initial model is generalized to:

$$y_t = \delta_0 + \delta_1 z_t + v_t \text{ where } v_t = \alpha_1 v_{t-1} + \epsilon_t \text{ with } \epsilon_t \underset{c}{\sim} \mathsf{IN}\left[0, \sigma_\epsilon^2\right]. \quad (6.31)$$

Least-squares requires finding values for $(\delta_0, \delta_1, \alpha_1)$ as the arguments which minimize:

$$\min_{\delta_0,\delta_1,\alpha_1} \sum_{t=2}^{T} \epsilon_t^2 = \min_{\delta_0,\delta_1,\alpha_1} \sum_{t=2}^{T} \left(y_t - \alpha_1 y_{t-1} - \delta_0 (1 - \alpha_1) - \delta_1 z_t - \delta_1 \alpha_1 z_{t-1}\right)^2. \quad (6.32)$$

Although the function to be minimized is non-linear in the arguments $(\delta_0, \delta_1, \alpha_1)$, it is easy to obtain the minimum by numerical optimization methods (see Ch.A5). Figure 6.5 records the shape of the residual sum of squares (denoted RSS) in (6.32) as α_1 varies over $(-1, 1)$, where the optimizing values of (δ_0, δ_1) are used at each point. The RSS function is close to a quadratic and the best fitting values are given by:

$$\begin{aligned} y_t &= \underset{(0.001)}{0.014}\, z_t + \underset{(0.07)}{3.11} \quad \text{where } \hat{\alpha}_1 = \underset{(0.08)}{0.30} \\ \hat{\sigma} &= 0.240 \end{aligned} \quad (6.33)$$

The residual autoregression coefficient is significantly different from zero, although the estimates of δ_0 and δ_1 are little altered. The residual correlogram from (6.33) is relatively flat (the value of the $\chi^2(12)$ test in Box and Pierce, 1970, is 16.5) so the remaining autocorrelation is much less than in (6.30), and the goodness of fit has improved as measured by the residual standard deviation. Since we know the source of the problem here (non-linearity), the apparent success of the correction is merely treating a symptom, not the cause — as claimed in (c). The analysis is complete, since we have established (d) *en route*, by developing a model with a white-noise error in (6.33). However, if the regressor z_t^2 is added to any of the estimated models above, its coefficient is significantly different from zero at the 1 per cent level, and the estimated autoregressive parameter becomes insignificant. Such a quadratic effect is easy to detect on a test for the residual variance being heteroscedastic in (6.30) (see White, 1980b). As we know, that is the correct route to follow here to rectify a functional form mis-specification. In practice, an investigator merely knows that a model has a potentially serious flaw if a diagnostic test rejects.

The moral of this cautionary tale, as ever in economics, is *caveat emptor* of empirical evidence. We have investigated a number of situations where the evidence does not have the meaning a researcher might wish to interpret it as having. In no case has the destructive power of the approach been impugned. One lesson is the potential value of indices of model adequacy: the significance of any one test invalidates a direct interpretation of any of the others, but the significance of any test cautions against mechanistically adopting its alternative. Conversely, the difficulties inherent in proceeding from simple models to more general ones are apparent, and hence we will consider the alternative of testing for valid simplifications of relatively general initial models.

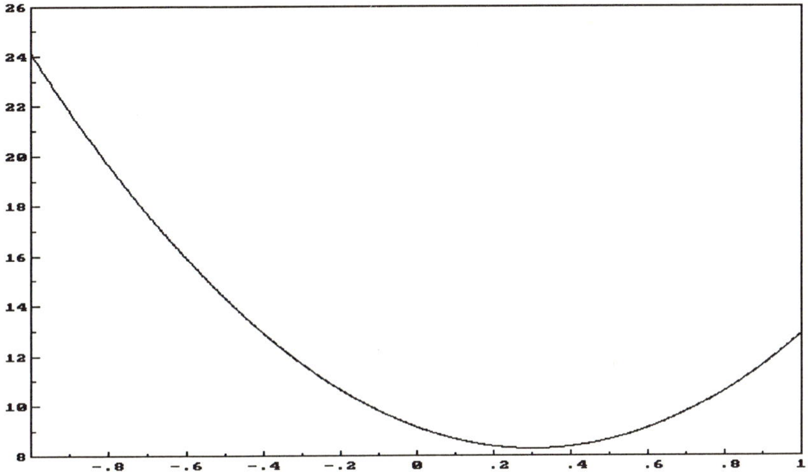

Fig. 6.5 Plot of $RSS(\alpha_1)$ for (6.33)

6.4 A simple dynamic model: AD(1,1)

We now combine dynamics and interdependence with the different interpretations underlying linear equations. The simplest example has the form (with $|\beta_2| < 1$):

$$y_t = \beta_0 + \beta_1 z_t + \beta_2 y_{t-1} + \beta_3 z_{t-1} + \epsilon_t \text{ where } \epsilon_t \sim \mathsf{IN}\left[0, \sigma_\epsilon^2\right]. \tag{6.34}$$

Equation (6.34) has an autoregressive component y_{t-1}, and an observable moving-average component z_t and z_{t-1}, which is called a distributed lag. Thus, (6.34) is called an autoregressive distributed-lag model, summarized as AD$(1,1)$, where the indices in parentheses refer to the maximum lags of y and z respectively. The AD$(1,1)$ class generalizes to AD(r, s) with maximum lags of r and s on y_t and z_t, or to AD$(r, s, p, \ldots, n)$ for additional variables with lag lengths of $p, \ldots, n$.

The error $\{\epsilon_t\}$ on (6.34) is an innovation against the available information and the serial independence of $\{\epsilon_t\}$ is part of the definition of an AD$(\cdot)$ model. The AD$(\cdot)$ class precludes models where the error $\{\epsilon_t\}$ is autocorrelated, and if models with error autocorrelation are to be part of this framework, they have to enter in some other way than by merely asserting that the error on (6.34) is autocorrelated. Since data densities can be sequentially factorized to have mean-innovation errors without loss of generality, only classes of models with innovation errors need be considered. In Chapter 7, models with autoregressive errors are shown to be a restriction of the initial class (not a generalization thereof); moving-average errors pose no difficulties in principle but do in practice. Either type of error may provide a convenient simplification of the dynamic reactions (see Jorgenson, 1966, and Hendry and Mizon, 1978). The normality and homoscedasticity assumptions are for convenience. Further, we will interpret y_t and z_t as $\log Y_t$ and $\log Z_t$ respectively, so that β_1 in (6.34) is an elasticity.

An intriguing feature of the AD(1, 1) model, despite its simplicity, is that virtually every type of single-equation model in empirical time-series econometrics is a special case of it. In the next chapter, we develop a typology of models with nine members from AD(1, 1), each of which manifests different behaviour in empirically important ways. Although the representatives of each type in the typology are schematic, the properties of the various types are not altered by multivariate generalizations. Chapter 7 analyses each of the nine types, and demonstrates that the forms of the restrictions they impose on the AD(1, 1) often entail certain empirical results, irrespective of how the data were generated. Thus, the results of some empirical studies are possibly as much a function of which member of the AD(1, 1) typology was chosen as a reflection of the data evidence, so may be an artefact of selecting a particular member of the typology. Chapter 8 extends the analysis to dynamic systems.

First, we classify (6.34) in terms of §6.1.1–§6.1.4 above. An important issue is the exogeneity status of z_t for $\boldsymbol{\beta} = (\beta_0 : \beta_1 : \beta_2 : \beta_3)'$. To simplify the exposition, assume that z_t is strongly exogenous for $\boldsymbol{\beta}$, so that (6.34) is a contingent plan. The essential features of the analysis are not affected if z_t is only weakly exogenous for $\boldsymbol{\beta}$, and can be generalized to z_t being endogenous. Letting $\boldsymbol{x}_t = (y_t : z_t)'$, take $\{\boldsymbol{x}_t; t = 1, \ldots, T\}$ to be generated by the stationary, sequential, joint-normal distribution:

$$\begin{pmatrix} y_t \\ z_t \end{pmatrix} \mid \boldsymbol{X}_{t-1} \sim \mathsf{N}_2 \left[\begin{pmatrix} \pi_{10} \\ \pi_{20} \end{pmatrix} + \begin{pmatrix} \pi_{11} & \pi_{12} \\ \pi_{21} & \pi_{22} \end{pmatrix} \begin{pmatrix} y_{t-1} \\ z_{t-1} \end{pmatrix}, \begin{pmatrix} \sigma_{11} & \sigma_{12} \\ \sigma_{12} & \sigma_{22} \end{pmatrix} \right]. \quad (6.35)$$

In (6.35), $\pi_{21} = 0$ precludes feedback from y_{t-1} on to z_t, in which case from Chapter 5:

$$\mathsf{E}\left[y_t \mid z_t, \boldsymbol{X}_{t-1}\right] = \pi_{10} + \pi_{11} y_{t-1} + \pi_{12} z_{t-1} + \sigma_{12}\sigma_{22}^{-1}\left(z_t - \pi_{20} - \pi_{22} z_{t-1}\right). \quad (6.36)$$

This can be rewritten as the model in (6.34), where $\beta_0 = (\pi_{10} - \gamma\pi_{20})$, $\beta_1 = \gamma$, $\beta_2 = \pi_{11}$ and $\beta_3 = (\pi_{12} - \gamma\pi_{22})$ when $\gamma = \sigma_{12}\sigma_{22}^{-1}$. Given strong exogeneity of z_t for $\boldsymbol{\beta}$:

$$\begin{pmatrix} y_t \\ z_t \end{pmatrix} \mid \boldsymbol{X}_{t-1} \sim \mathsf{N}_2 \left[\begin{pmatrix} \beta_0 + \beta_1\lambda_0 \\ \lambda_0 \end{pmatrix} + \begin{pmatrix} \beta_2 & \beta_3 + \beta_1\lambda_1 \\ 0 & \lambda_1 \end{pmatrix} \begin{pmatrix} y_{t-1} \\ z_{t-1} \end{pmatrix}, \begin{pmatrix} \sigma_{11} & \sigma_{12} \\ \sigma_{12} & \sigma_{22} \end{pmatrix} \right] \quad (6.37)$$

where $\lambda_0 = \pi_{20}$ and $\lambda_1 = \pi_{22}$. Consequently, $\sigma_\epsilon^2 = \sigma_{11} - \sigma_{12}^2\sigma_{22}^{-1}$. To ensure stationarity, impose the sufficient conditions that $|\lambda_1| < 1$, and $|\beta_2| < 1$. A more realistic situation is to allow for one unit root, namely $\lambda_1 = 1$, and Chapter 7 analyses that case once some additional tools have been developed.

To facilitate the Chapter 7 typology, we first discuss lag structures and their measurement in the AD(1, 1) class, which is the topic of the next section, and then investigate the properties of the model in (6.34), which is the subject of §6.6.

6.5 Lags and their measurement

6.5.1 Static solutions

The static or long-run solution of a dynamic, stochastic process denotes a hypothetical deterministic situation in which all change has ceased. For a stationary stochastic process like (6.34), the static solution corresponds to the expected value. As such, the concept does not necessarily denote a long run of time, but as will be seen in (6.43), the long-run solution has an effect on the outcome in every period. Rewrite (6.34) as:

$$(1-\beta_2 L)\, y_t = \beta_0 + (\beta_1 + \beta_3 L)\, z_t + \epsilon_t. \tag{6.38}$$

Let $\mathsf{E}[z_t] = z^*$ and $\mathsf{E}[y_t] = y^*\ \forall t$, which are constant due to the assumption of stationarity, then taking expectations in (6.38):

$$(1-\beta_2 L)\, \mathsf{E}[y_t] = \beta_0 + (\beta_1 + \beta_3 L)\, \mathsf{E}[z_t]. \tag{6.39}$$

Since $\mathsf{E}[y_t]$ and $\mathsf{E}[z_t]$ are constant, and a lag operator applied to a constant has no effect, (6.39) implies:

$$y^* = \frac{\beta_0}{(1-\beta_2)} + \left[\frac{(\beta_1+\beta_3)}{(1-\beta_2)}\right] z^* = K_0 + K_1 z^*. \tag{6.40}$$

Thus, AD(1, 1) models have linear static solutions, which are proportional if $\beta_0 = 0 = K_0$.

To generalize this result, consider an AD(p, q) model with lag polynomials $\gamma(L)$ and $\delta(L)$ of orders p and q operating on y_t and z_t respectively:

$$\gamma(L)\, y_t = \beta_0 + \delta(L)\, z_t + \epsilon_t. \tag{6.41}$$

When all the roots of $\gamma(L) = 1 - \sum_{i=1}^{p} \gamma_i L^i$ are stable, so that $\gamma(1) \neq 0$, the static solution is:

$$\gamma(1)\, y^* = \beta_0 + \delta(1)\, z^*,$$

in which case:

$$y^* = \frac{\beta_0}{\gamma(1)} + \left[\frac{\delta(1)}{\gamma(1)}\right] z^* = K_0 + K_1 z^*. \tag{6.42}$$

In a stationary world, (6.42) produces the same general form of long-run response of y to z as (6.40). This is an important result in as much as many economic theories have log-linear long-run equilibrium solutions, so we can mimic them in the AD($\cdot$) class. The concept of equilibrium in (6.42) is that of no inherent tendency to change, and any deviation of the form $(y^* - K_0 - K_1 z^*) \neq 0$ is a disequilibrium which should induce a change in $\{y_t\}$ in a later period.

A one–one transformation of (6.34) which highlights additional features of the lag structure is to re-express that equation in terms of growth rates of Y_t and Z_t and the equilibrium correction $(y - K_0 - K_1 z)_{t-1}$. This is often called an error correction following Davidson, Hendry, Srba and Yeo, 1978), but the correction only works within regimes, and does not 'correct' towards a changed equilibrium.

Subtract y_{t-1} from both sides of (6.34) using $\Delta y_t = (y_t - y_{t-1})$:

$$\begin{aligned}
\Delta y_t &= \beta_0 + \beta_1 z_t + (\beta_2 - 1)\, y_{t-1} + \beta_3 z_{t-1} + \epsilon_t \\
&= \beta_0 + \beta_1 (z_t - z_{t-1}) + (\beta_2 - 1)\, y_{t-1} + (\beta_1 + \beta_3)\, z_{t-1} + \epsilon_t \\
&= \beta_0 + \beta_1 \Delta z_t + (\beta_2 - 1)(y_{t-1} - K_1 z_{t-1}) + \epsilon_t \\
&= \beta_1 \Delta z_t + (\beta_2 - 1)(y - K_0 - K_1 z)_{t-1} + \epsilon_t
\end{aligned} \tag{6.43}$$

since from (6.40), $K_0(1-\beta_2)=\beta_0$ and $K_1(1-\beta_2)=(\beta_1+\beta_3)$. This transformation maps from $(\beta_0, \beta_1, \beta_2, \beta_3)$ to $(K_0, \beta_1, \beta_2, K_1)$ and maintains the number of parameters at four. From (6.43), the immediate impact of a change in z_t on y_t is β_1. Even when $\{\epsilon_t\}$ and $\{\Delta z_t\}$ are zero for a prolonged period, $\Delta y_t \neq 0$ until $y_t = K_0 + K_1 z_t$, matching the earlier interpretation of $(y^* - K_0 - K_1 z^*)$ as a disequilibrium. How rapidly Δy_t converges to zero, which is the equilibrium outcome, depends on the magnitude of $(\beta_2 - 1)$. That leads to our next topic.

6.5.2 Lag distributions

Having obtained the immediate and long-run responses of y to z in (6.34), we next trace out the dynamic path from one to the other. If (6.38) were deterministic, then starting from the impact $\beta_1 z_t$ on y_t in the current period, the effect would end at $K_1 z^*$, which is the eventual impact of z^* on y^* after time has run on indefinitely. Thus, the expected solution corresponds to the long-run-of-time solution in a deterministic world. To derive the adjustment path for (6.41) in response to an impulse change in z, express the relationship between y_t and z_t in terms of the weight function $w(L) = \delta(L)/\gamma(L)$:

$$y_t = \frac{\beta_0}{\gamma(L)} + \left[\frac{\delta(L)}{\gamma(L)}\right] z_t + \frac{\epsilon_t}{\gamma(L)} = K_0 + w(L) z_t + u_t, \tag{6.44}$$

where $\{u_t\}$ has a mean of zero and a constant variance when $\{\epsilon_t\}$ does, although in general $\{u_t\}$ will be autocorrelated unless $\gamma(L)$ has no terms involving L. From (6.44):

$$w(L) = \sum_{i=0}^{\infty} w_i L^i.$$

Given the strong exogeneity of z_t:

$$\frac{\partial y_t}{\partial z_{t-i}} = w_i, \; i = 0, 1, \ldots$$

Thus, the effect of z_t on y_t is w_0; the effect of z_t on y_{t+1} is w_1; and so on, where the long-run solution of (6.44) is:

$$K_1 = w(1) = \sum_{i=0}^{\infty} w_i = \frac{\delta(1)}{\gamma(1)}. \tag{6.45}$$

To calculate $(w_0, w_1, \ldots, w_n, \ldots)$ in terms of $\{\gamma_j\}$ and $\{\delta_i\}$, from $w(L)\gamma(L) = \delta(L)$:

$$\left(\sum_{i=0}^{\infty} w_i L^i\right)\left(\sum_{j=0}^{p} \gamma_j L^j\right) = \sum_{k=0}^{q} \delta_k L^k, \tag{6.46}$$

equate powers of L on the two sides of (6.46), noting that $\gamma_0 = 1$, to obtain:

$$w_0 = \delta_0; \; w_1 + w_0\gamma_1 = \delta_1; \; w_2 + w_1\gamma_1 + w_0\gamma_2 = \delta_2;$$

and so on. Hence:

$$w_0 = \delta_0;\ w_1 = \delta_1 - \delta_0\gamma_1;\ w_2 = \delta_2 - (\delta_1 - \delta_0\gamma_1)\,\gamma_1 - \delta_0\gamma_2; \text{ etc.}$$

It would be convenient to be able to map the ws onto a discrete probability distribution, to utilize existing mathematical tools. This can be achieved if $w(L)$ satisfies two conditions:

(i) $w(1) \neq 0$. If so, the sum of the weights can be normalized at unity with no loss of generality, so that:

$$w(1) = \sum_{i=0}^{\infty} w_i = K_1 = 1. \tag{6.47}$$

(ii) $0 \leq w_i \leq 1$.

If both (i) and (ii) are satisfied, the $\{w_i\}$ correspond to discrete probability weights and it makes sense to talk about mean and median lags as summary measures of the lag structure of (6.41), and hence (6.34). Given the mapping to discrete probabilities, and temporarily using $'$ to denote a derivative:

$$\text{Mean lag: } \mu = \frac{\sum_{i=0}^{\infty} i w_i}{\sum_{i=0}^{\infty} w_i} = \frac{1}{w(1)}\left(\frac{\partial w(L)}{\partial L}\Big\rfloor_{L=1}\right) = \frac{w'(1)}{w(1)}; \tag{6.48}$$

$$\text{Median lag: the smallest } m \text{ such that } \sum_{i=0}^{m-1} w_i \leq \tfrac{1}{2} \leq \sum_{i=0}^{m} w_i. \tag{6.49}$$

Thus, m is the first point at which the (normalized) sum of the weights exceeds 0.5. Although m often has to be worked out numerically from (6.49), the mean lag μ is open to general analysis.

Differentiate the ratio in (6.48) using (6.44):

$$w'(L) = \frac{\partial w(L)}{\partial L} = \frac{\delta'(L)}{\gamma(L)} - \frac{\delta(L)\,\gamma'(L)}{\gamma(L)^2} = w(L)\left(\frac{\delta'(L)}{\delta(L)} - \frac{\gamma'(L)}{\gamma(L)}\right). \tag{6.50}$$

Dividing by $w(1)$, the general formula for the mean lag becomes:

$$\mu = \frac{w'(1)}{w(1)} = \frac{\delta'(1)}{\delta(1)} - \frac{\gamma'(1)}{\gamma(1)}. \tag{6.51}$$

As an example, the mean lag for the AD(1, 1) follows from:

$$\delta(L) = \beta_1 + \beta_3 L \ \text{ and } \gamma(L) = 1 - \beta_2 L, \tag{6.52}$$

so that when $w(1) = K_1 = 1 = \sum_{i=1}^{3} \beta_i$, then:

$$\mu = \frac{w'(1)}{w(1)} = \frac{\beta_3}{(\beta_1 + \beta_3)} + \frac{\beta_2}{(1 - \beta_2)} = \frac{(\beta_2 + \beta_3)}{(1 - \beta_2)} = \frac{(1 - \beta_1)}{(1 - \beta_2)}. \tag{6.53}$$

Equation (6.53) is easy to interpret: the mean lag comprises whatever has not happened immediately, namely $(1-\beta_1)$, divided by the fraction of the disequilibrium carried forward in each period, namely $(1-\beta_2)$. As β_2 approaches unity, the mean lag tends to infinity. In the limit, for $\beta_2 = 1$, the model cannot reach equilibrium as no disequilibrium affects future behaviour. Conversely, the model appears to give a complete and immediate reaction if β_1 is unity since the mean lag becomes zero. However, that can occur even if β_2 and β_3 are non-zero, warning us that some of the w_i are negative and hence the formulae in (6.48) and (6.49) do not apply. Consequently, when (6.48) delivers a mean lag of zero, weights must be cancelling and the mathematics of discrete probability distributions are inapplicable.

For the median lag, reconsider the sequence of lag weights for (6.34):

$$\begin{aligned} w_0 &= \beta_1 \geq 0; && \text{(impact)} \\ w_1 &= \beta_2\beta_1 + \beta_3 = \phi \geq 0; && \text{(common factor)} \\ w_i &= \beta_2^{i-1}\phi \geq 0;\ i \geq 2 && \text{(exponential decay)} \end{aligned}$$

Thus, $\phi = 0$ implies that all later $w_i = 0$ also. Further, when $\sum_{i=1}^{3} \beta_i = 1$, then $\phi = (1-\beta_1)(1-\beta_2)$ and:

$$\begin{aligned} \sum_{j=0}^{m} w_j &= \beta_1 + \phi + \phi\beta_2 + \phi\beta_2^2 + \cdots + \phi\beta_2^{m-1} \\ &= \beta_1 + \phi\left(1-\beta_2^m\right)(1-\beta_2)^{-1} \\ &= \beta_1 + (1-\beta_1)\left(1-\beta_2^m\right) \\ &= 1 - \beta_2^m(1-\beta_1). \end{aligned} \tag{6.54}$$

Since $0 \leq \beta_2 < 1$, then $m = 0$ when $\beta_1 \geq \frac{1}{2}$ and when $\beta_1 < \frac{1}{2}$, m is:

$$m = -\frac{\log\left[2(1-\beta_1)\right]}{\log\beta_2}.$$

Figures 6.6a,b show a set of lag weights from an AD$(1,1,1)$ estimated for UK investment data (gross domestic fixed capital formation, seasonally adjusted) as a log-linear function of GNP and the interest rate on long bonds (denoted R_b). The distribution for GNP is skewed, and resembles an exponential shape, with the weights declining to zero by ten periods. From the same equation, however, the lag reaction to R_b rises at first then falls to zero. Figures 6.6c,d record the corresponding cumulative weights $\sum_{j=0}^{i} w_j$, both of which climb steadily to unity.

An important result due to Sims (1972) is that for any given lag distribution, there is another lag distribution that closely approximates it, where the first can have a small mean lag while the second can have a near-infinite mean lag. This warns us not to use the mean lag as the only summary statistic of a lag distribution: the median lag can provide useful additional information. This problem is due to expanding $\gamma(L)^{-1}$ as a power series in L to derive the $\{w_i\}$ in (6.46); such an expansion dies out slowly if β_2 is close to unity, so that the derived lag distribution can have fat tails. Even so, the median lag can be quite short: for example, $m = 0$ if $\beta_1 \geq \frac{1}{2}$, whereas μ could be large for small values of $(1 - \beta_2)$. A more complete description of the distributional shape is provided by the values of both the mean and median lag: in Fig. 6.6a, $\mu = 1.2$ and $m = 1$, whereas in Fig. 6.6b, $\mu = 1.7$ and $m = 1$, but the figures are even more informative than reporting μ and m.

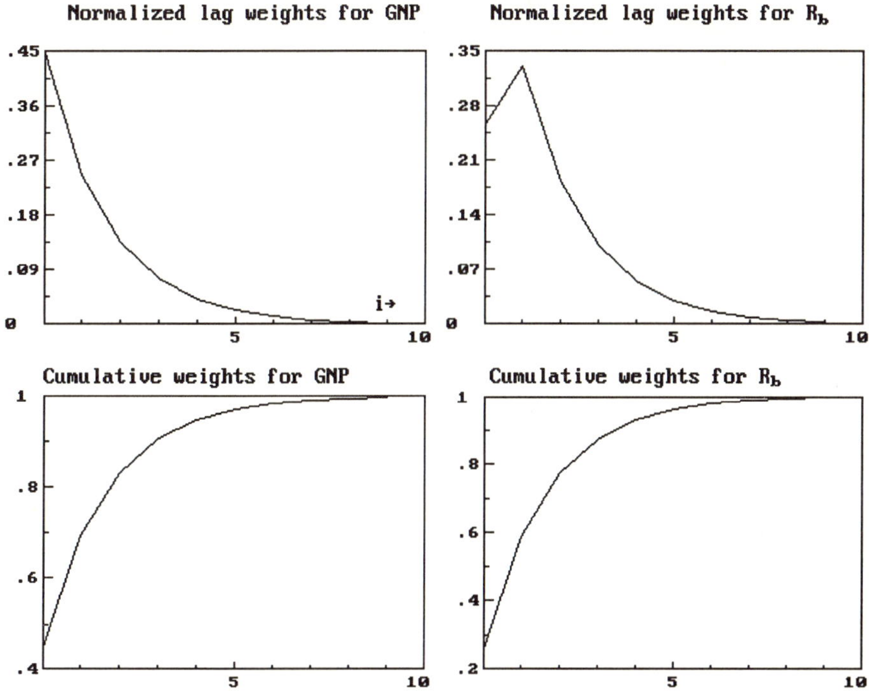

Fig. 6.6 Normalized and cumulative lag weights

Equations (6.52) and (6.54) highlight that different values of the parameters in $\gamma(L)$ and $\delta(L)$ impose restrictions on the calculated mean and the median lags, irrespective of the actual shape of the distribution. For example, if $\beta_3 = 0$, μ only depends on β_2, and imposes an exponential shape. Since the $\{\beta_i\}$ parameters generate different members of the model typology discussed below, some types of model may impose an incorrect lag shape on the data, and may not reveal that the wrong distributional shape has been imposed. Chapter 7 investigates that issue.

6.5.3 Interpreting empirical lag distributions

A natural question is whether economic analysis generally restricts the form of the lag polynomials $\gamma(L)$ and $\delta(L)$ in (6.41). Essentially, the answer must be negative since almost any pattern of signs is consistent with reasonable agent behaviour, as we now demonstrate for $\delta(L) z_t$. Polynomials are invariant to linear transformations such as:

$$\delta(L) = \sum_{i=0}^{n} \delta_i L^i = \sum_{i=0}^{n} \lambda_i (1-L)^i = \psi_0 + \sum_{i=1}^{n} \psi_i (1-L^i) = \omega_0 + \sum_{i=1}^{n-1} \omega_i (1-L) L^i.$$

Each expression corresponds to a different parameterization of the lag distribution, and agents may determine their plans in terms of any of these alternative forms. The implications are perhaps clearest in the following special cases:

(i) a difference generates a sign switch in levels:

$$\alpha \Delta z_t = \alpha z_t - \alpha z_{t-1};$$

(ii) an average growth generates a gap:

$$\alpha \left\{ \tfrac{1}{2} (\Delta z_t + \Delta z_{t-1}) \right\} = \tfrac{1}{2} \alpha z_t + 0.z_{t-1} - \tfrac{1}{2} \alpha z_{t-2} = \alpha \left(\tfrac{1}{2} \Delta_2 z_t \right);$$

(iii) a second difference (i.e. an acceleration) produces:

$$\alpha \Delta^2 z_t = \alpha z_t - 2\alpha z_{t-1} + \alpha z_{t-2};$$

(iv) a multi-period difference produces an average difference:

$$\alpha \Delta_4 z_t = \alpha \Delta z_t + \alpha \Delta z_{t-1} + \alpha \Delta z_{t-2} + \alpha \Delta z_{t-3} = \alpha \sum_{i=0}^{3} \Delta z_{t-i};$$

(v) a difference plus an acceleration produces:

$$\alpha \Delta z_t + \beta \Delta^2 z_t = (\alpha + \beta) \Delta z_t - \beta \Delta z_{t-1};$$

(vi) which in terms of the levels of the variables is:

$$(\alpha + \beta) z_t - (\alpha + 2\beta) z_{t-1} + \beta z_{t-2};$$

(vii) a level and a difference can induce apparent sign changes on lag-order switches:

$$\alpha \Delta z_t + \beta z_{t-1} = \beta z_t + (\alpha - \beta) \Delta z_t;$$

and so on. In each case, we merely re-parameterize the lag distribution. If agents respond to (linear combinations of) some or all differences up to the $(d+1)$st difference for a process which is I(1), then almost any coefficient pattern is conceivable. Should an economic theory not entail the observed lag distributions, this is probably because of implicit steady-state assumptions that led to ignoring higher-order differences of variables (e.g. perhaps because d was assumed constant at zero in the theory but was unity, or even varied, in reality). Such considerations suggest commencing from relatively unconstrained lag structures, transforming these to an interpretable but parsimonious parameterization using the reverse of the above mappings from differences to levels, then eliminating empirically irrelevant effects. Similar issues arise for $\gamma(L)$, noting that the first transform would usually be to an equilibrium correction as in (6.42), so that the remaining effects of the dependent variable would be expressed in differences and functions thereof. Chapter 16 illustrates the application of the above ideas to a dynamic model for money demand.

6.6 A Monte Carlo study of the AD(1,1) model

Section A3.7 develops the theory of least-squares estimation when it is valid to condition on the complete sample on all regressors. Section A4.8 extends estimation theory to dynamic processes, but using asymptotic distributions. We now investigate the relevance of such results to a finite sample from a dynamic process, applying recursive Monte Carlo to an experiment involving data generated from the AD(1, 1) DGP in (6.34) (see §3.6 for Monte Carlo methods). The set of parameter values used is based on empirical experience, namely:

$$\beta_0 = 0; \ \beta_1 = 0.5; \ \beta_2 = 0.9; \ \beta_3 = -0.4; \ \text{and} \ \sigma_\epsilon^2 = 1.$$

The intercept is imposed at zero for simplicity, and the variance is a scale normalization. For relevant empirical studies, see Hendry (1979b, 1984a).

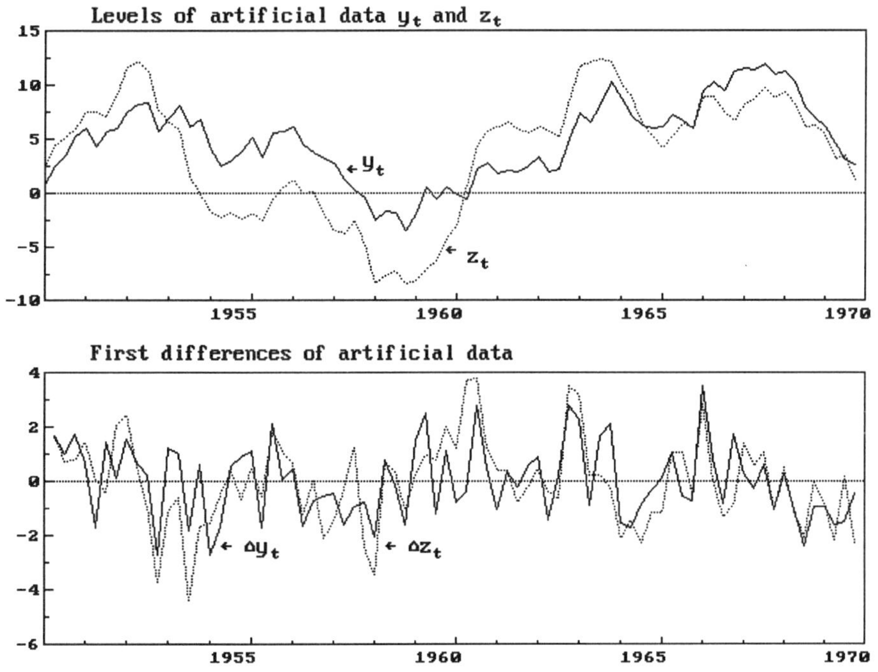

Fig. 6.7 Levels and differences of artificial data

The DGP is slightly more general than (6.37) in that z_t is generated by the AD(1, 0):

$$z_t = 0.95z_{t-1} + w_t + \nu_t \ \text{ where } \nu_t \sim \mathsf{IN}[0,1] \tag{6.55}$$

and

$$w_t = 0.25 + 0.75w_{t-1} + u_t \ \text{ where } u_t \sim \mathsf{IN}[0,1]. \tag{6.56}$$

The three error processes $\{\epsilon_t\}$, $\{\nu_t\}$ and $\{u_t\}$ are jointly independently distributed.

Since $\sum_{i=1}^{3} \beta_i = 1$, the long run entails $K_1 = 1$. The impact, β_1, in the first period is half of the total adjustment towards equilibrium, so the median lag is zero: $m = 0$. From (6.53), the mean lag is $\mu = 5$ so there is rapid short-run adjustment, but the long-run response is slow. The correct AD(1, 1) model is estimated by least-squares from a sample size of $T = 80$ in each of $M = 1000$ replications. Figures 6.7a,d show the time series of $\{y_t, z_t, \Delta y_t, \Delta z_t\}$ respectively from one randomly selected replication. The levels move gradually in line, and the differences are highly correlated.

We first consider the biases in the coefficient estimates as T changes, then examine the accuracy of the estimated standard errors, and conclude by investigating the size of the breakpoint Chow test for parameter constancy. The notation follows that established in §3.6.

6.6.1 Coefficient biases

If the theory in §A3.7 applied exactly, the coefficient estimates should be unbiased. Because of the dynamics, some biases may occur in finite samples even though the least-squares estimators are consistent for $\boldsymbol{\beta}$ in an AD(1, 1) DGP. The graphs of the sequences of the average coefficient biases from recursive estimation over sample sizes 20 to 80 reveal how the biases vary with sample size (if at all).

Figure 6.8a shows the mean biases when estimating the four β_i coefficients (of the intercept, z_t, y_{t-1}, and z_{t-1}). The estimates for β_1 start off slightly biased at $T = 20$, and converge gradually to an almost unbiased coefficient estimate at $T = 80$. Thus, even estimating β_1 unrestrictedly in an AD(1, 1) from a relatively small sample does not produce a badly biased coefficient estimate. The biases in β_2 are noticeable at small sample sizes, being around 10 per cent of the coefficient value, but die out quickly as the sample size increases. The biases in the estimates of β_3 are in the opposite direction to those of β_2. This last phenomenon arises because $K_1 = (\beta_1 + \beta_3) / (1 - \beta_2)$, so coefficient biases are offsetting to maintain the long-run outcome. The intercept is the least well determined. The largest bias in any of the other estimated coefficients is less than 0.02 at $T = 80$, which can be compared with a simulation standard error of less than 0.006, confirming the accuracy of the simulation estimates for a large replication sample.

By itself, this last finding is not necessarily reassuring. Generally in econometrics, estimation is only a step towards inference, and the latter measures coefficient estimates in relation to their standard errors, as in a t-test of H_0: $\beta = \beta^*$:

$$\mathsf{t}_{\beta=\beta^*} = \frac{\left(\hat{\beta} - \beta^*\right)}{\mathsf{SE}\left[\hat{\beta}\right]} = \frac{\left(\mathsf{E}\left[\hat{\beta}\right] - \beta\right)}{\mathsf{SE}\left[\hat{\beta}\right]} + \frac{(\beta - \beta^*)}{\mathsf{SE}\left[\hat{\beta}\right]} + \frac{\left(\hat{\beta} - \mathsf{E}\left[\hat{\beta}\right]\right)}{\mathsf{SE}\left[\hat{\beta}\right]}. \tag{6.57}$$

The first term in the final expression of (6.57) is the relative bias, and, when it is large, $\mathsf{t}_{\beta=\beta^*}$ could be large even when H_0 is true and the second term is zero. In the present example, however, the coefficient standard errors are much larger than 0.02, so the relative bias is small in the AD(1, 1) for the parameter values considered in this experiment.

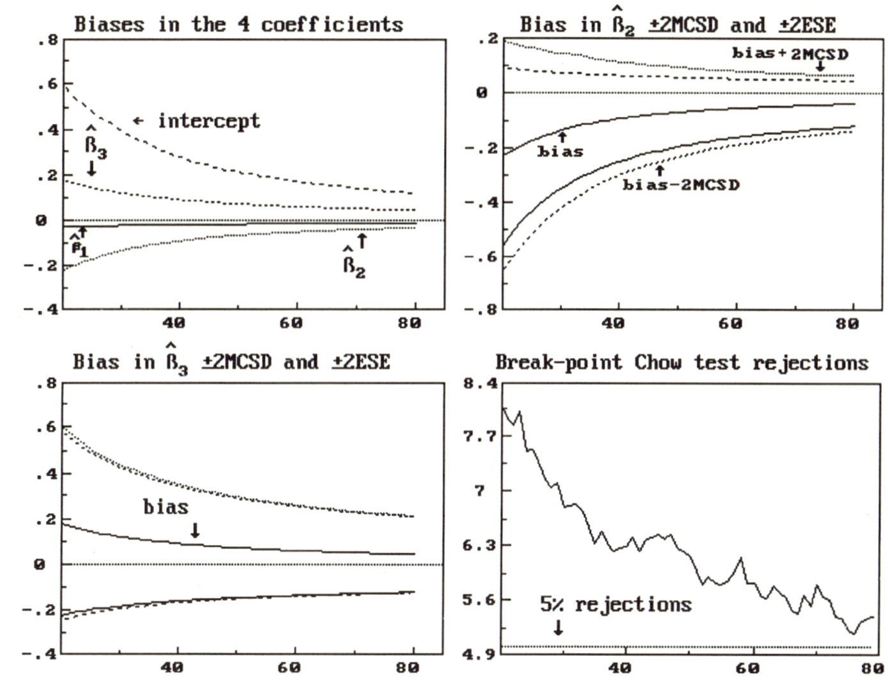

Fig. 6.8 Recursive Monte Carlo output

6.6.2 Coefficient standard errors

When regression coefficients are estimated, the computer-program formula for calculating the variances of the coefficient estimates for a sample of size t is:

$$\widehat{\mathsf{V}[\hat{\beta}_t]} = \hat{\sigma}_t^2 \left(\boldsymbol{X}_t^{1\prime} \boldsymbol{X}_t^1 \right)^{-1}, \tag{6.58}$$

where $\hat{\sigma}_t^2$ is the estimated equation error variance. The square roots of the diagonal of (6.58) are the coefficient standard errors (see §3.2). In deriving (6.58) analytically in the theoretical statistical model at level A, the model is assumed to be the DGP, and (6.58) is the correct formula only on the condition that the model is an adequate mimic of the DGP. In empirical research, (6.58) will not be the correct formula when the model does not adequately represent the DGP (see §4.9 for an example). There may also exist small-sample biases in estimating the variance in a dynamic process where (6.58) is an asymptotic approximation.

However, the correct variance can be computed in a Monte Carlo at any sample size using:

$$\mathcal{V}\left[\hat{\beta}_{jt}\right] = (M-1)^{-1} \sum_{i=1}^{M} \left(\hat{\beta}_{jit} - \bar{\beta}_{jt} \right)^2 \tag{6.59}$$

where $\bar{\beta}_{jt} = M^{-1} \sum_{i=1}^{M} \hat{\beta}_{jit}$, and $\hat{\beta}_{jit}$ is the estimate of β_j on the ith replication at sample size t. Formula (6.59) provides an unbiased estimator of the correct variance irrespective of model mis-specification, dynamics, etc. (see §3.6). The square roots of variances calculated from (6.58) are estimated standard errors, or ESE, whereas the square roots of the actual variances from (6.59) are Monte Carlo sampling standard deviations, or MCSD. The important question for the validity of inference is how close ESE is to the correct MCSD. Figure 6.8b reveals that for β_2, ESE $\simeq$ MCSD only for $T \geq 70$ and otherwise ESE underestimates MCSD, whereas Fig. 6.8c shows that ESE and MCSD are close for β_3. The outcomes for β_1 and β_3 are similar.

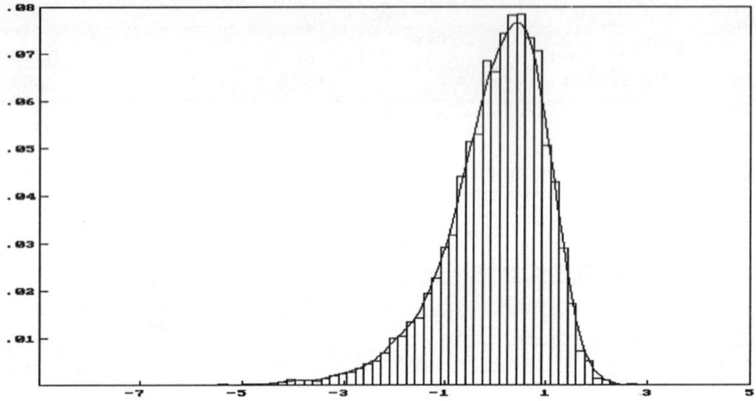

Fig. 6.9 Frequency distribution of $\hat{\beta}_2$

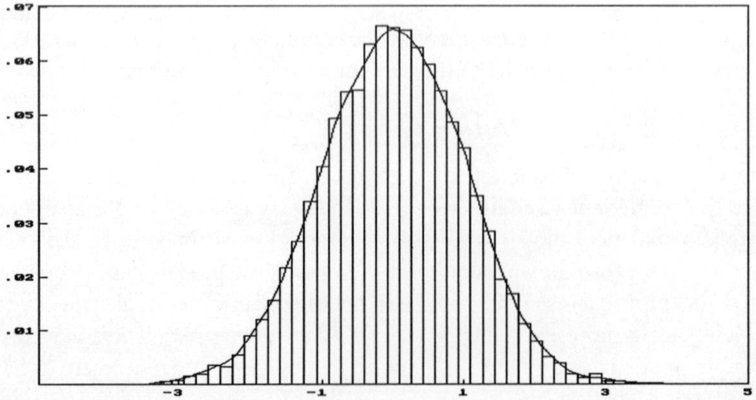

Fig. 6.10 Frequency distribution of $\hat{\beta}_1$

The standardized frequency distribution of the estimator of β_2 over the 1000 replications at $T = 80$ is shown in Fig. 6.9. The distribution is skewed with a long negative tail, which helps account for the bias in the ESE for the MCSD. The distributions of the estimators of β_1 and β_3 are close to normality, as Fig. 6.10 illustrates for the former. Overall, therefore, the conventional variance formula in (6.58) provides an adequate guide to the actual uncertainty in this class of dynamic models.

6.6.3 Parameter constancy tests

A bonus of recursive Monte Carlo is calculating every 1-step forecast error $\left(y_{t_j} - \hat{y}_{t_j}\right)$ for $T_j = T_0, T_0+1, \ldots, T$, given an initial sample size T_0. These forecast errors can be used to construct parameter constancy tests at (say) a 5 per cent critical value, and the rejection frequencies of the resulting tests can be reported graphically. The frequency of rejection will fluctuate for 1-step forecasts in a Monte Carlo: being an estimate of the probability p of rejecting the model, for M replications the estimated p has a standard error given by the binomial formula:

$$\mathsf{SE}\left[\hat{\mathsf{p}}\right] = \sqrt{\mathsf{p}\left(1 - \mathsf{p}\right)/M}.$$

When $\mathsf{p} = 0.05$, then $\mathsf{SE}\left[\hat{\mathsf{p}}\right] \simeq 0.218/\sqrt{M}$, so that M has to be large to get a standard error which is small relative to 0.05. For example, at $M = 1000$, a 95 per cent confidence interval based on the Monte Carlo standard error for $\mathsf{p} = 0.05$ is ± 0.014. Consequently, graphs of estimated probabilities will reveal considerable uncertainty until M becomes extremely large.

Because the breakpoint constancy test (see Chow, 1960, and §3.2.2 where this F-test is derived) is widely used in empirical econometrics, we compute it for every possible sub-sample: fit the model from 1 to T_1, forecast the outcome from $T_1 + 1$ to T and test whether the two are compatible, doing so for every possible T_1. Figure 6.8d records the rejection frequencies for a sequence of such tests, using a critical value as if only one test were calculated, designed to have a type I error of 5 per cent at each break point. The result should be interpreted as the size of the F-test at each possible break point within a fixed sample of $T = 80$ observations. On average, the test would have rejected the model about 5.6 per cent of the time at any point in time, with a standard error of 0.2 per cent, so the F-test rejects only a little too often when using dynamic data, under the null that the model has constant parameters.

Thus, the standard regression-theory results from Chapter A3 hold reasonably well despite the presence of dynamics. Although we have considered only one set of parameter values, similar findings hold over most of the relevant parameter space until β_2 is close to unity. On this basis, we proceed to the typology of nine members of the AD(1, 1) and contrast their Monte Carlo results with those for the AD(1, 1) parent.

6.7 An empirical illustration

To illustrate the AD(1, 1) model empirically, we consider UK quarterly, seasonally-adjusted data over 1963(1)–1989(2) from Hendry and Ericsson (1991b), on the (inverse) velocity of circulation of M1, given by $\log\left(M/PY\right)$ as a function of the net interest rate R_t (the differential between the 3-month local authority interest rate and the interest paid on retail sight deposits), where M denotes M1, Y is constant (1982) price total final expenditure, and P is the implicit deflator of Y. The net interest rate R_t has been learning adjusted as explained in Chapter 16. The basic AD(1, 1) model is interpreted as a money-demand equation and has the form:

$$\log\left(\frac{M}{PY}\right)_t = \beta_0 + \beta_1 R_t + \beta_2 \log\left(\frac{M}{PY}\right)_{t-1} + \beta_3 R_{t-1} + \epsilon_t. \tag{6.60}$$

This specification is to illustrate the estimation of an AD(1, 1) equation, and is knowingly mis-specified relative to the equations developed in earlier research (see e.g. Hendry, 1979b, 1985). Figure 6.11 shows the time series on $v_t = \{-\log(M/PY)_t\}$ and $\{R_t\}$, and reveals a degree of similarity in their time profiles.

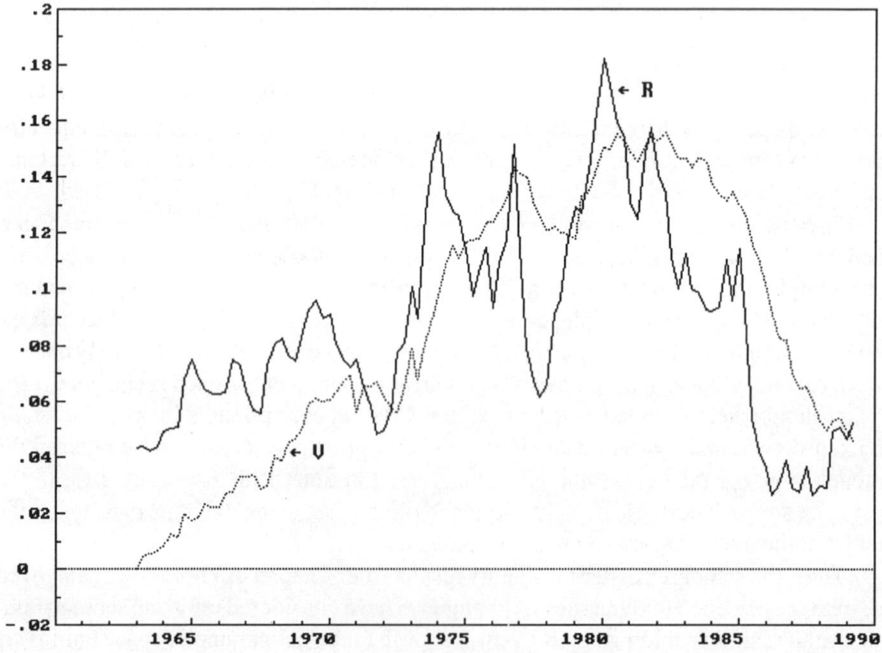

Fig. 6.11 Time series of velocity and the net interest rate

In common with the model in Hendry and Ericsson (1991b), the postulated equation imposes long-run homogeneity with respect to price and income, and adopts an appropriate measure of the opportunity cost of holding M1. However, it also imposes short-run price and income homogeneity (by excluding inflation and income growth as separate regressors), and excludes $\Delta \log(M/PY)_{t-1}$ (by focusing on one lag only): these restrictions are rejected by the data. Transforming the equation to a more interpretable parameterization, OLS estimation yields for $T = 1964(1) - 1989(2)$:

$$\Delta \widehat{\log \left(\frac{M}{PY}\right)_t} = \underset{(0.006)}{-0.006} - \underset{(0.15)}{0.79}\, \Delta R_t - \underset{(0.013)}{0.078} \log \left(\frac{M}{PY}\right)_{t-1} - \underset{(0.07)}{0.58}\, R_{t-1}$$

$$\mathrm{R}^2 = 0.47 \quad \hat{\sigma}^2 = 2.02\% \quad SC = -7.66 \quad AR\text{-}F(5,93) = 3.22 \quad ND\text{-}\chi^2(2) = 4.2. \tag{6.61}$$

The interpretation of (6.61) follows from (3.3.4) with the addition that SC denotes the Schwarz criterion, $AR\text{-}F\,(5,93)$ is an F-test for 5th-order residual autocorrelation and $ND\text{-}\chi^2\,(2)$ is a chi-square test for normality (see Doornik and Hendry, 1994b: the various tests are listed in Table 9.1 and their theory is presented in Part II). The intercept is small and insignificant, but the other three coefficient estimates are more than five times their estimated standard errors. The residual standard deviation is 2 per cent of M1 as against 1.3 per cent in Hendry and Ericsson (1991b), and the equation explains half of the variability in $\Delta \log{(M/PY)}_t$. There is some evidence of residual autocorrelation but little of non-normality.

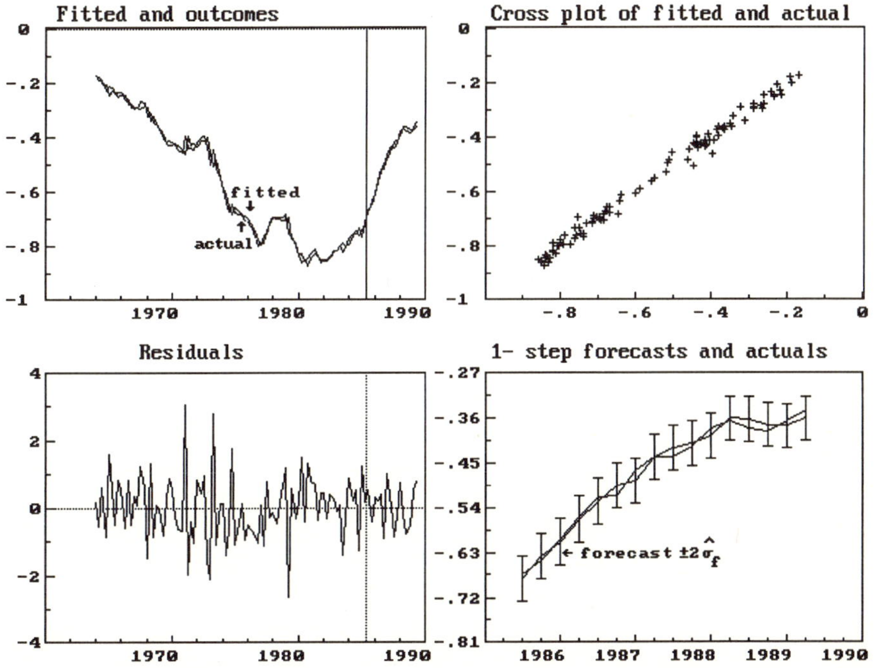

Fig. 6.12 UK M1 regression fits, forecasts and residuals

The hypothesis that $\beta_2 = 1$ can be rejected, so that the model has a long-run solution of the form:

$$\log\left(\frac{M}{PY}\right)^* + \underset{(0.9)}{7.4}\, R^* = -\underset{(0.08)}{0.08} \tag{6.62}$$

which yields a substantial interest (semi) elasticity (see Bårdsen, 1989, for the derivation of the standard errors). We have not yet established the tools to ascertain whether (6.61) can be interpreted as a demand equation, but will assume that it is.

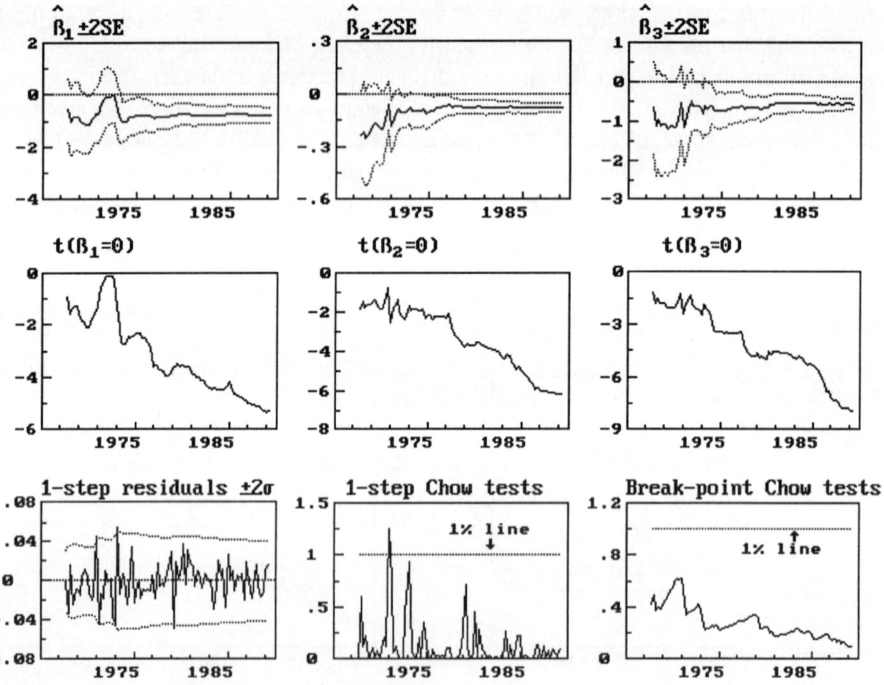

Fig. 6.13 Parameter constancy statistics

Although the coefficients β_1 and β_3 of R_t and R_{t-1} have different signs, the normalized lag weights derived from this AD(1, 1) are positive and monotonically decreasing with a mean lag of just over nine quarters. Figures 6.12a–d record the time series of fitted and actual values, the cross-plot of those, the full-sample residuals and the sequence of 1-step forecast errors together with $\pm 2\sigma\,(t)$ calculated recursively as explained in Chapter 3. Figures 6.13a–i show the sequences of estimates of $\{\hat{\beta}_i, i = 1, 2, 3\}$ (top row), the sequences of t-tests of $\mathsf{H}_0\colon \beta_i = 0$ (middle row), the 1-step residuals with $\pm 2\hat{\sigma}_t$, the 1-step constancy tests and the corresponding sequence of breakpoint Chow tests, both scaled by their 1 per cent critical values (bottom row). An F-test of constancy over the last sixteen quarters yields $F\,(6, 85) = 0.4$. Thus, the model is constant over the sample despite the mis-specifications and the large changes in monetary control rules which occurred in the 1970s and 1980s. Overall, the model tracks reasonably well despite its manifest drawbacks and will serve as an empirical benchmark for Chapter 7 to illustrate the comparative estimates and tests obtained in the nine special cases of the dynamic model typology.

6.8 A solved example

Consider the sequential conditional bivariate process for $t = 1, \ldots, T$:

$$\boldsymbol{x}_t | \boldsymbol{w}_t \sim \mathsf{N}_2 \left[\boldsymbol{\pi}_t \boldsymbol{w}_t, \boldsymbol{\Omega}_t \right] \text{ when } \boldsymbol{\Omega}_t = \begin{pmatrix} \omega_{11t} & \omega_{12t} \\ \omega_{21t} & \omega_{22t} \end{pmatrix}, \tag{6.63}$$

where $\boldsymbol{x}_t' = (y_t : z_t)$, $\boldsymbol{w}_t$ is a vector of k stationary variables which are strongly exogenous for $\{\boldsymbol{\pi}_t, \boldsymbol{\Omega}_t\}$, and $\boldsymbol{\Omega}_t = \{\omega_{ijt}\}$. The underlying economic behaviour is:

$$y_t = \beta_1 z_t + \boldsymbol{\beta}_2' \boldsymbol{w}_t + \epsilon_{1t} \tag{6.64}$$

$$z_t = \boldsymbol{\lambda}_t' \boldsymbol{w}_t + \epsilon_{2t} \tag{6.65}$$

where $\boldsymbol{\epsilon}_t = (\epsilon_{1t} : \epsilon_{2t})' \sim \mathsf{IN}_2 \left[\mathbf{0}, \boldsymbol{\Sigma}_t \right]$ with $\sigma_{11} = \mathsf{E}\left[\epsilon_{1t}^2\right]$ constant, and z_t is known to be super exogenous for $\boldsymbol{\beta}' = (\beta_1 : \boldsymbol{\beta}_2')$.

(a) Derive expressions for $\boldsymbol{\pi}_t$ and $\boldsymbol{\Omega}_t$ as functions of the parameters in (6.64) and (6.65).
(b) Consider the inverse of the regression in (6.64), in that the model is estimated by regressing z_t on y_t and $\boldsymbol{w}_t$. Obtain the parameters of this regression and prove that they cannot be invariants so long as $\boldsymbol{\lambda}_t$ and $\sigma_{22t} = \mathsf{E}\left[\epsilon_{2t}^2\right]$ are not constant.
(c) Comment on the economic implications of this finding. How might one test for the presence of this type of situation?

(Oxford M.Phil., 1985)

Solution

(a) Since the conditional process is $\boldsymbol{x}_t | \boldsymbol{w}_t \sim \mathsf{N}_2 \left[\boldsymbol{\pi}_t \boldsymbol{w}_t, \boldsymbol{\Omega}_t \right]$ then $\mathsf{E}\left[\boldsymbol{x}_t | \boldsymbol{w}_t\right] = \boldsymbol{\pi}_t \boldsymbol{w}_t$, and $\mathsf{V}\left[\boldsymbol{x}_t | \boldsymbol{w}_t\right] = \boldsymbol{\Omega}_t$. Thus, the process can be written as:

$$\boldsymbol{x}_t = \boldsymbol{\pi}_t \boldsymbol{w}_t + \boldsymbol{\nu}_t \text{ where } \mathsf{E}\left[\boldsymbol{\nu}_t \mid \boldsymbol{w}_t\right] = \mathbf{0} \text{ and } \mathsf{E}\left[\boldsymbol{\nu}_t \boldsymbol{\nu}_t' \mid \boldsymbol{w}_t\right] = \boldsymbol{\Omega}_t \tag{6.66}$$

so that $\mathsf{E}\left[\boldsymbol{x}_t \boldsymbol{\nu}_t' | \boldsymbol{w}_t\right] = \boldsymbol{\Omega}_t$ as well; these results also hold unconditionally for $\mathsf{E}\left[\boldsymbol{\nu}_t\right]$, $\mathsf{E}\left[\boldsymbol{\nu}_t \boldsymbol{\nu}_t'\right]$ and $\mathsf{E}\left[\boldsymbol{x}_t \boldsymbol{\nu}_t'\right]$.
In the model (6.64)+(6.65) of the process $\boldsymbol{x}_t'$, ϵ_{1t} and ϵ_{2t} must be independent since z_t is super exogenous for $\boldsymbol{\beta}$. Let:

$$\boldsymbol{\pi}_t = \begin{pmatrix} \boldsymbol{\pi}_{1t}' \\ \boldsymbol{\pi}_{2t}' \end{pmatrix}$$

where the π'_{it} are $1 \times k$, so that $\lambda_t = \pi_{2t}$. From conditioning in the normal distribution:

$$\beta_1 = \frac{\omega_{12t}}{\omega_{22t}}\ \forall t, \text{ so } \omega_{12t} = \beta_1 \omega_{22t}.$$

Also, on pre-multiplying (6.63) by $(1 : -\beta_1)$ and comparing coefficients with (6.64)+(6.65), then $\boldsymbol{\beta}_2 + \beta_1 \boldsymbol{\pi}_{2t} = \boldsymbol{\pi}_{1t}$ and $\omega_{11t} = \sigma_{11} + \beta_1^2 \sigma_{22t}$. Therefore:

$$\boldsymbol{\Omega}_t = \begin{pmatrix} \sigma_{11} + \beta_1^2 \sigma_{22t} & \beta_1 \sigma_{22t} \\ \beta_1 \sigma_{22t} & \sigma_{22} \end{pmatrix} \text{ and } \boldsymbol{\pi}_t = \begin{pmatrix} \boldsymbol{\beta}_2' + \beta_1 \boldsymbol{\lambda}_t' \\ \boldsymbol{\lambda}_t' \end{pmatrix}.$$

Note that $\mathsf{E}[\boldsymbol{x}_t \boldsymbol{x}_t'] = \boldsymbol{\pi}_t \boldsymbol{M}_{ww} \boldsymbol{\pi}_t' + \boldsymbol{\Omega}_t$ where $\mathsf{E}[\boldsymbol{w}_t \boldsymbol{w}_t'] = \boldsymbol{M}_{ww}$, but this is awkward to solve for the moments and hence for the regression relations required below.

(b) If z_t is weakly exogenous for β, then y_t cannot be so. This is shown by Engle, Hendry and Richard (1983) in the bivariate normal model. Here we examine the conditions under which parameter constancy in the model for y_t given z_t is compatible with parameter constancy in the reverse regression. At first sight, when $\beta_1 \neq 0$, inverting (6.64) seems innocuous since:

$$z_t = \beta_1^{-1} y_t - \beta_1^{-1} \boldsymbol{\beta}_2' \boldsymbol{w}_t - \beta_1^{-1} \epsilon_{1t}. \tag{6.67}$$

However, $\mathsf{E}[y_t \epsilon_{1t}] = \omega_{11t} \neq 0$ so (6.67) is not the reverse conditional regression, which is given by:

$$\begin{aligned} \mathsf{E}[z_t | y_t, \boldsymbol{w}_t] &= \boldsymbol{\pi}_{2t}' \boldsymbol{w}_t + \omega_{21t} \omega_{11t}^{-1} (y_t - \boldsymbol{\pi}_{1t}' \boldsymbol{w}_t) \\ &= \omega_{21t} \omega_{11t}^{-1} y_t + \left(\boldsymbol{\pi}_{2t} - \omega_{21t} \omega_{11t}^{-1} \boldsymbol{\pi}_{1t} \right)' \boldsymbol{w}_t \\ &= \alpha_{1t} y_t + \boldsymbol{\alpha}_{2t}' \boldsymbol{w}_t \end{aligned} \tag{6.68}$$

where $\alpha_{1t} = \beta_1 \sigma_{22t} / (\sigma_{11} + \beta_1^2 \sigma_{22t})$ and $\boldsymbol{\alpha}_{2t} = \boldsymbol{\lambda}_t - \alpha_{1t} (\boldsymbol{\beta}_2 + \beta_1 \boldsymbol{\lambda}_t)$. The expressions for α_{1t} and $\boldsymbol{\alpha}_{2t}$ cannot be constant when β_1 and $\boldsymbol{\beta}_2$ are constant unless both σ_{22t} and $\boldsymbol{\lambda}_t$ are constant. Therefore, the reverse regression does not deliver invariants since its parameters vary when σ_{22t} and $\boldsymbol{\lambda}_t$ alter. Moreover, let:

$$u_t = z_t - \alpha_{1t} y_t - \boldsymbol{\alpha}_{2t}' \boldsymbol{w}_t = \nu_{2t} - \alpha_{1t} \nu_{1t}. \tag{6.69}$$

Then:

$$\mathsf{E}\left[u_t^2\right] = \sigma_{22t} + \alpha_{1t}^2 \left(\sigma_{11} + \beta_1^2 \sigma_{22t}\right) - 2\alpha_{1t} \beta_1 \sigma_{22t} = \frac{\sigma_{11} \sigma_{22t}}{\sigma_{11} + \beta_1^2 \sigma_{22t}} \tag{6.70}$$

which is non-constant as well.

An alternative derivation follows from the technical definition of a regression. The theoretical regression of z_t on y_t and $\boldsymbol{w}_t$ can be viewed as needing two steps:

(i) partial the effects of $\boldsymbol{w}_t$ from y_t which implies that $\xi_t = y_t - \boldsymbol{\pi}_{1t}' \boldsymbol{w}_t$ is left;
(ii) regress z_t on ξ_t which implies a coefficient of $\omega_{12t}/\omega_{11t}$ as in (6.69) above.

Thus, the resulting coefficient is non-constant when $\boldsymbol{\Omega}_t$ varies. In the converse regression of y_t on $(z_t : \mathbf{w}_t)$, the first stage removes $\boldsymbol{\lambda}_t'\mathbf{w}_t$ from z_t leaving η_t (say) and the second delivers $\beta_1 = \omega_{21t}/\omega_{22t}$, which is constant.

(c) The economic implications are important: when the underlying process is not constant, perhaps due to changes in government control rules, then at most one direction of regression can be constant. Thus, it matters greatly whether e.g. money or prices are treated as exogenous in a claimed money demand function; or dividends or stock prices in a dividend model; or consumption or income in a savings analysis. Moreover, it is not valid to estimate a conditional model as in (6.64) then invert it to get (6.67) using the estimated parameters: the same mistake is being made, since the reverse model violates the orthogonality assumptions made at estimation, and hence alters the parameters and their constancy.
To test for this type of problem, the model could be estimated in both directions given knowledge that the marginal process (6.65) is non-constant. Alternatively, tests for super exogeneity could be used (see Ch.14), as could tests of the constancy of the parameters in (6.63). Thus, the direction of regression is unique here, and not open to arbitrary choice as in constant-parameter models (such as errors in variables, considered in Ch.12).

6.9 Exercises

6.1 Consider the model:

$$y_t = \beta_0 + \beta_1 z_t + \epsilon_t \text{ where } \epsilon_t \sim \mathsf{IN}\left[0, \sigma_\epsilon^2\right]. \tag{6.71}$$

Discuss four alternative interpretations of equation (6.71), commenting in each case on:

(a) the economic rationale;
(b) the statistical assumptions;
(c) discriminating between cases in which the exogeneity status of z_t for β_1 is different;
(d) testing for the potential invariance of β_1 to changes in the process generating z_t.

(Oxford M.Phil., 1989)

6.2 Consider the system:

$$y_{1t} = \beta_1 \mathsf{E}\left[y_{2t} \mid \mathcal{I}_{t-1}\right] + \gamma_1 z_{1t} + u_{1t} \tag{6.72}$$

$$y_{2t} = \beta_2 y_{1t} + \gamma_2 z_{2t} + u_{2t} \tag{6.73}$$

where $\mathbf{u}_t \sim \mathsf{IN}_2[\mathbf{0}, \boldsymbol{\Sigma}]$ and $z_{jt} = \alpha_j z_{jt-1} + v_{jt}$ with $\mathbf{v}_t \sim \mathsf{IN}_2[\mathbf{0}, \boldsymbol{\Omega}]$ and $\mathsf{E}[z_{jt}u_{kr}] = 0\ \forall j, k, t, r$. Here, $\mathcal{I}_{t-1}$ denotes all the information available at $(t-1)$ and agents are assumed to know the model structure, but not the population values of the parameters.

(a) Derive $\mathsf{E}[z_{jt}|\mathcal{I}_{t-1}]$ and hence obtain expressions for $(y_{1t} : y_{2t})$ as functions of z_{jt-1} and $y^e_{2t} = \mathsf{E}[y_{2t}|\mathcal{I}_{t-1}]$. Express y^e_{2t} in terms of the observable variables in the system, and show that the error of expectation $e_{2t} = y_{2t} - y^e_{2t}$ is uncorrelated with y^e_{2t}.

(b) Suggest a method of estimating the parameters of the first equation and show that your method is consistent. How might efficient estimates be obtained? Briefly describe how to test the claim that it is valid in (6.72) to replace y^e_{2t} by y_{2t}.

(Oxford M.Phil., 1985)

6.3 Consider the stationary DGP $\boldsymbol{x}_t|\boldsymbol{X}^1_{t-1} \sim \mathsf{N}_2[\boldsymbol{\pi}\boldsymbol{x}_{t-1}, \boldsymbol{\Omega}]$ of $\{\boldsymbol{x}_t; t = 1, \ldots, T\}$ when $\boldsymbol{X}^1_t = (\boldsymbol{x}_1, \ldots, \boldsymbol{x}_t)$ where:

$$\boldsymbol{x}_t = \begin{pmatrix} y_t \\ z_t \end{pmatrix}, \ \boldsymbol{\pi} = \begin{pmatrix} \alpha + \beta\lambda & 1 - \alpha - \beta\phi \\ \lambda & 1 - \phi \end{pmatrix} \text{ and } \boldsymbol{\Omega} = \begin{pmatrix} \omega_{11} & \omega_{12} \\ \omega_{21} & \omega_{22} \end{pmatrix}. \quad (6.74)$$

(a) Derive $\mathsf{E}[y_t|z_t, \boldsymbol{x}_{t-1}]$ and establish conditions under which z_t is weakly exogenous for (α, β). What type of model results when z_t is weakly exogenous for β? Derive its long-run solution.

(b) How would you test whether or not z_t is weakly exogenous for (α, β)?

(c) Establish when y does not Granger-cause z and describe how one might test that proposition. Hence comment on testing the strong exogeneity of z_t for (α, β).

(d) The long-run solution derived from (6.74) given the strong exogeneity of z_t is:

$$y^* = \frac{(1 - \alpha - \beta\phi)}{(1 - \alpha - \beta\lambda)} z^*. \quad (6.75)$$

Assuming that $\lambda \neq \phi$, explain how to reconcile this result with the solution obtained in (a). Is the case $\lambda = \phi$ of independent interest, and if so does it raise any problems?

(Adapted from Oxford M.Phil., 1988)

7

A Typology of Linear Dynamic Equations

Nine special cases of the AD(1, 1) model are analysed. Each focuses on a particular econometric problem, namely: static regressions associated with simple-to-general modelling in §7.2; autoregressive processes and the 'time-series versus econometrics' debate in §7.3; growth-rate models and potential theory inconsistency (§7.4); leading indicators and the problem of non-autonomy in §7.5; partial adjustment models and the role of expectations (§7.6); common-factor models and autocorrelation corrections (§7.7); finite distributed lags and multicollinearity in §7.8; dead-start models and derived equations (§7.9); and equilibrium correction and cointegration in §7.10. Monte Carlo and empirical studies are undertaken of each case. The different lag distributions imposed by each model are contrasted, revealing that empirical results may depend on the choice of model type.

7.1 Introduction

Chapter 6 discussed the properties of the AD(1, 1) model (denoted M_1) viewed as a DGP:

$$\mathsf{M}_1\colon\ y_t = \beta_0 + \beta_1 z_t + \beta_2 y_{t-1} + \beta_3 z_{t-1} + \epsilon_t \ \text{ where } \epsilon_t \sim \mathsf{IN}\left[0, \sigma_\epsilon^2\right] \tag{7.1}$$

with:

$$z_t = \lambda_0 + \lambda_1 z_{t-1} + \nu_t \ \text{ where } \nu_t \sim \mathsf{IN}\left[0, \sigma_\nu^2\right], \tag{7.2}$$

and $\mathsf{E}\left[\nu_t \epsilon_s\right] = 0 \ \forall t, s$. Also, $|\beta_2| < 1$ and $|\lambda_1| \leq 1$. The dynamics of (7.1) were analysed and a Monte Carlo study of the properties of least-squares estimators of β was conducted with satisfactory results. Building on Chapter 6, we consider each of the nine distinct types of model in Table 7.1, analytically and by means of Monte Carlo experiments. These models are special cases of (7.1) and demonstrate the consequences of picking a given type as the model, when the DGP is an AD(1, 1). For simplicity, we take $\beta_0 = \lambda_0 = 0$, leaving the generalizations to non-zero means as an exercise, and we interpret $\{y_t, z_t\}$ as the logs of $\{Y_t, Z_t\}$.

The statistical generating mechanism is given by (7.1) with zero means. Since the analysis is at level A, but is undertaken to assist research at level C where the DGP is unknown, each special case can be postulated as a stochastic economic model of a DGP which is unknown to the model's proprietor. When the model coincides with the DGP, then usually it will work well and deliver the anticipated results. The case of interest in practice is when the model does not coincide with the DGP, but is an invalid reduction of it, and most of the following results are relevant to that situation. We discriminate between the actual expectation $\mathsf{E}[\cdot]$ taken with respect to the joint sequential density $\mathsf{D}_{\mathsf{y,z}}(y_t, z_t|\cdot)$ of the random variables, and the asserted expectation $E[\cdot]$ believed by a model's proprietor. Further, many economic models fail to specify the complete distribution of all the random variables under analysis, due to implicit exogeneity assumptions and we consider this practice within models of (7.1), under the maintained assumption that z_t is strongly exogenous for $\boldsymbol{\beta}$.

Table 7.1 Autoregressive-distributed lag typology

Model, Section	Type	Equation[1]	Restrictions
M_1 §7.1	Autoregressive-distributed lag	$y_t = \beta_1 z_t + \beta_2 y_{t-1} + \beta_3 z_{t-1} + \epsilon_t$	None
M_2 §7.2	Static regression	$y_t = \beta_1 z_t + u_t$	$\beta_2 = \beta_3 = 0$
M_3 §7.3	Univariate time series	$y_t = \beta_2 y_{t-1} + \omega_t$	$\beta_1 = \beta_3 = 0$
M_4 §7.4	Differenced data	$\Delta y_t = \beta_1 \Delta z_t + \zeta_t$	$\beta_2 = 1, \beta_1 = -\beta_3$
M_5 §7.5	Leading indicator	$y_t = \beta_3 z_{t-1} + v_t$	$\beta_1 = \beta_2 = 0$
M_6 §7.6	Partial adjustment	$y_t = \beta_1 z_t + \beta_2 y_{t-1} + \eta_t$	$\beta_3 = 0$
M_7 §7.7	Common factor (autoregressive error)	$y_t = \beta_1 z_t + u_t,$ $u_t = \beta_2 u_{t-1} + e_t$	$\beta_3 = -\beta_1\beta_2$
M_8 §7.8	Finite distributed lag	$y_t = \beta_1 z_t + \beta_3 z_{t-1} + \xi_t$	$\beta_2 = 0$
M_9 §7.9	Dead start	$y_t = \beta_3 z_{t-1} + \beta_2 y_{t-1} + \nu_t$	$\beta_1 = 0$
M_{10} §7.10	Homogeneous equilibrium correction	$\Delta y_t = \beta_1 \Delta z_t +$ $(\beta_2 - 1)(y - z)_{t-1} + v_t$	$\sum_{i=1}^{3} \beta_i = 1$
M_{10}^* §7.11	General equilibrium correction[2]	$\Delta y_t = \beta_1 \Delta z_t +$ $(\beta_2 - 1)(y - K_1 z)_{t-1} + \epsilon_t$	None

From Chapters 3 and A4, the distributions of estimators and tests differ asymptotically between $|\lambda_1| < 1$ and $\lambda_1 = 1$. Consequently, we often treat those two cases

[1] The typology is illustrated by the AD(1, 1) model (7.1) with the constant term β_0 omitted for simplicity. For generalizations, see Hendry, Pagan and Sargan (1984).

[2] The general equilibrium-correction model is isomorphic to the autoregressive-distributed lag with $K_1 = (\beta_1 + \beta_3)/(1 - \beta_2)$ when $\beta_2 \neq 1$.

separately, although in finite samples it can be difficult to discriminate between $\lambda_1 = 1$ and λ_1 close to, but less than, unity. Further, the Monte Carlo results in Chapter 3 suggested that roots close to unity induced similar behaviour to unit roots, so the unit-root case will be used as a shorthand for near non-stationarity. Finally, the analysis will be conditional on the initial value $\boldsymbol{x}_0 = (y_0 : z_0)'$. Strictly speaking, the process is only asymptotically stationary for $|\lambda_1| < 1$, but we neglect this departure for tractability, and treat first and second moments as constant except when $\lambda_1 = 1$.

In each section we discuss an economic theoretic basis for the model form; derive its re-parameterization in terms of the parameters of (7.1), usually by explicit marginalization; note any general empirical implications; illustrate the model empirically using UK quarterly, seasonally-adjusted data over 1963(1)–1989(2) on the ratio of M1 to nominal income, given by $\log (M/PY)_t$ as a function of the net interest rate R_t; and finally, study the finite-sample behaviour of various statistics of the model using Monte Carlo. Chapter 6 reported the empirical illustration and results of the Monte Carlo study of (7.1) as an unrestricted equation.

7.2 Static regression

Many well-known economic theories are expressed in static form. For example, in the permanent income hypothesis (see Friedman, 1957), let c^p and i^p denote permanent consumption and permanent income respectively, and let ϕ denote the long-run propensity to consume such that:

$$c_t^p = \phi i_t^p.$$

If the measured variables are assumed to deviate randomly and independently from their respective permanent components according to:

$$c_t = c_t^p + e_{ct} \text{ and } i_t = i_t^p + e_{it},$$

the resulting economic model has the static form:

$$c_t = \phi i_t + v_t \text{ where } v_t = e_{ct} - \phi e_{it}.$$

In relation to the AD(1, 1) framework, a static regression is given by:

$$\mathsf{M}_2 : y_t = \gamma z_t + u_t \text{ where } E[z_t u_t] = 0 \tag{7.3}$$

where $E[\cdot]$ denotes an asserted expectation, imposed by choice of estimator. Equation (7.3) differs from the permanent income example only in assuming that z_t is orthogonal to the error, and could be generalized to account for endogenous regressors. The main feature of (7.3) of concern below is that y_t and z_t are asserted to be contemporaneously interdependent and not related at lagged values. Thus, (7.3) is an AD(0, 0).

There are several issues meriting comment. First, except in the special case when M_1 is indeed an AD(0, 0), $\{u_t\}$ will not be an innovation process and usually will be autocorrelated due to omitting the dynamics. Empirically, the phenomenon of residual autocorrelation is often found in estimated static models, and usually is a symptom of incorrect specification, especially dynamic mis-specification. We return in section 7.7 to analysing the consequences of removing residual autocorrelation in the AD(·) class by Cochrane–Orcutt autoregressive corrections. However, the results in §6.4 are not an encouraging precedent.

Secondly, γ in (7.3) is a function of all the parameters in the DGP. There are two ways of obtaining γ given the assertion that $E[z_t u_t] = 0$, namely as the plim of the regression coefficient estimate in (7.3) or from a formal reduction of (7.1) to (7.3). Naturally, these methods yield the same outcome. Under stationarity, the plim equals the expectation, so from the regression estimate:

$$\gamma = \operatorname*{plim}_{T\to\infty} \hat{\gamma} = \operatorname*{plim}_{T\to\infty} \left(\sum_{t=1}^{T} y_t z_t \Big/ \sum_{t=1}^{T} z_t^2 \right),$$

where the sample moments are calculated from the DGP as:

$$\begin{aligned} m_{zz} &= \mathsf{E}\left[z_t^2\right] &&= \lambda_1^2 \mathsf{E}\left[z_{t-1}^2\right] + \sigma_\nu^2 = \sigma_\nu^2 / \left(1 - \lambda_1^2\right) \\ m_{yz} &= \mathsf{E}\left[y_t z_t\right] &&= \beta_1 \mathsf{E}\left[z_t^2\right] + \beta_2 \mathsf{E}\left[y_{t-1} z_t\right] + \beta_3 \mathsf{E}\left[z_t z_{t-1}\right] \\ & &&= \beta_1 \mathsf{E}\left[z_t^2\right] + \beta_2 \lambda_1 \mathsf{E}\left[y_{t-1} z_{t-1}\right] + \beta_3 \lambda_1 \mathsf{E}\left[z_{t-1}^2\right]. \end{aligned} \tag{7.4}$$

Under stationarity, $\mathsf{E}[y_t z_t] = \mathsf{E}[y_{t-1} z_{t-1}]$, so collecting common terms:

$$\gamma = \frac{\beta_1 + \beta_3 \lambda_1}{1 - \beta_2 \lambda_1} = \beta_1 + \frac{\delta \lambda_1}{1 - \beta_2 \lambda_1} = K_1 - \frac{\delta (1 - \lambda_1)}{(1 - \beta_2 \lambda_1)(1 - \beta_2)} \tag{7.5}$$

where $\delta = \beta_1 \beta_2 + \beta_3$ (a parameter combination relevant to §7.7).

Next, consider the reduction route. To analytically marginalize a variable from a model entails first re-parameterizing to create the orthogonal component of that variable relative to the retained variables and then deleting it. For example, from the DGP in (7.1)–(7.2), $(z_t - \lambda_1 z_{t-1}) \perp z_{t-1}$ where $\perp$ denotes orthogonal in the sense that $\mathsf{E}[(z_t - \lambda_1 z_{t-1}) z_{t-1}] = 0$, which holds here because $(z_t - \lambda_1 z_{t-1}) = \nu_t$. However, $(z_t - \lambda_1 z_{t-1})$ and z_t are not orthogonal. If we define λ^* by $(z_t - \lambda^* z_{t-1}) \perp z_t$, then orthogonality is created by construction, with $\lambda^* = 1/\lambda_1$ provided $\lambda_1 \neq 0$. This result is readily extended to show that $(z_{t-1} - \lambda^* z_{t-2}) \perp z_t$ as well. To apply this technique to marginalizing (7.1) with respect to y_{t-1} and z_{t-1}, express y_t as:

$$y_t = (1 - \beta_2 L)^{-1} \left((\beta_1 + \beta_3 L) z_t + \epsilon_t \right) = \sum_{i=0}^{\infty} w_i z_{t-i} + e_t. \tag{7.6}$$

By strong exogeneity, $z_t \perp \epsilon_{t-j}\ \forall j$, and hence $z_t \perp e_t$. The $\{w_i\}$ can be obtained as in §6.5.2:

$$w_0 = \beta_1;\ w_1 = \beta_1 \beta_2 + \beta_3;\ w_2 = \beta_2 (\beta_1 \beta_2 + \beta_3);$$

and so on.

The remaining orthogonalization needed is between z_t and linear combinations of $\{z_{t-i},\ i=0,1\ldots\}$ of the form $(z_{t-i}-\lambda^* z_{t-i-1})$ from above, so using $\lambda^*=1/\lambda_1$:

$$y_t=\gamma z_t+\sum_{i=0}^{\infty}\tau_i\left(z_{t-i}-\lambda^* z_{t-i-1}\right)+e_t=\gamma z_t+u_t. \tag{7.7}$$

Matching coefficients between (7.6) and (7.7) yields:

$$\begin{aligned}
\gamma+\tau_0 &= w_0 &&= \beta_1;\\
\tau_1-\tau_0\lambda^* &= w_1 &&= \beta_1\beta_2+\beta_3;\\
\tau_2-\tau_1\lambda^* &= w_2 &&= \beta_2\left(\beta_1\beta_2+\beta_3\right);
\end{aligned}$$

and so on. Then:

$$\begin{aligned}
\gamma &= \beta_1-\tau_0\\
&= \beta_1-\lambda_1\left(\tau_1-\delta\right)\\
&= \beta_1+\lambda_1\delta-\lambda_1^2\left(\tau_2-\beta_2\delta\right)\\
&= \beta_1+\lambda_1\delta+\lambda_1^2\beta_2\delta-\lambda_1^2\tau_2=\cdots\\
&= \beta_1+\lambda_1\delta\left(1+\beta_2\lambda_1+\lambda_1^2\beta_2^2+\cdots\right)\\
&= \beta_1+\lambda_1\left(\beta_1\beta_2+\beta_3\right)/\left(1-\beta_2\lambda_1\right)\\
&= \left(\beta_1+\lambda_1\beta_3\right)/\left(1-\beta_2\lambda_1\right).
\end{aligned} \tag{7.8}$$

Although this is a longer derivation than the first, marginalization via orthogonalization is widely applicable in dynamic processes, and also reveals the precise structure of $\{u_t\}$. The value of γ depends on all of the parameters affecting the dynamics of the DGP, and implicitly on whether or not $\{z_t\}$ depends on y_{t-1}. Generally, therefore, γ is not interpretable as it is a mix which is neither the short-run impact β_1, nor the long-run outcome K_1 (see §6.4). From (7.5), $\gamma=K_1$ when $\lambda_1=1$ or $\delta=0$.

We can obtain an upper bound on the value of γ which is not directly dependent on (7.1). Since z_t is orthogonal to u_t by construction of γ, from (7.3):

$$\mathsf{V}\left[y_t\right]=\gamma^2\mathsf{V}\left[z_t\right]+\mathsf{V}\left[u_t\right].$$

Since $\mathsf{V}\left[u_t\right]>0$:

$$\frac{\mathsf{V}\left[y_t\right]}{\mathsf{V}\left[z_t\right]}>\gamma^2. \tag{7.9}$$

Consider applying this result to consumption and income in a stationary world. Empirically, the variance of consumption is less than that of income, so a downward-biased estimate of K_1 results from regressing current consumption on current income, even when the theory that consumption and income are proportional in the long run is true. From static regression in finite samples, we should not expect to find the long-run relationship that y is proportional to z, because the upper bound in (7.9) reveals that the relative variances of the two processes matter. However, when z is non-stationary (e.g. $\lambda_1=1$) and the sample is large, then the variances of both y and z tend to infinity: since

y and z are cointegrated by construction, the ratio of their variances converges to K_1. Thus, one set of conditions under which static regression delivers K_1 is that y and z are non-stationary but cointegrated.

These phenomena are apparent in early applied work relating consumption to income. In the 1940s, economists expected the marginal propensity to consume from consumption function estimates to be close to unity, and obtained numbers like 0.9. When the consumption function was fitted in first differences (a different member of the typology) since the growth rate of consumption is smooth while the growth rate of income is erratic, γ transpired to be small (around ½). Thus, the AD(1, 1) model entails results close to those in Kuznets (1946) in that the apparent short-run propensity to consume is low while the long-run propensity to consume is much higher, which led to the introduction of life-cycle and permanent-income models (see Spanos, 1989a, for a history). These changes in γ between equations in levels and differences have little to do with economics: economics is needed to explain why agents smooth consumption, but given that they do so for whatever reason, and that agents do not control their income, the relevant predictions of the permanent income hypothesis follow from the present framework (the AD(1, 1) also predicts that the savings rate will be highest in countries with the highest growth rate of income). These statistical models have nothing to say about consumption smoothing as yet, but some implications arise later in the typology.

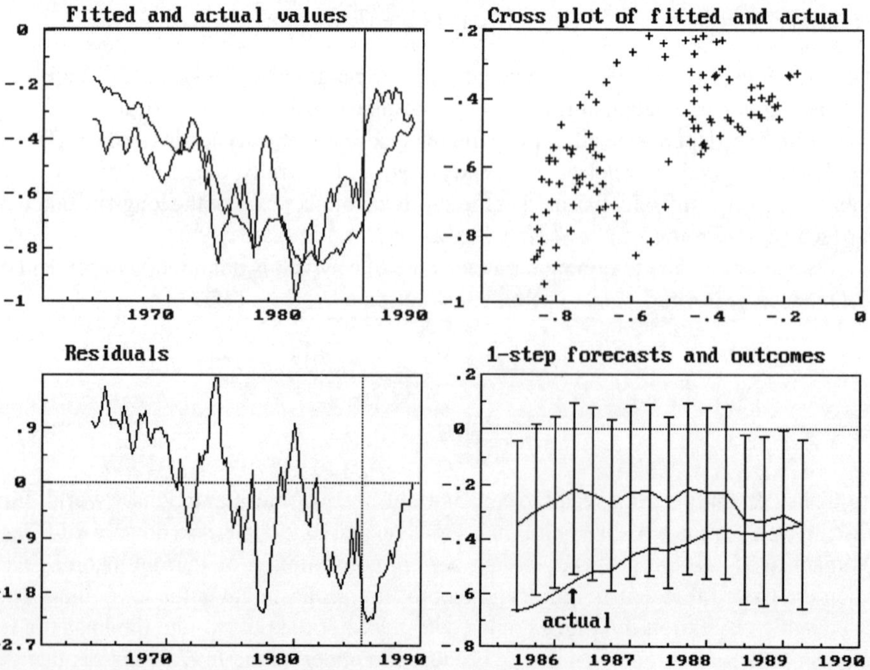

Fig. 7.1 Fitted values and outcomes from the static regression for M1

To illustrate the static equation, regress $\log(M/PY)_t$ on an intercept and R_t:

$$\widehat{\log\left(\frac{M}{PY}\right)_t} = \underset{(0.04)}{-\,0.22} - \underset{(0.42)}{3.80}\, R_t$$
$$\mathsf{R}^2 = 0.45\ \hat{\sigma} = 16\%\ \ SC = -3.62\ \ DW = 0.10 \qquad (7.10)$$
$$AR\text{-}F(5,99) = 144.5\ \ ND\text{-}\chi^2(2) = 5.8\ \ Chow\text{-}F(16,84) = 1.4.$$

The 'direct' estimates of the long run in (7.10) are poor relative to those obtained in Chapter 6, with the interest elasticity being about half the previous value. The AD(1, 1) model variance dominates the static equation by a factor of 64-fold, and the low R^2 cautions against appealing to the results in Engle and Granger (1987) to justify the estimates as a cointegrating regression (see Banerjee, Dolado, Hendry and Smith, 1986). The residual autocorrelation (AR-$F(5,99)$) is too severe to justify conventional constancy tests, but we note that most of the breakpoint Chow statistics reject the null at the 1 per cent level. Figure 7.1 shows the set of fitted and actual values, their cross-plot, the full-sample residuals and the 1-step forecasts over the final four years 1985(3)–1989(2). Figure 7.2 reports the recursive estimates of the coefficient of R_t, its t-values, the 1-step residuals with $0\pm2\hat{\sigma}_u$ and the sequence of breakpoint Chow tests scaled by their 1 per cent critical values. Figures for later models have the same form.

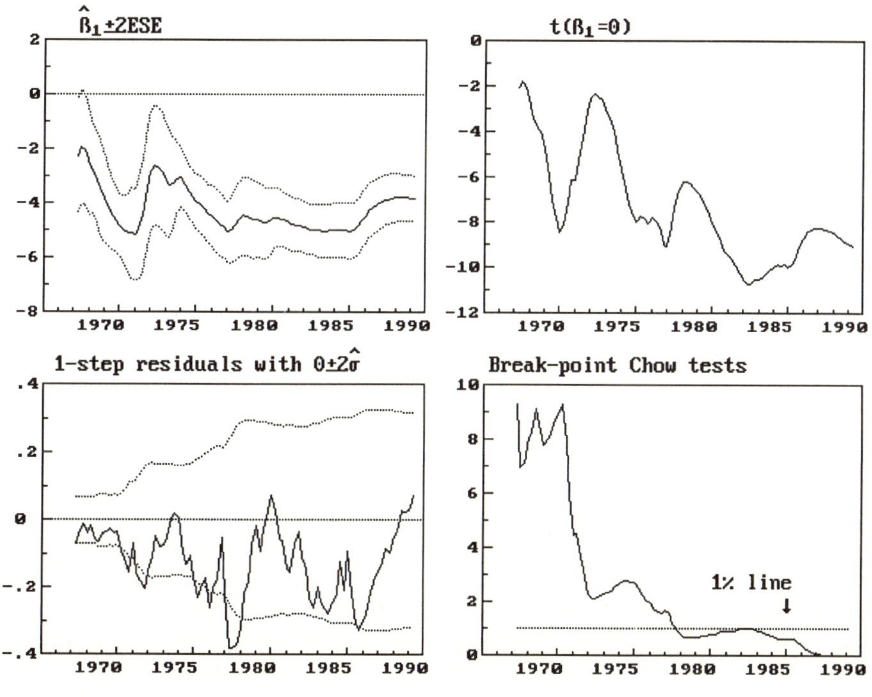

Fig. 7.2 Recursive statistics from the static regression for M1

To help interpret these empirical results, consider fitting the static regression model (7.3) when the DGP is the AD(1, 1) using the Monte Carlo experiment created in Chapter 6.[1] We wish to establish what an investigator would have found if the static (long-run) equation had been estimated. First, at a sample size of $T = 80$, the coefficient γ on z_t in (7.3) is estimated at about 0.89 (compared to the long-run K_1 of unity). In this particular DGP, the static regression coefficient is about 90 per cent of the long run and far removed from the short run of 0.5. Notice that the static model (7.3) imposes the mean and median lags at zero: $m = \mu = 0$. The bias problems when estimating K_1 are more or less severe depending on the extent to which the true values of m and μ deviate from zero and on the closeness of z_t to I(1). Since the true μ is 5, and m is zero, whereas $\lambda = 0.95$ (the w_t variable is also autoregressive), we would not anticipate serious problems, consistent with the estimated coefficient of around 0.9 when $K_1 = 1$. Nevertheless, the estimates are still 10 per cent biased relative to the true long-run solution, which could be quite important for policy. Figures 7.3 and 7.4 show the histograms and density functions for $\hat{\gamma}$ and the t-test of $\mathsf{H}_0\colon \gamma = 0$ respectively.

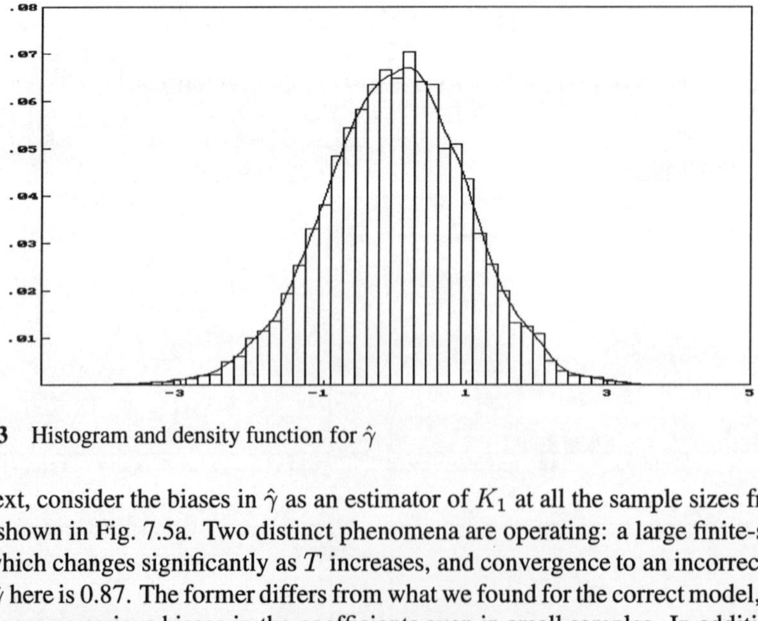

Fig. 7.3 Histogram and density function for $\hat{\gamma}$

Next, consider the biases in $\hat{\gamma}$ as an estimator of K_1 at all the sample sizes from 20 to 80 shown in Fig. 7.5a. Two distinct phenomena are operating: a large finite-sample bias which changes significantly as T increases, and convergence to an incorrect limit: plim $\hat{\gamma}$ here is 0.87. The former differs from what we found for the correct model, where there were no serious biases in the coefficients even in small samples. In addition, the estimated coefficient converges on 0.9, rather than 1 or 0.5. However, these biases are somewhat less than in the empirical illustration judged against the AD(1, 1) baseline.

The comparison between the uncertainty computed by a regression program, namely the ESE, and the correct value, i.e. MCSD, shown in Fig. 7.5b reveals that (6.6.58) is dramatically misleading here, and in an important direction: it greatly under-estimates the

[1] Remember that the Monte Carlo experiment created in Chapter 6 differs from (7.2) in that $\{z_t\}$ depends on a further autoregressive variable with a non-zero mean.

true uncertainty. The standard errors quoted for regression coefficients in empirical research are too small relative to the true uncertainty when there is positive residual serial correlation: by downward biasing the ESEs, upward biases in t-statistics are induced leading to excess rejection of correct null hypotheses.

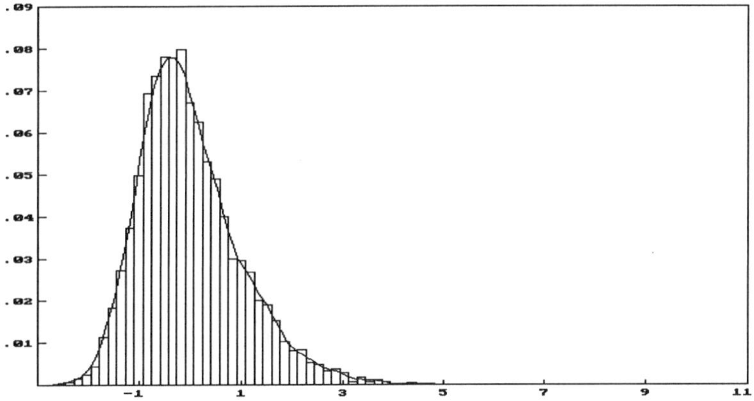

Fig. 7.4 Histogram and density function for the t-test of H_0: $\gamma = 0$

Although the DGP is constant, Figs. 7.5c and 7.5d, recording the graphs of $\hat{\sigma}_u$ and the sequence of breakpoint Chow tests, reveal considerable apparent non-constancy with rejection rates of about 60 per cent for a break at $T = 20$ when the critical value is for 5 per cent rejection under the null. The model fits increasingly poorly as the sample size increases, so the later the test period, the worse the model fits, and the harder it is to show from forecasts that the model is wrong. The full-sample estimate of σ_u is about 3.4 with plim $\hat{\sigma}_u = 3.6$, whereas $\sigma_\epsilon = 1$ in (7.1).[2]

Such an outcome raises an awkward methodological problem: the DGP is constant and hence the model should be constant in that there is no structural change, yet the Chow test rejects constancy much more than 5 per cent of the time. That problem is related to the structure of testing. A test is a statistic formulated under a null hypothesis in a maintained statistical model, with a known distribution under that null; a critical value is selected from the distribution to achieve a given rejection frequency when the null is true, and the test is conducted by rejecting the null when the test outcome exceeds the chosen critical value. However, apart from the possibility that the test will exceed the critical value a certain proportion of the time when the null is true, the fact that a test rejects is uninformative about what led to rejection since other departures from the null hypothesis can also induce rejection. For the Chow test here, the null of constant

[2] The graphs show $\bar{\sigma}_u$, which is the average equation standard error (i.e. $M^{-1}\sum_{i=1}^{M}(\hat{\sigma}_u)_i$), whereas the statistics in the text relate to $\sqrt{\bar{\sigma}_u^2}$, the square root of the average error variance (where $\bar{\sigma}_u^2 = M^{-1}\sum_{i=1}^{M}(\hat{\sigma}_u^2)_i$): the latter is a less downwards biased estimator of σ_u. The difference is noticable only when σ_u is large.

parameters is correct. The test rejects because the wrong formula is used for the variance of the coefficients as the residuals are autocorrelated due to fitting a static model instead of the correct dynamic model (see Chow and Corsi, 1982). A constancy test has no ostensible link with testing for residual autocorrelation, but can reject a model when the real mistake is ignoring residual autocorrelation. One cannot deduce that the alternative is true when the null is rejected: from rejection on a test — whether it is a constancy test or an autocorrelation test — one cannot infer that the ostensible objective of the test was the reason for rejection. Such a conclusion could be correct, but tests might also reject for almost any aspect of a wrong model: in a broader context, this is the Duhem–Quine thesis (see Cross, 1982). However, subject to the frequency of incorrect decisions corresponding to the choice of critical value, rejection entails that some aspects of the model and data are inconsistent. Chapter 13 discusses the technology of testing.

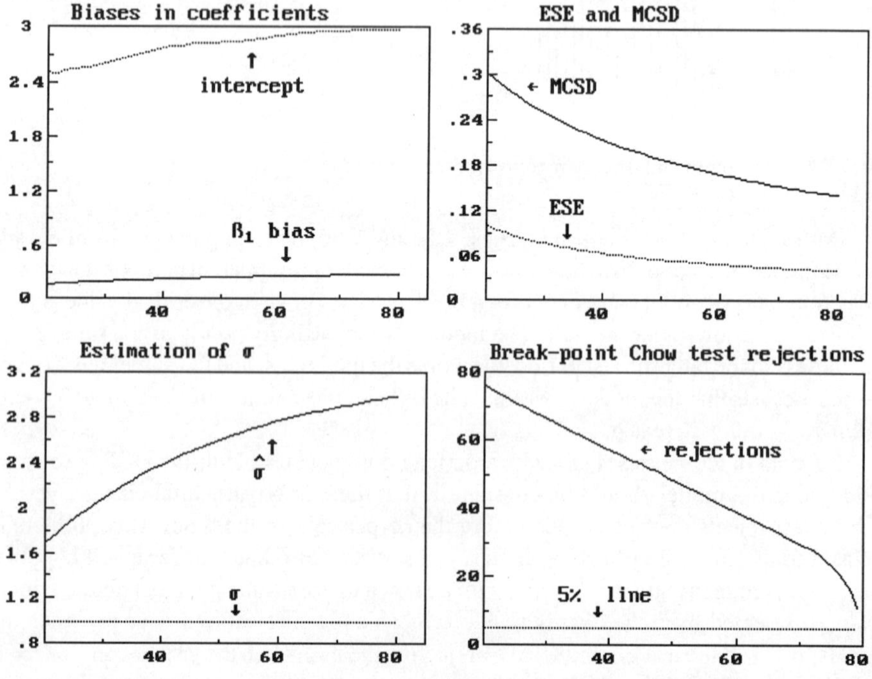

Fig. 7.5 Recursive Monte Carlo outcomes for the static regression

The importance of this analysis is that it precludes building models by starting from (say) static regressions, reviewing test evidence, and inferring from test rejections how to generalize models. One can imagine the mess if, from the outcome of the Chow test, the static regression was extended by letting the parameter γ change over time. When a model is wrong, a test rejection is a symptom of that mis-specification: there is no reliable way to patch a model, except to rethink the analysis and come up with a better model. It is not an appropriate methodology to begin from a simple equation, examine its failures on a set of tests (even if they cover the entire symptomatology of the basic textbooks), and extend the model in the directions corresponding to the alternative hypothesis of each test that rejects. Econometrics needs a more sustainable methodology than that.

7.3 Autoregression

A first-order autoregressive process takes the form discussed in Chapter 2:

$$\mathsf{M}_3 : y_t = \rho y_{t-1} + \omega_t. \tag{7.11}$$

This is a case of pure dynamics without interdependence. As a statistical model, autoregressions have arisen naturally from sequential factorizations above; and there is an economic theory basis for them from inter-temporal optimization as follows.

Reconsider the permanent income model from §7.2. Let i_t^p represent the return on the present discounted value of the expected future stream of income, given an information set $\mathcal{I}_t$, assuming that $i_t \in \mathcal{I}_t$ so that:

$$i_t^p = r\mathsf{E}\left[\sum_{j=1}^{\infty}(1+r)^{-j}\, i_{t+j} \mid \mathcal{I}_t\right], \tag{7.12}$$

where r is both the discount rate and the interest rate, assumed constant for simplicity. In static equilibrium where $i_t = i^* \;\forall t$, from (7.12), $i^p = i^*$ since $r\sum_{j=1}^{\infty}(1+r)^{-j} = 1$. Also:

$$i_{t+1}^p = r\mathsf{E}\left[\sum_{j=1}^{\infty}(1+r)^{-j}\, i_{t+j+1} \mid \mathcal{I}_{t+1}\right] = r\mathsf{E}\left[\sum_{j=2}^{\infty}(1+r)^{-j+1}\, i_{t+j} \mid \mathcal{I}_{t+1}\right],$$

and because $\mathcal{I}_t \subseteq \mathcal{I}_{t+1}$:

$$\begin{aligned}\mathsf{E}\left[i_{t+1}^p \mid \mathcal{I}_t\right] &= r\mathsf{E}\left[\mathsf{E}\left[\sum_{j=2}^{\infty}(1+r)^{-j+1}\, i_{t+j} \mid \mathcal{I}_{t+1}\right] \mid \mathcal{I}_t\right] \\ &= r\mathsf{E}\left[\sum_{j=2}^{\infty}(1+r)^{-j+1}\, i_{t+j} \mid \mathcal{I}_t\right]\end{aligned} \tag{7.13}$$

so that:

$$i_{t+1}^p - \mathsf{E}\left[i_{t+1}^p \mid \mathcal{I}_t\right] = r\sum_{j=2}^{\infty}(1+r)^{-j+1}\left\{\mathsf{E}\left[i_{t+j} \mid \mathcal{I}_{t+1}\right] - \mathsf{E}\left[i_{t+j} \mid \mathcal{I}_t\right]\right\} = \xi_t, \tag{7.14}$$

where $\mathsf{E}[\xi_t|\mathcal{I}_t] = 0$. Thus, revisions to permanent income are a martingale difference sequence:

$$\mathsf{E}\left[\Delta i^p_{t+1} \mid \mathcal{I}_t\right] = 0 \tag{7.15}$$

and hence $\{i^p_t\}$ is a martingale relative to $\mathcal{I}_t$. In such a case, since $c^p_t = \phi i^p_t$, permanent consumption would also be a martingale.

An alternative derivation is suggested by Hall (1978) as follows. Let $U(\cdot)$ be a strictly concave utility function, separable over time, and let an agent solve a life-cycle maximization problem for a horizon of H periods:

$$\max_{c_t \ldots c_{t+H}} \mathsf{E}\left[\sum_{j=0}^{H} (1+r)^{-j} U(c_{t+j}) \mid \mathcal{I}_t\right],$$

subject to the inter-temporal wealth constraint that:

$$\mathsf{E}\left[\sum_{j=0}^{H} (1+r)^{-j} (c_{t+j} - i_{t+j}) \mid \mathcal{I}_t\right] = W_t$$

where i_t denotes labour income and W_t is wealth. Using $U'(\cdot)$ to denote marginal utility, a necessary condition for a maximum is given by the first-order condition or Euler equation (for an excellent treatment, see Deaton (1992)):

$$\mathsf{E}[U'(c_{t+1}) \mid \mathcal{I}_t] = U'(c_t). \tag{7.16}$$

Equation (7.16) reveals that when the discount rate equals the interest rate and both are constant, marginal utility is equated over time, entailing that consumption is smoothed relative to earnings as envisaged in §7.2. Alternatively, the derivation delivers an optimal theory of habit, since on average an agent aims to repeat previous behaviour. While models like (7.16) are rejected empirically (see Davidson and Hendry, 1981), the lagged value of consumption explains more than 95 per cent of the variance of current consumption and it is difficult to predict changes in consumer's expenditure *ex ante*. However, other models are consistent with the evidence at this casual level, including many forms assuming adjustment costs. Finally, note that two versions of the same basic permanent-income theory have induced radically different model types in §7.2 and §7.3.

In empirical practice, autoregressive processes can be derived by valid or by invalid marginalization, as in the previous static regression type. If it is known that $\beta_1 = \beta_3 = 0$ so that $\rho = \beta_2$, then the autoregression (7.11) coincides with the DGP (7.1). More generally, it is feasible, if arbitrary, just to relate y_t to its lagged value irrespective of the data evidence, and this is perhaps the only route if the appropriate choice of z_t is not known or is unobserved. In some states of nature, invalid marginalization can be determined using the invariance arguments sketched in Chapter 5. The process for z_t from (7.1) can be rewritten as:

$$z_t = \frac{\nu_t}{(1 - \lambda_1 L)}. \tag{7.17}$$

Substitute (7.17) into the AD(1, 1) for y_t to eliminate z and all its lags when $|\lambda_1| < 1$:

$$\begin{aligned}(1-\beta_2 L)\, y_t &= (\beta_1 \nu_t) \,/\, (1-\lambda_1 L) + (\beta_3 \nu_{t-1}) \,/\, (1-\lambda_1 L) + \epsilon_t \\ &= [(\beta_1 + \beta_3 L) \,/\, (1-\lambda_1 L)]\, \nu_t + \epsilon_t.\end{aligned} \tag{7.18}$$

In the most favourable case for the validity of the autoregressive model that $\beta_3 = -\lambda_1\beta_1$, y_t becomes the autoregression:

$$y_t = \beta_2 y_{t-1} + (\epsilon_t + \beta_1 \nu_t) \tag{7.19}$$

with the correct coefficient $\rho = \beta_2$, where the error term is a composite of ϵ_t and ν_t which remains an innovation against all lagged information. More generally, $\rho = \beta_2 + \gamma\,(\beta_3 + \lambda_1\beta_1)\, s$ where $s = m_{zz}/m_{yy}$.

At first sight, the autoregression (7.19) appears to be a good representation of $\{y_t\}$. However, if σ^2_ν in (7.17) is non-constant, then (7.19) will reflect that non-constancy. Let z_t be determined by the government using (7.17) as a control rule, where the government can change the variance of z, then the error variance on the derived autoregression will not be constant even in a world in which the original *ADL* error variance is constant.

Moreover, when $\beta_3 \neq -\lambda_1\beta_1$, the autoregression will have an autocorrelated error due to lags in ν_t, and will not have constant parameters if λ_1 is not constant. We conclude that when the autoregression is autonomous it is an excellent model and will continue behaving constantly irrespective of other changes in the world. But a model derived by marginalizing with respect to z in the joint distribution of y and z will not be autonomous and will be susceptible to shifts at the points where the process generating z shifts. The potential lack of invariance in the derived process provides another approach to discovering whether a postulated model represents genuine features of reality or is just a descriptive derivation from a more complex process.

The finding that ARMA models appeared to forecast better for short-term horizons than large macro-econometric systems (see Cooper, 1972, and Nelson, 1972 in particular) led to a methodological debate about model forms — which should have been about modelling methods. Although ARMA models allow the error term to be a moving average rather than just white noise, as in AR, we saw from sequential factorization that white noise entails no loss of generality, so the use of an MA component concerns parsimony, not principle. In retrospect, by contrasting types §7.2 and §7.3, it is unsurprising that a time-series analyst might win a forecasting competition when an economist focuses on a static consumption function and tries to predict consumption given income with an error term that is large , while the time-series analyst predicts by an autoregression. This is partly because the economist has first to predict income in order to predict consumption via the static model; since the variance of income is larger than that of consumption the indirect prediction of consumption compounds the forecast errors. But it is also partly because dynamic mis-specification exacerbates the difficulty of accurate forecasting. The typology helps clarify this debate (see Trivedi, 1975, and §7.10).

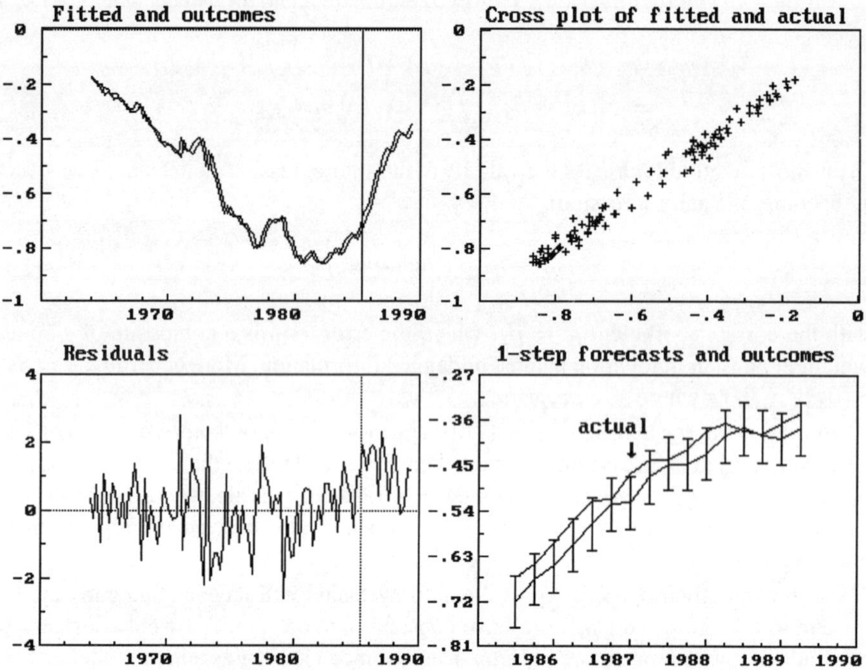

Fig. 7.6 Fitted values and outcomes from the autoregression for M1

Next consider the empirical findings when $\log(M/PY)_t$ is regressed on its own lagged value and an intercept, without any measure of the opportunity cost of holding money:

$$\widehat{\log\left(\frac{M}{PY}\right)_t} = \underset{(0.008)}{-\,0.01} + \underset{(0.013)}{0.98}\ \log\left(\frac{M}{PY}\right)_{t-1}$$

$$\mathsf{R}^2 = 0.98\ \ \hat{\sigma} = 2.7\%\ \ SC = -7.13\ \ DW = 1.65$$
$$AR\text{-}F(5,95) = 2.99\ \ ND\text{-}\chi^2(2) = 0.57\ \ Chow\text{-}F(16,84) = 1.71.$$

As anticipated, the autoregression explains the bulk of the variation in $\log(M/PY)_t$, see Fig. 7.6, but almost none of the variance in $\Delta\log(M/PY)_t$, noting that the hypothesis of a unit root cannot be rejected. The fit in terms of error variance is vastly better than §7.2, consistent with an Euler-equation view, but about 80 per cent worse than the AD(1, 1). Constancy is also much better than the static representation, with almost none of the breakpoint tests rejecting at the 1 per cent significance level (see Fig. 7.7).

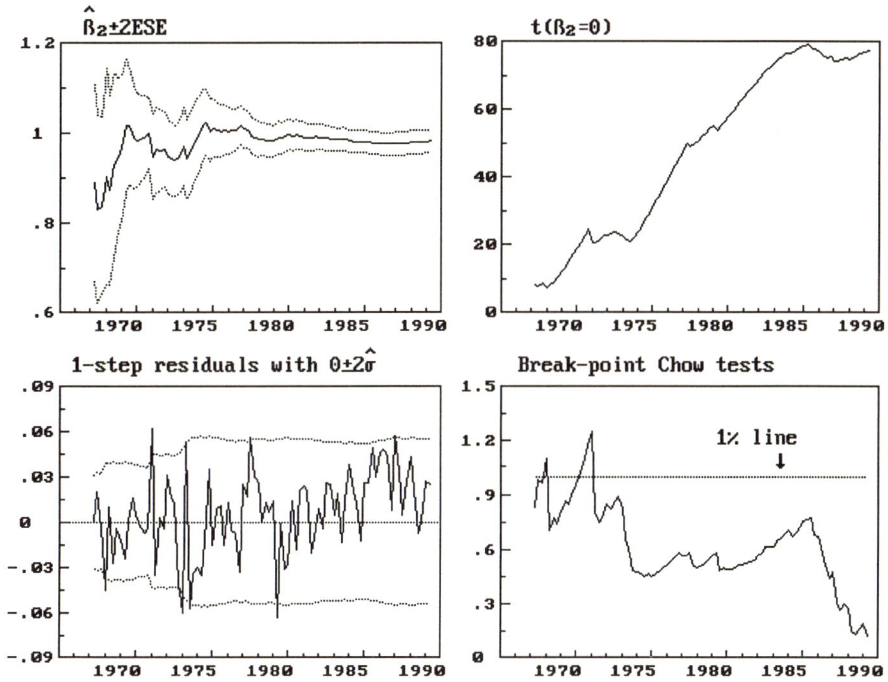

Fig. 7.7 Recursive statistics from the autoregression for M1

Finally, we turn to the Monte Carlo results. Figures 7.8 and 7.9 show the histograms and densities of $\hat{\rho}$ and of the t-test of H_0: $\rho = 0$. The former shows some skewness, but the latter is close to normality. Figure 7.10a graphs the bias in estimating ρ in (7.11) for $T = 20, \ldots, 80$, and reveals little bias (about 0.1), especially considering the initially small sample sizes. The true value of β_2 is 0.9 and the estimated value here is about unity, which is close to the plim of 0.992. Such a value is often found in empirical work but here the evidence cautions against differencing the data since $\{y_t\}$ is stationary. Figure 7.10b records the graph of the ESE and the associated MCSD. Apart from a discrepancy at small samples, the ESE and MCSD are close and would be very similar for more than a hundred observations, a common finding with time-series models. The residual standard deviation is about 1.44 and Fig. 7.10c shows it is estimated at a relatively constant value over T.

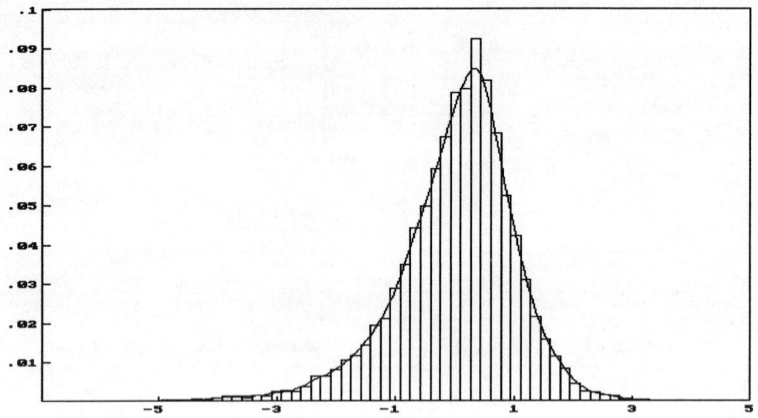

Fig. 7.8 Histogram and density for $\hat{\rho}$

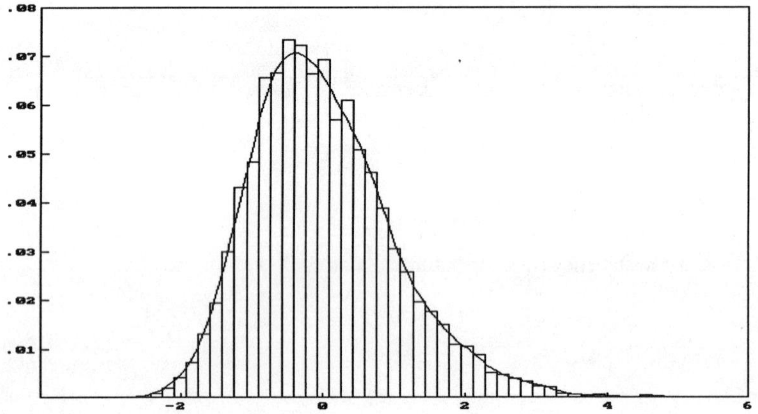

Fig. 7.9 Histogram and density for the t-test of H_0: $\rho = 0$

Figure 7.10d reports the rejection frequencies of the Chow test sequence. The Chow test does not behave at all like that in the static model despite the fact that (7.11) is misspecified for (7.1): it rejects the model less than 10 per cent of the time when $T = 20$ and by the end of the sample is around the one-off nominal rejection frequency of 5 per cent. This outcome supports the contention in §7.2 that omitting dynamics will lead to apparent predictive failure more often than omitting stationary explanatory variables (see Hendry, 1979b).

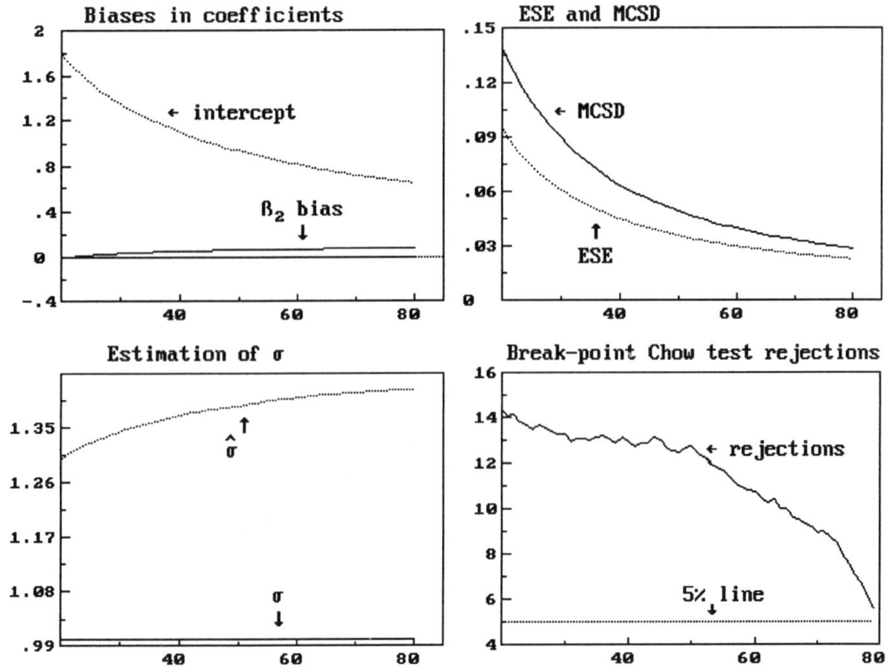

Fig. 7.10 Recursive Monte Carlo statistics for the autoregression

7.4 Differenced-data model

Growth-rate models arose early in the history of econometrics. Hooker (1901) analysed the impact of the state of the economy on marriage rates and differenced to remove common trends and thereby reveal the 'real relationship over the business cycle'. Tintner (1944) also stressed differencing to remove common trends. Consequently, when economists wanted to analyse (say) the relationship between consumption and income, so that the marginal and average propensity to consume were the parameters of interest, to estimate the former, they sometimes fitted models in first differences, or growth-rate models:

$$\mathsf{M}_4 : \Delta y_t = \phi \Delta z_t + \zeta_t \tag{7.20}$$

on the grounds that any common trends associated with the levels of the variables had thereby been removed. More recently, differencing has been used to circumvent non-stationarity problems viewed as unit roots rather than deterministic trends (see Granger and Newbold, 1974, building on Yule, 1926, and Ch.4).

An economic rationale for a differenced-data consumption model has been proposed by Campbell and Mankiw (1991), based on income-constrained consumers, following a similar analysis to Flemming (1973). They assume that a proportion of consumers are income constrained, and these receive a fraction ϕ of total income, with permanent-income consumers receiving the remaining $(1-\phi)$. This leads to an equation like (7.20):

$$\Delta c_t = \phi \Delta i_t + \zeta_t,$$

where ζ_t is the unpredictable innovation to permanent income (see §7.3 above).

Next, the derivation of (7.20) from (7.1) follows from the re-parameterization:

$$\Delta y_t = \beta_1 \Delta z_t + (\beta_2 - 1)(y - K_1 z)_{t-1} + \epsilon_t,$$

after marginalizing with respect to $(y - K_1 z)_{t-1}$, so that ϕ is the parameter value which ensures that $\Delta z_t \perp \zeta_t$. This is a more tedious marginalization to calculate, since we need the orthogonal component from regressing $(y - K_1 z)_{t-1}$ on Δz_t, which involves almost all the second moments of (7.1) (see (7.27) and (7.48) below for most of these). In fact:

$$\phi = \beta_1 - \frac{\delta(1-\lambda_1)}{2(1-\beta_2\lambda_1)}.$$

The mean lag μ in an AD(1, 1) model becomes infinite when the coefficient of the lagged dependent variable is unity and the conditional model in (7.20) implies that, once out of equilibrium in levels, the agent will stay out of equilibrium for ever. Presumably there are no costs attached to disequilibrium for equations like (7.20). Thus, growth-rate models entail the counter-intuitive prediction that agents do not try to remove disequilibria in levels. A possible argument in their favour is that economic time series are so highly autocorrelated that nothing useful can be learnt by analysing and predicting levels, but that claim will be shown to be misleading.

We can obtain (7.20) from (7.1) by setting $\beta_1 = -\beta_3$ and $\beta_2 = 1$ in the AD(1, 1) which avoids the problem of nonsense regressions, but at considerable cost: all the problems discussed in type §7.2 impinge again and some are even exacerbated. The variance-ratio upper bound on the magnitude of the coefficient ϕ becomes restrictive:

$$\frac{\mathsf{V}(\Delta y_t)}{\mathsf{V}(\Delta z_t)} > \phi^2. \tag{7.21}$$

In the UK, the variance of the change in aggregate income is between five and ten times the variance of the change in consumption, so a small value of ϕ will result when estimating the regression in changes, irrespective of the actual partial derivative of consumption with respect to income. That is an example of the claim that empirical results are often an artefact of the type of model chosen, so that the resulting evidence bears little on either the underlying economic theory or the data properties.

An internal inconsistency can arise in relating theory to data in differenced models, most easily seen for the permanent-income hypothesis, which is one potential long-run solution to the AD(1, 1) model, namely $y^* = K_1 z^*$. If that static, non-stochastic theory holds, it should also be true that:

$$\Delta y^* = K_1 \Delta z^*. \tag{7.22}$$

Assume we estimate the growth-rate model (7.20) to implement (7.22) and discover that $\{\zeta_t\}$ is white noise, reporting the estimated K_1 from (7.23):

$$\Delta y_t = K_1 \Delta z_t + \zeta_t. \tag{7.23}$$

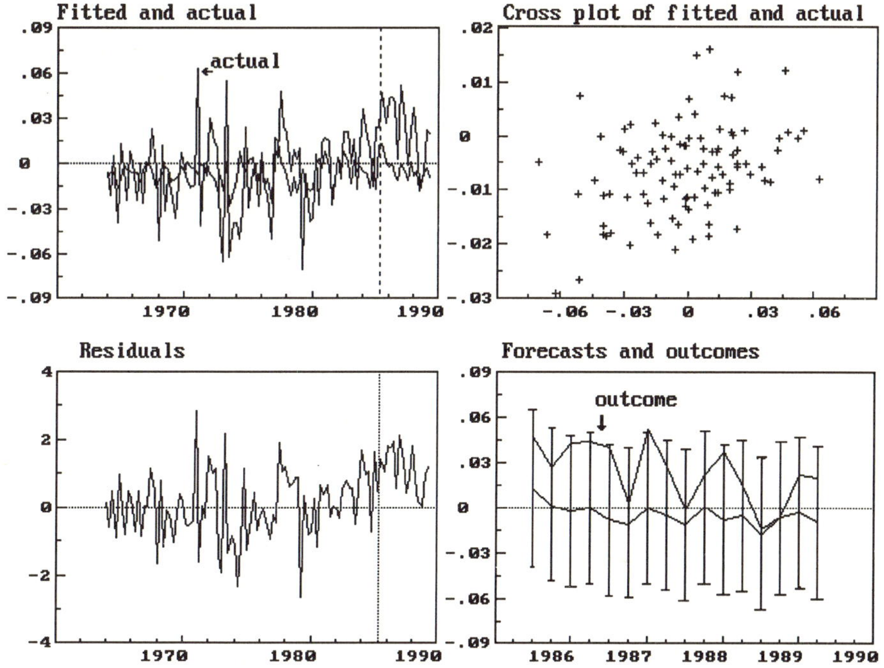

Fig. 7.11 Fitted and actual values for the growth-rate model of M1

This has refuted, rather than confirmed, the theory, because if (7.23) holds, then the only way to recover the levels equation is to integrate (7.23), which leads to:

$$y_t = K_0 + K_1 z_t + u_t \text{ where } u_t = u_{t-1} + \zeta_t, \tag{7.24}$$

and so the error is a random walk, accumulating ζ_t. It is difficult to attach meaning to a theory that claims y_t is proportional to z_t, yet can deviate from z_t by an infinite amount at any point in time. Thus, by finding a growth-rate model with a white-noise error, an internal inconsistency has developed between the starting point and the conclusion.

Part of the resolution to this conundrum lies in the problem of initial conditions. According to the description of the growth-rate processes (7.22) or (7.23), the same sequence $\{\Delta y_t\}$ should occur on average for a given sequence of $\{\Delta z_t\}$ (i.e. apart from a white-noise error) independently of when the sequence starts. Consequently, whether an analysis of consumption commences in 1945 or in 1985, if income growth is the same then the growth rate of consumption which results should be the same. However, the events prior to 1945 would probably have led to different consumer behaviour for a given stream of income growth than if the same stream of income growth arrived in the mid 1980s. The growth-rate model ignores such initial conditions. The problem of internal consistency and the problem of initial conditions have the same solution, and model type M_{10} in §7.10 will resolve this difficulty.

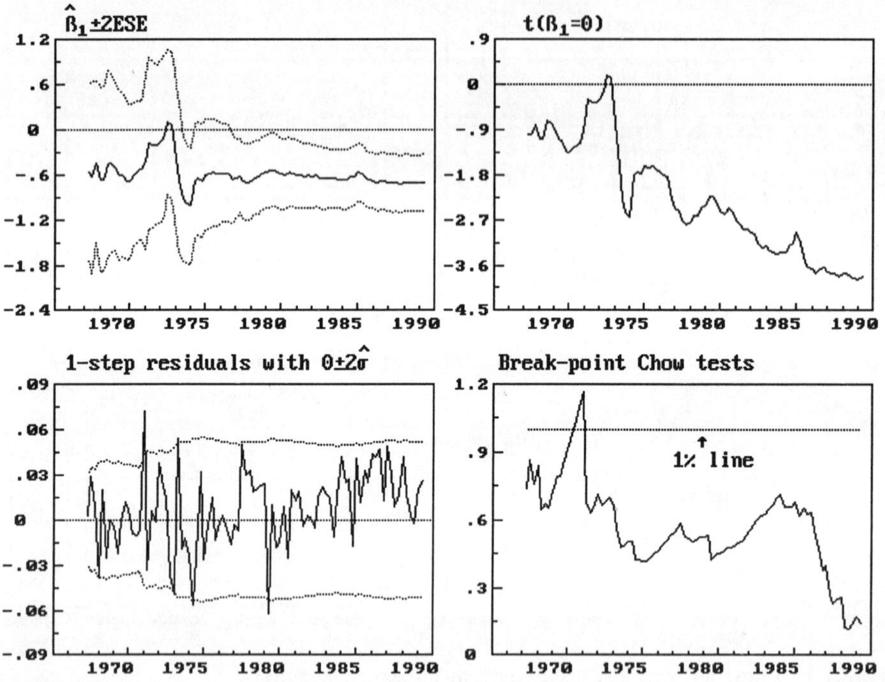

Fig. 7.12 Recursive statistics for the growth-rate model of M1

The empirical illustration produces results consistent with the above discussion. To estimate the differenced equation, regress $\Delta \log (M/PY)_t$ on an intercept and ΔR_t:

$$\widehat{\Delta \log \left(\frac{M}{PY}\right)_t} = \underset{(0.003)}{-\,0.002} - \underset{(0.19)}{0.71}\,\Delta R_t$$

$$\mathsf{R}^2 = 0.13\ \hat{\sigma} = 2.6\%\ \ SC = -7.25\ \ DW = 1.76$$
$$AR\text{-}F(5, 95) = 2.93\ ND\text{-}\chi^2(2) = 0.4\ \ Chow\text{-}F(16, 84) = 1.44.$$

As anticipated, the coefficient of ΔR_t matches the short-run effect from Chapter 6, and is only a tenth of the long-run outcome. However, $\hat{\sigma}$ is smaller than in either M_2 or M_3, and the diagnostic checks have improved somewhat. Constancy is close to that found for the AR equation in that few breakpoint tests reject. Figure 7.11 shows the statistics for goodness of fit and forecasting and Fig. 7.12 reports the recursive estimates and tests.

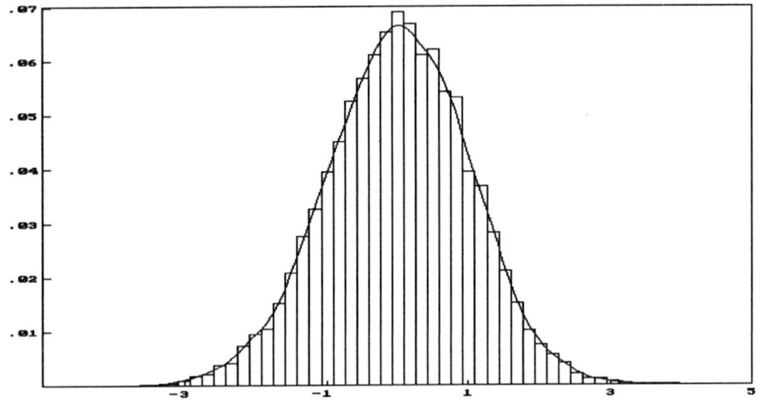

Fig. 7.13 Histogram and density for ϕ

Now consider the Monte Carlo results for the growth model. Figure 7.13 records the histogram and density of the estimate of ϕ. This is nearly symmetric and close to normal.

Figure 7.14a reports the graph of the bias in the estimate of ϕ where the true value of the short-run coefficient β_1 is 0.5. The bias in the estimate of ϕ around β_1 is only about 0.04 on average and is approximately constant. Thus, the estimated coefficient is not so far wrong as to lead to serious mistakes in either inferences or conditional predictions about the short run. Moreover, the equivalent graph in Fig. 7.14b of the estimated (ESE) and actual (MCSD) coefficient standard errors reveals that they are very close. The standard deviation of the regression residuals is only 1.05 in the growth-rate model, as against the true value of unity in the AD$(1, 1)$ so the differenced model might be thought to be an interesting one (see Fig. 7.14c). However, that outcome is partly due to the fact that in the Monte Carlo, Δz_t is designed to have a major impact on Δy_t, leading to $\mathsf{R}^2 = 0.44$ between Δy_t and Δz_t, so the Monte Carlo is somewhat biased in favour of the growth-rate model on this criterion.

The growth-rate model has an infinitely-long mean lag (as against 5 in the DGP) and generates an outcome unrelated to the actual long-run behaviour of the DGP, yet the estimated short-run coefficient is almost unbiased, as are the estimated standard errors. The median lag is also correctly estimated. A system built of equations like (7.22) would deliver uninterpretable results for long-run behaviour, but might function acceptably if used only for short-run forecasting. To check such a claim, consider the Chow test outcomes: the graph of the rejection frequencies shown in Fig. 7.14d reveals slightly less than 5 per cent rejections so that despite the model being wrong, the Chow tests would reject it at the nominal level for long forecast horizons. Further, the Durbin–Watson test rejects the null that the model has white-noise errors only 10 per cent of the time, even though ζ_t is a moving average in this case.

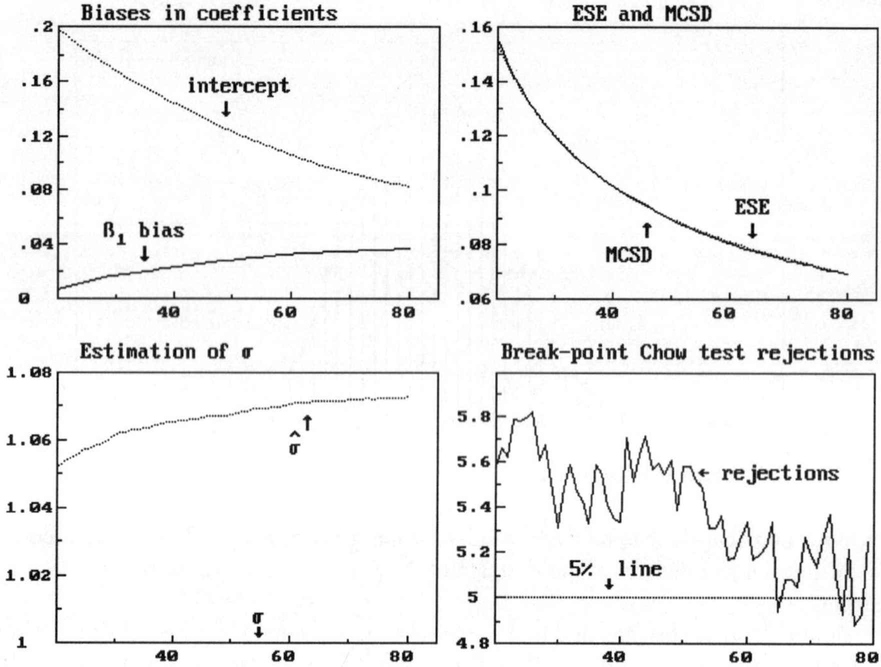

Fig. 7.14 Recursive Monte Carlo outcomes for the growth-rate model

Although it passes Chow and DW tests most of the time, the conditional growth-rate model has unacceptable economic implications. That is another methodological lesson: the fact that a model does not fail a range of tests does not prove that it is valid. It also reveals a further drawback to the methodology of starting from a simple equation and trying to generalize it according to which test rejections are encountered: tests may not reject false nulls and may fail to reveal serious mis-specifications which are only indirectly reflected in the chosen test statistics.

7.5 Leading indicator

The leading-indicator model is sometimes used for short-run forecasting, where last period's z explains this period's y:

$$\mathsf{M}_5 : y_t = cz_{t-1} + v_t. \tag{7.25}$$

In the forecasting context, primary concerns are the constancy of c and the goodness of fit of (7.25). There is no point in building a leading-indicator model if the link between what happens today and the previous value of the indicator will not persist over the relevant forecast horizon. But unless y and z actually are connected in a constant way there is no reason for c to be constant. Here, (7.25) imposes the restrictions $\beta_1 = 0$ and $\beta_2 = 0$ and so the constancy of c depends on that of every other parameter in the DGP.

The Thatcher government in the UK used various monetary measures as indicators of future inflation, but the arbitrary assumption that the equivalent to c in (7.25) was constant did not work well in monetary policy and is known as Goodhart's law after Goodhart (1978). When policy is changed to control y_t (e.g. inflation), given the value of the indicator z_t (e.g. money), that changes c, and hence $\{z_t\}$ ceases to indicate what is going to happen next. The result is that the impact of policy on y is not predictable by such equations, even if the government manages to control the indicator z. Two examples of leading indicator models are the Harvard Barometer A-B-C curves where leading indicators of economic activities were combined in the 1920s (see Persons, 1924), but their predictions for 1929 led to the Barometer being abandoned; and the model of US stock-market prices based on UK car output in Coen, Gomme and Kendall (1969). Frisch (1934) referred to such links as confluent, as opposed to autonomous, relationships (see §7.8 below).

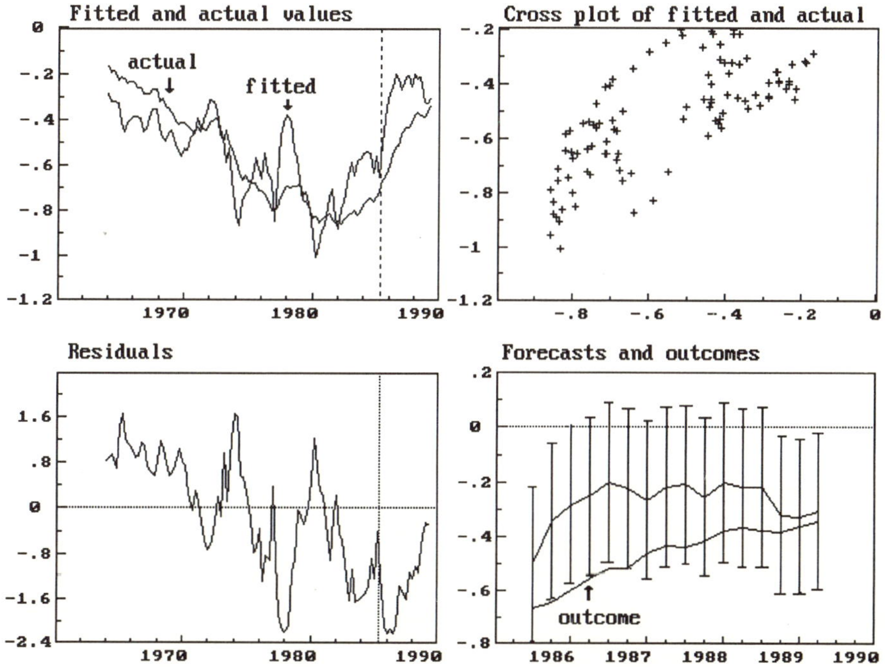

Fig. 7.15 Fitted and actual values for the leading indicator model of M1

There has been a recent resurgence of interest in leading indicators: see *inter alia* Neftci (1994), Lahiri and Moore (1991) and Stock and Watson (1989, 1992). The last authors seek to develop a statistical rationale for current and leading indicators based on dynamic latent variables, where an index is a restriction on a dynamic system, similar to factor analysis. However, the theory assumes constant coefficients and lag reactions and their follow-up demonstrates the inadvisability of such assumptions. Unless a leading-indicator model is structural, corresponding to how agents behave, and hence is interpretable in the light of a reasonable economic theory, it is unlikely be a useful way of modelling or forecasting (see Diebold and Rudebusch, 1991, Emerson and Hendry, 1994, and Clements and Hendry, 1995, for further discussion). There is no royal road to discovering autonomy, but bundling into an index model collections of series which happen to have previously exemplified some lead-lag connections seems among the less likely ways of doing so. Conversely, macro-econometric systems are just formalized leading-indicator structures.

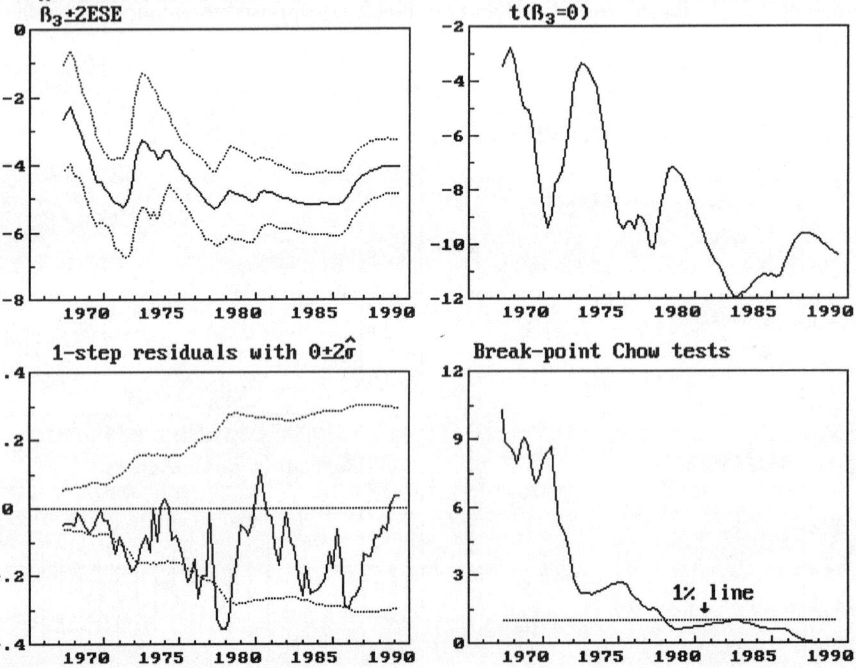

Fig. 7.16 Recursive statistics for the leading indicator model of M1

The derivation of (7.25) by marginalization from (7.1) is close to that in §7.2 and raises no new issues. Using the first approach:

$$c = \underset{T\to\infty}{\text{plim}}\ \hat{c} = \underset{T\to\infty}{\text{plim}} \sum_{t=1}^{T} y_t z_{t-1} \Big/ \sum_{t=1}^{T} z_{t-1}^2, \tag{7.26}$$

and the population moments are calculated as in (7.4):

$$\begin{aligned} \mathsf{E}\left[y_t z_{t-1}\right] &= \beta_1 \mathsf{E}\left[z_t z_{t-1}\right] + \beta_2 \mathsf{E}\left[y_{t-1} z_{t-1}\right] + \beta_3 \mathsf{E}\left[z_{t-1}^2\right] \\ &= \left(\beta_1 \lambda_1 + \beta_2 \gamma + \beta_3\right) \mathsf{E}\left[z_t^2\right]. \end{aligned} \tag{7.27}$$

From (7.5), $c = \gamma - (1 - \lambda_1)(\beta_1 - \delta/(1 - \beta_2\lambda_1))$, so when $\lambda_1 \simeq 1$, $c \simeq \gamma \simeq K_1$ and when $\delta = 0$, $c = \beta_1\lambda_1$.

The empirical illustration of (7.25) produces estimates that are similar to those of the static equation in §7.2:

$$\widehat{\log\left(\frac{M}{PY}\right)_t} = \underset{(0.04)}{-\,0.20} - \underset{(0.39)}{4.07}\, R_{t-1}$$

$$\mathsf{R}^2 = 0.52 \;\; \hat{\sigma} = 15\% \;\; SC = -3.75 \;\; DW = 0.14$$
$$AR\text{-}F(5,95) = 108.1 \;\; ND\text{-}\chi^2(2) = 5.9 \;\; Chow\text{-}F(16,84) = 1.48.$$

Using a lagged explanatory variable has had little effect on the fit or the coefficients, as might have been anticipated given that R_t is close to being a random walk. The residual autocorrelation again vitiates any constancy tests (which reject almost everywhere), so the usefulness of (7.25) is rather low: see Fig. 7.16.

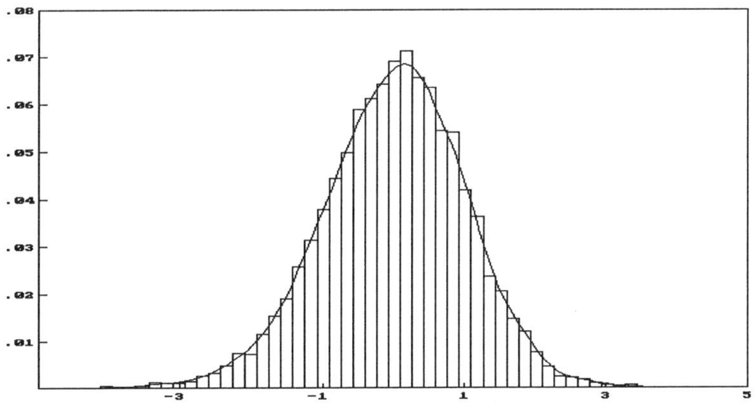

Fig. 7.17 Histogram and density for the leading indicator model

The Monte Carlo results for (7.25) are also almost identical to those for the static model in §7.2 as seen in Figs. 7.17 and 7.18: the estimate of c is skewed and has a changing bias, converging on the plim of 0.88; ESE is far from MCSD, but close to the asymptotic standard error; the equation standard error exceeds 3, with a plim of 3.3; and the Chow test rejection frequencies begin at almost 60 per cent, again due to substantial residual autocorrelation. We return in type §7.6 to whether correcting for residual autocorrelation is a sensible strategy.

The first four model types all involved only one parameter. We now consider two-parameter types beginning with a widely-used empirical form.

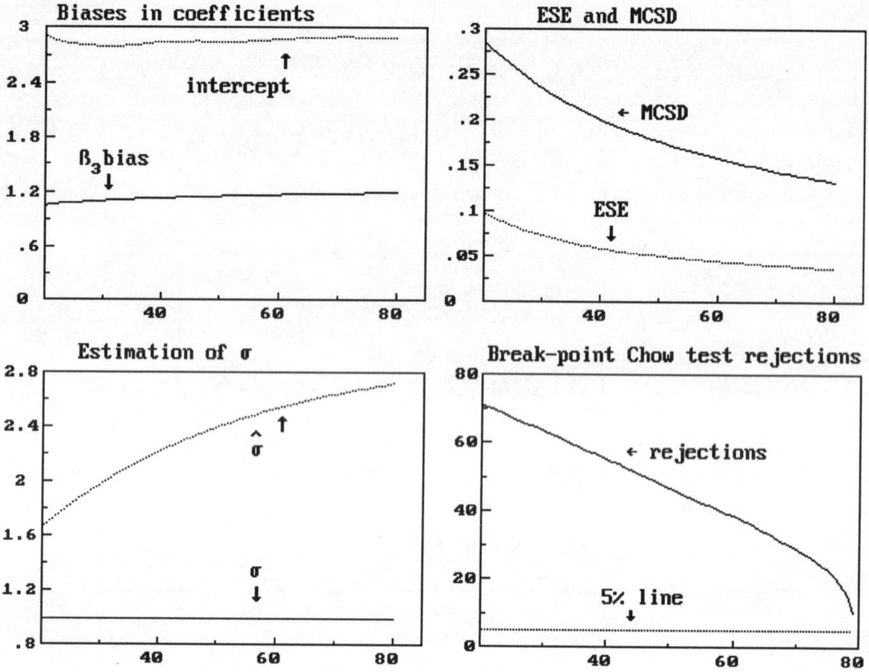

Fig. 7.18 Recursive Monte Carlo outcomes for the leading indicator model

7.6 Partial adjustment

Historically, this is perhaps the most popular type of model in two-parameter single equations. Partial adjustment is obtained by eliminating the distributed lag in AD(1, 1) making the assumption $\beta_3 = 0$ to get an AD(1, 0):

$$\mathsf{M}_6 : y_t = b_1 z_t + b_2 y_{t-1} + \eta_t. \tag{7.28}$$

As before, there are two ways in which (7.28) could arise: autonomous or derived. The former will usually work well but although the partial-adjustment principle has a respectable pedigree in economic analysis, imposing partial adjustment in a world where β_3 is not in fact zero will transpire to generate results which are an artefact of selecting a partial-adjustment process. Note the important distinction between the partial-adjustment principle and the actual implementation of partial adjustment often carried out: the following is not a critique of the principle but of the way that principle is implemented.

Suppose our 'economic theory' is of an agent with a target y^* who wants to minimize the costs C of not meeting that target when there are also costs to adjusting behaviour in order to achieve the target. For simplicity, we consider a one-period cost function (see Eisner and Strotz, 1963):

$$C_t = (y_t - y_t^*)^2 + \psi (y_t - y_{t-1})^2, \qquad (7.29)$$

where $\psi > 0$ is the relative weight accorded to adjustment costs in the cost function. On minimization of $C_t(y_t)$:

$$y_t - y_t^* + \psi y_t - \psi y_{t-1} = 0,$$

and hence:

$$\Delta y_t = (1+\psi)^{-1}(y_t^* - y_{t-1}) \quad \text{or} \quad y_t = \theta y_{t-1} + (1-\theta) y_t^*, \qquad (7.30)$$

where $\theta = \psi/(1+\psi) < 1$ for $\psi > 0$.[3] Thus, the higher the cost attached to adjustment, the slower the agent will adjust to a change in the target. In the limit, the agent will not change at all as ψ tends to infinity, since then $\theta \to 1$.

The mean and median lags in (7.28) only depend on b_2:

$$\mu = \frac{b_2}{(1-b_2)} \quad \text{and} \quad m = -\frac{\log(2b_2)}{\log(b_2)} \qquad (7.31)$$

because the imposed lag shape is an exponentially decreasing one. Thus, μ also tends to infinity as b_2 tends towards one, in which case adjustment is in terms of changes in y to the level of z. That is a serious drawback of M_6, because if $b_2 \simeq 1$, there would be a difference in the degrees of integration of the two sides in (7.28), which is unreasonable. Thus, values of b_2 close to unity suggest either a cointegration failure or the incorrect imposition of a long-tailed distribution.

Relating this analysis to consumption and income suggests another model of why agents might smooth the time path of consumption. According to the partial-adjustment explanation, if $\{y_t\}$ denotes consumption, agents have a target path for consumption, but attach costs to changing consumption, thereby smoothing it and only adjusting slowly in response to changes in the target. Certainly, if this description were actually what agents were doing, then the model would work well. But this argument is odd in the present context: in a growing world, where y_t^* has trended upwards on average for two centuries, agents will lag further and further behind their target if they attach costs to adjusting levels. Some alternative measure of the cost function is needed to model rational agents who consistently attain their targets.

One solution to that difficulty is to assume that y_t^* should incorporate predictions about its future level, which would require predicting the future values of determinants of y_{t+j}^* $(j > 0)$, such as future z (income in the example), which is hard for agents (or econometricians) to do very accurately. Nevertheless, reformulate (7.29) as an intertemporal optimization problem:

$$C_t = \mathsf{E}\left[\sum_{j=0}^{\infty} \delta^j \left((y_{t+j} - y_{t+j}^*)^2 + \psi (\Delta y_{t+j})^2 \right) \mid \mathcal{I}_t \right], \qquad (7.32)$$

[3] (7.30) is the plan rather than the outcome and an error term would reflect optimization mistakes.

where δ denotes an assumed constant discount rate. Differentiating C_t with respect to y_t involves terms at $j = 0$ and $j = 1$, (due to $\Delta y_{t+1} = y_{t+1} - y_t$), the latter reflecting the foresight that tomorrow will also have adjustment costs:

$$\frac{\partial C_t}{\partial y_t} = \mathsf{E}\left[2\left(y_t - y_t^*\right) + 2\psi\left(y_t - y_{t-1}\right) - 2\delta\psi\left(y_{t+1} - y_t\right) \mid \mathcal{I}_t\right] = 0. \tag{7.33}$$

Rearranging the terms in the middle expression of (7.33) and using E_t as a shorthand for $\mathsf{E}\left[\cdot|\mathcal{I}_t\right]$:

$$\mathsf{E}_t\left[\delta\psi y_{t+1} - \left\{1 + \psi\left(1+\delta\right)\right\} y_t + \psi y_{t-1}\right] = -\mathsf{E}_t\left[y_t^*\right], \tag{7.34}$$

or:

$$\mathsf{E}_t\left[\left(\delta\psi L^{-1} - \left\{1 + \psi\left(1+\delta\right)\right\} - \psi L\right) y_t\right] = -\mathsf{E}_t\left[y_t^*\right],$$

and hence:

$$\mathsf{E}_t\left[\left\{L^{-1} - \left(\frac{1+\psi\left(1+\delta\right)}{\delta\psi}\right) + \delta^{-1}L\right\} y_t\right] = -\frac{1}{\delta\psi}\mathsf{E}_t\left[y_t^*\right]. \tag{7.35}$$

The polynomial in L on the left-hand side in $\{\cdot\}$ can be expressed as:

$$\left(L^{-1} - \alpha\right)\left(1 - \theta L\right) \text{ where } \alpha\theta = \delta^{-1} \text{ and } \alpha + \theta = \frac{1+\psi\left(1+\delta\right)}{\delta\psi} = \frac{1}{\delta\psi} + 1 + \frac{1}{\delta}. \tag{7.36}$$

Consequently, for δ near unity, one of the roots (which we take to be θ) lies inside the unit circle, and the other (α) lies outside. Substitute (7.36) into (7.35) and cross-multiply by $\left(L^{-1} - \alpha\right)^{-1}$ to obtain:

$$\begin{aligned} \mathsf{E}_t\left[\left(1 - \theta L\right) y_t\right] &= -\tfrac{1}{\delta\psi}\mathsf{E}_t\left[\left(L^{-1} - \alpha\right)^{-1} y_t^*\right] \\ &= \tfrac{\delta\theta}{\delta\psi}\mathsf{E}_t\left[\left(1 - \delta\theta L^{-1}\right)^{-1} y_t^*\right] \\ &= \tfrac{\theta}{\psi}\mathsf{E}_t\left[\sum_{i=0}^{\infty}\left(\delta\theta\right)^i y_{t+i}^*\right], \end{aligned} \tag{7.37}$$

(using $\alpha = 1/\delta\theta$). From (7.36):

$$\frac{1}{\delta\psi} = \frac{1}{\delta\theta} + \theta - 1 - \frac{1}{\delta} \text{ so } \frac{\theta}{\psi} = 1 + \delta\theta^2 - \delta\theta - \theta = \left(1-\theta\right)\left(1-\delta\theta\right),$$

and hence:

$$\mathsf{E}_t\left[y_t\right] = \theta y_{t-1} + \left(1-\theta\right)\left\{\left(1-\delta\theta\right)\sum_{i=0}^{\infty}\left(\delta\theta\right)^i \mathsf{E}_t\left[y_{t+i}^*\right]\right\} = \theta y_{t-1} + \left(1-\theta\right) y_t^+, \tag{7.38}$$

where y_t^+ is the forward-looking target, appropriately discounted, in $\{\cdot\}$. However, (7.38) is identical in form to (7.30) for the appropriate interpretation of y_t^* and y_t^+ (see

Nickell, 1985, Pagan, 1985, and Kennan, 1979, *inter alia*). Worse still, agents now need to formulate forecasting rules for y^*_{t+i} $(i = 0, 1, \ldots, \infty)$, and form the weighted average of these to calculate y^+_t.

When z_t is generated by the stationary autoregression in (7.2) with $\lambda_0 = 0$, and $y^*_{t+i} = K_1 z^e_{t+i}$ is the rule for determining the target, assuming that z_t is known to the agent at planning time t:

$$z^e_{t+i} = \lambda^i_1 z_t, \tag{7.39}$$

and hence:

$$\sum_{i=0}^{\infty} (\delta\theta)^i \, \mathsf{E}_t \left[y^*_{t+i} \right] = K_1 \left(\sum_{i=0}^{\infty} (\delta\theta\lambda_1)^i \right) z_t = \frac{K_1}{1 - \delta\theta\lambda_1} z_t. \tag{7.40}$$

Substituting (7.40) into (7.38) and using $y^p_t = \mathsf{E}_t \left[y_t \right]$ as the agent's plan:

$$y^p_t = \theta y_{t-1} + (1 - \theta) K^* z_t \text{ where } K^* = \frac{K_1 (1 - \delta\theta)}{1 - \delta\theta\lambda_1}, \tag{7.41}$$

which reproduces (7.28) in form, but with the caveat that b_1 and b_2 are not invariants of the decision process, but are functions of $(\delta, \psi, \lambda_1, K_1)$ and will alter if any of these deeper parameters alter.

Empirical models tend to produce large estimates of θ, frequently larger than 0.85 in quarterly equations. Since $\delta \approx 1$ for such high-frequency data, we can solve for ψ from (7.36) using $\psi \simeq \theta / (1 - \theta)^2$. Thus, when $\theta = 0.9$, $\psi = 90$, which is implausible: why should it cost agents ninety times as much to adjust towards, as to deviate from, their desired target? Even if θ is as low as 0.8, $\psi = 20$. There seems little hope of rescuing the expectations interpretation of such partial-adjustment estimates.

The problem is the original choice of function assumed for the decision variable y in (7.29) or (7.32). For example, (7.29) could apply to y being the ratio of consumption to income, but the resulting empirical model would be quite different from that in which y was the level of consumption: the interpretation of adjustment costs would become more sensible if y were the ratio of consumption and income. In practice, y could be almost any function of the variable to be modelled and economic analysis is unclear as to which function to use. (7.28) could be a poor representation for one choice, yet be useful for another, with one clear implication: think carefully about how to choose any measure of y.

Unfortunately, we do not know which transformations economic agents use. Suppose a consumption–income model is estimated using (7.28). If the DGP were an AD(1, 1) with $K_1 = 1$, $\beta_1 = 0.5$ and $\beta_2 = 0.9$, we would predict an estimated value of b_2 of about unity (or more precisely, between unity and 0.8), so that b_1 must be small to ensure $b_1 / (1 - b_2) = 1$ as required for long-run homogeneity. Such an outcome implies that there are large costs of adjustment and a long adjustment lag. However, $\mu = 5$ and $m = 0$ in the Monte Carlo DGP, which suggests the possibility that long lags in partial adjustment may be an artefact of that type of model, independently of the actual process determining how agents behave.

By way of comparison, consider y as being the savings–income ratio S/I with $z = \Delta \log I$ where the long-run target is given by:

$$\frac{S^*}{I} = K(g) = k_0 + k_1 g \tag{7.42}$$

when g is the growth rate of real, after-tax income. Now (7.30) becomes (using $\Delta \log I_t$ for g_t):

$$\left(\frac{S^p}{I}\right)_t = \theta \left(\frac{S}{I}\right)_{t-1} + (1-\theta)\,\Delta \log I_t + \alpha \tag{7.43}$$

which is a well-known specification for savings behaviour (see e.g. Stone, 1966, 1973, and Hendry, 1983b). If $\log I_t$ is a random walk with drift g, given by:

$$\Delta \log I_t = g + \nu_t, \tag{7.44}$$

so that $z_t = \Delta \log I_t$ and $\lambda_1 = 0$ in (7.2), then (7.43) coincides in form with (7.30). Now a 90-fold higher cost of adjusting the long-term savings ratio as against responding to (perhaps transient) changes in income makes some sense.

At a methodological level, derivations such as (7.41) from (7.32) must be carefully appraised, since the properties of the latter depend entirely on how well the former encapsulates the salient aspects of dynamic decision-taking by economic agents. Why would agents wish to minimize a function such as (7.32)? At first sight, the desire to achieve a target seems unexceptionable and in many cases, symmetry is a useful approximation, so the term $(y_t - y_t^*)^2$ seems acceptable, as does the need to take account of future trajectories of y_t^* in deciding on today's action. Equally, penalizing too rapid change also seems acceptable, and if $\psi = 0$ then $y_t = y_t^* \ \forall t$. However, several difficulties must be confronted.

First, why does the agent select y_t^* before deciding to minimize (7.32)? A rational agent would surely optimize an overall criterion to make a plan and not undertake two-stage planning where, from (7.38), the actual target transpires to be y_t^{**} and not y_t^*. Secondly, the cost function C_t neglects the costs of information collection and processing needed to form the future expectations, an issue discussed in Chapter 6. Thirdly, how likely are K_1, δ and ψ to be invariant parameters? Here there is more room for alternative views, since there is little empirical evidence on which to draw, but I consider it unlikely that either δ or ψ are constant over time. Discount rates seem to change with income levels, probably respond to interest rates, and may well fluctuate over time (e.g. why do some motorists overtake on blind corners?). Equally, the relative weight of adjustment costs to target discrepancies will change with the degree of credit rationing, and transactions technology and may alter with the extent of disequilibrium existing at any point in time, as well as the variance of the uncontrolled processes which influence y_t^*.

As an analogy, consider attempting to shoot a target with a gun. When the target is stationary, rapid movement of the gun will induce a miss, hence one should penalize change in the neighbourhood of the target. At distances far from the target, rapid adjustment is desirable rather than costly. When the target is moving steadily, similar considerations apply with the two additional factors of needing to project where the target will be when the bullet arrives (so a lead time is required) and needing to continuously swing the gun to match the target's movement. Again, change *per se* should not be penalized, only unnecessary change away from the desired trajectory. Here, expectations about the target's future movements play an essential role in hitting it. Finally, when the target is moving erratically, it is far less clear how to move the gun. All the previous considerations apply but in some cases, such as when the target is zig-zagging around a mean path which is a straight line, it may pay to keep the gun still and await the arrival of the target. In such a situation, adjustment would slow down as the target's behaviour became more erratic.

As with all methodological issues concerning how to discover the way a process functions, it pays to think carefully about the specific problem under investigation. The derivation of an equation from an inter-temporal optimization approach does not by itself make it structural, or even sensible. Indeed, the first major problem is confronted again: without direct empirical evidence on how agents plan dynamically (i.e. on the structure of the DGP), we cannot know the appropriate class of model to use, and must return to an iteration between empirical evidence and theory, where each consolidates the knowledge acquired by the other.

Interestingly, the rational-expectations model of permanent income considered in §7.4 above is a partial-adjustment process. From (7.13) and (7.12):

$$\begin{aligned} \mathsf{E}\left[i^p_{t+1} \mid \mathcal{I}_t\right] &= r\mathsf{E}\left[\sum_{j=2}^{\infty}(1+r)^{-j+1}\, i_{t+j} \mid \mathcal{I}_t\right] \\ &= r\mathsf{E}\left[(1+r)\sum_{j=1}^{\infty}(1+r)^{-j}\, i_{t+j} - i_{t+1} \mid \mathcal{I}_t\right] \\ &= (1+r)\, i^p_t - r\mathsf{E}\left[i_{t+1} \mid \mathcal{I}_t\right]. \end{aligned} \tag{7.45}$$

Thus, $\Delta i^p_{t+1} = r\left(i^p_t - \mathsf{E}\left[i_{t+1}|\mathcal{I}_t\right]\right) + \xi_t$.

As usual, the next stage is to derive M_6 from (7.1) by appropriate marginalization operations. This involves eliminating the orthogonal component of z_{t-1} relative to $\boldsymbol{w}_t = (z_t \;\; y_{t-1})'$. Let:

$$z_{t-1} = \boldsymbol{\pi}'\boldsymbol{w}_t + \eta_t = \pi_1 z_t + \pi_2 y_{t-1} + \eta_t, \tag{7.46}$$

where $\eta_t \perp \boldsymbol{w}_t$ by construction since $\boldsymbol{\pi} = \left(\mathsf{E}\left[\boldsymbol{w}_t\boldsymbol{w}_t'\right]\right)^{-1}\mathsf{E}\left[\boldsymbol{w}_t z_{t-1}\right]$. Then from (7.1):

$$\begin{aligned} y_t &= \beta_1 z_t + \beta_2 y_{t-1} + \beta_3\left(\boldsymbol{\pi}'\boldsymbol{w}_t + \eta_t\right) + \epsilon_t \\ &= \left(\beta_1 + \beta_3\pi_1\right) z_t + \left(\beta_2 + \beta_3\pi_2\right) y_{t-1} + \beta_3\eta_t + \epsilon_t. \end{aligned} \tag{7.47}$$

The calculation of $\boldsymbol{\pi}$ requires all of the population second moments from (7.1), which can be derived as in §A4.8. These are as follows, in an obvious notation:

$$\begin{aligned}
m_{zz} &= \sigma_v^2 / \left(1-\lambda_1^2\right); \\
m_{zz_1} &= \lambda_1 m_{zz}; \\
m_{yz} &= \left(\beta_1+\beta_3\lambda_1\right) m_{zz} / \left(1-\beta_2\lambda_1\right) = \gamma m_{zz}; \\
m_{yz_1} &= \left[\beta_1\lambda_1+\beta_3+\beta_2\gamma\right] m_{zz} = \tau m_{zz}; \\
m_{y_1 z} &= \lambda_1 m_{yz} = \lambda_1 \gamma m_{zz}; \\
m_{yy} &= \left\{\left[\left(1-\beta_2\right)\left(1+\beta_2\lambda_1\right) K_1^2 - 2\beta_1\beta_3\left(1-\lambda_1\right)\right] m_{zz}\right\} / \\
&\quad \left(1-\beta_2\lambda_1\right)\left(1+\beta_2\right) + \sigma_\epsilon^2 / \left(1-\beta_2^2\right); \\
m_{yy_1} &= \left(\beta_1\lambda_1+\beta_3\right)\gamma m_{zz} + \beta_2 m_{yy}.
\end{aligned} \tag{7.48}$$

Letting $r = m_{zz}^{-1} m_{yy}$:

$$\begin{aligned}
\pi &= \begin{pmatrix} m_{zz} & m_{y_1 z} \\ m_{y_1 z} & m_{yy} \end{pmatrix}^{-1} \begin{pmatrix} m_{zz_1} \\ m_{yz} \end{pmatrix} = m_{zz}^{-1} \begin{pmatrix} 1 & \lambda_1\gamma \\ \lambda_1\gamma & r \end{pmatrix}^{-1} \begin{pmatrix} \lambda_1 m_{zz} \\ \gamma m_{zz} \end{pmatrix} \\
&= d^{-1} \begin{pmatrix} r & -\lambda_1\gamma \\ -\lambda_1\gamma & 1 \end{pmatrix} \begin{pmatrix} \lambda_1 \\ \gamma \end{pmatrix} = d^{-1} \begin{pmatrix} \lambda_1\left(r-\gamma^2\right) \\ \gamma\left(1-\lambda_1^2\right) \end{pmatrix},
\end{aligned} \tag{7.49}$$

where $d = \left(r - \lambda_1^2\gamma^2\right) \neq 0$. The analytic derivation does not simplify further except in special cases, although (7.49) is easy to calculate numerically. For the original model, therefore:

$$b = \begin{pmatrix} m_{zz} & m_{y_1 z} \\ m_{y_1 z} & m_{yy} \end{pmatrix}^{-1} \begin{pmatrix} m_{zy} \\ m_{y_1 y} \end{pmatrix} = \begin{pmatrix} \left(\beta_1+\beta_3\pi_1\right) \\ \left(\beta_2+\beta_3\pi_2\right) \end{pmatrix}.$$

We turn to the empirical illustration using $\log\left(M/PY\right)_t$ on $\log\left(M/PY\right)_{t-1}$ and R_t:

$$\begin{aligned}
\widehat{\log\left(\tfrac{M}{PY}\right)_t} &= \underset{(0.006)}{0.006} - \underset{(0.07)}{0.61}\, R_t + \underset{(0.01)}{0.92} \log\left(\tfrac{M}{PY}\right)_{t-1} \\
&\mathrm{R}^2 = 0.99 \;\; \hat{\sigma} = 2.0\% \;\; SC = -7.69 \;\; DW = 2.57 \\
&AR\text{-}F(5,94) = 2.6 \;\; ND\text{-}\chi^2(2) = 4.5 \;\; Chow - F(16,83) = 0.40.
\end{aligned} \tag{7.50}$$

This equation is in line with the results in Chapter 6, as R_{t-1} was not found to play an important role: the impact coefficient on R_t and that of the lagged dependent variable are similar to those of the general model, as is the goodness of fit. Figures 7.19 and 7.20 record the graphical output.

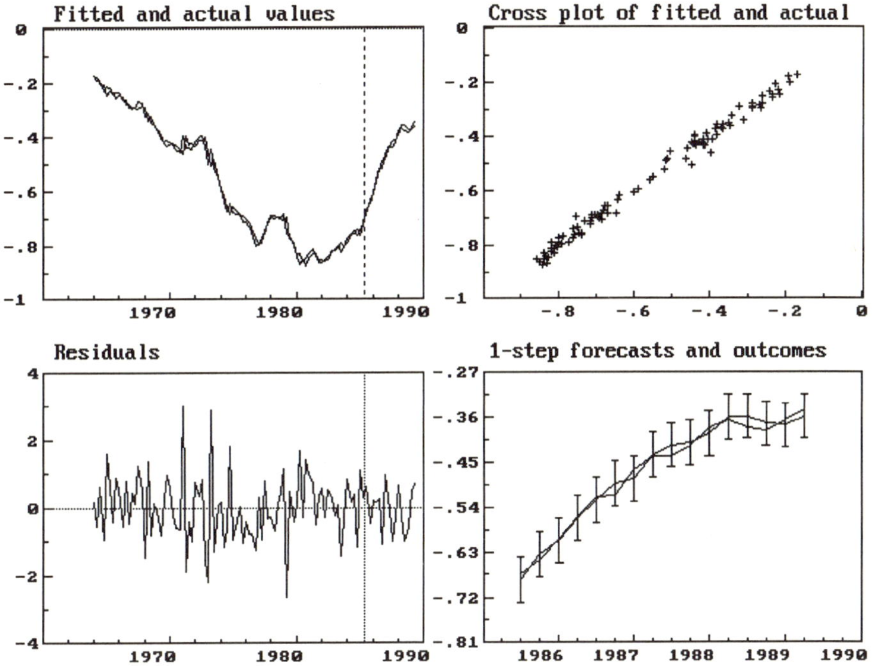

Fig. 7.19 Fitted and actual values from the partial adjustment model for M1

Now consider the Monte Carlo results of fitting M_6 to the AD$(1,1)$ DGP. The first finding is that the mean coefficients are close to their plims with $\mathsf{E}[\hat{b}_1] \simeq 0.2$ (plim $\hat{b}_1 = 0.18$), and $\mathsf{E}[\hat{b}_2] \simeq 0.8$ (plim $\hat{b}_2 = 0.81$), but badly biased for the true values $\beta_1 = 0.5$ and $\beta_2 = 0.9$. The model under-estimates the impact effect of z_t on y_t by not allowing z_{t-1} to enter the model, yet also under estimates the mean lag, which is four here instead of the true value of five. Conversely, partial adjustment over estimates the median lag, which is about three instead of the true value of zero. The policy implications of being wrong about lag responses are worrying. These results are not untypical of estimated partial-adjustment models, suggesting that some empirical findings may be an artefact of imposing that dynamic specification: standardizing for $K_1 = 1$, $\hat{b}_1$ often lies between $(0.1, 0.2)$ with $\hat{b}_2$ between $(0.8, 0.95)$ independently of the problem studied. Figures 7.21 and 7.22 show the histograms and densities for $\hat{b}_1$ and $\hat{b}_2$ at $T = 80$; and Fig. 7.23 the full-sample distribution of the t-test of H_0: $b_2 = \beta_2$.

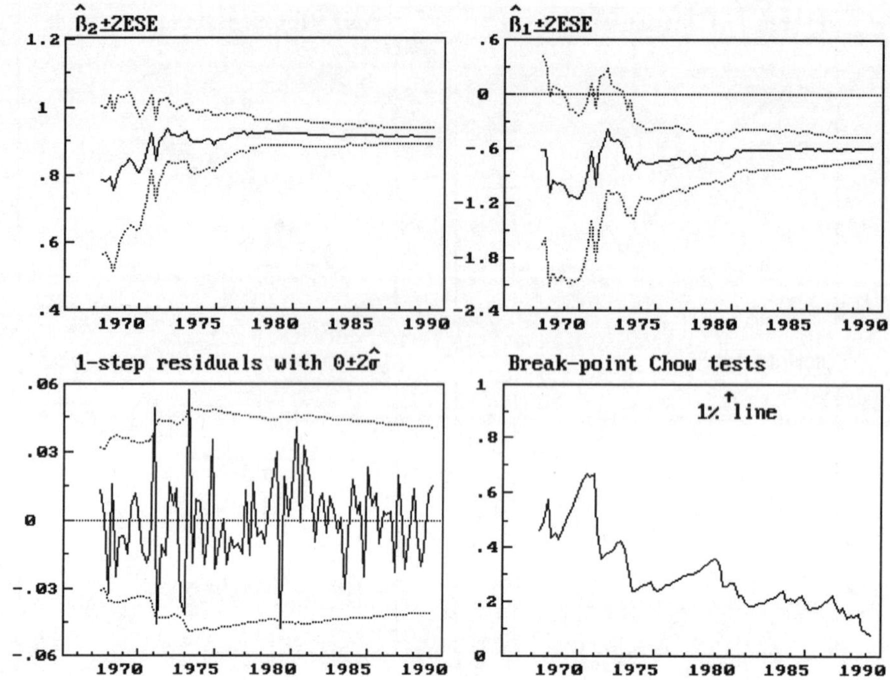

Fig. 7.20 Recursive statistics from the partial adjustment model for M1

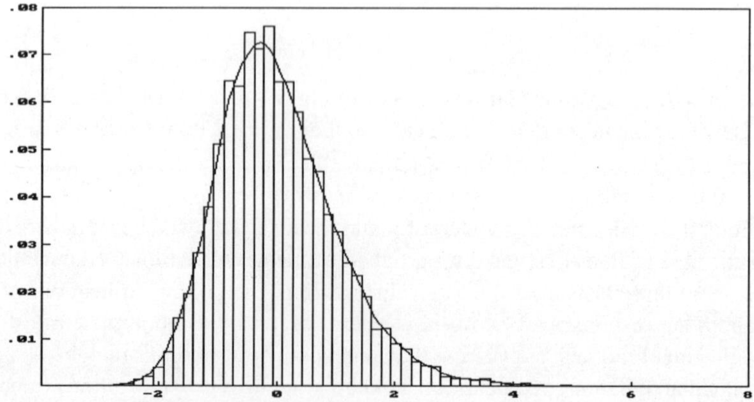

Fig. 7.21 Histogram and density for $\hat{b}_1$ in the Monte Carlo for partial adjustment

The graphs of the biases in $\hat{b}_1$ and $\hat{b}_2$ recursively estimated are shown in Fig. 7.24a. The bias in $\hat{b}_2$ for β_2 gradually flattens out at about -0.14, but the small-sample bias is large, so the estimate changes with the sample size, although the true coefficient is constant. However, the Chow test detects model change only about 12–13 per cent of the time, so we would not usually draw the wrong conclusion that the model has non-constant parameters (see Fig. 7.24d). The ESEs under estimate the true MCSDs by about 30–40 per cent as shown in Figs. 7.24b,c for $\hat{b}_1$ and $\hat{b}_2$, so the uncertainty in the model is seriously under estimated.

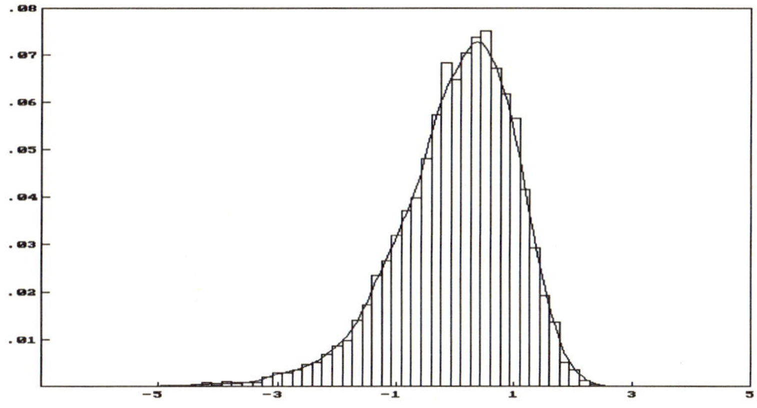

Fig. 7.22 Histogram and density for $\hat{b}_2$ in the Monte Carlo for partial adjustment

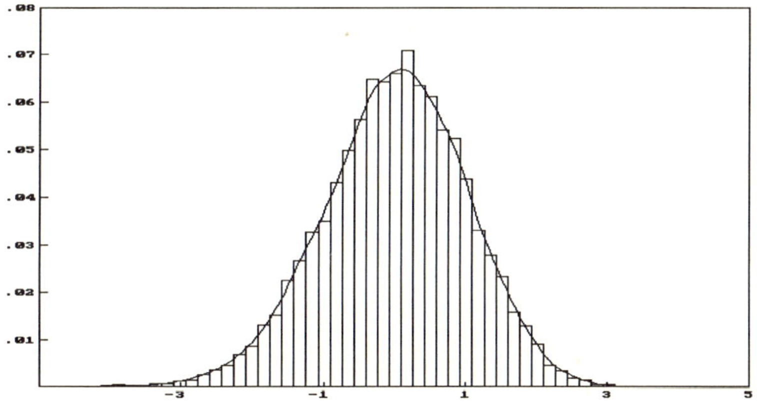

Fig. 7.23 Histogram and density for the t-test of H_0: $b_2 = \beta_2$

The DW statistic for the hypothesis of zero residual autocorrelation only marginally helps detect this last problem, as it rejects the null hypothesis 38 per cent of the time instead of 5 per cent, despite omitting a variable (z_{t-1}) with a coefficient of -0.4, which is 0.95 autoregressive.[4] In just over one-third of the samples, the DW test provides a

[4] DW is not a valid test here, however.

counter indicator to the specification, but it would be a mistake to 'correct' this residual autocorrelation. Although z_t is highly autoregressive, (7.46) shows that the omitted component is not as autoregressive as the data variable itself: regression mis-specifications only omit components which are orthogonal to those retained. Least-squares 'flattens' residual autocorrelation because of the composition of the error:

$$u_t = \epsilon_t + \beta_3 \eta_t. \tag{7.51}$$

The residual autocorrelation that should arise from omitting the autocorrelated variable z_{t-1} is masked by: (i) the white-noise process ϵ_t; (ii) η_t being less autocorrelated than z_{t-1}; and (iii) η_t being deflated by β_3. Thus, the residuals in this partial adjustment model are not strongly autocorrelated.

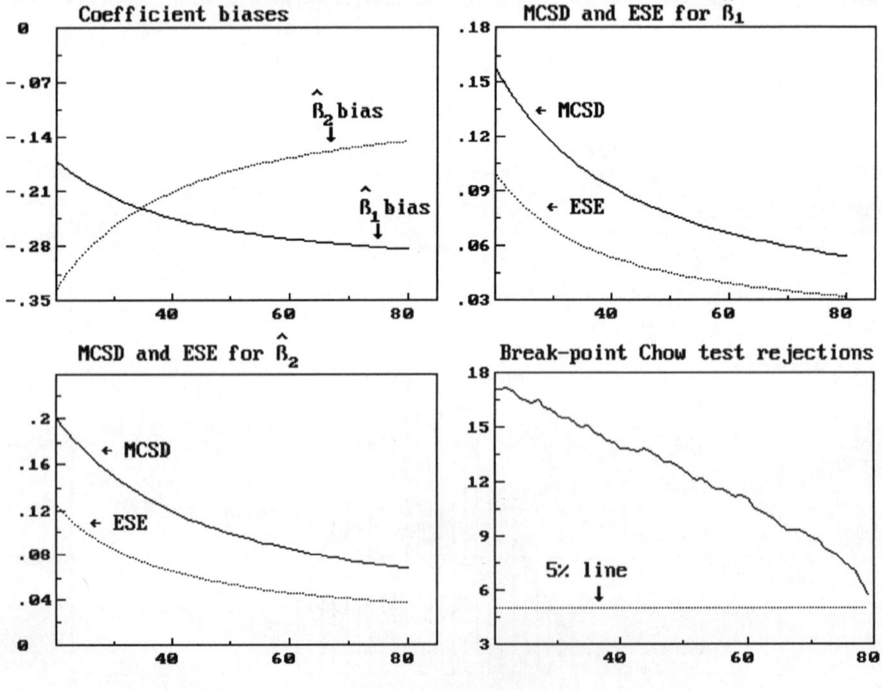

Fig. 7.24 Recursive Monte Carlo statistics for partial adjustment

7.7 Common factor

We next consider the case where an investigator decides to estimate an autocorrelated-error model:

$$y_t = dz_t + u_t \tag{7.52}$$

where:

$$u_t = \rho u_{t-1} + e_t, \tag{7.53}$$

and e_t is assumed to be white noise, so that (7.53) is a first-order autoregressive scheme. Belief in the validity of a model entails belief in all models which are isomorphic to it. Consequently, when (7.52)+(7.53) are the DGP, by substitution:

$$y_t - dz_t = \rho(y_{t-1} - dz_{t-1}) + e_t \tag{7.54}$$

or:

$$\mathsf{M}_7 : y_t = dz_t + \rho y_{t-1} - \rho dz_{t-1} + e_t. \tag{7.55}$$

Equation (7.55) is logically entailed by (7.52) and (7.53), so believing the autoregressive form entails accepting the general representative of the typology, namely the AD(1, 1) in (7.1), together with the restriction that the coefficient β_3 is $-\beta_1\beta_2$ where:

$$\beta_3 = -\rho d \text{ when } \beta_1 = d \text{ and } \beta_2 = \rho. \tag{7.56}$$

Repeat this analysis in the reverse order, beginning from the AD(1, 1) in (7.1) and imposing the restriction (7.56) in order to induce a model with an autocorrelated error. We consider the case when $\beta_1 \neq 0$, so that from (7.1):

$$(1 - \beta_2 L) y_t = \beta_1 \left(1 + \left[\frac{\beta_3}{\beta_1}\right] L\right) z_t + \epsilon_t. \tag{7.57}$$

Under the assumption in (7.56) that $\beta_3 = -\beta_1\beta_2$, (7.57) becomes:

$$(1 - \beta_2 L) y_t = \beta_1 (1 - \beta_2 L) z_t + \epsilon_t. \tag{7.58}$$

The lag polynomials on both sides of (7.58) have the factor $(1 - \beta_2 L)$ in common, which is where the name COMFAC, for common factor, comes from. Dividing by $(1 - \beta_2 L)$:

$$y_t = \beta_1 z_t + \frac{\epsilon_t}{(1 - \beta_2 L)} = \beta_1 z_t + u_t. \tag{7.59}$$

where $u_t = \epsilon_t / (1 - \beta_2 L)$. Multiplying u_t by $(1 - \beta_2 L)$ results in $(1 - \beta_2 L) u_t = \epsilon_t$ or:

$$u_t = \beta_2 u_{t-1} + \epsilon_t = \rho u_{t-1} + \epsilon_t, \tag{7.60}$$

which is the autoregressive error (7.53). Thus, (7.52)+(7.53) are isomorphic to (7.1)+(7.56): a first-order autoregressive error implies a common factor, and vice versa.

COMFAC is a statistical model, without a well-established economic-theory basis. One possible rationale is in terms of the persistence of good luck or bad luck, since from (7.52) and (7.53):

$$\mathsf{E}[y_t \mid z_t, y_{t-1}, z_{t-1}] = dz_t + \rho u_{t-1}. \tag{7.61}$$

In words, any chanced-upon state of nature affects the following period's conditional expectation. For example, if one is lucky (unlucky) and starts employment in a boom (recession), one's real wage may remain above (below) average for a considerable time. Another possibility is that agents confront autonomous shocks beyond their control, so adjust completely to the part they can control and partially to the part they cannot control. This matches the implication of (7.58) that the mean lag in a COMFAC model is zero for all values of the parameters. Also, from (7.61):

$$\mathsf{E}\left[y_t \mid z_t, y_{t-1}, z_{t-1}\right] = dz_t + \rho\left(y_{t-1} - dz_{t-1}\right). \tag{7.62}$$

Thus, the impact response, *d*, is the same as the long-run response. There are no a priori grounds for believing that such a model is realistic, and pragmatic grounds for suspecting claims to instant and complete adjustment. This point is especially forceful when y Granger-causes z, since then z_t and u_{t-1} must be correlated, making it difficult to interpret the sense in which $\{u_t\}$ is claimed to be autonomous. For forecasting, however, since u_{t-1} is the actual previous error, any systematic deviation can be partially mitigated by including the previous residual (see Hendry and Clements, 1992).

Turning to the derivation of COMFAC by marginalization from the AD(1, 1) model (7.1):

$$\begin{aligned} y_t &= \beta_1 z_t + \beta_3 z_{t-1} + \beta_2 y_{t-1} + \epsilon_t \\ &= \beta_1 z_t + \beta_2\left(y_{t-1} - \beta_1 z_{t-1}\right) + \left(\beta_1\beta_2 + \beta_3\right) z_{t-1} + \epsilon_t \\ &= dz_t + \rho\left(y_{t-1} - dz_{t-1}\right) + \xi_t, \end{aligned} \tag{7.63}$$

where, by appropriate choices of d and ρ, the disturbance ξ_t is orthogonalized with respect to the two regressors in the last line. The estimation of d and ρ involves non-linear optimization, and no closed analytic solution exists. The principle of orthogonalizing included and excluded components remains the same — it is just the implementation that is awkward. Hendry and Srba (1977) derive the plim of the normed likelihood function, and maximize that numerically to obtain values for the plims of the parameter estimators.

COMFAC analysis can be generalized to an AD($r, s, p, \ldots$), with lag polynomials of orders r, s, p, etc. When there are $n \leq \min\left(r, s, p, \ldots\right)$ common factors, such a model can be re-written as a more parsimonious regression equation with lag lengths $(r-n)$, $(s-n)$, $(p-n)$, etc., and with an autoregressive error of order n. Since the dynamics are represented by the autoregressive error, there is a one–one mapping: models with autoregressive errors correspond to common factors in an AD($\cdot$) model, and the general AD($\cdot$) model with common factors generates an autoregressive error (see Sargan, 1980b, Hendry and Mizon, 1978, and Mizon and Hendry, 1980).

Care is required in applying this analysis to the estimation of empirical models with residual autocorrelation. Assume we start by postulating (7.52) with a white-noise error, then find residual autocorrelation. Since (7.53) was estimated under the null hypothesis that $\{u_t\}$ was white noise, the appearance of an autocorrelated error reveals a misspecification, but does not reveal its cause. It is a *non sequitur* to assume that because the residuals are autocorrelated, they were generated by a common-factor member of the typology. There are many reasons why residuals are autocorrelated; two possibilities are:

(a) Wrong functional form: to correct this type of mistake by fitting an autocorrelated error process will generate another invalid model, where the symptoms of mis-specification will appear in a different form as shown in Chapter 6.
(b) Omitted lagged variables: that these generate autocorrelated residuals does not entail that the effects of the omitted lagged variables can be well approximated by an autoregressive error, which is the implication of asserting that the omitted lags correspond to common factors. This statement remains true even when the plim of the residual autocorrelation coefficient is β_2 (see the application by Hendry, 1975, of the test in Durbin, 1960).

Succinctly, residual autocorrelation does not entail error autoregression: and since the restriction in (7.56) is not a natural proposition in economics, the apparently common reporting of models with autoregressive errors almost certainly reflects the false assumption that residual autocorrelation implies common factors.

This problem is probably exacerbated by the invalid order of testing often adopted. Fitting a model then testing it for autocorrelated errors involves mis-specification testing (in the terminology of Mizon, 1977a). The only conclusion from a rejection on a mis-specification test is to reject the framework and begin again: we have already criticized the attempted constructive use of test rejection information. Detecting residual autocorrelation in a simple model like (7.52), and fitting a common-factor model in response, implicitly asserts that there were common factors in the general dynamic model, the omission of which generated the autocorrelated errors. If so, then the analysis should have begun with the more general member of the typology and proceeded by testing to see whether:

(i) there were common factors as in (7.52); in which case, whether
(ii) the common factor ρ was zero or not.

The second step tests for autoregressive errors conditional on the validity of the first step.

In an important sense, autoregressive errors are a restriction on a model, not a generalization as frequently presented in textbooks. That result arose in Chapter 2, since the DGP could be written without loss of generality in terms of an innovation error. While COMFAC models generate autoregressive errors, and vice versa, autocorrelated residuals *per se* could be due to a vast range of mistakes. The hypothesis that $\rho = 0$ cannot sensibly be tested unless the model has common factors to sustain the representation in (7.52) and (7.53), which here first requires testing (i) at the level of the AD(1, 1). To jump to the second step without testing the first step opens up the danger that $\rho \neq 0$ while $\beta_3 \neq -\beta_1\beta_2$.

In applied dynamic econometrics, coefficients of lagged variables in the AD($r, s, \ldots$) are often set to zero a priori. The information for doing that rarely has any basis beyond assumption, so until the issue is investigated empirically, the claimed models lack credibility. If such restrictions are rejected, the analysis falls foul of the general lesson that has recurred throughout this chapter, namely the dangers inherent in proceeding from simple models and attempting to generalize them from unfavourable diagnostic evidence. To make reliable progress requires beginning from the most general model entailed by the available theoretical and data information, and sequentially testing to see whether or not the claimed restrictions are satisfied by the evidence. Thus, of the two polar approaches to empirical econometrics: general-to-specific versus simple-to-general, a central message of this book is: do not use the latter.

A digression on the meaning of general-to-specific may be helpful. Simple and general are relative concepts. A simple model is one where its proprietor is not surprised to discover later that it needs to be generalized. For example, in a static regression estimated from economic time series, residual autocorrelation would be unsurprising and hence so would the need to generalize the initial model to take account of it. In that case, the approach is methodologically unsound, because many generalizations are possible. Perhaps the most persuasive argument is to begin with a simple model M_a, discover a flaw f_a, and generalize to M_b. Now discover a second flaw f_b in M_b, and try to generalize M_b to M_c. But how could any sense be attached to the interpretation of the first flaw f_a from which M_b was derived given that f_b reveals that M_b itself is flawed? From M_c, we cannot even deduce that the rejections which led from M_a to M_b were correctly interpreted. For example, f_a may have suggested autocorrelation corrections, but f_b then reveals non-constant parameters: both could well be due to non-linearities so that M_c (which patches both f_a and f_b) is hopelessly incorrect, and may even camouflage the correct solution. Every conclusion drawn is potentially wrong following a rejection at any point during the generalization, so the entire study collapses. Such a research strategy is liable to be inefficient. Complicated interactions between untreated problems can occur, since the consequences of resolving one difficulty are dependent on the unknown existence of other problems: see Hendry (1975).

Conversely, a general model is such that if a more general model was needed its proprietor would be surprised, and hence would have learnt something new by that discovery alone. For example, consider a study of money demand involving money, prices, income, and interest rates, where each variable could enter with many lags. If this general model proved inadequate (e.g. the parameters were non-constant), then we would have learnt that no member of this log-linear class could work, since the most general member fails. To proceed, we would need to think of some new idea or source of information not previously tried (e.g. perhaps income taxes on interest earnings matter; or financial innovation needs to be modelled). One should not proceed by some *ad hoc* generalization of the initial model. On any rejection, restart the analysis, albeit having gained genuine knowledge. However, in the simple-to-general approach, little is learnt from the fact that the simple model fails, though something might be if it succeeds.

Common-factor models highlight this methodological issue and show that a general model must satisfy at least four conditions:

(i) the model is sufficiently general that the need for a more general model should be a surprise;
(ii) its parameters must be estimable from the available data;
(iii) it must be identifiable, so that it is logically possible to learn about the parameters of interest using the model;
(iv) the model must characterize the joint distribution of all the variables at the outset.

These are difficult issues to resolve and point up the need for reduction methods, but they form a clear research agenda. The textbook symptomatology comprising the problems of autocorrelation, of heteroscedasticity, of multicollinearity, and so on, is itself partly a product of a simple-to-general viewpoint. Provided the initial model is sufficiently general to characterize the data, then problems like autocorrelation become simplifications which are valid in certain states of nature.

Mizon (1993a) highlights a key reason for commencing from the general characterization of the joint density of all the variables: contradictions can otherwise ensue. His example is one where $\{z_t\}$ is strongly exogenous for a parameter of interest β in a linear model, where $\mathsf{E}[y_t|z_t] = \beta z_t$ so:

$$y_t = \beta z_t + u_t \text{ with } u_t = \rho u_{t-1} + e_t \text{ and } e_t \sim \mathsf{IN}\left[0, \sigma_\epsilon^2\right]. \tag{7.64}$$

He shows that these assumptions are insufficient to sustain COMFAC estimation and advises against 'autocorrelation corrections'. Ignoring the autoregressive error, OLS estimation of β is consistent (due to strong exogeneity), yet least-squares estimation of (β, ρ) is not, since strong exogeneity does not ensure that $\mathsf{E}[z_{t-1}u_t] = 0$.

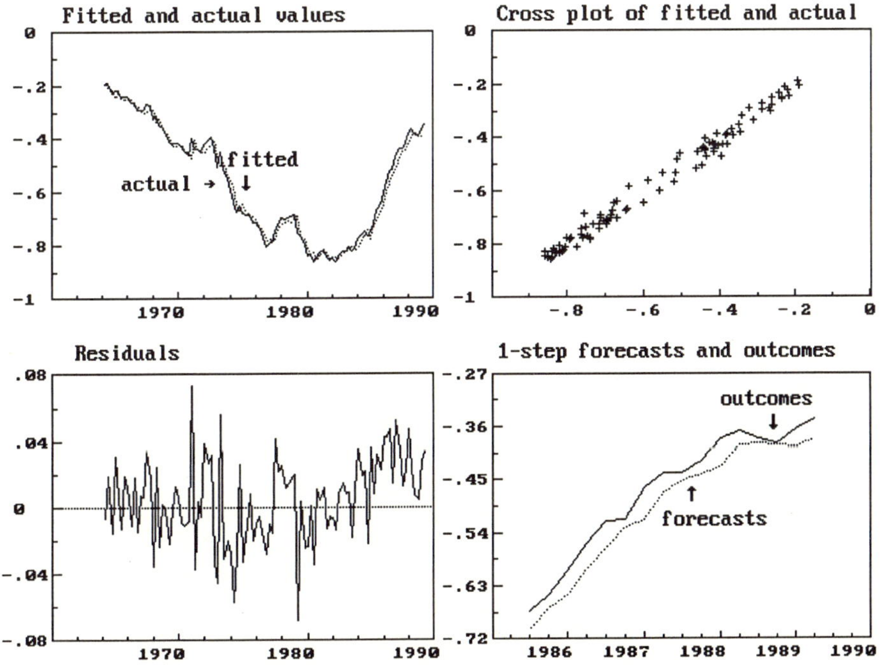

Fig. 7.25 Fitted values and outcomes for the COMFAC model of M1

In fact, the DGP which Mizon envisages is:

$$\begin{aligned} y_t &= \alpha y_{t-1} + w_{1t} \\ z_t &= w_{2t} \end{aligned} \quad \text{where } \boldsymbol{w}_t \sim \mathsf{IN}_2 \left[\begin{pmatrix} 0 \\ 0 \end{pmatrix}, \begin{pmatrix} \sigma_{11} & \sigma_{12} \\ \sigma_{12} & \sigma_{22} \end{pmatrix} \right]. \quad (7.65)$$

Then $\beta = \sigma_{12}\sigma_{22}^{-1}$, $\rho = \alpha$, and $e_t = v_t + \rho\beta w_{2t-1}$ where $v_t = w_{1t} - \beta w_{2t}$. Since $\mathsf{E}[v_t w_{2t}] = 0$ by construction of β and $v_t \sim \mathsf{IN}\left[0, \sigma_{11} - \sigma_{12}^2\sigma_{22}^{-1}\right]$ then $\mathsf{E}[e_t e_{t-i}] = 0\ \forall i > 0$ so $\{e_t\}$ is a white-noise process (and hence independent by normality) but is not an innovation. Thus, $\mathsf{E}[z_{t-1}u_t] = \mathsf{E}\left[z_{t-1}\left(\alpha y_{t-1} + v_t\right)\right] \neq 0$ as $\mathsf{E}\left[y_t|z_t\right] = \beta z_t$. In the transformed model $y_t = \beta z_t + \rho y_{t-1} - \rho\beta z_{t-1} + e_t$, $\mathsf{E}[z_{t-1}e_t] \neq 0$ so the least-squares estimator of (β, ρ) is inconsistent. Consequently, despite the model with $\rho = 0$ being nested in (7.64), a mis-specification analysis based on taking the assumptions justifying (7.64) as adequate would wrongly conclude that the OLS estimator of β should have the same plim.

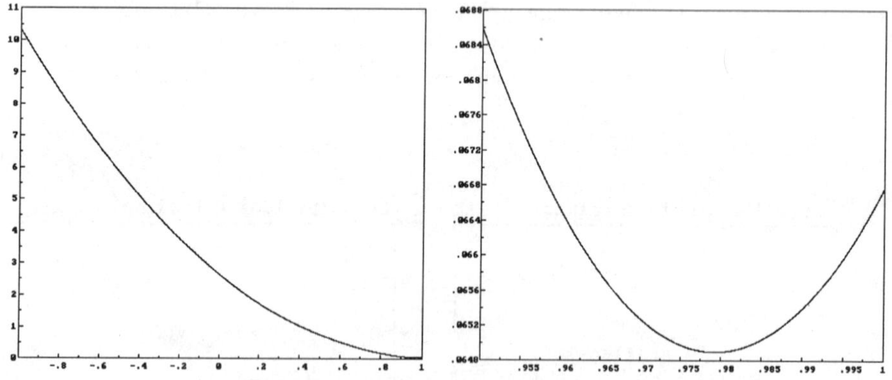

Fig. 7.26 RSS as a function of the autocorrelation parameter

The empirical illustration highlights several of these issues. COMFAC estimation yields:

$$\widehat{\log\left(\frac{M}{PY}\right)_t} = \underset{(0.13)}{-\,0.57} - \underset{(0.19)}{0.71}\, R_t + \underset{(0.01)}{0.98}\, u_{t-1}$$

$$\hat{\sigma} = 2.6\% \;\; CF_{LR}\text{-}\chi^2\,(1) = 59.6 \;\; CF_W\text{-}\chi^2\,(1) = 60.3 \;\; F\,(16, 82) = 1.47.$$

The common-factor restriction is strongly rejected by both the likelihood-ratio and Wald tests (see Ch.13), and the estimated value of ρ is close to unity. The imposed mean lag of zero contrasts with the unrestricted estimate (from Ch.6) of nine quarters. By forcing the long-run response to equal the impact effect, the former is badly under estimated. The coefficient of u_{t-1} is close to that of the lagged dependent variable in the AD(1, 1), which is not surprising given that the mistake in (7.63) of eliminating z_{t-1} imposes $\beta_3 + \beta_1\beta_2 = 0$, which forces a coefficient of -0.7 onto R_{t-1}. The estimates and goodness of fit are close to those obtained for the growth-rate model which imposes a common factor of unity.[5] Figure 7.26 shows two plots of the residual sum of squares as a function of the autocorrelation parameter, namely over $(-1.0, 1.0)$ and a 'zoom' onto $(0.95, 1.0)$. The function is unimodal, and falls almost monotonically over the former, but in close up is near a quadratic.

7.8 Finite distributed lags

A finite distributed lag is a model where y_t is explained by a sequence of past values of z, with the restriction that there are no lagged dependent variables, so that $\beta_2 = 0$:

$$\mathsf{M}_8 : y_t = w_1 z_t + w_2 z_{t-1} + \xi_t. \tag{7.66}$$

In longer-lag generalizations of (7.66), the coefficients are the weights $\{w_i\}$ at different lags, and if $\sum w_i = 1$ with $w_i > 0\ \forall i$, then each w_i is the proportional response due to z_{t-i}. Economists have sometimes been suspicious about using lagged dependent variables in models, questioning the adequacy of explaining today by what happened yesterday, and so preferring apparently extraneous variables such as z_t. However, if economic behaviour is dynamic, previous outcomes are a vital component of present decisions. Moreover, lagged dependent variables arise naturally in the sequential factorization of the joint density.

The worry about lagged dependent variables may arise in part from the commercialization of econometrics, where models are desired for multi-period predictions. To evaluate their performance, econometric models are often appraised using dynamic simulation (see Ch.8). However, that is an invalid evaluation method (see Chong and Hendry, 1986), which tends to drive model selection away from models with endogenous dynamics (i.e. lagged dependent variables) towards dynamics accounted for by non-modelled variables such as $\{z_t\}$ in (7.66). Their actual performance deteriorates by such a choice, but their performance as measured by the invalid yardstick of dynamic simulation appears to improve.

It is difficult to formulate economic-theory arguments for finite distributed lags, but a possible economic example follows. Consider using a finite distributed lag to analyse output in a coffee-price model like that discussed in Chapter 5. At first sight, (7.66) seems a reasonable possibility for describing the output of coffee $\{y_t\}$ as dependent on (say) the number of coffee trees planted in earlier years $\{z_t\}$. But at second sight, it is not so reasonable because the actual harvest levels must depend on current stocks of coffee beans, the price of coffee relative to cropping costs, and anticipated sales. The lagged dependent variable will reflect the first of these, as well as the past stock of trees. Equations like (7.66) can almost never be purely technical or mechanical in economics: a behavioural aspect is virtually certain to intrude. Even if farmers began by determining

[5] COMFAC models are non-linear in parameters and not covered by PcNaive, so no Monte Carlo evidence is offered here. For earlier studies, see Hendry and Trivedi (1972), Hendry and Srba (1977) and Mizon and Hendry (1980).

their decisions using (7.66), they would learn that lagged y was an excellent proxy for the past history of planting, and so summarize past information using y_{t-1}.

A similar analysis applies to the completions of new dwellings (d_t) given a history of housing starts (h_t). A finite distributed lag model relating d_t to h_t as in (7.66) initially looks sensible, but ignores the information that, once completed, a given start cannot logically influence other completions, although it will remain in the data for lagged starts. Hendry (1986a) offers a critical analysis of the AD$(0, n)$ in this context. In both cases, a model from the equilibrium-correction class in §7.10 seems preferable.

Marginalizing (7.1) with respect to y_{t-1} is relatively straightforward:

$$(1 - \beta_2 L)\, y_t = \beta_1 z_t + \beta_3 z_{t-1} + \epsilon_t, \tag{7.67}$$

so that:

$$\begin{aligned} y_t &= (1 - \beta_2 L)^{-1} (\beta_1 + \beta_3 L)\, z_t + (1 - \beta_2 L)^{-1} \epsilon_t \\ &= \left(1 + \beta_2 L + \beta_2^2 L^2 + \beta_2^3 L^3 + \cdots\right) (\beta_1 + \beta_3 L)\, z_t + u_t \\ &= \beta_1 z_t + \delta z_{t-1} + \beta_2 \delta L^2 (1 - \beta_2 L)^{-1} z_t + u_t \\ &= w_1 z_t + w_2 z_{t-1} + \xi_t, \end{aligned} \tag{7.68}$$

where $\delta = (\beta_1 \beta_2 + \beta_3)$ and $u_t = \beta_2 u_{t-1} + \epsilon_t$. Note that (7.68) will have an autocorrelated error when $\beta_2 \neq 0$, whereas $\delta = 0$ corresponds to COMFAC. The last stage of the orthogonalization of ξ_t with respect to (z_t, z_{t-1}) follows as in §7.2 above. Direct calculation of the regression as in (7.49) yields:

$$\begin{aligned} \boldsymbol{w} &= \begin{pmatrix} m_{zz} & m_{zz_1} \\ m_{z_1 z} & m_{zz} \end{pmatrix}^{-1} \begin{pmatrix} m_{zy} \\ m_{z_1 y} \end{pmatrix} \quad = m_{zz}^{-1} \begin{pmatrix} 1 & \lambda_1 \\ \lambda_1 & 1 \end{pmatrix}^{-1} \begin{pmatrix} \gamma m_{zz} \\ \tau m_{zz} \end{pmatrix} \\ &= \left(1 - \lambda_1^2\right)^{-1} \begin{pmatrix} 1 & -\lambda_1 \\ -\lambda_1 & 1 \end{pmatrix} \begin{pmatrix} \gamma \\ \tau \end{pmatrix} \quad = \left(1 - \lambda_1^2\right)^{-1} \begin{pmatrix} \gamma - \lambda_1 \tau \\ \tau - \lambda_1 \gamma \end{pmatrix}. \end{aligned} \tag{7.69}$$

From the moments in §7.6:

$$\gamma = \frac{(\beta_1 + \beta_3 \lambda_1)}{(1 - \beta_2 \lambda_1)} \quad \text{and} \quad \tau = \frac{\beta_3 + \beta_1 \lambda_1 + \beta_2 \beta_1 \left(1 - \lambda_1^2\right)}{(1 - \beta_2 \lambda_1)},$$

so that:

$$\gamma - \lambda_1 \tau = \beta_1 \left(1 - \lambda_1^2\right) \quad \text{and} \quad \tau - \lambda_1 \gamma = \frac{\delta \left(1 - \lambda_1^2\right)}{(1 - \beta_2 \lambda_1)},$$

leading to $w_1 = \beta_1$ and $w_2 = \delta / (1 - \beta_2 \lambda_1)$. The correlation of the longest lagged z with all omitted longer lagged variables raises its coefficient when all the β_i are positive, whereas a common factor would induce a zero coefficient.

If there are n lagged $\{z_{t-i}\}$ in a distributed-lag representation, and z_t is autocorrelated at 0.90 or higher, then the set $(z_t, \ldots, z_{t-n})$ will be highly inter-correlated. There might even be numerical instability problems in inverting the matrix of regressors for $n > 10$. The literature usually refers to this problem as multicollinearity, and we now digress to study that issue. Multicollinearity was a term coined by Frisch (1934) for a world of Walrasian general equilibrium, where every economic variable had a 'true' equilibrium value denoted by ζ_{it} for $i = 1, \ldots, N$, and $t = 1, \ldots, T$. In such an equilibrium, linear combinations of variables in the economy would satisfy:

$$\sum_{i=1}^{N} \beta_{ij} \zeta_{it} = 0 \text{ for } j = 1, \ldots, k, \tag{7.70}$$

where the ζs represent the latent structure of the economy and the βs the parameters of the autonomous equations. Such ζs are perfectly collinear by definition in (7.70). If there was one equation ($k = 1$), Frisch called the situation collinearity, and if there were many equations ($k > 1$), (7.70) was deemed to produce multicollinearity. Frisch was concerned that while the true values $\{\zeta_{it}\}$ satisfied many equations like (7.70), economists did not observe the equilibrium due to measurement and perturbation errors, but instead observed:

$$x_{it} = \zeta_{it} + \nu_{it}. \tag{7.71}$$

Consequently, he was concerned with what happened to estimated regressions like:

$$\sum_{i=1}^{N} \beta_{ij} x_{it} = u_{jt} \text{ where } \beta_{1j} = 1 \text{ for each } j. \tag{7.72}$$

Since the latent variables were perfectly collinear, Frisch showed that a standard regression analysis of (7.72) would yield nonsense. Substituting (7.71) into (7.72) and using (7.70):

$$\sum_{i=1}^{N} \beta_{ij} \nu_{it} = u_{jt}, \tag{7.73}$$

which involves regressing measurement errors on measurement errors. Such regressions entail nothing about the underlying economy and merely reflect the measurement structure of the economist. Multicollinearity in the Frisch sense is a serious problem in such a formulation. Since a Walrasian equilibrium might be something to which an economy tends, (7.70) could describe a long-run state, although it would be unreasonable in general to exclude lagged ζs and perhaps even lagged $x s$ from the behavioural equations of agents out of equilibrium.

Frisch developed a tool called confluence analysis, which he claimed could solve the problem of analysing (7.72). This tool is not now used, and is rarely an entry in econometric textbooks. There are actually many problems involved in analysing (7.72):

(a) There is a problem of perfect linear dependence between the ζs;
(b) there is a problem of identification, namely how to tell which equation is which, since every equation is a linear combination of ζs;
(c) there is a problem of simultaneity, since the ζs are jointly determined; and:
(d) there is a problem of measurement errors between the latent and observed variables.

To analyse (7.72) by regression involves normalizing one of the βs and usually setting others to zero. When the measurement errors are small and the exclusion restrictions break the collinearity, then regression could work reasonably well when the βs are identified: for example, regressing one x_{it} on a subset of the others could recover the associated βs.

The simultaneity, measurement error, and identification problems were each analysed separately by econometricians in the 1930s and 1940s, leaving the unsolved problem of multicollinearity. For reasons discussed in Hendry and Morgan (1989), the problem came to be associated with the xs in (7.72) being highly correlated, despite the fact that multicollinearity for Frisch could occur when the ζs were pair-wise orthogonal. In a later interpretation, high inter-correlations between xs were called multicollinearity in that $(\boldsymbol{X}'\boldsymbol{X})$ was close to singularity: $|\boldsymbol{X}'\boldsymbol{X}| = 0$ was already known as perfect collinearity. However, when $|\boldsymbol{X}'\boldsymbol{X}| \neq 0$, then there is no invariant measure for the degree of closeness to singularity. Textbooks often discuss the case of exact singularity and infer the consequences of multicollinearity as large standard errors and small t-values, due to:

$$(\boldsymbol{X}'\boldsymbol{X})^{-1} = \frac{ADJ(\boldsymbol{X}'\boldsymbol{X})}{|\boldsymbol{X}'\boldsymbol{X}|}. \tag{7.74}$$

Because a linear model is invariant under linear transformations, whereas multicollinearity is not, we cannot define 'near collinearity'. A given model may or may not have multicollinearity depending on which isomorphic representative is considered. For example, the distributed lag model is the same model if, instead of (7.66), it is written as:

$$y_t = w_1 \Delta z_t + (w_1 + w_2)\, z_{t-1} + \xi_t = b_1 \Delta z_t + b_2 z_{t-1} + \xi_t. \tag{7.75}$$

If z_t and z_{t-1} are highly correlated, then Δz_t and z_{t-1} are nearly orthogonal: (7.66) and (7.75) are isomorphic models yet one of them apparently has a collinearity problem and the other does not. One cannot say whether or not there is a collinearity problem from the presence or absence of regressor inter-correlations alone when $|\boldsymbol{X}'\boldsymbol{X}| \neq 0$.

A general treatment of linear models being invariant under linear transformations follows: denote the initial linear model for k regressors by the conventional form:

$$y_t = \boldsymbol{\beta}' \boldsymbol{z}_t + \epsilon_t \ \text{ where } \epsilon_t \sim \mathsf{IN}\left[0, \sigma_\epsilon^2\right] \tag{7.76}$$

and let $\boldsymbol{H}$ be any known $k \times k$ non-singular matrix, with $\boldsymbol{\gamma}$ a known $k \times 1$ vector. Subtract $\boldsymbol{\gamma}' \boldsymbol{z}_t$ (a known linear function of $\boldsymbol{z}_t$) from y_t in (7.76):

$$(y_t - \boldsymbol{\gamma}' \boldsymbol{z}_t) = (\boldsymbol{\beta} - \boldsymbol{\gamma})' \boldsymbol{z}_t + \epsilon_t; \tag{7.77}$$

this operation has already been used many times when transforming from y_t to (say) Δy_t in dynamic models. Next, since $\boldsymbol{H}^{-1}\boldsymbol{H} = \boldsymbol{I}_k$, from (7.77):

$$(y_t - \boldsymbol{\gamma}' \boldsymbol{z}_t) = \left\{(\boldsymbol{\beta} - \boldsymbol{\gamma})' \boldsymbol{H}^{-1}\right\} \boldsymbol{H} \boldsymbol{z}_t + \epsilon_t, \tag{7.78}$$

or:

$$y_t^* = \boldsymbol{\beta}^{*\prime} \boldsymbol{z}_t^* + \epsilon_t \ \text{ where } \boldsymbol{\beta}^* = \boldsymbol{H}^{-1} (\boldsymbol{\beta} - \boldsymbol{\gamma}). \tag{7.79}$$

We have merely re-parameterized the original model, and still have k unrestricted parameters β^*, k regressors (now z_t^*), and the original error $\{\epsilon_t\}$. It is irrelevant whether we estimate β and derive β^* or directly estimate β^* from the transformed model: the coefficient estimates and variances must be numerically equal. Let:

$$\hat{\beta}^* = \left(Z^{*\prime}Z^*\right)^{-1} Z^{*\prime}y^* \text{ and } \tilde{\beta}^* = H^{-1}\left(\hat{\beta} - \gamma\right),$$

then:

$$\begin{aligned} \hat{\beta}^* &= \left(Z^{*\prime}Z^*\right)^{-1} Z^{*\prime}y^* & &= \left(H'Z'ZH\right)^{-1} H'Z'\left(y - Z\gamma\right) \\ &= H^{-1}\left(Z'Z\right)^{-1} Z'\left(y - Z\gamma\right) & &= H^{-1}\left(\hat{\beta} - \gamma\right) \end{aligned} \tag{7.80}$$

so $\hat{\beta}^* \equiv \tilde{\beta}^*$. Also:

$$\mathsf{V}\left[\hat{\beta}^*\right] = \sigma_\epsilon^2 \left(H'Z'ZH\right)^{-1} = H^{-1}\mathsf{V}\left[\hat{\beta}\right] H'^{-1} = \mathsf{V}\left[\tilde{\beta}^*\right],$$

which could be a diagonal matrix irrespective of the near (but not perfect) singularity in $(Z'Z)$.

In terms of modelling, the advantage of near orthogonality is that deleting small or insignificant coefficients leaves the retained estimates almost unaltered numerically, as well as statistically, making simplification easier. This correspondes to the motto: transform to near orthogonality before deleting. If economic agents sensibly orthogonalize their own decision variables, β^* should be the parameter of interest. Just as the concept of exogeneity proved not to be a property of a variable *per se*, so collinearity is not a property of a set of regressors, but of a parameterization of a model (for a similar analysis, see Leamer, 1978). There are some sensible parameterizations, and there are some less sensible ones. The distributed lag in (7.66) is not among the former because it is difficult to interpret the lag coefficients. The parameterization in (7.75) seems more interpretable, since $b_1 = w_1$ shows the change in y_t for an impact change in Δz_t, so it describes the short-run effect, and the coefficient $b_2 = (w_1 + w_2)$ shows by how much a change in z will change y in the long-run.

Assume that there is a high correlation between z_t and z_{t-1}, and as a consequence that the ws in (7.66) have large standard errors. Since $b_1 = w_1$, its estimate must also have a large standard error, so consider the variance of the OLS estimate of b_2:

$$\mathsf{V}\left[\hat{b}_2\right] = \mathsf{V}\left[\hat{w}_1\right] + \mathsf{V}\left[\hat{w}_2\right] + 2\mathsf{C}\left[\hat{w}_1, \hat{w}_2\right]. \tag{7.81}$$

Due to the high positive correlation between z_t and z_{t-1}, both variances are large, but $\mathsf{C}\left[\hat{w}_1, \hat{w}_2\right]$ must also be large and negative. Consider $\left(Z'Z\right)^{-1}$ in the 2×2 case written as:

$$\begin{pmatrix} a & b \\ b & c \end{pmatrix}^{-1} = \frac{1}{(ac - b^2)} \begin{pmatrix} c & -b \\ -b & a \end{pmatrix}. \tag{7.82}$$

Since the off-diagonal element is $-b$, the covariance $\mathsf{C}\left[\hat{w}_1, \hat{w}_2\right]$ must be negative when the data have a positive covariance.

From (7.81) and (7.82), $\mathsf{V}[\hat{b}_2] = \sigma_\xi^2(a+c-2b)/(ac-b^2)$. If the original problem had a high degree of collinearity, and both coefficients had large variances, then $(ac - b^2)$ must be small, so that $ac \simeq b^2$. Since a is the variance of z_t and c is the variance of z_{t-1}, they are almost equal. But if $a \simeq c$, then $a \simeq b$, and:

$$\mathsf{V}\left[\hat{b}_2\right] \simeq \sigma_\xi^2 \frac{2\,(a-b)}{(a^2-b^2)} = \sigma_\xi^2 \frac{2}{(a+b)},$$

which will be small when a and b are the data variance and covariance of a dynamic process. Although the matrix in (7.82) is almost singular and difficult to invert, (7.81) will be small precisely because (7.66) has 'severe collinearity'.

The two w_i coefficients in (7.66) can be jointly statistically significant, yet either individually could be set to zero without loss. However, the remaining estimate might alter considerably on doing so. For example, dropping z_t in (7.66) will cause a large change in the estimate of the coefficient of z_{t-1} from $\hat{w}_2$ to $\hat{b}_2$. That is one aspect of the problem of high inter-correlations, namely a lack of robustness to a slight change in specification. There is one circumstance under which we can impose one coefficient and not affect another, which is when the variables are orthogonal. The transformation from (7.66) to (7.75), by switching from z_t and z_{t-1} to Δz_t and z_{t-1}, has nearly orthogonalized the variables. When Δz_t is orthogonal to z_{t-1}, the same estimate of b_2 results whether or not Δz_t is included. The advantage of the second parameterization (7.75) is that the coefficients are robust to auxiliary inclusions or exclusions of other variables.

It is not necessarily correct to associate small t-values with collinearity as can be illustrated by the distribution of an unbiased estimator. A large standard error implies that $\hat{w}_1$ has a dispersed distribution. However, the distribution has to integrate to unity and have a mean of w_1 so it must be very flat. Consequently, the value of $|\hat{w}_1|$ will often be large and big estimates for w_1 are quite likely. Conversely, small t-values will occur when $w_1 = 0$ even if there is no collinearity. If collinearity were a problem of high data inter-correlations, then such a problem should get worse on adding more variables that are highly correlated with the variables already in the model. However, it is easy to demonstrate analytically that despite adding highly inter-correlated variables, every t-value can increase in absolute value. This happens when the added variables are important in explaining the dependent variable; since estimated coefficient variances depend on $\hat{\sigma}_\epsilon^2\left(Z'Z\right)^{-1}$, standard errors will decrease when newly added variables reduce the error variance $\hat{\sigma}_\epsilon^2$ sufficiently, even if they worsen the collinearity, and $|\mathsf{t}|$ will increase if the $|\hat{\beta}_i|$ do not fall (see Davidson, Hendry, Srba and Yeo, 1978). Do not take collinearity as a justification for simplifying a model, since the symptoms are the same for a badly-fitting model as for a poor parameterization. The fact that t-values are small is no guidance as to whether to expand or contract a model: and the correlations between the zs in the original transformations are no guide to their information content, especially with $\mathsf{I}(1)$ data series. Exact linear dependencies must be eliminated, of course.

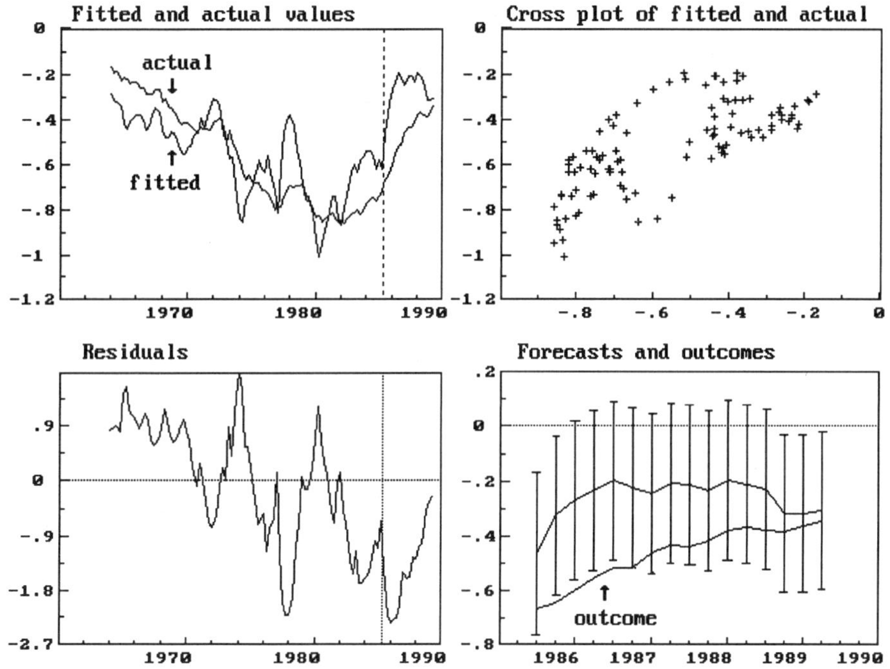

Fig. 7.27 Fitted and actual values for the distributed-lag model of M1

The empirical example again illustrates many of the analytical issues just discussed:

$$\widehat{\log\left(\frac{M}{PY}\right)_t} = \underset{(0.04)}{-0.20} + \underset{(1.09)}{0.01}\, R_t - \underset{(1.08)}{4.08}\, R_{t-1}$$
$$\mathsf{R}^2 = 0.52 \;\; \hat{\sigma} = 14.9\% \;\; SC = -3.71 \;\; DW = 0.14$$
$$AR\text{-}F(5,94) = 106.5 \;\; ND\text{-}\chi^2(2) = 5.9 \;\; F(16,83) = 1.55. \tag{7.83}$$

The goodness of fit is little better than the static model, severe residual autocorrelation persists, the coefficient standard errors are much larger than any seen hitherto, and comparison with the unrestricted AD(1, 1) reveals that adding $\log(M/PY)_{t-1}$ leads to a fall in all the estimated coefficient standard errors. Further, extending the length of the distributed lag does little to correct any of these problems, as (7.84) shows:

$$\widehat{\log\left(\frac{M}{PY}\right)_t} = \underset{(0.04)}{-0.17} - \underset{(1.05)}{0.81}\, R_t + \underset{(1.57)}{0.23}\, R_{t-1} - \underset{(1.05)}{3.80}\, R_{t-2}$$
$$\mathsf{R}^2 = 0.58 \;\; \hat{\sigma} = 14.2\% \;\; SC = -3.79 \;\; DW = 0.13$$
$$AR\text{-}F(5,93) = 105.0 \;\; ND\text{-}\chi^2(2) = 6.8. \tag{7.84}$$

Extending the lag distribution to twelve lags lowers $\hat{\sigma}$ to 7.4 per cent with the largest coefficient on R_{t-12}. When the largest coefficient occurs on the longest-lagged regressor, irrespective of lag length, the equation is almost certainly mis-specified by an extension of the formulation in (7.69), a result which will recur in the Monte Carlo. Figure 7.27 shows the fitted and actual values and Fig. 7.28 the recursive estimates.

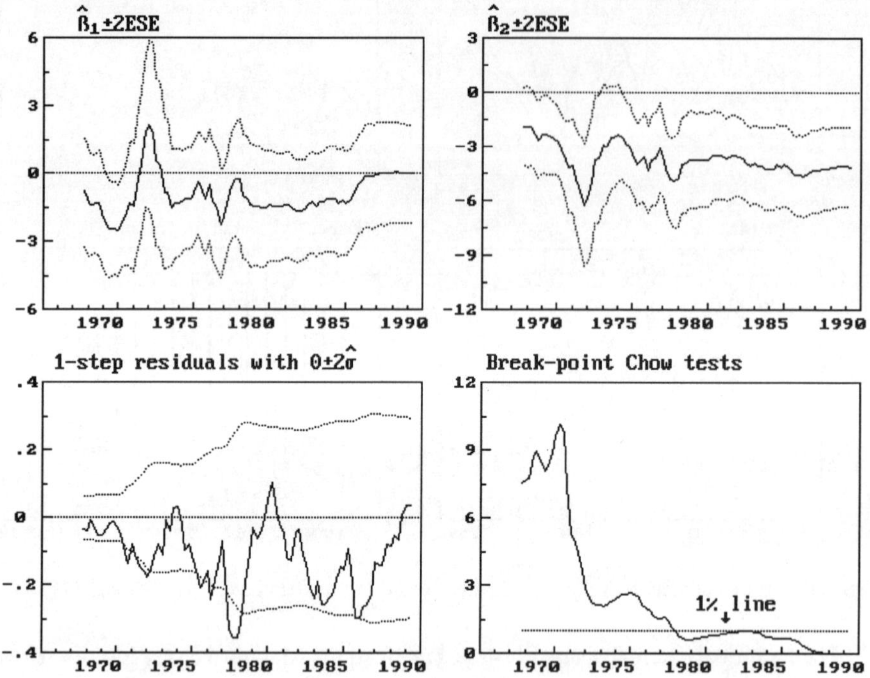

Fig. 7.28 Recursive statistics for the distributed-lag model of M1

Since Monte Carlo allows the properties of (7.66) to be studied in more complicated models than can be conveniently analysed, we estimate distributed lag models with one, two and three lags fitted to the earlier DGP.

Table 7.2 AD(0,3) mean coefficient estimates

Coefficient	Monte Carlo estimate	Derived value
w_1	0.48	0.50
w_2	−0.13	0.05
w_3	0.21	0.045
w_4	0.35	0.041

The derived value in Table 7.2 is the distributed-lag weight obtained from the second line of (7.68) solved indefinitely. The bias in the coefficient $\hat{w}_1$ of z_t as an estimator of β_1 is almost zero. The second coefficient estimate is -0.13 (whereas the derived coefficient of z_{t-1} is 0.05) and the fourth is 0.35. The lag weights start at about the correct value, fall, then rise at the end. This is a typical profile of the shape of distributed lags fitted to AD($\cdot$) processes and the increase in the final estimated lag weight matches that predicted earlier. Of course, diagnostic tests are a better index of a wrong model.

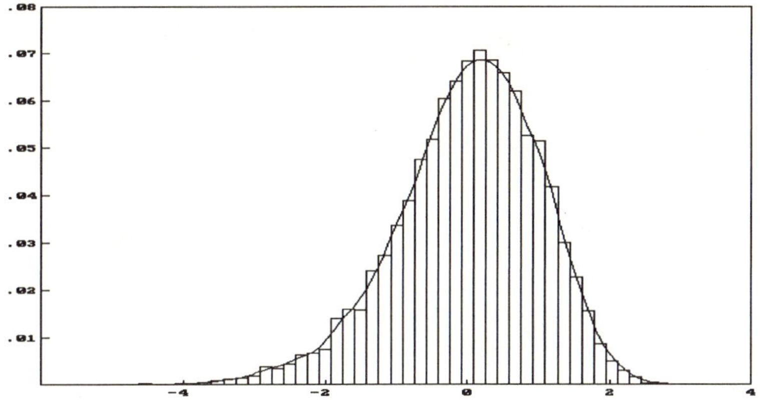

Fig. 7.29 Histogram and density function for $\hat{w}_1$

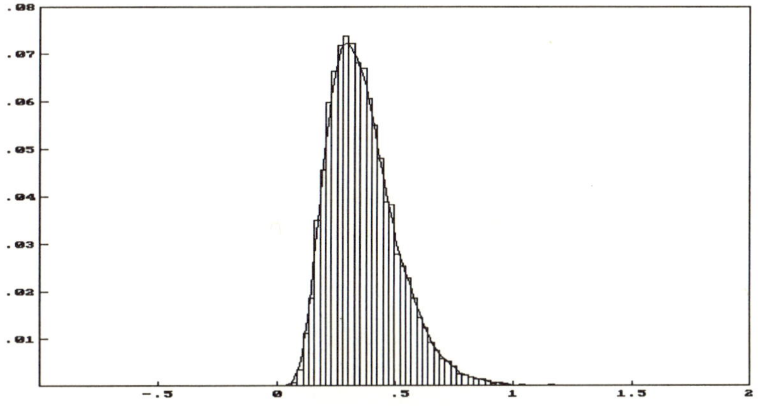

Fig. 7.30 Histogram and density function for the *DW* test

Next, since the first coefficient is almost 0.5, the median lag is estimated as zero. The second coefficient estimate of -0.13 violates the positivity condition needed to calculate a useful mean lag measure. Many investigators have found negative weights on fitting distributed-lag models unrestrictedly, usually regarded as the 'wrong sign', and 0.48, -0.13, 0.21, 0.35, 0.0 is a poor representation of the distribution of weights: 0.5, 0.05, 0.045, 0.041, 0.037, etc. The distributed-lag model is poor at capturing dynamics and the null of residual autocorrelation would be rejected 100 per cent of the time using the *DW* test: see Fig. 7.30. This finding also matches the empirical literature on distributed-lag equations, most of which reveal autocorrelated errors, often followed by fitting common-factor models without testing the validity of those restrictions.

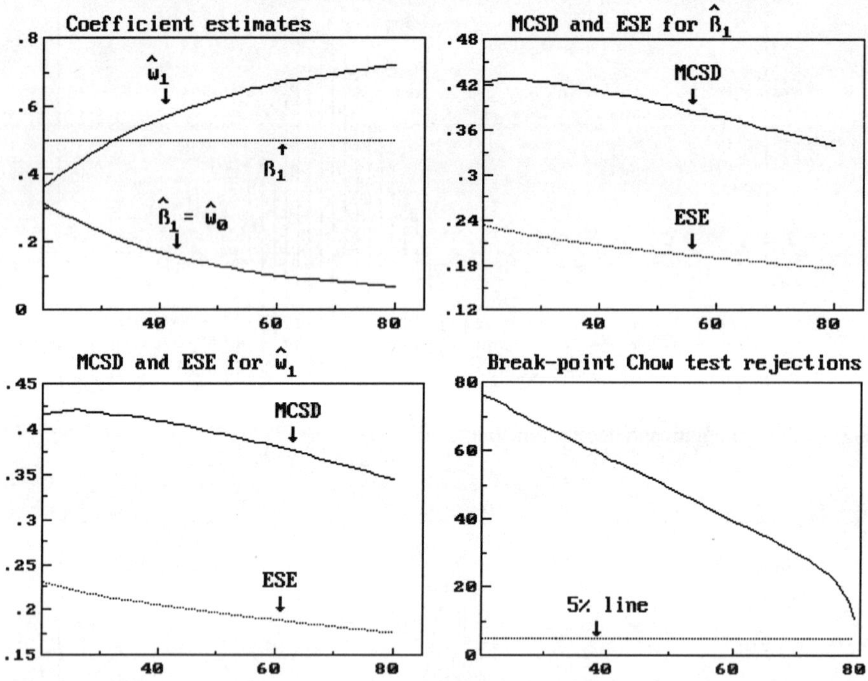

Fig. 7.31 Recursive Monte Carlo statistics for the distributed-lag model

Figure 7.31a shows the graph of the estimates of w_i in an AD(0, 2) as $T = 20, \ldots, 80$, and reveals that the coefficients change greatly as T increases, with offsetting changes in biases, suggesting apparent parameter non-constancy.[6] In the AD(0, 1) model, the plims of $\hat{w}_1$ and $\hat{w}_2$ are 0.5 and 0.34 respectively, which matched the Monte Carlo estimates at $T = 80$. Figures 7.31b,c record the estimates of the coefficient standard errors in the AD(0, 2) and reveal marked departures from the corresponding MCSDs. The break-point Chow tests in Fig. 7.31d reject the hypothesis that the parameters are constant 60 per cent of the time at $T = 20$, although the null is true, duplicating the problem of the static model. Similar results are obtained if AD(0, 3) or AD(0, 1) are used.

[6] When the corresponding β in the AD(1, 1) is zero, these are called biases in $\hat{w}_i$.

7.9 Dead-start models

The penultimate case is a model where the contemporaneous non-modelled variable is excluded:

$$\mathsf{M}_9 : y_t = d_2 y_{t-1} + d_3 z_{t-1} + \zeta_t. \tag{7.85}$$

Perhaps the most important practical issue is the constancy of the parameters in such a model. There are two ways in which a dead-start model could have arisen. It could be structural, and directly characterize the decision function of economic agents, but more often it is derived. For instance, y_t might depend on z_t, but z_t has been eliminated as a function of its past determinants. In that case, the coefficients d_2 and d_3 would become compounds of the original β_i coefficients in the DGP. For example, when the zs are generated by (7.2), d_3 would be $d_3 = \beta_3 + \beta_1\lambda_1$, and so would not be invariant to changes in λ_1. If the government changes the control rule determining, say, interest rates z and (7.85) is used as a money-demand equation, the model should exhibit parameter non-constancy when λ_1 alters. A model with non-constant parameters cannot be used for policy, for prediction, or even for testing theories. Thus, although $\{\zeta_t\}$ would be an innovation against the information used in (7.85) even when it was derived, that is an inadequate basis for selecting such an equation.

Some well-known derived equations are dead-start models. An example is the Hall (1978) consumption function discussed in §7.3. Hall argues from the permanent-income hypothesis together with rational expectations that the change in consumption is an innovation. However, when $\beta_1 = 0.5$, $\beta_3 = -0.4$, and $\lambda_1 = 0.90$ (say), $d_3 = 0.05$, and the incorrect conclusion might be reached that z_{t-1} did not affect y_t, especially if $\zeta_t = \epsilon_t + \beta_1\nu_t$ had a large variance. The issue of present concern is that an equation such as Hall's could not be the DGP, but must be a derived description. If $\Delta y_t = \zeta_t$ were the DGP, there would be a probability of observing negative consumption, since random walks eventually wander practically everywhere. In any theory model, many potential parameter non-constancies must build up as equations are derived from each other so the final result is no stronger than the weakest link in the theoretical derivation. This is the problem Frisch called a lack of autonomy in the resulting equation, i.e. any major perturbation in the economy will disrupt such an equation so it is not very interesting, either statistically or economically.

Conversely, if (7.85) were structural, it would be a partial-adjustment type and we could repeat the typology using lagged information only.

Empirically, the dead-start model for velocity is:

$$\widehat{\log\left(\frac{M}{PY}\right)_t} = \underset{(0.01)}{-\,0.00} - \underset{(0.08)}{0.54}\, R_{t-1} + \underset{(0.01)}{0.92} \log\left(\frac{M}{PY}\right)_{t-1}$$

$$\mathsf{R}^2 = 0.988 \;\; \hat{\sigma} = 2.28\% \;\; SC = -7.45 \;\; DW = 2.37$$
$$AR\text{-}F(5,94) = 0.78 \;\; ND\text{-}\chi^2(2) = 1.6 \;\; Chow\; F(16,83) = 0.60.$$

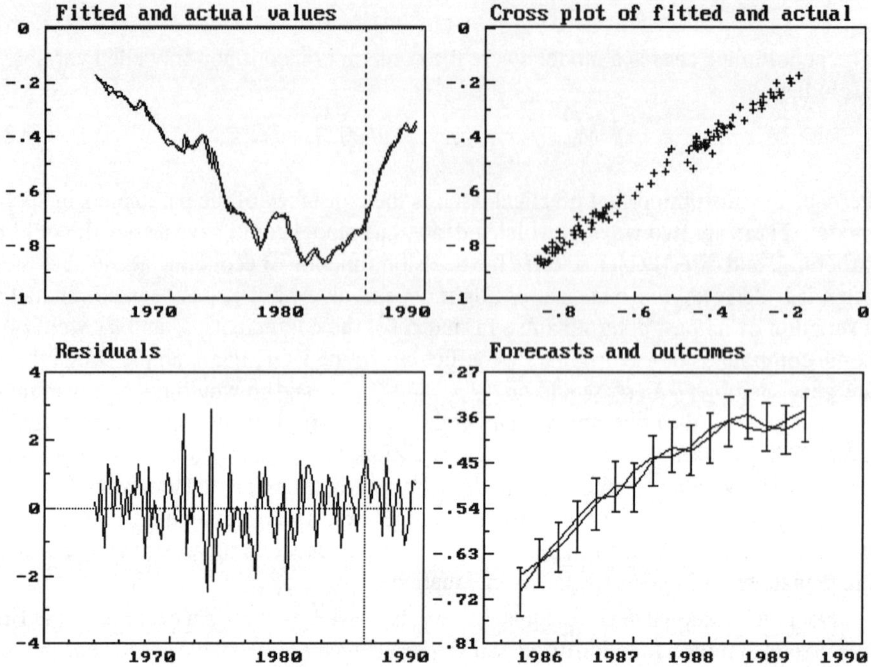

Fig. 7.32 Fitted and actual values for the dead-start model

The deterioration in fit over the unrestricted model (judged by $\hat{\sigma}$) is only about 15 per cent, and the long-run interest elasticity is estimated at -6.5, even though R_{t-1} was irrelevant when R_t was included. The closeness of the outcome to (7.50) arises because R_t is well described by a martingale. However, from the more general ADL model, the absence of residual autocorrelation can be seen to be a lack of power rather than an indication that (7.85) is a good characterization of agents' behaviour. Figure 7.32 shows the fitted and actual values and Fig. 7.33 the recursive estimates and associated statistics.

In the Monte Carlo, there is a noticeable finite-sample bias in the coefficient of y_{t-1} shown in Fig. 7.34, but little bias for the derived coefficient of z_{t-1}, which is centred around 0.08 and is rarely significantly different from zero, entailing a large bias for β_3.

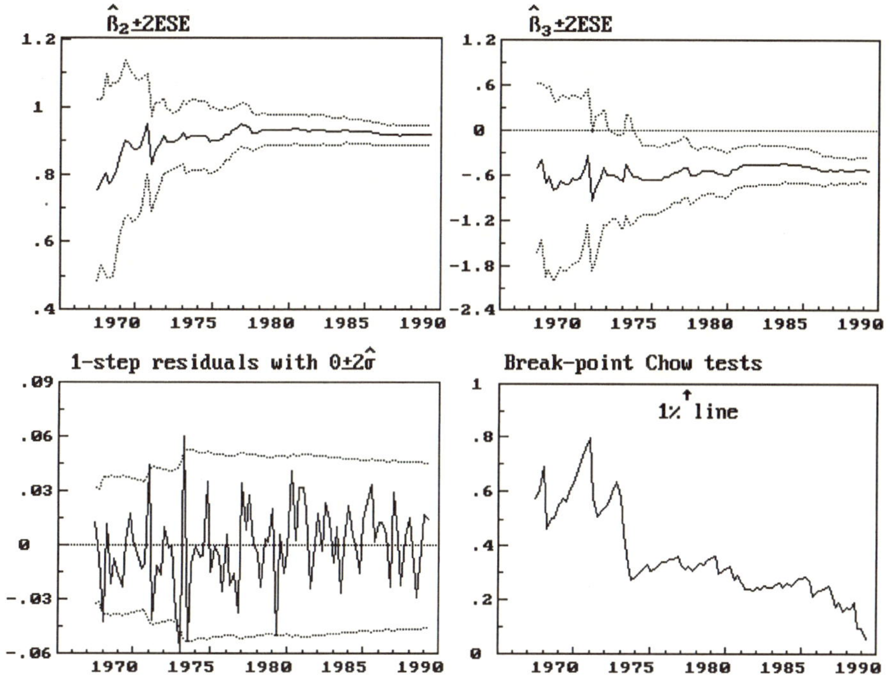

Fig. 7.33 Recursive statistics for the dead-start model

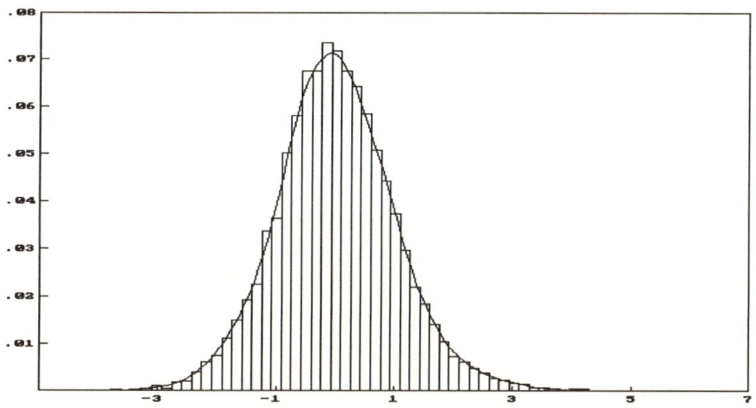

Fig. 7.34 Histogram and density function for $\hat{\beta}_2$

The plims of the estimated parameters are 0.84 and 0.15, so there are marked finite-sample effects as Fig. 7.35a reveals. However, it should be remembered that there is an additional determinant of z_t in the Monte Carlo, and, when z_t is regressed on z_{t-1} only, the plim of the resulting coefficient is 0.99. Thus, although the eigenvalues of the dynamics are 0.95, 0.90, and 0.75, the autoregressive representation of the marginal model has a root that is close to the unit circle, which may influence the small-sample behaviour of estimators. The ESE and MCSD in Fig. 7.35b, c are reasonably close to each other for both coefficients and Fig. 7.35d shows that the Chow test rejects at about its nominal level of 5 per cent. Overall, σ_ς is 1.1 so there is only a 10 per cent deterioration in fit from eliminating z_t, and, consistent with the earlier analysis, the DW test rejects 6 per cent of the time. Thus, without a regime shift to reveal the lack of parameter invariance, it would be difficult to detect that (7.85) was an incomplete representation: later, we will use encompassing tests to this end (see Davidson and Hendry, 1981, for an example).

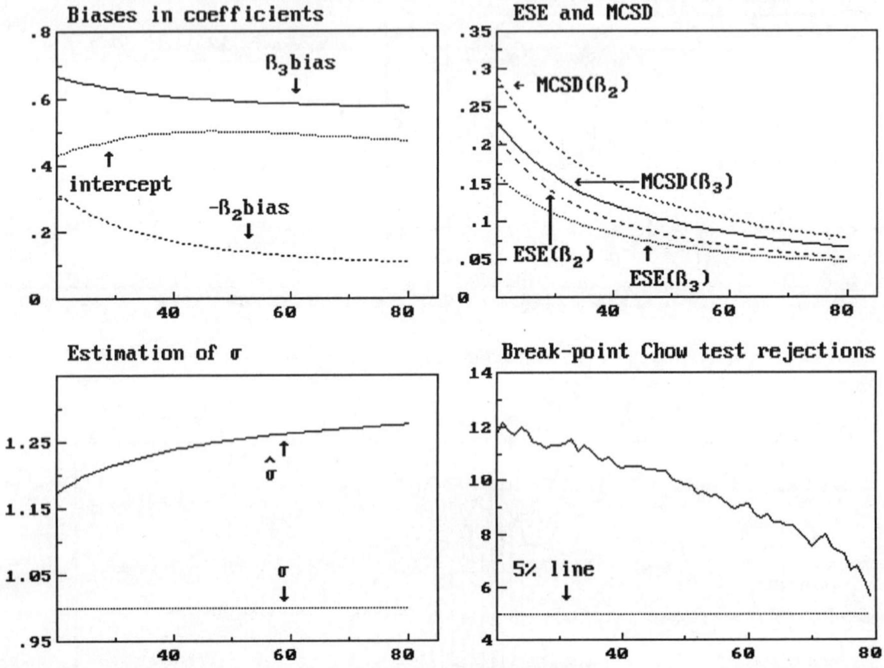

Fig. 7.35 Recursive Monte Carlo statistics for the dead-start model

7.10 Equilibrium correction

Reconsider the generic re-parameterization of the AD(1, 1) to parameters of interest defined by the impact effect and the long run. From (7.1), letting $\Delta y_t = y_t - y_{t-1}$, and mapping (z_t, z_{t-1}) to $(\Delta z_t, z_{t-1})$, we obtain the model in (6.6.43):

$$\mathsf{M}_7 : \Delta y_t = \beta_1 \Delta z_t + (\beta_2 - 1)\left(y - K_1 z\right)_{t-1} + \epsilon_t \qquad (7.86)$$

where the long-run expectation is given by:

$$\mathsf{E}\left[y_t - K_1 z_t\right] = 0 \text{ when } K_1 = \frac{(\beta_1 + \beta_3)}{(1 - \beta_2)}. \tag{7.87}$$

The model in (7.86) embodies the equilibrium-correction mechanism $(y - K_1 z)_{t-1}$ (denoted ECM), which captures departures from the long-run equilibrium in (7.87). When $\beta_2 \neq 1$, the first-differenced variables in (7.86) are not achieved by differencing as in the growth model: (7.86) is isomorphic to (7.1) in that no restrictions are imposed, just a re-parameterization from $(\beta_1, \beta_2, \beta_3)$ to $(\beta_1, \beta_2 - 1, K_1)$. Any member of the AD class can be written as an equilibrium-correction model, without loss of generality. The change in y is explained by the change in z, and the amount by which y_{t-1} differs from its long-run $K_1 z_{t-1}$, which measures the disequilibrium component.

The ECM parameterization is useful for six reasons. First, the two components Δz_t, namely the growth in z_t this period, and $(y - K_1 z)_{t-1}$, namely last period's deviation from equilibrium, are usually not highly correlated empirically. Thus, these parameters are easier to interpret and tests on them individually are meaningful.

Secondly, ECMs like (7.86) allow a flexible description of a unimodal lag shape, with potentially different values for the mean and median lags, subject to $\mu > m$: longer lags enable more complicated lag distributions to be characterized. From §6.5, when $0 \leq \beta_1 < 0.5, 0 < \beta_2 < 1$ and $K_1 = 1$:

$$\mu = \frac{1 - \beta_1}{1 - \beta_2} \text{ and } m = \frac{-\log\left(2\left(1 - \beta_1\right)\right)}{\log\left(\beta_2\right)}. \tag{7.88}$$

Thus, $m = 0$ occurs when $\beta_1 = 0.5$, although μ could be large for β_2 near unity, whereas when $\beta_1 \simeq 0$, then μ and m will be relatively close.

Next, (7.86) explains some of the problems about other members of the typology. For example, the growth-rate model corresponds to deleting the ECM $(\beta_2 - 1)(y - K_1 z)_{t-1}$, so long-run information is excluded; but because the included and omitted effects are nearly orthogonal, the coefficient of Δz_t is close to the short-run impact β_1. When $(y - K_1 z)$ is the deviation from long-run equilibrium in a rational plan, the omission of $(\beta_2 - 1)(y - K_1 z)_{t-1}$ will be hard to detect using residual autocorrelation tests, consistent with finding an apparently white-noise error (see Hendry and von Ungern-Sternberg, 1981). This result resolves the potential theory inconsistency: there is no need to integrate the model in §7.4 to return to levels, thus inducing a random-walk error, only a need to add back the omitted ECM term. Further, because of orthogonality, omitting the ECM need not induce parameter non-constancy, matching the relative constancy of the growth-rate model.

The COMFAC model can also be understood by rewriting it as a particular ECM. When the common-factor restriction $\beta_1 \beta_2 + \beta_3 = 0$ is valid, (7.63) can be rewritten as:

$$\Delta y_t = \beta_1 \Delta z_t + (\beta_2 - 1)\left(y_{t-1} - \beta_1 z_{t-1}\right) + \epsilon_t. \tag{7.89}$$

This is an ECM but with $K_1 = \beta_1$, so that imposing a common factor is equivalent to asserting that if any adjustment occurs, it occurs instantly or never. That is why (7.1) plus (7.56) forces $\mu = 0$, despite the equation being dynamic. Alternatively, growth-rate is COMFAC with a common factor of unity, but either constraint could be invalid empirically.

Continuing, we can understand some of the problems of the partial-adjustment model M_6 by re-expressing it in as an ECM:

$$\Delta y_t = (1-\theta)\,\Delta y_t^* + (1-\theta)\,(y^* - y)_{t-1} + \eta_t. \tag{7.90}$$

Asserting partial adjustment of y_t to y_t^* imposes the restriction that the impact coefficient equals the feedback coefficient, and it is this constraint which forces the skewed, right-tailed, lag distribution on the data. In (7.88) the mean lag μ depends on two relatively orthogonal parameters, whereas in (7.90), $\mu = \theta/(1-\theta)$ which only depends on the coefficient of the lagged dependent variable. Conversely, the ECM (7.86) is partial adjustment of $(y - K_1 z)$ to Δz, rather than of y to z.

We can even glean insights into static regression, leading indicator, and finite distributed-lag equations by rewriting them as ECMs. Since M_8 includes M_2 and M_5 as special cases, consider it; from (7.75):

$$\Delta y_t = b_1 \Delta z_t - 1\,(y - b_2 z)_{t-1} + \xi_t. \tag{7.91}$$

Thus, distributed-lag models are ECMs with an imposed feedback of -1; static regression adds the constraint that $b_1 = b_2$; whereas leading indicator sets $b_1 = 0$ with b_2 unrestricted. When such models intend to have behavioural content, it is important to allow for the possibility that agents try to correct present decisions in the light of previous disequilibria, so the size of the feedback coefficient is an empirical issue. This ability of the ECM to account for, or encompass, the difficulties apparent in cases M_2–M_8 would justify our interest in it. However, it has three further advantages as a baseline model type for empirical research:

1. ECMs have intimate links to the theory of cointegrated time series (§7.10.1);
2. ECMs have close links to servo-mechanisms arising from control theory (§7.10.2);
3. ECMs have experienced empirical success in modelling time series (§7.10.3).

We now consider these advantages more extensively.

7.10.1 Cointegration

The affinity of cointegration to the existence of a long-run solution is manifest since $y_t - K_1 z_t = u_t \sim \mathsf{I}(0)$ implies a well-behaved equilibrium, whereas when $u_t \sim \mathsf{I}(1)$, no equilibrium could be said to exist. In terms of the ECM reformulation in (7.86), $(\Delta y_t, \Delta z_t)$ are $\mathsf{I}(0)$ when their corresponding levels are $\mathsf{I}(1)$ with $\epsilon_t \sim \mathsf{I}(0)$, so the equation is balanced if and only if $(y - K_1 z)_t$ is $\mathsf{I}(0)$ as well. Thus, the nonsense-regressions problem arises from a failure of the integrated variables under analysis to cointegrate and its resolution is the converse, namely finding cointegration. The literature on cointegration is vast, and is the subject of a separate book in Banerjee, Dolado, Galbraith and Hendry (1993), so the treatment here is but the tip of a large iceberg.

Engle and Granger (1987) established the isomorphism between cointegration and equilibrium-correction models. Let $\boldsymbol{x}_t$ be an $n \times 1$ vector of I(1) time series, so that $\Delta\boldsymbol{x}_t \sim$ I(0). Then the components are cointegrated if $\boldsymbol{\beta}'\boldsymbol{x}_t$ is I(0) for some $\boldsymbol{\beta}$. For n elements in $\boldsymbol{x}_t$, when $\boldsymbol{\beta}$ is an $n \times r$ matrix there are r linearly-independent, cointegrating relationships between the xs, and $n-r$ combinations which are I(1). If $r = n$, then $\boldsymbol{x}_t$ must be I(0), so we exclude that case as $\boldsymbol{x}_t$ is I(1); similarly, if $r = 0$, there is no cointegration. When $r > 0$, the $\{\boldsymbol{x}_t\}$ process can be expressed in I(0) space in terms of r cointegrating combinations $\boldsymbol{\beta}'\boldsymbol{x}_t$ and $n-r$ first differences, denoted $\Delta\boldsymbol{x}_{at} = \boldsymbol{\beta}_{\perp}'\Delta\boldsymbol{x}_t$ where $\boldsymbol{\beta}_{\perp}$ is an $n \times (n-r)$ matrix of rank $(n-r)$ orthogonal to $\boldsymbol{\beta}$. In effect, we map $\boldsymbol{x}_t$ to $(\boldsymbol{\beta}'\boldsymbol{x}_t : \boldsymbol{\beta}_{\perp}'\boldsymbol{x}_t) = \boldsymbol{G}\boldsymbol{x}_t$ (say) where $\boldsymbol{G}$ is non-singular $n \times n$. The first block are I(0) and the second I(1), so need to be differenced to become I(0). This formalizes the fact that there are other ways to remove unit roots than differencing.

The simplest case is when $\boldsymbol{x}_t$ is generated by the first-order vector autoregression (VAR):

$$\boldsymbol{x}_t = \boldsymbol{\delta} + \boldsymbol{A}\boldsymbol{x}_{t-1} + \boldsymbol{e}_t \text{ where } \boldsymbol{e}_t \sim \mathsf{IN}_n\left[\mathbf{0}, \boldsymbol{\Sigma}\right]. \tag{7.92}$$

Since linear models are invariant to linear transformations, and lag functions of levels of $\boldsymbol{x}_t$ can be transformed to differences and a single levels vector, the VAR can be re-parameterized as:

$$\Delta\boldsymbol{x}_t = \boldsymbol{\delta} + (\boldsymbol{A} - \boldsymbol{I})\,\boldsymbol{x}_{t-1} + \boldsymbol{e}_t = \boldsymbol{\delta} + \boldsymbol{\pi}\boldsymbol{x}_{t-1} + \boldsymbol{e}_t. \tag{7.93}$$

When $r = 0$, no levels combinations of $\boldsymbol{x}_t$ are I(0) and since $\Delta\boldsymbol{x}_t$ and $\boldsymbol{e}_t$ are I(0), then $\boldsymbol{\pi}$ must be $\mathbf{0}$. Similarly, when $r = n$ and $\boldsymbol{x}_t$ is I(0), then $\boldsymbol{\pi}$ must be full rank n. Otherwise, $\boldsymbol{\pi}$ has rank r for $n > r > 0$, and so $\boldsymbol{\pi}$ can be expressed as the product of two $n \times r$ matrices of rank r, denoted by $\boldsymbol{\alpha}$, $\boldsymbol{\beta}$ so $\boldsymbol{\pi} = \boldsymbol{\alpha}\boldsymbol{\beta}'$. Thus, the system in (7.93) can be written as:

$$\Delta\boldsymbol{x}_t = \boldsymbol{\delta} + \boldsymbol{\alpha}\boldsymbol{\beta}'\boldsymbol{x}_{t-1} + \boldsymbol{e}_t, \tag{7.94}$$

where $\boldsymbol{\beta}'\boldsymbol{x}_{t-1}$ are the I(0) cointegrating combinations, or ECMs, so (7.94) provides a generalized ECM representation. Additional results of importance are:

(a) As rank$(\boldsymbol{\pi}) = r$ for r cointegrating vectors, by omitting $\boldsymbol{x}_{t-1}$, a VAR in differences omits important levels information incorporated in the ECMs;
(b) cointegrating vectors are not unique in the absence of a priori information because $\boldsymbol{\alpha}\boldsymbol{\beta}' = \boldsymbol{\alpha}\boldsymbol{P}\boldsymbol{P}^{-1}\boldsymbol{\beta}' = \boldsymbol{\alpha}^*\boldsymbol{\beta}^{*\prime}$ for all $r \times r$ non-singular matrices $\boldsymbol{P}$;
(c) The ECM terms $\boldsymbol{\beta}'\boldsymbol{x}_{t-1}$ may enter more than one equation, which would violate weak exogeneity of the variables in $\Delta\boldsymbol{x}_{at}$ for $\boldsymbol{\beta}$, and necessitate joint estimation for efficiency (see Phillips and Loretan, 1991, and Ch.5).
(d) When $\boldsymbol{y}$ and $\boldsymbol{z}$ are cointegrated, at least one must Granger-cause the other (see Granger, 1986). A sequence of 1-step forecasts conditioned on a proper information set, which includes lagged values of the variables to be forecast, are cointegrated with outcomes.

Further details on cointegration are provided in section §7.11 and Banerjee *et al.* (1993).

7.10.2 Servo-mechanistic control

Feedback control mechanisms are a common feature of everyday life, two obvious examples being thermostats and homeostasis. Phillips (1954, 1957) drew the attention of economists to this class of servo-mechanisms as models of dynamic control for economic policy. He noted the need for three elements: derivative, proportional, and integral controls, each having its own role, and associated problems. The ECM in (7.86) incorporates the first two in terms of Δz and $(y - K_1 z)$, but excludes integral control.

Just noting such an omission highlights a problem illustrated by the consumption-income example: when $y \neq K_1 z$, what happened to unspent income, and from where did over-spending receive its finance? Behind the scenes, an asset must be altering to absorb deviations, and we can define it implicitly by:

$$A_t \equiv A_{t-1} + Z_t - Y_t.$$

This in turn poses a problem of cointegration, since if z_t and y_t are I(1) and $\Delta A_t = (Z_t - Y_t)$, then either $Z_t - Y_t$ is I(0), and so these variables are cointegrated with $K_1 = 1$, or ΔA_t is I(1), in which case A_t is I(2). Since the other variables in (7.86) are I(0), to maintain balance, we need an I(0) measure. Thus, we assume that $(A_t - Z_t) = (A_{t-1} - Y_t)$ is I(0), requiring what is called multi-cointegration (see Granger and Lee, 1991), since the 'integral' variable A_t cointegrates with either of the components which also cointegrate with each other.

In practice, y and z are likely to be logs of the original variables (denoted by capitals), and a stock-flow, or integral-correction, mechanism (ICM) could be considered, based on approximating the identity:

$$\frac{A_t}{A_{t-1}} = 1 + \frac{(Z_t - Y_t)}{A_{t-1}},$$

by taking logs and using the approximations that $\log(1+\epsilon) \simeq \epsilon$:

$$\Delta a_t \simeq \log\left(1 + \left[\frac{Y_t}{A_{t-1}}\right]\left[\frac{Z_t - Y_t}{Y_t}\right]\right) \simeq \left(\frac{Y_t}{A_{t-1}}\right)\left(\frac{Z_t - Y_t}{Y_t}\right) \simeq B\left(z_t - y_t\right), \tag{7.95}$$

where $B = Y_t/A_{t-1}$ is taken to be constant in (7.95), and the last step uses the reverse approximation that $\exp(\epsilon) \simeq 1 + \epsilon$. The life-cycle hypothesis in its simplest form postulates that $Y_t = BA_{t-1}$, and hence entails multi-cointegration.

However, so long as $y_t \neq K_1 z_t$, then A_t must alter, so to allow for feedback onto behaviour, add the ECM $(y - a)_{t-1}$ to (7.86), leading to:

$$\Delta y_t = \phi_0 + \phi_1 \Delta z_t + \phi_2 \left(y - K_1 z\right)_{t-1} + \phi_3 \left(y - K_2 a\right)_{t-1} + \nu_t, \tag{7.96}$$

as a more general control rule, subject to possible restrictions on the K_i (see Hendry and von Ungern-Sternberg, 1981, and Salmon, 1982).

7.10.3 Empirical success of ECMs

Many empirical studies have utilized ECMs in the last decade, and a catalogue will not be attempted here. Most UK macro-econometric models are specified as ECM systems, a process started after Davidson *et al.* (1978) and accelerated following the developments relating cointegration to equilibrium correction. Econometric modelling of the demand for M1 in the UK helped establish the value of ECMs in developing constant-parameter, interpretable models (see Hendry and Mizon, 1993, and Hendry and Ericsson, 1991b, for recent evidence). Studies for other countries corroborate this view (see e.g. Johansen and Juselius, 1990).

Since ECMs are a general class of model isomorphic to cointegration, it is difficult to be specific about economic theory bases: rather, any economic theory about long-run relationships entails cointegration and equilibrium correction. This was noted above for the LCH, and applies to the PIH. Indeed, ECMs arose initially as a method for implementing long-run theory in econometric models (see Sargan, 1964, Hendry and Anderson, 1977, and Davidson *et al.*, 1978). As ever, care is required in translating theoretical information into an empirical model. From §7.2, the PIH specifies:

$$c_t^p = \phi i_t^p, \tag{7.97}$$

leading to an economic model in the original levels of the form $c_t = \phi i_t + v_t$. When $(c_t : i_t)$ are I(1), the PIH entails that these are cointegrated. However, a linear model with a non-trending error variance would eventually lead to an essentially deterministic relation. If measurement and behavioural errors have standard errors which are constant proportions of the levels, then a log-linear equation is more sensible, and is consistent with (7.97).

There has been some misunderstanding about the generality of the equilibrium-correction model, due to much of the early discussion restricting that name to the homogeneous case where $K_1 = 1$, when there is a loss of generality (see, however, Hendry and Anderson, 1977). If $K_1 \neq 1$, there will be an additional term, namely $(K_1 - 1)\, z_{t-1}$ relative to $(z - y)_{t-1}$. Many econometric models are based on theories that ensure long-run proportionality, so $K_1 = 1$ often occurs after a logarithmic transform, as with the log of the consumption-income ratio, money-income ratio, and capital-output ratio. However, the general ECM does not restrict K_1 to unity: it is merely that $K_1 = 1$ occurs widely in economics.

No marginalization is required to derive the ECM from an AD(1, 1), as it is a re-parameterization. Thus, we consider the empirical illustration relating $\log(M/PY)$ to R. Since the equivalent of K_1 above is not known for the interest elasticity of the velocity of circulation of M1, the ECM is merely a transform of the equation in Chapter 6 (the statistical theory of estimating cointegration vectors is considered in Ch.11). Here, the long-run coefficient of R_{t-1} is imposed in a two-step procedure derived from the long-run solution of the AD(1, 1):

$$\Delta \widehat{\log\left(\tfrac{M}{PY}\right)}_t = \underset{(0.002)}{0.006} - \underset{(0.14)}{0.79}\,\Delta R_t - \underset{(0.01)}{0.08}\left[\log\left(\tfrac{M}{PY}\right) - 7.4R\right]_{t-1}$$
$$\mathsf{R}^2 = 0.47 \;\; \hat{\sigma} = 2.0\% \;\; SC = -7.71 \;\; DW = 2.60$$
$$AR\text{-}F(5,94) = 3.2 \;\; ND\text{-}\chi^2(2) = 4.2 \;\; Chow\; F(16,83) = 0.36. \tag{7.98}$$

Such an imposition is valid, since from Chapter 3, the coefficients of I(1) variables are super-consistent (see Engle and Granger, 1987). The residual autocorrelation test reveals dynamic mis-specification (explained in Chapter 9), but otherwise the results are sensible, subject to $\log(M/PY)$ and R being I(1) and $(\log(M/PY) - 7.4R)$ being I(0). Figure 7.36 records the fitted and actual values from (7.98) and Fig. 7.37 shows the recursive statistics. Constancy is acceptable although $AR\text{-}F(\cdot)$ warns that the standard errors are not consistently estimated.

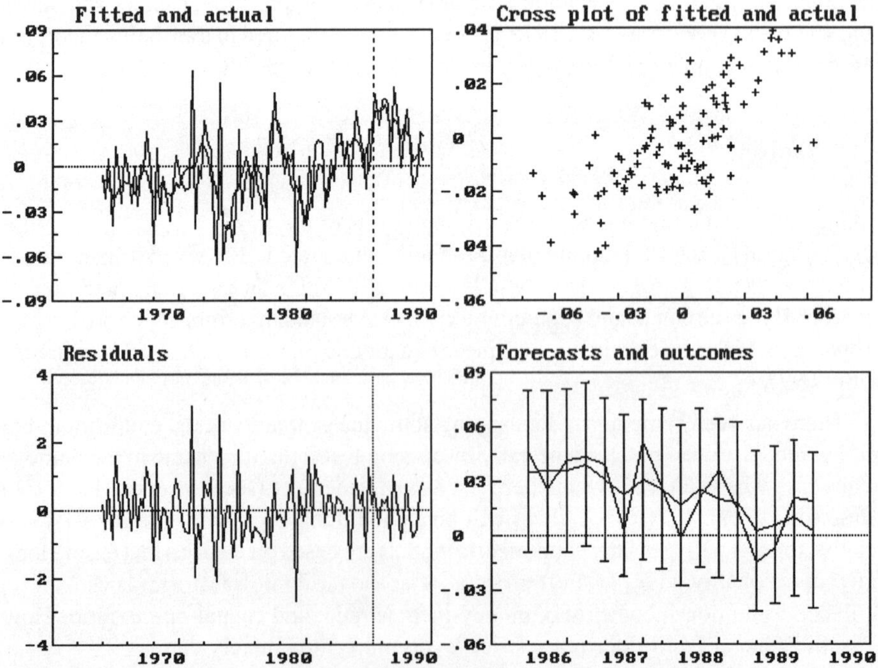

Fig. 7.36 Fitted and actual values from the equilibrium-correction model of M1

Now we turn to the Monte Carlo results for M_{10}. The coefficients on Δz_t and $(y-z)_{t-1}$ (using a priori knowledge of long-run homogeneity) are biased by less than 0.05 at any sample size, which is negligible: for correctly specified ECMs in this DGP, finite-sample biases are unimportant. Figure 7.38 shows the histogram and interpolated density for the ECM coefficient at $T = 80$. The distribution is nearly symmetric and approximately normal. Figure 7.39 plots the recursive Monte Carlo outcomes centred on -0.9 (as it is treated as a bias about β_2 by PcNaive): the vertical axis units reveal that the bias is small and only changes from -0.032 to -0.010 as T increases from 20 to 80, so the bias is negligible even in samples as small as size 20. For example, the true value of the β_1 coefficient is 0.5 and the bias is -0.015 at sample size 20.

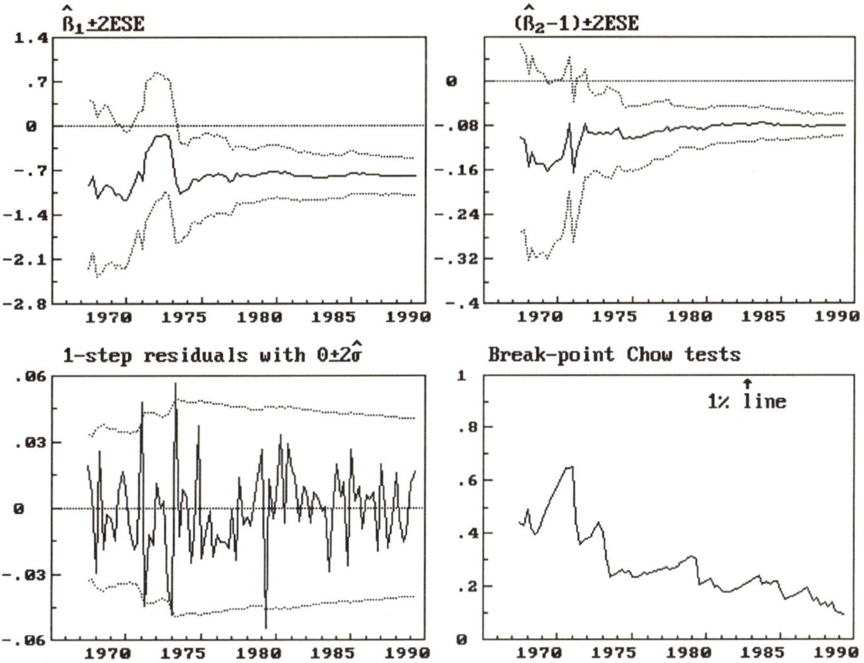

Fig. 7.37 Recursive statistics for the equilibrium-correction model of M1

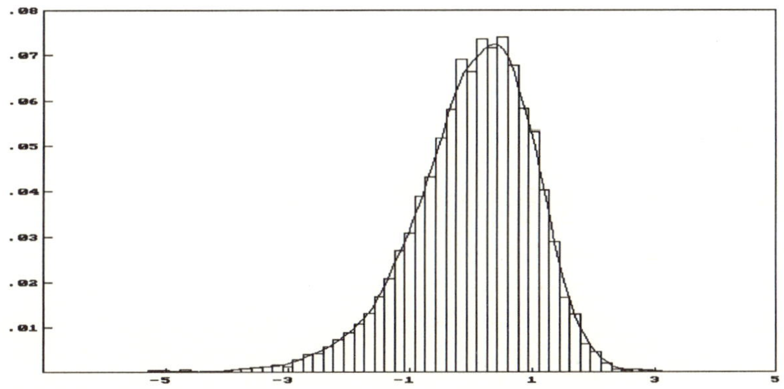

Fig. 7.38 Histogram and density function for $(\hat{\beta}_2 - 1)$

The graphs of ESE and MCSD in Fig. 7.39c,d show how close the least-squares standard errors are to the actual sampling standard deviations. The diagnostic tests also behave well: e.g. the *DW* rejects about 7 per cent of the time, only slightly higher than the nominal 5 per cent, although there is an implicit lagged dependent variable. Finally, the Chow test rejection frequencies are close to their nominal 5 per cent level, despite the dynamic nature of the data, but it must be remembered that the ECM coincides with the DGP in this experiment: Fig. 7.39d records the outcome.

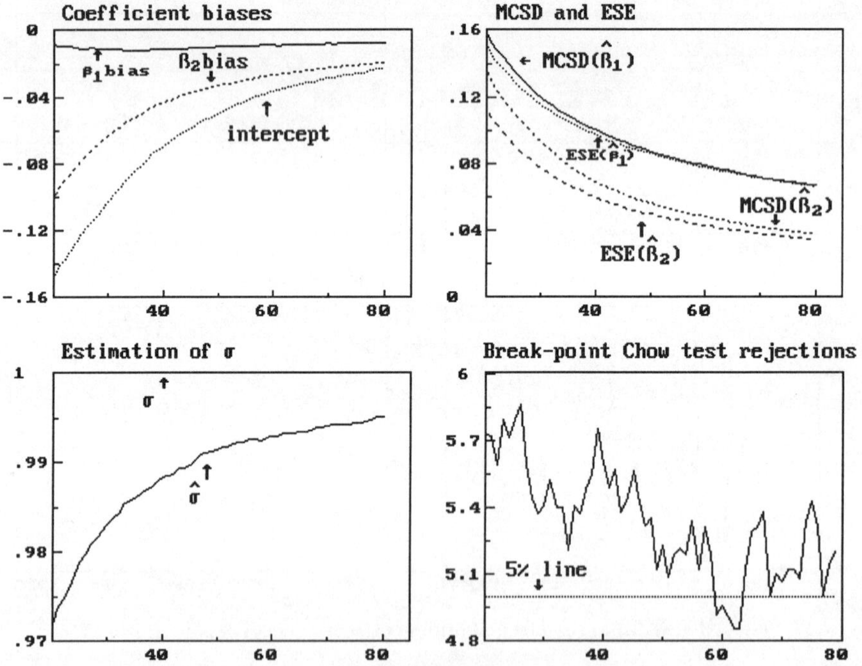

Fig. 7.39 Recursive Monte Carlo statistics for the equilibrium-correction model

7.11 Solved examples

7.11.1 Partial adjustment and equilibrium correction

Consider the AD(1, 1) model:

$$y_t = \beta_1 z_t + \beta_2 y_{t-1} + \beta_3 z_{t-1} + \epsilon_{1t} \tag{7.99}$$

where $|\beta_2| < 1$ and z_t is generated by:

$$z_t = \lambda z_{t-1} + \epsilon_{2t} \text{ where } |\lambda| < 1 \tag{7.100}$$

and

$$\epsilon_t = \begin{pmatrix} \epsilon_{1t} \\ \epsilon_{2t} \end{pmatrix} \sim \mathsf{IN}_2 \left[\begin{pmatrix} 0 \\ 0 \end{pmatrix}, \begin{pmatrix} \sigma_{11} & \sigma_{12} \\ \sigma_{12} & \sigma_{22} \end{pmatrix} \right] = \mathsf{IN}_2 \left[\mathbf{0}, \boldsymbol{\Sigma} \right],$$

with all parameters constant.

(a) Derive conditions under which z_t is weakly, and strongly, exogenous for the parameter vector $\boldsymbol{\beta}' = (\beta_1 : \beta_2 : \beta_3)$.
(b) What potential problems arise when seeking to estimate this model? When $\beta_1 + \beta_2 + \beta_3 = 1$, discuss the resulting class of model and sketch its properties.
(c) Another investigator hypothesizes:

$$y_t = b_1 z_t + b_2 y_{t-1} + u_t \text{ where } u_t \underset{c}{\sim} \mathsf{IN}\left[0, \tau^2\right]. \tag{7.101}$$

What class of model is this, how are its parameters related to (7.99) and (7.100), and under what conditions is z_t weakly exogenous for $\boldsymbol{b}' = (b_1 : b_2)$? Can z_t be weakly exogenous for $\boldsymbol{b}$ and $\boldsymbol{\beta}$ simultaneously?
(d) Is the choice of parameters of interest arbitrary between $\boldsymbol{b}$ and $\boldsymbol{\beta}$ and how would your answer be altered if λ was a policy parameter which changed?

(Oxford M.Phil., 1985)

Solution to 7.11.1 (a)

The DGP specification did not require that $\sigma_{12} = 0$. Consequently, (7.99) need not be the conditional expectation. The joint density takes the form $\boldsymbol{x}_t|\boldsymbol{x}_{t-1} \sim \mathsf{N}_2\left[\boldsymbol{\mu}_t, \boldsymbol{\Omega}\right]$ where $\boldsymbol{x}_t = (y_t \; z_t)'$ and:

$$\boldsymbol{\mu}_t = \begin{pmatrix} \beta_2 & \beta_3 + \beta_1\lambda \\ 0 & \lambda \end{pmatrix} \begin{pmatrix} y_{t-1} \\ z_{t-1} \end{pmatrix}, \; \boldsymbol{\Omega} = \begin{pmatrix} \sigma_{11} + \beta_1^2\sigma_{22} + 2\beta_1\sigma_{12} & \sigma_{12} + \beta_1\sigma_{22} \\ \sigma_{12} + \beta_1\sigma_{22} & \sigma_{22} \end{pmatrix}. \tag{7.102}$$

From (7.102), noting that $\omega_{12}\omega_{22}^{-1} = \sigma_{12}\sigma_{22}^{-1} + \beta_1 = \gamma + \beta_1$, the conditional model is given by:

$$\begin{aligned} \mathsf{E}\left[y_t | z_t, x_{t-1}\right] &= \omega_{12}\omega_{22}^{-1}\left(z_t - \lambda z_{t-1}\right) + \beta_2 y_{t-1} + \left(\beta_3 + \beta_1\lambda\right) z_{t-1} \\ &= \left(\beta_1 + \gamma\right) z_t + \left(\beta_3 - \gamma\lambda\right) z_{t-1} + \beta_2 y_{t-1}. \end{aligned} \tag{7.103}$$

The requirement for weak exogeneity is that $\gamma = \sigma_{12} = 0$, which is necessary and sufficient for (7.99) to be the conditional expectation, since when $\gamma \neq 0$, then $\boldsymbol{\beta}$ cannot be obtained from (7.103) as it would involve λ. Further, since z_t does not depend on past ys, strong exogeneity follows if and only if weak exogeneity holds.

Solution to 7.11.1 (b)

Many of the usual 'problems' could arise in special cases of the DGP, but not for (7.102) under weak exogeneity of z_t for $\boldsymbol{\beta}$. Simultaneity is precluded as $\sigma_{12} = 0$; the process is stationary, so cointegration is not an issue; there is no residual serial correlation; nor heteroscedasticity from the properties of $\{\epsilon_t\}$; and parameter change is precluded, so the remaining possibilities include:

(i) the incompleteness of the information set against marginalized IID variables;
(ii) finite-sample problems associated with dynamic models; and
(iii) the choice of parameterization as against:

$$\mathsf{M}_{10}^{*} : \Delta y_t = \alpha \Delta z_t + \delta \left(y - \kappa z\right)_{t-1} + \epsilon_{1t},$$

where $\alpha = \beta_1, \delta = \beta_2 - 1$, and $\kappa = (\beta_1 + \beta_3) / (1 - \beta_2)$.

Without further information on κ, there is little to choose between these specifications, but if $\beta_1 + \beta_2 + \beta_3 = 1$, then $\kappa = 1$, and the homogeneous ECM form is preferable, because then the ECM form captures cointegration. Since the regressors are usually nearly orthogonal, the parameters are easier to interpret and test individually. Derived parameters such as the mean lag $\mu = (1 - \alpha) / (1 - \beta_2)$ are not affected by this transformation. If $\sigma_{12} \neq 0$, the general ECM model M_{10}^{*} could still hold, but would not be the conditional expectation.

Solution to 7.11.1 (c)

This case is discussed in Hendry and Richard (1983). The model in (7.101) is a partial-adjustment. It can be derived from (7.99)+(7.100) by eliminating z_{t-1} using (7.100) if $\lambda \neq 0$, since then $z_{t-1} = (z_t - \epsilon_{2t}) / \lambda$; otherwise, if $\lambda = 0$, z_t is white noise and z_{t-1} can just be omitted to obtain (7.101). The first substitution delivers:

$$\begin{aligned} y_t &= \beta_1 z_t + \beta_2 y_{t-1} + \beta_3 (z_t - \epsilon_{2t}) / \lambda + \epsilon_{1t} \\ &= (\beta_1 + \beta_3/\lambda) z_t + \beta_2 y_{t-1} + (\epsilon_{1t} - (\beta_3/\lambda) \epsilon_{2t}) \qquad (7.104) \\ &= d_1 z_t + d_2 y_{t-1} + v_t \end{aligned}$$

where $v_t \sim \mathsf{IN}\left[0, \tau^2\right]$. Even if $\sigma_{12} = 0$, z_t is not weakly exogenous for $(d_1 : d_2)$ in (7.104), since $\mathsf{E}[z_t v_t] \neq 0$ as v_t contains ϵ_{2t}. However, z_t is weakly exogenous by construction for the parameters in:

$$\mathsf{E}[y_t \mid z_t, y_{t-1}] = \left(\beta_1 + \frac{\beta_3}{\lambda}\right) z_t + \beta_2 y_{t-1} - \left(\frac{\beta_3}{\lambda}\right) \mathsf{E}[\epsilon_{2t} \mid z_t, y_{t-1}]. \qquad (7.105)$$

The last term is obtained as usual for normal variates. Let $\epsilon_{2t} = \psi_1 z_t + \psi_2 y_{t-1} + \nu_t$ where $\mathsf{E}[z_t \nu_t] = \mathsf{E}[y_{t-1} \nu_t] = 0$ by construction: note the need to include y_{t-1} even though $\mathsf{E}[\epsilon_{2t} y_{t-1}] = 0$. Then, from normality, $\mathsf{E}[\epsilon_{2t} | z_t, y_{t-1}] = \psi_1 z_t + \psi_2 y_{t-1}$, so that:

$$\begin{aligned} \mathsf{E}[y_t | z_t, y_{t-1}] &= (\beta_1 + \beta_3 (1 - \psi_1) / \lambda) z_t + (\beta_2 - \beta_3 \psi_2 / \lambda) y_{t-1} \\ &= b_1 z_t + b_2 y_{t-1}. \end{aligned} \qquad (7.106)$$

Letting $u_t = y_t - \mathsf{E}[y_t | z_t, y_{t-1}]$, then u_t is orthogonal to (z_t, y_{t-1}).

By construction, therefore, z_t is weakly exogenous for $(b_1 : b_2)$ in the partial-adjustment model. Nevertheless, z_t cannot be weakly exogenous for both $\boldsymbol{\beta}$ and $\boldsymbol{b}$ unless $\beta_2 = 0$: if $\boldsymbol{\beta}$ is the parameter vector of interest, $\boldsymbol{b}$ cannot be derived from $\boldsymbol{\beta}$ without knowledge of (σ_{22}, λ); and in the reverse case, $\boldsymbol{\beta}$ is not identifiable from $\boldsymbol{b}$ without a further restriction.

Solution to 7.11.1 (d)

The choice between parameterizations is not arbitrary, since when $\beta_3 \neq 0$ and $|\lambda| < 1$:

$$\sigma_{11} \leq \tau^2 = \sigma_{11} + \sigma_{22}\beta_3^2 \leq \sigma_{11} + \sigma_{22}\left(\frac{\beta_3}{\lambda}\right)^2,$$

so residual variances can be ranked. Further, if λ did alter, at least one of $\boldsymbol{b}$ or $\boldsymbol{\beta}$ must alter.

7.11.2 Testing cointegration*

Consider the system:

$$\Delta y_t = \alpha_1 (z - y)_{t-1} + \epsilon_{1t} \tag{7.107}$$

$$\Delta z_t = \alpha_2 \Delta z_{t-1} + \epsilon_{2t} \tag{7.108}$$

where $\boldsymbol{\epsilon}_t = (\epsilon_{1t} : \epsilon_{2t})' \sim \mathsf{IN}_2 [\mathbf{0}, \boldsymbol{\Sigma}]$ for $t = 1, \ldots, T$.

(a) Establish the orders of integration $\mathsf{I}(d)$ of $\{y_t\}$ and $\{z_t\}$ and explain how you would test for $d = 0$. Could the values taken by α_1 and α_2 affect your conclusions?

(b) When $\alpha_2 = 0$, obtain the orders of magnitude in T of

$$T^{-1}\sum_{t=1}^{T} z_t^2,\ T^{-1}\sum_{t=2}^{T} z_t z_{t-1},\ \text{ and } T^{-1}\sum_{t=2}^{T} z_{t-1}\epsilon_{2t},$$

and comment on the implications of such results for the estimation of α_1.

(c) Derive the moving-average and autoregressive representations of the system (7.107) and (7.108) and the long-run relationship between y and z when $\alpha_2 = 0$.

(d) How would you test the hypothesis that y and z are not cointegrated?

(Oxford M.Phil., 1989)

Solution to 7.11.2 (a)

The numerical values of α_1 and α_2 are not stated but matter greatly. When $|\alpha_2| < 1$, then Δz_t is stationary, so $z_t \sim \mathsf{I}(1)$; but when $\alpha_2 = 1$, then $z_t \sim \mathsf{I}(2)$. We exclude the latter case in what follows, as we have not covered the analysis. If $z_t \sim \mathsf{I}(1)$ and $\alpha_1 \leq 0$, then from (7.107), $y_t \sim \mathsf{I}(1)$, as it is generated by a constant distributed lag of an $\mathsf{I}(1)$ variable. Also, from (7.107), when $\alpha_1 < 0$ then $(y_t - z_t)$ is $\mathsf{I}(0)$, and hence y and z are cointegrated in that y_t and z_t are individually $\mathsf{I}(1)$, but $\beta = 1$ in (7.94) delivers an $\mathsf{I}(0)$ combination, even though arbitrary linear combinations, such as $y_t - \gamma z_t$, will be $\mathsf{I}(1)$.

To test for $d = 0$ against $d = 1$ in $\mathsf{I}(d)$, the null is $d = 1$ to derive an appropriately sized test, with $d = 0$ as the stationary alternative which is adopted if $d = 1$ is rejected. To implement the test, regress Δy_t on y_{t-1} and test whether the regressor has a significant coefficient, noting that on the null of $d = 1$, the distribution is non-standard (see Dickey and Fuller, 1981 for tabulated values).

Solution to 7.11.2 (b)

$\alpha_2 = 0$ implies that z_t is a random walk, and its moments follow as in §3.7. There are no implications of these results for estimating α_1 when y and z are cointegrated, since then Δy_t and $(y_{t-1} - z_{t-1})$ are I(0) and conventional limiting-distribution theory holds. If $\alpha_1 = 0$, then y and z are not cointegrated, and $(y - z)_{t-1}$ is I(1), so that the material from Chapter 4 is relevant. If the cointegrating vector is unknown, the approach to be discussed in §11.5 is needed.

Solution to 7.11.2 (c)

The long-run solution when y and z are I(1) and cointegrated is given by $y^* = z^*$, on setting $\Delta y = \Delta z = 0$. The levels autoregressive representation is:

$$\begin{pmatrix} y_t \\ z_t \end{pmatrix} = \begin{pmatrix} (1-\alpha_1) & \alpha_1 \\ 0 & 1 \end{pmatrix} \begin{pmatrix} y_{t-1} \\ z_{t-1} \end{pmatrix} + \begin{pmatrix} \epsilon_{1t} \\ \epsilon_{2t} \end{pmatrix}. \tag{7.109}$$

In general, (7.109) can be written as $\boldsymbol{A}(L)\, \boldsymbol{x}_t = \boldsymbol{\epsilon}_t$, but the moving-average form cannot be obtained simply by inverting $\boldsymbol{A}(L)$ as there is a unit root. Thus, we need to express the MA first as $\boldsymbol{B}(L)\, \Delta \boldsymbol{x}_t = \boldsymbol{\epsilon}_t$, and then invert $\boldsymbol{B}(L)$. The long-run solution is :

$$\boldsymbol{A}(1) = \boldsymbol{\pi} = \begin{pmatrix} \alpha_1 & -\alpha_1 \\ 0 & 0 \end{pmatrix} = \begin{pmatrix} \alpha_1 \\ 0 \end{pmatrix} (1 : -1),$$

and hence has rank 1; also $\boldsymbol{\pi}^2 = \alpha_1 \boldsymbol{\pi}$ by direct multiplication. From (7.109), the system can be written as $(\boldsymbol{I}_2 - \boldsymbol{\pi} L/\Delta)\, \Delta \boldsymbol{x}_t = \boldsymbol{\epsilon}_t$, so that:

$$\Delta \boldsymbol{x}_t = \left(\boldsymbol{I} - \frac{\boldsymbol{\pi} L}{\Delta} \right)^{-1} \boldsymbol{\epsilon}_t = \boldsymbol{C}(L)\, \boldsymbol{\epsilon}_t = h(L)\, \boldsymbol{D}(L)\, \boldsymbol{\epsilon}_t,$$

say, where $h(L)$ is a scalar lag polynomial. To find $h(L)$ and $\boldsymbol{D}(L)$, use the definition of an inverse:

$$\boldsymbol{C}(L) \left(\boldsymbol{I}_2 - \frac{\boldsymbol{\pi} L}{\Delta} \right) = \boldsymbol{I}_2 \tag{7.110}$$

and equate coefficients of powers of L, setting:

$$\boldsymbol{C}(L) = \sum_{j=0}^{\infty} \boldsymbol{C}_j L^j \;\text{ where }\; \boldsymbol{C}_0 = \boldsymbol{I}_2,$$

and writing the expression to be solved as:

$$\boldsymbol{C}(L)\, (\boldsymbol{I}_2 (1 - L) - \boldsymbol{\pi} L) = (1 - L)\, \boldsymbol{I}_2. \tag{7.111}$$

On multiplying out, $\boldsymbol{I}_2 (1 - L)$ is equal to:

$$\boldsymbol{I}_2 (1 - L) + \boldsymbol{C}_1 L (1 - L) - \boldsymbol{\pi} L + \boldsymbol{C}_2 L^2 (1 - L) - \boldsymbol{C}_1 \boldsymbol{\pi} L^2 + \boldsymbol{C}_3 L^3 (1 - L) - \cdots \tag{7.112}$$

and hence $\boldsymbol{C}_1 = \boldsymbol{\pi}$; $\boldsymbol{C}_2 = \boldsymbol{\pi} + \boldsymbol{\pi}^2 = (1+\alpha_1)\,\boldsymbol{\pi}$; $\boldsymbol{C}_3 = (1+\alpha_1)^2\,\boldsymbol{\pi}$; and so on. Thus, for $\lambda = (1+\alpha_1)$:

$$\begin{aligned} \boldsymbol{C}(L) &= \left(\boldsymbol{I}_2 + \left(1 + \lambda L + \lambda^2 L^2 + \lambda^3 L^3 + \cdots\right)\boldsymbol{\pi} L\right) \\ &= \boldsymbol{I}_2 + \boldsymbol{\pi} L / (1-\lambda L) = (1-\lambda L)^{-1}\left[\boldsymbol{I}_2 + (\boldsymbol{\pi} - \lambda \boldsymbol{I}_2) L\right], \end{aligned} \tag{7.113}$$

and hence $h(L) = (1 - (1+\alpha_1) L)^{-1}$ and $\boldsymbol{D}(L) = [\boldsymbol{I}_2 + (\boldsymbol{\pi} - (1+\alpha_1)\boldsymbol{I}_2) L]$.

Solution to 7.11.2 (d)

There are many possible tests for cointegration and at this stage we only consider tests applied to the scalar AD$(1,1)$ class. Tests for the presence of genuine links between variables must take account of the outcome when there are no links. To check that a nonsense regression has not been estimated, it is possible to test that the residuals of the levels regression are a stationary process using for example, DW or Dickey–Fuller (DF) tests for a unit root. Kremers, Ericsson and Dolado (1992) argue that while such tests should reject nonsense regressions with probability one in large enough samples, they need not be optimal. Let $\hat{u}_t = y_t - \hat{\kappa} z_t$ where $\hat{\kappa}$ is the OLS estimate of the long-run parameter κ, then the DF statistic tests for H_0: $\rho = 0$ in:

$$\Delta\left(y_t - \hat{\kappa} z_t\right) = \rho\left(y_{t-1} - \hat{\kappa} z_{t-1}\right) + \omega_t. \tag{7.114}$$

A model like (7.114) based on $\hat{u}_t$ imposes a common factor on the dynamic structure. Kremers *et al.* (1992) contrast that approach with a direct test in the AD$(1,1)$:

$$\Delta y_t = \phi_1 \Delta z_t + \phi_2\left(y_{t-1} - \kappa z_{t-1}\right) + \omega_t, \tag{7.115}$$

where κ is not constrained to equal the short-run parameter ϕ_1. However, the resulting statistic is not similar and its null rejection frequency depends on the values of the 'nuisance' parameters (here ϕ_1 and σ_v^2). Kiviet and Phillips (1992) develop an approach for establishing similar tests which applies to cointegration tests with strongly exogenous regressors without a great sacrifice in power. In fact, their test is invariant to the values of ϕ_1 and σ_v^2, and coincides with the unrestricted AD$(1,1)$ variant of the Kremers *et al.* (1992) test. It is also the test computed in PcGive, so we consider the properties of both tests (see Park and Phillips, 1988, and Banerjee and Hendry, 1992, drawing on related work by Boswijk, 1992).

Under the null of no cointegration, the DGP in (7.107)+(7.108) is the bivariate $\mathsf{I}(1)$ process:

$$\begin{aligned} \Delta y_t &= \eta \Delta z_t + \omega_t \quad \text{where} \quad \omega_t \sim \mathsf{IN}\left[0, \sigma_\omega^2\right] \\ \Delta z_t &= \epsilon_{2t} \quad \text{with} \quad \epsilon_{2t} \sim \mathsf{IN}\left[0, \sigma_{22}\right]. \end{aligned} \tag{7.116}$$

In (7.116), $\omega_t = \epsilon_{1t} - \eta \epsilon_{2t}$ where $\mathsf{E}[\omega_t \epsilon_{2t}] = 0$. Thus, (7.115) is a re-parameterization of a bivariate normal distribution for Δy_t and Δz_t with covariance $\sigma_{12} = \eta \sigma_{22}$. Under the null of no cointegration ($\alpha_1 = 0$), $y_t - z_t = u_t = u_{t-1} + v_t$ is a random walk where $v_t = \omega_t + (\eta - 1)\,\epsilon_{2t}$ with variance $\sigma_v^2 = \sigma_\omega^2 + (\eta-1)^2\,\sigma_{22}$ and in (7.115), $\phi_1 = \eta$

and $\phi_2 = 0$. The parameter estimates in (7.115) then are:

$$\begin{pmatrix} \sqrt{T}\left(\hat{\phi}_1 - \eta\right) \\ T\left(\hat{\phi}_2\right) \end{pmatrix} = \begin{pmatrix} T^{-1}\sum_{t=1}^{T}\epsilon_{2t}^2 & T^{-\frac{3}{2}}\sum_{t=1}^{T}u_{t-1}\epsilon_{2t} \\ T^{-\frac{3}{2}}\sum_{t=1}^{T}u_{t-1}\epsilon_{2t} & T^{-2}\sum_{t=1}^{T}u_{t-1}^2 \end{pmatrix}^{-1} \begin{pmatrix} T^{-\frac{1}{2}}\sum_{t=1}^{T}\epsilon_{2t}\omega_t \\ T^{-1}\sum_{t=1}^{T}u_{t-1}\omega_t \end{pmatrix}$$

$$\Rightarrow \begin{pmatrix} \sigma_{22} & 0 \\ 0 & \sigma_v^2\int_0^1 W_v(r)^2 \mathrm{d}r \end{pmatrix}^{-1} \begin{pmatrix} \mathsf{N}\left[0, \sigma_{22}\sigma_\omega^2\right] \\ \sigma_v\sigma_\omega \int_0^1 W_v(r)\mathrm{d}W_\omega(r) \end{pmatrix} \tag{7.117}$$

using Table 3.2, where $W_\omega(r)$, $W_v(r)$, and $W_2(r)$ are constructed from the partial sums of ω_j/σ_ω, v_j/σ_v and $\epsilon_{2j}/\sqrt{\sigma_{22}}$ respectively:

$$T^{-\frac{1}{2}}\sum_{t=1}^{[Tr]}\frac{\omega_t}{\sigma_\omega} \Rightarrow W_\omega(r),\; T^{-\frac{1}{2}}\sum_{t=1}^{[Tr]}\frac{v_t}{\sigma_v} \Rightarrow W_v(r),\; T^{-\frac{1}{2}}\sum_{t=1}^{[Tr]}\frac{\epsilon_{2t}}{\sqrt{\sigma_{22}}} \Rightarrow W_2(r). \tag{7.118}$$

Since $\sigma_v\left(v_t/\sigma_v\right) = \sigma_\omega\left(\omega_t/\sigma_\omega\right) + (\eta - 1)\sqrt{\sigma_{22}}\left(\epsilon_{2t}/\sqrt{\sigma_{22}}\right)$:

$$\sigma_v W_v(r) = \sigma_\omega W_\omega(r) + (\eta - 1)\sqrt{\sigma_{22}}W_2(r) \tag{7.119}$$

where $W_\omega(r)$ and $W_2(r)$ are independent and so:

$$\sigma_v\int_0^1 W_v(r)\mathrm{d}W_\omega(r) = \sigma_\omega\int_0^1 W_\omega(r)\mathrm{d}W_\omega(r) + (\eta - 1)\sqrt{\sigma_{22}}\int_0^1 W_2(r)\mathrm{d}W_\omega(r). \tag{7.120}$$

The t-test of H_0: $\phi_2 = 0$ is given by $\mathsf{t}_{\phi_2=0} = \hat{\phi}_2/\mathsf{SE}\left(\hat{\phi}_2\right)$:

$$\Rightarrow \left(\sigma_v^2\int_0^1 W_v(r)^2\mathrm{d}r\right)^{-\frac{1}{2}}\left[\sigma_\omega\int_0^1 W_\omega(r)\mathrm{d}W_\omega(r) + (\eta - 1)\sqrt{\sigma_{22}}\int_0^1 W_2(r)\mathrm{d}W_\omega(r)\right]. \tag{7.121}$$

The first term in $\{\cdot\}$ in (7.121) leads to a Dickey–Fuller type of distribution and the second to a normal distribution, again using Table 3.2. Equation (7.121) shows that the Kremers *et al.* (1992) test differs notably from that based on (7.114) and confirms that the test is not similar since the outcome varies with η and $\sqrt{\sigma_{22}}/\sigma_\omega$ *inter alia*.

To create a similar test, the level z_{t-1} (a redundant regressor) must be added to (7.115), which also avoids the need to know the cointegrating vector. The equation to be estimated becomes:

$$\Delta y_t = \kappa_1\Delta z_t + \kappa_2\left(y_{t-1} - z_{t-1}\right) + \kappa_3 z_{t-1} + \omega_t. \tag{7.122}$$

When $\kappa_2 \neq 0$, the cointegrating vector can be obtained from solving (7.122) for $(1 : 1 - \kappa_3/\kappa_2)$ (the second element in that vector could be zero, which would imply that y_t was I(0) but unrelated to the level of z). The cointegration test is a pseudo t-test of H_0: $\kappa_2 = 0$. Under the null, $\mathsf{t}_{\kappa_2=0}$ is a functional of Wiener distributions but is invariant to $(\eta, \sigma_\omega^2, \sigma_{22})$ and hence is similar when z_t is strongly exogenous for $\boldsymbol{\kappa}$ (see Kiviet and Phillips, 1992). The estimates of (7.122) are:

$$\begin{pmatrix} \sqrt{T}(\hat{\kappa}_1 - \kappa_1) \\ T(\hat{\kappa}_2) \\ T(\hat{\kappa}_3) \end{pmatrix} =$$

$$\begin{pmatrix} T^{-1}\sum_{t=1}^T \epsilon_{2t}^2 & T^{-\frac{3}{2}}\sum_{t=1}^T u_{t-1}\epsilon_{2t} & T^{-\frac{3}{2}}\sum_{t=1}^T z_{t-1}\epsilon_{2t} \\ T^{-\frac{3}{2}}\sum_{t=1}^T u_{t-1}\epsilon_{2t} & T^{-2}\sum_{t=1}^T u_{t-1}^2 & T^{-2}\sum_{t=1}^T u_{t-1}z_{t-1} \\ T^{-\frac{3}{2}}\sum_{t=1}^T z_{t-1}\epsilon_{2t} & T^{-2}\sum_{t=1}^T u_{t-1}z_{t-1} & T^{-2}\sum_{t=1}^T z_{t-1}^2 \end{pmatrix}^{-1} \begin{pmatrix} T^{-\frac{1}{2}}\sum_{t=1}^T \epsilon_{2t}\omega_t \\ T^{-1}\sum_{t=1}^T u_{t-1}\omega_t \\ T^{-1}\sum_{t=1}^T z_{t-1}\omega_t \end{pmatrix}$$

and so tend to:

$$\begin{pmatrix} \sigma_{22} & 0 & 0 \\ 0 & \sigma_v^2\int_0^1 W_v(r)^2\mathrm{d}r & \sigma_v\sqrt{\sigma_{22}}\int_0^1 W_v(r)W_2(r)\mathrm{d}r \\ 0 & \sigma_v\sqrt{\sigma_{22}}\int_0^1 W_v(r)W_2(r)\mathrm{d}r & \sigma_{22}\int_0^1 W_2(r)^2\mathrm{d}r \end{pmatrix}^{-1} \times$$

$$\begin{pmatrix} \mathsf{N}\left[0, \sigma_{22}\sigma_\omega^2\right] \\ \sigma_v\sigma_\omega\int_0^1 W_v(r)\mathrm{d}W_\omega(r) \\ \sigma_\omega\sqrt{\sigma_{22}}\int_0^1 W_2(r)\mathrm{d}W_\omega(r) \end{pmatrix}.$$

By partitioned inversion, $T\hat{\kappa}_2$ tends to:

$$\frac{\sigma_\omega\left(\int_0^1 W_2(r)^2\mathrm{d}r\int_0^1 W_v(r)\mathrm{d}W_\omega(r) - \int_0^1 W_v(r)W_2(r)\mathrm{d}r\int_0^1 W_2(r)\,\mathrm{d}W_\omega(r)\right)}{\sigma_v\left[\int_0^1 W_v(r)^2\mathrm{d}r\int_0^1 W_2(r)^2\mathrm{d}r - \left(\int_0^1 W_v(r)W_2(r)\mathrm{d}r\right)^2\right]}.$$

The estimated standard error of $T\hat{\kappa}_2$ tends to:

$$\frac{\sigma_\omega\left(\int_0^1 W_2(r)^2\mathrm{d}r\right)^{\frac{1}{2}}}{\sigma_v\left[\int_0^1 W_v(r)^2\mathrm{d}r\int_0^1 W_2(r)^2\mathrm{d}r - \left(\int_0^1 W_v(r)W_2(r)\mathrm{d}r\right)^2\right]^{\frac{1}{2}}}.$$

Thus, $\mathsf{t}_{\kappa_2=0}$ tends to:

$$\frac{\int_0^1 W_2(r)^2\mathrm{d}r\int_0^1 W_v(r)\mathrm{d}W_\omega(r) - \int_0^1 W_v(r)W_2(r)\mathrm{d}r\int_0^1 W_2(r)\mathrm{d}W_\omega(r)}{\left(\int_0^1 W_2(r)^2\mathrm{d}r\right)^{\frac{1}{2}}\left[\int_0^1 W_v(r)^2\mathrm{d}r\int_0^1 W_2(r)^2\mathrm{d}r - \left(\int_0^1 W_v(r)W_2(r)\mathrm{d}r\right)^2\right]^{\frac{1}{2}}}$$

which equals:

$$\frac{\int_0^1 W_\omega(r)\mathrm{d}W_\omega(r) - \int_0^1 W_\omega(r)W_2(r)\mathrm{d}r \left(\int_0^1 W_2(r)^2\mathrm{d}r\right)^{-1} \int_0^1 W_2(r)\mathrm{d}W_\omega(r)}{\left(\int_0^1 W_\omega(r)^2\mathrm{d}r\right)^{\frac{1}{2}} \left[1 - \left(\int_0^1 W_\omega(r)W_2(r)\mathrm{d}r\right)^2 \left(\int_0^1 W_2(r)^2\mathrm{d}r\right)^{-1} \left(\int_0^1 W_\omega(r)^2\mathrm{d}r\right)^{-1}\right]^{\frac{1}{2}}} \tag{7.123}$$

using (7.119), and the related result that:

$$\begin{aligned}\sigma_v^2 \int_0^1 W_v(r)^2\mathrm{d}r &= \sigma_v\sigma_\omega \int_0^1 W_\omega(r)W_v(r)\mathrm{d}r + b\sigma_v \int_0^1 W_2(r)W_v(r)\mathrm{d}r \\ &= \sigma_\omega^2 \int_0^1 W_\omega(r)^2\mathrm{d}r + 2b\sigma_\omega \int_0^1 W_\omega(r)W_2(r)\mathrm{d}r + b^2 \int_0^1 W_2(r)^2\mathrm{d}r.\end{aligned}$$

This confirms the similarity of the test to η, σ_ω^2 and σ_{22}.

An alternative expression based on (7.123) is enlightening. Let R denote the limiting form of Yule's correlation for the nonsense regression linking the levels of y_t and z_t when $\eta = 0$ (i.e. under the null of no relation) namely:

$$y_t = \beta z_t + u_t, \tag{7.124}$$

so that from Phillips (1986):

$$\mathsf{R} \Rightarrow \frac{\left(\int_0^1 W_\omega(r)W_2(r)\mathrm{d}r\right)}{\left(\int_0^1 W_\omega(r)^2\,\mathrm{d}r \int_0^1 W_2(r)^2\mathrm{d}r\right)^{\frac{1}{2}}}, \tag{7.125}$$

then:

$$\mathsf{t}_{\kappa_2=0} \Rightarrow \frac{(DF - \mathsf{R}\cdot\mathsf{N}[0,1])}{(1-\mathsf{R}^2)^{\frac{1}{2}}}. \tag{7.126}$$

This demonstrates that the test differs from the Dickey–Fuller distribution, so its critical values need separate tabulation. The exact and limiting distributions respectively are derived in Kiviet and Phillips (1992) and Boswijk (1992) (also see Park and Phillips, 1988, Sims, Stock and Watson, 1990, and Campos, Ericsson and Hendry, 1993).

Similarity is easily verified in a Monte Carlo by simulating the distribution at different parameter values using the same random numbers. The critical values under the null for this test and for the ADF(1) (also a similar test) for regressions like (7.122) were computed in Banerjee *et al.* (1993) by simulating the model (7.116). Local alternatives can be analysed using the near-integrated regressors approach discussed in Phillips (1988b) and applied in Kremers *et al.* (1992). At small values of κ_2, Banerjee *et al.* (1993) find that the power of the ADF test is close to that of the $\mathsf{t}_{\kappa_2=0}$ test, although both tests perform poorly. The power of $\mathsf{t}_{\kappa_2=0}$ relative to the ADF increases with $|\kappa_2|$, the signal-noise ratio $(1-\kappa_1)\,\sigma_{22}/\sigma_\omega^2$ and T, but slowly when κ_2 is small, matching the results in Kremers *et al.* (1992). When the dynamics are close to satisfying a common-factor restriction, the ADF test does relatively well. When a common-factor approximation is poor, in that the ADF test suffers a large increase in the residual standard error, the ADF test does badly.

Similarity depends on the strong exogeneity of z_t, which requires that there is no feedback from lagged y onto current z, and that the ECM only enters the y equation. When z_t is not weakly exogenous, the test just studied is potentially a rather poor way of detecting cointegration. However, the Wald test in Boswijk (1992) (based on testing for a common factor of unity) is asymptotically similar when no cointegration exists, and sustains individual equation analyses without presumptions about exogeneity.

7.11.3 Cointegration representations

Consider the following DGP for the cointegrated random variables z_t and y_t:

$$(1-L)\begin{pmatrix} y_t \\ z_t \end{pmatrix} = (1-0.4L)^{-1}\begin{pmatrix} 1-0.8L & 0.8L \\ 0.1L & 1-0.6L \end{pmatrix}\begin{pmatrix} e_{1t} \\ e_{2t} \end{pmatrix} \quad (7.127)$$

where $\boldsymbol{e}_t = (e_{1t} : e_{2t})' \sim \mathsf{IN}_2[\mathbf{0}, \boldsymbol{I}]$, with $z_0 = y_0 = 0$. Obtain the autoregressive and equilibrium-correction representations of the DGP. Hence, or otherwise, deduce the long-run relation between z and y.

(Oxford M.Phil., 1987)

Solution to 7.11.3

To find the autoregressive representation, let:

$$\begin{pmatrix} 1-0.8L & 0.8L \\ 0.1L & 1-0.6L \end{pmatrix} = \boldsymbol{C}(L) = (1-0.4L)\,\boldsymbol{D}(L).$$

Since $\boldsymbol{C}(L)$ is non-singular, by direct inversion:

$$\boldsymbol{C}(L)^{-1} = \frac{1}{|\boldsymbol{C}(L)|} ADJ(\boldsymbol{C}(L)),$$

where $|\boldsymbol{C}(L)| = (1-L)(1-0.4L)$, so

$$(1-0.4L)^{-1}\,\boldsymbol{C}(L)^{-1} = (1-L)^{-1}\begin{pmatrix} 1-0.6L & -0.8L \\ -0.1L & 1-0.8L \end{pmatrix}.$$

Thus:

$$\begin{pmatrix} 1-0.6L & -0.8L \\ -0.1L & 1-0.8L \end{pmatrix}\begin{pmatrix} y_t \\ z_t \end{pmatrix} = \begin{pmatrix} e_{1t} \\ e_{2t} \end{pmatrix},$$

or $\boldsymbol{A}(L)\boldsymbol{x}_t = \boldsymbol{e}_t$, which is the autoregressive representation.

For the ECM form, express the DGP as:

$$(1-L)\begin{pmatrix} y_t \\ z_t \end{pmatrix} = -\begin{pmatrix} \alpha_1 \\ \alpha_2 \end{pmatrix}(\beta_1 y_{t-1} - \beta_2 z_{t-1}) + \begin{pmatrix} e_{1t} \\ e_{2t} \end{pmatrix},$$

where $(\beta_1 : \beta_2)$ solves $(\beta_1 : \beta_2)\boldsymbol{D}(1) = (0 : 0)$, which implies (after normalizing) that $\beta_1 = 1$ and $\beta_2 = -2$. Then, $(\alpha_1 : \alpha_2)$ solves $\boldsymbol{D}(1)\boldsymbol{\alpha} = \mathbf{0}$, and so $\alpha_1 = 0.4$ and

$\alpha_2 = -0.1$. Alternatively, from the autoregressive representation:

$$\begin{aligned}
\begin{pmatrix} 1-0.6L & -0.8L \\ -0.1L & 1-0.8L \end{pmatrix} &= \begin{pmatrix} 1-L+0.4L & -0.8L \\ -0.1L & 1-L+0.2L \end{pmatrix} \\
&= \begin{pmatrix} 1-L & 0 \\ 0 & 1-L \end{pmatrix} + \begin{pmatrix} 0.4L & -0.8L \\ -0.1L & 0.2L \end{pmatrix} \\
&= \Delta \boldsymbol{I}_2 + \begin{pmatrix} 0.4 \\ -0.1 \end{pmatrix} (1:-2)\, L \\
&= \Delta \boldsymbol{I}_2 + \boldsymbol{\alpha\beta}' L.
\end{aligned} \tag{7.128}$$

From the ECM solution, the long-run solution is $y = 2z$.

7.12 Summary and conclusion

There are many ways to summarize this long chapter but we only focus on two:

(i) comparative goodness of fit as measured by $\hat{\sigma}$, the equation standard error; and
(ii) the different lag shapes imposed by the nine model forms.

7.12.1 Goodness of fit

The values of $\hat{\sigma}$ in the nine models across the Monte Carlo at $T = 80$ are as follows:[7]

Model	M_2	M_3	M_4	M_5	M_6	M_7	M_8	M_9	M_{10}	$AD(1,1)$
$\hat{\sigma}$	3.40	1.44	1.05	3.20	1.12	1.07	2.92	1.28	1.00	1.00
plim $\hat{\sigma}$	3.60	1.43	1.14	3.30	1.15	*na*	3.30	1.31	1.00	1.00

Apart from M_4, M_6 and M_7, all other models are more than 25 per cent worse, and three are about 300 per cent worse, than the DGP. Variance dominance alone would allow selection across such tightly parameterized types as those in the present typology.

7.12.2 Distributed-lag shapes

Figure 7.40 records the distributed-lag weights $\{w_i\}$ for all but M_3, which has $w_i = 0\,\forall i$. It is clear that a wide variety of shapes has been imposed on the data, most bearing little relationship to the actual lag distribution of the DGP. It is imperative to commence from a relatively unrestricted lag distribution to avoid such needless mis-specifications and actually learn from the data what the lag shape is like.

The major purpose of this chapter has been to illustrate the various types of dynamic single equations which occur regularly in the empirical literature, and discuss their properties and relative merits in relation to data analysis and investigating economic theories. For clarity of exposition, only special cases have been discussed, and while the situation is less clear cut when more general lag models are considered, nevertheless many of the

[7] M_7 is based on one replication only and the plim of its equation standard error is not available; as discussed earlier, $\sqrt{\bar{\sigma}_u^2}$ is used in the second row.

features noted above apply in a modified form. In practice, a more important complication is that neither the form of the model nor the relevant lag lengths are known and some model-selection process has to be used. Since equation types which have similar goodness of fit can differ markedly in their derived lag distributions, data-based selection criteria alone are insufficient and economic theoretical considerations and/or prior information often must be invoked as well.

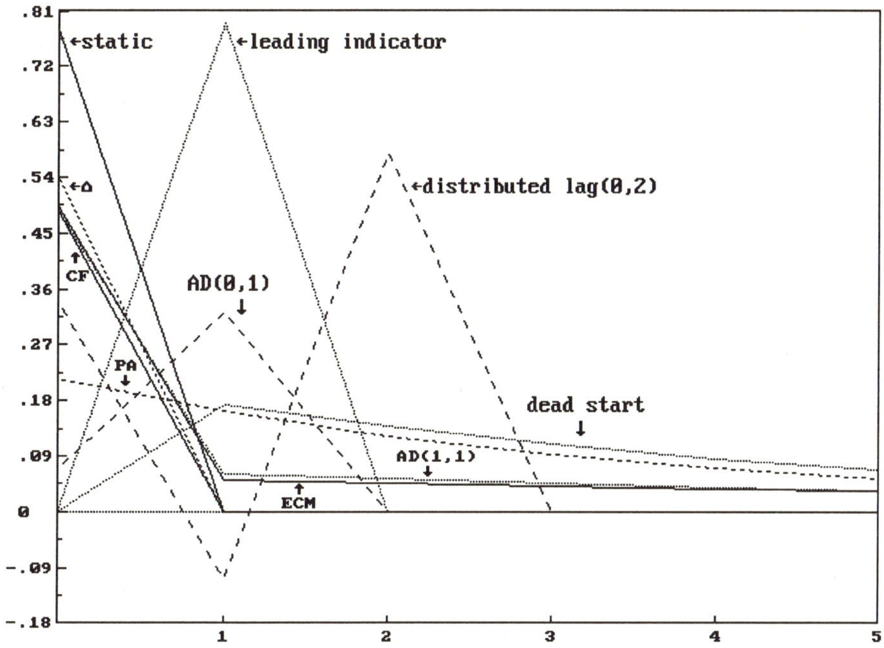

Fig. 7.40 Lag weights in the Monte Carlo study of the model typology

The main choice of model type depends on the issue of long-run properties between the variables under study, since an ECM is the most appropriate type when cointegration holds. In other cases, an analogue of equilibrium correction may be useful, but it is not necessarily the best choice. Despite its advantages, ECM is not a panacea for econometric ills. First, it is important to adopt an appropriate methodology and hence rigorously test whichever type is postulated: remember Fig. 7.40. Secondly, there are many situations in which other model forms are more appropriate (see e.g. Muellbauer, 1979). This is especially important when the long-run equilibrium has shifted (as after financial deregulation), in which case the ECM will worsen forecast performance. Finally, while we have focused on dynamic specification issues in this chapter, many other problems are at least as important in practice, and alternative approximations to unknown DGPs may prove more robust to mis-specification, and hence could provide more lasting constant-parameter models for economic time series. The next chapter extends the typology to dynamic systems and the final chapter of Part I considers the theory of reduction as a basis for the origin of empirical models, and develops a taxonomy of information against which models can be evaluated.

7.13 Exercises

7.1 Consider the model:

$$y_t = \beta_0 + \beta_1 z_t + \beta_2 z_{t-1} + \beta_3 y_{t-1} + \epsilon_t \tag{7.129}$$

where $\epsilon_t \sim \mathsf{IN}\left[0, \sigma_\epsilon^2\right]$ when $0 \leq \beta_3 < 1$, $\beta_1 \geq 0$, and $(\beta_2 + \beta_1\beta_3) \geq 0$, when z_t is strongly exogenous for $\boldsymbol{\beta}$.

(a) Derive the mean lag μ of the reaction of y_t to a change in z_t.

(b) For the three cases: (i) $\beta_2 = 0$; (ii) $\beta_2 = -\beta_1\beta_3$; (iii) $\beta_2 = 1 - \beta_1 - \beta_3$, reparameterize (7.129) in an unrestricted form, discussing which 'type' of model results, what its merits and drawbacks are, and what happens to μ in each case.

(c) Consider the distributed-lag equation:

$$y_t = \sum_{i=0}^{\infty} w_i z_{t-i} + v_t \tag{7.130}$$

derived from (7.129): obtain a formula for the median lag J given by:

$$\sum_{i=0}^{J-1} w_i < \tfrac{1}{2} \sum_{i=0}^{\infty} w_i \leq \sum_{i=0}^{J} w_i \tag{7.131}$$

as a function of $(\beta_1 : \beta_2 : \beta_3)$.

(d) Briefly discuss how to estimate μ and an asymptotically-valid standard error for $\hat{\mu}$.

(Oxford M.Phil., 1982)

7.2 Consider the process:

$$y_t = \beta_0 + \beta_1 z_t + \beta_2 y_{t-1} + \beta_3 z_{t-1} + \epsilon_t \tag{7.132}$$

where $\epsilon_t \sim \mathsf{IN}\left[0, \sigma_\epsilon^2\right]$, $\mathsf{E}\left[z_t \epsilon_s\right] = 0 \ \forall t, s$ and $|\beta_2| < 1$.

(a) Explain how to test the common-factor restriction that $\beta_3 = -\beta_1\beta_2$. What model results if the restriction is imposed?

(b) Discuss alternative numerical maximization procedures which could be applied to obtain maximum likelihood estimators of the parameters in the model where the common-factor restriction is imposed. Is it worth iterating beyond the first step?

(c) Evaluate the potential problems which might arise if the restriction is invalidly imposed. Does it matter if z_t is only weakly exogenous for β?

(Oxford M.Phil., 1986)

7.3 Consider the AD(1, 1) model:

$$y_t = \beta_0 + \beta_1 z_t + \beta_2 z_{t-1} + \beta_3 y_{t-1} + \epsilon_t \tag{7.133}$$

where $\epsilon_t \sim \mathsf{IN}\left[0, \sigma_\epsilon^2\right]$.

(a) When z_t is strongly exogenous for $\boldsymbol{\beta}' = (\beta_0, \beta_1, \beta_2, \beta_3)$, develop nine distinct types of model, commenting briefly on their special characteristics. How are each of these affected (taken in turn) if z_t is stationary, but only weakly exogenous for $\boldsymbol{\beta}$, noting two cases where the properties of least-squares estimation are radically altered?

(b) If the exogeneity status of z_t for $\boldsymbol{\beta}$ is unknown, develop at least three different economic hypotheses which lead to a model looking like AD(1, 1) but with different interpretations and implications.

(c) Given the properties of the nine types for a stationary world, ascertain for each type the extent to which empirical results obtained are an artefact of the type selected.

(d) If $z_t \sim \mathsf{I}(1)$, how are your conclusions in (c) modified?

(e) If it is now revealed that the marginal model for z_t is:

$$z_t = \gamma_0 + \gamma_1 z_{t-1} + \gamma_{2t} x_t + \nu_t \tag{7.134}$$

where $\nu_t \sim \mathsf{IN}\left[0, \omega_t^2\right]$, when γ_{2t} and ω_t^2 are policy-determined parameters and x_t is strongly exogenous for $(\boldsymbol{\beta} : \boldsymbol{\gamma})$, how are your conclusions in (a)–(d) affected (if at all)?

(f) Using the UKM1 data with $\log(M/PY)$ as y_t and R as z_t, empirically implement each type, briefly describe the results, and comment on the extent to which the findings match the theoretical analysis.

7.4 Show that the partial autocorrelation at lag k of a stationary time series generated by an autoregressive process of order m is equal to zero if $k > m$.
A stationary process $\{x_t\}$ is governed by the equation:

$$x_t = \alpha x_{t-1} + u_t - \beta u_{t-1},$$

for $t = 1, 2, \ldots, T$ where $-1 < \alpha, \beta < 1$ and the random variables $\{u_t\}$ are $\mathsf{IID}\left[0, \sigma_u^2\right]$.

(a) Determine the autocorrelation and partial autocorrelation functions. Comment briefly on what happens when $\alpha = \beta$.

(b) Describe the relationship between the autocorrelation and partial autocorrelation functions for an ARMA(m, n) process and those for an ARMA(n, m) process, with particular reference to AR(m) and MA(m) processes.

(Oxford M.Phil., 1989)

7.5 Consider the following DGP (see Engle and Granger, 1987):

$$x_t + \beta y_t = u_{1t} \text{ where } u_{1t} = u_{1t-1} + \epsilon_{1t} \tag{7.135}$$

$$x_t + \alpha y_t = u_{2t} \text{ where } u_{2t} = \rho u_{2t-1} + \epsilon_{2t} \tag{7.136}$$

and:

$$\begin{pmatrix} \epsilon_{1t} \\ \epsilon_{2t} \end{pmatrix} \sim \mathsf{IID}_2 \left[\begin{pmatrix} 0 \\ 0 \end{pmatrix}, \begin{pmatrix} \sigma_{11} & \sigma_{12} \\ \sigma_{12} & \sigma_{22} \end{pmatrix} \right]. \tag{7.137}$$

(a) Derive the integration properties of the two series x_t and y_t. Do your results depend on any restrictions on the values of α, β, and ρ?
(a) When are x_t and y_t cointegrated, and, if so, what is their cointegrating parameter?
(b) Under the specification that x_t and y_t are cointegrated, derive (i) the moving-average; (ii) the autoregressive; (iii) the equilibrium-correction representations of the process. Are all cointegrated series representable in this fashion?
(c) Derive $\mathsf{E}\left[y_t | x_t, y_{t-1}, x_{t-1}\right]$, and comment on the form of this equation.
(d) How general is the DGP in this question?

(Oxford M.Phil., 1988)

7.6 The desired level y_t^* of a random variable y at time t is related to a variable x_t by:

$$y_t^* = \beta x_t. \tag{7.138}$$

However, only a fraction γ of the disequilibrium between the outcome y_t and y_t^* is removed by partial adjustment each period through a reaction function of the form:

$$y_t - y_{t-1} = \gamma(y_t^* - y_{t-1}) + \epsilon_t \tag{7.139}$$

where $\epsilon_t \underset{c}{\sim} \mathsf{IN}\left[0, \sigma_\epsilon^2\right]$ and $0 < \gamma < 1$, when $\underset{c}{\sim}$ denotes that the error is claimed to be distributed as shown.

(a) Compare this model with the adaptive-expectations model in which:

$$y_t = \beta x_{t+1}^e + v_t \tag{7.140}$$

when $v_t \underset{c}{\sim} \mathsf{IN}\left[0, \sigma_v^2\right]$ where x_{t+1}^e is the expected value of x_{t+1} generated by:

$$x_{t+1}^e - x_t^e = \lambda \left(x_t - x_t^e\right) \tag{7.141}$$

with $0 < \lambda < 1$.

(b) If (7.138)+(7.139) comprise the DGP with $\epsilon_t \sim \mathsf{IN}\left[0, \sigma_\epsilon^2\right]$, show that regressing y_t on y_{t-1} and x_t will yield fully-efficient estimates of the parameters of (7.138)+(7.139), but inconsistent estimates of the parameters in (7.140)+(7.141).
(c) Comment on this difference and suggest how to test which model is appropriate.
(d) How are your results affected by x_t being integrated of first order?

(Oxford M.Phil., 1992)

8

Dynamic Systems

Linear dynamic systems are formulated for stationary and integrated data processes. Both open and closed systems are noted. General-to-specific modelling of the joint data-density function is reviewed. A typology of linear dynamic systems is developed, extending that for individual dynamic equations in Chapter 7. Alternative models of systems are derived from three operations on systems, namely contemporaneous and intertemporal transforms, and conditioning. Methods for analysing econometric systems are discussed.

8.1 Introduction

This chapter formulates systems of linear dynamic equations to represent the joint data-density function of a set of related variables. A dynamic system is any time-dependent representation of the endogenous variables in terms of available information, and so is the Haavelmo distribution (see Haavelmo, 1944, and Spanos, 1986). The dynamic statistical system is defined by the variables of interest, their distributions, which variables are modelled and non-modelled (the latter may be absent, as in a VAR), and their lag polynomials. Since the dynamic system is the maintained statistical model, its initial specification is crucial to the success of any empirical analysis. A typology of linear dynamic systems is developed, extending the typology for individual dynamic equations in Chapter 7, to reveal the properties of various specifications.

Once a well-specified system is available, an econometric model of it can be developed. An econometric model imposes a structure on a statistical system, intended to isolate autonomous, parsimonious relationships interpretable by economic theory. A system is therefore a model of itself and in fact all models which impose no (over-identifying) restrictions on a common set of variables correspond to the same system. Once the initial system adequately characterizes the data evidence, the model must account for the results obtained by the system. Economic theory often formulates the economic mechanism in terms of sets of simultaneous equations which impose restrictions on the dynamic system, and any such representation is a model of the system. Simultaneous equations models have been criticized from a number of viewpoints (see *inter alia* Wold and Juréen, 1953, Liu, 1960, Sims, 1980, and Hendry, Neale and Srba, 1988). Such criticisms arise in part because dynamic system modelling usually commences from an assumed known structural form of the process generating the data, from which the system (reduced form) is derived (see e.g. Judge, Griffiths, Hill, Lütkepohl and Lee, 1985, Ch.14). That approach raises numerous difficulties: in particular, by not first testing the validity of the reduced form, the credibility of the model's parameter estimates is unclear. A more methodical approach to linear dynamic system modelling circumvents many of the extant criticisms (see Hendry and Mizon, 1993, and Hendry and Doornik, 1994). The analysis, therefore, considers joint-density modelling even when the objective may be a single relation of interest. Since proceeding from general to simple enforces a systems approach, and hence necessitates a large modelling burden, reasons for general-to-specific modelling are discussed.

Alternative systems, and models thereof, are described to clarify relationships between ostensibly different closed, open, complete, and incomplete models of systems for I(0), I(1), and I(2) processes, including such model forms as vector autoregressions, vector equilibrium-correction models, simultaneous equations, reduced forms, causal models, block-recursive systems, and triangular systems. Finally, we address the issue of how each model form can be analysed. The chapter draws on Klein (1969), Zellner and Palm (1974), Prothero and Wallis (1976), Palm and Zellner (1980), Kmenta and Ramsey (1981), Hendry *et al.* (1988), Hendry and Ericsson (1991b), Hendry and Mizon (1993), Engle and Hendry (1993), Hendry and Doornik (1994) and Hendry (1994c).

8.2 Statistical formulation

Consider the joint data-density function $\mathsf{D_X}(\cdot)$ for T observations on a vector of n observable, real random variables $\boldsymbol{x}_t = (x_{1t} \ldots x_{nt})'$ for the complete sample $\boldsymbol{X}_T^1$:

$$\mathsf{D_X}\left(\boldsymbol{X}_T^1 \mid \boldsymbol{X}_0, \boldsymbol{Q}_T^1, \boldsymbol{\theta}\right) \quad \text{where } \boldsymbol{\theta} \in \Theta \subseteq \mathbb{R}^p \tag{8.1}$$

when $\boldsymbol{X}_0$ denotes the pre-sample initial conditions, $\boldsymbol{Q}_T^1 = (\boldsymbol{q}_1 \ldots \boldsymbol{q}_T)$ is a set of m deterministic conditioning variables (such as constant, seasonals, trend, and dummy variables — see Ch.15), and there are ρ parameters in $\boldsymbol{\theta}$. Writing the sequential conditional density as $\mathsf{D_x}\left(\boldsymbol{x}_t | \boldsymbol{X}_{t-1}^1, \boldsymbol{Q}_T^1, \boldsymbol{\theta}\right)$, from (8.1):

$$\mathsf{D_X}\left(\boldsymbol{X}_T^1 \mid \boldsymbol{X}_0, \boldsymbol{Q}_T^1, \boldsymbol{\theta}\right) = \prod_{t=1}^{T} \mathsf{D_x}\left(\boldsymbol{x}_t \mid \boldsymbol{X}_{t-1}, \boldsymbol{Q}_T^1, \boldsymbol{\theta}\right). \tag{8.2}$$

In (8.2), $\boldsymbol{\theta}$ may contain transient parameters, (e.g. parameters of dummy variables, perhaps interactive with lagged elements of $\boldsymbol{x}_t$). The parameters of interest comprise a subset $\boldsymbol{\psi} \in \Psi$ of $\boldsymbol{\lambda} = \boldsymbol{f}(\boldsymbol{\theta})$ where $\boldsymbol{f}(\cdot)$ is a one–one function of $\boldsymbol{\theta}$. Since:

$$\mathsf{D_X}\left(\boldsymbol{X}_T^1 \mid \boldsymbol{X}_0, \boldsymbol{Q}_T^1, \boldsymbol{\theta}\right) = \mathsf{D_X}\left(\boldsymbol{X}_T^1 \mid \boldsymbol{X}_0, \boldsymbol{Q}_T^1, \boldsymbol{\lambda}\right), \tag{8.3}$$

$\mathsf{D_X}(\cdot)$ is invariant under such parameter transformations, and the resulting class of densities is isomorphic. Such a result is regularly used in derivations (e.g. switching between a variance and a standard deviation).

The deterministic nature of Q_T^1 does not entail that future values of q_t are known with certainty. Polynomials in time are predictable, but dummy variables for special events (such as an oil crisis or regime shift) can only be created *post hoc*. In analyses of dynamic systems (including dynamic simulation), the treatment of such dummies can play a crucial role in the ostensible performance, and, as shown below, the way q_t is treated matters for the system properties and for parameter estimators. In practice, we only require valid conditioning on q_t, which is a weaker (albeit not unexceptional) assumption, so the following reduction is sufficient for modelling:

$$\mathsf{D_x}\left(\boldsymbol{x}_t \mid \boldsymbol{X}_{t-1}, \boldsymbol{Q}_T^1, \boldsymbol{\theta}\right) = \mathsf{D_x}\left(\boldsymbol{x}_t \mid \boldsymbol{X}_{t-1}, \boldsymbol{q}_t, \boldsymbol{\theta}\right). \quad (8.4)$$

Thus, only contemporaneous (or lagged) information on the deterministic terms is used. However, a major assumption is hidden in this reduction, namely, that the parameterization $\boldsymbol{\theta}$ is known, and this is unlikely to be the case for regime shifts etc.

Finally, a maximum lag length, or memory, of s periods is imposed for tractability: it may prove possible in practice to obtain more parsimonious representations using moving-average components but that aspect will not be considered here. Combining all of these ingredients, we represent the Haavelmo distribution as:

$$\mathsf{D_X}\left(\boldsymbol{X}_T^1 \mid \boldsymbol{X}_0, \boldsymbol{Q}_T^1, \boldsymbol{\theta}\right) = \prod_{t=1}^{T} \mathsf{D_x}\left(\boldsymbol{x}_t \mid \boldsymbol{X}_{t-1}^{t-s}, \boldsymbol{q}_t, \boldsymbol{\lambda}\right). \quad (8.5)$$

Many possible model forms could be adopted to characterize the behaviour of the $\{\boldsymbol{x}_t\}$ and learn about $\boldsymbol{\psi}$. To formulate these, we first note four major categorisations common to all such models, namely whether the model is open or closed (meaning that all variables are modelled), whether it is complete or incomplete (i.e. whether there are fewer equations than variables to be modelled), whether the model is linear or non-linear, and whether the data are stationary, I(0), or are integrated (I(1) or I(2)). Other forms of non-stationarity (such as regime shifts) are assumed to be adequately accounted for by the introduction of transient parameters. We are mainly concerned with systems which are linear in the variables, although the generic form of model in macro-econometrics must be non-linear due to linear accounting identities, multiplicative price, quantity and value relations, and (usually) log-linear behavioural equations (see Ch.A6). Further, we only analyse complete models, since incomplete models can be obtained by omitting some of the equations remembering that the associated variables are endogenous to the system and are determined by a subset of non-modelled or lagged variables (see Hendry and Richard, 1983). Finally, the initial formulation is the general one, with I(1) or I(2) being generated by restrictions on the basic form, as shown below.

8.3 Theoretical formulation

Using a framework of inter-temporal optimization by rational agents, empirical research in economics often faces the issue of jointly modelling systems of relationships of the form (ignoring deterministic factors):

$$\mathsf{E}\left[\boldsymbol{A}(L)\,\boldsymbol{\xi}_t \mid \mathcal{I}_t\right] = \mathbf{0}, \tag{8.6}$$

where $\boldsymbol{\xi}_t$ is an $n \times 1$ vector of theoretical variables of interest, for which $\boldsymbol{x}_t$ is the observed counterpart, $\mathsf{E}\left[\cdot|\mathcal{I}_t\right]$ is the conditional expectation, and $\mathcal{I}_t$ denotes the information set assumed available to agents at the start of decision time-period t. As before, the lag operator L maps $\boldsymbol{\xi}_t$ into $\boldsymbol{\xi}_{t-1}$. In (8.6), $\boldsymbol{A}(L)$ is a polynomial matrix of the form discussed in Chapter A1. When only finite lags are involved, $\boldsymbol{A}(L)$ can be written as:

$$\boldsymbol{A}(L) = \sum_{k=0}^{s} \boldsymbol{A}_k L^k = \sum_{k=0}^{s} \left\{ a_{ij,k} L^k \right\}$$

where s is the maximum lag length and some of the $\{\boldsymbol{A}_k\}$ and/or individual $\{a_{ij,k}\}$ may be zero: $\boldsymbol{A}_0$ can be a unit matrix. Thus, the ith equation in (8.6) is a generalization of the equation types in Chapter 7, such that when $\boldsymbol{A}_0 = \boldsymbol{I}_n$ and $s = 1$, there are n equations like:

$$\xi_{it} + \sum_{j=1}^{n} a_{ij,1} \xi_{j,t-1} = \epsilon_{it} \;\; \text{where} \;\; \mathsf{E}\left[\epsilon_{it} \mid \mathcal{I}_t\right] = 0.$$

When $\boldsymbol{A}(\cdot)$ involves leads (L^{-1} etc.), the latent constructs become expectations of future variables.

Although economic theory may offer a useful initial framework, theory is too abstract to be definitive and should not constitute a strait-jacket to empirical research: theory models should not simply be imposed on data. If an empirical counterpart to a theory is imposed on data, it will exclude many phenomena and it is valid to test such restrictions under the assumption that the theory is correct. However, for any inferences concerning $\boldsymbol{A}(\cdot)$ to be sustainable, accurate estimates of the inferential uncertainty are required. This necessitates establishing the innovation variance for $\boldsymbol{x}_t$ given the available information and a set of invariants $\boldsymbol{\theta}$ (on which $\boldsymbol{A}(\cdot)$ depends) that characterize the data density (see e.g. Hendry and Mizon, 1993).

When $\boldsymbol{x}_t$ is an accurate measure of $\boldsymbol{\xi}_t$ (i.e. assuming $\boldsymbol{x}_t = \boldsymbol{\xi}_t$), and future expectations do not affect outcomes, the counterpart of (8.6) in terms of observable variables becomes the vector autoregression:

$$\mathsf{E}\left[\boldsymbol{x}_t \mid \boldsymbol{x}_{t-1}, \ldots, \boldsymbol{x}_{t-s}\right] = \sum_{j=1}^{s} \boldsymbol{A}_j \boldsymbol{x}_{t-j}. \tag{8.7}$$

Measurement errors will induce a vector moving-average error process and are discussed more generally in Chapter 12. The observable system in (8.7) comprises the most unrestricted (closed) system to be entertained and is discussed in the following section. Further:

$$\boldsymbol{\nu}_t = \boldsymbol{x}_t - \mathsf{E}\left[\boldsymbol{x}_t \mid \boldsymbol{x}_{t-1}, \ldots, \boldsymbol{x}_{t-s}\right] \tag{8.8}$$

must be a mean-innovation process against the available information and is assumed to have a positive-definite (symmetric) variance matrix $\mathsf{E}\left[\boldsymbol{\nu}_t \boldsymbol{\nu}_t'\right] = \boldsymbol{\Omega}$. Tests for $\{\boldsymbol{\nu}_t\}$

being homoscedastic and white noiseare feasible, and the value of continued modelling requires that satisfactory outcomes result from such tests, as well as from tests of parameter constancy. If so, the system is data coherent and it is worth developing a parsimonious model. The main advantage of first formulating the statistical model is that later tests (e.g. of over-identifying restrictions) can be conducted against a valid background, so awkward circles of the kind arising in simple-to-general searches are avoided. These issues are considered in greater detail below.

8.4 Closed linear systems

8.4.1 Formulation

Given the restriction of the analysis to linear, finite-lag systems, the basic closed form of $\mathsf{D_x}(\boldsymbol{x}_t|\cdot)$ in (8.5) is a VAR: no issue of principle is involved in extending this to have vector moving-average errors but estimation and identification are less easy (see e.g. Lütkepohl, 1991). The typologies below consider special cases of the VAR formulation. Assuming that joint normality is a good approximation to $\mathsf{D_x}(\cdot)$, consistent with linearity of conditional models, and retaining the deterministic terms, the initial system is the stochastic version of (8.7):

$$\boldsymbol{x}_t = \sum_{j=1}^{s} \boldsymbol{A}_j \boldsymbol{x}_{t-j} + \boldsymbol{K}\boldsymbol{q}_t + \boldsymbol{\nu}_t \text{ where } \boldsymbol{\nu}_t \sim \mathsf{IN}_n[\mathbf{0}, \boldsymbol{\Omega}]. \tag{8.9}$$

Despite the presence of deterministic non-modelled variables in (8.9), we refer to it as a closed system. To keep the notation simple, we have not explicitly allowed for interactions between the $\boldsymbol{q}_t$ and lagged $\{\boldsymbol{x}_{t-j}\}$, and have assumed that the parameters $(\boldsymbol{A}_1, \ldots, \boldsymbol{A}_s, \boldsymbol{K}, \boldsymbol{\Omega})$ are constant in the postulated representation. In practice, interactions such as $q_{it}x_{j,t-l}$ may be used, especially when q_{it} is a regime-shift dummy (so that $q_{it}x_{j,t-l}$ may be zero for a proportion of the sample), but little is gained in a level A theoretical treatment by their retention. Then relative to (8.1), $\rho = n(ns + m + (n+1)/2)$ so that even for (e.g.) two equations with two lags and two dummies, $\rho = 15$; for four equations with four lags and five dummy variables, $\rho = 90$, and hence the dimensionality of the parameter space rises rapidly. This curse of dimensionality is a major driving force behind the desire to develop more parsimonious representations of the initial specification as discussed in §8.8.

8.4.2 Invariance under linear transformations

We now consider the set of non-singular linear transformations of (8.9) which are isomorphic in that they retain the same basic innovation process $\{\boldsymbol{\nu}_t\}$. This also generates the class of all equivalent models of (8.9). We take $s = 2$ for simplicity, so the system can be written as:

$$\boldsymbol{x}_t = \boldsymbol{A}_1 \boldsymbol{x}_{t-1} + \boldsymbol{A}_2 \boldsymbol{x}_{t-2} + \boldsymbol{K}\boldsymbol{q}_t + \boldsymbol{\nu}_t. \tag{8.10}$$

Let $\boldsymbol{f}_t' = \left(\boldsymbol{x}_t' : \boldsymbol{x}_{t-1}' : \boldsymbol{x}_{t-2}' : \boldsymbol{q}_t'\right)$ and rewrite (8.10) as:

$$\boldsymbol{G}\boldsymbol{f}_t = \boldsymbol{\nu}_t \tag{8.11}$$

where $\boldsymbol{G} = (\boldsymbol{I} : -\boldsymbol{A}_1 : -\boldsymbol{A}_2 : -\boldsymbol{K})$. Longer lags merely extend $\boldsymbol{f}_t$. Two types of linear transforms are feasible. Let $\boldsymbol{M}$ and $\boldsymbol{P}$ be known $n \times n$ and $p \times p$ non-singular matrices where $p = (s+1)\,n + m$, and consider:

$$\boldsymbol{M}\boldsymbol{G}\boldsymbol{P}^{-1}\boldsymbol{P}\boldsymbol{f}_t = \boldsymbol{M}\boldsymbol{\nu}_t \text{ or } \boldsymbol{G}^{\star}\boldsymbol{f}_t^{\star} = \boldsymbol{\nu}_t^{\star}, \tag{8.12}$$

where $\boldsymbol{f}_t^{\star} = \boldsymbol{P}\boldsymbol{f}_t$ and $\boldsymbol{\nu}_t^{\star} \sim \mathsf{IN}_n[\boldsymbol{0}, \boldsymbol{M\Omega M}']$ such that (see Ericsson, 1993a):

$$\boldsymbol{P} = \begin{pmatrix} \boldsymbol{I}_n & \boldsymbol{P}_{12} \\ \boldsymbol{0} & \boldsymbol{P}_{22} \end{pmatrix},$$

and:

$$\boldsymbol{G}^{\star} = \boldsymbol{M}\boldsymbol{G}\boldsymbol{P}^{-1} = (\boldsymbol{M} : -\boldsymbol{A}_1^{\star} : -\boldsymbol{A}_2^{\star} : -\boldsymbol{K}^{\star}).$$

Clements and Hendry (1993) refer to these as M- and P-transforms. No restrictions are imposed by these reversible transforms, so the systems (8.11) and (8.12) are isomorphic. M-transforms combine contemporaneous elements of $\boldsymbol{x}_t$ and can induce simultaneity. The restriction that abs$\,|\boldsymbol{M}| = 1$ preserves the scale. When elements of $\boldsymbol{M}$ are unknown, statistical equivalence need not hold, and such cases are discussed in §8.8: in particular, there must be sufficient restrictions on the resulting coefficient matrices to ensure unique identification (see Koopmans, 1950a, and Fisher, 1966; for an example, see Hendry and Mizon, 1993). P-transforms induce inter-temporal data combinations, such as creating differences. All types of closed model are generated by alternative choices for $\boldsymbol{M}$ and $\boldsymbol{P}$.

A transformation to levels and differences is achievable by P-transforms and so leaves the system invariant. One useful reformulation of the system in equation (8.9) is (see Hendry, Pagan and Sargan, 1984, Engle and Granger, 1987, Johansen, 1988, and Banerjee, Dolado, Galbraith and Hendry, 1993):

$$\Delta\boldsymbol{x}_t = \sum_{j=1}^{s-1} \boldsymbol{A}_j^{*}\Delta\boldsymbol{x}_{t-j} + \boldsymbol{\pi}\boldsymbol{x}_{t-1} + \boldsymbol{K}\boldsymbol{q}_t + \boldsymbol{\nu}_t. \tag{8.13}$$

No restrictions are imposed by this transform and the resulting system is called a vector equilibrium correction. Its parameterization is more orthogonal than that in (8.9) since the variables are usually less inter-correlated after transformation from levels to differences and differentials: the resulting parameters are often more interpretable. When $s = 2$, (8.13) becomes:

$$\Delta\boldsymbol{x}_t = \boldsymbol{A}_1^{*}\Delta\boldsymbol{x}_{t-1} + \boldsymbol{\pi}\boldsymbol{x}_{t-1} + \boldsymbol{K}\boldsymbol{q}_t + \boldsymbol{\nu}_t. \tag{8.14}$$

A 'structural' representation of the closed system requires an M-transform of (8.14) to yield:

$$\boldsymbol{M}\Delta\boldsymbol{x}_t = \boldsymbol{M}_1^{*}\Delta\boldsymbol{x}_{t-1} + \boldsymbol{\pi}^{*}\boldsymbol{x}_{t-1} + \boldsymbol{K}^{*}\boldsymbol{q}_t + \boldsymbol{\nu}_t^{*}. \tag{8.15}$$

We refer to (8.15) as a structural VAR, although its actual structurality remains to be established. When $\boldsymbol{M}$ is known, we can transform the $\boldsymbol{x}_t$ to obtain:

$$\Delta \boldsymbol{x}_t^0 = \boldsymbol{A}_1^0 \Delta \boldsymbol{x}_{t-1}^0 + \boldsymbol{\pi}^0 \boldsymbol{x}_{t-1}^0 + \boldsymbol{K}^0 \boldsymbol{q}_t^0 + \boldsymbol{\nu}_t^0 \qquad (8.16)$$

where $\boldsymbol{x}_t^0 = \boldsymbol{M}\boldsymbol{x}_t$, $\boldsymbol{q}_t^0 = \boldsymbol{M}\boldsymbol{q}_t$, $\boldsymbol{A}_1^0 = \boldsymbol{M}\boldsymbol{A}_1^* \boldsymbol{M}^{-1}$, $\boldsymbol{\pi}^0 = \boldsymbol{M}\boldsymbol{\pi}\boldsymbol{M}^{-1}$, $\boldsymbol{K}^0 = \boldsymbol{M}\boldsymbol{K}\boldsymbol{M}^{-1}$ and $\boldsymbol{\nu}_t^0 = \boldsymbol{\nu}_t^* \sim \mathsf{IN}_n\left[\mathbf{0}, \boldsymbol{M}\boldsymbol{\Omega}\boldsymbol{M}'\right]$. In effect, the $\boldsymbol{x}_t^0$ are the linear data combinations of economic interest. Although the resulting system is invariant, its parameterization is equivariant: for example, any linear estimator $\hat{\boldsymbol{\pi}}^0$ of $\boldsymbol{\pi}^0$ is equal to $\boldsymbol{M}\hat{\boldsymbol{\pi}}\boldsymbol{M}^{-1}$ and hence varies in line with the parameter transforms. Both M- and P-transforms are used below.

8.4.3 Cointegration

The data $\{\boldsymbol{x}_t\}$ are $\mathsf{I}(d)$ when the maximal order of integration of any element is d. This formulation accommodates the invariance of linear systems to linear transforms. When the data $\{\boldsymbol{x}_t\}$ are $\mathsf{I}(1)$, then $\Delta\boldsymbol{x}_t$ is $\mathsf{I}(0)$ and the system specification in (8.13) is balanced only if $\boldsymbol{\pi}\boldsymbol{x}_{t-1}$ is $\mathsf{I}(0)$: otherwise, there arises a contradiction between the left- and right-hand sides. Clearly $\boldsymbol{\pi}$ cannot be full rank since that would contradict the assumption that $\boldsymbol{x}_t$ was $\mathsf{I}(1)$, so $\text{rank}(\boldsymbol{\pi}) = r < n$. Then $\boldsymbol{\pi} = \boldsymbol{\alpha}\boldsymbol{\beta}'$ where $\boldsymbol{\alpha}$ and $\boldsymbol{\beta}$ are $n \times r$ matrices of rank r, and $\boldsymbol{\beta}'\boldsymbol{x}_t$ comprises r cointegrating $\mathsf{I}(0)$ relations, inducing a restricted $\mathsf{I}(0)$ representation as in 7, so (8.14) has the form (see Engle and Granger, 1987, and Johansen, 1988):

$$\Delta \boldsymbol{x}_t = \boldsymbol{A}_1^* \Delta \boldsymbol{x}_{t-1} + \boldsymbol{\alpha}\left(\boldsymbol{\beta}'\boldsymbol{x}_{t-1}\right) + \boldsymbol{K}\boldsymbol{q}_t + \boldsymbol{\nu}_t. \qquad (8.17)$$

This is called the $\mathsf{I}(0)$ vector equilibrium-correction model (VECM).

To ensure that $\boldsymbol{x}_t$ is not $\mathsf{I}(2)$, a further requirement is that:

$$\text{rank}\left(\boldsymbol{\alpha}_\perp \boldsymbol{\Phi}\boldsymbol{\beta}'_\perp\right) = n - r \quad \text{when} \quad \boldsymbol{\Phi} = -\sum_{j=1}^{s} j\boldsymbol{A}_j$$

so $\boldsymbol{\Phi}$ is the mean-lag matrix, where $\boldsymbol{\alpha}_\perp$ and $\boldsymbol{\beta}_\perp$ are $n \times (n-r)$ matrices such that $\boldsymbol{\alpha}'_\perp\boldsymbol{\alpha} = \boldsymbol{\beta}'_\perp\boldsymbol{\beta} = \mathbf{0}$ with $(\boldsymbol{\alpha} : \boldsymbol{\alpha}_\perp)$ and $(\boldsymbol{\beta} : \boldsymbol{\beta}_\perp)$ full-rank (n) matrices. Should the analysis commence in $\mathsf{I}(2)$ space, then $\boldsymbol{\alpha}_\perp\boldsymbol{\Phi}\boldsymbol{\beta}'_\perp = \boldsymbol{\gamma}\boldsymbol{\delta}'$ is also reduced rank, so some linear combinations first cointegrate from $\mathsf{I}(2)$ to $\mathsf{I}(1)$ and then r others (perhaps with $\mathsf{I}(1)$ differences of $\mathsf{I}\,(2)$ variables) cointegrate to $\mathsf{I}(0)$ (see Johansen, 1992b). Thus, both $\mathsf{I}(2)$ and $\mathsf{I}(1)$ impose reduced-rank restrictions on the initial formulation in (8.13), and the former imposes further restrictions on (8.17).

The behaviour of the system depends greatly on the properties of $\boldsymbol{K}\boldsymbol{q}_t$. We consider the case where $\boldsymbol{q}'_t = (1, t)$ so that $\boldsymbol{K}\boldsymbol{q}_t = \boldsymbol{k}_1 + \boldsymbol{k}_2 t$. When $\boldsymbol{k}_2$ is unrestricted, there will be a quadratic trend in the levels of the variables in (8.17), so to ensure only a linear trend, we must force t to enter the cointegration space: i.e. $\boldsymbol{k}_2 = \boldsymbol{\alpha}\boldsymbol{\varphi}$ say, where $\boldsymbol{\varphi}$ is $r \times 1$. Then (8.17) becomes:

$$\Delta \boldsymbol{x}_t = \boldsymbol{A}_1^* \Delta \boldsymbol{x}_{t-1} + \boldsymbol{\alpha}\left(\boldsymbol{\beta}'\boldsymbol{x}_{t-1} + \boldsymbol{\varphi}t\right) + \boldsymbol{k}_1 + \boldsymbol{\nu}_t. \qquad (8.18)$$

There is at most a linear trend in levels in (8.18). A similar treatment could be given to the intercept, and would force driftless processes on any variables which did not cointegrate: this might be acceptable for interest rates, but not for say GNP (see §8.8.2).

8.5 Open linear systems

8.5.1 Conditional systems

Let $\boldsymbol{x}_t' = (\boldsymbol{y}_t' : \boldsymbol{z}_t')$ where $\boldsymbol{y}_t$ and $\boldsymbol{z}_t$ are $n_1 \times 1$ and $n_2 \times 1$ vectors of endogenous and non-modelled variables respectively with $n_1 + n_2 = n$. Partition $\boldsymbol{\lambda}' = (\boldsymbol{\lambda}_1' : \boldsymbol{\lambda}_2')$ in (8.3) conformably with $(\boldsymbol{y}_t' : \boldsymbol{z}_t')$ and factorize the joint sequential density (conditional on $\boldsymbol{q}_t$) as:

$$\mathsf{D_x}\left(\boldsymbol{x}_t \mid \boldsymbol{X}_{t-1}^{t-s}, \boldsymbol{q}_t, \boldsymbol{\lambda}\right) = \mathsf{D_{y|z}}\left(\boldsymbol{y}_t \mid \boldsymbol{z}_t, \boldsymbol{X}_{t-1}^{t-s}, \boldsymbol{q}_t, \boldsymbol{\lambda}_1\right) \mathsf{D_z}\left(\boldsymbol{z}_t \mid \boldsymbol{X}_{t-1}^{t-s}, \boldsymbol{q}_t, \boldsymbol{\lambda}_2\right). \quad (8.19)$$

The validity of conditioning depends on the weak exogeneity of $(\boldsymbol{z}_t : \boldsymbol{q}_t)$ for the parameters of interest $\boldsymbol{\psi}$ in (8.19), so as discussed in Chapter 5, we need (i) $\boldsymbol{\psi} = \boldsymbol{f}(\boldsymbol{\lambda}_1)$ alone and (ii) $\Lambda = \Lambda_1 \times \Lambda_2$ where $\boldsymbol{\lambda}_1 \in \Lambda_1$ and $\boldsymbol{\lambda}_2 \in \Lambda_2$.

Keeping to linear systems conditional on $\boldsymbol{z}_t$ and $\boldsymbol{q}_t$:

$$\boldsymbol{y}_t = \boldsymbol{\Gamma}_0 \boldsymbol{z}_t + \boldsymbol{\Gamma}_1 \boldsymbol{z}_{t-1} + \cdots + \boldsymbol{\Gamma}_s \boldsymbol{z}_{t-s} + \boldsymbol{\Phi}_1 \boldsymbol{y}_{t-1} + \cdots + \boldsymbol{\Phi}_s \boldsymbol{y}_{t-s} + \boldsymbol{\Xi} \boldsymbol{q}_t + \boldsymbol{u}_t. \quad (8.20)$$

Given data up to and including time $t-1$ on $(\boldsymbol{Y}_{t-1}^0 : \boldsymbol{Z}_{t-1}^0)$ together with $(\boldsymbol{z}_t : \boldsymbol{q}_t)$ and the values of the parameters $(\boldsymbol{\Gamma}_0, \boldsymbol{\Gamma}_1 \ldots \boldsymbol{\Gamma}_s, \boldsymbol{\Phi}_1 \ldots . \boldsymbol{\Phi}_s, \boldsymbol{\Xi})$, the next value of $\boldsymbol{y}_t$ is generated by equation (8.20). When $s = 1$:

$$\boldsymbol{y}_t = \boldsymbol{\Gamma}_0 \boldsymbol{z}_t + \boldsymbol{\Gamma}_1 \boldsymbol{z}_{t-1} + \boldsymbol{\Phi}_1 \boldsymbol{y}_{t-1} + \boldsymbol{\Xi} \boldsymbol{q}_t + \boldsymbol{u}_t. \quad (8.21)$$

One lag is fully general and is the only case we need to consider: the relevant matrix algebra is sketched in Chapter A1. Let $\bar{\boldsymbol{y}}_t' = (\boldsymbol{y}_t' : \boldsymbol{y}_{t-1}' : \cdots : \boldsymbol{y}_{t-s+1}')$ and $\bar{\boldsymbol{z}}_t' = (\boldsymbol{z}_t' : \boldsymbol{z}_{t-1}' : \cdots : \boldsymbol{z}_{t-s}')$, then stack the coefficients in the second line of (8.20) in conformable $(n_1 s \times n_2(s+1))$ and $n_1 s \times n_1 s$ matrices:

$$\boldsymbol{\Gamma}^+ = \begin{pmatrix} \boldsymbol{\Gamma}_0 & \boldsymbol{\Gamma}_1 & \cdots & \boldsymbol{\Gamma}_s \\ \mathbf{0} & \mathbf{0} & \cdots & \mathbf{0} \\ \mathbf{0} & \mathbf{0} & \cdots & \mathbf{0} \\ \vdots & \vdots & \ddots & \vdots \\ \mathbf{0} & \cdots & \mathbf{0} & \mathbf{0} \end{pmatrix} \text{ and } \boldsymbol{\Phi}^+ = \begin{pmatrix} \boldsymbol{\Phi}_1 & \boldsymbol{\Phi}_2 & \cdots & \boldsymbol{\Phi}_{s-1} & \boldsymbol{\Phi}_s \\ \boldsymbol{I} & \mathbf{0} & \cdots & \mathbf{0} & \mathbf{0} \\ \mathbf{0} & \boldsymbol{I} & \cdots & \mathbf{0} & \mathbf{0} \\ \vdots & \vdots & \ddots & \vdots & \vdots \\ \mathbf{0} & \mathbf{0} & \cdots & \boldsymbol{I} & \mathbf{0} \end{pmatrix}.$$

By direct multiplication, when $\boldsymbol{\Xi} = \mathbf{0}$, it can be checked that (8.20) maps into (for $\bar{\boldsymbol{u}}_t = (\boldsymbol{u}_t' : \mathbf{0}' : \ldots : \mathbf{0}')'$):

$$\bar{\boldsymbol{y}}_t = \boldsymbol{\Gamma}^+ \bar{\boldsymbol{z}}_t + \boldsymbol{\Phi}^+ \bar{\boldsymbol{y}}_{t-1} + \bar{\boldsymbol{u}}_t,$$

where the top block delivers (8.20), augmented by identities of the form $\boldsymbol{y}_{t-j} \equiv \boldsymbol{y}_{t-j}$. In some respects the resulting notation can be awkward, so we concentrate on one lag in both typology expositions. Equally, two-equation systems will be used to illustrate the later model analyses.

8.5.2 Simultaneous equations

Interest in economics often centres on a simultaneous representation such as:

$$\boldsymbol{B}_0 \boldsymbol{y}_t + \boldsymbol{B}_1 \boldsymbol{y}_{t-1} + \cdots + \boldsymbol{B}_s \boldsymbol{y}_{t-s} = \boldsymbol{C}_0 \boldsymbol{z}_t + \boldsymbol{C}_1 \boldsymbol{z}_{t-1} + \cdots + \boldsymbol{C}_s \boldsymbol{z}_{t-s} + \boldsymbol{\Upsilon} \boldsymbol{q}_t + \boldsymbol{\epsilon}_t \quad (8.22)$$

where $\boldsymbol{B}_0$ is the $n_1 \times n_1$ matrix of coefficients of all the endogenous variables, $\boldsymbol{B}_1$ is the coefficient matrix of the one-lagged endogenous variables . . . , $\boldsymbol{C}_0$ is the $n_2 \times n_2$ matrix of the current dated non-modelled variables etc., and $\boldsymbol{\epsilon}_t \sim \mathsf{IN}_{n_1}[\mathbf{0}, \boldsymbol{\Sigma}]$. As it stands, (8.22) is a partial, or incomplete, model unless supplemented by a marginal model for the $\{\boldsymbol{z}_t\}$ process. For $s = 1$ lag:

$$\boldsymbol{B}_0 \boldsymbol{y}_t + \boldsymbol{B}_1 \boldsymbol{y}_{t-1} = \boldsymbol{C}_0 \boldsymbol{z}_t + \boldsymbol{C}_1 \boldsymbol{z}_{t-1} + \boldsymbol{\Upsilon} \boldsymbol{q}_t + \boldsymbol{\epsilon}_t. \quad (8.23)$$

The condition $|\boldsymbol{B}_0| \neq 0$ is needed to ensure that the system of equations is complete (i.e. as many independent equations as endogenous variables) and that the equations are mutually consistent, with none redundant. Sufficient restrictions on the coefficient matrices are required to ensure a unique representation. The model in (8.22) is a special case of a structural form, which claims to model the decision equations of the relevant agents: as before, the structurality of the representation is a claim that must be established.

The reduced, or solved, form expresses $\boldsymbol{y}_t$ as a function of the parameters, non-modelled variables, and lagged variables:

$$\boldsymbol{y}_t = \boldsymbol{f}\left(\boldsymbol{y}_{t-1}, \ldots, \boldsymbol{y}_{t-s}, \boldsymbol{z}_t, \boldsymbol{z}_{t-1}, \ldots, \boldsymbol{z}_{t-s}, \boldsymbol{q}_t, \boldsymbol{u}_t\right). \quad (8.24)$$

When the system is linear and $\boldsymbol{B}_0$ is non-singular, the solution to (8.22) is:

$$\begin{aligned} \boldsymbol{y}_t &= \boldsymbol{B}_0^{-1} \sum_{j=0}^{s} \boldsymbol{C}_j \boldsymbol{z}_{t-j} - \boldsymbol{B}_0^{-1} \sum_{i=1}^{s} \boldsymbol{B}_i \boldsymbol{y}_{t-i} + \boldsymbol{B}_0^{-1} \boldsymbol{\Upsilon} \boldsymbol{q}_t + \boldsymbol{B}_0^{-1} \boldsymbol{\epsilon}_t \\ &= \sum_{j=0}^{s} \boldsymbol{\Gamma}_j \boldsymbol{z}_{t-j} + \sum_{i=1}^{s} \boldsymbol{\Phi}_i \boldsymbol{y}_{t-i} + \boldsymbol{\Xi} \boldsymbol{q}_t + \boldsymbol{u}_t \end{aligned} \quad (8.25)$$

which returns us to a restricted version of the original conditional system and reveals the implicit, testable restrictions imposed by the simultaneous formulation (Monfort and Rabemananjara, 1990, analyse open stationary systems).

8.5.3 Cointegration

In practice, $\boldsymbol{y}_t$ and $\boldsymbol{z}_t$ are often I(1) and the balance of (8.23) must be checked since combinations of orders of integration for ys and zs need not be mutually consistent with the claim that $\boldsymbol{\epsilon}_t$ is I(0). For example, when $\boldsymbol{y}_t$ is I(1) and $s = 1$, the unit roots must cancel between $\{\boldsymbol{B}_0 \boldsymbol{y}_t\}$ and $\{\boldsymbol{C}_0 \boldsymbol{z}_t + \boldsymbol{C}_1 \boldsymbol{z}_{t-1} - \boldsymbol{B}_1 \boldsymbol{y}_{t-1}\}$. One possibility is when $\boldsymbol{B}_1 = -\boldsymbol{B}_0$ and $\boldsymbol{C}_1 = -\boldsymbol{C}_0$ so (8.23) holds in differences:

$$\boldsymbol{B}_0 \Delta \boldsymbol{y}_t = \boldsymbol{C}_0 \Delta \boldsymbol{z}_t + \boldsymbol{\Upsilon} \boldsymbol{q}_t + \boldsymbol{\epsilon}_t. \quad (8.26)$$

All terms are I(0) when the levels data are I(1), so balance occurs. However, the system has not been ‘differenced’: rather, the model happens to satisfy coefficient restrictions which sustain a differenced representation. In particular, its error process remains

$\mathsf{IN}_{n_1}[\mathbf{0}, \boldsymbol{\Sigma}]$ and no negative moving average has been induced as would occur when the data are differenced. This is an important practical issue and can be clarified by expressing the system in lag-operator notation as:

$$(\boldsymbol{B}_0 + \boldsymbol{B}_1 L)\,\boldsymbol{y}_t = (\boldsymbol{C}_0 + \boldsymbol{C}_1 L)\,\boldsymbol{z}_t + \boldsymbol{\Upsilon}\boldsymbol{q}_t + \boldsymbol{\epsilon}_t \tag{8.27}$$

so $(\boldsymbol{B}_0 + \boldsymbol{B}_1 L)$ and $(\boldsymbol{C}_0 + \boldsymbol{C}_1 L)$ are examples of polynomial matrices. Imposing the parameter restrictions that $\boldsymbol{B}_1 = -\boldsymbol{B}_0$ and $\boldsymbol{C}_1 = -\boldsymbol{C}_0$ yields:

$$(\boldsymbol{B}_0 - \boldsymbol{B}_0 L)\,\boldsymbol{y}_t = (\boldsymbol{C}_0 - \boldsymbol{C}_0 L)\,\boldsymbol{z}_t + \boldsymbol{\Upsilon}\boldsymbol{q}_t + \boldsymbol{\epsilon}_t,$$

or:

$$\boldsymbol{B}_0\,(1 - L)\,\boldsymbol{y}_t = \boldsymbol{C}_0\,(1 - L)\,\boldsymbol{z}_t + \boldsymbol{\Upsilon}\boldsymbol{q}_t + \boldsymbol{\epsilon}_t \tag{8.28}$$

leading to (8.26). As a consequence, the reduced form (8.21) becomes:

$$\boldsymbol{y}_t = \boldsymbol{\Gamma}_0\boldsymbol{z}_t - \boldsymbol{\Gamma}_0\boldsymbol{z}_{t-1} + \boldsymbol{y}_{t-1} + \boldsymbol{\Upsilon}\boldsymbol{q}_t + \boldsymbol{u}_t. \tag{8.29}$$

This is obviously a restrictive parameterization, and when the highest order of polynomial in time in $\boldsymbol{q}_t$ is h, then (8.29) includes a polynomial of order $h + 1$.

More generally, when $\boldsymbol{y}_t$ and $\boldsymbol{z}_t$ are I(1) and cointegrate (see Engle and Granger, 1987), then some linear combinations are I(0): we denote these by $(\boldsymbol{y}_t - \boldsymbol{\Psi}\boldsymbol{z}_t)$. Many possibilities arise depending on the dimensionality of $\boldsymbol{y}_t$ and $\boldsymbol{z}_t$ (n_1 and n_2) and the number of cointegrating relations. We assume complete cointegration for simplicity here, so the system can be written as (see Davidson and Hall, 1991):

$$\boldsymbol{B}_0\Delta\boldsymbol{y}_t = \boldsymbol{C}_0\Delta\boldsymbol{z}_t - \boldsymbol{D}_0\,(\boldsymbol{y}_{t-1} - \boldsymbol{\Psi}\boldsymbol{z}_{t-1}) + \boldsymbol{\Upsilon}\boldsymbol{q}_t + \boldsymbol{\epsilon}_t, \tag{8.30}$$

where every term is I(0), $\boldsymbol{D}_0 - \boldsymbol{B}_0 = \boldsymbol{B}_1$, and $\boldsymbol{D}_0\,\boldsymbol{\Psi} = \boldsymbol{C}_0 + \boldsymbol{C}_1$. When $\boldsymbol{D}_0$ induces a full-rank stable process, the system adjusts to the equilibrium or steady-state path $(\boldsymbol{y}^* - \boldsymbol{\Psi}\boldsymbol{z}^*) = \boldsymbol{\phi}(\boldsymbol{q})$ driven by the equilibrium correction $(\boldsymbol{y}_{t-1} - \boldsymbol{\Psi}\boldsymbol{z}_{t-1})$, so the resulting system is again an I(0) VECM. If only a subset ($< n_1$) of equations cointegrates, then these alone have 'levels equilibria' and the remaining variables have steady-state growth rates (of the form $\mathsf{E}[\Delta y_{it}] = g_i$). The behaviour of the system depends on $\boldsymbol{\Upsilon}\boldsymbol{q}_t$ as in the closed case.

We now consider why system modelling may be required and how it can be organized, then investigate the possible model forms in a system typology.

8.6 Modelling dynamic systems

General-to-specific methods have played a major role in recent econometric modelling practice. Past analyses of that approach have focused its research efficiency, and important earlier arguments for commencing from the general system include the benefits of directed research over directionless strategies; interpreting intermediate test results such that later results would not vitiate these; avoiding the *non sequitur* of having to adopt the alternative hypothesis when a test rejects; determining the baseline innovation error at the outset; and avoiding the dangers of correcting flaws in a model which was not congruent. Our concern here is with the logical and methodological basis for general-to-specific modelling from the joint density, additional to these previous reasons. In the extreme, the joint density should comprise all relevant economic variables, but a major avenue for an investigator's value added is appropriate specifications of the sets of variables necessitating joint modelling. Hendry and Doornik (1994) discuss ten inter-related reasons for commencing econometric analyses of economic time series from the joint density and we note several of their main arguments here.

8.6.1 The economy is a system

This is the most obvious reason for joint modelling, and was the basis for the advances in econometrics precipitated by Haavelmo (1944). To understand how a system functions, its components and framework both require modelling. Potentially all variables are endogenously determined by the economic mechanism and these interact in many ways. In a Walrasian general-equilibrium setting, all variables influence each other in the long run (like a water-bed, which oscillates in all directions when disturbed anywhere). It may happen that some sectors or variables can be decoupled, but that is an empirical matter which can only be decided after the event, although to make progress some such assumption may be essential at the outset. Thus, implicitly, all analyses are on reductions of the DGP due to marginalizing with respect to omitted variables.

8.6.2 To test marginalization

Should it prove desirable to check the validity of marginalization with respect to a set of variates, then their joint density must be modelled. Let $\boldsymbol{w}_t$ denote the vector of potentially irrelevant variables, then since:

$$\begin{aligned}&\mathsf{D}_{\mathsf{W,X}}\left(\boldsymbol{W}_T^1, \boldsymbol{X}_T^1 \mid \boldsymbol{W}_0, \boldsymbol{X}_0, \boldsymbol{Q}_T^1, \boldsymbol{\phi}\right)\\&= \mathsf{D}_{\mathsf{W|X}}\left(\boldsymbol{W}_T^1 \mid \boldsymbol{X}_T, \boldsymbol{W}_0, \boldsymbol{Q}_T^1, \boldsymbol{\phi}_1\right) \mathsf{D}_{\mathsf{X}}\left(\boldsymbol{X}_T^1 \mid \boldsymbol{X}_0, \boldsymbol{Q}_T^1, \boldsymbol{\phi}_2\right)\end{aligned} \tag{8.31}$$

the conditions required for a fully-efficient analysis from $\mathsf{D}_{\mathsf{X}}(\cdot)$ alone mirror those of weak exogeneity (see Engle, Hendry and Richard, 1983, and Ericsson, 1992a) namely:

$\boldsymbol{\psi}$ is a function of $\boldsymbol{\phi}_2$ alone and $(\boldsymbol{\phi}_1, \boldsymbol{\phi}_2) \in \Psi_1 \times \Psi_2$ and hence are variation free.

In such a case, $\boldsymbol{\phi}_2 = \boldsymbol{\theta}$, and there is no loss of relevant information about $\boldsymbol{\psi}$ from analysing only the marginal density. A necessary condition for the validity of such a reduction is that $\boldsymbol{W}_{t-1}^1$ does not Granger-cause $\boldsymbol{x}_t$ (see Granger, 1969, Ch.9, and Cook and Hendry, 1993). Such a condition can be tested from the joint density $\mathsf{D}_{\mathsf{W,X}}(\cdot)$.

8.6.3 Simultaneity

Simultaneity, or contemporaneous relationships between variables, is a system property and, although individual equation, or limited information, methods exist (see Ch.11), these can lose valuable information about contemporaneous interactions. The curse of dimensionality relative to data availability remains a limitation, but computational problems no longer provide an excuse for avoiding system methods (see Doornik and Hendry, 1994a).

8.6.4 To test weak exogeneity

Frequently, investigators wish to condition on a subset of stochastic variables denoted $z_t \subset x_t$, and not model the determination of z_t within the system. To test the legitimacy of weak exogeneity requires modelling z_t, then testing that the marginal density does not contain information of relevance to the parameters of interest, matching the analysis in (8.19) above. Elements of ψ (such as cointegration vectors) can occur in λ_2, which would violate weak exogeneity, and could induce serious distortions of inference in I(1) systems (see Ch.5).

8.6.5 To check identification

Identification here denotes uniqueness of the representation. Previous necessary and sufficient criteria (such as the famous rank condition in simultaneous systems developed in Koopmans, 1950a) depended on the (unknown) values of the parameters, although generic identification could be checked by using random values for parameters (which ensured that there was not 'global unidentification'). Johansen (1993) proposed an operational check on identification of parameters in linear models by linear restrictions. The restrictions are said to be identifying, and the parameters to be identified, by the restrictions. White (1984) showed that checking the rank of $(X'Z)$, when X is the regressor matrix and Z is the matrix of instruments, provided a necessary and sufficient condition in finite samples.

8.6.6 Cointegration is a system property

The rank r of π can only be determined by considering the complete vector of variables x_t which necessitates modelling the joint density either explicitly (as in Johansen, 1988) or implicitly (as in Phillips, 1991). Similarly, determining the matrix β of cointegration vectors involves a system analysis. This requirement interacts with the issue of testing weak exogeneity, since α determines whether elements of the form $\beta_i' x_{t-1}$ from the ith equation enter any other equation, thereby violating weak exogeneity for parameters of interest which include β. Tests on the structure of the α matrix can be conducted and have conventional (χ^2) distributions asymptotically providing that the cointegration rank is preserved.

8.6.7 To test cross-equation dependencies

Cross-equation dependencies might include cross-equation restrictions, cross-equation serial correlation, and so on. Any test for system mis-specification logically requires system analysis. The most important such test is probably that of over-identifying restrictions (see Koopmans, 1950a, and Hendry and Mizon, 1993, who show that this is equivalent to a test of whether the restricted model parsimoniously encompasses the VAR: see Ch.14).

8.6.8 To investigate system dynamics

The stability and convergence (or otherwise) of a system can only be assessed validly in a system context. There are interesting illustrations where an equation in a system seems to be unstable (e.g. because the coefficient on the equilibrium correction is positive), but in fact the complete system is stable due to relationships between the differenced variables. As discussed in Chapter A1, the eigenvalues μ_i of $\boldsymbol{\Phi}^+$ must lie inside the unit circle: §8.8.1 provides a two-equation illustration.

Any one of these reasons by itself is sufficient justification for commencing an econometric analysis from the joint density. Together, they constitute an overwhelming case for joint modelling, without resolving how general the starting-point must be. Data limitations preclude beginning with more than a relatively small number of variables, but the issue here is one of modelling principles, not practice. In particular, knowledge accumulation tends to be progressive rather than once-for-all crucial discoveries that permanently resolve a modelling problem by forging an empirical 'law'. Thus, the relevant question is not whether the postulated model is 'true' or 'complete' — with all the attendant philosophical difficulties we have discussed in earlier chapters — but whether useful empirical knowledge can be gleaned from an incomplete analysis. Chapter 15 follows up this analysis.

8.7 A typology of open linear dynamic systems

We now consider the typology of open linear systems. At most one lag is allowed (generalizations may change the resultant type) and deterministic factors are omitted (depending on how they enter as discussed above, no major surprises result from their inclusion). From the preceding analysis, conditioning induces a reduction in the system from an n-dimensional to an n_1-dimensional density and weak exogeneity ensures that such a reduction is without loss of information about the parameters of interest. Thus, the closed system in $\boldsymbol{x}_t$ is the most general under consideration and the open system in $\boldsymbol{y}_t$ conditional on $\boldsymbol{z}_t$ is a special case; naturally, the closed system in $\boldsymbol{y}_t$ is even more specialized and does not entail that an open system (which includes $\boldsymbol{z}_t$) is somehow more general than a closed one. Further, the imposition of a 'structure' via simultaneity also entails restrictions on the system and again is less general. These points are important in understanding the typologies below.

The conditional SGM is given by (8.32) without deterministic components:

$$\boldsymbol{y}_t = \boldsymbol{\Gamma}_0 \boldsymbol{z}_t + \boldsymbol{\Gamma}_1 \boldsymbol{z}_{t-1} + \boldsymbol{\Phi}_1 \boldsymbol{y}_{t-1} + \boldsymbol{u}_t. \tag{8.32}$$

where $\boldsymbol{u}_t \sim \mathsf{IN}_{n_1}[\mathbf{0}, \boldsymbol{\Omega}]$. We refer to (8.32) as a vector autoregressive-distributed lag system, denoted by VAD$(1,1;n_1,n_2)$ where the first two arguments show the maximum lags and the second two the dimensions of the $\boldsymbol{y}_t$ and $\boldsymbol{z}_t$ vectors; information on the detailed lags of each variable is lost. Each system is postulated as a stochastic economic model of a DGP which is unknown to the system's proprietor. When the system coincides with the DGP, then usually it will work well, and estimation and forecasting will deliver the anticipated results. The case of interest in practice is when the system does not coincide with the DGP, but is an invalid reduction of it.

Many economic models fail to specify the complete distribution of all the random variables under analysis, due to implicit exogeneity assumptions. A necessary condition for valid analysis of (8.32) is that z_t is weakly exogenous for the parameters of interest ψ. Such a requirement already precludes many possible systems since no cointegration vector relevant to (8.32) may enter the marginal process for z_t. The systems are 'reduced forms': pre-multiply by $B_0 \neq I$ to obtain the simultaneous form. This ease of transform between system types and corresponding model types is one reason why the second typology below overlaps. Nevertheless, as will be seen, models of systems raise new issues.

The distributions of estimators and tests often differ asymptotically between I(0) and I(1) processes (see Sims, Stock and Watson, 1990), so these need separate consideration as in Chapter 7. The analysis is conditional on the initial value $x_0 = (y_0 : z_0)'$ so the process is only asymptotically stationary for I(0). As can be seen from Table 8.1, the system typology is an exact analogy of the individual-equation one. The restrictions as listed are dependent on maintaining the contents of $(y_t : z_t)$: as stressed above, the VAR nests the VAD when $y_t = x_t$. We comment briefly on each system type in turn.

Table 8.1 Vector autoregressive-distributed lag system typology

Type	System[1]	Restrictions
VAD	$y_t = \Gamma_0 z_t + \Gamma_1 z_{t-1} + \Phi_1 y_{t-1} + u_t$	None
VECM	$\Delta y_t = \Gamma_0 \Delta z_t - D_0(y_{t-1} - \Psi z_{t-1}) + u_t$	None
Static system	$y_t = \Gamma_0 z_t + e_t$	$\Phi_1 = \Gamma_1 = 0$
Levels VAR	$y_t = \Phi_1 y_{t-1} + \nu_t$	$\Gamma_0 = \Gamma_1 = 0$
Differenced system	$\Delta y_t = \Gamma_0 \Delta z_t + v_t$	$\Phi_1 = I, \Gamma_1 = -\Gamma_0$
Leading indicator	$y_t = \Gamma_1 z_{t-1} + \xi_t$	$\Phi_1 = \Gamma_0 = 0$
Partial adjustment	$y_t = \Gamma_0 z_t + \Phi_1 y_{t-1} + \varepsilon_t$	$\Gamma_1 = 0$
Common factor	$y_t = \Gamma_0 z_t + w_t,$ $w_t = \Phi_1 w_{t-1} + \zeta_t$	$\Gamma_1 = -\Phi_1 \Gamma_0$
Finite distributed lag	$y_t = \Gamma_0 z_t + \Gamma_1 z_{t-1} + \eta_t$	$\Phi_1 = 0$
Dead start	$y_t = \Gamma_1 z_{t-1} + \Phi_1 y_{t-1} + \varsigma_t$	$\Gamma_0 = 0$

8.7.1 Vector equilibrium-correction system

The unrestricted VECM is isomorphic to the VAD with $D_0 \Psi = \Gamma_1 + \Gamma_0$ and $D_0 = I - \Phi_1$. We have discussed its forms and related problems in §8.5.3 above. When z_t is

[1] For simplicity, the typology is illustrated by a VAD$(1, 1; n_1, n_2)$ without deterministic elements.

weakly exogenous for ψ, then the cointegration vectors $(\boldsymbol{I}_{n_1} : -\boldsymbol{\Psi})(\boldsymbol{y}_t' : \boldsymbol{z}_t')' = \boldsymbol{\beta}_1'\boldsymbol{x}_t$ must coincide with a non-singular linear transformation of those in the VAR for $\boldsymbol{x}_t$, other than vectors entering only the marginal process.

8.7.2 Static system

Such a system might be used to investigate cointegration (see Engle and Granger, 1987, and Phillips, 1991), with $\{e_t\}$ generally being highly autocorrelated. This type recurs in the second typology as part of a triangular-system representation.

8.7.3 Vector autoregression

When the information set is restricted to $\{\boldsymbol{y}_t\}$ alone, a VAR is unlikely to provide a dominant system form. Allowing the information to be $\{\boldsymbol{x}_t\}$ often leads to a system that accurately characterizes the available data, albeit with a profligate parameterization. There are several solutions to that dilemma, including constructing parsimonious VARs (see Clements and Mizon, 1991) and imposing exact or loose prior information as in Bayesian VARs (see Doan, Litterman and Sims, 1984). A possible problem arising from including $\boldsymbol{z}_t$ is apparent parameter change in the marginal process: this is likely to occur when $\boldsymbol{z}_t$ includes policy-determined variables which are not well represented by linear autoregressions. The appropriate solution need not be to condition on variables which are difficult to model, and hope that weak exogeneity is not violated; instead, modelling the regime shifts (e.g. by dummy variables) allows tests for the absence from the conditional system of the additional variables in the marginal system, and hence evaluates an aspect of super exogeneity (see Engle and Hendry, 1993).

8.7.4 Differenced system

Estimating a system in levels entails estimating any unit roots that may be present and may require the use of Dickey and Fuller (1979) type critical values for hypothesis tests (see Sims *et al.*, 1990). Consequently, some investigators consider systems in the first differences of the original variables, thereby imposing all the unit roots and sustaining conventional inference when the levels are I(1). However, as noted above, if a subset of the levels cointegrate, then the differenced system excludes these, which may induce a negative moving-average error that reflects the loss of long-run information. Clements and Hendry (1993) find that such a loss can be important for forecasting in two-dimensional systems.

8.7.5 Leading indicator

Leading-indicator systems are discussed in, *inter alia,* Neftci (1979), Stock and Watson (1989, 1992), Diebold and Rudebusch (1991), and Artis, Bladen-Hovell, Osborn, Smith and Zhang (1993). The evidence that there exist systematic leading and lagging links that can be exploited for forecasting without econometric modelling of the relevant system is scanty (e.g. see Emerson and Hendry, 1994). Conversely, the VAD is just a generalized 'leading-indicator' system which incorporates both economic theory and empirical information.

8.7.6 Partial adjustment

The exclusion of lagged non-modelled variables can be seen in the system context to be an unwarranted restriction, dependent on the timing of measurements and the length of observation intervals. The rationale for the partial-adjustment principle is discussed in Chapter 7 and relative to a VECM does not seem sustainable. Should the lag-length restrictions on non-modelled variables be valid, commencing from the VAD$(1,1;\cdot,\cdot)$ allows them to be tested.

8.7.7 Common factor

As in individual equations, autoregressive errors impose common-factor restrictions on the dynamics and do not represent a generalization of the system. The common factor (that $\boldsymbol{\Gamma}_1 = -\boldsymbol{\Phi}_1 \boldsymbol{\Gamma}_0$) can be seen using lag-operator notation, since:

$$(\mathbf{I}_{n_1} - \boldsymbol{\Phi}_1 L)\, \mathbf{y}_t = (\boldsymbol{\Gamma}_0 + \boldsymbol{\Gamma}_1 L)\, \mathbf{z}_t + \mathbf{u}_t = (\mathbf{I}_{n_1} - \boldsymbol{\Phi}_1 L)\, \boldsymbol{\Gamma}_0 \mathbf{z}_t + \mathbf{u}_t \tag{8.33}$$

or:

$$\begin{aligned} \mathbf{y}_t &= \boldsymbol{\Gamma}_0 \mathbf{z}_t + \mathbf{w}_t \\ \mathbf{w}_t &= \boldsymbol{\Phi}_1 \mathbf{w}_{t-1} + \boldsymbol{\zeta}_t \end{aligned} \tag{8.34}$$

which holds only if the lag polynomial matrices $(\mathbf{I}_{n_1} - \boldsymbol{\Phi}_1 L)$ and $(\boldsymbol{\Gamma}_0 + \boldsymbol{\Gamma}_1 L)$ have the matrix common factor $(\mathbf{I}_{n_1} - \boldsymbol{\Phi}_1 L)$. Further, $\boldsymbol{\Phi}_1 = \mathbf{I}_{n_1}$ is the restriction for no cointegration, and hence induces a differenced representation (see e.g. Mizon, 1993b).

8.7.8 Finite distributed lag

Again, the system context suggests that the restriction of excluding all lagged endogenous information is untenable: $\mathbf{y}_{t-1}$ is almost certain to matter in time-series economics. Arguments for long lags on non-modelled variables may be based on a misconception about dynamic simulation, discussed in §8.9.4.

8.7.9 Dead start

The presence or absence of the contemporaneous value of $\mathbf{z}_t$ turns on three considerations. First, whether $\mathbf{z}_t$ is weakly exogenous for $\boldsymbol{\psi}$ in the resulting system; secondly, if so, whether the coefficient matrix $\boldsymbol{\Gamma}_0 \neq \mathbf{0}$; finally, if so whether $\boldsymbol{\Gamma}_0$ is constant over time and across regimes. A positive answer to all three points entails that the dead-start model is a reduced form and hence it may omit important information if theory testing is an objective of the analysis. Interestingly, a negative answer to the first two also precludes the possibility that dead start is a structural representation in its own right, noting that the presence or absence of $\mathbf{z}_t$ in the conditional model is irrelevant to its exogeneity status.

Much more could be written about each of the typology forms, their empirical performance, specification tests, and detailed interpretations as we did in Chapter 7. Most of the criticisms of each type as a single-equation model carry over to the system context when that type does not coincide with the DGP. Some of these issues will arise in the typology concerned with alternative model representations of linear systems.

8.7.10 An empirical illustration

We conclude this section with an empirical illustration, jointly modelling $\log (M/PY)_t$ and $\{R_t\}$ from Chapter 6. Again, we stress the strong restrictions imposed to map to a two-dimensional system: Chapter 15 presents a less restricted VAR for the four variables $(M_t, P_t, Y_t, R_t)_t$ which are implicitly being modelled. Estimation is by OLS applied to each equation in ECM form, and the sample remains 1964(1)–1989(2):

$$\widehat{\Delta \log \left(\tfrac{M}{PY}\right)_t} = \underset{(0.006)}{-0.003} - \underset{(0.18)}{0.26}\, \Delta R_{t-1} - \underset{(0.10)}{0.28}\, \Delta \log \left(\tfrac{M}{PY}\right)_{t-1} - \underset{(0.016)}{0.097} \log \left(\tfrac{M}{PY}\right)_{t-1} - \underset{(0.10)}{0.66}\, R_{t-1}. \tag{8.35}$$

$$\widehat{\Delta R_t} = \underset{(0.004)}{-0.008} + \underset{(0.11)}{0.22}\, \Delta R_{t-1} - \underset{(0.063)}{0.004}\, \Delta \log \left(\tfrac{M}{PY}\right)_{t-1} - \underset{(0.010)}{0.0005} \log \left(\tfrac{M}{PY}\right)_{t-1} - \underset{(0.063)}{0.088}\, R_{t-1}. \tag{8.36}$$

Table 8.2 records some summary statistics for each equation and the system.

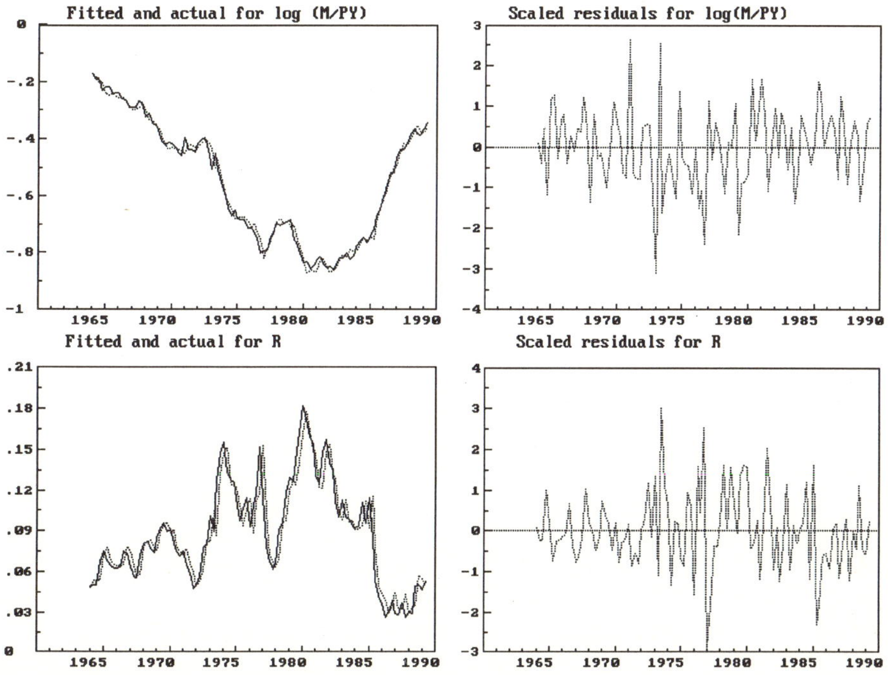

Fig. 8.1 Fitted and actual values and residuals

Table 8.2 Summary statistics for the VAR

equation	$\hat{\sigma}$	R	$\log\|\hat{\Omega}\|$	R^2	r
$\log(M/PY)$	2.2%	0.61	–	–	–
R	1.4%	0.29	–	–	–
system	–	–	−16.6	0.50	−0.48

In Table 8.2, $\hat{\sigma}$ denotes the residual standard deviation of each equation, R is the correlation between fitted and actual values, the system R^2 is one of several possible measures (see Doornik and Hendry, 1994a) and r is the contemporaneous correlation between the residuals on the two equations. There is no evidence of vector residual serial correlation of up to fifth order ($F(20, 172) = 0.71$) or non-normality ($\chi^2(4) = 6.3$) but some evidence of heteroscedasticity ($F(24, 250) = 1.6$). The coefficients in the $\log(M/PY)$ equation are well determined, but few are significant in the R equation. Figure 8.1 shows the fitted and actual values and the residuals, whereas Fig. 8.2 records the residual correlograms and densities.

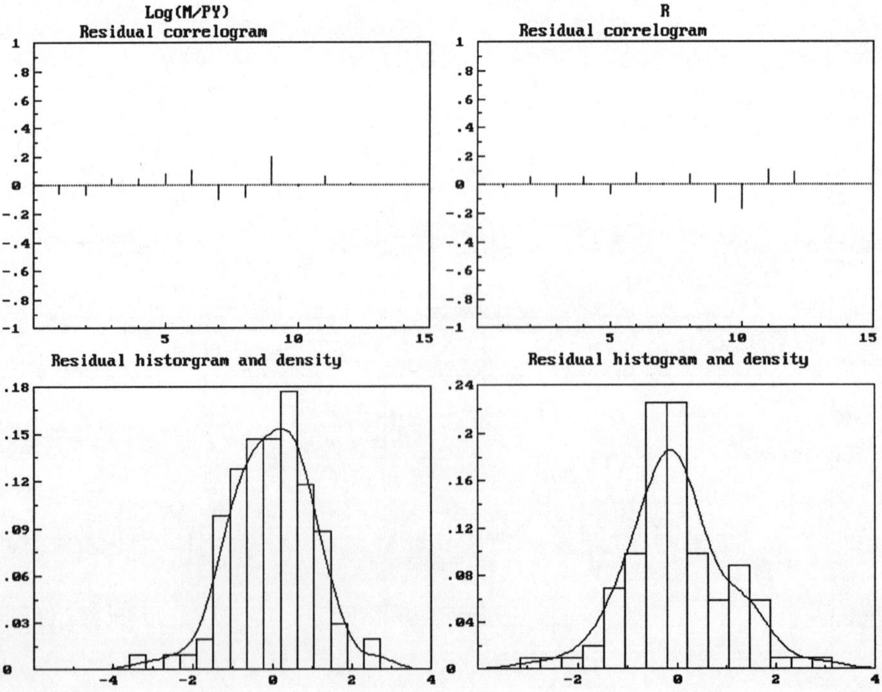

Fig. 8.2 Residual correlograms and densities

Turning to the dynamic analysis of the system, the long-run matrix π is:

$$\pi = \begin{pmatrix} -0.097 & -0.66 \\ -0.001 & -0.088 \end{pmatrix}.$$

The matrix π has two real eigenvalues with modulus 0.12 and 0.07, neither of which is very far from zero. Nevertheless, the procedure proposed by Johansen (1988) (explained in Ch.11) detects one cointegrating vector $\beta' x$ given by:

$$\log\left(\frac{M}{PY}\right) = -7.73R + 0.11,$$

with the corresponding α' vector of $(-0.087 : 0.008)$. Figure 8.3 shows the time series for the computed cointegration vector.

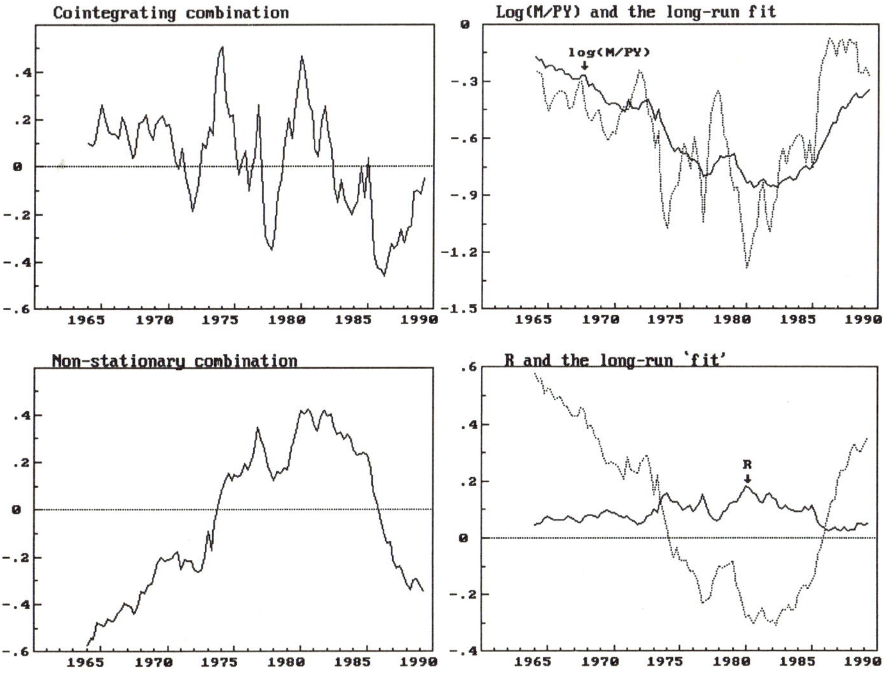

Fig. 8.3 Cointegrating vector time series

Testing the relevance of the cointegrating vector in the R equation and imposing $\text{rank}(\pi) = 1$ produces a test statistic of $\chi^2(1) = 1.62$, which is insignificant and so does not reject the weak exogeneity of R for the (long-run) parameters of the $\log(M/PY)$ equation. The restricted cointegrating vector is barely altered:

$$\log\left(\frac{M}{PY}\right) = -7.54R + 0.09,$$

with $\alpha' = (-0.097 : 0)$. When these relations are imposed and the resulting system re-estimated, we obtain:

$$\begin{aligned}\widehat{\Delta \log \left(\tfrac{M}{PY}\right)_t} = \; & \underset{(0.003)}{0.008} - \underset{(0.18)}{0.28}\, \Delta R_{t-1} - \underset{(0.10)}{0.29}\, \Delta \log \left(\tfrac{M}{PY}\right)_{t-1} \\ & - \underset{(0.013)}{0.089} \left(\log \left(\tfrac{M}{PY}\right) + 7.54 R\right)_{t-1}.\end{aligned} \tag{8.37}$$

$$\begin{aligned}\widehat{\Delta R_t} = \; & \underset{(0.002)}{0.001} + \underset{(0.11)}{0.24}\, \Delta R_{t-1} + \underset{(0.064)}{0.003}\, \Delta \log (M/PY)_{t-1} \\ & - \underset{(0.008)}{0.010} \left(\log \left(\tfrac{M}{PY}\right) + 7.54 R\right)_{t-1}.\end{aligned} \tag{8.38}$$

The values of $\hat{\sigma}$ are essentially unaltered.

Finally, Fig. 8.4 reports the outcomes from recursive estimation of the dynamic system.

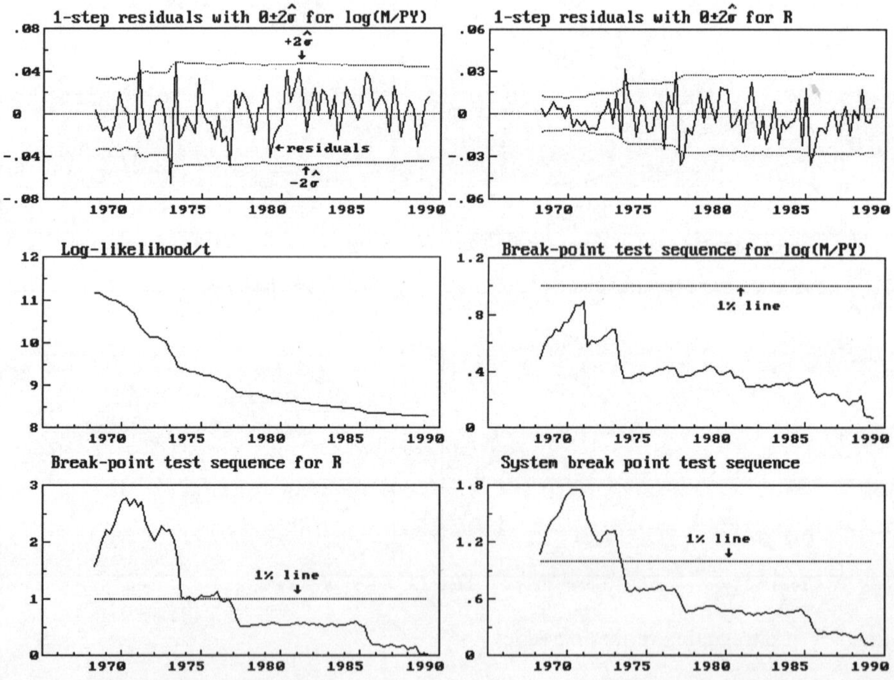

Fig. 8.4 Recursive outcomes

As can be seen, the first equation is constant whereas that for R is not, as Fig. 8.4b shows a considerable increase in residual variance over the sample. The use of $\log R$ helps correct that problem but induces a non-linear system, and so is beyond the scope of the present analysis.

8.8 Models of linear systems

Reconsider the formulation of the I(0) VAR in (8.9) when $s = 1$ written as:

$$\boldsymbol{x}_t = \boldsymbol{A}\boldsymbol{x}_{t-1} + \boldsymbol{K}\boldsymbol{q}_t + \boldsymbol{\nu}_t \text{ where } \boldsymbol{\nu}_t \sim \mathsf{IN}_n[\boldsymbol{0}, \boldsymbol{\Omega}]. \tag{8.39}$$

There are a number of different models of this basic VAR, including equilibrium-correction models, open and closed simultaneous systems, conditional models, causal chains, block-recursive models and triangular representations. These alternatives are generated by the operations of conditioning and M- and P-transforms. Whereas members of the system typology were not equivalent to each other, many model types are isomorphic in a world of constant parameters. In each case, we will note the number of parameters and hence whether restrictions are or are not being imposed.

A two-equation maquette will illustrate each type. Although the equations in each model form could be any type from the single-equation typology, we focus on unrestricted VAD$(1, 1; \cdot, \cdot)$ forms. The basic system is when $n = 2$ and there is only one deterministic component, namely an intercept, so that (8.39) can be expressed as:

$$\boldsymbol{x}_t = \boldsymbol{A}\boldsymbol{x}_{t-1} + \boldsymbol{k} + \boldsymbol{\nu}_t,$$

or:

$$\begin{pmatrix} x_{1t} \\ x_{2t} \end{pmatrix} = \begin{pmatrix} a_{11} & a_{12} \\ a_{21} & a_{22} \end{pmatrix} \begin{pmatrix} x_{1t-1} \\ x_{2t-1} \end{pmatrix} + \begin{pmatrix} k_1 \\ k_2 \end{pmatrix} + \begin{pmatrix} \nu_{1t} \\ \nu_{2t} \end{pmatrix} \tag{8.40}$$

where:

$$\begin{pmatrix} \nu_{1t} \\ \nu_{2t} \end{pmatrix} \sim \mathsf{IN}_2 \left[\begin{pmatrix} 0 \\ 0 \end{pmatrix}, \begin{pmatrix} \omega_{11} & \omega_{12} \\ \omega_{12} & \omega_{22} \end{pmatrix} \right]. \tag{8.41}$$

There are nine parameters in (8.40) and (8.41) $(a_{11}, a_{12}, a_{21}, a_{22}; k_1, k_2; \omega_{11}, \omega_{12}, \omega_{22})$, and these are assumed to be variation free. The parameter values differ across the model types, but all parameter spaces are subspaces of $\mathbb{R}^9$, with $\omega_{11} > 0$, $\omega_{22} > 0$ and $\omega_{12}^2 < \omega_{11}\omega_{22}$. The values taken by $(a_{11}, a_{12}, a_{21}, a_{22})$ determine whether the system is I(1) or I(0). We now consider each type in turn.

8.8.1 Vector autoregressive representation

Under the present assumptions, both (8.39) and the specialization in (8.40) are first-order VARs. There is no conditioning, $\boldsymbol{M} = \boldsymbol{I}$ and $\boldsymbol{P} = \boldsymbol{I}$. The system is stationary when the latent roots μ_i of $\boldsymbol{A}$ are within the unit circle (subject to appropriate initial condition distributions), given by solving $|\mu \boldsymbol{I} - \boldsymbol{A}| = 0$ or:

$$\begin{vmatrix} \mu - a_{11} & -a_{12} \\ -a_{21} & \mu - a_{22} \end{vmatrix} = (\mu - a_{11})(\mu - a_{22}) - a_{12}a_{21} = \mu^2 - tr(\boldsymbol{A})\mu + |\boldsymbol{A}| = 0.$$

This yields the quadratic equation $\mu^2 - (a_{11} + a_{22})\mu + (a_{11}a_{22} - a_{12}a_{21}) = 0$ with roots:

$$\frac{(a_{11} + a_{22}) \pm \sqrt{\left[(a_{11} + a_{22})^2 - 4(a_{11}a_{22} - a_{12}a_{21})\right]}}{2}.$$

When either a_{12} or a_{21} is zero, the roots are simply a_{11} and a_{22}, so for stationarity we require $|a_{11}| < 1$ and $|a_{22}| < 1$. The condition $a_{21} = 0$ entails that x_1 does not Granger-cause x_2 (vice versa for $a_{12} = 0$: see Granger, 1969). More generally, when the latent roots of $\boldsymbol{A}$ lie within the unit circle, the matrix $(\boldsymbol{I} - \boldsymbol{A})$ is non-singular, so on average:

$$\mathsf{E}[\boldsymbol{x}_t] = (\boldsymbol{I}_n - \boldsymbol{A})^{-1}\boldsymbol{k}. \tag{8.42}$$

Thus, a stationary VAR converges on a unique equilibrium point, or steady-state growth path if a linear deterministic trend is allowed. To consider non-stationarity, we turn to the next member of the typology.

8.8.2 Vector equilibrium correction

Re-express (8.40) in a vector equilibrium-correction form as ($\boldsymbol{M} = \boldsymbol{I}$ but $\boldsymbol{P}$ differs from a unit matrix by $-\boldsymbol{I}$ as its top-right block):

$$\begin{pmatrix} \Delta x_{1t} \\ \Delta x_{2t} \end{pmatrix} = \begin{pmatrix} a_{11}-1 & a_{12} \\ a_{21} & a_{22}-1 \end{pmatrix} \begin{pmatrix} x_{1t-1} \\ x_{2t-1} \end{pmatrix} + \begin{pmatrix} k_1 \\ k_2 \end{pmatrix} + \begin{pmatrix} \nu_{1t} \\ \nu_{2t} \end{pmatrix} \tag{8.43}$$

which is a special case of (8.13) where $\boldsymbol{\pi} = (\boldsymbol{A} - \boldsymbol{I}_n)$. Thus, rank$(\boldsymbol{\pi}) = 2$ is necessary for stationarity and matches (8.42). When $a_{11} \neq 1$ and $a_{21} \neq 0$ (assumptions made for convenience of normalization), (8.43) can be written as:

$$\begin{pmatrix} \Delta x_{1t} \\ \Delta x_{2t} \end{pmatrix} = \begin{pmatrix} (a_{11}-1)(x_{1t-1} - \kappa_1 x_{2t-1}) \\ a_{21}(x_{1t-1} - \kappa_2 x_{2t-1}) \end{pmatrix} + \begin{pmatrix} k_1 \\ k_2 \end{pmatrix} + \begin{pmatrix} \nu_{1t} \\ \nu_{2t} \end{pmatrix} \tag{8.44}$$

where $\kappa_1 = a_{12}/(1 - a_{11})$ and $\kappa_2 = (1 - a_{22})/a_{21}$. This is the equilibrium-correction form, and with nine unrestricted parameters, remains isomorphic to (8.40) (other than the non-zero requirements for normalizing). The static equilibrium, defined by taking unconditional expectations, yields two equations linking x_1 and x_2 inducing a point as the solution as in (8.42).

When $\kappa_1 = \kappa_2$, weak exogeneity of either regressor for the parameters of interest of the other equation is violated, and the system becomes I(1) since rank$(\boldsymbol{\pi}) = 1$ (see Boswijk, 1992, and Johansen, 1992c). Explicitly:

$$\begin{pmatrix} \Delta x_{1t} \\ \Delta x_{2t} \end{pmatrix} = \begin{pmatrix} (a_{11}-1) \\ a_{21} \end{pmatrix} (x_{1t-1} - \kappa x_{2t-1}) + \begin{pmatrix} k_1 \\ k_2 \end{pmatrix} + \begin{pmatrix} \nu_{1t} \\ \nu_{2t} \end{pmatrix}, \tag{8.45}$$

and letting $g_i = \mathsf{E}[\Delta x_{it}]$, the long-run solution is the relation:

$$\mathsf{E}[x_{1t} - \kappa x_{2t}] = \frac{(g_1 - k_1)}{(a_{11} - 1)} = \frac{(g_2 - k_2)}{a_{21}} = \delta. \tag{8.46}$$

By differencing, (8.46) also entails that $\mathsf{E}[\Delta x_{1t}] = \kappa \mathsf{E}[\Delta x_{2t}]$, so $g_1 = \kappa g_2$ and hence x_{2t} grows at the rate:

$$g_2 = \frac{a_{21}k_1 - (a_{11}-1)k_2}{\kappa a_{21} - (a_{11}-1)}, \tag{8.47}$$

with x_{1t} growing at κ times this rate. Thus, the I(1) solution set is a line, rather than the point that results for I(0). However, (8.44) also becomes I(1) under other restrictions which do not violate weak exogeneity (such as when $a_{22} = 1$ and $a_{21} = 0$), so the presence or absence of weak exogeneity conditions is not tied to the degree of integration. Finally, from (8.47) and (8.46):

$$\delta = \frac{k_1 - \kappa k_2}{(a_{11} - 1) - \kappa a_{21}},$$

which is proportional to the cointegrating combination of the intercepts.

In (8.46), when $k_1 = (a_{11} - 1)\varphi$ and $k_2 = a_{21}\varphi$ then $g_2 = 0$ from (8.47) and (8.45) is:

$$\begin{pmatrix} \Delta x_{1t} \\ \Delta x_{2t} \end{pmatrix} = \begin{pmatrix} (a_{11} - 1) \\ a_{21} \end{pmatrix} (x_{1t-1} - \kappa x_{2t-1} + \varphi) + \begin{pmatrix} \nu_{1t} \\ \nu_{2t} \end{pmatrix}.$$

Thus, the system exhibits no growth when the intercept vector lies in the cointegration space: as noted above, such a restriction might hold for variables like interest rates or the acceleration of the price level ($\Delta^2 p_t$), but seems unlikely for real flow magnitudes like income.

In general, letting $\boldsymbol{\pi} = \boldsymbol{\alpha\beta}'$ where $\boldsymbol{\alpha}$ and $\boldsymbol{\beta}$ are $n \times r$ matrices of rank $r < n$, the general VECM was noted above as:

$$\Delta \boldsymbol{x}_t = \sum_{j=1}^{s-1} \boldsymbol{A}_j^* \Delta \boldsymbol{x}_{t-j} + \boldsymbol{\alpha} \left(\boldsymbol{\beta}' \boldsymbol{x}_{t-1}\right) + \boldsymbol{K} \boldsymbol{q}_t + \boldsymbol{\nu}_t. \tag{8.48}$$

This model form is in I(0) space when correctly formulated, so inference about the parameters can be conducted using conventional procedures. Identification restrictions must be imposed on $\boldsymbol{\beta}$ to ensure uniqueness of $\boldsymbol{\alpha}$ and $\boldsymbol{\beta}$. The parameterization in terms of short-run dynamics and long-run disequilibria is closer to orthogonality than in (8.39), but the innovation process is unaltered. Restricting $\boldsymbol{K}\boldsymbol{q}_t$ to lie in the cointegration space by $\boldsymbol{K} = \boldsymbol{\alpha}\boldsymbol{\varphi}$ when $q_t = 1$ (an intercept) yields an ECM of $\boldsymbol{\alpha} \left(\boldsymbol{\beta}' \boldsymbol{x}_{t-1} + \boldsymbol{\varphi}\right)$ so has zero long-run growth, as seen for the two-equation illustration.

8.8.3 Simultaneous-equations model

Haavelmo (1943) described how to estimate this representation, which is often adopted to capture the structure of economic agents' decision rules. A non-diagonal $n \times n$ matrix $\boldsymbol{B}_0$ pre-multiplies $\Delta \boldsymbol{x}_t$ to allow contemporaneous connections between the variables. Since the system remains isomorphic for all non-singular matrices, normalization and identification requirements must be imposed on the model to ensure a unique representation. Here, identification involves all three attributes of uniqueness, interpretability given the prior theory, and correspondence to the agents' decision rules. The first can be imposed by arbitrary restrictions (perhaps suggested by theory) but is then unlikely to correspond to autonomous relations. This problem led Sims (1980) to suggest that such restrictions were 'incredible', but Hendry and Mizon (1993) argue that his critique lacks force, since even the VAR is a model and there are almost bound to be valid restrictions between elements of the $\{\boldsymbol{A}_i\}$: cointegration restrictions are one possible example. More usefully, the first-order VAR is defined by:

$$\mathsf{E}\left[\boldsymbol{x}_t \mid \boldsymbol{x}_{t-1}\right] = \boldsymbol{A}\boldsymbol{x}_{t-1} + \boldsymbol{k} \tag{8.49}$$

and we construe modelling as attempting to represent this conditional expectation more parsimoniously (see Clements and Mizon, 1991). One possibility, among many others, is that $\boldsymbol{A} = -\boldsymbol{B}^{-1}\boldsymbol{C}$ say, where $\{\boldsymbol{B}, \boldsymbol{C}\}$ are sparse matrices. In the two-equation I(0) case, consider:

$$\begin{pmatrix} 1 & b_{12} \\ 0 & 1 \end{pmatrix} \begin{pmatrix} \Delta x_{1t} \\ \Delta x_{2t} \end{pmatrix} = \begin{pmatrix} c_{11} & 0 \\ c_{21} & c_{22} \end{pmatrix} \begin{pmatrix} x_{1t-1} \\ x_{2t-1} \end{pmatrix} + \begin{pmatrix} k_1^* \\ k_2^* \end{pmatrix} + \begin{pmatrix} \nu_{1t} \\ \nu_{2t} \end{pmatrix}. \tag{8.50}$$

This model is one just-identified representation of (8.9) but may be more interpretable. Under stationarity, it is observationally equivalent to the VAR, but it may be valid to impose (say) $c_{21} = 0$. For an I(1) system mapped to I(0), an interesting possibility is:

$$\begin{pmatrix} 1 & b_{12} \\ 0 & 1 \end{pmatrix} \begin{pmatrix} \Delta x_{1t} \\ \Delta x_{2t} \end{pmatrix} = \begin{pmatrix} c_{11}^* \\ c_{22}^* \end{pmatrix} (x_{1t-1} - \kappa x_{2t-1}) + \begin{pmatrix} k_1^* \\ k_2^* \end{pmatrix} + \begin{pmatrix} \nu_{1t} \\ \nu_{2t} \end{pmatrix}. \tag{8.51}$$

However, this 'triangular' system is unidentified without further restrictions (it has nine parameters for a cointegrated representation with only eight), and e.g. $c_{11}^* = 0$ corresponds to (8.50) when $\boldsymbol{x}_t$ is I(1).

The general simultaneous-equations form is:

$$\boldsymbol{B}_0 \Delta \boldsymbol{x}_t = \sum_{j=1}^{s-1} \boldsymbol{B}_j \Delta \boldsymbol{x}_{t-j} + \boldsymbol{\alpha}^* \left(\boldsymbol{\beta}' \boldsymbol{x}_{t-1}\right) + \boldsymbol{K}^* \boldsymbol{q}_t + \boldsymbol{v}_t \quad \text{where} \quad \boldsymbol{v}_t \sim \mathsf{IN}_n\left[\boldsymbol{0}, \boldsymbol{\Sigma}\right]. \tag{8.52}$$

Notice that $\boldsymbol{\beta}$ is unaffected by the switch of model form, and is an invariant of the transformation, but that all other parameters are transformed, including $\boldsymbol{\alpha}^*$. Such a formulation can be more interpretable than (8.48) yet use fewer parameters, allowing tests of over-identifying restrictions by checking whether (8.52) parsimoniously encompasses (8.48) (see Hendry and Richard, 1989, and Hendry and Mizon, 1993).

8.8.4 Conditional model

A conditional model corresponds to the special case (taking x_{2t} as the conditioning variable from the two-equation VAR):

$$\begin{pmatrix} 1 & c \\ 0 & 1 \end{pmatrix} \begin{pmatrix} x_{1t} \\ x_{2t} \end{pmatrix} = \begin{pmatrix} d_{11} & d_{12} \\ d_{21} & d_{22} \end{pmatrix} \begin{pmatrix} x_{1t-1} \\ x_{2t-1} \end{pmatrix} + \begin{pmatrix} k_1^0 \\ k_2^0 \end{pmatrix} + \begin{pmatrix} \epsilon_{1t} \\ \epsilon_{2t} \end{pmatrix} \tag{8.53}$$

where:

$$\begin{pmatrix} \epsilon_{1t} \\ \epsilon_{2t} \end{pmatrix} \sim \mathsf{IN}_2\left[\begin{pmatrix} 0 \\ 0 \end{pmatrix}, \begin{pmatrix} \sigma_{11} & 0 \\ 0 & \omega_{22} \end{pmatrix}\right]. \tag{8.54}$$

There are still nine parameters, so an isomorphic representation again results prior to imposing further restrictions. When the system is a cointegrated VAR, we have:

$$\begin{pmatrix} 1 & c \\ 0 & 1 \end{pmatrix}\begin{pmatrix} \Delta x_{1t} \\ \Delta x_{2t} \end{pmatrix} = \begin{pmatrix} \alpha_{11}^0 \\ \alpha_{21}^0 \end{pmatrix}(x_{1t-1} - \kappa x_{2t-1}) + \begin{pmatrix} k_1^0 \\ k_2^0 \end{pmatrix} + \begin{pmatrix} \epsilon_{1t} \\ \epsilon_{2t} \end{pmatrix} \quad (8.55)$$

which is just identified (eight parameters). However, conditioning is valid only when $\alpha_{11}^0\alpha_{21}^0 = 0$, which entails a restriction that can be evaluated against the data evidence. When it is acceptable, the resulting model yields an ECM as its first equation, with the I(1) completing model of the conditioning variable being a random walk with drift.

From (8.9) conditional on z_t:

$$\Delta y_t = C_0 \Delta z_t + \sum_{j=1}^{s-1} C_j \Delta x_{t-j} + \alpha_0 (\beta' x_{t-1}) + K_0 q_t + \epsilon_{1t} \quad (8.56)$$

where $\epsilon_{1t} \sim \mathsf{IN}_{n_1}[\mathbf{0}, \Sigma_{11}]$ and Σ_{11} depends on the elements of Ω_v. As it stands, (8.56) is a partial or incomplete model, but could be supplemented by marginal models for the $\{z_t\}$ process. The validity of conditioning depends on the weak exogeneity of z_t for the parameters of interest in (8.56) as discussed above. As before, β remains an invariant of the reformulated system.

8.8.5 Conditional simultaneous model

It is not possible to represent this case in a two-equation typology, since this model combines the two preceding types in the form:

$$B_0 \Delta y_t = G_0 \Delta z_t + \sum_{j=1}^{s-1} G_j \Delta x_{t-j} + \alpha_0^* (\beta' x_{t-1}) + K_0^* q_t + \epsilon_{1t}^* \quad (8.57)$$

where $\epsilon_{1t}^* \sim \mathsf{IN}_{n_1}[\mathbf{0}, \Sigma_{11}^*]$. The simultaneity is between elements of Δy_t, and the conditioning is on elements of Δz_t, so a three-variable system is the smallest that can manifest both characteristics. The generic 'structural simultaneous system' is usually written in the form of (8.57). Often (8.56) is referred to as the reduced form of (8.57). Sometimes, models such as (8.57) have been postulated a priori without checking the validity of the entailed reductions from the joint sequential density, then tested against their own derived reduced form, when the latter may not be congruent. Such an approach seems unlikely to deliver useful representations of the economy. It is, of course, proceeding from simple to general and either relies on an initial correct specification, or on a sequential testing process that hopes to uncover a congruent specification *en route*.

8.8.6 Causal chain

Wold and Juréen (1953) placed considerable emphasis on this representation which they argued was closer to the autonomous decision rules of economic agents than the simultaneous system of Haavelmo (1943). They proved that a causal chain could always be developed, but did not show that the resulting model embodied the underlying structure. Indeed, since their proof also applies to arbitrary orderings of equations, some other criterion must be used to select between the resulting isomorphic forms. In the two-equation, I(0) illustration, one possible causal chain is:

$$\begin{pmatrix} 1 & 0 \\ h & 1 \end{pmatrix}\begin{pmatrix} x_{1t} \\ x_{2t} \end{pmatrix} = \begin{pmatrix} \tau_{11} & \tau_{12} \\ \tau_{21} & \tau_{22} \end{pmatrix}\begin{pmatrix} x_{1t-1} \\ x_{2t-1} \end{pmatrix} + \begin{pmatrix} k_1^\star \\ k_2^\star \end{pmatrix} + \begin{pmatrix} \eta_{1t} \\ \eta_{2t} \end{pmatrix} \tag{8.58}$$

where:

$$\begin{pmatrix} \eta_{1t} \\ \eta_{2t} \end{pmatrix} \sim \mathsf{IN}_2\left[\begin{pmatrix} 0 \\ 0 \end{pmatrix}, \begin{pmatrix} \omega_{11} & 0 \\ 0 & \omega_{22} \end{pmatrix}\right]. \tag{8.59}$$

As before, there remain nine parameters, although some of the $\{\tau_{ij}\}$ could be restricted. In the I(1) system with cointegration:

$$\begin{pmatrix} 1 & 0 \\ h & 1 \end{pmatrix}\begin{pmatrix} \Delta x_{1t} \\ \Delta x_{2t} \end{pmatrix} = \begin{pmatrix} \alpha_{11}^\star \\ \alpha_{21}^\star \end{pmatrix}(x_{1t-1} - \kappa x_{2t-1}) + \begin{pmatrix} k_1^\star \\ k_2^\star \end{pmatrix} + \begin{pmatrix} \eta_{1t} \\ \eta_{2t} \end{pmatrix} \tag{8.60}$$

so no testable restrictions are imposed relative to the corresponding VAR. Weak exogeneity of the first variable for the parameters of the second equation requires $\alpha_{11}^\star = 0$.

In general, let $\boldsymbol{\Omega}^{-1} = \boldsymbol{H}\boldsymbol{H}'$ where the $\boldsymbol{H}$ matrix is upper triangular. Pre-multiply (8.9) by $\boldsymbol{H}'$:

$$\boldsymbol{H}'\boldsymbol{x}_t = \sum_{j=1}^{s} \boldsymbol{H}'\boldsymbol{A}_j\boldsymbol{x}_{t-j} + \boldsymbol{H}'\boldsymbol{K}\boldsymbol{q}_t + \boldsymbol{H}'\boldsymbol{\nu}_t \ \text{ where } \ \boldsymbol{H}'\boldsymbol{\nu}_t = \boldsymbol{\eta}_t \sim \mathsf{IN}_n\left[\mathbf{0}, \boldsymbol{I}\right]. \tag{8.61}$$

Then (8.61) provides a causal chain in that the error covariance matrix is diagonal (and normalized for simplicity) and each equation in the representation can treat contemporaneous variables as previously determined. However, none of the resulting systems need satisfy weak exogeneity of each equation's contemporaneous variables for the parameters of interest (see Engle *et al.*, 1983). If so, no equation will in fact embody structure. Implicitly, causal chains impose conditioning in a recursive order over equations.

8.8.7 Block-recursive representation

Both (8.58) and (8.53) are in fact block recursive, in that one of the (single-equation) blocks can be taken as determined prior to the other. In a larger system, subsystems could be simultaneous internally, but block recursive externally. Thus, this is an intermediate step towards a causal chain. In general (for two blocks only, to save cumbersome notation):

$$\begin{pmatrix} \boldsymbol{B}_{11} & \boldsymbol{B}_{12} \\ \mathbf{0} & \boldsymbol{B}_{22} \end{pmatrix}\begin{pmatrix} \Delta \boldsymbol{y}_t \\ \Delta \boldsymbol{z}_t \end{pmatrix} = \sum_{j=1}^{s-1} \boldsymbol{C}_j^\diamond \Delta\boldsymbol{x}_{t-j} + \boldsymbol{\alpha}_0^\diamond(\boldsymbol{\beta}'\boldsymbol{x}_{t-1}) + \boldsymbol{K}_0^\diamond\boldsymbol{q}_t + \boldsymbol{\epsilon}_t^\diamond \tag{8.62}$$

where:

$$\begin{pmatrix} \boldsymbol{\epsilon}_{1t}^\diamond \\ \boldsymbol{\epsilon}_{2t}^\diamond \end{pmatrix} \sim \mathsf{IN}_n\left[\begin{pmatrix} \mathbf{0} \\ \mathbf{0} \end{pmatrix}, \begin{pmatrix} \boldsymbol{\Sigma}_{11}^\diamond & 0 \\ 0 & \boldsymbol{\Sigma}_{22}^\diamond \end{pmatrix}\right], \tag{8.63}$$

is a possible block-recursive system, with $\Delta\boldsymbol{z}_t$ being predetermined (see Fisher, 1965).

8.8.8 Triangular representation

Phillips (1991) considers this as a basic formulation for examining long-run relations. Omitting deterministic factors, a triangular representation has the form:

$$\begin{pmatrix} x_{1t} \\ \Delta x_{2t} \end{pmatrix} = \begin{pmatrix} \beta_2' x_{2t} \\ \mathbf{0} \end{pmatrix} + \begin{pmatrix} \xi_{1t} \\ \xi_{2t} \end{pmatrix}, \tag{8.64}$$

where ξ_t is assumed to be a stationary process which satisfies suitable homogeneity and memory conditions (such as mixing). However, (8.64) only focuses on the long run and does not consider modelling the short-run dynamics as well. When $\{\xi_t\}$ has a finite autoregressive representation, as assumed for the other members of the typology above, such that $R(L)\xi_t = u_t$ where $R_0 = I$ then for $\beta' x_t = x_{1t} - \beta_2' x_{2t}$:

$$R(L)\begin{pmatrix} \beta' x_t \\ \Delta x_{2t} \end{pmatrix} = u_t \sim \mathsf{IN}_n[\mathbf{0}, \Omega_u]. \tag{8.65}$$

This expresses the system in terms of the two sets of I(0) variables, $\beta' x_t$ and Δx_{2t} and lagged values thereof, but could be re-parameterized to a VECM by rearranging lags and differences.

In the two-equation example when $R(L)\xi_t = u_t$ and there is only one lag:

$$\begin{pmatrix} x_{1t} - \kappa x_{2t} \\ \Delta x_{2t} \end{pmatrix} = \begin{pmatrix} r_{11} & 0 \\ r_{21} & 0 \end{pmatrix} \begin{pmatrix} x_{1t-1} - \kappa x_{2t-1} \\ \Delta x_{2t-1} \end{pmatrix} + \begin{pmatrix} k_1 \\ k_2 \end{pmatrix} + \begin{pmatrix} u_{1t} \\ u_{2t} \end{pmatrix}, \tag{8.66}$$

where:

$$\begin{pmatrix} u_{1t} \\ u_{2t} \end{pmatrix} \sim \mathsf{IN}_2\left[\begin{pmatrix} 0 \\ 0 \end{pmatrix}, \begin{pmatrix} \sigma_{11} & \sigma_{12} \\ \sigma_{12} & \sigma_{22} \end{pmatrix}\right]. \tag{8.67}$$

This imposes the one cointegration vector, but without additional restrictions (such as $r_{21} = 0$), the system requires joint analysis and no direction of weak exogeneity holds. (8.66) is readily seen to be a re-parameterization of (8.45).

8.8.9 Empirical illustrations

There are few distinct examplars of model types with the present bivariate system for $\log(M/PY)$ and R. However, the two illustrations that can be discussed provide some useful insights.

8.8.9.1 Vector equilibrium correction

First, we consider the restricted VECM estimates in (8.68) and (8.69):

$$\widehat{\Delta \log\left(\tfrac{M}{PY}\right)_t} = \underset{(0.003)}{0.009} - \underset{(0.09)}{0.27}\, \Delta \log\left(\tfrac{M}{PY}\right)_{t-1} - \underset{(0.01)}{0.10}\, \left(\log\left(\tfrac{M}{PY}\right) + 7.54R\right)_{t-1}. \tag{8.68}$$

$$\widehat{\Delta R_t} = \underset{(0.001)}{0.0001} + \underset{(0.09)}{0.11}\, \Delta R_{t-1}. \tag{8.69}$$

Table 8.3 Summary statistics for VECM

equation	$\hat{\sigma}$	R	$\log\lvert\hat{\Omega}\rvert$	R^2	r
$\log(M/PY)$	2.2%	0.61	–	–	–
R	1.4%	0.29	–	–	–
system	–	–	−16.5	0.50	−0.50

Table 8.3 records some summary statistics for each equation and the parsimonious system as a whole.

The goodness of fit is essentially unaltered and again there is no evidence of vector residual serial correlation of up to 5th order ($F(20, 178) = 0.87$) or non-normality ($\chi^2(4) = 6.1$), but there is some evidence of ARCH in the R equation ($F(4, 90) = 3.1$). The likelihood-ratio test of the over-identifying restrictions yields $\chi^2(3) = 4.15$, so the simplified system is acceptable. Figure 8.5 shows the fitted and actual values and the residuals.

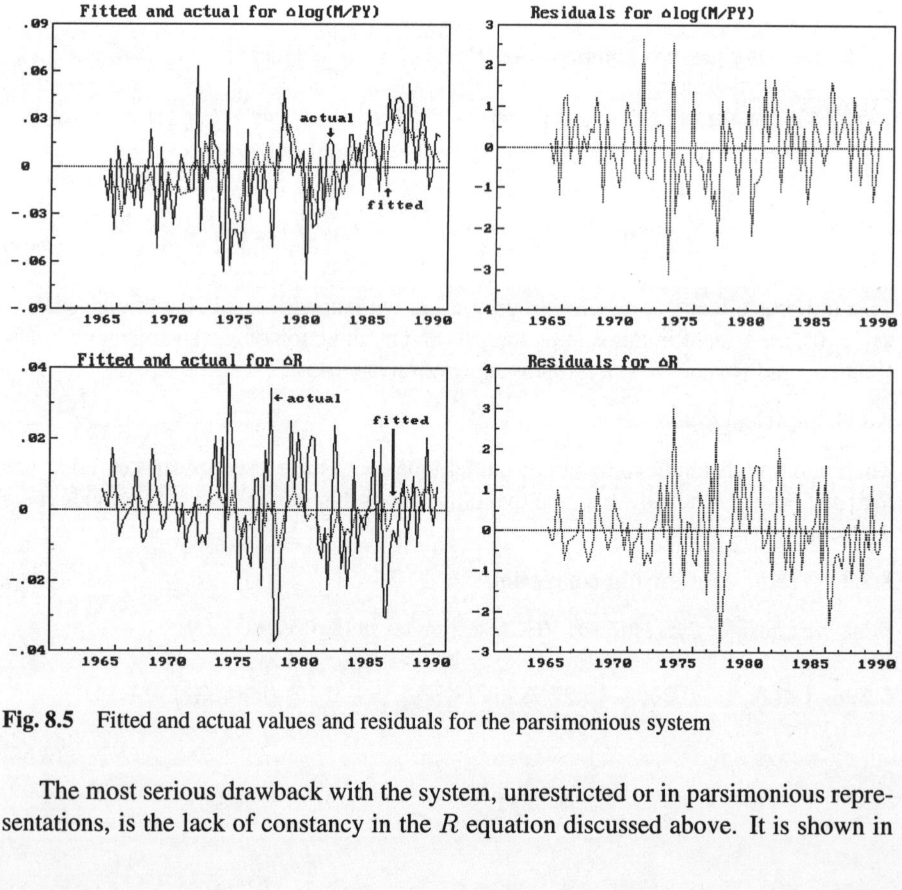

Fig. 8.5 Fitted and actual values and residuals for the parsimonious system

The most serious drawback with the system, unrestricted or in parsimonious representations, is the lack of constancy in the R equation discussed above. It is shown in

Chapter 11 that recursive estimators are as easily applied to multivariate systems as to any equation thereof, so no new difficulties arise in investigating constancy of systems or models. Conversely, it is imperative to be aware of the empirical characteristics of any proposed model or system, including its constancy or otherwise.

8.8.9.2 Simultaneous model

Since we have not yet discussed maximum likelihood estimation of simultaneous equations models of dynamic systems, the empirical results for this type are discussed in Chapter 11.

8.8.9.3 Conditional model

Finally, we consider the conditional estimates where $\log(M/PY)$ is conditioned on R, and both equations are estimated by OLS:

$$\widehat{\Delta \log \left(\frac{M}{PY}\right)_t} = \underset{(0.002)}{0.009} - \underset{(0.14)}{0.81}\, \Delta R_t - \underset{(0.09)}{0.28}\, \Delta \log \left(\frac{M}{PY}\right)_{t-1} - \underset{(0.012)}{0.099} \left(\log \left(\frac{M}{PY}\right) + 7.54R\right)_{t-1}. \tag{8.70}$$

$$\widehat{\Delta R_t} = \underset{(0.10)}{0.18}\, \Delta R_{t-1}. \tag{8.71}$$

The estimates are close to those of the $\log(M/PY)$ equation reported in Chapter 7. Table 8.4 records the summary statistics for each equation.

Table 8.4 Summary statistics for (8.70)–(8.71)

equation	$\hat{\sigma}$	R^2	$\log\lvert\hat{\Omega}\rvert$
$\log(M/PY)$	1.9%	0.52	−7.94
R	1.4%	0.03	−8.60

All of the single-equation diagnostics were acceptable, except for some evidence of ARCH in the R equation, and its lack of constancy. The insignificance of $\widehat{\Delta R_t}$ (or ΔR_{t-1}) when added to the conditional model supports the hypothesis that R can be treated as weakly exogenous for the parameters of the $\log(M/PY)$ equation, as in Chapter 7, but this is not a powerful test given the fragility of the R equation.

8.9 Analysing dynamic systems

The key element of 'choice' between the preceding representations must be which one captures the invariants of the economic mechanism, and there do not seem to be high-level considerations for any form being dominant, although some forms (such as VARs) seem more likely to be derived than autonomous. Once a form is selected as optimal given the theory and data process, the issue of how to analyse it arises. In particular, closed models entail that contemporaneous partial derivatives are hard to interpret, it being far from obvious which experiment could feasibly hold all other things constant to examine the link in question. When conditioning is valid, analysis of the conditional system is straightforward in that derivatives of the form:

$$\frac{\partial \boldsymbol{y}_t}{\partial \boldsymbol{z}'_{t-j}},$$

are well defined as shown below. Here we consider possible methods for closed systems which have non-diagonal error covariance matrices.

Write the original formulation in (8.17) in lag polynomial triangular form as in (8.65), but retaining deterministic terms, and under stationarity invert $\boldsymbol{R}(L) = \sum_{j=1}^{s} \boldsymbol{R}_j L^j$ to obtain:

$$\begin{pmatrix} \boldsymbol{\beta}' \boldsymbol{x}_t \\ \Delta \boldsymbol{x}_{2t} \end{pmatrix} = \boldsymbol{R}(L)^{-1} (\boldsymbol{K}\boldsymbol{q}_t + \boldsymbol{u}_t) = \boldsymbol{S}(L) \boldsymbol{K}\boldsymbol{q}_t + \boldsymbol{\xi}_t, \tag{8.72}$$

where $\boldsymbol{\xi}_t = \boldsymbol{S}(L) \boldsymbol{u}_t$ and $\boldsymbol{S}(L) = \boldsymbol{R}(L)^{-1}$. When $\boldsymbol{\Omega}_u$ is non-diagonal, the reformulation underlying a causal chain could be used by writing $\boldsymbol{\Omega}_u^{-1} = \boldsymbol{H}_u \boldsymbol{H}'_u$ (say) and treating each element of $\boldsymbol{w}_t = \boldsymbol{H}'_u \boldsymbol{u}_t$ as analysing 'autonomous' changes in w_{it}. This introduces conditioning indirectly, and camouflages the resulting loss of structurality should the selected ordering not coincide with that underlying the economic mechanism. In particular, although the invariance of $\boldsymbol{S}(L)$ derives from that of the parameters of the structural mechanism, they are no longer structural and changes in any element of the structure are liable to alter many elements of $\boldsymbol{S}(L)$ (see Hendry and Mizon, 1993, for further details). Valid conditional models are easier to analyse from this perspective.

The analysis of simultaneous models has also posed problems for some commentators (see e.g. Pearl, 1993, for a summary of recent debates). Granted that conditioning on contemporaneous variables is admissible, then the simultaneous system is a model of the conditional expectation of the endogenous vector given the weakly exogenous and lagged variables as discussed above. However, when the $\{x_{it}\}$ are jointly dependent, one cannot consider the first equation as being (say) $\mathsf{E}[\Delta x_{1t} | \Delta x_{2t}, \boldsymbol{x}_{t-1}]$.

Nevertheless, (8.50) for example, corresponds to the system:

$$\begin{pmatrix} \Delta x_{1t} \\ \Delta x_{2t} \end{pmatrix} = \begin{pmatrix} c_{11} - b_{12}c_{21} & -b_{12}c_{22} \\ c_{21} & c_{22} \end{pmatrix} \begin{pmatrix} x_{1t-1} \\ x_{2t-1} \end{pmatrix} + \begin{pmatrix} k_1^0 \\ k_2^0 \end{pmatrix} + \begin{pmatrix} \nu_{1t}^0 \\ \nu_{2t}^0 \end{pmatrix}. \tag{8.73}$$

There is a hidden proportionality between the two equations, most easily seen when $c_{11} = 0$. There are then nine coefficients in (8.73), whereas the simultaneous representation has eight parameters: more dramatic 'savings' result in larger systems. Further, 'simultaneity' is not invariant under linear transformations; when x_{1t}, x_{2t} represent (say) consumption and income with $b_{12} = \kappa$ then the first equation in (8.51) becomes saving, leading to the model:

$$\begin{pmatrix} \Delta (x_{1t} - \kappa x_{2t}) \\ \Delta x_{2t} \end{pmatrix} = \begin{pmatrix} c_{11}^* \\ c_{22}^* \end{pmatrix} (x_{1t-1} - \kappa x_{2t-1}) + \begin{pmatrix} k_1^* \\ k_2^* \end{pmatrix} + \begin{pmatrix} \nu_{1t} \\ \nu_{2t} \end{pmatrix}, \tag{8.74}$$

which is not simultaneous even when (8.51) is, but could be structural. Once one understands how to analyse (8.74), then (8.50) should not prove problematical by following the reverse steps.

8.9.1 Dynamic multipliers

In §8.5, we established that only $s = 1$ need be considered, and from (8.21):

$$\frac{\partial \boldsymbol{y}_t}{\partial \boldsymbol{z}_t'} = \boldsymbol{\Gamma}_0,$$

which is called an impact multiplier. However, the model also holds one period earlier, so that from (8.21) lagged:

$$\begin{aligned}\boldsymbol{y}_t &= \boldsymbol{\Gamma}_0 \boldsymbol{z}_t + \boldsymbol{\Gamma}_1 \boldsymbol{z}_{t-1} + \boldsymbol{\Phi}_1 \left(\boldsymbol{\Gamma}_0 \boldsymbol{z}_{t-1} + \boldsymbol{\Gamma}_1 \boldsymbol{z}_{t-2} + \boldsymbol{\Phi}_1 \boldsymbol{y}_{t-2} + \boldsymbol{\nu}_{t-1}\right) + \boldsymbol{\nu}_t \\ &= \boldsymbol{\Gamma}_0 \boldsymbol{z}_t + \left(\boldsymbol{\Gamma}_1 + \boldsymbol{\Phi}_1 \boldsymbol{\Gamma}_0\right) \boldsymbol{z}_{t-1} + \boldsymbol{\Phi}_1 \boldsymbol{\Gamma}_1 \boldsymbol{z}_{t-2} + \boldsymbol{\Phi}_1^2 \boldsymbol{y}_{t-2} + \boldsymbol{\nu}_t + \boldsymbol{\Phi}_1 \boldsymbol{\nu}_{t-1}.\end{aligned} \tag{8.75}$$

Thus:

$$\frac{\partial \boldsymbol{y}_t}{\partial \boldsymbol{z}_{t-1}'} = \boldsymbol{\Gamma}_1 + \boldsymbol{\Phi}_1 \boldsymbol{\Gamma}_0,$$

which is called an interim multiplier (here for one lag).

When the autoregressive component of the model is dynamically stable, $\boldsymbol{\Phi}_1^t \to \mathbf{0}$ as $t \to \infty$ so that:

$$\begin{aligned}\boldsymbol{y}_t &= \boldsymbol{\Gamma}_0 \boldsymbol{z}_t + \left(\boldsymbol{\Gamma}_1 + \boldsymbol{\Phi}_1 \boldsymbol{\Gamma}_0\right) \boldsymbol{z}_{t-1} + \boldsymbol{\Phi}_1 \boldsymbol{\Upsilon} \boldsymbol{z}_{t-2} + \cdots + \boldsymbol{\nu}_t + \boldsymbol{\Phi}_1 \boldsymbol{\nu}_{t-1} + \boldsymbol{\Phi}_1^2 \boldsymbol{\nu}_{t-2} + \cdots \\ &= \boldsymbol{\Gamma}_0 \boldsymbol{z}_t + \boldsymbol{\Upsilon} \boldsymbol{z}_{t-1} + \boldsymbol{\Phi}_1 \boldsymbol{\Upsilon} \boldsymbol{z}_{t-2} + \cdots + \sum_{i=0}^{\infty} \boldsymbol{\Phi}_1^i \boldsymbol{\nu}_{t-i} \\ &= \boldsymbol{\Gamma}_0 \boldsymbol{z}_t + \sum_{i=0}^{\infty} \boldsymbol{\Phi}_1^i \boldsymbol{\Upsilon} \boldsymbol{z}_{t-i-1} + \sum_{i=0}^{\infty} \boldsymbol{\Phi}_1^i \boldsymbol{\nu}_{t-i},\end{aligned} \tag{8.76}$$

where $\boldsymbol{\Upsilon} = \boldsymbol{\Gamma}_1 + \boldsymbol{\Phi}_1 \boldsymbol{\Gamma}_0$. The condition $\boldsymbol{\Phi}_1^t \to \mathbf{0}$ as $t \to \infty$ is needed to ensure that the effects of past shocks die out rather than cumulate explosively or persist indefinitely. Then, due to the dynamics, $\boldsymbol{y}_t$ is the cumulation of all past $\boldsymbol{z}$s and $\boldsymbol{\nu}$s with declining weights. Define a static equilibrium by $\mathsf{E}[\boldsymbol{z}_t] = \boldsymbol{z}^* \; \forall t$ when $\{\boldsymbol{z}_t\}$ is stationary. Then, taking expected values in (8.76):

$$\boldsymbol{y}^* = \boldsymbol{\Gamma}_0 \boldsymbol{z}^* + \sum_{i=0}^{\infty} \boldsymbol{\Phi}_1^i \boldsymbol{\Upsilon} \boldsymbol{z}^* = \boldsymbol{\Psi} \boldsymbol{z}^*, \text{ say.} \tag{8.77}$$

Since from (8.21):

$$\boldsymbol{y}^* = \left(\boldsymbol{\Gamma}_0 + \boldsymbol{\Gamma}_1\right) \boldsymbol{z}^* + \boldsymbol{\Phi}_1 \boldsymbol{y}^*, \tag{8.78}$$

then:

$$\boldsymbol{y}^* = \left(\boldsymbol{I} - \boldsymbol{\Phi}_1\right)^{-1} \left(\boldsymbol{\Gamma}_0 + \boldsymbol{\Gamma}_1\right) \boldsymbol{z}^* = \boldsymbol{\Psi} \boldsymbol{z}^*. \tag{8.79}$$

The expressions in (8.77) and (8.79) must be the same, and define what is called the long-run multiplier:

$$\frac{\partial \boldsymbol{y}^*}{\partial \boldsymbol{z}^{*\prime}} = \boldsymbol{\Psi}.$$

This shows the total effect of a change in $\boldsymbol{z}$ on $\boldsymbol{y}$.

Interim multipliers for the effects of past shocks on current outcomes can be calculated, treating $\boldsymbol{\nu}_t$ as an unobserved extraneous variable. When $\boldsymbol{\nu}_t$ is not in fact autonomous to the economic system, but is treated as exogenous, incorrect results will be obtained. An example of this mistake is the treatment of incomes policies as exogenous shocks when they are an endogenous response to developments in the economy. More subtle examples occur in the analyses of closed systems (i.e. with no $\boldsymbol{z}$ variables so that (8.20) becomes a VAR) which seek to attribute the effects of shocks to different endogenous variables.

8.9.2 Final forms

An alternative expression of interest from (8.21) is to express each endogenous variable as a function of lagged values of non-modelled variables and error terms. Using the lag operator L:

$$(\boldsymbol{I} - \boldsymbol{\Phi}_1 L)\, \boldsymbol{y}_t = (\boldsymbol{\Gamma}_0 + \boldsymbol{\Gamma}_1 L)\, \boldsymbol{z}_t + \boldsymbol{\nu}_t. \tag{8.80}$$

The matrix $(\boldsymbol{I} - \boldsymbol{\Phi}_1 L)$ is a polynomial matrix in the operator L and providing all of its latent roots are inside the unit circle, can be inverted using the expression:

$$(\boldsymbol{I} - \boldsymbol{\Phi}_1 L)^{-1} = \frac{1}{|\boldsymbol{I} - \boldsymbol{\Phi}_1 L|} \mathrm{Adj}\,(\boldsymbol{I} - \boldsymbol{\Phi}_1 L) = \frac{\boldsymbol{G}\,(L)}{|\boldsymbol{I} - \boldsymbol{\Phi}_1 L|} \text{ say.}$$

The determinant $|\boldsymbol{I} - \boldsymbol{\Phi}_1 L|$ is a high-order scalar polynomial in L and $\boldsymbol{G}\,(L)$ is a polynomial matrix of finite order in L. Thus:

$$\gamma\,(L)\, \boldsymbol{y}_t = \boldsymbol{G}\,(L) \left\{ (\boldsymbol{\Gamma}_0 + \boldsymbol{\Gamma}_1 L)\, \boldsymbol{z}_t + \boldsymbol{\nu}_t \right\}, \tag{8.81}$$

where $\gamma\,(L) = |\boldsymbol{I} - \boldsymbol{\Phi}_1 L|$. This is called the final form, and shows that every endogenous variable in a system obeys the same autoregressive process (subject to possible cancellation of roots in common to both sides of (8.81)), but with different, and possibly complicated, moving-average errors.

8.9.3 Non-linearity

Explicit solution as in (8.25) is not usually feasible in a non-linear model, so that system consistency is harder to check and systems have to be solved numerically:

$$\boldsymbol{f}\left(\hat{\boldsymbol{y}}_t \mid \boldsymbol{y}_{t-1}, \boldsymbol{z}_t, \boldsymbol{z}_{t-1}; \hat{\boldsymbol{\theta}} \right) = \boldsymbol{0} \tag{8.82}$$

where $\hat{\boldsymbol{\theta}}$ denotes the vector of estimated parameters. There are many algorithms for doing so, but Gauss–Seidel is the most common: given

$$y_{1,t}^{i+1}, \ldots, y_{j,t}^{i+1}, y_{j+1,t}^{i}, \ldots, y_{j+n,t}^{i},$$

solve for $y_{j+1,t}^{i+1}$ and update recursively. Usually, this iterative algorithm can be made to converge by minor adaptations, and is fast in practice.

To calculate a multiplier analogue, proceed as follows, although care is needed since the numerical size of multipliers depends on the state of the system. Let one z, say z_{jt}, change by an amount δ_{jt}. Then, for an impact multiplier, using a first-order Taylor approximation:

$$\frac{\partial \boldsymbol{y}_t}{\partial z_{jt}} \simeq \frac{\boldsymbol{f}\left(\boldsymbol{y}_t \mid \boldsymbol{y}_{t-1}, \boldsymbol{z}_t + \delta_{jt}\boldsymbol{\iota}, \boldsymbol{z}_{t-1}\right) - \boldsymbol{f}\left(\cdot\right)}{\delta_{jt}}$$

where $\boldsymbol{\iota}$ is a zero vector with unity in the jth position. The procedure is: solve for $\boldsymbol{y}_t$, change or perturb $\boldsymbol{z}_t$, solve again for the changed $\boldsymbol{y}_t$, and use $\Delta y_{it}/\delta_{jt}$ as the multiplier. In practice, large models seem close to linearity locally, so this method works reasonably well.

8.9.4 Dynamic simulation

$\boldsymbol{y}_t$ can be generated dynamically when the errors are set to their expectations of zero, by successively calculating ys and feeding back past generated ys as in:

$$\tilde{\boldsymbol{y}}_1 = \boldsymbol{\Gamma}_0 \boldsymbol{z}_1 + \boldsymbol{\Gamma}_1 \boldsymbol{z}_0 + \boldsymbol{\Phi}_1 \boldsymbol{y}_0,$$

so that:

$$\tilde{\boldsymbol{y}}_2 = \boldsymbol{\Gamma}_0 \boldsymbol{z}_2 + \boldsymbol{\Gamma}_1 \boldsymbol{z}_1 + \boldsymbol{\Phi}_1 \tilde{\boldsymbol{y}}_1,$$

and so on, leading to:

$$\tilde{\boldsymbol{y}}_t = \boldsymbol{\Gamma}_0 \boldsymbol{z}_t + \boldsymbol{\Gamma}_1 \boldsymbol{z}_{t-1} + \boldsymbol{\Phi}_1 \tilde{\boldsymbol{y}}_{t-1}. \tag{8.83}$$

Subtracting (8.83) from the reduced form in (8.21) (for $\boldsymbol{\Xi} = \mathbf{0}$) yields:

$$\boldsymbol{y}_t - \tilde{\boldsymbol{y}}_t = \boldsymbol{\Phi}_1 \left(\boldsymbol{y}_{t-1} - \tilde{\boldsymbol{y}}_{t-1}\right) + \boldsymbol{u}_t \quad \text{where} \quad \boldsymbol{u}_t = \boldsymbol{B}_0^{-1}\boldsymbol{\epsilon}_t. \tag{8.84}$$

For stochastic systems, $\tilde{\boldsymbol{y}}$ will differ from $\boldsymbol{y}$ (sometimes drastically, as the example later shows), and the stochastic simulation error follows the same autoregressive process as the model. Consequently:

$$\boldsymbol{y}_t - \tilde{\boldsymbol{y}}_t = \tilde{\boldsymbol{v}}_t = \sum_{i=0}^{t} \boldsymbol{\Phi}_1^i \boldsymbol{u}_{t-i}. \tag{8.85}$$

This expression shows that the $\{\tilde{\boldsymbol{v}}_t\}$ process is autocorrelated and heteroscedastic, and hence is a poor basis for inference. In particular, the correlation between $\boldsymbol{y}_t$ and $\tilde{\boldsymbol{y}}_t$ will depend on how much of the variability of $\boldsymbol{y}_t$ is explained by the $\{\boldsymbol{z}_t\}$ process: the two extreme cases are when there are no non-modelled conditioning variables (so $\boldsymbol{y}_t$ is a VAR), and the correlation tends to zero as the sample size increases, and when $\boldsymbol{\Phi}_1 = \mathbf{0}$ so the simulation track is as good as the 1-step fit. In other words, the more the explanation of $\boldsymbol{y}_t$ is attributed to the $\boldsymbol{z}_t$, the better the simulation, irrespective of the validity of that attribution (see Hendry and Richard, 1982, Chong and Hendry, 1986, and Pagan, 1989). Estimation of the parameters will exacerbate the poor fit of a dynamic simulation for a VAR.

The parsimonious dynamic system in §8.8.9 provides a convenient illustration. We estimate both closed and open systems, and Figs. 8.6a–d show the dynamic simulation performance for the money-demand equation under both assumptions, for I(1) and I(0) representations. A glance at the figures reveals the incredibly 'better' performance of the open model — but it is hardly surprising that had the complete future trajectory of interest rates been known in the 1960s, rather better forecasts of money demand would have resulted. It must be stressed that all the evidence supports the weak and strong exogeneity of R for the money demand parameters: the validity of conditioning is not at issue. Nevertheless, the operational characteristics of the system cannot be judged by the simulation performance of the open variant unless future interest rates would be known in practice, and selecting a model by its simulation behaviour is prone to this problem.

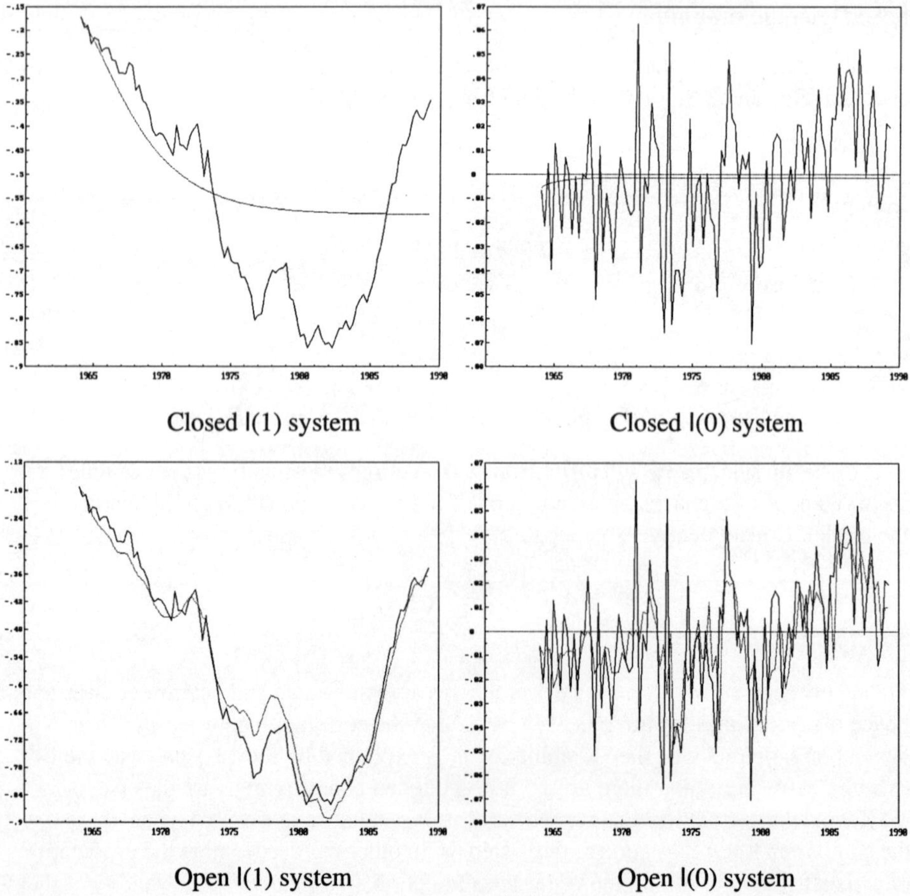

Closed I(1) system | Closed I(0) system

Open I(1) system | Open I(0) system

Fig. 8.6 Dynamic simulation of closed and open I(1) and I(0) systems

8.10 Exercises

8.1 Consider the following simple macro-model:

$$
\begin{aligned}
y_t &= \bar{y} + \epsilon_{1t} && \text{aggregate supply} \\
y_t &= \alpha\left(m_t - p_t\right) - \beta\left\{r_t - \left(\mathsf{E}_t\left[p_{t+1}\right] - p_t\right)\right\} + \epsilon_{2t} && \text{aggregate demand} \\
m_t &= \bar{m} && \text{money supply} \\
m_t &= y_t + p_t - \gamma\left(r_t - z_t\right) + \epsilon_{3t} && \text{money demand}
\end{aligned}
$$

where y is output, m is the level of money balances, p is the price level (all in logarithms), r is the nominal rate of interest, and z is the return on an alternative asset which is strongly exogenous. The disturbances ϵ_{1t}, ϵ_{2t} and ϵ_{3t} are serially independent and are mutually uncorrelated. $\mathsf{E}_t\left[\cdot\right]$ denotes the conditional expectation given available information.
Show that the price level p satisfies: $p_t = \theta\mathsf{E}_t\left[p_{t+1}\right] + k + \omega_t$ where k is a constant and $0 \le \theta \le 1$. Hence, deduce the form of the general solution for the price process under rational expectations. Discuss identification of the parameters of the model and indicate how you could obtain consistent estimates for those parameters which are identified.

(Oxford M.Phil., 1989)

8.2 The DGP is the same as in example B of §5.12:

$$y_t = \beta\mathsf{E}\left[z_t \mid \mathcal{I}_{t-1}\right] + \epsilon_{1t} \;\; \text{(private sector behaviour)} \tag{8.86}$$

$$z_t = \lambda y_{t-1} + \epsilon_{2t} \;\; \text{(policy rule)} \tag{8.87}$$

$$\epsilon_t \sim \mathsf{IN}_2\left[\begin{pmatrix} 0 \\ 0 \end{pmatrix}, \begin{pmatrix} \sigma_{11} & \sigma_{12} \\ \sigma_{12} & \sigma_{22} \end{pmatrix}\right], \tag{8.88}$$

where $\mathcal{I}_{t-1}$ is available information, and β is invariant to the distribution of $\{z_t\}$. Describe how to estimate β when the form of the policy rule is: (i) known; (ii) unknown.

Solution Hints

(i) Instrumental variables (IV) are an appropriate method to estimate rational expectations models when the policy rule is known (see §A4.9). If generated variables such as regression predictions are used to estimate unobserved expectations in a two-step procedure, then the inference based on the OLS standard errors in the second step is not reliable. An appropriate correction is derived in Pagan (1984a).

(ii) If the policy rule is not known, then IV estimators can be computed using the errors-in-variables approach (see McCallum, 1976, and Ch.12).

9

The Theory of Reduction

This chapter draws together the preceding analyses. Twelve stages of reduction are delineated from the actions of agents in the economy to an econometric model of a subset thereof. The first stage is the actual measurement process which induces the DGP. The next three preliminary steps are data transformations and aggregation; formulating parameters of interest; and partitioning the data. These do not involve actual reductions, but transform the parameterization. However, marginalization, sequential factorization, the mapping to $\mathsf{I}(0)$, and conditional factorization can involve considerable loss of information if inappropriately implemented. Next, constancy, lag truncation, and functional form are discussed, leading to the derived model. Most of the main concepts of econometrics arise as measures of 'no loss of information' about parameters of interest during a reduction. The reduction sequence also entails a taxonomy of information sets relevant to model evaluation. These clarify the relation of model-selection criteria to the null hypotheses of test statistics. Implicit model design is criticized in favour of an explicit approach which seeks to exhaust the available information. The analysis concludes with a discussion of congruence.

9.1 Introduction

We now consolidate the implications of the previous chapters, reviewing the stages of analysis, determining the origins of the concepts discussed, and investigating the status of the resulting framework.[1]

Initially, we focus on the context of model discovery, where the truth is not known a priori to the investigator, and then turn to the context of model evaluation. The discussion treats the investigator as operating at level C, but accords the reader the privilege of knowledge at level A to clarify the consequences of each decision. The approach is called the theory of reduction as it seeks to explain the origin of empirical models in terms of reduction operations conducted implicitly on the DGP to induce the relevant empirical model (see Hendry and Richard, 1982, Florens, Mouchart and Rolin, 1990).

[1] This chapter is based on Cook and Hendry (1993).

The analysis begins with the complete set of random variables $\{u_t^*\}$ relevant to the economy under investigation over a time span $t = 1, \ldots T$, where the superscript * denotes a perfectly measured variable $U_T^{*1} = (u_1^*, \ldots, u_T^*)$, defined on the probability space $(\Omega, \mathcal{F}, \mathsf{P})$. The assumption that economic events are measurable is not unreasonable: Schumpeter (1933) argued that economics was inherently the most quantitative of the sciences since its measures arose from the ordinary business of life. The $\{u_t^*\}$ comprise all the potential variables from the economic mechanism under study which operates at the level of U_T^{*1}, and hence the vector u_t^* comprises details of every economic action of every agent at time t in all the regions of the geographical space relevant to the analysis. However, many of the $\{u_{it}^*\}$ variables are either unobserved or badly measured, so the term data is not strictly applicable to u_t^*. The mapping from the economic mechanism to the data-generation process through the measurement system is the first reduction, which can lose a vast amount of information, and introduce inaccuracy but leads to a data-set which is denoted by $\{u_t\}$. At a conceptual level, all variables $\{u_{it}^*\}$ are assumed to be measured as $\{u_{it}\}$ although for some variables, the level of quantification may be low, possibly even an artificial entry of zero. The probability space $(\Omega, \mathcal{F}, \mathsf{P})$ is transformed by the measurement process (usually markedly), but little is gained by changing notation to reflect this. Measurement is the subject of Chapter 12 and will not be considered further here despite its essential role in a viable empirical econometrics.

The DGP then induces $U_T^1 = (u_1 \ldots u_T)$, so U_T^1 remains unmanageably large. Consequently, operational models are defined by a sequence of data reductions, which are organized into a further eleven stages. Although some stages are not uniquely ordered, in that there is no logical requirement for some to precede others, it does not matter in which order they are investigated, since the result is independent of the path taken at such stages. The important point is that empirical relationships must arise from these reductions of the DGP, an issue stressed earlier when viewing empirical models as derived entities.

Since the primary purpose of the theory of reduction is to account for the status of empirical models as derived entities, the first focus is on their reduction from the DGP.[2] Reduction steps, and necessary preliminaries, are described and linked to the relevant earlier chapters. This aspect is intended to clarify the importance of various modelling decisions in practice as well as clothe the skeletal framework evolved in previous chapters.

Next, we discuss the fact that the salient concepts of econometrics — including exogeneity, innovation, Granger non-causality, identification, parameters of interest, invariance, common factors, and cointegration — arise in a natural way in the theory of

[2] Model-reduction theory differs from Fisher's notion of data reduction (see Fisher, 1922b), although both are related to general-to-specific modelling. Model reduction must occur no matter what approach is adopted, whereas Fisher was concerned with data reduction to summarize the information content of a given data-set. However, one route to developing congruent models is general-to-specific modelling, which is the practical correspondence of model reduction, and is closely related to Fisher's data-reduction notions. Concepts of sufficiency from Fisher's approach also arise in model-reduction theory in the context of valid reductions when marginalizing.

reduction, and correspond to when a given reduction entails no loss of relevant information. Thirdly, the reduction steps also provide a taxonomy of evaluation information, which structures the set of possible null hypotheses for diagnostic tests, and relates these to criteria for model selection. The concept of model design is thereby clarified, and implicit design approaches are criticized in favour of explicitly designing empirical models to exhaust the information in the available data. A possible justification for diagnostic testing is discussed. Finally, the concept of congruence is considered as a basis for empirical modelling and related to progressive research strategies where it acts as an operational substitute for the lack of a criterion for empirical truth.

9.2 Data transformations and aggregation

Consider a one–one mapping of $\boldsymbol{U}_T^1$ to a new data set $\boldsymbol{W}_T^1 : \boldsymbol{U}_T^1 \leftrightarrow \boldsymbol{W}_T^1$. Some of the $\boldsymbol{W}_T^1$ are measured aggregates to be analysed, and the rest are disaggregates or other aggregates which are deemed to be irrelevant. All information is retained, and nothing is eliminated at this stage. To calculate the aggregates across agents of every one of a given set of $j = 1, \ldots, J$ variables $\{u_{jnt}\}$ for $n = 1, \ldots, N$ agents over $t = 1, \ldots, T$ time periods, the mapping is from:

$$\{u_{11t} \ldots u_{J1t}, \ldots, u_{1Nt} \ldots u_{JNt}\} \text{ to } \left\{\sum_{n=1}^{N} u_{1nt} \ldots \sum_{n=1}^{N} u_{Jnt}, u_{12t} \ldots u_{JNt}\right\},$$

which becomes the provisional set of $\{w_{kit}\}$. Aggregating across the nominal values of a subset of commodities (e.g. consumers' goods and services) induces a further mapping:

$$\left\{\sum_{n=1}^{N} u_{1nt} \ldots \sum_{n=1}^{N} u_{Jnt}, u_{12t} \ldots u_{JNt}\right\} \text{ to } \left\{\sum_{j \in \mathcal{J}} w_{j1t}, w_{21t} \ldots w_{J1t}, w_{12t} \ldots w_{JNt}\right\}$$

and so on. If action time is a second, and observed time a month, then time aggregation is also required. For example, aggregate quarterly consumers' expenditure at time t in the United Kingdom is the total flow over that quarter of the sum of all individual consumers' expenditures across all final consumers' goods and services throughout the UK.

The economist's concern about aggregation transformations arises from their impact on the respective parameter vectors of the untransformed and transformed densities. Let the DGP of $\boldsymbol{U}_T^1$, and so of $\boldsymbol{W}_T^1$, be characterized by the joint density:

$$\mathsf{D_U}\left(\boldsymbol{U}_T^1 \mid \boldsymbol{U}_0, \boldsymbol{\psi}_T^1\right) = \mathsf{D_W}\left(\boldsymbol{W}_T^1 \mid \boldsymbol{W}_0, \boldsymbol{\phi}_T^1\right) \tag{9.1}$$

where $\boldsymbol{\psi}_T^1 \in \boldsymbol{\Psi}$ and $\boldsymbol{\phi}_T^1 \in \boldsymbol{\Phi}$. The first density $\mathsf{D_U}(\cdot)$ is a high-dimensional function over all the relevant variables $\boldsymbol{U}_T^1$, with initial conditions $\boldsymbol{U}_0$. The parameterization $\boldsymbol{\psi}_T^1$ potentially allows for transient parameters and structural change, and is an element of the parameter space $\boldsymbol{\Psi}$. The transformed density $\mathsf{D}_{\mathsf{W}}(\cdot)$ of $\boldsymbol{W}_T^1$ is a possibly different distribution, albeit one which is a function of $\mathsf{D}_{\mathsf{U}}(\cdot)$. Individual decision variables often behave erratically over time, and need not be normally distributed. However, from the central limit theorem, the aggregate of a large number N of independent random variables from a non-normal distribution will be approximately normal (see Ch.A4), so a possible benefit from analysing aggregates is that they are closer to normal random variates.

The transformation from $\boldsymbol{U}$ to $\boldsymbol{W}$ also affects the parameter space, so $\boldsymbol{\Psi}$ is transformed into $\boldsymbol{\Phi}$. The new parameters in $\boldsymbol{\phi}$ may be more or less interpretable than the old, and fewer or more of them may be constant than in $\boldsymbol{\psi}$. An under-researched area of econometrics is what happens to the time variability of parameters at the aggregate level which are non-constant for individuals over time in different, but perhaps offsetting, ways. Chapter 2 discussed aggregation and the impact of logarithmic transformations on data densities.

In terms of a simple example, if at each t, $u_{jnt} \sim \mathsf{ID}\left[\mu_{jn}, \sigma^2_{jn}\right]$, independently across the N individuals, but with the restriction that the means and variances are constant over time, then:

$$\bar{u}_{j.t} = N^{-1} \sum_{n=1}^{N} u_{jnt} \underset{app}{\sim} \mathsf{N}\left[\bar{\mu}_{j.}, N^{-1}\bar{\sigma}^2_{j.}\right],$$

where:

$$\bar{\mu}_{j.} = N^{-1} \sum_{n=1}^{N} \mu_{jn} \text{ and } \bar{\sigma}^2_{j.} = N^{-1} \sum_{n=1}^{N} \sigma^2_{jn}.$$

When the $\bar{\mu}_{k.}$ are the parameters of interest (e.g. the aggregate propensities to spend if the u_{jnt} are consumption–income ratios), then conditional on retaining $\{\bar{u}_{j.t}\}$, the remaining $\{u_{jnt}\}$ for $n = 2, \ldots, N$, will be an order of magnitude less informative about $\bar{\mu}_{k.}$ than is $\bar{u}_{j.t}$, despite the fact that the $\{\mu_{jn}\}$ may differ across the N individuals.

Similar issues arise with respect to aggregation over time to weeks, months, quarters, or years. Information usually will be lost, and it is always worth contemplating the costs of its loss. Little is known about the relationship between agents' decision periods and conventional observation intervals, but Phillips (1988a) shows that equilibrium-correction formulations hold accurately in discrete time if decisions are made continuously.

Finally, functional-form transformations also alter the parameters and can induce or lose constancy. This is true even of monotonic transforms: for example, in $\mathsf{I}(1)$ processes, taking logs of positive variables may remove or induce heteroscedasticity over time (see Ermini and Hendry, 1991).

9.3 Parameters of interest

There is no point in undertaking a statistical analysis unless we expect to learn something useful concerning a relevant problem. It is difficult to conceptualize and understand the world without having parameters (in the broad sense) as a basis, so it is important to specify the parameters of interest at the outset. Such parameters might be the marginal propensity to consume; the government's impact on rates of inflation from changing its deficit; the interest elasticity of the demand for money; or some functions of tastes and technology which are believed to parameterize a given problem. 'At the outset' involves taking account of all previous empirical and theoretical information, although the current fashion in economics is to base models primarily on theoretical derivations. Either way, denote the parameters of interest by $\boldsymbol{\mu} \in \mathcal{M}$. It is assumed that these are identifiable, and invariant to an interesting class of interventions: such assumptions may well be false in any specific empirical setting but are open to evaluation later.

To learn about parameters of interest, they must be identifiable, in the sense of the uniqueness of the parameterization, rather than its interpretation, correspondence, or its discovery (Koopmans, 1950a, Hood and Koopmans, 1953, and Ch.11 discuss conditions for uniquely determining the parameters in simultaneous-equations systems). The other senses also occur, as noted earlier: to identify a given equation as a demand curve entails not only that its parameters be uniquely defined, but also that it can be interpreted as a demand relation, and that it does not correspond to a supply schedule (say). Finally, in time-series analysis, identification denotes learning from the data (see Box and Jenkins, 1976). For example, a given process might be identified as an ARMA(1, 1) from examining its correlogram and partial correlogram. These senses are common in everyday use — a lost painting might be identified as a Miro. At level C, all three senses are involved and are important aspects of $\boldsymbol{\mu}$.

The other primary attribute of parameters of interest is their potential invariance over time and to interventions in the economy. There is a fundamental difference between formulating $\boldsymbol{\mu}$ at levels A and C. Events in the real world will almost certainly never be perfectly predictable from information available to human beings, and so it is useful to characterize the DGP as a joint distribution over random variables, as we have done throughout level A. When developing an econometric theory at level A, we simply assumed that the DGP was characterized by a set of parameters $\boldsymbol{\theta} \in \Theta$ (say), and then endowed $\boldsymbol{\theta}$ with whatever properties were desired. The level B analysis of estimating $\boldsymbol{\theta}$ then follows elegantly, as will be seen in Part II. These are necessary steps even within an approach which emphasizes the econometric problem as one of modelling at level C, rather than estimation at level B.

However, the relevance to data analysis of arbitrarily postulated DGPs with constant parameters $\boldsymbol{\theta}$ is open to question, since it is not obvious that there need exist any parameters in the empirical representations which economists consider. Consequently, the parameters at level C can only be a conjecture in a theoretical model of the DGP. For example, there may not be a marginal propensity to consume for any agents, any society, or any entities, however many theories postulate its central role, or data analyses claim its determination. I believe such constructions do exist, because (e.g.) the aggregate marginal propensity to consume apparently can be altered by changing taxes. Moreover, a substantial number of econometric relationships seem to persist through time. Finally, human behaviour, at both the individual and the social level, evolves slowly relative to the time-span of most econometric studies. Just as there is no criterion of truth for empirical models, so we cannot verify that parameters of interest exist to be discovered. Nevertheless, parameters of interest motivate and structure a study to come to a better understanding of the world in which we live. Historically, the existence of the initially postulated parameters may not be essential to scientific progress since, in the process of analysis, a better framework may emerge. Conversely, faster progress is likely if the selected parameters do reflect salient and constant features of reality. Parameters which prove to be constant empirically seem naturally to be of interest; in Chapter 14, we will analyse their potential invariance.[3]

Economists generally use economic theory to suggest their parameters of interest. Such a methodology raises questions concerning mapping theoretically-based entities, which are explicitly cognitive in nature, on to empirically-based entities, which are functions of physically existing quantities. Several correspondence conditions are involved:

(a) between theoretical latent variables and the corresponding empirical-data constructs (e.g. from permanent income to some measured values thereof);
(b) between theory decision-time periods and empirical time intervals (e.g. from 't' to months or quarters);
(c) between a theory's *ceteris paribus* assumptions about everything not included in the theory model, and the actual irrelevance in practice of the excluded influences; and
(d) between the constants of the theory model and the coefficients of the empirical model.

Economic theory with its associated theoretical concepts and models provides an essential component of our cognitive structure, in that it is difficult to think about economic events without invoking aspects of existing theory. The internal consistency and generality of economic theory endow it with considerable power as a first-order description of individual economic behaviour in relatively static circumstances. As discussed in Chapter 1, however, theories are abstractions which only focus on the salient phenomena and consider these in isolation from other potential influences. Even at their best, they are incomplete descriptions.

Frisch (1938) and Haavelmo (1944) were concerned about the four correspondence problems above, and although technical developments in continuous time analysis, dynamic economic theory, and econometrics have alleviated some of their original concerns, they have not entirely removed them. There remains a large gap between an abstract theory of an unrationed inter-temporal optimizing individual agent and an empirical model of the supposedly corresponding aggregate behaviour. Consequently, other

[3] From the history of science (see e.g. Mason, 1962, and Losee, 1980), considerable progress has been made searching for parameters of interest that do not exist given present knowledge. As examples, seeking phlogiston as a material to explain combustion led to the discovery of some of the principles of modern thermodynamics; searching for an 'integer' theory to explain chemical weights led to isotopic theory and later to an improved atomic theory of chemical behaviour; alchemy, which was an abortive attempt to transduce base metals into gold, was a precursor of chemistry, and now can be implemented in modern particle accelerators (see Hendry, 1980). All of these examples involved searching for entities that we now believe do not exist, but nevertheless were productive of scientific development. In practice, parameters of interest may arise during a study as a result of discoveries or models which explain previous anomalies.

sources of information and forms of reasoning than just economic theory are admissible in formulating and analysing parameters of interest.

The final step prior to any actual reductions is to isolate that subset of information from $\boldsymbol{W}_T^1$ which is believed relevant to the parameters of interest. Both theory and past evidence again play important roles in this selection, which is the major precursor to the largest reduction — due to marginalization.

9.4 Data partition

Partition $\boldsymbol{W}_T^1$ into the two sets:

$$\boldsymbol{W}_T^1 = (\boldsymbol{X}_T^1 : \boldsymbol{V}_T^1) \tag{9.2}$$

where the $\boldsymbol{X}_T^1$ matrix is $T \times n$. The objective of the partition in (9.2) is to ensure that everything about μ can be learnt from analysing the $\boldsymbol{X}_T^1$ alone, so that $\boldsymbol{V}_T^1$ is not essential to inference about μ. While the choice of the elements to include in $\boldsymbol{X}_T^1$ is only based on conjecture, as in any science, the final model will be testable and so provide evidence on the adequacy of the selected partition. In any practical application, $\boldsymbol{V}_T^1$ will not be fully specified and its contents are usually defined by default, as everything not explicitly included in $\boldsymbol{X}_T^1$.

Steps §9.3 and §9.4 are the stages at which an investigator's value added enters. For productive research, one must think of parameters μ that are actually interesting, in that they correspond to relatively constant behavioural propensities, and of the data set that will deliver those parameters of interest when properly analysed. Theoretical reasoning is frequently of immense help in doing so, despite being neither necessary nor sufficient, but how one discovers useful knowledge remains an art rather than a science.

In any event, given the specification of μ and the choice of $\boldsymbol{X}_T^1$, the next step is to reduce $\mathsf{D}_\mathsf{W}(\cdot)$ in (9.1) to manageable proportions by concentrating the analysis on $\boldsymbol{X}_T^1$ and marginalizing with respect to the remainder of $\boldsymbol{W}_T^1$.

9.5 Marginalization

The reduction path is not unique at this stage, in that the order of §9.5 and §9.6 is irrelevant. The particular path of §9.5 then §9.6, which we follow first, is the easier in terms of analytical derivations, but the less helpful for understanding the consequences, so we briefly consider the alternative order in step §9.6 below.

To marginalize the joint density in (9.1) with respect to all the elements of $\boldsymbol{V}_T^1$ involves the following density factorization:

$$\mathsf{D}_\mathsf{W}\left(\boldsymbol{W}_T^1 \mid \boldsymbol{W}_0, \phi_T^1\right) = \mathsf{D}_{\mathsf{V}|\mathsf{X}}\left(\boldsymbol{V}_T^1 \mid \boldsymbol{X}_T^1, \boldsymbol{W}_0, \boldsymbol{\Lambda}_{aT}^1\right) \mathsf{D}_\mathsf{X}\left(\boldsymbol{X}_T^1 \mid \boldsymbol{W}_0, \boldsymbol{\Lambda}_{bT}^1\right). \tag{9.3}$$

We can eliminate $\boldsymbol{V}_T^1$ by discarding the conditional density $\mathsf{D}_{\mathsf{V}|\mathsf{X}}(\boldsymbol{V}_T^1|\boldsymbol{X}_T^1, \boldsymbol{W}_0, \boldsymbol{\Lambda}_{aT}^1)$ in (9.3), while retaining the marginal density $\mathsf{D}_\mathsf{X}(\boldsymbol{X}_T^1|\boldsymbol{W}_0, \boldsymbol{\Lambda}_{bT}^1)$. This operation corresponds to throwing away the data on $\boldsymbol{V}_T^1$, although, in general, the data on $\boldsymbol{V}_T^1$ were probably not collected, so 'throwing away' all of the V_T^1 is a logical rather than a physical issue. Henceforth, an investigation only concerns the marginal (joint) distribution of the X_T^1 as a function of their parameters Λ_{bT}^1, and the initial conditions W_0 of the DGP. After this stage, unless one believes in omniscience, $\mathsf{D}_X(\cdot)$ is no longer the DGP, merely the most general joint distribution under consideration, and so it constitutes the Haavelmo distribution for the analysis.

While (9.3) clarifies the implications of only analysing X_T^1, it entails important assumptions as discussed in Chapter 8. The conditions closely parallel those of weak exogeneity, but applied to a global factorization where the marginal rather than the conditional distribution is of interest. Thus, μ must be a function of Λ_{bT}^1 alone, given by $\mu = f(\Lambda_{bT}^1)$, so it must be possible to learn μ from Λ_{bT}^1, without there being any information about μ in Λ_{aT}^1. Secondly, there must be nothing to learn about Λ_{bT}^1 from Λ_{aT}^1, otherwise information is being ignored. As in Chapter 5, a cut is required, so that $(\Lambda_{aT}^1 : \Lambda_{bT}^1) \in \Lambda_a \times \Lambda_b$. It is valid to discard V_T^1 only if everything of relevance can be learnt from analysing Λ_{bT}^1 alone.

Conventionally in econometrics, the problem of invalidly marginalizing with respect to relevant V_T^1 is called omitted-variables bias. There is a set of parameters of interest μ such that, when all the relevant variables are not included, then the resulting parameter estimates are biased, or perhaps inconsistent, for μ. However, this is not the most useful mode of analysis for two reasons. First, the key issue is not that biased or inconsistent estimates of μ are obtained, but that the wrong parameters are calculated. Instead of estimating μ, a different parameter α, say, is estimated which is mistakenly interpreted as μ. This view helps account for the literature on so-called wrong signs. For example, consider modelling money demand by regressing real money on interest rates. Say a positive coefficient is calculated as the estimate of α — then it has the wrong sign relative to most theories of money demand. But α does not have the wrong sign for that model on that data-set: what is incorrect is the interpretation of α as corresponding to the interest elasticity of the demand for money in the theory model, namely μ. Having marginalized the problem with respect to whatever variables are omitted, the correct parameter is no longer obtained.[4]

The second aspect of invalid marginalization is really an implication of the first. In $\mathsf{D}_W(\cdot)$, μ may well have been a constant function of ϕ_T^1, yet when the distribution (9.1) is factorized as in (9.3), $\alpha = f(\Lambda_{bT}^1)$ might vary over time. Consequently, if the wrong marginalization is chosen, constant parameters might not be discovered even when the relevant aspect of the world has constant parameters in an appropriate formulation. Reduction by marginalization is complicated because it is difficult to write down what function Λ_{bT}^1 is of ϕ_T^1 in order to analyse the preservation or loss of constancy. That issue will be clearer after one more factorization.

When Λ_{aT}^1 provides information about μ, even though μ can be recovered in principle from Λ_{bT}^1, the usual problem which results from ignoring V_T^1 is that μ ceases to be constant. Thus, when we remark that a more informative analysis is possible from the

[4] $\hat{\alpha} > 0$ could occur when $\alpha < 0$ due to sampling, but here we are concerned with the logical issue and assume throughout this section that T is very large.

joint density, the extent of that additional information may be the difference between a useful and an unhelpful analysis.

9.6 Sequential factorization

Assume that we can learn everything required about $\boldsymbol{\mu}$ from $\mathbf{X}_T^1$ via $\boldsymbol{\Lambda}_{bT}^1$ by analysing $\mathsf{D}_X(\cdot)$ in (9.3). To create the innovation process required for statistical inference, the fifth step is to sequentially factorize $\mathbf{X}_T^1$ as follows:

$$\mathsf{D}_X\left(\mathbf{X}_T^1 \mid \mathbf{W}_0, \boldsymbol{\Lambda}_{bT}^1\right) = \prod_{t=1}^{T} \mathsf{D}_x\left(\mathbf{x}_t \mid \mathbf{X}_{t-1}^1, \mathbf{W}_0, \boldsymbol{\lambda}_{bt}\right). \tag{9.4}$$

Chapters 2 and 4 described how this factorization of the joint distribution into sequential distributions generated a mean-innovation error process $\boldsymbol{\epsilon}_t = \mathbf{x}_t - \mathsf{E}\left[\mathbf{x}_t | \mathbf{X}_{t-1}^1\right]$, so we will not discuss that aspect any further. Instead, let us backtrack and conduct stages §9.5 and §9.6 in the opposite order to see a hidden complication in (9.3).

9.6.1 Sequential factorization of $\mathbf{W}_T^1$

Sequential factorization at the level of the DGP in (9.1) produces:

$$\mathsf{D}_W\left(\mathbf{W}_T^1 \mid \mathbf{W}_0, \boldsymbol{\phi}_T^1\right) = \prod_{t=1}^{T} \mathsf{D}_w\left(\mathbf{w}_t \mid \mathbf{W}_{t-1}, \boldsymbol{\delta}_t\right). \tag{9.5}$$

The right-hand side again generates an MIP, given by $\boldsymbol{\eta}_t = \mathbf{w}_t - \mathsf{E}\left[\mathbf{w}_t | \mathbf{W}_{t-1}^1\right]$.

9.6.2 Marginalizing with respect to $\mathbf{V}_T^1$

Marginalizing the sequential distributions in (9.5) with respect to $\mathbf{V}_T^1$ involves two distinct conditions highlighted by the following factorization:

$$\mathsf{D}_w\left(\mathbf{w}_t \mid \mathbf{W}_{t-1}, \boldsymbol{\delta}_t\right) = \mathsf{D}_{v|x}\left(\mathbf{v}_t \mid \mathbf{x}_t, \mathbf{W}_{t-1}, \boldsymbol{\delta}_{at}\right) \mathsf{D}_x\left(\mathbf{x}_t \mid \mathbf{V}_{t-1}^1, \mathbf{X}_{t-1}^1, \mathbf{W}_0, \boldsymbol{\delta}_{bt}\right), \tag{9.6}$$

noting that $\mathbf{W}_{t-1}$ is made up of $\left\{\mathbf{V}_{t-1}^1, \mathbf{X}_{t-1}^1, \mathbf{W}_0\right\}$. The first condition is that $\boldsymbol{\mu}$ can be obtained from $\{\boldsymbol{\delta}_{bt}\}$ alone, so that the set $\{\boldsymbol{\delta}_{at}\}$ must be irrelevant. Moreover, at every t, the second density on the right in (9.6) must be marginalized with respect to $\mathbf{V}_{t-1}^1$:

$$\mathsf{D}_x\left(\mathbf{x}_t \mid \mathbf{V}_{t-1}^1, \mathbf{X}_{t-1}^1, \mathbf{W}_0, \boldsymbol{\delta}_{bt}\right) = \mathsf{D}_x\left(\mathbf{x}_t \mid \mathbf{X}_{t-1}^1, \mathbf{W}_0, \boldsymbol{\delta}_{bt}^*\right). \tag{9.7}$$

There will be no loss of information if and only if $\boldsymbol{\delta}_{bt} = \boldsymbol{\delta}_{bt}^* \; \forall t$, which requires that the conditional, sequential distribution of $\{\mathbf{x}_t\}$ does not depend on $\mathbf{V}_{t-1}^1$. This condition of Granger non-causality (GNC) is hidden in (9.4), and (9.7) highlights that the lagged values of the $\mathbf{v}$s should not affect the current values of the $\mathbf{x}$s: see Granger (1969) and Engle, Hendry and Richard (1983). The requirement that, conditional on $\mathbf{X}_{t-1}^1$, $\mathbf{V}_{t-1}^1$ does not Granger-cause $\mathbf{x}_t$ reveals the strength of the marginalization condition in (9.4).

The desired function of the parameters of the DGP will be recovered only if, conditional on the variables retained, the variables omitted from the analysis actually are irrelevant, which is an all too obvious statement.

Since $\mathsf{E}[\eta_t | \boldsymbol{W}_{t-1}^1] = \mathbf{0}$ in (9.5), a necessary condition for no information loss from reducing (9.5) to (9.7) is that $\mathsf{E}[\epsilon_t | \boldsymbol{W}_{t-1}^1] = \mathsf{E}[\epsilon_t | \boldsymbol{V}_{t-1}^1, \boldsymbol{X}_{t-1}^1] = \mathbf{0}$ whereas we only know that $\mathsf{E}[\epsilon_t | \boldsymbol{X}_{t-1}^1]$ is zero. Thus, we deduce the weaker necessary condition that $\mathsf{E}[\epsilon_t | \boldsymbol{V}_{t-1}^1] = \mathbf{0}$ if sequential marginalization is to be valid. It is probably at the marginalization stage that most empirical research goes wrong by over-enthusiastic elimination of potentially-relevant variables. In part, this is due to the common methodological practice of commencing from simple models, which are generalized only after rejection; in part, it depends on assuming the empirical validity of some, perhaps implicit, *ceteris paribus* clause in a theory model; and in part, it may be the result of a collection of beliefs about the information content of time-series samples, the prevalence of collinearity and of identification problems, and the virtues of parsimony. After conducting many empirical studies, I consider that the most likely cause of predictive failure in applied research is a change in the data properties of a relevant, but omitted, variable. We return to this issue in Chapter 14.

For the order of reduction to be irrelevant, the two distributions in (9.4) and (9.7) must be the same:

$$\mathsf{D}_{\mathsf{x}}\left(\boldsymbol{x}_t \mid \boldsymbol{X}_{t-1}^1, \boldsymbol{W}_0, \boldsymbol{\lambda}_{bt}\right) = \mathsf{D}_{\mathsf{x}}\left(\boldsymbol{x}_t \mid \boldsymbol{X}_{t-1}^1, \boldsymbol{W}_0, \boldsymbol{\delta}_{bt}^*\right).$$

This requires that $\boldsymbol{\lambda}_{bt}$ is isomorphic to $\boldsymbol{\delta}_{bt}^*$; since these apparently different parameterizations sustain the same conditional distributions and are assumed to be identifiable, we take them to be in one–one correspondence.

The role of GNC at stage 9.6.1 is purely associated with marginalizing. This result contrasts with Sims (1972), who defined exogeneity in terms of Granger non-causality, confounding issues of marginalization with those of conditioning. As discussed in Chapter 5, GNC is neither necessary nor sufficient for weak exogeneity, but is necessary to eliminate the past values of variables deemed irrelevant. Thus, GNC is an important aspect of marginalization, not of conditioning.

9.7 Mapping to I(0)

A consistent theme in earlier chapters is that economic data appear to be integrated. For a coherent analysis, an important reduction is the elimination of linear combinations of integrated, but not cointegrated, variables. Relative to the terminology in Chapter 4, these are the nonsense relationships. Integrated processes can be expressed in terms of cointegrated and differenced variables without loss of information, but with a reduction in the dimension of the parameter vector, so a gain is feasible from doing so (see Phillips, 1991, Banerjee, Dolado, Galbraith and Hendry, 1993, and Chs. 7 and 8). At the completion of these two operations, all variables will be I(0), and a conventional statistical analysis can be implemented. The generic type of linear model, therefore, is an equilibrium-correction form, which links changes to cointegrating combinations, relating the analysis to that in the two previous chapters. Information about the levels of some variables will not be ostensibly retained, but can be recovered if needed by integrating the differenced data given the initial conditions on the levels.

When variables are retained in an integrated form, many inferences remain valid, but it may not always be clear which tests require conventional, and which require Dickey–Fuller, critical values (see Sims, Stock and Watson (1990) and Chs. 3–5). For other uses of empirical models, such as forecasting, retaining integrated variables may be more or less satisfactory. Engle and Yoo (1987) find that an unrestricted VAR in levels performs less well at long forecast horizons than an ECM, but Clements and Hendry (1994) show that for mean-square forecast errors in differences and/or cointegrating combinations, the opposite ranking can occur depending on how the ECM is estimated.

We now assume that a mapping to a set of suitably differenced and cointegrated variables has been achieved, but will not modify the notation to reflect the outcome. We return to the estimation of cointegrating vectors in Chapter 11.

9.8 Conditional factorization

Much applied econometric research is concerned with explaining one set of variables $\boldsymbol{y}_t$ given another set $\boldsymbol{z}_t$. To analyse this aspect, factorize the density of $\boldsymbol{x}_t$ into sets of n_1 and n_2 variables where $n_1 + n_2 = n$:

$$\boldsymbol{x}'_t = (\boldsymbol{y}'_t : \boldsymbol{z}'_t)\,, \tag{9.8}$$

where the $\boldsymbol{y}_t$ are endogenous and the $\boldsymbol{z}_t$ are non-modelled. Factorizing the sequential density of $\boldsymbol{x}_t$ in (9.4) into a conditional and a marginal density associated with $\boldsymbol{y}_t$ and $\boldsymbol{z}_t$ respectively yields:

$$\mathsf{D_x}\left(\boldsymbol{x}_t \mid \boldsymbol{X}^1_{t-1}, \boldsymbol{W}_0, \boldsymbol{\lambda}_{bt}\right) = \mathsf{D_{y|z}}\left(\boldsymbol{y}_t \mid \boldsymbol{z}_t, \boldsymbol{X}^1_{t-1}, \boldsymbol{W}_0, \boldsymbol{\theta}_{at}\right) \mathsf{D_z}\left(\boldsymbol{z}_t \mid \boldsymbol{X}^1_{t-1}, \boldsymbol{W}_0, \boldsymbol{\theta}_{bt}\right). \tag{9.9}$$

From Chapter 5, $\boldsymbol{z}_t$ is weakly exogenous for $\boldsymbol{\mu}$ if (i) $\boldsymbol{\mu} = \boldsymbol{f}(\boldsymbol{\theta}_{at})$ alone; and (ii) $(\boldsymbol{\theta}_{at}, \boldsymbol{\theta}_{bt}) \in \boldsymbol{\Theta}_a \times \boldsymbol{\Theta}_b$. Under the conditions in (i) and (ii), there is no need to analyse the marginal distribution $\mathsf{D_z}(\boldsymbol{z}_t|\boldsymbol{X}^1_{t-1}, \boldsymbol{W}_0, \boldsymbol{\theta}_{bt})$ of $\boldsymbol{z}_t$ in (9.9) to efficiently analyse $\boldsymbol{\mu}$. The problem can be reduced to analysing only the conditional distribution $\mathsf{D_{y|z}}(\boldsymbol{y}_t|\boldsymbol{z}_t, \boldsymbol{X}^1_{t-1}, \boldsymbol{W}_0, \boldsymbol{\theta}_{at})$ of $\boldsymbol{y}_t$ given $\boldsymbol{z}_t$, thereby increasing the robustness of inference to incorrect formulations of $\mathsf{D_z}(\cdot)$, as well as reducing the complexity of the analysis. More importantly, the model-selection problem is greatly simplified by valid reductions: valid conditioning is especially useful when $\boldsymbol{\theta}_{at}$ is constant and $\boldsymbol{\theta}_{bt}$ is not.

This step is almost the converse of step §9.5, in that we now discard the marginal distribution, and retain the conditional. However, since we have already established the relevant concepts, and discussed weak exogeneity extensively, we will not pursue conditioning reductions any further.

9.9 Constancy

This reduction concerns the time homogeneity of the process through the constancy of its parameters. Even at stage §9.8 in the reduction, the formulation is virtually vacuous, since there are potentially as many parameters as data points. To progress, some assumptions are needed about the homogeneity over time of the process being observed, since little can be learnt from analysing data drawn from a process which is completely different at every point in time. Consider the extreme case of complete parameter constancy:

$$\boldsymbol{\theta}_{at} = \boldsymbol{\theta}_a \ \forall t \tag{9.10}$$

where $\boldsymbol{\theta}_a \in \Theta_a$, so that $\boldsymbol{\mu}$ is a function of $\boldsymbol{\theta}_a$: $\boldsymbol{\mu} = \boldsymbol{f}(\boldsymbol{\theta}_a)$. This is a large reduction when it is valid, and for at least a subset of the parameters, it is an essential reduction if progress is to be made in empirical modelling.

As discussed in Chapter 2, by taking the parameter vector $\boldsymbol{\theta}_a$ as constant, any regime changes which occurred must be modelled. The discovery problem is to establish which function of the xs delivers the constant $\boldsymbol{\mu}$, or alternatively expressed, to find the constancies of the DGP. There is an intimate link between how the data are modelled and the reasonableness of assuming that the corresponding parameters are constant. The assumption of constant parameters does not preclude technical progress, learning, regime shifts, adaptation, changing shocks, and so on. What it does require is that such factors are potentially open to being modelled as functions of more basic parameters that are constant in turn. Clearly, (9.10) is intended to apply to these basic parameters.

Random-parameter models, such as:

$$\boldsymbol{\theta}_{at} = \boldsymbol{\theta}_{at-1} + \boldsymbol{\omega}_t \ \text{ where } \boldsymbol{\omega}_t \sim \mathsf{ID}_k\left[\mathbf{0}, \boldsymbol{\Sigma}_\omega\right] \ \text{ and } \ \boldsymbol{\theta}_{a0} \ \text{ is fixed,} \tag{9.11}$$

were related to constancy in Chapter 2, and shown to be constant-parameter models with unobservable variables. There is no a priori reason to believe that the representation postulated in (9.11) is better than other constant-parameter representations. In a linear model with random parameters, say:

$$y_t = \boldsymbol{\theta}'_{at} \mathbf{z}_t + \eta_t,$$

substituting (9.11) solved backwards to $t = 0$, yields:

$$y_t = \boldsymbol{\theta}'_{a0} \mathbf{z}_t + \eta_t + \mathbf{z}'_t \sum_{i=0}^{t} \boldsymbol{\omega}_{t-i} = \boldsymbol{\beta}' \mathbf{z}_t + e_t,$$

where $\{e_t\}$ is heteroscedastic and possibly autocorrelated, but $\boldsymbol{\beta} = \boldsymbol{\theta}_{a0}$ is constant. The correct choice of parameterization is an empirical issue, open to evaluation, which depends on appropriately modelling learning and adjustments to regime shifts, making sensible decisions about functional forms, and the inclusion of relevant variables, and on the structure of the unknown DGP. When (9.11) captures constant features of the DGP in a parsimonious way then it is useful; but nothing guarantees in any given instance that it will do so. We cannot avoid having some constant parameters which are the entities on which to base the analysis.

When the constancy reduction is valid, the conditional density in (9.9) becomes:

$$\prod_{t=1}^{T} \mathsf{D}_{\mathsf{y}|\mathsf{z}} \left(y_t \mid z_t, \boldsymbol{X}_{t-1}^1, \boldsymbol{W}_0, \boldsymbol{\theta}_a \right) \tag{9.12}$$

with $\boldsymbol{\theta}_a \in \boldsymbol{\Theta}$. The model in (9.12) is still non-operational even with constant parameters over time, because the history retained in $\boldsymbol{X}_{t-1}^1$ is increasing with the sample size, and so the model dimension is diverging to infinity. Hence a further reduction is needed to capture the model form conventionally adopted. An alternative approach is to allow the model size to increase as the sample grows, but at a slower rate. If the number of parameters per endogenous variable is K_T then it is possible to let $K_T \to \infty$ as $T \to \infty$, such that $K_T/T \to 0$ sufficiently quickly that standard limiting distributions obtain. A reasonable justification for this possibility is that standard errors of estimated coefficients decline as the sample size grows, and hence the significance of an effect may not show up until a large sample has accrued, especially when the significance level is also declining towards zero (see e.g. White, 1990). The number of endogenous variables can also be allowed to increase with the sample size as in Sargan (1975).

9.10 Lag truncation

The relevance of past history declines as time proceeds in processes with limited memory, and an important practical reduction is accomplished by fixing the extent of the history of $\boldsymbol{X}_{t-1}^1$ in (9.12) at s earlier periods:

$$\mathsf{D}_{\mathsf{y}|\mathsf{z}} \left(y_t \mid z_t, \boldsymbol{X}_{t-1}^1, \boldsymbol{W}_0, \boldsymbol{\theta}_a \right) = \mathsf{D}_{\mathsf{y}|\mathsf{z}} \left(y_t \mid z_t, \boldsymbol{X}_{t-1}^{t-s}, \boldsymbol{W}_0, \boldsymbol{\delta} \right). \tag{9.13}$$

The concept that sustains this reduction is that $\{\epsilon_t\}$ defined by (9.4) remains an innovation process, since otherwise the reduction loses important information. Reconsider the model typology, where many of the criticisms of specific model types were due to arbitrarily excluding the history of some of the variables: all terms in $\boldsymbol{X}_{t-1}^1$ were excluded in static models; some were excluded in autoregressions, partial adjustments, and distributed lags; or were entered in restricted ways in common-factor representations. Invalid exclusions usually induce a non-innovation error because of the limited retention of the history of the process. Thus, in empirical research, examine the residuals to see whether the limited-memory assumption is valid for any given choice of s. This reduction requires that the error remains a mean innovation against the available information.

9.11 Functional form

Constancy, functional form, and distributional assumptions are intimately related. As a contrived example, when the log of consumption c_t is a constant linear function of the log of income i_t, given by $c_t = \alpha_0 + \alpha_1 i_t + \epsilon_t$ with $\alpha_1 \neq 1$, and the income process is non-stationary, then the coefficient of income in the regression of the level of consumption on the level of income will not be constant since:

$$C_t = K I_t^{\alpha_1} \exp(\epsilon_t) \neq \beta_0 + \beta_1 I_t + \xi_t. \tag{9.14}$$

Thus, a researcher could find a constant parameterization in logs of variables and a non-constant parameterization in levels. The reduction here also refers to the form of the distribution $\mathsf{D}_{\mathsf{y}|\mathsf{z}}(\cdot)$. It would be convenient if we could choose simple functional forms for y_t and z_t and their retained history that simultaneously induced constant parameters and made $\mathsf{D}_{\mathsf{y}|\mathsf{z}}(\cdot)$ correspond approximately to a normal distribution. The reason for such a desire is obvious, since in a normal distribution, the conditional relationship is linear, so such a reduction would entail a linear model in the transformed space of the appropriate functions of y_t and z_t. Thus, the functional-form issue concerns, on the one hand, linearity, and on the other, normality, subject to the caveat that there is no point in postulating a linear, normal model if it loses constancy in the parameters. It is difficult, and sometimes impossible, to think of a function with properties that satisfy all our requirements.

One cost of inappropriate functional-form choice is often the creation of an apparently heteroscedastic error. The usual message of not 'correcting' symptoms holds: procedures exist for inducing homoscedastic errors but unless the heteroscedasticity is a property of the error, and not just a reflection of another mistake, removing it may do little good.

To carry out the functional-form reduction, map y_t into $y_t^* = h(y_t)$, and z_t into $z_t^* = g(z_t)$, and denote the resulting data by X^*. Assume that y_t^* and z_t^* simultaneously make $\mathsf{D}_{\mathsf{y}^*|\mathsf{z}^*}(\cdot)$ approximately normal and homoscedastic, denoted $\mathsf{N}_{n_1}[\eta_t, \Upsilon]$:

$$\mathsf{D}_{\mathsf{y}|\mathsf{z}}\left(y_t \mid z_t, X_{t-1}^{t-s}, W_0, \delta\right) = \mathsf{D}_{\mathsf{y}^*|\mathsf{z}^*}\left(y_t^* \mid z_t^*, X^{*}{}_{t-1}^{t-s}, W_0, \gamma\right). \tag{9.15}$$

When (9.15) holds with normality, a linear model for y_t^* is obtained in terms of z_t^*; otherwise, linearity is required as an additional assumption after transformation, which may not deliver a useful model (see Ch.6). Rather, it is better to select transforms such that parameters result which are potentially constant, then conduct inference relative to the empirical form of the resulting error distribution. The positivity of many economic variables make logs admissible, and in practice, log transforms often help to achieve all the aims of this reduction.

9.12 The derived model

The initial conditions W_0 are unobservable, and will be taken as given. Providing the history retained in (9.15) is adequate to create an innovation error, the parameter of the reduced conditional density will remain γ. The actual historical time may matter for non-stationary processes, especially just after major events such as wars, but such effects should fade as time increases. Many empirical models have the property that after transformations and modelling regime shifts, the variables are nearly stationary, and initial conditions do not have a large effect. Henceforth, we suppose this is the case, so that after the reductions, the model takes the form:

$$\boldsymbol{A}(L)\boldsymbol{y}_t^* = \boldsymbol{B}(L)\boldsymbol{z}_t^* + \boldsymbol{\epsilon}_t \tag{9.16}$$

where $\boldsymbol{\epsilon}_t \underset{app}{\sim} \mathsf{N}_{n_1}[\boldsymbol{0}, \boldsymbol{\Sigma}_\epsilon]$, and $\boldsymbol{A}(L)$ and $\boldsymbol{B}(L)$ are polynomial matrices of order s in the lag operator L.

The complete sequence of reductions here has led to a vector autoregressive-distributed lag model, VAD$(s, s, \ldots, s)$, in the variables in $\boldsymbol{h}(\boldsymbol{y}_t)$ and $\boldsymbol{g}(\boldsymbol{z}_t)$, although the lag length s might need to be long to ensure an innovation error.[5] The resulting model is, of course, the conventional formulation adopted in econometrics precisely because we have asserted at each reduction stage that the relevant conditions are valid. A major point of the reduction analysis is to highlight the conditions necessary to sustain models like (9.16). Below, we consider the obverse issue of evaluating (9.16) for relevant losses of information against the various reduction steps, but before doing so, a number of comments on (9.16) and its derivation are worthwhile.

First, if no zs are present, (9.16) is a VAR in the space of $\boldsymbol{h}(\boldsymbol{y}_t)$, so all of the implicit restrictions in stages 9.2–9.11 apply to that class. Secondly, the typologies in Chapters 7 and 8 revealed that innovation errors do not preclude models with autocorrelated errors as simplifications of the general VAD$(\cdot)$. In this sense, common factors do not arise naturally, but as simplifications, reiterating the earlier point that autoregressive errors are a restriction on a model, not a generalization. The VAD$(s, s, \ldots, s)$ model describes a generic class in that almost every known type of linear model used in empirical econometrics is a special case of that class: other classes arise from making other assumptions or approximations (e.g. the structured time-series models noted in Chapter 2). For I(1) data, (9.16) will be an ECM, so it becomes the most general form. Thirdly, Chapter 6 described four possible interpretations of (9.16) for scalar $h(y_t)$: whether it is a regression equation; a least-squares approximation; a contingent plan; or a behavioural plan. Given the validity of every reduction here, it is the first three of these at once when $\boldsymbol{z}_t$ is weakly exogenous for $\boldsymbol{\mu}$. More importantly, we confirm a feature asserted in Chapter 1: ϵ_t is a derived, and not an autonomous, process, being defined by:

$$\boldsymbol{\epsilon}_t = \boldsymbol{A}(L)\boldsymbol{y}_t^* - \boldsymbol{B}(L)\boldsymbol{z}_t^*. \tag{9.17}$$

The only condition under which $\{\boldsymbol{\epsilon}_t\}$ can be regarded as autonomous is that there is no loss of information in any reduction required to obtain (9.17) from (9.1). In that case, $\{\boldsymbol{\epsilon}_t\}$ is the DGP error process, which makes all the reductions vacuous in that (9.17) must also be the DGP. Otherwise, $\{\boldsymbol{\epsilon}_t\}$ is entailed by the reductions. That is a vital insight, because if $\{\boldsymbol{\epsilon}_t\}$ is derived and entailed by the reductions, different error processes

[5] Moving-average error representations are not excluded in principle, and in practice can be approximated by autoregressions of the same lag length: see Hendry and Trivedi (1972), Hendry (1977) and Chapter 15. Thus, we only consider members of the VAD$(\cdot)$ class here.

must result from different reductions. Thus, some reductions will correspond to more informative empirical models than others.

Without an assumption of omniscience, there is no escaping the implication that all empirical econometric models are designed according to criteria specified by their proprietors. Since the error is inevitably derived, it is a human artefact susceptible to design, unless the model is the DGP (see Hendry, 1987). The interesting issue is not whether or not models should be designed, but how they should be designed, and thus how the gap between theory and empirical evidence should be bridged. A further consequence is to question any interpretation of the 'errors' on econometric models: when $\{\epsilon_t\}$ is derived, it is a compound of many reduction losses and cannot sustain claims to be a 'demand' shock or a 'monetary innovation'. This remains true even when μ can be determined from the same model: a simple example is when omitted effects are large and variable, but orthogonal to retained variables so μ can be estimated consistently.

Before analysing model design in detail, we consider an important property of the theory of reduction. For any claimed model, the reduction process can be reversed to determine the loss of information from each reduction. The resulting analysis clarifies the status of empirical models, and more surprisingly, casts light on the primary concepts of econometric analysis discussed in earlier chapters.

9.13 Econometric concepts as measures of no information loss

Previous sections implicitly established how to measure the loss of information at each reduction stage, namely from the specific conditions needed to validate that reduction. Reviewing these, almost every major econometric concept discussed so far is a measure of when there is no loss of information from the associated reduction. We consider the concepts in relation to the order of reductions in sections 9.2–9.12:

§9.2 Aggregation entails no loss of information on marginalizing with respect to disaggregates when the retained information comprises a set of sufficient statistics for the parameters of interest μ.

§9.3 Transformations *per se* do not entail any associated reduction, but directly introduce the concept of parameters of interest, and indirectly the notions that parameters should be invariant and identifiable.

§9.4 Data partition is a preliminary to §9.5, although the decision about which variables to include and which to omit is perhaps the most fundamental determinant of the success or otherwise of empirical modelling.

§9.5 Marginalizing with respect to $\boldsymbol{v}_t$ is without loss providing the remaining data are sufficient for μ, whereas marginalizing with respect to $\mathbf{V}_{t-1}^1$ without loss entails both Granger non-causality for $\boldsymbol{x}_t$ and that the parameters satisfy a cut.

§9.6 Sequential factorization involves no loss when the derived error process is an innovation relative to the history of the random variables, and via the notion of common factors, reveals that autoregressive errors are a restriction and not a generalization.

§9.7 Integrated-data systems can be reduced to I(0) by suitable combinations of cointegration and differencing, allowing conventional inference procedures to be applied to more parsimonious relationships.

§9.8 Conditional factorization reductions, which eliminate marginal processes, lead to no loss of information relative to the joint analysis when the conditioning variables are weakly exogenous for the parameters of interest.

§9.9 This stage introduces the requirement of parameter constancy, and implicitly relates to invariance as constancy across interventions which affect the marginal processes.

§9.10 Lag truncation involves no loss when the error process remains an innovation despite excluding some of the past of relevant variables.

§9.11 Functional-form approximations are one of the few reductions without a separate name. This may be because no reduction need be involved (as when taking logs of log-normally distributed variables): in general, there will be no loss of information when the two densities in (9.15) are equal. However, when y_t and z_t characterize a complete economic system, linearity in any space (y_t^*, z_t^*) seems unlikely due to the presence of multiplicative identities linking nominal values to the products of prices and quantities, together with additive identities defining (say) GNP in nominal terms.

§9.12 The derived model, being a reduction of the DGP, is nested within that DGP and its properties are fully explained by the reduction process: knowledge of the DGP entails knowledge of all reductions thereof, although in practice, the mathematics of any given reductions might be tedious. The issue arises as to whether that property holds for any two models: does knowledge of the first (say) entail knowledge of the second? If so, the first is said to encompass the second. Since all models are reductions of the DGP, they are potentially comparable to see which encompasses which: this will be the subject of Chapter 14, once we have discussed the theory of testing.

The more natural question is the obverse of nesting: does the model encompass the Haavelmo distribution? This is denoted parsimonious encompassing. If so, then no loss of information occurred from the entire reduction sequence, and in that sense, parsimonious encompassing characterizes a valid limit to model reduction (see §9.16 below).

The fact that we can reinterpret many of the concepts that have arisen separately in econometrics as corresponding to when reductions involve no loss of information endows reduction theory with excess content. The theory arose as an explanation for the origin of empirical models and the associated 'problems' approach to empirical econometric modelling. It is an important bonus that it integrates and clarifies most previously established concepts. There is further excess content to come, once we have discussed model design both as an implicit and an explicit process.

9.14 Implicit model design

Consider a model designed by any process in the spectrum of modelling methods from theoretical assertion to data mining. Another investigator could attempt to evaluate that model by retracing the reductions, and checking whether there was any observable loss of information against a more general formulation. At this juncture, we could branch in either one of two directions, both of which are facets of the theory of reduction.

The first is implicit design, or the symptomatology approach in econometrics, which comprises testing for problems like autocorrelation, heteroscedasticity, multicollinearity, omitted variables, non-constant parameters, etc., and correcting these problems as they are ascertained. It is clear why one should be concerned about such problems; it is less clear whether the problems are worse than the supposed cure. From reduction analysis, if a set of variables y_t is selected to be explained by another set of variables z_t using a limited history, then the derived error will not in general satisfy many of the assumptions that are conventionally made. Consequently, problems are likely to arise. That is because, implicitly, reductions are imposed merely by writing down a model like (9.16). This may seem a novel view of model formulation, but reduction appears to be the only way to derive an empirical model.

All too often, empirical practice embodies a methodology of extended implicit design, whereby diagnostic tests are used as selection criteria in model building, successively extending a model to remove each significant test rejection by assuming the validity of the ostensible alternative hypothesis of the corresponding test. Once models are built according to such criteria, it is vacuous to test the models using the same criteria. Since we have already established the drawbacks of a simple-to-general approach in Chapter 7, we turn to the other approach: explicit model design.

9.15 Explicit model design

The explicit design approach seeks to mimic reduction theory in practical research by employing the concepts in §9.13 to minimize the losses due to the reductions selected. It begins from a statistical model corresponding to the Haavelmo distribution, also called the general unrestricted model (GUM). This is the most general, estimable, statistical model that can reasonably be postulated initially, given the present sample of data, previous empirical and theoretical research, and any institutional and measurement information available. By estimable is meant that its parameters can be uniquely determined from the evidence. The GUM is also formulated to contain the parsimonious, interpretable, and invariant econometric model at which it is hoped the modelling exercise will end. For example, in analysing consumers' expenditure, the GUM might comprise the current values and n lags of each of logs of consumption, income, and past wealth, perhaps involving the decomposition of wealth into liquid and illiquid assets and debt; interest rates; measures of demographic structure, including family size, age, and composition; inflation; indices of taxation structure; proxies for major financial innovations; and so on. Allow for everything at the outset that might matter at least logically, if not necessarily empirically in the event, but structured by a careful theoretical analysis — the GUM is not simply the mindless repository of the contents of some large socio-economic databank. Then investigate whether and how this initial general model can be reduced without significant loss of information about the parameters of interest.

Since the general model comprises many highly inter-correlated variables, an immediate worry might be multicollinearity, but we analysed that in §7.8. There is no well-defined concept of multicollinearity, although there are clever parameterizations and less useful parameterizations. While the GUM often has a collinear parameterization initially, we are not interested in its parameters *per se*, but in functions of its parameters, and so do not care about the uncertainty attached to individual parameter estimates, except when that misleads our modelling efforts. The primary role of the GUM is to define the innovation process in the statistical analysis characterized in Chapter 2, and to determine the variance of that innovation process such that no other model on the same data dominates. While the GUM is itself a reduction, it ought to be able to account for all previous results produced when analysing the same data-set. Thus, in addition to defining the innovation process, the GUM should also encompass pre-existing evidence.

To add further structure to this analysis, assume that an econometric model has been constructed by reduction from the corresponding GUM: how can its validity be evaluated? Answering that question will clarify the model-building process, and deliver the third bonus from the theory of reduction: a taxonomy of evaluation information that is complete and exhaustive, corresponding to the reduction process but followed in the opposite direction. Thus, we now consider the information losses that might have occurred at each reduction stage, and classify potential information losses in terms of the taxonomy. Unsurprisingly, in this context of evaluation, precisely the same concepts recur as discussed in §9.13, but related to notions of testing, rather than designing, models.

9.16 A taxonomy of evaluation information

Partition the data $\mathbf{X}_T^1$ used in modelling into the three information sets of past data (§9.16.1), present data (§9.16.2), and future data (§9.16.3). This idea is based on the adage that the past is immutable; we live in the present; and the future is uncertain, which is most of economics in a nutshell. We will check the immutability of the model in the past, the validity of it in the present, and the uncertainty of it into the future. To do so, the data-set under analysis is written in the following partition:

$$\mathbf{X}_T^1 = \left(\mathbf{X}_{t-1}^1 : \mathbf{x}_t : \mathbf{X}_T^{t+1}\right), \tag{9.18}$$

where the classification into the past, present, and future is a relative matter and changes with t. This aspect was reflected in the theory of recursive estimation: whichever time period was selected as t, the sample was divided into the three sections past, current, and future. Additional available information includes theory information (see §9.16.4),[6]

[6] All information sets require dating in a general framework since theories evolve over time, as do measurement systems such as national accounts.

measurement information (§9.16.5), and data of rival models, which could be analysed into past, present, and future in turn (§9.16.6).

Evaluation proceeds by formulating a null hypothesis corresponding to a valid reduction for the corresponding information set, with the associated concept in §9.13, then constructing relevant or interesting alternatives against which to test the model. The following null hypotheses correspond to the above classes of information.

9.16.1 Past data

To check that a model is valid against the past, the null hypothesis is that its error is a homoscedastic innovation against the available information. Testing that there is no loss of information against the past is equivalent to testing that the ignored information is constantly irrelevant over time. In a model which has a homoscedastic innovation error against the data history, there is nothing left to explain in the past, so the model is historically comprehensive. Earlier, we demonstrated that white noise need not be an innovation; that the Durbin–Watson statistic is not a test for an innovation error, but only a test for white noise (and in fact has power mainly against first-order autocorrelation); and that the difference between an innovation and white noise may be due to imposing an invalid common factor (see Ch.2 and §7.7).

9.16.2 Present data

For validation against present data, the contemporaneous conditioning variables in $\boldsymbol{y}_t$, given $\boldsymbol{z}_t$ and $\boldsymbol{X}_{t-1}^{t-s}$, are those in $\boldsymbol{z}_t$. Thus, the model will be valid when $\boldsymbol{z}_t$ is weakly exogenous for the parameters of interest $\boldsymbol{\mu}$. Since there is no loss of information from only analysing a conditional model when $\boldsymbol{z}_t$ is weakly exogenous for $\boldsymbol{\mu}$, the validity of the model in the present maps one–one on to the concept of weak exogeneity, and the relevant evaluation test is for the null hypothesis of weak exogeneity (see Ch.5).

9.16.3 Future data

For future data, the obvious concept is constancy. However, underlying that notion is the more fundamental idea of invariance which requires that the parameters stay constant irrespective of how the $\{\boldsymbol{z}_t\}$ process changes, perhaps within a class of interventions. Invariance, and the closely related concept of super exogeneity, were also discussed in Chapter 5. While harder to test than constancy, aspects of invariance are testable using recursivity combined with super exogeneity and encompassing. Because of its importance as a critique of the use of empirical models for economic policy, the 'Lucas critique' is the subject of analysis following encompassing in Chapter 14.

9.16.4 Theory information

Theory often is a creative stimulus in economics, and one of the most important aspects of theory information is to help specify $\boldsymbol{\mu}$, the vector of parameters of interest. This determines the formal model specification, but does not preclude the possibility that $\boldsymbol{\mu}$ might come from a data-instigated model. Another theory-related concept is identification, namely whether it is possible to uniquely determine the parameters given the model and the form of the evidence (see Ch.11 for a review). The final main concept here is theory consistency, so that there is no evaluation conflict between the model and the theory interpretation. Many over-identified models, corresponding to different ostensible parameters of interest, could be consistent both logically and statistically with a given theory. However, this observational equivalence is of little practical relevance in worlds with regime shifts, as Chapter 14 will clarify.

9.16.5 Measurement information

Measurement information includes price-index theory, constructed identities (such as consumption equals income minus savings), and knowledge about data collection and processing. The main concepts are data accuracy and admissibility. The former is analysed in Chapter 12 and concerns the closeness of the correspondence between the latent constructs that occur in the economic mechanism and the observed magnitudes in the empirical study. A model is data admissible if its predictions automatically satisfy all known data constraints. Inadmissible models are logically inconsistent with the data even though that does not necessarily entail that they are poor empirical representations: for example, the heights of individuals are approximately normally distributed even though height must be positive. However, it would be reasonable to worry if consumption plus saving was supposed to equal income but did not.

9.16.6 Rival models

Rival models on common data lead to the concept of encompassing. One of the more powerful predictions from the theory of reduction is that all models are comparable: when all models are reductions of a common DGP they are comparable by retracing the reduction process far enough to find the process from which they were all reduced. Thus, while models may be non-nested relative to one another, all models are nested in the DGP.

The concept of encompassing asks of each model M_i, 'can M_i explain the results of other models $\mathsf{M}_j (i \neq j)$?' Consider a simple example: the DGP is M_0: $x_t \sim \mathsf{IN}[\mu, \sigma^2]$; model 1 is M_1: $x_t \sim \mathsf{IN}[\phi, 1]$; and model 2 is M_2: $x_t \sim \mathsf{IN}[0, \omega^2]$. The two models M_1 and M_2 are non-nested in the sense that they are not special cases of each other when $(\mu, \sigma) \neq (0, 1)$. At the same time, they are both special cases of M_0. What would somebody who believed in M_1 expect to find when they fitted M_2? Because the variance becomes the mean-square error when a zero mean is enforced, they would expect to find that $\omega^2 = (1 + \phi^2)$ in the fitted M_2. Thus, from the distribution in M_1, one can work out what will be found in M_2 even though M_2 is not nested in M_1. Conversely, what would one expect to find in M_1 on the basis of the model M_2? We must expect to find $\phi = 0$ in M_1. Encompassing occurs with respect to the relevant parameter when the prediction is correct. The first prediction requires that $\sigma^2 = 1$; and the second that $\mu = 0$. When the models are non-nested, both cannot occur; but the models are isomorphic in a DGP where $(\mu, \sigma) = (0, 1)$.

Consequently, encompassing is anti-symmetric: if M_1 explains M_2, M_2 cannot explain M_1 unless either the two models are isomorphic or the distribution is degenerate. To understand that result, note that M_1 must be able to explain M_0 in order to explain M_2. In many widely-assumed stochastic processes, a necessary and sufficient condition for M_1 to encompass M_2 is that M_1 can correctly predict the outcome for the initial general model M_0 that nests both M_1 and M_2: if M_1 can predict M_0, then M_1 can predict M_2. If M_1 cannot predict M_2, it cannot predict M_0 when that is the nesting model of M_1 and M_2. Thus, encompassing is really asking the question, 'Can the reduced model explain the results of the general model from which the reduction started?'; this was called parsimonious encompassing above. In the evaluation context, encompassing requires a model to act like a pseudo-DGP with the property that it can explain all the findings in the analysis.

Encompassing ensures that there is no loss of information in the reduction as a whole, and hence the final question is to ask of the selected econometric model, 'Does it parsimoniously encompass the initial unrestricted model?' When it does, the reductions are valid and a final product which satisfies all six criteria is a valid, simplified, and interpretable econometric model of the statistical mechanism. Such a model goes beyond corroboration given the data evidence, as measured by satisfying various tests — some of which may have low power relative to the GUM — by accounting for the results of other models, and predicting the results of those models without actually estimating them. Encompassing, therefore, is both predicted by reduction theory and explains when to stop a reduction sequence, namely, when a simplification cannot encompass the general model, because at that point important information is lost: see Chapter 14 for statistical details. Table 9.1 on page 366 records the design criteria. We can summarize the six main criteria as:

- §9.16.1 homoscedastic, innovation errors;
- §9.16.2 weakly exogenous conditioning variables for the parameters of interest;
- §9.16.3 constant, invariant parameters of interest;
- §9.16.4 theory-consistent, identifiable structures;
- §9.16.5 data admissible formulations on accurate observations; and
- §9.16.6 encompassing rival models.

Models which satisfy the first five information sets are said to be congruent: by analogy with one triangle which matches another in all respects, the model matches the evidence in all measured respects. An encompassing congruent model satisfies all six criteria.

A congruent model is not necessarily true. As seen in Chapter 4, an innovation is relative to its information set but may be predictable from other information. Thus, a sequence of congruent models could be developed, each of which encompassed all previous models. Satisfying all six criteria thereby sustains a progressive research strategy. Moreover, true models, if such can be conceived, would be congruent, so it is useful to exclude non-congruent models. Further, congruency or its absence can be ascertained from the available evidence, subject to the usual caveats about incorrect test-rejection decisions, and hence it provides an operational criterion, unlike truth in an empirical science. An important methodological implication of this chapter, therefore, is the advantage of substituting the joint requirements of encompassing and congruency for truth as the final decision criteria for empirical modelling.

Table 9.1 Evaluation and design criteria

Information Set	Null Hypothesis	Alternative Hypothesis	Sources
relative past of own data	innovation errors	first-order residual autocorrelation	Durbin and Watson (1950, 1951)
"	"	j^{th}-order residual autocorrelation	Box and Pierce (1970), Godfrey (1978), Harvey (1981a)
"	"	invalid parameter restrictions	Johnston (1972)
"	"	j^{th}-order ARCH	Engle (1982a)
"	"	heteroscedasticity quadratic in regressors	White (1980a), Nicholls and Pagan (1983)
"	"	j^{th}-order RESET	Ramsey (1969)
"	normality of the errors	skewness and excess kurtosis	Jarque and Bera (1980), Doornik and Hansen (1994)
relative present	weakly exogenous regressors	invalid conditioning	Sargan (1958, 1980a), Engle *et al.* (1983)
relative future	constant parameters; adequate forecasts	parameter non-constancy; predictive failure	Fisher (1922a), Chow (1960), Brown, Durbin and Evans (1975), Hendry (1979b)
economic theory	theory consistency; cointegration	'implausible' coefficients; no cointegration	Engle and Granger (1987)
measurement system	data accuracy, admissibility	'impossible' observables	Hendry and Richard (1982)
relative past of rival data	variance dominance	relative poor fit	Hendry and Richard (1982)
"	variance encompassing	inexplicable observed error variance	Cox (1961, 1962), Pesaran (1974), Hendry (1983a)
"	parameter encompassing	significant additional variables	Johnston (1963), Mizon and Richard (1986)
relative present	exogeneity encompassing	inexplicable valid conditioning	Hendry (1988)
relative future	MSFE dominance	poor relative forecasts	
"	forecast encompassing	informative forecasts from alternative model	Chong and Hendry (1986)
"	forecast-model encompassing	alternative model regressors valuable in forecasting	Ericsson (1992b)

As ever, new problems arise by doing so. For example, later models reveal that earlier models were non-congruent, and hence false. Arguing from false propositions can generate contradictions and the apparent ability to prove any desired proposition: is there a danger of such an outcome here? The answer seems to be negative, since empirical models are not sets of propositions. In particular, a model could be non-congruent by being incomplete rather than inconsistent with reality.

Conversely, some older problems are given a new slant. In the process of reduction to a claimed sufficient representation, information can be discarded conditional on the validity of the reduction. Such information can provide the basis for diagnostic testing without contaminating specification testing, precisely because it could be discarded: in principle, a different agency could undertake the diagnostic testing on the discarded data. For example, when $x_t \sim \mathsf{IN}[\mu, \sigma^2]$ and $(x_1 \dots x_T)$ are observed, $(\bar{x}, s^2)$ are sufficient statistics for (μ, σ^2) and the remaining data can be ignored. However, those data (in effect, $T - 2$, scaled, 1-step residuals) can be used to test the assumptions of independence, normality, homoscedasticity, and so on. Providing that the maintained model is correct, such tests will sustain that outcome (when properly controlled for overall rejection frequencies); when it is not correct, tests will reveal that problem (subject to Type II errors). For the large sample sizes envisaged at level A, both errors can be made negligibly small. Then non-rejection sustains the initial inferences about (μ, σ^2) from $(\bar{x}, s^2)$ as if testing had not occurred, whereas rejection warns that the framework is invalid: the independent testing agency should alert the original investigator in such a state of nature. It is to protect ourselves against an inappropriate framework, when specification testing may go awry, that diagnostic testing is so valuable (for an excellent analysis, see Mayo, 1981). An advantage of time series is the constant accrual of new information to allow evaluation of past decisions, emphasizing that econometric modelling is a continuing activity, not a 'one-off' forging of empirical laws (see Pagan, 1987).

The primary objective of this part of the book was to analyse the concepts, models, and processes underpinning the development of congruent empirical econometric models. That task has been achieved as far as we can go without further technology, so, in Part II, we develop additional tools and return to apply the analysis to level C in Part III.

9.17 Exercises

9.1 Describe the main steps in the theory of reduction from a vector time series $\boldsymbol{w}_t$ of k variables, where $\boldsymbol{W}_T^1 = \{\boldsymbol{w}_1 \dots \boldsymbol{w}_T\}$, to a conditional econometric model involving $n + 1$ variables $\{y_t : \boldsymbol{z}_t\}$ where there are $n \ll k$ variables in $\boldsymbol{z}$. In your answer, carefully explain the main potential losses of information from reduction steps, the associated econometric concepts, and how you would investigate the validity of each reduction.

9.2 Consider the $AD(1,1)$ model:

$$y_t = \beta_0 + \beta_1 z_t + \beta_2 z_{t-1} + \beta_3 y_{t-1} + \epsilon_t \tag{9.19}$$

with $\epsilon_t \sim \mathsf{IN}\left[0, \sigma_\epsilon^2\right]$.

(a) Derive encompassing predictions for (9.19) from at least three model types from Chapter 7 when the $AD(1,1)$ is the DGP and z_t is strongly exogenous for $\boldsymbol{\beta}$.
(b) How would you test the weak exogeneity of z_t for $\boldsymbol{\beta}$ in (9.19) if its exogeneity status is unknown?
(c) How would you test the super exogeneity of z_t for $\boldsymbol{\beta}$ in (9.19) if the marginal model for z_t is:

$$z_t = \gamma_0 + \gamma_1 z_{t-1} + \gamma_{2t} x_t + \nu_t \qquad (9.20)$$

where $\nu_t \sim \mathsf{IN}[0, \omega_t^2]$, γ_{2t} and ω_t^2 are policy-determined parameters, and x_t is strongly exogenous for $(\boldsymbol{\beta}, \gamma_t)$?
(d) Derive one recursively computable test of the $AD(1,1)$ model.
(e) Compare three members of the typology on an empirical data-set, considering their mutual encompassing predictions.

9.3 Briefly summarize the main issues arising in the theory of model design. Include in your discussion, the interpretations of models, their derivation, evaluation, and alteration in the light of sample information.

9.4 What is the taxonomy of information and what purposes does it serve? Delineate the main information sets, their role as model evaluation criteria, and the associated econometric concepts.

Part II

Statistical Tools for Econometric Analysis

10

Likelihood

The analysis in Part I provides the framework for level B. The statistical model, estimation criteria, and four approaches to estimation methods are noted, before focusing on likelihood-based methods. The likelihood function is the obverse of the data-density function, and summaries thereof are discussed, leading to maximum likelihood estimation. The first derivative of the log-likelihood, called the score, plays a central role in estimation and inference so its properties are described, followed by a discussion of maximum likelihood estimation and its properties, especially in large samples. Two solved examples illustrate the analysis. Misleading inferences due to incorrect variance estimation and possible solutions thereof are investigated. Derived distributions, asymptotic equivalencies of other methods to maximum likelihood, the concentrated (or profile) likelihood function, and marginal and conditional distributions are discussed, leading to the concept of an estimator generating equation which will play a major role in Chapter 11.

10.1 Review of Part I

Part I developed the econometric analysis at level A, namely when the data-generation process was known in every respect, and explored the implications of alternative model specifications for different data processes (DGPs). The economic mechanism was construed as a high-dimensional, integrated but cointegrated, dynamic system, expressed in the form of the statistical generating mechanism (SGM) $\mathsf{D}_{\mathsf{X}}(\boldsymbol{X}_T^1|\boldsymbol{X}_0,\boldsymbol{\theta})$, given a set of initial conditions $\boldsymbol{X}_0$, where $\boldsymbol{X}_T^1 = (\boldsymbol{x}_1 \ldots \boldsymbol{x}_T)'$ is the observation matrix on the set of n random variables $\{\boldsymbol{x}_t\}$ of relevance, and $\boldsymbol{\theta} \in \Theta \subseteq \mathbb{R}^k$ is the parameter vector in a parameter space Θ which is a subset of k-dimensional real space.

Chapter 2 focused on sequential factorization of $\mathsf{D}_{\mathsf{X}}(\boldsymbol{X}_T^1|\boldsymbol{X}_0,\boldsymbol{\theta})$, leading to innovation processes, which are related to martingale difference sequences (MDS). Innovation errors were shown to be derived, rather than autonomous, processes, but able to sustain econometric modelling, and autoregressive errors were a restriction on a model rather than a generalization. Chapter A4 presents a more technical treatment of asymptotic distribution theory, based on the weaker assumption of the errors being an MDS. Chapter 3 extended the analysis to integrated data processes.

Chapter 4 then analysed dynamic processes, emphasizing the issues of unit roots and nonsense regressions, where the latter are interpreted in terms of an inadequate sequential factorization of the DGP. Having completed a first round of analysis of dynamics, Chapter 5 turned to a study of contemporaneous conditioning and hence the concepts of weak, strong, and super exogeneity and their relation to Granger non-causality. Chapter 6 discussed the interpretation of linear equations, as a framework for analyses of expectations, autocorrelation corrections, simple dynamic models, and lag structures, leading to the typology in Chapter 7. Chapter 8 extended the analysis to dynamic systems and econometric models thereof. Finally, Chapter 9 integrated the various aspects of Part I in the theory of reduction, explaining empirical models as derived entities susceptible to design, either implicitly or explicitly, but open to evaluation against a wide range of information. Empirical models of a (transformed) subset of the original variables $\boldsymbol{x}_t$ arise as reductions of the DGP, from aggregation, data transformation, cointegration, marginalization, sequential factorization, conditioning, lag truncation, and linearization operations on $\mathsf{D}_{\mathsf{X}}(\boldsymbol{X}_T^1|\boldsymbol{X}_0, \boldsymbol{\theta})$ to produce linear conditional dynamic systems of the form $\boldsymbol{y}_t = \boldsymbol{\pi} \boldsymbol{z}_t + \boldsymbol{\epsilon}_t$ where $\boldsymbol{\pi} = \boldsymbol{g}(\boldsymbol{\theta})$. The typologies of single equations and systems highlighted their economic and statistical interpretations, the reductions entailed, and their often restrictive implications. The importance of reduction theory, beyond explaining the origin and status of empirical models, is that it also clarifies existing econometric concepts such as exogeneity, non-causality, innovations, invariance etc., by relating them to reduction operations, and leads to a taxonomy of information sets and associated model-selection criteria. Part III will resume the analysis of model design at level C, drawing on these developments: in this part, we first study the theory of estimation and inference when the precise form, structure, and specification of $\mathsf{D}_{\mathsf{X}}(\boldsymbol{X}_T^1|\boldsymbol{X}_0, \boldsymbol{\theta})$ is known, but the location of the population value $\boldsymbol{\theta}_p \in \Theta$ (the numerical value of every $\{\theta_i\}$ for the relevant mechanism) is unknown.

So far we have worked with least-squares methods and now develop more general tools for analysing economic data and econometric models. Despite the artificiality at level B of a formulation where we assume knowledge of the DGP $\mathsf{D}_{\mathsf{X}}(\boldsymbol{X}_T^1|\boldsymbol{X}_0, \boldsymbol{\theta})$ but not of the value of $\boldsymbol{\theta}_p$, this step is needed in order to derive methods for estimating $\boldsymbol{\theta}$; we investigate testing hypotheses about functions of $\boldsymbol{\theta}$ in Chapter 13.

It is important to keep in perspective the role of estimation as a model-building tool. If level B were realistic, so that the DGP was known except for the value $\boldsymbol{\theta}_p$ of $\boldsymbol{\theta}$, then we would probably proceed differently from the approach to be described below. When knowledge that $\boldsymbol{\theta}_p$ is the correct vector of parameters includes knowing that all of its elements are constant and non-zero, we could simply estimate $\boldsymbol{\theta}$ in a way deemed optimal given the criterion function. However, even when a model has a known parameterization, there may exist features that are highly uncertain. In particular, some θ_i may be zero, but if we do not know a priori which ones are zero, we may want to act differently between the zero and the non-zero elements prior to obtaining final estimates (e.g., eliminating zero-valued parameters). Such an approach leads to the problem known as pre-testing. Conversely, specifying $\boldsymbol{\theta}$ usually entails imposing zero values on myriads of other potential parameters, and some of these might be tested for their relevance during a modelling exercise. The need for either form of testing casts doubt on the claim that $\mathsf{D}_{\mathsf{X}}(\cdot)$ is characterized by $\boldsymbol{\theta}$. An implicit assumption of level B discourse is that all elements of $\boldsymbol{\theta}$ are relevant, although some may be of greater interest than others. Eliminating the zero elements in $\boldsymbol{\theta}$ on the basis of data evidence to achieve a more parsimonious set of parameters, when it is unclear that $\mathsf{D_X}(\cdot)$ is actually characterized by $\boldsymbol{\theta}_p$, as occurs in level C, raises model-selection problems of a different kind. To understand this last difficulty, we need estimation tools which work well when $\boldsymbol{\theta}_p$ does characterize $\mathsf{D_X}(\cdot)$, so we first proceed to that topic.

10.2 The statistical model

Although there is a large range of possible statistical principles that could be used, the only one that we will discuss in detail is that based on the likelihood function, which follows naturally in a reduction framework. In particular, we have conceptualized the SGM as:

$$\mathsf{D_X}\left(\boldsymbol{X}_T^1 \mid \boldsymbol{X}_0, \boldsymbol{\theta}\right) = \prod_{t=1}^{T} \mathsf{D_x}\left(\boldsymbol{x}_t \mid \boldsymbol{X}_{t-1}, \boldsymbol{\theta}\right) \tag{10.1}$$

where $\boldsymbol{\theta}_p \in \Theta$ is the value in the population from which the sample of $\boldsymbol{X}_T^1$ was generated. This does not entail that $\boldsymbol{\theta}_p$ is the true value in any useful sense, as will be seen later.

The first simplification concerns the sampling procedure under which the $\{\boldsymbol{x}_t\}$ are obtained, and we assume that $\boldsymbol{\nu}_t = \boldsymbol{x}_t - \mathsf{E}[\boldsymbol{x}_t|\boldsymbol{X}_{t-1}^{t-n}]$ is an IID error. While the IID assumption is too strong to be reasonable for error processes in time-series economics, essentially the same results can be proved using the sequential factorization of $\mathsf{D_X}(\cdot)$ in (10.1) which constructs a martingale difference sequence as the basic innovation process (see Ch.2). However, martingales would necessitate the more powerful asymptotic theory discussed in Chapter A4, without yielding a great deal of extra insight. Consequently, we will note difficulties which arise when it is too restrictive to assume that $\{\boldsymbol{\nu}_t\}$ is IID, even for the tools that we will be using, but otherwise in Part II we ignore the issue of how the data were sampled.

We also require assumptions to eliminate strong time dependence in the $\{\boldsymbol{x}_t\}$ process, and assume that it is stationary and ergodic in most derivations of the properties of methods of estimating $\boldsymbol{\theta}$. Although inferences can go wrong when $\{\boldsymbol{x}_t\}$ is not stationary, it is difficult to consider the distributions of all available methods of estimating $\boldsymbol{\theta}$, for all possible DGPs. In particular, allowing for I(1) processes would be too complicated at this stage. We appeal to the results in Chapter 7, showing that models can be reduced to I(0) by appropriate transformations, and assume that all relevant equations are expressed in that form from the outset. Chapter 3 considered the distributions which result when I(1) data occur in models, and Chapter 11 will consider the modelling of cointegrated processes.

Combining these two claims, there will be little loss in this chapter by assuming that the $\{\boldsymbol{x}_t\}$ themselves are IID, and we reserve generalizations to heterogeneous and/or dynamic processes for Chapter A4 and specialized subsections.

There are three cases to consider: (i) one observation; (ii) a sample of size T; (iii) the population. Most of the time, we deal with one observation when deriving basic results about likelihood functions, then consider a sample and finally examine how the sample relates to the population from which it might have been drawn. An IID assumption is restrictive in this context since all observations are assumed to be alike, but generalizations to allow for heterogeneity are noted.

The final preamble concerns the simultaneous status of the $\mathbf{x}_t$, and functions thereof, as observed numbers and as random variables: in asymptotic situations (i.e. $T \to \infty$), we also think of past outcomes as numbers and potential future outcomes as random variables. Because of the need to use capital letters for matrices, it would complicate the notation unduly to retain a notational distinction between random variables and their realizations, and for the most part at level B, whether variables can be regarded as random or as outcomes depends on the context. A Monte Carlo analogy may help: draw a sample $\mathbf{X}_T^1$ from $\mathsf{D_X}(\mathbf{X}_T^1|\mathbf{X}_0, \boldsymbol{\theta}_p)$ and compute the values of any relevant statistics. After drawing $\mathbf{X}_T^1$, that matrix is a set of numbers; but we can draw again as often as desired, each time calculating the statistics. This generates the distributions of the statistics, equivalent to those which would be obtained by treating $\mathbf{X}_T^1$ as a random matrix. Since an estimator is a computational rule for mapping random variables into statistics, and estimate is the outcome on any given sample, the same notion applies.

For the remainder of this chapter, therefore, the SGM and DGP are given by:

$$\prod_{t=1}^{T} \mathsf{D_x}(\mathbf{x}_t \mid \boldsymbol{\theta}_p) \text{ where } \boldsymbol{\theta}_p \in \Theta,$$

and the objective is to develop 'good' methods of estimating the unknown value $\boldsymbol{\theta}_p$ of $\boldsymbol{\theta}$ from a sample realization on $\{\mathbf{x}_t\}$.

10.3 Estimation criteria and estimation methods

Given the specification of level B, the problem is to obtain the 'best' estimation method for $\boldsymbol{\theta}$ when $\boldsymbol{\theta}_p$ could be any value in Θ. However, that transpires to be a difficult problem, mainly because what is the best in one context need not be best in another. The rules that statisticians have developed for selecting good estimators of $\boldsymbol{\theta}$ involve either laying down criteria, or postulating methods. The first approach provides a list of criteria which good estimators of $\boldsymbol{\theta}$ should satisfy, such as unbiasedness, minimum variance in a certain class, consistency and so on. Such criteria are open to question, as is whether the class of problems satisfying such criteria is interesting. We will not be able to obtain unbiased estimators in general in econometrics, nor minimum variance estimators even in restrictive classes. Indeed, we are frequently driven to require weak properties for estimators viewed from the perspective of the criterion approach. Moreover, the criteria can conflict with each other: the only unbiased estimator may not be the minimum-variance linear estimator, so choice becomes arbitrary, or criteria must be combined, as with minimum-variance (or best) linear unbiased estimators (usually denoted BLUE).

Also, there are many sensible estimators in econometrics whose low-order moments such as means or variances do not exist, and we would never pick any of these estimators on (say) a minimum-variance criterion. Nevertheless, the non-existence of a variance does not entail that such estimators are necessarily poor in other senses, and they may have a higher probability of being in any reasonable neighbourhood of the population parameter value than estimators with finite variances. Chapter A3 offers a background discussion.

More usually in time-series econometrics, large-sample criteria are used, such as consistency or asymptotic efficiency. These will provide the main estimator choice criteria here, primarily to select between otherwise equivalent methods. Chapter A4 describes the various concepts. Consistency alone is weak, since from reduction theory, any empirical model has a parameter β_p (say) which is a function of θ_p, and it is usually easy to obtain consistent estimators of β_p, without these necessarily being of any interest economically.

The second approach to selecting between estimators is to postulate a general method for estimating θ and then ask about its properties. There are four methods in general use.

(a) The method of moments, including least squares, instrumental variables, and generalized method of moments (GMM). These will be treated as approximations to the preferred approach in (d);
(b) Bayesian methods, where both x_t and θ are treated as random variables, so θ is no longer a fixed number, and is an entity in the mind rather than a feature of the world. The uncertainty about the population value of θ at the start of the analysis is represented by a density over θ, called the prior density, which incorporates everything supposedly known about θ. Then the posterior distribution of θ is calculated from Bayes theorem. As more information accrues, the posterior is updated. Here, we will only focus on the elements of Bayesian methods in common with the fourth method below.[1]
(c) Non-parametric and semi-parametric methods make few assumptions about the underlying parameterization, and try to infer relationships directly from the data. They are a promising technique in many areas, but will not be discussed here due to present limitations on the dimensions of the multivariate problems they can handle (see §A3.6 for the scalar case).
(d) Likelihood based methods, which are the focus of this chapter. Likelihood methods are more demanding in terms of informational requirements than the method of moments since distributional assumptions are required, and less demanding than Bayesian methods since a definite prior distribution is not needed. Moreover, they follow naturally from the approach in Part I, in that if different values of θ generate different observations on x_t, that evidence on x_t should in turn yield information about θ.

[1] See Hendry, Leamer and Poirier (1990) for an extensive discussion of Bayesian and classical methods.

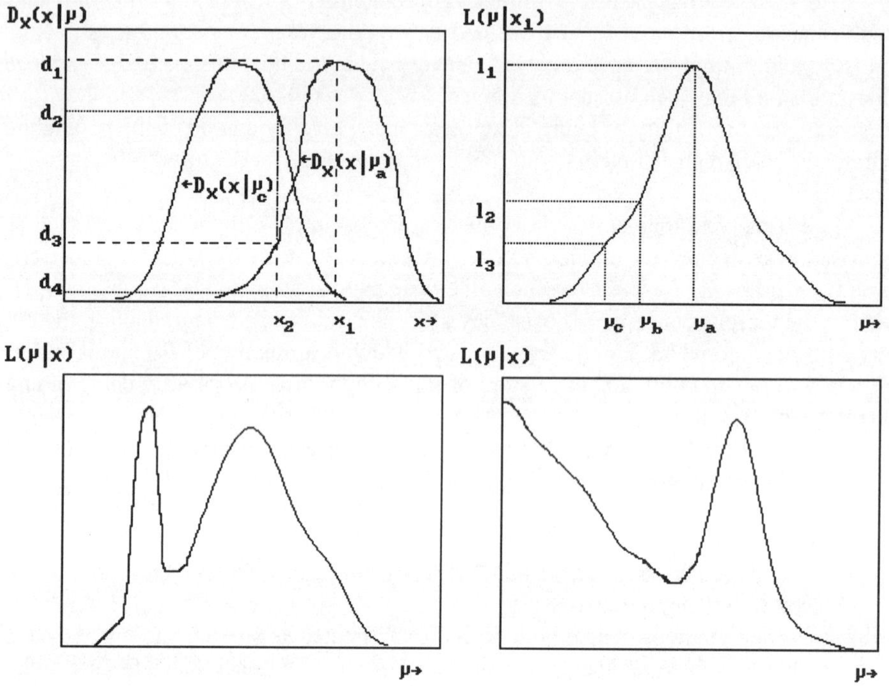

Fig. 10.1 Density and likelihood functions

The simplest example is:

$$x_t \sim \mathsf{IN}\left[\mu, 1\right] \tag{10.2}$$

so that larger values of x_t correspond on average to larger values of μ. When $\mu = 0$, then x_t should be located around zero (as $\mathsf{E}[x_t] = 0$), whereas, when $\mu = 10$, samples of x_t will on average be centred around ten. When the standard deviation of the distribution is 100, however, it would be difficult to discriminate between these two values of μ except in large samples. The essence of estimation is to invert the problem between levels A and B: in the former, we deduce the probability structure of data samples given $\boldsymbol{\theta}_p$, whereas in the latter, from the observed outcomes, we try to determine the most likely parameter value to have generated the particular sample of xs. The central idea of the likelihood approach can be understood from Fig. 10.1a which shows two density functions $\mathsf{D}_{\mathsf{x}}(x|\mu)$ for different values of μ in (10.2). Suppose that μ takes the value μ_a, and the sample value is x_1. When $\mathsf{D}_{\mathsf{x}}(x|\mu_a)$ is the DGP, the probability of observing x_1 is high, especially in comparison to the probability of observing x_2. But that is not the case when μ takes the value μ_c and the distribution becomes $\mathsf{D}_{\mathsf{x}}(x|\mu_c)$, in which case x_1 has a low probability, whereas x_2 has a high probability. While x_2 could have come from either $\mathsf{D}_{\mathsf{x}}(x|\mu_a)$ or $\mathsf{D}_{\mathsf{x}}(x|\mu_c)$, it is more likely to have come from the latter. Data evidence reflects the underlying state of nature and this is formalized in the likelihood function.

10.4 The likelihood function

At level A, the problem is one of deducing the probability of observing certain values of the xs given the value $\boldsymbol{\theta}_p$ of $\boldsymbol{\theta}$; at level B, it is one of inferring the likely value of $\boldsymbol{\theta}$ given a sample of xs. To relate these formally, we define the likelihood of $\boldsymbol{\theta}$ given $\boldsymbol{x}$ as $\mathsf{L}(\boldsymbol{\theta}|\boldsymbol{x})$ where:

$$\mathsf{D}_{\mathsf{X}}\left(\boldsymbol{X}_T^1 \mid \boldsymbol{\theta}\right) = \phi\left(\boldsymbol{X}_T^1\right) \mathsf{L}\left(\boldsymbol{\theta} \mid \boldsymbol{X}_T^1\right), \tag{10.3}$$

when $\phi(\cdot)$ does not depend on $\boldsymbol{\theta}$ (and will be normalized at unity below). Thus, $\mathsf{D}_{\mathsf{X}}(\boldsymbol{X}|\boldsymbol{\theta})$ and $\mathsf{L}(\boldsymbol{\theta}|\boldsymbol{X})$ are essentially the same function, but interpreted differently. On the right-hand side, $\boldsymbol{\theta}$ is an argument of the function $\mathsf{L}(\cdot)$, and the $\boldsymbol{X}_T^1$ are taken at their observed values (a semi-colon following $\boldsymbol{X}_T^1$ would denote that $\boldsymbol{X}_T^1$ was conditional on something else, such as the initial conditions $\boldsymbol{X}_0$ in a dynamic setting). In Fig. 10.1b, the xs are observed numbers, and we seek the most likely value of μ, which for x_1 in Fig. 10.1a corresponds to μ_a (here, x_1 is the maximum of the function in Fig. 10.1a, which occurs at μ_a). Conversely, as μ_b corresponds to a density for which x_2 is the most probable drawing (not shown), μ_b is relatively unlikely, and μ_c is very unlikely, to be the population parameter value when the observation is x_1. We could calculate the 'likeliness' of the μs for other observations: had x_2 been sampled, a different location of the function would have resulted from that shown. From equation (10.3), all information about x is contained in the likelihood, so there is no more information about θ, (unless we introduce prior information), and in a scalar parameterization, we could almost complete the statistical analysis at this stage by graphing $\mathsf{L}(\theta|x_T^1)$.

However, if $\boldsymbol{\theta}$ is a high-dimensional parameter, then it is impossible to plot $\mathsf{L}(\boldsymbol{\theta}|\cdot)$, and we must summarize the information in the likelihood function. There are many ways of summarizing $\mathsf{L}(\boldsymbol{\theta}|\cdot)$ in terms of moments, ranges, its derivatives, and so on. Since the most likely $\boldsymbol{\theta}$ is of interest, a convenient summary is in terms of the point where the tangent at the maximum occurs together with the curvature of $\mathsf{L}(\cdot)$ in that neighbourhood, corresponding to the first and second derivatives of the likelihood function. The first derivative helps locate the maximum and the second derivative helps separate functions by their steepness or shallowness around the maximum point. The value of $\boldsymbol{\theta}$ is better determined when the function curves steeply than when the function is flat, although the maximizing value of $\boldsymbol{\theta}$ may be the same. Conversely, two derivatives alone are uninformative when the likelihood function is not well behaved, as in the problematic examples shown in Figs. 10.1c and 10.1d. To describe the likelihood function in terms of only its first two derivatives at a point is a travesty of the information content in these situations.

Although pathological examples are relatively easy to construct, in many situations of practical relevance the likelihood function is well behaved in large samples so that maximum likelihood has become a major technique for estimating unknown parameters. Some attention has also been paid to related estimators, such as Bayesian methods, or methods which integrate over the likelihood to calculate the average value of $\boldsymbol{\theta}$ — rather than the modal value — weighting the different values of $\boldsymbol{\theta}$ by their likeliness; and to methods which modify the function to be maximized to ensure better-behaved estimators. We briefly note some results about such developments in the next chapter.

10.5 Maximum likelihood estimation

The maximum likelihood estimator (MLE) $\hat{\boldsymbol{\theta}}$ of a parameter $\boldsymbol{\theta}$ is defined by:

$$\hat{\boldsymbol{\theta}} = \underset{\boldsymbol{\theta}\in\Theta}{\operatorname{argmax}} \left\{ \mathsf{L}(\hat{\boldsymbol{\theta}}) \right\}.$$

We first consider the MLE for the example in (10.2), where the density function for an IID sample with T observations is:

$$\prod_{t=1}^{T} \mathsf{D_x}(x_t \mid \mu) = (2\pi)^{-\frac{T}{2}} \exp\left[-\sum_{t=1}^{T} \frac{(x_t-\mu)^2}{2} \right] = \prod_{t=1}^{T} \mathsf{L}(\mu \mid x_t) = \mathsf{L}\left(\mu \mid \boldsymbol{x}_T^1\right). \tag{10.4}$$

Then $\mathsf{L}(\mu|\boldsymbol{x}_T^1)$ is the likelihood function for μ conditional on the xs, and μ is an argument. Using the Monte Carlo analogy in §10.4 above, think of the xs as random variables, so that the likelihood function itself is a random variable.

Because of the exponential in functions like (10.4), the log-likelihood function is often more convenient, and is denoted by:

$$\ell\left(\mu \mid \boldsymbol{x}_T^1\right) = \log \mathsf{L}\left(\mu \mid \boldsymbol{x}_T^1\right) = \sum_{t=1}^{T} \ell\left(\mu \mid x_t\right) = \sum_{t=1}^{T} \ell_t\left(\mu\right), \tag{10.5}$$

for IID variables. The maxima of $\mathsf{L}(\cdot)$ and $\ell(\cdot)$ occur at the same value of the parameters, so first-derivative information is unaffected, and it will turn out that the second derivative of $\ell(\cdot)$ has a useful role as well. When $\{x_t\}$ is not an IID process, $\ell_t(\boldsymbol{\theta}) = \log \mathsf{D_x}(x_t|\boldsymbol{X}_{t-1}^{t-s}, \boldsymbol{\theta})$, and so from (10.1), equation (10.3) still reduces to a sum as in (10.5).

In many statistical problems under reasonable (but not unrestrictive) assumptions, $\ell(\cdot)$ is a continuously-differentiable function of $\boldsymbol{\theta}$, and the maximum can be computed from equating the first derivatives to zero. Since $\ell(\cdot)$ is a function of a set of random variables, so is the derivative of $\ell(\cdot)$ with respect to $\boldsymbol{\theta}$. The first derivative is known as the score, and for a single observation will be denoted by the $k \times 1$ vector $\boldsymbol{q}_t(\cdot)$:

$$\frac{\partial \ell_t(\hat{\boldsymbol{\theta}})}{\partial \boldsymbol{\theta}} = \frac{\partial \ell\left(\boldsymbol{\theta}|\boldsymbol{x}_t\right)}{\partial \boldsymbol{\theta}} = \boldsymbol{q}_t(\hat{\boldsymbol{\theta}}) \text{ for } t = 1, \ldots, T. \tag{10.6}$$

Since the qs are random variables when the xs are random variables, they have a derived distribution which is obtained below. Given a set $(\boldsymbol{q}_1(\hat{\boldsymbol{\theta}}) \ldots \boldsymbol{q}_T(\boldsymbol{\theta}))$ corresponding to a sample of xs, there is an average score denoted by:

$$\bar{\boldsymbol{q}}_{(T)}(\hat{\boldsymbol{\theta}}) = T^{-1} \sum_{t=1}^{T} \boldsymbol{q}_t(\hat{\boldsymbol{\theta}}) = T^{-1} \frac{\partial \ell(\hat{\boldsymbol{\theta}})}{\partial \boldsymbol{\theta}} = T^{-1} \boldsymbol{q}(\hat{\boldsymbol{\theta}}). \tag{10.7}$$

Unless ambiguity arises, $\boldsymbol{q}_t(\hat{\boldsymbol{\theta}})$ is often denoted by $\boldsymbol{q}_t$. As a necessary condition, the maximizing value $\hat{\boldsymbol{\theta}}$ satisfies $\bar{\boldsymbol{q}}_{(T)}(\hat{\boldsymbol{\theta}}) = \mathbf{0}$.

The second derivative, called the Hessian, is denoted by H_t. When $\boldsymbol{\theta}$ is a $k \times 1$ vector, $\boldsymbol{H}_t$ will be a $k \times k$ matrix. In the scalar case of (10.2), for example:

$$\frac{\partial^2 \ell\left(\mu|x_t\right)}{\partial \mu^2} = \frac{\partial q_t\left(\mu|x_t\right)}{\partial \mu} = H\left(\mu \mid x_t\right) = H_t\left(\mu\right). \tag{10.8}$$

Further, $H_t(\mu)$ is random when x_t is random, and there is a set $(H_1(\mu)\ldots H_T(\mu))$ of Hessians for a sample of xs with:

$$\bar{H}_{(T)}\left(\mu\right) = T^{-1}\sum_{t=1}^{T} H_t\left(\mu\right). \tag{10.9}$$

Again, $H_t(\mu)$ is often written as H_t. When $\boldsymbol{\theta}$ is a vector:

$$\frac{\partial^2 \ell\left(\boldsymbol{\theta}|\boldsymbol{x}_t\right)}{\partial \boldsymbol{\theta}\partial \boldsymbol{\theta}'} = \frac{\partial \boldsymbol{q}_t(\hat{\boldsymbol{\theta}})}{\partial \boldsymbol{\theta}'} = \boldsymbol{H}\left(\boldsymbol{\theta} \mid \boldsymbol{x}_t\right) = \boldsymbol{H}_t(\hat{\boldsymbol{\theta}}), \tag{10.10}$$

with average:

$$\bar{\boldsymbol{H}}_{(T)}(\hat{\boldsymbol{\theta}}) = T^{-1}\sum_{t=1}^{T} \boldsymbol{H}_t(\hat{\boldsymbol{\theta}}) = T^{-1}\boldsymbol{H}(\boldsymbol{\theta}). \tag{10.11}$$

When $\bar{\boldsymbol{H}}_{(T)}(\hat{\boldsymbol{\theta}})$ is negative definite, $\bar{\boldsymbol{q}}_{(T)}(\hat{\boldsymbol{\theta}}) = \mathbf{0}$ defines a maximum.

10.6 Properties of the score

We next examine the properties of the $\{\boldsymbol{q}_t\}$ as random variables, then turn to determining the behaviour of solutions $\hat{\boldsymbol{\theta}}$ to $\bar{\boldsymbol{q}}_{(T)}(\hat{\boldsymbol{\theta}}) = \mathbf{0}$. In the following proofs for vector $\boldsymbol{\theta}$, we often omit subscripts relating to sample (or random variable) points, justifying that by the fact that $\{\boldsymbol{x}_t\}$ is IID here. Also, $\boldsymbol{q}(\boldsymbol{\theta}_p|\boldsymbol{x})$ is $\boldsymbol{q}(\boldsymbol{\theta}|\boldsymbol{x})$ evaluated at $\boldsymbol{\theta}_p$.

Property 1. The expectation of $\boldsymbol{q}(\boldsymbol{\theta}_p|\boldsymbol{x})$ is zero under the assumptions that:

(a) the range of integration in calculating the expectation does not depend upon $\boldsymbol{\theta}$;
(b) derivatives and integrals can be exchanged (heuristically $\partial \int = \int \partial$);
(c) $\mathsf{D_x}(\boldsymbol{x}|\boldsymbol{\theta}_p) = \mathsf{L}(\boldsymbol{\theta}_p|\boldsymbol{x})$ (we comment on this later);
(d) there are only a finite number of parameters θ_i (to exclude considering cases of an infinite number of — perhaps incidental — parameters).[2]

The first assumption rules out many of the cases which invalidate the second assumption. The scalar case is analysed in Chapter A3, and the basic results established therein are assumed in the following analysis.

[2] This is unnecessarily restrictive and we could allow for ever-increasing numbers of parameters provided their number is vanishingly small relative to the sample size.

Proof. From (10.7), $q(\theta_p|x)$ is:

$$q(\theta_p \mid x) = \frac{\partial \ell(\theta|x)}{\partial \theta}\rfloor_{\theta_p},$$

so the expectation of $q(\theta_p|x)$ for $x \in \mathcal{X}$ is:

$$\mathsf{E}[q(\theta_p \mid x)] = \int_{\mathcal{X}} q(\theta_p \mid x)\mathsf{D}_{\mathsf{X}}(x \mid \theta_p)dx = \int_{\mathcal{X}} \left(\frac{\partial \ell(\theta|x)}{\partial \theta}\rfloor_{\theta_p}\right) \mathsf{D}_{\mathsf{X}}(x \mid \theta_p)dx. \tag{10.12}$$

Since the integral of a density function over its range is unity:

$$\int_{\mathcal{X}} \mathsf{D}_{\mathsf{X}}\left(x \mid \theta_p\right) dx = 1. \tag{10.13}$$

Differentiating (10.13) with respect to θ using assumption (b):

$$\int_{\mathcal{X}} \left(\frac{\partial \mathsf{D}_{\mathsf{X}}(x|\theta)}{\partial \theta}\rfloor_{\theta_p}\right) dx = \mathbf{0}. \tag{10.14}$$

Since the functions $\mathsf{L}(\cdot)$ and $\mathsf{D}_{\mathsf{X}}(\cdot)$ are the same by assumption (c):

$$\frac{\partial \ell(\theta|x)}{\partial \theta}\rfloor_{\theta_p} = \frac{1}{\mathsf{L}(\theta_p|x)}\frac{\partial \mathsf{L}(\theta|x)}{\partial \theta}\rfloor_{\theta_p} = \frac{1}{\mathsf{D}_{\mathsf{X}}(x|\theta_p)}\frac{\partial \mathsf{D}_{\mathsf{X}}(x|\theta)}{\partial \theta}\rfloor_{\theta_p}, \tag{10.15}$$

so that using (10.13) and (10.15) in (10.12):

$$\begin{aligned}\mathsf{E}[q(\theta_p \mid x)] &= \int_{\mathcal{X}} \frac{1}{\mathsf{D}_{\mathsf{X}}(x|\theta_p)}\left(\frac{\partial \mathsf{D}_{\mathsf{X}}(x|\theta)}{\partial \theta}\rfloor_{\theta_p}\right) \mathsf{D}_{\mathsf{X}}\left(x \mid \theta_p\right) dx \\ &= \int_{\mathcal{X}} \left(\frac{\partial \mathsf{D}_{\mathsf{X}}(x|\theta)}{\partial \theta}\rfloor_{\theta_p}\right) dx\end{aligned} \tag{10.16}$$

which is zero by (10.14). This is a basic justification for MLE: since $\hat{\theta}$ corresponds to the point at which $\bar{q}_{(T)}(\hat{\theta}) = \mathbf{0}$, it is important that on average $q_t(\hat{\theta})$ should equal zero at θ_p. Equally, under the auxiliary assumption that:

$$\mathsf{D}_{\mathsf{X}}(x \mid \theta_1) \neq \mathsf{D}_{\mathsf{X}}(x \mid \theta_2) \text{ if and only if } \theta_1 \neq \theta_2, \tag{10.17}$$

the proof shows that $\mathsf{E}[q(\theta_1|x)] \neq \mathbf{0}$ when $\theta_1 \neq \theta_p$. This result is important below given the role the score plays in hypothesis testing between different parameter values. As discussed in Chapter 2, (10.17) involves two conditions: (i) the 'if condition', is an identification condition, which implies that different parameter values will generate different data samples; (ii) the 'only if condition', which entails a sufficient parameterization, in that θ completely characterizes the distribution and no more parameters are needed, in which case, when $\mathsf{D}_{\mathsf{X}}(x|\theta_1)$ is not equal to $\mathsf{D}_{\mathsf{X}}(x|\theta_2)$ then $\theta_1 \neq \theta_2$. The sufficiency condition is discussed by Madansky (1976), but it is often implicitly assumed that the parameterization is sufficient. The identification condition is important in Chapter 11.

Property 2. The variance of the score is given by the information matrix:

$$\mathsf{E}\left[q\left(\theta_p \mid x\right) q\left(\theta_p \mid x\right)'\right] = \mathcal{I}\left(\theta_p \mid x\right) = \mathcal{I}\left(\theta_p\right).$$

Also $\mathcal{I}(\theta_p) = -\mathsf{E}[H(\theta_p)]$ under assumption (c) that the likelihood is based on the DGP (i.e. $\mathsf{D_X}(\cdot) = \mathsf{L}(\cdot)$).

Proof. Differentiate (10.12), which equals zero by property 1, with respect to θ and use assumption (b) above:

$$\int_{\mathcal{X}} \left(\frac{\partial q\left(\theta|x\right)}{\partial \theta'}\rfloor_{\theta_p}\right) \mathsf{D_X}\left(x \mid \theta_p\right) \mathrm{d}x + \int_{\mathcal{X}} q\left(\theta_p \mid x\right) \left(\frac{\partial \mathsf{D_X}\left(x|\theta\right)}{\partial \theta'}\rfloor_{\theta_p}\right) \mathrm{d}x = \mathbf{0}. \tag{10.18}$$

Since:

$$\frac{\partial \mathsf{D_X}\left(x|\theta\right)}{\partial \theta'}\rfloor_{\theta_p} = \mathsf{D_X}\left(x \mid \theta_p\right) \frac{\partial \ell\left(\theta|x\right)}{\partial \theta'}\rfloor_{\theta_p} = q\left(\theta_p \mid x\right)' \mathsf{D_X}\left(x|\theta_p\right),$$

using (10.15) in (10.18):

$$\int_{\mathcal{X}} H\left(\theta_p \mid x\right) \mathsf{D_X}\left(x \mid \theta_p\right) \mathrm{d}x + \int_{\mathcal{X}} q\left(\theta_p \mid x\right) q\left(\theta_p \mid x\right)' \mathsf{D_X}\left(x \mid \theta_p\right) \mathrm{d}x = \mathbf{0}.$$

Thus, in a shorthand notation, $\mathsf{E}[H] + \mathsf{E}[qq'] = \mathbf{0}$ or:

$$\mathsf{E}\left[q\left(\theta_p \mid x\right) q\left(\theta_p \mid x\right)'\right] = \mathcal{I}\left(\theta_p\right) = -\mathsf{E}\left[H(\theta_p)\right]. \tag{10.19}$$

Consequently, the variance of the score, or the information, on average equals the negative of the Hessian.

Property 3. The $\{q_t(\theta_p)\}$ are independently distributed when the $\{\ell(\theta_p|x_t)\}$ are independent.

This holds (e.g.) for (10.4), since the xs are assumed to be independently drawn, and the $\{q_t(\theta_p)\}$ are continuous functions of them. Thus, $\mathsf{E}[q_t(\theta_p)q_s'(\theta_p)] = \mathbf{0}$ for $t \neq s$ when the xs are independent (or more generally, when $x_t - \mathsf{E}[x_t|X_{t-1}^{t-n}] = \nu_t$ is an MDS). To sum up, when $x_t \sim \mathsf{ID}(\cdot)$ and $\mathsf{D_X}(x_t|\theta_p) = \mathsf{L}(\theta_p|x_t)$, then:

$$q_t\left(\theta_p\right) \sim \mathsf{ID}\left[\mathbf{0}, \mathcal{I}_t\left(\theta_p\right)\right] \quad \text{where } \mathcal{I}_t\left(\theta_p\right) = -\mathsf{E}\left[H_t(\theta_p)\right].$$

Since the assumption of a known DGP is unrealistic, these three properties can be misleading in empirical econometrics at level C: the likelihood function is formulated from a model, and expectations calculated under the model need not coincide with expectations under the DGP. Property 2, in particular, is dependent on the validity of assumption (c), and can fail when the model is not the DGP. Thus, $\mathcal{I}(\theta_p) = -\mathsf{E}[H(\theta_p)]$ need not hold in general at level C, and $\mathcal{I}(\theta_p) + \mathsf{E}[H(\theta_p)]$ will turn out to be a potential test statistic for model mis-specification. An appropriate generalization of assumption (c), which is valid for modelling, is that the model is congruent. Thus, $\boldsymbol{\theta}_p$ may correspond to a valid reduction of a more general joint density, and congruence can sustain $\mathsf{E}[\boldsymbol{q}_t(\boldsymbol{\theta}_p)] = \mathbf{0}\ \forall t$, $\mathsf{E}[\boldsymbol{q}_t(\boldsymbol{\theta}_p)\boldsymbol{q}_s'(\boldsymbol{\theta}_p)] = \mathbf{0}$ for $t \neq s$ and $\mathcal{I}_t(\boldsymbol{\theta}_p) = -\mathsf{E}[\boldsymbol{H}_t(\boldsymbol{\theta}_p)]$. Section 10.10 discusses the issues.

A sketch of $q(\mu)$ for a scalar parameter is shown in Fig. 10.2. Notice that: (a) $\hat{\mu}$ is a root of $\bar{q}(\mu)$, namely a point at which the score equation cuts the zero axis; and, (b) different scores arise from different samples as well as from different populations.

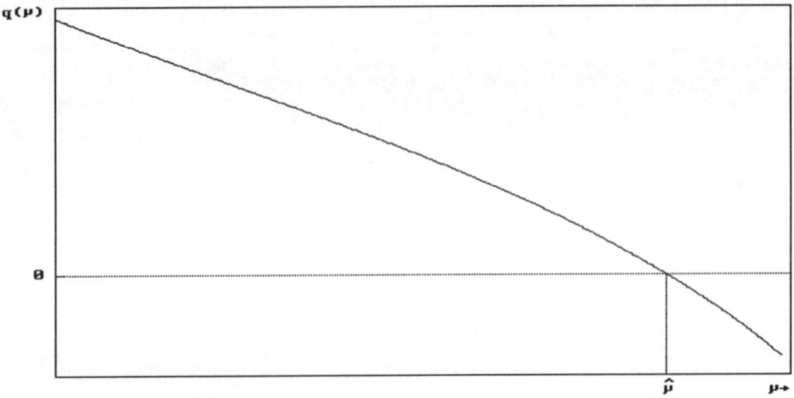

Fig. 10.2 Score equation

10.7 Properties of maximum likelihood estimators

Next, we consider the properties of MLEs like $\hat{\boldsymbol{\theta}}$ in terms of such criteria as unbiasedness, minimum variance, etc., focusing on large-sample behaviour in §10.8. For a vector of parameters $\ell(\boldsymbol{\theta}|\boldsymbol{X}_T^1; \boldsymbol{X}_0)$, in well-defined problems (e.g. continuously differentiable likelihood functions), solving the score equation $\bar{\boldsymbol{q}}(\boldsymbol{\theta}) = \mathbf{0}$ for the MLE $\hat{\boldsymbol{\theta}}$ yields:

$$\hat{\boldsymbol{\theta}} = \underset{\boldsymbol{\theta}\in\Theta}{\operatorname{argmax}}\, \ell\left(\boldsymbol{\theta} \mid \boldsymbol{X}_T^1; \boldsymbol{X}_0\right). \tag{10.20}$$

First, we discuss the important property of equivariance of MLEs, which entails that certain other properties cannot hold. By equivariance is meant that the estimator of a transformed parameter is the transformed estimator. The density $\mathsf{D_x}(\boldsymbol{x}|\boldsymbol{\theta})$ is unaffected by one–one transformations of $\boldsymbol{\theta} \mapsto \boldsymbol{g}(\boldsymbol{\theta}) = \boldsymbol{\psi}$, so the likelihood is invariant under such transformations:

$$\mathsf{L}(\boldsymbol{\theta} \mid \boldsymbol{x}) = \mathsf{L}(\boldsymbol{g}(\boldsymbol{\theta}) \mid \boldsymbol{x}) = \mathsf{L}(\boldsymbol{\psi} \mid \boldsymbol{x}). \tag{10.21}$$

Consequently, MLEs are equivariant under $\boldsymbol{g}(\cdot)$, in that when $\hat{\boldsymbol{\theta}}$ is the MLE of $\boldsymbol{\theta}$, then $\boldsymbol{g}(\hat{\boldsymbol{\theta}})$ is the MLE of $\boldsymbol{g}(\boldsymbol{\theta})$ for a class of well-behaved functions $\boldsymbol{g}(\cdot)$.

Instead of estimating $\hat{\boldsymbol{\theta}}$ directly, maximize $\ell(\cdot)$ with respect to $\boldsymbol{\psi} = \boldsymbol{g}(\boldsymbol{\theta})$, solving:

$$\frac{\partial \ell\left(\boldsymbol{\psi}|\boldsymbol{x}\right)}{\partial \boldsymbol{\psi}} = \mathbf{0}.$$

Since:

$$\frac{\partial \ell\left(\boldsymbol{\theta}|\boldsymbol{x}\right)}{\partial \boldsymbol{\theta}} = \frac{\partial \boldsymbol{\psi}'}{\partial \boldsymbol{\theta}} \frac{\partial \ell\left(\boldsymbol{\theta}|\boldsymbol{x}\right)}{\partial \boldsymbol{\psi}} = \frac{\partial \boldsymbol{\psi}'}{\partial \boldsymbol{\theta}} \frac{\partial \ell\left(\boldsymbol{\psi}|\boldsymbol{x}\right)}{\partial \boldsymbol{\psi}} = \mathbf{0},$$

yields $\hat{\boldsymbol{\theta}}$, when:

$$\frac{\partial \boldsymbol{\psi}'}{\partial \boldsymbol{\theta}} = \frac{\partial \boldsymbol{g}(\boldsymbol{\theta})'}{\partial \boldsymbol{\theta}} = \boldsymbol{G}(\boldsymbol{\theta}),$$

has full rank k, the two solutions coincide such that $\hat{\boldsymbol{\psi}} = \boldsymbol{g}(\hat{\boldsymbol{\theta}})$. Some estimation methods do not have the property of equivariance, and it is an important attribute of likelihood-based methods.

Since expectations are not invariant to non-linear transformations, then in general:

$$\mathsf{E}\left[g(\hat{\boldsymbol{\theta}})\right] \neq g\left(\mathsf{E}\left[\hat{\boldsymbol{\theta}}\right]\right), \tag{10.22}$$

so that MLEs are usually biased, although there may exist an unbiased maximum likelihood function $\boldsymbol{\phi} = \boldsymbol{h}(\hat{\boldsymbol{\theta}})$ such that $\mathsf{E}[\hat{\boldsymbol{\phi}}] = \boldsymbol{\phi}$.

Next, consider minimum variance. Suppose that there exists an unbiased MLE $\hat{\boldsymbol{\theta}}$, so $\mathsf{E}[\hat{\boldsymbol{\theta}}] = \boldsymbol{\theta}$. Take any other unbiased estimator $\boldsymbol{s}$ of $\boldsymbol{\theta}$: $\mathsf{E}[\boldsymbol{s}] = \boldsymbol{\theta}$. We will prove that:

(i) the variance of $\boldsymbol{s}$ is never less than $\mathcal{I}^{-1}(\boldsymbol{\theta}_p)$; and
(ii) in a range of important special cases, the variance of the MLE $\hat{\boldsymbol{\theta}}$ is $\mathcal{I}^{-1}(\boldsymbol{\theta}_p)$.

The first claim is one of the fundamental results in the theory of MLE, known as the Cramér–Rao bound, and Chapter A3 considers the second for quadratic functions $\ell(\cdot)$ of a scalar parameter. Here, we consider the generalization to a vector of k parameters.

Proof: (i) From the definition of unbiasedness:

$$\mathsf{E}\left[\boldsymbol{s}\right] = \int_{\mathcal{X}} \boldsymbol{s} \mathsf{D}_{\mathsf{X}}\left(\boldsymbol{x} \mid \boldsymbol{\theta}_p\right) \mathrm{d}\boldsymbol{x} = \boldsymbol{\theta}_p \tag{10.23}$$

Taking the derivative of the integral in (10.23) with respect to $\boldsymbol{\theta}$, under the previously stated assumption (b):

$$\frac{\partial\left(\int_{\mathcal{X}} \boldsymbol{s}\mathsf{D}_{\mathsf{X}}\left(\boldsymbol{x}|\boldsymbol{\theta}\right)\mathrm{d}\boldsymbol{x}\right)}{\partial \boldsymbol{\theta}}\Big\rfloor_{\boldsymbol{\theta}_p} = \int_{\mathcal{X}} \boldsymbol{s}\left(\frac{\partial \mathsf{D}_{\mathsf{X}}\left(\boldsymbol{x}|\boldsymbol{\theta}\right)}{\partial \boldsymbol{\theta}}\right)\Big\rfloor_{\boldsymbol{\theta}_p} \mathrm{d}\boldsymbol{x} = \boldsymbol{I}_k. \tag{10.24}$$

Hence, as in (10.14)–(10.16), using $\mathsf{L}(\boldsymbol{\theta}|\boldsymbol{x}) = \mathsf{D}_{\mathsf{X}}(\boldsymbol{x}|\boldsymbol{\theta})$, then:

$$\int_{\mathcal{X}} \boldsymbol{s} \cdot \boldsymbol{q}\left(\boldsymbol{\theta}_p \mid \boldsymbol{x}\right) \mathsf{D}_{\mathsf{X}}\left(\boldsymbol{x} \mid \boldsymbol{\theta}_p\right) \mathrm{d}\boldsymbol{x} = \boldsymbol{I}_k.$$

Since $\mathsf{E}[\boldsymbol{q}(\boldsymbol{\theta}_p|\boldsymbol{x})] = \mathbf{0}$, then $\mathsf{C}[\boldsymbol{s}, \boldsymbol{q}(\boldsymbol{\theta}_p|\boldsymbol{x})] = \boldsymbol{I}_k$, a remarkable result in itself. Thus, the variance-covariance matrix of $\boldsymbol{q}(\boldsymbol{\theta}_p|\boldsymbol{x})$ and $\boldsymbol{s}$ is:

$$\mathsf{V}\begin{bmatrix} \boldsymbol{q}(\boldsymbol{\theta}_p|\boldsymbol{x}) \\ \boldsymbol{s} \end{bmatrix} = \begin{pmatrix} \mathcal{I}(\boldsymbol{\theta}_p) & \boldsymbol{I}_k \\ \boldsymbol{I}_k & \mathsf{V}[\boldsymbol{s}] \end{pmatrix}.$$

Since a variance matrix must be non-negative definite, denoted by $\mathsf{V}[\cdot] \succeq \mathbf{0}$, applying the partitioned-inversion formula (see Ch.A1), the lower-right block yields the conditional variance of $\boldsymbol{s}$ given $\boldsymbol{q}(\boldsymbol{\theta}_p|\boldsymbol{x})$, namely:

$$\mathsf{V}[\boldsymbol{s}] - \mathcal{I}^{-1}(\boldsymbol{\theta}_p) \succeq \mathbf{0}. \tag{10.25}$$

Consequently, no unbiased estimator has a variance less than the inverse information matrix, which is the Cramér–Rao bound (we do not require that there always exists an $\boldsymbol{s}$ which attains this lower bound).

(ii) We next prove that in certain cases, the variance of the MLE does attain the lower bound of $\mathcal{I}^{-1}(\boldsymbol{\theta}_p)$. In general, MLEs are non-linear functions and hence awkward to analyse in finite samples. However, when $\ell(\cdot)$ is quadratic in $\boldsymbol{\theta}$, $\boldsymbol{q}(\boldsymbol{\theta}|\boldsymbol{x})$ is linear and $\boldsymbol{H}$ is a constant, full-rank matrix independent of $\boldsymbol{\theta}$, so we first consider that case. In section 10.8, a related result will be shown for large samples. Expand $\boldsymbol{q}(\hat{\boldsymbol{\theta}}|\boldsymbol{x}) = \mathbf{0}$ in a Taylor series around $\boldsymbol{\theta}_p$, noting that higher-order derivatives vanish:

$$\boldsymbol{q}(\hat{\boldsymbol{\theta}} \mid \boldsymbol{x}) = \mathbf{0} = \boldsymbol{q}(\boldsymbol{\theta}_p \mid \boldsymbol{x}) + \boldsymbol{H}\left(\hat{\boldsymbol{\theta}} - \boldsymbol{\theta}_p\right),$$

so:

$$\hat{\boldsymbol{\theta}} - \boldsymbol{\theta}_p = -\boldsymbol{H}^{-1}\boldsymbol{q}(\boldsymbol{\theta}_p \mid \boldsymbol{x}).$$

Since $\mathsf{E}[\boldsymbol{q}(\boldsymbol{\theta}_p|\boldsymbol{x})] = \mathbf{0}$ and $\boldsymbol{H}$ is fixed, $\mathsf{E}[\hat{\boldsymbol{\theta}}] = \boldsymbol{\theta}_p$. Further, by direct multiplication, since $\boldsymbol{H}$ is symmetric:

$$\begin{aligned} \mathsf{E}\left[\left(\hat{\boldsymbol{\theta}} - \boldsymbol{\theta}_p\right)\left(\hat{\boldsymbol{\theta}} - \boldsymbol{\theta}_p\right)'\right] &= \mathsf{E}\left[\boldsymbol{H}^{-1}\boldsymbol{q}_p(\boldsymbol{\theta} \mid \boldsymbol{x})\, \boldsymbol{q}(\boldsymbol{\theta}_p \mid \boldsymbol{x})'\, \boldsymbol{H}^{-1}\right] \\ &= \boldsymbol{H}^{-1}\mathcal{I}(\boldsymbol{\theta}_p)\,\boldsymbol{H}^{-1} = \mathcal{I}^{-1}(\boldsymbol{\theta}_p) \end{aligned}$$

using (10.19). Thus, the MLE attains the Cramér–Rao variance bound in this case.

10.8 Large-sample properties of MLEs

More generally, when the likelihood function is not quadratic, the Taylor-series (strictly, mean-value) expansion of $\boldsymbol{q}(\hat{\boldsymbol{\theta}})$ around $\boldsymbol{q}(\boldsymbol{\theta}_p)$ (dropping the explicit conditioning on $\boldsymbol{x}$) is:

$$\bar{\boldsymbol{q}}_{(T)}\left(\hat{\boldsymbol{\theta}}\right) = \mathbf{0} = \bar{\boldsymbol{q}}(\boldsymbol{\theta}_p) + \bar{\boldsymbol{H}}_{(T)}(\bar{\boldsymbol{\theta}})\left(\hat{\boldsymbol{\theta}} - \boldsymbol{\theta}_p\right) \tag{10.26}$$

where $\bar{\boldsymbol{\theta}}$ lies in $(\hat{\boldsymbol{\theta}}, \boldsymbol{\theta}_p)$. Since $\bar{\boldsymbol{q}}_{(T)}(\boldsymbol{\theta}_p) = T^{-1}\sum_{t=1}^{T} \boldsymbol{q}_t(\boldsymbol{\theta}_p)$, from the weak law of large numbers (see §A4.4), the average score converges to zero in probability:

$$\bar{\boldsymbol{q}}_{(T)}(\boldsymbol{\theta}_p) \xrightarrow{P} \mathbf{0} = \mathsf{E}\left[\boldsymbol{q}_t(\boldsymbol{\theta}_p)\right], \tag{10.27}$$

where $\xrightarrow{P}$ denotes convergence in probability (see §A4.3). Taking plims in (10.26), the consistency of $\hat{\boldsymbol{\theta}}$ for $\boldsymbol{\theta}_p$ follows when $\text{plim}_{T\to\infty}\ \bar{\boldsymbol{H}}_{(T)}(\bar{\boldsymbol{\theta}})$ is finite and non-singular.

However, to derive a limiting distribution, we need to know how close $\bar{\boldsymbol{H}}_{(T)}(\bar{\boldsymbol{\theta}})$ in (10.26) is to $\bar{\boldsymbol{H}}_{(T)}(\boldsymbol{\theta}_p)$ so that we can replace the former by the latter. To do so heuristically, we first show by an alternative route that $\hat{\boldsymbol{\theta}}$ converges to $\boldsymbol{\theta}_p$ and continuous functions of $\hat{\boldsymbol{\theta}}$ converge to the corresponding function of $\boldsymbol{\theta}_p$, so that the 'interval' $(\hat{\boldsymbol{\theta}}, \boldsymbol{\theta}_p)$ tends to zero and $\bar{\boldsymbol{\theta}}$ must converge to $\boldsymbol{\theta}_p$. The argument borrows from the logic of the proof in Wald (1949) that MLEs converge to their population values under weak conditions, but makes no attempt at mathematical rigour. In any given sample, by definition of MLE:

$$\ell(\hat{\boldsymbol{\theta}}) \geq \ell(\boldsymbol{\theta})\ \forall \boldsymbol{\theta} \in \Theta. \tag{10.28}$$

When the MLE is unique (ruling out multi-modal likelihood functions, which is a strong assumption not valid for all cases):

$$\ell(\hat{\boldsymbol{\theta}}) > \ell(\boldsymbol{\theta})\ \forall \boldsymbol{\theta} \neq \hat{\boldsymbol{\theta}}. \tag{10.29}$$

Consequently:

$$\bar{\ell}(\hat{\boldsymbol{\theta}}) > \bar{\ell}(\boldsymbol{\theta})\ \forall \boldsymbol{\theta} \neq \hat{\boldsymbol{\theta}}, \tag{10.30}$$

where $\bar{\ell}(\cdot) = T^{-1}\sum_{t=1}^{T}\ell_t$.

Denote the standardized population log-likelihood by ℓ_p, where by definition of $\boldsymbol{\theta}_p$:

$$\ell_p(\boldsymbol{\theta}_p) > \ell_p(\boldsymbol{\theta})\ \forall \boldsymbol{\theta} \neq \boldsymbol{\theta}_p. \tag{10.31}$$

Let the sample size tend to infinity, so $\bar{\ell}(\cdot)$ tends to $\ell_p(\cdot)$. A contradiction must emerge between (10.30) and (10.31) unless $\hat{\boldsymbol{\theta}}$ converges to $\boldsymbol{\theta}_p$. So we have:

$$\hat{\boldsymbol{\theta}} \xrightarrow{P} \boldsymbol{\theta}_p. \tag{10.32}$$

R.A. Fisher argued for a likelihood approach in part because of a property related to (10.32), called 'Fisher consistency': if a statistical rule used in a sample is the same as the rule used in the population, then the statistic calculated from the sample should coincide with that calculated from the population when the sample becomes the population. That is the essence of the argument, but there are many tricky mathematical issues which we are side-stepping, and the above claims are potentially subject to counter-examples unless careful assumptions are made. A formal definition of $\xrightarrow{P}$ is provided in Chapter A4, which also includes the following theorem due to Slutsky:

$$\text{If } \hat{\boldsymbol{\theta}} \xrightarrow{P} \boldsymbol{\theta}_p \text{ and } \boldsymbol{g}(\cdot) \text{ is continuous at } \boldsymbol{\theta}_p \text{ then } \boldsymbol{g}(\hat{\boldsymbol{\theta}}) \xrightarrow{P} \boldsymbol{g}(\boldsymbol{\theta}_p).$$

Consequently as $T \to \infty$:

$$\bar{\boldsymbol{H}}_{(T)}(\bar{\boldsymbol{\theta}}) \xrightarrow{P} \boldsymbol{H}_p(\boldsymbol{\theta}_p),$$

where $\boldsymbol{H}_p(\boldsymbol{\theta}_p)$ is the Hessian of $\ell_p(\boldsymbol{\theta}_p)$. Given (10.32), (10.26) becomes:

$$\bar{\boldsymbol{q}}_{(T)}(\boldsymbol{\theta}_p) + \boldsymbol{H}_p(\boldsymbol{\theta}_p)\left(\hat{\boldsymbol{\theta}} - \boldsymbol{\theta}_p\right) \simeq \boldsymbol{0}. \tag{10.33}$$

Note that standard regression estimators have the property that $\bar{\boldsymbol{H}}_{(T)}(\bar{\boldsymbol{\theta}}) = \bar{\boldsymbol{H}}_{(T)}(\boldsymbol{\theta}_p)$, and that the consistency of $\widehat{\boldsymbol{\theta}}$ for $\boldsymbol{\theta}_p$ only requires that $\boldsymbol{H}_p(\boldsymbol{\theta}_p)$ is finite and non-singular. Solving the expression in (10.33) for $\widehat{\boldsymbol{\theta}}$:

$$\widehat{\boldsymbol{\theta}} \simeq \boldsymbol{\theta}_p - \boldsymbol{H}_p\left(\boldsymbol{\theta}_p\right)^{-1} \bar{\boldsymbol{q}}_{(T)}\left(\boldsymbol{\theta}_p\right), \tag{10.34}$$

which is a basic result for both computation and distributional derivations.

The point of establishing the distribution of $\bar{\boldsymbol{q}}_{(T)}(\boldsymbol{\theta}_p)$ above becomes clear: given the (asymptotically valid) approximation of $\bar{\boldsymbol{H}}(\bar{\boldsymbol{\theta}})$ by $\boldsymbol{H}_p(\boldsymbol{\theta}_p)$, then $\widehat{\boldsymbol{\theta}}$ deviates from $\boldsymbol{\theta}_p$ by a function which depends only on $\bar{\boldsymbol{q}}_{(T)}(\boldsymbol{\theta}_p)$; so the distribution of $\widehat{\boldsymbol{\theta}}$ can be derived from the distribution of $\boldsymbol{q}(\cdot)$. However, we currently only know that $\boldsymbol{q}_t(\boldsymbol{\theta}_p) \sim \mathsf{ID}[\mathbf{0}, \mathcal{I}_t(\boldsymbol{\theta}_p)]$ and need a central-limit theorem to obtain the form of its distribution.

Since the first two moments of $\boldsymbol{q}_t(\boldsymbol{\theta}_p)$ exist, and the $\{\boldsymbol{q}_t(\boldsymbol{\theta}_p)\}$ are ID, assuming condition (ii) of the Lindeberg–Feller central-limit theorem holds (see §A4.5):

$$\sqrt{T}\bar{\boldsymbol{q}}_{(T)}\left(\boldsymbol{\theta}_p\right) \xrightarrow{D} \mathsf{N}_k\left[\mathbf{0}, \mathcal{I}_p\left(\boldsymbol{\theta}_p\right)\right], \tag{10.35}$$

where $\mathcal{I}_p(\boldsymbol{\theta}_p) = \lim_{T\to\infty} T^{-1}\sum_{t=1}^{T}\mathcal{I}_t(\boldsymbol{\theta}_p)$, and $\xrightarrow{D}$ denotes convergence in distribution. Thus, $\bar{\boldsymbol{q}}_{(T)}(\boldsymbol{\theta}_p)$ tends to a normal distribution as $T \to \infty$. Since $\boldsymbol{H}_t(\boldsymbol{\theta}_p) \sim \mathsf{ID}_{k^2}[\mathsf{E}[\boldsymbol{H}_t(\boldsymbol{\theta}_p)], \cdot]$, the weak law of large numbers confirms the earlier result:

$$\bar{\boldsymbol{H}}_{(T)}\left(\boldsymbol{\theta}_p\right) \xrightarrow{P} \boldsymbol{H}_p\left(\boldsymbol{\theta}_p\right) = \lim_{T\to\infty} T^{-1}\sum_{t=1}^{T}\mathsf{E}\left[\boldsymbol{H}_t\left(\boldsymbol{\theta}_p\right)\right]. \tag{10.36}$$

Thus, the average Hessian at $\boldsymbol{\theta}_p$ converges on the population Hessian. From Slutsky's theorem, $\bar{\boldsymbol{H}}_{(T)}(\widehat{\boldsymbol{\theta}})$ is a consistent estimator of $\boldsymbol{H}_p(\boldsymbol{\theta}_p)$, and this allows us to estimate the large-sample variance of $\widehat{\boldsymbol{\theta}}$; other possible estimators will be noted below.

The final result we need is for stochastic functions of asymptotically normal random variables (see Ch.A4), namely Cramér's theorem. Consider the random linear vector function:

$$\boldsymbol{Y}_T = \boldsymbol{A}_T\boldsymbol{X}_T, \tag{10.37}$$

where $\boldsymbol{Y}_T$, $\boldsymbol{A}_T$ and $\boldsymbol{X}_T$ are $m\times 1, m\times n$, and $n\times 1$ respectively. When $\boldsymbol{X}_T \xrightarrow{D} \mathsf{N}_n[\boldsymbol{\mu}, \boldsymbol{\Sigma}]$ and $\boldsymbol{A}_T \xrightarrow{P} \boldsymbol{A}$, then:

$$\boldsymbol{Y}_T \xrightarrow{D} \mathsf{N}_m\left[\boldsymbol{A\mu}, \boldsymbol{A\Sigma A}'\right]. \tag{10.38}$$

In the limit, therefore, although $\boldsymbol{A}_T$ is stochastic and varying, $\boldsymbol{Y}_T$ behaves like the random variable $\boldsymbol{Y}_T^* = \boldsymbol{A}\boldsymbol{X}_T$ in which $\boldsymbol{A}$ is fixed. To interpret this theorem, if $\boldsymbol{X}_T$ has a limiting distribution, and $\boldsymbol{A}_T$ converges to $\boldsymbol{A}$, the extent to which $\boldsymbol{A}_T$ varies as it converges does not affect the limiting distribution of $\boldsymbol{Y}_T$ (not even the variance of that limiting distribution). Thus, we can replace $\boldsymbol{A}_T$ by $\boldsymbol{A}$ in such derivations. Alternatively, the random variable:

$$\boldsymbol{Y}_T - \boldsymbol{Y}_T^* = \left(\boldsymbol{A}_T - \boldsymbol{A}\right)\boldsymbol{X}_T \xrightarrow{P} \mathbf{0},$$

and has a limiting variance dependent on $(\boldsymbol{A}_T - \boldsymbol{A})^2$ (which is $O_p(T^{-1})$ when $(\boldsymbol{A}_T - \boldsymbol{A})$ is $O_p(T^{-\frac{1}{2}})$) and so vanishes rapidly.

In the case of $\hat{\boldsymbol{\theta}}$, $\boldsymbol{A}_T$ is $-\bar{\boldsymbol{H}}_{(T)}^{-1}$, $\boldsymbol{X}_T$ is $\bar{\boldsymbol{q}}_{(T)}(\boldsymbol{\theta}_p)$ and $\boldsymbol{Y}_T$ is $(\hat{\boldsymbol{\theta}} - \boldsymbol{\theta}_p)$, so from (10.26) and (10.36):

$$\sqrt{T}\left(\hat{\boldsymbol{\theta}} - \boldsymbol{\theta}_p\right) \xrightarrow{D} \mathsf{N}_k\left[\mathbf{0}, \boldsymbol{H}_p^{-1}(\boldsymbol{\theta}_p)\,\mathcal{I}_p(\boldsymbol{\theta}_p)\,\boldsymbol{H}_p^{-1}(\boldsymbol{\theta}_p)\right] = \mathsf{N}_k\left[\mathbf{0}, \boldsymbol{V}(\boldsymbol{\theta}_p)\right]. \quad (10.39)$$

Here, $\mathcal{I}_p^{-1}(\boldsymbol{\theta}_p) = -\boldsymbol{H}_p^{-1}(\boldsymbol{\theta}_p)$, so $\boldsymbol{V}(\boldsymbol{\theta}_p) = \boldsymbol{H}_p^{-1}(\boldsymbol{\theta}_p)$ where:

$$\boldsymbol{H}_p(\boldsymbol{\theta}_p) = \operatorname*{plim}_{T\to\infty} T^{-1}\frac{\partial^2 \ell(\boldsymbol{\theta}|\boldsymbol{x})}{\partial\boldsymbol{\theta}\partial\boldsymbol{\theta}'}\rfloor_{\boldsymbol{\theta}_p}.$$

Thus, given our (somewhat restrictive) assumptions, MLEs are asymptotically normally distributed and attain the Cramér–Rao bound asymptotically.

10.9 Two solved examples

Example A

Consider the model $y_t|z_t \sim \mathsf{N}[\beta z_t, \sigma_\epsilon^2]$.

(a) Derive the joint density for an independent sample $\boldsymbol{y}' = (y_1 \dots y_T)$ when $\{z_t\}$ is strongly exogenous for β, so the model has the form $\boldsymbol{y}|\boldsymbol{z} \sim \mathsf{N}_T[\boldsymbol{z}\beta, \sigma_\epsilon^2\boldsymbol{I}]$ where $\boldsymbol{z}' = (z_1 \dots z_T)$.

(b) Obtain the log-likelihood function $\ell(\beta|\boldsymbol{y};\boldsymbol{z})$ when $\sigma_\epsilon^2 = 1$ is known. Express $\ell(\beta|\boldsymbol{y};\boldsymbol{z})$ as a function of $q(\beta|\boldsymbol{y};\boldsymbol{z})$ (the score) and $H(\beta|\boldsymbol{y};\boldsymbol{z})$ (the Hessian matrix, here 1×1), where:

$$\frac{\partial \ell(\beta|\boldsymbol{y};\boldsymbol{z})}{\partial\beta} = q(\beta \mid \boldsymbol{y};\boldsymbol{z}) \quad\text{and}\quad \frac{\partial^2 \ell(\beta|\boldsymbol{y};\boldsymbol{z})}{\partial\beta^2} = H(\beta \mid \boldsymbol{y};\boldsymbol{z}),$$

and obtain the MLE $\hat{\beta}$ of β.

(c) Hence show that the Newton–Raphson algorithm:

$$\left(\hat{\beta} - \beta_a\right) = -\left[H(\beta_a \mid \boldsymbol{y};\boldsymbol{z})\right]^{-1} q(\beta_a \mid \boldsymbol{y};\boldsymbol{z})$$

yields the OLS/MLE estimator of β in one step, no matter what value is selected for β_a. Comment on why this result holds here.

(d) By direct evaluation, show that if $q_t(\beta) = \partial\ell_t(\beta)/\partial\beta$ then:

$$\mathsf{E}\left[q_t(\beta)\right] = 0 \quad\text{and}\quad \mathsf{E}\left[q_t(\beta)^2\right] = -\mathsf{E}\left[H_t(\beta)\right].$$

(e) Do the results in (c) and (d) generalize for σ_ϵ^2 unknown?

(f) Show that $\hat{\beta}$ is unbiased for β, conditionally on z, and that $\hat{\beta}$ is consistent for β.

(g) What is the variance of the limiting distribution of $(\hat{\beta} - \beta)$? Discuss the need to re-normalize to obtain a non-degenerate distribution. Derive the exact variance of $\hat{\beta}$, its order of magnitude, and hence the order in probability of $(\hat{\beta} - \beta)$.
(h) Derive the limiting distribution of $\sqrt{T}(\hat{\beta} - \beta)$.
(i) Obtain the information matrix $\mathcal{I}(\boldsymbol{\theta})$, where $\boldsymbol{\theta}' = (\beta, \sigma_\epsilon^2)$, and hence explain how (h) could be answered without deriving the distribution of $\hat{\sigma}_\epsilon^2$.
(j) Prove that $\hat{\sigma}_\epsilon^2$ is consistent for σ_ϵ^2.
(k) What is the MLE of $\gamma = 1/\beta$ $(\beta \neq 0)$? Is $\hat{\gamma} = 1/\hat{\beta}$ unbiased for $\gamma = 1/\beta$? Derive the limiting distribution of $\sqrt{T}(\hat{\gamma} - \gamma)$ and comment on the moments of that distribution.

Solution to example A

(a) Denoting $(z_1 \ldots z_T)$ by $\boldsymbol{z}_T^1$ and $(y_1 \ldots y_T)$ by $\boldsymbol{y}_T^1$, given that sampling is independent, the joint density $\mathsf{D}_{\mathsf{Y},\mathsf{Z}}(\boldsymbol{y}_T^1, \boldsymbol{z}_T^1|\boldsymbol{\psi})$ for a sample of size T can be factorized as:

$$\prod_{t=1}^{T} \mathsf{D}_{\mathsf{y}|\mathsf{z}} \left(y_t \mid \boldsymbol{y}_{t-1}^1, \boldsymbol{z}_t^1, \boldsymbol{\theta}\right) \mathsf{D}_{\mathsf{z}} \left(z_t \mid \boldsymbol{z}_{t-1}^1, \boldsymbol{\lambda}\right) = \prod_{t=1}^{T} \mathsf{D}_{\mathsf{y}|\mathsf{z}} \left(y_t \mid z_t, \boldsymbol{\theta}\right) \mathsf{D}_{\mathsf{z}} \left(z_t \mid \boldsymbol{\lambda}\right), \tag{10.40}$$

where $\boldsymbol{\psi} = \boldsymbol{f}(\boldsymbol{\theta}, \boldsymbol{\lambda})$ is one–one. Because z_t is strongly exogenous for β, (10.40) can be rewritten as:

$$\mathsf{D}_{\mathsf{Y},\mathsf{Z}} \left(\boldsymbol{y}_T^1, \boldsymbol{z}_T^1 \mid \boldsymbol{\psi}\right) = \mathsf{D}_{\mathsf{Y}|\mathsf{Z}} \left(\boldsymbol{y}_T^1 \mid \boldsymbol{z}_T^1, \boldsymbol{\theta}\right) \mathsf{D}_{\mathsf{Z}} \left(\boldsymbol{z}_T^1 \mid \boldsymbol{\lambda}\right). \tag{10.41}$$

Since β does not enter $\mathsf{D}_{\mathsf{Z}}(\boldsymbol{z}_T^1|\boldsymbol{\lambda})$, and can be learned from $\boldsymbol{\theta}$ alone, we can disregard the marginal model and concentrate on the conditional sub-model for inference about β, namely:

$$\mathsf{D}_{\mathsf{Y}|\mathsf{Z}}(\boldsymbol{y}_T^1 \mid \boldsymbol{z}_T^1, \boldsymbol{\theta}).$$

(b) To simplify notation, we let $\boldsymbol{y}$ denote $\boldsymbol{y}_T^1$, and $\boldsymbol{z}$ denote $\boldsymbol{z}_T^1$, then $\mathsf{D}_{\mathsf{Y}|\mathsf{Z}}(\boldsymbol{y}_T^1|\boldsymbol{z}_T^1, \boldsymbol{\theta})$ equals the conditional likelihood $\mathsf{L}(\beta, \sigma_\epsilon^2|\boldsymbol{y}; \boldsymbol{z})$ where:

$$\mathsf{L}\left(\beta, \sigma_\epsilon^2 \mid \boldsymbol{y}; \boldsymbol{z}\right) = (2\pi)^{-\frac{T}{2}} \left(\sigma_\epsilon^2\right)^{-\frac{T}{2}} \exp\left[-\frac{(\boldsymbol{y} - \boldsymbol{z}\beta)'(\boldsymbol{y} - \boldsymbol{z}\beta)}{2\sigma_\epsilon^2}\right]. \tag{10.42}$$

When $\sigma_\epsilon^2 = 1$:

$$\ell\left(\beta \mid \boldsymbol{y}; \boldsymbol{z}\right) = -\frac{T}{2}\log\left(2\pi\right) - \tfrac{1}{2}\left(\boldsymbol{y} - \boldsymbol{z}\beta\right)'\left(\boldsymbol{y} - \boldsymbol{z}\beta\right). \tag{10.43}$$

Since:

$$\frac{\partial \ell\left(\beta|\boldsymbol{y}; \boldsymbol{z}\right)}{\partial \beta} = q\left(\beta\right) = \boldsymbol{z}'\boldsymbol{y} - \boldsymbol{z}'\boldsymbol{z}\beta$$

and:

$$\frac{\partial^2 \ell\left(\beta|\boldsymbol{y}; \boldsymbol{z}\right)}{\partial \beta^2} = H\left(\beta\right) = -\boldsymbol{z}'\boldsymbol{z},$$

we can write $\ell(\beta|\boldsymbol{y};\boldsymbol{z})$ as:

$$\ell(\beta \mid \boldsymbol{y}; \boldsymbol{z}) = -\frac{T}{2}\log(2\pi) - \tfrac{1}{2}\boldsymbol{y}'\boldsymbol{y} + \beta q(\beta) - \tfrac{1}{2}\beta^2 H(\beta), \qquad (10.44)$$

and the maximum occurs at $\hat{\beta} = (\boldsymbol{z}'\boldsymbol{z})^{-1}\boldsymbol{z}'\boldsymbol{y}$, so $q(\hat{\beta}) = 0$.

(c) The Newton–Raphson algorithm is:

$$\left(\hat{\beta} - \beta_a\right) = -H(\beta_a)^{-1} q(\beta_a) = (\boldsymbol{z}'\boldsymbol{z})^{-1}(\boldsymbol{z}'\boldsymbol{y} - \boldsymbol{z}'\boldsymbol{z}\beta_a) = (\boldsymbol{z}'\boldsymbol{z})^{-1}\boldsymbol{z}'\boldsymbol{y} - \beta_a \qquad (10.45)$$

and hence:

$$\hat{\beta} = (\boldsymbol{z}'\boldsymbol{z})^{-1}\boldsymbol{z}'\boldsymbol{y}\ \forall \beta_a. \qquad (10.46)$$

Thus, (10.45) holds in one step, wherever the algorithm is started, because despite the notation, $H(\beta)$ does not depend on β, and hence is independent of β_a.

(d) We have:

$$q_t(\beta) = z_t y_t - z_t^2\beta = z_t\epsilon_t, \qquad (10.47)$$

so $\mathsf{E}[q_t(\beta)] = \mathsf{E}[z_t\epsilon_t] = 0$. Further, since $\sigma_\epsilon^2 = 1$:

$$\mathsf{E}\left[q_t(\beta)^2\right] = \mathsf{E}\left[z_t^2\epsilon_t^2\right] = z_t^2\mathsf{E}\left[\epsilon_t^2\right] = z_t^2 = -H_t(\beta) = -\mathsf{E}\left[H_t(\beta)\right]. \qquad (10.48)$$

(e) At first sight, the results seem to depend on the assumption of a known variance for the residuals. When σ_ϵ^2 is unknown, the Hessian $\boldsymbol{H}(\hat{\boldsymbol{\theta}})$ is given by:

$$\frac{1}{\sigma_\epsilon^2}\begin{pmatrix} -\boldsymbol{z}'\boldsymbol{z} & \frac{1}{\sigma_\epsilon^2}(\boldsymbol{z}'\boldsymbol{z}\beta - \boldsymbol{z}'\boldsymbol{y}) \\ \frac{1}{\sigma_\epsilon^2}(\boldsymbol{z}'\boldsymbol{z}\beta - \boldsymbol{z}'\boldsymbol{y}) & \frac{T}{2\sigma_\epsilon^2} - \frac{1}{\sigma_\epsilon^4}(\boldsymbol{y} - \boldsymbol{z}\beta)'(\boldsymbol{y} - \boldsymbol{z}\beta) \end{pmatrix} =$$

$$\frac{1}{\sigma_\epsilon^2}\begin{pmatrix} -\boldsymbol{z}'\boldsymbol{z} & -\frac{1}{\sigma_\epsilon^2}\boldsymbol{z}'\boldsymbol{\epsilon} \\ -\frac{1}{\sigma_\epsilon^2}\boldsymbol{z}'\boldsymbol{\epsilon} & \frac{T}{2\sigma_\epsilon^2} - \frac{1}{\sigma_\epsilon^4}\boldsymbol{\epsilon}'\boldsymbol{\epsilon} \end{pmatrix},$$

which does depend on $\boldsymbol{\theta}$. However, the log-likelihood function $\ell(\beta, \sigma^2|\boldsymbol{y};\boldsymbol{z})$ is:

$$-\frac{T}{2}\log(2\pi) - \frac{T}{2}\log\left(\sigma_\epsilon^2\right) - \frac{(\boldsymbol{y} - \boldsymbol{z}\beta)'(\boldsymbol{y} - \boldsymbol{z}\beta)}{2\sigma_\epsilon^2}, \qquad (10.49)$$

and if (10.49) is maximized with respect to σ_ϵ^2, the conditional maximum is:

$$\left(\sigma_\epsilon^2\right)_c = T^{-1}(\boldsymbol{y} - \boldsymbol{z}\beta)'(\boldsymbol{y} - \boldsymbol{z}\beta).$$

Eliminating σ_ϵ^2 in (10.49) using $(\sigma_\epsilon^2)_c$ yields the concentrated log-likelihood function (CLF):

$$\ell^0\left(\beta \mid \left(\sigma_\epsilon^2\right)_c, \boldsymbol{y}; \boldsymbol{z}\right) = -\frac{T}{2}\left\{\log(2\pi) + 1 - \log T + \log(\boldsymbol{y} - \boldsymbol{z}\beta)'(\boldsymbol{y} - \boldsymbol{z}\beta)\right\} \qquad (10.50)$$

so maximizing $\ell^0(\cdot)$ is equivalent to minimizing $(\boldsymbol{y} - \boldsymbol{z}\beta)'(\boldsymbol{y} - \boldsymbol{z}\beta)$, which relates the problem to that when σ_ϵ^2 is known, with the same score and Hessian.

(f)–(h) and (j) are textbook problems which should pose no difficulties for the reader to solve.

(i) $\mathcal{I}(\boldsymbol{\theta}_p)$ is obtained by direct calculation from the variance of $\boldsymbol{q}(\boldsymbol{\theta}_p|\boldsymbol{y};\boldsymbol{z})$. The expected or (asymptotic) information matrix is diagonal, and therefore the estimators of β and σ_ϵ^2 are (asymptotically) independent.

(k) By the equivariance of MLE to one–one re-parameterizations, the MLE of $\gamma = 1/\beta$ is:

$$\hat{\gamma} = \frac{1}{\hat{\beta}}.$$

Although $\hat{\beta}$ is unbiased for β, $\hat{\gamma}$ is not unbiased for γ. Indeed, $\mathsf{E}[\hat{\gamma}]$ does not exist since $\hat{\beta} \sim \mathsf{N}[\beta, \sigma_\epsilon^2(\boldsymbol{z}'\boldsymbol{z})^{-1}]$, and hence $\hat{\beta}$ has a non-zero probability of lying in a neighbourhood of zero. Nevertheless, the limiting distribution of $\hat{\gamma}$ is well behaved provided $\beta \neq 0$, as follows. From the results on non-linear functions of MLEs (see Ch.A4):

$$\sqrt{T}\,(\hat{\gamma} - \gamma) \xrightarrow{D} \mathsf{N}\left[0, \frac{\mathsf{AV}\left[\hat{\beta}\right]}{\beta^4}\right], \tag{10.51}$$

where $\mathsf{AV}[\hat{\beta}]$ is the variance of the limiting distribution of $\hat{\beta}$. The distribution in (10.51) has all of its moments finite when $\beta \neq 0$.

Example B

For the model:

$$\boldsymbol{y} = \boldsymbol{Z\beta} + \boldsymbol{u} \text{ where } \boldsymbol{u} \sim \mathsf{N}_T\left[\boldsymbol{0}, \sigma_u^2 \boldsymbol{I}\right] \text{ and } \mathsf{E}\left[\boldsymbol{Z}'\boldsymbol{u}\right] = \boldsymbol{0},$$

when $\boldsymbol{\beta}$ is $k \times 1$, using the fact that $(\boldsymbol{y} - \boldsymbol{Z\beta}) = \boldsymbol{Q}_Z\boldsymbol{y} - \boldsymbol{Z}(\boldsymbol{\beta} - \hat{\boldsymbol{\beta}})$ where $\boldsymbol{Q}_Z = \boldsymbol{I}_T - \boldsymbol{Z}(\boldsymbol{Z}'\boldsymbol{Z})^{-1}\boldsymbol{Z}'$, when σ_u^2 is unknown, show that the CLF:

$$T^{-1}\ell^0\left(\boldsymbol{\beta} \mid \left(\sigma_u^2\right)_c\right)$$

is given by:

$$-\tfrac{1}{2}\left[1 + \log(2\pi)\right] - \tfrac{1}{2}\log\left(\frac{\boldsymbol{y}'\boldsymbol{Q}_Z\boldsymbol{y}}{T} + \left(\boldsymbol{\beta} - \hat{\boldsymbol{\beta}}\right)'\left(\frac{\boldsymbol{Z}'\boldsymbol{Z}}{T}\right)\left(\boldsymbol{\beta} - \hat{\boldsymbol{\beta}}\right)\right).$$

When $k = 2$, $(\sigma_u^2)_c = 1$ (which implies that $T^{-1}\boldsymbol{y}'\boldsymbol{Q}_Z\boldsymbol{y} = 1$), $\hat{\boldsymbol{\beta}} = \boldsymbol{0}$, and $T^{-1}\boldsymbol{Z}'\boldsymbol{Z} = \boldsymbol{I}_2$, sketch iso-likelihood contours of the form $T^{-1}\ell^0(\cdot) = c$ in (β_1, β_2) space. What shape are these functions?

Solution to example B

The log-likelihood function is:

$$\ell\left(\boldsymbol{\beta}, \sigma_u^2 \mid \boldsymbol{y}; \boldsymbol{Z}\right) = -\frac{T}{2}\log(2\pi) - \frac{T}{2}\log\sigma_u^2 - \frac{(\boldsymbol{y} - \boldsymbol{Z\beta})'(\boldsymbol{y} - \boldsymbol{Z\beta})}{2\sigma_u^2}. \tag{10.52}$$

By equating the score for σ_u^2 to zero:

$$\left(\sigma_u^2\right)_c = T^{-1}\left(y - Z\beta\right)'\left(y - Z\beta\right). \tag{10.53}$$

Therefore, the concentrated log-likelihood function (CLF) for β is:

$$\ell^0\left(\beta \mid \left(\sigma_u^2\right)_c, y; Z\right) = -\frac{T}{2}\left[\log\left(2\pi\right) + 1\right] - \frac{T}{2}\log\left[T^{-1}\left(y - Z\beta\right)'\left(y - Z\beta\right)\right]. \tag{10.54}$$

The matrix Q_Z is an idempotent matrix orthogonal to Z, so that $Q_Z Z = \mathbf{0}$ and hence (see Ch.A3):

$$\left(y - Z\beta\right) = Q_Z y - Z\left(\beta - \hat{\beta}\right).$$

Thus, the CLF $T^{-1}\ell^0(\beta|(\sigma_u^2)_c, y; Z)$ becomes:

$$-\tfrac{1}{2}\left[1 + \log\left(2\pi\right)\right] - \tfrac{1}{2}\log\left[\frac{y'Q_Z y}{T} + \left(\beta - \hat{\beta}\right)'\left(\frac{Z'Z}{T}\right)\left(\beta - \hat{\beta}\right)\right]. \tag{10.55}$$

Under the stated conditions on the MLEs as $\log e = 1$:

$$T^{-1}\ell^0\left(\beta \mid \left(\sigma_u^2\right)_c, y; Z\right) = -\tfrac{1}{2}\log\left[2\pi e\left(1 + \beta'\beta\right)\right] = c.$$

This can be re-expressed in the form $\beta'\beta = K$. Thus, the iso-likelihood contours are all the combinations of $\beta_1^2 + \beta_2^2$ equal to a constant, and are highest at zero, so they describe the equations of circles centred at the origin.

10.10 Misleading inference when $V \neq \mathcal{I}^{-1}$

Equation (10.39) holds for stationary stochastic processes after sequential factorization, but a number of methodological issues are raised by the assumption of 'correct specification', whereby $\mathsf{D}_{\mathsf{X}}(x \mid \theta) = \mathsf{L}(\theta \mid x)$ and $\mathcal{I}(\theta_p) = -\mathsf{E}[H(\theta_p)]$ so that $V(\theta_p) = -(\mathsf{E}[H(\theta_p)])^{-1}$.

First, conventional computer programs do not usually calculate the formula in (10.39), namely:

$$V\left(\hat{\theta}\right) = H\left(\hat{\theta}\right)^{-1}\mathcal{I}\left(\hat{\theta}\right)H\left(\hat{\theta}\right)^{-1},$$

but instead report $-H^{-1}(\hat{\theta})$ as the estimated variance matrix of $\hat{\theta}$. When $V(\theta_p) \neq -H(\theta_p)^{-1}$, or $\mathcal{I}(\theta_p) + \mathsf{E}[H(\theta_p)] \neq \mathbf{0}$, inappropriate parameter-variance estimates are calculated, and incorrect inferences may result. Second, $\mathsf{D}_{\mathsf{X}}(x|\theta) = \mathsf{L}(\theta|x)$ is not necessary for $V(\theta_p) = -H(\theta_p)^{-1}$, since $\mathsf{D}_{\mathsf{X}}(x|\theta)$ and $\mathsf{L}(\theta|x)$ could differ in ways that do not affect the relationship between the information matrix and the Hessian. In particular, congruent models with valid weak exogeneity and homoscedastic, innovation errors, given their information sets, will suffice as follows. The score vector $q(\theta_p)$ equals $\sum_{t=1}^{T} q_t(\theta_p)$, so that:

$$\mathcal{I}(\theta_p) = \mathsf{E}\left[q(\theta_p)q(\theta_p)'\right] = \mathsf{E}\left[\sum_{t=1}^{T} q_t(\theta_p)\sum_{s=1}^{T} q_s'(\theta_p)\right] = \mathsf{E}\left[\sum_{t=1}^{T}\sum_{s=1}^{T} q_t(\theta_p)q_s'(\theta_p)\right].$$

Provided $\mathsf{E}[\boldsymbol{q}_t(\boldsymbol{\theta}_p)\boldsymbol{q}_s(\boldsymbol{\theta}_p)'] = \mathbf{0}$ for $t \neq s$, and $\mathsf{E}[\boldsymbol{q}_t(\boldsymbol{\theta}_p)\boldsymbol{q}_t(\boldsymbol{\theta}_p)'] = -T^{-1}\mathsf{E}[\boldsymbol{H}(\boldsymbol{\theta}_p)]$, and is constant $\forall t$, then $\mathcal{I}(\boldsymbol{\theta}_p) + \mathsf{E}[\boldsymbol{H}(\boldsymbol{\theta}_p)] = \mathbf{0}$.

As an illustration of the effects of non-congruency, we consider heteroscedastic-consistent standard errors (HCSEs) discussed by Eicker (1967) and White (1980a). Relative to the usual standard errors reported in regression estimation, HCSEs allow the estimated coefficient variances to reflect heteroscedasticity in the residuals. Consider OLS estimation in:

$$y_t = \boldsymbol{z}_t'\boldsymbol{\beta} + \epsilon_t \text{ where } \epsilon_t \sim \mathsf{IN}\left[0, \sigma_t^2\right] \tag{10.56}$$

and $\mathsf{E}[\boldsymbol{z}_t\epsilon_s] = \mathbf{0}\ \forall t, s$. However, the investigator believes $\epsilon_t \underset{c}{\sim} \mathsf{IN}[0, \sigma_\epsilon^2]$ (where $\underset{c}{\sim}$ denotes 'is claimed to be distributed as') so that the log-likelihood is formulated as in (10.52) and is believed to induce the score equation:

$$\boldsymbol{q}(\boldsymbol{\beta}) = \sigma_\epsilon^{-2}\sum_{t=1}^{T} \boldsymbol{q}_t(\boldsymbol{\beta}) = \sigma_\epsilon^{-2}\sum_{t=1}^{T} \boldsymbol{z}_t\epsilon_t.$$

Then conditional on the zs:

$$\mathsf{E}[\boldsymbol{q}(\boldsymbol{\theta}_p)\boldsymbol{q}(\boldsymbol{\theta}_p)'] = \mathsf{E}\left[\sum_{t=1}^{T}\boldsymbol{q}_t(\boldsymbol{\theta}_p)\sum_{s=1}^{T}\boldsymbol{q}_s(\boldsymbol{\theta}_p)'\right] = \mathsf{E}\left[\sum_{t=1}^{T}\sum_{s=1}^{T}\frac{\boldsymbol{z}_t\epsilon_t\epsilon_s\boldsymbol{z}_s'}{\sigma_\epsilon^4}\right] = \sum_{t=1}^{T}\frac{\sigma_t^2\boldsymbol{z}_t\boldsymbol{z}_t'}{\sigma_\epsilon^4}, \tag{10.57}$$

and hence $\mathcal{I}(\boldsymbol{\theta}_p)$ involves a weighted average of the zs, whereas the conventional Hessian is calculated as:

$$\boldsymbol{H}(\boldsymbol{\beta}_p) = -\sigma_\epsilon^{-2}\sum_{t=1}^{T}\boldsymbol{z}_t\boldsymbol{z}_t'.$$

In (10.57), the weights are proportional to the error variances at each observation. If these weights are not constant over the sample, the inverse of the Hessian and the information matrix will not cancel as assumed in the last step of (10.39).

At first sight, the unknown error variances $\{\sigma_t^2\}$ seem inestimable because there are T of them. A surprising aspect of the result in White (1980a) is that we can replace the σ_t^2 by $\hat{\epsilon}_t^2$ in (10.57) to estimate the information matrix (the middle term in (10.58)):

$$\hat{\boldsymbol{V}} = (\boldsymbol{Z}'\boldsymbol{Z})^{-1}\left(\sum_{t=1}^{T}\hat{\epsilon}_t^2\boldsymbol{z}_t\boldsymbol{z}_t'\right)(\boldsymbol{Z}'\boldsymbol{Z})^{-1} = \hat{\boldsymbol{H}}^{-1}\mathcal{I}\left(\hat{\boldsymbol{\beta}}\right)\hat{\boldsymbol{H}}^{-1}. \tag{10.58}$$

The conventional estimator of $\boldsymbol{V}$ is the special case that all σ_t are constant when $\mathsf{E}[\epsilon_t^2] = \sigma_\epsilon^2$. White proves that $\hat{\boldsymbol{V}}$ in (10.58) is consistent for $\boldsymbol{V}$ (also see White, 1984). In the present illustration, we need only show that $T^{-1}(\mathcal{I}(\hat{\boldsymbol{\beta}}) - \mathcal{I}(\boldsymbol{\beta}_p))$ converges to zero, and since $\text{plim}_{T\to\infty}\,\hat{\boldsymbol{\beta}} = \boldsymbol{\beta}_p$:

$$\hat{\epsilon}_t = y_t - \boldsymbol{z}_t'\hat{\boldsymbol{\beta}} = \boldsymbol{z}_t'(\boldsymbol{\beta}_p - \hat{\boldsymbol{\beta}}) + \epsilon_t = \epsilon_t + O_p(T^{-\frac{1}{2}}),$$

then letting $\boldsymbol{P}_t = \boldsymbol{z}_t\boldsymbol{z}_t'$:

$$T^{-1}\sum_{t=1}^{T}(\hat{\epsilon}_t^2 - \sigma_t^2)\boldsymbol{z}_t\boldsymbol{z}_t' = T^{-1}\sum_{t=1}^{T}(\epsilon_t^2 - \sigma_t^2)\boldsymbol{P}_t + O_p(T^{-1}) \xrightarrow{P} 0,$$

because of the weak law of large numbers applied to the product of $(\epsilon_t^2 - \sigma_t^2)$ and $\boldsymbol{P}_t$. Note that this proof did not require that σ_t^2 was non-constant, and still holds when $\sigma_t^2 = \sigma_\epsilon^2$. However, $\mathcal{I}(\widehat{\beta})^{-1}$ will be biased for $\widehat{\boldsymbol{H}}^{-1}\mathcal{I}(\widehat{\beta})\widehat{\boldsymbol{H}}^{-1}$ unless congruency holds.

Thus, the more general form of $\boldsymbol{V}$ in (10.58) is estimable for some error processes and helps generalize the region of valid inference to models with unknown and untreated heteroscedasticity. In programming, the variance-covariance matrix could take the form of (10.58), rather than $\widehat{\sigma}_\epsilon^2(\boldsymbol{Z}'\boldsymbol{Z})^{-1}$, and is often used in the generalized method of moments (GMM) class. Further generalizations to allow for autocorrelated residuals and so on are possible, but raise methodological issues about the status of the postulated model, as well as the efficiency of estimation and inference in non-congruent models.

Next, when $\mathsf{D}_\mathsf{X}(\boldsymbol{x}|\boldsymbol{\theta}) \neq \mathsf{L}(\boldsymbol{\theta}|\boldsymbol{x})$, then $\widehat{\boldsymbol{\theta}}$ is no longer the maximum likelihood estimator, since the likelihood function is incorrect for the density, but is a 'pseudo-MLE'. We consider its consistency and efficiency in such cases, and begin with the former. Earlier, we proved that MLEs are consistent for the population parameter. Sometimes, the population value $\boldsymbol{\theta}_p$ is called the 'true' value, but that does not entail that $\boldsymbol{\theta}_p$ corresponds to an economic parameter of interest (see e.g. Hendry, 1979a): the present statistical formulation is almost too general (see Ch.A4). If $\widehat{\boldsymbol{\theta}}$ converges to $\boldsymbol{\theta}^*$ say, then by redefining that convergent value as the population parameter $\boldsymbol{\theta}_p$, convergent MLEs are consistent for $\boldsymbol{\theta}_p = \boldsymbol{\theta}^*$, which does not guarantee that $\boldsymbol{\theta}_p$ is a parameter of interest. Further, Chapter 4 showed that estimators in spurious regression models need not converge to constants.

When $\boldsymbol{\theta}_p = \text{plim}_{T\to\infty}\, \widehat{\boldsymbol{\theta}}$ holds by definition (sometimes called a pseudo-true value), where $\boldsymbol{\theta}_p$ maximizes a log-likelihood based on an incorrect specification of the density function (factorized to a martingale difference sequence), then even though the DGP errors are heteroscedastic, and correlated with the zs, $\widehat{\boldsymbol{\theta}}$ will be approximately normal around $\boldsymbol{\theta}_p$ with a variance-covariance matrix which is estimable by $\boldsymbol{V}$ (but incorrectly estimated by $-\widehat{\boldsymbol{H}}^{-1}$). Even if $\boldsymbol{V}$ is used for inference, however, $\widehat{\boldsymbol{\theta}}$ will usually be inefficient — if the latter concept has meaning in the present context.

Unfortunately, this situation may be typical in much empirical research. An investigator does not know if the problem as formulated has a meaningful $\boldsymbol{\theta}_p$ in reality, although the general form of asymptotic normal distribution in (10.39) will often apply. Thus, the fact that reasonable estimates are obtained for the claimed parameters and variances (using $-\widehat{\boldsymbol{H}}^{-1}$) cannot ensure that we do not end with inconsistent estimates and misleading inferences. Consequently, we must proceed beyond estimation to careful and rigorous testing of postulated relationships.

10.11 Derived distributions

Often the objective of estimation is not $\boldsymbol{\theta}$ itself but a function of $\boldsymbol{\theta}$, such as the long-run outcome as discussed in Chapter 6. One of the major reasons for adopting MLE is its equivariance property noted in §10.7: when $\boldsymbol{\phi} = \boldsymbol{g}(\boldsymbol{\theta})$, then the MLE of $\boldsymbol{\phi}$ is $\widehat{\boldsymbol{\phi}} = \boldsymbol{g}(\widehat{\boldsymbol{\theta}})$ when $\widehat{\boldsymbol{\theta}}$ is the MLE of $\boldsymbol{\theta}$. To conduct inference about $\boldsymbol{\phi}$ requires a general method of obtaining $\mathsf{V}[\hat{\phi}]$. Consider a Taylor-series approximation to $\hat{\phi} = g(\hat{\theta})$:

$$\begin{aligned} g(\hat{\theta}) &= g(\theta_p) + \frac{\partial g}{\partial \theta}'\rfloor_{\theta_p} \left(\hat{\theta} - \theta_p\right) + O_p\left(T^{-1}\right) \\ &\simeq g(\theta_p) + G(\theta_p)\left(\hat{\theta} - \theta_p\right), \end{aligned} \tag{10.59}$$

where $G(\theta_p)$ is the Jacobian mapping from θ to ϕ evaluated at θ_p. We could use $G(\theta^*)$ in place of $G(\theta_p)$ and drop the approximation, where θ^* lies between $\hat{\theta}$ and θ_p; since $\hat{\theta} \xrightarrow{P} \theta_p$, then $\theta^* \xrightarrow{P} \theta_p$ and so $G(\theta^*) \xrightarrow{P} G(\theta_p)$ as the sample size tends to infinity. From (10.59), letting $G(\theta_p) = G_p$, when $|G_p| \neq 0$:

$$\sqrt{T}\left(g(\hat{\theta}) - g(\theta_p)\right) \simeq G_p\sqrt{T}\left(\hat{\theta} - \theta_p\right), \tag{10.60}$$

and hence from Cramér's theorem, since $g(\theta_p) = \phi_p$, when $\sqrt{T}(\hat{\theta} - \theta_p) \xrightarrow{D} \mathsf{N}_k[\mathbf{0}, V]$ then:

$$\sqrt{T}\left(\hat{\phi} - \phi_p\right) \xrightarrow{D} \mathsf{N}_k\left[\mathbf{0}, G_p V G_p'\right]. \tag{10.61}$$

Again, (10.61) is technically correct, but its utility depends how rapidly the relevant function converges to normality, since there will be some functions $g(\cdot)$ for which (10.61) is a poor approximation (although Monte Carlo can be used as a check in important cases). For example, $\hat{\theta}$ and $\hat{\theta}^2$ are both normal according to (10.61), but when $\hat{\theta}$ is normal, $\hat{\theta}^2$ is distributed as χ^2.

10.12 Asymptotic equivalence

A related issue arises when instead of working with the MLE $\hat{\theta}$, an estimator $\tilde{\theta}$ is chosen instead such that:

$$\tilde{\theta} = \hat{\theta} + O_p\left(T^{-1}\right), \tag{10.62}$$

such that the difference between $\tilde{\theta}$ and $\hat{\theta}$ when multiplied by T is bounded in probability (see §A4.2). Terms of $O_p(T^{-1})$, or the root of that — or indeed any inverse function of the sample size — tend to zero as the sample size tends to infinity. When the difference in (10.62) is multiplied by $\sqrt{T}$, for example, then:

$$\sqrt{T}\left(\tilde{\theta} - \hat{\theta}\right) = O_p\left(T^{-\frac{1}{2}}\right), \tag{10.63}$$

and since $O_p(T^{-\frac{1}{2}}) \to 0$ as $T \to \infty$, then $\text{plim}_{T\to\infty} \sqrt{T}(\tilde{\theta} - \hat{\theta}) = \mathbf{0}$.

Estimators like $\tilde{\theta}$ are said to be asymptotically equivalent to MLE, and have the same limiting distribution (such as (10.39)). Any differences between the distributions of two estimators which are asymptotically equivalent to order $O_p(T^{-1})$ disappear, so we do not necessarily need MLEs in (10.39). There is an infinitely large class of estimators $\tilde{\theta}$ which differ from the corresponding MLE $\hat{\theta}$ by stochastic functions that vanish at $O_p(T^{-1})$ and so are asymptotically equivalent to MLE. We return to a characterization of that class in §10.15.

10.13 Concentrated likelihood functions

It is useful for both theoretical derivations and computer programming to know some tricks about likelihood functions. Often, the likelihood is not just a function of one set of parameters, but of two: $\boldsymbol{\theta} = (\boldsymbol{\theta}_1 : \boldsymbol{\theta}_2)$ so that $\mathsf{L}(\boldsymbol{\theta}) = \mathsf{L}(\boldsymbol{\theta}_1 : \boldsymbol{\theta}_2)$ where $\boldsymbol{\theta}_1$ is a set of parameters of interest, and $\boldsymbol{\theta}_2$ is a set of nuisance parameters (such as seasonal dummy variables, variance-covariance matrix parameters, etc.). To calculate the MLE, maximize $\mathsf{L}(\hat{\boldsymbol{\theta}})$ which is a problem defined by:

$$\max_{\boldsymbol{\theta}_1,\boldsymbol{\theta}_2} \mathsf{L}(\boldsymbol{\theta}) = \max_{\boldsymbol{\theta}_1} \left[\max_{\boldsymbol{\theta}_2} \mathsf{L}(\boldsymbol{\theta}_1 : \boldsymbol{\theta}_2) \right] = \max_{\boldsymbol{\theta}_1} \mathsf{L}^*(\boldsymbol{\theta}_1), \tag{10.64}$$

where the $\mathsf{L}^*(\boldsymbol{\theta}_1)$ function in square brackets is the concentrated likelihood function (denoted by CLF above). In statistics, the CLF is more usually called the profile likelihood function. Assuming the usual regularity conditions, differentiate $\ell(\boldsymbol{\theta})$ with respect to $\boldsymbol{\theta}_2$ and equate to zero for a local maximum:

$$\frac{\partial \ell(\boldsymbol{\theta}_1 : \boldsymbol{\theta}_2)}{\partial \boldsymbol{\theta}_2} = \mathbf{q}_2(\boldsymbol{\theta}_1 : \boldsymbol{\theta}_2) = \mathbf{0}. \tag{10.65}$$

Solve (10.65) for $\boldsymbol{\theta}_2$, which yields the function $(\boldsymbol{\theta}_2)_c = \boldsymbol{h}(\boldsymbol{\theta}_1)$. From the equivariance property of maximum likelihood estimators, once $\hat{\boldsymbol{\theta}}_1$ is known:

$$\hat{\boldsymbol{\theta}}_2 = \boldsymbol{h}\left(\hat{\boldsymbol{\theta}}_1\right). \tag{10.66}$$

Thus, we only need $\hat{\boldsymbol{\theta}}_1$ to calculate the maximum of the log-likelihood function after maximizing $\ell(\boldsymbol{\theta}_1 : \boldsymbol{\theta}_2)$ over $\boldsymbol{\theta}_2$. This is achieved by substituting $\boldsymbol{h}(\boldsymbol{\theta}_1)$ for $\boldsymbol{\theta}_2$ since:

$$\max_{\boldsymbol{\theta}_2} \ell(\boldsymbol{\theta}_1 : \boldsymbol{\theta}_2) = \ell(\boldsymbol{\theta}_1 : \boldsymbol{h}(\boldsymbol{\theta}_1)) = \ell^*(\boldsymbol{\theta}_1). \tag{10.67}$$

The MLE of $\boldsymbol{\theta}_1$ is now obtained by maximizing $\ell^*(\boldsymbol{\theta}_1)$ with respect to $\boldsymbol{\theta}_1$. We have used this result several times before, as when eliminating the error variance σ^2 from the likelihood in regression: differentiate $\ell(\cdot)$ with respect to σ^2 and substitute that formula into $\ell(\cdot)$ which yields a monotonic function of the residual sum of squares to be minimized with respect to $\boldsymbol{\beta}$. Obtaining $(\sigma^2)_c$ corresponds to the first step in the CLF theorem above; obtaining $\hat{\boldsymbol{\beta}}$ assumes that the theorem is true. Given $\hat{\boldsymbol{\beta}}$, the MLE of σ^2 uses $\boldsymbol{h}(\hat{\boldsymbol{\beta}})$.

The importance of the CLF result relates to obtaining $\hat{\boldsymbol{\theta}}_1$ from $\partial\ell^*(\cdot)/\partial\boldsymbol{\theta}_1$ using:

$$\frac{\partial \ell^*(\boldsymbol{\theta}_1)}{\partial \boldsymbol{\theta}_1} \equiv \frac{\partial \ell(\hat{\boldsymbol{\theta}})}{\partial \boldsymbol{\theta}_1}\Big\rfloor_{\boldsymbol{h}(\boldsymbol{\theta}_1)} = \mathbf{0}. \tag{10.68}$$

Either compute the CLF and then differentiate that with respect to $\boldsymbol{\theta}_1$, solving for $\boldsymbol{\theta}_1$; or differentiate the original likelihood function with respect to $\boldsymbol{\theta}_1$ and substitute $\boldsymbol{h}(\boldsymbol{\theta}_1)$

for $\boldsymbol{\theta}_2$. The equality in (10.68) holds because of the implicit function theorem, using (10.65):

$$\frac{\partial \ell\left(\boldsymbol{\theta}_1 : \boldsymbol{h}\left(\boldsymbol{\theta}_1\right)\right)}{\partial \boldsymbol{\theta}_1} = \frac{\partial \ell(\widehat{\boldsymbol{\theta}})}{\partial \boldsymbol{\theta}_1}\Big\rfloor_{\boldsymbol{h}(\boldsymbol{\theta}_1)} + \frac{\partial \boldsymbol{h}'}{\partial \boldsymbol{\theta}_1}\frac{\partial \ell\left(\cdot\right)}{\partial \boldsymbol{h}} = \frac{\partial \ell(\widehat{\boldsymbol{\theta}})}{\partial \boldsymbol{\theta}_1}\Big\rfloor_{\boldsymbol{h}(\boldsymbol{\theta}_1)} \text{ since } \frac{\partial \ell\left(\cdot\right)}{\partial \boldsymbol{h}} = \mathbf{0}. \tag{10.69}$$

As a consequence of (10.64)–(10.69), when $\ell^*(\cdot)$ is a simple function of $\boldsymbol{\theta}_1$, use:

$$\frac{\partial \ell^*(\boldsymbol{\theta}_1)}{\partial \boldsymbol{\theta}_1} = \boldsymbol{q}_1^*(\boldsymbol{\theta}_1) = \mathbf{0}, \tag{10.70}$$

to solve for $\widehat{\boldsymbol{\theta}}_1$; whereas when $\ell(\cdot)$ is a simple function of $\boldsymbol{\theta}_1$, solve:

$$\frac{\partial \ell(\widehat{\boldsymbol{\theta}})}{\partial \boldsymbol{\theta}_1}\Big\rfloor_{\boldsymbol{h}(\boldsymbol{\theta}_1)} = \mathbf{0}. \tag{10.71}$$

The choice between (10.70) and (10.71) can greatly facilitate computation in complicated or high-dimensional estimation problems (for an example, see Hendry, 1971).

10.14 Marginal and conditional distributions

Above, we established the following approximation in finite samples (where $\boldsymbol{V}$ is normalized by T^{-1}):

$$\begin{pmatrix} \widehat{\boldsymbol{\theta}}_1 \\ \widehat{\boldsymbol{\theta}}_2 \end{pmatrix} \underset{app}{\sim} \mathsf{N}_k\left[\begin{pmatrix} \boldsymbol{\theta}_1 \\ \boldsymbol{\theta}_2 \end{pmatrix}, \begin{pmatrix} \boldsymbol{V}_{11} & \boldsymbol{V}_{12} \\ \boldsymbol{V}_{21} & \boldsymbol{V}_{22} \end{pmatrix}\right]. \tag{10.72}$$

From (10.72), the marginal distribution of $\widehat{\boldsymbol{\theta}}_1$ is:

$$\widehat{\boldsymbol{\theta}}_1 \underset{app}{\sim} \mathsf{N}_{k_1}\left[\boldsymbol{\theta}_1, \boldsymbol{V}_{11}\right]. \tag{10.73}$$

However, since $\boldsymbol{V} = \mathcal{I}^{-1}$ when $\mathsf{L}(\cdot) = \mathsf{D_x}(\cdot)$, using partitioned inversion:

$$\boldsymbol{V}_{11} = \left(\mathcal{I}_{11} - \mathcal{I}_{12}\mathcal{I}_{22}^{-1}\mathcal{I}_{21}\right)^{-1} \quad \text{where } \mathcal{I} = \begin{pmatrix} \mathcal{I}_{11} & \mathcal{I}_{12} \\ \mathcal{I}_{21} & \mathcal{I}_{22} \end{pmatrix}. \tag{10.74}$$

Thus, $\boldsymbol{V}_{11}$ is not the inverse of the information matrix $\mathcal{I}_{11}$ unless $\mathcal{I}_{12} = \mathbf{0}$, in which case $\widehat{\boldsymbol{\theta}}_1$ and $\widehat{\boldsymbol{\theta}}_2$ are uncorrelated. Since $\boldsymbol{V}_{12} = -\boldsymbol{V}_{11}\mathcal{I}_{12}\mathcal{I}_{22}^{-1}$ then $\boldsymbol{V}_{12}$ is null if and only if $\mathcal{I}_{12} = \mathbf{0}$.

Next, consider the conditional distribution:

$$\widehat{\boldsymbol{\theta}}_1 \mid \widehat{\boldsymbol{\theta}}_2 \underset{app}{\sim} \mathsf{N}_{k_1}\left[\boldsymbol{\theta}_1 + \boldsymbol{V}_{12}\boldsymbol{V}_{22}^{-1}\left(\widehat{\boldsymbol{\theta}}_2 - \boldsymbol{\theta}_2\right), \left(\boldsymbol{V}_{11} - \boldsymbol{V}_{12}\boldsymbol{V}_{22}^{-1}\boldsymbol{V}_{21}\right)\right], \tag{10.75}$$

where the last term is the conditional variance matrix of $\widehat{\boldsymbol{\theta}}_1$, and (again from partitioned inversion) is equal to $\mathcal{I}_{11}^{-1}$. If $\widehat{\boldsymbol{\theta}}_1$ and $\widehat{\boldsymbol{\theta}}_2$ are correlated so that $\boldsymbol{V}_{12} \neq \mathbf{0}$, then it holds that $\left(\boldsymbol{V}_{11} - \boldsymbol{V}_{12}\boldsymbol{V}_{22}^{-1}\boldsymbol{V}_{21}\right) \preceq \boldsymbol{V}_{11}$, so calculating the standard errors of $\widehat{\boldsymbol{\theta}}_1$ for given values of $\widehat{\boldsymbol{\theta}}_2$ can under-estimate the uncertainty in $\widehat{\boldsymbol{\theta}}_1$, perhaps seriously. Some computer programs do this without warning for autocorrelation corrections.

10.15 Estimator generating equations

Almost all econometric estimators follow from solving one subset of the score equation either exactly or approximately, given the solution to another subset, again perhaps approximately. Consider the complete score equation:

$$\begin{aligned} q_1(\theta_1 : \theta_2) &= \mathbf{0} \\ q_2(\theta_1 : \theta_2) &= \mathbf{0}. \end{aligned} \tag{10.76}$$

Assume we are interested in estimating θ_1 and not so much interested in θ_2. The MLE for θ_2 solves $q_2(\cdot) = \mathbf{0}$ as a function of θ_1, and conversely the MLE for θ_1 is obtained by solving for $\hat{\theta}_1$ from:

$$q_1\left(\theta_1 : \hat{\theta}_2\right) = \mathbf{0}, \tag{10.77}$$

where $\hat{\theta}_2$ is the MLE of θ_2. However, the result in (10.77) holds asymptotically on replacing $\hat{\theta}_2$ by $\tilde{\theta}_2 = \hat{\theta}_2 + O_p(T^{-1})$, in that the derived $\tilde{\theta}_1$ has the same limiting distribution as $\hat{\theta}_1$. Consequently, consider a method of estimation determined by conditioning the estimate of θ_1 on that of $\tilde{\theta}_2$, namely solve for $\tilde{\theta}_1$ from:

$$q_1\left(\theta_1 \mid \tilde{\theta}_2\right) = \mathbf{0}. \tag{10.78}$$

Equation (10.78) generates estimators of θ_1 as functions of the estimators chosen for θ_2: as the rule for estimating θ_2 changes, different methods are generated for estimating θ_1, and so it is called an estimator generating equation (EGE).

A major reason why (10.78) is interesting is that in linear systems of simultaneous equations (the subject of Ch.11), with or without measurement errors, with or without dynamics, and with or without error autocorrelation, every known econometric estimator is a special case of (10.78). Moreover, every method can be obtained from (10.78) in a straightforward way (see Hendry, 1976).

To understand why, reconsider (10.72) and (10.74). When $\mathcal{I}_{12} = \mathbf{0}$ in (10.74), then although $\tilde{\theta}_2$ is needed to calculate $\hat{\theta}_1$, the distribution of $\hat{\theta}_1$ does not depend on that of $\tilde{\theta}_2$. The condition for $\mathcal{I}_{12} = \mathbf{0}$ is:

$$\mathsf{E}\left[\frac{\partial q_1(\theta)}{\partial \theta_2'}\right] = \mathbf{0}, \tag{10.79}$$

which states that changes in θ_2 do not affect the score for θ_1 on average. If (10.79) holds, instead of requiring $\tilde{\theta}_2$ in (10.78) to be asymptotically equivalent to $\hat{\theta}_2$, and hence asymptotically efficient, a consistent estimator of θ_2 in (10.78) will generate an asymptotically efficient estimator of θ_1. When $\tilde{\theta}_2 \xrightarrow{P} \theta_{2p}$ (using θ_{2p} to denote the population value), then $\tilde{\theta}_1$ is as efficient asymptotically as the MLE: $(\tilde{\theta}_1 - \hat{\theta}_1) \xrightarrow{D} \mathbf{0}$. Indeed, if $\mathcal{I}_{12} = \mathbf{0}$, even an inconsistent but convergent estimator of θ_2 (say $\tilde{\theta}_2 \xrightarrow{P} \theta_2^* \neq \theta_{2p}$) generates a consistent $\tilde{\theta}_1 : \tilde{\theta} \xrightarrow{P} \theta_1$. Thus, the EGE highlights minimum conditions on $\tilde{\theta}_2$ to obtain consistent or efficient estimators of θ_1, as well as summarizing the structure of a vast range of estimators. In Chapter 11, we turn to a detailed consideration of this result for simultaneous-equations estimators. First, we consider an example based on a common-factor dynamic equation to illustrate the various steps involved.

10.16 An EGE for common-factor dynamics

Consider the model:

$$y_t = \beta' z_t + u_t \tag{10.80}$$

for $t = 0, 1, \ldots, T$, where z_t is strongly exogenous for β and:

$$u_t = \rho u_{t-1} + \epsilon_t \tag{10.81}$$

with $|\rho| < 1$ and $\epsilon_t \sim \mathsf{IN}\left[0, \sigma_\epsilon^2\right]$. It is proposed to estimate (β, ρ) in (10.80)+(10.81) using the following EGE:

$$\begin{pmatrix} \sum_{t=1}^{T} (z_t - \rho z_{t-1})\,\epsilon_t \\ \sum_{t=1}^{T} u_{t-1}\epsilon_t \end{pmatrix} = \mathbf{0}. \tag{10.82}$$

Explain the origin of the EGE in (10.82) given (10.80)+(10.81), and show how to solve (10.82) for estimators of β and ρ. Develop both an asymptotically efficient, and a consistent but inefficient estimator of β, discussing whether or not iterating is useful.

(Adapted from Oxford M.Phil., 1987)

Solution

From the definition of the model, substituting (10.81) into (10.80):

$$y_t - \beta' z_t = \rho\,(y_{t-1} - \beta' z_{t-1}) + \epsilon_t \tag{10.83}$$

with $\epsilon_t \sim \mathsf{IN}[0, \sigma_\epsilon^2]$. Neglecting the initial conditions and the Jacobian (both of which are asymptotically negligible although they could matter greatly in finite samples), the log-likelihood is:

$$\ell\left(\beta, \rho, \sigma_\epsilon^2\right) = -\frac{T}{2}\log(2\pi) - \frac{T}{2}\log\sigma_\epsilon^2 - \frac{1}{2\sigma_\epsilon^2}\sum_{t=1}^{T}\left(y_t - \beta' z_t - \rho y_{t-1} + \rho\beta' z_{t-1}\right)^2. \tag{10.84}$$

From equation (10.81), the last term in (10.84) can also be interpreted as $\sum_{t=1}^{T}\epsilon_t^2$ or as $\sum_{t=1}^{T}(u_t - \rho u_{t-1})^2$ by invariance. The score equations for β and ρ are:

$$q_1(\beta) = \frac{1}{\sigma_\epsilon^2}\sum_{t=1}^{T}(z_t - \rho z_{t-1})(y_t - \beta' z_t - \rho y_{t-1} + \rho\beta' z_{t-1}) = \frac{1}{\sigma_\epsilon^2}\sum_{t=1}^{T}(z_t - \rho z_{t-1})\epsilon_t \tag{10.85}$$

and:

$$q_2(\rho) = \frac{1}{\sigma_\epsilon^2} \sum_{t=1}^{T} (y_{t-1} - \beta' z_{t-1})(y_t - \beta' z_t - \rho y_{t-1} + \rho\beta' z_{t-1}) = \frac{1}{\sigma_\epsilon^2} \sum_{t=1}^{T} u_{t-1}\epsilon_t. \tag{10.86}$$

Equating these to zero delivers (10.82). The expectation of both scores is zero since they are implicitly evaluated at the population parameter values.

To solve the EGE, provisional estimates of β and ρ are required. Two cases arise, namely, (a) $y_{t-s} \notin \{z_{it}\}$; and (b) $y_{t-s} \in \{z_{it}\}$ where $s \geq 1$. The crucial difference between these is that in (a), which holds when z_t is strongly exogenous, $\mathsf{E}[z_t u_{t-r}] = \mathbf{0}\,\forall r$, whereas in (b) the lagged dependent variable is a regressor and must be correlated with the corresponding lagged value of the autoregressive error. This determines whether or not $\mathcal{I}_{12}$ is zero, since from (10.85) and (10.86):

$$\mathsf{E}\left[q_1(\beta)q_2(\rho)\right] = \frac{1}{\sigma_\epsilon^4} \sum_{t=1}^{T}\sum_{s=1}^{T} \mathsf{E}\left[z_t u_{s-1}\epsilon_t\epsilon_s - \rho z_{t-1} u_{s-1}\epsilon_t\epsilon_s\right].$$

In both (a) and (b), $\mathsf{E}[z_t\epsilon_s] = \mathbf{0}\,\forall t \geq s$, but only under strong exogeneity will $\mathsf{E}[z_t u_{t-r}] = \mathbf{0}\,\forall r$. The original problem assumed (a), so we follow that here.

An obvious first estimator of β is OLS, which solves the first equation of the EGE in (10.82) when $\rho = 0$. The consistency of OLS depends on $\mathcal{I}_{12} = \mathbf{0}$, but the result is inefficient if in fact $\rho \neq 0$, and the OLS variance formula is incorrect. However, a consistent estimator of β induces 'consistent' residuals $\hat{u}_{t-1}$ which can be used in the second EGE equation to provide a consistent and asymptotically efficient estimator of ρ, since (10.79) holds. Using the resulting value of $\hat{\rho}$, the first equation can be solved again for a consistent and asymptotically efficient estimator of β. Continued iteration is feasible and leads to the MLE, which may improve inference in finite samples, but yields no gain in asymptotic efficiency.

Under (b), consistent initial values can be obtained in many ways, perhaps the simplest being based on (10.83), involving regressing y_t on the non-redundant elements in (z_t, y_{t-1}, z_{t-1}) and getting β as the coefficient of z_t. Iteration is required to obtain the MLE in (b), at least conducting two steps for asymptotic efficiency (see Rothenberg and Leenders, 1964, and Hendry, 1976). The iterated COMFAC estimator was applied to the conditional model of velocity given the net interest rate in Chapter 7.

10.17 Exercises

10.1 Consider the process:

$$\begin{pmatrix} y_t \\ z_t \end{pmatrix} \sim \mathsf{IN}_2\left[\begin{pmatrix} 0 \\ 0 \end{pmatrix}, \begin{pmatrix} \sigma_t^2 & \varphi \\ \varphi & \omega^2 \end{pmatrix}\right] \quad \text{for } t = 1, \ldots, T. \tag{10.87}$$

You wish to estimate the parameter β in a conditional linear model relating y_t to z_t.

(a) Derive β as a function of the parameters of (10.87). Find its maximum likelihood estimator $\hat{\beta}$ and the limiting distribution of $\hat{\beta}$ when $\{\sigma_t^2\}$ is a known sequence. Is $\hat{\beta}$ computable when $\{\sigma_t^2\}$ is unknown?

(b) Obtain the least-squares estimator $\tilde{\beta}$ of β, prove it is consistent for β, and derive a consistent estimator of its limiting variance when $\{\sigma_t^2\}$ is unknown.

(c) Using the fact that the arithmetic mean is no less than the harmonic mean, show that $\hat{\beta}$ is at least as efficient as $\tilde{\beta}$ when $\{\sigma_t^2\}$ is known.

(Oxford M.Phil., 1984)

10.2 Derive the MLE for the parameters of the stationary process:

$$y_t = \boldsymbol{z}_t'\boldsymbol{\beta} + u_t, \tag{10.88}$$

where $u_t = \rho u_{t-1} + \epsilon_t$ with $|\rho| < 1$ and $\epsilon_t \sim \mathsf{IN}\left[0, \sigma_\epsilon^2\right]$, when $\boldsymbol{z}_t$ is weakly, but not strongly exogenous, for $\boldsymbol{\beta}$. Obtain the score and the information matrix, and show that the MLEs $\hat{\boldsymbol{\beta}}$ and $\hat{\rho}$ are not independent. Briefly describe how to calculate your estimator.

(Oxford M.Phil., 1983)

10.3 An investigator asserts the model:

$$y_t = \alpha z_t + \epsilon_t, \tag{10.89}$$

where $\epsilon_t \underset{c}{\sim} \mathsf{IN}\left[0, \sigma_\epsilon^2\right]$ and $\mathsf{E}\left[z_t\epsilon_s\right] = 0\ \forall t, s$, and $\underset{c}{\sim}$ is a claimed distribution.

(a) Derive the log-likelihood function for $\boldsymbol{\theta}' = (\alpha, \sigma_\epsilon^2)$, its first and second derivatives $\boldsymbol{q}(\hat{\boldsymbol{\theta}})$ and $\boldsymbol{H}(\boldsymbol{\theta})$, and the maximum likelihood estimator $\tilde{\boldsymbol{\theta}}$ of $\boldsymbol{\theta}$.

(b) In fact:

$$\epsilon_t = u_t - \lambda u_{t-1} \tag{10.90}$$

where $u_t \sim \mathsf{IN}[0, \sigma_u^2]$ and $|\lambda| < 1$. Obtain: $\mathsf{E}[\boldsymbol{q}(\hat{\boldsymbol{\theta}})]$, $\mathsf{E}[\boldsymbol{H}(\hat{\boldsymbol{\theta}})]$, and $\mathsf{E}[\boldsymbol{q}(\hat{\boldsymbol{\theta}})\boldsymbol{q}(\boldsymbol{\theta})']$ for the asserted model (10.89) when (10.90) holds. How could $\mathsf{V}[\tilde{\alpha}]$ be consistently estimated when $\lambda \neq 0$? Comment on the adequacy of this treatment of autocorrelation, and consider how robust your analysis is to z_t not being strictly exogenous.

(Oxford M.Phil., 1985)

10.4 An investigator hypothesizes the model:

$$\begin{pmatrix} y_t | z_t \\ z_t \end{pmatrix} \underset{c}{\sim} \mathsf{IN}_2\left[\begin{pmatrix} \beta z_t \\ 0 \end{pmatrix}, \begin{pmatrix} \sigma_\epsilon^2 & 0 \\ 0 & \omega^2 \end{pmatrix}\right] \quad \text{for } t = 1, \ldots, T, \tag{10.91}$$

when, in fact:

$$y_t - \mathsf{E}\left[y_t \mid z_t\right] = e_t \sim \mathsf{IN}\left[0, \sigma_t^2\right] \tag{10.92}$$

and $\underset{c}{\sim}$ is a claimed distribution; σ_t^2 is not constant over t.

(a) Formulate the log-likelihood function believed by the investigator, given (10.91), its score $\boldsymbol{q}(\cdot)$, Hessian $\boldsymbol{H}(\cdot)$, and the maximum likelihood estimator $\hat{\beta}$.

(b) Obtain both the correct information matrix $\mathcal{I}(\cdot)$, when (10.92) holds, and the expected value of $\boldsymbol{H}(\cdot)$.

(c) Derive the limiting distribution of (an appropriately normalized) $\hat{\beta}$ given (10.92) and show that the conventional variance estimator is not a consistent estimator of the variance $\boldsymbol{V}$ of that limiting distribution. Explain how to consistently estimate $\boldsymbol{V}$ irrespective of the constancy of σ_t^2.

(d) Comment on what happens when T is finite, and suggest an estimator of $\boldsymbol{V}$ which is consistent when $\sigma_t^2 \neq \sigma_\epsilon^2\ \forall t$, and is unbiased when $\sigma_t^2 = \sigma_\epsilon^2\ \forall t$.

(Oxford M.Phil., 1983)

10.5 Consider the model which asserts:

$$y_t = \phi z_t + u_t \text{ for } t = 1, \ldots, T \tag{10.93}$$

where $u_t \underset{c}{\sim} \mathsf{IN}[0, \sigma_u^2]$ with $E[z_t u_s] = 0\ \forall t, s$, when $E[\cdot]$ denotes an asserted expectation based on a model and $\underset{c}{\sim}$ is a claimed distribution.

(a) Derive the likelihood function for (ϕ, σ_u^2), the score, the Hessian, and information matrix, and the maximum likelihood estimator (MLE) $\hat{\phi}$ of ϕ.

(b) The actual DGP can be expressed as:

$$y_t \mid z_t, y_{t-1}, z_{t-1} \sim \mathsf{N}\left[\alpha z_t + \rho y_{t-1} - \alpha\rho z_{t-1}, \sigma_u^2\right] \tag{10.94}$$

where $|\rho| < 1$, and:

$$z_t \mid y_{t-1}, z_{t-1} \sim \mathsf{N}\left[\gamma z_{t-1}, \sigma_v^2\right] \tag{10.95}$$

with $|\gamma| < 1$. Derive the expected value of the score, Hessian, and information matrix for $\hat{\phi}$ obtained in (a) when (b) holds.

(c) Discuss how to estimate the Hessian and information matrix consistently, even though (b) holds, and comment on whether this is a sensible approach to handling the mis-specification in (10.94) and (10.95).

(d) Discuss in what ways, if any, your analysis would change if z_t were not strictly exogenous in (10.95).

(Oxford M.Phil., 1984)

10.6 An investigator asserts the following model when $(z_1 \ldots z_T)$ are a set of fixed numbers:

$$y_t = \beta z_t + \epsilon_t \tag{10.96}$$

where $\epsilon_t \underset{c}{\sim} \mathsf{IN}[0, \sigma_\epsilon^2]$ and $\mathsf{E}[z_t \epsilon_s] = 0\ \forall t, s$, and $\underset{c}{\sim}$ is a claimed distribution. The actual data-generation process is:

$$y_t = \beta_t z_t + u_t \tag{10.97}$$

where $u_t \sim \mathsf{IN}[0, \sigma_u^2]$ with $\mathsf{E}[z_t u_s] = 0\ \forall t, s$ and:

$$\beta_t = \beta_0 + k_t \tag{10.98}$$

where $k_t \sim \mathsf{IN}[0, \sigma_k^2]$ for $t = 1, \ldots, T$.

(a) Derive the distribution of the least-squares estimator $\hat{\beta}$ of β when (10.96) is assumed to be valid.
(b) Obtain the distribution of $\hat{\beta}$ when (10.97) is correct, showing that $\{\epsilon_t\}$ is heteroscedastic, carefully stating any assumptions which you make.
(c) Derive the bias in the conventional variance estimator of $\hat{\beta}$ (which assumes (10.96) is true) for the actual variance (when (10.97) holds).
(d) Obtain a heteroscedastic-consistent variance estimator for $\hat{\beta}$.
(e) How could the mis-specification in this question be detected in practice?

(Oxford M.Phil., 1986)

10.7 A variable y_t is generated by:

$$y_t = \boldsymbol{z}_t'\boldsymbol{\beta} + u_t \tag{10.99}$$

$$u_t = \rho u_{t-1} + \epsilon_t \tag{10.100}$$

where $|\rho| < 1$ with $\epsilon_t \sim \mathsf{IN}[0, \sigma_\epsilon^2]$ when y_{t-1} is one of the variables in $\boldsymbol{z}_t$. Consistent initial estimates $(\tilde{\boldsymbol{\beta}}, \tilde{\rho})$ are available. Consider the formulation:

$$y_t = \boldsymbol{z}_t'\boldsymbol{\beta} + \rho\tilde{u}_{t-1} + e_t, \tag{10.101}$$

where $(\boldsymbol{\beta}, \rho)$ are to be estimated by least squares when:

$$\tilde{u}_{t-1} = y_{t-1} - \boldsymbol{z}_{t-1}'\tilde{\boldsymbol{\beta}}. \tag{10.102}$$

By comparing this estimator of $\boldsymbol{\beta}$ with that from the non-linear least-squares (approximate maximum likelihood) estimator of $(\boldsymbol{\beta}, \rho)$ show that this 'lagged residual' estimator is not fully efficient. Explain why the problem of inefficiency arises. Would iterating the 'lagged residual' estimator to convergence solve the problem?

(Oxford M.Phil., 1982)

10.8 An investigator postulates the following economic model:

$$y_t = \beta z_t + u_t \tag{10.103}$$

where $\mathsf{E}[z_t u_s] = 0\ \forall t, s$ and $u_t \underset{c}{\sim} \mathsf{IN}[0, \sigma_u^2]$, when $\underset{c}{\sim}$ denotes 'is claimed to be distributed as'.
(a) Derive the log-likelihood function for $\boldsymbol{\theta} = (\beta, \sigma_u^2)'$, its first and second derivatives $\boldsymbol{q}(\hat{\boldsymbol{\theta}})$ and $\boldsymbol{H}(\hat{\boldsymbol{\theta}})$, and the maximum likelihood estimator $\tilde{\boldsymbol{\theta}}$ of $\boldsymbol{\theta}$, assuming the claims in (10.103) are valid. Obtain the large-sample distribution of $\sqrt{T}(\tilde{\boldsymbol{\theta}} - \boldsymbol{\theta})$ from those of $\boldsymbol{q}(\hat{\boldsymbol{\theta}})$ and $\boldsymbol{H}(\hat{\boldsymbol{\theta}})$.
(b) Unknown to the investigator, the structure of the DGP induces:

$$u_t = \rho u_{t-1} + \epsilon_t \tag{10.104}$$

where $\epsilon_t \sim \mathsf{IN}[0, \sigma_\epsilon^2]$ and $|\rho| < 1$. Obtain the actual expectations $\mathsf{E}[\boldsymbol{q}(\hat{\boldsymbol{\theta}})]$, $\mathsf{E}[\boldsymbol{H}(\boldsymbol{\theta})]$, and $\mathsf{E}[\boldsymbol{q}(\hat{\boldsymbol{\theta}})\boldsymbol{q}(\hat{\boldsymbol{\theta}})']$ for the postulated model in (10.103) when (10.104) is true. Derive the large-sample distribution of $\sqrt{T}(\tilde{\beta} - \beta)$. How could $\mathsf{V}[\tilde{\beta}]$ be consistently estimated when $\rho \neq 0$? How adequate is this treatment of autocorrelation and is it robust to the assumption that z_t is strictly exogenous?

(Oxford M.Phil., 1991)

10.9 In the following stationary process, z_t is strongly exogenous for (α, β):

$$y_t = \alpha y_{t-1} + \beta z_t + u_t \tag{10.105}$$

with $|\alpha| < 1$:

$$u_t = \rho u_{t-1} + \epsilon_t \tag{10.106}$$

when $|\rho| < 1$ and $\epsilon_t \sim \mathsf{IN}[0, \sigma_\epsilon^2]$ for $t = 1, \ldots, T$.

(a) Show how a consistent estimator of (α, β) can be obtained by the method of instrumental variables. Can consistent estimates of (α, β) be obtained by subtracting ρy_{t-1} from both sides of (10.105) and applying ordinary least squares?

(b) Derive the log-likelihood function for the parameters when y_1 and y_2 are fixed. Show that the MLE is equivalent to non-linear least squares.

(c) Evaluate the large-sample information matrix $\mathcal{I}(\cdot)$, using the result that:

$$\mathcal{I}(\cdot) = \sigma_\epsilon^{-2} \operatorname*{plim}_{T\to\infty} T^{-1} \sum_{t=1}^{T} \frac{\partial \epsilon_t}{\partial \psi} \frac{\partial \epsilon_t}{\partial \psi'} \tag{10.107}$$

where $\psi' = (\alpha, \beta, \rho)$. You may use in your proof the results that:

$$\begin{aligned}
\operatorname*{plim}_{T\to\infty} T^{-1} \sum_{t=1}^{T} (y_{t-1} - \rho y_{t-2})^2 &= m_{aa} \\
\operatorname*{plim}_{T\to\infty} T^{-1} \sum_{t=1}^{T} (z_t - \rho z_{t-1})^2 &= m_{bb} \\
\operatorname*{plim}_{T\to\infty} T^{-1} \sum_{t=1}^{T} (y_{t-1} - \rho y_{t-2})(z_t - \rho z_{t-1}) &= m_{ab}.
\end{aligned}$$

Hence prove that the MLEs $\hat{\alpha}$ and $\hat{\rho}$ are not independently distributed even in large samples.

(d) Show how the MLEs may be found by Gauss–Newton and construct an efficient two-step estimator. Compare this result with the usual Cochrane–Orcutt two-step estimator and comment in the light of the outcome in (c).

(Oxford M.Phil., 1992)

10.10 Consider the stationary second-order autoregressive process:

$$y_t = \alpha_1 y_{t-1} + \alpha_2 y_{t-2} + \epsilon_t \tag{10.108}$$

when $\epsilon_t \sim \mathsf{IN}[0, \sigma_\epsilon^2]$ for $t = 1, \ldots, T$.

(a) Construct the log-likelihood function for the model given that $y_0 = y_{-1} = 0$, and hence derive the MLE of (α_1, α_2).

(b) Consider the alternative model:

$$\begin{aligned} y_t &= \gamma y_{t-1} + u_t \\ u_t &= \rho u_{t-1} + \epsilon_t \end{aligned} \tag{10.109}$$

where $\epsilon_t \sim \mathsf{IN}[0, \sigma_\epsilon^2]$ for $t = 1, \ldots, T$. Show that this is equivalent to a second-order autoregressive process for y_t. Is it possible to solve uniquely for (γ, ρ) given (α_1, α_2) from the model in (a)? Consider estimating the model in (10.109) by maximum likelihood. What can you deduce about the shape of the likelihood function, and does it relate to the problem of identifying (γ, ρ)?

(c) An investigator estimates the model:

$$y_t = \delta y_{t-1} + v_t \text{ where } v_t \underset{c}{\sim} \mathsf{IN}\left[0, \sigma_v^2\right], \tag{10.110}$$

and $\underset{c}{\sim}$ denotes 'is claimed to be distributed as'. When (10.108) is the DGP, show that the inconsistency in estimating δ by least squares is:

$$\underset{T\to\infty}{\text{plim}} \left(\hat{\delta} - \gamma\right) = \underset{T\to\infty}{\text{plim}} \left(\frac{T^{-1} \sum_{t=2}^{T} y_t y_{t-1}}{T^{-1} \sum_{t=2}^{T} y_{t-1}^2} \right) - \gamma = \frac{\rho\left(1 - \gamma^2\right)}{(1 + \gamma\rho)}. \tag{10.111}$$

Discuss the source of this inconsistency, and describe a way of eliminating it.

(d) How would you construct a Lagrange-multiplier test of H_0: $\alpha_2 = 0$ after estimating (10.110)?

(Oxford M.Phil., 1993)

10.11 Consider the system:

$$\begin{aligned} y_t &= \lambda z_t + u_t \\ u_t &= \rho u_{t-1} + \epsilon_t \\ \Delta z_t &= \omega_t \end{aligned} \quad \text{when} \quad \begin{pmatrix} \epsilon_t \\ \omega_t \end{pmatrix} \sim \mathsf{IN}_2 \left[\begin{pmatrix} 0 \\ 0 \end{pmatrix}, \begin{pmatrix} \sigma_{11} & 0 \\ 0 & \sigma_{22} \end{pmatrix} \right] \tag{10.112}$$

where $|\rho| < 1$. An investigator estimates the following model:

$$\Delta y_t = \phi_1 \Delta z_t + \phi_2 \left(y_{t-1} - \hat{\lambda} z_{t-1}\right) + v_t \tag{10.113}$$

where $\hat{\lambda}$ is the first-stage estimate of λ from regressing y_t on z_t.

(a) Show that $\text{plim}_{T\to\infty} \sqrt{T}(\hat{\lambda} - \lambda) = 0$.

(b) Let $\phi = (\phi_1 : \phi_2)'$. Prove that the distribution of $\sqrt{T}(\hat{\phi} - \phi)$ from (10.113) is the same as if λ is known. Obtain the variance matrix of the joint normal limiting distribution.

(c) Discuss the effect on estimating ϕ of adding z_{t-1} as a regressor in (10.113).

(d) Comment on the appropriateness of this approach to estimating the parameters of (10.112).

(Oxford M.Phil., 1993)

11

Simultaneous Equations Systems

Linear system modelling is structured in ten stages from the general to the specific. Chapter 8 considered the form and implications of dynamic systems — the estimation of their unknown parameters is now considered. The dynamic statistical system is the maintained model, defined by the variables of interest, their distributions, whether they are modelled or non-modelled, and their lag polynomials. System formulation, the status of its variables, dynamic specification, integration and cointegration, estimation, and evaluation are discussed in §11.2–§11.6. At that stage, a congruent system is available against which any postulated econometric model can be evaluated. An econometric model is a (possibly) simultaneous-equations entity, which is treated as a model of the system intended to isolate autonomous, parsimonious relationships based on economic theory. The model must adequately characterize the data evidence and account for the results obtained by the system. Model formulation, identification, estimation (using an estimator generating equation), encompassing, and evaluation are considered in §11.8–§11.13. Numerical optimization is often needed for model estimation and is discussed in Chapter A5. The related errors-in-variables model is considered in Chapter 12.

11.1 Introduction

During the last decade, simultaneous equations models have been criticized from a number of viewpoints (see *inter alia* Sims, 1980, and Hendry, Neale and Srba, 1988). Dynamic system modelling usually commences from (an assumed known) structural form of the process generating the data, from which the reduced form is derived (see e.g. Judge, Griffiths, Hill, Lütkepohl and Lee, 1985, Ch.14). Such an approach raises numerous difficulties: in particular, by not first testing the validity of the reduced form, which constitutes the baseline for the test of over-identifying restrictions, the credibility of the structural-parameter estimates is unclear.

Linear system modelling can be conducted in a more structured approach, and in this chapter we distinguish ten distinct modelling stages from the general to the specific, including evaluation. This formulation is based on the analyses in Hendry *et al.* (1988), Hendry and Mizon (1993) and Doornik and Hendry (1994a), who provide operational details. These ten stages are investigated in §11.2–§11.6, §11.8–§11.10, and §11.12 and

§11.13. The analysis is illustrated in sections 11.7 and 11.14 by the consumption–income model discussed in Haavelmo (1943).

The dynamic system is the maintained statistical model, and a simultaneous equations structure is a model of that system (see e.g. Spanos, 1986). Given linearity, the system is defined by the set of variables of interest, their distributions, whether they are modelled or not, and the lag polynomials applicable to every variable. Section 11.2 discusses system formulation and the status of its variables; §11.3 considers the specification of the system dynamics to ensure that the residuals are innovation processes; §11.4 considers system estimation; then §11.5 discusses reducing the degree of integration of the original variables to I(0); and §11.6 concludes with system evaluation. At that stage, a congruent system is available against which any postulated econometric model can be evaluated. The one awkward aspect of the exposition is that section 11.4 assumes stationarity prior to the analysis of cointegration, but the benefit is introducing the main tools in a more familiar context. Section 11.7 illustrates.

An econometric model imposes a structure on a statistical system to try and isolate autonomous relationships with parsimonious interpretations based on economic theory. Necessary conditions for a valid model are that the system adequately characterizes the data evidence (congruency) and that the model accounts for the results obtained by the system (encompassing, discussed in Ch.14). The former is the focus of §11.2–§11.6 as just described; the latter is the subject of §11.8–§11.13. Thus, §11.8 considers model formulation; §11.9 describes rank and order conditions for identification; model estimation is discussed in §11.10 using the estimator generating equation approach noted in Chapter 10; §11.12 considers model evaluation by testing its encompassing of the system; and §11.13 discusses model evaluation using derived statistics and auxiliary calculations.

This sequence of stages aims to structure the empirical modelling of small linear dynamic systems, and represents the steps needed to ensure valid parsimonious representations of the DGP within a general-to-specific modelling methodology (see Mizon, 1977b, and Pagan, 1987). While level B knowledge is assumed, the approach considers the likely utility of the various procedures in the practical arena of level C. Chapter 16 presents a modelling illustration.

11.2 The statistical system

The statistical system is the Haavelmo distribution defined by specifying the variables of interest, their status (modelled or not), their degree of integration, data transformations, the history of the process, and the sample period. Let $\{x_t\}$ be the complete vector of N observable variables of interest, suggested by previous research, economic theory, and the objectives of the analysis, where for a sample period of size T, $X_T^1 = (x_1 \dots x_T)$. The statistical generating mechanism is $\mathsf{D}_X(X_T^1|X_0, \theta)$, where X_0 is the set of initial conditions and $\theta \in \Theta \subseteq \mathbb{R}^m$ is the parameter vector in an m-dimensional parameter space Θ, where θ is defined to allow for any necessary transients. Then $\mathsf{D}_X(\cdot)$ is sequentially factorized as:

$$\mathsf{D_X}\left(\boldsymbol{X}_T^1 \mid \boldsymbol{X}_0, \boldsymbol{\theta}\right) = \prod_{t=1}^{T} \mathsf{D_x}\left(\boldsymbol{x}_t \mid \boldsymbol{X}_{t-1}, \boldsymbol{\theta}\right). \tag{11.1}$$

Let $\boldsymbol{x}_t' = (\boldsymbol{y}_t' : \boldsymbol{z}_t')$ and $\boldsymbol{X}_T^{1\prime} = (\boldsymbol{Y}_T^{1\prime} : \boldsymbol{Z}_T^{1\prime})$ where $\boldsymbol{y}_t$ is an $n \times 1$ vector of endogenous variables and $\boldsymbol{z}_t$ is a $k \times 1$ vector of variables which will not be modelled, with $n + k = N$.[1] From Chapter 5, treating $\boldsymbol{z}_t$ as a valid conditioning vector requires that $\boldsymbol{z}_t$ be weakly exogenous for the parameters of interest $\boldsymbol{\phi}$. If weak exogeneity holds, inference in the conditional distribution of $\boldsymbol{y}_t$, given $\boldsymbol{z}_t$ and the history of the process, involves no loss of information relative to analysing the joint distribution of $\boldsymbol{x}_t$. From (11.1), and Chapter 5:

$$\prod_{t=1}^{T} \mathsf{D_x}\left(\boldsymbol{x}_t \mid \boldsymbol{X}_{t-1}, \boldsymbol{\theta}\right) = \prod_{t=1}^{T} \mathsf{D_{y|z}}\left(\boldsymbol{y}_t \mid \boldsymbol{z}_t, \boldsymbol{X}_{t-1}, \boldsymbol{\lambda}_1\right) \mathsf{D_z}\left(\boldsymbol{z}_t \mid \boldsymbol{X}_{t-1}, \boldsymbol{\lambda}_2\right) \tag{11.2}$$

where $\boldsymbol{\phi} = \boldsymbol{f}(\boldsymbol{\lambda}_1)$ and $(\boldsymbol{\lambda}_1, \boldsymbol{\lambda}_2) \in \Lambda_1 \times \Lambda_2$. This formulation is a direct application of the principles established in Chapter 9 for transforming a joint process to a conditional and marginal representation.

Finally, since we restrict attention to linear systems, the $\{\boldsymbol{x}_t\}$ will generally have been transformed from the original raw data such that linearity is a reasonable approximation.

Consequently, at level C, we commence by selecting $\boldsymbol{y}_t$ and $\boldsymbol{z}_t$, and specifying the statistical structure as in (11.2). The level C econometric model then seeks to isolate the autonomous relationships with interpretable parameters, having an economic theory basis, while remaining consistent with the system (an issue discussed in detail in Ch.16 and noted in Ch.7 above).

11.3 System dynamic specification

Having assumed linearity, specified the menu comprising $\{\boldsymbol{x}_t\}$, and classified the variables into $\{\boldsymbol{y}_t\}$ and $\{\boldsymbol{z}_t\}$, the conditional system formulation is complete when the degrees and roots of every lag polynomial are specified.[2] Let:

$$\boldsymbol{y}_t \mid \boldsymbol{z}_t, \boldsymbol{X}_{t-1} \sim \mathsf{N}_n \left[\boldsymbol{P}_0 \boldsymbol{z}_t + \sum_{i=1}^{h} \boldsymbol{P}_i \boldsymbol{x}_{t-i}, \boldsymbol{\Omega} \right], \tag{11.3}$$

so that the longest lag is h periods and the conditional system of n linear equations is:

$$\boldsymbol{y}_t = \sum_{j=0}^{l} \boldsymbol{\pi}_{1j} \boldsymbol{z}_{t-j} + \sum_{i=1}^{s} \boldsymbol{\pi}_{2i} \boldsymbol{y}_{t-i} + \boldsymbol{\nu}_t \text{ where } \boldsymbol{\nu}_t \sim \mathsf{IN}_n \left[\boldsymbol{0}, \boldsymbol{\Omega}\right], \tag{11.4}$$

[1] The system may be closed as in a VAR, in which case there are no non-modelled variables $\boldsymbol{z}_t$.

[2] For estimation, models of the system need not be complete but must be fully specified (see Richard, 1984).

and $h = \max(l, s)$, noting that $\boldsymbol{P}_0 = \boldsymbol{\pi}_{10}$ and $\boldsymbol{P}_i = (\boldsymbol{\pi}_{1i} : \boldsymbol{\pi}_{2i})$ for $i = 1, \ldots, h$. In (11.4), $\boldsymbol{\pi}_{1i}$ is $n \times k$, $\boldsymbol{\pi}_{2i}$ is $n \times n$, and $\boldsymbol{\Omega}$ is $n \times n$. A subset of the variables in $\boldsymbol{y}_t$ can be linked by identities, but otherwise $\boldsymbol{\Omega}$ is symmetric, positive-definite and unrestricted. Then (11.4) is the general, unrestricted, conditional dynamic system once l and s are specified. Let $\boldsymbol{\Pi} = (\boldsymbol{\pi}_{10} \ldots \boldsymbol{\pi}_{1l}, \boldsymbol{\pi}_{21} \ldots \boldsymbol{\pi}_{2s})$ where $\boldsymbol{\Pi}$ (which is $n \times (k(l+1)+ns)$) and $\boldsymbol{\Omega}$ are variation free given the assumption of multivariate normality, and are the parameters of interest in the conditional distribution, though not necessarily the parameters of interest in the overall analysis. When (11.4) is correctly specified, its parameters may be estimated by least squares (see §11.4), but the limiting distributions of the estimators and tests depend on the degree of integrability of the variables, an issue considered in §11.5.

At this stage, the main requirement is that the system in (11.4) should be a congruent representation of the data, since it will be the specification against which all other simplifications are tested, and hence is the baseline for encompassing. From Chapter 9, congruency requires that:

(i) $\{\boldsymbol{\nu}_t\}$ is a homoscedastic innovation process against $\boldsymbol{X}_{t-1}$;
(ii) $\boldsymbol{z}_t$ is weakly exogenous for $(\boldsymbol{\Pi}, \boldsymbol{\Omega})$; and
(iii) $(\boldsymbol{\Pi}, \boldsymbol{\Omega})$ is constant $\forall t$.

The first of these depends on specifying the lag structure adequately (see Hendry, Pagan and Sargan, 1984). Particular system tests can be constructed for vector residual autocorrelation (e.g. for dependence between $\boldsymbol{\nu}_t$ and $\boldsymbol{\nu}_{t-1}$) or dynamic mis-specification (the significance of the next lag $(\boldsymbol{y}_{t-s-1}, \boldsymbol{z}_{t-l-1})$). Weak exogeneity can be investigated by modelling $\boldsymbol{z}_t$ as a function of $(\boldsymbol{y}_{t-i}, \boldsymbol{z}_{t-i}; i = 1, \ldots, h)$ and perhaps further lagged non-modelled variables, then testing cross-equation independence from the $\boldsymbol{y}_t$ system. Finally constancy can be studied using recursive procedures based on the approach described in Chapter 3. Weak exogeneity is also indirectly testable via $(\boldsymbol{\Pi}, \boldsymbol{\Omega})$ being constant when the marginal process alters (see §11.6). Some of the $\boldsymbol{z}_t$ could be dummy variables so that the corresponding parameters are transients (see §A4.11). Normality is useful but not essential in a linear formulation, and is also testable. Chapter 13 considers the formal theory of testing and Doornik and Hendry (1994a) discuss the relevant tests in detail.

Once the system is congruent, a structural model of that system can be developed. Although the system (11.1) corresponds to what is often called the unrestricted reduced form (URF), it is the initial formulation, and not a derived representation based on a prior structural specification. This is an important difference, since if the system is mis-specified, due to residual autocorrelation, parameter non-constancy, or other problems, further restrictions on it will be invalid, and tests thereof will be against an invalid baseline. In an approach where the structural model is estimated first, tests of the structural over-identifying restrictions against the URF are conditional on untested assumptions about the validity of the latter, and these are often of a stringent nature.

The selection of l and s is usually data based, given a prior maximum lag length. Since (11.4) is a statistical model, parsimony is not essential at this stage, whereas ensuring that the $\{\nu_t\}$ are innovations is important for later inferences. This argument supports commencing with an over-parameterized representation (see Ch.8).

The next issue of importance for valid inference concerns the degree of integrability of the time series in $\{x_t\}$ since the correct critical values of tests depend on the orders of integration. Moreover, equilibrium-correction feedbacks (cointegration) may play a role in stabilizing economic behaviour and attaining long-run targets, as well as implementing insights from economic theory in dynamic statistical analyses. To introduce the main techniques, we first discuss estimation when the system is in I(0) space, then consider cointegration.

11.4 System estimation

Assume that the variables in the system have been reduced to I(0) by differencing or taking κ linear cointegrating combinations of the form $\beta' x_t$. The general specification is a closed system in all the variables x_t, but when z_t is weakly exogenous for the parameters of interest in the conditional system, then we can rewrite (11.4) as:

$$\Delta y_t = \Pi w_t + \nu_t \tag{11.5}$$

where Δy_t is the first difference of the original dependent variable, and w_t is the $p \times 1$ I(0) transformation $(\Delta z_t' \ldots \Delta z_{t-l+1}', \Delta y_{t-1}' \ldots \Delta y_{t-s+1}', \beta' x_{t-1})$ of the original variables, where $p = (k \times l + n \times (s-1) + \kappa)$. Let $\Delta Y' = (\Delta y_1 \ldots \Delta y_T)$ and $W' = (w_1 \ldots w_T)$, then the system (11.5) can be written compactly as:

$$\Delta Y = W\Pi' + V, \tag{11.6}$$

which is a multivariate linear regression model with a common set of regressors in each equation (see Anderson, 1984, and Lütkepohl, 1991). Under the assumptions in §11.1–§11.3, the log-likelihood function $\ell(\Pi, \Omega | \Delta Y, W)$ depends on the multivariate normal distribution:

$$\begin{aligned} \ell(\Pi, \Omega \mid \Delta Y, W) &= -\tfrac{Tn}{2}\log 2\pi - \tfrac{T}{2}\log|\Omega| - \tfrac{1}{2}\sum_{t=1}^{T} \nu_t' \Omega^{-1} \nu_t \\ &= K + \tfrac{T}{2}\log\left|\Omega^{-1}\right| - \tfrac{1}{2} tr\left[\Omega^{-1} V' V\right] \end{aligned} \tag{11.7}$$

where tr[$\cdot$] is the trace. The sample is $t = 1, \ldots, T$ after creating all necessary lags.

We first concentrate $\ell(\cdot)$ with respect to Ω, which involves differentiating (11.7) with respect to Ω^{-1} and equating the score to $\mathbf{0}$, taking explicit account of symmetry due to $\omega_{ij} = \omega_{ji}$. For a non-symmetric matrix, the following two matrix differentiation results can be confirmed by comparing corresponding elements on both sides (see Ch.A1):

$$\frac{\partial \log|D|}{\partial D} = D^{-1\prime} \text{ and } \frac{\partial \mathrm{tr}(DC)}{\partial D} = C'. \tag{11.8}$$

When $\boldsymbol{D}$ is symmetric, there are two sets of off-diagonal terms on both sides which cancel. Applying (11.8):

$$2\boldsymbol{V}'\boldsymbol{V} - dg(\boldsymbol{V}'\boldsymbol{V}) = 2T\boldsymbol{\Omega} - Tdg(\boldsymbol{\Omega}) \tag{11.9}$$

where $dg(\boldsymbol{\Omega}) = diag(\omega_{11} \ldots \omega_{nn})$, yielding the conditional maximum:

$$\boldsymbol{\Omega}_c = T^{-1} \sum_{t=1}^{T} \boldsymbol{v}_t \boldsymbol{v}_t' = T^{-1} \boldsymbol{V}'\boldsymbol{V} \tag{11.10}$$

where the subscript $_c$ denotes a concentrated likelihood estimator, such that the MLE is obtained from the relevant formula when the MLE of the right-hand side is known. (11.10) is a natural result, as $\mathsf{E}[T^{-1}\boldsymbol{V}'\boldsymbol{V}] = \boldsymbol{\Omega}$. The resulting CLF $\ell_c(\boldsymbol{\Pi}|\Delta\boldsymbol{Y}, \boldsymbol{W}; \boldsymbol{\Omega})$ is:

$$\begin{aligned} \ell_c(\boldsymbol{\Pi} \mid \Delta\boldsymbol{Y}, \boldsymbol{W}; \boldsymbol{\Omega}) &= K - \tfrac{T}{2}\log|\boldsymbol{V}'\boldsymbol{V}| + \tfrac{Tn\log T}{2} - \tfrac{Tn}{2} \\ &= K^* - \tfrac{T}{2}\log\left|(\Delta\boldsymbol{Y}' - \boldsymbol{\Pi}\boldsymbol{W}')(\Delta\boldsymbol{Y} - \boldsymbol{W}\boldsymbol{\Pi}')\right|. \end{aligned} \tag{11.11}$$

Since $\boldsymbol{\Pi}$ is unrestricted, its MLE is obtained by differentiating $\ell_c(\boldsymbol{\Pi}|\cdot)$ with respect to $\boldsymbol{\Pi}$, and equating the score to zero:

$$\hat{\boldsymbol{\Pi}}' = (\boldsymbol{W}'\boldsymbol{W})^{-1}\boldsymbol{W}'\Delta\boldsymbol{Y} \tag{11.12}$$

and hence

$$\hat{\boldsymbol{\Omega}} = T^{-1}\hat{\boldsymbol{V}}'\hat{\boldsymbol{V}} = T^{-1}(\Delta\boldsymbol{Y}'Q_W\Delta\boldsymbol{Y}). \tag{11.13}$$

In (11.13), $Q_W = (\boldsymbol{I}_T - \boldsymbol{W}(\boldsymbol{W}'\boldsymbol{W})^{-1}\boldsymbol{W}')$ is the symmetric, idempotent matrix which annihilates $\boldsymbol{W}$, and the residuals are defined by:

$$\hat{\boldsymbol{V}} = \Delta\boldsymbol{Y} - \boldsymbol{W}\hat{\boldsymbol{\Pi}}' = Q_W\Delta\boldsymbol{Y}. \tag{11.14}$$

The maximizing value of $\ell(\cdot)$ is:

$$\hat{\ell} = \frac{-Tn}{2}(1 + \log 2\pi) - \frac{T}{2}\log\left|\hat{\boldsymbol{\Omega}}\right|. \tag{11.15}$$

These are multivariate least squares (MLS) estimators, which are special cases of those derived *en route* in §11.10.

Formulae for parameter and equation standard errors, test statistics, etc. are generalized analogues of those in OLS. To derive parameter estimator variances, we first review some algebra conventions. As in Chapter A1, when $\boldsymbol{A} = (\boldsymbol{a}_1 \ldots \boldsymbol{a}_m)$, let $(\cdot)^v$ denote the vectoring operator:

$$\boldsymbol{A}^v = \begin{pmatrix} \boldsymbol{a}_1 \\ \vdots \\ \boldsymbol{a}_m \end{pmatrix} = \boldsymbol{a}, \tag{11.16}$$

so $(\cdot)^v$ stacks the columns of a matrix as a vector. Also, $\otimes$ denotes the Kronecker product of two matrices defined by $\boldsymbol{C} \otimes \boldsymbol{D} = (d_{ij}\,\boldsymbol{C})$: when $\boldsymbol{C}$ is $n_1 \times n_2$ and $\boldsymbol{D}$ is $n_3 \times n_4$, then $\boldsymbol{C} \otimes \boldsymbol{D}$ is $n_1 n_3 \times n_2 n_4$, comprising the product of every element of $\boldsymbol{C}$ with every element of $\boldsymbol{D}$ in the order shown (i.e. the first row is $[d_{11}c_{11}\; d_{11}c_{12}\; d_{11}c_{13} \ldots d_{11}c_{1n_2}]$). Combining these operations, when the three matrices $\boldsymbol{A}$, $\boldsymbol{C}$, and $\boldsymbol{D}$ conform appropriately in size, direct evaluation of the two expressions shows that:

$$(\boldsymbol{CAD})^v = (\boldsymbol{C} \otimes \boldsymbol{D}')\,\boldsymbol{A}^v. \tag{11.17}$$

The definitions preserve the order of the matrix products on vectoring.

Applying $(\cdot)^v$ to (11.5) induces $\Delta\boldsymbol{y}_t = (\boldsymbol{I}_n \otimes \boldsymbol{w}_t')\boldsymbol{\Pi}^v + \boldsymbol{\nu}_t$ or:

$$(\Delta\boldsymbol{Y}')^v = (\boldsymbol{I}_n \otimes \boldsymbol{W})\,\boldsymbol{\Pi}^v + (\boldsymbol{V}')^v$$

From (11.12):

$$\hat{\boldsymbol{\Pi}}^v = \left(\boldsymbol{I}_n \otimes (\boldsymbol{W}'\boldsymbol{W})^{-1}\boldsymbol{W}'\right)(\Delta\boldsymbol{Y}')^v = \boldsymbol{\Pi}^v + \left(\boldsymbol{I}_n \otimes (\boldsymbol{W}'\boldsymbol{W})^{-1}\boldsymbol{W}'\right)(\boldsymbol{V}')^v. \tag{11.18}$$

When $\boldsymbol{W}$ is fixed in repeated samples, the variance matrix follows from:

$$\mathsf{V}\left[\hat{\boldsymbol{\Pi}}^v\right] = \mathsf{E}\left[\left(\hat{\boldsymbol{\Pi}}^v - \boldsymbol{\Pi}^v\right)\left(\hat{\boldsymbol{\Pi}}^v - \boldsymbol{\Pi}^v\right)'\right],$$

and as $\boldsymbol{\Omega} = \boldsymbol{\Omega} \otimes 1$:

$$\mathsf{V}\left[\hat{\boldsymbol{\Pi}}^v\right] = \left(\boldsymbol{I}_n \otimes (\boldsymbol{W}'\boldsymbol{W})^{-1}\boldsymbol{W}'\right)\boldsymbol{\Omega}\left(\boldsymbol{I}_n \otimes (\boldsymbol{W}'\boldsymbol{W})^{-1}\boldsymbol{W}'\right) = \boldsymbol{\Omega} \otimes (\boldsymbol{W}'\boldsymbol{W})^{-1}. \tag{11.19}$$

In I(0) dynamic processes, the equivalent asymptotic result from the methods in Chapter A4 is:

$$\sqrt{T}\left(\hat{\boldsymbol{\Pi}}^v - \boldsymbol{\Pi}^v\right) \xrightarrow{D} \mathsf{N}_{np}\left[\boldsymbol{0}, \boldsymbol{\Omega} \otimes \boldsymbol{M}_W^{-1}\right] \tag{11.20}$$

where $\boldsymbol{M}_W = \text{plim}_{T\to\infty} T^{-1}\boldsymbol{W}'\boldsymbol{W}$. The estimated variance matrix of the coefficient estimator is:

$$\widehat{\mathsf{V}\left[\hat{\boldsymbol{\Pi}}^v\right]} = \hat{\boldsymbol{\Omega}} \otimes (\boldsymbol{W}'\boldsymbol{W})^{-1}. \tag{11.21}$$

The recursive version of MLS is the system analogue of recursive least squares (RLS), and involves little additional computation over the method discussed in Chapter 3, since the relevant formulae for updating $(\boldsymbol{W}_t'\boldsymbol{W}_t)^{-1}$ are identical due to the common regressors:

$$(\boldsymbol{W}_{t+1}'\boldsymbol{W}_{t+1})^{-1} = (\boldsymbol{W}_t'\boldsymbol{W}_t)^{-1} - \frac{\boldsymbol{\psi}_{t+1}\boldsymbol{\psi}_{t+1}'}{(1 + \boldsymbol{\psi}_{t+1}'\boldsymbol{w}_{t+1})} \tag{11.22}$$

where $\boldsymbol{\psi}_{t+1} = (\boldsymbol{W}_t'\boldsymbol{W}_t)^{-1}\boldsymbol{w}_{t+1}$. From (11.22), $\hat{\boldsymbol{\Pi}}_{t+1}$ and $\hat{\boldsymbol{\Omega}}_{t+1}$ can be calculated by repeated application of (11.12) and (11.13). For example, to update $\hat{\boldsymbol{\Omega}}_t$, define the innovations $\boldsymbol{e}_t$ and the standardized innovations or recursive residuals (see Harvey, 1990) $\boldsymbol{i}_t$:

$$\boldsymbol{e}_t = \Delta\boldsymbol{y}_t - \hat{\boldsymbol{\Pi}}_{t-1}\boldsymbol{w}_t \quad\text{and}\quad \boldsymbol{i}_t = \frac{\boldsymbol{e}_t}{\sqrt{1 + \boldsymbol{w}_t'\boldsymbol{\psi}_t}} \tag{11.23}$$

so:

$$\hat{V}'_{t+1}\hat{V}_{t+1} = \hat{V}'_t\hat{V}_t + i_{t+1}i'_{t+1} \tag{11.24}$$

from which $\hat{\Omega}_{t+1}$ can be derived. The 1-step residuals at $t+1$ are $\Delta y_{t+1} - \hat{\Pi}_{t+1}w_{t+1}$. Sequences of parameter constancy tests are readily computed and their use is discussed in §11.6.

11.5 System cointegration estimation

The degree of integration of any element in $\{x_t\}$ depends on the properties of the complete system, so that cointegration must be analysed at the level of the joint density. It may happen that a subset of variables is almost certain to be weakly exogenous for (Π, Ω) so that a conditional analysis is feasible from the outset, but we will not consider that case here. Equally, the number and location of the unit roots may be known in some cases, but again we will not assume that knowledge. Rather, we let the data evidence influence the cointegration specification, using available theoretical models to appraise the selection and identify the cointegration space. Extensive treatments are provided in Johansen (1995) and Banerjee, Dolado, Galbraith and Hendry (1993).

Reconsider the complete system in (11.1), written in linear form as:

$$x_t = \sum_{i=1}^{h} R_i x_{t-i} + v_t$$

where $v_t \sim \mathsf{IN}_N[\mathbf{0}, \Phi]$, or:

$$\Delta x_t = \sum_{i=1}^{h-1} A_i \Delta x_{t-i} + \pi x_{t-1} + v_t = \Psi f_t + \pi x_{t-1} + v_t \tag{11.25}$$

when $f_t = (\Delta x'_{t-1} \ldots \Delta x'_{t-h+1})'$ and $\Psi = (A_1 \ldots A_{h-1})$. Equation (11.25) corresponds to $\mathsf{D_x}(x_t | X^{t-h}_{t-1}, \theta)$ re-parameterized into levels and differences, so that θ comprises the elements of (Ψ, π, Φ). Alternatively, (11.25) is the closed version of (11.4).[3]

The first step is determining the number of cointegrating vectors $0 \leq \kappa \leq n + k$. If we underestimate κ, then empirically-relevant equilibrium-correction mechanisms (ECMs) will be omitted, whereas if we overestimate κ, the distributions of statistics will be non-standard as discussed in Chapter 3, so that incorrect inferences will result from using conventional critical values in tests. Forecasts will also be less accurate due to retaining any I(1) components, which are analogous to nonsense combinations.

A test for κ cointegrating vectors can be based on the maximum likelihood approach proposed by Johansen (1988). The test is equivalent to testing whether $\pi = \gamma\beta'$, where β and γ are $N \times \kappa$ of rank κ ($N = n + k$), and hence tests for π having a reduced rank. Once κ is known, we can proceed to estimate β and γ. Deterministic components,

[3] The conditions required to ensure that x_t is not I(2) are discussed in Ch.8 (see Johansen, 1992b).

such as intercepts or seasonal dummy variables, can be included in (11.25) and influence the resulting distributions, but to explain the basic procedure will be omitted in what follows.

Under the assumptions that (11.25) is the DGP, and that all the coefficient matrices are constant, the log-likelihood function $\ell(\boldsymbol{\Psi}, \boldsymbol{\pi}, \boldsymbol{\Phi}|\boldsymbol{X}_T^1)$ depends on the multivariate normal distribution:[4]

$$\begin{aligned} & -\tfrac{TN}{2}\log 2\pi - \tfrac{T}{2}\log|\boldsymbol{\Phi}| - \tfrac{1}{2}\sum_{t=1}^{T}\boldsymbol{v}_t'\boldsymbol{\Phi}^{-1}\boldsymbol{v}_t \\ = & \; K - \tfrac{T}{2}\log|\boldsymbol{\Phi}| - \tfrac{1}{2}\text{tr}\left[\boldsymbol{\Phi}^{-1}\boldsymbol{V}'\boldsymbol{V}\right] \\ = & \; K + \tfrac{T}{2}\log\left|\boldsymbol{\Phi}^{-1}\right| - \tfrac{1}{2}\text{tr}\left[\boldsymbol{\Phi}^{-1}(\Delta\boldsymbol{X}' - \boldsymbol{\Psi}\boldsymbol{F}' - \boldsymbol{\pi}\boldsymbol{X}_h')(\Delta\boldsymbol{X} - \boldsymbol{F}\boldsymbol{\Psi}' - \boldsymbol{X}_h\boldsymbol{\pi}')\right] \end{aligned} \tag{11.26}$$

where $\Delta\boldsymbol{X}' = (\Delta\boldsymbol{x}_1 \dots \Delta\boldsymbol{x}_T)$, $\boldsymbol{X}_h' = (\boldsymbol{x}_0 \dots \boldsymbol{x}_{T-1})$, and $\boldsymbol{F}' = (\boldsymbol{f}_1 \dots \boldsymbol{f}_T)$, which are $N \times T$, $N \times T$, and $N(h-1) \times T$ respectively.[5] Note the use of the equivariance theorem to express $\ell(\cdot)$ in these equivalent forms.

We first derive the cointegration rank estimator from a conventional concentrated likelihood approach as in Banerjee and Hendry (1992), then relate that to the original analysis in Johansen (1988). Concentrate $\ell(\cdot)$ by applying (11.8) to the derivative of (11.26) with respect to $\boldsymbol{\Phi}^{-1}$, taking account of its symmetry ($\phi_{ij} = \phi_{ji}$):

$$\boldsymbol{\Phi}_c = T^{-1}\sum_{t=1}^{T}\boldsymbol{v}_t\boldsymbol{v}_t' = T^{-1}\boldsymbol{V}'\boldsymbol{V}. \tag{11.27}$$

The resulting CLF $\ell^0(\boldsymbol{\Psi}, \boldsymbol{\pi}|\boldsymbol{X}_T^1; \boldsymbol{\Phi})$ is:

$$\begin{aligned} \ell^0(\cdot) &= K_1 - \tfrac{T}{2}\log|\boldsymbol{V}'\boldsymbol{V}| \\ &= K_1 - \tfrac{T}{2}\log\left|(\Delta\boldsymbol{X}' - \boldsymbol{\Psi}\boldsymbol{F}' - \boldsymbol{\pi}\boldsymbol{X}_h')(\Delta\boldsymbol{X} - \boldsymbol{F}\boldsymbol{\Psi}' - \boldsymbol{X}_h\boldsymbol{\pi}')\right|. \end{aligned} \tag{11.28}$$

Next, we remove the I(0) variables from (11.28) to focus on the matrix $\boldsymbol{\pi}$, which requires concentrating $\ell^0(\cdot)$ with respect to $\boldsymbol{\Psi}$. As usual, this is most easily achieved by differentiating $\ell(\cdot)$ with respect to $\boldsymbol{\Psi}$ and evaluating the result at the MLE of $\boldsymbol{\Phi}$. The trace term in (11.26) is $\text{tr}\{\boldsymbol{D}\boldsymbol{\Phi}^{-1}\}$ where $\boldsymbol{D}$ is given by:

$$\left(\Delta\boldsymbol{X}' - \boldsymbol{\pi}\boldsymbol{X}_h'\right)\left(\Delta\boldsymbol{X} - \boldsymbol{X}_h\boldsymbol{\pi}'\right) - \boldsymbol{\Psi}\boldsymbol{F}'\left(\Delta\boldsymbol{X} - \boldsymbol{X}_h\boldsymbol{\pi}'\right) - \left(\Delta\boldsymbol{X}' - \boldsymbol{\pi}\boldsymbol{X}_h'\right)\boldsymbol{F}\boldsymbol{\Psi}' + \boldsymbol{\Psi}\boldsymbol{F}'\boldsymbol{F}\boldsymbol{\Psi}' \tag{11.29}$$

Differentiate (11.29) with respect to $\boldsymbol{\Psi}$ using (11.8):

$$\frac{\partial\ell(\cdot)}{\partial\boldsymbol{\Psi}} = \boldsymbol{\Phi}^{-1}\left[\left(\Delta\boldsymbol{X}' - \boldsymbol{\pi}\boldsymbol{X}_h'\right)\boldsymbol{F} - \boldsymbol{\Psi}\boldsymbol{F}'\boldsymbol{F}\right]. \tag{11.30}$$

[4] To avoid notational complexity, sufficient pre-sample observations are assumed to be available to allow all summations to extend over $t = 1, \dots, T$.

[5] The form $\boldsymbol{X}_h'$ is used because the specification is invariant in essential respects to the lag length of the level variable.

Thus, evaluation at $\boldsymbol{\Phi}_c$ from (11.27) is irrelevant, and equating (11.30) to zero yields:

$$\boldsymbol{\Psi}_c = \left(\Delta \boldsymbol{X}' - \boldsymbol{\pi} \boldsymbol{X}_h'\right) \boldsymbol{F} \left(\boldsymbol{F}'\boldsymbol{F}\right)^{-1}, \tag{11.31}$$

leading to the CLF $\ell^*(\boldsymbol{\pi}|\boldsymbol{X}_T^1; \boldsymbol{\Phi}, \boldsymbol{\Psi}) - K_1$ given by:

$$\begin{aligned} & -\tfrac{T}{2}\log\left|(\Delta \boldsymbol{X}' - \boldsymbol{\pi}\boldsymbol{X}_h' - [\Delta \boldsymbol{X}' - \boldsymbol{\pi}\boldsymbol{X}_h'] \boldsymbol{H}_F)(\Delta \boldsymbol{X} - \boldsymbol{X}_h\boldsymbol{\pi}' - \boldsymbol{H}_F[\Delta \boldsymbol{X} - \boldsymbol{X}_h\boldsymbol{\pi}'])\right| \\ = \; & -\tfrac{T}{2}\log\left|(\Delta \boldsymbol{X}' - \boldsymbol{\pi}\boldsymbol{X}_h')\left(\boldsymbol{I}_T - \boldsymbol{F}\left(\boldsymbol{F}'\boldsymbol{F}\right)^{-1}\boldsymbol{F}'\right)(\Delta \boldsymbol{X} - \boldsymbol{X}_h\boldsymbol{\pi}')\right| \\ = \; & -\tfrac{T}{2}\log\left|\Delta \boldsymbol{X}'\boldsymbol{Q}_F\Delta \boldsymbol{X} - \boldsymbol{\pi}\boldsymbol{X}_h'\boldsymbol{Q}_F\Delta \boldsymbol{X} - \Delta \boldsymbol{X}'\boldsymbol{Q}_F\boldsymbol{X}_h\boldsymbol{\pi}' + \boldsymbol{\pi}\boldsymbol{X}_h'\boldsymbol{Q}_F\boldsymbol{X}_h\boldsymbol{\pi}'\right| \end{aligned} \tag{11.32}$$

where $\boldsymbol{Q}_F = (\boldsymbol{I}_T - \boldsymbol{F}(\boldsymbol{F}'\boldsymbol{F})^{-1}\boldsymbol{F}') = \boldsymbol{I}_T - \boldsymbol{H}_F$ is the matrix which annihilates $\boldsymbol{F}$. Terms such as $\boldsymbol{Q}_F\Delta\boldsymbol{X}$ and $\boldsymbol{Q}_F\boldsymbol{X}_h$ are the residuals from regressing $\Delta\boldsymbol{X}$ and $\boldsymbol{X}_h$ respectively on $\boldsymbol{F}$.

The second-moment matrices of the residuals in (11.32) are denoted $\boldsymbol{S}_{00}$, $\boldsymbol{S}_{0h}$, $\boldsymbol{S}_{h0}$, and $\boldsymbol{S}_{hh}$ where $\boldsymbol{S}_{00} = T^{-1}(\Delta\boldsymbol{X}'\boldsymbol{Q}_F\Delta\boldsymbol{X})$, $\boldsymbol{S}_{0h} = T^{-1}(\Delta\boldsymbol{X}'\boldsymbol{Q}_F\boldsymbol{X}_h)$, and $\boldsymbol{S}_{hh} = T^{-1}\boldsymbol{X}_h'\boldsymbol{Q}_F\boldsymbol{X}_h$. Substituting these into (11.32), the CLF $\ell^*(\boldsymbol{\pi})$ becomes:

$$\ell^*(\boldsymbol{\pi}) = K_2 - \tfrac{T}{2}\log\left|\boldsymbol{S}_{00} - \boldsymbol{S}_{0h}\boldsymbol{\pi}' - \boldsymbol{\pi}\boldsymbol{S}_{h0} + \boldsymbol{\pi}\boldsymbol{S}_{hh}\boldsymbol{\pi}'\right|. \tag{11.33}$$

When $\boldsymbol{\pi}$ is unrestricted, maximization yields:

$$\widehat{\boldsymbol{\pi}} = \boldsymbol{S}_{0h}\boldsymbol{S}_{hh}^{-1}.$$

However, we are interested in solutions where we impose the reduced-rank restriction that $\boldsymbol{\pi} = \boldsymbol{\gamma}\boldsymbol{\beta}'$. From (11.33), $\ell^*(\boldsymbol{\gamma}, \boldsymbol{\beta}) - K_2$ is:

$$\begin{aligned} & -\tfrac{T}{2}\log\left|\boldsymbol{S}_{00} - \boldsymbol{S}_{0h}\boldsymbol{\beta}\boldsymbol{\gamma}' - \boldsymbol{\gamma}\boldsymbol{\beta}'\boldsymbol{S}_{h0} + \boldsymbol{\gamma}\boldsymbol{\beta}'\boldsymbol{S}_{hh}\boldsymbol{\beta}\boldsymbol{\gamma}'\right| \\ = \; & -\tfrac{T}{2}\log\left|\Delta\boldsymbol{X}'\boldsymbol{Q}_F\Delta\boldsymbol{X} - \Delta\boldsymbol{X}'\boldsymbol{Q}_F\boldsymbol{X}_h\boldsymbol{\beta}\boldsymbol{\gamma}' - \boldsymbol{\gamma}\boldsymbol{\beta}'\boldsymbol{X}_h'\boldsymbol{Q}_F\Delta\boldsymbol{X} + \boldsymbol{\gamma}\boldsymbol{\beta}'\boldsymbol{X}_h'\boldsymbol{Q}_F\boldsymbol{X}_h\boldsymbol{\beta}\boldsymbol{\gamma}'\right|. \end{aligned} \tag{11.34}$$

The second line is in terms of (11.32), and suggests that the next step is notionally to form the I(0) linear combinations $\boldsymbol{X}_h\boldsymbol{\beta}$, and then concentrate $\ell^*(\boldsymbol{\gamma}, \boldsymbol{\beta})$ with respect to $\boldsymbol{\gamma}$. This will yield an expression for the MLE of $\boldsymbol{\gamma}$ as a function of $\boldsymbol{\beta}$, as in Chapter 10, and a further CLF that depends only on $\boldsymbol{\beta}$. Once the MLE of $\boldsymbol{\beta}$ is found, we solve backwards for estimators of all the other unknown parameters as functions of the MLE of $\boldsymbol{\beta}$. Differentiating with respect to $\boldsymbol{\gamma}$ in (11.34), using the CLF theorem in Chapter 10:

$$\frac{\partial \ell^*(\boldsymbol{\gamma}, \boldsymbol{\beta})}{\partial \boldsymbol{\gamma}} = \mathbf{0} \text{ implies } \boldsymbol{S}_{0h}\boldsymbol{\beta} - \boldsymbol{\gamma}\boldsymbol{\beta}'\boldsymbol{S}_{hh}\boldsymbol{\beta} = \mathbf{0},$$

so that:

$$\boldsymbol{\gamma}_c = \boldsymbol{S}_{0h}\boldsymbol{\beta}\left(\boldsymbol{\beta}'\boldsymbol{S}_{hh}\boldsymbol{\beta}\right)^{-1}. \tag{11.35}$$

Substituting the expression for $\boldsymbol{\gamma}_c$ in (11.35) into (11.34) yields the final CLF $\ell^{**}(\boldsymbol{\beta})$:

$$\ell^{**}(\boldsymbol{\beta}) = K_2 - \tfrac{T}{2}\log\left|\boldsymbol{S}_{00} - \boldsymbol{S}_{0h}\boldsymbol{\beta}\left(\boldsymbol{\beta}'\boldsymbol{S}_{hh}\boldsymbol{\beta}\right)^{-1}\boldsymbol{\beta}'\boldsymbol{S}_{h0}\right|. \tag{11.36}$$

Differentiating $\ell^{**}(\beta)$ with respect to β looks formidable, but the algebra is close to that underlying the LIML estimator for individual simultaneous equations derived in Koopmans (1950a) and noted below; both depend on reduced-rank restrictions being imposed. Taking determinants of a 2×2 block matrix (see Ch.A1):

$$\begin{vmatrix} A & B \\ C & D \end{vmatrix} = \begin{vmatrix} I & -BD^{-1} \\ 0 & I \end{vmatrix} \begin{vmatrix} A & B \\ C & D \end{vmatrix} = \begin{vmatrix} A - BD^{-1}C & 0 \\ C & D \end{vmatrix} = \left|A - BD^{-1}C\right| |D|. \tag{11.37}$$

Repeating these operations in the alternative direction establishes that:

$$\left|A - BD^{-1}C\right| |D| = |A| \left|D - CA^{-1}B\right|. \tag{11.38}$$

Apply this result to (11.36):

$$\begin{aligned} \ell^{**}(\beta) &= K_2 - \tfrac{T}{2} \log \left|\beta' S_{hh} \beta\right|^{-1} |S_{00}| \left|\beta' S_{hh} \beta - \beta' S_{h0} S_{00}^{-1} S_{0h} \beta\right| \\ &= K_2 - \tfrac{T}{2} \log \left|\beta' S_{hh} \beta\right|^{-1} |S_{00}| \left|\beta' \left(S_{hh} - S_{h0} S_{00}^{-1} S_{0h}\right) \beta\right|. \end{aligned} \tag{11.39}$$

Since $|S_{00}|$ is a constant relative to β, maximizing $\ell^{**}(\beta)$ with respect to β corresponds to minimizing the generalized variance ratio, which in our notation becomes:

$$\frac{\left|\beta' \left(S_{hh} - S_{h0} S_{00}^{-1} S_{0h}\right) \beta\right|}{\left|\beta' S_{hh} \beta\right|} = \frac{\left|\beta' S_{hh}^{*} \beta\right|}{\left|\beta' S_{hh} \beta\right|} \tag{11.40}$$

or:

$$\frac{\left|\beta' \left(X_h' Q_F Q_{\Delta X}^{*} Q_F X_h\right) \beta\right|}{\left|\beta' X_h' Q_F X_h \beta\right|},$$

where $Q_{\Delta X}^{*} = (I_T - Q_F \Delta X (\Delta X' Q_F \Delta X)^{-1} \Delta X' Q_F)$, the symmetric idempotent matrix which creates residuals from a regression on $Q_F \Delta X$. The expression for γ_c in (11.35) can now be seen to involve regressing $Q_F \Delta X$ on $Q_F X_h \beta$. Then (11.40) involves the ratio of determinants of idempotent quadratic forms, such that the denominator matrix (S_{hh}) exceeds that in the numerator (S_{hh}^{*}) by a non-negative definite matrix $(S_{h0} S_{00}^{-1} S_{0h})$.

At this stage, we turn an apparent drawback to an advantage: $\pi = \gamma \beta'$ is not unique since if G is any $\kappa \times \kappa$ non-singular matrix, then $\pi = \gamma G G^{-1} \beta' = \gamma^{*} \beta^{*\prime}$. One important consequence is that the present procedure determines the cointegrating dimension rather than the actual cointegrating vectors. A second implication is that to find the maximum of $\ell^{**}(\beta)$, we must impose a normalization on β to select a unique outcome, from which other choices can be derived by linear transformations, and it is convenient to use $\beta' S_{hh} \beta = I_\kappa$. The MLE, therefore, requires minimizing:

$$\left|\beta' S_{hh}^{*} \beta\right| \quad \text{subject to } \beta' S_{hh} \beta = I_\kappa. \tag{11.41}$$

This has translated the minimization into an eigenvalue problem:

$$\left|\lambda S_{hh} - S_{h0} S_{00}^{-1} S_{0h}\right| = 0, \tag{11.42}$$

to solve for the κ largest eigenvalues $\lambda_1 \geq \ldots \geq \lambda_\kappa \geq \ldots \geq \lambda_N$ and the corresponding eigenvectors:

$$\widehat{\boldsymbol{\beta}} = (\boldsymbol{g}_1 \ldots \boldsymbol{g}_\kappa) \tag{11.43}$$

given by solving:

$$\left(\lambda_i \boldsymbol{S}_{hh} - \boldsymbol{S}_{h0} \boldsymbol{S}_{00}^{-1} \boldsymbol{S}_{0h}\right) \boldsymbol{g}_i = \boldsymbol{0} \ \text{ for } i = 1, \ldots, \kappa, \tag{11.44}$$

subject to the normalization $\widehat{\boldsymbol{\beta}}' \boldsymbol{S}_{hh} \widehat{\boldsymbol{\beta}} = \boldsymbol{I}_\kappa$. Given $\widehat{\boldsymbol{\beta}}$, all the other intermediate MLEs can be obtained. To check that the largest eigenvalues should be selected to minimize (11.41), pre-multiply (11.44) by $\boldsymbol{g}_i'$, and let $\lambda_i = 1 + \mu_i$ to obtain:

$$\mu_i \boldsymbol{g}_i' \boldsymbol{S}_{hh} \boldsymbol{g}_i + \boldsymbol{g}_i' \boldsymbol{S}_{hh}^* \boldsymbol{g}_i = 0$$

so that

$$\mu_i = -\frac{\boldsymbol{g}_i' \boldsymbol{S}_{hh}^* \boldsymbol{g}_i}{\boldsymbol{g}_i' \boldsymbol{S}_{hh} \boldsymbol{g}_i}.$$

The smallest value of the last ratio yields the largest μ_i and hence the largest λ_i.

The problem in (11.42) requires calculating the eigenvalues of $\boldsymbol{S}_{hh}^*$ in the metric of $\boldsymbol{S}_{hh}$ rather than $\boldsymbol{I}$. Since $\boldsymbol{S}_{hh}$ is symmetric and positive-definite for finite T, its inverse can be factorized as $\boldsymbol{S}_{hh}^{-1} = \boldsymbol{H}\boldsymbol{H}'$ where $\boldsymbol{H}$ is non-singular. Substituting that expression into (11.42) produces the standard eigenvalue problem:

$$\left|\lambda \boldsymbol{I}_N - \boldsymbol{H}' \boldsymbol{S}_{h0} \boldsymbol{S}_{00}^{-1} \boldsymbol{S}_{0h} \boldsymbol{H}\right| = 0, \tag{11.45}$$

since $\boldsymbol{H}' \boldsymbol{S}_{hh} \boldsymbol{H} = \boldsymbol{I}_N$. Thus, only conventional numerical tools are needed. From (11.44) written in matrix form, and the normalization $\boldsymbol{G}' \boldsymbol{S}_{hh} \boldsymbol{G} = \boldsymbol{I}_N$ where $\boldsymbol{G} = (\boldsymbol{g}_1 \ldots \boldsymbol{g}_N)$:

$$\boldsymbol{S}_{h0} \boldsymbol{S}_{00}^{-1} \boldsymbol{S}_{0h} \boldsymbol{G} = \boldsymbol{S}_{hh} \boldsymbol{G} \boldsymbol{\Lambda}, \tag{11.46}$$

where $\boldsymbol{\Lambda}$ is the $N \times N$ diagonal matrix of eigenvalues, so that:

$$\boldsymbol{G}' \boldsymbol{S}_{h0} \boldsymbol{S}_{00}^{-1} \boldsymbol{S}_{0h} \boldsymbol{G} = \boldsymbol{G}' \boldsymbol{S}_{hh} \boldsymbol{G} \boldsymbol{\Lambda} = \boldsymbol{\Lambda}. \tag{11.47}$$

Consequently, from (11.39) and (11.47), $\ell^{**}(\boldsymbol{\beta})$ evaluated at $\widehat{\boldsymbol{\beta}}$ becomes:

$$\begin{aligned} \ell^{**}\left(\widehat{\boldsymbol{\beta}}\right) &= K_2 - \tfrac{T}{2} \log \left| \widehat{\boldsymbol{\beta}}' \left(\boldsymbol{S}_{hh} - \boldsymbol{S}_{h0} \boldsymbol{S}_{00}^{-1} \boldsymbol{S}_{0h}\right) \widehat{\boldsymbol{\beta}} \right| \\ &= K_2 - \tfrac{T}{2} \log \left| \boldsymbol{I}_\kappa - \boldsymbol{\Lambda}_\kappa \right| \\ &= K_2 - \tfrac{T}{2} \sum_{i=1}^{\kappa} \log\left(1 - \lambda_i\right) \end{aligned} \tag{11.48}$$

where $\boldsymbol{\Lambda}_\kappa$ is the sub-matrix of $\boldsymbol{\Lambda}$ corresponding to the κ largest eigenvalues. When $\boldsymbol{\pi}$ is unrestricted, all N eigenvalues are retained, so the unrestricted maximum of the likelihood corresponds to:

$$\ell^{**}\left(\boldsymbol{G}\right) = K_2 - \tfrac{T}{2} \sum_{i=1}^{N} \log\left(1 - \lambda_i\right). \tag{11.49}$$

The analysis so far has been conditional on knowing κ. Since the κ largest eigenvalues deliver the cointegration vectors, and since $\lambda_{\kappa+1} \dots \lambda_N$ should be zero for the non-cointegrating combinations (i.e. unit roots), tests of the hypothesis that there are κ cointegrating vectors ($0 \leq \kappa < N$) can be based on:

$$\eta(\kappa) = -T \sum_{i=\kappa+1}^{N} \log(1-\lambda_i) \quad \text{for } \kappa = 0, 1, \dots, N-1. \tag{11.50}$$

Thus, $\eta(\kappa)$ is twice the log of the likelihood ratio between (11.48) and (11.49). To test the hypothesis of κ cointegrating vectors within the maintained model, testing proceeds seriatim from $\eta(0)$, $\eta(1), \dots,$ $\eta(N-1)$. Then κ is selected as the last significant statistic $\eta(\kappa-1)$, or zero if $\eta(0)$ is not significant. This is called the trace statistic.

Alternatively, a test of κ cointegrating vectors within $\kappa+1$ could be based on the largest eigenvalue $\lambda_{\kappa+1}$ using $\xi(\kappa) = -T\log(1-\lambda_{\kappa+1})$, called the max statistic. Both $\eta(\kappa)$ and $\xi(\kappa)$ have non-standard distributions which are functionals of Wiener processes (see Ch.3), but critical values for these tests have been tabulated by Johansen (1988), Johansen and Juselius (1990) and Osterwald-Lenum (1992) *inter alia*, and are included in PcGive.

To relate the above analysis to Johansen (1988), we can partial out the effects of $\boldsymbol{f}_t$ from $\Delta \boldsymbol{x}_t$ and $\boldsymbol{x}_{t-1}$ in (11.32) by regression since $\boldsymbol{\Psi}$ is unrestricted, to obtain the residuals:

$$\boldsymbol{R}_{0t} = \Delta \boldsymbol{x}_t - \tilde{\boldsymbol{\Psi}} \boldsymbol{f}_t \quad \text{where} \quad \tilde{\boldsymbol{\Psi}} = \Delta \boldsymbol{X}' \boldsymbol{F} (\boldsymbol{F}'\boldsymbol{F})^{-1},$$

and:

$$\boldsymbol{R}_{ht} = \boldsymbol{x}_{t-1} - \bar{\boldsymbol{\Psi}} \boldsymbol{f}_t \quad \text{where} \quad \bar{\boldsymbol{\Psi}} = \boldsymbol{X}_h{}' \boldsymbol{F} (\boldsymbol{F}'\boldsymbol{F})^{-1},$$

so that $\boldsymbol{R}_0 = \boldsymbol{Q}_F \Delta \boldsymbol{X}$ and $\boldsymbol{R}_h = \boldsymbol{Q}_F \boldsymbol{X}_h$. The CLF $\ell^*(\boldsymbol{\pi})$ now only depends on $(\boldsymbol{R}_0, \boldsymbol{R}_h)$ and is:

$$\ell^*(\boldsymbol{\pi}) = K_1 - \tfrac{T}{2} \log \left| (\boldsymbol{R}_0 - \boldsymbol{R}_h \boldsymbol{\pi}')' (\boldsymbol{R}_0 - \boldsymbol{R}_h \boldsymbol{\pi}') \right|. \tag{11.51}$$

The second-moment matrices of the residuals in (11.32) are seen to be:

$$\boldsymbol{S}_{ij} = T^{-1} \sum_{t=1}^{T} \boldsymbol{R}_{it} \boldsymbol{R}'_{jt} \quad \text{for } i, j = 0 \text{ and } h. \tag{11.52}$$

Substituting these into (11.51) yields (11.33) from which the remaining analysis follows as earlier.

Once the degree of cointegration has been established, the cointegrating combinations are given by:

$$\hat{\boldsymbol{u}}_t = \hat{\boldsymbol{\beta}}' \boldsymbol{x}_t \tag{11.53}$$

and these linear combinations of the data are the estimated ECMs. Moreover, $\hat{\boldsymbol{\gamma}}$ reveals the importance of each cointegrating combination in each equation, and is related to the speed of adjustment of the system to a disequilibrium. If a given ECM enters more than one equation, the parameters are inherently cross-linked between such equations, and hence their dependent variables cannot be weakly exogenous in the related equations. This entails that joint estimation is needed for fully efficient estimation.

The above results are presented for the simplest model to clarify the analysis. There are many possible extensions, including the presence of deterministic variables in equations. Under the null of no cointegrating vectors, non-zero intercepts would generate trends. However, in equations with ECMs, two possibilities arise, namely the intercept enters only in the ECM (to adjust its mean value), or it enters as separately in some equations. Both cases are considered by Johansen and Juselius (1990). Other potential dummy variables include a linear deterministic trend t and a set of seasonals in quarterly or monthly data. When a trend is included in the system but none of the variables manifests a quadratic trend in levels, it must enter only the cointegration space: this formulation is discussed in Chapter 8 (for a more extensive treatment, see Banerjee *et al.*, 1993).

Another generalization concerns testing linear restrictions on $\boldsymbol{\beta}$ and γ, corresponding to prior theories about the cointegration vectors, and their roles in different equations. Conditional on κ being the number of cointegrating relationships, and the model therefore being transformed to I(0) space, the relevant hypothesis tests generally involve standard χ^2 distributions (again see Johansen and Juselius, 1990). Consider testing linear restrictions on $\boldsymbol{\beta}$ of the form $\boldsymbol{\beta} = \boldsymbol{D\Upsilon}$ where $\boldsymbol{D}$ is a known $N \times p$ matrix and $\boldsymbol{\Upsilon}$ is $p \times \kappa$ where $p < \kappa$. Maximization of the likelihood function is unaltered until equation (11.41), which becomes:

$$\min_{\boldsymbol{\Upsilon}} \left| \boldsymbol{\Upsilon}'\boldsymbol{D}' \left(\boldsymbol{S}_{hh} - \boldsymbol{S}_{h0}\boldsymbol{S}_{00}^{-1}\boldsymbol{S}_{0h} \right) \boldsymbol{D\Upsilon} \right| .$$

In place of (11.42) we solve for the eigenvalues λ_i^* from:

$$\left| \lambda^* \boldsymbol{D}'\boldsymbol{S}_{hh}\boldsymbol{D} - \boldsymbol{D}'\boldsymbol{S}_{h0}\boldsymbol{S}_{00}^{-1}\boldsymbol{S}_{0h}\boldsymbol{D} \right| = 0,$$

so no principles are altered. A likelihood-ratio test against the unrestricted value of $\boldsymbol{\beta}$ can be calculated, and results in an asymptotic χ^2 distribution. Similar principles apply for testing the hypothesis that a subset of $\boldsymbol{\beta}$ equals a known matrix. Hendry and Doornik (1994) apply these cointegration tests to UK money demand (also see Ch.16).

11.6 System evaluation

If system residuals are not innovations, or parameters are statistically non-constant over time, then the distributions of hypothesis tests will not correspond to those conventionally assumed, even after the transformation to I(0) variables. Restricting the parameterization by structural formulations of the system, without changing the conditioning or lag assumptions, cannot remove, but could camouflage, such problems. System evaluation seeks to reduce the chances of imposing restrictions on a system, only to discover at a later stage that the framework cannot provide an adequate representation of the data.

There is a wide range of hypotheses to be investigated corresponding to the basic information sets delineated in the taxonomy of Chapter 9, applied to the system as a whole. The earlier focus on one-equation conditional systems was to clarify the models, concepts, and processes of the approach, but that did not limit the applicability of the methodology to single equations. Rather, the general modelling procedures and tests are vector analogues of those arising for single equations albeit that modelling a system is much more difficult than modelling a single conditional relationship. For example, the various constancy statistics from recursive MLS match those from RLS closely, so the analysis of Chapter 3 applies to e.g. break-point tests of one equation from the system or the system as a whole. The formulae for forecast statistics also are similar, and are presented below for a model of the system, but can be specialized to the system by considering an unrestricted (i.e. just-identified) model.

Subject to a correct specification of the marginal model for z_t, one test for the weak exogeneity of z_t for the parameters of interest is that the errors on the conditional system are uncorrelated with those on the marginal processes. The difficulty lies in appropriately formulating the marginal model, especially when conditioning is desired because of anticipated non-constancy in the marginal processes. A useful direct test is for the presence of the cointegrating vectors in both marginal and conditional models.

11.7 Empirical cointegration illustration

To illustrate cointegration analysis empirically, we reconsider the earlier example of money demand and interest rates. While not all issues can arise in a bivariate system, several important aspects do occur. The estimated unrestricted VAR in levels for two lags on each of $\log(M/PY)$ and R with a constant was presented in Chapter 8. The extent of cointegration is investigated here, and reveals that there is one unit root, so that the system is I(1). The cointegrating combination is close to that found in Chapter 6. As the cointegration vector is absent from the R equation, weak exogeneity of R for the parameters of the conditional model is not rejected System diagnostic tests for the absence of serial independence, homoscedasticity, and normality are acceptable. The earlier recursive estimation revealed that the VAR was not constant over the sample, but this is less of a problem with the I(0) representation.

The estimated unrestricted long-run matrix from the dynamic analysis of the bivariate system is:

$$\hat{\pi} = \begin{pmatrix} -0.097 & -0.66 \\ -0.001 & -0.088 \end{pmatrix},$$

which has (conventional) eigenvalues of -0.12 and -0.07. These are neither large nor negligible, so a more precise statistical analysis, based on Johansen (1988) is in order. The conventional eigenvalues of the companion matrix (see Ch.8) are all real with one close to unity and the others small.

Turning to the cointegration analysis, the Johansen eigenvalues and associated test statistics are:

rank $(\pi) = \kappa$	ℓ	λ_i	$-T\log(1-\lambda_i)$	$-T\sum_{i=1}^{\kappa}\log(1-\lambda_i)$
0	817.2			
1	844.8	0.42	55.22**	58.36**
2	846.4	0.03	3.15	3.15

Thus, H_0: rank$(\pi) = 0$ is rejected in favour of $\kappa = 1$ at the 1 per cent level, whereas $\kappa = 1$ cannot be rejected in favour of $\kappa = 2$, consistent with one unit root and one cointegrating vector. The latter is given by $\log(M/PY) = -7.73R$, close to that found in Chapter 6, since:

$$\hat{\alpha} = \begin{pmatrix} -0.09 & 0.01 \\ -0.01 & -0.01 \end{pmatrix}, \; \hat{\beta}' = \begin{pmatrix} 1 & 7.73 \\ -1.60 & 1 \end{pmatrix}.$$

The long-run matrix $\alpha\beta'$ of rank one is:

$$\hat{\alpha}\hat{\beta}' = \begin{pmatrix} -0.10 & -0.66 \\ -0.00 & -0.09 \end{pmatrix}.$$

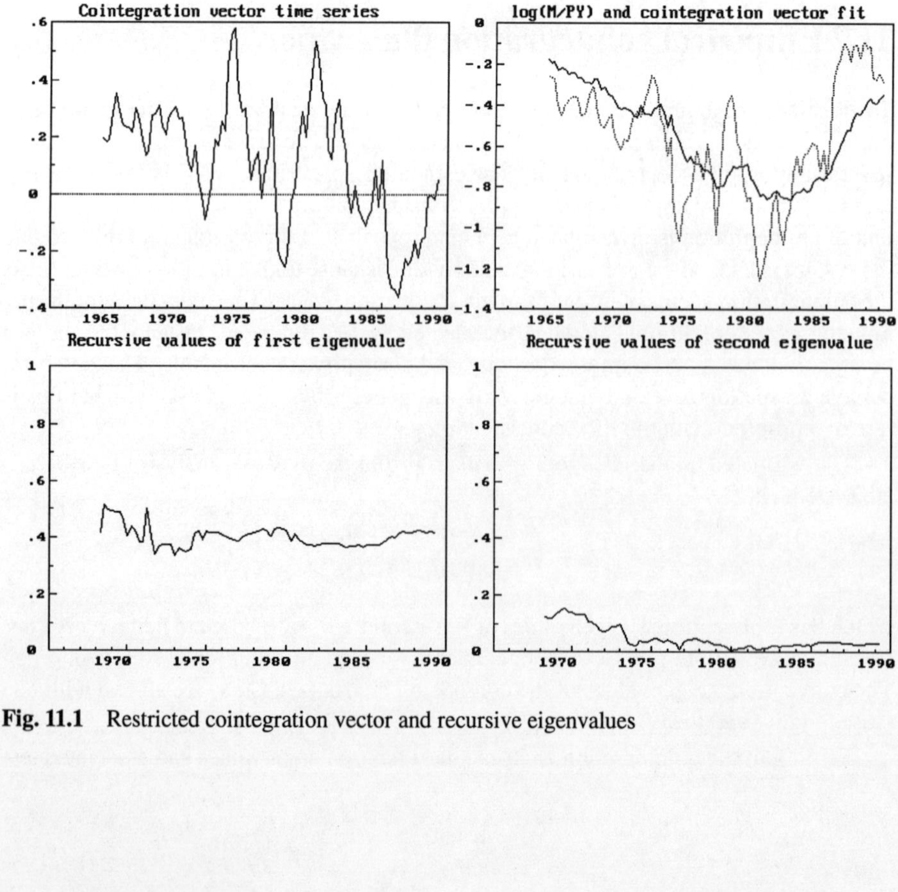

Fig. 11.1 Restricted cointegration vector and recursive eigenvalues

Imposing rank$(\boldsymbol{\pi}) = 1$ and restricting $\boldsymbol{\alpha}' = (\alpha_{11} : 0)$ — to test for the absence of the ECM from the R equation — leads to the restricted cointegrating vector: $\log(M/PY) = -7.54R$ with $\hat{\alpha}_{11} = -0.097$. The associated test of the necessary condition for the weak exogeneity of R for the money-demand parameters is $\chi^2(1) = 1.66$, which does not reject. Figure 8.3 showed the time series of the unrestricted cointegrating vector, and Fig. 11.1 shows the time-series plot of the restricted cointegration vector, the match between $-7.54R_t$ and $\log(M/PY)_t$, and the two eigenvalues estimated recursively over the sample. The system can now be reduced to I(0) space by mapping to differences and the cointegrating vector $CI = \log(M/PY) + 7.73R$.

Since the system has been formulated, estimated, and tested, we turn to formulating a model of the system (11.4).

11.8 The econometric model

The main criterion for the validity of the system is its congruence, since that is a necessary condition for efficient statistical estimation and inference. An econometric model is a restricted version of a congruent system which sustains an economic interpretation, consistent with the associated theory. All linear structural models of (11.4) can be obtained by pre-multiplying (11.4) by a non-singular matrix $\boldsymbol{B}$, which generates:

$$\boldsymbol{B}\boldsymbol{y}_t = \sum_{i=0}^{l} \boldsymbol{B}\boldsymbol{\pi}_{1i}\boldsymbol{z}_{t-i} + \sum_{j=1}^{s} \boldsymbol{B}\boldsymbol{\pi}_{2j}\boldsymbol{y}_{t-j} + \boldsymbol{B}\boldsymbol{\nu}_t. \tag{11.54}$$

Let $\boldsymbol{B}_j = -\boldsymbol{B}\boldsymbol{\pi}_{2j}$ for $j = 1, \ldots, s$ and $\boldsymbol{C}_i = -\boldsymbol{B}\boldsymbol{\pi}_{1i}$ for $i = 0, \ldots, l$ with $\boldsymbol{u}_t = \boldsymbol{B}\boldsymbol{\nu}_t$, then:

$$\sum_{j=0}^{s} \boldsymbol{B}_j \boldsymbol{y}_{t-j} + \sum_{i=0}^{l} \boldsymbol{C}_i \boldsymbol{z}_{t-i} = \boldsymbol{u}_t \quad \text{where} \quad \boldsymbol{u}_t \sim \mathsf{IN}\left[\mathbf{0}, \boldsymbol{\Sigma}\right] \tag{11.55}$$

with $\boldsymbol{\Sigma} = \boldsymbol{B}\boldsymbol{\Omega}\boldsymbol{B}'$ and $\boldsymbol{B}_0 = \boldsymbol{B}$. Let $\boldsymbol{C} = (\boldsymbol{B}_1 \ldots \boldsymbol{B}_s, \boldsymbol{C}_0 \ldots \boldsymbol{C}_l)$, with $\boldsymbol{A} = (\boldsymbol{B} : \boldsymbol{C})$ and $\boldsymbol{X} = (\boldsymbol{Y} : \boldsymbol{W})$, the matrices of all the coefficients and all of the observations respectively: this changes the definition of $\boldsymbol{x}_t$ but retains the idea of 'all the variables'. We drop sample subscripts on data matrices and assume that the diagonal of $\boldsymbol{B}$ is normalized at unity to ensure a unique scaling in every equation: other normalizations are feasible. Then (11.55) can be written in compact notation as $\boldsymbol{A}\boldsymbol{X}' = \boldsymbol{U}'$. When identities are present, the corresponding elements of $\{\boldsymbol{u}_t\}$ are precisely zero, so the model can be written as:

$$\boldsymbol{A}\boldsymbol{X}' = \begin{pmatrix} \boldsymbol{A}_1 \\ \boldsymbol{A}_2 \end{pmatrix} \boldsymbol{X}' = \begin{pmatrix} \boldsymbol{U}_1 \\ \mathbf{0} \end{pmatrix} \tag{11.56}$$

where $n = n_1 + n_2$ for n_1 stochastic equations and n_2 identities. The elements of $\boldsymbol{A}_2$ are known so do not need estimation, but we set $n_2 = 0$ for simplicity below; for notational ease, we assume that the system is stationary.

Given the system formulation, the model involves stating the mapping between the unknown coefficients in the matrix $\boldsymbol{A}$ and the parameters of interest $\boldsymbol{\phi}$. This mapping can be achieved in many different notations, and the one which follows is natural in a computer-programming context, and is that used in PcFiml. Let $(\cdot)^u$ denote a selection operator which retains only unrestricted elements, so that $(\boldsymbol{A}^v)^u = \boldsymbol{a}^u = \boldsymbol{\phi}$. Other than the r elements of $\boldsymbol{\phi}$, and the normalization on the diagonal of $\boldsymbol{B}$, the remaining elements of $\boldsymbol{A}$ are zero, and $(\cdot)^u$ merely records where in $\boldsymbol{A}$ the unrestricted elements occur. Thus, $(\cdot)^u$ could be viewed as location information. For example, if the first non-zero, non-normalized element of $\boldsymbol{A}$ is in the first row, fourth column, the second in the second row, first column and so on, then $(\cdot)^u$ codes (1,4), (2,1), etc. Let ^{v_u} denote the joint operator, then since the order is immaterial, $(\boldsymbol{A}^u)^v = \boldsymbol{A}^{v_u} = \boldsymbol{a}^u = \boldsymbol{\phi}$: this notation is convenient below.

11.9 Identification

Without some restrictions, the coefficients in $\boldsymbol{A}$ in (11.56) cannot be identified in the sense of uniqueness. The matrix $\boldsymbol{B}$ used to multiply the system to obtain the model could in turn be multiplied by an arbitrary non-singular matrix, $\boldsymbol{D}$ say, and still produce a linear model, but with different coefficients. To resolve such arbitrariness, we need to know something about the form of $\boldsymbol{A}$ in advance, and $\boldsymbol{A}$ must be sufficiently restricted that the only admissible $\boldsymbol{D}$ matrix is $\boldsymbol{I}_n$.

The order condition for identification concerns the number of unrestricted coefficients in $\boldsymbol{A}$. Since $\boldsymbol{\Pi}$ in (11.5) is $n \times p$, where $p = k \times l + n \times (s-1) + \kappa$ is the number of variables in $\boldsymbol{w}_t$ in the $\mathsf{I}(0)$ notation, no more than p regressors can enter any equation, with no more than $r \leq np$ unknowns in $\boldsymbol{\phi}$. The order condition is easily checked by counting the number of unrestricted elements in every equation of $\boldsymbol{A}$. Since $\boldsymbol{A}$ is $n \times (n+p)$ with the diagonal of $\boldsymbol{B}$ normalized at unity, there must be at least $n(n-1)$ restrictions. However, these need to be located in the appropriate positions such that no equation can be obtained as a linear combination of other equations. This requires the exclusion of some variables and the inclusion of others in different ways in every equation. From (11.4), let $\boldsymbol{R} = (\boldsymbol{I}_n : -\boldsymbol{\Pi})$ so that in matrix form, the system is $\boldsymbol{R}\boldsymbol{X}' = \boldsymbol{V}'$. Comparing with $\boldsymbol{A}\boldsymbol{X}' = \boldsymbol{U}'$, we must have $\boldsymbol{B}\boldsymbol{R} = \boldsymbol{A}$. This is usually expressed as $\boldsymbol{B}\boldsymbol{\Pi} + \boldsymbol{C} = \boldsymbol{0}$, but a more convenient form is obtained by letting $\boldsymbol{Q}' = (\boldsymbol{\Pi}' : \boldsymbol{I}_p)$ so that $\boldsymbol{A}\boldsymbol{Q} = \boldsymbol{0}$. In fact, $\boldsymbol{Q}$ is the $(n+p) \times p$ matrix of the conditional expectation of $\boldsymbol{x}_t$ given $\boldsymbol{w}_t$:

$$\mathsf{E}[\boldsymbol{x}_t \mid \boldsymbol{w}_t] = \mathsf{E}\left[\begin{pmatrix} \boldsymbol{y}_t \\ \boldsymbol{w}_t \end{pmatrix} \mid \boldsymbol{w}_t\right] = \begin{pmatrix} \boldsymbol{\Pi} \\ \boldsymbol{I}_p \end{pmatrix} \boldsymbol{w}_t = \boldsymbol{Q}\boldsymbol{w}_t \tag{11.57}$$

and hence $\boldsymbol{Q}$ is unique. Thus, the identification of $\boldsymbol{A}$ rests on being able to uniquely solve for $\boldsymbol{A}$ from $\boldsymbol{A}\boldsymbol{Q} = \boldsymbol{0}$, such that there is no other matrix $\boldsymbol{A}^* \neq \boldsymbol{A}$ satisfying $\boldsymbol{A}^*\boldsymbol{Q} = \boldsymbol{0}$. The order condition ensures a sufficient number of equations, and the rank condition ensures that these equations are linearly independent. The rank condition is determined on a probability-one basis: if a variable is included in an equation, then its associated coefficient a_{ij} is assumed to be non-zero, although in practice an estimate may be zero or there may exist linear combinations of coefficients which are collinear and hence lower the rank. An implication of this analysis is that any linear system like (11.4) can also be interpreted as the unrestricted reduced form of a just-identified structural econometric model.

When a model is just identified, it is possible to solve uniquely for $\hat{\boldsymbol{A}}$ from $\hat{\boldsymbol{B}}\hat{\boldsymbol{\Pi}} + \hat{\boldsymbol{C}} = \mathbf{0}$ in any finite sample without restricting the elements of $\boldsymbol{\Pi}$; under-identification provides too few equations for a unique solution; and over-identification provides too many, so inconsistent solutions can be obtained. The resolution in the last case is to restrict the estimate of $\boldsymbol{\Pi}$ using the information from $\boldsymbol{B\Pi} + \boldsymbol{C} = \mathbf{0}$ and that leads to simultaneous equations methods.

11.10 An EGE for simultaneous equations estimation

Estimation methods are summarized by the estimator generating equation (EGE) described in Chapter 10; for discussions of simultaneous equations estimation, see e.g. Judge *et al.* (1985, Ch.15) or Spanos (1986, Ch.15). Consider the system of n structural simultaneous equations in (11.55), written as:

$$\boldsymbol{B}\boldsymbol{y}_t + \boldsymbol{C}\boldsymbol{w}_t = \boldsymbol{A}\boldsymbol{x}_t = \boldsymbol{u}_t \text{ with } \boldsymbol{u}_t \sim \mathsf{IN}_n\left[\mathbf{0}, \boldsymbol{\Sigma}\right], \tag{11.58}$$

for n endogenous variables $\boldsymbol{y}_t$ and p weakly exogenous or lagged variables $\boldsymbol{w}_t$, where the r parameters of interest $\boldsymbol{\phi}$ in (11.58) are identified, and $|\boldsymbol{B}| \neq 0$. As in (11.55), we write the model in compact notation with $\boldsymbol{A} = (\boldsymbol{B} : \boldsymbol{C})$ and $\boldsymbol{x}_t' = (\boldsymbol{y}_t' : \boldsymbol{w}_t')$. In this section, we only consider models in which $\boldsymbol{A}$ is a linear function of $\boldsymbol{\phi}$.

In fact, (11.58) is a useful way to view the claims of econometrics: a stochastic vector $\boldsymbol{x}_t$ with a complicated, evolving, high-dimensional, dynamic, and perhaps integrated distribution, when multiplied by the correct constant matrix $\boldsymbol{A}$, is asserted to be a homoscedastic, normally-distributed innovation process $\boldsymbol{u}_t$. Expressed in that form, the claim is ambitious, and yields insight into econometrics as filtering data $\boldsymbol{x}_t$ through a matrix $\boldsymbol{A}$ to produce an unpredictable component $\boldsymbol{u}_t \sim \mathsf{IN}_n[\mathbf{0}, \boldsymbol{\Sigma}]$. Large macro-econometric models are generally non-linear in both variables and parameters, so are only approximated by (11.58), but in practice linearity is a reasonable first approximation.

The statistical structure of (11.58) is expressed in (11.57) through the conditional expectation:

$$\mathsf{E}\left[\boldsymbol{x}_t \mid \boldsymbol{w}_t\right] = \boldsymbol{Q}\boldsymbol{w}_t \tag{11.59}$$

where $\boldsymbol{Q}' = (\boldsymbol{\Pi}' : \boldsymbol{I}_p)$ and we interpret $\boldsymbol{\Pi}$ as $-\boldsymbol{B}^{-1}\boldsymbol{C}$ so that:

$$\boldsymbol{y}_t \mid \boldsymbol{w}_t \sim \mathsf{N}_n\left[\boldsymbol{\Pi}\boldsymbol{w}_t, \boldsymbol{\Omega}\right] \text{ with } \boldsymbol{\Omega} = \boldsymbol{B}^{-1}\boldsymbol{\Sigma}\boldsymbol{B}'^{-1}. \tag{11.60}$$

These relationships are the inverses of those associated with (11.55). The likelihood function is the multivariate normal distribution dependent on $(\boldsymbol{\Pi}, \boldsymbol{\Omega}) = \boldsymbol{f}(\boldsymbol{\phi}, \boldsymbol{\Sigma})$ and we need to maximize $\ell(\cdot)$ with respect to $\boldsymbol{\phi}$ (which corresponds to $\boldsymbol{\theta}_1$ in Chapter 10), and $\boldsymbol{\Sigma}$ (which corresponds to $\boldsymbol{\theta}_2$). Departing somewhat from the earlier treatment of EGEs, $\boldsymbol{Q}$ will also be part of $\boldsymbol{\theta}_2$, but the result will materialize correctly.

As an intuitive background, consider the condition:

$$\mathsf{E}\left[\boldsymbol{w}_t \boldsymbol{u}_t'\right] = \mathbf{0} \tag{11.61}$$

entailed by the fact that the $\boldsymbol{w}_t$ are the conditioning variables and are uncorrelated with the $\boldsymbol{u}_t$. Then (11.60) implies that $\boldsymbol{Q}\boldsymbol{w}_t$, which from (11.59) is the best predictor of $\boldsymbol{x}_t$ given $\boldsymbol{w}_t$, is also uncorrelated with $\boldsymbol{u}_t$:

$$\mathsf{E}\left[\boldsymbol{Q}\boldsymbol{w}_t \boldsymbol{u}_t'\right] = \mathbf{0}. \tag{11.62}$$

Since $\boldsymbol{u}_t' = \boldsymbol{x}_t' \boldsymbol{A}_t'$, (11.62) becomes:

$$\mathsf{E}\left[\boldsymbol{Q}\boldsymbol{w}_t \boldsymbol{x}_t' \boldsymbol{A}'\right] = \mathbf{0}. \tag{11.63}$$

As $\boldsymbol{u}_t$ is heteroscedastic across equations (it is homoscedastic over time), and its variance matrix is $\boldsymbol{\Sigma}$, post-multiply $\boldsymbol{u}_t$ by $\boldsymbol{\Sigma}^{-1}$ to obtain a suitably weighted function:

$$\mathsf{E}\left[\boldsymbol{Q}\boldsymbol{w}_t \boldsymbol{x}_t' \boldsymbol{A}' \boldsymbol{\Sigma}^{-1}\right] = \mathbf{0}. \tag{11.64}$$

Finally (11.64) has to hold for all t. Sum over the sample using $\boldsymbol{X}'\boldsymbol{W} = \sum_{t=1}^{T} \boldsymbol{x}_t \boldsymbol{w}_t'$, and transpose the result for convenience:

$$\mathsf{E}\left[\boldsymbol{\Sigma}^{-1} \boldsymbol{A} \boldsymbol{X}' \boldsymbol{W} \boldsymbol{Q}'\right] = \mathbf{0}. \tag{11.65}$$

Dropping the expectations operator, (11.65) is in fact $q_1(\boldsymbol{\theta}_1|\boldsymbol{\theta}_2)$, where $\boldsymbol{\theta}_1$ corresponds to $\boldsymbol{A}(\boldsymbol{\phi})$ and $\boldsymbol{\theta}_2$ to $(\boldsymbol{\Sigma}, \boldsymbol{Q})$. All known linear simultaneous-equations estimation methods are generated by special cases of (11.65). This includes full-information maximum likelihood (FIML: see Koopmans, 1950a), full-information instrumental variables (FIVE: see Brundy and Jorgenson, 1971), three-stage least squares (3SLS: see Zellner and Theil, 1962), limited-information maximum likelihood (LIML: see Anderson and Rubin, 1949), two-stage least squares (2SLS: see Basmann, 1957, and Theil, 1961), instrumental variables (IV: see e.g. Sargan, 1958), limited-information instrumental variables (LIVE), k-class estimators (see Theil, 1961), fix-point estimators (see Mosbaek and Wold, 1970), ordinary least squares and reduced-form estimators.

A formal derivation now follows. The log-likelihood $\ell(\boldsymbol{\Pi}, \boldsymbol{\Omega})$ is:

$$\begin{aligned} & -\tfrac{Tn}{2}\log 2\pi - \tfrac{T}{2}\log|\boldsymbol{\Omega}| - \tfrac{1}{2}\sum_{t=1}^{T}\left(\boldsymbol{y}_t - \boldsymbol{\Pi}\boldsymbol{w}_t\right)'\boldsymbol{\Omega}^{-1}\left(\boldsymbol{y}_t - \boldsymbol{\Pi}\boldsymbol{w}_t\right) \\ = \;& K - \tfrac{T}{2}\log|\boldsymbol{\Omega}| - \tfrac{1}{2}tr\left[\boldsymbol{\Omega}^{-1}\left(\boldsymbol{Y}'\boldsymbol{Y} - \boldsymbol{Y}'\boldsymbol{W}\boldsymbol{\Pi}' - \boldsymbol{\Pi}\boldsymbol{W}'\boldsymbol{Y} + \boldsymbol{\Pi}\boldsymbol{W}'\boldsymbol{W}\boldsymbol{\Pi}'\right)\right]. \end{aligned} \tag{11.66}$$

Since $\boldsymbol{\Omega}^{-1} = \boldsymbol{B}'\boldsymbol{\Sigma}^{-1}\boldsymbol{B}$ and $\boldsymbol{\Pi} = -\boldsymbol{B}^{-1}\boldsymbol{C}$, substituting these into (11.66), $\ell(\boldsymbol{\Pi}, \boldsymbol{\Omega})$ can be rewritten as $\ell(\boldsymbol{B}, \boldsymbol{C}, \boldsymbol{\Sigma})$ which equals:

$$K + \frac{T}{2}\log\left|\boldsymbol{\Sigma}^{-1}\right| + T\log\|\boldsymbol{B}\| - \tfrac{1}{2}\mathrm{tr}\left[\boldsymbol{\Sigma}^{-1}\left(\boldsymbol{B}\boldsymbol{Y}' + \boldsymbol{C}\boldsymbol{W}'\right)\left(\boldsymbol{Y}\boldsymbol{B}' + \boldsymbol{W}\boldsymbol{C}'\right)\right]. \tag{11.67}$$

The last term is also:

$$-\tfrac{1}{2}\mathrm{tr}\left[\boldsymbol{\Sigma}^{-1}\boldsymbol{U}'\boldsymbol{U}\right] = -\tfrac{1}{2}\mathrm{tr}\left[\boldsymbol{\Sigma}^{-1}\boldsymbol{A}\boldsymbol{X}'\boldsymbol{X}\boldsymbol{A}'\right],$$

where $||\boldsymbol{B}||$ is the modulus of $|\boldsymbol{B}|$. If $\boldsymbol{B}$ is singular, as in an incompletely specified system with fewer than n equations, the term $(T/2)\log|\boldsymbol{B}'\boldsymbol{\Sigma}^{-1}\boldsymbol{B}|$ is retained in place of the two middle terms in (11.67).

Concentrating $\ell(\boldsymbol{B}, \boldsymbol{C}, \boldsymbol{\Sigma})$ with respect to $\boldsymbol{\Sigma}$ requires differentiating (11.67) with respect to $\boldsymbol{\Sigma}^{-1}$ as in (11.27). Equating to zero as a necessary condition for a maximum:

$$\boldsymbol{\Sigma}_c = T^{-1}\boldsymbol{U}'\boldsymbol{U} = T^{-1}\boldsymbol{A}\boldsymbol{X}'\boldsymbol{X}\boldsymbol{A}',$$

(compare $\boldsymbol{\theta}_2 = \boldsymbol{h}(\boldsymbol{\theta}_1)$) with the resulting CLF:

$$\ell^0\left(\boldsymbol{A}(\boldsymbol{\phi})\right) = K_1 - \tfrac{T}{2}\log|\boldsymbol{A}\boldsymbol{X}'\boldsymbol{X}\boldsymbol{A}'| + T\log||\boldsymbol{B}||. \tag{11.68}$$

To maximize $\ell^0(\boldsymbol{\phi})$ with respect to $\boldsymbol{\phi}$, differentiate $\ell(\boldsymbol{B}, \boldsymbol{C}, \boldsymbol{\Sigma})$ with respect to $\boldsymbol{B}$ and $\boldsymbol{C}$, retaining only those terms corresponding to $\boldsymbol{\phi}$, and evaluate the outcome at $\boldsymbol{\Sigma}_c = T^{-1}\boldsymbol{A}\boldsymbol{X}'\boldsymbol{X}\boldsymbol{A}'$, as established in the CLF theorem in Chapter 10. This is most easily done using the operator notation introduced above since:

$$\left(\frac{\partial \ell}{\partial \boldsymbol{A}}\right)^{v_u} = \left(\frac{\partial \ell}{\partial (\boldsymbol{A})^{v_u}}\right) = \frac{\partial \ell}{\partial \boldsymbol{\phi}} = \boldsymbol{q}_1(\boldsymbol{\phi}), \tag{11.69}$$

and hence:

$$\left(\left(\frac{\partial \ell}{\partial \boldsymbol{A}}\right)_{\rfloor \boldsymbol{\Sigma}=T^{-1}\boldsymbol{A}\boldsymbol{X}'\boldsymbol{X}\boldsymbol{A}'}\right)^{v_u} = \left(\frac{\partial \ell^0}{\partial \boldsymbol{A}}\right)^{v_u} = \frac{\partial \ell^0}{\partial \boldsymbol{\phi}} = \boldsymbol{q}_1^0(\boldsymbol{\phi}), \tag{11.70}$$

as required. Differentiating $\ell(\boldsymbol{\phi})$ with respect to $\boldsymbol{B}$ and $\boldsymbol{C}$ in turn, using (11.8) yields:

$$\left(\left(\frac{\partial \ell}{\partial \boldsymbol{B}}\right)_{\rfloor \boldsymbol{\Sigma}=T^{-1}\boldsymbol{A}\boldsymbol{X}'\boldsymbol{X}\boldsymbol{A}'}\right)^{v_u} = \left((T\boldsymbol{B}^{-1\prime} - \boldsymbol{\Sigma}^{-1}\boldsymbol{U}'\boldsymbol{Y})_{\rfloor \boldsymbol{\Sigma}=T^{-1}\boldsymbol{A}\boldsymbol{X}'\boldsymbol{X}\boldsymbol{A}'}\right)^{v_u}, \tag{11.71}$$

and:

$$\left(\left(\frac{\partial \ell}{\partial \boldsymbol{C}}\right)_{\rfloor \boldsymbol{\Sigma}=T^{-1}\boldsymbol{A}\boldsymbol{X}'\boldsymbol{X}\boldsymbol{A}'}\right)^{v_u} = -\left((\boldsymbol{\Sigma}^{-1}\boldsymbol{U}'\boldsymbol{W})_{\rfloor \boldsymbol{\Sigma}=T^{-1}\boldsymbol{A}\boldsymbol{X}'\boldsymbol{X}\boldsymbol{A}'}\right)^{v_u}. \tag{11.72}$$

The trick to solving these two equations together was discovered by Durbin (1963), published as Durbin (1988). From the function for $\boldsymbol{\Sigma}_c$ at the first step:

$$\boldsymbol{\Sigma}_c = T^{-1}\boldsymbol{A}\boldsymbol{X}'\boldsymbol{X}\boldsymbol{A}', \tag{11.73}$$

which on pre-multiplication of both sides by $\boldsymbol{\Sigma}_c^{-1}$ implies that:

$$\boldsymbol{I}_n = T^{-1}\boldsymbol{\Sigma}_c^{-1}\boldsymbol{A}\boldsymbol{X}'\boldsymbol{X}\boldsymbol{A}'. \tag{11.74}$$

Next, post-multiply both sides of (11.74) by $TB^{-1\prime}$:

$$TB^{-1\prime} = \Sigma_c^{-1} AX'XR', \tag{11.75}$$

where $R = B^{-1}A = (I_n : -\Pi)$, and hence $XR' = (Y - W\Pi') = V$ is the matrix of reduced-form errors as in §11.4. Thus, using (11.75) in (11.71), since $AX' = U'$:

$$\begin{aligned} TB^{-1\prime} - \Sigma_c^{-1} U'Y &= \Sigma_c^{-1} U'XR' - \Sigma_c^{-1} U'Y \\ &= \Sigma_c^{-1} U' \left(Y - W\Pi' - Y \right) \\ &= -\Sigma_c^{-1} U'W\Pi'. \end{aligned} \tag{11.76}$$

Combining the two derivatives in (11.71) and (11.72) using (11.76):

$$\begin{aligned} \left(\frac{\partial \ell^0}{\partial \phi}\right) &= -\left((\Sigma^{-1} U'W\Pi' : \Sigma^{-1} U'W) \rfloor_{\Sigma = T^{-1}AX'XA'; \Pi = -B^{-1}C} \right)^{v_u} \\ &= -\left((\Sigma^{-1} AX'WQ') \rfloor_{\Sigma = T^{-1}AX'XA'; Q' = (-C'B^{-1\prime} : I_n)} \right)^{v_u}, \end{aligned} \tag{11.77}$$

which is the EGE discussed in (11.65) above, with the selection, vectorizing, and evaluation operators explicitly present. Then $\hat{\phi}$ solves the last expression equated to zero.

The variance of $\hat{\phi}$ depends on $-T^{-1}$ times the inverse Hessian:

$$\begin{aligned} -T^{-1}\left(\frac{\partial^2 \ell^0(\cdot)}{\partial \phi \partial \phi'}\right) &= -T^{-1}\left(\frac{\partial q_1^0(\phi)}{\partial \phi'}\right) \\ &= \left(\frac{\partial \left(\Sigma^{-1} A \left[T^{-1} X'W\right] Q'\right)}{\partial \phi'} \rfloor_{\Sigma, Q}\right)^{v_u} \\ &= \left(\frac{\partial \left(\Sigma^{-1} \left[T^{-1} U'W\right] Q'\right)}{\partial \phi'} \rfloor_{\Sigma, Q}\right)^{v_u}, \end{aligned} \tag{11.78}$$

which must take account of the dependence of Q and Σ on ϕ. However, the central term in $q_1^0(\phi)$ is $[T^{-1}U'W]$, which has an expectation and a plim of zero. Thus, the effects of changing ϕ on Σ and Q are negligible asymptotically, since the resulting terms are multiplied by a term which vanishes. The only non-negligible derivative asymptotically is that due to A^{v_u}, which is a unit matrix. Further, since $\text{plim}_{T\to\infty} T^{-1}U'W = 0$:

$$\underset{T\to\infty}{\text{plim}}\, T^{-1} X'W = \underset{T\to\infty}{\text{plim}}\, T^{-1} QW'W.$$

Thus, letting $M_W = \text{plim}_{T\to\infty} T^{-1} W'W$, the asymptotic variance matrix of $\sqrt{T}(\hat{\phi} - \phi)$ is:

$$\mathsf{AV}\left[\sqrt{T}\left(\hat{\phi} - \phi\right)\right] = \left[\left(\Sigma^{-1} \otimes QM_W Q'\right)^u\right]^{-1}. \tag{11.79}$$

Consequently, it does not matter for asymptotic efficiency what estimates of Σ^{-1} or Q are used in evaluating the EGE, providing they converge to their population values. Even inappropriate estimators $\tilde{Q}$ or $\tilde{\Sigma}^{-1}$ will suffice for consistent estimates of A in (11.77), providing they converge to non-zero, finite values $\boldsymbol{Q}^*$ and $\boldsymbol{\Sigma}^{*-1}$, since such choices cannot affect the fact that $\boldsymbol{w}_t$ is uncorrelated with $\boldsymbol{u}_t$. There is an infinite number of estimators generated by choosing different $\tilde{\boldsymbol{Q}}$ and $\tilde{\boldsymbol{\Sigma}}$.

As an example, consider 2SLS, which is a special case of IV. In 2SLS, the variance-covariance matrix is ignored by setting $\tilde{\boldsymbol{\Sigma}}^{-1} = \boldsymbol{I}_n$, which is certainly inconsistent, and potentially could be very different from $\boldsymbol{\Sigma}$. However, because $\boldsymbol{\Sigma}$ is part of $\boldsymbol{\theta}_2$, its inconsistency does not affect the consistency of $\boldsymbol{\theta}_1$ so long as $\tilde{\boldsymbol{\Sigma}}$ converges (as it does here). Further, 2SLS estimates $\boldsymbol{Q}$ by regression:

$$\tilde{\boldsymbol{Q}} = \boldsymbol{X}'\boldsymbol{W}\left(\boldsymbol{W}'\boldsymbol{W}\right)^{-1}, \tag{11.80}$$

which is often called the first stage of 2SLS. The predicted value of $\boldsymbol{X}$ is given by:

$$\tilde{\boldsymbol{X}} = \tilde{\boldsymbol{Q}}\boldsymbol{W}. \tag{11.81}$$

Solve the EGE expression (11.77) for $\boldsymbol{A}$ using (11.80) and $\tilde{\boldsymbol{\Sigma}} = \boldsymbol{I}_n$ to obtain:

$$\left(\boldsymbol{A}\boldsymbol{X}'\boldsymbol{W}\left(\boldsymbol{W}'\boldsymbol{W}\right)^{-1}\boldsymbol{W}'\boldsymbol{X}\right)^{v_u} = \boldsymbol{0}, \tag{11.82}$$

which is 2SLS applied simultaneously to every equation. The asymptotic distribution of 2SLS could be established directly (see Ch.A4 for IV), but is easily obtained from EGE theory. Write (11.82) as:

$$\left(\boldsymbol{A}\boldsymbol{X}'\boldsymbol{W}\tilde{\boldsymbol{Q}}'\right) = \left(\boldsymbol{U}'\boldsymbol{W}\tilde{\boldsymbol{Q}}'\right) = \boldsymbol{0}.$$

Then, 2SLS is consistent and has an asymptotic variance matrix given by $\sigma_{ii}(\boldsymbol{QMQ}')^{-1}$ for the ith equation.

Next, we examine the FIML estimator, which requires $\hat{\boldsymbol{\theta}}_2$, and bases $\hat{\boldsymbol{\theta}}_1$ explicitly on $\boldsymbol{h}(\hat{\boldsymbol{\theta}}_2)$. However, $\hat{\boldsymbol{\theta}}_2$ requires $\hat{\boldsymbol{Q}}$ which requires $\hat{\boldsymbol{\Pi}}$, which requires $\hat{\boldsymbol{B}}$ and $\hat{\boldsymbol{C}}$, which obviously require $\boldsymbol{A}(\hat{\boldsymbol{\phi}})$. Likewise, $\hat{\boldsymbol{\Sigma}}$ is quadratic in $\boldsymbol{A}$, because the MLE from (11.73) is:

$$\hat{\boldsymbol{\Sigma}} = T^{-1}\boldsymbol{A}\left(\hat{\boldsymbol{\phi}}\right)\boldsymbol{X}'\boldsymbol{X}\boldsymbol{A}\left(\hat{\boldsymbol{\phi}}\right)'. \tag{11.83}$$

Therefore, both $\boldsymbol{Q}$ and $\boldsymbol{\Sigma}$ are complicated non-linear functions of $\boldsymbol{A}(\boldsymbol{\phi})$ and we have to solve the whole EGE expression (11.77) for $\boldsymbol{A}(\hat{\boldsymbol{\phi}}) = (\hat{\boldsymbol{B}} : \hat{\boldsymbol{C}})$ simultaneously:

$$\left[\left(\boldsymbol{A}(\boldsymbol{\phi})\left[\frac{\boldsymbol{X}'\boldsymbol{X}}{T}\right]\boldsymbol{A}(\boldsymbol{\phi})'\right)^{-1}\boldsymbol{A}(\boldsymbol{\phi})\boldsymbol{X}'\boldsymbol{W}\left(-\boldsymbol{C}(\boldsymbol{\phi})'\boldsymbol{B}(\boldsymbol{\phi})'^{-1} : \boldsymbol{I}_p\right)\right]^{v_u} = \boldsymbol{0}. \tag{11.84}$$

Trying to solve that highly non-linear problem slowed the progress of econometrics, because FIML seemed too complicated to apply with existing computational facilities. As a result, econometrics digressed to invent methods that were easier to compute, and have since transpired to be other EGE solutions. The revolution in computer power has rendered most of these shortcut solutions otiose, although 3SLS remains a convenient method for calculating initial values for FIML, and has different finite-sample properties.

The concept of an EGE in simultaneous equations systems is not tied to a linear mapping from $\boldsymbol{A}$ to $\boldsymbol{\phi}$, and we briefly note two cases of empirical concern, namely:

(i) when $\boldsymbol{A}(\boldsymbol{\phi})$ is a non-linear function of the parameters $\boldsymbol{\phi}$ (see Hausman, 1975); and

(ii) when there is a vector autoregressive error, which satisfies system COMFAC restrictions (see Hendry, 1976, and Hendry and Anderson, 1977).

11.10.1 Non-linear parameters

Reconsider the model in (11.58):

$$\boldsymbol{A}(\boldsymbol{\phi})\,\boldsymbol{x}_t = \boldsymbol{u}_t \sim \mathsf{IN}_n\left[\mathbf{0}, \boldsymbol{\Sigma}\right].$$

The log-likelihood is given by (11.67), namely:

$$\ell(\boldsymbol{\theta}, \boldsymbol{\Sigma}) = K + \frac{T}{2}\log\left|\boldsymbol{\Sigma}^{-1}\right| + T\log\left|\left|\boldsymbol{B}(\boldsymbol{\phi})\right|\right| - \tfrac{1}{2}\mathrm{tr}\left(\boldsymbol{\Sigma}^{-1}\boldsymbol{A}(\boldsymbol{\phi})\,\boldsymbol{X}'\boldsymbol{X}\boldsymbol{A}(\boldsymbol{\phi})'\right).$$

When the mapping from $\boldsymbol{A}$ to $\boldsymbol{\phi}$ cross-relates elements, the score equation cannot be written generally, but it remains similar to that obtained before. Differentiate $\ell(\cdot)$ with respect to ϕ_i:

$$\frac{\partial \ell}{\partial \phi_i} = \mathrm{tr}\left[T\boldsymbol{B}'(\boldsymbol{\phi})^{-1}\frac{\partial \boldsymbol{B}(\boldsymbol{\phi})}{\partial \phi_i} - \boldsymbol{\Sigma}^{-1}\boldsymbol{A}(\boldsymbol{\phi})\,\boldsymbol{X}'\boldsymbol{X}\frac{\partial \boldsymbol{A}(\boldsymbol{\phi})'}{\partial \phi_i}\right] = 0, \qquad (11.85)$$

since:

$$\frac{\partial \log\left|\left|\boldsymbol{B}(\boldsymbol{\phi})\right|\right|}{\partial b_{ij}} = b^{ji} = \mathrm{tr}\left(\boldsymbol{B}^{-1\prime}\frac{\partial \boldsymbol{B}}{\partial b_{ij}}\right).$$

Further, as in (11.75):

$$T\boldsymbol{B}'(\boldsymbol{\phi})^{-1} = \boldsymbol{\Sigma}_c^{-1}\boldsymbol{A}(\boldsymbol{\phi})\,\boldsymbol{X}'\left(\boldsymbol{Y} - \boldsymbol{W}\boldsymbol{\Pi}'\right).$$

Thus, we obtain an expression similar to that of the previous EGE:

$$\mathrm{tr}\left(\boldsymbol{\Sigma}^{-1}\boldsymbol{A}(\boldsymbol{\phi})\,\boldsymbol{X}'\boldsymbol{W}\boldsymbol{Q}'\boldsymbol{J}'_{i}\right) = 0, \qquad (11.86)$$

where $\boldsymbol{J}_i = \partial\boldsymbol{A}(\boldsymbol{\phi})/\partial\phi_i$ for $i = 1, \ldots, r$.

The earlier analysis of linear restrictions set $\boldsymbol{J}_i$ equal to a matrix that was zero except for unity in the position associated with the relevant parameter. Thus, the same analysis goes through, but both the symbols and the solution are somewhat more awkward.

11.10.2 Vector autoregressive errors

We now assume that a first-order vector autoregressive error is a valid data reduction, and hence the model can be written as:

$$\boldsymbol{A}\boldsymbol{x}_t = \boldsymbol{u}_t = \boldsymbol{R}\boldsymbol{u}_{t-1} + \epsilon_t \text{ where } \epsilon_t \sim \mathsf{IN}_n\left[\mathbf{0}, \boldsymbol{\Sigma}\right],$$

or letting $\boldsymbol{x}_t^* = (\boldsymbol{x}_t' : \boldsymbol{x}_{t-1}')'$ and $\boldsymbol{A}^* = (\boldsymbol{A} : -\boldsymbol{R}\boldsymbol{A})$:

$$\boldsymbol{A}\boldsymbol{x}_t - \boldsymbol{R}\boldsymbol{A}\boldsymbol{x}_{t-1} = \boldsymbol{A}^*\boldsymbol{x}_t^* = \epsilon_t. \tag{11.87}$$

The log-likelihood function $\ell(\phi, \boldsymbol{\Sigma}, \boldsymbol{R})$ follows from the multivariate normal distribution as:

$$K + \frac{T}{2}\log\left|\boldsymbol{\Sigma}^{-1}\right| + T\log\left|\left|\boldsymbol{B}\left(\phi\right)\right|\right| - \tfrac{1}{2}\mathrm{tr}\left(\boldsymbol{\Sigma}^{-1}\boldsymbol{A}^*\left(\phi\right)\sum_{t=1}^{T}\boldsymbol{x}_t^*\boldsymbol{x}_t^{*\prime}\boldsymbol{A}^*\left(\phi\right)'\right).$$

Concentrating with respect to $\boldsymbol{\Sigma}^{-1}$ using $\partial\ell(\cdot)/\partial\boldsymbol{\Sigma}^{-1} = \mathbf{0}$ implies that:

$$\boldsymbol{\Sigma}_c = T^{-1}\sum_{t=1}^{T}\epsilon_t\epsilon_t' = T^{-1}\boldsymbol{E}'\boldsymbol{E}.$$

Similarly, concentrating with respect to $\boldsymbol{R}$:

$$\left(\frac{\partial\ell}{\partial\boldsymbol{R}}\right)^{v_u} = \left(\boldsymbol{\Sigma}_c^{-1}\boldsymbol{E}'\boldsymbol{U}_1\right)^{v_u}.$$

When $\boldsymbol{R}$ is unrestricted, equating the score to zero:

$$\boldsymbol{R}_c = \left(\boldsymbol{U}'\boldsymbol{U}_1\right)\left(\boldsymbol{U}_1'\boldsymbol{U}_1\right)^{-1} = \left(\boldsymbol{A}\boldsymbol{X}'\boldsymbol{X}_1\boldsymbol{A}'\right)\left(\boldsymbol{A}\boldsymbol{X}_1'\boldsymbol{X}_1\boldsymbol{A}'\right)^{-1}. \tag{11.88}$$

If $\boldsymbol{R}$ is restricted (e.g. diagonal), then the solution takes the form:

$$\left[\boldsymbol{\Sigma}_c^{-1}\left(\boldsymbol{U}' - \boldsymbol{R}_c\boldsymbol{U}_1'\right)\boldsymbol{U}_1\right]^{v_u} = \mathbf{0}, \tag{11.89}$$

or:

$$\left(\boldsymbol{R}_c\right)^{v_u} = \left(\left[\boldsymbol{\Sigma}^{-1}\otimes\boldsymbol{U}_1'\boldsymbol{U}_1\right]^u\right)^{-1}\left[\boldsymbol{\Sigma}^{-1}\otimes\boldsymbol{U}_1'\right]^u\left(\boldsymbol{U}'\right)^v. \tag{11.90}$$

Finally, differentiating $\ell(\cdot)$ with respect to ϕ and considering the simple linear mapping again, $(\partial\ell/\partial\boldsymbol{A})^{v_u} = \mathbf{0}$ implies:

$$\begin{aligned}&\big[T\boldsymbol{B}^{-1\prime} - \boldsymbol{\Sigma}_c^{-1}(\boldsymbol{A}\boldsymbol{X}'\boldsymbol{X} - \boldsymbol{R}_c\boldsymbol{A}\boldsymbol{X}_1'\boldsymbol{X})\\ &-\boldsymbol{R}_c'\boldsymbol{\Sigma}_c^{-1}\boldsymbol{A}\boldsymbol{X}'\boldsymbol{X}_1 + \boldsymbol{R}_c'\boldsymbol{\Sigma}_c^{-1}\boldsymbol{R}_c\boldsymbol{A}\boldsymbol{X}_1'\boldsymbol{X}_1\big]^{v_u} = \mathbf{0}.\end{aligned}$$

After the usual Durbin transformation, this can be written in the more felicitous form:

$$\left(T^{-1}\boldsymbol{\Sigma}_c^{-1}\boldsymbol{E}'\boldsymbol{W}^*\boldsymbol{Q}^{*\prime} - T^{-1}\boldsymbol{R}_c'\boldsymbol{\Sigma}_c^{-1}\boldsymbol{E}'\boldsymbol{X}_1\right)^{v_u} = \mathbf{0},$$

where $\boldsymbol{W}^* \boldsymbol{Q}^{*\prime}$ is the reduced form of the autoregressive transformed model (see Bhargava, 1989). Combining the two score equations for $\boldsymbol{A}$ and $\boldsymbol{R}$ yields:

$$\begin{pmatrix} T^{-1}\boldsymbol{\Sigma}_c^{-1}\boldsymbol{E}'\boldsymbol{W}^*\boldsymbol{Q}^{*\prime} - T^{-1}\boldsymbol{R}'\boldsymbol{\Sigma}_c^{-1}\boldsymbol{E}'\boldsymbol{X}_1 \\ T^{-1}\boldsymbol{\Sigma}_c^{-1}\boldsymbol{E}'\boldsymbol{U}_1 \end{pmatrix}^{v_u} = \mathbf{0}. \tag{11.91}$$

Unsurprisingly, the result in (11.91) is an extension of both the preceding EGE for simultaneous systems and for single-equation COMFAC models as in Chapter 10. In general, the only fully efficient solutions for dynamic models will involve iterating to determine $\hat{\boldsymbol{A}}$ and $\hat{\boldsymbol{R}}$ jointly. In special cases, such as static models with strictly exogenous regressors, non-iterative asymptotically-efficient solutions exist.

11.11 A solved example

Consider the simple Keynesian model:[6]

$$C_t = \alpha I_t + u_t \;\text{ where }\; u_t \sim \mathsf{IN}\left[0, \sigma^2\right] \tag{11.92}$$

$$I_t \equiv C_t + E_t \;\text{ with }\; \mathsf{E}\left[E_t u_s\right] = 0 \;\forall t, s \tag{11.93}$$

where C_t is consumption, I_t is income, and E_t is autonomous investment. Also, $\mathsf{E}[E_t] = \mu > 0$ and:

$$\mathsf{E}\left[E_t^2\right] = \operatorname*{plim}_{T\to\infty} T^{-1}\sum_{t=1}^{T} E_t^2 = \tau \text{ where } 0 < \tau < \infty.$$

(a) Derive the joint data density of C_t and I_t conditional on E_t and hence obtain $\mathsf{E}[C_t|E_t]$. Let $\boldsymbol{\theta} = (\alpha : \sigma^2)'$. Noting that the data density is singular, derive the log-likelihood function $\ell(\boldsymbol{\theta}|\,\boldsymbol{C}_T^1, \boldsymbol{E}_T^1)$ from the conditional model for C_t (given a sample of size T) and re-express this in terms of $\ell(\boldsymbol{\theta}|\,\boldsymbol{C}_T^1, \boldsymbol{I}_T^1)$.

(b) Obtain the score from $\ell(\boldsymbol{\theta}|\,\boldsymbol{C}_T^1, \boldsymbol{I}_T^1)$, and derive the asymptotic information matrix in terms of $(\boldsymbol{\theta}, \mu, \tau)$. Find the maximum likelihood estimator of α (using $\sigma_c^2 = T^{-1}\sum_{t=1}^{T} u_t^2$) and calculate its asymptotic variance (appropriately normalized).

(c) Show that the instrumental variables estimator:

$$\tilde{\alpha} = \frac{\sum_{t=1}^{T} C_t E_t}{\sum_{t=1}^{T} I_t E_t} \tag{11.94}$$

is asymptotically efficient.

[6] I am grateful to Tom Rothenberg for suggesting this example, cited in Hendry *et al.* (1988).

Solution to (a)

E_t is assumed to be strongly exogenous for $\boldsymbol{\theta} = (\alpha : \sigma^2)'$. Solving to remove the simultaneity in (11.92):

$$C_t = \frac{\alpha E_t}{(1-\alpha)} + \frac{u_t}{(1-\alpha)} \text{ and } I_t = \frac{E_t}{(1-\alpha)} + \frac{u_t}{(1-\alpha)}. \quad (11.95)$$

The joint density is:

$$\begin{pmatrix} C_t \\ I_t \end{pmatrix} \mid E_t \sim \mathsf{N}_2\left[\begin{pmatrix} \alpha(1-\alpha)^{-1} E_t \\ (1-\alpha)^{-1} E_t \end{pmatrix}, \frac{\sigma^2}{(1-\alpha)^2}\begin{pmatrix} 1 & 1 \\ 1 & 1 \end{pmatrix}\right]. \quad (11.96)$$

Then $\mathsf{E}[C_t|E_t] = \alpha(1-\alpha)^{-1}E_t$ is the conditional mean from (11.96). Because I_t is determined by an identity, it could be eliminated by substitution, reducing the system to a univariate conditional representation of the density $\prod_{t=1}^{T} \mathsf{D}_c(C_t|E_t, \boldsymbol{\theta})$. Since the identity parameters are known, the log-likelihood can be transformed back to one involving C_t and I_t. In terms of a general representation based on (11.56):

$$\ell(\boldsymbol{A}_1, \boldsymbol{\Sigma}) = K + \tfrac{T}{2}\log\left|\boldsymbol{\Sigma}^{-1}\right| + T\log||\boldsymbol{B}|| - \tfrac{1}{2}\mathrm{tr}\left[\boldsymbol{\Sigma}^{-1}\boldsymbol{A}_1\boldsymbol{X}'\boldsymbol{X}\boldsymbol{A}_1\right] \quad (11.97)$$

involving the complete $\boldsymbol{B}$ matrix, but the variance matrix $\boldsymbol{\Sigma}$ of the stochastic equations only. Thus, although the error variance matrix in (11.96) is singular, the log-likelihood $\ell(\boldsymbol{\theta}|\,\boldsymbol{C}_T^1; \boldsymbol{E}_T^1)$ is obtained from the first equation of (11.96):

$$K_0 - \frac{T}{2}\log\left(\frac{\sigma^2}{(1-\alpha)^2}\right) - \left(\frac{(1-\alpha)^2}{2\sigma^2}\right)\sum_{t=1}^{T}\left(C_t - \frac{\alpha}{1-\alpha}E_t\right)^2. \quad (11.98)$$

Using (11.93), the log-likelihood for the model becomes:

$$\ell\left(\boldsymbol{\theta}|\,\boldsymbol{C}_T^1, \boldsymbol{I}_T^1\right) = K_0 - \frac{T}{2}\log\sigma^2 + T\log(1-\alpha) - \frac{1}{2\sigma^2}\sum_{t=1}^{T}(C_t - \alpha I_t)^2, \quad (11.99)$$

matching $||\boldsymbol{B}|| = (1-\alpha)$ and $\boldsymbol{\Sigma} = \sigma^2$.

Solution to (b)

Since the model is just identified, the system and model likelihoods coincide, and the latter arises without any Jacobian transformation (see Richard, 1984). The score equation from (11.99) is:

$$\frac{\partial \ell(\boldsymbol{\theta})}{\partial \boldsymbol{\theta}} = \boldsymbol{q}(\boldsymbol{\theta}) = \begin{pmatrix} -T(1-\alpha)^{-1} + \sigma^{-2}\sum_{t=1}^{T} I_t u_t \\ -\frac{1}{2}T\sigma^{-2} + \frac{1}{2}\sigma^{-4}\sum_{t=1}^{T} u_t^2 \end{pmatrix}. \quad (11.100)$$

As $\mathsf{E}[I_t u_t] = \sigma^2(1-\alpha)^{-1}$ and $\mathsf{E}[I_t^2] = (\tau + \sigma^2)(1-\alpha)^{-2} = \rho$, the expected Hessian or information matrix is:

$$\mathsf{E}\left[-T^{-1}\frac{\partial^2 \ell(\boldsymbol{\theta})}{\partial \boldsymbol{\theta} \partial \boldsymbol{\theta}'}\right] = \mathcal{I}(\boldsymbol{\theta}) = \frac{1}{\sigma^2}\begin{pmatrix} \sigma^2(1-\alpha)^{-2} + \rho & (1-\alpha)^{-1} \\ (1-\alpha)^{-1} & \frac{1}{2}\sigma^{-2} \end{pmatrix}. \tag{11.101}$$

The diagonality of $\mathcal{I}(\boldsymbol{\theta})$ for error-variance parameters, familiar from OLS, is absent.

Next, setting $\boldsymbol{q}(\boldsymbol{\theta}) = \mathbf{0}$, the second element in (11.100) yields:

$$\sigma_c^2 = T^{-1}\sum_{t=1}^{T} u_t^2, \tag{11.102}$$

which matches (11.73). Substituting (11.102) into the first element of $\boldsymbol{q}(\boldsymbol{\theta}) = \mathbf{0}$:

$$-\sigma_c^{-2}\left[\sum_{t=1}^{T}\frac{u_t^2}{(1-\alpha)} - \sum_{t=1}^{T} I_t u_t\right] = \sigma_c^{-2}\left(\sum_{t=1}^{T} u_t\left[I_t - \frac{u_t}{(1-\alpha)}\right]\right) = \frac{\sum_{t=1}^{T} E_t u_t}{\sigma_c^2(1-\alpha)} = 0 \tag{11.103}$$

from (11.95). Equivalently, the MLE of α is obtained by solving $\sum_{t=1}^{T} E_t u_t = 0$ which, as $u_t = C_t - \alpha I_t$, is:

$$\hat{\alpha} = \frac{\sum_{t=1}^{T} C_t E_t}{\sum_{t=1}^{T} I_t E_t}. \tag{11.104}$$

The asymptotic variance of $\sqrt{T}(\hat{\alpha} - \alpha)$ can be obtained directly from (11.104) or from (11.101), and is given by the $(1,1)$ element of $\mathcal{I}(\boldsymbol{\theta})^{-1}$:

$$\mathcal{I}(\boldsymbol{\theta})^{-1} = \frac{2\sigma^4}{\tau}\begin{pmatrix} \frac{1}{2}\sigma^{-2}(1-\alpha)^2 & -(1-\alpha) \\ -(1-\alpha) & \tau + 2\sigma^2 \end{pmatrix},$$

so that:

$$\mathsf{AV}\left[\sqrt{T}(\hat{\alpha} - \alpha)\right] = \frac{\sigma^2(1-\alpha)^2}{\tau}. \tag{11.105}$$

In fact, (11.103) is the earlier EGE, as can be seen by letting $\boldsymbol{w}_t' = E_t$, $\boldsymbol{W} = \boldsymbol{E}$, $\boldsymbol{Q}' = (1-\alpha)^{-1}$ (since there are no exogenous structural regressors), and $\boldsymbol{u}' = \boldsymbol{A}_1\boldsymbol{X}'$ where $\boldsymbol{A}_1 = (1 : -\alpha)$:

$$\left(\sigma_c^{-2}\frac{\boldsymbol{u}'\boldsymbol{E}}{(1-\alpha)}\right)^{v_u} = \left[\boldsymbol{\Sigma}_c^{-1}\boldsymbol{A}_1\boldsymbol{X}'\boldsymbol{W}\boldsymbol{Q}'\right]^{v_u}. \tag{11.106}$$

When the model is just-identified, $\boldsymbol{Q}'$ is non-singular and unrestricted. Further, (11.105) also equals the outcome from $[(\boldsymbol{\Sigma}^{-1} \otimes \boldsymbol{Q}\boldsymbol{M}_W\boldsymbol{Q}')^u]^{-1}$ in (11.79).

This example of the derivation of the EGE clarifies the roles of the Jacobian term $T\log(1-\alpha)$ in (11.99), Durbin's insight for re-expressing (11.100) as (11.103), and the handling of singular densities due to identities. Numerical calculation reveals that 2SLS and FIML estimates of α are identical, with the score vector being zero when evaluated at the initial values of 2SLS, as holds for just-identified models. Thus, there is no test for over-identification, and the model automatically encompasses the system irrespective of how badly specified the model or system are.

Solution to (c)

Comparison of (11.94) and (11.104) reveals that the IV estimator is the MLE here, and hence is asymptotically efficient. As shown in Chapter A4, however, it has no moments in finite samples.

Chapter 8 discussed model types and the derivations of multipliers and of reduced forms. Having obtained (11.65) formally, conditional on $\boldsymbol{\Sigma}$ and $\boldsymbol{Q}$, the expression is linear in $\boldsymbol{A}$ and so is easy to solve (leading to 3SLS or FIVE). However, that does not mean that iterating an algorithm based on the score will be computationally efficient (Ch.A5 discusses numerical optimization).

11.12 Simultaneous equations modelling

By assuming that the structural form of the DGP was known, the preceding analysis was conducted at level B. Textbook presentations of simultaneous equations estimation usually treat the mapping $\boldsymbol{A}(\boldsymbol{\phi})$ as given, and derive the reduced form from the structure (see §11.10 above). However, since the reduced form has many more parameters than there are in $\boldsymbol{\phi}$, at level C, such an approach is simple to general and so is open to all the difficulties discussed above (Hendry *et al.*, 1988, provide a more detailed analysis). Moreover, by not first testing the validity of the reduced form, which is the basis of the test of over-identifying restrictions used to validate the structural form, all inferences are doubtful (see Sims, 1980, Spanos, 1986, and Hendry, 1987). The approach here is within the general-to-specific modelling methodology proposed in earlier chapters, extended to allow for the complications of multi-equations and identification.

Given that the system is a congruent representation of the data, the model must parsimoniously encompass the system to be valid. This aspect is discussed more fully in Chapter 14, but in the present context can be checked by a likelihood-ratio test for over-identifying restrictions. Using the analogue of (11.7), the CLF, $\ell_1(\cdot)$, for the system is:

$$\ell_1\left(\hat{\boldsymbol{\Pi}}, \hat{\boldsymbol{\Omega}}\right) = K - \frac{T}{2}\log\left|T^{-1}\hat{\boldsymbol{V}}_1'\hat{\boldsymbol{V}}_1\right| = K - \frac{T}{2}\log\left|\hat{\boldsymbol{R}}\left(T^{-1}\boldsymbol{X}'\boldsymbol{X}\right)\hat{\boldsymbol{R}}'\right|, \quad (11.107)$$

where K_0 is a constant, $\boldsymbol{R} = (\boldsymbol{I}_n : -\boldsymbol{\Pi})$, and $\hat{\boldsymbol{V}}_1$ denotes the matrix of residuals for the n_1 stochastic equations, excluding identities. The CLF $\ell_0(\hat{\boldsymbol{\phi}}, \hat{\boldsymbol{\Sigma}})$ for the complete model from (11.68) is:[7]

$$\ell_0\left(\hat{\boldsymbol{\phi}}, \hat{\boldsymbol{\Sigma}}\right) = K - \frac{T}{2}\log\left|\hat{\boldsymbol{A}}_1\left(T^{-1}\boldsymbol{X}'\boldsymbol{X}\right)\hat{\boldsymbol{A}}_1'\right| + T\log\left||\hat{\boldsymbol{B}}|\right|, \quad (11.108)$$

where $\hat{\boldsymbol{A}}_1$ and $\hat{\boldsymbol{B}}$ are the relevant maximum likelihood estimates. The test is computed by:

$$\xi\left(M - n_1^2\right) = 2\left(\ell_1 - \ell_0\right) \underset{a}{\sim} \chi^2\left(M - n_1^2\right) \quad (11.109)$$

[7] Here we consider complete systems with $|\boldsymbol{B}| \neq 0$; more generally, see Richard, 1984.

for M a priori restrictions on $\boldsymbol{A}$. If $\xi(\cdot)$ is significant, the model fails to encompass the system. Thus, that particular implementation of the underlying theory should be rejected.

There may be several models consistent with the identification restrictions, even if all are highly over-identified. In particular, this is true for just-identified models when $M = n_1^2$, so that $\xi(\cdot)$ is not computable. More generally, however, satisfying the test in (11.109) is manifestly insufficient to justify a model, especially if the system is itself not rigorously tested for congruency.

11.13 Derived statistics

When a model is a congruent reduction of the system, other derived statistics can usefully highlight its properties. Such statistics include forecast tests, the computation of the restricted reduced form, long-run and interim multipliers, and stochastic-dynamic simulation to ascertain the data moments predicted by the model; however, the last is not a valid model-evaluation technique (see Chong and Hendry, 1986 and Ch.8).

From the model estimator, the MLE of the restricted reduced form is:

$$\tilde{\boldsymbol{\Pi}} = -\hat{\boldsymbol{B}}^{-1}\hat{\boldsymbol{C}}. \qquad (11.110)$$

The covariance matrix of the restricted reduced-form residuals for the subset of stochastic equations is obtained by letting:

$$\boldsymbol{B}^{-1} = \begin{pmatrix} \boldsymbol{B}^{11} & \boldsymbol{B}^{12} \\ \boldsymbol{B}^{21} & \boldsymbol{B}^{22} \end{pmatrix}, \qquad (11.111)$$

where $\boldsymbol{B}^{ij}$ is $n_i \times n_j$. Then:

$$\boldsymbol{\Omega} = \boldsymbol{B}^{11}\boldsymbol{\Sigma}\boldsymbol{B}^{11\prime}. \qquad (11.112)$$

The variance-covariance matrix of the restricted reduced-form coefficients is:

$$\mathsf{V}\left[\left(\tilde{\boldsymbol{\Pi}}\right)^{v}\right] = \boldsymbol{J}\mathsf{V}\left[\hat{\boldsymbol{\phi}}\right]\boldsymbol{J}' \text{ where } \boldsymbol{J} = \frac{\partial \boldsymbol{\Pi}^{v}}{\partial \boldsymbol{\phi}'} = -\left[\boldsymbol{B}^{-1} \otimes (\boldsymbol{\Pi}' : \boldsymbol{I}_p)\right], \qquad (11.113)$$

and the estimated variances of the elements of $\hat{\boldsymbol{\phi}}$ are given by:

$$\mathsf{V}\left[\hat{\boldsymbol{\phi}}\right] = \left[\left(\hat{\boldsymbol{\Sigma}}^{-1} \otimes \hat{\boldsymbol{Q}}\boldsymbol{Z}'\boldsymbol{Z}\hat{\boldsymbol{Q}}'\right)^{u}\right]^{-1}, \qquad (11.114)$$

where, before inversion, we choose the rows and columns of the right-hand side corresponding to unrestricted elements of $\boldsymbol{A}_1$ only.

Variables which are included unrestrictedly in all equations of the model, such as dummy variables for the constant term, seasonal shift factors, or trend, can be concentrated out of the likelihood function. This reduces the dimensionality of the parameter vector and enhances numerical optimization. The stochastic part of the model is written as:

$$\boldsymbol{A}_1\boldsymbol{X}' + \boldsymbol{D}\boldsymbol{S}' = \boldsymbol{U}', \qquad (11.115)$$

where $\boldsymbol{D}$ is the $n_1 \times q$ unconstrained matrix of coefficients and $\boldsymbol{S}$ is the $T \times q$ matrix of observations on the unrestricted variables. Then (see Hendry, 1971), the log-likelihood $\ell(\boldsymbol{A}_1, \boldsymbol{D}, \boldsymbol{\Sigma})$ is:

$$K + T\log||\boldsymbol{B}|| - \frac{T}{2}\log|\boldsymbol{\Sigma}| - \tfrac{1}{2}\mathrm{tr}\left(\boldsymbol{\Sigma}^{-1}\left(\boldsymbol{A}_1\boldsymbol{X}'\boldsymbol{X}\boldsymbol{A}_1' + 2\boldsymbol{A}_1\boldsymbol{X}'\boldsymbol{S}\boldsymbol{D}' + \boldsymbol{D}\boldsymbol{S}'\boldsymbol{S}\boldsymbol{D}'\right)\right). \tag{11.116}$$

Since $\boldsymbol{D}$ is unrestricted, maximizing $\ell(\cdot)$ with respect to $\boldsymbol{D}$ yields:

$$\boldsymbol{D}_c = \boldsymbol{A}_1\boldsymbol{X}'\boldsymbol{S}\left(\boldsymbol{S}'\boldsymbol{S}\right)^{-1}. \tag{11.117}$$

Let $\boldsymbol{X}^* = (\boldsymbol{I}_T - \boldsymbol{S}(\boldsymbol{S}'\boldsymbol{S})^{-1}\boldsymbol{S}')\boldsymbol{X}$ denote the 'de-seasonalized' data, namely the residuals from the regression of $\boldsymbol{X}$ on $\boldsymbol{S}$, then the concentrated likelihood function is:

$$\ell^*(\cdot) = K + T\log||\boldsymbol{B}|| - \frac{T}{2}\log|\boldsymbol{\Sigma}| - \tfrac{1}{2}\mathrm{tr}\left(\boldsymbol{\Sigma}^{-1}\left(\boldsymbol{A}_1\boldsymbol{X}^{*\prime}\boldsymbol{X}^*\boldsymbol{A}_1'\right)\right). \tag{11.118}$$

From (11.117), the variance-covariance matrix of the $\hat{\boldsymbol{D}}$ coefficients is:

$$\mathsf{V}\left[\left(\hat{\boldsymbol{D}}\right)^v\right] = \hat{\boldsymbol{\Sigma}} \otimes \left(\boldsymbol{S}'\boldsymbol{S}\right)^{-1} + \boldsymbol{J}_s\mathsf{V}\left[\hat{\boldsymbol{\phi}}\right]\boldsymbol{J}_s', \tag{11.119}$$

where $\boldsymbol{J}_s = (\boldsymbol{I}_{n_1} \otimes (\boldsymbol{S}'\boldsymbol{S})^{-1}\boldsymbol{S}'\boldsymbol{X})$.

To test for predictive failure, 1-step forecast errors $\hat{\boldsymbol{\nu}}_{T+i,1} = \boldsymbol{y}_{T+i} - \hat{\boldsymbol{y}}_{T+i,1}$ are calculated as (see Doornik and Hendry, 1994a):

$$\hat{\boldsymbol{\nu}}_{T+i,1} = \boldsymbol{\Pi}\boldsymbol{w}_{T+i} + \boldsymbol{\nu}_{T+i} - \hat{\boldsymbol{\Pi}}\boldsymbol{w}_{T+i} = \left(\boldsymbol{I}_n \otimes \boldsymbol{w}_{T+i}'\right)\left(\boldsymbol{\Pi}^v - \hat{\boldsymbol{\Pi}}^v\right) + \boldsymbol{\nu}_{T+i}, \tag{11.120}$$

since $\hat{\boldsymbol{\nu}}_{T+i,1}$ is $(n \times 1)$. To a first approximation, $\hat{\boldsymbol{\Pi}}$ is an unbiased estimator of $\boldsymbol{\Pi}$, so we take $\mathsf{E}[\hat{\boldsymbol{\nu}}_{T+i,1}] = \boldsymbol{0}$. From (11.19):

$$\begin{aligned}\mathsf{V}\left[\hat{\boldsymbol{\nu}}_{T+i,1}\right] &= \boldsymbol{\Omega} + \left(\boldsymbol{I}_n \otimes \boldsymbol{w}_{T+i}'\right)\mathsf{V}\left[\hat{\boldsymbol{\Pi}}^v\right]\left(\boldsymbol{I}_n \otimes \boldsymbol{w}_{T+i}\right) \\ &= \boldsymbol{\Omega}\left(1 + \boldsymbol{w}_{T+i}'\left(\boldsymbol{W}'\boldsymbol{W}\right)^{-1}\boldsymbol{w}_{T+i}\right) \qquad = \boldsymbol{\Psi}_{T+i} \text{ (say)},\end{aligned} \tag{11.121}$$

so that:

$$\hat{\boldsymbol{\nu}}_{T+i} \underset{app}{\sim} \mathsf{IN}_n\left[\boldsymbol{0}, \boldsymbol{\Psi}_{T+i}\right], \tag{11.122}$$

where $\boldsymbol{\Psi}_{T+i}$ reflects both innovation and parameter uncertainty (see e.g. Calzolari, 1981, Chong and Hendry, 1986, and Clements and Hendry, 1994). The derivation assumes constant parameters and homoscedastic innovation errors over the forecast period, which may be invalid assumptions in practice — see Clements and Hendry (1995) on the general issue of forecasting under conditions of parameter change.

To derive forecast accuracy, and constancy, tests requires the joint (inter-temporal) variance matrix of all forecast errors. Stacking the H rows over a forecast horizon of H periods and vectorizing, (11.120) yields:

$$\hat{\boldsymbol{\nu}} = \left(\boldsymbol{I}_H \otimes \boldsymbol{W}_H\right)\left(\boldsymbol{\Pi}^v - \hat{\boldsymbol{\Pi}}^v\right) + \left(\boldsymbol{V}_H\right)^v, \tag{11.123}$$

where $\boldsymbol{W}_H$ is the $(H \times p)$ matrix of data for the forecast period $T+1, \ldots, T+H$. Again $\mathsf{E}[\hat{\boldsymbol{\nu}}] \simeq \mathbf{0}$ and:

$$\mathsf{V}[\hat{\boldsymbol{\nu}}] = \boldsymbol{\Omega} \otimes \left(\boldsymbol{I}_H + \boldsymbol{W}_H \left(\boldsymbol{W}'\boldsymbol{W} \right)^{-1} \boldsymbol{W}_H' \right) = \boldsymbol{\Psi}. \tag{11.124}$$

Under the null of no parameter change, tests can be based on the approximate test statistic:

$$\eta = \hat{\boldsymbol{\nu}}' \hat{\boldsymbol{\Psi}}^{-1} \hat{\boldsymbol{\nu}} \underset{app}{\sim} \chi^2 (nH). \tag{11.125}$$

In an operational context, when the forecast horizon H exceeds unity, *ex ante* statements about an economy require knowledge of all the conditioning variables, which necessitates a closed system. To illustrate the approach, after transforming to I(0) variables, let $\boldsymbol{x}_t^* = (\boldsymbol{y}_t' : \boldsymbol{w}_t')'$ be the vector of all the variables less the longest lag in the sub-systems determining $(\boldsymbol{y}_t : \boldsymbol{z}_t)$. Then the closed system can be written in companion form as:

$$\boldsymbol{x}_t^* = \boldsymbol{\Gamma} \boldsymbol{x}_{t-1}^* + \boldsymbol{\zeta}_t \text{ where } \boldsymbol{\zeta}_t \sim \mathsf{IN}_{Nh} \left[\mathbf{0}, \boldsymbol{\Lambda} \right], \tag{11.126}$$

so that $\boldsymbol{\zeta}_t$ is an innovation against $\boldsymbol{x}_{t-1}^*$. Then (11.126) is a stacked version of (11.25) in I(0) space. $\boldsymbol{\Gamma}$ depends on all the parameters of that system, which we denote by the vector of parameters $\boldsymbol{\delta}$ (to distinguish from the structural parameters $\boldsymbol{\phi}$). Since MLEs are equivariant to functional transformations, the MLE of $\boldsymbol{\Gamma}$ is given by $\hat{\boldsymbol{\Gamma}} = \boldsymbol{\Gamma}(\hat{\boldsymbol{\delta}})$, from which $\mathsf{V}[\hat{\boldsymbol{\Gamma}}^v]$ can be derived as in (11.113). The optimal predictor of a mean-zero martingale difference sequence is zero, so $\mathsf{E}[\boldsymbol{\zeta}_{T+i}] = \mathbf{0} \, \forall i \geq 1$. Consequently, once $\boldsymbol{x}_T^*$ is known, the best predictor of $\boldsymbol{x}_{T+i}^*$ for $i > 0$ is:

$$\hat{\boldsymbol{x}}_{T+i}^* = \hat{\boldsymbol{\Gamma}}^i \boldsymbol{x}_T^* \text{ with forecast errors } \hat{\boldsymbol{\zeta}}_{T+i} = \boldsymbol{x}_{T+i}^* - \hat{\boldsymbol{x}}_{T+i}^*. \tag{11.127}$$

The properties of this predictor, and a derivation of its variance matrix $\mathsf{V}[\hat{\boldsymbol{\zeta}}_{T+i}]$ are provided in Clements and Hendry (1995) *inter alia*. The model must characterize the economy as accurately in the forecast period as it did over the estimation sample if the prediction errors are to be from the same distribution as that assumed in (11.126), namely $\mathsf{IN}[\mathbf{0}, \boldsymbol{\Lambda}]$ (ignoring the sampling variation due to estimating $\boldsymbol{\Gamma}$). This is a strong requirement, and seems unlikely to be met unless $\boldsymbol{\Gamma}$ is constant within sample: the further condition that $\boldsymbol{\Gamma}$ is invariant to any regime changes out-of-sample is considered in Chapter 14. Even if $\boldsymbol{\Gamma}$ is both constant and invariant, $\mathsf{V}[\sum_{i=0}^{j-1} \boldsymbol{\Gamma}^i \boldsymbol{\zeta}_{T+i+1}]$ will generally increase quite rapidly with j. Also, the forecast errors are heteroscedastic and serially correlated, so care is required in interpreting multi-step forecast errors.

11.14 Empirical model estimates

A restricted simultaneous model in the three variables $(\Delta \log(M/PY)_t, \Delta R_t, CI_t)$ was developed for the parsimonious VECM in Chapter 8. The empirical estimates are by FIML over 1964(1)–1989(2) for the over-identified representation shown in (11.128). Although there is a redundancy in the representation using these three variables, since

$(\Delta R_t, CI_t)$ alone would suffice, a more interpretable model results from retaining both of the differenced variables, with the equilibrium correction defined by the identity:

$$CI_t \equiv CI_{t-1} + \Delta \log (M/PY) + 7.54\Delta R_t.$$

Introducing CI_t also facilitates dynamic forecasts as shown below.

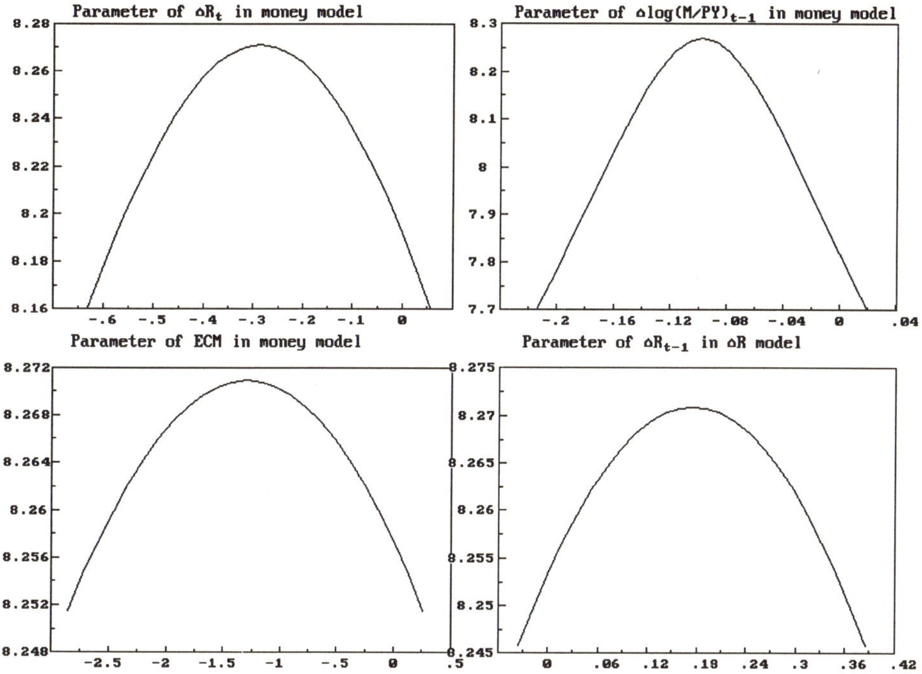

Fig. 11.2 Log-likelihood grids

The money-demand equation is well determined, but the uncertainty about ΔR_t has risen substantially due to that variable being endogenized, illustrating the potential advantages of valid weak exogeneity information. The other coefficients are similar to the earlier estimates reported in Chapter 8. However, the R_t equation is nearly null and suggests that interest rates are close to a random walk.

$$\widehat{\Delta \log \left(\frac{M}{PY}\right)_t} = \underset{(0.002)}{0.009} - \underset{(0.91)}{1.30}\, \Delta R_t - \underset{(0.09)}{0.29}\, \Delta \log \left(\frac{M}{PY}\right)_{t-1} - \underset{(0.012)}{0.097}\, \left(\log \left(\frac{M}{PY}\right) + 7.54R\right)_{t-1}. \quad (11.128)$$

$$\widehat{\Delta R_t} = \underset{(0.001)}{0.0001} + \underset{(0.10)}{0.18}\, \Delta R_{t-1}. \quad (11.129)$$

Figure 11.2 shows the log-likelihood grids for each estimated parameter, holding all other parameters fixed at their MLE; this checks for the presence of flat likelihoods or multiple optima, if any exist. Here, the functions reveal no difficulties and have well-defined maxima. Table 11.1 records some summary statistics for each equation and the model.

Table 11.1 Summary statistics

equation	$\hat{\sigma}$	R	$\log\|\hat{\Omega}\|$	R^2	r
$\log(M/PY)$	2.0%	0.61	–	–	–
R	1.4%	0.29	–	–	–
model	–	–	−16.5	0.50	0.34

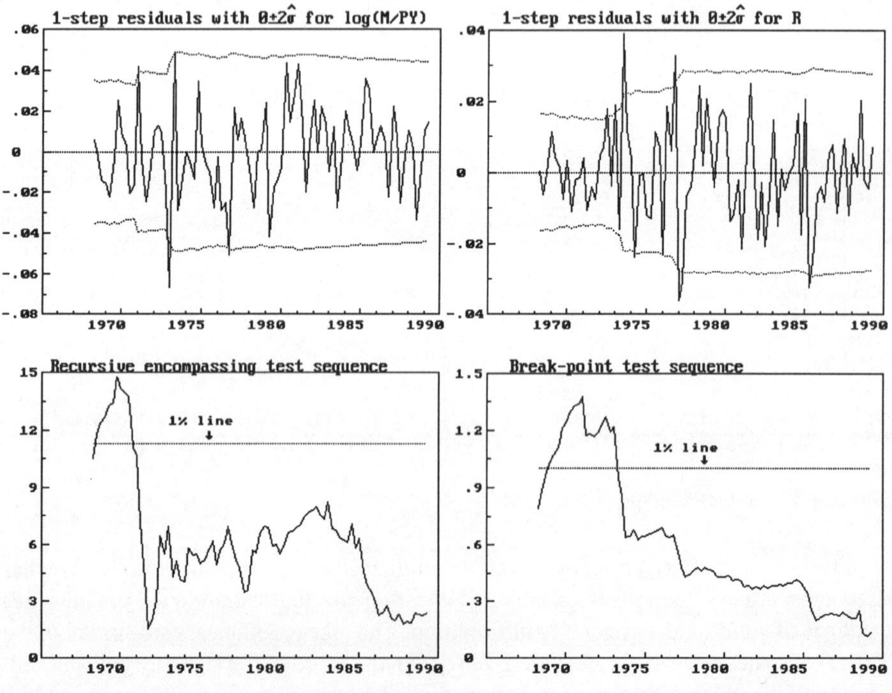

Fig. 11.3 Model recursive estimates

The likelihood-ratio test of the over-identifying restrictions is $\chi^2(2) = 2.35$. However, the simultaneity is adding little to the explanation in this instance, although the cross-equation residual correlation is radically altered. The diagnostic tests and graphs were similar to those for the VECM, and Fig. 11.3 reports recursive statistics for the model estimates (obtained using PcFiml). The equation for $\log(M/PY)$ is constant, but the equation for R is not. This induces an overall failure of constancy for the model, and an associated apparent failure of the model to encompass the system at the start of the estimation sample.

Figure 11.4 plots 12-quarter-ahead forecasts from the model; the error bars allow for the uncertainty from $\boldsymbol{\Lambda}$, but not from $\widehat{\boldsymbol{\Gamma}}$. There is almost no increase in uncertainty for the two equations in differences, but a marked increase for the cointegrating vector.

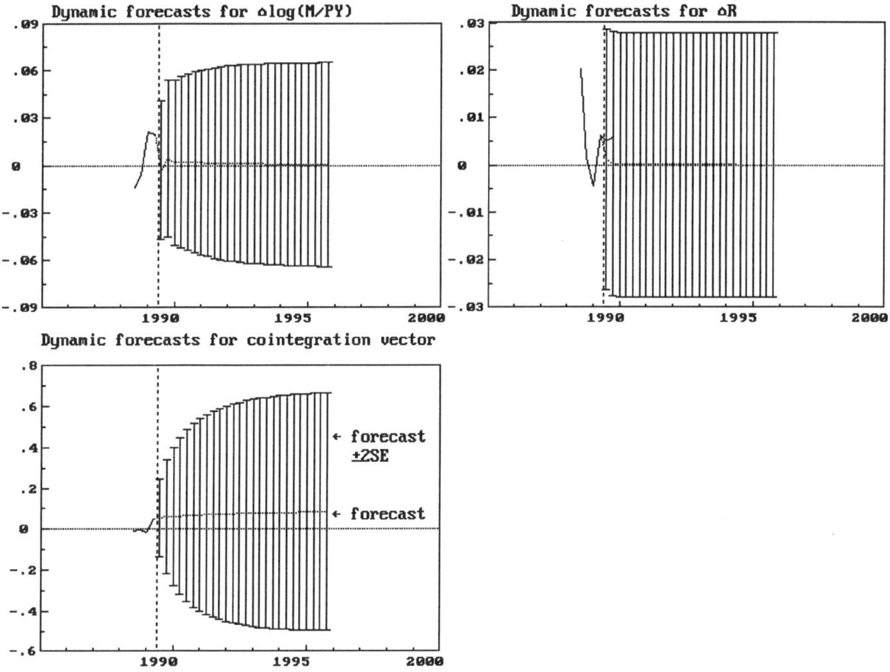

Fig. 11.4 12-quarter ahead forecasts

That concludes our discussion of estimation and associated tools. To estimate new models, formulate their likelihood function, derive the relevant estimator generating equation for the class of possible methods, and select appropriate members either on computational grounds or because of their particular statistical properties. Locating the maximum numerically is feasible with modern computers, and is discussed in Chapter A5, although selecting congruent representations may be more difficult for complicated data processes. The next set of issues concern what the estimated numbers might mean, and how the models might be evaluated: in particular, how we can learn whether models are congruent. An important aspect of interpreting empirical results is the measurement accuracy of the data and its correspondence to the theoretically desired magnitude, so Chapter 12 considers measurement problems before we turn to the theory of testing and evaluation in Chapter 13.

11.15 Exercises

11.1 Consider the simultaneous equations model:

$$\boldsymbol{B}\boldsymbol{y}_t + \boldsymbol{C}\boldsymbol{z}_t = \boldsymbol{\epsilon}_t \text{ where } \mathsf{E}[\boldsymbol{z}_t\boldsymbol{\epsilon}_s'] = \mathbf{0}\ \forall t, s. \tag{11.130}$$

In (11.130), $\boldsymbol{y}_t$ is endogenous and $\boldsymbol{z}_t$ is strongly exogenous for $(\boldsymbol{B}, \boldsymbol{C})$. The detailed specification of the equations is:

$$y_{1t} + \beta_{12}y_{2t} + \beta_{13}y_{3t} + \gamma_{11}z_{1t} + \gamma_{13}z_{3t} = \epsilon_{1t} \tag{11.131}$$

$$\beta_{21}y_{1t} + y_{2t} + \gamma_{21}z_{1t} + \gamma_{22}z_{2t} = \epsilon_{2t} \tag{11.132}$$

$$\beta_{31}y_{1t} + y_{3t} + \gamma_{33}z_{3t} = \epsilon_{3t}. \tag{11.133}$$

(a) Discuss the identification of the parameters in terms of rank and order conditions.
(b) How would you estimate any identifiable unknown parameters if $\boldsymbol{\epsilon}_t \sim \mathsf{IN}_3[\mathbf{0}, \boldsymbol{\Sigma}]$?
(c) How would you test any available over-identifying restrictions?

11.2 Consider the linear over-identified simultaneous equations model:

$$\boldsymbol{A}\boldsymbol{x}_t = \boldsymbol{B}\boldsymbol{y}_t + \boldsymbol{C}\boldsymbol{z}_t = \boldsymbol{\epsilon}_t \sim \mathsf{IN}_n[\mathbf{0}, \boldsymbol{\Sigma}], \tag{11.134}$$

where $\boldsymbol{A}^{v_u} = \boldsymbol{\theta}$ are the p unrestricted parameters, $(\cdot)^{v_u}$ is a combined vectoring and selection operator, and $\boldsymbol{z}_t$ is strongly exogenous for $\boldsymbol{\theta}$ with:

$$\mathsf{E}[\boldsymbol{x}_t \mid \boldsymbol{z}_t] = \boldsymbol{P}\boldsymbol{z}_t \text{ when } \boldsymbol{P}' = (\boldsymbol{\Pi}' : \boldsymbol{I}) \text{ and } \boldsymbol{\Pi} = -\boldsymbol{B}^{-1}\boldsymbol{C}. \tag{11.135}$$

Using $\boldsymbol{X}' = (\boldsymbol{x}_1 \ldots \boldsymbol{x}_T)$, etc.), the score vector is:

$$\left(\boldsymbol{\Sigma}_c^{-1}\boldsymbol{A}\boldsymbol{X}'\boldsymbol{Z}\boldsymbol{P}_c'\right)^{v_u} = \mathbf{0} \quad (p \text{ equations to be solved for } \boldsymbol{\theta}) \tag{11.136}$$

with:

$$\boldsymbol{\Sigma}_c = T^{-1}\boldsymbol{A}\boldsymbol{X}'\boldsymbol{X}\boldsymbol{A}' \text{ and } \boldsymbol{P}_c' = \left(-\boldsymbol{C}'\boldsymbol{B}^{-1\prime} : \boldsymbol{I}\right). \tag{11.137}$$

(a) Explain why it is sensible to solve an expression like (11.136) for $\boldsymbol{\theta}$ given (11.134).
(b) Under what conditions are solutions to (11.136) as efficient as FIML and why?
(c) Describe three solutions to (11.136) which yield consistent estimates of $\boldsymbol{\theta}$, not all of the same asymptotic efficiency, and derive the limiting distribution of one of these.

(Oxford M.Phil., 1982, 1989)

11.3 Consider the system:

$$\boldsymbol{y} = \boldsymbol{X}\boldsymbol{\beta} + \boldsymbol{\epsilon} \tag{11.138}$$

where $\boldsymbol{y}' = (y_1 \ldots y_T)$ and $\boldsymbol{X}' = (\boldsymbol{x}_1 \ldots \boldsymbol{x}_T)$. However, $\mathsf{E}[\boldsymbol{x}_t\epsilon_t] \neq \mathbf{0}$ when:

$$\boldsymbol{X} = \boldsymbol{Z}\boldsymbol{\Pi}' + \boldsymbol{V} \tag{11.139}$$

where $\boldsymbol{Z}' = (\boldsymbol{z}_1 \ldots \boldsymbol{z}_T)$, $\mathsf{E}[\boldsymbol{Z}'\boldsymbol{\epsilon}] = \mathbf{0}$, and $\mathsf{E}[\boldsymbol{z}_t\boldsymbol{v}_s'] = \mathbf{0}\ \forall t, s$ when $\boldsymbol{x}_t$ and $\boldsymbol{z}_t$ are $k \times 1$ and $n \times 1$ respectively, with $k \leq n$, and $\text{rank}(\boldsymbol{\Pi}) = k$.

(a) Show that the two-stage least-squares (2SLS) estimator $\hat{\beta}$ of β can be obtained by:

$$\underset{\beta}{\operatorname{argmin}}\, \epsilon' Z \left(Z'Z\right)^{-1} Z'\epsilon. \tag{11.140}$$

(b) Derive the limiting distribution of $\hat{\beta}$, stating any assumptions and theorems required.

(c) Show that a loss of asymptotic efficiency results if only a subset Z_a of Z is used in (11.140).

(Oxford M.Phil., 1982)

11.4 Consider the structural equation:

$$y_{1t} = \beta y_{2t} + \nu_t \text{ where } \nu_t \sim \mathsf{IN}\left[0, \sigma_\nu^2\right] \tag{11.141}$$

when there are $k > 1$ valid instrumental variables z_t which can be used for an instrumental variables estimator (IV) $\hat{\beta}$ of β. Alternatively, the same model could have been formulated as:

$$y_{2t} = \gamma y_{1t} + \epsilon_t \text{ where } \epsilon_t \sim \mathsf{IN}\left[0, \sigma_\epsilon^2\right] \tag{11.142}$$

with the IV estimator $\hat{\gamma}$ again based on z_t. Prove that $\hat{\beta}\hat{\gamma} \leq 1$. Discuss this result, considering whether or not the estimator $1/\hat{\gamma}$ of β is consistent. Is any method of estimating β independent of the normalization choice between (11.141) and (11.142)?

(Oxford M.Phil., 1983, 1989)

11.5 In the simultaneous system:

$$\begin{aligned} \boldsymbol{y}_1 - \beta \boldsymbol{y}_2 &= \boldsymbol{u}_1 \\ \boldsymbol{y}_2 - \gamma \boldsymbol{z} &= \boldsymbol{u}_2 \end{aligned} \quad \text{where} \begin{pmatrix} u_{1t} \\ u_{2t} \end{pmatrix} \sim \mathsf{IN}_2\left[\mathbf{0}, \boldsymbol{\Sigma}\right] \text{ for } t = 1, \ldots, T,$$

$\boldsymbol{y}_1$ and $\boldsymbol{y}_2$ are $T \times 1$ vectors of observations on endogenous variables, $\boldsymbol{z}$ is a $T \times 1$ vector of observations on a variable strongly exogenous for (β, γ), and $\boldsymbol{u}_1$ and $\boldsymbol{u}_2$ are $T \times 1$ vectors of errors with an unrestricted covariance matrix $\boldsymbol{\Sigma}$, which is symmetric and positive definite.

(a) Derive the reduced-form equations, and obtain least-squares estimators of their coefficients and error variance matrix.

(b) Show that the indirect and two-stage least-squares estimators of β are equivalent.

(c) Another estimator of β is obtained by minimizing the determinant of the reduced-form error variance matrix, and solving for β from the resulting estimates of the reduced form coefficients. What is this estimator? Is it also equivalent to the estimators in (a)?

(d) Briefly describe one other equivalent estimator. Are all of these estimators equivalent when it is known that $\boldsymbol{\Sigma}$ is diagonal?

(Oxford M.Phil., 1992)

12

Measurement Problems in Econometrics

This chapter considers four measurement problems. First, the errors-in-variables model is discussed, then methods are investigated for estimating models subject to data measurement errors. An estimator generating equation is derived, which has weighted least squares and instrumental variables as solutions. Next, dynamic latent-variables models are analysed. A Monte Carlo simulation technique for evaluating likelihood functions is described, based on artificial factorizations of the sequential joint density of the observables and latent variables. An application to a one-parameter dynamic min-condition model is discussed and extensions to models with weakly exogenous variables are noted. Then the effects of data revisions in I(1) processes are studied. Finally, the impact of measurement errors in an equilibrium-correction model is investigated.

12.1 Introduction

One of the few econometric problems not to have surfaced during the typology in Chapter 7 was that of measurement errors. Models with errors in variables due to measurement errors, and models with errors in equations were equally prominent in the early history of econometrics (see Morgan, 1989). For example, Frisch (1934) proposed the method of Confluence Analysis to study systems of economic relationships subject to errors of measurement and Koopmans (1937) included both sources of error in his time-series framework. Since the formalization of modern econometrics in Haavelmo (1944) and Koopmans (1950a), however, the major focus of attention has been on errors in equations, and so far this book has been no exception.

In many respects, the demise of the errors-in-variables model (EVM) as a standard paradigm is surprising, because Haavelmo (1944) stressed the distinctions between the latent variables of economic theories, their correctly measured empirical counterparts and the error-ridden observed values available to the econometrician. Also, Morgenstern (1950) highlighted the poor quality of many economic data series so that the absence of EVM analyses cannot be attributed to either the negligible importance of measurement errors or to ignorance about their presence. Thus, the low profile of EVM in present econometrics is more due to a lack of useful ideas than an absence of important data measurement errors. As shown in Hendry and Morgan (1989) *inter alia*, the Frisch Confluence Analysis model (and EVM generally) raises a host of difficulties, but it is inappropriate to ignore measurement errors merely because they are awkward to handle. At one level, the errors-in-variables notion is too broad as it includes all deviations between latent variables and observables, from the Frisch Confluence model noted in section 7.8, through the DHSY explanation of the rise in the saving ratio as due to mismeasurement of income, to all notions of expectations formation. At another level, we can never determine the extent of measurement errors, although we often do have an idea about the range or variance of such errors, as well as information about the extent of revisions or cross-comparisons, as with GNP identities. Chapter A2 briefly considers measurability and scales of measurement.

Four econometric measurement problems are now considered. In the next section, the errors-in-variables model is discussed, then the implications of data measurement errors are analysed. The EVM is related to the simultaneous-equations model (SEM), and an estimator generating equation which applies to both types of model is obtained. Next, in section 12.3, dynamic latent-variables models are considered. A Monte Carlo simulation technique for evaluating likelihood functions is described, based on artificial factorizations of the sequential joint density of the observables and latent variables, and is applied to a simple dynamic min-condition model. Extensions to models with weakly exogenous variables are noted. Then in section 12.4, the effects of data revisions in I(1) processes are studied. Finally, section 12.5 describes the impact in finite samples of measurement errors on estimating an equilibrium-correction model.

12.2 Errors in variables

Consider an m-dimensional stationary stochastic process $\{\omega_t\}$ with joint sequential density $\mathsf{D}_\omega(\omega_t|\boldsymbol{\Omega}_{t-1}, \boldsymbol{\rho})$, for $\boldsymbol{\rho}_p \in \mathbb{R}^l$, given by:

$$\omega_t \mid \boldsymbol{\Omega}_{t-1} \sim \mathsf{N}_m \left[\boldsymbol{\Upsilon}\omega_{t-1}, \boldsymbol{\Phi}\right], \tag{12.1}$$

where $\boldsymbol{\Omega}_{t-1} = (\omega_1 \ldots \omega_{t-1})$, and all the latent roots of $\boldsymbol{\Upsilon}$ are inside the unit circle. Rewriting (12.1) in model form:

$$\omega_t = \boldsymbol{\Upsilon}\omega_{t-1} + \epsilon_t \;\text{ with }\; \epsilon_t \sim \mathsf{IN}_m \left[\mathbf{0}, \boldsymbol{\Phi}\right], \tag{12.2}$$

where $\mathsf{E}[\omega_t|\boldsymbol{\Omega}_{t-1}] = \boldsymbol{\Upsilon}\omega_{t-1}$ and $\mathsf{E}[\omega_{t-1}\epsilon_t'] = \mathbf{0}$. Let $\omega_t' = (\eta_t : \chi_t' : \xi_t')$, where the dimensions of the sub-vectors χ_t and ξ_t are $n \times 1$ and $k \times 1$, so that $m = 1 + n + k$. Factorize $\mathsf{D}_\omega(\omega_t|\boldsymbol{\Omega}_{t-1}, \boldsymbol{\rho})$ as:

$$\mathsf{D}_{\eta|\chi,\xi}\left(\eta_t \mid \chi_t, \xi_t, \boldsymbol{\Omega}_{t-1}, \boldsymbol{\mu}_1\right) \mathsf{D}_{\chi|\xi}\left(\chi_t \mid \xi_t, \boldsymbol{\Omega}_{t-1}, \boldsymbol{\mu}_2\right) \mathsf{D}_{\xi}\left(\xi_t \mid \boldsymbol{\Omega}_{t-1}, \boldsymbol{\mu}_3\right), \tag{12.3}$$

where $\boldsymbol{\mu} = \boldsymbol{f}(\boldsymbol{\rho})$ supports the factorization and:

$$(\boldsymbol{\mu}_1 : \boldsymbol{\mu}_2 : \boldsymbol{\mu}_3) \in \mathcal{M}_1 \times \mathcal{M}_2 \times \mathcal{M}_3 \subseteq \mathbb{R}^l. \tag{12.4}$$

The relationship of concern to the economist is a linear model between η_t and χ_t given by:

$$\eta_t = \beta'\chi_t + \nu_t \text{ with } \nu_t \mid \Omega_{t-1} \sim \mathsf{N}\left[0, \sigma_v^2\right], \tag{12.5}$$

where χ_t is weakly exogenous for the parameter of interest β, and $\mathsf{E}[\chi_t\nu_t] = \mathbf{0}$. Let $\gamma' = (1 : -\beta' : \mathbf{0}')$ such that:

$$\gamma'\omega_t = \eta_t - \beta'\chi_t = \nu_t, \tag{12.6}$$

so from (12.2):

$$\gamma'\omega_t = \gamma'\Upsilon\omega_{t-1} + \gamma'\epsilon_t = \nu_t. \tag{12.7}$$

Since ν_t is an innovation relative to Ω_{t-1}, then $\gamma'\Upsilon = \mathbf{0}'$, so $\gamma'\epsilon_t = \nu_t$ and $\sigma_v^2 = \gamma'\Phi\gamma$. In terms of (12.3), $\mathsf{D}_\omega(\omega_t|\Omega_{t-1}, \rho)$ simplifies to:

$$\mathsf{D}_{\eta|\chi}\left(\eta_t \mid \chi_t, \mu_1\right) \mathsf{D}_{\chi|\xi}\left(\chi_t \mid \xi_t, \Omega_{t-1}, \mu_2\right) \mathsf{D}_{\xi}\left(\xi_t \mid \Omega_{t-1}, \mu_3\right), \tag{12.8}$$

where $\mathsf{E}[\eta_t|\chi_t] = \beta'\chi_t$ and $(\chi_t : \xi_t)$ are weakly exogenous for β. So far, the DGP is typical of those discussed in Part I.

When $\{\omega_t\}$ is an observable process, β can be estimated by regression from (12.5). However, we allow for the possibility that the observed process $w_t = (y_t : x_t' : g_t')'$ differs from ω_t by a vector of measurement errors u_t:

$$w_t = \omega_t + u_t \text{ where } u_t \sim \mathsf{IN}_m\left[\mathbf{0}, \Gamma\right]. \tag{12.9}$$

For simplicity, we consider the case where $\{u_t\}$ is serially independent and $\mathsf{E}[\omega_t u_t'] = \mathbf{0}\,\forall t$, so that $\mathsf{E}[\epsilon_t u_t'] = \mathbf{0}$ as well. In practice, measurement errors may be systematic and may be dependent on the latent variables ω_t; in either case, progress in understanding the DGP would depend on developing useful models of such systematic dependencies. If any ω_t were measured without error, the corresponding row and column of Γ would be zero. Intercepts could be incorporated in the analysis by letting one of the χ_t be unity, with the associated u_t being zero, but at the cost of letting one of the roots of Υ be unity; below, we will retain a zero mean. Super-imposing the measurement process (12.9) onto (12.2) induces:

$$w_t = \Upsilon w_{t-1} + \epsilon_t + u_t - \Upsilon u_{t-1}, \tag{12.10}$$

which is a vector autoregressive-moving average process for the observed data. It is not easy to calculate $\mathsf{E}[y_t|x_t, g_t, W_{t-1}]$, but in general it is not equal to $\beta' x_t$.

There are several econometric issues. First, (12.3) and (12.8) may lead an economist to analyse only the corresponding conditional density, namely:

$$\mathsf{D}_{y|x}\left(y_t \mid x_t, W_{t-1}, \phi_1\right),$$

and hence try to learn β from the conditional equation $\mathsf{E}[y_t|x_t]$; we consider the properties of this approach below.

Second, a major difficulty in any EVM is the interpretation of the latent variables, and hence of the measurement errors. If (12.2) is the DGP of $\{\omega_t\}$ and corresponds to how economic agents actually behave, then the agents must be observing $\{\omega_t\}$, and so only the econometrician has the problem of analysing the mis-measured variables $\{w_t\}$. This paradigm could occur when η_t was a plan and χ_t a vector of expectations held by agents when forming the plan: with observed outcomes y_t and x_t, the analysis generalizes section 6.1.4. However, when the data $\{w_t\}$ actually collected differs from the true values $\{\omega_t\}$ (due to omissions, arithmetical mistakes, recording errors etc.), so that $\{u_t\}$ is a pure measurement error, then it is less reasonable to maintain that agents can observe $\{\omega_t\}$ but the econometrician cannot. At one extreme, each economic agent may perceive their real income correctly, but the econometrician may mis-measure aggregate real income, which would be consistent with a DGP like (12.2); at the other extreme, since the only available measure of the balance of payments deficit is common to both agents and the observing econometrician, it is unimaginable that the behaviour of agents could depend directly on Ω_{t-1} (as opposed to W_{t-1}) in such a case. Consequently, we will interpret ω_t as a vector of latent variables like plans and expectations, and w_t as the associated measured values of the outcomes.

Finally, the role of the complete joint density of the observables must be investigated since important information may be obtainable from g_t, even though ξ_t is irrelevant when η_t and χ_t are correctly observed.

12.2.1 Analysing the errors-in-variables model

The first consequence of observing w_t rather than ω_t is that although χ_t is weakly exogenous for β, x_t is not. Let S be a selection matrix such that $Sw_t = x_t$, and pre-multiply (12.10) by γ', noting from (12.7) that $\gamma'\Upsilon = 0'$, then (see Ch.A4):

$$\gamma' w_t = y_t - \beta' x_t = \gamma' (\epsilon_t + u_t) = e_t, \tag{12.11}$$

(say) where $e_t \sim \mathsf{IN}[0, \sigma_e^2]$ with $\sigma_e^2 = \gamma'(\Phi + \Gamma)\gamma$. However, $\gamma'\epsilon_t = \nu_t$ and:

$$\mathsf{E}[x_t\nu_t] = \mathsf{E}[\chi_t\nu_t] + S\mathsf{E}[u_t\epsilon_t']\gamma = 0,$$

so that:

$$\mathsf{E}[x_te_t] = \mathsf{E}[x_t\nu_t + x_tu_t'\gamma] = S\mathsf{E}[w_tu_t']\gamma = S\Gamma\gamma = \delta \neq 0, \tag{12.12}$$

in general. Let $\mathsf{E}[e_t|x_t] = \psi' x_t$ where $\psi = M_{xx}^{-1}\delta$ when $M_{xx} = \mathsf{E}[x_tx_t']$, then:

$$\mathsf{E}[y_t \mid x_t] = \beta' x_t + \mathsf{E}[e_t \mid x_t] = x_t'\left(\beta + M_{xx}^{-1}\delta\right) = x_t'(\beta + \psi), \tag{12.13}$$

and so the least-squares estimator of β from regressing y_t on x_t is inconsistent: β cannot be obtained from only analysing the conditional model of y_t given x_t.

Let $W = (w_1 \dots w_T)$ denote the sample of T observations available on the $\{w_t\}$ process. From (12.10), due to stationarity and the zero mean assumption, $\mathsf{E}[\omega_t] = 0$ and so $\mathsf{E}[w_t] = 0$ also. From (12.2):[1]

$$\mathsf{E}[\omega_t\omega_t'] = M = \Upsilon M \Upsilon' + \Phi = \Sigma + \Phi,$$

[1] The subscripts on $M_{\omega\omega}$ have been omitted to avoid confusion with the typographically similar subscripts on M_{ww}.

and from (12.9):

$$\mathsf{E}\left[T^{-1}\boldsymbol{W}'\boldsymbol{W}\right] = \boldsymbol{M}_{ww} = \boldsymbol{M} + \boldsymbol{\Gamma},$$

with $\boldsymbol{M}_{xx} = \boldsymbol{S}\boldsymbol{M}_{ww}\boldsymbol{S}'$. Combining these two results:

$$\boldsymbol{M}_{ww} = \boldsymbol{\Upsilon}\boldsymbol{M}\boldsymbol{\Upsilon}' + (\boldsymbol{\Phi} + \boldsymbol{\Gamma}) = \boldsymbol{\Sigma} + \boldsymbol{\Lambda}, \tag{12.14}$$

(say). Since $\boldsymbol{\gamma}'\boldsymbol{\Upsilon} = \mathbf{0}'$, then $\boldsymbol{\gamma}'\boldsymbol{\Sigma} = \mathbf{0}'$.

From (12.14), when $\boldsymbol{M}_{ww}$ is known, or estimated from the sample using $T^{-1}\boldsymbol{W}'\boldsymbol{W}$, knowledge of either $\boldsymbol{\Sigma}$ or $\boldsymbol{\Lambda}$ entails knowledge of the other. Thus, the EVM leads to the problem of decomposing the observed-data covariance matrix $\boldsymbol{M}_{ww}$ into two component covariance matrices $\boldsymbol{\Sigma}$ and $\boldsymbol{\Lambda}$, such that $\boldsymbol{\gamma}$, and hence its component of interest $\boldsymbol{\beta}$, can be obtained from solving:

$$(\boldsymbol{M}_{ww} - \boldsymbol{\Lambda})\boldsymbol{\gamma} = \boldsymbol{\Sigma}\boldsymbol{\gamma} = \mathbf{0}, \tag{12.15}$$

subject to the normalization $\gamma_1 = 1$. We refer to approaches which use information about $\boldsymbol{\Lambda}$ as EVM analyses (see e.g. Koopmans, 1937, Kendall and Stuart, 1977, Ch.25, and Malinvaud, 1966, Ch.10), since these lead to variants of weighted-regression estimators. Approaches which try to estimate $\boldsymbol{\Sigma}$ directly tend to be instrumental-variables methods (see e.g. Reiersøl, 1945, Sargan, 1958, and Blalock, 1961). Since the last k elements of $\boldsymbol{\gamma}$ are zero, EVM analysis usually restricts attention to the $(n+1)$ variables $(y_t : \boldsymbol{x}_t)$ even though $\boldsymbol{g}_t$ is part of the joint density. We consider such an approach first, and return in section 12.2.2 to investigate the role of the remaining k variables $\boldsymbol{g}_t$ in relation to $\boldsymbol{\Sigma}$. Since the $\boldsymbol{g}_t$ have zero coefficients in $\boldsymbol{\gamma}$, it is convenient to set k to zero and let $\boldsymbol{f}_t = (y_t : \boldsymbol{x}_t')'$, and we do so for the remainder of this sub-section.

At first sight, there seems little to choose between obtaining $\boldsymbol{\gamma}$ by estimating $\boldsymbol{\Sigma}$ via $\hat{\boldsymbol{\Sigma}} = \hat{\boldsymbol{M}}_{ww} - \hat{\boldsymbol{\Lambda}}$ from information $\hat{\boldsymbol{\Lambda}}$ about $\boldsymbol{\Lambda}$, or from direct estimates $\hat{\boldsymbol{\Sigma}}$ of $\boldsymbol{\Sigma}$ obtained in some other way; surprisingly, it will transpire that the two approaches are far from equivalent. Let $\hat{\boldsymbol{\Lambda}}$ denote a consistent estimator of $\boldsymbol{\Lambda}$ such that $\hat{\boldsymbol{\Lambda}} = \boldsymbol{\Lambda} + o_p(1)$, which is intended to include the possibility that some elements of $\boldsymbol{\Lambda}$ are known a priori. Since $k = 0$, $\boldsymbol{f}_t = \boldsymbol{w}_t$, and to avoid a major change of notation, we continue to let:

$$\hat{\boldsymbol{\Sigma}} = \hat{\boldsymbol{M}}_{ww} - \hat{\boldsymbol{\Lambda}} \quad \text{where} \quad \hat{\boldsymbol{M}}_{ww} = T^{-1}\boldsymbol{W}'\boldsymbol{W}. \tag{12.16}$$

Since $\boldsymbol{\Sigma}\boldsymbol{\gamma} = \mathbf{0}$, it seems reasonable to solve for $\hat{\boldsymbol{\gamma}}$ from $\hat{\boldsymbol{\Sigma}}\hat{\boldsymbol{\gamma}} = \mathbf{0}$. Thus, we consider the properties of such an estimator.

While $\boldsymbol{\Sigma}$ must be singular because $\boldsymbol{\Sigma}\boldsymbol{\gamma} = \mathbf{0}$, $\hat{\boldsymbol{\Sigma}}$ need not be, so that the EVM estimator in practice solves:

$$\left(\hat{\boldsymbol{M}}_{ww} - \hat{\alpha}\hat{\boldsymbol{\Lambda}}\right)\hat{\boldsymbol{\gamma}} = \mathbf{0}, \tag{12.17}$$

where $\hat{\alpha}$ is the smallest eigenvalue of $|\hat{\boldsymbol{M}}_{ww} - \alpha\hat{\boldsymbol{\Lambda}}| = 0$, subject to the normalization $\gamma_1 = 1$. From (12.16), (12.17) is equivalent to:

$$\left(\hat{\boldsymbol{\Sigma}} + (1 - \hat{\alpha})\,\hat{\boldsymbol{\Lambda}}\right)\hat{\boldsymbol{\gamma}} = \mathbf{0}, \tag{12.18}$$

and the correction of $(1-\hat{\alpha})\hat{\boldsymbol{\Lambda}}$ to $\hat{\boldsymbol{\Sigma}}$ ensures that the resulting $\hat{\boldsymbol{\gamma}}$ minimizes the variance ratio:

$$\hat{\alpha} = \frac{\hat{\boldsymbol{\gamma}}'\hat{\boldsymbol{M}}_{ww}\hat{\boldsymbol{\gamma}}}{\hat{\boldsymbol{\gamma}}'\hat{\boldsymbol{\Lambda}}\hat{\boldsymbol{\gamma}}} \geq 1, \tag{12.19}$$

as can be seen from pre-multiplying (12.17) by $\hat{\boldsymbol{\gamma}}'$. Consequently, $\hat{\boldsymbol{\gamma}}$ is the eigenvector corresponding to the smallest eigenvalue of $\hat{\boldsymbol{M}}_{ww}$ in the metric of $\hat{\boldsymbol{\Lambda}}$.

Since $\operatorname{plim} \hat{\boldsymbol{\Lambda}} = \boldsymbol{\Lambda}$ and $\operatorname{plim} \hat{\boldsymbol{M}}_{ww} = \boldsymbol{M}_{ww}$, then $\operatorname{plim} \hat{\boldsymbol{\Sigma}} = \boldsymbol{\Sigma}$ from (12.16). But $\boldsymbol{\Sigma}$ is singular, so if $\alpha_l = \operatorname{plim} \hat{\alpha}$, and $\boldsymbol{\gamma}_l = \operatorname{plim} \hat{\boldsymbol{\gamma}}$, the equation:

$$\operatorname*{plim}_{T\to\infty} \left(\hat{\boldsymbol{\Sigma}} + (1-\hat{\alpha})\,\hat{\boldsymbol{\Lambda}}\right)\hat{\boldsymbol{\gamma}} = (\boldsymbol{\Sigma} + (1-\alpha_l)\,\boldsymbol{\Lambda})\,\boldsymbol{\gamma}_l = \mathbf{0},$$

has the solution $\alpha_l = 1$ and $\boldsymbol{\gamma}_l = \boldsymbol{\gamma}$. Since $\hat{\alpha} \geq 1$, $\operatorname{plim} \hat{\alpha} \geq 1$, so $\alpha_l = 1$ is the minimizing solution, and hence $\boldsymbol{\gamma}_l = \boldsymbol{\gamma}_p$, so $\hat{\boldsymbol{\gamma}}$ is consistent for $\boldsymbol{\gamma}_p$.

An important converse to the above proof that $\hat{\boldsymbol{\gamma}}$ is consistent for $\boldsymbol{\gamma}_p$ when $\hat{\boldsymbol{\Lambda}}$ is consistent for $\boldsymbol{\Lambda}$, is that an inconsistent estimator $\tilde{\boldsymbol{\Lambda}}$ of $\boldsymbol{\Lambda}$ usually generates an inconsistent estimator $\tilde{\boldsymbol{\gamma}}$ of $\boldsymbol{\gamma}_p$. To establish this converse, let $\operatorname{plim} \tilde{\boldsymbol{\Lambda}} = \boldsymbol{\Lambda}_l \neq \boldsymbol{\Lambda}$. Then the limit of (12.17) yields:

$$(\boldsymbol{M}_{ww} - \alpha_l \boldsymbol{\Lambda}_l)\,\boldsymbol{\gamma}_l = (\boldsymbol{\Sigma} + \boldsymbol{\Lambda} - \alpha_l \boldsymbol{\Lambda}_l)\,\boldsymbol{\gamma}_l = \mathbf{0}. \tag{12.20}$$

Except in the special case that $\boldsymbol{\Lambda}_l$ and $\boldsymbol{\Lambda}$ are multiples of a common matrix, such as $\boldsymbol{I}_m$, there is no value of α_l such that $\boldsymbol{\Lambda} - \alpha_l \boldsymbol{\Lambda}_l = \mathbf{0}$, and hence $\boldsymbol{\gamma}_l$ will not correspond to a solution of $\boldsymbol{\Sigma}\boldsymbol{\gamma} = \mathbf{0}$. Consequently, the consistency of $\hat{\boldsymbol{\Lambda}}$ for $\boldsymbol{\Lambda}$ is essential for the consistency of $\hat{\boldsymbol{\gamma}}$ for $\boldsymbol{\gamma}_p$. Such an outcome contrasts with the robustness of the EGE solutions for simultaneous systems to inconsistent estimators of the error covariance matrix.

When $\boldsymbol{\Lambda}$ is diagonal, the method of estimating $\boldsymbol{\gamma}$ by solving (12.17) is called weighted least squares (WLS), because if $\hat{\boldsymbol{\gamma}}' = (1 : -\hat{\boldsymbol{\beta}}')$ is substituted into (12.17), noting that $\boldsymbol{w}_t' = (y_t : \boldsymbol{x}_t')$, then letting $\boldsymbol{y}' = (y_1 \ldots y_T)$ and $\boldsymbol{X}' = (\boldsymbol{x}_1 \ldots \boldsymbol{x}_T)$:

$$\left[T^{-1}\begin{pmatrix} \boldsymbol{y}'\boldsymbol{y} & \boldsymbol{y}'\boldsymbol{X} \\ \boldsymbol{X}'\boldsymbol{y} & \boldsymbol{X}'\boldsymbol{X} \end{pmatrix} - \hat{\alpha}\begin{pmatrix} \lambda_{11} & \mathbf{0}' \\ \mathbf{0} & \boldsymbol{\Lambda}_{11} \end{pmatrix}\right]\begin{pmatrix} 1 \\ -\hat{\boldsymbol{\beta}} \end{pmatrix} = \mathbf{0}. \tag{12.21}$$

Consequently, $\hat{\boldsymbol{\beta}}$ is given by:

$$\hat{\boldsymbol{\beta}} = (\boldsymbol{X}'\boldsymbol{X} - T\hat{\alpha}\boldsymbol{\Lambda}_{11})^{-1}\,\boldsymbol{X}'\boldsymbol{y}. \tag{12.22}$$

For diagonal $\boldsymbol{\Lambda}_{11}$, (12.22) down-weights the diagonal of the matrix to be inverted, to offset its 'inflation' from the measurement-error variance: remember that for regression to work, the regressors usually need corrected (see Ch.A4).

OLS is the special case $\boldsymbol{\Lambda}_{11} = \mathbf{0}$ and $\lambda_{11} = \sigma^2$, so that every variable but y_t is error free. Thus, (12.17) is an EGE for estimators of $\boldsymbol{\beta}$, generated by alternative estimators of $\boldsymbol{\Lambda}$: OLS, WLS, and several other well-known methods are special cases. For example, $\hat{\boldsymbol{\Lambda}} = \sigma^2 \boldsymbol{I}_m$ generates principal components since (12.17) becomes:

$$\left(\hat{\boldsymbol{M}}_{ww} - (\hat{\alpha}\sigma^2)\,\boldsymbol{I}_m\right)\hat{\boldsymbol{\gamma}} = \left(\hat{\boldsymbol{M}}_{ww} - \kappa \boldsymbol{I}_m\right)\hat{\boldsymbol{\gamma}} = \mathbf{0}, \tag{12.23}$$

where κ is the smallest eigenvalue of $\hat{\boldsymbol{M}}_{ww}$, and $\hat{\boldsymbol{\gamma}}$ is the matching eigenvector. This method corresponds to orthogonal regression (see Anderson, 1976(eq.3.5)); other directions of regression result from alternative specifications of $\boldsymbol{\Lambda}$ having only one non-zero element.

Nevertheless, care is required in specifying $\boldsymbol{\Lambda}$. For example, the OLS specification:

$$\boldsymbol{\Lambda} = \begin{pmatrix} \lambda_{11} & \mathbf{0}' \\ \mathbf{0} & \mathbf{0} \end{pmatrix},$$

entails that agents condition on $\boldsymbol{x}_t$ rather than χ_t. Alternatively, $\boldsymbol{\Lambda} = \sigma^2 \boldsymbol{I}_m$ (equal error variances) requires either a natural set of units for all of the variables, or careful scaling. The assumption that the measurement-error variance matrix is diagonal is not easy to sustain in linear models of economic behaviour. It is rare in economics that the original variables are analysed in their untransformed state: more usually, a range of transformations is undertaken (from values to quantities, nominal to real magnitudes, total to per-capita measures, levels to growth rates and differentials, etc.), and in time-series studies, several lags of variables frequently occur. It is hard to see why $\boldsymbol{\Lambda}$ should be diagonal for the particular transformations selected. For example, if in the set of consumption, income, and saving, the first two have unrelated measurement errors, the second and third cannot since savings $\equiv$ income $-$ consumption. If levels of variables have independent errors of measurement (both over time and between variables), then differences and equilibrium-correction mechanisms cannot. Thus, it is difficult to see how appropriate prior information about the diagonality of $\boldsymbol{\Lambda}$ could be obtained, or about the relative size of its diagonal elements, or indeed about the serial independence or homoscedasticity of the $\{\boldsymbol{u}_t\}$.

Since (12.11) is a linear model, it is invariant under non-singular linear transforms of the form (see Ch.6):

$$\boldsymbol{\gamma}'\boldsymbol{w}_t = \left(\boldsymbol{\gamma}'\boldsymbol{D}^{-1}\right)\boldsymbol{D}\boldsymbol{w}_t = \boldsymbol{\gamma}^{*\prime}\boldsymbol{w}_t^*, \tag{12.24}$$

where $\boldsymbol{D}$ is $m \times m$ of rank m, subject to appropriate re-normalization to retain $\gamma_1^* = 1$. However, from (12.9):

$$\boldsymbol{w}_t^* = \boldsymbol{D}\boldsymbol{\omega}_t + \boldsymbol{D}\boldsymbol{u}_t = \boldsymbol{\omega}_t^* + \boldsymbol{u}_t^* \text{ where } \boldsymbol{u}_t^* \sim \mathsf{IN}_m\left[\mathbf{0}, \boldsymbol{\Gamma}^*\right], \tag{12.25}$$

and $\boldsymbol{\Gamma}^* = \boldsymbol{D}\boldsymbol{D}'$. Thus, $\boldsymbol{\Gamma}^*$ is not diagonal when $\boldsymbol{\Gamma}$ is, unless $\boldsymbol{D}$ is also diagonal.

The important implication of this last result arises from its interaction with the previous finding that $\hat{\boldsymbol{\gamma}}$ is generally consistent for $\boldsymbol{\gamma}$ if and only if $\hat{\boldsymbol{\Lambda}}$ is consistent for $\boldsymbol{\Lambda}$ (barring special cases). Unless every data transformation has a known impact on the structure of the measurement errors, and the resulting complete variance-covariance matrix $\boldsymbol{\Lambda}^*$ is either known or consistently estimable, then it will prove difficult to consistently estimate $\boldsymbol{\gamma}$ by solving the EVM estimator generating equation. Nevertheless, the EVM route is not the only one for tackling errors-in-variables in econometric models, so we next consider the approach first proposed by Reiersøl (1945).

12.2.2 Instrumental variables

In the above discussion, we set k to zero to focus on the usual EVM estimators, so $\{w_t\}$ comprised only the observable variables actually included in the equation under study leading to the regression (for $\lambda = \beta + \psi$):

$$y_t = \lambda' x_t + e_t. \tag{12.26}$$

However, the original DGP included y_t, x_t, and g_t (for $k > 0$), and since weak exogeneity of x_t for β is violated, then the joint density of W must be analysed. For time series, doing so will reintroduce w_{t-1} (or longer lags) as determinants of x_t even when g_t is absent. In economics, however, the vector $f_t' = (y_t : x_t')$ will not usually be determined by a closed system, so that some g_t will be present. Reiersøl (1945) proposed using a set of such additional variables as 'instruments' by which to obtain a solution to the EVM estimating equation (in the context of Frisch's Bunch Maps approach to Confluence Analysis; interestingly, Reiersøl also suggested using w_{t-1} as the instrument set). With hindsight, since the simultaneous-equations problem and the errors-in-variables problem both induce $\mathsf{E}[x_t e_t] \neq \mathbf{0}$ in linear equations like (12.26), it is unsurprising that both have instrumental-variables solutions.

Let $z_t = (g_t' : w_{t-1}')'$ denote all the available instruments namely, valid conditioning variables whether contemporaneous or lagged (see Ch.A4 for an introduction to IV). The specification of z_t depends on economic analysis and previous empirical evidence, but if e_t is an innovation against w_{t-1}, then all relevant lags are admissible instruments. The two essential requirements of an instrument are that it should be a determinant of χ_t (and hence of x_t), yet be independent of e_t (i.e. of $\gamma'\epsilon_t$ and u_t). Thus, when contemporaneous variables are used as instruments, their measurement errors (if any) must be independent of those of f_t: such a property is invariant to linear transformations within z_t or within f_t. When w_{t-1} are used as instruments, then ϵ_t and u_t must be innovation processes, entailing that systematic measurement errors must be modelled to leave an innovation residual.

Given a set $\{z_t\}$ with the required properties, but assuming only one lag is relevant for simplicity:

$$\prod_{t=1}^{T} \mathsf{D_w}(f_t, g_t \mid w_{t-1}, \varphi) = \prod_{t=1}^{T} \mathsf{D_{f|g}}(f_t \mid z_t, \theta_1)\, \mathsf{D_g}(g_t \mid w_{t-1}, \theta_2), \tag{12.27}$$

where weak exogeneity of g_t for β requires that β is a function of θ_1 only, and θ_1 and θ_2 are variation free. If so, retaining linearity and normality, the conditional process is denoted by:

$$f_t = \Pi z_t + v_t \quad \text{where} \quad \mathsf{E}[v_t v_t'] = \Delta \quad \text{and} \quad \mathsf{E}[z_t v_t'] = \mathbf{0}, \tag{12.28}$$

where (12.28) derives by conditioning on g_t in (12.10), so:

$$\begin{pmatrix} f_t \\ g_t \end{pmatrix} = w_t = \begin{pmatrix} \Pi \\ I_k \; \mathbf{0} \end{pmatrix} z_t + \begin{pmatrix} v_t \\ \mathbf{0} \end{pmatrix} = \Pi^* z_t + v_t^*. \tag{12.29}$$

Thus, from (12.11) and (12.29):

$$\gamma' \boldsymbol{w}_t = \gamma' \boldsymbol{\Pi}^* \boldsymbol{z}_t + \gamma' \boldsymbol{v}_t^* = e_t, \tag{12.30}$$

and so $\gamma' \boldsymbol{\Pi}^* = \mathbf{0}'$ for a linearly independent set $\{\boldsymbol{z}_t\}$, with $\sigma_e^2 = \gamma' \boldsymbol{\Delta}^* \gamma$ where $\mathsf{E}[\boldsymbol{v}_t^* \boldsymbol{v}_t^{*\prime}] = \boldsymbol{\Delta}^*$. In contrast to (12.12), $\mathsf{E}[\boldsymbol{z}_t e_t] = \mathbf{0}$.

Since $\boldsymbol{z}_t$ is $(m+k) \times 1$, where $m = n + k + 1$, and $\boldsymbol{w}_t$ is $m \times 1$, then $\boldsymbol{\Pi}^*$ is $m \times (m+k)$ of rank $(n+k)$ when rank$(\boldsymbol{M}_{xz}) = n$ (see White, 1984). Consequently, γ could be derived from $\boldsymbol{\Pi}^*$ in a similar way to the EVM approach of obtaining γ from $\boldsymbol{\Sigma}$ in (12.18). Indeed, from (12.29):

$$\boldsymbol{M}_{ww} = \boldsymbol{\Pi}^* \boldsymbol{M}_{zz} \boldsymbol{\Pi}^{*\prime} + \boldsymbol{\Delta}^*, \tag{12.31}$$

since $\mathsf{E}[\boldsymbol{z}_t \boldsymbol{v}_t^{*\prime}] = \mathbf{0}$, and hence:

$$\boldsymbol{\Pi}^* \boldsymbol{M}_{zz} \boldsymbol{\Pi}^{*\prime} + \boldsymbol{\Delta}^* = \boldsymbol{\Sigma} + \boldsymbol{\Lambda}. \tag{12.32}$$

In terms of the sample data, from (12.29):

$$\hat{\boldsymbol{\Pi}}^* = (\boldsymbol{W}'\boldsymbol{Z})(\boldsymbol{Z}'\boldsymbol{Z})^{-1} = \hat{\boldsymbol{M}}_{wz} \hat{\boldsymbol{M}}_{zz}^{-1},$$

and:

$$\hat{\boldsymbol{M}}_{ww} = \hat{\boldsymbol{\Pi}}^* \hat{\boldsymbol{M}}_{zz} \hat{\boldsymbol{\Pi}}^{*\prime} + \hat{\boldsymbol{\Delta}}^* = \hat{\boldsymbol{M}}_{wz} \hat{\boldsymbol{\Pi}}^{*\prime} + \hat{\boldsymbol{\Delta}}^*. \tag{12.33}$$

Since plim $\hat{\boldsymbol{\Pi}}^* = \boldsymbol{\Pi}^*$ by construction of (12.29), a consistent estimator of γ (and so of β) could be obtained by solving $\hat{\boldsymbol{\Pi}}^{*\prime} \hat{\gamma} = \mathbf{0}$. Also, $\hat{\boldsymbol{\Delta}}^*$ can be estimated from the sample evidence. Thus, the key difference from EVM is not the presence of $\boldsymbol{g}_t$, but the fact that the systematic variance (corresponding to $\boldsymbol{\Sigma}$) is being modelled, not the error variance (corresponding to $\boldsymbol{\Lambda}$). Indeed, in (12.32), $\boldsymbol{M}_{fz} \boldsymbol{\Pi}' \neq \boldsymbol{\Sigma}$ in general, nor is $\boldsymbol{\Delta}$ equal to $\boldsymbol{\Lambda}$, yet a consistent estimator of γ results.

The final step is to relate these results to the EGE in (12.18). Consider (12.33) generalized to:

$$\left(\hat{\boldsymbol{M}}_{wz} \hat{\boldsymbol{\Pi}}^{*\prime} - (1 - \hat{\alpha}) \hat{\boldsymbol{\Delta}}^* \right) \hat{\gamma} = \mathbf{0}. \tag{12.34}$$

Since $\boldsymbol{\Pi}^{*\prime} \gamma = \mathbf{0}$, (12.34) has a consistent solution for γ_p using $\hat{\alpha} = 1$. Consequently, although inconsistency in $\hat{\boldsymbol{\Lambda}}$ for $\boldsymbol{\Lambda}$ induced inconsistency in $\hat{\gamma}$ for γ_p in (12.18), inconsistency in $\hat{\boldsymbol{\Delta}}^*$ for $\boldsymbol{\Delta}^*$ does not do so in (12.34). Indeed, providing that $\mathsf{E}[\boldsymbol{z}_t e_t] = \mathbf{0}$ and $\boldsymbol{M}_{xz}$ has rank n, then plim$\hat{\alpha} = 1$ irrespective of the estimator $\tilde{\boldsymbol{\Delta}}^*$ for $\boldsymbol{\Delta}^*$ in (12.34). Specific choices for the estimators $\tilde{\boldsymbol{\Pi}}^*$, $\tilde{\alpha}$, and $\tilde{\boldsymbol{\Delta}}^*$ in (12.34) deliver the EGE of Chapter 11 for estimating a single equation from a system. For example, $\tilde{\alpha} = 1$ and $\tilde{\boldsymbol{\Pi}}^* = \hat{\boldsymbol{\Pi}}^*$ generates 2SLS (compare (11.82)); and LIML corresponds to:

$$\tilde{\boldsymbol{\Delta}}^* = T^{-1} \boldsymbol{W}' \boldsymbol{Q}_Z \boldsymbol{W}, \tag{12.35}$$

where $\tilde{\alpha}$ is the smallest eigenvalue of $|\hat{\boldsymbol{M}}_{ww} - \alpha \tilde{\boldsymbol{\Delta}}^*| = \mathbf{0}$, $\tilde{\gamma}$ is the corresponding eigenvector, and $\boldsymbol{Q}_Z = (\boldsymbol{I}_T - \boldsymbol{Z}(\boldsymbol{Z}'\boldsymbol{Z})^{-1}\boldsymbol{Z}')$ so that:

$$\tilde{\boldsymbol{\Pi}}^{*\prime} = \boldsymbol{W}' \boldsymbol{Q}_{\tilde{e}} \boldsymbol{Z} (\boldsymbol{Z}' \boldsymbol{Q}_{\tilde{e}} \boldsymbol{Z})^{-1}, \tag{12.36}$$

where $\tilde{e} = W\tilde{\gamma}$, with a similar definition to Q_Z for $Q_{\tilde{e}}$, and hence $\tilde{\gamma}'\tilde{\Pi}^* \equiv \mathbf{0}$, so $\tilde{\Pi}'\tilde{\beta} = \mathbf{0}$ as required. Notice that IV does not satisfy that last requirement, yet provides a consistent estimator of β. The difference between the implications of assumptions about Σ and Λ is now apparent: knowledge that ω_t depends on k observables g_t such that $\mathsf{E}[g_t e_t] = \mathbf{0}$ is sufficient for estimating β consistently, even when g_t is an incomplete subset of the determinants of ω_t. This remarkable difference between the modelling of Λ and the modelling of Σ seems to underpin the successful development of econometrics. Little progress could be achieved when complete and exact information about all error variances was essential for even consistent estimation; much is possible if information about a few determinants of Σ suffices. One consequence has been the historical focus on instrumental-variables methods, which in economics are selected on the basis of system characteristics and prior theory.

12.3 Dynamic latent-variables models

Dynamic latent-variables (DLV) models include variables, such as expectations, confidence, consumption, and permanent income, which are not directly observable (see e.g. Aigner, Hsiao, Kapteyn and Wansbeek, 1984).[2] Latent variables play a major role in economic theories of agent behaviour, and often enter the formulation of an econometric model. Many latent variables are inherently dynamic, especially in models involving inter-temporal optimization, search or duration processes, equilibrium-correction mechanisms, models of habit formation, learning, or persistence, and state dependence. Important examples are discrete choice models (Heckman, 1981) and min-condition models (see Quandt, 1988, 1989).

Unfortunately, the likelihood functions of DLV models are often analytically intractable, because the elimination of the latent variables by marginalization requires high-dimensional integration. Techniques have been developed to improve tractability, including simplifying the dynamic structure (e.g., autocorrelated errors in static supply–demand min-condition models as in Laffont and Monfort, 1979), and the use of observable surrogates for latent variables (e.g., price-adjustment equations in min-condition models as in Quandt, 1982, 1988, or Maddala, 1984, or the use of fixed-effects formulations as in Heckman and McCurdy, 1980). Although the likelihood functions associated with DLV models may be intractable, the models themselves are often amenable to joint simulation of the latent and observable processes. Hence, the method of simulated moments (MSM) (see e.g. McFadden, 1989, or Pakes and Pollard, 1989), is applicable to DLV models. So far in this book, we have used Monte Carlo to simulate distributions of statistics, and to establish properties of econometric methods; now we consider evaluating likelihood functions by simulation, thereby using Monte Carlo for estimation. Simulation estimation techniques are computationally demanding, but are general and have the potential for preserving the dynamic structure of the model under analysis.

[2] This section is based on Hendry and Richard (1991).

At first sight, using random numbers for estimation of empirical models seems paradoxical. However, Monte Carlo methods are a technique for obtaining integrals by solving an equivalent stochastic problem. Since many statistical techniques are likelihood based, as discussed in Chapter 10, marginalizing with respect to unobservables corresponds to integrating them out of the joint density. Thus, by clever reformulation, simulation can solve the marginalization problem to produce the correct likelihood in terms of observables only. The difficulty lies in the fact that the joint distribution of the latent variables, conditional on the observables is generally not known for DLV models. An approximating distribution, called an importance function, can be selected as a random-number generator in an approach close to that of Monte Carlo integration (see e.g. Geweke, 1988, for technical details and references).

To establish the basic ideas, let $\boldsymbol{y}_t$ denote a vector of n observable random variables at time t, and $\boldsymbol{s}_t$ a vector of k unobservable variables, where $\boldsymbol{Y}_{t-1} = (\boldsymbol{y}_1 \ldots \boldsymbol{y}_{t-1})$ and $\boldsymbol{S}_{t-1} = (\boldsymbol{s}_1 \ldots \boldsymbol{s}_{t-1})$. Let $\mathsf{D}_{\mathsf{Y}}(\boldsymbol{Y}, \boldsymbol{S}|\boldsymbol{\theta})$ denote the joint density of $\boldsymbol{Y}$ and $\boldsymbol{S} \in \mathcal{S}$ for a sample of size T, where exogenous variables are omitted for simplicity, and $\boldsymbol{\theta} \in \boldsymbol{\Theta} \subseteq \mathbb{R}^l$. The likelihood function $\mathsf{L}(\boldsymbol{\theta}|\, \boldsymbol{Y})$ is proportional to the marginal data density:

$$\mathsf{L}(\boldsymbol{\theta} \mid \boldsymbol{Y}) \propto \mathsf{D}_{\mathsf{Y}}(\boldsymbol{Y} \mid \boldsymbol{\theta}) = \int \cdots \int_{\mathcal{S}} \mathsf{D}_{\mathsf{Y,S}}(\boldsymbol{Y}, \boldsymbol{S} \mid \boldsymbol{\theta})\, \mathrm{d}\boldsymbol{S}, \tag{12.37}$$

where the dimension of integration depends on that of $\boldsymbol{S}$. Implicitly, a model exists relating the observed and latent variables, but no particular specification is required at this stage.

For $\boldsymbol{X}_{t-1} = (\boldsymbol{Y}_{t-1}, \boldsymbol{S}_{t-1})$, sequentially and conditionally factorize the joint density $\mathsf{D}_{\mathsf{Y,S}}(\boldsymbol{Y}, \boldsymbol{S}|\boldsymbol{\theta})$ as:

$$\mathsf{D}_{\mathsf{Y,S}}(\boldsymbol{Y}, \boldsymbol{S} \mid \boldsymbol{\theta}) = \prod_{t=1}^{T} \mathsf{D}_{\mathsf{y|s}}(\boldsymbol{y}_t \mid \boldsymbol{s}_t, \boldsymbol{X}_{t-1}, \boldsymbol{\mu}_1)\, \mathsf{D}_{\mathsf{s}}(\boldsymbol{s}_t \mid \boldsymbol{X}_{t-1}, \boldsymbol{\mu}_2), \tag{12.38}$$

to create a latent process $\{\boldsymbol{s}_t|\boldsymbol{X}_{t-1}, \boldsymbol{\mu}_2\}$ combined with a conditional measurement process that determines the observables $\{\boldsymbol{y}_t|\boldsymbol{s}_t, \boldsymbol{X}_{t-1}, \boldsymbol{\mu}_1\}$. We can also factorize $\mathsf{D}_{\mathsf{Y,S}}(\boldsymbol{Y}, \boldsymbol{S}|\boldsymbol{\theta})$ into the product of a function $g_Y(\boldsymbol{S}|\boldsymbol{\theta})$, and a remainder function $h(\boldsymbol{Y}, \boldsymbol{S}|\boldsymbol{\theta})$ using:

$$\mathsf{D}_{\mathsf{Y,S}}(\boldsymbol{Y}, \boldsymbol{S} \mid \boldsymbol{\theta}) = h(\boldsymbol{Y}, \boldsymbol{S} \mid \boldsymbol{\theta})\, g_Y(\boldsymbol{S} \mid \boldsymbol{\theta}). \tag{12.39}$$

In (12.39), $g_Y(\cdot)$ can be any suitable auxiliary distribution constructed to help estimate the integral:

$$\mathsf{D}_{\mathsf{Y}}(\boldsymbol{Y} \mid \boldsymbol{\theta}) = \int \cdots \int_{\mathcal{S}} h(\boldsymbol{Y}, \boldsymbol{S} \mid \boldsymbol{\theta})\, g_Y(\boldsymbol{S} \mid \boldsymbol{\theta})\, \mathrm{d}\boldsymbol{S}, \tag{12.40}$$

so $g_Y(\cdot)$ need not be a valid reduction of $\mathsf{D}_{\mathsf{Y,S}}(\boldsymbol{Y}, \boldsymbol{S}|\boldsymbol{\theta})$, nor coincide with the conditional distribution $\mathsf{D}_{\mathsf{S|Y}}(\boldsymbol{S}|\, \boldsymbol{Y}, \boldsymbol{\lambda})$. However,

$$\int \cdots \int_{\mathcal{S}} h(\boldsymbol{Y}, \boldsymbol{S} \mid \boldsymbol{\theta})\, g_Y(\boldsymbol{S} \mid \boldsymbol{\theta})\, \mathrm{d}\boldsymbol{S} = \mathsf{E}_g\left[h(\boldsymbol{Y}, \boldsymbol{S} \mid \boldsymbol{\theta})\right],$$

so the key to obtaining $\mathsf{D}_Y(\boldsymbol{Y}|\boldsymbol{\theta})$ from (12.40) is to formulate $g_Y(\cdot)$ such that the expectation $\mathsf{E}_g[\cdot]$ can be evaluated by Monte Carlo using the mean of random samples of $\boldsymbol{S}$ drawn from $g_Y(\boldsymbol{S} \mid \boldsymbol{\theta})$:

$$\mathsf{E}_g\left[h\widehat{(\boldsymbol{Y}, \boldsymbol{S} \mid \boldsymbol{\theta})}\right] = \frac{1}{M}\sum_{i=1}^{M} h(\boldsymbol{Y}_i, \boldsymbol{S}_i \mid \boldsymbol{\theta}),$$

From (12.38), a natural choice for $g_Y(\cdot)$ is:

$$g_Y(\boldsymbol{S} \mid \boldsymbol{\theta}) = \prod_{t=1}^{T} \mathsf{D}_\mathsf{s}(\boldsymbol{s}_t \mid \boldsymbol{X}_{t-1}, \boldsymbol{\mu}_2), \qquad (12.41)$$

and so:

$$h(\boldsymbol{Y}, \boldsymbol{S} \mid \boldsymbol{\theta}) = \prod_{t=1}^{T} \mathsf{D}_{\mathsf{y}|\mathsf{s}}(\boldsymbol{y}_t \mid \boldsymbol{s}_t, \boldsymbol{X}_{t-1}, \boldsymbol{\mu}_1). \qquad (12.42)$$

Thus, at any time t, given $\boldsymbol{X}_{t-1}$, and any admissible value of $\boldsymbol{\theta}$, it must be possible to draw from $\mathsf{D}_\mathsf{s}(\boldsymbol{s}_t \mid \boldsymbol{X}_{t-1}, \boldsymbol{\mu}_2)$: the latent variable $\boldsymbol{s}_t$ is drawn conditionally on the actual values of the observables $\boldsymbol{Y}_{t-1}$ and previously simulated values of $\boldsymbol{S}_{t-1}$ for a given $\boldsymbol{\theta}$. This process is conducted sequentially for $t = 1, \ldots, T$. Then M independent replications of the entire procedure are carried out, and the average value of $h(\boldsymbol{Y}, \boldsymbol{S}|\boldsymbol{\theta})$ is computed, which is the numerical estimate of $\mathsf{D}_Y(\boldsymbol{Y}|\boldsymbol{\theta})$ from (12.40). Repeating over different $\boldsymbol{\theta}$ generates the likelihood function even though $\boldsymbol{S}$ was never observed. The maximum can be obtained by comparison, or using a more sophisticated approach also incorporating numerical optimization. This avenue is computer intensive, but is capable of solving some difficult problems. Moreover, having established the logic of the method, numerous variants occur, such as applying the idea to scores, or moments etc. The main element in (12.40) is that the expectations need not be taken over the actual stochastic process that generated the data, but can be with respect to an artificial process, allowing the latter to be selected to facilitate a solution. The sequential processes in (12.41) and (12.42) arise due to the dynamic nature of the DGP.

Section 12.3.1 considers the MSM approach which historically came before simulated likelihood (see Pakes, 1986); the selection of importance functions is discussed in §12.3.2; an application to a simple DLV model is noted in §12.3.3; and the treatment of exogenous variables is examined in §12.3.4.

12.3.1 Method of simulated moments

We first abstract from the dynamic structure of the model. The likelihood function $\mathsf{L}(\boldsymbol{\theta}; \boldsymbol{Y})$ of the observables in (12.37) suggests that both analytical and numerical integration are generally intractable for DLV models due to the high dimensionality of the problem — namely a multiple of sample size (see McFadden, 1989, and Pakes and Pollard, 1989). In contrast, simulation techniques have been applied with success in high-dimensional problems. Their application to (12.37) for any given value of $\boldsymbol{\theta}$ requires that a random-number generator be available for $\boldsymbol{S}$ with $\boldsymbol{Y}$ being held fixed. This would be the case if the distribution of $(\boldsymbol{Y}, \boldsymbol{S})$, given θ could be factorized as in:

$$\mathsf{D}_{\mathsf{Y,S}}(\boldsymbol{Y}, \boldsymbol{S} \mid \theta) = \mathsf{D}_{\mathsf{S|Y}}(\boldsymbol{S} \mid \boldsymbol{Y}, \theta_a)\, \mathsf{D}_{\mathsf{Y}}(\boldsymbol{Y} \mid \theta_b). \tag{12.43}$$

Then $\mathsf{D}_{\mathsf{S|Y}}(\boldsymbol{S} | \boldsymbol{Y}, \theta_a)$ would suffice. Unfortunately, DLV models are generally specified in the form of a dynamic process as in (12.41) and (12.42), whereby variables are generated at time t conditionally on the past history of the process. The transformation from such a sequential factorization of the model into a global distribution for $\boldsymbol{S}$ given $\boldsymbol{Y}$ as in (12.43) is often intractable (exceptions include linear Gaussian models, where the joint distribution of $\boldsymbol{Y}$ and $\boldsymbol{S}$ is also Gaussian; and models where the latent variables do not feedback onto the observables, namely, with Granger non-causality).

Random-number generators are often available for the sequential distribution of $\{\boldsymbol{y}_t\}$ and $\{\boldsymbol{s}_t\}$, which can be used to draw random samples from the joint distribution. Hence integrals of the form:

$$\boldsymbol{H}(\boldsymbol{\theta}) = \int \cdots \int_{\mathcal{S},\mathcal{Y}} \boldsymbol{h}(\boldsymbol{Y}, \boldsymbol{S} \mid \boldsymbol{\theta})\, \mathsf{D}_{\mathsf{Y,S}}(\boldsymbol{Y}, \boldsymbol{S} \mid \boldsymbol{\theta})\, \mathrm{d}\boldsymbol{S}\mathrm{d}\boldsymbol{Y}, \tag{12.44}$$

where $\boldsymbol{h}(\cdot)$ is an appropriate vector function, can be estimated by simulation for a range of dynamic models. Such integrals as (12.44) are instrumental in the derivation of generalized method-of-moments estimators (see Hansen, 1982), and on the lines of Chapter 11, (12.44) can be construed as an EGE. Specifically, when $\boldsymbol{\theta}_p$ denotes the population value of $\boldsymbol{\theta}$, the statistical formulation of econometric models suggests choosing $\boldsymbol{h}(\cdot)$ for which $\boldsymbol{H}(\boldsymbol{\theta}_p) = \boldsymbol{0}$. Typical examples are orthogonality conditions and score vectors. Alternatively, $\boldsymbol{h}(\cdot)$ can be any function such that a point estimate, $\hat{\boldsymbol{H}}$, is available for $\boldsymbol{H}(\boldsymbol{\theta})$.

MSM uses simulation techniques to evaluate $\boldsymbol{H}(\boldsymbol{\theta})$ for different values of $\boldsymbol{\theta}$. A value of $\boldsymbol{\theta}$ is then selected that minimizes a suitable distance between the estimate $\hat{\boldsymbol{H}}$ and the predicted value $\boldsymbol{H}(\boldsymbol{\theta}_p)$. This approach has been applied to a number of problems (see Lerman and Manski, 1981, Pakes, 1986, Hajivassiliou, 1989, McFadden, 1989, and Hajivassiliou and McFadden, 1989). Considerable theoretical progress has also been achieved in the investigation of the properties of these simulation estimators (see Andrews, 1989, Duffie and Singleton, 1989, and Pakes and Pollard, 1989). Attractions of MSM are its conceptual simplicity and ease of adaptation to a range of models. Its application to integrals of the form in (12.37) requires that $\boldsymbol{Y}$ be kept fixed in the simulation, which raises an additional layer of complexity that has not yet been fully resolved for DLV models. Hajivassiliou and McFadden (1989) condition on the observables in limited dependent-variable models where $\boldsymbol{y}$ is a discrete, many-to-one, transform $\boldsymbol{\tau}(\cdot)$ of the latent variable $\boldsymbol{s}$. They do not evaluate the likelihood function itself, but construct a random-number generator based on Gibbs resampling technique (see e.g. Geman and Geman, 1984) that enables them to draw directly from the distribution of $\boldsymbol{s}$, truncated to the event $A(\boldsymbol{y}) = \{\boldsymbol{s} | \boldsymbol{y} = \boldsymbol{\tau}(\boldsymbol{s})\}$. These random numbers are then used to construct a Monte Carlo estimate of the score function. As an alternative, we consider constructing importance functions to approximate the conditional distribution of $\boldsymbol{s}$ given $\boldsymbol{y}$, in a way which is applicable to DLV models.

12.3.2 Simulated likelihood functions

We now take explicit account of the dynamic structure of the model, and use factorizations of the joint data density as in (12.38). Initial conditions are assumed known or included in $\boldsymbol{S}$, depending on the context. As in (12.37), the likelihood function is proportional to the marginal data density where the dimensions of integration can be high (the simple disequilibrium model below requires T-dimensional integration). The crucial step in estimating by Monte Carlo techniques consists in factorizing the joint density into the product of the importance function $g_Y(\boldsymbol{S}|\boldsymbol{\theta})$, from which samples can be drawn at random, and the remainder function $h(\boldsymbol{Y}, \boldsymbol{S}|\boldsymbol{\theta})$, defined in (12.39), where $g_Y(\cdot)$ is any auxiliary distribution constructed for evaluating the integral in (12.40). Throughout the integration, the $\boldsymbol{Y}$s are treated as fixed constants, and the choice of $g_Y(\cdot)$ may depend on the observed values.

Under the factorization (12.39), the integral in (12.40) was rewritten as:

$$\mathsf{D}_{\mathsf{Y}}(\boldsymbol{Y} \mid \boldsymbol{\theta}) = \mathsf{E}_g\left[h(\boldsymbol{Y}, \boldsymbol{S} \mid \boldsymbol{\theta})\right], \tag{12.45}$$

to be evaluated by Monte Carlo as the average when sampling from $g_Y(\cdot)$, using the sequential factorization of $\mathsf{D}_{\mathsf{Y,S}}(\boldsymbol{Y}, \boldsymbol{S}|\boldsymbol{\theta})$ in (12.38), from which (12.41) and (12.42) were obtained:

$$\mathsf{D}_{\mathsf{Y,S}}(\boldsymbol{Y}, \boldsymbol{S} \mid \boldsymbol{\theta}) = \prod_{t=1}^{T} \mathsf{D}_{\mathsf{y,s}}(\boldsymbol{y}_t, \boldsymbol{s}_t \mid \boldsymbol{X}_{t-1}, \boldsymbol{\theta}). \tag{12.46}$$

Since DLV models are inherently sequential, assumptions are directly formulated in terms of one of two additional factorizations. If $\boldsymbol{s}$ does not Granger-cause $\boldsymbol{y}$ (see Ch.5), then we use:

$$\mathsf{D}_{\mathsf{Y,S}}(\boldsymbol{Y}, \boldsymbol{S} \mid \boldsymbol{\theta}) = \mathsf{D}_{\mathsf{S|Y}}(\boldsymbol{S} \mid \boldsymbol{Y}, \boldsymbol{\theta})\, \mathsf{D}_{\mathsf{Y}}(\boldsymbol{Y} \mid \boldsymbol{\theta}),$$

where:

$$\mathsf{D}_{\mathsf{Y}}(\boldsymbol{Y} \mid \boldsymbol{\theta}) = \prod_{t=1}^{T} \mathsf{D}_{\mathsf{y}}(\boldsymbol{y}_t \mid \boldsymbol{X}_{t-1}, \boldsymbol{\varphi}_1) = \prod_{t=1}^{T} \mathsf{D}_{\mathsf{y}}(\boldsymbol{y}_t \mid \boldsymbol{Y}_{t-1}, \boldsymbol{\varphi}_1), \tag{12.47}$$

and:

$$\mathsf{D}_{\mathsf{S|Y}}(\boldsymbol{S} \mid \boldsymbol{Y}, \boldsymbol{\theta}) = \prod_{t=1}^{T} \mathsf{D}_{\mathsf{s|y}}(\boldsymbol{s}_t \mid \boldsymbol{y}_t, \boldsymbol{X}_{t-1}, \boldsymbol{\varphi}_2). \tag{12.48}$$

An alternative factorization of individual terms in (12.46) was shown in (12.38) as:

$$\mathsf{D}_{\mathsf{y,s}}(\boldsymbol{y}_t, \boldsymbol{s}_t \mid \boldsymbol{X}_{t-1}, \boldsymbol{\theta}) = \mathsf{D}_{\mathsf{y|s}}(\boldsymbol{y}_t \mid \boldsymbol{s}_t, \boldsymbol{X}_{t-1}, \boldsymbol{\mu}_1)\, \mathsf{D}_{\mathsf{s}}(\boldsymbol{s}_t \mid \boldsymbol{X}_{t-1}, \boldsymbol{\mu}_2). \tag{12.49}$$

The factorization (12.49) is often used, but the transformation from expression (12.49) to (12.47)+(12.48) is straightforward, as illustrated in the example below.

Based on the factorizations in (12.49) and (12.48), two general choices for $g_Y(\cdot)$ and $h(\cdot)$ are:[3]

$$\begin{aligned} g_Y(\boldsymbol{S} \mid \boldsymbol{\theta}) &= \prod_{t=1}^{T} \mathsf{D}_{\mathsf{s|y}}(s_t \mid y_t, \boldsymbol{X}_{t-1}, \varphi_2) \\ \text{and} & \\ h(\boldsymbol{Y}, \boldsymbol{S} \mid \boldsymbol{\theta}) &= \prod_{t=1}^{T} \mathsf{D}_{\mathsf{y}}(y_t \mid \boldsymbol{X}_{t-1}, \varphi_1), \end{aligned} \tag{12.50}$$

or:

$$\begin{aligned} g_Y(\boldsymbol{S} \mid \boldsymbol{\theta}) &= \prod_{t=1}^{T} \mathsf{D}_{\mathsf{s}}(s_t \mid \boldsymbol{X}_{t-1}, \mu_2) \\ \text{and} & \\ h(\boldsymbol{Y}, \boldsymbol{S} \mid \boldsymbol{\theta}) &= \prod_{t=1}^{T} \mathsf{D}_{\mathsf{y|s}}(y_t \mid s_t, \boldsymbol{X}_{t-1}, \mu_1). \end{aligned} \tag{12.51}$$

In either case, the random draws of $\boldsymbol{S}$ are organized sequentially: at time t, the latent variable s_t is drawn conditionally on the actual values of the observables ($\boldsymbol{Y}_t$ in (12.50) and $\boldsymbol{Y}_{t-1}$ in (12.51)), and the available simulated values $\boldsymbol{S}_{t-1}$.

Minimizing the sampling variance of the residual function $h(\cdot)$ favours the factorization in (12.50), since the densities whose product defines $h(\cdot)$ depend only on the lagged values of $\{s_t\}$, while in (12.51) they also depend on its current value. When s does not Granger-cause y, the Monte Carlo sampling variance of $h(\boldsymbol{Y}, \boldsymbol{S})$ is zero (see (12.47)) and so the choice of $g_Y(\cdot)$ in (12.50) is optimal. Other practical considerations regarding the choice of $g_Y(\cdot)$ concern the possible use of acceleration techniques: when more efficient techniques are available for the factorization in (12.51) than that in (12.50), the ranking of the $g_Y(\cdot)$s could be reversed.

12.3.3 A dynamic min-condition model

Disequilibrium behaviour, such as that due to rationing, is often represented by min-condition models (see Quandt, 1982, 1988, 1989, and Ch.A6). However, their statistical structure and the difficulties raised by unobservable dynamic variables have limited their applicability. Since such models are meant to capture adjustment out of equilibrium, they are inherently dynamic, yet truly dynamic versions of these models exhibit complex non-linearities and cannot be estimated by conventional techniques. Because Monte Carlo simulation techniques offer one potential solution, we illustrate the analysis for a simple dynamic disequilibrium model in which all elements other than lagged variables are omitted.

Let $\boldsymbol{q}_t' = (q_{1t} : q_{2t})$ denote a bivariate random variable whose conditional sampling distribution for $t = 1, \ldots, T$ is given by:

$$q_t \mid q_{t-1} \sim \mathsf{N}_2\left[\boldsymbol{A}\boldsymbol{q}_{t-1}, \boldsymbol{\Sigma}\right]. \tag{12.52}$$

Hendry and Richard (1991) considered the special case where $\boldsymbol{A}\boldsymbol{q}_{t-1} = \{\alpha_i q_{it-1}\}$ with $|\alpha_i| < 1$ and $\boldsymbol{\Sigma} = \boldsymbol{I}_2$. The initial conditions q_{i0} are given by:

$$\begin{pmatrix} q_{10} \\ q_{20} \end{pmatrix} \sim \mathsf{IN}_2\left[\begin{pmatrix} 0 \\ 0 \end{pmatrix}, \begin{pmatrix} [1-\alpha_1^2]^{-1} & 0 \\ 0 & [1-\alpha_2^2]^{-1} \end{pmatrix}\right].$$

[3] Other factorizations of $\mathsf{D}_{\mathsf{y,s}}(y_t, s_t \mid \boldsymbol{X}_{t-1}, \cdot)$ than these may lead to different choices of $g_Y(\cdot)$.

The only observable is:

$$y_t = \min\left(q_{1t}, q_{2t}\right).$$

The latent variables are a binary variable δ_t which equals i if $y_t = q_{it}$, and:

$$\lambda_t = \max\left(q_{1t}, q_{2t}\right).$$

In terms of the earlier notation, $s_t = (\lambda_t, \delta_t)'$.

Both factorizations in (12.50) and (12.51) are available, based on the algebra of the min operator applied to the bivariate normal density (see Johnson and Kotz, 1970a, and Quandt, 1988). Let $\phi(\cdot)$ denote the standardized normal density, where $\Phi(\cdot)$ is the corresponding distribution function. Conditionally on (y_{t-1}, λ_{t-1}) and $\delta_{t-1} = 1$, the elements of the factorization in (12.51) are:

$$\begin{aligned}\mathsf{D}_\lambda\left(\lambda_t \mid \boldsymbol{X}_{t-1}\right) = {} & \phi\left(\lambda_t - \alpha_1 y_{t-1}\right)\Phi\left(\lambda_t - \alpha_2\lambda_{t-1}\right) \\ & + \phi\left(\lambda_t - \alpha_2\lambda_{t-1}\right)\Phi\left(\lambda_t - \alpha_1 y_{t-1}\right)\end{aligned} \tag{12.53}$$

$$\mathsf{P}\left(\delta_t = 1 \mid \lambda_t, \boldsymbol{X}_{t-1}\right) = \frac{\phi\left(\lambda_t - \alpha_2\lambda_{t-1}\right)\Phi\left(\lambda_t - \alpha_1 y_{t-1}\right)}{\mathsf{D}_\lambda\left(\lambda_t \mid \boldsymbol{X}_{t-1}\right)} \tag{12.54}$$

$$\mathsf{D}_{\mathsf{y}|\lambda}\left(y_t \mid \lambda_t, \delta_t = 1, \boldsymbol{X}_{t-1}\right) = \begin{cases} \dfrac{\phi\left(y_t - \alpha_1 y_{t-1}\right)}{\Phi\left(\lambda_t - \alpha_1 y_{t-1}\right)} & \text{if } y_t \leq \lambda_t \\ 0 & \text{otherwise.} \end{cases} \tag{12.55}$$

Similar expressions are available conditionally on $\delta_{t-1} = 2$, with λ_{t-1} and y_{t-1} being interchanged in the formulae. The simulation is based sequentially on (12.53) and (12.54). At step t for $t = 1, \ldots, T$, draw λ_t which, from (12.53), is the maximum of a bivariate normal distribution. Conditionally on λ_t, generate a Bernoulli drawing for δ_t. The function $h(\boldsymbol{Y}, \boldsymbol{S})$ is the product of T factors of the form in (12.55). In practice, however, this algorithm generates a large number of sequences for which at least one λ_t is lower than the corresponding y_t, and as $h(\boldsymbol{Y}, \boldsymbol{S})$ is zero, its efficiency is low.

Conditionally on (y_{t-1}, λ_{t-1}) and $\delta_{t-1} = 1$, the factorization in (12.50) yields:

$$\mathsf{P}\left(\delta_t = 1 \mid y_t, \boldsymbol{X}_{t-1}\right) = \frac{\phi\left(y_t - \alpha_1 y_{t-1}\right)\left[1 - \Phi\left(y_t - \alpha_2\lambda_{t-1}\right)\right]}{\mathsf{D}_{\mathsf{y}}\left(y_t \mid \boldsymbol{X}_{t-1}\right)} \tag{12.56}$$

$$\begin{aligned}\mathsf{D}_{\mathsf{y}}\left(y_t \mid \boldsymbol{X}_{t-1}\right) = {} & \phi\left(y_t - \alpha_1 y_{t-1}\right)\left[1 - \Phi\left(y_t - \alpha_2\lambda_{t-1}\right)\right] \\ & + \phi\left(y_t - \alpha_2\lambda_{t-1}\right)\left[1 - \Phi\left(y_t - \alpha_1 y_{t-1}\right)\right]\end{aligned} \tag{12.57}$$

$$\mathsf{D}_{\lambda|\mathsf{y}}\left(\lambda_t \mid \delta_t = 1, y_t, \boldsymbol{X}_{t-1}\right) = \frac{\phi\left(\lambda_t - \alpha_2\lambda_{t-1}\right)}{1 - \Phi\left(y_t - \alpha_2\lambda_{t-1}\right)}, \quad \lambda_t \geq y_t \tag{12.58}$$

$$\mathsf{D}_{\lambda|\mathsf{y}}\left(\lambda_t \mid \delta_t = 2, y_t, \boldsymbol{X}_{t-1}\right) = \frac{\phi\left(\lambda_t - \alpha_1 y_{t-1}\right)}{1 - \Phi\left(y_t - \alpha_1 y_{t-1}\right)}, \quad \lambda_t \geq y_t. \tag{12.59}$$

Similar expressions are available conditionally on $\delta_{t-1} = 2$, with λ_{t-1} and y_{t-1} being interchanged in formulae (12.56) through (12.59). The function $h(\boldsymbol{Y}, \boldsymbol{S}|\boldsymbol{\theta})$ is the product of T factors of the form in (12.57). The simulation is based on (12.56), (12.58), and (12.59) and again proceeds sequentially. At step t for $t = 1, \ldots, T$, generate a Bernoulli drawing for δ_t with probabilities as given in (12.56). Conditionally on δ_t, draw λ_t from a truncated normal distribution given in either (12.58) or (12.59), depending on whether δ_t equals one or two.

The distributions $g_Y(\cdot)$ are artificial in that they only approximate the actual distribution of $\boldsymbol{S}$ given $\boldsymbol{Y}$. Thus, the sampling process in (12.56), (12.58), and (12.59) can be modified at will, at the cost of appropriately redefining the remainder factor in (12.57). We can, for example, leave (12.58) and (12.59) unchanged, but replace (12.56) by:

$$\mathsf{P}\left(\delta_t = 1 \mid y_t, \boldsymbol{X}_{t-1}\right) = \frac{\phi\left(y_t - \alpha_1 y_{t-1}\right)}{\phi\left(y_t - \alpha_1 y_{t-1}\right) + \phi\left(y_t - \alpha_2 \lambda_{t-1}\right)}. \tag{12.60}$$

The function $h(\boldsymbol{Y}, \boldsymbol{S}|\boldsymbol{\theta})$ is redefined accordingly as the product of T factors for $\mathsf{D_y}(y_t \mid \boldsymbol{X}_{t-1})$ of the form:

$$\begin{cases} \phi\left(y_t - \alpha_2 \lambda_{t-1}\right)\left(\phi\left(y_t - \alpha_1 y_{t-1}\right) + \phi\left(y_t - \alpha_2 \lambda_{t-1}\right)\right) \text{ if } \delta_t = 1 \\ \phi\left(y_t - \alpha_1 y_{t-1}\right)\left(\phi\left(y_t - \alpha_1 y_{t-1}\right) + \phi\left(y_t - \alpha_2 \lambda_{t-1}\right)\right) \text{ if } \delta_t = 2. \end{cases} \tag{12.61}$$

Hendry and Richard (1991) applied this approach to a one-parameter example with $\alpha_1 = \alpha_2 = \alpha$, and generated the likelihood function for $\alpha = 0.60$ and $T = 50$, based on 10 000 Monte Carlo drawings from the random-number generator characterized by equations (12.56), (12.58), and (12.59). The Monte Carlo coefficients of variation associated with the individual points were of the order of 1.5 per cent or less, using common random numbers for different values of α. Their example could be extended by the relaxation of the parameter restrictions, the introduction of additional regressors, or a price-adjustment equation as an indicator of disequilibrium.

12.3.4 Exogeneity issues

In a dynamic context, simulation under fixed exogenous variables requires that the latter be strongly exogenous, and hence both weakly exogenous and not Granger-caused by the latent variables. Let z_t denote the vector of variables weakly exogenous for the parameters of interest, where $\boldsymbol{Z}_{t-1} = (z_1 \ldots z_{t-1})$, and $\boldsymbol{W}_{t-1} = (\boldsymbol{S}_{t-1}, \boldsymbol{Z}_{t-1}, \boldsymbol{Y}_{t-1})$ regroups the lagged values of all relevant variables. The symbol $\perp$ denotes independence in probability, or conditional independence when followed by the conditioning operator $|$. To validate conditional likelihood simulation, we need the following result. If:

$$z_t \perp \boldsymbol{S}_{t-1} \mid \boldsymbol{Z}_{t-1}, \boldsymbol{Y}_{t-1}, \tag{12.62}$$

when $\boldsymbol{Z}$ is a matrix of weakly exogenous variables, the likelihood function of the observables $(\boldsymbol{Y}, \boldsymbol{Z})$ is given by:

$$\mathsf{L}\left(\boldsymbol{\theta} \mid \boldsymbol{Y}, \boldsymbol{Z}\right) = \int \cdots \int \left[\prod_{t=1}^{T} \mathsf{D_{y,s}}\left(y_t, s_t \mid z_t, \boldsymbol{W}_{t-1}, \boldsymbol{\theta}\right)\right] \mathrm{d}s_1 \ldots \mathrm{d}s_T. \tag{12.63}$$

Since (12.62) implies that $\mathsf{D}_{\mathsf{z}}(z_t | \boldsymbol{W}_{t-1}, \cdot) \equiv \mathsf{D}_{\mathsf{z}}(z_t | \boldsymbol{Y}_{t-1}, \cdot)$, the result holds as the latter density does not depend on the latent variables, and so factors out of the integral in (12.63).

Comparing (12.63) with (12.46) shows that under condition (12.62), the exogenous variables are kept fixed at their observed values in the evaluation of (12.63). If, instead, assumption (12.62) does not hold, then the exogenous process also belongs to the integral in (12.63). For MSM techniques in dynamic models with exogenous variables, when both the latent and the observable endogenous variables are subject to simulation, assumption (12.62) has to be replaced by the stronger condition that:

$$z_t \perp (\boldsymbol{S}_{t-1}, \boldsymbol{Y}_{t-1}) \mid \boldsymbol{Z}_{t-1}. \tag{12.64}$$

Overall, therefore, simulation-based methods for evaluating likelihood functions of dynamic latent-variables models offer a promising route to solving previously intractable problems. Extensions to min-condition models where prices respond to past disequilibria and to non-stationary processes, including cointegrated systems, may prove feasible.

12.4 Revisions to I(1) data

When data for an unchanged theoretical concept are revised, both the initial and final estimates cannot be correct. Usually, the revised value is closer to the desired latent variable, although there is no necessity that this be so. Revisions may alter the concept being measured, as when the banking sector is redefined, for example, and later measures may be worse approximations to the new concept than the earlier were to their concept. Revisions to nominal magnitudes are presumably due to new information accruing, whereas revisions to price deflators often arise from changing the baseline basket of goods and services. When the raw series are I(1), the revisions are likely to be so as well. For example, Hendry (1994a) compares the original series used in DHSY with a later vintage (revised in 1992 at 1985 prices) and finds revisions of more than 5 per cent to real expenditure. The standard deviation of the revisions to the consumption–income ratio is 1.7 per cent (the residual standard deviation in DHSY was only 0.5 per cent), changing the ratio by more than 7 percentage points over the sample. Smith and Weale (1992) also find significant measurement errors. Since the original and revised constant-price consumption series are not cointegrated, I(1) measurement errors can pose serious problems for modelling cointegrated data (see Nowak, 1991). However, the impacts of data revisions on econometric analyses when the underlying data are I(1) do not seem to have been thoroughly investigated despite their manifest practical importance, so we now consider some of the issue that arise. This section considers theoretically and empirically the impact of a change in a price index when the component prices are I(1).

12.4.1 Revisions to price indices

A central example of data revisions is the change in a price index when the basket of goods is altered (see Ch.A6 for an introduction). Let p_{it}, q_{it} be the price and quantity of the ith commodity ($i = 1, \ldots, N$) in a price index at time t. Consider a Laspeyres price index, denoted $P_t(q_0)$, with base period 0, and implicit reference period 1, defined as a weighted average of the price relatives $\rho_{it} = p_{it}/p_{i1}$:

$$P_t(q_0) = \frac{\sum_{i=1}^{N} q_{i0} p_{it}}{\sum_{j=1}^{N} q_{j0} p_{j1}} = \sum_{i=1}^{N} w_{i0} \rho_{it}, \tag{12.65}$$

where:

$$w_{i0} = \frac{q_{i0} p_{i1}}{\sum_{j=1}^{N} q_{j0} p_{j1}} \text{ so that } \sum_{i=1}^{N} w_{i0} = 1. \tag{12.66}$$

and hence $P_1(q_0) \equiv 1$. The base and reference periods could be the same, but altering the reference period with a fixed base period merely rescales the index so will not be analysed. The important change is altering the base period from 0 to a (say) with a fixed reference period. From (12.65):

$$\frac{P_t(q_a)}{P_t(q_0)} = \frac{\sum_{i=1}^{N} w_{ia} \rho_{it}}{\sum_{i=1}^{N} w_{i0} \rho_{it}}, \tag{12.67}$$

where both sets of weights $\{w_{i0}\}$ and $\{w_{ia}\}$ sum to unity. Consequently, changes in the price index are due to changes in the relative weights, or the shares in total expenditure of the commodities in the basket, scaled by the price relative corresponding to that weight.

Since the time-series properties of price indices are functions of their components, we decompose the price-index changes into changes in the weights and in the individual prices. Let V_{at} denote the nominal value of real expenditure in base period a at current prices:

$$V_{at} = \sum_{j=1}^{N} q_{ja} p_{jt}. \tag{12.68}$$

From (12.66):

$$w_{i0} = \frac{q_{i0} p_{i0}}{\sum_{j=1}^{N} q_{j0} p_{j0}} = \frac{q_{i0} p_{i0}}{V_{00}}, \tag{12.69}$$

where V_{00} is actual nominal expenditure in the base period. Then using (12.65):

$$P_{t-1}(q_0) = \frac{\sum_{i=1}^{N} q_{i0} p_{it-1}}{V_{00}} = \sum_{i=1}^{N} w_{i0} \rho_{it-1}, \tag{12.70}$$

and so:

$$P_t(q_0) - P_{t-1}(q_0) = V_{00}^{-1} \sum_{i=1}^{N} q_{i0} (p_{it} - p_{it-1}). \tag{12.71}$$

Thus:

$$\frac{\Delta P_t(q_0)}{P_{t-1}(q_0)} = \frac{\sum_{i=1}^{N} q_{i0} \Delta p_{it}}{\sum_{i=1}^{N} q_{i0} p_{it-1}} = \frac{\sum_{i=1}^{N} q_{i0} \Delta p_{it}}{V_{0t-1}}. \tag{12.72}$$

The left-hand side of (12.72) is approximately $\Delta \log P_t(q_0)$. Similarly:

$$\Delta \log P_t(q_a) = \frac{\sum_{i=1}^{N} q_{ia}\Delta p_{it}}{\sum_{i=1}^{N} q_{ia}p_{it-1}} = \frac{\sum_{i=1}^{N} q_{ia}\Delta p_{it}}{V_{at-1}}. \tag{12.73}$$

Since $\Delta \log[P_t(q_a)/P_t(q_0)] = \Delta \log P_t(q_a) - \Delta \log P_t(q_0)$:

$$\begin{aligned}\Delta \log\left[\frac{P_t(q_a)}{P_t(q_0)}\right] &= V_{at-1}^{-1}\left[\sum_{i=1}^{N} q_{ia}\Delta p_{it}\right] - V_{0t-1}^{-1}\left[\sum_{i=1}^{N} q_{i0}\Delta p_{it}\right] \\ &= \sum_{i=1}^{N}(W_{iat-1} - W_{i0t-1})\Delta \log p_{it},\end{aligned} \tag{12.74}$$

where $W_{iat-1} = q_{ia}p_{it-1}/V_{at-1}$. Thus, $\Delta \log[P_t(q_a)/P_t(q_0)]$ is a variable-weighted average of the $\Delta \log p_{it}$, with weights which sum to unity. Let $\delta_{ia0t} = W_{iat} - W_{i0t}$, so that $\sum_{i=1}^{N} \delta_{ia0t} = 0$.

Assume that the individual prices series are not revised, and that each $\Delta \log p_{it}$ is a non-zero mean, white-noise process ϵ_{it} (say), so that:

$$\Delta \log p_{it} = \alpha_i + \epsilon_{it} \text{ where } \epsilon_{it} \sim \mathsf{IID}[0, \sigma_{ii}], \tag{12.75}$$

then:

$$\Delta \log\left[\frac{P_t(q_a)}{P_t(q_0)}\right] = \sum_{i=1}^{N} \alpha_i\delta_{ia0t} + \sum_{i=1}^{N} \delta_{ia0t}\epsilon_{it}.$$

Conditional on information at $t-1$, denoted $\mathcal{I}_{t-1}$:

$$\mathsf{E}\left[\Delta \log\left[\frac{P_t(q_a)}{P_t(q_0)}\right] \mid \mathcal{I}_{t-1}\right] = \sum_{i=1}^{N} \alpha_i\delta_{ia0t}. \tag{12.76}$$

If $\mathsf{E}[\epsilon_{it}\epsilon_{jt}] = \sigma_{ii}$ for $i = j$, and 0 otherwise:

$$\mathsf{V}\left[\Delta \log\left[\frac{P_t(q_a)}{P_t(q_0)}\right] \mid \mathcal{I}_{t-1}\right] = \sum_{i=1}^{N} \sigma_{ii}\delta_{ia0t}^2. \tag{12.77}$$

When revisions to the weights are uncorrelated with the 'inherent inflation rates' of the individual price series, or all $\alpha_i = 0$, then (12.76) vanishes. Thus, when individual prices are random walks, the revisions induce a heteroscedastic white-noise error on the difference between the measured growth rates of the price indices. Otherwise, the revisions induce systematic effects in inflation rates.

12.4.2 An empirical illustration

US quarterly seasonally-adjusted data on prices were substantially revised in the late 1980s between a 1972 and a 1982 basis. Figures 12.1a–b show the effects of the price revisions on the levels and quarterly inflation rates of the seasonally-adjusted GNP deflator over 1959–85, denoted p_t^o (for old) and p_t^n (for new), using lower case for logs, and $\{\Delta p_t\}$ for inflation. Figure 12.1c shows the difference $\{p_t^n - p_t^o\}$, and reveals a series similar to a random walk. The standard deviation of $\{p_t^n - p_t^o\}$ is 0.027 compared to 0.007 for $\{\Delta p_t^n\}$ or 0.011 for revisions to the real money stock $\{\Delta(m-p)_t^n\}$, as measured by M1 (itself unrevised). The changes shown in these graphs may not seem too large at first glance, but their impact on the real money stock is large, changing the ratio of $(M/P)_t^o$ to $(M/P)_t^n$ by more than 10 percentage points over the sample: the original and revised constant-price money series have a correlation of only 0.85. Figure 12.1d shows the two time series. As Baba, Hendry and Starr (1992) note, despite these changes, essentially the same empirical money-demand model describes both datasets equally well.

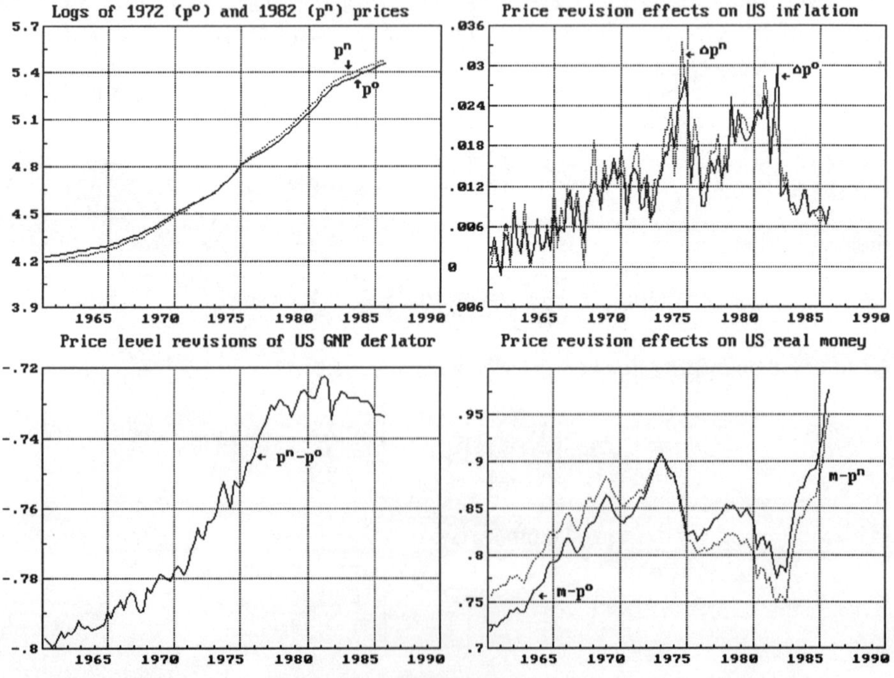

Fig. 12.1 Price index revisions to the US GNP deflator

As Fig. 12.1b suggests, the price-index revisions have the effect of adding a small variance, white-noise perturbation to the differences of the original series as shown in the following OLS regression for 1960(1)–1985(4):

$$\Delta p_t^n = \underset{(0.0004)}{0.00034} + \underset{(0.033)}{1.031}\ \Delta p_t^o - \underset{(0.002)}{0.012}\ D81(4)$$
$$\mathsf{R}^2 = 0.908,\ \hat{\sigma} = 0.22\%,\ DW = 1.96,\ SC = -12.13. \tag{12.78}$$

Standard errors are shown in parentheses; SC denotes the Schwarz criterion: all calculations used PcGive. Congruency tests for autocorrelation, parameter constancy, normality, ARCH, heteroscedasticity, and functional form were satisfactory, with the last two being borderline significant at the 5 per cent level; an outlier in 1981(4) was removed by the dummy $D81(4)$.

The key result is that the residuals on (12.78) are homoscedastic white noise: matching Fig. 12.1c, the revisions to the price levels are indeed a random walk so the two price-index measures are not cointegrated with each other. I(1) measurement errors in at least one of the two vintages is a serious problem which needs further investigation. The theory sketched above suggests one explanation of the outcome, but a more detailed analysis is required.

A similar result is reported for the UK in Hendry (1994a): the data revisions to consumers' expenditure added a white-noise perturbation to the first differences of the annual changes in the original series. The unexplained residual standard error in the equivalent regression to (12.78) was almost as large as the equation standard error in DHSY, and neither the two levels nor the two annual change measures of consumers' expenditure were cointegrated with each other.

A test for investigating which vintage is the more accurate can be based by analogy on the seasonality encompassing test in Ericsson, Hendry and Tran (1994). Under the null hypothesis that the DHSY model is valid and that their data set is accurate, the revisions are irrelevant noise so should not contribute to the explanation, whereas the revisions should help explain the DHSY specification fitted to the recent vintage. Conversely, under the rival hypothesis that the recent vintage is more accurate, and that its model is correct, the revisions should be irrelevant for that model. Applying the test, Hendry (1994a) found an inconclusive outcome, somewhat favouring DHSY.

12.5 The impact of measurement errors on ECMs

Most data series have some errors of measurement, so we now investigate the impact of adding errors to the non-modelled variable in an AD(1, 1) model (see Ch.7 for details). An algebraic analysis is tedious, since a moving-average error is created as in (12.10), so we exploit Monte Carlo. The analysis is restricted to I(0) measurement errors on I(0) variables. If the data are I(1) and the errors of measurement are I(0), their impact must be negligible, so such a case does not merit attention. It seems unlikely that the growth rates of economic variables could be mis-measured by more than an I(0) variable, with a variance that is smaller than the observed unconditional data variance. Although I(1) errors on levels are likely, as discussed in the previous section, they will not be investigated here.

Let $z_t^o = z_t + v_t$ be the observed value of a strongly exogenous variable z_t when y_t is generated by a homogeneous AD$(1, 1)$ where the long-run parameter is $K_1 = 1$. An investigator postulates the correct model form but with incorrectly measured data:

$$\Delta y_t = \beta_1 \Delta z_t^o + (\beta_2 - 1)(y - z^o)_{t-1} + e_t. \tag{12.79}$$

By comparison with the DGP equation (see (7.1)):

$$\Delta y_t = \beta_1 \Delta z_t + (\beta_2 - 1)(y - z)_{t-1} + \epsilon_t,$$

the error on (12.79) is:

$$e_t = \epsilon_t - \beta_1 \Delta v_t - (1 - \beta_2) v_{t-1}.$$

Under strong exogeneity and assuming all errors are IID and mutually uncorrelated:

$$\mathsf{E}[z_t^o e_t] = -\beta_1 \mathsf{E}[z_t^o v_t] - (1 - \beta_1 - \beta_2) \mathsf{E}[z_t^o v_{t-1}] < 0,$$

in general and:

$$\mathsf{E}[e_t e_{t-1}] = -\beta_1 (1 - \beta_1 - \beta_2) \sigma_v^2 \neq 0,$$

so (12.79) is mis-specified both by (negative) residual autocorrelation and by correlations between the regressors and the error when formulated to have the parameters $(\beta_1 : [\beta_2 - 1])$. Regression will of course orthogonalize the latter effect and thereby create different coefficients.

The DGP for z_t in the Monte Carlo includes two strongly exogenous, autoregressive determinants, which are observed without error, to be used as instrumental variables for estimating (12.79). IV estimators are consistent here, and because there are more instruments than mis-measured variables, sensible finite-sample estimates will be obtained: see section A4.9. Thus, the $\{z_t\}$ process is given by:

$$z_t = \lambda_1 z_{t-1} + \lambda_2 w_{1t} + \lambda_3 w_{2t} + \nu_t \tag{12.80}$$

where $\lambda_1 = 0.85$ and:

$$w_{jt} = \rho_j w_{jt-1} + \omega_{jt} \tag{12.81}$$

with the coefficients λ_j of the additional w_{jt} variables being unity in (12.80), $\rho_j = 0.8$ for $j = 1, 2$, and $\omega_{jt} \sim \mathsf{IN}[0, 1]$. Otherwise, the same parameter values were retained as used for the Monte Carlo in Chapter 7. The measurement error on z_t is uniform over $(-1.5, 1.5)$, so the mean is zero and standard deviation is 0.87. The resulting R^2 from fitting (12.79) is 0.53 on average. When Δz_t^o is treated as endogenous, the set of instruments is w_{1t}, w_{2t}, and $(y - z^o)_{t-1}$.

The first stage is to investigate the impact of the measurement errors on the estimated long-run coefficient K_1 derived by solving the estimated unrestricted levels equation. It might be anticipated that over a long sweep of time, the unconditional variance of z_t^o would be so large that little bias would ensue on the long-run coefficient even though the growth rate might contain substantial errors of measurement. Such a conjecture receives support in that from samples of size 40 to 80, $\hat{K}_1 > 0.9$ despite the process being stationary. Since the Monte Carlo and estimated standard errors were 0.1 or larger, H_0: $K_1 = 1$ would not be rejected. Of course, $\hat{K}_1$ has no finite moments of any order (see Chs. 7 and A4), so outliers occur with non-negligible frequency. These outcomes are similar to those found for $\hat{K}_1$ when there are no errors of measurement.

Table 12.1 ECM measurement error biases

	$\hat{\beta}_1$	$(\hat{\beta}_2 - 1)$
OLS	-0.110 (0.002)	$-.025$ (0.001)
IV	0.020 (0.002)	$-.024$ (0.001)

Next, K_1 is imposed at its population value of unity to examine the effects on the I(0) representation. Table 12.1 reports the biases in $\hat{\beta}_1$ and $(\hat{\beta}_2 - 1)$ for OLS and IV at $T = 80$.

The numbers in parentheses are the Monte Carlo standard errors of the biases for 1 000 replications. OLS estimates of β_1 are significantly downwards biased (by about 20 per cent) whereas all the other biases are relatively small.

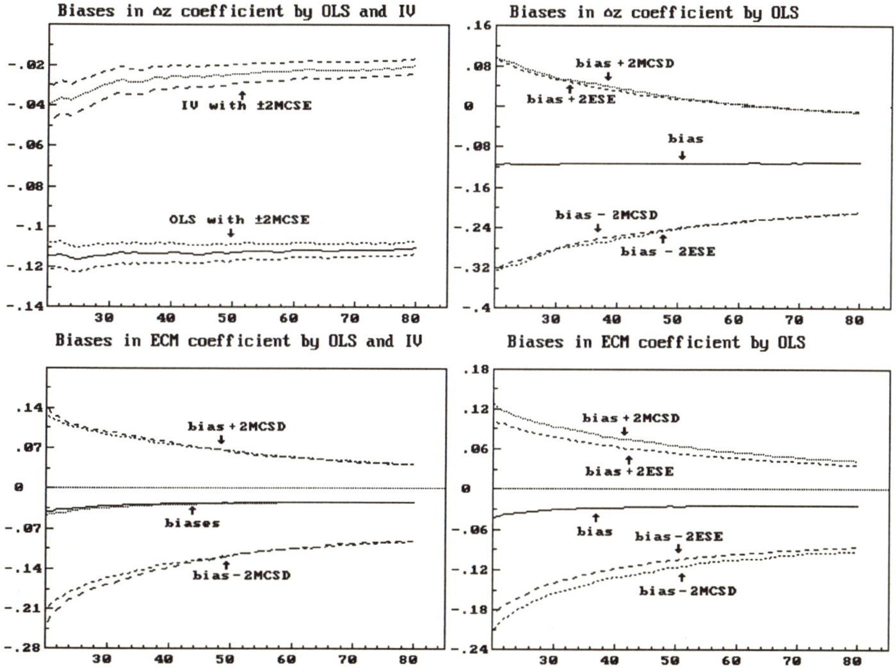

Fig. 12.2 Monte Carlo recursive biases from measurement errors

Figures 12.2a–d show the recursive estimates of the biases and standard errors. In Fig. 12.2a, the biases in $\hat{\beta}_1$ by OLS are large and only change by a small amount as T increases from 20 to 80, whereas the IV biases are always close to zero. The small MCSEs show that these outcomes are precisely determined. Despite the bias, the ESE and MCSD are close for $\hat{\beta}_1$ by OLS as Fig. 12.2b shows (as they are for IV). By way of contrast, the ECM coefficients by OLS and IV are both similar with biases close to zero as can be seen in Fig. 12.2c, which also reveals that the MCSDs are close for both estimators. Finally, Fig. 12.2d confirms that ESE and MCSD are close for $\hat{\beta}_2$ by OLS. Unsurprisingly, the OLS equation standard error is somewhat smaller than that for IV, and increases slightly with T. Finally, the negative moving-average error is detected about 25 per cent of the time by IV but rarely by OLS.

Overall, these results are encouraging: the measurement error would have increased the conditional variance of z_t by 85 per cent so it is non-trivial, although it is manifestly only one specific form. Nevertheless, the main bias is 20 per cent in the impact coefficient β_1 which, being that of a first difference, has a lower signal/noise ratio than the levels variables; the feedback coefficient is almost unbiased, the long-run is unaffected by construction, and the ESEs would have reliably estimated the correct SDs.

12.6 Exercises

12.1 Consider the model:

$$y_t = \alpha \mathsf{E}\left[y_{t+1} \mid \mathcal{I}_t\right] + \beta z_t + \epsilon_{1t} \tag{12.82}$$

when:

$$z_t = \lambda z_{t-1} + \epsilon_{2t} \text{ where } |\lambda| \leq 1 \tag{12.83}$$

and:

$$\epsilon_t = \begin{pmatrix} \epsilon_{1t} \\ \epsilon_{2t} \end{pmatrix} \sim \mathsf{IN}_2\left[\begin{pmatrix} 0 \\ 0 \end{pmatrix}, \begin{pmatrix} \sigma_{11} & 0 \\ 0 & \sigma_{22} \end{pmatrix}\right] \tag{12.84}$$

where $\mathcal{I}_t$ is available information.

(a) Discuss the identification or lack of identification of this model and propose some solutions for the second case.

(b) Assuming that $|\alpha| < 1$, sketch the patterns of effects on y_t of permanent, temporary, and gradual phase-out unanticipated unit shocks in z_t.

(c) Comment on limited and full information methods for estimating the model in (12.82)–(12.84).

(d) Explain under what conditions the regression of y_t on z_t will yield a consistent estimator of the long-run elasticity $(1-\alpha)^{-1}\beta$ and discuss whether these conditions are likely to be hold in practice.

(Oxford M.Phil., 1987)

12.2 Consider the model:

$$y_t^0 = \beta x_t^0 \text{ where } x_t^0 \sim \mathsf{IN}\left[0, \sigma_{22}\right] \tag{12.85}$$

with:

$$\begin{pmatrix} y_t \\ x_t \end{pmatrix} = \begin{pmatrix} y_t^0 \\ x_t^0 \end{pmatrix} + \begin{pmatrix} \epsilon_t \\ \nu_t \end{pmatrix}, \tag{12.86}$$

when

$$\begin{pmatrix} \epsilon_t \\ \nu_t \end{pmatrix} \sim \mathsf{IN}_2\left[\begin{pmatrix} 0 \\ 0 \end{pmatrix}, \begin{pmatrix} \omega_{11} & 0 \\ 0 & \omega_{22} \end{pmatrix}\right], \tag{12.87}$$

independently of (y_t^0, x_t^0). However, only (y_t, x_t) are observed for $t = 1, \ldots, T$.

(a) Show that the OLS estimator $\hat{\beta}$ of β from regressing y_t on x_t is inconsistent despite (12.85).

(b) If ω_{22} is known, show that β is uniquely defined (identifiable).

(c) Show that $(x_t y_t - \beta\sigma_{22}) \sim \mathsf{IID}[0, (\beta^2\sigma_{22}(2\sigma_{22}+\omega_{22})+\omega_{11}(\sigma_{22}+\omega_{22}))]$. Hence derive the limiting distribution of $\hat{\beta}$, appropriately normalized.

(d) Derive the limiting distribution of any consistent estimator $\tilde{\beta}$ of β, when ω_{22} is known. Comment on the resulting asymptotic variances of $\hat{\beta}$ and $\tilde{\beta}$.

(Oxford M.Phil., 1982)

12.3 Consider the over-identified structural equation:

$$y_t = \boldsymbol{x}_t'\boldsymbol{\beta} + \epsilon_t \tag{12.88}$$

where $\epsilon_t \sim \mathsf{IN}[0, \sigma_\epsilon^2]$ for $t = 1, \ldots, T$, when $\boldsymbol{\beta}$ is $k \times 1$, but $\mathsf{E}[\boldsymbol{x}_t\epsilon_t] \neq \mathbf{0}$ due to measurement errors. However, there exists a vector of $m > k$ stationary instrumental variables $\boldsymbol{z}_t$ which satisfy $\mathsf{E}[\boldsymbol{z}_t\epsilon_t] = \mathbf{0}\ \forall t$ such that:

$$\boldsymbol{x}_t = \boldsymbol{\pi}\boldsymbol{z}_t + \boldsymbol{\nu}_t \tag{12.89}$$

where $\mathsf{E}[\boldsymbol{z}_t\boldsymbol{\nu}_t'] = \mathbf{0}\ \forall t$. The solved version of the equation given (12.88) is written as:

$$y_t = \boldsymbol{z}_t'\boldsymbol{\delta} + \omega_t \tag{12.90}$$

and $\mathsf{E}[\boldsymbol{z}_t\omega_t] = \mathbf{0}\ \forall t$.

(a) Derive an estimator generating equation for this class of problem.

(b) Obtain the limiting distribution of the general instrumental-variables estimator $\hat{\boldsymbol{\beta}}$ of $\boldsymbol{\beta}$, carefully stating all the assumptions and theorems you use.

(c) Obtain a statistic for testing the validity of the instruments $\boldsymbol{z}_t$ used for estimation, corresponding to H_0: $\mathsf{E}[\boldsymbol{z}_t\epsilon_t] = \mathbf{0}$, and show that your proposed test is equivalent to testing the hypothesis that $\boldsymbol{\delta} = \boldsymbol{\pi}'\boldsymbol{\beta}$.

(d) How does the EGE in (a) relate to that obtained for simultaneous equations?

13

Testing and Evaluation

After reviewing the statistical framework at level B for testing one parametric hypothesis against another, the non-central χ^2 distribution associated with many hypothesis testing situations is introduced. The large-sample properties of tests for sequences of local alternatives are analysed. An approximation to the non-central χ^2 distribution reveals the determinants of test power for tests that depend only on the distance of the null from the alternative, and are invariant to the direction of the departure. Likelihood ratio, Wald, and Lagrange-multiplier tests are introduced and compared, the last being illustrated by a solved example. The behaviour of these tests for non-linear restrictions is considered and some of the methodological implications of the analysis for evaluation are highlighted.

13.1 The statistical framework

As with the theory of estimation discussed in Chapters 10 and 11, the analysis is at level B, based on the sequentially factorized joint data-density function:

$$\mathsf{D_X}\left(\boldsymbol{X}_T^1 \mid \boldsymbol{X}_0, \boldsymbol{\theta}\right) = \prod_{t=1}^{T} \mathsf{D_x}\left(\boldsymbol{x}_t \mid \boldsymbol{X}_{t-1}^1, \boldsymbol{\theta}\right) \text{ with } \boldsymbol{\theta} \in \Theta \subseteq \mathbb{R}^k. \tag{13.1}$$

The likelihood function $\mathsf{L}(\boldsymbol{\theta}|\cdot)$ follows as in Chapter 10, and we assume the validity of the results established there and in Chapters A3 and A4 for the limiting distribution of the MLE $\widehat{\boldsymbol{\theta}}$, namely:

$$\sqrt{T}\left(\widehat{\boldsymbol{\theta}} - \boldsymbol{\theta}_p\right) \underset{a}{\sim} \mathsf{N}_k\left[\mathbf{0}, \boldsymbol{V}\right], \tag{13.2}$$

where $\boldsymbol{\theta}_p$ denotes the population value of $\boldsymbol{\theta}$, and $\boldsymbol{V}$ is the variance-covariance matrix of the limiting distribution. In finite samples, we approximate the distribution in (13.2) by:

$$\widehat{\boldsymbol{\theta}} \underset{app}{\sim} \mathsf{N}_k\left[\boldsymbol{\theta}_p, T^{-1}\boldsymbol{V}\right]. \tag{13.3}$$

Many situations in economics involve tests concerning conjectured numerical values of the parameter $\boldsymbol{\theta}$ or subsets thereof. For example, we may want to check whether some particular θ_i is zero, or whether two elements θ_i and θ_j are equal. Tests of this form are called specification tests, since they concern aspects of the model as specified (see Mizon, 1977b). In other situations, we wish to check on the adequacy of a model as a data description, and so embed the model in a larger model to check whether it is a valid reduction. Tests of this form are called mis-specification tests, or diagnostic checks if they concern model evaluation following a sequential reduction. Chapter 9 delineated the relevant criteria for model evaluation as corresponding to no loss of information from reductions. In the present chapter, we consider the statistical theory of hypothesis testing: Chapter A3 provides the relevant background.

The general analysis is formulated as follows. The statistical model within which all testing will take place is called the maintained hypothesis, H_m: $\boldsymbol{\theta} \in \Theta$. It is essential that the model sustaining H_m be congruent if the tests are to yield valid inferences. We wish to know which of two hypotheses holds within H_m, namely, the null hypothesis denoted by H_0: $\boldsymbol{\theta} \in \Theta_0$ where Θ_0 is a subset of the parameter space Θ, or the alternative hypothesis H_1: $\boldsymbol{\theta} \notin \Theta_0$, corresponding to $\boldsymbol{\theta} \in \Theta - \Theta_0$. The properties of the resulting tests depend on maintaining that $\boldsymbol{\theta}$ is an element in the overall parameter space Θ, and that granted, we test to see in which of the two conjectured regions of Θ the population value of $\boldsymbol{\theta}$ lies. In order to conduct a test of H_0 against H_1 conditional on $\boldsymbol{\theta} \in \Theta$, we partition the observation space $\mathcal{X}$ of the relevant random variable X into two regions such that when we observe certain values of X, we decide to accept that $\boldsymbol{\theta} \in \Theta_0$, but when we observe other values of X, we decide to reject $\boldsymbol{\theta} \in \Theta_0$. Thus, before observing the data, partition $\mathcal{X}$ into the two regions $\mathcal{R}$ and $\mathcal{X} - \mathcal{R} = \mathcal{R}^c$ such that when $\boldsymbol{X}_T^1 \in \mathcal{R}$, reject H_0, whereas when $\boldsymbol{X}_T^1 \notin \mathcal{R}$ (i.e. $\boldsymbol{X}_T^1 \in \mathcal{R}^c$), do not reject H_0.

$\mathcal{R}$ is called the critical region. Since X is a random variable, it could lie in $\mathcal{R}$ even when H_0 is true. Consequently, we would like to set a small probability α such that:

$$\mathsf{P}\left(\boldsymbol{X}_T^1 \in \mathcal{R} \mid \mathsf{H}_0\right) = \alpha\left(T, \boldsymbol{\theta}\right), \qquad (13.4)$$

where α is called the significance level of the test. A test is called similar when $\alpha(T, \boldsymbol{\theta})$ does not depend on $\boldsymbol{\theta}$, since it behaves the same at all points in $\boldsymbol{\theta}$, in which case $\alpha(T)$ is called the size of the test. When H_0 is true, the outcome that $\boldsymbol{X}_T^1 \in \mathcal{R}$ is called a Type I error, so such a mistake occurs with probability $\alpha(T)$.

At the same time, we would like to have a high probability $\mathcal{P}(\cdot)$ such that:

$$\mathsf{P}\left(\boldsymbol{X}_T^1 \in \mathcal{R} \mid \mathsf{H}_1\right) = \mathcal{P}\left(T, \boldsymbol{\theta}_p, \Theta_0, \alpha\right), \qquad (13.5)$$

where $\mathcal{P}$ is called the power of the test, and generally depends on T and $\boldsymbol{\theta}_p$ as well as on α and Θ_0. When H_1 is true but $\boldsymbol{X}_T^1 \notin \mathcal{R}$, we are said to make a Type II error. Both α and $\mathcal{P}$ vary as the choice of $\mathcal{R}$ is changed. Tests with $\alpha(\cdot) = 0$ and $\mathcal{P}(\cdot) = 1$ for all values of T and $\boldsymbol{\theta}$ would be optimal, but because X is random, Type I and Type II errors are inevitable unless T is essentially infinite.

Since $\boldsymbol{X}_T^1$ usually has a complicated distribution in economics, at first sight the problem of choosing $\mathcal{R}$ and calculating α and $\mathcal{P}$ looks insoluble. The trick is to take a scalar function of $\boldsymbol{X}_T^1$ denoted by $g(\boldsymbol{X})$ such that we seek:

$$\mathsf{P}\left(g\left(\boldsymbol{X}_T^1\right) \in r\right) = \mathsf{P}\left(\boldsymbol{X}_T^1 \in \mathcal{R}\right) \qquad (13.6)$$

where r is an interval of $\mathbb{R}$. In (13.6), $g(\boldsymbol{X}_T^1)$ is a function of the data only, and does not depend directly on $\boldsymbol{\theta}$, although the probability that $g(\boldsymbol{X}_T^1)$ lies in r must depend on $\boldsymbol{\theta}$ if we wish to discriminate H_0 from H_1 using data evidence. In practice, α is usually set, and we derive the corresponding r_α (say) for functions $g(\boldsymbol{X}_T^1)$ with known distributions when H_0 is true, then determine the behaviour of the statistic under the alternative, which is the power function of the test.

Consider the example of a scalar parameter θ, where the MLE has a known variance:

$$\hat{\theta} \sim \mathsf{N}\left[\theta_p, \sigma^2\right]. \tag{13.7}$$

From (13.7), on the null hypothesis H_0 that $\theta_p = \theta_0$:

$$\eta_0 = \frac{\left(\hat{\theta} - \theta_0\right)^2}{\sigma^2} \sim \chi^2(1). \tag{13.8}$$

When H_0: $\theta_p = \theta_0$ is true, $(\hat{\theta} - \theta_0)^2/\sigma^2$ depends only on the data, and so is a potential solution to the test derivation problem. Since η_0 has no unknowns under H_0: $\theta_p = \theta_0$, and the probability distribution of $\chi^2(1)$ is known, the probabilities of η_0 exceeding certain values c_α (say) can be calculated. Moreover, in this case, α does not depend on T or θ since:

$$\mathsf{P}\left(\chi^2(1) \geq c_\alpha \mid \mathsf{H}_0\right) = \alpha, \tag{13.9}$$

when c_α is the appropriate critical value based on the upper α-tail of the $\chi^2(1)$ distribution. Conventionally, α is set at 0.05 but we will comment on that later. To test an hypothesis such as H_0: $\theta_p = \theta_0$, in effect we replace θ_p by θ_0 in (13.7) and compare the outcome η_0 with the $\chi^2(1)$ table. When H_0 is false, so the true but unknown value θ_p differs from θ_0, then from (13.8), the test statistic is equal to:

$$\frac{\left(\hat{\theta} - \theta_0\right)^2}{\sigma^2} = \frac{\left[\left(\hat{\theta} - \theta_p\right) - (\theta_0 - \theta_p)\right]^2}{\sigma^2}. \tag{13.10}$$

To calculate the power of the test under H_1, we need some results on central and non-central $\chi^2(\cdot)$ distributions, and these are presented in the next section.

13.2 Non-central χ^2 distributions

Let $\chi^2(k)$ denote a random variable from the central chi-square distribution with k degrees of freedom. When $\boldsymbol{V}$ is a known $k \times k$ non-singular matrix, a quadratic form in (13.3) leads to the test statistic $\eta_0(k)$ on H_0: $\boldsymbol{\theta}_p = \boldsymbol{\theta}_0$, where:

$$\eta_0(k) = T\left(\hat{\boldsymbol{\theta}} - \boldsymbol{\theta}_0\right)' \boldsymbol{V}^{-1}\left(\hat{\boldsymbol{\theta}} - \boldsymbol{\theta}_0\right) \underset{\mathsf{H}_0}{\sim} \chi^2(k). \tag{13.11}$$

The notation '$\underset{\mathsf{H}_0}{\sim}$' denotes that the distribution takes the form shown only when H_0 is true. When H_0: $\boldsymbol{\theta}_p = \boldsymbol{\theta}_0$ is true for the conjectured value $\boldsymbol{\theta}_0$ of $\boldsymbol{\theta}_p$, the function on the left-hand side in (13.11) again depends only on the data, and we can choose α such that:

$$\mathsf{P}\left(\chi^2(k) \geq c_{\alpha,k} \mid \mathsf{H}_0\right) = \alpha, \tag{13.12}$$

where $c_{\alpha,k}$ is the critical value based on the upper α-tail of the $\chi^2(k)$ distribution. When H_0 is false, and $\boldsymbol{\theta}_p \neq \boldsymbol{\theta}_0$, then from (13.3):

$$\left(\hat{\boldsymbol{\theta}} - \boldsymbol{\theta}_0\right) \sim \mathsf{N}_k\left[(\boldsymbol{\theta}_p - \boldsymbol{\theta}_0), T^{-1}\boldsymbol{V}\right], \tag{13.13}$$

and this switches from a mean-zero, or central, normal distribution to a non-central normal distribution.

To obtain the power function of $\eta_0(k)$, we need two theorems:

THEOREM **1.** *If* $(\hat{\boldsymbol{\theta}} - \boldsymbol{\theta}_0)$ *is distributed as:*

$$\left(\hat{\boldsymbol{\theta}} - \boldsymbol{\theta}_0\right) \sim \mathsf{N}_k\left[(\boldsymbol{\theta}_p - \boldsymbol{\theta}_0), \boldsymbol{\Omega}\right], \tag{13.14}$$

where $\boldsymbol{\Omega}$ *is a* $k \times k$ *non-singular variance matrix, then letting* $\boldsymbol{\Omega}^{-1} = \boldsymbol{K}\boldsymbol{K}'$ *such that* $\boldsymbol{K}'\boldsymbol{\Omega}\boldsymbol{K} = \boldsymbol{I}_k$*:*

$$\boldsymbol{K}'\left(\hat{\boldsymbol{\theta}} - \boldsymbol{\theta}_0\right) \sim \mathsf{N}_k\left[\boldsymbol{\mu}, \boldsymbol{I}_k\right], \tag{13.15}$$

where $\boldsymbol{\mu} = \boldsymbol{K}'(\boldsymbol{\theta}_p - \boldsymbol{\theta}_0)$ *is the non-centrality parameter.*

THEOREM **2.** *If* $\boldsymbol{w} \sim \mathsf{N}_k[\boldsymbol{b}, \boldsymbol{I}_k]$*, then* $\boldsymbol{w}'\boldsymbol{w} \sim \chi^2(k, \boldsymbol{b}'\boldsymbol{b})$*.*

Thus, when $\boldsymbol{w}$ has a non-central k-dimensional normal distribution, then $\boldsymbol{w}'\boldsymbol{w}$ has a non-central χ^2 distribution with non-centrality parameter $\boldsymbol{b}'\boldsymbol{b}$ and k degrees of freedom. In other words, if the normal random variable has a non-zero mean $\boldsymbol{b}$ and an identity variance matrix, then its quadratic form is a non-central χ^2: §13.4 analyses non-central $\chi^2(\cdot)$ distributions. Below, $\chi^2(k)$ is also written as $\chi^2(k, 0)$ where the second argument denotes a zero non-centrality.

From (13.13), applying the two theorems, we have:

$$\boldsymbol{K}'\left(\hat{\boldsymbol{\theta}} - \boldsymbol{\theta}_0\right) \sim \mathsf{N}_k\left[\boldsymbol{K}'(\boldsymbol{\theta}_p - \boldsymbol{\theta}_0), \boldsymbol{I}_k\right] = \mathsf{N}_k\left[\boldsymbol{\mu}, \boldsymbol{I}_k\right], \tag{13.16}$$

and hence on H_1: $\boldsymbol{\theta}_p \neq \boldsymbol{\theta}_0$, then $\eta_0(k) \sim \chi^2(k, \psi^2)$ where:

$$\psi^2 = \boldsymbol{\mu}'\boldsymbol{\mu} = (\boldsymbol{\theta}_p - \boldsymbol{\theta}_0)'\boldsymbol{K}\boldsymbol{K}'(\boldsymbol{\theta}_p - \boldsymbol{\theta}_0) = T(\boldsymbol{\theta}_p - \boldsymbol{\theta}_0)'\boldsymbol{V}^{-1}(\boldsymbol{\theta}_p - \boldsymbol{\theta}_0). \tag{13.17}$$

We deduce that when H_0 is true, $\psi^2 = 0$, and otherwise ψ^2 is the same type of quadratic form as the test statistic, with the MLE replaced by the population parameter value.

To illustrate the above analysis in terms of regression theory from Chapter A4, when $\text{plim}\,\hat{\boldsymbol{\beta}} = \boldsymbol{\beta}_p$:

$$\sqrt{T}\left(\hat{\boldsymbol{\beta}} - \boldsymbol{\beta}_p\right) \sim \mathsf{N}_k\left[\boldsymbol{0}, \sigma^2\boldsymbol{M}^{-1}\right]. \tag{13.18}$$

From theorems 1 and 2 applied to (13.18) when $\sigma^2 \boldsymbol{M}^{-1}$ is known, and $\boldsymbol{M}$ is non-singular:

$$T\sigma^{-2}\left(\hat{\boldsymbol{\beta}} - \boldsymbol{\beta}_p\right)' \boldsymbol{M}\left(\hat{\boldsymbol{\beta}} - \boldsymbol{\beta}_p\right) \sim \chi^2(k).$$

In practice, $\boldsymbol{\beta}_p$ is unknown, so the test statistic is calculated by replacing $\boldsymbol{\beta}_p$ by an assumed value $\boldsymbol{\beta}_0$, so that on H_0: $\boldsymbol{\beta}_p = \boldsymbol{\beta}_0$:

$$\eta_0(k) = T\sigma^{-2}\left(\hat{\boldsymbol{\beta}} - \boldsymbol{\beta}_0\right)' \boldsymbol{M}\left(\hat{\boldsymbol{\beta}} - \boldsymbol{\beta}_0\right) \underset{\mathsf{H}_0}{\sim} \chi^2(k). \tag{13.19}$$

The middle expression in (13.19) is called a pivotal quantity, in that having replaced the unknown $\boldsymbol{\beta}_p$ by the conjectured value $\boldsymbol{\beta}_0$ to be tested, there are no unknowns in the test statistic. Under the null H_0: $\boldsymbol{\beta}_p = \boldsymbol{\beta}_0$, the test statistic $\eta_0(k)$ is distributed as $\chi^2(k)$ and hence we can calculate $c_{\alpha,k}$ for any desired α from (13.12). Under the alternative that H_1: $\boldsymbol{\beta}_p \neq \boldsymbol{\beta}_0$, we can calculate the power function $\mathcal{P}(\cdot)$ for various T and $\boldsymbol{\beta}_p$ using theorems 1 and 2:

$$\mathsf{P}\left(\chi^2\left(k, \psi^2\right) \geq c_{\alpha,k} \mid \mathsf{H}_1\right) = \mathcal{P}\left(\psi^2, \alpha\right), \tag{13.20}$$

where:

$$\psi^2 = T\sigma^{-2}\left(\boldsymbol{\beta}_p - \boldsymbol{\beta}_0\right)' \boldsymbol{M}\left(\boldsymbol{\beta}_p - \boldsymbol{\beta}_0\right).$$

Thus, in this instance, the power of the test depends on the hypothesis, the sample size, the error variance, and the values of the parameters only through the non-centrality parameter ψ^2.

13.3 Large-sample properties of tests

When the variance matrix $\boldsymbol{V}$ in (13.2), or $\sigma^2 \boldsymbol{M}^{-1}$ in (13.19), is non-singular but unknown, it must be replaced by a consistent estimator, such that $\hat{\boldsymbol{V}} \xrightarrow{P} \boldsymbol{V}$, or $\hat{\sigma}^2 \hat{\boldsymbol{M}}^{-1} \xrightarrow{P} \sigma^2 \boldsymbol{M}^{-1}$. Using Slutsky's theorem (see Ch.A4), for the general case of a parameter $\boldsymbol{\theta}$ estimated by $\hat{\boldsymbol{\theta}}$, in large samples on H_0: $\boldsymbol{\theta}_p = \boldsymbol{\theta}_0$:

$$\eta_0(k) = T\left(\hat{\boldsymbol{\theta}} - \boldsymbol{\theta}_0\right)' \hat{\boldsymbol{V}}^{-1}\left(\hat{\boldsymbol{\theta}} - \boldsymbol{\theta}_0\right) \underset{\mathsf{H}_0}{\overset{D}{\rightarrow}} \chi^2(k). \tag{13.21}$$

The size α of this $\eta_0(k)$ test is based on the asymptotic $\chi^2(k)$ distribution, usually called the nominal size, which may differ from the actual null rejection frequency in small samples.

Tests of the form in (13.21) occur regularly in econometrics, are readily computed, and have a number of useful properties. Under the alternative hypothesis H_1: $\boldsymbol{\theta}_p \neq \boldsymbol{\theta}_0$, from theorems 1 and 2 above, $\eta_0(k)$ has a non-central χ^2 distribution in large samples. However, we have to be careful how that limiting non-central distribution is derived. If we merely replace $\boldsymbol{\theta}_p$ by $\boldsymbol{\theta}_0$, then the non-centrality of the approximate normal distribution in (13.13) becomes $\sqrt{T}(\boldsymbol{\theta}_p - \boldsymbol{\theta}_0)$, so that when $\boldsymbol{\theta}_p \neq \boldsymbol{\theta}_0$, the non-centrality tends to infinity with T. The resulting test distribution which is the same for most tests, and is uninterpretable, except that it confirms the consistency of $\eta_0(k)$ for $\boldsymbol{\theta}_p \neq \boldsymbol{\theta}_0$, as shown below. Consequently, instead of fixed alternatives of the form $\boldsymbol{\theta}_0 \neq \boldsymbol{\theta}_p$, we consider a sequence of local alternatives given by:

$$\mathsf{H}_T\colon \boldsymbol{\theta}_p = \boldsymbol{\theta}_0 + T^{-\frac{1}{2}}\boldsymbol{\delta}. \tag{13.22}$$

In (13.22), $\boldsymbol{\delta}$ is taken to be fixed as T tends to infinity. The resulting sequence provides local alternatives, so-called because the difference between $\boldsymbol{\theta}_p$ and $\boldsymbol{\theta}_0$ becomes arbitrarily close to 0 for ever larger amounts of information. Of course, we can pick $\boldsymbol{\delta}$ as large or as small as desired to consider large or small departures of $\boldsymbol{\theta}_0$ from $\boldsymbol{\theta}_p$ at any given sample size. From (13.22):

$$\sqrt{T}\left(\boldsymbol{\theta}_p - \boldsymbol{\theta}_0\right) = \boldsymbol{\delta}, \tag{13.23}$$

and hence from §13.2:

$$\sqrt{T}\left(\hat{\boldsymbol{\theta}} - \boldsymbol{\theta}_0\right) \underset{a}{\sim} \mathsf{N}_k\left[\boldsymbol{\delta}, \mathbf{V}\right], \tag{13.24}$$

so in (13.24), $\boldsymbol{\delta}$ is the non-centrality parameter of the limiting normal distribution. The null hypothesis characterized by H_0: $\boldsymbol{\delta} = \mathbf{0}$ corresponds to $\boldsymbol{\theta}_0 = \boldsymbol{\theta}_p$, and we consider sequences of local alternatives for non-zero $\boldsymbol{\delta}$ which nevertheless converge on the null as T increases without bound.

Although we are testing $\boldsymbol{\theta}_0$ as a local alternative to $\boldsymbol{\theta}_p$ relative to ever-increasing amounts of information, we can still use (13.22) to investigate behaviour for fixed alternatives. If in fact $\boldsymbol{\theta}_0$ differs from $\boldsymbol{\theta}_p$ by a fixed amount, then $\boldsymbol{\delta} = \sqrt{T}(\boldsymbol{\theta}_p - \boldsymbol{\theta}_0)$ will tend to infinity with the sample size. Thus, (13.24) becomes a normal distribution with an infinitely large non-centrality, and hence we will be able to reject any fixed false null with certainty. That leads to the first criterion for selecting a test statistic, namely consistency.

Denote a generic χ^2-test by η with the decision rule: reject H_0 when $\eta > c_\alpha$, where the probability of that event under H_0 is:

$$\mathsf{P}\left(\eta > c_\alpha \mid \mathsf{H}_0\right) = \alpha. \tag{13.25}$$

Here, η is the scalar statistic which corresponds to $g(\cdot)$ in the original formulation in (13.6) above, and r is the interval (c_α, ∞). Then the test η is consistent if:

$$\mathsf{P}\left(\eta > c_\alpha \mid \mathsf{H}_1\right) = \mathcal{P}\left(\cdot\right) \underset{T\to\infty}{\to} 1, \tag{13.26}$$

so the probability of rejecting H_0 when it is false becomes unity as the sample size tends to infinity.

Since the probability of falsely rejecting H_0 is α according to (13.25), and the probability of correctly rejecting H_0 is $\mathcal{P}(\cdot)$ by (13.26), a second criterion for selecting tests is that $\mathcal{P}(\cdot) \geq \alpha$ for all values of T and $\boldsymbol{\theta}$, in which case, the test is said to be unbiased.

To apply (13.26) to the pivotal-quantity test $\eta_0(k)$ in (13.21), compute:

$$\eta_0\left(k\right) = T\left(\hat{\boldsymbol{\theta}} - \boldsymbol{\theta}_0\right)' \hat{\mathbf{V}}^{-1}\left(\hat{\boldsymbol{\theta}} - \boldsymbol{\theta}_0\right) \underset{\mathsf{H}_T}{\overset{D}{\to}} \chi^2\left(k, \psi_\eta^2\right), \tag{13.27}$$

on H_T: $\boldsymbol{\theta}_p = \boldsymbol{\theta}_0 + \boldsymbol{\delta}/\sqrt{T}$. Here, ψ^2_η is the non-centrality parameter given by conversion from the non-centrality $\boldsymbol{\delta}$ of the associated normal distribution as in theorem 2, namely:

$$\psi^2_\eta = \boldsymbol{\delta}' \mathbf{V}^{-1} \boldsymbol{\delta} = T\left(\boldsymbol{\theta}_p - \boldsymbol{\theta}_0\right)' \mathbf{V}^{-1}\left(\boldsymbol{\theta}_p - \boldsymbol{\theta}_0\right). \tag{13.28}$$

Under the alternative (13.22) for pivotal tests of this χ^2 form, we obtain a non-central χ^2. However, when $\boldsymbol{\theta}_p \neq \boldsymbol{\theta}_0$ for a fixed $\boldsymbol{\theta}_0$, then ψ^2_η tends to infinity as T grows, which shows that $\eta_0(k)$ is consistent.

The initial decision rule for a test $\eta_0(k)$ derived on H_0: $\boldsymbol{\theta}_p = \boldsymbol{\theta}_0$ is a plan to reject H_0 if:

$$\mathsf{P}\left[\chi^2(k, 0) > c_{\alpha,k}\right] = \alpha. \tag{13.29}$$

With this rule, rejection of H_0 occurs in large samples with probability α when H_0 is true. When α is small and the event $\eta_0(k) > c_{\alpha,k}$ occurs, we must conclude that either an unlikely outcome happened or that H_0 is false. Under the alternative, H_T: $\boldsymbol{\theta}_p = \boldsymbol{\theta}_0 + \boldsymbol{\delta}/\sqrt{T}$, what we are in fact computing is the probability:

$$\mathsf{P}\left[\chi^2\left(k, \psi^2_\eta\right) > c_{\alpha,k}\right] = \mathcal{P}\left(\psi^2_\eta, T, \alpha\right). \tag{13.30}$$

α (which may depend on T in practice) is the Type-I error, and $1 - \mathcal{P}(\psi^2_\eta, T, \alpha)$ is the Type-II error, so the test will be useful if for small α, the Type-II error is small. The final step is to show that the probability of a non-central χ^2 being larger than $c_{\alpha,k}$ is greater than the probability of the original central χ^2 exceeding $c_{\alpha,k}$, and so a $\chi^2(k, \psi^2_\eta)$ with a non-zero non-centrality parameter ψ^2_η is everywhere larger than the equivalent $\chi^2(k, 0)$. The next section demonstrates that result, and shows that $\mathcal{P}(\cdot) \geq \alpha$, so that the χ^2-test in (13.29) and (13.30) is unbiased and consistent, although $\eta_0(k)$ may be biased in small samples when it is not exactly distributed as χ^2.

To recap the discussion so far: we need to derive the distribution of any proposed test under the null hypothesis, as is satisfied by the t, F, and χ^2 tests commonly used. Secondly, we need to obtain the distribution of the test under a relevant class of alternatives to establish that the test is more likely to reject when the null is false than when it is true. Thirdly, we would like a test with a non-centrality parameter which tends to infinity for any fixed alternative so that the probability of rejection tends to unity. Finally, we would like a test with the highest power to reject false null hypotheses locally, as well as fixed incorrect conjectures. Often, we can only establish results which hold in large samples, so approximate distributions and Monte Carlo simulations may be used to study departures from asymptotic behaviour.

13.4 Understanding the non-central χ^2 distribution

Because many widely-used tests have non-central χ^2 distributions when H_0 is false, it will be useful to gain some insight into the properties of that distribution. First, its mean and variance are given by:

$$\mathsf{E}\left[\chi^2\left(k, \psi^2\right)\right] = k + \psi^2, \tag{13.31}$$

so that the non-centrality parameter and the degrees of freedom are simply added; and:

$$\mathsf{V}\left[\chi^2\left(k,\psi^2\right)\right] = 2\left(k + 2\psi^2\right). \tag{13.32}$$

For detailed derivations, see Johnson and Kotz (1970b). Since (13.31) and (13.32) hold for $\psi^2 = 0$, the central χ^2 has mean k and variance $2k$. From (13.32), as $\psi \to \infty$, the standard deviation of $\chi^2(k,\psi^2)$ increases roughly as ψ, whereas, from (13.31), the mean increases as ψ^2, so that the ratio of the mean to the standard deviation tends to infinity. To understand why testing procedures, it is useful to relate the non-central χ^2 distribution to that of the central χ^2, which we do by approximating the non-central χ^2 by a proportion of a central χ^2:

$$\chi^2\left(k,\psi^2\right) = h\chi^2\left(m,0\right), \tag{13.33}$$

where $h > 0$ and $m > 0$ are selected to ensure that the approximating distribution $h\chi^2(m,0)$ has the same first two moments as $\chi^2(k,\psi^2)$. Equating the non-central χ^2 mean and variance to the proportions of the central χ^2 with mean hm and variance $2h^2m$ using (13.31) and (13.32), we obtain:

$$\psi^2 + k = hm, \tag{13.34}$$

and:

$$2\left(k + 2\psi^2\right) = 2h^2m. \tag{13.35}$$

Solving for h by dividing (13.35) by (13.34) yields:

$$h = \frac{k + 2\psi^2}{k + \psi^2} = 1 + \frac{\psi^2}{k + \psi^2} \geq 1, \tag{13.36}$$

and then m is given by:

$$m = \frac{k + \psi^2}{h} = \frac{\left(k + \psi^2\right)^2}{k + 2\psi^2} = k + \frac{\psi^4}{k + 2\psi^2} \geq k. \tag{13.37}$$

When $\psi = 0$, then $h = 1$ and $m = k$. Thus, (13.36) and (13.37) reveal several features of the approximation in (13.33):

(i) $h \geq 1$, so that the non-central χ^2 is always a proportion greater than unity times the central χ^2;
(ii) $m \geq k$, so that the derived central χ^2 never has smaller degrees of freedom than the original non-central χ^2;
(iii) as ψ^2 tends to infinity, h tends to 2, so that $2 \geq h \geq 1$;
(iv) as $\psi^2 \to \infty$, then $m \to \infty$, so that $k \leq m \leq \infty$.

To a good approximation, a non-zero non-centrality parameter ensures that, although we look up critical values based on $\chi^2(k,0)$ under the null, the actual distribution is a proportion larger than unity of a central χ^2 with degrees of freedom greater than k. Since

χ^2 distributions have larger critical value for larger degrees of freedom, the non-central χ^2 always delivers a greater number, and hence a higher probability of rejection for false hypotheses, in sufficiently large samples.

To calculate the power function of the $\eta_0(k)$ test in (13.27), use the approximation:

$$\begin{aligned} \mathsf{P}\left[\eta_0(k) > c_{\alpha,k} \mid \mathsf{H}_1\right] &\simeq \mathsf{P}\left[\chi^2\left(k, \psi_\eta^2\right) > c_{\alpha,k} \mid \mathsf{H}_1\right] \\ &= \mathsf{P}\left[h\chi^2(m,0) > c_{\alpha,k} \mid \mathsf{H}_1\right] \\ &= \mathsf{P}\left[\chi^2(m,0) > h^{-1}c_{\alpha,k} \mid \mathsf{H}_1\right] \\ &= \int_s^\infty \mathrm{d}\chi^2(m,0), \end{aligned} \tag{13.38}$$

where $s = c_{\alpha,k}/h$, and:

$$\int_a^b \mathrm{d}\chi^2(n,0) = \int_a^b \mathsf{f}_{\chi^2(n)}(x)\,\mathrm{d}x$$

is the area from a to b under the $\chi^2(n,0)$ distribution. Thus, the integral in (13.38) is evaluated over the interval $[c_{\alpha,k}/h \le c_{\alpha,k}, \infty)$, when the integral:

$$\int_s^\infty \mathrm{d}\chi^2(m,0) \ge \int_{c_{\alpha,k}}^\infty \mathrm{d}\chi^2(k,0) = \alpha, \tag{13.39}$$

so that the non-central approximation includes more of the distribution and has larger values at each point. In the limit, as $\psi_\eta^2 \to \infty$, then $c_{\alpha,k}/h \to c_{\alpha,k}/2$ and $m \to \infty$, so all the mass of the distribution lies to the right of the lower bound and $\mathcal{P}(\cdot)$ tends to unity. This analysis explains why χ^2 tests in econometrics have power to reject false hypotheses.

13.5 Test power

All tests are inconsistent against some alternatives, and, conversely, there are many consistent tests of a given null. To illustrate the latter, consider a consistent estimator $\tilde{\boldsymbol{\theta}}$ of $\boldsymbol{\theta}$ with the asymptotic distribution:

$$\sqrt{T}\left(\tilde{\boldsymbol{\theta}} - \boldsymbol{\theta}_p\right) \xrightarrow{D} \mathsf{N}_k\left[\mathbf{0}, \mathbf{V}^*\right] \text{ where } \tilde{\boldsymbol{\theta}} \xrightarrow{P} \boldsymbol{\theta}_p. \tag{13.40}$$

Construct a test $\zeta_0(k)$ of H_0: $\boldsymbol{\theta}_p = \boldsymbol{\theta}_0$ using $(\tilde{\boldsymbol{\theta}}, \tilde{\mathbf{V}}^*)$ instead of $(\hat{\boldsymbol{\theta}}, \hat{\mathbf{V}})$ using (13.21). The test is consistent but would be practically useless if $\mathbf{V}^*$ were (say) a thousand times as large as $\mathbf{V}$ in (13.2). Therefore, consistency is a weak property of a test, just as it is a weak property of an estimator: we need to choose the 'best' from all the consistent tests. When the variance matrices are non-singular, consider the non-centrality parameters of the two proposed tests, $\eta_0(k)$ and $\zeta_0(k)$ given by:

$$\psi_\eta^2 = \boldsymbol{\delta}'\mathbf{V}^{-1}\boldsymbol{\delta} \text{ and } \psi_\zeta^2 = \boldsymbol{\delta}'\mathbf{V}^{*-1}\boldsymbol{\delta}. \tag{13.41}$$

The relative power of $\zeta_0(k)$ would be low when (say) $V^* = 1000\,V$. Consequently, we select tests according to their local non-centrality parameters, and for given degrees of freedom k, choose the test with the largest local non-centrality parameter. Asymptotically both tests have infinite non-centralities for fixed alternatives, and so reject fixed false null hypotheses with probability unity, but ψ^2_η is much larger than ψ^2_ζ, so never delivers lower power.

Unbiasedness, consistency, and highest power given k seem to be unequivocally good properties of tests. However, so far we have only considered tests that are invariant to the direction of departure between null and alternative: in the metric of V, the non-centrality ψ^2_η is quadratic in δ and so does not depend on the direction in which the hypothesis is wrong. In particular, consider an orthogonal transformation of (13.2) by a matrix R such that $R^{-1} = R'$:

$$\sqrt{T}\left(R\hat{\theta} - R\theta_p\right) \overset{D}{\to} \mathsf{N}_k\left[\mathbf{0}, RVR'\right]. \tag{13.42}$$

The test $\eta_0(k)$ in (13.21) is unaffected by this transformation since:

$$T\left(\hat{\theta} - \theta_0\right)'\hat{V}^{-1}\left(\hat{\theta} - \theta_0\right) = T\left(R\hat{\theta} - R\theta_0\right)'\left(R\hat{V}R'\right)^{-1}\left(R\hat{\theta} - R\theta_0\right).$$

The non-centrality parameter is also unaffected:

$$\psi^2_\eta = \delta' R'\left(RVR'\right)^{-1} R\delta = \delta' V^{-1}\delta. \tag{13.43}$$

Invariance under (say) orthogonal transformations narrows the class of admissible tests, and so helps select the best one within that narrower class, but it is not so obviously a good property in general. Consider a simple example, using a t-distribution. We will develop two tests of a scalar hypothesis H_0: $\theta_p = 0$ against H_1: $\theta_p > 0$, both of which have 5 per cent rejection frequencies under the null: test (a) will reject when the statistic $Z_0 > 1.64$, which is a one-tail test; whereas test (b) will reject when $|Z_b| > 1.96$, which is a two-tail test. The choice between the two tests depends upon the likely value under the alternative of the parameter to be tested. When $\theta_p > 0$ is true, then Z_0 is preferable to Z_b; whereas when θ_p is negative, then Z_b is preferable to Z_0. Which test should be used depends on an unknown state of the world. Unfortunately, the major reason for testing is precisely because we do not know the state of the world, so we cannot get a uniformly good test for even this simple directional problem. What we might be able to develop for some problems are locally asymptotically most powerful invariant (LAMPI) tests like η_0 above. Such tests correspond to tests with the largest non-centrality parameters in our χ^2 framework. The next section concerns how to find such tests.

13.6 Likelihood-ratio, Wald, and Lagrange-multiplier tests

Three ways of finding LAMPI tests are used in econometrics. The pivotal illustration in (13.21) above is a well-known example of how to find a LAMPI test when one exists.

More generally, we consider three test principles: likelihood-ratio (LR), Wald (W), and Lagrange-multiplier (LM), or efficient-score, tests. Useful references are Breusch and Pagan (1980), Engle (1984), Pagan (1984b) and Godfrey (1988).

13.6.1 Likelihood-ratio tests

The hypotheses are set up as before under $\mathsf{H}_m\colon \boldsymbol{\theta}_p \in \Theta$, namely:

$$\mathsf{H}_0\colon \boldsymbol{\theta}_p = \boldsymbol{\theta}_0 \text{ or } \boldsymbol{\theta}_p \in \Theta_0 \text{ versus } \mathsf{H}_1\colon \boldsymbol{\theta}_p \neq \boldsymbol{\theta}_0 \text{ or } \boldsymbol{\theta}_p \notin \Theta_0.$$

The likelihood ratio λ is given by:

$$0 \leq \lambda = \frac{\max_{\boldsymbol{\theta}\in\Theta_0} \mathsf{L}(\boldsymbol{\theta})}{\max_{\boldsymbol{\theta}\in\Theta} \mathsf{L}(\boldsymbol{\theta})} \leq 1. \tag{13.44}$$

The numerator in (13.44) is the best representative of the null hypothesis and, being maximum likelihood, provides the most favourable evidence for H_0. We contrast that with the best evidence over all possible values of $\boldsymbol{\theta}$ by comparing the relative likeliness of $\boldsymbol{\theta} = \boldsymbol{\theta}_0$ with all alternatives, and do not reject H_0 when λ is close to unity. Conversely, when the numerator (restricting $\boldsymbol{\theta}$ to Θ_0) is a small percentage of the denominator, the evidence seems strongly against the null being true. If you do not want to tie yourself to pure testing, think of model evaluation along such lines, maintaining a broad perspective for appraising evidence in which statistics are indices of model adequacy (see Pagan, 1981).

Now a third theorem can be invoked:

THEOREM 3. *If* H_m *is true, then under the regularity conditions discussed in Chapter 10, when* H_0 *holds and imposes* n *restrictions* (see Silvey, 1970):

$$-2\log\lambda \underset{\mathsf{H}_0}{\overset{D}{\to}} \chi^2(n, 0). \tag{13.45}$$

Three assumptions are involved in deriving this theorem. First, that H_m is 'true'. Secondly, that there is sufficient regularity that the Chapter 10 theorems about likelihood hold. Thirdly, that H_0 holds within H_m. Theorem 3 then provides a general way of deriving test statistics: compute the maximum of the likelihood under the null, compute it under the alternative, then minus twice the log of that ratio can be compared to a $\chi^2(n, 0)$ on H_0. A range of tests in econometrics takes that form. Intuitively, the test makes sense: $\log\lambda$ is a negative number close to zero when $\lambda \simeq 1$; with n degrees of freedom more in the denominator than in the numerator, the likelihood of the former will be higher than that of the latter even when H_0 is valid. On average, that de-restriction in $-2\log\lambda$ space will induce an increase of about a $\chi^2(n, 0)$.

As an analogy, consider adding an irrelevant variable in a linear regression, which induces a t-distribution on H_0. Since t^2 corresponds to $\chi^2(1, 0)$, adding a variable induces a $\chi^2(1, 0)$, which is the amount of change that we expect on average in the log-likelihood from adding a variable that does not matter (see Ch.A3). Since $\mathsf{E}[\chi^2(1, 0)] = 1$, we anticipate a t-statistic of unity for an irrelevant variable, in which case the estimated error variance is unchanged.

How much change should we expect in the log-likelihood from adding variables that do matter? The answer is a non-central χ^2, although the non-centrality is a little more awkward to derive here. We use the following result. Let:

$$\tilde{\boldsymbol{\theta}} = \underset{\boldsymbol{\theta} \in \Theta_0}{\operatorname{argmax}} \, \mathsf{L}(\boldsymbol{\theta}) \quad \text{and} \quad \hat{\boldsymbol{\theta}} = \underset{\boldsymbol{\theta} \in \Theta}{\operatorname{argmax}} \, \mathsf{L}(\boldsymbol{\theta}).$$

When the null is true, $\tilde{\boldsymbol{\theta}}$ should be close to $\hat{\boldsymbol{\theta}}$. Using a Taylor-series expansion of $\ell(\tilde{\boldsymbol{\theta}})$ around $\hat{\boldsymbol{\theta}}$ on H_0:

$$\begin{aligned} \ell(\tilde{\boldsymbol{\theta}}) &\simeq \ell(\hat{\boldsymbol{\theta}}) + \boldsymbol{q}(\hat{\boldsymbol{\theta}})' \left(\tilde{\boldsymbol{\theta}} - \hat{\boldsymbol{\theta}}\right) + \tfrac{1}{2} \left(\tilde{\boldsymbol{\theta}} - \hat{\boldsymbol{\theta}}\right)' \boldsymbol{H}(\hat{\boldsymbol{\theta}}) \left(\tilde{\boldsymbol{\theta}} - \hat{\boldsymbol{\theta}}\right) \\ &= \ell(\hat{\boldsymbol{\theta}}) + \tfrac{1}{2} \left(\tilde{\boldsymbol{\theta}} - \hat{\boldsymbol{\theta}}\right)' \boldsymbol{H}(\hat{\boldsymbol{\theta}}) \left(\tilde{\boldsymbol{\theta}} - \hat{\boldsymbol{\theta}}\right), \end{aligned} \tag{13.46}$$

since $\boldsymbol{q}(\hat{\boldsymbol{\theta}}) = \mathbf{0}$. Thus:

$$-2\left[\ell(\tilde{\boldsymbol{\theta}}) - \ell(\hat{\boldsymbol{\theta}})\right] \simeq -\left(\tilde{\boldsymbol{\theta}} - \hat{\boldsymbol{\theta}}\right)' \boldsymbol{H}(\hat{\boldsymbol{\theta}}) \left(\tilde{\boldsymbol{\theta}} - \hat{\boldsymbol{\theta}}\right), \tag{13.47}$$

which is a quadratic form similar to the earlier χ^2, with the main difference of using two estimators rather than $(\tilde{\boldsymbol{\theta}} - \boldsymbol{\theta}_p)$, and resulting in a $\chi^2(n)$ rather than a $\chi^2(k)$ since $(\tilde{\boldsymbol{\theta}} - \hat{\boldsymbol{\theta}})$ has a singular distribution. Nevertheless, (13.47) reveals why the result might be a χ^2, why we need a factor of two, and why a large outcome results if $\tilde{\boldsymbol{\theta}}$ is far from $\hat{\boldsymbol{\theta}}$. In the limit, $\hat{\boldsymbol{\theta}}$ converges to $\boldsymbol{\theta}_p$, and $T^{-1}\boldsymbol{H}(\hat{\boldsymbol{\theta}})$ converges to the population Hessian. Since $\tilde{\boldsymbol{\theta}}$ is inconsistent for $\boldsymbol{\theta}_p$ on H_1, then $-T(\tilde{\boldsymbol{\theta}} - \hat{\boldsymbol{\theta}})'(T^{-1}\boldsymbol{H}(\hat{\boldsymbol{\theta}}))(\tilde{\boldsymbol{\theta}} - \hat{\boldsymbol{\theta}})$ converges to a non-centrality parameter which tends to infinity as T tends to infinity. Section 13.7 provides a more formal analysis, once we have derived the distribution of $\tilde{\boldsymbol{\theta}}$.

13.6.2 Wald tests

This is the pivotal test extensively discussed above, which only uses the H_m estimator $\hat{\boldsymbol{\theta}}$. It is the basis for computing F and t-tests of null hypotheses from a regression, based on the results that:

$$T\hat{\sigma}^{-2}\left(\hat{\boldsymbol{\beta}} - \boldsymbol{\beta}_0\right)' \hat{\boldsymbol{M}} \left(\hat{\boldsymbol{\beta}} - \boldsymbol{\beta}_0\right) \overset{D}{\rightarrow} \chi^2(k, 0) \ \text{ on } \mathsf{H}_0\text{: } \boldsymbol{\beta}_p = \boldsymbol{\beta}_0, \tag{13.48}$$

and from (13.18):

$$\frac{T\left(\hat{\beta}_i - \beta_{0i}\right)^2}{\hat{\sigma}^2 \hat{m}^{ii}} \overset{D}{\rightarrow} \chi^2(1, 0) \ \text{ on } \mathsf{H}_0\text{: } \beta_{pi} = \beta_{0i},$$

where $\hat{m}^{ii}$ is the ith diagonal element of $\hat{\boldsymbol{M}}^{-1}$. We have already shown that a non-central χ^2 results when the null is false but the maintained is true.

13.6.3 Lagrange-multiplier or efficient-score tests

The LM test only needs the H_0 estimator $\tilde{\boldsymbol{\theta}}$, and we first derive this as an efficient-score test without introducing Lagrange multipliers (see Rao, 1952). We established in Chapter 10 that:

$$\sqrt{T}\bar{\boldsymbol{q}}_{(T)}(\boldsymbol{\theta}_p) \xrightarrow{D} \mathsf{N}_k\left[\mathbf{0}, \mathcal{I}(\boldsymbol{\theta}_p)\right], \tag{13.49}$$

on H_0, and hence:

$$T\bar{\boldsymbol{q}}_{(T)}(\boldsymbol{\theta}_p)'\mathcal{I}(\boldsymbol{\theta}_p)^{-1}\bar{\boldsymbol{q}}_{(T)}(\boldsymbol{\theta}_p) \xrightarrow{D} \chi^2(k, 0). \tag{13.50}$$

We also know that $\boldsymbol{q}(\hat{\boldsymbol{\theta}}) = \mathbf{0}$ but $\boldsymbol{q}(\tilde{\boldsymbol{\theta}}) \neq \mathbf{0}$.

Consider a test of H_0 based on a quadratic form in $\bar{\boldsymbol{q}}_{(T)}(\tilde{\boldsymbol{\theta}})$:

$$\zeta_{0,k} = T\bar{\boldsymbol{q}}_{(T)}(\tilde{\boldsymbol{\theta}})'\mathcal{I}(\tilde{\boldsymbol{\theta}})^{-1}\bar{\boldsymbol{q}}_{(T)}(\tilde{\boldsymbol{\theta}}). \tag{13.51}$$

The ζ test is checking if restricting $\boldsymbol{\theta}$ to Θ_0 via $\tilde{\boldsymbol{\theta}}$ leaves the restricted score close to zero, given that $\bar{\boldsymbol{q}}(\hat{\boldsymbol{\theta}}) = \mathbf{0}$ and, in the limit, $\bar{\boldsymbol{q}}(\boldsymbol{\theta}_p) = \mathbf{0}$. Then $\bar{\boldsymbol{q}}(\tilde{\boldsymbol{\theta}}) \simeq \mathbf{0}$ suggests that the restricted $\tilde{\boldsymbol{\theta}}$ is indeed close to $\hat{\boldsymbol{\theta}}$. If $\tilde{\boldsymbol{\theta}}$ is far from $\hat{\boldsymbol{\theta}}$, then $\boldsymbol{q}(\tilde{\boldsymbol{\theta}})$ should be far from zero. Equation (13.47) has the same non-centrality as the statistic in (13.51), as can be seen by expanding $\bar{\boldsymbol{q}}_{(T)}(\tilde{\boldsymbol{\theta}})$ around $\bar{\boldsymbol{q}}_{(T)}(\hat{\boldsymbol{\theta}})$, since under H_0:

$$\bar{\boldsymbol{q}}_{(T)}(\tilde{\boldsymbol{\theta}}) \simeq \bar{\boldsymbol{q}}_{(T)}(\hat{\boldsymbol{\theta}}) + \bar{\boldsymbol{H}}(\hat{\boldsymbol{\theta}})\left(\tilde{\boldsymbol{\theta}} - \hat{\boldsymbol{\theta}}\right) \simeq \bar{\boldsymbol{H}}(\tilde{\boldsymbol{\theta}})\left(\tilde{\boldsymbol{\theta}} - \hat{\boldsymbol{\theta}}\right). \tag{13.52}$$

Substituting (13.52) into (13.51), produces a similar expression to (13.47) for the LR test under the null (see Aitchison and Silvey, 1960). Specific tests are discussed in (e.g.) Doornik and Hendry (1994b).

13.7 Comparing the tests

If two tests η_1 and η_2 have the same critical value and plim $|\eta_1 - \eta_2| = 0$ for both the null hypothesis and local alternatives, then $\eta_1 \xrightarrow{D} \eta_2$. Such tests become perfectly correlated as $T \to \infty$, and hence are asymptotically equivalent. To compare the three tests in §13.6, first consider the case where $\ell(\boldsymbol{\theta})$ is a quadratic function, as in regression, namely:

$$\ell(\boldsymbol{\theta}) = h_0 + \boldsymbol{h}_1'\boldsymbol{\theta} + \tfrac{1}{2}\boldsymbol{\theta}'\boldsymbol{H}\boldsymbol{\theta}, \tag{13.53}$$

so that $\boldsymbol{q}(\boldsymbol{\theta}) = \boldsymbol{h}_1 + \boldsymbol{H}\boldsymbol{\theta}$, and as $\boldsymbol{q}(\hat{\boldsymbol{\theta}}) = \mathbf{0}$, then $\hat{\boldsymbol{\theta}} = -\boldsymbol{H}^{-1}\boldsymbol{h}_1$. Further:

$$\boldsymbol{q}(\tilde{\boldsymbol{\theta}}) = \boldsymbol{q}(\hat{\boldsymbol{\theta}}) + \boldsymbol{H}\left(\tilde{\boldsymbol{\theta}} - \hat{\boldsymbol{\theta}}\right) = \boldsymbol{H}\left(\tilde{\boldsymbol{\theta}} - \hat{\boldsymbol{\theta}}\right), \tag{13.54}$$

so that $\tilde{\boldsymbol{\theta}} = \hat{\boldsymbol{\theta}} + \boldsymbol{H}^{-1}\boldsymbol{q}(\tilde{\boldsymbol{\theta}})$. Denote the LR, W, and LM (score) tests of H_0: $\boldsymbol{\theta} \in \Theta_0$ by R, W, and S respectively. Since H_0: $\boldsymbol{\theta}_p \in \Theta_0$ is a region rather than a point, we translate H_0 into a set of functional restrictions on $\boldsymbol{\theta}$, such as $\boldsymbol{g}(\boldsymbol{\theta}) = \mathbf{0}$, or, in the linear case, $\boldsymbol{G\theta} = \mathbf{0}$. Then $\boldsymbol{G}\tilde{\boldsymbol{\theta}} = \mathbf{0}$ for $\boldsymbol{\theta} \in \Theta_0$ whereas $\boldsymbol{G}\hat{\boldsymbol{\theta}} \neq \mathbf{0}$ in general. Indeed:

$$\boldsymbol{G}\tilde{\boldsymbol{\theta}} = \boldsymbol{G}\hat{\boldsymbol{\theta}} + \boldsymbol{G}\boldsymbol{H}^{-1}\boldsymbol{q}(\tilde{\boldsymbol{\theta}}) \text{ so that } \boldsymbol{G}\hat{\boldsymbol{\theta}} = -\boldsymbol{G}\boldsymbol{H}^{-1}\boldsymbol{q}(\tilde{\boldsymbol{\theta}}).$$

Finally, $\tilde{\boldsymbol{\theta}}$ is obtained by solving the Lagrangean $\ell(\boldsymbol{\theta}) - \boldsymbol{\lambda}'\boldsymbol{G\theta}$, which yields $\boldsymbol{q}(\tilde{\boldsymbol{\theta}}) = \boldsymbol{G}'\tilde{\boldsymbol{\lambda}}$, so that:

$$\boldsymbol{G}\hat{\boldsymbol{\theta}} = -\boldsymbol{G}\boldsymbol{H}^{-1}\boldsymbol{G}'\tilde{\boldsymbol{\lambda}} \text{ or } \tilde{\boldsymbol{\lambda}} = -\left(\boldsymbol{G}\boldsymbol{H}^{-1}\boldsymbol{G}'\right)^{-1}\boldsymbol{G}\hat{\boldsymbol{\theta}}.$$

Hence, $\tilde{\boldsymbol{\lambda}}$ is a linear function of $\boldsymbol{G}\hat{\boldsymbol{\theta}}$. The solved example in section 13.8 amplifies these relationships and section 13.9 considers non-linear restrictions.

In the linear case, the formulae for the three tests of H_0: $\boldsymbol{G\theta} = \mathbf{0}$ in (13.53) are:

$$\begin{aligned} R = 2\left[\ell(\hat{\theta}) - \ell(\tilde{\theta})\right] &= 2\boldsymbol{h}_1'\left(\hat{\boldsymbol{\theta}} - \tilde{\boldsymbol{\theta}}\right) + \hat{\boldsymbol{\theta}}'\boldsymbol{H}\hat{\boldsymbol{\theta}} - \tilde{\boldsymbol{\theta}}'\boldsymbol{H}\tilde{\boldsymbol{\theta}} \\ &= -2\hat{\boldsymbol{\theta}}'\boldsymbol{H}\left(\hat{\boldsymbol{\theta}} - \tilde{\boldsymbol{\theta}}\right) + \hat{\boldsymbol{\theta}}'\boldsymbol{H}\hat{\boldsymbol{\theta}} - \tilde{\boldsymbol{\theta}}'\boldsymbol{H}\tilde{\boldsymbol{\theta}} \\ &= -\left(\hat{\boldsymbol{\theta}} - \tilde{\boldsymbol{\theta}}\right)'\boldsymbol{H}\left(\hat{\boldsymbol{\theta}} - \tilde{\boldsymbol{\theta}}\right). \end{aligned} \tag{13.55}$$

Since $\mathcal{I} = -\boldsymbol{H}$ here, as both are fixed, from (13.54):

$$S = \boldsymbol{q}(\tilde{\boldsymbol{\theta}})'\mathcal{I}^{-1}\boldsymbol{q}(\tilde{\boldsymbol{\theta}}) = -\left(\tilde{\boldsymbol{\theta}} - \hat{\boldsymbol{\theta}}\right)'\boldsymbol{H}\left(\tilde{\boldsymbol{\theta}} - \hat{\boldsymbol{\theta}}\right) = R. \tag{13.56}$$

The Wald test is based on checking $\boldsymbol{G\theta} = \mathbf{0}$ using $\hat{\boldsymbol{\theta}}$, which leads to:

$$\begin{aligned} W &= -\hat{\boldsymbol{\theta}}'\boldsymbol{G}'\left(\boldsymbol{G}\boldsymbol{H}^{-1}\boldsymbol{G}'\right)^{-1}\boldsymbol{G}\hat{\boldsymbol{\theta}} \\ &= \tilde{\boldsymbol{\lambda}}'\boldsymbol{G}\boldsymbol{H}^{-1}\boldsymbol{G}'\left(\boldsymbol{G}\boldsymbol{H}^{-1}\boldsymbol{G}'\right)^{-1}\boldsymbol{G}\boldsymbol{H}^{-1}\boldsymbol{G}'\tilde{\lambda} \\ &= -\tilde{\boldsymbol{\lambda}}'\boldsymbol{G}\boldsymbol{H}^{-1}\boldsymbol{G}'\tilde{\boldsymbol{\lambda}} \\ &= -\boldsymbol{q}(\tilde{\boldsymbol{\theta}})'\boldsymbol{H}^{-1}\boldsymbol{q}(\tilde{\boldsymbol{\theta}}) = S. \end{aligned} \tag{13.57}$$

Consequently, the three tests are numerically identical at all sample sizes for a quadratic log-likelihood subject to linear restrictions. If $\ell(\boldsymbol{\theta})$ is more non-linear than quadratic then the three tests usually differ numerically, since the formula for W stays essentially the same asymptotically (see Ch.10); that for R includes the higher-order functions of $\boldsymbol{\theta}$ from $\ell(\cdot)$; and $\boldsymbol{q}(\tilde{\boldsymbol{\theta}})$ ceases to be a linear function of $(\tilde{\boldsymbol{\theta}} - \hat{\boldsymbol{\theta}})$ alone.

In a scalar case, the LR test corresponds to twice the integral under the score $q(\theta)$ over the interval between the restricted and unrestricted estimates:

$$R = 2\int_{\tilde{\theta}}^{\hat{\theta}} q(\theta)\mathrm{d}\theta = 2\left[\ell(\hat{\theta}) - \ell(\tilde{\theta})\right]. \tag{13.58}$$

The Wald test measures the difference between the two estimates relative to the Hessian evaluated at $\hat{\theta}$, which is the tangent to $q(\theta)$ at $\hat{\theta}$:

$$W = \left(\hat{\theta} - \tilde{\theta}\right)^2 \frac{\partial q(\theta)}{\partial \theta}\rfloor_{\hat{\theta}}, \tag{13.59}$$

whereas the LM test scales the score using the Hessian evaluated at $\tilde{\theta}$, which is the tangent to $q(\theta)$ at $\tilde{\theta}$:

$$S = q(\tilde{\theta})^2 \left[\frac{\partial q(\theta)}{\partial \theta} \rfloor_{\tilde{\theta}} \right]^{-1}. \tag{13.60}$$

When the score is a straight line, these three tests are identical. Otherwise, the three tests differ. What matters for the LR test is the area under the score, which depends on how rapidly the score slopes, as well as on how far apart $\hat{\theta}$ and $\tilde{\theta}$ are. A small LR test would result if the score was small, so the LR test depends on how informative the data are. The Wald test depends on how much the score curves at $\hat{\theta}$, and so could be misled by a score which is flat at $\hat{\theta}$ then turns down rapidly, giving a large projection. Since the Wald test tries to infer the shape of the score purely from calculating $\hat{\theta}$, we require that the shape of the score at $\hat{\theta}$ is like its shape everywhere else. That is the linearity approximation, namely, the assumption that the Hessian is constant between $\hat{\theta}$ and $\tilde{\theta}$. The LM test, conversely, depends on how rapidly the score is changing at $\tilde{\theta}$, and can be fooled, in an analogous way to the Wald test, by a score that changes little at $\tilde{\theta}$. However, the three tests yield the same results asymptotically under both the null hypothesis and local alternatives since the log-likelihood function is quadratic asymptotically.

13.8 A solved example

Consider the stationary DGP:

$$\mathsf{D}_{\mathsf{X}}\left(\mathbf{X}_T^1 \mid \boldsymbol{\theta}\right) = \prod_{t=1}^{T} \mathsf{D}_{\mathsf{x}}\left(\mathbf{x}_t \mid \boldsymbol{\theta}\right) \text{ where } \boldsymbol{\theta} \in \Theta \subseteq \mathbb{R}^k, \tag{13.61}$$

with population value $\boldsymbol{\theta}_p$.Under H_0: $\mathbf{G}\boldsymbol{\theta} = \mathbf{0}$, where $\mathbf{G}$ is a known $n \times k$ matrix ($n < k$), show that the restricted MLE $\tilde{\boldsymbol{\theta}}$ of $\boldsymbol{\theta}$ obtained from the Lagrangean satisfies:

$$\sqrt{T}\left(\tilde{\boldsymbol{\theta}} - \boldsymbol{\theta}_p\right) \xrightarrow{D} \mathsf{N}_k\left[\mathbf{0}, \left(\mathcal{I}_p^{-1} - \mathcal{I}_p^{-1}\mathbf{G}'\left(\mathbf{G}\mathcal{I}_p^{-1}\mathbf{G}'\right)^{-1}\mathbf{G}\mathcal{I}_p^{-1}\right)\right], \tag{13.62}$$

where:

$$\mathcal{I}_p = \mathsf{E}\left[\mathbf{q}_t(\boldsymbol{\theta}_p)\mathbf{q}_t'(\boldsymbol{\theta}_p)\right] \text{ and } \mathbf{q}_t(\boldsymbol{\theta}_p) = \frac{\partial \log \mathsf{D}_{\mathsf{x}}\left(\mathbf{x}_t|\boldsymbol{\theta}\right)}{\partial \boldsymbol{\theta}} \rfloor_{\boldsymbol{\theta}_p}. \tag{13.63}$$

If $\boldsymbol{\lambda}$ is the associated Lagrange multiplier, also show that under H_0:

$$\frac{\tilde{\boldsymbol{\lambda}}}{\sqrt{T}} \xrightarrow{D} \mathsf{N}_n\left[\mathbf{0}, \left(\mathbf{G}\mathcal{I}_p^{-1}\mathbf{G}'\right)^{-1}\right], \tag{13.64}$$

and hence derive a test of $\mathbf{G}\boldsymbol{\theta} = \mathbf{0}$.

(Oxford M.Phil., 1983)

Solution

The restricted MLE of $\boldsymbol{\theta}$ is derived by maximizing the log-likelihood function under the constraint $\boldsymbol{G\theta} = \mathbf{0}$. Denote the log-likelihood function by $\ell(\boldsymbol{\theta})$; then, the Lagrangean associated with this problem is:

$$\ell(\boldsymbol{\theta}) - (\boldsymbol{G\theta})' \boldsymbol{\lambda}, \tag{13.65}$$

where $\boldsymbol{\lambda}$ is the $n \times 1$ vector of Lagrange multipliers measuring the 'costs' of imposing the parametric restrictions. From (13.65), the first-order conditions to optimize $\ell(\boldsymbol{\theta})$ with respect to $\boldsymbol{\theta}$ subject to the constraints are:

$$\boldsymbol{q}(\tilde{\boldsymbol{\theta}}) - \boldsymbol{G}'\tilde{\boldsymbol{\lambda}} = \mathbf{0}, \tag{13.66}$$

and:

$$\boldsymbol{G}\tilde{\boldsymbol{\theta}} = \mathbf{0}, \tag{13.67}$$

where $\boldsymbol{q}(\tilde{\boldsymbol{\theta}})$ is the score vector. The solutions to (13.66) and (13.67) are denoted $\tilde{\boldsymbol{\theta}}$ and $\tilde{\boldsymbol{\lambda}}$.

To determine the asymptotic distribution of these estimators under the null hypothesis, we exploit the fact that (13.61) entails an independent identical distribution for $\boldsymbol{x}_t$ and expand (13.66) and (13.67) around $\boldsymbol{\theta}_p$ to obtain:

$$\boldsymbol{q}(\tilde{\boldsymbol{\theta}}) = \boldsymbol{q}(\boldsymbol{\theta}_p) + \boldsymbol{H}\left(\tilde{\boldsymbol{\theta}} - \boldsymbol{\theta}_p\right) \quad \text{where} \quad \boldsymbol{H} = \frac{\partial^2 \ell(\cdot)}{\partial \boldsymbol{\theta} \partial \boldsymbol{\theta}'}, \tag{13.68}$$

and $\boldsymbol{H}$ is evaluated at $\boldsymbol{\theta}_1$ between $\tilde{\boldsymbol{\theta}}$ and $\boldsymbol{\theta}_p$. After suitably scaling by functions of T, we obtain:

$$T^{-\frac{1}{2}}\boldsymbol{q}(\boldsymbol{\theta}_p) + T^{-1}\boldsymbol{H}\sqrt{T}\left(\tilde{\boldsymbol{\theta}} - \boldsymbol{\theta}_p\right) - T^{-\frac{1}{2}}\boldsymbol{G}'\tilde{\boldsymbol{\lambda}} = \mathbf{0}, \tag{13.69}$$

and from (13.67):

$$\sqrt{T}\boldsymbol{G}\left(\tilde{\boldsymbol{\theta}} - \boldsymbol{\theta}_p\right) = \mathbf{0}. \tag{13.70}$$

Equations (13.69)–(13.70) can be stacked in matrix form as:

$$\begin{pmatrix} -T^{-1}\boldsymbol{H} & \boldsymbol{G}' \\ \boldsymbol{G} & \mathbf{0} \end{pmatrix} \begin{pmatrix} \sqrt{T}\left(\tilde{\boldsymbol{\theta}} - \boldsymbol{\theta}_p\right) \\ T^{-\frac{1}{2}}\tilde{\boldsymbol{\lambda}} \end{pmatrix} = \begin{pmatrix} T^{-\frac{1}{2}}\boldsymbol{q}(\boldsymbol{\theta}_p) \\ \mathbf{0} \end{pmatrix}. \tag{13.71}$$

Using partitioned inversion:

$$\begin{pmatrix} \sqrt{T}\left(\tilde{\boldsymbol{\theta}} - \boldsymbol{\theta}_p\right) \\ T^{-\frac{1}{2}}\tilde{\boldsymbol{\lambda}} \end{pmatrix} = \begin{pmatrix} -T\boldsymbol{R} & \boldsymbol{H}^{-1}\boldsymbol{G}'\boldsymbol{B} \\ \boldsymbol{BGH}^{-1} & \mathbf{0} \end{pmatrix} \begin{pmatrix} T^{-\frac{1}{2}}\boldsymbol{q}(\boldsymbol{\theta}_p) \\ \mathbf{0} \end{pmatrix}, \tag{13.72}$$

where $\boldsymbol{B} = (\boldsymbol{GH}^{-1}\boldsymbol{G}')^{-1}$ and $\boldsymbol{R} = (\boldsymbol{H}^{-1} - \boldsymbol{H}^{-1}\boldsymbol{G}'\boldsymbol{BGH}^{-1})$. On replacing $-T^{-1}\boldsymbol{H}$ by its asymptotic equivalent $\mathcal{I}_p$ in (13.72):

$$\sqrt{T}\left(\tilde{\boldsymbol{\theta}} - \boldsymbol{\theta}_p\right) = \left[\mathcal{I}_p^{-1} - \mathcal{I}_p^{-1}\boldsymbol{G}'\left(\boldsymbol{G}\mathcal{I}_p^{-1}\boldsymbol{G}'\right)^{-1}\boldsymbol{G}\mathcal{I}_p^{-1}\right]T^{-\frac{1}{2}}\boldsymbol{q}(\boldsymbol{\theta}_p) + o_p(1) \tag{13.73}$$

and:

$$T^{-\frac{1}{2}}\tilde{\lambda} = \left[\left(G\mathcal{I}_p^{-1} G' \right)^{-1} G\mathcal{I}_p^{-1} \right] T^{-\frac{1}{2}} q(\theta_p) + o_p(1). \tag{13.74}$$

Equation (13.74) was used in §13.7 to relate the Lagrange multiplier to the score. Since:

$$T^{-\frac{1}{2}} q(\theta_p) \underset{a}{\sim} \mathsf{N}_k [\mathbf{0}, \mathcal{I}_p],$$

by applying Cramér's theorem to (13.73) and (13.74):

$$\sqrt{T}\left(\tilde{\theta} - \theta_p\right) \xrightarrow{D} \mathsf{N}_k \left[\mathbf{0}, \mathcal{I}_p^{-1} - \mathcal{I}_p^{-1} G' \left(G\mathcal{I}_p^{-1} G' \right)^{-1} G\mathcal{I}_p^{-1} \right] = \mathsf{N}_k [\mathbf{0}, J_p], \tag{13.75}$$

and:

$$T^{-\frac{1}{2}}\tilde{\lambda} \xrightarrow{D} \mathsf{N}_n \left[\mathbf{0}, \left(G\mathcal{I}_p^{-1} G' \right)^{-1} \right]. \tag{13.76}$$

Hence the quantity $\eta_n = T^{-1}\tilde{\lambda}' G\mathcal{I}_p^{-1} G'\tilde{\lambda}$ is asymptotically distributed as $\chi^2(n)$ on H_0, so η_n can be used to test the null. In practice, it is convenient to retain $-T^{-1}\tilde{H}$ rather than $\mathcal{I}_p$. Since $q(\tilde{\theta}) = G'\tilde{\lambda}$, rewrite η_n as $S = -\tilde{q}'\tilde{H}^{-1}\tilde{q}$, where $\tilde{q} = q(\tilde{\theta})$, and use S instead of η_n to test H_0.

Several incidental results are worth noting. First, under the present assumptions, the unrestricted MLE is known from Chapter 10 to be distributed as:

$$\sqrt{T}\left(\hat{\theta} - \theta_p\right) \xrightarrow{D} \mathsf{N}_k \left[\mathbf{0}, \mathcal{I}_p^{-1} \right].$$

Next, in (13.75), J_p is 'smaller' than $\mathcal{I}_p^{-1}$ in that J_p equals $\mathcal{I}_p^{-1}$ minus a non-negative definite matrix. Letting $\mathcal{I}_p^{-1} = KK'$ then:

$$\mathcal{I}_p^{-1} - \mathcal{I}_p^{-1} G' \left(G\mathcal{I}_p^{-1} G' \right)^{-1} G\mathcal{I}_p^{-1} = K \left[I_k - K'G' \left(GKK'G' \right)^{-1} GK \right] K',$$

or $K(I_k - Q)K'$ where Q is a symmetric idempotent matrix of rank n. Thus, J_p is $k \times k$ of rank $k - n$, so imposing the restrictions $G\theta = \mathbf{0}$ reduces the asymptotic variance matrix in that sense. Further:

$$\sqrt{T}\left(\hat{\theta} - \theta_p\right) \xrightarrow{D} -(TH)^{-1} T^{-\frac{1}{2}} q(\theta_p) \simeq \mathcal{I}_p^{-1} T^{-\frac{1}{2}} q(\theta_p),$$

and hence:

$$\begin{aligned}
\sqrt{T}\left(\tilde{\theta} - \hat{\theta}\right) &\simeq \left(J_p - \mathcal{I}_p^{-1} \right) T^{-\frac{1}{2}} q(\theta_p) \\
&= \left(\mathcal{I}_p^{-1} G' \left(G\mathcal{I}_p^{-1} G' \right)^{-1} G\mathcal{I}_p^{-1} \right) T^{-\frac{1}{2}} q(\theta_p) \\
&= A T^{-\frac{1}{2}} q(\theta_p),
\end{aligned}$$

where $A = KQK'$. Consequently, on H_0:

$$\sqrt{T}\left(\tilde{\theta} - \hat{\theta}\right) \xrightarrow{D} \mathsf{N}_k \left[\mathbf{0}, A\mathcal{I}_p A \right] = \mathsf{N}_k [\mathbf{0}, A].$$

Since G is an $n \times k$ matrix of rank $n < k$, A is singular of rank n. This is unsurprising as we imposed n restrictions on $\tilde{\theta}$ and none on $\hat{\theta}$, but resolves the technical difficulty which precluded an easy proof of (13.47) having a $\chi^2(n)$ distribution. A generalized inverse (such as Moore–Penrose: see e.g. Dhrymes, 1984) can be used to establish the result.

Finally, when the imposed restrictions are false, and $G\theta_p \neq \mathbf{0}$, the distribution of $\hat{\theta}$ is unaffected (consistent under H_0 and H_1, but inefficient when H_0 is true), whereas $\tilde{\theta}$ becomes inconsistent (but was consistent and efficient on H_0). Tests based directly on the difference between two such estimators are discussed in Durbin (1954) and Hausman (1978).

13.9 Non-linear restrictions

Consider an economic theory which specifies $g(\theta) = \mathbf{0}$, where θ is $k \times 1$ and there are n restrictions in $g(\cdot)$, so that $k - n$ parameters ϕ_i remain unrestricted. Let:

$$f(\theta) = (g(\theta) : h(\theta))' = (\delta : \phi)', \tag{13.77}$$

where $f(\cdot)$ is a continuous one–one function mapping θ onto $(\delta : \phi)$ such that under H_0, $\delta = \mathbf{0}$. When H_0 is true, then by equivariance:

$$\ell(\theta) = \ell(f(\theta)) = \ell(g(\theta), \phi) \underset{\mathsf{H}_0}{=} \ell(\mathbf{0}, \phi) = \ell_1(\phi). \tag{13.78}$$

As before, we distinguish unrestricted estimates, $\hat{\theta}$, obtained without restricting θ, from restricted estimates $\tilde{\theta}$, based on imposing $g(\theta) = \mathbf{0}$, so that $g(\tilde{\theta}) = \mathbf{0}$.

Evidence about the validity of $g(\theta) = \mathbf{0}$ depends on how large $\mathsf{L}(\hat{\theta})/\mathsf{L}(\tilde{\theta})$ is relative to unity, leading to a likelihood-ratio based approach. Under H_m, we get $\hat{\theta}$ from $q(\hat{\theta}) = \mathbf{0}$ and can evaluate $g(\hat{\theta})$ to see how close to zero this restrictions vector is, leading to a Wald approach. Finally, under H_0, we compute only $\tilde{\theta} = (\mathbf{0}' : \tilde{\phi}')'$, the restricted maximum likelihood estimator (RMLE) from the Lagrangean $\ell(\theta) - \lambda' g(\theta)$, leading to the score equation:

$$q(\tilde{\theta}) - G(\tilde{\theta})'\tilde{\lambda} = \mathbf{0} \quad \text{where} \quad G = \frac{\partial g(\theta)}{\partial \theta'}, \tag{13.79}$$

from which $q(\tilde{\theta}) = G(\tilde{\theta})'\tilde{\lambda}$. Under H_0, $g(\hat{\theta}) \neq \mathbf{0}$ although $g(\theta_p) = \mathbf{0}$, and $q(\hat{\theta}) \neq \mathbf{0}$ but $g(\tilde{\theta}) = \mathbf{0}$.

It is useful to work with the re-parameterized problem $f(\theta)$, and to distinguish three possibilities about the parameters of interest when testing hypotheses about δ, see Table 13.1.

Case (a) corresponds to a test of the validity of the specification for a model estimated assuming that $\delta = \mathbf{0}$, as with tests based on residuals; case (b) involves testing hypotheses about parameters in the face of nuisance parameters, and uses the concentrated likelihood function discussed in Chapter 10 to eliminate the latter; case (c) is illustrated by the subset tests discussed in Chapter A4.

Table 13.1 Hypothesis forms

Test	Interest	Nuisance	Objective
(a): LM	ϕ	δ	Estimate ϕ and test $\delta = \mathbf{0}$
(b): W	δ	ϕ	Concentrate with respect to ϕ, and test δ
(c): LR	δ, ϕ	–	Test a subset of the parameters

Given the widespread occurrence of the RMLE and tests based thereon in empirical econometrics, we will obtain the relevant limiting distributions here. For simplicity, we assume identical independent distributions, since appropriate generalizations follow as in Chapter 10. As noted in (13.79) above, the score equation is:

$$q(\tilde{\theta}) - G(\tilde{\theta})'\tilde{\lambda} = \mathbf{0}, \tag{13.80}$$

where:

$$g(\tilde{\theta}) = \mathbf{0}. \tag{13.81}$$

We obtain the limiting distributions by dropping asymptotically negligible terms. Since $\tilde{\theta}$ is consistent for θ_p under H_0, we take their difference to be $O_p(T^{-\frac{1}{2}})$, so that quadratic terms in their difference (schematically denoted by $(\tilde{\theta} - \theta_p)^2$ below) are $O_p(T^{-1})$:

$$\mathbf{0} = g(\theta_p) = g(\tilde{\theta}) + G(\tilde{\theta})\left(\tilde{\theta} - \theta_p\right) + O_p\left[\left(\tilde{\theta} - \theta_p\right)^2\right]. \tag{13.82}$$

Since $g(\tilde{\theta}) = \mathbf{0}$, then $G(\tilde{\theta})(\tilde{\theta} - \theta_p) \simeq \mathbf{0}$, leading asymptotically to $G(\theta_p)(\tilde{\theta} - \theta_p) = \mathbf{0}$. Also:

$$q(\tilde{\theta}) = q(\theta_p) + H(\theta_p)\left(\tilde{\theta} - \theta_p\right) + O_p\left[\left(\tilde{\theta} - \theta_p\right)^2\right], \tag{13.83}$$

so that, to the approximations involved:

$$q(\theta_p) + H(\theta_p)\left(\tilde{\theta} - \theta_p\right) - G'(\tilde{\theta})\tilde{\lambda} = \mathbf{0}. \tag{13.84}$$

Writing these results in matrix form:

$$\begin{pmatrix} -T^{-1}H(\theta_p) & G'(\theta_p \\ G(\theta_p) & \mathbf{0} \end{pmatrix} \begin{pmatrix} \sqrt{T}\left(\tilde{\theta} - \theta_p\right) \\ T^{-\frac{1}{2}}\tilde{\lambda} \end{pmatrix} = \begin{pmatrix} T^{-\frac{1}{2}}q(\theta_p) \\ \mathbf{0} \end{pmatrix} \tag{13.85}$$

as in (13.71). Inverting the left-hand side matrix, replacing $-T^{-1}H(\theta_p)$ by its asymptotic equivalent $\mathcal{I}(\theta_p)$, and denoting evaluation at θ_p by the subscript $_p$ alone:

$$\begin{pmatrix} \sqrt{T}\left(\tilde{\theta} - \theta_p\right) \\ T^{-\frac{1}{2}}\tilde{\lambda} \end{pmatrix} = \begin{pmatrix} J_p & \mathcal{I}_p^{-1}G_p'B_p^{-1} \\ B_p^{-1}G_p\mathcal{I}_p^{-1} & B_p^{-1} \end{pmatrix} \begin{pmatrix} T^{-\frac{1}{2}}q_p \\ \mathbf{0} \end{pmatrix}, \tag{13.86}$$

as in section 13.8 above, where $J_p = \mathcal{I}_p^{-1}(I - G_p' B_p^{-1} G_p \mathcal{I}_p^{-1})$. Using the partitioned inversion theorem:

$$\begin{pmatrix} \mathcal{I}_p & G_p' \\ G_p & \mathbf{0} \end{pmatrix}^{-1} = \begin{pmatrix} \mathcal{I}_p^{-1}\left[I - G_p' B_p^{-1} G_p \mathcal{I}_p^{-1}\right] & \mathcal{I}_p^{-1} G_p' B_p^{-1} \\ B_p^{-1} G_p \mathcal{I}_p^{-1} & B_p^{-1} \end{pmatrix}, \qquad (13.87)$$

when $B_p = (G_p \mathcal{I}_p^{-1} G_p')$. Thus, the asymptotic variance of the vector in (13.86) is:

$$V = \mathsf{V}\begin{bmatrix} \sqrt{T}\left(\tilde{\theta} - \theta_p\right) \\ T^{-\frac{1}{2}}\tilde{\lambda} \end{bmatrix},$$

or:

$$\begin{pmatrix} J_p & \mathcal{I}_p^{-1} G_p' B_p^{-1} \\ B_0^{-1} G_p \mathcal{I}_p^{-1} & B_p^{-1} \end{pmatrix} \begin{pmatrix} \mathcal{I}_p & \mathbf{0} \\ \mathbf{0} & \mathbf{0} \end{pmatrix} \begin{pmatrix} J_p & \mathcal{I}_p^{-1} G_p' B_p^{-1} \\ B_0^{-1} G_p \mathcal{I}_p^{-1} & B_p^{-1} \end{pmatrix}$$
$$= \begin{pmatrix} J_p & \mathbf{0} \\ \mathbf{0} & B_p^{-1} \end{pmatrix}. \qquad (13.88)$$

This corresponds closely to the linear restrictions problem in section 13.8. The normalization on $\tilde{\lambda}$ remains $T^{-\frac{1}{2}}$ with an asymptotic variance matrix of $(G_p \mathcal{I}_p^{-1} G_p)^{-1}$. There is asymptotically independent information in $(\tilde{\theta} - \theta_p)$ and $\tilde{\lambda}$ since the covariance of $\mathsf{C}(\tilde{\theta} - \theta_p, \tilde{\lambda})$ is zero, despite the non-diagonality of the matrix in (13.86). As before, there is an efficiency gain since:

$$J(\theta_p) = \mathcal{I}_p^{-1} - \mathcal{I}_p^{-1} G_p \left(G_p \mathcal{I}_p^{-1} G_p\right)^{-1} G_p \mathcal{I}_p^{-1} \leq \mathcal{I}_p^{-1},$$

noting that $J_p \mathcal{I}_p J_p = J_p$.

13.10 Some methodological considerations

The preceding analysis leaves open a number of important considerations for empirical research. These concern the broad issues of: the null hypothesis (§13.10.1); the alternative hypothesis (§13.10.2); the test statistics (§13.10.3); the significance level (§13.10.4); and multiple testing (§13.10.5).

13.10.1 The null hypothesis

Chapter 9 delineated null hypotheses in terms of no loss of information from reductions, and these constituted the criteria for model selection in the context of discovery. and for model evaluation in the context of justification. Such nulls relate to potential model mis-specifications. Null hypotheses based on prior theoretical reasoning could take almost any form, but in parametric models often can be expressed as functional restrictions on a basic set of parameters as in section 13.9. Different issues are raised when testing inequality restrictions (such as positivity) or testing on boundaries of the parameter space, or when some parameters become unidentified under the null: for examples of the technical problems arising, see Davies (1979), Breusch (1986), Gourieroux, Monfort and Trognon (1984), and Quandt (1988).

In practice, a test may have a larger null space than that envisaged by its derivation; this is called the implicit null (see Mizon and Richard, 1986). Such a problem arises when there exist parameter values different from the null against which the test has no power. For example, Engle, Hendry and Trumbull (1985) show that the Durbin–Watson test has power in finite samples to detect ARCH errors, but has no power to do so asymptotically, so parameter values generating conditional heteroscedasticity fall in its implicit null space in large samples.

13.10.2 The alternative hypothesis

The χ^2 tests described above were justified by having highest asymptotic local power in the class of invariant tests. In one sense, this formulation camouflaged the issue of the choice of alternative since the DGP was assumed known and fully parameterized by $\boldsymbol{\theta}$. Thus, the local alternatives arose after the specification of the model, given $\boldsymbol{\theta}$. In practice, for mis-specification tests, there is no unique alternative to a given null until it has been precisely defined in terms of nuisance parameters, such as $\boldsymbol{\delta}$ above. For example, deviations from a white-noise residual could be due to a first-order autoregressive process; to a first-order moving average; a higher-order form of either; or a mixture; or omitted variables; or dynamic mis-specification; or incorrect functional form; and so on. Tests are designed to have highest power against a given alternative, but may have more or less power against related alternatives, and some are equivalent under local alternatives. Thought should be given to potentially important directions of departure from the null, but pragmatic researchers tend to compute a variety of indices of model adequacy, which raises issues of multiple testing, and the independence of the statistics, as discussed below.

As stressed before, it is a *non sequitur* to accept the alternative when the null is rejected: what we learn from rejection is that the null is false, with a probability α of an incorrect decision. At best, the alternative can suggest ideas for rethinking the modelling exercise in ways which later research may show to be more or less fruitful. Worse still is the implicit simple-to-general approach of patching a model for the alternative, as occurs with residual-autoregressive corrections: it is important to return to the general formulation before proceeding (see DHSY and the corrective in Hendry and von Ungern-Sternberg, 1981). Alternatively expressed, tests usually have power to reject against departures from the null other than those for which they were explicitly designed. Such departures may take very different forms, such as incorrect functional form reflected in residual autocorrelation, as discussed in Chapter 6.

13.10.3 The test statistics

In stationary processes, LM, LR, and W tests are asymptotically equivalent under H_0 and local alternatives H_1 within H_m (see Engle, 1984, for a survey). That does not imply that a choice between them is irrelevant. First, depending on the DGP and the departure involved, the three tests are not equally robust to H_m being false. In particular, it can matter in LM and W tests whether the Hessian or the information matrix is used as the metric, even though they are asymptotically equivalent under the null. White (1980a) proposed an information matrix test based on the difference between the estimated Hessian and an estimate of the information matrix formula derived under the null (see Ch.10). Conversely, it is easy to modify LM and W tests for, say, HCSEs or other consistent variance estimators, whereas LR modifications are less clear.

Secondly, in small samples the accuracy of the $\chi^2(k, 0)$ approximation can vary across the tests. Since they produce different outcomes in finite samples for non-linear or multivariate problems, then whether we do or do not reject a hypothesis could vary with the test used (see Berndt and Savin, 1977). In other words, the actual critical values of the selected tests may not be close to their nominal values based on $\chi^2(k, 0)$ in a finite sample. This suggests checking the accuracy of the χ^2 approximation by Monte Carlo if the decision varies between test choices. Degree-of-freedom adjustments to asymptotic χ^2 criteria are discussed by Harvey (1981a) and Kiviet (1985), and used for most of the statistics in this book.

Since the Wald test is susceptible to the precise formulation of the restrictions being tested, a related controversy has occurred under the issue of 'How long is a piece of string?' (see Gregory and Veale, 1985). For example, consider testing the null H_0: $\beta_1 = \beta_2$. A natural way of testing this is to switch to a null H_0^*: $(\beta_1 - \beta_2) = 0$. Alternatively, we could also test H_0^{**}: $\beta_1/\beta_2 - 1 = 0$; but imagine what happens when β_2 is close to zero. Because the variance of the Wald statistic is an asymptotic approximation and involves the Jacobian of the transformation from the ratio β_1/β_2, large variances could result, inducing very different outcomes for different forms of the same Wald test, even when the null is true. This is really an aspect of the previous point, and reinforces the advice to check the accuracy of any χ^2 approximations, as well as suggesting care in formulating the null hypothesis.

A further ground for choosing between LM, LR, and W tests is computational ease. An LR test requires the estimation of both null and alternative. In many settings, this is straightforward, although it is easy to construct examples where one is easy and the other hard. If H_0 is rejected, H_m will anyway be required, and in a simplification approach commencing from H_m, valid restrictions will lead to the selection of H_0, so the need to estimate both models is not a compelling objection.

As noted above, the LM test sustains mis-specification and diagnostic testing (see Mizon, 1977b), because the model is only estimated under the null, from which the evidence about the validity of that null is examined. A standard example involving an LM test is fitting a regression model and then testing for residual autocorrelation. LM tests turn up regularly in such a context, and well-known examples include the Durbin and Watson (1950) statistic, the Durbin (1970) h-test, the test in Godfrey (1978) for residual autocorrelation, the Sargan (1959) IV test, and so on, all of which correspond to checking outside the original model whether or not a postulated mis-specification occurs (see Godfrey, 1988, for a general treatment).

Conversely, the W test is suitable for specification tests, within a general-to-specific testing framework, since it needs only $\hat{\boldsymbol{\theta}}$. Thus, one can easily construct tests to see whether elements of $\boldsymbol{\theta}$ can be combined, simplified, or eliminated using the following result. Given a nested sequence $\mathsf{H}_{k_1} \subset \mathsf{H}_{k_2}$ with $k_1 < k_2$, tested by the χ^2 statistics $W(k_1)$ and $W(k_2)$, then, when H_{k_1} is valid:

$$W(k_2) - W(k_1) \sim \chi^2(k_2 - k_1, 0), \tag{13.89}$$

and is distributed independently of $W(k_1) \sim \chi^2(k_1, 0)$. That basic result for W tests underlies the COMFAC procedure checking for common factors in lag polynomials proposed by Sargan (1980b) (also see Hendry and Mizon, 1978). The COMFAC test in PcGive computes a sequence of Wald tests given the unrestricted dynamic model. Either the individual tests $W(k_i)$, or the changes in the W-tests in the form of (13.89), can be calculated. Thus, Wald procedures tend to sustain general-to-specific modelling or sequential testing.

13.10.4 The significance level

Since no theory is precisely true, care is required in rejecting hypotheses when T is large: overwhelming evidence can be mounted against a null even when it is an excellent approximation. For example, a hypothesis that $\theta_0 = 1$ would eventually be rejected against $\theta_p = 0.9999$, even if the deviation were of no practical relevance. There are two ways to avoid this possible danger:

(a) Derive tests against local alternatives as above, and so only consider how good a test is at detecting alternatives close to the null for a fixed α;
(b) Consider a vanishing Type I error $\alpha \to 0$ at some fixed rate as $T \to \infty$, so that $\mathcal{P}(T, \boldsymbol{\theta}_p, \alpha)$ does not converge on unity even for fixed alternatives.

It does not seem sensible to fix α independently of T since the balance between Type I and II errors should alter with the weight of evidence (see the discussion in Hendry, Leamer and Poirier, 1990). Thus, an approach based on a fixed alternative and a fixed significance level has little to recommend it as part of a progressive research strategy: as information accumulates, more precise statements should be possible.

Rules of the form $\alpha = cT^{-0.8}$ match conventional choices at usual sample sizes when $c = 4.7$, namely, 10 per cent at $T = 20$, 5 per cent at $T = 50$, 2.5 per cent at about $T = 100$ and 1 per cent at about $T = 350$, dropping to 0.01 per cent at $T = 2000$. Such rules do not affect the consistency of the test strategy, and seem to offer a reasonable balance between Type I and Type II errors when the actual cost of either mistake cannot be assigned.

13.10.5 Multiple testing

Most practical modelling exercises involve testing a multitude of hypotheses, some of which are reported, others perhaps not even consciously noticed by the investigator. If a significance level of, say, $\alpha = 0.05$ is used throughout, and N tests are conducted all with valid null hypotheses, then the overall size of the test procedure is likely to be large (see Savin, 1984). When the dependence between the tests is unknown, a bound on the probability of not falsely rejecting any of the hypotheses tested is provided by the Bonferroni inequality. Consider a set of events $\{\mathcal{A}_i,\ i = 1, \ldots, N\}$ where $\mathcal{A}_i^c$ corresponds to rejecting the null for the ith test with $\mathsf{P}(\mathcal{A}_i^c) = \alpha$. Chapter A2 establishes that

$\mathsf{P}(\cup\mathcal{A}_i) \leq \sum \mathsf{P}(\mathcal{A}_i)$ since $\mathsf{P}(\cap\mathcal{A}_i) \geq 0$. Also, $\mathsf{P}(\mathcal{A}_i) = 1 - \mathsf{P}(\mathcal{A}_i^c)$ and $(\cap\mathcal{A}_i)^c = \cup\mathcal{A}_i^c$. Thus:

$$\mathsf{P}\left(\bigcap_{i=1}^{N}\mathcal{A}_i\right) = 1 - \mathsf{P}\left(\left(\bigcap_{i=1}^{N}\mathcal{A}_i\right)^c\right) = 1 - \mathsf{P}\left(\bigcup_{i=1}^{N}\mathcal{A}_i^c\right) \geq 1 - \sum_{i=1}^{N}\mathsf{P}\left(\mathcal{A}_i^c\right) = 1 - N\alpha.$$

The probability of not rejecting on any test by the Bonferroni bound is $\alpha^+ \leq N\alpha$. If α is small and N is not too large, the bound is reasonably accurate (see Miller and Orr, 1966).

When all the tests are independent, $\mathsf{P}(\cap\mathcal{A}_i) = \prod_{i=1}^{N}\mathsf{P}(\mathcal{A}_i)$, so the probability of not falsely rejecting any of the hypotheses tested, when the $\mathsf{P}(\mathcal{A}_i^c)$ are all equal to α, is given by:

$$\alpha^* = \left[1 - \prod_{i=1}^{N}(1-\alpha)\right] = \left[1 - (1-\alpha)^N\right].$$

For $\alpha = 0.05$ and $N = 10$, then $\alpha^* = 0.4$, so the overall Type I error is large. The Bonferroni bound from α^+ is 0.5 in this case. For multiple testing, therefore, individual test sizes of 5 per cent seem too high. By way of contrast, when $\alpha = 0.01$, then α^* becomes 0.10 for $N = 10$, which is also the upper bound for α^+; $N = 50$ would be needed to raise the Type I error to 0.4. For $\alpha = 0.001$, we obtain $\alpha^* = 0.01$ and also $\alpha^+ \leq 0.01$ at $N = 10$, and increasing N to 50 only raises the Type I error to 0.05. Thus, the overall Type I error can be controlled at relatively low levels even for a large number of tests by using an individual test size of $\alpha = 0.001$ (0.1 per cent), perhaps using different significance levels on different types of test (e.g. 5 per cent for key diagnostic tests, and 0.1 per cent for specification tests).

A natural reaction to a proposal to set α as low as 0.001 is to worry about the consequences of low test power. To the extent that normality is a reasonable approximation for the distributions of statistics, and hence tests are close to t or F distributions, such a worry need not cause any loss of sleep. The critical values from the t(50) distribution at small significance levels highlight this point (see Table 13.2).

Table 13.2 Significance levels for t(50)

α	0.05	0.01	0.005	0.001
c_α	2.0	2.7	3.1	3.5

We refer to this phenomenon as 'tight tails', since the probability mass in the tails of the distribution dies out so rapidly that only a small increase in the t-statistic is needed to allow a small Type I error rate on individual tests. As casual perusal of many empirical time-series studies reveals, t-values often exceed 3.5 in absolute value, suggesting that incorrect rejection of the null due to an excessive number of tests is unlikely to be the explanation. We return to the issue of 'data mining' in Chapter 15.

13.11 Exercises

13.1 Consider the following process conditional on $(z_1 \ldots z_T)$:

$$y_t \mid z_t \sim \mathsf{IN}\left[z_t\beta, 1\right] \quad \text{for } t = 1, \ldots, T, \tag{13.90}$$

where z_t is strongly exogenous for β.

(a) Derive a χ^2-test η_0 of H_0: $\beta = 0$ against H_1: $\beta \neq 0$. Show that $\text{sign}(\beta)\sqrt{\eta_0} = \eta_1 \sim \mathsf{N}[0,1]$ on H_0.

(b) Obtain the distribution of η_1 when H_2: $\beta = \beta_0/\sqrt{T}$ and β_0 is fixed. Show that η_1 is consistent against H_4: $\beta = \beta_0 \neq \beta_p$, the population parameter.

(c) Explain the concepts of size and power of a test. What is the power of η_1 when $T = 100$ and (i) $\beta_p = 1.0$; (ii) $\beta_p = 0.1$ if $\sum_{t=1}^{T} z_t^2 = 10$?

(Oxford M.Phil., 1983)

13.2 Throughout, consider the model:

$$y_t = \beta x_t + \epsilon_t \text{ where } \epsilon_t \sim \mathsf{IN}\left[0, \sigma_\epsilon^2\right] \tag{13.91}$$

with $\mathsf{E}[x_t\epsilon_s] = 0 \ \forall t, s$.

(a) Obtain the asymptotic standard error of $\hat{\beta}$ (the MLE of β) and hence derive the asymptotic standard error of $1/\hat{\beta}$ when $\beta \neq 0$.

(b) Obtain Wald, LR, and LM tests of H_0: $\beta = 0$, denoted by ξ_w, ξ_r, and ξ_m. Show that $\xi_w \geq \xi_r \geq \xi_m$.

(c) Derive the exact distribution of ξ_w and hence of functions of ξ_r and ξ_m for a test whose significance level is α. Comment on why the inequality in (b) occurs.

(d) Obtain the limiting distribution of ξ_w for H_0: $\beta = 0$ against H_T: $\beta = \delta/\sqrt{T}$ with $\delta \neq 0$, when H_T is true.

(e) If $\beta = 1.0$ when $T = 100$, $\sigma_\epsilon^2 = 25$, and $\sigma_x^2 = \mathsf{E}[x_t^2] = 1$, what is the power of ξ_w to reject H_0: $\beta = 0$ at the 5 per cent significance level? (Use $\chi^2(3,0)$ as an approximation).

(f) What happens to the power as $T \to \infty$? Does this contradict the result in (d)?

13.3 Consider the model:

$$y_t = \boldsymbol{x}_t'\boldsymbol{\beta} + u_t \text{ where } u_t = \rho u_{t-1} + \epsilon_t \tag{13.92}$$

with $|\rho| < 1$ and $\epsilon_t \sim \mathsf{IN}[0, \sigma_\epsilon^2]$.

(a) When $\boldsymbol{x}_t$ is strongly exogenous for $\boldsymbol{\beta}$, derive an LM (or efficient-score) test of H_0: $\rho = 0$ against H_1: $\rho \neq 0$ and obtain its large-sample distribution under H_0.

(b) Does this test cease to be appropriate if $y_{t-1} \in \{\boldsymbol{x}_t\}$? If so, how can an appropriate test be constructed?

(c) Show that the MLEs of $\boldsymbol{\beta}$ and ρ are not independent when $y_{t-1} \in \{\boldsymbol{x}_t\}$. Describe how to obtain a likelihood-ratio test of the hypothesis H_0: $\rho = 0$ against H_1: $\rho \neq 0$ in that case.

(Oxford M.Phil., 1982)

13.4 Consider the first-order autoregressive process for $t = 1, \ldots, T$:

$$y_t = \beta y_{t-1} + \epsilon_t \text{ where } |\beta| < 1 \text{ and } \epsilon_t \underset{c}{\sim} \mathsf{IN}\left[0, \sigma_\epsilon^2\right] \tag{13.93}$$

when $\underset{c}{\sim}$ denotes that the error is claimed to be distributed as shown.

(a) Derive the population second moments of the data, and the plims of the least-squares estimators $\tilde{\beta}$ and $\tilde{\sigma}^2$ of the parameters β and σ_ϵ^2 assuming that (13.93) is true.

(b) An investigator concerned at possible mis-specification in (13.93) wishes to test for the importance of a second lag with coefficient γ. Show that an F-test of the hypothesis H_0: $\gamma = 0$ is asymptotically distributed as $\chi^2(1)$ when the null is true.

(c) In fact, the data-generation process is given by:

$$y_t = \theta y_{t-1} + \lambda y_{t-2} + \zeta_t \text{ where } \zeta_t \sim \mathsf{IN}\left[0, \sigma_\zeta^2\right]. \tag{13.94}$$

Obtain (a) the plim of the data second moments; and (b) the population parameters $\beta_p = \text{plim}\, \tilde{\beta}$ and $\sigma_p^2 = \text{plim}\, \tilde{\sigma}^2$.

(d) Under local alternatives of the form:

$$\mathsf{H}_T\colon \lambda = T^{-\frac{1}{2}}\phi \tag{13.95}$$

where ϕ is a fixed finite number and T is the sample size, show that the F-test in (b) becomes a non-central $\chi^2(1, \mu^2)$, and derive μ^2. Hence, or otherwise, explain how to calculate the power of the test to reject H_0 when it is false.

(Oxford M.Phil., 1991)

13.5 It is desired to test the following fitted model for possible mis-specifications:

$$\boldsymbol{y} = \boldsymbol{Z}\hat{\boldsymbol{\beta}} + \hat{\boldsymbol{\epsilon}}. \tag{13.96}$$

(a) Discuss potential information sets against which tests might be constructed.

(b) Derive an LM test against the alternative that an additional set of variables $\boldsymbol{W}$ has been omitted from the model.

(c) By deriving the distribution of $\boldsymbol{W}'\hat{\boldsymbol{\epsilon}}$ under the null that $\boldsymbol{y} = \boldsymbol{Z}\boldsymbol{\beta} + \boldsymbol{\epsilon}$, where $\boldsymbol{\epsilon} \sim \mathsf{N}_T[\boldsymbol{0}, \sigma_\epsilon^2 \boldsymbol{I}_T]$, obtain a residual diagnostic test for the fitted model against the alternative in (b).

(d) Compare the tests in (b) and (c) and comment on their usefulness in finite samples; does either approach generalize to other mis-specifications?

(Oxford M.Phil., 1984)

13.6 For the autoregressive process over $t = 1, \ldots, T$:

$$y_t = \beta y_{t-1} + \epsilon_t \text{ where } |\beta| < 1, \epsilon_t \sim \mathsf{IN}\left[0, \sigma_\epsilon^2\right] \text{ and } y_0 = 0. \tag{13.97}$$

(a) Derive the likelihood function and the MLE $\hat{\beta}$ of β, obtaining its limiting distribution as a function of the parameters (β, σ^2).

(b) Describe how to construct Wald and likelihood-ratio tests of $\mathsf{H}_0\colon \beta = 0$ against $\mathsf{H}_1\colon \beta \neq 0$, and derive the large-sample distribution of the Wald test under the sequence of local alternatives: $\mathsf{H}_T\colon \beta = \delta/\sqrt{T}$ for fixed finite δ.

(c) Hence prove that the Wald test is consistent, and explain how to calculate the approximate power of the test.

(d) How would the condition that $y_0 \sim \mathsf{N}[0, \sigma_\epsilon^2/(1-\beta^2)]$ affect your analysis? (Hint: how is the likelihood function formulated in that case?).

(Oxford M.Phil., 1984)

13.7 Explain how the LM test statistic is defined for a general set of constraints on a statistical model and specialize your result to the case of zero restrictions on a subset of coefficients. Consider the model:

$$\boldsymbol{y} = \boldsymbol{X}\boldsymbol{\beta} + \boldsymbol{u} \;\text{ where }\; \boldsymbol{u} \sim \mathsf{N}_T\left[\boldsymbol{0}, \boldsymbol{\Omega}(\rho)\right] \tag{13.98}$$

where:

$$\operatorname*{plim}_{T\to\infty}\left(T^{-1}\boldsymbol{X}'\boldsymbol{u}\right) = \boldsymbol{0}, \;\; \operatorname*{plim}_{T\to\infty}\left(T^{-1}\boldsymbol{X}'\boldsymbol{X}\right) = \boldsymbol{M}. \tag{13.99}$$

Here, $\boldsymbol{y}$ and $\boldsymbol{u}$ are $T \times 1$ vectors, $\boldsymbol{\beta}$ is a $k \times 1$ vector, $\boldsymbol{X}$ is a $T \times k$ matrix, $\boldsymbol{M}$ is positive definite, and $\boldsymbol{\Omega}(\rho)$ has typical element ω_{ts} of the form:

$$\omega_{ts} = \frac{\rho^{|t-s|}}{1-\rho^2}. \tag{13.100}$$

(a) Derive the log-likelihood function $\ell(\boldsymbol{\beta}, \rho)$ and the score at $\rho = 0$.

(b) Obtain the LM test of $\mathsf{H}_0\colon \rho = 0$. Note that $|\boldsymbol{\Omega}| = (1-\rho^2)^{-1}$ and:

$$\boldsymbol{\Omega}(\rho)^{-1} = \begin{pmatrix} 1 & -\rho & 0 & \cdots & 0 & 0 \\ -\rho & 1+\rho^2 & -\rho & \cdots & 0 & 0 \\ 0 & -\rho & 1+\rho^2 & \ddots & \vdots & \vdots \\ 0 & 0 & -\rho & \ddots & -\rho & 0 \\ \vdots & \vdots & \ddots & \ddots & 1+\rho^2 & -\rho \\ 0 & 0 & 0 & \cdots & -\rho & 1 \end{pmatrix}. \tag{13.101}$$

(Oxford M.Phil., 1987)

13.8 Consider the model:

$$\begin{aligned} y_t &= \beta x_t + u_t \\ x_t &= \lambda x_{t-1} + v_t \end{aligned} \quad \text{where} \begin{pmatrix} u_t \\ v_t \end{pmatrix} \sim \mathsf{IN}_2\left[\begin{pmatrix} 0 \\ 0 \end{pmatrix}, \begin{pmatrix} \sigma_{11} & \sigma_{12} \\ \sigma_{12} & \sigma_{22} \end{pmatrix}\right],$$

when $|\lambda| < 1, \sigma_{12} \neq 0$, and $t = 1, \ldots, T$.

(a) Derive the population first and second moments of the variables $\{y_t\}$ and $\{x_t\}$, and obtain the limiting distribution of the instrumental variables estimator of β, using x_{t-1} as an instrument.

(b) Develop a test of the null hypothesis H_0: $\beta = \beta_0$, against the sequence of local alternatives H_T: $\beta = \beta_0 + \delta/\sqrt{T}$ for δ fixed. Show that your test is consistent against a fixed (rather than a local) alternative.

(c) Explain how to derive the asymptotic local power of your test.

(Oxford M.Phil., 1986)

13.9 The following theory-based economic model is to be estimated from a sample of T time-series observations on $\{y_t, \boldsymbol{x}_t\}$:

$$y_t = \boldsymbol{x}_t'\boldsymbol{\beta} + u_t \tag{13.102}$$

where it is claimed that $u_t \sim \mathsf{IN}[0, \sigma_u^2]$, and that $\boldsymbol{\beta}$ is constant over time.

(a) What is the status of the model in (13.102)? Against what information sets can it be evaluated?

(b) Develop an LM test of the alternative hypothesis that H_1: $\boldsymbol{\beta} = \boldsymbol{\beta}_0 + z_t\boldsymbol{\beta}_1$ where z_t is an observable variable. If H_0: $\boldsymbol{\beta} = \boldsymbol{\beta}_0$ is rejected against H_1, what should be concluded?

(c) If z_t is a dummy variable which is zero till $T_1 < T$ and then unity thereafter, precisely what is H_1 testing?

(Oxford M.Phil., 1986)

13.10 An investigator wishes to test the performance of the model:

$$\begin{aligned} y_t &= \alpha z_t + \beta y_{t-1} + \epsilon_{1t} \\ z_t &= \lambda z_{t-1} + \epsilon_{2t} \end{aligned} \quad \text{where } \boldsymbol{\epsilon}_t \sim \mathsf{IN}_2\left[\mathbf{0}, \boldsymbol{\Sigma}\right].$$

(a) When the parameters are known, derive the *ex ante* 1-step-ahead forecast error in predicting (y_{T+1}, z_{T+1}) given (y_T, z_T), and obtain a formula for its variance matrix under the null hypothesis that the model stays unaltered in the forecast period. Hence derive a χ^2 test of that null.

(b) In fact, at time $T+1$ a permanent shift $\boldsymbol{\mu}$ occurs to the mean of the system such that $\boldsymbol{\epsilon}_t \sim \mathsf{IN}_2[\boldsymbol{\mu}, \boldsymbol{\Sigma}]$ for $t = T+1, \ldots, T+n$. What is the non-centrality of the test in (a)?

(c) Generalize this result to two 1-step-ahead forecasts, obtaining a χ^2 test for constancy over $T+1$ and $T+2$, still with known parameters over $t = 1, \ldots, T$. What is the distribution of this test for $\boldsymbol{\mu} \neq \mathbf{0}$?

(d) Compare this test with a single 2-step-ahead forecasting procedure, derive the mean and the variance of the 2-step forecast errors, and hence propose a χ^2 test based on these which only uses information up to time T. Derive the non-centrality parameter of this test, and comment on its relation to that of the two 1-step-ahead forecasts.

(e) Discuss how your results might be affected by having to estimate the parameters of the system.

(Oxford M.Phil., 1985)

13.11 Explain how you would design and analyse a Monte Carlo study to determine the power function $\mathcal{P}_T(\theta|\psi)$ of a test statistic η of H_0: $\theta = 0$ which is asymptotically distributed as a $\chi^2(1, 0)$ under H_0 for a DGP dependent on the parameter vector (θ, ψ, T) for T observations. Discuss:

(a) the non-null asymptotic distribution of η.

(b) the Monte Carlo estimation of $\mathcal{P}_T(\theta|\psi)$ for given (θ, ψ, T).

(c) how you would formulate and test a response surface approximation to $\mathcal{P}_T(\theta|\psi)$ when the number of replications per experiment is (i) $M = 1$; (ii) $M > 100$.

(Oxford M.Phil., 1988)

13.12 Consider the over-identified structural model:

$$y_t = \boldsymbol{x}_t'\boldsymbol{\beta} + \epsilon_t \ \text{ where } \ \epsilon_t \sim \mathsf{IN}\left[0, \sigma_\epsilon^2\right] \tag{13.103}$$

for $t = 1, \ldots, T$, when $\mathsf{E}[\boldsymbol{x}_t\epsilon_t] \neq \mathbf{0}$, $\boldsymbol{\beta}$ is $k \times 1$, and there is a set of $m > k$ instrumental variables $\boldsymbol{z}_t$ believed to satisfy $\mathsf{E}[\boldsymbol{z}_t\epsilon_t] = \mathbf{0}\ \forall t$. Let:

$$\boldsymbol{x}_t = \boldsymbol{\pi}\boldsymbol{z}_t + \boldsymbol{v}_t \tag{13.104}$$

where $\mathsf{E}[\boldsymbol{z}_t\boldsymbol{v}_t'] = \mathbf{0}\ \forall t$, with the reduced form of (13.103) being:

$$y_t = \boldsymbol{z}_t'\boldsymbol{\gamma} + w_t \ \text{ and } \ \mathsf{E}\left[\boldsymbol{z}_t w_t\right] = \mathbf{0}\ \forall t. \tag{13.105}$$

Derive a Wald test of the hypothesis that H_0: $\boldsymbol{\gamma} = \boldsymbol{\pi}'\boldsymbol{\beta}$, and show that this is equivalent to testing the validity of the instruments $\boldsymbol{z}_t$ used for estimation (i.e. H_1: $\mathsf{E}[\boldsymbol{z}_t\epsilon_t] = \mathbf{0}$).

(Oxford M.Phil., 1983)

13.13 Consider the following fixed-regressor model:

$$\boldsymbol{y} = \boldsymbol{X}\boldsymbol{\beta} + \boldsymbol{\epsilon} \ \text{ where } \ \boldsymbol{\epsilon} \sim \mathsf{N}_T\left[\mathbf{0}, \sigma_\epsilon^2\boldsymbol{\Sigma}\right] \ \text{ subject to } \ \boldsymbol{R}\boldsymbol{\beta} = \boldsymbol{r} \tag{13.106}$$

when $\boldsymbol{X}$ and $\boldsymbol{R}$ are $T \times k$ and $q \times k$ of rank k,and q respectively, $\boldsymbol{\Sigma}$ is positive definite with $tr(\boldsymbol{\Sigma}) = T$, and $\boldsymbol{\Sigma}$, $\boldsymbol{R}$, and $\boldsymbol{r}$ are known.

(a) Derive the restricted generalized least-squares (GLS) estimator of $\boldsymbol{\beta}$ in (13.106). Show that the estimator $\widehat{\boldsymbol{\lambda}}$ of the Lagrange multiplier vector $\boldsymbol{\lambda}$ $(q\times 1)$ is distributed as:

$$\widehat{\boldsymbol{\lambda}} \sim \mathsf{N}_q\left[\mathbf{0}, 4\sigma_\epsilon^2\left(\boldsymbol{R}\left(\boldsymbol{X}'\boldsymbol{\Sigma}^{-1}\boldsymbol{X}\right)^{-1}\boldsymbol{R}'\right)^{-1}\right]. \tag{13.107}$$

(b) Obtain an F-test of the hypothesis H_0: $\boldsymbol{R}\boldsymbol{\beta} = \boldsymbol{r}$ against the alternative H_1: $\boldsymbol{R}\boldsymbol{\beta} \neq \boldsymbol{r}$.

(c) Consider the following modification of (13.106):

$$\boldsymbol{y} = \boldsymbol{X}\boldsymbol{\beta} + \boldsymbol{\epsilon} \ \text{ where } \ \boldsymbol{\epsilon} \sim \mathsf{N}_T\left[\mathbf{0}, \sigma_\epsilon^2\boldsymbol{I}_T\right] \tag{13.108}$$

subject to

$$\boldsymbol{r} = \boldsymbol{R}\boldsymbol{\beta} + \boldsymbol{v} \ \text{ when } \ \boldsymbol{v} \sim \mathsf{N}_q\left[\mathbf{0}, \tau^2\boldsymbol{I}_T\right],$$

and ϵ and $\boldsymbol{v}$ are independent of each other. Estimate the following model by GLS:

$$\begin{pmatrix} \boldsymbol{y} \\ \boldsymbol{r} \end{pmatrix} = \begin{pmatrix} \boldsymbol{X} \\ \boldsymbol{R} \end{pmatrix} \boldsymbol{\beta} + \begin{pmatrix} \boldsymbol{\epsilon} \\ \boldsymbol{v} \end{pmatrix}$$

to obtain $\widehat{\boldsymbol{\beta}}_{GLS}$. Letting $\omega^2 = \sigma^2/\tau^2$, interpret the polar cases $\omega^2 \to \infty$ induced by (i) $\sigma_\epsilon^2 \to \infty$, and (ii) $\tau^2 \to 0$. What happens when $\omega^2 \to 0$?

(Oxford M.Phil., 1992)

13.14 Consider the following model:

$$y_t = \boldsymbol{\beta}' \mathbf{z}_t + u_t \tag{13.109}$$

where:

$$u_t = \rho u_{t-1} + \epsilon_t \tag{13.110}$$

when $|\rho| < 1$ and $\epsilon_t \sim \mathsf{IN}[0, \sigma_\epsilon^2]$. In (13.109)+(13.110), $\mathbf{z}_t$ is a $k \times 1$ vector of variables strongly exogenous for $\boldsymbol{\beta}$.

(a) This model can be regarded as a special case of an autoregressive-distributed lag equation:

$$y_t = \boldsymbol{\gamma}_1' \mathbf{z}_t + \gamma_2 y_{t-1} + \boldsymbol{\gamma}_3' \mathbf{z}_{t-1} + \epsilon_t. \tag{13.111}$$

Use the Wald test principle to construct a test statistic for testing the validity of the restrictions implied by the hypothesized process in (13.109) and (13.110) when none of the variables in $\mathbf{z}_t$ is redundant when lagged.

(b) Derive a Lagrange multiplier (LM) test of H_0: $\rho = 0$ based on:

$$r_1 = \frac{\sum \hat{u}_{t-1} \hat{u}_t}{\sum \hat{u}_{t-1}^2} \tag{13.112}$$

when the $\hat{u}_t$ are the residuals from the least-squares estimation of (13.109) ignoring (13.110).

(c) Are the hypotheses tested in (a) and (b) the same? If so, are there any reasons for preferring one test to the other? If not, explain what each hypothesis is testing and whether there is a preferred order in which they should be tested.

(d) Briefly explain how to derive the power function of one of these tests.

(Oxford M.Phil., 1992)

Part III

Empirical Modelling

14
Encompassing

Since the form of the DGP is unknown at level C, there often exists a multiplicity of empirical models for the same data-set. Encompassing seeks to resolve the proliferation of rival models by requiring any given model to account for, or explain, the results obtained by other models. Because rejection is not final, and corroboration is not definitive, encompassing augments the conventional testing strategy, building on antecedents in the theory of mis-specification. The notion is formalized through the encompassing relation $\mathcal{E}$, and its properties are examined; it is reflexive and anti-symmetric, but not necessarily transitive. Various levels of analysis are described, leading to the concept of parsimonious encompassing, denoted $\mathcal{E}_p$. This is transitive, and so supplants the original concept. Invariance to isomorphic re-specification is used to choose between alternative tests of encompassing implications. The approach is illustrated by a simple example, before relating encompassing to nesting. The main focus is on encompassing in linear regression models and in stationary scalar and vector processes. Finally, the Lucas critique for feedback against expectational models is analysed in terms of encompassing and super exogeneity, which make the critique refutable as well as confirmable.

14.1 Introduction

Part II utilized the conceptual framework established in Part I to develop the theory of estimation and inference when the form of the DGP was known, but the numerical population value of the parameter vector was unknown. The sequential joint data density $\mathsf{D}_{\mathsf{x}}(\boldsymbol{x}_t|\boldsymbol{X}_{t-1},\boldsymbol{\theta})$ was reinterpreted as the likelihood function $\mathsf{L}(\boldsymbol{\theta}|\boldsymbol{x}_t;\boldsymbol{X}_{t-1})$, from which maximum likelihood estimators and a range of test statistics were derived. Part III investigates empirical modelling at level C, when the form of the DGP is unknown. This introduces the possibility that there may be a multiplicity of empirical models of the same data-set. Conversely, once there exists more than one model of a given data process, a level B analysis is infeasible, since at least one of the investigators cannot have known the form of the DGP. Thus, it is natural to commence our study of level C with the encompassing principle, which helps analyse, and offers one resolution of, the problem of a proliferation of rival empirical models of a common data-set. The need for a concept like encompassing arises in part from the non-experimental nature of aggregate economics, which entails that many investigators analyse the same data, but from different perspectives.

Chapter 13 discussed the theory of testing in terms of formulating a null hypothesis, deriving a statistic whose distribution is known under the null, finding an appropriate critical value given the relative costs of Type I and Type II errors, and then computing the relevant statistic to see whether or not the null could be maintained in light of the evidence from the particular data-set under study. The tests explicitly derived were direction free, usually being quadratic forms asymptotically distributed as non-central χ^2 statistics under the alternative. Many testing situations take such a form, but some do not. In particular, consider attempting to test between two models of the consumption function, one of which assumed that consumption depended on income (say), while the other assumed that consumption depended on wealth (see Pesaran and Deaton, 1978). It is not immediately obvious how to develop a χ^2 test to choose between these models.

The proliferation of rival explanations of empirical phenomena raises several interesting methodological issues. First, when there are two or more contradictory explanations for a phenomenon, at least one of them must be wrong — and possibly all are. Secondly, because every model is a reduction of the data-generation process, empirical models are just reduced re-combinations of the data. Thus, if a model M_1 claims to explain the data, then M_1 ought to be able to explain the re-combinations of that same data which other investigators use, namely rival models. Consequently, a natural question to ask of any empirical model M_1 is whether it can explain why another model M_2 found the results which M_2 reports. That idea leads directly to the encompassing principle. Thirdly, when the rival empirical models have prior theory-model bases, then either there co-exist competing theoretical paradigms between which testing is required, or the given theory framework does not have unique empirical implications. These three issues recur below.

Encompassing arose as the intuitive idea of trying to explain the results obtained by rival models as seen from the viewpoint of a given model (see Hendry, 1975, Hendry and Anderson, 1977, and Davidson, Hendry, Srba and Yeo, 1978). The notion was proposed to reduce the proliferation of rival explanations, and was initially implemented partly by standardizing the rival models and partly by embedding them in a common framework. However, the conceptual basis of encompassing has since been formalized and related to the theory of non-nested hypothesis testing (see *inter alia* Cox, 1961, 1962, Pesaran, 1974, Hendry and Richard, 1982, 1989, Mizon, 1984, Mizon and Richard, 1986, Govaerts, Hendry and Richard, 1993, and Florens, Hendry and Richard, 1994).

The analysis is at level C hereafter in the sense that we do not endow the investigator with knowledge of the DGP. Encompassing operates over models, but to develop solutions to theoretical problems, we return to level A for distribution theory and concepts, and to level B for estimators. This has been our implicit approach throughout: map an empirical problem into a theoretical one, solve the theory problem, and map that back as the solution to the empirical difficulty. So far, such a methodology needed little comment as we operated at levels A and B where the adequacy of the solution could be judged immediately. At level C, the adequacy of the solution is less clear, and we can only judge the first three steps by reference to assumed DGPs. The iterative nature of our whole enterprise must be remembered — the evidence we accrue may suggest a complete reformulation of the initial assumptions of the edifice. Nevertheless, this chapter yields some new payoffs to the general theory we have constructed above. First, despite its very different origins, encompassing transpires to be a natural implication of the theory of reduction as presaged in Chapter 9. Secondly, the conjunction of super exogeneity and encompassing helps resolve the nature of the 'Lucas' critique noted on several occasions above.

The chapter is organized as follows. First, because rejection on a test is not final nor corroboration definitive, the intuitive role of encompassing in augmenting the conventional testing strategy is discussed in section 14.2. Then, in §14.3, we relate encompassing to the theory of mis-specification. In section 14.4, the notion is formalized through the encompassing relation $\mathcal{E}$ which is reflexive and anti-symmetric, but not necessarily transitive. Levels of encompassing analysis are described in §14.5, leading to the concept of parsimonious encompassing, denoted $\mathcal{E}_p$ which is transitive, and so supplants the original concept. The approach is illustrated by a simple example in §14.7 before focusing on encompassing in linear regression models and stationary processes in §14.9–§14.10. Section 14.13 considers encompassing the VAR. The Lucas critique for feedback and expectational models is analysed in §14.14–§14.17 in terms of encompassing and super exogeneity. The combination of these two tools makes the critique refutable as well as confirmable, attenuating its sometimes nihilistic application. Finally, §14.18 provides an empirical illustration.

14.2 Augmenting the conventional testing strategy

There are two reasons for augmenting the conventional testing strategy, described in Chapter 13, by a principle such as encompassing: rejection is not final, and corroboration is not definitive.

14.2.1 Rejection is not final

When a model is tested and the test rejects, it is nevertheless nearly always possible to rescue a version of that model, appropriately patched to offset the earlier rejection evidence. An obvious example is the use of residual autocorrelation corrections to ensure a white-noise error. More generally, in any model-building strategy where modelling continues until no rejections occur, theories can never be rejected by counter-evidence. This is partly a problem of data mining in so far as only an investigator can know how an empirical model was developed, and hence whether reported statistics were used in selection or were genuine tests.

We have also previously noted the difficulty of deducing from a test rejection what induced that outcome, since it is a *non sequitur* to attribute the problem to the alternative against which the test was constructed. This is an aspect of the Duhem–Quine problem: if a combination of postulates has an incorrect implication, then the group as a whole is in doubt, but any individual postulate can be retained by sufficient adjustment of other postulates (see e.g. Losee, 1980). Moreover, it is naïve to abandon a previously successful framework because of a small number of counter-instances or anomalies: these may transpire to be due to incorrect measurement, or an inappropriate interpretation. Rather, anomalies often co-exist for long periods with prevailing theories until the appearance of new theories which are more successful at explaining both the anomalies and the pre-existing evidence (see Ch.1). Finally, theories are rarely tested directly in economics, and are usually first formulated as theory models. Rejecting a model, or even a sequence of models, does not entail that the theory is incorrect. Thus, theories are rarely rejected, and at best are supplanted by better theories which have fewer remaining anomalies or rejection instances.

14.2.2 Corroboration is not definitive

A claim, such as a theory or an hypothesis, is said to be 'corroborated' by evidence which is consistent with an implication of that claim, when the evidence could have refuted the claim. As such, excess corroborated content is a necessary ingredient to endow a theory with credibility. However, corroboration is insufficient to 'verify' a theory, and in practice only offers weak support for a theory. This is obviously true when the theory is formed to explain evidence previously obtained. Further, it is possible to formulate a rather silly theory, search for evidence to confirm it, and duly find support for the initial theory: remember the 'pink elephant' problem discussed in Chapter 5.

There are many 'paradoxes' of corroboration. These include the following oft-cited example. Since the proposition 'all As are Bs' entails 'all not-Bs are not-As', then every 'not-B' that is also a 'not-A' corroborates the initial assumption (e.g. a student's white shirt thereby corroborates the claim that 'all crows are black'). However, there are more pernicious difficulties. Consider a theory that has at least one corroborating instance. A second item of evidence is then discovered that by itself also corroborates the theory. One might feel that the theory is even better supported, but in fact the two items together could refute the theory: successive corroboration can entail refutation. A simple example is provided by a theory with two parameters α and β which are predicted to satisfy $\alpha + \beta < 0$ and $\alpha > 0$. First, we observe $\beta = -1$. That is corroborating evidence, because β has to be negative according to the theory if $\alpha + \beta$ is to be negative yet α is positive. Moreover, the evidence would have rejected the theory had β been positive. Next, observe $\alpha = 2$. This element alone is also corroborating since α has to be positive and a negative α would have rejected the theory. However, the theory is refuted by the combination of the two corroborating items, because $\alpha + \beta$ is not negative. Thus, two items, each of which individually corroborates, jointly can refute (see Ericsson and Hendry, 1989, for a formalization).

As always in empirical research, the requirements of corroboration and non-rejection are necessary but not sufficient: if they are not satisfied, then the theory is deemed inadequate, but satisfying them need not imply that the theory is adequate. Since rejection is not final and corroboration is not definitive, proceeding by just postulating models and either corroborating or rejecting them cannot constitute a complete methodology. The encompassing principle is an attempt to improve that research strategy in the context of a progressive approach, by building on earlier findings and thereby trying to explain more and more of the world with a given model. It explicitly recognizes that only necessary criteria are available for model validity, and that theories are only replaced by better theories and are not simply accepted or rejected. We will have to revise that idea as we proceed, but a closely related and less flawed notion will emerge as a concomitant of reduction theory.

14.3 Encompassing and mis-specification analysis

Encompassing is related to conventional mis-specification analysis, and is how the idea originally arose. Given any DGP and a false model thereof, the mis-specifications in the model can be predicted from knowledge of the DGP. These mis-specifications must occur when the algebra of the analysis is correct.

For example, let the DGP (denoted M_0) be a trivariate normal distribution for $(y_t : x_{1t} : x_{2t})$ with the conditional representation:

$$\mathsf{M}_0\colon\ y_t = \beta_1 x_{1t} + \beta_2 x_{2t} + \epsilon_t, \tag{14.1}$$

corresponding to $\mathsf{E}[y_t|x_{1t}, x_{2t}]$, whereas a model M_1 assumes:

$$\mathsf{M}_1\colon\ y_t = \alpha x_{1t} + v_t, \tag{14.2}$$

representing $\mathsf{E}[y_t|x_{1t}]$. M_1 is nested in (14.1). Reformulate M_0 in (14.1) as:

$$y_t = (\beta_1 + \beta_2 b_{21})\, x_{1t} + \beta_2\, (x_{2t} - b_{21} x_{1t}) + \epsilon_t = \alpha x_{1t} + \nu_t, \tag{14.3}$$

where $b_{21} = m_{21} m_{11}^{-1}$ when $m_{ij} = \mathsf{E}[x_{it} x_{jt}]$ so $x_{1t} \perp (x_{2t} - b_{21} x_{1t})$. Then marginalizing with respect to x_{2t} is equivalent to eliminating $(x_{2t} - b_{21} x_{1t})$ (i.e., imposing $\beta_2 = 0$), which generates M_1. From the DGP (14.1), we can correctly predict in (14.2) that:

$$\alpha = \beta_1 + \beta_2 b_{21}. \tag{14.4}$$

This formula explains the numerical value of α, or why α might have the opposite sign to that anticipated for β_1. For example, when $\beta_2 < 0$ and $b_{21} > 0$ by a sufficient amount to ensure that $|\beta_2 b_{21}| > \beta_1$, then $\alpha < 0$ even though $\beta_1 > 0$. Chapter 9 showed that knowledge of the DGP entails knowledge of the model, and hence the former must encompass the latter.

Encompassing requires of any model that it should mimic the DGP in exactly the same way. A valid model M_1 ought to be able to predict the parameter values in other models $\{\mathsf{M}_i\}$, because under the hypothesis that M_1 is congruent, the other models are reduced parameterizations of M_1. Since M_1 is playing the role of the DGP, it should accurately predict the outcomes as in (14.4). When it does so, the other models are redundant. However, unlike mis-specification analysis at level A, M_1 may not in fact mimic the DGP, so the predictions from M_1 about the other models may turn out to be wrong, in which case we learn that M_1 is incorrect. Thus, encompassing has a natural interpretation as a test principle. Consider a second model M_2 of M_0 in (14.1):

$$\mathsf{M}_2\colon\ y_t = \delta x_{2t} + u_t, \tag{14.5}$$

which models $\mathsf{E}[y_t|x_{2t}]$. Using an equivalent form to (14.3), from M_0:

$$y_t = \beta_1 (x_{1t} - b_{12}x_{2t}) + (\beta_2 + \beta_1 b_{12}) x_{2t} + \epsilon_t = \delta x_{2t} + u_t, \tag{14.6}$$

where $b_{12} = m_{12}m_{22}^{-1}$. Then M_0 entails:

$$\delta = \beta_2 + \beta_1 b_{12}. \tag{14.7}$$

The encompassing question is whether or not M_1 can explain the parameter value δ of M_2. To proceed to an evaluation, the two models must share a common probability space, and otherwise are not commensurable. This can be achieved if the proprietor of M_1 views that model as complete, and hence interprets M_1 as $\mathsf{E}[y_t|x_{1t}, x_{2t}]$ subject to the restriction that $\beta_2 = 0$. Then a sufficient condition for M_1 to account for the results of M_2 is that $\beta_2 = 0$, which entails $\alpha = \beta_1$ from (14.4), and hence that M_1 coincides with M_0: because M_0 can explain δ, M_1 can as well, and both predict δ to be $\beta_1 b_{12} = \alpha b_{12}$, which we denote by δ_α.

Conversely, when $\beta_2 \neq 0$, M_1 should fail to explain M_2. This can be seen by noting that δ_α remains αb_{12} which now equals $(\beta_1 + \beta_2 b_{21})b_{12}$ from (14.4), whereas $\delta = \beta_2 + \beta_1 b_{12}$. Thus, $\delta \neq \delta_\alpha$ unless $b_{12}b_{21} = 1$, which requires a perfect correlation between x_{2t} and x_{1t}, so that M_1 is isomorphic to M_2 (see Ch.2). Finally, even when $\beta_2 = 0$, (14.6) entails that the relation between y_t and x_{2t} alone in (14.5) is well defined, although the DGP only involves a relation between y_t and x_{1t}, and (14.5) is not ostensibly nested in (14.2).

14.4 Formalizing encompassing

More generally, consider two models M_1 and M_2 of a random variable y, neither model necessarily being the DGP (M_0), where their respective families of density functions are given by:

$$\mathsf{M}_1\colon \mathsf{D}_1 (\mathbf{y} \mid \boldsymbol{\alpha}),\ \boldsymbol{\alpha} \in \mathcal{A} \subseteq \mathbb{R}^k \tag{14.8}$$

$$\mathsf{M}_2\colon \mathsf{D}_2 (\mathbf{y} \mid \boldsymbol{\delta}),\ \boldsymbol{\delta} \in \mathcal{D} \subseteq \mathbb{R}^n \tag{14.9}$$

$$\mathsf{M}_0\colon \mathsf{D}_\mathsf{y} (\mathbf{y} \mid \boldsymbol{\theta}),\ \boldsymbol{\theta} \in \Theta \subseteq \mathbb{R}^p. \tag{14.10}$$

Two models M_1 and M_2 are isomorphic when their parameters are one–one transformations of each other, so they are the same model in different parameterizations, denoted by $\mathsf{M}_1 \doteq \mathsf{M}_2$ (see Ch.2). We assume that M_1 and M_2 are not isomorphic. From the theory of reduction in Chapter 9, M_1 and M_2 are nested in M_0, denoted by $\mathsf{M}_1 \subseteq \mathsf{M}_0$, etc. For nested models, there exist transformations $\mathbf{t}_\lambda(\boldsymbol{\theta}) = \boldsymbol{\lambda} = (\boldsymbol{\lambda}_1' : \boldsymbol{\lambda}_2')'$, such that M_1 is derived by imposing $\boldsymbol{\lambda}_2 = \mathbf{0}$, and hence $\boldsymbol{\lambda}_1 = \boldsymbol{\alpha}$. There is no loss from reducing M_0 to M_1 when $\boldsymbol{\lambda}_2$ is in fact zero, but there is no necessity that $\boldsymbol{\lambda}_2 = \mathbf{0}$. Similarly, $\mathbf{t}_\mu(\boldsymbol{\theta}) = \boldsymbol{\mu} = (\boldsymbol{\mu}_1' : \boldsymbol{\mu}_2')'$ delivers M_2 when $\boldsymbol{\mu}_2 = \mathbf{0}$ with $\boldsymbol{\mu}_1 = \boldsymbol{\delta}$. Since some parameters of a model may be zero, when M_3 is the extension of M_1 which potentially allows $\boldsymbol{\lambda}_2 \neq \mathbf{0}$ even though $\boldsymbol{\lambda}_2$ is zero, then we define the two models to be equivalent, denoted $\mathsf{M}_1 \approx \mathsf{M}_3$. Thus, $\mathsf{M}_1 \doteq \mathsf{M}_3$ implies $\mathsf{M}_1 \approx \mathsf{M}_3$. Equivalent models need not have the same number of parameters, but in a minimal-sufficient parameterization, would be isomorphic.

Since M_1 and M_2 are nested in M_0, their parameters are functions of those of the DGP, denoted by $\boldsymbol{\alpha} = \boldsymbol{\alpha}(\boldsymbol{\theta})$ and $\boldsymbol{\delta} = \boldsymbol{\delta}(\boldsymbol{\theta})$: (14.7) is an example of such a mapping. In practice, M_1 and M_2 may not be nested with respect to each other, despite being nested in $\mathsf{D}_{\mathsf{y}}(\cdot)$, and one aim of encompassing is to compare their parameters irrespective of nesting. However, when M_1 is the DGP, then $\mathsf{M}_2 \subseteq \mathsf{M}_1$ despite its appearance, so that $\boldsymbol{\delta}$ must be a function of $\boldsymbol{\alpha}$. We denote this function by $\boldsymbol{\delta}_{\alpha} = \boldsymbol{\phi}_{21}(\boldsymbol{\alpha})$, where $\boldsymbol{\phi}_{21} : \mathcal{A} \mapsto \mathcal{D}$, and the subscripts record between which models the mapping occurs. Thus, as in the previous example, $\boldsymbol{\delta}_{\alpha}$ is what M_1 predicts M_2 should find as the value of the parameter of $\mathsf{D}_2(\boldsymbol{y}|\cdot)$. Even though $\boldsymbol{\theta}$ is unknown, we can compare the predicted value $\boldsymbol{\phi}_{21}(\boldsymbol{\alpha}(\boldsymbol{\theta}))$ with the value $\boldsymbol{\delta} = \boldsymbol{\delta}(\boldsymbol{\theta})$ which M_2 actually finds.

The population encompassing difference between M_2 and the prediction of M_2 based on M_1 is:

$$\boldsymbol{\psi}_{\delta}\left(\boldsymbol{\theta}_p\right) = \boldsymbol{\delta}\left(\boldsymbol{\theta}_p\right) - \boldsymbol{\phi}_{21}\left(\boldsymbol{\alpha}\left(\boldsymbol{\theta}_p\right)\right). \tag{14.11}$$

Now we can define encompassing formally.

DEFINITION 1. *Model 1 encompasses model 2, denoted by* $\mathsf{M}_1\mathcal{E}\mathsf{M}_2$, *with respect to* $\boldsymbol{\delta}$ *if* $\boldsymbol{\psi}_{\delta} = \mathbf{0}$.

Encompassing is an exact property in the population, but is a contingent relation, unlike concepts such as bias: it cannot be expected to hold for all values of $\boldsymbol{\theta}$. Indeed, we could have $\mathsf{M}_1\mathcal{E}\mathsf{M}_2$ when $\boldsymbol{\theta} = \boldsymbol{\theta}_1$ whereas $\mathsf{M}_2\mathcal{E}\mathsf{M}_1$ when $\boldsymbol{\theta} = \boldsymbol{\theta}_2$. This would pose no problems if a unique value $\boldsymbol{\theta}_p$ existed, but regime shifts and innovations occur, so we must anticipate establishing encompassing relations only for a class of empirical models over some epoch. Looking back, we can see that this is a generic problem that affects all estimation and testing applications in empirical economics.

For $\boldsymbol{\psi}_{\delta}$ to vanish (apart from probability-zero events), $\boldsymbol{\alpha}(\boldsymbol{\theta})$ must be a sufficient re-parameterization of $\boldsymbol{\theta}$ in so far as $\boldsymbol{\delta}$ is concerned. Encompassing will not be possible if there are aspects of $\boldsymbol{\theta}$ on which $\boldsymbol{\delta}$ depends but $\boldsymbol{\alpha}$ does not. Therefore, letting $\mathcal{E}^c$ denote 'does not encompass', we deduce the converse that if $\mathsf{M}_1\mathcal{E}^c\,\mathsf{M}_2$, then M_2 must reflect specific features of the DGP that are not included in M_1. That leads to our first theorem.

THEOREM 1. *If* $\mathsf{M}_1\mathcal{E}\,\mathsf{M}_2$ *then either* $\mathsf{M}_2\mathcal{E}^c\,\mathsf{M}_1$ *or the two models are equivalent.*

To prove theorem 1, first consider the possibility that both $\mathsf{M}_2\mathcal{E}\mathsf{M}_1$ and $\mathsf{M}_1\mathcal{E}\mathsf{M}_2$ hold. The former implies $\boldsymbol{\alpha} = \boldsymbol{\phi}_{12}(\boldsymbol{\delta})$, and hence that:

$$\boldsymbol{\psi}_{\alpha} = \boldsymbol{\alpha}\left(\boldsymbol{\theta}_p\right) - \boldsymbol{\phi}_{12}\left(\boldsymbol{\delta}\left(\boldsymbol{\theta}_p\right)\right) = \mathbf{0}.$$

Since $\boldsymbol{\psi}_{\delta} = \mathbf{0}$, then $\boldsymbol{\delta} = \boldsymbol{\phi}_{21}(\boldsymbol{\alpha})$ as well, so that:

$$\boldsymbol{\delta} = \boldsymbol{\phi}_{21}\left(\boldsymbol{\phi}_{12}\left(\boldsymbol{\delta}\right)\right) \text{ and hence } \boldsymbol{\phi}_{21}\boldsymbol{\phi}_{12} = \mathbf{I}_n. \tag{14.12}$$

Thus, after suitable re-parameterizations and the elimination of redundant parameters, the models M_1 and M_2 are isomorphic. Conversely, when $\boldsymbol{\psi}_{\delta} = \mathbf{0}$ and $\boldsymbol{\psi}_{\alpha} \neq \mathbf{0}$ then $\mathsf{M}_2\mathcal{E}^c\,\mathsf{M}_1$.

We next introduce the concept of a minimal nesting model, M_m, with parameter vector $\gamma \in \Gamma \subseteq \mathbb{R}^m$, such that $\mathsf{M}_1 \subseteq \mathsf{M}_m$ and $\mathsf{M}_2 \subseteq \mathsf{M}_m$, and no smaller model with integer dimension less than m nests both M_1 and M_2. Beginning from two models M_1 and M_2, there may exist an infinity of models with the same number of parameters which nest M_1 and M_2, and in that sense, the concept of a minimal nesting model is arbitrary. In the theory of reduction, however, M_m occurred *en route* before separating into M_1 and M_2, and M_m is a valid reduction of the DGP when either of M_1 or M_2 is, so in that sense is not arbitrary. Indeed, M_m could be a valid reduction when neither M_1 nor M_2 is valid. The apparently arbitrary nature of M_m arises on going from simple to general, confirming that it is a poor modelling strategy.

A number of propositions about encompassing can now be established. First, we examine whether encompassing implements the notion of a progressive research strategy: a model-building strategy in which knowledge is gradually accumulated as codified, reproducible information about the world. To achieve that objective, encompassing must have three properties which seem natural requirements in any science, namely that it is reflexive, anti-symmetric, and transitive, and hence defines a partial ordering across models:

(a) Reflexivity: $\mathsf{M}_1 \mathcal{E} \mathsf{M}_1$. This requirement is automatically satisfied by definition 1.
(b) Anti-symmetry: if $\mathsf{M}_1 \mathcal{E} \mathsf{M}_2$ and $\mathsf{M}_2 \mathcal{E} \mathsf{M}_1$, then $\mathsf{M}_1 \approx \mathsf{M}_2$. Definition 1 also satisfies this property, as shown by theorem 1 above.
(c) Transitivity: if $\mathsf{M}_1 \mathcal{E} \mathsf{M}_2$ and $\mathsf{M}_2 \mathcal{E} \mathsf{M}_3$, then $\mathsf{M}_1 \mathcal{E} \mathsf{M}_3$. Definition 1 does not necessarily satisfy this requirement, as shown below, but a modification of encompassing will.

Let the parameters of M_3 be $\boldsymbol{\rho}$, then the first two conditions in (c) entail that $\boldsymbol{\delta}(\boldsymbol{\theta}) = \boldsymbol{\phi}_{21}(\boldsymbol{\alpha}(\boldsymbol{\theta}))$ and $\boldsymbol{\rho}(\boldsymbol{\theta}) = \boldsymbol{\phi}_{32}(\boldsymbol{\delta}(\boldsymbol{\theta}))$ so that:

$$\boldsymbol{\rho}(\boldsymbol{\theta}) = \boldsymbol{\phi}_{32}\left[\boldsymbol{\phi}_{21}(\boldsymbol{\alpha}(\boldsymbol{\theta}))\right], \tag{14.13}$$

which is insufficient to prove that $\boldsymbol{\rho}(\boldsymbol{\theta}) = \boldsymbol{\phi}_{31}(\boldsymbol{\alpha}(\boldsymbol{\theta}))$. Rather, (14.13) is a condition of 'intermediary' transitivity, whereby, using M_2 as a vehicle, M_1 can account for the results of M_3 even though it cannot do so directly. A transitive variant of encompassing is developed in section 14.6 below.

The absence of transitivity is related to the earlier corroboration paradox: both arise in going from the simple to the general. Consider a sequence where M_3 is built first, and M_2 can explain its results, so $\mathsf{M}_2 \mathcal{E} \mathsf{M}_3$; when we find $\mathsf{M}_1 \mathcal{E} \mathsf{M}_2$, this need not entail that $\mathsf{M}_1 \mathcal{E} \mathsf{M}_3$. Information is dropped by moving from M_3 to M_2 to M_1, unless all the information in the union of M_2 and M_3 is retained. The reason that successive corroboration can imply refutation is the failure to retain all of the information that accrues: an item of information arrives and the model is successfully tested against it, which expands the information set. Testing against the second item alone may also indicate successful corroboration, but what should have occurred at that stage is a test of the model against the expanded information set incorporating both previous items of information. A failure to do so allows non-rejection in the earlier paradox, whereas testing against the original information plus the second item of information would show rejection.

Similarly, the fact that M_2 can explain M_3, and M_1 can explain M_2 does not entail that M_1 can explain the union of M_2 and M_3, because information in M_3 was dropped when moving to M_2 alone. The issue is not merely a theoretical possibility but has occurred empirically. Davidson *et al.* (1978) tested their model for a unit elasticity of consumption with respect to income in an equation without liquid assets, and accepted that restriction; later, they tested the restricted model for the significance of the level of liquid assets and accepted its absence; but Hendry and von Ungern-Sternberg (1981) found a significant role for the level of liquid assets when the unit income elasticity was not imposed.

Encompassing also throws light on the problem of model comparison. In particular, simplification should stop at the point that further simplification induces an invalid reduction. Thus, the model at the last valid reduction should be able to account for all results prior to the reduction, since no information has been lost. Hence, the point at which we can no longer encompass is the point at which reduction is no longer valid, so that non-encompassing defines the limit to model reduction. Moreover, we need not consider non-nested hypotheses tests separately since they are indirectly nested tests. The theory of reduction treats all models as special cases of the DGP irrespective of whether or not they are mutually non-nested. In fact, encompassing provides a test generating equation which is the mirror image in testing theory of the EGE in estimation, namely a formula for generating an infinity of possible tests for the same hypotheses, with power against different alternatives and perhaps no power in certain states of the world: see Mizon and Richard (1986). Finally, encompassing supports inference in mis-specified models. Nothing said above about comparing M_1 and M_2 required that either of them was correct, and providing one of them is congruent, we should be able to make useful statements about them, including using the models to mutually reject each other. Given that no empirical models are 'true', it is important to have a set of tools that do not depend on the truth of at least one of the underlying models.

To build congruent models, we need criteria which detect inappropriate modelling decisions. Encompassing helps here because the other models against which we test our own model are built by researchers with different world views, who likewise are trying to build the best models they can. Thus, when we have exhausted the direct data evidence by a general-to-specific search procedure, it is a stringent check on a model, to test against outside models, which involve variables not included in our own research: encompassing provides fresh evidence for evaluating models. Prior to continuing with the formal analysis, we digress to discuss the levels at which an encompassing relation could be developed.

14.5 Levels of analysis

Encompassing can be conducted at three different levels of analysis: specification, mis-specification, and selection.

14.5.1 Specification encompassing

This concerns the question of whether M_1 can correctly predict the parameters of another model M_2. For example, assume that the second model relates consumption to income, whereas M_1 regresses consumption on lagged wealth. Given M_1's results, we can derive a prediction for the relation of consumption to income. This is an attempt to encompass the specification adopted. The analysis of $\boldsymbol{\delta} - \boldsymbol{\delta}_\alpha$ above concerns specification encompassing.

14.5.2 Mis-specification encompassing

As an example at this level, the proprietor of M_1 might also notice that the relationship between income and wealth is not constant over the sample. If M_1 is constant over the sample, then it is impossible for M_2 also to be constant over the sample when M_1 is the DGP. Therefore, M_1 must predict such a mis-specification in M_2, namely that M_2 should suffer predictive failure at any point where the relation between income and wealth alters. A second example is predicting residual autocorrelation in other models: if a variable in M_1 depends on an integral of past behaviour, models which do not at least implicitly include that integral cannot avoid residual autocorrelation (see Hendry, 1986a). Researchers might difference the data to remove the integral, which should create a negatively autocorrelated residual. Such mis-specification predictions are testable, and this level of encompassing helps in understanding the Lucas critique, discussed later in the chapter. Referring back, when M_1 is the DGP, $\boldsymbol{\theta} = \boldsymbol{t}_\lambda^{-1}(\boldsymbol{\alpha} : \mathbf{0})$ and so $\boldsymbol{t}_\mu(\boldsymbol{\theta}) = \boldsymbol{t}_\mu(\boldsymbol{t}_\lambda^{-1}(\boldsymbol{\alpha} : \mathbf{0})) = (\boldsymbol{\delta} : \boldsymbol{\mu}_2)$ hence M_1 should also be able to predict the value of $\boldsymbol{\mu}_2$ from $\boldsymbol{\alpha}$ and thereby reveal flaws in M_2.

14.5.3 Selection encompassing

This level has yet to be formalized. If M_1 is the correct model, can it explain why other researchers picked different models and what led them to choose the wrong model? Model choices are partly due to methodological assumptions which bias selection against models of certain forms. For example, DHSY argued that UK consumption functions in the 1970s suffered predictive failure partly because investigators believed it was incorrect to fit general models (due to problems labelled data mining, collinearity, etc.), thereby excluding the model class needed to explain that data.

These three levels can be undertaken for each of the following distinct data partitions:

(i) *Historical encompassing*: $\mathsf{D}_\mathsf{X}(\boldsymbol{x}_t|\boldsymbol{X}_{t-1}^1, \cdot)$. Here, one model tries to explain the past values of parameters in alternative models, given that lagged information is legitimate. To date, this has been the main area of interest.

(ii) *Contemporaneous encompassing*: $\mathsf{D}_\mathsf{X}(\boldsymbol{y}_t|\boldsymbol{z}_t, \boldsymbol{X}_{t-1}^1, \cdot)$. This extends (i), taking account of the, perhaps conflicting, exogeneity classifications in alternative models. Exogeneity encompassing is difficult, because it is hard to maintain identification. If M_1 tries to explain the results obtained by another model which conditions on a data-set $\boldsymbol{Z}$ while itself conditioning on a set $\boldsymbol{W}$, M_1 may need to endogenize both $\boldsymbol{Z}$ and $\boldsymbol{W}$, but to do so might lose identification.

(iii) *Forecast encompassing*: $\mathsf{D}_{\mathsf{X}}(\boldsymbol{X}_T^{t+1}|\boldsymbol{X}_t^1,\cdot)$. In this last case, M_1 tries to explain prediction errors or parameter non-constancy outside sample in alternative models. Forecast encompassing clarifies forecast pooling, whereby a better forecast is sought by using a weighted average of two other forecasts, with weights based on the historical accuracy of each forecast. In an encompassing framework, two models based on common information are both wrong when the weights are not unity and zero, because then the outside sample outcomes cannot be explained by either model alone (see Clements and Hendry, 1995, and Ericsson, 1992b).

14.6 Parsimonious encompassing

When M_1 is nested in M_2, then M_2 must encompass M_1: $\mathsf{M}_1 \subseteq \mathsf{M}_2$ implies $\mathsf{M}_2\mathcal{E}\mathsf{M}_1$. A general model must encompass a special case thereof: indeed, mis-specification analysis could not work without this result. Thus, encompassing apparently could always be achieved by building a large nesting model. To counter this difficulty, we define parsimonious encompassing (denoted $\mathcal{E}_p$):

DEFINITION 2. M_1 *parsimoniously encompasses* M_2, *written as* $\mathsf{M}_1\mathcal{E}_p\mathsf{M}_2$, *if* $\mathsf{M}_1 \subseteq \mathsf{M}_2$ *and* $\mathsf{M}_1\mathcal{E}\mathsf{M}_2$.

Parsimonious encompassing requires a small model to explain the results of a larger model within which it is nested, whereas encompassing allows the possibility of a larger model explaining the results of a smaller model. In fact, $\mathcal{E}_p$ is a natural consequence of the theory of reduction: having reduced a model to the smallest representation that is not an invalid reduction, the final model must still explain the initial one and therefore should parsimoniously encompass it. The initial model nests the final one and by construction encompasses it.

Once parsimonious encompassing has been introduced, a number of advantages become apparent. First, statistical-theory derivations are often simpler when M_1 is nested in M_2. Even if M_1 and M_2 are non-nested, there is a minimal nesting model M_m within which M_1 and M_2 are nested at an earlier stage of reduction. Secondly, parsimonious encompassing is related to the original concept of encompassing via a refinement of the notion of the M_m. Since M_m cannot contain any information additional to that in M_1 and M_2 if it is to be minimal, we have:

$$\mathsf{M}_m = \mathsf{M}_1 \cup \mathsf{M}_2^{\perp}$$

where $\mathsf{M}_2^{\perp}$ denotes the model which represents all aspects of M_2 that do not overlap with M_1. Then we have the following theorem:

THEOREM 2. *When* $\mathsf{M}_1 \subseteq \mathsf{M}_m$ *and* $\mathsf{M}_1\mathcal{E}_p\,\mathsf{M}_m$ *then* $\mathsf{M}_1 \approx \mathsf{M}_m$.

Since $\mathsf{M}_1 \subseteq \mathsf{M}_m$ implies that $\mathsf{M}_m\mathcal{E}\mathsf{M}_1$, and by definition 2, $\mathsf{M}_1\mathcal{E}_p\mathsf{M}_m$ implies $\mathsf{M}_1\mathcal{E}\mathsf{M}_m$, then by theorem 1, M_1 and M_2 are equivalent. Thus we can establish the theorem:

THEOREM 3. *If* $\mathsf{M}_1 \subseteq \mathsf{M}_m$ *and* $\mathsf{M}_2 \subseteq \mathsf{M}_m$, *then* $\mathsf{M}_1\mathcal{E}\,\mathsf{M}_2$ *if and only if* $\mathsf{M}_1\mathcal{E}_p\,\mathsf{M}_m$.

From theorem 2 when $\mathsf{M}_1 \subseteq \mathsf{M}_m$, if $\mathsf{M}_1\mathcal{E}_p\mathsf{M}_m$, then $\mathsf{M}_m \approx \mathsf{M}_1$; and as $\mathsf{M}_2 \subseteq \mathsf{M}_m \approx \mathsf{M}_1$, then $\mathsf{M}_1\mathcal{E}\mathsf{M}_2$. Conversely, if $\mathsf{M}_1\mathcal{E}_p^c\mathsf{M}_m$ when $\mathsf{M}_1 \subseteq \mathsf{M}_m = \mathsf{M}_1 \cup \mathsf{M}_2^{\perp}$, since $\mathsf{M}_1\mathcal{E}\mathsf{M}_1$, then M_2 must contain additional information to that in M_1, and hence $\mathsf{M}_1\mathcal{E}^c\,\mathsf{M}_2$. Intuitively, if M_m is a valid reduction of the DGP and M_1 parsimoniously encompasses M_m, then M_1 is a valid reduction of the DGP and therefore it is still equivalent to the DGP. If so, M_1 can explain M_2 even if M_2 is a different model.

The minimal nesting model M_m is needed for proving the 'only if' part; for the 'if' part, when $\mathsf{M}_1\mathcal{E}_p\mathsf{M}_4$ (say), then $\mathsf{M}_2 \subseteq \mathsf{M}_4$ entails $\mathsf{M}_1\mathcal{E}\mathsf{M}_2$. The theorem is proved in a Bayesian framework by Florens *et al.* (1994).

The primary reason for introducing parsimonious encompassing is that $\mathcal{E}_p$ is transitive, so no information is lost in model comparisons. If $\mathsf{M}_1\mathcal{E}_p\mathsf{M}_m$ and $\mathsf{M}_m\mathcal{E}_p\mathsf{M}_g$, then $\mathsf{M}_1\mathcal{E}_p\mathsf{M}_g$: a valid reduction of a valid reduction remains a valid reduction. Thus, parsimonious encompassing is transitive in an almost trivial, but nevertheless important, sense. When parsimonious encompassing is part of a reduction sequence, later models explain the same by fewer parameters; when the initial information set is enlarged to M_g within which M_m is nested, and parsimonious encompassing still results, acceptable models explain more data information. Either way, we have the basis for a progressive research strategy.

14.7 A simple example

The following example from Hendry and Richard (1989), noted in Chapter 9, captures many features of encompassing theory. Consider the DGP:

$$\mathsf{M}_0\colon\ y_t \sim \mathsf{IN}\left[\gamma, \omega^2\right] \quad \text{where } \gamma \in \mathbb{R} \text{ and } \omega^2 \in \mathbb{R}_+ \tag{14.14}$$

which is claimed to be represented by each of the two rival models:

$$\mathsf{M}_1\colon\ y_t \sim \mathsf{IN}\left[\mu, 1\right] \quad \text{such that } \mathsf{E}\left[y_t\right] = \mu \in \mathbb{R}; \tag{14.15}$$

$$\mathsf{M}_2\colon\ y_t \sim \mathsf{IN}\left[0, \sigma^2\right] \quad \text{meaning that } \mathsf{E}\left[y_t^2\right] = \sigma^2 \in \mathbb{R}_+. \tag{14.16}$$

Providing that $\mu \neq 0$ and $\sigma^2 \neq 1$, M_1 and M_2 are ostensibly non-nested, but are both nested within M_0. Under M_0, $\mu = \gamma$ and $\sigma^2 = \omega^2 + \gamma^2$, so relative to M_0, testable restrictions on the nested models are $\omega^2 = 1$ on M_1 and $\gamma = 0$ on M_2. Further, taking the two models in turn as the DGP entails for $\boldsymbol{\theta} = (\gamma : \omega^2)'$ that:

$$\text{on } \mathsf{M}_1\colon\ \sigma_\mu^2 = \phi_{21}\left\{\mu\left(\boldsymbol{\theta}\right)\right\} = 1 + \mu^2;$$

and:

$$\text{on } \mathsf{M}_2\colon\ \mu_{\sigma^2} = \phi_{12}\left\{\sigma^2\left(\boldsymbol{\theta}\right)\right\} = 0.$$

We now obtain the various statistics of all three models and derive their distributions for a sample $(y_1 \ldots y_T)$ from (14.14). The estimators are denoted by $\hat{\alpha}$, $\tilde{\alpha}$, and $\bar{\alpha}$ for any parameter α under M_1, M_2 and M_0 respectively:

$$\hat{\mu} = T^{-1}\sum_{t=1}^{T} y_t \sim \mathsf{N}\left[\mu, T^{-1}\right] \text{ on } \mathsf{M}_1; \tag{14.17}$$

$$\tilde{\sigma}^2 = T^{-1}\sum_{t=1}^{T} y_t^2 \sim \sigma^2 T^{-1}\chi^2(T) \text{ on } \mathsf{M}_2. \tag{14.18}$$

Finally, treating the DGP as the nesting model M_m:[1]

$$\bar{\gamma} = T^{-1}\sum_{t=1}^{T} y_t \sim \mathsf{N}\left[\mu, T^{-1}\omega^2\right] \text{ on } \mathsf{M}_m \tag{14.19}$$

and:

$$\bar{\omega}^2 = T^{-1}\sum_{t=1}^{T}(y_t - \bar{\gamma})^2 = T^{-1}\sum_{t=1}^{T} y_t^2 - \bar{\gamma}^2 \sim T^{-1}\omega^2\chi^2(T-1) \text{ on } \mathsf{M}_m. \tag{14.20}$$

14.7.1 Can $\mathsf{M}_1\mathcal{E}\mathsf{M}_2$?

Suppose we believed M_1, then we would anticipate:

$$\mathsf{E}_1\left[\tilde{\sigma}^2\right] = \mathsf{E}_1\left[y_t^2\right] = 1 + \mu^2, \tag{14.21}$$

where $\mathsf{E}_1[\cdot]$ denotes an expectation calculated assuming M_1 is the DGP. From (14.18) and (14.21), the sample encompassing difference is:

$$\tilde{\psi}_{\sigma^2} = \tilde{\sigma}^2 - \left(1 + \hat{\mu}^2\right) = \bar{\omega}^2 - 1. \tag{14.22}$$

There are two ways of testing whether or not M_1 can explain the results of M_2. One is directly to test M_1 against M_2 using M_2's calculation of the variance minus unity plus the mean squared under M_1. Alternatively, test whether $\bar{\omega}^2$ is unity in the nesting model. Here, whether we test M_1 against the general model or the rival model, we obtain the same numerical results, consistent with the claim that $\mathsf{M}_1\mathcal{E}\mathsf{M}_2$ if and only if $\mathsf{M}_1\mathcal{E}_p\mathsf{M}_m$. When M_1 tries to explain the general model, it must predict that:

$$\mathsf{E}_1\left[\bar{\gamma}\right] = \mu \text{ and } \mathsf{E}_1\left[\bar{\omega}^2\right] = 1. \tag{14.23}$$

The corresponding population and sample encompassing differences for $\mathsf{M}_1\mathcal{E}_p\mathsf{M}_m$ are:

$$\psi_\gamma = \gamma - \mu \equiv 0 \text{ with } \hat{\psi}_\gamma = \bar{\gamma} - \hat{\mu} \equiv 0 \tag{14.24}$$

(which holds irrespective of the validity of M_1) and:

$$\psi_{\omega^2} = \omega^2 - 1 \text{ with } \hat{\psi}_{\omega^2} = \bar{\omega}^2 - 1. \tag{14.25}$$

[1] While $\bar{\omega}^2$ is a biased estimator of ω^2, the algebra is simpler if T^{-1} is the divisor rather than $(T-1)^{-1}$.

In this example, therefore, $\mathsf{M}_1\mathcal{E}\mathsf{M}_2$ if and only if $\omega^2 = 1$, and hence if and only if $\mathsf{M}_1\mathcal{E}_p\mathsf{M}_m$. Let H_0 denote $\mathsf{M}_1\mathcal{E}\mathsf{M}_2$. A test of H_0 can be based on (14.25), and although the models are non-nested, the test statistic is a conventional χ^2, equivalent to a nested test since:

$$\bar{\omega}^2 \underset{\mathsf{H}_0}{\widetilde{\ }} T^{-1}\chi^2(T-1). \tag{14.26}$$

This distribution follows from (14.20) when $\omega^2 = 1$.

14.7.2 Can $\mathsf{M}_2\mathcal{E}\mathsf{M}_1$?

Suppose now that we believed M_2. We would expect that:

$$\mathsf{E}_2[\hat{\mu}] = \mathsf{E}_2[\bar{\gamma}] = 0 \tag{14.27}$$

and so would expect the sample mean to be close to zero irrespective of seeking to encompass M_1 or M_m. At first sight, it looks as though there is another hypothesis we could test, namely whether:

$$\mathsf{E}_2\left[\bar{\omega}^2\right] = \sigma^2. \tag{14.28}$$

However, from (14.20), the sample encompassing difference against M_m is:

$$\hat{\psi}_{\omega^2} = \bar{\omega}^2 - \hat{\sigma}^2 = -\bar{\gamma}^2 \tag{14.29}$$

and so is equivalent to testing whether $\mu = 0$. As before, $\mathsf{M}_2\mathcal{E}\mathsf{M}_1$ if and only if $\mathsf{M}_2\mathcal{E}_p\mathsf{M}_m$ since both correspond to $\mu = 0$. Again, the test is a conventional one, namely a t-test for the mean being zero. Let H_1 denote $\mathsf{M}_2\mathcal{E}\mathsf{M}_1$, then under H_1:

$$\hat{\mu} \sim \mathsf{N}\left[0, \sigma^2 T^{-1}\right] \text{ and so } \frac{\sqrt{T}(\hat{\mu}-0)}{\hat{\sigma}} \underset{\mathsf{H}_1}{\widetilde{\ }} \mathsf{t}(T-1). \tag{14.30}$$

Hence, the fact that the two models are ostensibly non-nested does not affect the tests being conventional t or χ^2 statistics.

14.8 Nesting and encompassing

When conditional models are to be compared, a completing model is needed to link their unmodelled variables. Two reductions have been involved: the conditioning on the joint set of 'exogenous' variables; and the marginalizations of each model with respect to the variables retained by their rival. The completing model implicitly recovers the joint density of all the variables. Comparisons between the models are possible only if they lie in a common probability space: otherwise, both of them could represent valid, if perhaps incomplete, claims. For example, when y_t, $\boldsymbol{x}_t$, and $\boldsymbol{z}_t$ are jointly normally distributed, then:

$$\mathsf{E}[y_t \mid \boldsymbol{x}_t] = \boldsymbol{x}_t'\boldsymbol{\beta} \text{ and } \mathsf{E}[y_t \mid \boldsymbol{z}_t] = \boldsymbol{z}_t'\boldsymbol{\gamma}, \tag{14.31}$$

so that both M_1 and M_2 correctly characterize these conditional expectations, providing their parameters of interest are deemed to be $\boldsymbol{\beta}$ and $\boldsymbol{\gamma}$ respectively. However, at least one must be incomplete, and hence an invalid reduction, in that information has been lost relative to the joint distribution.

In the theory of reduction, and the associated theory of congruence, asserting that M_1 is a congruent model entails that adding $\boldsymbol{z}_t$ to M_1 should contribute negligibly to the explanation of y_t. The implicit nesting model for the joint normal distribution is:

$$\mathsf{M}_m\colon y_t = \boldsymbol{x}_t'\boldsymbol{b} + \boldsymbol{z}_t'\boldsymbol{c} + \epsilon_t \text{ where } \epsilon_t \sim \mathsf{IN}\left[0,\omega^2\right] \tag{14.32}$$

so that $\boldsymbol{b} = \mathbf{0}$ delivers M_2 and $\boldsymbol{c} = \mathbf{0}$ yields M_1, when we assume no common variables for algebraic convenience. M_m provides a common probability space for comparing M_1 and M_2.

To relate the unmodelled variables in the rival claims in (14.31), we use a completing model M_c, the specification of which can affect the robustness of encompassing tests in conditional models (see §14.10). Such an outcome seems inevitable, and places the analysis within the theory of reduction, despite the initial formulation involving ostensibly non-nested models. For example, to conduct a Monte Carlo study of non-nested hypothesis tests involves implicitly creating a nesting model, which corresponds to augmenting M_1 and M_2 by the completing model M_c relating $\boldsymbol{x}_t$ to $\boldsymbol{z}_t$, such that the two models are reductions of the joint density.

As discussed in Chapter 2, there are other characterizations of nesting than that the parameter space of the nested model is a subset of that of the nesting model (see, e.g., Pesaran, 1987 and Gourieroux and Monfort, 1991). Nesting must be decided at the level of the joint density, and was defined to ensure a close relationship with encompassing. The following analysis is based on Gourieroux and Monfort (1992), Govaerts *et al.* (1993) and Mizon (1993a).

Consider a claimed conditional linear single-equation model of the form:

$$y_t = \delta_1 z_{1t} + \delta_2 z_{2t} + e_t. \tag{14.33}$$

The model in (14.33) is to be interpreted as $\mathsf{E}\left[y_t|z_{1t}, z_{2t}\right] = \delta_1 z_{1t} + \delta_2 z_{2t}$. A second investigator postulates the conditional equation:

$$y_t = \kappa_1 z_{1t} + \zeta_t. \tag{14.34}$$

Again, the equation has the interpretation that $\mathsf{E}\left[y_t|z_{1t}, z_{2t}\right] = \kappa_1 z_{1t}$. In both cases, the parameter spaces are unrestricted, so $\boldsymbol{\delta} \in \mathbb{R}^2$ and $\kappa_1 \in \mathbb{R}$, and hence the second parameter space is a subset of the first. At first sight, the equation in (14.34) appears to be a special case of the equation in (14.33), obtained by restricting δ_2 to zero, and as such should be nested in (14.33). However, the first investigator (falsely) believes that z_{1t} is orthogonal to z_{2t}, both in the sense that they are uncorrelated on average, and that the sample values satisfy $\boldsymbol{z}_1'\boldsymbol{z}_2 = 0$. Consequently, an encompassing 'test' of the hypothesis that (14.33) encompasses (14.34) could check whether $\delta_1 = \kappa_1$. When in fact $\boldsymbol{z}_1'\boldsymbol{z}_2 \neq 0$, such a test will reject, seeming to imply that nesting is insufficient to ensure encompassing.

The paradox arises because the nesting relation is unaltered by the auxiliary claim that the variables are orthogonal, whereas encompassing is affected. In the terminology of Govaerts *et al.* (1993), part of the completing model in (14.33) is invalid (namely $z_1'z_2 = 0$), and such a mis-specification leads to a non-robust and inconsistent encompassing test, although completing models exist which ensure consistent tests: see §14.10.

Reconsider the analysis from the perspective of the joint density:

$$\mathsf{D}_{\mathsf{y,z}}\left(y_t, z_t \mid \boldsymbol{\theta}\right) = \mathsf{D}_{\mathsf{y|z}}\left(y_t \mid z_t, \boldsymbol{\theta}_1\right) \mathsf{D}_{\mathsf{z}_1|\mathsf{z}_2}\left(z_{1t} \mid z_{2t}, \boldsymbol{\mu}_1\right) \mathsf{D}_{\mathsf{z}_2}\left(z_{2t} \mid \boldsymbol{\mu}_2\right) \tag{14.35}$$

where $\boldsymbol{\theta} \in \Theta$ and $(\boldsymbol{\theta}_1, \boldsymbol{\mu}_1, \boldsymbol{\mu}_2) = \boldsymbol{f}(\boldsymbol{\theta})$. The equation in (14.33) enforces the reduction:

$$\mathsf{D}_{\mathsf{z}_1|\mathsf{z}_2}\left(z_{1t} \mid z_{2t}, \boldsymbol{\mu}_1\right) = \mathsf{D}_{\mathsf{z}_1}\left(z_{1t} \mid \boldsymbol{\mu}_1\right), \tag{14.36}$$

leading to the (invalid) factorization of $\mathsf{D}_{\mathsf{y,z}}\left(y_t, z_t|\boldsymbol{\theta}\right)$ as:

$$\mathsf{D}_{\mathsf{y}|\mathsf{z}_1,\mathsf{z}_2}\left(y_t \mid z_{1t}, z_{2t}, \boldsymbol{\theta}_1\right) \mathsf{D}_{\mathsf{z}_1}\left(z_{1t} \mid \boldsymbol{\mu}_1\right) \mathsf{D}_{\mathsf{z}_2}\left(z_{2t} \mid \boldsymbol{\mu}_2\right). \tag{14.37}$$

The model in (14.34), however, is obtained by the alternative reduction that the entire analysis is marginalized with respect to z_2:

$$\mathsf{D}_{\mathsf{y|z}}\left(y_t \mid z_t, \boldsymbol{\theta}_1\right) = \mathsf{D}_{\mathsf{y}|\mathsf{z}_1}\left(y_t \mid z_{1t}, \boldsymbol{\tau}_1\right) \tag{14.38}$$

leading to the factorization of $\mathsf{D}_{\mathsf{y,z}}(y_t, z_t|\boldsymbol{\theta})$ as:

$$\mathsf{D}_{\mathsf{z}_2|\mathsf{y},\mathsf{z}_1}\left(z_{2t} \mid y_t, z_{1t}, \boldsymbol{\tau}_2\right) \mathsf{D}_{\mathsf{y}|\mathsf{z}_1}\left(y_t \mid z_{1t}, \boldsymbol{\tau}_1\right) \mathsf{D}_{\mathsf{z}_1}\left(z_{1t} \mid \boldsymbol{\mu}_1\right). \tag{14.39}$$

The models in (14.37) and (14.39) are no longer nested, and only the latter is a complete representation.

Such paradoxes cannot arise when analyses commence with the joint density, and check encompassing by testing parsimonious encompassing of the initial general model by later reductions. Section 14.10 shows that the choice of completing model is irrelevant to parsimonious encompassing tests. Here (14.37) would be rejected against (14.35) when the orthogonality of z_{1t} to z_{2t} was invalid. Conversely, when (14.37) is accepted, there exists a valid test for eliminating z_{2t} from the conditional model.

14.9 Encompassing in linear regression

Linear regression has been the main arena for the application of encompassing tests, so we consider this case in some detail. Section 14.3 provided an introduction, and section 14.10 generalizes the analysis to models of greater interest in time-series econometrics. Consider the two models:

$$\mathsf{M}_1\colon\ \boldsymbol{y} = \boldsymbol{X\beta} + \boldsymbol{u} \ \text{ where } \ \boldsymbol{u} \sim \mathsf{N}_T\left[\boldsymbol{0}, \sigma^2\boldsymbol{I}\right] \tag{14.40}$$

with the $(k+1) \times 1$ parameter vector $\boldsymbol{\alpha} = (\boldsymbol{\beta}, \sigma^2)$; and:

$$\mathsf{M}_2\colon\ \boldsymbol{y} = \boldsymbol{Z\gamma} + \boldsymbol{v} \ \text{ where } \ \boldsymbol{v} \sim \mathsf{N}_T\left[\boldsymbol{0}, \tau^2\boldsymbol{I}\right] \tag{14.41}$$

with the $(n+1) \times 1$ parameter vector $\boldsymbol{\delta} = (\boldsymbol{\gamma}, \tau^2)$. When the regressor sets $\boldsymbol{x}_t$ and $\boldsymbol{z}_t$ contain some distinct variables, and hence neither is a linear transform of a subset of the other, these models are non-nested. Think of the first model as a Keynesian hypothesis and the second one as a monetarist hypothesis, say.

Chapter 13 discussed tests for the validity of reductions; here, we focus on the logic of testing encompassing. First, consider the relationship between $\boldsymbol{x}_t$ and $\boldsymbol{z}_t$ in terms of the completing model M_c which introduces an auxiliary equation system linking $\boldsymbol{x}_t$ and $\boldsymbol{z}_t$ with the form:

$$\mathsf{M}_c\colon \boldsymbol{x}_t = \boldsymbol{\Pi} \boldsymbol{z}_t + \boldsymbol{w}_t \text{ where } \boldsymbol{w}_t \sim \mathsf{IN}_k\left[\mathbf{0}, \boldsymbol{\Omega}\right]. \tag{14.42}$$

Although (14.42) is written as a model with parameters $(\boldsymbol{\Pi}, \boldsymbol{\Omega})$, a projection of $\boldsymbol{X}'$ on $\boldsymbol{Z}'$ would suffice for the statistical analysis, namely $\boldsymbol{X}' = \boldsymbol{P}\boldsymbol{Z}' + \boldsymbol{W}'$ where $\boldsymbol{Z}'\boldsymbol{W} = \mathbf{0}$ using:

$$\boldsymbol{P} = \boldsymbol{X}'\boldsymbol{Z}\left(\boldsymbol{Z}'\boldsymbol{Z}\right)^{-1} \text{ and } \boldsymbol{W} = \boldsymbol{Q}_Z \boldsymbol{X}, \tag{14.43}$$

with $\boldsymbol{Q}_Z = (\boldsymbol{I}_T - \boldsymbol{Z}(\boldsymbol{Z}'\boldsymbol{Z})^{-1}\boldsymbol{Z}')$. To obtain parametric results of interest, we assume (14.42) holds. For investigating $\mathsf{M}_2 \mathcal{E} \mathsf{M}_1$, equations (14.42) and (14.43) must be formulated in the opposite direction (projecting $\boldsymbol{Z}$ on $\boldsymbol{X}$).

By substituting (14.42) into M_1, an investigator who believed that M_1 and M_c were both correct would derive the predicted form of M_2 as:

$$\boldsymbol{y} = \boldsymbol{Z}\boldsymbol{\Pi}'\boldsymbol{\beta} + \boldsymbol{u} + \boldsymbol{W}\boldsymbol{\beta} = \boldsymbol{Z}\boldsymbol{\gamma}_\alpha + \boldsymbol{v} \text{ where } \boldsymbol{\gamma}_\alpha = \boldsymbol{\Pi}'\boldsymbol{\beta}, \tag{14.44}$$

so that from $\mathsf{M}_1 + \mathsf{M}_c$, $\boldsymbol{\gamma}_\alpha = \boldsymbol{\phi}_{21}(\boldsymbol{\alpha}^*)$ where $\boldsymbol{\alpha}^* = (\boldsymbol{\alpha}, \boldsymbol{\Pi}, \boldsymbol{\Omega})$. Equation (14.44) could be denoted M_2^* as it is the linear regression equation relating $\boldsymbol{y}$ to $\boldsymbol{Z}$ which is anticipated under M_1. Comparison of (14.44) with (14.41) reveals that M_1 also predicts:

$$\boldsymbol{v} = \boldsymbol{u} + \boldsymbol{W}\boldsymbol{\beta} \text{ and hence that } \tau_\alpha^2 = \sigma^2 + \boldsymbol{\beta}'\boldsymbol{\Omega}\boldsymbol{\beta}, \tag{14.45}$$

using $\mathsf{E}[\boldsymbol{w}_t u_t] = \mathbf{0}$ from (14.40) and (14.42). There are direct and indirect ways of estimating both $\boldsymbol{\gamma}$ and τ^2. The former can be obtained by regressing $\boldsymbol{y}$ on $\boldsymbol{Z}$ (yielding $\boldsymbol{\gamma}$); or by regressing $\boldsymbol{y}$ on $\boldsymbol{X}$ and $\boldsymbol{X}$ on $\boldsymbol{Z}$ (yielding $\boldsymbol{\gamma}_\alpha$). When M_1 is a valid reduction, the two procedures should give the same answer, because (14.44) is what the direct method is estimating.

Under H_0: $\mathsf{M}_1 \mathcal{E} \mathsf{M}_2$, then $\boldsymbol{\gamma}_\alpha = \boldsymbol{\Pi}'\boldsymbol{\beta}$ so that

$$\boldsymbol{\psi}_\gamma = \boldsymbol{\gamma} - \boldsymbol{\gamma}_\alpha = \boldsymbol{\gamma} - \boldsymbol{\Pi}'\boldsymbol{\beta};$$

also, $\tau_\alpha^2 = \sigma^2 + \boldsymbol{\beta}'\boldsymbol{\Omega}\boldsymbol{\beta}$ so that:

$$\psi_{\tau^2} = \tau^2 - \tau_\alpha^2 = \tau^2 - \sigma^2 - \boldsymbol{\beta}'\boldsymbol{\Omega}\boldsymbol{\beta}.$$

A Wald encompassing test (WET) of H_0 based on $\boldsymbol{\psi}_\gamma$ is due to Mizon and Richard (1986), and a test based on ψ_{τ^2} is related to a Cox (1961) test for non-nested hypotheses. The former is obtained below. The latter delineates a class of one-degree-of-freedom tests which check whether the variance of M_1 can encompass the variance of M_2 (also see Cox, 1962, Pesaran, 1974, and Davidson and MacKinnon, 1981). Since $\boldsymbol{\beta}'\boldsymbol{\Omega}\boldsymbol{\beta}$ is positive semi-definite, σ^2 must be smaller than τ^2 if τ^2 is to equal τ_α^2. Thus, a model must variance dominate its rival as a necessary condition for encompassing, providing a variance ranking across models: if M_1 is to encompass M_2, it must begin by fitting at least as well as M_2.

The methodological implications of the preceding analysis are interesting. The strategy of selecting the best-fitting model is not generally a good one: the fact that a model fits best does not mean that it can forecast well or that its parameters are interpretable or invariant and so on. Encompassing reveals what is wrong with choosing a model on fit alone: variance dominance is a necessary but not a sufficient condition for encompassing. Being best fitting does not guarantee that a model will encompass rival evidence. Further, the fact that a model satisfies a variance-encompassing test does not entail parameter encompassing. However, an encompassing model variance dominates its rivals, and hence is the best fitting.

There are other tests for parameter encompassing, including a simplification encompassing test (SET) which tests the hypothesis $\boldsymbol{c} = \boldsymbol{0}$ in (14.32) for testing $\mathsf{M}_1\mathcal{E}_p\mathsf{M}_m$ with respect to $\boldsymbol{\alpha}$; or $\boldsymbol{b} = \boldsymbol{0}$ for testing $\mathsf{M}_2\mathcal{E}_p\mathsf{M}_m$ with respect to $\boldsymbol{\delta}$ (again, see Mizon and Richard, 1986).[2] Alternatively, a Hausman encompassing test (HET: see Hausman, 1978) can be used for the hypothesis $\boldsymbol{b} = \boldsymbol{\beta}$, which also tests $\mathsf{M}_1\mathcal{E}_p\mathsf{M}_m$; or $\boldsymbol{c} = \boldsymbol{\gamma}$ for $\mathsf{M}_2\mathcal{E}_p\mathsf{M}_m$. Care is required with HETs in this framework, since $\boldsymbol{X}$ can be made orthogonal to $\boldsymbol{Z}$ in the design of M_1, so that $\boldsymbol{b}$ could equal $\boldsymbol{\beta}$, yet $\boldsymbol{c}$ still be highly significant.

In fact, the SET and the WET are functions of the F-test in the linear regression framework. On M_2, $\boldsymbol{\gamma}$ is estimated by OLS as:

$$\widehat{\boldsymbol{\gamma}} = \left(\boldsymbol{Z}'\boldsymbol{Z}\right)^{-1}\boldsymbol{Z}'\boldsymbol{y}. \tag{14.46}$$

To estimate $\boldsymbol{\Pi}$ on M_c, MLS is valid:

$$\widehat{\boldsymbol{\Pi}}' = \left(\boldsymbol{Z}'\boldsymbol{Z}\right)^{-1}\boldsymbol{Z}'\boldsymbol{X} \tag{14.47}$$

which equals $\boldsymbol{P}$ above; and finally, $\boldsymbol{\beta}$ can be estimated by OLS on M_1:

$$\widehat{\boldsymbol{\beta}} = \left(\boldsymbol{X}'\boldsymbol{X}\right)^{-1}\boldsymbol{X}'\boldsymbol{y}. \tag{14.48}$$

From (14.47) and (14.48), the estimate of $\boldsymbol{\gamma}_\alpha = \boldsymbol{\Pi}'\boldsymbol{\beta}$ is $\widehat{\boldsymbol{\gamma}}_\alpha = \widehat{\boldsymbol{\Pi}}'\widehat{\boldsymbol{\beta}}$ so:

$$\widehat{\boldsymbol{\gamma}}_\alpha = \left(\boldsymbol{Z}'\boldsymbol{Z}\right)^{-1}\boldsymbol{Z}'\boldsymbol{X}\left(\boldsymbol{X}'\boldsymbol{X}\right)^{-1}\boldsymbol{X}'\boldsymbol{y} = \left(\boldsymbol{Z}'\boldsymbol{Z}\right)^{-1}\boldsymbol{Z}'\left(\boldsymbol{I}_T - \boldsymbol{Q}_X\right)\boldsymbol{y}. \tag{14.49}$$

The sample encompassing difference between (14.46) and (14.49) is $\widehat{\boldsymbol{\psi}}_\gamma = \widehat{\boldsymbol{\gamma}} - \widehat{\boldsymbol{\gamma}}_\alpha$ or:

$$\left(\boldsymbol{Z}'\boldsymbol{Z}\right)^{-1}\boldsymbol{Z}'\boldsymbol{y} - \left(\boldsymbol{Z}'\boldsymbol{Z}\right)^{-1}\boldsymbol{Z}'\left(\boldsymbol{I}_T - \boldsymbol{Q}_X\right)\boldsymbol{y} = \left(\boldsymbol{Z}'\boldsymbol{Z}\right)^{-1}\boldsymbol{Z}'\boldsymbol{Q}_X\boldsymbol{y} = \boldsymbol{A}\widehat{\boldsymbol{u}} \tag{14.50}$$

[2] Smith (1993) considers likelihood-ratio tests.

where $A = (Z'Z)^{-1}Z'$ and $Q_X y = \hat{u}$ is the vector of residuals from regressing y on X. Thus, encompassing tests are also residual diagnostic tests (see Pagan, 1984b): to test whether or not the encompassing difference is significant, take the residuals from M_1 and regress them on Z. Since $Q_X y = Q_X u$, the distribution of the encompassing difference in (14.50) is:

$$\hat{\psi}_\gamma = A Q_X u \underset{\mathsf{H}_0}{\sim} \mathsf{N}_n\left[0, \sigma^2 A Q_X A'\right] = \mathsf{N}_n\left[0, \sigma^2 V\right]. \tag{14.51}$$

The variance matrix in (14.51) is the difference between the variance matrices of the direct and indirect estimators since:

$$\begin{aligned} A Q_X A' &= \sigma^2 (Z'Z)^{-1} Z' \left(I_T - X (X'X)^{-1} X'\right) Z (Z'Z)^{-1} \\ &= \sigma^2 (Z'Z)^{-1} - \sigma^2 \hat{\Pi}' (X'X)^{-1} \hat{\Pi} \\ &= \mathsf{V}[\hat{\gamma}] - \hat{\Pi}'\mathsf{V}\left[\hat{\beta}\right]\hat{\Pi}. \end{aligned} \tag{14.52}$$

Estimating the general model M_m by OLS yields the following estimator for c:

$$\hat{c} = (Z'Q_X Z)^{-1} Z'Q_X y = KA\hat{u}, \tag{14.53}$$

where $K = (Z'Q_X Z)^{-1} Z'Z$ is a fixed non-singular matrix. Therefore, an F-test for $c = 0$ is just K times a Wald test of $\psi_\gamma = 0$: as there is only one hypothesis to be tested, the two tests are linked by a non-singular linear mapping. From (14.51) and (14.52):

$$\eta_1 = \hat{\psi}_\gamma' \mathsf{V}\left[\hat{\psi}_\gamma\right]^{-1} \hat{\psi}_\gamma = \frac{u'Q_X A' (A Q_X A')^{-1} A Q_X u}{\hat{\sigma}^2} \underset{\mathsf{H}_0}{\sim} \chi^2(q) \tag{14.54}$$

where q is the rank of $\mathsf{V}[\cdot]$, so there are q extra variables in M_2 (a generalized inverse is needed if there are variables in common). The statistic in (14.54) can be adjusted for the degrees of freedom to produce the correct size for the test, and turned into an F-test by deriving the independent χ^2 distribution for $\hat{\sigma}^2$:

$$\eta_2 = \frac{\hat{u}'Z (Z'Q_X Z)^{-1} Z'\hat{u}}{q\hat{\sigma}^2} \underset{\mathsf{H}_0}{\sim} F(q, T - k - q), \tag{14.55}$$

when there are k variables in x_t.

Since $\mathsf{M}_1 \mathcal{E} \mathsf{M}_2$ is equivalent to $\mathsf{M}_1 \mathcal{E}_p (\mathsf{M}_1 \cup \mathsf{M}_2^{\perp})$, then it ought to be possible to add any subset of variables from M_1 to M_2 to create another rival model M_2^* (say) and still require M_1 to encompass M_2^*. For example, suppose M_1 is a regression of consumption on income and lagged consumption, and M_2 models consumption by wealth. When $\mathsf{M}_1 \mathcal{E} \mathsf{M}_2$, then $\mathsf{M}_1 \mathcal{E}_p \mathsf{M}_m$ so M_1 should still explain a model of consumption regressed on wealth and lagged consumption. In particular, we must avoid reaching one conclusion if one subset of the variables from M_1 is added to M_2, and a different conclusion for another. Translating that into a testing principle, we require tests of encompassing to be invariant to adding subsets of M_1 to M_2.

There is only one invariant test for linear models, namely the F-test, or simplification encompassing test.[3] That the F-test is invariant for pairs of models follows because it tests M_1 against $\mathsf{M}_1 \cup \mathsf{M}_2^{\perp}$ and is not concerned with the specification of M_2 beyond the fact that it contains $\mathsf{M}_2^{\perp}$. This is not true for tests of variance dominance, or subsets of parameters. Further, the invariance of the F-test in binary comparisons confirms that the encompassing relation $\mathcal{E}$ is not necessarily transitive for triples of models: relative to $\mathsf{M}_2 \cup \mathsf{M}_3^{\perp}$, $\mathsf{M}_1 \mathcal{E} \mathsf{M}_2^{\perp}$ and $\mathsf{M}_2 \mathcal{E} \mathsf{M}_3^{\perp}$ correspond to tests on subsets for which invariance does not hold.

14.10 Encompassing in stationary stochastic processes

We now consider encompassing for the linear equations (14.40) and (14.41) in stationary stochastic processes. Let $\mathsf{D}_{\mathsf{s}}(y_t, \boldsymbol{x}_t, \boldsymbol{z}_t | \boldsymbol{S}_{t-1}, \boldsymbol{\theta})$ denote the sequential joint density of $\boldsymbol{s}_t = (y_t : \boldsymbol{x}_t' : \boldsymbol{z}_t')'$, where $\boldsymbol{x}_t$ and $\boldsymbol{z}_t$ are strongly exogenous for $\boldsymbol{\alpha}$ under M_1, and $\boldsymbol{z}_t$ is strongly exogenous for $\boldsymbol{\delta}$ under M_2. Our treatment draws on Govaerts *et al.* (1993). Factorize $\mathsf{D}_{\mathsf{s}}(y_t, \boldsymbol{x}_t, \boldsymbol{z}_t | \boldsymbol{S}_{t-1}, \boldsymbol{\theta})$ as:

$$\mathsf{D}_{\mathsf{y}|\mathsf{x},\mathsf{z}}\left(y_t \mid \boldsymbol{x}_t, \boldsymbol{z}_t, \boldsymbol{S}_{t-1}, \boldsymbol{\mu}\right) \mathsf{D}_{\mathsf{x}|\mathsf{z}}\left(\boldsymbol{x}_t \mid \boldsymbol{z}_t, \boldsymbol{S}_{t-1}, \boldsymbol{\lambda}\right) \mathsf{D}_{\mathsf{z}}\left(\boldsymbol{z}_t \mid \boldsymbol{S}_{t-1}, \boldsymbol{\kappa}\right). \tag{14.56}$$

Under M_1, the conditional distribution of y_t given $\boldsymbol{x}_t$ and $\boldsymbol{z}_t$ can be marginalized with respect to $\boldsymbol{z}_t$ without loss, so M_1 views (14.56) as:

$$\mathsf{D}_{\mathsf{y}|\mathsf{x},\mathsf{z}}\left(y_t \mid \boldsymbol{x}_t, \boldsymbol{S}_{t-1}, \boldsymbol{\alpha}\right) \mathsf{D}_{\mathsf{x}|\mathsf{z}}\left(\boldsymbol{x}_t \mid \boldsymbol{z}_t, \boldsymbol{S}_{t-1}, \boldsymbol{\lambda}\right) \mathsf{D}_{\mathsf{z}}\left(\boldsymbol{z}_t \mid \boldsymbol{S}_{t-1}, \boldsymbol{\kappa}\right). \tag{14.57}$$

The completing model M_c above corresponds to the density $\mathsf{D}_{\mathsf{x}|\mathsf{z}}(\boldsymbol{x}_t | \boldsymbol{z}_t, \boldsymbol{S}_{t-1}, \boldsymbol{\lambda})$ which arises naturally from a conditional factorization under M_1. The factorization under M_2 follows in a similar way to produce:

$$\mathsf{D}_{\mathsf{y}|\mathsf{x},\mathsf{z}}\left(y_t \mid \boldsymbol{z}_t, \boldsymbol{S}_{t-1}, \boldsymbol{\delta}\right) \mathsf{D}_{\mathsf{z}|\mathsf{x}}\left(\boldsymbol{z}_t \mid \boldsymbol{x}_t, \boldsymbol{S}_{t-1}, \boldsymbol{\rho}\right) \mathsf{D}_{\mathsf{x}}\left(\boldsymbol{x}_t \mid \boldsymbol{S}_{t-1}, \boldsymbol{\varphi}\right).$$

Since the variables are generated by stationary stochastic processes, the population second moments of the strongly-exogenous variables are defined by:

$$\boldsymbol{\Sigma}_{zz} = \mathsf{E}_{\mathsf{DGP}}\left[T^{-1}\boldsymbol{Z}'\boldsymbol{Z}\right] = \operatorname*{plim}_{T\to\infty}\left(T^{-1}\boldsymbol{Z}'\boldsymbol{Z}\right) \tag{14.58}$$

$$\boldsymbol{\Sigma}_{zx} = \mathsf{E}_{\mathsf{DGP}}\left[T^{-1}\boldsymbol{Z}'\boldsymbol{X}\right] = \operatorname*{plim}_{T\to\infty}\left(T^{-1}\boldsymbol{Z}'\boldsymbol{X}\right). \tag{14.59}$$

Therefore, under $\mathsf{M}_1 + \mathsf{M}_c$, $\boldsymbol{\gamma}_\alpha$ is given by:

$$\boldsymbol{\gamma}_\alpha = \boldsymbol{\Sigma}_{zz}^{-1}\boldsymbol{\Sigma}_{zx}\boldsymbol{\beta}, \tag{14.60}$$

[3] The SET is not always the F-test, as we will see later for models with weakly exogenous regressors, but in many cases, the SET coincides with F.

and hence the sample predicted value is:

$$\hat{\gamma}_\alpha = \hat{\Sigma}_{zz}^{-1}\hat{\Sigma}_{zx}\hat{\beta}. \tag{14.61}$$

Thus, the encompassing difference $\tilde{\psi}_\gamma = (\hat{\gamma} - \hat{\gamma}_\alpha)$ in a stochastic linear-models framework is:

$$\begin{aligned} \tilde{\psi}_\gamma &= (Z'Z)^{-1} Z'y - \hat{\Sigma}_{zz}^{-1}\hat{\Sigma}_{zx}\hat{\beta} \\ &= (Z'Z)^{-1} Z'Q_X y + \left[(Z'Z)^{-1} Z'X - \hat{\Sigma}_{zz}^{-1}\hat{\Sigma}_{zx}\right]\hat{\beta} \\ &= \hat{\psi}_\gamma + \left[\hat{\Pi} - \hat{\Sigma}_{zz}^{-1}\hat{\Sigma}_{zx}\right]\hat{\beta}. \end{aligned} \tag{14.62}$$

The expression in (14.62) leads to a potentially different encompassing test. When z_t is treated as strongly exogenous, the term in square brackets disappears since the parameter Π can be estimated unrestrictedly by regression, and so the prediction from $\mathsf{M}_1 + \mathsf{M}_c$ of the second moment of z_t is always correct:

$$\hat{\Pi} = \hat{\Sigma}_{zz}^{-1}\hat{\Sigma}_{zx}. \tag{14.63}$$

However, when z_t is not strongly exogenous for α, M_1 may restrict the second-moment matrix of z_t.

Consider an example where M_1 and M_2 are given by:

$$\mathsf{M}_1\colon y_t = \beta y_{t-1} + u_t \text{ when } |\beta| < 1 \text{ and } u_t \sim \mathsf{IID}\left[0, \sigma_u^2\right] \tag{14.64}$$

and:

$$\mathsf{M}_2\colon y_t = \rho y_{t-2} + \nu_t \text{ with } |\rho| < 1. \tag{14.65}$$

Here, we cannot arbitrarily choose the completing model M_c to relate x_t and z_t, since M_1 forces as M_c the model:

$$\mathsf{M}_c\colon y_{t-1} = \pi y_{t-2} + \omega_t. \tag{14.66}$$

Then (14.66) is M_1 lagged one period, and hence M_1 entails the value of Σ_{zz}, namely $\Sigma_{zz} = \beta\sigma_u^2/(1-\beta^2)$. Consequently, without strong exogeneity, M_1 may entail the values of some of the parameters of M_c. If by doing so M_c restricts Σ_{zz} or Σ_{zx}, encompassing tests will differ from the F-test, since the F-test does not exploit the fact that the second term in (14.62) may be non-zero.

In fact, there are four possible states for the $[\cdot]$ term in the last line of (14.62):

(i) when $[\cdot] = 0$ and (14.63) holds, the WET is the F-test;
(ii) when $[\cdot]$ is non-zero, but is $O_p(T^{-1})$, the WET converges in distribution to the F-test under the null hypothesis and local alternatives, called strong asymptotic equivalence;
(iii) when $[\cdot]$ is $O_p(1/\sqrt{T})$, the WET converges in probability to the F-test only under the null, called weak asymptotic equivalence;

(iv) when $[\cdot]$ is $O_p(1)$, the WET differs asymptotically from the F-test, so the two tests are not equivalent asymptotically.

The choice of M_c matters in determining which of (i)–(iv) holds, as shown by the following example taken from Govaerts (1986). Let:

$$\mathsf{M}_1\colon y_t = \beta x_t + u_t \text{ where } u_t \underset{c}{\sim} \mathsf{IN}\left[0, \sigma_u^2\right] \tag{14.67}$$

$$\mathsf{M}_2\colon y_t = \gamma y_{t-1} + \nu_t \text{ where } \nu_t \underset{c}{\sim} \mathsf{IN}\left[0, \sigma_v^2\right] \tag{14.68}$$

and:

$$\mathsf{M}_m\colon y_t = b x_t + c y_{t-1} + \epsilon_t \text{ where } \epsilon_t \sim \mathsf{IN}\left[0, \sigma_\epsilon^2\right]. \tag{14.69}$$

Consider the following two possible ways of completing M_1 and M_2:

$$\mathsf{M}_c\,(1)\colon x_t = \rho y_{t-1} + e_t \tag{14.70}$$

or:

$$\mathsf{M}_c\,(2)\colon x_t = e_t. \tag{14.71}$$

In both (14.70) and (14.71), e_t is assumed by the investigator to be white noise. When using $\mathsf{M}_c(2)$ as the completing model, the assumption that x_t is white noise entails that y_t is white noise in M_1. Thus, M_1 must predict $\gamma_\beta = 0$ in M_2. That is an incorrect prediction when x_t is not in fact white noise: for example, when $\mathsf{M}_c(1)$ is the DGP for x_t then M_1 predicts $\gamma_\beta = \rho\beta$. Thus, it is possible to fail an encompassing test by choosing the wrong completing model, as case (iv) suggested. Rules for choosing completing models are discussed in Govaerts *et al.* (1993) who show that a minimal completing model can be chosen which guarantees robustness: there always exists an M_c such that case (iii) is the worst possible outcome, so the encompassing decision under the null is not affected asymptotically by the specification of M_c.

When formulating local alternatives under which to derive powers of encompassing tests, care must be exercised to avoid contradicting the baseline model. For example, if M_m in (14.69) is used with $c = \lambda/\sqrt{T}$, then the error term $\{u_t\}$ on (14.67) must be autocorrelated, violating the assumptions under which the test should be applied. In such circumstances, the encompassing test has lower local power than the corresponding F-test, even though for other local alternatives, such as the omission of an innovation variable, the power is equal to that of the F-test.

Parsimonious encompassing does not suffer from this difficulty, and in fact simplifies the analysis even in dynamic models. Consider estimating M_m in (14.32):

$$\begin{pmatrix} \hat{b} \\ \hat{c} \end{pmatrix} = \begin{pmatrix} X'X & X'Z \\ Z'X & Z'Z \end{pmatrix}^{-1} \begin{pmatrix} X'y \\ Z'y \end{pmatrix}. \tag{14.72}$$

When the DGP is a jointly stationary stochastic process, the predicted values under M_1

are estimated by:

$$\begin{pmatrix} \hat{b}_\alpha \\ \hat{c}_\alpha \end{pmatrix} = \begin{pmatrix} \hat{\Sigma}_{xx} & \hat{\Sigma}_{xz} \\ \hat{\Sigma}_{zx} & \hat{\Sigma}_{zz} \end{pmatrix}^{-1} \begin{pmatrix} \hat{\Sigma}_{xx}\hat{\beta} \\ \hat{\Sigma}_{zx}\hat{\beta} \end{pmatrix}$$
$$= \begin{pmatrix} \hat{\Sigma}_{xx} & \hat{\Sigma}_{xz} \\ \hat{\Sigma}_{zx} & \hat{\Sigma}_{zz} \end{pmatrix}^{-1} \begin{pmatrix} \hat{\Sigma}_{xx} & \hat{\Sigma}_{xz} \\ \hat{\Sigma}_{zx} & \hat{\Sigma}_{zz} \end{pmatrix} \begin{pmatrix} \hat{\beta} \\ \mathbf{0} \end{pmatrix} \tag{14.73}$$
$$= \begin{pmatrix} \hat{\beta} \\ \mathbf{0} \end{pmatrix},$$

a result which holds independently of how the $\boldsymbol{\Sigma}$s are estimated. The sample encompassing difference is, therefore:

$$\begin{pmatrix} \hat{b} \\ \hat{c} \end{pmatrix} - \begin{pmatrix} \hat{b}_\alpha \\ \hat{c}_\alpha \end{pmatrix} = \begin{pmatrix} \hat{b} - \hat{\beta} \\ \hat{c} \end{pmatrix}. \tag{14.74}$$

The first row yields the HET and the second row the SET, and the $\boldsymbol{\Sigma}s$ do not enter the tests. Local alternatives based on M_m with $c = \lambda/\sqrt{T}$ pose no methodological problems.

14.11 A solved example

Consider the three hypotheses:

$$\mathsf{H}_a\colon y_t = x_t\beta + \epsilon_t \text{ where } \epsilon_t \underset{c}{\sim} \mathsf{IN}\left[0, \sigma_\epsilon^2\right] \text{ and } \mathsf{E}\left[x_t\epsilon_s\right] = 0\,\forall t, s \tag{14.75}$$

$$\mathsf{H}_b\colon y_t = z_t\gamma + v_t \text{ where } v_t \underset{c}{\sim} \mathsf{IN}\left[0, \sigma_v^2\right] \text{ and } \mathsf{E}\left[z_tv_s\right] = 0\,\forall t, s \tag{14.76}$$

$$\mathsf{H}_c\colon x_t = \pi z_t + w_t \text{ with } \mathsf{E}\left[z_tw_t\right] = 0 \text{ and } \mathsf{E}\left[w_tw_s\right] = \delta_{ts}\sigma_w^2. \tag{14.77}$$

Prove the following claims.

(a) If H_a and H_c are true: $\gamma = \pi\beta$ and $\sigma_v^2 = \sigma_\epsilon^2 + \beta^2\sigma_w^2$.
(b) In the joint 'nesting' model:

$$\mathsf{H}_d\colon y_t = x_tb + z_tc + u_t, \tag{14.78}$$

an F-test of $\mathsf{H}_0\colon c = 0$ is given by:

$$\eta = \left(\frac{\hat{\boldsymbol{\epsilon}}'\hat{\boldsymbol{\epsilon}} - \hat{\mathbf{u}}'\hat{\mathbf{u}}}{\hat{\mathbf{u}}'\hat{\mathbf{u}}} \times \frac{(T-2)}{1}\right) \sim F^1_{T-2}. \tag{14.79}$$

(c) A Wald test of $\mathsf{H}_1\colon \delta = \gamma - \pi\beta = 0$ can be expressed as a function of η when H_a and H_c are true.
(d) Comment on the role of this last encompassing test, and hence on the criticism that H_d artificially nests H_a and H_b.

Solution to (a)

When H_a and H_c are true, by substituting H_c in H_a:

$$y_t = \pi\beta z_t + \{\beta w_t + \epsilon_t\}, \tag{14.80}$$

from which equation, the restriction $\gamma = \pi\beta$ in H_b is immediate. Further, $\sigma_v^2 = \sigma_\epsilon^2 + \beta^2\sigma_w^2$ follows from (14.75) and (14.77) given the assumptions on the variance-covariance matrix of ϵ_t, w_t, and v_t, since:

$$\mathsf{E}\left[w_t\epsilon_t\right] = \mathsf{E}\left[(x_t - \pi z_t)\,\epsilon_t\right] = 0.$$

Solution to (b)

By representing H_d as a partitioned regression model in matrix form:

$$\begin{pmatrix} \boldsymbol{x}'\boldsymbol{x} & \boldsymbol{x}'\boldsymbol{z} \\ \boldsymbol{z}'\boldsymbol{x} & \boldsymbol{z}'\boldsymbol{z} \end{pmatrix}\begin{pmatrix} \hat{b} \\ \hat{c} \end{pmatrix} = \begin{pmatrix} \boldsymbol{x}'\boldsymbol{y} \\ \boldsymbol{z}'\boldsymbol{y} \end{pmatrix}, \tag{14.81}$$

we can write:

$$\hat{c} = \left(\boldsymbol{z}'\boldsymbol{Q}_x\boldsymbol{z}\right)^{-1}\boldsymbol{z}'\boldsymbol{Q}_x\boldsymbol{y} \quad \text{where} \quad \boldsymbol{Q}_x = \boldsymbol{I}_T - \boldsymbol{x}\left(\boldsymbol{x}'\boldsymbol{x}\right)^{-1}\boldsymbol{x}'. \tag{14.82}$$

Under the null hypothesis H_0, $\boldsymbol{Q}_x\boldsymbol{y} \sim \mathsf{N}_T[\boldsymbol{0}, \sigma_\epsilon^2\boldsymbol{Q}_x]$, and therefore:

$$\hat{c} \sim \mathsf{N}\left[0, \sigma_\epsilon^2\left(\boldsymbol{z}'\boldsymbol{Q}_x\boldsymbol{z}\right)^{-1}\right] \quad \text{so that} \quad \frac{\hat{c}^2\left(\boldsymbol{z}'\boldsymbol{Q}_x\boldsymbol{z}\right)}{\sigma_\epsilon^2} \underset{\mathsf{H}_0}{\widetilde{\ }} \chi^2(1). \tag{14.83}$$

Let $s^2 = \hat{\boldsymbol{u}}'\hat{\boldsymbol{u}}/(T-2)$, then:

$$\frac{(T-2)\,s^2}{\sigma_\epsilon^2} \sim \chi^2(T-2).$$

Since $\hat{c}$ and s^2 are independent:

$$\frac{(T-2)\,\hat{c}^2\left(\boldsymbol{z}'\boldsymbol{Q}_x\boldsymbol{z}\right)}{s^2} = \eta \underset{\mathsf{H}_0}{\widetilde{\ }} F^1_{T-2}. \tag{14.84}$$

Alternatively, letting $\boldsymbol{z}^* = \boldsymbol{Q}_x\boldsymbol{z}$, $\boldsymbol{Q}_{z*} = (\boldsymbol{I}_T - \boldsymbol{z}^*(\boldsymbol{z}^{*\prime}\boldsymbol{z}^*)^{-1}\boldsymbol{z}^{*\prime})$, and:

$$\boldsymbol{Q} = \boldsymbol{Q}_{z*}\boldsymbol{Q}_x = \left(\boldsymbol{Q}_x - \boldsymbol{Q}_x\boldsymbol{z}\left(\boldsymbol{z}'\boldsymbol{Q}_x\boldsymbol{z}\right)^{-1}\boldsymbol{z}'\boldsymbol{Q}_x\right),$$

then $(T-2)\eta$ is given by:

$$\frac{\boldsymbol{y}'\boldsymbol{Q}_x\boldsymbol{z}\left(\boldsymbol{z}'\boldsymbol{Q}_x\boldsymbol{z}\right)^{-1}\left(\boldsymbol{z}'\boldsymbol{Q}_x\boldsymbol{z}\right)\left(\boldsymbol{z}'\boldsymbol{Q}_x\boldsymbol{z}\right)^{-1}\boldsymbol{z}'\boldsymbol{Q}_x\boldsymbol{y}}{\boldsymbol{y}'\boldsymbol{Q}\boldsymbol{y}} = \frac{\boldsymbol{y}'\boldsymbol{Q}_x\boldsymbol{y} - \boldsymbol{y}'\boldsymbol{Q}\boldsymbol{y}}{\boldsymbol{y}'\boldsymbol{Q}\boldsymbol{y}}. \tag{14.85}$$

Since:

$$\boldsymbol{Q}_x\boldsymbol{y} = \boldsymbol{Q}_x\boldsymbol{z}\boldsymbol{b} + \boldsymbol{Q}_x\boldsymbol{u} = \boldsymbol{z}^*\boldsymbol{b} + \boldsymbol{Q}_x\boldsymbol{u} = \hat{\boldsymbol{\epsilon}}$$

then $\boldsymbol{Q}\boldsymbol{y} = \boldsymbol{Q}\boldsymbol{u} = \hat{\boldsymbol{u}}$, and hence:

$$\eta = \left(\frac{\hat{\boldsymbol{\epsilon}}'\hat{\boldsymbol{\epsilon}} - \hat{\boldsymbol{u}}'\hat{\boldsymbol{u}}}{\hat{\boldsymbol{u}}'\hat{\boldsymbol{u}}} \times \frac{(T-2)}{1}\right) \underset{\mathsf{H}_0}{\widetilde{\ }} F^1_{T-2}.$$

Solution to (c)

To show the result, consider the sample encompassing difference:

$$\hat{\psi}_\gamma = \hat{\gamma} - \hat{\gamma}_\alpha \tag{14.86}$$

where $\hat{\gamma}$ is the estimate of γ under H_b and $\hat{\gamma}_\alpha$ is the sample prediction of γ under $\mathsf{H}_a + \mathsf{H}_c$:

$$\hat{\psi}_\gamma = (z'z)^{-1} z'y - (z'z)^{-1} z'x (x'x)^{-1} x'y = (z'z)^{-1} z' Q_x y = K\hat{c} \tag{14.87}$$

when $K = (z'z)^{-1} z' Q_x z$. Thus, $\hat{\psi}_\gamma$ is a linear function of $\hat{c}$, with $\mathsf{V}[\hat{\psi}_\gamma] = K^2 \mathsf{V}[\hat{c}]$, and the F-test follows as in (b).

Solution to (d)

At first sight, H_d seems an artificial nesting model given H_a and H_b, and from the latter alone, it is not obvious that H_d need be either unique or optimal in any sense. However, (c) establishes that the Wald encompassing test (transformed to obtain an exact finite-sample distribution) is identical to the F-test in the nesting model. As before, the non-uniqueness problem stems from going from the simple to the general (H_a and H_b to H_d), and not following the reduction sequence, where H_d should have arisen prior to either simplification.

14.12 An empirical illustration

To illustrate encompassing tests empirically, we reconsider the UKM1 data over the sample period 1963(1)–1989(2) on $\log(M/PY)$ and R_t. The rival models have the form of an 'econometric' equation denoted M_1, and a 'time-series' model, M_2:

$$\Delta \log \left(\frac{M}{P}\right)_t = \beta_0 + \beta_1 \Delta R_t + \beta_2 \Delta \log Y_t + \beta_3 \Delta \log \left(\frac{M}{P}\right)_{t-1} + \epsilon_{1t} \tag{14.88}$$

and:

$$\Delta \log M_t = \gamma_0 + \gamma_1 \Delta \log M_{t-1} + \epsilon_{2t}. \tag{14.89}$$

These specifications are illustrative, and are in differences because the data are $\mathsf{I}(1)$. The econometric model (14.88) relates the growth rate of real money to that of income and the change in the opportunity cost of holding M1, with a lagged-dependent variable, whereas the time-series equation (14.89) is just an autoregression in the growth rate of nominal money. Such specifications might occur in a debate about real versus nominal money: (14.88) imposes short-run homogeneity of money with respect to prices, and (14.89) does not.

The models can be transformed to equations with the same dependent variable, $\Delta \log(M/P)_t$, provided $\Delta \log P_t$ is included as a regressor in (14.89) with a coefficient of minus unity: the unrestricted estimate is close to that value. The minimal nesting model M_c includes the regressors:

$$\mathsf{M}_c\text{: } 1,\ \Delta R_t,\ \Delta \log Y_t,\ \Delta \log \left(\frac{M}{P}\right)_{t-1},\ \Delta \log P_t,\ \Delta \log M_{t-1}.$$

In Table 14.1 we only report summary statistics related to fit, constancy and encompassing (see Chs. 6–8 and 16 for equation estimates): JS denotes the parameter constancy test in Hansen (1992a).

Table 14.1 Summary statistics

Model	M_c	M_1	M_2	M_{2a}
R^2	0.52	0.38	0.45	0.52
σ	0.019	0.021	0.019	0.018
DW	2.46	2.59	2.23	2.45
SC	−7.77	−7.60	−7.77	−7.77
JS	2.4**	1.4	2.5**	2.2**

There is little to choose between the models in terms of σ, with M_1 fitting somewhat worse. However, the general equation does not fully characterize the data as there is some evidence of parameter non-constancy and residual autocorrelation. Table 14.2 reports the diagnostic test outcomes.

Table 14.2 Diagnostic test outcomes

Test	Outcome
$AR1-5 \quad F(5,92)$	7.7**
ARCH 4 $\quad F(4,89)$	0.07
$ND \quad \chi^2(2)$	0.15
$X_i^2 \quad F(10,86)$	0.72
$X_i \times X_j \quad F(20,76)$	1.11
RESET $\quad F(1,96)$	0.59

The encompassing test statistics are shown in Table 14.3 together with the asymptotic distribution form of the test under the null, and its source. Both models are rejected against each other, and against M_c.

It may happen that the economist does not care about inclusion of R in the time-series model, since it is not germane to the debate about modelling nominal or real money. The summary statistics for this revised version of M_2, denoted M_{2a}, are also shown in Table 14.1. The fit is marginally better. Table 14.4 reports the new encompassing-test values.

As can be seen, the F-test (which is the SET and equals the test of the validity of (14.88) as a reduction of M_c) is unaltered, but the Cox and IV tests change, so are not

Table 14.3 Encompassing test statistics

Test	Form	M_1 v M_2	M_2 v M_1
Cox (1961)	$\mathsf{N}(0,1)$	-9.1	-3.3
Ericsson (1983) IV	$\mathsf{N}(0,1)$	7.7	3.1
Sargan (1959)	$\chi^2(2)$	22.3	12.2
Joint Model	$F(2,97)$	14.1	4.5

Table 14.4 Revised encompassing test statistics

Test	Form	M_1 v M_2	M_2 v M_1
Cox	$\mathsf{N}(0,1)$	-8.3	0.51
Ericsson IV	$\mathsf{N}(0,1)$	7.0	-0.51
Sargan	$\chi^2(2)$	22.3	0.35
Joint Model	$F(2,97)$	14.1	0.17

invariant to the specification of the rival hypothesis. Both sets of restrictions are rejected by the data in the first formulation, but M_{2a} suggests that short-run price homogeneity is at fault, as M_{2a} is not rejected in Table 14.4.

14.13 Encompassing the VAR

Consider a VAR defined for a vector $\boldsymbol{f}_t$ of N variables by:

$$\boldsymbol{f}_t = \boldsymbol{\Pi} \boldsymbol{f}_{t-1} + \boldsymbol{v}_t \quad \text{where} \quad \boldsymbol{v}_t \sim \mathsf{IN}_N \left[\mathbf{0}, \boldsymbol{\Omega}_v\right]. \tag{14.90}$$

The VAR may be in companion form, and is in I(0) space to ensure that the correct critical values of tests are used, so all the eigenvalues of $\boldsymbol{\Pi}$ are inside the unit circle.[4] The second moments of $\boldsymbol{f}_t$ from (14.90) are:

$$\mathsf{E}\left[\boldsymbol{f}_t \boldsymbol{f}_{t-1}'\right] = \boldsymbol{\Pi} \mathsf{E}\left[\boldsymbol{f}_{t-1} \boldsymbol{f}_{t-1}'\right] = \boldsymbol{\Pi M} \quad \text{where} \quad \boldsymbol{M} = \boldsymbol{\Pi M \Pi}' + \boldsymbol{\Omega}_v.$$

There are two rival complete simultaneous-equations models (SEMs) of the form:

$$\mathsf{H}_a\colon \boldsymbol{\Phi}_a \boldsymbol{f}_t = \boldsymbol{u}_{at} \quad \text{and} \quad \mathsf{H}_b\colon \boldsymbol{\Phi}_b \boldsymbol{f}_t = \boldsymbol{u}_{bt}, \tag{14.91}$$

which are (over)identified relative to the congruent statistical system (14.90), where $\boldsymbol{\Phi}_a$ and $\boldsymbol{\Phi}_b$ are $n \times N$ (see Ch.11). The error covariance matrices of each SEM in (14.91) are given by $\boldsymbol{\Sigma}_{aa} = \boldsymbol{\Phi}_a \boldsymbol{M} \boldsymbol{\Phi}_a'$ and $\boldsymbol{\Sigma}_{bb} = \boldsymbol{\Phi}_b \boldsymbol{M} \boldsymbol{\Phi}_b'$ respectively, so that H_a dominates H_b in generalized variance (or likelihood) if $\det(\boldsymbol{\Sigma}_{aa}) \leq \det(\boldsymbol{\Sigma}_{bb})$, which is necessary

[4] This section draws on Hendry and Mizon (1993).

but not sufficient for $\mathsf{H}_a \mathcal{E}\, \mathsf{H}_b$. The VAR (14.90) defines the common probability space, so provides the framework within which the properties of H_a and H_b can be evaluated. Both H_a and H_b are nested within the VAR (14.90), which we denote by $\mathsf{H}_i \subset$VAR. The VAR encompasses H_i by virtue of each H_i being a reduction of the VAR. The issue is whether either of H_a or H_b encompasses the VAR. If so, since a reduced model is accounting for the results of the more general model within which it is nested, we are testing $\mathsf{H}_a \mathcal{E}_p$ VAR, or $\mathsf{H}_b \mathcal{E}_p$ VAR.

The main difficulty in establishing encompassing theorems about SEMs is that their exogeneity assumptions may differ, so that the models are not in a common probability space. This problem does not arise with closed systems if either H_a or H_b asserts that $\mathsf{E}_i[\boldsymbol{u}_{it}\boldsymbol{f}'_{t-1}] = \mathbf{0}$ for $i = a, b$ where E_i denotes expectations with respect to model i. Consider the case $i = a$. Since $\mathsf{E}_a[\boldsymbol{u}_{at}\boldsymbol{f}'_{t-1}] = \mathbf{0}$ implies that the derived error $\{\boldsymbol{u}_{at}\}$ is an innovation against the past of the process in (14.91):

$$\mathsf{E}_a[\boldsymbol{u}_{at}\boldsymbol{f}'_{t-1}] = \boldsymbol{\Phi}_a \mathsf{E}\left[\boldsymbol{f}_t\boldsymbol{f}'_{t-1}\right] = \boldsymbol{\Phi}_a \boldsymbol{\Pi} \boldsymbol{M} = \mathbf{0}\,\forall t, \tag{14.92}$$

and hence:

$$\boldsymbol{\Phi}_a \boldsymbol{\Pi} = \mathbf{0}. \tag{14.93}$$

Such a condition entails correct dynamic specification. When (14.93) holds, then H_a is a valid reduction of the VAR, and hence $\mathsf{H}_a \mathcal{E}_p$ VAR. Conversely, if (14.93) does not hold, H_a cannot encompass the VAR, and can be rejected against the VAR since elements of $\boldsymbol{f}_{t-1}$ must be relevant to H_a in addition to the variables included in (14.91). If neither modeller accepts the validity of the instruments used by the other, or there are insufficient instruments to identify the nesting hypothesis, cross-model encompassing may not be testable: see Ericsson (1983). Thus, conditional on the proprietor of H_a accepting lagged variables as legitimate potential instruments, we have:

THEOREM **4.** $\mathsf{H}_a \mathcal{E}$ VAR *if and only if* $\boldsymbol{\Phi}_a \boldsymbol{\Pi} = \mathbf{0}$.

A consequence of theorem 4, is:

THEOREM **5.** *If* $\mathsf{H}_a \mathcal{E}_p$VAR *and* $\mathsf{H}_i \subset$VAR, *then* $\mathsf{H}_a \mathcal{E}\, \mathsf{H}_i$.

Thus, the VAR is a catalyst for encompassing comparisons between SEMs. The converse of theorem 5 is false in that $\mathsf{H}_a \mathcal{E}\, \mathsf{H}_i$ could hold without $\mathsf{H}_a \mathcal{E}_p$VAR (e.g., because $\mathsf{H}_i \subset \mathsf{H}_a$), but by requiring congruence, H_a would be rejected against the VAR. Hence, to encompass rival models, it is sufficient for H_a to be congruent and $\mathsf{H}_a \mathcal{E}_p$VAR.

Since $\boldsymbol{\Pi}$ is singular when the lag length exceeds unity, the set $\{\boldsymbol{\Phi}_i | \boldsymbol{\Phi}_i \boldsymbol{\Pi} = \mathbf{0}; i = a, b\}$ will usually have more than one element, and hence several models could satisfy the encompassing property in theorem 4, and be mutually encompassing. Thus, that theorem defines an equivalence class of mutually encompassing models, which could correspond to apparently antagonistic theoretical specifications, all of which could be identifiable by their a priori restrictions. In this sense, therefore, the claim in Sims (1980) that structural identifying information is 'incredible' is sustainable: since the equivalence class members are observationally equivalent, it is unclear how 'prior' information about particular members could ever be acquired.

The resolution to this conundrum rests on the applicability of the Lucas critique discussed below. Moreover, such a resolution supplies a constructive application of what is often used as a destructive empirical criticism. Specifically, coefficient matrices $\boldsymbol{\Phi}_i$ in the set $\{\boldsymbol{\Phi}_i | \boldsymbol{\Phi}_i \boldsymbol{\Pi} = \mathbf{0}\}$ (which are not merely re-parameterizations of each other) cannot all be invariant to changes in the parameters of the DGP, since they are different functions of those parameters. Thus, policy-regime changes will induce changes in some of the parameter sets, destroying the observational equivalence, and hence preventing the mutual encompassing which might have held in a constant parameter world: when nature experiments enough, only that representation which corresponds to the actual structure of behaviour can remain constant.

14.14 Testing the Lucas critique

As we have seen at several stages above, there is a long history of doubt about almost every facet of the empirical econometric enterprise by both critics and contributors.[5] Many of those doubts have related to the potential non-constancy of the coefficients of econometric equations under changed states of nature (see *inter alia* Robbins, 1932, Ch.5, Frisch, 1938, Keynes, 1939, Haavelmo, 1944, Marschak, 1953, Hurwicz, 1962, Lucas, 1976, Hendry, 1979b, and Engle, Hendry and Richard, 1983). Despite the importance of earlier contributions, the recent debate has referred to the issue as 'the Lucas critique' (see Aldrich, 1989, for a history of the converse concept of autonomy). The Lucas critique is explicitly of the use of econometric models for policy analysis as exemplified by the following syllogism:

> 'Given that the structure of an econometric model consists of optimal decision rules for economic agents, and that optimal decision rules vary systematically with changes in the structure of series relevant to the decision maker, it follows that any change in policy will systematically alter the structure of econometric models.' Lucas (1976, p.41).

If correct, the assertion is a damaging criticism of any econometric research which fails to model the expectations formation of economic agents and their behavioural plans separately: confounding the two is claimed to lead to predictive failure when the stochastic processes of the determining series alter (see e.g., Wallis, 1980). Conversely, the Lucas critique is also testable, and hence it is possible to discriminate between models affected by the critique and models which can be used under certain conditions for policy simulation analyses.

First, we interpret the critique as a potential denial of invariance of parameters of interest to a (perhaps unspecified) class of interventions affecting the economy. Secondly, we consider the critique in terms of whether any given assertion about its presence or absence can be corroborated or refuted. Finally, we discriminate three levels of applicability of the critique.

[5] This section is based on research with Rob Engle and Carlo Favero, and was first presented as the A. W. Phillips Lecture at the 1989 Australasian Meeting of the Econometric Society: see Favero and Hendry (1992) and Engle and Hendry (1993).

(a) agents' plans depend on the environment;
(b) agents' plans depend on the control rules of others;
(c) agents' plans depend on expectations.

Level (a) corresponds to the fact that invariance to all possible changes in the environment is not achievable in a social science: econometric models estimated from observations before a radical change in the world cannot in general be expected to function equally well after the change has occurred (e.g. after a nuclear war). This point is essential to the relevance of economics, as otherwise agents would not respond to changes in the world. A critique at level (a) entails that there may exist a sufficiently large change such that no previous empirical evidence is relevant. Thus, level (a) is generically confirmable since any given claimed instance could potentially be corroborated, and by doing so reject invariance. Conversely, it is only specifically refutable in that failing to confirm one instance (and thereby 'refuting' the assertion of variation in response to the claimed changes) cannot preclude that future instances will be confirmed. To the extent that level (a) of the critique is testable, it coincides with the procedures for level (b), and hence will not be considered further.

Level (b) concerns the variation in parameters with changes in the distributions of variables which are outside the direct control of the agents being modelled. In such a case, the parameters of interest μ are not invariant or, for a conditional model, the regressors are not super exogenous for μ (see Ch.5). Super exogeneity may be violated by the dependence of model parameters on policy agency control rules or on the distributions of the conditional variables. Like (a), this level is generically confirmable but only specifically refutable, since future changes in other variables may alter μ. The class of alternative hypotheses under which μ may vary must be specified for a viable test statistic, and failure to reject invariance is compatible with low power due to a poor selection of alternatives. A class of super-exogeneity tests proposed by Engle and Hendry (1993) is discussed below. The discussion follows Hendry (1988) and Favero and Hendry (1992) who apply these methods to test the model proposed by Baba, Hendry and Starr (1992). Hendry, Muellbauer and Murphy (1990) also test the invariance of the DHSY model.

Level (c) is a critique of the use of a 'backward-looking' econometric specification when the behaviour of economic agents follows forward-looking rules: in this case, the regression coefficients are not the parameters of interest, as they are mixtures of behavioural and expectations parameters (see Ch.6). This possibility applies when expectations are relevant, and a typical example is the use of a feedback consumption function when agents behave according to a forward-looking permanent-income/life-cycle hypothesis. An important additional feature of this level is the inherent presence of two rival hypotheses: feedback and expectations. Consequently, encompassing comparisons are feasible as well as invariance tests, and as shown below, the two requirements allow generic confirmation and generic refutation.

The next section reviews a theoretical case where the critique may be applicable, then §14.16 describes tests for super exogeneity and invariance, followed by encompassing comparisons between feedback and feedforward models in §14.17.

From Chapters 5 and 9, all the empirical models are treated as derived entities obtained by reduction from the DGP. Data reductions entail transformations on the original parameters of that DGP and hence potentially involve losing constancy or invariance even if either property is present in the DGP. The set of variables of relevance is denoted by $\{w_t, t = 1, \ldots, T\}$, with the Haavelmo distribution $\mathsf{D_W}(w_1 \ldots w_T | W_0, \theta)$ where W_0 is the set of initial conditions, and $\theta \in \Theta$ is the $p \times 1$ vector of parameters characterizing $\mathsf{D_W}(\cdot)$. Conditionally on $W_{t-1} = (W_0, w_1, \ldots, w_{t-1})$:

$$\mathsf{D_W}\left(W_T^1 \mid W_0, \theta\right) = \prod_{t=1}^{T} \mathsf{D_w}\left(w_t \mid W_{t-1}, \theta\right) \tag{14.94}$$

creating the innovation process $\nu_t = w_t - \mathsf{E}[w_t | W_{t-1}]$ relative to (the σ-field generated by) W_{t-1}. Let $w_t' = (y_t' : z_t')$, where y_t is the $n \times 1$ vector of variables to be modelled, and z_t is the $k \times 1$ vector not to be modelled (see Ch.5) so:

$$\mathsf{D_w}\left(w_t \mid W_{t-1}, \theta\right) = \mathsf{D_y}\left(y_t \mid z_t, W_{t-1}, \lambda_1\right) \mathsf{D_z}\left(z_t \mid W_{t-1}, \lambda_2\right). \tag{14.95}$$

If agents form expectations about z_t when planning y_t, then λ_1 will depend on λ_2 and consequently λ_1 will alter if λ_2 changes. When z_t is not observable by the agent at the time the plan is formulated, then the first density must be marginalized with respect to z_t, or z_t must be modelled. Both conditional and expectational models can be derived from the sequential joint density of w_t.

The resulting model is assumed to be the vector autoregressive-distributed lag system (see Ch.8):

$$B(L)\, y_t + C(L)\, z_t = \epsilon_t \text{ where } \epsilon_t \underset{app}{\sim} \mathsf{IN}\left[\mathbf{0}, \Sigma_\epsilon\right] \tag{14.96}$$

and $B(L)$ and $C(L)$ are polynomials of order m in the lag operator L. When y_t and z_t are $\mathsf{I}(d)$, they are assumed to be cointegrated in levels (see Engle and Granger, 1987, and Ch.11). As shown in Chapter 8, models like (14.96) lead naturally to equilibrium-correction formulations on re-parameterizing in terms of differences and lagged levels, and the latter will be relevant when (perhaps subsets of) y_t and z_t are cointegrated.

14.15 The applicability of the critique

To illustrate the applicability of the critique, we illustrate level (c) by a conditional consumption function when agents behave according to the PIH/LCH hypothesis. The estimated consumption function is:

$$C_t = \gamma_0 + \gamma_1 Y_t + u_t \tag{14.97}$$

whereas consumers plan consumption C_t according to:

$$C_t = \psi Y_t^p + v_t,$$

where permanent income Y_t^p is given by:

$$Y_t^p = \sum_{i=1}^{\infty} \delta^i \mathsf{E}\left[Y_{t+i} \mid \mathcal{I}_t\right] \qquad (14.98)$$

where δ is the discount factor, and $\mathcal{I}_t$ denotes available information. When Y_t follows the process:

$$Y_t = \rho Y_{t-1} + \epsilon_t,$$

then:

$$Y_t^p = \frac{Y_t}{1 - \rho\delta}, \qquad (14.99)$$

so in (14.97), $\gamma_0 = 0$ and $\gamma_1 = \psi/(1 - \rho\delta)$. If we change the generating process of Y_t from (14.98) by assuming that an economic policy stabilizes output at its natural level $\bar{Y}_t$:

$$Y_t = \bar{Y}_t,$$

then:

$$Y_t^p = \frac{\bar{Y}_t}{1 - \delta} \qquad (14.100)$$

and the coefficients in (14.97) become $\gamma_0 = \bar{Y}_t/(1 - \delta)$ with $\gamma_1 = 0$. Policy analysis of (14.97) cannot be validly performed because of the failure to model the feedforward mechanism determining permanent income. The estimated parameters in (14.97) are mixtures of expectations parameters and plan parameters, and so vary when a new policy regime changes agents' expectations. The same comment applies if expectations or plans are incorrectly modelled.

Since the above models have different policy implications yet differ only in their interpretations, the importance of distinguishing autonomous from derived parameters is obvious and applies more widely than just the context of feedback versus feedforward econometric specifications. Fortunately, the apparent observational equivalence of the two estimated models derived from competing theories can be solved precisely because of their differing susceptibilities to regime changes, and the necessary existence of two models which thereby allows encompassing comparisons. Section 14.17 is devoted to that issue.

14.16 Tests for super exogeneity

The three concepts of weak exogeneity, constancy, and invariance clarify tests for the potential independence of agents' plans from policy control rules. From the factorization of the joint sequential density in (14.95), z_t is weakly exogenous for the parameter of interest μ if (i) μ is a function of λ_1 alone; and (ii) λ_1 and λ_2 are variation free. When z_t is weakly exogenous for μ, there is no loss of information from analysing μ in the conditional model without modelling the marginal process determining z_t. This seems a necessary condition for not having to model the expectations processes.

Constancy is time-independence of parameters, and invariance is constancy across interventions (see Ch.2). Further, from Chapter 5, z_t is super exogenous for $\boldsymbol{\mu}$ if z_t is weakly exogenous for $\boldsymbol{\mu}$, and $\boldsymbol{\lambda}_1$ is invariant to changes in $\boldsymbol{\lambda}_2$. Thus, super exogeneity of the conditioning variables for the parameters of interest is necessary to justify using a conditional model for policy analyses and relates to the level (b) critique.

Consider the joint distribution (14.95) for a bivariate normally-distributed random variable $\boldsymbol{w}_t$ when $\mathsf{E}[\boldsymbol{w}_t|\mathcal{I}_t] = \boldsymbol{\omega}_t$, and $\mathcal{I}_t$ depends on both $\boldsymbol{W}_{t-1}$ and other valid conditioning variables $\{\boldsymbol{\xi}_j,\ j = 1,\ldots,t\}$. As above, $\boldsymbol{w}_t$ is factorized into y_t and z_t (now scalars), and (14.96) holds, but with $\boldsymbol{\Sigma}_\epsilon$ non-constant (denoted by $\boldsymbol{\Sigma}_t$). Each of $\boldsymbol{\omega}_t$ and $\boldsymbol{\Sigma}_t$ may depend on $\mathcal{I}_t$, but need not do so. The conditional expectation of y_t is:

$$\mathsf{E}\left[y_t \mid z_t, \mathcal{I}_t\right] = \omega_t^y + \beta_t\left(z_t - \omega_t^z\right) \ \text{ where } \beta_t = \frac{\sigma_t^{yz}}{\sigma_t^{zz}} \tag{14.101}$$

with conditional variance:

$$\mathsf{E}\left[\left(y_t - \mathsf{E}\left[y_t|z_t,\mathcal{I}_t\right]\right)^2 \mid z_t, \mathcal{I}_t\right] = \tau_t = \left(\sigma_t^{yy} - \frac{\left(\sigma_t^{yz}\right)^2}{\sigma_t^{zz}}\right).$$

The parameters of interest are α and $\boldsymbol{\gamma}$ in the theoretical model:

$$\omega_t^y = \alpha\omega_t^z + \boldsymbol{\gamma}'\boldsymbol{\xi}_t \tag{14.102}$$

although α could vary under some set of interventions. From (14.101) and (14.102):

$$y_t = \alpha z_t + \boldsymbol{\gamma}'\boldsymbol{\xi}_t + \left(\beta_t - \alpha\right)\left(z_t - \omega_t^z\right) + \epsilon_t \tag{14.103}$$

where $\epsilon_t = y_t - \mathsf{E}[y_t|z_t,\mathcal{I}_t]$, given (14.102).

To estimate α and $\boldsymbol{\gamma}$ efficiently from (14.103) requires:

(i) $(z_t : \boldsymbol{\xi}_t')$ must be weakly exogenous for $(\alpha : \boldsymbol{\gamma}')$, so that ω_t^z does not appear in (14.103);

(ii) β_t must be constant, and if τ_t is also to be constant, then σ_t^{yy} must equal $(\tau + \beta\sigma_t^{zz})$;

(iii) α must be invariant to potential changes in the processes generating z_t and $\boldsymbol{\xi}_t$.

These requirements entail $\alpha = \beta_t\ \forall t$, and all three conditions are needed for a constant parameter, invariant, conditional equation. For example, if (ii) is not satisfied, then weak exogeneity will fail as well as constancy since either $\alpha \neq \beta_t$, or α is non-constant and ω_t^z enters the conditional model. Conversely, granted all three conditions, (14.103) simplifies to the regression:

$$y_t = \alpha z_t + \boldsymbol{\gamma}'\boldsymbol{\xi}_t + \epsilon_t. \tag{14.104}$$

Let $u_t = z_t - \omega_t^z$, then $\mathsf{E}[\epsilon_t u_t] = 0$ assuming (i)–(iii); but if $\mathsf{E}[\epsilon_t u_t] \neq 0$, so weak exogeneity does not hold, non-constancy may result if the marginal process generating $(z_t : \boldsymbol{\xi}_t')$ alters. To relate the analysis to level (c), interpret ω_t^z as the expectation formed about z_t.

Engle and Hendry (1993) examine the impact on a model like (14.103) of changes in the moments $(\omega_t^z, \sigma_t^{zz})$ of $\{z_t\}$, using a linear expansion of the form:

$$\alpha\left(\omega_t^z, \sigma_t^{zz}\right) = \alpha_0 + \alpha_1 \omega_t^z + \alpha_2 \sigma_t^{zz} + \alpha_3 \frac{\sigma_t^{zz}}{\omega_t^z} \text{ when } \omega_t^z \neq 0. \tag{14.105}$$

If invariance holds, $\alpha_i = 0$ for $i = 1, 2, 3$, and $\alpha_0 = \alpha$, so the issue becomes that of testing for weak exogeneity as in (i) (see Wu, 1973, Hausman, 1978, and Engle, 1982b). Tests for constancy as in (ii) can be based on recursive estimation. Finally, if $\alpha_i \neq 0$, invariance (iii) fails even if β is constant. Tests for super exogeneity can be constructed by substituting (14.105) for α in (14.103) and replacing the unobservable values of ω_t^z (or equivalently u_t) and σ_t^{zz} (i.e. $\mathsf{E}[u_t^2]$) by proxies based on models of the process generating z_t. Engle and Hendry (1993) propose a variety of proxies for $(\omega_t^z, \sigma_t^{zz})$ including models of $\{u_t\}$ based on ARCH processes (see Engle, 1982a), and allow for non-constant σ_t^{zz} to capture changes in regimes. They also relate their approach to testing whether the restricted specification (14.104) can encompass the unrestricted regression of y_t on all of the instruments and proxies[6] (see Hendry and Richard, 1982, Mizon, 1984, Mizon and Richard, 1986, and Hendry and Richard, 1989); this aspect will be central to section 14.17. Another closely related class of tests is of the variance encompassing hypothesis $\sigma_v^2 = \sigma_\epsilon^2 + \alpha^2 \sigma_u^2$ where σ_v^2 is estimated from the unrestricted regression and σ_ϵ^2 is the constant error variance of (14.104), leading to one-degree-of-freedom tests (see Cox, 1961, Pesaran, 1974, and Ericsson, 1983; and Favero, 1989, for an application; Charemza and Kiraly, 1986, suggest recursive analogues of such tests).

14.17 Encompassing implications of feedback versus feedforward models

In contrasting feedback with feedforward models, we compare a contingent specification with a model that includes expectations together with an auxiliary system for expectations formation (see Ch.6). To clarify the encompassing implications of the two alternatives, we refer to a generic dependent variable y_t, and to a vector of k forcing variables $\boldsymbol{x}_t$, letting $\boldsymbol{\Psi}_t^{ij} = \mathsf{E}[\boldsymbol{x}_{t+i} | \mathcal{I}_{t-j}]$ denote the expectation of $\boldsymbol{x}_{t+i}$ using information available at time $t - j$. Hendry (1988) considers the case $\boldsymbol{\Psi}_t^{01}$, so we analyse the case in which the explanatory variables in the feedforward model are the expectations for $\boldsymbol{x}_{t+1}$ conditional on $\mathcal{I}_t$ (i.e. $\boldsymbol{\Psi}_t^{10}$).

The feedback, or conditional, sub-model denoted H_b is:

$$\mathsf{H}_f\colon y_t = \boldsymbol{\gamma}' \boldsymbol{x}_t + v_t \text{ where } \mathsf{E}_b\left[\boldsymbol{x}_t v_t\right] = \mathbf{0}. \tag{14.106}$$

The feedforward, or expectations, model H_e is:

$$\mathsf{H}_e\colon y_t = \boldsymbol{\delta}' \mathsf{E}\left[\boldsymbol{x}_{t+1} \mid \mathcal{I}_t\right] + \epsilon_t \text{ where } \mathsf{E}_e\left[\boldsymbol{x}_t \epsilon_t\right] = \mathbf{0} \tag{14.107}$$

6 These tests are equivalent to the test of independence of instruments and errors in e.g. Sargan (1964).

and the marginal completing model is:

$$\boldsymbol{x}_t = \boldsymbol{\pi}_t \boldsymbol{x}_{t-1} + \boldsymbol{\eta}_t \text{ with } \boldsymbol{\eta}_t \sim \mathsf{ID}_k\left[\mathbf{0}, \boldsymbol{\Omega}_t\right], \tag{14.108}$$

which depends on time through $\boldsymbol{\Omega}_t$ and $\boldsymbol{\pi}_t$, and entails that the only information relevant to predicting $\boldsymbol{x}_{t+1}$ is $\boldsymbol{x}_t$. We explore the encompassing predictions of each hypothesis H_b and H_e for the other, i.e. $\mathsf{H}_b \mathcal{E} \mathsf{H}_e$ and vice versa.

14.17.1 Does $\mathsf{H}_b \mathcal{E} \mathsf{H}_e$?

When (14.108) and (14.106) are a congruent representation of the DGP, the following implications hold.

(i) When $\boldsymbol{\pi}_t$ and $\boldsymbol{\Omega}_t$ are non-constant, the projection of y_t on $\boldsymbol{x}_{t-1}$ is also non-constant, and by substituting from (14.108) into (14.106):

$$\mathsf{E}_b\left[y_t \mid \boldsymbol{x}_{t-1}\right] = \boldsymbol{\gamma}' \boldsymbol{\pi}_t \boldsymbol{x}_{t-1}.$$

The error-variance is non-constant since:

$$y_t - \mathsf{E}_b\left[y_t \mid \boldsymbol{x}_{t-1}\right] = \boldsymbol{\gamma}' \boldsymbol{\eta}_t + v_t = \phi_t$$

with:

$$\mathsf{E}_b\left[\phi_t^2\right] = \sigma_{\phi_t}^2 = \sigma_v^2 + \boldsymbol{\gamma}' \boldsymbol{\Omega}_t \boldsymbol{\gamma}.$$

(ii) The projection of y_t on $\boldsymbol{x}_{t-1}$ should fit worse than the behavioural model, since $\sigma_\phi^2 \geq \sigma_v^2$ as $\boldsymbol{\gamma}' \boldsymbol{\Omega}_t \boldsymbol{\gamma} \geq 0$.

(iii) The behavioural model (14.106) should be constant.

14.17.2 Does $\mathsf{H}_e \mathcal{E} \mathsf{H}_b$?

When (14.107) and (14.108) are a congruent representation of the DGP, different implications hold.

(i) The conditional model cannot be constant when $\boldsymbol{\pi}_t$ is sufficiently variable, since:

$$\mathsf{E}_e\left[y_t \mid \boldsymbol{x}_t\right] = \boldsymbol{\alpha}_t' \boldsymbol{x}_t \text{ where } \boldsymbol{\alpha}_t = \left(\mathsf{E}_e\left[\boldsymbol{x}_t \boldsymbol{x}_t'\right]\right)^{-1} \mathsf{E}_e\left[\boldsymbol{x}_t y_t\right] = \boldsymbol{\pi}_{t+1}' \boldsymbol{\delta}. \tag{14.109}$$

(ii) The projection of y_t on $\boldsymbol{x}_{t-1}$ is non-constant but with parameter vector $\boldsymbol{\pi}_t' \boldsymbol{\pi}_{t+1}' \boldsymbol{\delta}$.

(iii) No error variance ranking arises since:

$$y_t - \mathsf{E}_e\left[y_t \mid \boldsymbol{x}_t\right] = \epsilon_t,$$

as in (14.107).

14.17.3 Incomplete information

Before drawing the conclusions of this analysis, we analyse the case of incomplete information, i.e. of under-parameterization of the marginal model for $\boldsymbol{x}_t$. Assume that $\boldsymbol{x}_t$ is only a subset of the information set $\mathcal{I}_t = (\boldsymbol{x}_t : \boldsymbol{z}_t)$ used by agents, when the DGP of $\boldsymbol{x}_t$ has constant parameters $\boldsymbol{\kappa}$:

$$\boldsymbol{x}_t = \boldsymbol{\kappa}_1 \boldsymbol{x}_{t-1} + \boldsymbol{\kappa}_2 \boldsymbol{z}_{t-1} + \boldsymbol{\nu}_t \quad \text{where} \quad \boldsymbol{\nu}_t \sim \mathsf{ID}_k \left[\mathbf{0}, \boldsymbol{\Phi}\right],$$

when $\boldsymbol{z}_t$ is $r \times 1$. Given (14.108), the relationship between $\boldsymbol{x}_t$ and $\boldsymbol{z}_t$ cannot be constant, and we must have:

$$\boldsymbol{z}_t = \boldsymbol{\Gamma}_t \boldsymbol{x}_t + \boldsymbol{\zeta}_t \quad \text{with} \quad \boldsymbol{\zeta}_t \sim \mathsf{ID}_r \left[\mathbf{0}, \boldsymbol{\Upsilon}_t\right],$$

so that:

$$\boldsymbol{\pi}_t = \boldsymbol{\kappa}_1 + \boldsymbol{\kappa}_2 \boldsymbol{\Gamma}_t \quad \text{and} \quad \boldsymbol{\Omega}_t = \boldsymbol{\Phi} + \boldsymbol{\kappa}_2 \boldsymbol{\Upsilon}_t \boldsymbol{\kappa}_2'.$$

If $\boldsymbol{\Gamma}_t$ were constant, a contradiction would result from the implication that $\boldsymbol{\pi}_t$ must also be constant. Consequently, the regression of y_t on $\boldsymbol{x}_t$ cannot be constant under H_e:

$$\mathsf{E}_e \left[y_t \mid \boldsymbol{x}_t\right] = \boldsymbol{\alpha}_t' \boldsymbol{x}_t \quad \text{where} \quad \boldsymbol{\alpha}_t = \left(\boldsymbol{\kappa}_1 + \boldsymbol{\kappa}_2 \boldsymbol{\Gamma}_{t+1}\right)' \boldsymbol{\delta}.$$

14.17.4 Implications

Combining §14.17.1 and §14.17.2 yields the following proposition. When

1 the model $y_t = \boldsymbol{\gamma}' \boldsymbol{x}_t + v_t$ has $\boldsymbol{\gamma}$ constant; and
2 the model $y_t = \boldsymbol{\delta}' \mathsf{E}[\boldsymbol{x}_{t+1} | \boldsymbol{x}_t] + \epsilon_t$ has $\boldsymbol{\delta}$ constant; but
3 the model $\boldsymbol{x}_t = \boldsymbol{\pi}_t \boldsymbol{x}_{t-1} + \boldsymbol{\eta}_t$ does not have $\boldsymbol{\pi}_t$ constant:

then the feedback model cannot be derived from a feedforward structure.

This is almost precisely the Lucas critique, but applied in the opposite direction to delineate situations when conditional models cannot have an expectations interpretation. The result is unaffected by the lack of complete information on the process by which $\boldsymbol{x}_t$ was generated, or by which expectations were formed. The information set in (14.108) is a proper one in that, even if the elements of $\boldsymbol{x}$ are $\mathsf{I}(1)$, forecasts and outcomes remain cointegrated when $\boldsymbol{\pi}$ is constant. The result holds in the population, as is essential for a clear specification of the hypotheses under consideration, so that finite-sample issues remain in terms of the size and power of any particular test implementation. Nevertheless, a high degree of constancy in a contingent plan equation is inconsistent with the joint claim of an expectations interpretation and non-constant expectations formation (Ericsson and Hendry, 1989, analyse the impact of this finding on approaches that stress empirical corroboration of theory models).

Having established the background to testing invariance, exogeneity, and expectations-based models, we consider an empirical illustration of these procedures.

14.18 Empirical testing of invariance

Both super-exogeneity tests and encompassing tests will be considered.

14.18.1 Testing super exogeneity

As usual, we investigate the velocity model for UKM1 over 1964(1)–1989(3), and begin by developing a dummy variable for policy shocks to the interest rate equation. Since the objective is to obtain the most powerful test of the invariance of the money-demand equation to regime shifts in interest rates, the dummy is based on known institutional and historical knowledge, and on data evidence as to periods when an autoregressive equation for ΔR_t manifested predictive failure. This resulted in a dummy, called *Pol*, taking the value unity in 1973(3), 1976(4), and 1985(1); minus one in 1977(1) and 1985(2); and 0.5 in 1979(3) and 1979(4). Adding *Pol* to the equation for ΔR_t yields:

$$\Delta R_t = \underset{(0.08)}{0.29}\ \Delta R_{t-1} + \underset{(0.005)}{0.035}\ Pol_t$$
$$\mathsf{R}^2 = 0.37\ \sigma = 0.011\ DW = 2.15\ JS = 0.64\ SC = -8.95. \tag{14.110}$$

The dummy is highly significant, and markedly improves the stability over time of the error variance (*VS* $= 0.44$: see Hansen, 1992a).

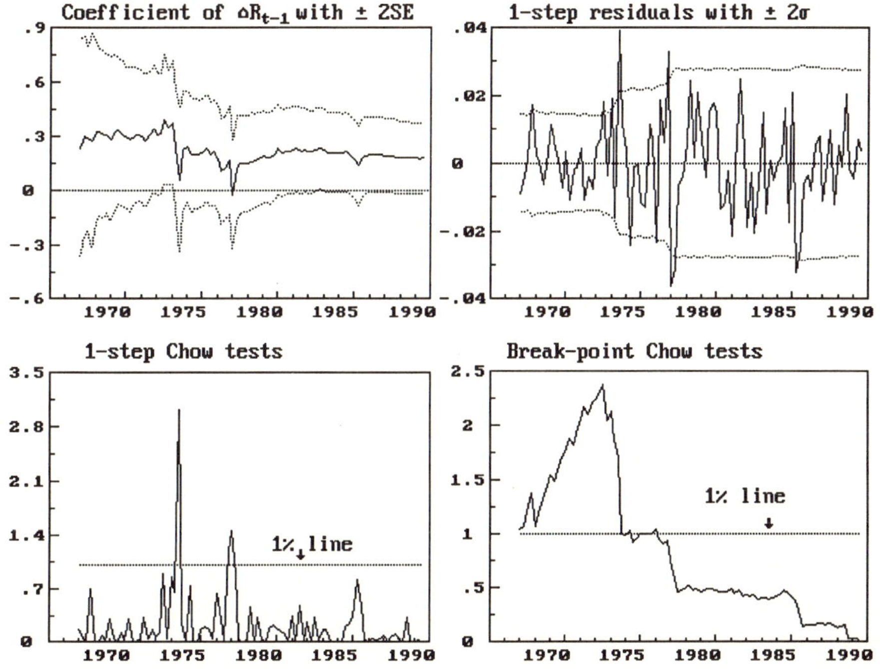

Fig. 14.1 Recursive graphical statistics for ΔR

The test of super exogeneity corresponds to adding *Pol* to the ECM equation for $\Delta \log(M/PY)$ in Chapter 7, which yields (using $ECM = \log(M/PY + 7.4R)$ as in Ch.7):

$$\Delta \log \left(\frac{M}{PY}\right)_t = \underset{(0.002)}{0.006} - \underset{(0.17)}{0.76}\ \Delta R_t - \underset{(0.010)}{0.078}\ ECM_{t-1} - \underset{(0.010)}{0.003}\ Pol_t$$

$$\mathsf{R}^2 = 0.47\ \sigma = 0.020\ DW = 2.60\ JS = 0.86\ SC = -7.66. \tag{14.111}$$

Most of the diagnostic tests produced satisfactory outcomes, with evidence of residual autocorrelation and non-normality (AR_{1-5}-$F(5, 94) = 3.3^{**}$ and normality-$\chi^2(2) = 6.3^{*}$). Thus, in the conditional model, the dummy is insignificant at any reasonable test size. If the residuals from (14.110) are added as well, the two variables remain insignificant. Such an outcome strongly supports the validity of conditioning on ΔR_t.

14.18.2 Testing encompassing

The tests here are based on checking the constancy of the conditional model in the face of a non-constant marginal model. The outcomes are reported graphically for the equations matching (14.110) and (14.111), but excluding the dummy *Pol.* Figures 14.1a–d show the outcomes for the interest-rate equation: the coefficient of ΔR_{t-1} is relatively constant, but the error variance is not, resulting in rejection on the constancy statistics in Figs. 14.1c–d for much of the sample, even at the one per cent level.

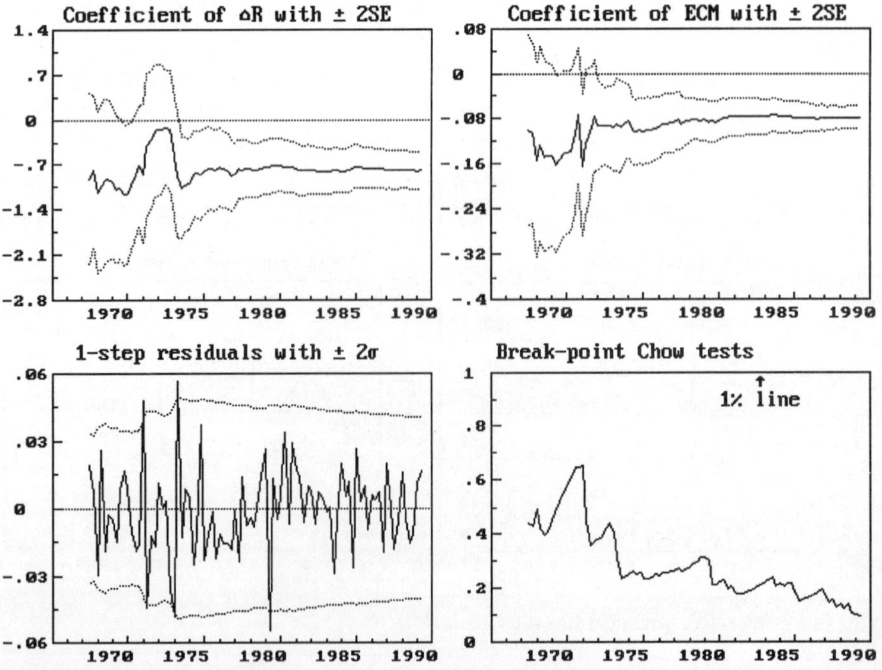

Fig. 14.2 Recursive graphical statistics for $\Delta \log M/PY$

The velocity equation, however, does not fail the same breakpoint constancy test at any point in the sample, at one-off critical values (again, of one per cent). This is consistent with agents being unable to predict changes in interest rates. If they used the type of predictor discussed in Chapter 6, it would have to be $\Delta^2 R_{t+1} = 0$ or $\Delta R_{t+1} = \Delta R_t$. This seems unlikely, and suggests that money-demand behaviour is contingent on the short-term interest rate confronting agents at the time their decisions are taken.

Thus, asserting that an empirical model which has not modelled expectations is liable to suffer from parameter change when expectations alter is not adequate grounds for its dismissal. Evidence must be presented to sustain any such claim, and the attempt to glean that evidence could lead to the opposite outcome in some instances. The class of data-based expectations processes in Chapter 6 helps explain why some econometric equations are less susceptible to predictive failure deriving from changes in expectations formation than might be anticipated, but the possibility of contingent behaviour cannot be excluded either.

14.19 Exercises

14.1 Two investigators hypothesize the following models for an observable series $\{y_t\}$:

$$\mathsf{M}_1\colon\ y_t \sim \mathsf{IN}\left[\mu, 1\right]$$

$$\mathsf{M}_2\colon\ y_t \sim \mathsf{IN}\left[0, \sigma^2\right].$$

(a) State conditions on the parameters under which M_1 encompasses M_2 (denoted $\mathsf{M}_1 \mathcal{E} \mathsf{M}_2$) and $\mathsf{M}_2 \mathcal{E} \mathsf{M}_1$. Formulate a minimal nesting model M_m which nests both M_1 and M_2, and hence show that $\mathsf{M}_1 \mathcal{E}\ \mathsf{M}_2$ if and only if $\mathsf{M}_1 \mathcal{E}_p \mathsf{M}_m$, where $\mathcal{E}_p$ denotes parsimonious encompassing.

(b) Assuming that M_1 is the DGP, obtain tests of the hypotheses $\mathsf{M}_1 \mathcal{E} \mathsf{M}_2$ and $\mathsf{M}_1 \mathcal{E}_p\ \mathsf{M}_m$, and derive their sampling distributions.

(c) Repeat (b) with the roles of M_1 and M_2 interchanged.

(d) If M_m is the DGP and comprises $y_t \sim \mathsf{IN}[\theta, \omega^2]$, where $\theta \neq 0$ and $\omega^2 \neq 1$, derive the distribution of your test that $\mathsf{M}_1 \mathcal{E}_p \mathsf{M}_m$ for a sample of size T, explaining why your test has power to reject the false encompassing claim.

(Oxford M.Phil., 1987)

14.2 Consider the two rival models:

$$\mathsf{M}_1\colon\ y_t = \beta x_t + \epsilon_t \text{ with } \epsilon_t \underset{c}{\sim} \mathsf{IN}\left[0, \sigma_\epsilon^2\right] \text{ and } \mathsf{E}\left[x_t \epsilon_t\right] = 0$$

$$\mathsf{M}_2\colon\ y_t = \gamma x_{t-1} + \nu_t \text{ with } \nu_t \underset{c}{\sim} \mathsf{IN}\left[0, \sigma_\nu^2\right] \text{ and } \mathsf{E}\left[x_{t-1} \nu_t\right] = 0,$$

where $\underset{c}{\sim}$ denotes 'is claimed to be distributed as', and both model builders accept that:

$$\mathsf{M}_3\colon\ x_t = \lambda x_{t-1} + u_t \text{ where } u_t \sim \mathsf{IN}\left[0, \sigma_u^2\right].$$

(a) What implications does M_1 have for the parameters of M_2 when M_1 and M_3 are true? Derive the converse implications of $\mathsf{M}_2 + \mathsf{M}_3$ for M_1.
(b) Explain how you would test the claim that $\mathsf{M}_1 \mathcal{E} \mathsf{M}_2$ given M_3.
(c) Prove that $\mathsf{M}_1 \mathcal{E} \mathsf{M}_2$ if and only if $\mathsf{M}_1 \mathcal{E}_p \mathsf{M}_4$ where:

$$\mathsf{M}_4\colon\ y_t = \theta_1 x_t + \theta_2 x_{t-1} + v_t \text{ where } v_t \sim \mathsf{IN}\left[0, \sigma_v^2\right].$$

(d) Is the test of $\mathsf{H}_0\colon \theta_2 = 0$ a test of $\mathsf{M}_1 \mathcal{E} \mathsf{M}_2$? Do any additional problems arise when testing $\mathsf{M}_2 \mathcal{E} \mathsf{M}_1$? Prove that if $\mathsf{M}_1 \mathcal{E} \mathsf{M}_2$, then M_2 cannot encompass M_1.
(e) Would your results be affected by discovering that y Granger-caused x?

(Oxford M.Phil., 1989)

14.3 An investigator using the model:

$$y_t = \beta z_t + u_t \tag{14.112}$$

$$u_t = \rho u_{t-1} + \epsilon_t \text{ where } \epsilon_t \sim \mathsf{IN}\left[0, \sigma_\epsilon^2\right] \tag{14.113}$$

when $|\rho| < 1$ for $t = 1, \ldots, T$, wishes to parsimoniously encompass the rival, more general model:

$$y_t = \gamma_1 z_t + \gamma_2 y_{t-1} + \gamma_3 z_{t-1} + \eta_t \text{ where } \eta_t \sim \mathsf{IN}\left[0, \sigma_\eta^2\right]. \tag{14.114}$$

The common-factor restriction on (14.114) needed to yield (14.112)+(14.113) is:

$$\mathsf{H}_0\colon\ \gamma_1 + \gamma_2\gamma_3 = 0. \tag{14.115}$$

(a) Derive a likelihood ratio test of H_0.
(b) Explain how to test H_0 by embedding (14.112)+(14.113) in a more general model H_m and testing against H_m.
(c) Describe how you might test H_0 using a Wald encompassing test based on comparing $\tilde{\beta}\tilde{\rho}$ from (14.112)+(14.113) with $\hat{\gamma}_3$ from (14.114).
(d) Briefly discuss the relative advantages, if any, of these alternative testing approaches.

(Oxford M.Phil., 1984)

14.4 Derive a Wald test W of $\mathsf{H}_0\colon \beta = 0$ against $\mathsf{H}_1\colon \beta \neq 0$ for the model:

$$\mathsf{M}_1\colon\ y_t = \beta z_t + \epsilon_t \text{ for } t = 1, \ldots, T \tag{14.116}$$

where:

$$z_t = \lambda z_{t-1} + v_t \text{ with } |\lambda| < 1 \tag{14.117}$$

when:

$$\begin{pmatrix} \epsilon_t \\ v_t \end{pmatrix} \sim \mathsf{IN}\left[\begin{pmatrix} 0 \\ 0 \end{pmatrix}, \begin{pmatrix} \sigma_{11} & 0 \\ 0 & \sigma_{22} \end{pmatrix}\right].$$

(a) Obtain the distribution under H_0 of W: (i) conditional on $(z_1 \dots z_T)$; (ii) unconditionally in large samples.

(b) Derive the large-sample distribution of W under the sequence of local alternatives H_T: $\beta = \delta/\sqrt{T}$ for fixed δ, and show that your test is consistent if $\delta = O(\sqrt{T})$.

(c) The contending hypothesis is postulated that:

$$\mathsf{M}_2\colon y_t = \gamma z_{t-1} + u_t \quad \text{where} \quad u_t \underset{c}{\sim} \mathsf{IN}\left[0, \sigma_{33}\right] \tag{14.118}$$

when $\underset{c}{\sim}$ denotes 'is distributed as claimed'. Obtain a Wald test of the hypothesis that (14.116) encompasses (14.118) (denoted $\mathsf{M}_1\mathcal{E}\ \mathsf{M}_2$), in the sense that H_3: $\gamma = \beta\lambda$ is true.

(d) Show that, when H_3 is true, then (14.118) cannot encompass (14.116). What could be concluded from the information that $\sigma_{33} > \sigma_{11}$?

(e) What other implications of (14.118) are entailed by (14.116)+(14.117), and how might an encompassing test of these by obtained ?

(Oxford M.Phil., 1982)

14.5 Two investigators disagree about whether an additive or a multiplicative model should be used for the ratio Y_t of consumption to income, where $Y_t > 0\ \forall t = 1, \dots, T$:

$$\mathsf{M}_1\colon Y_t = \beta \exp\left(\epsilon_t\right) \quad \text{with } \epsilon_t \underset{c}{\sim} \mathsf{IN}\left[0, \sigma^2\right],$$

$$\mathsf{M}_2\colon Y_t = \gamma + \nu_t \quad \text{with } \nu_t \underset{c}{\sim} \mathsf{IN}\left[0, \omega^2\right]$$

where β and γ are positive.

(a) Obtain estimators $(\hat{\beta}, \hat{\sigma}^2)$ for $\boldsymbol{\alpha} = (\beta, \sigma^2)'$ under M_1 and $(\tilde{\gamma}, \tilde{\omega}^2)$ for $\boldsymbol{\delta} = (\gamma, \omega^2)'$ under M_2 and derive their probability limits under their own hypotheses.

(b) Under M_1 obtain the following as functions of $\boldsymbol{\alpha}$:

$$\underset{T\to\infty}{\text{plim}}\ \left(\tilde{\gamma}, \tilde{\omega}^2\right) = \left(\gamma_\alpha, \omega_\alpha^2\right).$$

(c) Derive a test for $\mathsf{M}_1\mathcal{E}\mathsf{M}_2$. Show that a necessary condition is $\sigma < \omega_\alpha/\gamma_\alpha$.

(Oxford M.Phil., 1988)

14.6 Consider the rival dynamic models:

$$\mathsf{M}_1\colon y_t = \beta y_{t-1} + \epsilon_{1t} \quad \text{where } \epsilon_{1t} \underset{c}{\sim} \mathsf{IN}\left[0, \sigma_1^2\right]$$

$$\mathsf{M}_2\colon y_t = \gamma y_{t-2} + \epsilon_{2t} \quad \text{with } \epsilon_{2t} \underset{c}{\sim} \mathsf{IN}\left[0, \sigma_2^2\right],$$

when $|\beta| < 1$ and $|\gamma| < 1$ to ensure stationarity, where $\underset{c}{\sim}$ denotes that each modeller claims that the error is distributed as shown.

(a) What implications does M_1 have for the parameters of M_2 when M_1 is true? Obtain the plim of the least-squares estimator of γ in M_2 when M_1 is true. Derive the converse implications of M_2 for M_1.

(b) Explain how you would test the claim that M_1 encompasses M_2.

(c) Prove that if $\mathsf{M}_1\mathcal{E}\mathsf{M}_2$ then M_2 cannot encompass M_1.

(d) Let $\mathcal{E}_p$ denote parsimonious encompassing and consider the nesting model:

$$\mathsf{M}_3\colon\ y_t = \theta_1 y_{t-1} + \theta_2 y_{t-2} + \nu_t \text{ where } \nu_t \sim \mathsf{IN}\left[0, \sigma_\nu^2\right].$$

Obtain a test of the hypothesis that $\mathsf{M}_1\mathcal{E}_p\mathsf{M}_3$. Prove that $\mathsf{M}_1\mathcal{E}\mathsf{M}_2$ if and only if $\mathsf{M}_1\mathcal{E}_p\mathsf{M}_3$.

(e) Is the test of $\mathsf{H}_0\colon\ \theta_1 = 0$ in M_3 a test of $\mathsf{M}_2\mathcal{E}\mathsf{M}_1$? Do any additional problems arise when testing $\mathsf{M}_2\mathcal{E}\mathsf{M}_1$?

(Oxford M.Phil., 1991)

14.7 In the linear over-identified structural equation for $t = 1, \ldots, T$:

$$y_t = \boldsymbol{x}_t'\boldsymbol{\beta} + \epsilon_t \text{ where } \epsilon_t \sim \mathsf{IN}\left[0, \sigma^2\right] \tag{14.119}$$

when $\boldsymbol{\beta}$ is $k \times 1$, but $\mathsf{E}[\boldsymbol{x}_t\epsilon_t] \neq \mathbf{0}$. However, there exists a vector of $m > k$ stationary instrumental variables $\boldsymbol{z}_t$ which satisfy $\mathsf{E}[\boldsymbol{z}_t\epsilon_t] = \mathbf{0}\ \forall t$ such that:

$$\boldsymbol{x}_t = \boldsymbol{\pi}\boldsymbol{z}_t + \boldsymbol{\nu}_t \text{ where } \mathsf{E}\left[\boldsymbol{z}_t\boldsymbol{\nu}_t'\right] = \mathbf{0}\ \forall t. \tag{14.120}$$

The solved version of the structural equation (14.119), given (14.120), is:

$$y_t = \boldsymbol{z}_t'\boldsymbol{\delta} + \omega_t \text{ and } \mathsf{E}\left[\boldsymbol{z}_t\omega_t\right] = \mathbf{0}\ \forall t. \tag{14.121}$$

Derive a Wald encompassing test for the hypothesis that $\boldsymbol{\delta} = \boldsymbol{\pi}'\boldsymbol{\beta}$ and show that this is equivalent to testing the validity of the instruments $\boldsymbol{z}_t$ used for estimation, corresponding to $\mathsf{H}_0\colon\ \mathsf{E}[\boldsymbol{z}_t\epsilon_t] = \mathbf{0}$.

(Oxford M.Phil., 1991)

14.8 Two rival models are assumed by their proprietors to take the form:

$$\begin{aligned}\mathsf{M}_1\colon\ y_t &= \beta z_t + \epsilon_{1t} \text{ where } \epsilon_{1t} \underset{c}{\sim} \mathsf{IN}\left[0, \sigma_1^2\right],\\ \mathsf{M}_2\colon\ y_t &= \gamma y_{t-1} + \epsilon_{2t} \text{ with } \epsilon_{2t} \underset{c}{\sim} \mathsf{IN}\left[0, \sigma_2^2\right],\end{aligned}$$

for $|\gamma| < 1$ when $\underset{c}{\sim}$ denotes that each model claims its error to be distributed as shown. The sample size T may be taken to be arbitrarily large.

(a) What is meant by the claim that M_1 encompasses M_2, denoted $\mathsf{M}_1\mathcal{E}\mathsf{M}_2$? Explain how to derive the encompassing implications of M_1 for the parameters of M_2 when M_1 is true, and how to test the hypothesis $\mathsf{H}_0\colon\ \mathsf{M}_1\mathcal{E}\mathsf{M}_2$ without risking incorrectly rejecting either model.

(b) Derive the converse encompassing implications of M_2 for M_1. Prove that if $\mathsf{M}_1\mathcal{E}\mathsf{M}_2$ then either M_2 cannot encompass M_1 or the two models are isomorphic.

(c) Explain how your tests in (a) and (b) relate to simplification F-tests in the nesting model:

$$\mathsf{M}_3\colon\ y_t = \theta_1 z_t + \theta_2 y_{t-1} + \nu_t \text{ where } \nu_t \sim \mathsf{IN}\left[0, \sigma_\nu^2\right].$$

Is the test of $\mathsf{H}_0\colon\ \theta_2 = 0$ in M_3 a test of $\mathsf{M}_1\mathcal{E}\mathsf{M}_2$? Do any additional problems arise when testing $\mathsf{M}_2\mathcal{E}\mathsf{M}_1$?

(Oxford M.Phil., 1992)

14.9 Derive encompassing predictions for at least three members of the typology in Chapter 7, both against the AD(1, 1) DGP, and against each other. Write the AD(1, 1) model as:

$$y_t = \beta_0 + \beta_1 z_t + \beta_2 z_{t-1} + \beta_3 y_{t-1} + \epsilon_t \text{where } \epsilon_t \sim \mathsf{IN}[0, \sigma^2]. \qquad (14.122)$$

(a) How would you test the weak exogeneity of z_t for β in (14.122)?
(b) How would you test the super exogeneity of z_t for β in (14.122)?
(c) Derive a recursively computable test of the validity of the AD(1, 1) model when (14.122) holds. Describe how to use a recursive approach to testing the claim that z_t is super exogenous for β. Apply your proposed test using the UKM1 data with $\log(M/(PY))$ as y_t, and R as z_t.
(d) What conclusions can be drawn about the validity of a claim that the parameters of your 'money demand' model are immune to the Lucas critique?
(e) Compare three members of the typology on the data-set DATA, considering their mutual encompassing predictions, and testing recursively for any super exogeneity claims you might wish to entertain.

14.10 An investigator wishes to ascertain which (if either) of the following two models is valid:

$$\mathsf{M}_1\colon \mathsf{E}[y_t \mid x_t] = \beta x_t,$$

or:

$$\mathsf{M}_2\colon \mathsf{E}[y_t \mid z_t] = \beta \mathsf{E}[x_t \mid z_t],$$

when the joint distribution of $\boldsymbol{w}_t = (y_t : x_t : z_t)'$ is:

$$\boldsymbol{w}_t \mid \boldsymbol{w}_{t-1} \sim \mathsf{N}_3[\boldsymbol{\Pi} \boldsymbol{w}_{t-1}, \boldsymbol{\Omega}],$$

where

$$\boldsymbol{\Pi} = \begin{pmatrix} 0 & \alpha & \mu \\ 0 & \gamma & \delta \\ 0 & \phi & \lambda \end{pmatrix} \text{ and } \boldsymbol{\Omega} = \begin{pmatrix} \omega_{11} & \omega_{12} & \omega_{13} \\ \omega_{21} & \omega_{22} & \omega_{23} \\ \omega_{31} & \omega_{32} & \omega_{33} \end{pmatrix}.$$

(a) Under what conditions are (i) x_t; and (ii) z_t, weakly exogenous for β?
(b) Taking M_1 and M_2 in turn as the DGP, where $\mathcal{E}$ denotes encompassing:
   (i) Obtain a variance ranking between the rival specifications.
   (ii) Under what conditions on $(\boldsymbol{\Pi}, \boldsymbol{\Omega})$ does $\mathsf{M}_1 \mathcal{E} \mathsf{M}_2$?
   (iii) Under what conditions on $(\boldsymbol{\Pi}, \boldsymbol{\Omega})$ does $\mathsf{M}_2 \mathcal{E} \mathsf{M}_1$?
   (iv) Derive two tests of the hypothesis that $\mathsf{M}_1 \mathcal{E} \mathsf{M}_2$ and one of the hypothesis that $\mathsf{M}_2 \mathcal{E} \mathsf{M}_1$.
   (v) Carefully explain how your answer would be altered by the discovery that δ varied over a sample $t = 1, \ldots, T$.

(Adapted from Oxford M.Phil., 1988)

15
Modelling Issues

This chapter takes up the analysis of many problems noted at earlier stages. Data mining is shown to have three distinct meanings, and is detectable when it denotes ignoring, or camouflaging, conflicting evidence in a prejudiced search for an acceptable model. The twin dangers of excessive theory dependence versus sample dependence of models are investigated. This leads to a discussion of progressive research strategies and the ability of alternative approaches to determine structure when it exists. Then we look again at the converse problem (Pyrrho's lemma), namely, that one can obtain any desired regression outcome by the addition of one more regressor to any model. This is potentially the extreme of data mining, and an aspect of the fact that empirical models can be formulated in-sample to satisfy design criteria.

Next, we consider the more practical concerns of the properties of dummy variables, and the impacts of seasonal adjustment on integrated-cointegrated data when used in modelling dynamic systems. The adequacy of approximating moving-average processes by autoregressive schemes is investigated. Finally, we turn to modelling second moments, and the relation between population and sample analyses, emphasising the need for a clear distinction to interpret data evidence.

15.1 Data mining

'Data mining' is an accusation sometimes used to dismiss results where empirical evidence is deemed to have played an excessive role in modelling. We consider three possible senses (see Leamer, 1978, and Ch.1).

The first meaning is that of a prejudiced search for an acceptable model, a problem which may be believed to vitiate any substantive role for empirical evidence in economics. Since models can be designed to satisfy selection criteria, we must distinguish that legitimate productive activity from one of 'torturing data till a false confession is obtained'. Following Gilbert (1986), we distinguish weak data mining, whereby corroboration is sought for a prior belief, from strong data mining in which conflicting evidence is camouflaged, ignored, or not reported. Weak data mining is prone to paradoxes of corroboration as discussed in Chapter 14. However, a model-search process which deliberately ignores or camouflages conflicting results, as in strong data mining, is unscientific. Both are open to adversarial scrutiny which checks how well the resulting model accounts for the findings of rival studies. The resolution of potential data-mining criticisms in these senses is to explain the *Gestalt* of empirical evidence: strong fails immediately as there is already known conflicting evidence; weak will fail when other models cannot be encompassed — and if they can, then an undominated model results, so the criticism fails.

The second sense of 'data mining' arises because empirical models are often accompanied by test statistics which appear to assess their adequacy, yet tests can be made insignificant by iteratively revising models in the light of adverse data evidence, as demonstrated in Chapters 1 and 6. A clear reporting distinction is needed between test statistics which are used as model-design criteria (indices which reflect the exploitation of data evidence) and tests in the Neyman–Pearson sense (which use previously unavailable evidence). The former concern the adequacy of model design; the latter the adequacy of the model: implicit-design strategies may mislead as to the interpretation of diagnostic tests. Since the investigator alone knows whether the reported statistics were used in model selection or were genuine tests, the only real solution to the second sense is post-sample testing on new data, against new rival models, or by applying new tests.

The third sense is one in which the uncertainty in the reported results does not reflect the true uncertainty in the study. One of the methodological worries sometimes expressed about general-to-specific modelling, is that it is just 'sophisticated data mining'. As an analogy, imagine a 'hyper non-parametric estimator', which, given a large class of distribution functions, an array of possible functional forms and lag lengths, and a large set of potential regressors, estimates a unique model, and properly calibrates the estimation uncertainty in its reported unconditional standard errors. Such an approach is strongly data based, but, as an extension of conventional estimation methods, is hardly data mining. By way of contrast, the approach in this book would have selected a model by reduction, and reported the final — conditional — estimates and their associated uncertainty. The reported standard errors are those that would arise from one-off estimation of the selected specification, and do not reflect the selection process. I regard it as a virtue of the reduction approach that it conditions on the final model, when that selection is congruent: the validity of the model is an intrinsic property, neither impugned nor sustained by the discovery path (see Ch.1). As argued in Chapter 10, following Mayo (1981), diagnostic test information is effectively independent of the sufficient statistics, so 'discounting' for such tests is not necessary. The conditioning involved is more complicated than in a regression context, but, when valid, delivers a more precise outcome, just as weak exogeneity does for single-equation estimates. Conversely, it is essential that the model be a valid reduction to sustain the conditioning. The proposed solution in Leamer (1983) of his extreme-bounds analysis can be understood from this viewpoint as an attempt to infer the implicit uncertainty from published estimates alone, without knowing the search path; unfortunately, it has technical drawbacks discussed in McAleer, Pagan and Volker (1985), Breusch (1990) and Ericsson (1993b).

Encompassing throws light on all these senses of 'data mining'. To borrow the example in Gilbert (1986), take all the output of any empirical study and separate it into two piles, where the first contains every result that is redundant because it is parsimoniously encompassed by the finally selected model, and the second contains all other interim findings. If the second pile has any members, then there has been data mining. Many of the models used in extreme bounds analysis to evaluate the uncertainty are invalid reductions that are encompassed by the reported estimates, so support, rather than detract from, the final selection (see Hendry and Mizon, 1990). When all results are encompassed by a parsimonious, data coherent, and interpretable empirical model which has constant parameters historically, then that model constitutes a useful addition to empirical understanding of the economic mechanism under investigation, as part of a progressive accumulation of knowledge. The cycle is completed by testing the model against new data, and consolidating the resulting knowledge in a theoretical framework which also accounts for other phenomena of interest.

15.2 Theory dependence versus sample dependence

Theory dependence is construed as the problem that the 'empirical' results are merely a quantified theory model, and are therefore no more, nor less, valid than the initial theory. Sample dependence is the opposite extreme where the results are subject to important sampling vagaries, so data mining might be seen as likely to induce a high degree of sample dependence. Spanos (1990) provides an excellent overview on the relation of theory and evidence in econometric modelling.

15.2.1 Theory-driven approaches

In one approach to empirical economics, a theoretical model is postulated, and data evidence is used to calibrate its parameters; little testing is done and little is learnt from the data, possibly because of concerns with pre-test problems (see Ch.10). Such 'theory-driven' approaches, where a model is derived from a priori theory and calibrated from data evidence, suffer from theory dependence. The credibility of the resulting models depends on the credibility of the theory from which they arose, and when that theory is discarded, so is the associated evidence (see Kydland and Prescott, 1991). Since economic theory is progressing rapidly, theory dependence is likely to induce transient and non-structural evidence.

A particular problem for this approach (though it occurs in a less extreme form in all approaches) is how to proceed when the empirical evidence cannot be made consistent with the theoretical model. If the empirical implementation is rejected, the theory must lose credibility as it cannot explain the empirical results; whereas if the implementation is not rejected, the theory must be altered to avoid maintaining two contradictory propositions. If the theory is revised to match the evidence, then it may become *ad hoc*. Of course, the phenomena that induced rejection may be unrelated to the ostensible nature of the test used: for example, the measurement process may be at fault. Evidence that this is so must be adduced to 'rescue' the theory model. In practice, the empirical model, the measurement instruments and the theory may be revised till consistency is achieved (see Ch.1). Depending on how model design is implemented, the result may or may not lack credibility. Postulating an endless sequence of models and theories that get rejected in turn fails to incorporate learning from the evidence. The proposed solution here is to conduct research in a progressive framework of successively encompassing congruent models consolidated by empirically relevant theories.

15.2.2 Data-driven approaches

An alternative approach abandons structural modelling, and estimates data descriptive models such as ARIMAs or VARs. 'Data-driven' approaches, where models are developed just to describe the data, suffer from sample dependence, in that accidental and transient data features are embodied as tightly in the model as permanent aspects, so that extensions of the data-set may reveal predictive failure. Restrictions are sometimes imposed to offset this problem. These could be data-based as in Box and Jenkins (1976) modelling, with its data 'identification' procedures; or may claim an extraneous source as in the 'Minnesota prior' which 'shrinks' lagged-dependent variable parameters towards unity, and others towards zero relative to the data evidence (see Doan, Litterman and Sims, 1984). However, such restrictions will deliver structure only if the resulting parameters are indeed invariant aspects of the underlying autonomous relations. Section 15.1 discussed the related problem of data mining.

15.2.3 Bayesian approaches

Bayesians consider internal coherence of inference to be a dominant requirement, and while some claim to embody all available evidence in their approach, this assumes away the more basic problems as to what constitutes legitimate evidence, and how it was acquired (see Leamer, 1978, and contrast Florens, Mouchart and Rolin, 1990). For individual decision taking, such an issue is not pertinent; but in a public process like science aimed at progressive discovery, it is a major lacuna (see the debate in Hendry, Leamer and Poirier, 1990). In particular, any interdict against testing can reduce the chances of discovering structure. Otherwise, there seem to be no issues of principle between classical and Bayesian inference concerning the roles of economic theory and evidence, and many of the procedures discussed earlier have close Bayesian counterparts (see Florens *et al.*, 1990, and Florens, Hendry and Richard, 1994).

15.2.4 Data modelling using economic theory guidelines

The approach advocated in this book attempts to merge inference from data with guidelines from economic theory, emphasizing empirical models as reductions which can be designed to be congruent. It seeks to characterize data parsimoniously in a general economic theoretical framework, as well as providing a statistical baseline against which other models can be evaluated, so the drawbacks of data mining and theory calibration do not apply to such an approach.

All approaches in econometrics base their conclusions on a mixture of theory and evidence, but accord different weights to the components, and often have different constructions of admissible theory. These major differences in approach reflect genuine difficulties in empirical economics and are not merely fads. There are obvious dangers in trying to learn more from combining an abstract, idealised, incomplete and evolving theory model with a relatively short, autocorrelated, non-homogeneous, non-stationary, imprecise and inaccurate data sample than it can reasonably yield. Theory-based models are unlikely to describe the data, whereas data-selected models are more likely to fail in social, than natural, sciences when new observations appear. The problem of sample dependence of findings is especially acute in practice, because all aspects of an empirical model can be designed to satisfy pre-assigned criteria, including parameter constancy, highlighting the distinction between explanation and prediction (see Hendry and Starr, 1993). The need to identify structural relations if congruent and invariant models are to be developed and weak exogeneity maintained, highlights one role for economic analysis but necessitates that theory can in fact deliver ideas about permanent relationships. The major issue remains the respective weights to be accorded to theory dependence and sample dependence of econometric evidence.

Consider the following simplified model of money demand where m, p, y, and R respectively denote logs of nominal money, the price level, aggregate income, and the level of the interest rate, expressed in restricted form as:

$$\Delta m_t = \rho_0 - \rho_1 \Delta (m - p - y)_{t-1} - \rho_2 (m - p - y)_{t-2} - \rho_3 R_t + \epsilon_t. \qquad (15.1)$$

The model embodies unit long-run, but zero short-run, price and income elasticities, and is postulated to have 4 structural parameters $(\rho_0, \rho_1, \rho_2, \rho_3)$. Once such a formulation is known, it is trivial to estimate, but the exact specification of the dynamic reactions is unlikely to be known, so we contrast (15.1) with an initial unrestricted equation of the form:

$$m_t = \gamma_0 + \sum_{i=0}^{2} \gamma_{1+i} p_{t-i} + \sum_{i=1}^{2} \gamma_{3+i} m_{t-i} + \sum_{i=0}^{2} \gamma_{6+i} y_{t-i} + \sum_{i=0}^{2} \gamma_{9+i} R_{t-i} + e_t. \quad (15.2)$$

Then:

$$\begin{aligned}&\gamma_0 = \rho_0;\ \gamma_1 = 0;\ \gamma_2 = \rho_1;\ \gamma_3 = -\rho_1 + \rho_2;\ \gamma_4 = 1 - \rho_1;\ \gamma_5 = \rho_1 - \rho_2;\\ &\gamma_6 = 0;\ \gamma_7 = \rho_1;\ \gamma_8 = -\rho_1 + \rho_2;\ \gamma_9 = -\rho_3;\ \gamma_{10} = 0;\ \gamma_{11} = 0.\end{aligned}$$

It is hard to imagine the sample dependence of the coefficients in (15.2) not exceeding that of the parameters in (15.1), since the presence of many free regressors allows the general equation to capture accidental features of the sample. In such a case, simplification to (15.1) clearly reduces sample dependence.

To illustrate the analysis empirically, we consider the UK money-demand model in Hendry and Ericsson (1991b) which de-restricts the earlier velocity equation from Chapter 6 (this model is also studied by Boswijk, 1992, Ericsson, Campos and Tran, 1990, Ericsson, Hendry and Tran, 1994, Hendry and Mizon, 1993, and Johansen, 1992c). The complete vector analysed over 1964(1)–1989(2) is $\boldsymbol{x}_t = (m_t - p_t, y_t, \Delta p_t, R_t)$: long-run price homogeneity was imposed in order to reduce the analysis from I(2) to I(1). The resulting series are I(1) for most of the sample, but the degree of integration is not an inherent property of a time series: before 1984, R_t is an I(1) level variable, whereas after 1984, it is a stationary differential. While such 'regime shifts' affect some approaches more than others, an analysis which concludes with an I(0) congruent, invariant and encompassing explanation is not dependent on assuming a constant degree of integration.

The unrestricted estimates are recorded in Table 15.1, and the restricted estimates from (15.1) in Table 15.2. The restricted model has more precise estimates, yet is consistent with the unrestricted formulation. The PcGive unit-root test was −6.0** (see Ch.7), confirming cointegration, and the long-run solved equation from (15.2) with price homogeneity imposed was:

$$\underset{}{(m-p)} = -\underset{(1.5)}{0.74} + \underset{(0.13)}{1.09}\ y - \underset{(1.9)}{7.1}\ \Delta p - \underset{(0.7)}{7.3}\ R.$$

This is consistent with the earlier ECM (see Ch.6), but shows an important role for inflation.

Table 15.1 Unrestricted money-demand equation

	0	1	2	Σ
$m-p$	-1	0.66	0.24	-0.09
		(0.16)	(0.09)	(0.02)
y	-0.01	0.23	-0.12	0.10
	(0.10)	(0.13)	(0.10)	(0.01)
Δp	-0.91	-0.02	0.23	-0.66
	(0.19)	(0.23)	(0.19)	(0.15)
R	-0.46	-0.26	0.03	-0.68
–	(0.11)	(0.17)	(0.12)	(0.10)
1	-0.06	–	–	-0.06
–	(0.13)	–	–	(0.13)

Table 15.2 Restricted money-demand equation

	0	1	2	Σ
$m-p$	-1	0.71	0.20	-0.09
		(0.06)	–	(0.01)
y	0.00	0.29	-0.20	0.09
	–	(0.06)	–	(0.01)
Δp	-1.00	0.00	0.00	-1.00
	–	–	–	–
R	-0.56	0.00	0.00	-0.56
–	(0.05)	–	–	(0.05)
1	-0.02	–	–	-0.02
–	(0.01)	–	–	(0.01)

Simplification could also exacerbate sample dependence if the influences of accidental aspects are captured more 'significantly' by linear combinations of the variables. When many regressors are included, as may occur in the unrestricted formulation, combinations of these can act, in effect, as dummies for chance coincidences with 'blips' in the dependent variable. This difficulty may be offset by reference to a theory model, but anyway is a transient problem since an extended data sample will reveal the accidental nature of the earlier effects by their becoming less significant. Recursive estimates should increase in significance as the sample extends, and a failure to do so suggests carefully considering the role of the associated regressors. A major focus of empirical modelling must be to mitigate the sample dependence of findings by linking evidence and theory. The next section addresses this issue.

15.3 Progressive research strategies

The value of research based on an imperfect model is addressed in this section. Economies are subject to regime shifts, and technological and financial innovations which force adaptation and learning by economic agents. Such changes induce different forms of non-stationarity, which require careful empirical modelling if invariant parameters are to be established. In practice, empirical studies in econometrics are limited in scope over time and information sets, often comprising a restricted set of variables relative to the potentially important determinants of any economic phenomena. Thus, it is unsurprising that evidence in economics is less secure than in natural sciences, a difficulty exacerbated by the tiny allocation of resources to data collection in economics.

In Chapter 2, the concept of structure was defined as the set of invariant attributes of the economic mechanism. Thus, $\boldsymbol{\theta} \in \Theta$ defines a structure if it is invariant under all extensions of the information set (over time, variables, and interventions) and directly characterizes the relations of the economy under analysis (i.e. is not derived from more basic parameters). When $\boldsymbol{\theta} \in \Theta$ is structural and $\boldsymbol{\gamma} = \boldsymbol{f}(\boldsymbol{\theta})$ then $\boldsymbol{\gamma}$ is not structural even when it is invariant to all three extensions of information, since it is a derived parameter. On such a conceptualization, economic theory is not necessary to define structure and is certainly not sufficient: the property that a theory parameter is 'structural' within a given theory is not sufficient to make it structural in a rival theory, or in any empirical model. Conversely, the empirical invariance of a parameter is also insufficient.

An important implication of this conceptual framework is that when structure exists, it can be determined in a progressive research strategy, so that partial knowledge of structure could be acquired without complete knowledge in advance of what structure actually comprises. Without such a result, no genuine knowledge could be acquired till everything was known, vitiating the concept of a science: historical scientific progress supports the view that partial knowledge is feasible (see Ch.1). We do not claim that the world must satisfy the strong assumptions needed to sustain the existence of a structure, merely that when it does so, a progressive research strategy can acquire empirical knowledge without complete prior information as to the nature of that structure. That logic is now applied to analyse six aspects of econometric modelling.

15.3.1 Identified cointegration vectors

Given the information set $\{\boldsymbol{x}_t\}$ and cointegration space, $\boldsymbol{\alpha\beta}' \equiv \boldsymbol{\alpha PP}^{-1}\boldsymbol{\beta}' = \boldsymbol{\alpha}^*\boldsymbol{\beta}^{*\prime}$, so without further restrictions any coordinate system is acceptable. For example, in Phillips (1991), reduced-form cointegration vectors are made unique by expressing $\boldsymbol{\beta}'$ as $[\boldsymbol{I}_r : \boldsymbol{\beta}_a']$. However, unless valid identifying restrictions are imposed, the set of cointegrating vectors will not correspond to a structural relation, and need not be interpretable in the light of theory. When the empirical analysis yields $\alpha^*\beta^{*\prime}$ instead of $\alpha\beta'$, let the first vector be $\beta_1^{*\prime}x_{t-1} = \beta_1' x_{t-1} + \beta_2' x_{t-1}$. This has two consequences. First, by using $\beta_1^{*\prime}x_{t-1}$ rather than $\beta_1' x_{t-1}$, the unwanted I(0) combination $\beta_2' x_{t-1}$ makes the resulting equation non-structural. Secondly, if $\beta_2' x_{t-1}$ enters any other equation, weak exogeneity will be violated with the adverse implications for inference noted above.

Conversely, consider the cointegrating matrix β. Once sufficient valid restrictions are imposed to ensure unique identification of every element, such that the resulting characterization of the long run matches that of the DGP and is constant over prolonged periods of time, then β constitutes structural knowledge. To identify the structural cointegration vectors β necessitates both careful formulation of the long-run economic analysis and thorough testing of the requisite restrictions on the eigenvectors. Johansen and Juselius (1990) show the latter aspect in operation, and Hendry and Mizon (1993) investigate the former. Once an identifiable β is determined, it is unique under extensions of the information set. This follows because $\beta' x_t$ is I(0), and once β is identifiable then that is not affected by the presence of additional (I(0) or I(1)) variables. Indeed, in a linear system, β is an invariant, and cointegration could be defined by that property. For example (see Banerjee, Dolado, Galbraith and Hendry, 1993), pre-multiply (8.13) by any non-singular $n \times n$ matrix H:

$$\begin{aligned} H\Delta x_t &= \sum_{i=1}^{s-1} HA_i^*\Delta x_{t-i} + H\pi x_{t-1} + HKq_t + H\nu_t \\ &= \sum_{i=1}^{s-1} A_i^\diamond \Delta x_{t-i} + \alpha^\diamond \beta' x_{t-1} + K^\diamond q_t + \nu_t^\diamond . \end{aligned}$$

The adjustment coefficients are altered to $\alpha^\diamond = H\alpha$, whereas $\beta' x_t$ remain the cointegrating vectors. This result extends to I(2) processes, and to conditional models of y_t given z_t, where the transformation $\Sigma_{12}\Sigma_{22}^{-1}$ again only affects α. As shown in section 15.6, β is invariant to seasonal adjustment, so it is worth establishing identified β.

To illustrate this analysis, consider the VAR of the vector x_t analysed in section 15.2 above. Basing the specification on Hendry and Mizon (1993), a constant, linear trend t, and dummy variables $DOUT$ and $DOIL$ for major government and oil shocks are included; t only enters the cointegration space as otherwise it would induce a quadratic trend (see Ch.8). The cointegration statistics are shown in Table 15.3 (Ch.11 discusses the estimation theory).

Table 15.3 Four-variable cointegration analysis

$\hat{\beta}'$	$m-p$	y	Δp	R_n	t
$m-p$	1	−1.0	7.0	7.0	0
y	0	1	−3.4	1.8	−0.0063

r	1	2	3	4
μ_r	0.56	0.40	0.12	0.06
Max	74.9**	47.6**	12.2	5.9
Tr	140.6**	65.7**	18.1	5.9

There are two identified cointegration vectors. The first corresponds to the long-run money-demand function (closely similar to that above). The second is interpretable as an excess-demand relation connecting the deviation of output from trend ($y^* = y - 0.006t$) to the rate of interest and inflation. The eigenvalues are denoted by μ_r, and Max and Tr are the maximal and trace tests from Johansen (1988), adjusted for degrees of freedom, using critical values from Osterwald-Lenum (1992).

When $(m - p)$ is omitted from the analysis, the excess-demand relation remains, showing its invariance to the extension of the information set to include real money. When y_t is omitted, a long-run money relation still emerges, but as a non-structural cointegration relation which does not conform to any transactions-demand theory. Table 15.4 reports the estimates.

Table 15.4 Three-variable cointegration analysis

$$\begin{bmatrix} \hat{\beta}' & y & \Delta p & R_n & t \\ y & 1 & -0.4 & 1.9 & -0.0066 \end{bmatrix} \quad \begin{bmatrix} \hat{\beta}' & m-p & \Delta p & R_n & t \\ m-p & 1 & 5.8 & 8.8 & -0.0075 \end{bmatrix}$$

$$\begin{bmatrix} r & 1 & 2 & 3 \\ \mu_r & 0.52 & 0.11 & 0.05 \\ Max & 71.9^{**} & 11.6 & 4.9 \\ Tr & 88.5^{**} & 16.6 & 4.9 \end{bmatrix} \quad \begin{bmatrix} r & 1 & 2 & 3 \\ \mu_r & 0.55 & 0.10 & 0.06 \\ Max & 78.4^{**} & 10.4 & 6.4 \\ Tr & 95.1^{**} & 16.8 & 6.4 \end{bmatrix}$$

Apart from the much smaller coefficient of inflation on excess demand, the cointegrating outcomes are similar between the tables.

15.3.2 Orthogonal parameters

A second example is a linear conditional model with variables which are super exogenous for the parameters,are mutually orthogonal, and are orthogonal to excluded functions of information. Again, extending the information set over time, across regime shifts or by additional variables will not alter the knowledge achieved, and by being invariant and constant, such parameters satisfy all the testable attributes of structurality. When economic agents also orthogonalize information in their decision rules, the entailed model could capture structural information. The parameters may not in fact correspond to the actual hidden structure, but meta-considerations would be needed to decide on that issue. The point is one of principle: regression parameters could embody structure. In practice, conditional models with nearly orthogonal parameters have proved surprisingly durable and robust. A possible example is provided by the sequence of studies on the UK consumption function from DHSY through Hendry, Muellbauer and Murphy (1990), Harvey and Scott (1993) and Hendry (1994a), who find the initial dynamic and equilibrium-correction parameters recurring in extended information sets, and over longer time periods, despite regime shifts.

By way of contrast, other modelling approaches seem to need an additional assumption of omniscience (or axiom of correct specification: see Leamer, 1978) to justify a claim to structurality. We consider three examples.

15.3.3 Inappropriate estimation

Perhaps the greatest worry from using 'inconsistent' estimators is that they deliver different parameters in the empirical model than those which could have been obtained by more appropriate methods applied to the SGM. Consequently, structure could be lost despite a clever prior analysis. For example, as shown in Campos, Ericsson and Hendry (1993), if the 2-step method proposed by Engle and Granger (1987) is used when the imposed COMFAC restrictions are invalid (see Kremers, Ericsson and Dolado, 1992 , and Ch.7), breaks in marginal distributions are carried into the estimates, and structurality can be lost in the model despite its presence in reality. Thus, the operating characteristics of our instruments merit careful analysis to ensure that econometric procedures do not lose hard-earned insights. Since so-called 'calibration' methods have been subjected to little formal analysis, and what exists is rather critical (see Canova, Finn and Pagan, 1992, and Kim and Pagan, 1993), one must be concerned that implementations of the resulting models could be non-structural even when the theory happened to capture some structural aspects of reality.

15.3.4 Common trends

A common-trend function of the data, such as $\beta'_{\perp} x_t$, will usually be altered when I(1) variables z_t are added to an analysis, and hence cannot be structural in general — without the added assumption of omniscience. This result is a direct implication of empirical models being derived by reduction, so that their errors contain everything not yet modelled. Unless the system within which the common trends are determined is complete and constant, so no marginalization has in fact occurred, additional variables will alter the combinations labelled as common trends.

15.3.5 Residual analysis

The same difficulty plagues attempts to interpret errors in other ways, such as in impulse response analyses (see Sims, 1980), or as corresponding to 'supply' or 'demand' shocks (see Blanchard and Quah, 1989). It is worth stressing that a model could embody (partial) structure in its parameters yet have non-structural errors. Focusing on the unmodelled component in an analysis seems unlikely to be as productive as seeking to interpret what has been explicitly modelled.

15.3.6 Expectations and structure

A mixed possibility arises in the final example. The concept of generic refutation discussed in Chapter 14 is most powerfully implemented by using mutual counter-examples as the encompassing contenders against which to test (see Boland, 1989, and Favero and Hendry, 1992). The Lucas (1976) critique of the dependence of econometric model parameters on changing expectations processes automatically leads to a counter-example to a claimed invariant conditional model. Since the converse also holds, a 'crucial' test between them is feasible: there are automatically two mutually-inconsistent theories when expectations are involved (see Hendry, 1988). When no member of one class can encompass a congruent representative of the other, then that class is in grave doubt. The approach used is not a formal statistical test, and the Type I error (falsely rejecting the expectations null) is unknown. A more formal testing approach may be possible, deriving the distribution of the constancy tests of the conditional model when the null is true and the marginal processes alter, although it would have to resolve the issue of successive tests being dependent (suggesting the use of 1-step statistics).

Favero and Hendry (1992) show that the powers of tests to reject mis-specified conditional models for coefficient or error-variance changes in expectations processes are low. However, the same tests have high powers to detect the omission of relevant variables which are subject to interventions. Thus, if the relevant policy metric is the closeness of the outcome to the target, the Lucas critique may lack force in practice (see the evidence in Ericsson and Irons, 1994). Chapter 14 also showed that such an implication holds even when expectations-formation processes are incompletely specified. We conclude that the possible role of expectations in agent behaviour may, but need not, preclude learning about the economic structure from data evidence.

15.4 Pyrrho's lemma

The force of this lemma was discussed by Wold and Juréen (1953), but named and extended by Dijkstra (1992). Pyrrho's lemma is the result that, by the addition of one more regressor to a linear model, one can obtain any desired regression outcome for the size and sign of coefficients, and goodness of fit, as well as satisfy in-sample forecast tests. While apparently inimical to the empirical enterprise, the lemma is closely related to the notion that models are designed, and confirms the methodological imperative to test results outside their design context.

Write a regression model in standard notation as:

$$\boldsymbol{y} = \boldsymbol{X\beta} + \boldsymbol{u}, \tag{15.3}$$

where $\boldsymbol{X}$ is $T \times k$ and $\boldsymbol{\beta}$ is $k \times 1$. The OLS estimator of $\boldsymbol{\beta}$ is:

$$\widehat{\boldsymbol{\beta}} = (\boldsymbol{X}'\boldsymbol{X})^{-1} \boldsymbol{X}'\boldsymbol{y}. \tag{15.4}$$

If an additional regressor $\boldsymbol{z}$ is added, then the regression becomes:

$$\boldsymbol{y} = \boldsymbol{Xb} + \boldsymbol{z}c + \boldsymbol{v} = \boldsymbol{W\lambda} + \boldsymbol{v}, \tag{15.5}$$

where $\boldsymbol{W} = (\boldsymbol{X} : \boldsymbol{z})$ and $\boldsymbol{\lambda}' = (\boldsymbol{b}' : c)$. Consider the following specific choice of the regressor $\boldsymbol{z}$:

$$\boldsymbol{z} = \boldsymbol{X\alpha} + \left(\boldsymbol{y} - \boldsymbol{X}\widehat{\boldsymbol{\beta}}\right)\gamma + \boldsymbol{d}, \tag{15.6}$$

where $\boldsymbol{d}$ is $T \times 1$ and orthogonal to $\boldsymbol{X}$ by construction. $\boldsymbol{y} - \boldsymbol{X}\widehat{\boldsymbol{\beta}} = \widehat{\boldsymbol{u}}$ comprises the new information in z relative to X. Since $X'd = 0 = X'\hat{u}$, when estimating (15.5):

$$\begin{pmatrix} \hat{b} \\ \hat{c} \end{pmatrix} = \begin{pmatrix} X'X & X'z \\ z'X & z'z \end{pmatrix}^{-1} \begin{pmatrix} X'y \\ z'y \end{pmatrix} = \begin{pmatrix} X'X & X'X\alpha \\ \alpha'X'X & \alpha'X'X\alpha + h \end{pmatrix}^{-1} \begin{pmatrix} X'y \\ z'y \end{pmatrix} \tag{15.7}$$

where $h = \gamma^2\hat{u}'\hat{u} + d'd$. Using partitioned inversion:

$$\begin{pmatrix} X'X & X'X\alpha \\ \alpha'X'X & \alpha'X'X\alpha + h \end{pmatrix}^{-1} = \begin{pmatrix} (X'X)^{-1} + \alpha\alpha'h^{-1} & \alpha h^{-1} \\ -\alpha'h^{-1} & h^{-1} \end{pmatrix}, \tag{15.8}$$

then as $\hat{u}'y = \hat{u}'\hat{u}$ (see Ch.A3):

$$\begin{pmatrix} \hat{b} \\ \hat{c} \end{pmatrix} = \begin{pmatrix} (X'X)^{-1} + \alpha\alpha'h^{-1} & \alpha h^{-1} \\ -\alpha'h^{-1} & h^{-1} \end{pmatrix} \begin{pmatrix} X'y \\ \alpha'X'y + \gamma\hat{u}'y + d'y \end{pmatrix} = \begin{pmatrix} \hat{\beta} - \alpha\hat{c} \\ h^{-1}(\gamma\hat{u}'\hat{u} + d'y) \end{pmatrix}.$$

Thus, by appropriate choice of α in the construction of z, while ensuring $\hat{c} \neq 0$, we can make $\hat{b}$ equal to any desired value. The RSS value from (15.3) is:

$$RSS_X = \hat{u}'\hat{u} = y'Q_X y,$$

where $Q_X = (I_T - X(X'X)^{-1}X')$. From (15.5) and (15.6):

$$\hat{v} = y - X\left(\hat{\beta} - \alpha\hat{c}\right) - z\hat{c} = Q_X y + (X\alpha - z)\hat{c} = (1 - \hat{c}\gamma)\hat{u} - \hat{c}d, \tag{15.9}$$

so the RSS from (15.5) is:

$$RSS_W = \hat{v}'\hat{v} = y'Q_W y,$$

which can be made as small as desired by selecting γ and d.

For 'post-estimation' prediction given X_h, Dijkstra (1992) uses:

$$\tilde{y}_h = X_h\left(\hat{\beta} - \alpha\hat{c}\right) + \hat{c}z_h, \tag{15.10}$$

and hence any desired predictions can be obtained as well by choice of z_h. Since one needs to know the outcome y_h to ensure that $\tilde{y}_h \simeq y_h$, (15.10) is only applicable within sample. Genuine forecast tests cannot be manipulated this way.

These results may seem artificial at first sight, since z depends on $\hat{u}$. However, the existence of a vector of regressor observations such that any desired coefficients, fit, and forecasts can be derived is not dependent on knowing $\hat{u}$. Consider the interpretation that:

$$z = \underset{\text{collinearity}}{X\alpha} + \underset{\text{simultaneity}}{y\gamma} + \underset{\text{new information}}{d}.$$

The two 'classic' econometric problems of collinearity and simultaneity (or measurement errors) interact to determine the manipulability of regression evidence in practice. The former can be offset, as we have seen, by appropriate re-parameterizations to induce near orthogonality. The latter entails a failure of weak exogeneity and re-emphasises the importance of that condition for conditional inference.

Hendry and Starr (1993) discuss the same issues from the standpoint of model design. Consider commencing with a thorough literature search to ascertain all rival models; forming the (linear) nesting monster model of all variables (which ensures parsimonious encompassing); then simplifying to the minimal-dimension representation that preserves data coherence (innovation errors, but perhaps heteroscedastic). Such a model can now be designed to be empirically constant in-sample against a wide range of tests as follows. As in Chapter 3 write the regression model as:

$$\boldsymbol{y}_t^1 = \boldsymbol{X}_t^1 \boldsymbol{\beta} + \boldsymbol{\epsilon}_t^1 \;\text{ for }\; t = 1, \ldots, T, \tag{15.11}$$

where there are k regressors and $\hat{\boldsymbol{\beta}}_t$ is the recursively estimated value at sample point t. From the sequence of coefficient estimates, generate the 1-step residuals:

$$\nu_t = y_t - \boldsymbol{x}_t' \hat{\boldsymbol{\beta}}_{t-1} \;\text{ with }\; RSS_t = RSS_{t-1} + \frac{\nu_t^2}{\omega_t}, \tag{15.12}$$

where:

$$\boldsymbol{\lambda}_{t+1} = \left(\boldsymbol{X}_t^{1\prime} \boldsymbol{X}_t^1\right)^{-1} \boldsymbol{x}_{t+1} \quad\text{and}\quad \omega_t = \left(1 + \boldsymbol{x}_t' \boldsymbol{\lambda}_t\right). \tag{15.13}$$

The $\{\nu_t\}$ in (15.12) are the basis for Chow tests, and changes in their variances are crucial since:

$$RSS_T = \sum_{t=M}^{T} \frac{\nu_t^2}{\omega_t}. \tag{15.14}$$

It is possible to 'stabilize' the variances of the $\{\nu_t\}$ over the sample by parameter restrictions which remove the power of constancy tests, just as COMFAC transforms remove the power of low-order tests for residual autocorrelation (as in Ch.6). Denote the full-sample residuals by:

$$\hat{\epsilon}_t = y_t - \boldsymbol{x}_t' \hat{\boldsymbol{\beta}}_T = \nu_t - \left(\hat{\boldsymbol{\beta}}_T - \hat{\boldsymbol{\beta}}_{t-1}\right)' \boldsymbol{x}_t, \tag{15.15}$$

then from Chapter 3:

$$RSS_T = \sum_{t=1}^{T} \hat{\epsilon}_t^2. \tag{15.16}$$

Consider an example where $\hat{\boldsymbol{\beta}}_t$ changes in every sub-sample, and the $\{\nu_t\}$ reflect this non-constancy. Fix $\boldsymbol{\beta}$ at $\hat{\boldsymbol{\beta}}_T$ so no free parameters remain to estimate. By construction, RSS_T cannot alter by imposing such a restriction, (15.14) shows that the cumulated 1-step residuals do not change, and (15.15) reveals that $\hat{\epsilon}_t$ is forced to equal ν_t. The resulting $\hat{\epsilon}_t$ may be heteroscedastic, but we know how to transform these to homoscedasticity.

Thus, both parameter and variance non-constancy can be camouflaged in part, either inadvertently, or deliberately if that is a design aim: such an outcome may or may not be 'spurious' (see Smith, 1991). In-sample empirical constancy of a model can be achieved by design, even when the underlying process is not constant. In practice, it may be hard to determine the precise restrictions required, but in principle it seems to be possible.

That leaves only the need to design weak exogeneity. A casual reading of Chapter 5 may have left the impression that merely by re-defining the parameters of interest, weak exogeneity was trivial to achieve. Section 5.13 demonstrated that such a view is false: in cointegrated processes, cross-linking of cointegration parameters violates weak exogeneity, and affects inference even asymptotically, yet cannot be removed by any re-definition of parameters of interest. Thus, we reach the surprising conclusion that weak exogeneity is the only feature that cannot be designed automatically. Nevertheless, the conclusion is clear: even ignoring moral-hazard problems, whether design was deliberate or inadvertent, the only genuine test of a model is against evidence that was not available when the model was developed. This is the basis for the claim in Hendry (1980) that the three golden rules of econometrics are 'test, test, and test'.

15.5 Dummy variables

Dummy variables play many roles in econometric modelling, and here we consider three aspects: their interaction with parameter non-constancy; the validity of conditioning on dummies; and the justification for intercepts and trends.

Dummy variables of an impulse or step form are often used to 'model' parameter non-constancy. In many economic processes, a VAR for a set of n variables, $\boldsymbol{x}_t$, will not manifest constant parameters because it is a derived rather than a structural representation, so its equations involve functions of the more basic parameters of agents' decision rules. When one of the agents is a policy maker, regime shifts are liable to occur, and hence a constant parameterization will be insufficient to capture the data behaviour. Thus, some dummy variables may be needed to make a system approximately constant in practice. This also applies to econometric models which include policy equations, or are estimated over samples subject to regime shifts (such as changes in credit rationing).

Dummies are denoted by the $m \times 1$ vector $\boldsymbol{q}_t = (1, t, \boldsymbol{s}_t, \boldsymbol{d}_t)$, where $\boldsymbol{s}_t$ and $\boldsymbol{d}_t$ are dummies for seasonals (see §15.6) and special factors respectively: the latter may need to be interactive with lagged elements of stationary combinations of $\boldsymbol{x}_t$, especially in equations for policy variables, but this issue will not be considered. An investigator may not wish to model policy variables, but conditioning on them without first testing for super exogeneity runs the risk that the resulting model will not sustain policy analysis, and may be inadequate for forecasting during economic-policy changes. One of the approaches considered in Engle and Hendry (1993) was to develop constant-parameter representations of the marginal policy processes, and then test the irrelevance of the created variables in the conditional equations of interest. This is most usefully conducted in a system context, in which case a natural generalization of their test is the significance of the additional variables from the joint marginal model in the joint conditional model under analysis: Chapter 16 provides an empirical example.

Both approaches requires conditioning on the dummy variables. However, despite their being deterministic, it is unclear that the elements of $\boldsymbol{Q}_T^1 = (q_1 \dots q_T)$ are valid conditioning variables in general, so we consider the roles of the constant, a linear trend, seasonal dummies, and dummy variables for policy changes. The future values of the first three variables are known with certainty, so the issue is the role they play in the model, not whether their values are altered by other economic variables. Dummy variables for special events such as the oil crisis, or financial de-regulation, are not known in advance, and may reflect endogenous responses.

The treatment of dummies in cointegrated systems is important for long-run behaviour (see Chs.8 and 11). For example, the VECM in (8.13) is:

$$\Delta \boldsymbol{x}_t = \sum_{j=1}^{s-1} \boldsymbol{A}_j^* \Delta \boldsymbol{x}_{t-j} + \boldsymbol{\alpha}\boldsymbol{\beta}' \boldsymbol{x}_{t-1} + \boldsymbol{K}\boldsymbol{q}_t + \boldsymbol{\nu}_t, \tag{15.17}$$

where $\boldsymbol{\nu}_t \sim \mathsf{IN}_n[\mathbf{0}, \boldsymbol{\Omega}]$. Let $\boldsymbol{K} = \boldsymbol{\alpha}\boldsymbol{\gamma}' + \boldsymbol{\alpha}_{\perp}\boldsymbol{\delta}'$, where $\boldsymbol{\alpha}, \boldsymbol{\alpha}_{\perp}, \boldsymbol{\gamma}$, and $\boldsymbol{\delta}$ are $n \times r$, $m \times r$, $n \times (n-r)$, and $m \times (n-r)$ respectively. The system can be expressed as:

$$\Delta \boldsymbol{x}_t = \sum_{j=1}^{s-1} \boldsymbol{A}_j^* \Delta \boldsymbol{x}_{t-j} + \boldsymbol{\alpha} (\boldsymbol{\beta}' \boldsymbol{x}_{t-1} + \boldsymbol{\gamma}' \boldsymbol{q}_t) + \boldsymbol{\alpha}_{\perp}\boldsymbol{\delta}' \boldsymbol{q}_t + \boldsymbol{\nu}_t. \tag{15.18}$$

When q_t is just the constant, $\delta = 0$ precludes autonomous growth, so the intercept can only be restricted to lie in the cointegration space if no variable manifests growth.[1] Growth of real output has been about 2.5 per cent p.a. in the UK, whereas inflation and interest rates should have zero long-run growth, and hence need no separate intercepts. Conversely, the formulation in (15.18) imposes a constant and autonomous growth rate, which is a strong restriction (see Pagan, 1985 , and Salmon, 1988).

When $\boldsymbol{q}_t$ also contains a trend, $\boldsymbol{\delta} = \mathbf{0}$ allows growth when $\gamma_2 \neq 0$. Generally, t must only enter the cointegration space, as otherwise it would induce a quadratic trend in the levels, for which there is little evidence. A linear deterministic trend in real output proxies the slow and steady evolution of total human capital, embodying knowledge accumulation, experience growth, and improved education, implemented by cohort arrivals and departures in the labour force. Those departing have considerable experience, but were educated many years previously, whereas the latest arrivals lack experience, but benefit from the greater knowledge embodied in more recent education. As such, due to aggregation across many millions of individuals at all stages of their life cycles, smooth growth should occur in the total effective labour force. Human capital operates on the total physical capital stock, which again embodies technical progress across many vintages of investment, slow depreciation and obsolescence, and reflects the human capital in investment industries. Even if such effects were stochastic, as in random walks with positive drifts dependent on the level of scientific progress and R&D, the variance of

[1] q_t can be restricted to the cointegration space only if that constraint is valid for all equations.

the aggregate should be small compared to mean growth,so real-output variables could appear to be well-approximated by trend stationarity.

Major shocks, such as natural resource availability scientific breakthroughs, and changes in institutions or regulations, will influence the trend, so a constant coefficient over a prolonged sample seems unlikely: this will affect the intercept when that determines mean growth. Clements and Hendry (1995) argue that the most important parameter changes causing forecasting failures are in intercepts, so attention should be paid to check the constancy of the 'constant'. This comment applies forcefully to ECM specifications, where the constant also represents the equilibrium level of the relationship: a change in that level entails that the existing ECM does not 'error correct' towards the new equilibrium but still converges on the old. An example is provided in DHSY, who find the ECM specification fails when inflation is omitted from their model, which then equilibrates to the wrong savings ratio (see Clements and Hendry, 1995, for further discussion).

Seasonal adjustment is considered in the next section, so here we merely note the constancy assumptions embodied in fixed, or constantly evolving, seasonal patterns. Although summer is unlikely to become winter, economic behaviour can change greatly in response to seasons: witness the large switch in electricity consumption to summer months with air conditioning. As ever, endogenous responses are likely, and careful thought may be needed to represent seasonal factors (see, e.g., Hylleberg, 1992).

Finally, policy changes, including major regime shifts, are endogenous responses to economic circumstances. Dummy variables for these may also be endogenous, and are rarely predictable. For example, Wallis (1971) argues that incomes-policy dummies are endogenous, and that conditioning on them may induce incorrect inferences. This suggests that the use of data-based dummies for super-exogeneity tests may reject too often.

15.6 Seasonal adjustment

Seasonal variations are 'regular' patterns of variability recurring across years: well-known examples are increased expenditure on soft drinks during the summer and on heating during the winter. There are many potential causes of seasonal fluctuations from weather cycles over the year, religious festivals, statutory holidays etc. The effects of seasonality on the economy have been the subject of analysis for more than a century (see e.g. Jevons, 1884 , and Hylleberg, 1986). Figures 15.1a–d show the time series of the log of quarterly consumers' expenditure (c_t) in the UK from 1961(1)–1992(4); its seasonal pattern estimated by regression on the seasonal dummies $\{s_{it}\}$ and $\{s_{it}t\}$; growth in seasonally adjusted (SA) and unadjusted UKM1 (Δm_t, as analysed above, with the adjustment procedure being X–11, and Δm_t^u); and their difference ($m_t^u - m_t$).[2] A strongly trending seasonal is evident for c_t, and a marked and rather regular seasonal pattern for m_t. Figures 15.2a–d plot c_t against real personal disposable income (y_t)

[2] SA also denotes 'seasonal adjustment' depending on the context, and NSA denotes unadjusted.

where the four quarters are denoted by the first four digits; the consumption–income ratio $(c_t - y_t)$; the time series of both c_t and y_t (matched to have the same means and ranges); and the annual differences $(\Delta_4 c_t, \Delta_4 y_t)$. Not only is c_t at its highest in the fourth quarter, so is its ratio to income; the level of c_t shows greater short-run variability than that of y_t, whereas the opposite is true of the annual changes.

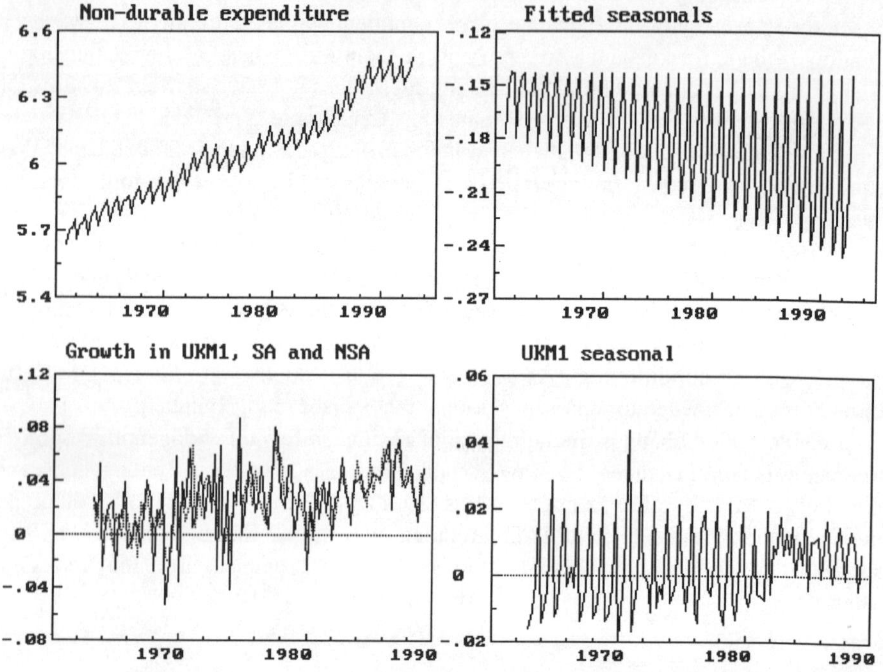

Fig. 15.1 Seasonal behaviour of UK consumption and money stock

Seasonal patterns are partly extraneous (such as the effects of temperature changes on energy demand, or rainfall in agriculture) and partly social (e.g. Christmas spending, and summer holidays), but both lead to adaptation by economic agents to reduce the costs of the fluctuations. Thus, we might anticipate that seasonal patterns evolve over time (imagine the mid-winter diets of northern Europeans five centuries ago in contrast to today). This makes the handling of seasonality in econometric modelling less than straightforward.

Four main approaches can be distinguished. First, dummy variables for the seasons are often added to models to parametrically adjust for seasonality: a constant (or steadily evolving) pattern is assumed, and is subject to the caveats of the preceding paragraph. Secondly, endogenous dynamics are used to model the seasonality: for example, Box and Jenkins (1976) use annual differences, and DHSY augment those with an annual equilibrium correction. Thirdly, an evolving pattern has been proposed for consumers' expenditure by Harvey and Scott (1993), given the evidence noted above. Finally, filters are applied to seasonal time series to remove components at seasonal frequencies. The resulting SA data are then analysed. We have conducted most of the empirical analyses in this book using such data, but for simplicity of exposition, rather than any view that prior seasonal adjustment is justifiable. Section 15.6.1 discusses the impact of SA on cointegrated time series, following Ericsson *et al.* (1994). Integration and cointegration may also occur at seasonal frequencies and are discussed by Dickey, Hasza and Fuller (1984), Hylleberg, Engle, Granger and Yoo (1990), Ghysels, Lee and Noh (1991), Beaulieu and Miron (1993) and Osborn (1988), Birchenhall, Bladen-Hovell, Chui, Osborn and Smith (1989) *inter alia*.

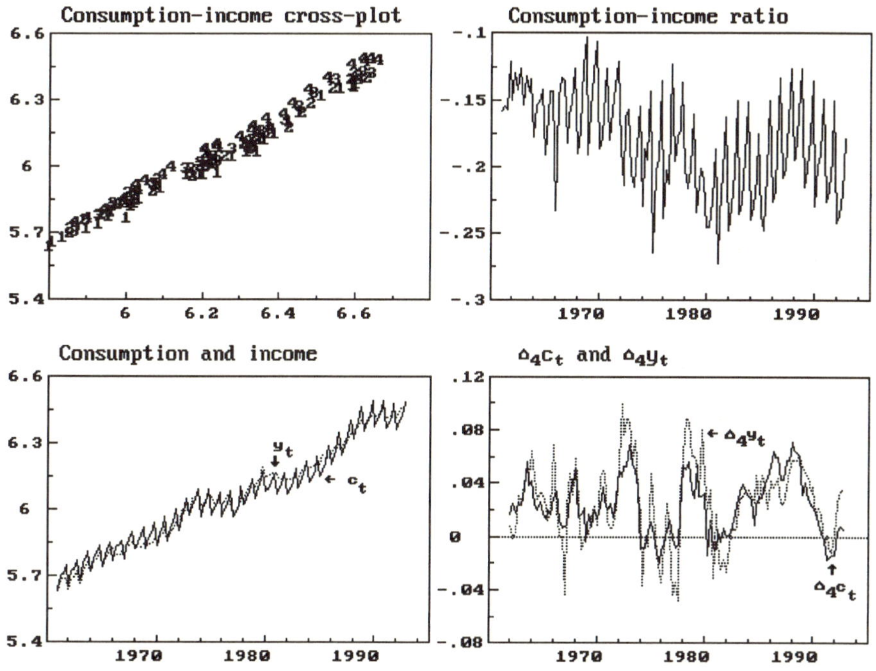

Fig. 15.2 UK consumption and income

15.6.1 Seasonal filters

One widely-used method of seasonal adjustment is the X–11 procedure (see *inter alia* Lovell, 1963, Nerlove, 1964, Wallis, 1974, Sims, 1974, Kenny and Durbin, 1982, Hylleberg, 1986, and Maravall and Pierce, 1987, on the properties of this and related methods). There is a vast literature on seasonal adjustment, and other relevant references include Burridge and Wallis (1984), Cleveland and Tiao (1976), Granger (1978) and Grether and Nerlove (1970). Most SA series in governmental data-bases have been adjusted by this approach. It can be sensible to filter a time series to remove or highlight certain of its components — for example, the 'trend' in unemployment may not be easily discerned when there are important seasonal changes superimposed.

However, conducting econometric analyses on data that have been subjected to any adjustments raises modelling issues. Sims (1974) and Wallis (1974) examined the effects of seasonal adjustment on econometric relationships from two perspectives. Sims investigated estimation where the relation was in terms of non-seasonal components, but unadjusted data were used. Wallis considered the converse of using SA data when the economic relation was in terms of unadjusted data. In both cases, the empirical model is mis-specified (also see Wallis, 1978).

We follow Wallis (1974) in using a two-sided, linear-filter approximation to investigate the consequences of SA on econometric analyses:

$$x_t^a = f(L)x_t, \tag{15.19}$$

where the SA series is $\{x_t^a\}$ and $f(L)$ is the two-sided linear filter in the lag operator L:

$$f(L) = \sum_{i=-n}^{n} f_i L^i \tag{15.20}$$

with half-length $n < \infty$, and fixed, finite weights $\{f_i\}$. Some f_i could be zero, so $f(L)$ could be a one-sided filter in practice. Express $f(L)$ as:

$$f(L) = f(1) + f^*(L)\Delta = f(1) + f^*(1)\Delta + f^{**}(L)\Delta^2 \dots \tag{15.21}$$

where the recursion can be repeated to any order. In (15.21), $f^*(L)$ and $f^{**}(L)$ are finite-order, fixed-weight, two-sided linear filters with coefficients $\{f_i^*\}$ and $\{f_i^{**}\}$. The sum of the coefficients in successive lag polynomials can be obtained recursively from:

$$f^*(1) = -\frac{\partial f(L)}{\partial L}\rfloor_{L=1} \text{ and } f^{**}(1) = -\frac{\partial f^*(L)}{\partial L}\rfloor_{L=1}, \tag{15.22}$$

so that the sums $f^*(1)$ and $f^{**}(1)$ are $-\sum_{i=-n}^{n} i \cdot f_i$ and $-\sum_{i=-n}^{n-1} i \cdot f_i^*$. This analogue model seems to provide a good approximation to the X–11 procedure (see Wallis, 1982, 1983).[3]

15.6.2 Properties of seasonal filters

The SA filter in (15.20) is assumed to satisfy three conditions. First, $f(1) = 1$, so $f(L) = 1 + f^*(L)\Delta$. This represents a normalization to ensure that x_t^a and x_t are in the same units. Otherwise, from (15.21), $f(1) = 0$ would entail that x_t^a was a distributed lag of Δx_t, and hence would be integrated of a different order, whereas SA is meant to leave long-run properties unaffected.

[3] The linear filter ignores several features of X–11: graduation of extreme values; constraints on calendar-year totals; corrections at the ends of series; and multiplicative models of SA.

Next, $f(L)$ is symmetric in L, namely $f(L) = f(L^{-1})$, and hence, $f_i = f_{-i}, i = 1, \ldots, n$. From (15.22), this implies that $f^*(1) = 0$, and so $f(L) = 1 + f^{**}(L)\Delta^2$. Symmetry is sufficient for $f^*(1) = 0$, but is not necessary. For example, a unit root in $f^*(L)$ ensures $f^*(1) = 0$, but does not imply symmetry (see Osborn, 1993, and Wallis, 1993).

Finally, a fixed seasonal pattern can be represented by $d(L)s_{1t}$, where $d(L)$ is a $(p-1)$th-order polynomial when p is the periodicity of seasonality (e.g. $p = 4$ for quarterly data), and s_{it} is the mean-adjusted dummy for the ith season.[4] Then, if $f(L) = f^{\diamond}(L)m(L)$, where $m(L)$ is the summation operator:

$$m(L) = p^{-1} \sum_{i=0}^{p-1} L^i,$$

since $m(L)s_{1t} = 0$:

$$f(L)d(L)s_{1t} = f^{\diamond}(L)m(L)d(L)s_{1t} = f^{\diamond}(L)d(L)m(L)s_{1t} = 0. \qquad (15.23)$$

Thus, $f(L)$ annihilates seasonal dummies.[5]

The first application of these properties is to cointegration between the series x_t^a and x_t when x_t is $\mathsf{I}(d)$. Since:

$$x_t^a = f(L)x_t = x_t + f^{**}(L)\Delta^2 x_t \qquad (15.24)$$

then $x_t^a - x_t$ is (at most) $\mathsf{I}(d-2)$. Thus, x_t^a and x_t certainly cointegrate with a unit coefficient when $d \leq 2$. However, the expectation of $x_t^a - x_t$ need not be zero (assuming it exists) although it is desirable to have the adjusted and unadjusted series equal 'on average'. Because fixed seasonal patterns are non-ergodic, mean equality is defined as:

$$\mathsf{E}\left[m(L)\left(x_t^a - x_t\right)\right] := 0.$$

Let $\Delta_p = (1 - L^p)$ be the annual-difference operator, then $\Delta m(L) = p^{-1}\Delta_p$ and so from (15.24) when the filter is symmetric:

$$\begin{aligned} \mathsf{E}\left[m(L)\left(x_t^a - x_t\right)\right] &= \mathsf{E}\left[m(L)f^{**}(L)\Delta^2 x_t\right] \\ &= \mathsf{E}\left[f^{**}(L)\Delta^2 m(L)x_t\right] \\ &= p^{-1}\mathsf{E}\left[f^{**}(L)\Delta\Delta_p x_t\right]. \end{aligned} \qquad (15.25)$$

When $d = 1$, $\mathsf{E}[\Delta\Delta_p x_t] = 0$, so x_t^a and x_t will be mean equal.

15.6.3 Cointegration

We now generalize the analysis to a vector of n $\mathsf{I}(1)$ time series $\boldsymbol{x}_t^a$ and $\boldsymbol{x}_t$ satisfying the relationship:

$$\boldsymbol{x}_t^a = \boldsymbol{F}(L)\boldsymbol{x}_t \text{ where } \boldsymbol{F}(L) = \boldsymbol{I}_n + \boldsymbol{F}^{**}(L)\Delta^2 \qquad (15.26)$$

[4] This is how PcGive creates its set of centred seasonals.

[5] An SA filter with a factor of $m(L)$ will also eliminate any seasonal unit roots in x_t, and otherwise will be similar to over-differencing: see Maravall (1993).

(as for $f(L)$ above), when $\boldsymbol{F}(L)$ is the $n \times n$ diagonal matrix of scalar polynomials, diag$[f_1(L)\ldots f_n(L)]$, such that $x^a_{jt} = f_j(L)x_{jt}$ for $j = 1, \ldots, n$. Thus, each x^a_{jt} depends only on the corresponding unadjusted series, but different filters may be used for different series. When $\boldsymbol{\beta}$ is an $n \times r$ cointegrating matrix for $\boldsymbol{x}_t$, then $\boldsymbol{\beta}$ is also the cointegrating matrix for $\boldsymbol{x}^a_t$ (and vice versa) so SA affects only the dynamics of a process, and not its long-run properties. To see this result, pre-multiply (15.26) by $\boldsymbol{\beta}'$:

$$\boldsymbol{\beta}'\boldsymbol{x}^a_t = \boldsymbol{\beta}'\boldsymbol{x}_t + \boldsymbol{\beta}'\boldsymbol{F}^{**}(L)\Delta^2\boldsymbol{x}_t. \tag{15.27}$$

Since $\boldsymbol{x}_t$ is I(1), $\boldsymbol{\beta}'\boldsymbol{x}_t$ is I(0), and $\Delta^2\boldsymbol{x}_t$ is I(−1) (i.e. over-differenced), so $\boldsymbol{\beta}'\boldsymbol{x}^a_t$ is also I(0), and hence $\boldsymbol{\beta}$ is the cointegrating matrix for $\boldsymbol{x}^a_t$, and conversely. Consequently, $\boldsymbol{x}_t$ and $\boldsymbol{x}^a_t$ must have the same number of cointegrating vectors. Moreover, $\boldsymbol{\beta}'\boldsymbol{x}^a_t$ and $\boldsymbol{\beta}'\boldsymbol{x}_t$ will be mean equal (Ericsson *et al.*, 1994, show how close they are empirically). Conversely, if the conditions in section 15.6.2 are not satisfied, the cointegrating vectors for $\boldsymbol{x}_t$ and $\boldsymbol{x}^a_t$ need not be the same, affecting long-run, as well as short-run, relationships between the series (see Bartelsman and Cleveland, 1993).

When $\boldsymbol{x}_t$ is generated by an I(1), sth-order Gaussian VAR (as in Johansen, 1988), inference from the SA data $\boldsymbol{x}^a_t$ generally is affected, even though $\boldsymbol{\beta}$ and r are invariant to the transformation from $\boldsymbol{x}_t$ to $\boldsymbol{x}^a_t$. As discussed in Hendry and Mizon (1978) and DHSY, series may be filtered, but not relationships: the relationship for the SA data is obtained by filtering each NSA series individually (potentially using different filters) and then combining the filtered (SA) data. For example, re-consider (15.17) written as:

$$\boldsymbol{A}(L)\Delta\boldsymbol{x}_t = \boldsymbol{\alpha}\boldsymbol{\beta}'\boldsymbol{x}_{t-1} + \boldsymbol{K}\boldsymbol{q}_t + \boldsymbol{\nu}_t \tag{15.28}$$

where $\boldsymbol{A}(L) = \boldsymbol{I}_n - \sum_{j=1}^{s-1}\boldsymbol{A}^*_j L^j$, and there are sufficient a priori restrictions on $\boldsymbol{\alpha}$ and $\boldsymbol{\beta}$ to identify them uniquely. Pre-multiply (15.28) by $\boldsymbol{F}(L)$:

$$\boldsymbol{F}(L)\boldsymbol{A}(L)\Delta\boldsymbol{x}_t = \boldsymbol{F}(L)\boldsymbol{\alpha}\boldsymbol{\beta}'\boldsymbol{x}_{t-1} + \boldsymbol{F}(L)\boldsymbol{K}\boldsymbol{q}_t + \boldsymbol{F}(L)\boldsymbol{\nu}_t. \tag{15.29}$$

Next, substitute the identity $\boldsymbol{x}^a_t + (\boldsymbol{x}_t - \boldsymbol{x}^a_t)$ for $\boldsymbol{x}_t$:

$$\boldsymbol{F}(L)\boldsymbol{A}(L)\Delta\boldsymbol{x}_t = \boldsymbol{F}(L)\boldsymbol{A}(L)\Delta\boldsymbol{x}^a_t + \boldsymbol{F}(L)\boldsymbol{A}(L)\Delta(\boldsymbol{x}_t - \boldsymbol{x}^a_t). \tag{15.30}$$

Then $\Delta(\boldsymbol{x}_t - \boldsymbol{x}^a_t)$ is I(−1) since $\boldsymbol{x}_t$ and $\boldsymbol{x}^a_t$ cointegrate with a unit coefficient. Further, when $q_{1t} = 1$, $\boldsymbol{F}(L)\boldsymbol{k}_1 = \boldsymbol{k}_1$; similarly, a linear deterministic trend is preserved; and if there are seasonal dummies, these vanish in (15.29) as in (15.23). Finally:

$$\begin{aligned}\boldsymbol{F}(L)\boldsymbol{\alpha}\boldsymbol{\beta}'\boldsymbol{x}_{t-1} &= \boldsymbol{F}(L)\boldsymbol{\alpha}\boldsymbol{\beta}'\boldsymbol{x}^a_{t-1} + \boldsymbol{F}(L)\boldsymbol{\alpha}\boldsymbol{\beta}'(\boldsymbol{x}_{t-1} - \boldsymbol{x}^a_{t-1}) \\ &= \boldsymbol{\alpha}\boldsymbol{\beta}'\boldsymbol{x}^a_{t-1} + \boldsymbol{F}^{**}(L)\boldsymbol{\alpha}\boldsymbol{\beta}'\Delta^2\boldsymbol{x}^a_{t-1} + \boldsymbol{F}(L)\boldsymbol{\alpha}\boldsymbol{\beta}'(\boldsymbol{x}_{t-1} - \boldsymbol{x}^a_{t-1}).\end{aligned} \tag{15.31}$$

Other than $\boldsymbol{\alpha}\boldsymbol{\beta}'\boldsymbol{x}^a_{t-1}$, all remaining terms are I(−1). Thus, by substitution and rearrangement of terms, (15.29) may be written in the form:

$$\boldsymbol{B}(L)\Delta\boldsymbol{x}^a_t = \boldsymbol{\alpha}\boldsymbol{\beta}'\boldsymbol{x}^a_{t-1} + \boldsymbol{K}\boldsymbol{q}^*_t + \boldsymbol{u}_t \tag{15.32}$$

where $B(L)$ is in general a two-sided polynomial. Importantly, u_t is not an innovation even when ν_t is, which could distort inference (see Wallis, 1974, and Ghysels and Perron, 1993). The cointegrating vectors β are invariant to the type of data (NSA or SA), but since $\beta' x^a_{t-1}$ is therefore I(0), its correlation with u_t entails that α is not invariant. When $B(L)$ is a two-sided, non-diagonal polynomial matrix, the conditional representation of (15.32) confounds dynamics from future Δx^a with $\beta' x^a_{t-1}$, and dynamics in u_t with lagged dynamics in Δx^a. Both affect α, and so may affect weak exogeneity for β: whether or not a set of variables is weakly exogenous then depends upon which type of data is used. Despite the invariance of cointegration, the empirical power of cointegration tests on SA and on NSA data may differ (see Lee and Siklos, 1991, 1993).

15.7 Approximating moving-average processes

Chapter 2 introduced autoregressive (AR), moving average (MA), and autoregressive-moving average (ARMA) processes. So far, we have only allowed for autoregressive processes and ignored moving-average components. This section comments on that potential limitation since a closer representation of a data series or error process may be obtained for a given number of parameters by using the ARMA class than just autoregressions (see Hannan and Deistler, 1988, for a general analysis).

An ARMA(r, s) is:

$$y_t = \lambda + \sum_{i=1}^{r} \alpha_i y_{t-i} + \epsilon_t + \sum_{j=1}^{s} \gamma_j \epsilon_{t-j} \tag{15.33}$$

with $\epsilon_t \sim \mathsf{IN}[0, \sigma^2_\epsilon]$. In (15.33), $\{\epsilon_t\}$ must be white noise, but normality is inessential. Unit roots should be imposed, and we will interpret y_t as the resulting stationary variable. Finally, there should be no redundant common factors, so writing (15.33) in lag polynomial form:

$$\alpha(L)\, y_t = \lambda + \gamma(L)\, \epsilon_t,$$

where:

$$\alpha(Z) = \prod_{i=1}^{r} \left(1 - \rho_i Z^i\right) \text{ and } \gamma(Z) = \prod_{j=1}^{s} \left(1 - \lambda_j Z^j\right),$$

then no ρ_i can equal any λ_j. This problem led Box and Jenkins (1976) to argue for parsimonious representations using low orders of r and s.

Many models generate apparent moving-average errors, due to aggregation over time or over dynamic variables, seasonal adjustment, latent variables, and data measurement errors. For example, consider the AR(1) process for a latent variable y^*_t measured as y_t:

$$y^*_t = \alpha y^*_{t-1} + v_t \text{ where } y_t = y^*_t + \xi_t,$$

so:

$$y_t = \alpha y_{t-1} + v_t + \xi_t - \alpha \xi_{t-1} = \alpha y_{t-1} + \epsilon_t + \gamma \epsilon_{t-1},$$

where the MA(1) coefficient follows from equating the current and lagged moments of $\{v_t + \xi_t - \alpha\xi_{t-1}\}$ and $\{\epsilon_t + \gamma\epsilon_{t-1}\}$, so that:

$$\sigma_v^2 + (1+\alpha^2)\,\sigma_\xi^2 = (1+\gamma^2)\,\sigma_\epsilon^2 \text{ and } -\alpha\sigma_\xi^2 = \gamma\sigma_\epsilon^2. \tag{15.34}$$

Hence $\gamma = -\alpha\sigma_\xi^2/\sigma_\epsilon^2$, and unless σ_ξ^2 is small relative to σ_v^2, there is a near-redundant common factor.

We now consider the costs of using only AR processes. In a multivariate context, the presence of MA errors in univariate representations does not entail MA errors in structural equations. The analysis in Chapter 8 showed that systems of dynamic equations with white-noise errors would have final forms with moving-average errors. However, several of the previous arguments favouring MA errors could apply directly to structural equations.

Theory and simulation suggest that approximating a low-order ARMA process by an AR processes of the same combined order yields a good match in terms of fit, especially given the multitude of other mistakes likely to be involved in empirical studies (see Hendry and Trivedi, 1972, and Hendry, 1977). However, the parameters need not match closely. The analysis proceeds as follows for the stationary and invertible ARMA(1, 1):

$$y_t = \alpha y_{t-1} + \epsilon_t + \gamma\epsilon_{t-1} \tag{15.35}$$

versus an AR(2), interpreted as an AR(1) data process with an AR(1) error:

$$y_t = \delta y_{t-1} + u_t \text{ where } u_t = \phi u_{t-1} + v_t \tag{15.36}$$

or:

$$y_t = (\delta + \phi)\, y_{t-1} - \delta\phi y_{t-2} + v_t. \tag{15.37}$$

Since:

$$(1+\gamma L)^{-1} \equiv \left[1 - \gamma L + \frac{\gamma^2 L^2}{(1+\gamma L)}\right], \tag{15.38}$$

rewrite (15.35) as:

$$(1+\gamma L)^{-1}\,(y_t - \alpha y_{t-1}) = \epsilon_t,$$

so that using (15.38):

$$(1-\gamma L)\,(y_t - \alpha y_{t-1}) + \gamma^2 L^2 \epsilon_t = \epsilon_t,$$

and hence:

$$y_t = (\gamma+\alpha)\, y_{t-1} - \gamma\alpha y_{t-2} + \epsilon_t - \gamma^2\epsilon_{t-2} = (\gamma+\alpha)\, y_{t-1} - \gamma\alpha y_{t-2} + w_t. \tag{15.39}$$

Since $\mathsf{E}[y_{t-1}v_t] = \mathsf{E}[y_{t-2}v_t] = 0$ in (15.37) by definition of the parameters, whereas $\mathsf{E}[y_{t-2}w_t] = -\gamma^2\sigma_\epsilon^2 \neq 0$, then $v_t \neq w_t$, but (15.39) suggests why the match in fit might be close. Indeed, as $(\delta : \phi)$ achieve the best fit in (15.36):

$$\sigma_v^2 \leq \sigma_w^2 = (1+\gamma^4)\,\sigma_\epsilon^2.$$

Even for $|\gamma| = 0.8$, the residual standard deviation increases by less than 19 per cent, and for $|\gamma| = 0.5$ induces a 3 per cent increase (for example, when $\alpha = 0.9$ and $\sigma_\xi^2 = \sigma_v^2$ in (15.34), then $\gamma = -0.45$).

Next we consider the parameter match. Let $\mathsf{E}[y_t y_{t-1}] = \sigma_{yy_1}$, then from (15.35):

$$\sigma_{yy_1} = \alpha\sigma_y^2 + \gamma\sigma_\epsilon^2 \text{ and } \sigma_y^2 = \sigma_\epsilon^2 \frac{1 + 2\alpha\gamma + \gamma^2}{(1-\alpha^2)},$$

so that:

$$\rho = \frac{\sigma_{yy_1}}{\sigma_y^2} = \alpha + \theta \text{ where } \theta = \gamma^* \frac{(1-\alpha^2)}{(1+2\alpha\gamma^*)} \text{ and } \gamma^* = \frac{\gamma}{(1+\gamma^2)}.$$

Project w_t onto $(y_{t-1} : y_{t-2})$ to orthogonalize these, which thereby produces the error v_t in (15.36):

$$w_t = \begin{pmatrix} y_{t-1} & y_{t-2} \end{pmatrix} \begin{pmatrix} a_1 \\ a_2 \end{pmatrix} + v_t, \tag{15.40}$$

where comparison of (15.37) with (15.39) reveals that :

$$\begin{pmatrix} a_1 \\ a_2 \end{pmatrix} = \begin{pmatrix} (\delta + \phi) - (\gamma + \alpha) \\ \gamma\alpha - \delta\phi \end{pmatrix}. \tag{15.41}$$

Since from (15.40) by population regression:

$$\begin{aligned} \begin{pmatrix} a_1 \\ a_2 \end{pmatrix} &= \begin{pmatrix} \sigma_y^2 & \sigma_{yy_1} \\ \sigma_{yy_1} & \sigma_y^2 \end{pmatrix}^{-1} \begin{pmatrix} 0 \\ -\gamma^2\sigma_\epsilon^2 \end{pmatrix} \\ &= \frac{1}{\sigma_y^2(1-\rho^2)} \begin{pmatrix} 1 & -\rho \\ -\rho & 1 \end{pmatrix} \begin{pmatrix} 0 \\ -\gamma^2\sigma_\epsilon^2 \end{pmatrix} \\ &= \frac{\gamma\theta}{(1-\rho^2)} \begin{pmatrix} \rho \\ -1 \end{pmatrix}, \end{aligned} \tag{15.42}$$

then by comparing (15.41) and (15.42) we obtain the relation:

$$\begin{pmatrix} \delta + \phi \\ -\delta\phi \end{pmatrix} = \begin{pmatrix} \gamma + \alpha \\ -\gamma\alpha \end{pmatrix} + \frac{\gamma\theta}{(1-\rho^2)} \begin{pmatrix} \rho \\ -1 \end{pmatrix}.$$

Thus, the 'inconsistency' in the individual AR parameters need not be small even when there is a close match in terms of fit: because $\gamma\theta > 0$, both parameters tend to be magnified in absolute value, although their sum is usually well estimated, with a bias of $-\gamma(\rho - \alpha)/(1+\rho)$.

A different issue raised by MA processes is that near cancellation of $\alpha = 1$ and $\gamma = -1 + \mu$ in an ARMA(1, 1) generates a 'long memory' property in what is otherwise apparently a white-noise process. For example, (15.35) then becomes:

$$y_t - y_{t-1} = \epsilon_t - \epsilon_{t-1} + \mu\epsilon_{t-1} \text{ or } \Delta y_t = \Delta\epsilon_t + \mu\epsilon_{t-1}. \tag{15.43}$$

When $\mu = 0$, the factor of $\Delta = (1 - L)$ cancels, revealing that $\{y_t\}$ is white noise; for $\mu \simeq 0$, near cancellation occurs (see e.g. Molinas, 1986, and Schwert, 1989). Assuming an initial time of $t = 0$ before which all $\{\epsilon_{t-i}\}$ are zero:

$$y_t = \epsilon_t + \mu \sum_{j=1}^{t-1} \epsilon_{t-j}. \tag{15.44}$$

Consequently $\mathsf{E}[y_t^2] = \sigma_\epsilon^2(1 + \mu^2 t)$ which would increase slowly for small μ. Also, for $k \geq 1$:

$$\begin{aligned}\mathsf{E}\left[y_t y_{t-k}\right] &= \mathsf{E}\left[\left(\epsilon_t + \mu \sum_{j=1}^{t-1} \epsilon_{t-j}\right)\left(\epsilon_{t-k} + \mu \sum_{j=1}^{t-1-k} \epsilon_{t-j-k}\right)\right] \\ &= \mu\sigma_\epsilon^2 \left[1 + \mu\left(t - 1 - k\right)\right],\end{aligned}$$

so that:

$$\mathsf{corr}\left[y_t, y_{t-k}\right] = \frac{\mu + \mu^2\left(t - 1 - k\right)}{\left(1 + \mu^2 t\right)}. \tag{15.45}$$

Thus (15.45) will decrease slowly as k increases, although it will start at a small value for small μ. A white-noise model is likely to be chosen when μ is small, missing the 'long-memory' component.

These properties of MA errors suggest advantages to including them in a general modelling strategy. The major difficulty with doing so was alluded to above, namely that a general-to-specific approach is precluded by the problem of redundant common factors, forcing a parsimonious (usually data-based) start, generalized in the light of observed data mis-matches. Consequently, we continue to focus on AR representations at the cost of perhaps some parsimony.

15.8 A solved example: modelling second moments

There seem to be as many possibilities for characterising second moments as there were for first. To date, economic theory of agent behaviour has mainly focused on first moments, but as shown in Chapter 5, exogeneity often depends on the links between unconditional first moments and data second moments. Since the topic of modelling second moments merits a book on its own, the aim of this section is simply to exploit the remarkable number of important distinctions that are highlighted by ARCH processes, using a solved example. Engle and Bollerslev (1987) and Bollerslev, Chou and Kroner (1992) survey much of the literature on ARCH and related processes; Harvey and Shephard (1993) discuss stochastic-variance models. Figure 15.3a–d show monthly data over 1950–1989 for the first difference ΔR_{bt} of the US long-term interest rates R_{bt} (twenty-year bond rate); the squares $(\Delta R_{bt})^2$; absolute values $|\Delta R_{bt}|$; and the correlogram of $|\Delta R_{bt}|$. The first differences are close to weak white noise but with greatly changing variability. The squares $(\Delta R_{bt})^2$ and absolute values $|\Delta R_{bt}|$ are both highly positively autocorrelated for many lags, and the correlogram of $|\Delta R_{bt}|$ suggests that the autocorrelations die out slowly. We return in the final section to an analysis of that last issue: here we focus on the properties of ARCH.

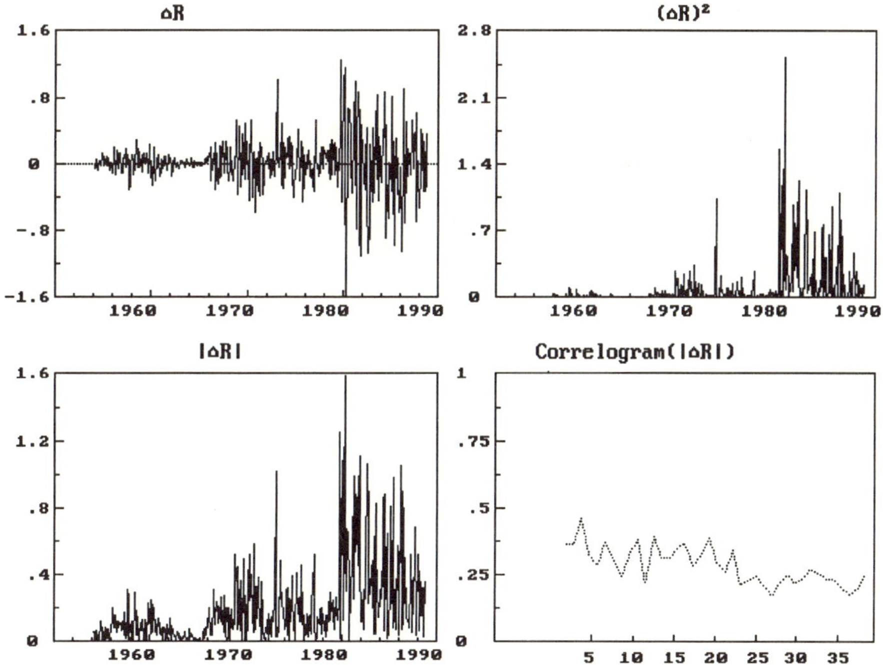

Fig. 15.3 Functions of monthly US long-term interest rates

Consider a data-generation process of the form for $t = 1, \dots, T$:

$$y_t = \beta z_t + \epsilon_t \;\text{ where }\; \mathsf{E}\left[z_t \epsilon_s\right] = 0 \;\forall t, s \tag{15.46}$$

when $\{\epsilon_t\}$ is the first-order ARCH process (see Engle, 1982a):

$$\epsilon_t = \eta_t \sqrt{\alpha_0 + \alpha_1 \epsilon_{t-1}^2} \tag{15.47}$$

subject to the positivity and stationarity conditions $\alpha_0 > 0$ and $0 < \alpha_1 < 1$, when $\epsilon_0 = 0$ and $\eta_t \sim \mathsf{IN}[0, 1]$. The $\{z_t\}$ can be treated as fixed in repeated samples.

(a) Show that:

$$\mathsf{E}\left[\epsilon_t^2 \mid \epsilon_{t-1}\right] = \alpha_0 + \alpha_1 \epsilon_{t-1}^2.$$

Hence obtain $\mathsf{E}[\epsilon_t]$ and $\mathsf{E}[\epsilon_t^2] = \sigma_\epsilon^2$, and show that $\{\epsilon_t\}$ is not autocorrelated.

(b) Show that the least-squares estimator of β in (15.46) is unbiased, and establish that it is the best linear unbiased estimator (BLUE) of β. Also show that the conventional least-squares variance formula is unbiased.

(c) Show that an LM test of H_0: $\alpha_1 = 0$ against H_1: $\alpha_1 > 0$ can be based on the least-squares residual diagnostic regression:

$$\hat{\epsilon}_t^2 = \alpha_0 + \alpha_1 \hat{\epsilon}_{t-1}^2 + \nu_t \;\text{ where }\; \hat{\epsilon}_t = y_t - \hat{\beta} z_t. \tag{15.48}$$

(d) Derive the MLE $\tilde{\beta}$ of β when α_0 and α_1 are known. Hence show that the MLE is unbiased.
(e) If $\bar{\beta}$ is a pre-test estimator based on using OLS when the LM test in (c) is not significant, and MLE when it is, prove that $\bar{\beta}$ is unbiased for β.
(f) Show that the BLUE is asymptotically inefficient when $\alpha_1 > 0$.

(Adapted from Oxford M.Phil., 1985)

Solution to (a)

Much of the following analysis is derived from Engle, Hendry and Trumbull (1985) and Hendry (1986b). From (15.47):

$$\mathsf{E}\left[\epsilon_t^2 \mid \epsilon_{t-1}\right] = \mathsf{E}\left[\eta_t^2\left(\alpha_0 + \alpha_1\epsilon_{t-1}^2\right) \mid \epsilon_{t-1}\right] = \alpha_0 + \alpha_1\epsilon_{t-1}^2 > 0, \qquad (15.49)$$

since $\mathsf{E}[\eta_t^2] = 1$. Next:

$$\mathsf{E}\left[\epsilon_t^2 \mid \epsilon_{t-1}\right] = \mathsf{E}\left[\eta_t\sqrt{\alpha_0 + \alpha_1\epsilon_{t-1}^2} \mid \epsilon_{t-1}\right] = \mathsf{E}\left[\eta_t\right]\sqrt{\alpha_0 + \alpha_1\epsilon_{t-1}^2} = 0, \quad (15.50)$$

as $\mathsf{E}[\eta_t] = 0$, and so $\mathsf{E}[\epsilon_t] = 0$. Thus, (15.50) also proves that $\{\epsilon_t\}$ is not first-order autocorrelated. Similarly, $\mathsf{E}[\epsilon_t|\epsilon_{t-j}] = 0 \ \forall j > 0$. Finally, setting $\mathsf{E}[\epsilon_t^2] = \sigma_\epsilon^2$ and taking expectations in (15.49) assuming weak stationarity:

$$\sigma_\epsilon^2 = \mathsf{E}\left[\epsilon_t^2\right] = \alpha_0 + \alpha_1\mathsf{E}\left[\epsilon_{t-1}^2\right] = \alpha_0 + \alpha_1\sigma_\epsilon^2 = \frac{\alpha_0}{1-\alpha_1} > 0. \qquad (15.51)$$

Alternatively, since $|\alpha_1| < 1$, construct sequentially:

$$\mathsf{E}[\epsilon_1^2] = \alpha_0; \ \mathsf{E}[\epsilon_2^2] = (1+\alpha_1)\alpha_0; \ \mathsf{E}[\epsilon_t^2] = \alpha_0\sum_{i=1}^{t}\alpha_1^{i-1} \to \frac{\alpha_0}{1-\alpha_1}.$$

Unconditionally, therefore, $\{\epsilon_t\}$ is homoscedastic. Moreover, ϵ_t is conditionally normal, and is not autocorrelated. Nevertheless, the vector $\epsilon' = (\epsilon_1 \dots \epsilon_T)$ is neither jointly normal, nor are its elements independent, as is obvious from (15.47). Finally, ϵ_t is not marginally normal, but has 'fat' tails due to the ARCH effect. Thus, this example illustrates that lack of correlation does not entail independence when the component normals do not sustain a joint normal.

Solution to (b)

The OLS estimator in (15.46) is:

$$\hat{\beta} = \beta + \left(\sum_{t=1}^{T} z_t^2\right)^{-1}\sum_{t=1}^{T} z_t\epsilon_t \qquad (15.52)$$

and since $\{z_t\}$ is strictly exogenous and fixed in repeated samples:

$$\mathsf{E}\left[\hat{\beta}\right] = \beta + \left(\sum_{t=1}^{T} z_t^2\right)^{-1}\sum_{t=1}^{T} z_t\mathsf{E}\left[\epsilon_t\right] = \beta,$$

with:

$$\mathsf{V}\left[\widehat{\beta}\right]=\left(\sum_{t=1}^{T}z_t^2\right)^{-2}\sum_{t=1}^{T}z_t z_s \mathsf{E}\left[\epsilon_t\epsilon_s\right]=\sigma_\epsilon^2\left(\sum_{t=1}^{T}z_t^2\right)^{-1}=\sigma_\epsilon^2 m_{zz}^{-1}. \tag{15.53}$$

Further, $\widehat{\beta}$ is a linear function of $\{y_t\}$. Consider any other linear unbiased estimator:

$$\breve{\beta}=\sum_{t=1}^{T}w_t y_t,$$

where:

$$\mathsf{E}\left[\breve{\beta}\right]=\mathsf{E}\left[\sum_{t=1}^{T}w_t\left(\beta z_t+\epsilon_t\right)\right]=\beta\mathsf{E}\left[\sum_{t=1}^{T}w_t z_t\right],$$

so $\mathsf{E}[\breve{\beta}]=\beta$ only if $\sum_{t=1}^{T}w_t z_t=1$. In that case:

$$\mathsf{V}\left[\breve{\beta}\right]=\mathsf{E}\left[\sum_{t=1}^{T}w_t w_s\epsilon_t\epsilon_s\right]=\sigma_\epsilon^2\sum_{t=1}^{T}w_t^2.$$

This is precisely the form which a proof of the Gauss–Markov theorem would follow (see Ch.A3), since the ARCH aspect of the error plays no role. Indeed, $\mathsf{E}[y_t|z_t]=\beta z_t$ because $\mathsf{E}[\epsilon_t]=0$ and $\mathsf{V}[y_t|z_t]=\mathsf{E}[\epsilon_t^2]=\sigma_\epsilon^2$. Hence the minimum variance is when $w_t=m_{zz}^{-1}z_t$, which yields $\widehat{\beta}$ as the BLUE despite the ARCH error. From (15.51) and (15.53), since $\widehat{\boldsymbol{\epsilon}}=\boldsymbol{y}-\widehat{\beta}\boldsymbol{z}=\boldsymbol{Q}_Z\boldsymbol{\epsilon}$ where $\boldsymbol{Q}_Z=(\boldsymbol{I}_T-\boldsymbol{z}(\boldsymbol{z}'\boldsymbol{z})^{-1}\boldsymbol{z}')$:

$$\mathsf{E}\left[\widehat{\sigma}_\epsilon^2\right]=(T-1)^{-1}\mathsf{E}\left[\sum_{t=1}^{T}\widehat{\epsilon}_t^2\right]=(T-1)^{-1}\mathsf{E}\left[\boldsymbol{\epsilon}'\boldsymbol{Q}_Z\boldsymbol{\epsilon}\right]=\sigma_\epsilon^2,$$

and so the conventional OLS variance formula is also unbiased. This would not be true if one of the regressors was the lagged-dependent variable.

Solution to (c)

Since $\epsilon_t|\epsilon_{t-1}\sim\mathsf{N}[0,v_t^2]$ where $v_t^2=\alpha_0+\alpha_1\epsilon_{t-1}^2$, and the likelihood function is the product of the sequential densities of the $\{\epsilon_t\}$, then:

$$\mathsf{D}_\epsilon\left(\epsilon_1\ldots\epsilon_T\right)=\prod_{t=1}^{T}\frac{1}{\sqrt{2\pi v_t^2}}\exp\left(-\frac{\epsilon_t^2}{2v_t^2}\right) \tag{15.54}$$

Note that $\{v_t^2-\epsilon_t^2\}$ is a mean-zero, serially-independent process. The log-likelihood is:

$$\ell\left(\alpha_0,\alpha_1,\beta\mid\cdot\right)=-\tfrac{1}{2}\log 2\pi-\tfrac{1}{2}\sum_{t=1}^{T}\log v_t^2-\sum_{t=1}^{T}\frac{\left(y_t-\beta z_t\right)^2}{2v_t^2}. \tag{15.55}$$

To derive an LM test of $\mathsf{H}_0\colon \alpha_1 = 0$ against $\mathsf{H}_1\colon \alpha_1 > 0$, we need the scores of (15.55), then evaluate these under the null. A signed square-root will deliver the required one-sided test. Since:

$$\frac{\partial v_t^2}{\partial \alpha_0} = \frac{\partial \left(\alpha_0 + \alpha_1 \epsilon_{t-1}^2\right)}{\partial \alpha_0} = 1 \text{ and } \frac{\partial v_t^2}{\partial \alpha_1} = \frac{\partial \left(\alpha_0 + \alpha_1 \epsilon_{t-1}^2\right)}{\partial \alpha_1} = \epsilon_{t-1}^2, \tag{15.56}$$

whereas:

$$\frac{\partial v_t^2}{\partial \beta} = \alpha_1 \frac{\partial \left(y_{t-1} - \beta z_{t-1}\right)^2}{\partial \beta} = -2\alpha_1 \epsilon_{t-1} z_{t-1}, \tag{15.57}$$

and $\partial \epsilon_t^2 / \partial \alpha_i = 0$, then the relevant scores are:

$$\frac{\partial \ell\left(\cdot\right)}{\partial \alpha_0} = -\sum_{t=1}^{T} \frac{1}{2v_t^2} + \sum_{t=1}^{T} \frac{\epsilon_t^2}{2v_t^4} = \frac{1}{2} \sum_{t=1}^{T} \left(\frac{\epsilon_t^2}{v_t^2} - 1\right) \frac{\partial \log v_t^2}{\partial \alpha_0},$$

and:

$$\frac{\partial \ell\left(\cdot\right)}{\partial \alpha_1} = -\sum_{t=1}^{T} \frac{\epsilon_{t-1}^2}{2v_t^2} + \sum_{t=1}^{T} \frac{\epsilon_t^2 \epsilon_{t-1}^2}{2v_t^4} = \frac{1}{2} \sum_{t=1}^{T} \left(\frac{\epsilon_t^2}{v_t^2} - 1\right) \frac{\partial \log v_t^2}{\partial \alpha_1}, \tag{15.58}$$

since

$$\frac{\partial \log v_t^2}{\partial \alpha_i} = \frac{1}{v_t^2} \frac{\partial v_t^2}{\partial \alpha_i}.$$

Finally:

$$\frac{\partial \ell\left(\cdot\right)}{\partial \beta} = \frac{1}{2} \sum_{t=1}^{T} \left(\frac{\epsilon_t^2}{v_t^2} - 1\right) \frac{\partial \log v_t^2}{\partial \beta} + \sum_{t=1}^{T} \frac{z_t \epsilon_t}{v_t^2}, \tag{15.59}$$

which differs from the usual generalized least-squares formula. Since the score for β is a linear function of $\{\epsilon_t\}$ (see (15.57)), whereas those for α_0 and α_1 are functions of $\{\epsilon_t^2\}$ from (15.56), their MLEs are independent. Since α_0 corresponds to the mean, we can imagine partialling it out to leave a mean-zero component.

The relevant information matrix term for α_1 is based on:

$$\frac{\partial^2 \ell\left(\cdot\right)}{\partial \alpha_1^2} = \frac{1}{2} \sum_{t=1}^{T} \left(\frac{\epsilon_t^2}{v_t^2} - 1\right) \frac{\partial^2 \log v_t^2}{\partial \alpha_1^2} - \frac{1}{2} \sum_{t=1}^{T} \frac{\epsilon_t^2}{v_t^2} \left(\frac{\partial \log v_t^2}{\partial \alpha_1}\right)^2.$$

The first term has zero expectation conditional on the information at $t-1$. Thus:

$$\mathsf{E}\left[-T^{-1} \frac{\partial^2 \ell\left(\cdot\right)}{\partial \alpha_1^2}\right] = \frac{1}{2} \mathsf{E}\left[\frac{\epsilon_t^2}{v_t^2} \left(\frac{\epsilon_{t-1}^2}{v_t^2}\right)^2\right].$$

Under $\mathsf{H}_0\colon \alpha_1 = 0$, $v_t^2 = \alpha_0 = \sigma_\epsilon^2$, the MLE of β is OLS, and $\hat{\alpha}_0 = T^{-1} \sum_{t=1}^{T} \hat{\epsilon}_t^2$. Since $\mathsf{E}[\epsilon_t^4] = 3\alpha_0^2$:

$$\mathcal{I}\left(\alpha_1\right)_{\rfloor \alpha_1 = 0} = \frac{3\alpha_0^3}{2\alpha_0^3} = \frac{3}{2}.$$

Thus, from (15.58):

$$\mathsf{LM} = \frac{1}{T}\left(\frac{\partial \ell(\cdot)}{\partial \alpha_1}\rfloor_{\alpha_1=0}\right)^2 \left(\mathcal{I}(\alpha_1)_{\rfloor \alpha_1=0}\right)^{-1} = \left(\frac{1}{3T}\sum_{t=1}^{T}\left(\frac{\epsilon_t^2}{\alpha_0}-1\right)\frac{\epsilon_{t-1}^2}{\alpha_0}\right)^2,$$

which for estimated values depends on:

$$\frac{1}{T}\left[\sum_{t=1}^{T}\hat{\epsilon}_{t-1}^2\left(\hat{\epsilon}_t^2-\hat{\alpha}_0\right)\right]^2,$$

where $\hat{\epsilon}_t = y_t - \hat{\beta} z_t$, so the LM test can be based on the least-squares residual diagnostic regression:

$$\hat{\epsilon}_t^2 = \alpha_0 + \alpha_1 \hat{\epsilon}_{t-1}^2 + \nu_t.$$

An AR error process induces ARCH effects, so Engle *et al.* (1985) consider the Durbin–Watson test and show that it has power to detect ARCH in small samples, but is an inconsistent test.

Solution to (d)

The MLE requires iterative solution, since equating to zero the scores for α_0 and α_1 yields expressions of the form:

$$\sum_{t=1}^{T}\left(\frac{v_t^2-\epsilon_t^2}{v_t^4}\right) = 0 \text{ and } \sum_{t=1}^{T}\left(\frac{v_t^2-\epsilon_t^2}{v_t^4}\right)\epsilon_{t-1}^2 = 0,$$

where $\epsilon_t = y_t - \beta z_t$ and is dependent on the α_i. However, when α_0 and α_1 are known, since $\epsilon_t \sim \mathsf{N}[0, v_t^2]$, map the problem to least squares on the transformed model:

$$\frac{y_t}{v_t} = \beta\frac{z_t}{v_t} + \frac{\epsilon_t}{v_t}. \tag{15.60}$$

The solution to the MLE is still non-linear, since $v_t^2 = \alpha_0 + \alpha_1 \epsilon_{t-1}^2$, with:

$$\tilde{\beta} = \left(\sum_{t=1}^{T}\frac{z_t^2}{v_t^2}\right)^{-1}\sum_{t=1}^{T}\frac{z_t y_t}{v_t^2} = \beta + \left(\sum_{t=1}^{T}\frac{z_t^2}{v_t^2}\right)^{-1}\sum_{t=1}^{T}\frac{z_t \epsilon_t}{v_t^2}.$$

However ϵ_t is symmetric, and v_t^2 is an even function of the $\{\epsilon_t\}$, so for fixed z_t, $\tilde{\beta}$ is invariant to a sign change in $\{\epsilon_t\}$. Thus, antithetic variates (see Ch.3) prove that $\tilde{\beta}$ is unbiased for β. The MLE here is a non-linear but unbiased estimator. When α_0 and α_1 are unknown, they are also even functions of $\{\epsilon_t\}$, so the MLE remains unbiased.

Solution to (e)

The pre-test estimator $\bar{\beta}$ is based on using $\hat{\beta}$ when the LM test in (c) is not significant, and $\tilde{\beta}$ when it is. Both underlying estimators are unbiased, and hence so is any weighted average of them, implying that $\bar{\beta}$ is unbiased for β provided the probability of rejection on the LM test is independent of $(\hat{\beta} - \tilde{\beta})$. Thus, pre-testing need not induce biased estimates.

Solution to (f)

The final step is to show that the BLUE is asymptotically inefficient when $\alpha_1 > 0$, and has a larger variance in its asymptotic distribution than the (non-linear unbiased) MLE. The second derivative of the log-likelihood follows from (15.59), and it is left as an exercise to derive that outcome and show that it is smaller than the OLS variance in (15.53). Thus, OLS may be BLUE but it is not efficient. Indeed, Engle (1982a) shows that the efficiency loss can be large. As remarked at the start of this section, ARCH illustrates many distinctions in econometric theory that may otherwise appear otiose. The analysis generalises to both GARCH, and higher-order, processes.

15.9 Populations and samples

The distinction between the sample (level C) and the population (level A) is of paramount importance in understanding data evidence. A simple example, relating autocorrelation and independence in a process subject to a regime shift, will illustrate. Consider an independently distributed process $\{y_t\}$ subject to a change in its mean β at time T_1:

$$y_t \sim \mathsf{IN}\left[\beta_1, \sigma^2\right] \text{ for } t = 1, \dots, T_1 \text{ and } y_t \sim \mathsf{IN}\left[\beta_2, \sigma^2\right] \text{ for } t = T_1 + 1, \dots, T.$$

Denote the two regimes by $j = 1, 2$ and let $J = \{1, 2\}$. The $\{y_t\}$ process is independent by construction and:

$$\mathsf{E}\left[\left(y_t - \mathsf{E}\left[y_t\right]\right)\left(y_{t-1} - \mathsf{E}\left[y_{t-1}\right]\right)\right] = 0. \tag{15.61}$$

A similar result holds for longer autocovariances being zero, irrespective of the dependence on the regimes. Nevertheless, this is cold comfort for a modeller at level C who is unaware of the regime shift in β. Let the sample mean be $\hat{\beta} = T^{-1}\sum_{t=1}^{T} y_t$, then:

$$\mathsf{E}\left[\hat{\beta}\right] = T^{-1}\mathsf{E}\left[\sum_{t=1}^{T_1} y_t + \sum_{t=T_1+1}^{T} y_t\right] = \frac{T_1}{T}\beta_1 + \left(\frac{T - T_1}{T}\right)\beta_2 \tag{15.62}$$

which is a weighted average of β_1 and β_2. Let $K = T_1/T$ and $\phi = \beta_2 + K(\beta_1 - \beta_2)$. The expected sample autocovariance at one lag is:

$$\mathsf{C}\left[y_t, y_{t-1}\right] = T^{-1}\mathsf{E}\left[\sum_{t=1}^{T}\left(y_t - \hat{\beta}\right)\left(y_{t-1} - \hat{\beta}\right)\right] \simeq T^{-1}\mathsf{E}\left[\sum_{t=1}^{T}\left(y_t - \phi\right)\left(y_{t-1} - \phi\right)\right]$$

and so:

$$\begin{aligned}\mathsf{C}\left[y_t, y_{t-1}\right] &\simeq T^{-1}\mathsf{E}\left[\sum_{t=1}^{T_1}\left(y_t - \phi\right)\left(y_{t-1} - \phi\right) + \sum_{t=T_1+1}^{T}\left(y_t - \phi\right)\left(y_{t-1} - \phi\right)\right] \\ &\simeq K\left(1 - K\right)\left(\beta_1 - \beta_2\right)^2 > 0\end{aligned} \tag{15.63}$$

since $\phi - \beta_1 = (K-1)(\beta_1 - \beta_2)$ and:

$$T^{-1}\mathsf{E}\left[\sum_{t=1}^{T_1}(y_t - \beta_1)(y_{t-1} - \beta_1) + \sum_{t=T_1+1}^{T}(y_t - \beta_2)(y_{t-1} - \beta_2)\right] = 0,$$

from (15.61). A similar result holds at longer lags, and hence the unmodelled regime shift induces apparent positive serial dependence. The formula in (15.63) is symmetric in the length of the two regimes and the changes in means (see Hendry and Neale, 1991, and Perron, 1989). The implication is the usual one when a model induces adverse evidence: the model as a whole is rejected, but there are many reasons why that may have occurred, and we know that here the errors are in fact independent. Thus, population independence by itself does not ensure sample independence.

Similarly, interpreting heteroscedasticity at level C raises difficulties, and we illustrate that using an example similar to (15.61) (see Ding, Granger and Engle, 1993, and Hall and Sola, 1993). Consider a heteroscedastic, but independent error process $\{\epsilon_t\}$:

$$\epsilon_t \sim \mathsf{IN}\left[0, \sigma_1^2\right] \text{ for } t = 1, .., T_1 \text{ and } \epsilon_t \sim \mathsf{IN}\left[0, \sigma_2^2\right] \text{ for } t = T_1 + 1, \ldots, T.$$

Then:

$$\epsilon_t^2 \sim \sigma_j^2 \chi^2(1) \text{ for } j \in J.$$

Such $\{\epsilon_t^2\}$ remain independent, since for a constant choice of j:

$$\mathsf{E}\left[\epsilon_t^2\right] = \sigma_j^2 \text{ and } \mathsf{V}\left[\epsilon_t^2\right] = \mathsf{E}\left[\left(\epsilon_t^2 - \sigma_j^2\right)^2\right] = 2\sigma_j^4,$$

so that:

$$\mathsf{E}\left[\left(\epsilon_t^2 - \sigma_j^2\right)\left(\epsilon_{t-1}^2 - \sigma_j^2\right)\right] = 0. \tag{15.64}$$

Nevertheless, the sample covariance can be far from zero for a sample comprising substantial numbers of drawings from the two regimes:

$$\begin{aligned}\mathsf{E}\left[T^{-1}\sum_{t=1}^{T}\epsilon_t^2\right] &= \mathsf{E}\left[T^{-1}\left(\sum_{t=1}^{T_1}\epsilon_t^2 + \sum_{t=T_1+1}^{T}\epsilon_t^2\right)\right] \\ &= K\sigma_1^2 + (1-K)\sigma_2^2 = \mu.\end{aligned}$$

Letting $\mathsf{C}[\epsilon_t^2, \epsilon_{t-1}^2] = \mathsf{E}[T^{-1}\sum_{t=1}^{T}(\epsilon_t^2 - \mu)(\epsilon_{t-1}^2 - \mu)]$, then $\mathsf{C}[\epsilon_t^2, \epsilon_{t-1}^2]$ equals:

$$\begin{aligned}&T^{-1}\mathsf{E}\left[\sum_{t=1}^{T_1}\left(\epsilon_t^2\epsilon_{t-1}^2 - \mu\left(\epsilon_t^2 + \epsilon_{t-1}^2\right) + \mu^2\right) + \sum_{t=T_1+1}^{T}\left(\epsilon_t^2\epsilon_{t-1}^2 - \mu\left(\epsilon_t^2 + \epsilon_{t-1}^2\right) + \mu^2\right)\right] \\ &\simeq T^{-1}\left[\sum_{t=1}^{T_1}\left(\sigma_1^4 - 2\mu\sigma_1^2 + \mu^2\right) + \sum_{t=T_1+1}^{T}\left(\sigma_2^4 - 2\mu\sigma_2^2 + \mu^2\right)\right] \\ &= K(1-K)\left(\sigma_1^2 - \sigma_2^2\right)^2 \geq 0.\end{aligned} \tag{15.65}$$

Thus, $\mathsf{C}[\epsilon_t^2, \epsilon_{t-1}^2] > 0$, suggesting an ARCH error. This outcome contrasts with (15.64) and is analogous to (15.63): an unmodelled change in unconditional variance can be mistaken for ARCH or persistence of shocks.

A possible empirical example of this analysis is provided by the US long-term interest rate data shown in Fig. 15.3 above. As noted, the squares $(\Delta R_t)^2$ and absolute values $|\Delta R_t|$ are highly positively autocorrelated for many lags: Fig. 15.3d reveals that all the autocorrelations of $|\Delta R_t|$are positive for up to 40 lags, even though those of $\{\Delta R_t\}$are in fact near to zero at all lags. At level C, it is impossible to be certain as to the cause of the observed outcome, but Fig. 15.3a is consistent with three 'regimes' for $\{\Delta R_t\}$, namely, from 1954–1966, 1966–1980, and 1980–1989 within which epochs the variance is relatively constant, but it changes between epochs. This could reflect ARCH or related processes at work.

It is intrinsically difficult to determine when a process is weakly stationary (perhaps after differencing to remove any unit roots) and when it is subject to non-stationary effects. For example, apparent regime changes may be drawings from a constant distribution of rare events (e.g., a Poisson process) impinging on an otherwise stationary process; and ARCH reveals that conditional heteroscedasticity can be consistent with unconditional homoscedasticity. However, an intensive analysis of all the implications of a data-set, as in Ding *et al.* (1993), can help reveal which hypotheses are the most sustainable, and which face conflicting evidence.

15.10 Exercises

15.1 What implications might the finding that data revisions are $\mathsf{I}(1)$ have for:

(a) the estimation of models with measurement errors; and

(b) empirical econometric modelling?

15.2 Prove that OLS in §15.8 satisfies the Gauss–Markov theorem despite the ARCH error.

15.3 Consider how to generalize the results in §15.8 to a GARCH error process of the form:

$$\epsilon_t | (\epsilon_{t-1} \dots \epsilon_{t-k}) \sim \mathsf{N}\left[0, v_t^2\right],$$

where

$$v_t^2 = \alpha_0 + \alpha_1 \epsilon_{t-1}^2 + \beta_1 v_{t-1}^2,$$

with α_1 and β_1 non-negative. Does the case $\alpha_1 + \beta_1 = 1$ raise problems?

15.4 What are the implications of structural breaks in dynamic processes on tests for unit roots?

16

Econometrics in Action

The methods, approaches and principles are now applied to modelling the transactions demand for money in the UK over 1963–1989. Financial innovations affecting money demand are investigated, and their impact on the opportunity cost of holding money is captured in a learning-adjusted interest rate differential. The data are first described by graphs of time series, cross-plots, densities, and correlograms to highlight the main features requiring modelling, and matching between series, to deliver a congruent model. A VAR is examined for cointegration, and potential long-run weak exogeneity. A small monetary system is formulated. This sustains a single-equation model of transactions demand, so commencing from a general linear autoregressive-distributed lag representation, a simplified congruent model is developed as an exercise in practical data modelling.

16.1 The transactions demand for money

The demand for the transactions medium, or narrow money, plays a major role in many macro-economic theories, both because it is essential to the efficient functioning of modern economies, and because some economists view money as an important determinant of the price level. Consequently, empirical econometric models of the demand for money, of which M1 equations in both the UK and the US are now classic examples, have been a major focus of interest since the early 1970s.[1] The M1 measure comprises notes and coin in circulation plus balances in checking accounts, and modelling its behaviour is the focus of this chapter.

A standard postulate is (see e.g. Goldfeld, 1973):

$$M^d = f(P, I, r), \tag{16.1}$$

[1] For the UK, see Hacche (1974), Courakis (1978), Hendry and Mizon (1978), Coghlan (1978), Hendry (1979b, 1985), Desai (1981), Trundle (1982), Hendry and Richard (1983), Lubrano, Pierse and Richard (1986), Cuthbertson (1988), Hendry (1988), Hall, Henry and Wilcox (1990), Hendry and Mizon (1993), and Hendry and Ericsson (1991a, 1991b). For the US, see Judd and Scadding (1982), Laidler (1985), and Goldfeld and Sichel (1990) for surveys, and Friedman (1956), Goldfeld (1973, 1976), Gordon (1984), Rose (1984), and Baba, Hendry and Starr (1992) *inter alia* for empirical studies. The references in the surveys provide a more extensive bibliography.

where M^d is the demand for the transactions medium, P is the price level, I is a measure of real transactions volume, and $\boldsymbol{r}$ is a vector of interest rates, representing the net opportunity costs of holding money as against alternative interest-bearing assets. In (16.1), $f(\cdot)$ implicitly includes dynamic adjustment and expectations formation, with only the long-run determinants being explicitly noted. Frequently, price homogeneity is imposed on the grounds that the units of a currency are irrelevant, so that the model becomes:

$$\frac{M^d}{P} = f(I, \boldsymbol{r}). \tag{16.2}$$

However, the analysis in Chapter 7 cautions against imposing restrictions which may inadvertently affect short-run dynamics.

Despite its importance for inference, forecasting, and policy, it has proved difficult to establish M1 equations with constant parameters. Many estimated money-demand equations suffered predictive failure during the periods known as 'missing money' in the mid-1970s, the 'great velocity decline' in the early 1980s, and the recent explosion in M1. Non-constant empirical equations do not preclude a constant underlying money-demand function, but in the absence of a constant-parameter econometric model, an unresolved issue is whether predictive failure is due to shifts in the function, or mis-specification in the econometric model. Further, mis-specification is necessary, but not sufficient, for parameter non-constancy.

The magnitude of the task confronting the applied econometrician is illustrated in Figs. 16.1a–d, which graph the logs of nominal M1 (m) with the price level (p), and real M1 ($m - p$) with real total final expenditure (TFE) (i) for the UK and real GNP for the US, through 1989 and 1993 respectively. The variability in real M1 prior to 1984 was sufficient to reject previous models, yet is dwarfed by the end-of-sample increases in both countries. Real M1 increased by more than fifty per cent in the second half of the 1980s in both countries, so the claim that 'money causes inflation' makes modelling these series of considerable interest. However, the series are strongly trended, and must be treated as integrated, evolutionary processes, so the low visual correlation between $m - p$ and their main determinant i confirms that the task will not be easy.

The chapter first reviews economic theories of money demand in section 16.2, then discusses the econometric formulation for the UK data series to be investigated in §16.3. The issue of financial innovation is considered in §16.4, then the data are described in detail in §16.5. Next, cointegration is examined in a system context in §16.6. The outcome suggests that there are two identifiable cointegrating vectors, corresponding to long-run money demand, and excess demand for goods and services, and these are imposed. A small monetary model of the system is developed in §16.8, which supports the weak exogeneity for the parameters of the money-demand equation of expenditure, inflation, and the opportunity-cost measure. This allows a conditioning reduction to a dynamic empirical analogue of (16.1), which is modelled in section 16.10 from a general autoregressive-distributed lag relation to a parsimonious model. The simplification and transformation steps are explained and tested in §16.11. Post-modelling evaluation is undertaken in §16.12, followed by tests of the Lucas critique and invertibility in §16.13.

Finally, some policy implications of the analysis are discussed in §16.15. The precise data definitions are presented in §16.16.

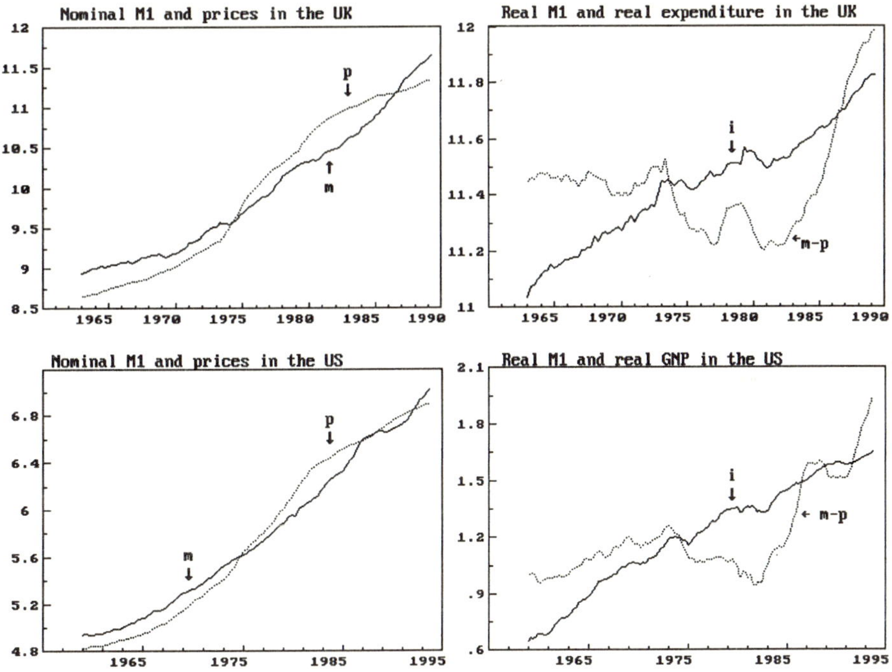

Fig. 16.1 UK and US money stocks, output, and prices

The present exercise aims to illustrate the modelling issues analysed in earlier chapters, and is based on Hendry (1979b, 1985), Hendry and Ericsson (1991b), Hendry and Mizon (1993) and Hendry and Doornik (1994). It is as apt for highlighting the limitations of the approach as for demonstrating its advantages. Since the data are highly informative, by their having rejected most earlier contenders, powerful tests of super exogeneity and invariance claims are feasible for any claimed constant parameter representation (see Ch.14). Conversely, many facets of any empirical analysis involve conjecture and discovery. While this makes model design difficult, and initial inferences hazardous, claims can be tested on later data. As stressed in Chapter 15, partial knowledge can be acquired.

16.2 Economic theories of money demand

There are three conceptually-distinct justifications for holding money: transactions demand, with money held as a medium of exchange; precautionary demand, where money is a liquid reserve for contingencies; and asset (or speculative) demand, with money being one of several assets in which wealth is held. In practice, money demand seems to depend on all three factors.

Transactions-demand theory is based on the need for money to smooth timing differences between income and expenditure streams. Thus, the aggregate real quantity of money demanded, M^d/P as in (16.2), is taken to be an increasing function of the volume of real transactions (I). Real GNP and TFE are the two measures commonly used (as in Fig. 16.1). Money demand declines as the opportunity costs of holding money increase, where the latter depend upon the returns to alternative assets such as bills, bonds, and deposit accounts in banks or other financial intermediaries.[2] Often, a log-linear specification is adopted for (16.2):

$$m^d - p = \delta i + \gamma' \boldsymbol{r}, \tag{16.3}$$

where the parameters in γ are negative for competing rates, and positive for own rates. The choice of $\log M$ for the dependent variable, and the positivity of M, P, and I, allows easy switching between m, $(m - p)$, $(m - p - \delta i)$, or time-differences of any of these. Theories differ about the anticipated value of the long-run income (or expenditure) elasticity δ, which takes the value 0.5 in Baumol and Tobin's transactions demand theory, and unity in Friedman's quantity theory of money.[3] Credit facilities may also affect the transactions demand for money.

Precautionary demands depend on the need for a liquid balance to meet unexpected expenses, the scale of which is probably a function of income.

In the portfolio-balance approach, money is one of many alternative forms of holding wealth, and each asset has its own explicit return (interest plus capital gain) and implicit return (non-pecuniary, including convenience and liquidity). For money, transactions services are included in the latter. Different assets have different expected returns and different degrees of uncertainty associated with their return. Individuals are assumed to choose the composition of their portfolio (including money) to maximize the expected returns, balancing more certain, but lower, returns with higher, but riskier, ones.[4] The resulting money-demand function is similar to (16.3), but wealth, rather than income or expenditure, is the 'scale' variable, and some measure of the volatility of alternative assets' returns enters in addition to their expected returns (see Tobin, 1958, and Walsh, 1984). In some theories (e.g. Ando and Shell, 1975), money is a dominated asset, but this result need not hold if borrowing and lending interest rates differ (see Baba *et al.*, 1992).

The determinants of money demand are central to modelling observed money holdings, but the 'money supply' is also involved. Often in macroeconomic models, an

[2] See Baumol (1952) and Tobin (1956) for the detailed development of transactions-demand theory. Miller and Orr (1966), Clower (1967), Ando and Shell (1975), Akerlof (1973, 1979), Gale (1982, 1983), Milbourne (1983), and Smith (1986) *inter alia* provide further developments, including 'cash-in-advance' models which give rise to transactions demands. Laidler (1984) has a related discussion of money as a 'buffer stock'.

[3] The difference in the value of δ is only one of many contrasts between these two theories. Friedman and Schwartz (1982) also describes Friedman's version of the quantity theory of money.

[4] Individuals may have different attitudes towards risk.

observed money stock (supposedly set by policy makers) is equated to money demand, from which prices (or interest rates, or income) are determined. When the money stock is deemed fixed, or the supply M^s is 'exogenous', equating the demand and supply yields:

$$M^d = M^s = f\left(P, I, \mathbf{r}\right),$$

thereby forcing one of P, I, or any element of $\mathbf{r}$ to adjust to changes in M^s, by 'inverting' the money-demand function. For example, Barro (1987) inverts to obtain a price equation in a theoretical supply and demand model; and Edison, Marquez and Tryon (1987) and Fair (1984) invert to obtain interest-rate equations in large empirical macro-models. Alternatively, a policy reaction function may make some interest rate endogenous. However, as discussed in Chapter A6, equating M^d to M^s conflates equilibrium with causality, and is not a firm basis for empirical modelling.

Here, we assume agents control their mean desired levels of M^d by substitution between assets of relatively similar liquidity and return characteristics (e.g. deposit accounts, or short-term bills). The monetary authority is deemed to control the discount (or similar) interest rate, the weak exogeneity of which for the parameters of $f(\cdot)$ needs investigation. The underlying theoretical framework draws on the 'target-bounds' literature.[5] In its simplest incarnation, economic agents formulate long-run upper and lower bands for their real-money balances, based on long-run real expenditure plans and precautionary anticipations. These long-run bands are rarely revised. Given the prevailing price level, the real bands translate into nominal bands, and when nominal balances fall below their lower band, they are increased to near the mean; similarly, when they rise above the upper band, they are reduced to near the mean. This model entails short-run movements of nominal money relative to targets set for longer-run considerations.

A range of issues must be resolved to translate an embryonic theoretical model like (16.2) into a useful relationship between observables. Alternative decisions could be made at almost every stage during modelling, so that different scholars could legitimately follow different routes and conclude with disparate models. Most models must be invalid, although each could capture important aspects of the overall picture. Since we are trying to discover an empirical relationship, such proliferation is neither surprising nor worrying: rather, a diverse set of congruent empirical models provides a challenging encompassing exercise. Any particular empirical study is part of the research progression, not the final word on the relevant subject. As discussed in Chapter 15, the discovery route cannot affect the validity of the product, though it might affect the credibility placed in it prior to rigorous external evaluation.

16.3 Econometric formulation

Rather than seek direct empirical correspondences to the theoretical entities in (16.1), we use that equation as a guide to the empirical analysis. Since most previous empirical

[5] For formal dynamic derivations, see, *inter alia*, Miller and Orr (1966), Akerlof (1973, 1979), Milbourne (1983), and Smith (1986).

models of money demand have been constructed by grafting empirical flesh onto skeletal theories like (16.1), yet appear to have experienced predictive failure at some points in the last quarter century, it cannot be claimed that such approaches have proved uniformly successful. Thus, a *prima-facie* case exists for trying an alternative approach.

The M1 measure of money, which we will model, is a simple aggregate of cash and current-account holdings.[6] Since decisions by central banks, especially the US Federal Reserve System, concerning monetary control rules have had major impacts on the domestic and the world economy during the 1980s, M1 deserves study from policy, theory, and data-analytic viewpoints. The choice of M1 does not entail that it corresponds precisely to M^d in (16.1), but does require that (16.1) remains relevant to the demand for M1 (so $f(\cdot)$ must capture the salient demand factors), which in turn requires careful consideration of how the associated P, I, and r should be measured. For example, since components of M1 became interest bearing during the historical period, the opportunity costs of holding M1 have altered, so the specification of r must be considered in that light.

The model relates M1 to TFE (I), and its implicit deflator (P). These are conventional, rather than optimal, choices since UK M1 is almost certainly not the only vehicle for financing imports (suggesting continued evaluation of any selected model as European integration proceeds). Money and expenditure are in £million, the deflator is unity in 1985, and the interest rate is annual, in fractions. The full sample is 1963(1)–1989(2) but after allowing for lags, estimation is usually over 1964(3)–1989(2), which yields 100 observations. Since M, P and I are separately seasonally adjusted, the caveats noted in Chapter 15 apply.[7] The interest-rate vector is the subject of the next section.

The econometric specification of the 'target-bounds' model uses a log-linear equilibrium-correction mechanism to determine the long-run bands, and, relative to these, agents move nominal money into and out of their accounts according to the changes in the short-run regressors. Individual agents await the crossing of their reaction thresholds before adjusting, so dynamic regressors reflect the probabilities of such crossings. The setting of the bands and thresholds depends on real transactions expenditures, and the opportunity costs of leaving money idle, which effects are captured by the measures of interest rates and inflation in the model. Actual 'adjustment costs' seem relatively negligible, so lagged reactions reflect the small benefits of adjusting rather than the large costs (see Akerlof, 1979): for example, when average holdings are £1 000, a three-month delay in adjusting to a two-percentage point change in competitive interest rates foregoes under £4, after tax of 25 per cent. Consequently, for M1, the pay-offs from forming expectations about future values of any potential conditioning variable seem small, except perhaps future inflation.

The dynamic money-demand model is the contingent planning equation:

[6] It is a major exercise to measure the transactions medium: see Simpson and Porter (1980), and Barnett (1980) for an index-number theory approach.

[7] Ericsson, Hendry and Tran (1994) analyse the corresponding seasonally unadjusted data and develop encompassing tests between models based on the two data sets.

$$\Delta(m-p)_t = \phi_0 + \phi_1(L)\Delta(m-p)_{t-1} + \phi_2(L)\Delta p_t + \phi_3(L)\Delta i_t + \phi_4(L)'\Delta \mathbf{r}_t + \phi_5\left[\left(m^d - p\right)_{t-1} - (m-p)_{t-1}\right] + \epsilon_t, \tag{16.4}$$

where the $\phi_i(L)$ for $i = 1, \ldots, 4$ are polynomials in L, ϵ_t is the deviation of the outcome from the plan, and m^d_{t-1} denotes the long-run target value m^d in (16.3) evaluated at $p_{t-1}, i_{t-1}, \mathbf{r}_{t-1}$. The choice of money as the dependent variable is justified by the claim that agents control its mean value. Equation (16.4) allows separate reaction speeds to the various determinants of money demand (reflecting different costs of adjustment or disequilibrium), yet ensures that the long-run target (16.3) is achieved in steady state. Relative to the economic theory, the short-run factors determine money movements given desired bands, whereas the longer-run factors in the ECM influence the levels of the bands. To be interpretable as a demand equation, $\phi_2(1) \leq 0, \phi_3(1) \geq 0$, and $\phi_{4j}(1) \leq 0$ for r_j on assets outside M1, with $\phi_{4j}(1) \geq 0$ for r_j on assets inside M1; and for cointegration $\phi_5 < 0$.[8] The signs, magnitudes, and numbers of individual lag-polynomial coefficients must be data-based, since economic theory is uninformative on such aspects. The intercept value ϕ_0 should preclude autonomous growth in velocity.

Money demand is part of the economic system, and interacts with many variables. Thus, as argued in Chapter 8, the analysis must commence from the joint density of m, p_t, i_t, and $\mathbf{r}_t$. In turn, that requires the specification of those variables, of which the remaining problem is the opportunity-cost measure, which is discussed in section 16.4. Once we have selected the measured variables, we can consider the dynamic specification of the empirical system, check its cointegration and congruency, simplify it to an interpretable econometric equation, test whether it encompasses previous models, and then evaluate it rigorously.

16.4 Financial innovation

The United Kingdom has witnessed numerous financial innovations over the last thirty years (see Desai and Low, 1987, and Hall *et al.*, 1990), starting in 1971 with the change in regulations called Competition and Credit Control, which abolished what had previously been a banking cartel. During the 1980s, building societies (the main UK mortgage lenders, equivalent to Savings and Loans institutions) and commercial banks both introduced checkable interest-bearing accounts, but with accounts at the former being outside of M1, and those at the latter within. Building societies were gradually de-regulated, allowing them to function more like banks (one of the largest societies changed status in 1989).[9] Modelling learning about, and adjustment to, innovation is the objective of this section, which leads to a specification of the opportunity-cost measure.

[8] This is sufficient, but not necessary, as discussed in Ch.8.

[9] For an empirical model of building society behaviour, see Hendry and Anderson (1977) and Anderson and Hendry (1984).

For new assets to influence behaviour, agents must learn about their existence and characteristics. Baba *et al.* (1992) (denoted by BHS) argued that, at the margin, an economic agent substituting from M1 into a near-money asset would select the highest-yielding asset, conditional on its liquidity profile and risk. In the UK, deposit accounts in building societies are a competitive alternative with high liquidity, but as Anderson and Hendry (1984) found that they set their rates in response to the interest rate on three-month local authority bills, R_{3t}, that is the measure selected here. When transactions balances can earn interest at a rate R_{ot}, the opportunity cost of 'idle' balances falls, so agents will desire to hold larger M1 balances. However, they first have to learn about the new asset, probably due to a slowly-spreading 'epidemic' of knowledge about its existence and advantages. There was no sudden explosion in M1 holdings when they became eligible to earn interest, although M1 later grew rapidly. The appropriate economic-policy reaction to such growth hinges on whether it was a portfolio adjustment, or an indicator of excess demand in the economy. An econometric model is needed to determine the answer, and success in doing so would provide an empirical rebuttal of the claims in Summers (1991) that econometrics has failed to deliver substantive economic knowledge.

To 'learning adjust' interest rates on newly-introduced assets, we follow the approach in BHS. Denote the interest rate on a new asset a by R_a, and the best rate on the existing asset choice by R_e for $R_a > R_e$. Then the learning-adjusted rate is:

$$R_{at}^{l} = R_{et} + w_{at}\left(R_{at} - R_{et}\right), \tag{16.5}$$

where $0 \leq w_{at} \leq 1$ is the weight at time t reflecting learning about asset a. BHS postulated an ogive-shaped learning curve spread over five years, representing the proportion of the relevant population willing to invest in the new asset at time t (zero till t_0, when the asset was introduced), given by the logistic function:

$$w_t = \left[1 + \exp\left(\alpha - \beta s\right)\right]^{-1} \quad \text{where } s = \left(t - t_0 + 1\right), \tag{16.6}$$

and α and β correspond to initial knowledge and rate of learning. BHS set $\alpha = 7$ and $\beta = 0.8$ for the US, but as interest-bearing retail sight deposits appeared in the UK subsequently (t_0 = 1984(3)), Hendry and Ericsson (1991b) set $\alpha = 5$ and $\beta = 1.2$. These values imply higher initial knowledge and more rapid learning, with $w_t = 0.50$ after one year and $w_t = 0.99$ after two years. The important feature of this weighting scheme is to down-weight the early returns on a new asset, when few agents knew to invest in it, and the precise choice of weights is not essential (see §16.12). Fig. 16.2 shows the weighting function.

Interest rates weighted by this function are denoted by a superscript '*l*' for learning, so the learning-adjusted own-interest rate for checking accounts, R_{ot}^{l}, uses (16.5) with $R_{et} \equiv 0$, namely, $R_{ot}^{l} = w_t R_{ot}$. Then the opportunity cost of holding M1 is:

$$R_t = R_{3t} - R_{ot}^{l}, \tag{16.7}$$

which neglects implicit service costs and benefits on existing checking accounts. As there were no major innovations outside M1, R_t is the only element in $\mathbf{r}_t$.

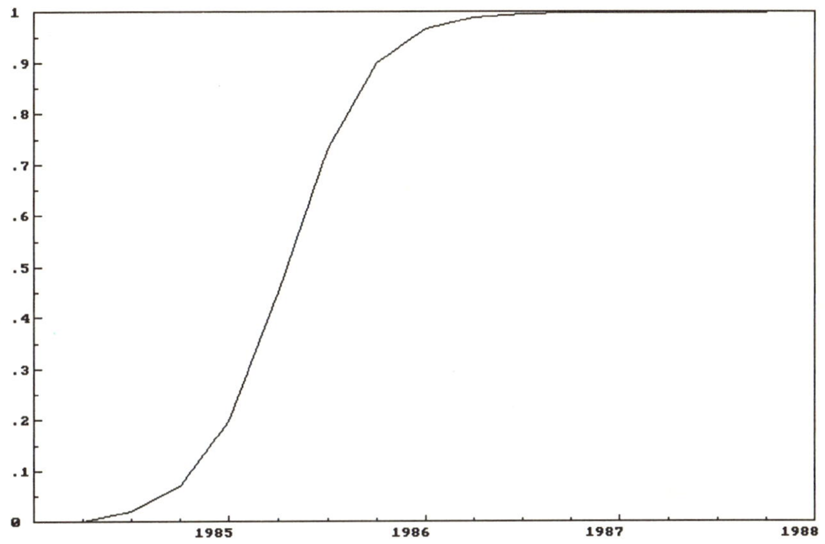

Fig. 16.2 Weighting function for learning adjustment of interest rates

Figs. 16.3a–b show the time series of the two interest-rate components, R_{3t} and R_{ot}, and ΔR_t. The interest rate has been quite volatile, and increased substantially over the period. The own rate rose rapidly at first, then stabilised between six and eight per cent, entailing a sharp fall in the differential.

16.5 Data description

Precise definitions of the data series are provided in section 16.16. Figs. 16.3c–d show the time series of real money and expenditure growth, and annual inflation.

Both $\Delta(m-p)$ and Δi are erratic, but show little correlation. Inflation was high and persistent over much of the period, rising substantially then falling to 1960s' levels by the end of the period. Figs. 16.1a,c recorded the time series of m and p for the UK and US: visually, these may seem highly correlated, but the variables are in logs, so there are considerable percentage departures between them. These can be seen more clearly from the time series for real money $(m - p)$ plotted in Figs. 16.1b,d with i, which reveal large changes in real money over the sample. Notice the rapid fall between 1972 and 1974 (Goldfeld, 1976, calls this episode 'missing money' in the US), and the rapid rise from 1980–2 (called the 'great velocity decline' in the US, and associated with a period of monetary control known as the New Operating Procedures). Finally, there is a virtual explosion in $(m - p)$ following the introduction of interest-bearing checking accounts (called NOW accounts in the US, and introduced there in 1981). The whole sample provides a severe test of any money-demand model, especially the periods from 1974 to 1980, when the stock of real money fell by about 15 per cent although the two economies grew fairly substantially, inducing a marked economization on transactions balances; and between 1983–87 when balances increased by large amounts relative to incomes.

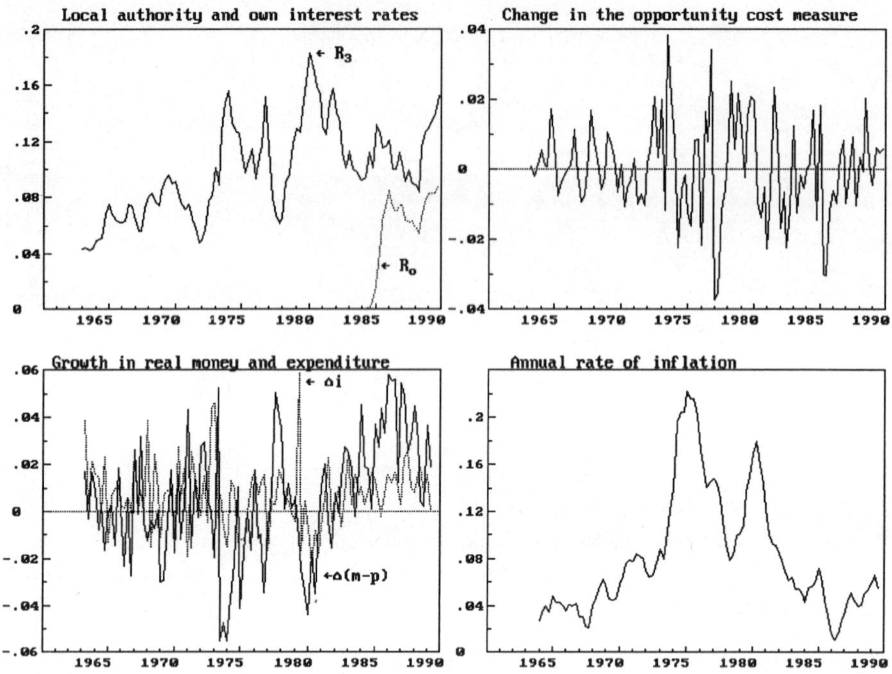

Fig. 16.3 Interest rates, real money and expenditure growth, and inflation

When Δm_t and Δp_t are cross-plotted as in Fig. 16.4a, there is no correlation between them, in marked contrast to the levels graph in Fig. 16.1. Such phenomena are typical of integrated series: Fig. 16.1a no more establishes that money causes prices, than Fig. 16.4a proves there is no relation. Rather, there is evidence for long-run price homogeneity, but not for short run, although partialling out the effects of other variables might alter both statements. Indeed, the interest rate and inflation do not move closely in line as seen in Fig. 16.4b, so the former could explain the lack of a simple correlation between Δm_t and Δp_t. Inflation was above the interest rate for much of the middle 1970s. Irrespective of whether this phenomenon reflects changes in the real interest rate, or in the covariance between interest and inflation, the interest rate could not have provided an equally good hedge against inflation at all times: consequently, the nominal interest rate is not the only opportunity cost of holding money.

Moreover, inflation is not tax deductible, whereas individuals pay taxes on interest earnings. Consider two groups of agents, one paying taxes, the other not, initially in equilibrium at a given real interest rate.[10] When inflation rises, changes in the nominal interest rate cannot bring the real interest rate back to the same level for both groups. On all these grounds, money-demand functions require inflation as a separate argument from nominal interest rates. Inflation alters the relative advantages of all financial assets compared to goods, and when agents reduce their financial asset holdings, they would *ceteris paribus* reduce money holdings, reflected in a negative inflation coefficient.

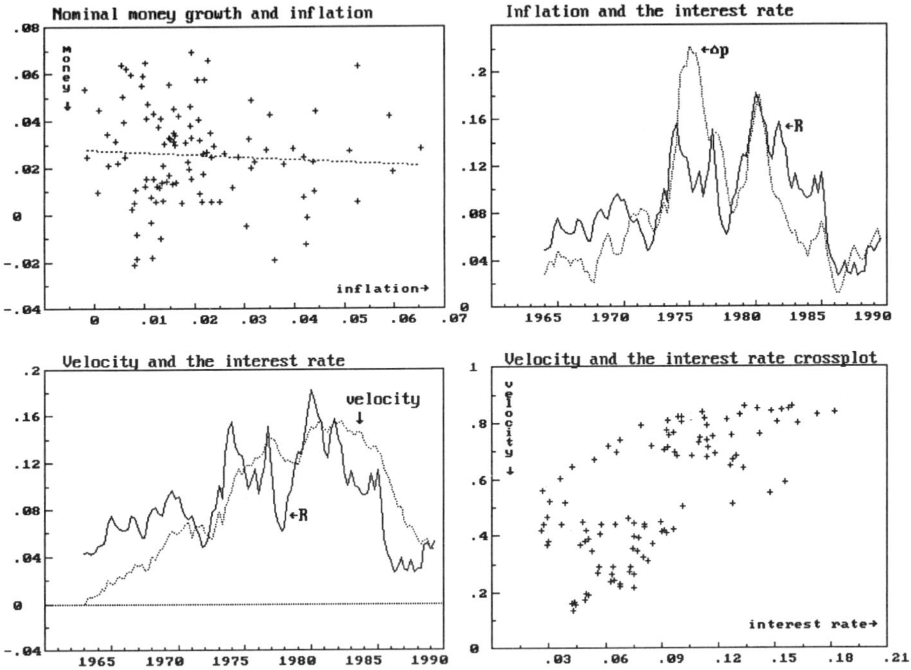

Fig. 16.4 Money growth, inflation, velocity and interest rates

The velocity of circulation of money $c_t = (i_t + p_t - m_t)$ (modelled in Chs.6–8) is shown in Fig. 16.4c with the interest rate R_t; the two series are positively correlated over the sample, as their cross-plot in Fig. 16.4d confirms. Incidentally, the time series of c_t is similar to that for the US over the same historical period: c_t increased substantially until the early 1980s, then decreased till the end of the sample.

Graphs like those in Figs. 16.1a and 16.4a have been claimed respectively to demonstrate that money does (does not) cause inflation. However, as argued in Chapter 5, causal inferences cannot be drawn from correlations alone. To make causality claims requires at least:

[10] Financial institutions, such as insurance companies and pension funds, do not pay tax on interest earnings.

(i) a theoretical model in which cause is well defined;
(ii) a deduction of what the correlation structure ought to be like when causality does and does not hold;
(iii) a discernable difference between causality being present or absent;
(iv) a test of the empirical model comparing the observed with the anticipated correlation structure; and
(v) persistence of the claimed link across regime changes.

Even when an empirical model satisfies these criteria, it has merely not rejected the claimed causal link; future evidence may do so.

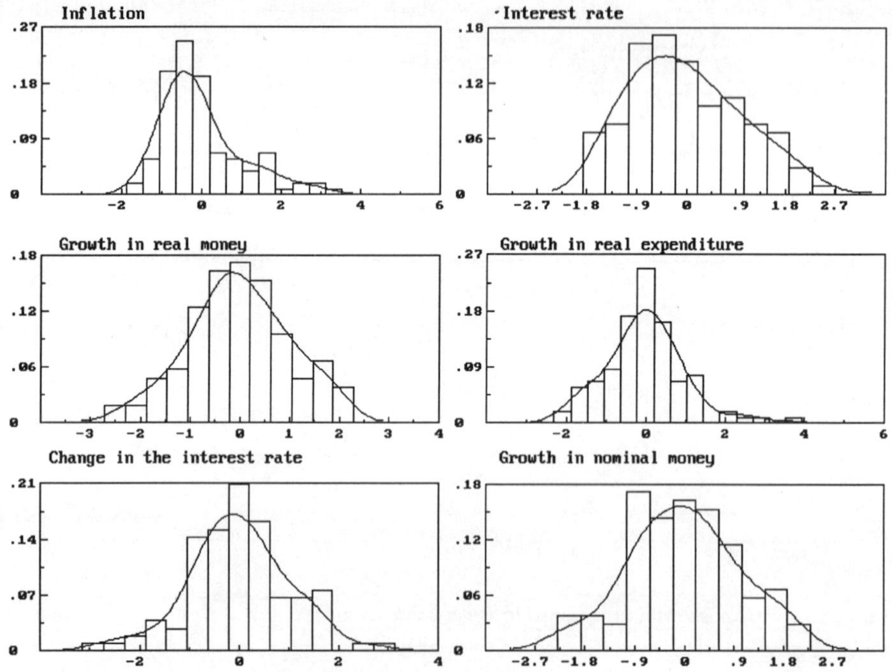

Fig. 16.5 Data densities for money, inflation, income and interest rates

Glancing back at the above figures, the time-series properties of the various series differ markedly. Alternative portrayals of this phenomenon are provided by graphs of the data densities and histograms, and the correlograms of the series. Figures 16.5a–f show the former for (Δp_t, R_t, $\Delta(m_t - p_t)$, Δi_t, ΔR_t, and Δm_t). The distributions are unimodal without too much excess kurtosis (except perhaps Δp_t), although none of the variables is precisely normally distributed. Their changes are closer to normality than their levels, but there are considerable differences between the distributional shapes of these variables even though they are to be linearly combined to form the money-demand model: such differences must 'cancel' if the residuals are to be approximately normal.

Similarly, the correlograms shown in Figs. 16.6a–h differ vastly: consider the I(1) pattern for real income, the high positive autocorrelations for velocity, the slowly changing autocorrelations for real money, the similar patterns for the growth in real and nominal money, and the near white-noise behaviour of ΔR_t and Δi_t.

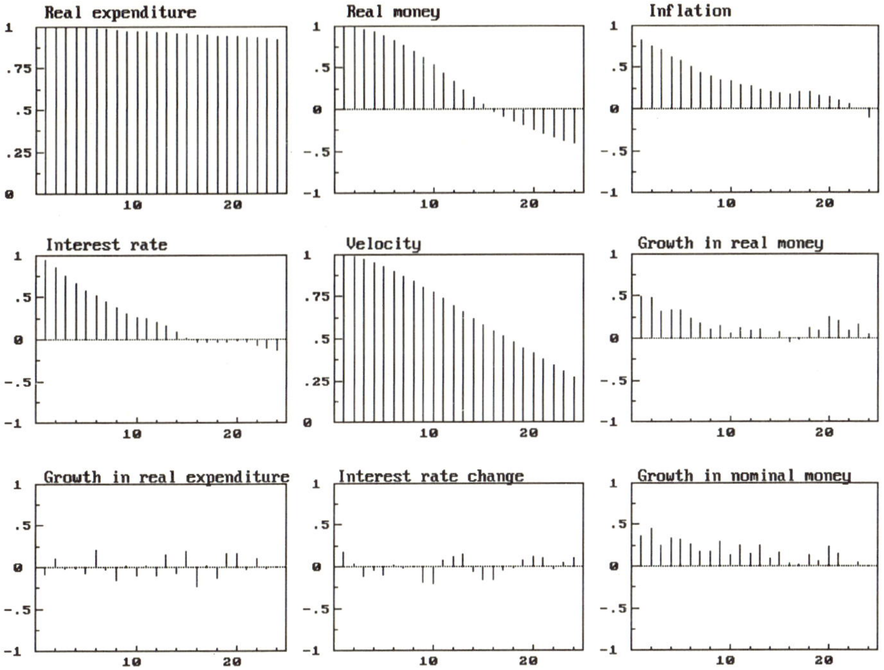

Fig. 16.6 Correlograms for money, inflation, income and interest rates

These descriptive graphs reveal many facets of the series putatively included in the demand-for-money function. Since economic theory is far from being a complete and correct characterization of reality, apart from a few unknown coefficient values, it is essential to examine the relevant data carefully before modelling any economic process. Theory itself is a function of what we know about the world, and regular predictive failure in empirical econometrics reveals that we do not yet know enough. In line with level C of Chapter 2, the only way to learn more about an empirical process is to study it, so research begins by examining the data to see what needs to be modelled and how it might be modelled. Graphs are only one way of doing so, but have the advantage of drawing attention to the salient data features needing to be captured by models (trends; changing levels, variances, and correlations; the presence or absence of correlations; and so on), which are aspects that will have to be encompassed later.

Each graph is implicitly based on a simple model (usually a linear, one-parameter model), but the entailed correlation may (and often does) change over time. Such graphs can help exclude many potential contending explanations, as some models will have difficulty encompassing certain of the data features. For example, the scatter in Fig. 16.4a poses problems for the class of theory models in which the short-run demand for money is homogeneous of degree one in prices: if it were, we should find a correlation near to plus one between the growth rate of money and the rate of inflation. The same figure also poses problems for models in which a short-run increase in the rate of money growth should increase the rate of inflation. After modelling, check that the results explain why graphs took the form they did. For example, one encompassing feature noted above is the apparent long-run unit dependence of money on prices, suggesting a cointegration formulation. Also, any useful model must explain the marked rises and falls in velocity: specifically, why agents first reduced their real-money holdings relative to real income to the extent they did, over the last thirty years, then increased them again. The mix of variables must correctly blend the different (scalar) time-series properties if a congruent multivariate model is to result.

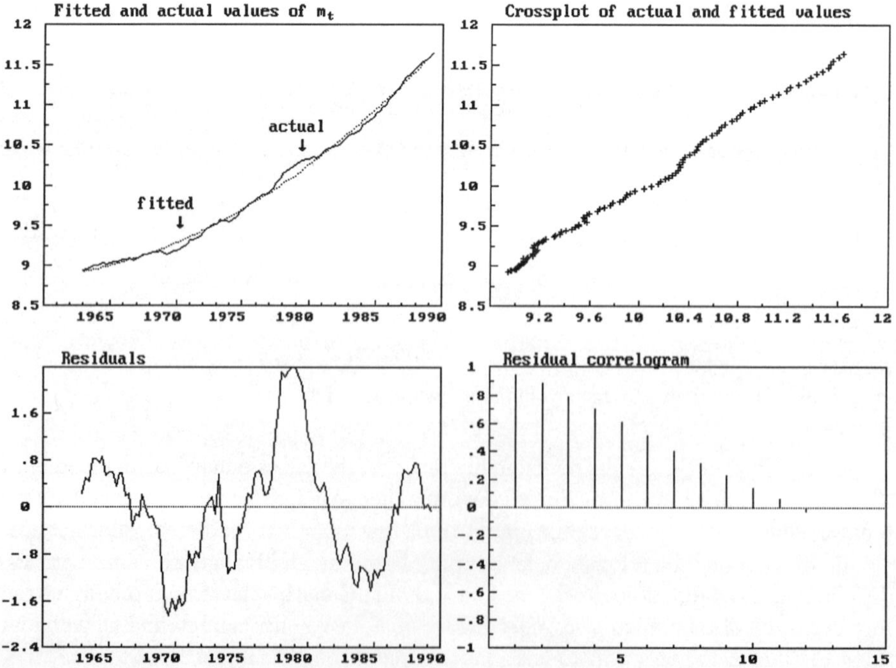

Fig. 16.7 Fitted and actual values for trend equation

Finally, a recurrent issue in recent macro-economic debates is whether time series are stationary around a trend or are integrated. To investigate this issue for m_t, regress it on a constant, trend, and trend squared:

$$\underset{}{m_t} = \underset{(0.028)}{8.84} + \underset{(0.0009)}{0.0022}\, t + \underset{(0.000006)}{0.00017}\, t^2 \tag{16.8}$$
$$\mathsf{R}^2 = 0.995 \; \hat{\sigma} = 0.055 \; DW = 0.10.$$

Fig. 16.7a–d reports the fitted and actual values, their cross-plot, the residuals from (16.8), and the residual correlogram. To the eye, the fit is impressive. Unfortunately, appearances are deceptive, as we might expect from the analysis in Chapter 4: the null hypothesis of a unit root in the residuals cannot be rejected, and because of the residual autocorrelation, the regression coefficients appear non-constant over the sample. The series is so smooth that it looks more like I(2) than I(1), and Johansen (1992c) concludes that it is I(2). If the data on m and p are indeed I(2), the relation in (16.3) need not cointegrate, as it may need inflation (an I(1) variable when p is I(2)) to be reduced to I(0).

16.6 A small monetary system

We have now examined the relevant variables graphically in at least one representation. The restriction on the opportunity cost of holding money in (16.7) is imposed since the data period for R_{ot} is too short to do much else. Thus, R_t demonstrates that the order of integration is not an inherent property of a time series, since R_{3t} is initially I(1), but after 1984 as a differential between competing interest rates, R_t is almost certainly I(0). While such 'regime shifts' affect some approaches more than others, an analysis which concludes with an I(0), congruent, invariant, and encompassing explanation is not dependent on assumed constancy of the degree of integration *inter alia*. Since $\{m_t\}$ seems to be I(2), whereas $\{m_t - p_t\}$ is I(1), long-run price homogeneity was imposed. Thus the vector of variables in the joint density comprises:

$$(m_t - p_t, \Delta p_t, i_t, R_t)\,.$$

It is feasible to distinguish between the interest rate R_{3t} and the opportunity cost of holding M1 R_t, since the former should affect the demand for output, whereas the latter influences the demand for money, but for simplicity we only use R_t. No modelling decision is irrevocable, as all are open to later evaluation, but those just made are purely pragmatic, and violate the principle of proceeding from general to specific.

The variables provide little information about the determination of TFE, interest rates or inflation, so the present exercise is best seen as studying the transactions-demand for money by commencing from the joint density, and testing the reductions needed to validate single-equation models. The system context also provides some interesting economic insights on the other variables being modelled, and illustrates the reduction approach in Hendry, Neale and Srba (1988), Hendry and Mizon (1993) and Hendry and Doornik (1994). This section closely follows those last authors. The graphs shown below are as they would appear during modelling with PcFiml, and they aim to summarize large amounts of information by highlighting salient features, rather than offer detailed appraisal or valid test statistics.

In addition to the four stochastic variables $m - p$, i, Δp, and R, the system contains a constant and trend. Basing the specification on Hendry and Mizon (1993) and Engle and Hendry (1993), we included the dummy variables D_y and D_o which the first authors created.[11] Conditioning on such dummies is discussed in Chapter 15, and how they enter the system in Chapter 8. Here, the intercept cannot be restricted to lie in the cointegration space due to growth in TFE, although Δp, and R should have zero intercepts. D_o should probably have no long-run effects (due to substitution, new discoveries, new energy sources, etc.), but D_y could have long-run effects from changing the stocks of physical and human capital during booms and recessions. They are both entered unrestrictedly, like the intercept. Finally, t only enters the cointegration space to avoid a quadratic trend in the levels (Ch.15 also discusses the rationale for linear deterministic trends).[12]

The next step is to determine the lag length for the vector autoregression. Since the data are quarterly, given the number of variables and the sample size ($T = 100$), a lag length of four was selected as the maximum, and retained for the cointegration analysis. The initial general system, therefore, had ninety (unrestricted) coefficients (including the error covariances). The two dummies, which proxy regime shifts in the other equations than money, were entered unrestrictedly to allow reduction tests corresponding to the invariance of the money-demand parameters with respect to the dummies. Simplification tests of the initial system lag length suggested that two lags sufficed, so this reduction was implemented (using likelihood-ratio tests adjusted for 'degrees of freedom', the statistic is $F(32, 285) = 1.2$).[13]

The ordering for testing hypotheses is unclear in the present context. The two considerations of avoiding conditioning on hypotheses to be tested at a later stage, and working in I(0) space conflict: to be meaningful, cointegration requires the constancy of the long-run parameters under analysis, but constancy tests on the initial system will not be in I(0) space.[14] We adopt the strategy of first ensuring system congruency against the historical data, then analysing constancy. When a satisfactory outcome has been achieved, cointegration is investigated, followed by tests of potential long-run weak exogeneity of inflation, income and interest rates for the parameters of the money demand function. That step determines the mapping to I(0) space, the extent of feasible conditioning reductions, and hence the size of the system to be jointly modelled. It happens that a single-equation model is practical, so we then turn to modelling that by reduction of lag length, and transformation to a more interpretable parameterization.

[11] D_y is zero except for unity in 1972(4), 1973(1) and 1979(2); D_o is zero except for unity in 1973(3), 1973(4) and 1979(3). These impulses adjust for the largest residuals, which Hendry and Mizon attribute to the 'Heath-Barber ' boom and subsequent strikes, and the effects of the first Thatcher government for output; and the two oil crises, and the VAT increase for inflation.

[12] The outcome of the cointegration analysis is dependent on these choices. When all four dummies are in the short run (unrestricted), one cointegration vector emerges, whereas two emerge for the choice in the text (or no regime dummies), and three appear if all four dummies are restricted to the long run.

[13] These are implemented in PcFiml following Anderson (1958) and Rao (1952).

[14] Hansen (1992b) proposes a constancy test that is applicable to I(1) data, so this technical constraint will soon be removed.

To see the extent to which the variables interact, the residual correlations for the system are reported in Table 16.1. There are large negative correlations between real money and both inflation and the interest rate which merit modelling, especially since the latter two are not themselves highly correlated.

Table 16.1 Residual correlations

	$m-p$	i	Δp	R
i	−0.05	–	–	–
Δp	−0.49	−0.02	–	–
R	−0.48	0.12	0.30	–

Table 16.2 records the estimates of the VAR parameters, and their standard errors, other than the dummies (mp denotes $m-p$).

Table 16.2 Unrestricted VAR estimates

	mp_{t-1}	mp_{t-2}	i_{t-1}	i_{t-2}	Δp_{t-1}	Δp_{t-2}	R_{t-1}	R_{t-2}
$m-p$	0.56	0.35	0.17	− 0.12	− 0.54	0.02	− 0.82	0.15
	(0.13)	(0.12)	(0.14)	(0.14)	(0.28)	(0.25)	(0.15)	(0.15)
i	− 0.11	0.01	0.68	0.19	− 0.03	0.17	− 0.11	− 0.10
	(0.08)	(0.07)	(0.09)	(0.09)	(0.18)	(0.16)	(0.10)	(0.10)
Δp	0.04	− 0.05	0.04	0.04	0.50	0.19	0.06	− 0.00
	(0.05)	(0.05)	(0.06)	(0.06)	(0.11)	(0.10)	(0.06)	(0.06)
R	0.08	− 0.10	0.07	− 0.02	0.09	− 0.00	1.09	− 0.22
	(0.10)	(0.09)	(0.11)	(0.11)	(0.22)	(0.20)	(0.12)	(0.12)

Most individual coefficients are not significant at even the 5 per cent level, so considerable simplification should be possible after suitable transforms designed to facilitate the interpretation of this multi-dimensional evidence.

Table 16.3 Lag length and dynamics

statistic	$m-p$	i	Δp	R				
$F_{s=1}(4,88)$	9.87**	16.31**	5.04**	24.05**				
$F_{s=2}(4,88)$	2.33	1.60	1.46	1.13				
$\lvert\lambda_a\rvert$	0.39	0.17	0.07	0.07				
$\lvert\lambda_b\rvert$	0.96	0.96	0.68	0.68	0.34	0.32	0.24	0.24

Table 16.3 reports statistics on lag length and dynamic specification, where $F_j(\cdot,\cdot)$ denotes an F-test for the hypothesis of an i-period lag ($F_{s=i}$); $|\lambda_a|$ denotes the modulus of the eigenvalues of the π matrix; and $|\lambda_b|$ the modulus of the eigenvalues of the companion matrix of the dynamics (see Ch.8). The two-period lag is not significant.

The long-run matrix has two eigenvalues λ_a close to zero, and two rather larger ones, suggesting there are two non-stationary combinations, and possibly two cointegrating vectors. Matching this, two of the eigenvalues λ_b of the companion matrix of the dynamics are close to unity, and otherwise none is on or outside the unit circle, consistent with I(1) processes.

Figs. 16.8a–l present a condensed view of the descriptive power of the system, showing the four sets of fitted and actual values, their cross-plots and the scaled residuals for each equation. Despite the (deliberate) lack of fine detail in the figure, the differences in goodness-of-fit between the four equations are apparent to the eye, especially the greater scatter for Δp and R, as well as 'outliers' of about three standard deviations in several of residual series. Due to the non-stationarity, the fits look good, but more usefully, the residuals seem to be white noise. Fig. 16.10 confirms the latter in terms of the residual correlograms and densities: the former are fairly flat, and the latter are quite close to normality. Consequently, this aspect of congruency seems satisfactory.

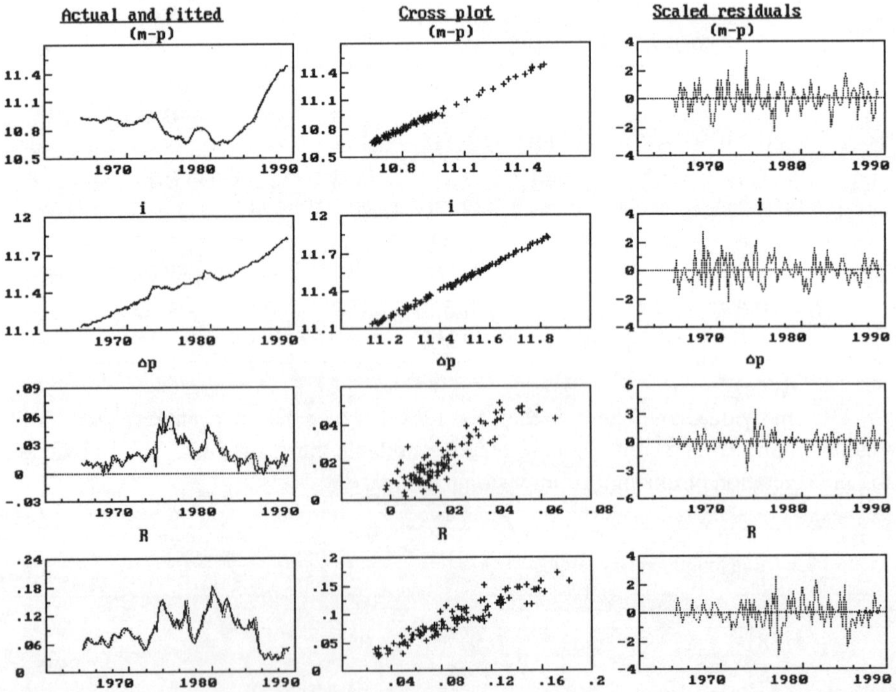

Fig. 16.8 System fitted and actual values, and residuals

Table 16.4 records statistical information about the VAR, namely, equation residual standard deviations (denoted $\hat{\sigma}$: the value for R_t is in percentage points); single-equation evaluation statistics for no serial correlation (F_{ar}, against fifth-order residual autoregression); no ARCH (F_{arch}, against fourth order); no heteroscedasticity (F_{het}: see White,

1980a); and a test for normality (χ^2_{nd}: see Doornik and Hansen, 1994); analogous system (vector) tests are denoted by ^{v} (see Doornik and Hendry, 1994a). Finally, * and ** denote significance at the 5 per cent and 1 per cent levels respectively. The baseline innovation variances are small, although there is evidence of ARCH and non-normality.

Table 16.4 Goodness of fit and evaluation

Statistic	$m-p$	i	Δp	R	VAR
$\hat{\sigma}$	1.65%	1.04%	0.68%	1.3	
$F_{ar}(5,83)$	1.64	1.03	1.69	1.20	
$F_{arch}(4,80)$	0.65	0.64	3.39*	5.69**	
$F_{het}(20,67)$	0.84	1.00	0.92	1.39	
$\chi^2_{nd}(2)$	4.81	1.23	13.2**	4.44	
$F^v_{ar}(80,258)$					1.21
$F^v_{het}(180,548)$					0.90
$\chi^{2\,v}_{nd}(8)$					19.4*

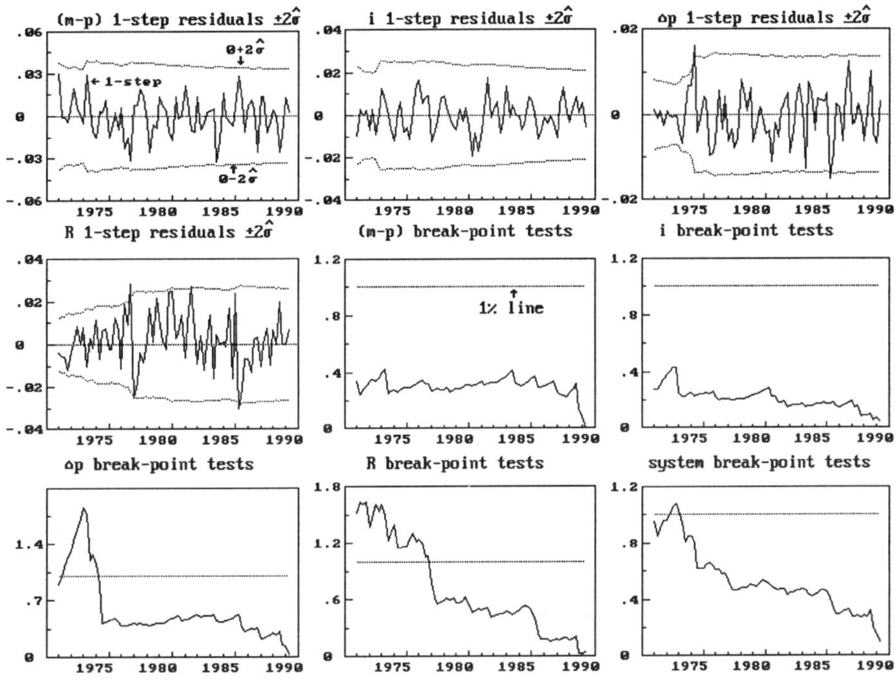

Fig. 16.9 System recursive evaluation statistics

The next important facet is parameter constancy, and we use recursive estimation to examine this. Since the data are non-stationary, constancy statistics are descriptive, rather than inferential, although the outcomes in practice are close to those obtained for the I(0) representation formulated below. Figure 16.9 reports the 1-step residuals with $0 \pm 2\hat{\sigma}$ for each equation, then the corresponding sequences of breakpoint Chow tests (scaled by their 1 per cent significance levels), and finally a system breakpoint test sequence. The equations for $(m-p)_t$ and i_t are constant, whereas, even with the dummies included, those for R_t and Δp_t are rejected at the 1 per cent level (selected because more than sixty tests are conducted): the system statistic is above the 1 per cent line at one point. However, for investigating cointegration, when we seek to condition on R_t in due course, this evidence suffices to let us proceed.

Fig. 16.10 shows the graphical representation of the single-equation diagnostics for serially-correlated residuals (correlograms), and normality (the residual histograms with non-parametric densities, and the distributions plotted against N[0,1]: see Ch.A3). These graphs, and the formal system tests reported in Table 16.4, suggest few major specification problems at this stage. Should any of the present tests reject (when correctly calibrated for the system under analysis), then an enlarged specification must be developed, and the analysis recommenced with the new more general system. As yet the influence on later inferences of discovering a serious mis-specification and recommencing are unclear, but should the re-specification yield a congruent representation, restarting seems likely to be less harmful than persevering with a knowingly mis-specified system.

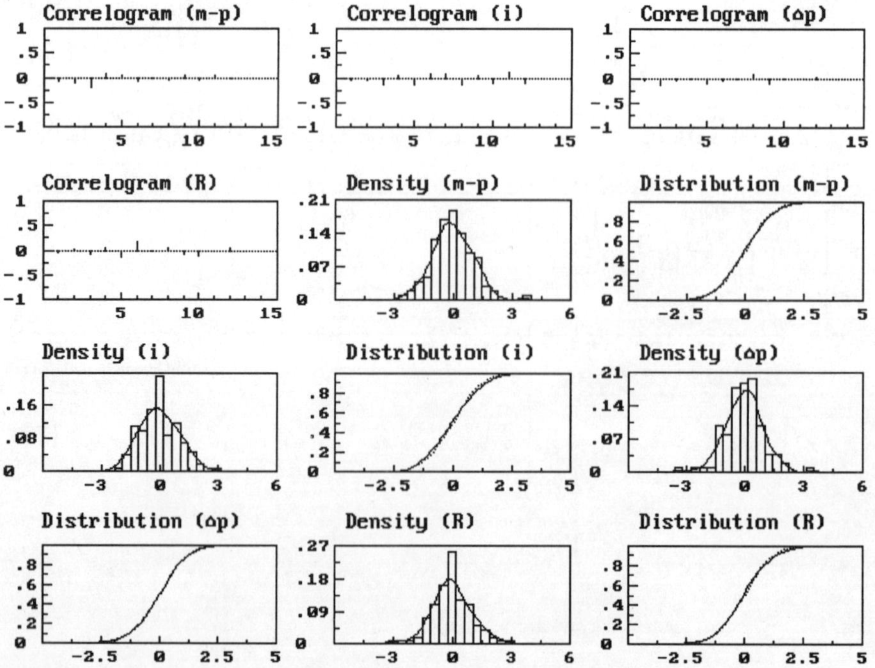

Fig. 16.10 Graphical diagnostic information

16.7 Cointegration analysis

Assuming that the VAR is adequately specified, we investigate cointegration in the four-equation system. Table 16.5 reports the log-likelihood values (ℓ), eigenvalues (μ), and associated maximum eigenvalue (*Max*) and trace (*Tr*) statistics as discussed in Chapter 11.[15] The test statistics are adjusted for degrees-of-freedom following Reimers (1992), and the critical values are from Osterwald-Lenum (1992). The outcome formally supports the hypothesis that there is only one cointegrating vector. However, when the dummies are dropped from the analysis altogether, or are entered restrictedly, then two cointegrating combinations are obtained, matching those in Hendry and Mizon (1993). The results are based on two cointegrating vectors, estimated with unrestricted regime dummies and intercept, but forcing the trend to lie in the cointegration space. Table 16.6 records the adjustment coefficients and the estimated cointegrating vectors.

Table 16.5 Cointegration statistics

	1	2	3	4
ℓ	1838	1846	1850	1853
μ	0.55	0.13	0.08	0.06
Max	72.9**	13.3	7.9	5.7
Tr	99.9**	26.9	13.6	5.7

Table 16.6 Cointegration analysis

$\hat{\alpha}$	1	2	3	4
$m-p$	−0.09	−0.01	0.05	0.04
i	−0.02	−0.10	−0.04	0.02
Δp	−0.00	0.08	−0.02	−0.02
R	−0.00	−0.06	−0.02	−0.08

$\hat{\beta}'$	$m-p$	i	Δp	R	t
1	1.00	−1.00	7.34	7.65	−0.0005
2	−0.06	1.00	−3.38	0.86	−0.0059
3	−0.29	0.69	1.00	−0.63	−0.0025
4	0.30	−1.58	1.10	1.00	0.0097

The first $\hat{\beta}$ vector in Table 16.6 is recognizably the money-demand relation in Hendry and Ericsson (1991b), with an unrestricted income elasticity of unity, large negative effects from inflation and the interest rate, and a negligible trend. The second $\hat{\beta}$ vector is like an 'excess-demand' equation, with the deviation of output from trend having a large positive relation to inflation, and a negative one to the interest rate (although that is a differential after 1984).

[15] There was little change in these statistics as the lag length was reduced from four to two.

Figs. 16.11a–l plot the estimated disequilibria $\hat{\boldsymbol{\beta}}'\boldsymbol{x}_t$ for the two cointegration vectors in Table 16.6, and the remaining two non-stationary components, together with their fitted and actual values, and the eigenvalues estimated recursively (but partialling out the full-sample short-run dynamics and unrestricted variables: see Hansen and Johansen, 1992). Denoting the normalized element of the ith row of $\boldsymbol{\beta}$ by β_{ii}, then x_{it} is the 'actual' and $-\sum_{j\neq i}\hat{\beta}_{ij}x_{jt}$ is the 'fitted'.

The disequilibria in money demand are large (sometimes over 70 per cent) consistent with the small benefits of adjusting interacting with the large shocks experienced by the economy. Much smaller disequilibria are observed for the 'excess-demand' vector, also consistent with the observed recessions and booms of the last third of the century. The first recursive eigenvalue is constant (conditional on the full-sample dynamic estimates), whereas the second (supposedly non-zero) recursive eigenvalue is less constant, and not very large. The remaining two components seem distinctly non-stationary, and their associated eigenvalues are always close to zero.

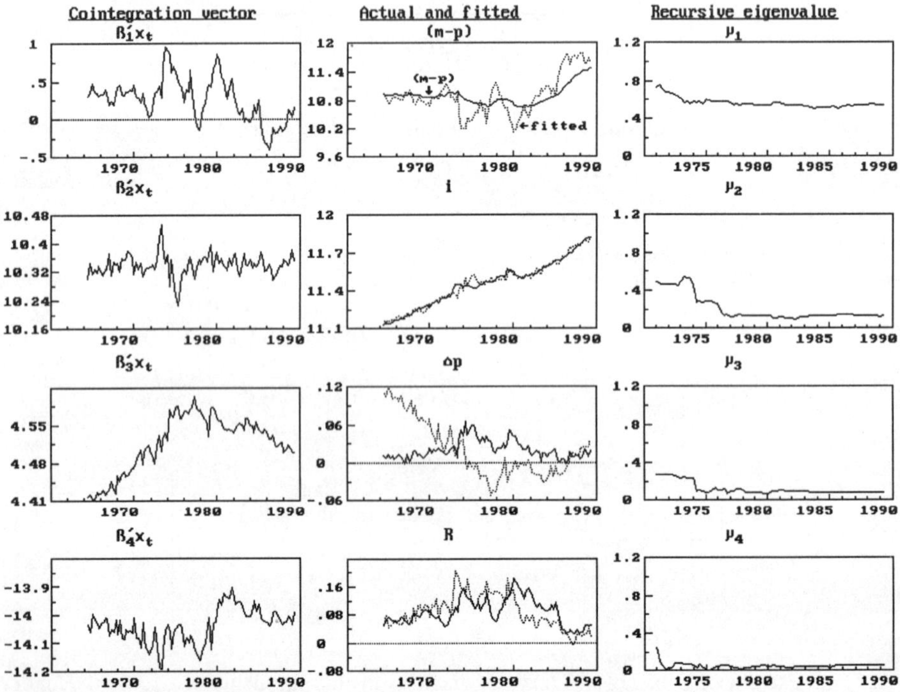

Fig. 16.11 $\hat{\boldsymbol{\beta}}'\boldsymbol{x}_t$ and recursive eigenvalues

The cointegration vectors from Table 16.6 were made unique as follows: for long-run money demand, a unit income elasticity, equal effects from Δp_t and R_t, and a zero trend, matching (16.3); and for output, the trend coefficient was imposed at the value from regressing i_t on t (equal to the sample mean of $\{\Delta i_t\}$), with no effect from real money, and coefficients of -3.4 and 1.8 on Δp_t and R_t.[16]

The restricted cointegration vectors were tested for lying in the cointegration space, jointly with testing for i_t, Δp_t, and R_t being long-run weakly exogenous for the money-demand parameters (see Johansen, 1992c) when the excess-demand vector was excluded from the first equation. This involved checking whether the first column of α had the form $(*, 0, 0, 0)'$, when β was identified as described, and the second was $(0, *, *, *)'$. The test is a conventional $\chi^2(\cdot)$, since the hypothesis is linear, the cointegration rank is preserved, and the system is in I(0) space, yielding $\chi^2(12) = 9.7$, which is insignificant at the 5 per cent level.

The data are now mapped to I(0) linear combinations, defining the ECMs by:

$$\begin{aligned} c_{1t} &= m_t - p_t - i_t + 7.0\Delta p_t + 7.0R_t - 0.21 \\ &\text{and} \\ c_{2t} &= i_t - 0.0063t - 3.4\Delta p_t + 1.8R_t - 11.2. \end{aligned} \tag{16.9}$$

Since the units of P_t are arbitrary, c_{1t} and c_{2t} were adjusted to have mean zero by subtracting their sample means, which by itself does not impose any restrictions.

The I(0) system determines the six variables $\Delta(m-p)_t$, Δi_t, $\Delta^2 p_t$, ΔR_t, c_{1t}, and c_{2t}. Two of the variables are redundant, in that c_{1t}, c_{2t}, $\Delta^2 p_t$, and ΔR_t would suffice, but retaining the differences of the four original variables together with the two ECMs defined by the identities in (16.10) will prove useful:

$$\begin{aligned} c_{1t} &\equiv c_{1t-1} + \Delta\left(m-p\right)_t - \Delta i_t + 7.0\Delta^2 p_t + 7.0\Delta R_t \\ &\text{and} \\ c_{2t} &\equiv c_{2t-1} + \Delta\left(i_t - 0.0063t\right) - 3.4\Delta^2 p_t + 1.8\Delta R_t. \end{aligned} \tag{16.10}$$

Table 16.7 PVAR estimates

	$\Delta(m-p)_{t-1}$	Δi_{t-1}	$\Delta^2 p_{t-1}$	ΔR_{t-1}	c_{1t-1}	c_{2t-1}
$\Delta(m-p)$	− 0.34	0.07	0.07	− 0.16	− 0.10	0.01
	(0.12)	(0.13)	(0.25)	(0.15)	(0.01)	(0.06)
Δi	− 0.00	− 0.22	− 0.18	0.13	− 0.02	− 0.08
	(0.07)	(0.08)	(0.16)	(0.09)	(0.01)	(0.04)
$\Delta^2 p$	0.05	− 0.01	− 0.23	0.03	− 0.01	0.04
	(0.05)	(0.06)	(0.10)	(0.06)	(0.01)	(0.02)
ΔR	0.08	0.10	− 0.08	0.23	0.00	− 0.07
	(0.09)	(0.11)	(0.20)	(0.12)	(0.01)	(0.04)

The available information set comprises $(\Delta(m-p)_{t-1}, \Delta i_{t-1}, \Delta^2 p_{t-1}, \Delta R_{t-1}, c_{1t-1}, c_{2t-1})$ together with D_y, D_o and an intercept, which entails a reduction to an I(0)

[16] Dale Henderson has suggested that the excess-demand equation is a relation between y^* and a measure of the real interest rate, since in annual units, $y^* + 1.8(R - \Delta_4 p) = 0$. This idea requires using R_3 rather than R, and merits exploration.

'parsimonious' VAR (PVAR) in nine explanatory variables with forty-six unrestricted coefficients (including error covariances). The correlations between actual and fitted values for the four stochastic variables in the PVAR are 0.80, 0.70, 0.62, and 0.43 respectively. The validity of the cointegration reduction cannot be tested by a conventional likelihood-ratio test, but was already tested by the validity of suppressing the two non-cointegrating vectors (in Table 16.5), and restricting the trend (twelve restrictions in total). Table 16.7 records the estimates of the I(0) VAR.

Despite imposing forty-four (data acceptable) restrictions, the dimensionality of this PVAR remains high, and many coefficients are insignificant, so we turn to modelling it.

16.8 Modelling the I(0) PVAR

The main reasons for modelling the I(0) PVAR are to enhance its interpretability, and reduce its sample dependence, or increase its invariance to regime changes. High dimensional parameter vectors induce dependence on transient empirical phenomena (see Ch.15), so we seek to re-parameterize in terms of autonomous relations which eliminate accidental features. The best order of hypothesis tests is again unclear, but we have already found long-run weak exogeneity of $(i_t, \Delta p_t, R_t)$ for the parameters of the first cointegrating relation, and if the exercise were aimed purely at modelling money demand, a conditional factorization could be the next test.

For the moment, we persevere with system modelling, and postulate a 'structure' based on the evidence in Hendry and Mizon (1993). This allows us to test the post-sample constancy of a close analogue of their model. To define the money-demand equation, we exclude Δi_{t-1}, $\Delta^2 p_{t-1}$, ΔR_{t-1}, D_o, D_y, and c_{2t-1}, and include Δi_t, $\Delta^2 p_t$, ΔR_t. To restrict the other equations, c_{1t-1} is excluded from all three, and $\Delta(m-p)_{t-1}$, $\Delta^2 p_{t-1}$, ΔR_{t-1}, and D_o from Δi_t; Δi_{t-1}, D_y, 1, and ΔR_{t-1} from $\Delta^2 p_t$; and $\Delta(m - p)_{t-1}$, Δi_{t-1}, D_y, 1 and $\Delta^2 p_{t-1}$ from ΔR_t. These restriction are based on the accumulated evidence, the earlier theoretical analysis, and the data evidence in Table 16.7. It transpired that in the money-demand relation, the coefficients of $\Delta(m - p)_{t-1}$ and Δi_{t-1} were nearly equal magnitude, opposite sign, and so were combined into a change in velocity term, $\Delta(m - p - i)_{t-1}$.

The resulting equations, estimated by FIML, are shown in Table 16.8. Associated ancillary information is presented in Table 16.9. The test of over-identifying restrictions ($\chi^2_{or}(20) = 21.8$, p $= 0.35$) does not reject, so the model parsimoniously encompasses the PVAR.

The estimates of the money-demand function are close to those found by previous investigators, despite endogenising the contemporaneous regressors. The equation for TFE confirms the role of the excess-demand cointegration vector, and the impact of D_y: the absolute value of the 't-test' on c_{2t-1} exceeds 4.5, and it also enters the equations for $\Delta^2 p_t$ and ΔR_t, so it plays a significant role in the system. The change in inflation is negatively autocorrelated, somewhat affected by real money and influenced by D_o. Finally the interest-rate equation depends on excess demand, lagged changes in R_t, and D_o. The coefficients of $\Delta^2 p_t$ and ΔR_t in the first equation were restricted to be equal by Hendry and Mizon (1993), and below we test the equality of the intercepts in the first two equations.

Table 16.8 FIML model estimates

$$\Delta(m-p)_t = -\underset{(0.06)}{0.19}\,\Delta(m-p-i)_{t-1} - \underset{(0.32)}{0.66}\,\Delta^2 p_t - \underset{(0.28)}{0.78}\,\Delta R_t - \underset{(0.01)}{0.09}\,c_{1t-1} + \underset{(0.001)}{0.005}$$

$$\Delta i_t = \underset{(0.01)}{0.05}\,D_{yt} - \underset{(0.08)}{0.12}\,i_{t-1} - \underset{(0.02)}{0.11}\,c_{2t-1} + \underset{(0.001)}{0.007}$$

$$\Delta^2 p_t = -\underset{(0.09)}{0.23}\,\Delta^2 p_{t-1} + \underset{(0.005)}{0.02}\,D_{ot} + \underset{(0.03)}{0.06}\,\Delta(m-p)_{t-1} + \underset{(0.02)}{0.04}\,c_{2t-1}$$

$$\Delta R_t = \underset{(0.09)}{0.20}\,\Delta R_{t-1} + \underset{(0.01)}{0.03}\,D_{ot} - \underset{(0.03)}{0.07}\,c_{2t-1}$$

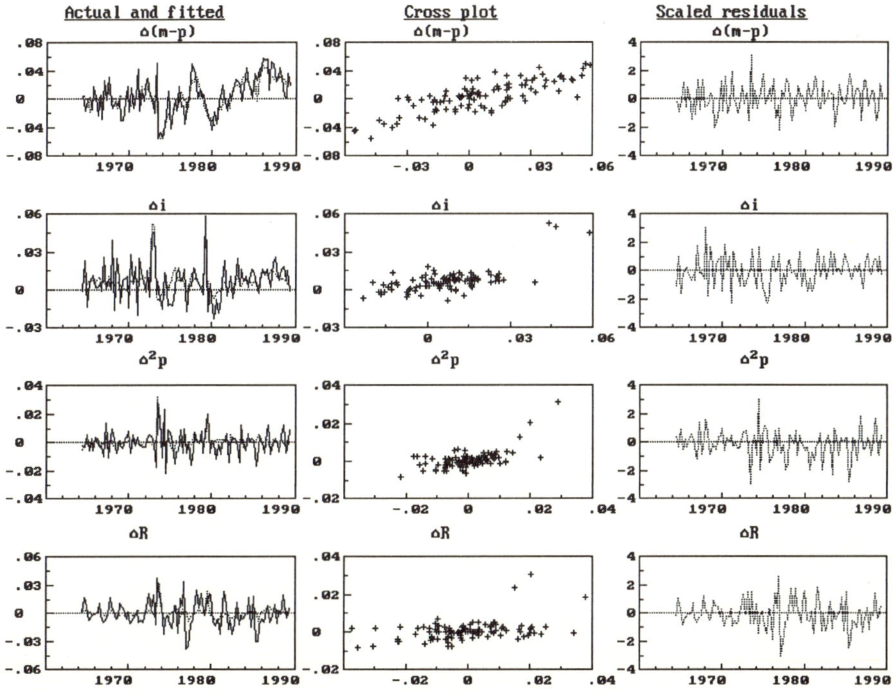

Fig. 16.12 Fitted values, outcomes and residuals for the model

Fig. 16.12 shows the fitted and actual values, their cross plots and the scaled residuals. The poor fit relative to Fig. 16.8 is due to analysing stationary variables, but the explanatory power for $\Delta^2 p_t$ and ΔR_t is low. Estimating the original system using differences as the dependent variables would have revealed that at the outset.

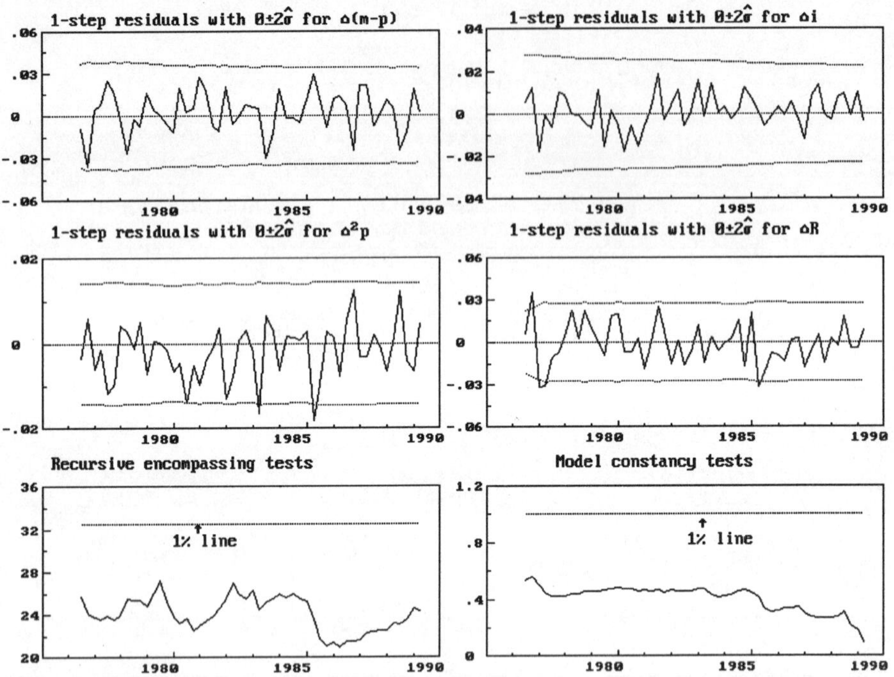

Fig. 16.13 Recursive FIML statistics

Fig. 16.13 records recursive FIML estimates over the longest feasible sample (using 48 initial values): this is computed by calculating FIML at each successive sample size, commencing the iterations from the previous estimates. Such a procedure highlights the constancy of the model over the later part of the sample, using 1-step residuals $\pm 2\hat{\sigma}_j$, a recursively computed parsimonious-encompassing statistic (here, the over-identification test), and an overall model-constancy test. At no point in the latter part of the period would the model have failed a test for encompassing the PVAR, nor for non-constant parameters.

Figure 16.14 shows the one-dimensional projections of the full-sample likelihood surface for each of the sixteen parameters. The graphs show that the likelihood is unimodal in the neighbourhood of the optimum. From these statistics at least, the model seems well specified.

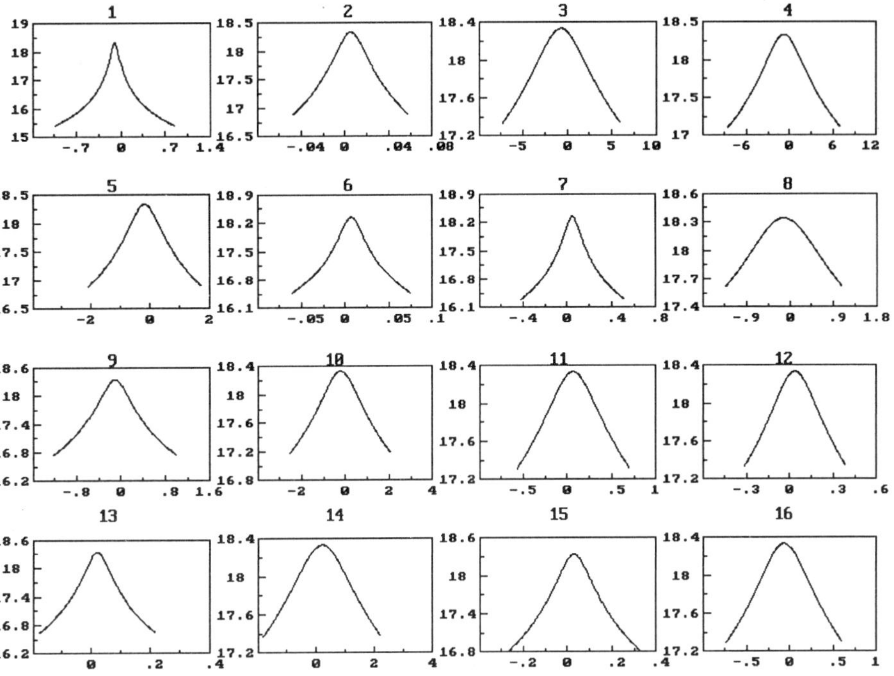

Fig. 16.14 One-dimensional projections of the likelihood surface

Overall, there are only eleven coefficients for stochastic variables, five for the dummies — including intercepts — and ten error covariances in $\hat{\Sigma}$. These last are shown in Table 16.9 as correlations below the diagonal, with residual standard deviations on the diagonal, and reveal low correlations between the structural residuals, so $\hat{\Sigma}$ is nearly diagonal. The reduced-form correlations based on $\hat{\Omega}$ are shown above the diagonal, and reproduce the correlation structure seen in Table 16.1, so the model offers a structural explanation of this data feature.

Table 16.9 FIML residual correlations

	$\Delta(m-p)_t$	Δi_t	$\Delta^2 p_t$	ΔR_t
$\Delta(m-p)_t$	1.34%	−0.08	−0.51	−0.50
Δi_t	0.01	1.10%	0.05	0.12
$\Delta^2 p_t$	−0.02	0.05	0.69%	0.33
ΔR_t	0.26	0.12	0.33	1.31

The model diagnostics in Table 16.10, denoted by F^m_{ar} etc., are all insignificant (including the additional test, $F^m_{fn}(\cdot)$, for model functional-form mis-specification), matching the valid reduction from the congruent PVAR. Finally, the I(0) system was analysed by the Johansen cointegration algorithm to check stationarity, and yielded four large eigenvalues as anticipated. We conclude that the model is a data-coherent, constant representation that parsimoniously encompasses the PVAR, which in turn parsimoniously encompasses the VAR, allowing for the reduction to I(0) requiring Wiener-based critical values.

Table 16.10 Model diagnostic tests

$F^m_{ar}(80, 290)$	1.21
$F^m_{het}(160, 616)$	1.13
$\chi^{2\,m}_{nd}(8)$	11.0
$F^m_{fn}(390, 485)$	0.92

16.9 Evaluating the model

To illustrate the explanatory power of the model over the sample not available to Hendry and Mizon (1993), Fig. 16.15 reports the 1-step forecast statistics for 1984(3)–1989(2), together with a small pre-forecast sample. The data have been revised since their study (note the analysis in Ch.15), interest-bearing checking accounts were introduced, and the price index base was changed, so from that perspective the constancy test is a demanding one. Conversely, the model has been revised, in that the interest rate R_{3t} has been replaced by the opportunity-cost measure $R_{3t} - R^l_{ot}$, although it is otherwise the same.[17] Consistent with the recursive analysis, constancy is easily accepted, with almost every forecast lying well inside the individual 95 per cent confidence bars, the overall test yielding $F(80, 77) = 0.74$. This is not an 'operational' forecasting test, since it incorporates knowledge of the regime shift due to R_o becoming non-zero, but as Hendry and Ericsson (1991b) note, the learning adjustment was formulated by 1985, and the parameter values remain close to their pre-1984 estimates.

Too much cannot be expected of multi-step forecasting, however, since R_t is essentially a random walk. Fig. 16.16 shows a sequence of one through eight steps-ahead forecasts from 1989(3) onwards, with error bars for 95 per cent confidence intervals (asymptotically valid, but neglecting parameter uncertainty). The forecasts converge on their unconditional means, and the error bars on the unconditional stationary data variances (see Clements and Hendry, 1995). There is little genuine information beyond the first few periods for ΔR_t and $\Delta^2 p_t$, but the uncertainty in $\Delta(m-p)_t$ doubles over eight-steps ahead, and that for Δi_t increases by more than 50 per cent. We comment on the graphs for the equilibrium corrections below.

A feature of Fig. 16.16 is that the long-run forecasts for $\Delta^2 p_t$ and ΔR_t converge to zero. This occurs even when the intercepts are not restricted to zero. Solving for the

[17] The replacement of log R_{3t} by R_{3t} does not seem crucial.

long-run outcome of the unrestricted dynamic system as a function of the deterministic variables, the intercepts are near zero for all variables except $\Delta(m-p)_t$ and Δi_t, whereas these have nearly equal values, close to the sample mean growth-rate of TFE of 0.0063. Since velocity $(p+y-m)_t$ should not have an autonomous trend, such an outcome makes good sense, and suggests the reduction of restricting the intercepts in the first two equations to equal 0.0063: the test thereof yields $\chi^2(2) = 0.82$.

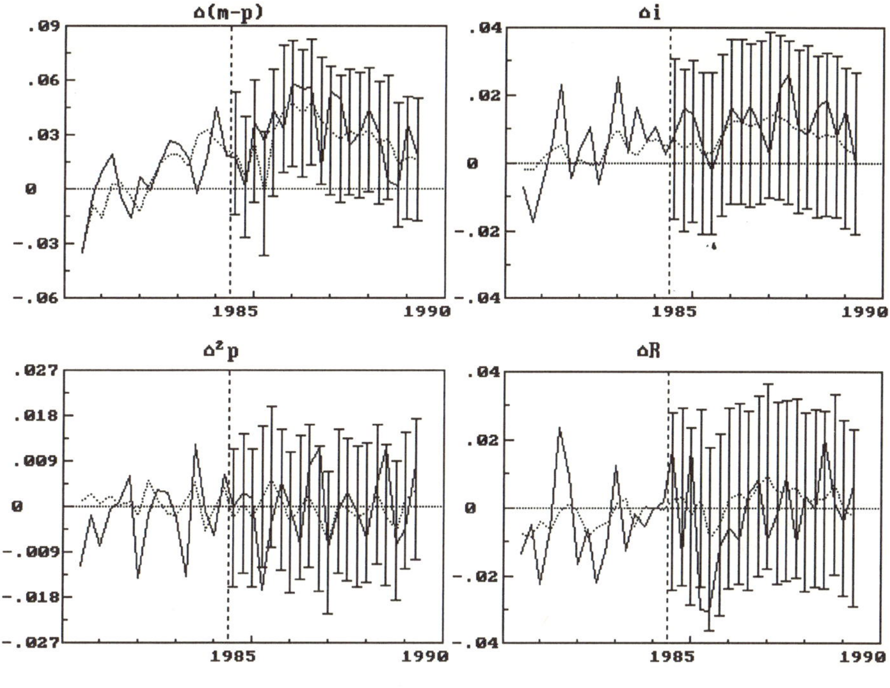

Fig. 16.15 One-step model-based forecasts

The apparent explanatory power of a linear model depends on the transformations inspected, as shown by comparing Figs. 16.8 and 16.12. Here, the correlations between the actual and fitted values of the entailed equations for c_{1t} and c_{2t} are 0.92 and 0.77, and their residual standard deviations are 0.11 and 0.03 respectively, although the basic explanation is unaltered. Fig. 16.16 also records their multi-step forecasts, which gradually deteriorate in accuracy as the horizon increases, and show the convergence of the disequilibria to their long-run means of zero.

Finally, to investigate the super exogeneity of $(i_t, \Delta p_t, R_t)$ for the parameters of the money-demand equation, the four step-dummy variables used in Engle and Hendry (1993) were tested for significance, yielding $F(16, 257) = 0.66$ (p > 0.8). Thus, their irrelevance cannot be rejected at the 5 per cent level. Since we have already tested the irrelevance of D_y and D_o from the money relation, despite their important role in the system, super exogeneity is accepted. This validates conditioning, so we proceed to consider single-equation modelling.

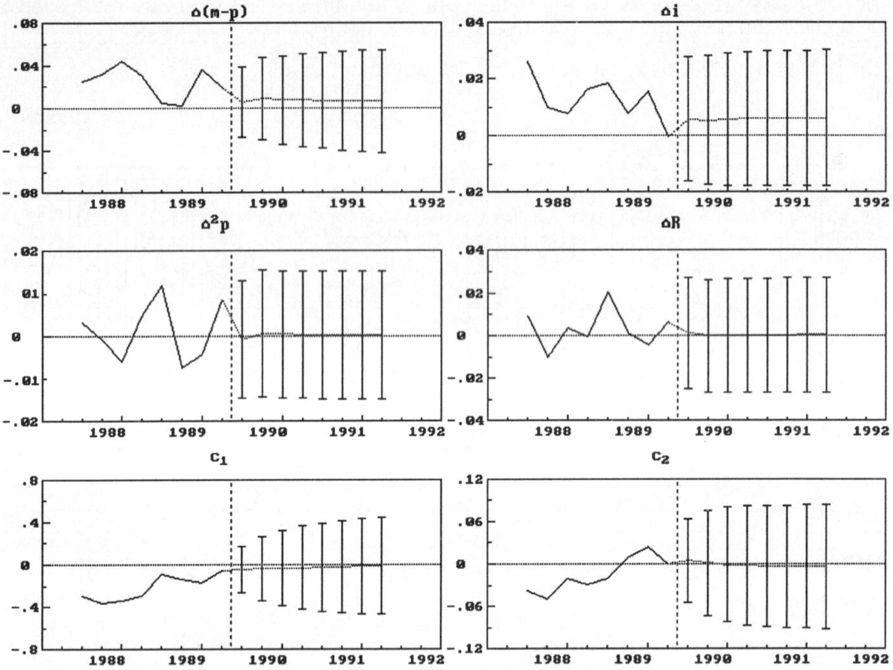

Fig. 16.16 Dynamic model-based forecasts

16.10 A single-equation money-demand model

We now focus on the conditional density of m_t given the other three variables, and the history of the process. This corresponds to the assertion that, given $\boldsymbol{X}_{t-1}$, the set of variables (p_t, i_t, R_t) are weakly exogenous for the parameters of the money-demand model, which thereby is a contingent-plan equation. For sequential factorization, to avoid an excessively long sequence, we use an initial lag length of two for all variables, and estimated this general ADL model by least squares.

First, some descriptive statistics. Table 16.11 records the correlations between the levels of the main variables over 1963(1)–1989(2). The levels variables, other than R_t, are highly intercorrelated, as one might expect under non-stationarity. The transformation to real money and inflation already clarifies the picture and delivers more interpretable correlations: as argued in Chapter 7, multicollinearity is not simply a problem of high correlations.

Table 16.11 Data correlation matrices

$$\begin{bmatrix} & m & p & i \\ p & 0.97 & - & - \\ i & 0.96 & 0.95 & - \\ R & -0.03 & 0.15 & 0.09 \end{bmatrix}, \quad \begin{bmatrix} & m-p & \Delta p \\ \Delta p & -0.42 & - \\ i & 0.34 & 0.14 \\ R & -0.72 & 0.68 \end{bmatrix}$$

As Table 16.12 below shows, many t-values in the single-equation general unrestricted model (GUM) exceed the conventional (absolute) value of two, even though the GUM spreads whatever is to be explained across a large number of variables, some of which probably do not actually affect behaviour. One discovery aspect, therefore, is to reduce the equation to an interpretable form which isolates the data functions that do explain behaviour, and eliminates those that do not. There are two approaches to doing so. One is based on the insignificance of t-tests at some level (e.g. 5 per cent), so first eliminates variables with small t-values. The other first transforms variables to highlight relevant features, then eliminates irrelevant functions of variables after those transformations. One frequently helpful technique is to transform a time-series into a level and a change, or simple moving averages of these; another is to switch to differentials (such as interest rate spreads, already implemented in the construction of R_t), or ECMs. Reduction to $\mathsf{I}(0)$ usually accomplishes many of these transforms simultaneously.

Information criteria, which adjust the equation standard error to allow for potentially over-parameterizing the model, are also reported. Such model-selection criteria penalize extra variables to induce a parsimonious explanation of data phenomena. The Schwarz criterion is defined by $SC = \log \tilde{\sigma}^2 + K(\log T)/T$ for K regressors, where $\tilde{\sigma}^2$ is the unadjusted residual variance. SC can record a model as 'improved' even when the equation fits worse as measured by $\hat{\sigma}$.

The initial GUM with two lags, but not imposing price homogeneity, has $\hat{\sigma} = 1.33$ per cent with $SC = -8.21$, for twelve variables and $T = 100$ observations. The unit-root test is significant at the one per cent level, rejecting a lack of cointegration. The long-run solved equation is (see Ch.6):

$$m = \underset{(3.77)}{-4.03} + \underset{(0.32)}{1.37}\, i + \underset{(0.09)}{0.91}\, p - \underset{(0.92)}{6.39}\, R. \tag{16.11}$$

We do not present these initial GUM estimates, merely noting the acceptability of long-run price homogeneity. This is imposed henceforth, transforming from (m, p) to $(m - p, \Delta p)$ to eliminate the price-level effect, and creating the baseline GUM with nineteen variables. OLS estimation yields $\hat{\sigma} = 1.28$ per cent with $SC = -8.07$, and the long-run solution:

$$m - p = \underset{(1.46)}{-0.68} + \underset{(0.13)}{1.09}\, i - \underset{(1.97)}{7.49}\, \Delta p - \underset{(0.69)}{7.11}\, R. \tag{16.12}$$

The solution in (16.12) is close to the cointegration vector in Table 16.6, consistent with weak exogeneity. The expenditure elasticity is close to unity, and the rates of interest and inflation both have a large coefficients which are quite well determined, and so are highly significant. The inflation response lies in the range found by Cagan (1956) from analysing hyper-inflations, so it could represent a structural response.

The linear combination defined in (16.12) could be used to create the ECM, but to make the model more interpretable, the unit-expenditure elasticity was imposed, inducing the modified long-run solution:

$$m - p - i = \underset{(0.06)}{0.25} - \underset{(1.7)}{11.2\Delta i} - \underset{(1.43)}{6.67\,\Delta p} - \underset{(0.55)}{6.92\,R}. \qquad (16.13)$$

This was the form adopted as the ECM in the I(0) representation, but without the growth of expenditure; note the great reduction in the uncertainty about the intercept compared to the two earlier solutions.

The unrestricted estimates from the baseline model are shown in Table 16.12. Estimation yields $\hat{\sigma} = 1.32$ per cent, with $SC = -8.28$.

Table 16.12 Money-demand GUM

Lag	0	1	2	$\sum$
$m - p$	− 1	0.66	0.24	− 0.09
	–	(0.10)	(0.09)	(0.02)
i	0.00	0.22	− 0.12	0.10
	(0.10)	(0.13)	(0.11)	(0.01)
Δp	− 0.85	0.15	–	− 0.70
	(0.18)	(0.20)		(0.15)
R	− 0.48	− 0.26	0.08	− 0.66
	(0.11)	(0.17)	(0.12)	(0.09)
1	− 0.06	–	–	− 0.06
	(0.13)			(0.13)

As with the VAR earlier, the presence of many coefficients makes it hard to discern patterns, and impossible to interpret the GUM in any detail. Since sequential simplification is essential, we digress to reconsider one aspect of 'data mining' (see Ch.15). Consider a theoretical statistical model to determine the number of significant outcomes that would arise by chance on fitting a regression to (say) twenty variables using one-hundred observations, when all the regressors are unrelated to the dependent variable. On average, several t-values will exceed the conventional critical value of two, a few will exceed a critical value of three, but almost none will by chance exceed a critical value of four or over. A similar argument applies to the F-test, although the critical values now vary with the degrees of freedom of both numerator and denominator. The reason discussed in Chapter 13 is that the tail of a t- or an F-distribution dies out rapidly outside three standard deviations. Larger critical values are required for significance when processes are I(1), but even so, 'data mining' alone cannot explain four t-values with $p < 0.005$. Transforming, then selecting the most important of the resulting combinations, will entail larger critical values than conventional, as will an allowance for the number of tests to be conducted. Thus, given the sample size, and assuming we will not conduct more than twenty tests, a 0.005 per cent level seems reasonable for each test to protect against spurious significance without too great a risk of model mis-specification.

Next, we turn to the analysis of the lag structure using the methods discussed in Chapters 6 and 7.

Table 16.13 Tests of significance of each variable

Variable	F(num,denom)	Value	Unit-root t-test
$m - p$	$F(2, 91)$	2100**	−6.0**
i	$F(3, 91)$	27.6**	8.6**
Δp	$F(2, 91)$	16.6**	−4.6**
R	$F(3, 91)$	25.9**	−7.0**

The F-tests in Table 16.13 are tests of the joint significance of the associated variables, with all their lags, and provide tests for deleting each variable completely from the model: every F-test is highly significant. The unit-root t-tests of whether the variable in question enters as a level or as a difference (i.e., checking for an eigenvalue of unity in each lag polynomial: see Ch.7), confirm that every variable enters the long-run solution.

Finally, we consider the importance of the various lag lengths, using F-tests on the significance of the first-order lag, then the second-order lag. Table 16.14 reports the outcomes.

Table 16.14 Tests of significance of each lag

Lag	F(num,denom)	Value
1	$F(4, 91)$	19.3**
2	$F(3, 91)$	3.0*

The second lag does not matter greatly, but before deleting variables from a model, transform to an interpretable, preferably orthogonal, parameterization, and then consider deletions. The cumulative lag weights show similar latencies for the three regressors, being roughly 60 per cent converged after ten quarters.

Fig. 16.17 shows the fitted and actual values of $(m_t - p_t)$, the scaled residuals from the model in Table 16.12, a plot of the residual correlogram, and the residual density and histogram. The residuals show evidence of third-order autocorrelation (and perhaps seventh), and there are several outliers, especially those in 1969(1) and 1971(1).

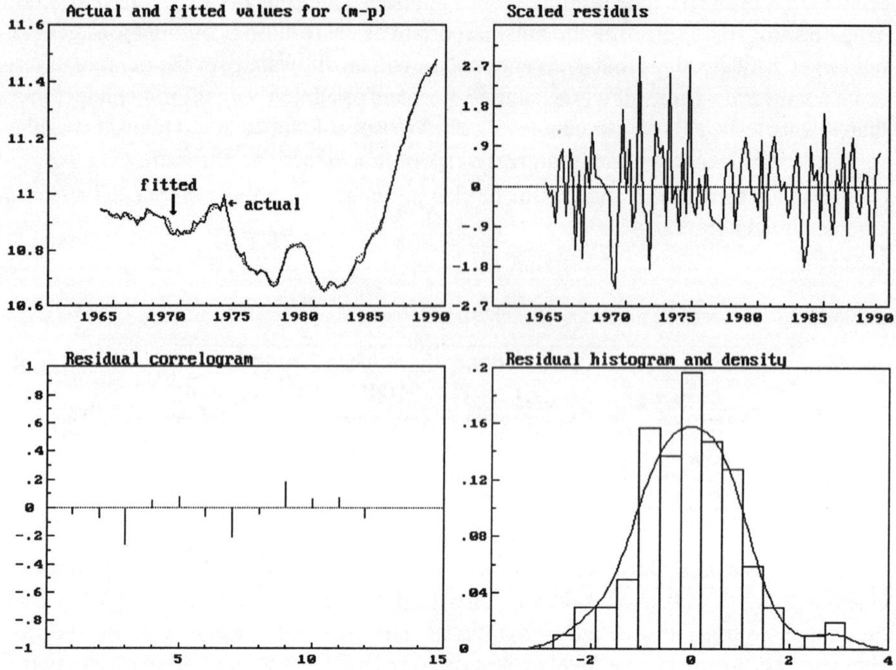

Fig. 16.17 Graphical evaluation statistics for M1-demand GUM

More formal checks on whether the model is data coherent are provided by testing for residual autocorrelation (fifth-order), ARCH (fourth-order), non-normality, and functional form mis-specification. Table 16.15 records the outcomes.

Table 16.15 Mis-specification tests

Alternative	Test	Value
autocorrelation	$F(5, 86)$	2.4*
ARCH	$F(4, 83)$	0.5
non-normality	$\chi^2(2)$	4.3
RESET	$F(1, 90)$	0.1

These results confirm the graphical evidence of residual autocorrelation, and detailed study reveals that $\Delta(m-p)_{t-3}$ and Δp_{t-3} are significant if the reduction commences at four lags. While this is a good illustration of the dangers of not commencing with the most general model, for the present exposition we will proceed on the assumption that the residual autocorrelation is a Type-I error, and continue with the equation in Table 16.12. The GUM often over-fits, resulting in negatively autocorrelated residuals; if that is the source of the problem, then it will reduce as we proceed. Positive residual autocorrelation would necessitate a re-formulation.

The tests for parameter and variance constancy within sample, using the approach in Hansen (1992a), reveal no problems (variance instability test: 0.28; joint parameter instability test: 1.44). Thus, we tentatively conclude that the GUM provides a cointegrated and data congruent, if non-parsimonious, representation of money demand.

16.11 Transformation and reduction

The next stage is to transform the GUM in Table 16.12 to a more interpretable form. The principles are similar to the reductions conducted above on the system. Imposing an equilibrium correction, and otherwise mapping to differences, to ensure an I(0) representation not only induces a substantial parameter reduction, which we know to be valid from the cointegration analysis, it moves towards a more orthogonal representation. It is also helpful for graphical illustrations, as it enforces a switch in the dependent variable to growth rates of real money. A number of other transformations will be tried as we proceed: in particular, we seek to represent the model in terms of a lagged growth rate of velocity, changes in interest rates and acceleration of inflation. At each stage, we re-estimate to show the orthogonalization impact; if we are successful in highlighting the main determinants of behaviour, then we can delete the newly redundant combinations of variables; if not, we continue transforming.

We have already imposed long-run price homogeneity without loss of fit, and now map to the cointegration vector, eliminating all levels of real money by transforming to differences. The test of the validity of that reduction (from I(1) to I(0)) was satisfied above. The ECM could be entered at any lag, and here we adopt one lag, as it will transpire to simplify the analysis. The I(0) reduction for the individual conditional equation generates the outcomes in (16.14): the reduction test yields $F(3,94) = 0.08$.

$$
\begin{aligned}
\Delta \widehat{(m-p)}_t = \underset{(0.002)}{0.000} - \underset{(0.09)}{0.24}\,\Delta(m-p)_{t-1} - \underset{(0.10)}{0.00}\,\Delta i_t + \underset{(0.10)}{0.12}\,\Delta i_{t-1} \\
- \underset{(0.17)}{0.83}\,\Delta^2 p_t - \underset{(0.10)}{0.49}\,\Delta R_t - \underset{(0.11)}{0.05}\,\Delta R_{t-1} - \underset{(0.01)}{0.10}\, ECM_{t-1}
\end{aligned}
$$

$$\mathsf{R}^2 = 0.77 \;\; \hat{\sigma} = 1.30\% \;\; SC = -8.41 \;\; VS = 0.27 \;\; JS = 1.30. \tag{16.14}$$

Interestingly, the diagnostic test outcomes in Table 16.16 no longer show significant residual autocorrelation, consistent with the earlier interpretation of slight over-fitting creating negative autocorrelation.

It is often difficult in a high-dimensional problem to visualize the impact of any given transform, and I may spend days mentally experimenting with alternatives that might simplify the problem. Chapter 6 described some of the many forms of dynamic combinations that can be interpreted, yet capture several effects in one parameter. While (16.14) is only one way to summarize the evidence, it is more easily interpreted than the GUM in Table 16.12. However, it still contains three redundant regressors, namely Δi_t, ΔR_{t-1}, and the intercept, all of which have negligible coefficients, so we delete these.

Table 16.16 I(0)-model diagnostic tests

Alternative	Test	Value
autocorrelation	$F(5,89)$	2.1
ARCH	$F(4,86)$	0.5
non-normality	$\chi^2(2)$	4.0
heteroscedasticity	$F(14,79)$	0.7
RESET	$F(1,93)$	0.01

The final simplification step is less obvious and took several years to realize. The coefficients of the lagged growth rates of real money and real expenditure have similar magnitudes and opposite signs, and combining them under that assumption would create the change in lagged velocity, namely, $\Delta v_{t-1} = \Delta(p+i-m)_{t-1}$. That would retain a positive impact from expenditure changes in an interpretable form. Re-estimation produces:

$$\Delta\widehat{(m-p)}_t = \underset{(0.06)}{0.18}\,\Delta v_{t-1} - \underset{(0.17)}{0.84}\,\Delta^2 p_t - \underset{(0.10)}{0.51}\,\Delta R_t - \underset{(0.01)}{0.10}\;ECM_{t-1}$$

$$\tilde{\mathsf{R}}^2 = 0.78\;\; \hat{\sigma} = 1.29\%\;\; SC = -8.56\;\; VS = 0.28\;\; JS = 0.77. \qquad (16.15)$$

The F-test of the last simplification yields $F(4,94) = 0.28$. All parameters are significant at the 0.5 per cent level or higher, have interpretable signs, and reveal highly elastic interest-rate and inflation responses in both the short and long run. Accelerating inflation quickly erodes money demand, but financial innovation has had a large attractive effect on M1 holdings. The ECM induces ten per cent adjustment per period, with intermediate adjustments captured by the difference terms. Current inflation enters with a near minus unit coefficient, implying that (16.15) could be rewritten with Δm_t as the dependent variable, without current inflation mattering for determining money in the short-run. Almost eighty per cent of the change in real money is explained by the model ($\tilde{\mathsf{R}}$ does not allow for a mean).

Fig. 16.18 shows the fitted and actual values of $\Delta(m_t - p_t)$, the scaled residuals, the residual correlogram, and their density and histogram. The tracking is close for a series with a range of twelve percentage points, although the residuals now show clear evidence of third-order autocorrelation: an LM test yields $F(1,97) = 7.2^{**}$ (it may represent an artefact due to separate seasonal adjustment of each series). The outliers are somewhat attenuated, but still visible in the residual histogram. Even so, the diagnostic tests remain insignificant as shown in Table 16.17.

Despite their appearance, the residuals show no ARCH effects, even though two of the significant explanatory variables (Δp_t and R_t) had highly significant ARCH tests in the VAR. Thus, the volatility of interest rates and inflation are correctly reflected in the model.

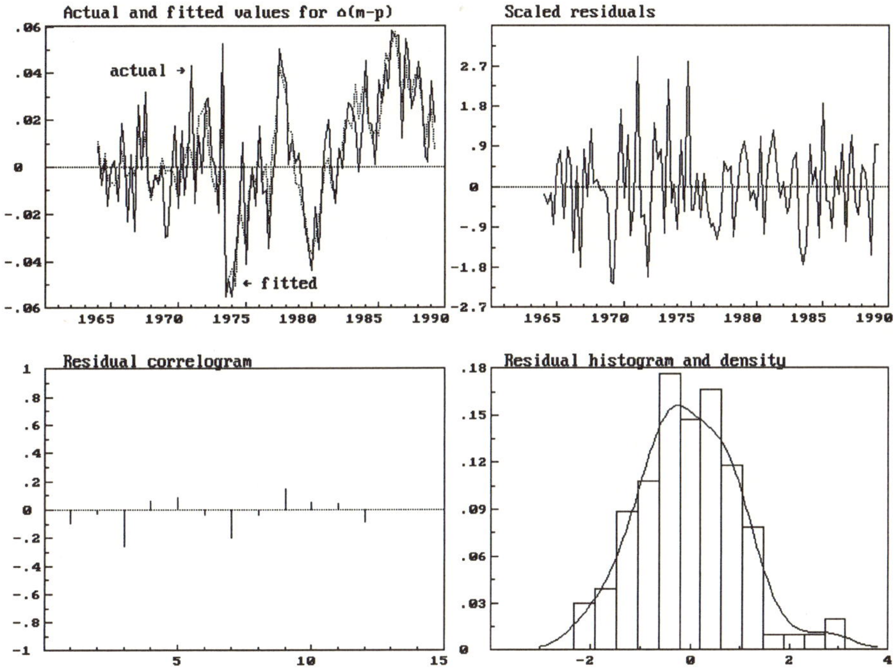

Fig. 16.18 Graphical evaluation statistics for M1-demand equation

Table 16.17 Final M1-equation diagnostic tests

Alternative	Test	Value
autocorrelation	$F(5, 93)$	1.9
ARCH	$F(4, 90)$	0.6
non-normality	$\chi^2(2)$	2.9
heteroscedasticity	$F(14, 83)$	0.6
RESET	$F(1, 97)$	0.01

Fig. 16.19 shows the recursively estimated coefficients, the 1-step residuals and the breakpoint Chow tests scaled by their 1 per cent significance values. The estimated parameters are constant, and significant over most of the sample period, and no test statistic is near the significance level at any point in the sample.

Equation (16.15) is the final simplified model choice. The demand for real money is explained by the change in velocity in the previous quarter, the current change in inflation and in the learning-adjusted opportunity cost of holding money, and the previous disequilibrium from the long-run demand relation in (16.13). The results are consistent with the theoretical analysis of the 'target-bounds' model, with the long-run demand theory, and with the data evidence. The equation parsimoniously encompasses the GUM by construction of the simplification process, is constant and data coherent. The conditional estimates are more precise than the FIML values reported in Table 16.8, as anticipated. We have tested various aspects of weak exogeneity, but section 16.13 will reconsider super exogeneity.

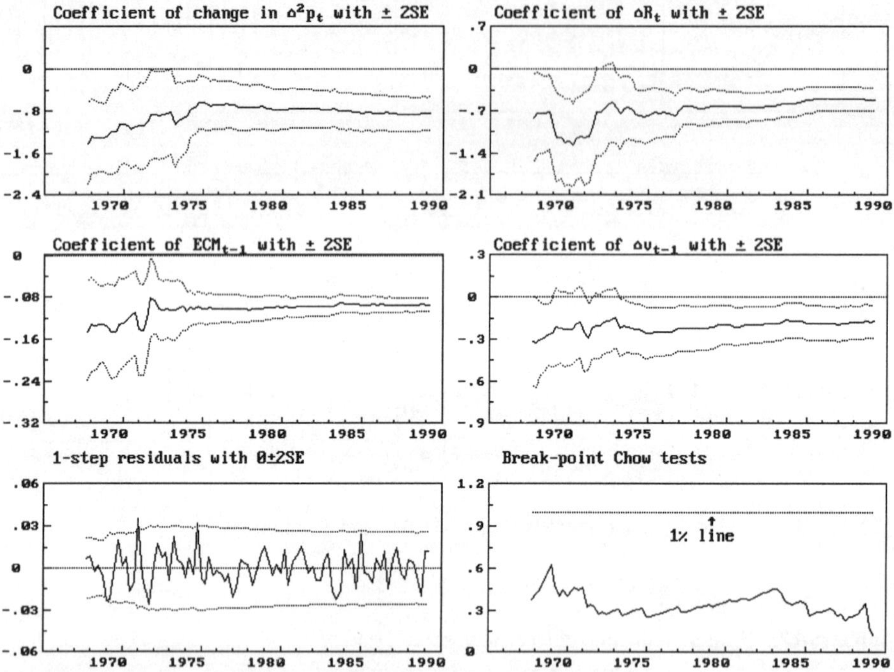

Fig. 16.19 Recursive OLS statistics for M1-demand equation

16.12 Post-modelling evaluation

Table 16.18 records the correlations between the regressors, and reveals the extent to which an orthogonal parameterization has been achieved. The second column shows the simple correlations of each regressor with the dependent variable, and the third the partial correlation. The latter are all greater in absolute value than the former, except for Δv_t which changed sign, so the structure of the money demand equation is better revealed by the multi-variable model. Conversely, therefore, complete orthogonality cannot have been achieved.

The correlations between the regressors in the last three columns are small except between ECM_{t-1} and Δv_{t-1}, so we have achieved a relatively orthogonalized model, while retaining most of the explanatory power in a few data functions. Such an outcome is consistent with (16.15) representing a contingent plan for agents who partition available information into conceptually separate entities. The coefficient of the own rate identifies the model as a demand, rather than a supply, equation.

Table 16.18 Correlation matrix after transformations

	Simple	Partial	$\Delta^2 p_t$	ΔR_t	ECM_{t-1}
$\Delta^2 p_t$	−0.29	−0.47	–	–	–
ΔR_t	−0.31	−0.46	0.36	–	–
ECM_{t-1}	−0.74	−0.84	−0.12	−0.07	–
Δv_{t-1}	0.36	−0.29	0.12	0.02	−0.64

16.12.1 Learning adjustment

Conditional on retaining the basic specification of (16.15), we can estimate the parameters α and β of the learning function in (16.6). Non-linear least-squares yields:

$$\hat{\alpha} = \underset{(2.68)}{4.66} \quad \text{and} \quad \hat{\beta} = \underset{(0.55)}{-\,1.04}\,.$$

Neither parameter is very accurately determined, but they have similar values to those initially assumed, and the weighting function is little altered. Now, $\hat{\sigma} = 1.30$ per cent, with $SC = -8.47$, so there is almost no change in fit.

16.12.2 Constancy

The formulation in (16.15) can be estimated from any sub-period, and yields similar estimates and goodness of fit. Estimating it separately from the first, middle and last thirty-three observations (actually, the last sub-sample is thirty-four) yields $\hat{\sigma}$ values of 1.53 per cent, 1.25 per cent and 1.09 per cent respectively. The coefficients are recognizable in each period, but often are not statistically significant. This suggests that it is important to allow for 'model expansion' as information accrues over time. Here the fit has improved over time, rather than deteriorated as is often found, even though (16.15) is similar to the estimated equations published before the introduction of interest-bearing checking accounts. For example, for a sample ending in 1982(4), from Hendry (1985):

$$\begin{aligned}\Delta\widehat{(m-p)}_t &= \underset{(0.13)}{0.37}\,\Delta i_{t-1} - \underset{(0.12)}{0.80}\,\Delta p_t - \underset{(0.07)}{0.58}\,R_{3t} \\ &\quad - \underset{(0.01)}{0.10}\,(m-p-i)_{t-2} - \underset{(0.07)}{0.28}\,\Delta(m-p)_{t-1} - \underset{(0.01)}{0.04} \qquad (16.16)\end{aligned}$$

$R^2 = 0.71 \;\; \hat{\sigma} = 1.3\%$.

The model was already fitting better than in earlier samples. Of course, if R_{3t} alone is used in longer samples, the equation shows signs of predictive failure, and no longer cointegrates. Thus constancy seems to hold more at the level of decision taking, than at the phenomenological level.

16.12.3 Encompassing

There are no formal rival models against which to test, but the final estimates can be expressed in levels to check that they are close to those in Table 16.12, and so do indeed represent an interpretation of the complicated dynamic structure of the GUM. Specifically, solving back to the levels from (16.15) yields the outcome in Table 16.19.

Table 16.19 Restricted levels representation

Lag	0	1	2	$\sum$
$m-p$	-1	0.73	0.17	-0.10
i	0	0.27	-0.17	0.10
Δp	-0.84	0.20	0	-0.64
R	-0.51	-0.15	0	-0.66
1	0.02	–	–	0.02

The match is reasonable, so the eleven coefficients in Table 16.12 are 'explained' by the four regressors in (16.15).

16.13 Testing the Lucas critique

Tests of the Lucas critique were discussed Chapter 14, and here we implement two aspects of those ideas, using similar tests to those that Favero and Hendry (1992) apply to the model in Baba *et al.* (1992). First, the model of money demand conditional on inflation in (16.15) is constant over the sample period. The VAR estimates above suggested that the marginal model for inflation was not constant, and entails that the reverse regression of inflation on money, 'inverting' (16.15) should be non-constant: super exogeneity is not invariant to re-normalization. The estimates are:

$$\widehat{\Delta p_t} = \underset{(0.06)}{0.05}\,\Delta m_t + \underset{(0.06)}{0.25}\,\Delta R_t + \underset{(0.09)}{0.71}\,\Delta p_{t-1} + \underset{(0.007)}{0.013}\,ECM_{t-1} + \underset{(0.04)}{0.04}\,\Delta v_{t-1} - \underset{(0.002)}{0.006} \tag{16.17}$$

$$\mathsf{R}^2 = 0.73\ \hat{\sigma} = 0.76\%\ SC = -9.56\ VS = 0.25\ JS = 1.11.$$

Most of the explanation is due to the lagged inflation variable. Table 16.20 reports the diagnostic tests, and Fig. 16.20 shows the recursive statistics. Almost every diagnostic test is failed, and the parameter estimates are much less constant than in (16.15), although *VS* and *JS* do not reject.

Table 16.20 Inflation-equation diagnostic tests

Alternative	Test	Value
autocorrelation	$F(5,89)$	3.4**
ARCH	$F(4,86)$	2.8*
non-normality	$\chi^2(2)$	9.7**
heteroscedasticity	$F(10,83)$	3.4**
RESET	$F(1,93)$	0.07

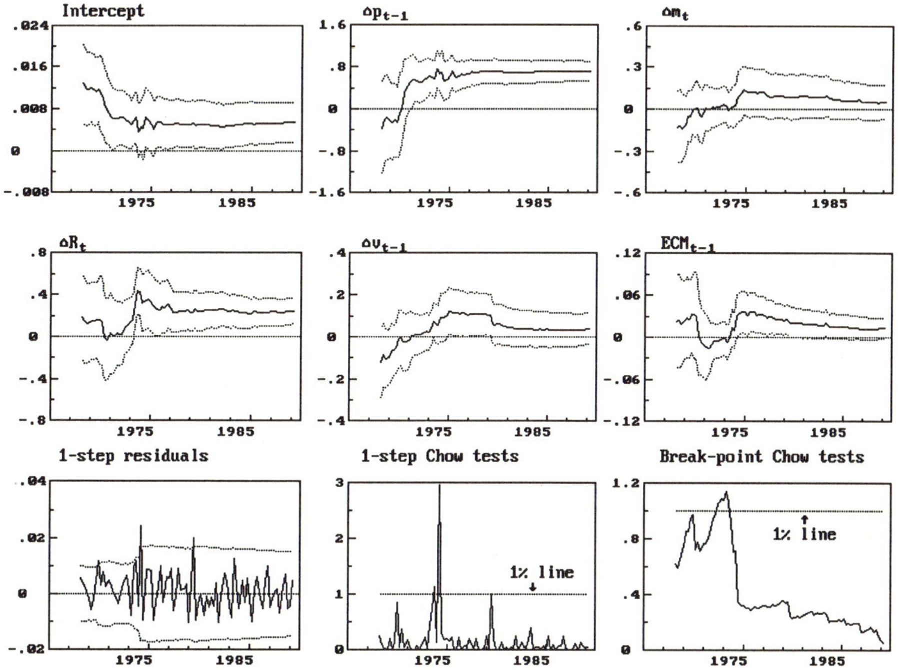

Fig. 16.20 Recursive statistics for the inflation equation

The interest rate equation obtained by inversion delivers a similar outcome: the coefficients are less constant, but only the ARCH test rejects.

The super exogeneity test checks whether the parameters of the conditional model are invariant to changes in the parameters in the marginal processes, so determinants of those processes' non-constancies should be statistically insignificant when added to the conditional model as in Engle and Hendry (1993).[18] In modelling the system, two

[18] That the constancy tests differ from the invariance tests reveals the difference between the two concepts.

dummy variables were needed to establish the constancy of the marginal processes for output, inflation and interest rates. These dummies do enter the marginal processes, and should not enter the conditional model under the hypothesis of super exogeneity. The omitted-variable test of their irrelevance yields $F(2, 94) = 0.11$; and using the component impulse dummies yields $F(6, 90) = 0.40$. Such outcomes sustain the hypothesis that the model in (16.15) is a valid conditional model with invariant parameters of interest. Had the regressor variables been proxies for expectations, (16.15) should have manifested changes in its parameters when the expectations processes altered during the sample; it did not, so the evidence favours agents using data-based expectations of the form discussed in Chapter 6. The high degree of differencing in the final equation is consistent with that proposition.

16.14 Post-sample evaluation

A genuine test of the model requires an update of the data set from 1989. As noted, however, due to changes in the composition of the banking sector, data on M1 are no longer collected, a point of some significance in the next section. Equation (16.15) is unlikely to be the final word on the demand for M1 in the UK, but should provide a useful basis for future research should a consistent data-set be collated.

16.15 Policy implications

The final issue in this analysis concerns policy implications, of which there are many. First, the econometric equation (16.15) has constant parameters, but the resulting determinants of money demand entail huge shifts in the policy-relevant space of P_t and R_{3t}. One explanation for M1 demand equations being constant is that the stock of M1 is endogenously determined by private-sector behaviour, with the central bank determining the interest rate. That transactions money is a responsive variable in the UK economy, rather than a causal autonomous factor, brings into question elementary textbook treatments in which the price level is determined by the intersection of the (constant) demand for money function with an extraneously determined nominal money stock. Had the Bank of England raised interest rates to suppress the large increases in M1 recorded in the second half of the 1980s, to offset an 'anticipated upturn in inflation', they would have significantly misunderstood the portfolio adjustment behaviour of the private sector, and unnecessarily reduced output. In the event, they correctly read the evidence. Indeed, the monetary authority must have decided that M1 is now an epiphenomenon — they have stopped collecting the data on it (see section 16.16).

Next, the opportunity cost of holding M1 has become a differential, which makes it impossible to control M1 by manipulating the level of interest rates. Thirdly, excess demand for output affects, and is affected by, inflation and by the interest rate. Thus, raising interest rates to control inflation will operate in the UK by lowering output. The behaviour of money demand is due to incidental side effects from (possible) increases in the interest differential and falls in income lowering money demand, followed later by a rise due to lower inflation. The price level here is the result of cumulative inflation shocks, with inflation increasing or falling with the state of excess demand.

Finally, the conditional money demand equation cannot be 'inverted' to determine P, and the ensuing equation is non-constant. We have subjected the model to the Lucas-critique tests in §16.12, and, as we find no evidence for the critique, the model offers a viable basis for policy. Economically, 'non-invertibility' implies that some policy implications do not follow from the existence of a constant money-demand equation such as (16.15): for example, the equation determines money holdings, and not inflation or the interest rate.

The selected model of money demand in the UK has been constant and well-specified in the presence of data revisions and financial innovations, and has survived the accrual of new data which differed greatly from the previous within-sample observations. Even so, the historical development of the equation highlights the need for econometric models to be as adaptive to their environment as economic agents are. Since the model proved to be constant and invariant over a considerable extension of the sample period and against additional information, it satisfies two of the attributes of structure, and suggests that a progressive research strategy can work in practice.

16.16 Data definitions

The data begin in 1963(1), the earliest date for which the Bank of England calculated detailed monetary statistics, and end in 1989(2), due to a major change in the institutions included as banks. In July 1989, the Abbey National Building Society converted to a public limited company, so was classified as a bank, increasing M1 by sixteen per cent overnight. The Bank of England stopped reporting total M1, although it can still be constructed from its components. See the *Bank of England Quarterly Bulletin* (August 1989, pp. 352-353) and Healey, Mann, Clews and Hoggarth (1990) for further details.

M_t	=	M1, £million, seasonally adjusted
P_t	=	deflator of TFE, seasonally adjusted (base 1985)
I_t	=	real TFE, £million, seasonally adjusted
R_{3t}	=	three-month local authority bill rate, fraction p.a.
R_t	=	$R_{3t} - R^l_{0t}$
R^l_{0t}	=	learning-adjusted retail sight deposit interest rate
v_t	=	log velocity: $p_t + i_t - m_t$
Δx_t	=	$(x_t - x_{t-1})$ for any variable x_t
$\Delta^2 x_t$	=	$\Delta x_t - \Delta x_{t-1}$
D_{ot}	=	Dummy: unity in 1972 (4) ; 1973 (1) ; 1979(2)
D_{yt}	=	Dummy: unity in 1973 (3) ; 1973 (4) ; 1979(3).

Part IV

Appendices

A1
Matrix Algebra

Following an overview of the six appendix chapters, the properties of matrices and the most common operations of matrix algebra are reviewed. The concept of a matrix array is related to the formulation of a simple econometric model, then the main algebraic operations on matrices and vectors are described. Relations between operations are noted, including vector and matrix differentiation. The final extension to polynomial matrices is useful for analysing dynamic systems.

A1.1 Summary of the appendix chapters

The objective of the appendix is to explain the technical background to how econometrics develops tools for modelling empirical economic phenomena, establishing the values of any unknowns in models of distributions, and testing conjectures about the mechanisms generating the outcomes, given the nature of economic behaviour. The six chapters cover matrix algebra; probability and distributions; statistical theory; asymptotic distribution theory for stationary processes; numerical optimization methods; and macro-econometric models.

To summarize their contents, Chapter A1 introduces the concept of a matrix as an ordered array, then draws together the elements of matrix algebra used in the main text. The most common properties and operations are reviewed, then extended to polynomial matrices which are useful for analysing dynamic systems.

Next, Chapter A2 commences with the outcomes of a random experiment, which determines what events can occur. A probability calculus is developed to characterize events, which also handles the probabilities of joint events, and of some events conditional on others occurring. Then the concept of a random variable is formulated as a mapping from events to numerical measures thereof, so that outcomes become real numbers which cannot be perfectly predicted in advance. The behaviour of random variables is described by their distribution functions, although it is often more convenient to work with density functions when they exist. These are the theoretical counterparts of empirical distributions and densities. The resulting framework sustains the specification of probability models, which comprise families of possible distributions for random variables. These families are indexed by parameters: given a distributional form, the parameters determine its characteristics. Properties of random variables and their distributions, such as expectations, or average values, variances, and higher moments are analysed. Moments help describe the shapes of distributions and often yield values which are directly related to the parameters of the distributions. In practice, the values of parameters are unknown and need to be determined from data evidence.

That last step focuses the problem of modelling random processes on specifying an appropriate family of distributions and estimating the values of its parameters from observed data. This issue is taken up in Chapter A3 on statistics. Sample observations are summarized in terms of statistics and their distributions, with the likelihood function linking parameters to statistics, leading to the method of maximum likelihood for estimation. In turn, the distributions of estimators must be obtained. Even in simple cases, exact distributions are difficult to derive, suggesting a need for some form of approximation, an issue tackled in Chapter A4. The next topic concerns testing, or evaluating, theories or conjectures about the functioning of the stochastic (economic) mechanism, and attempts to develop powerful test procedures. The important special case of linear regression is discussed in detail.

Chapter A4 confronts the difficulty that even when the correct member of the family of probability distributions is known, deriving the distributions of statistics often proves difficult. A standard approach is to investigate what happens in indefinitely large samples, so asymptotic distribution theory is considered in detail, progressing from the simplest case of an independent, identically distributed scalar random variable through to a dynamic, stationary vector process, with errors described by mixing or martingale processes. The extension to stochastic processes (time-dated random variables) is an important move towards making probability theory applicable in economics. As a result, approximations are provided for the distributions in finite samples of most statistics of interest to the economist analysing stationary time-series data. The theory is applied to instrumental variables and maximum likelihood estimators, and illustrated by several solved examples. The main text considers distributions for non-stationary data, as well as ways of evaluating the accuracy of the asymptotic approximations in small samples using Monte Carlo simulation methods.

Chapter A5 analyses numerical optimization techniques which are used extensively in practical econometric modelling. Many likelihood functions are sufficiently non-linear that their optima cannot be determined analytically. This contrasts with least squares where a quadratic criterion leads to a linear estimator. In any application, however, numerical methods can locate the optimum. Scalar and vector optimization methods are described, focusing on numerically efficient methods. Issues of multiple optima, convergence criteria, iterative rules, and efficiency are considered. Four categories of multivariate optimization methods are distinguished: gradient-based procedures; step-wise; conjugate directions, and variable metric, where the last is the preferred option. The main text also discusses the links between efficient statistical procedures and efficient numerical methods (see Ch.11).

Finally, Chapter A6 introduces the terminology and structure of macro-econometric models for readers approaching this text from a non-economics background. The main types of variables and kinds of equations are explained, and a schematic macro-model is formulated in steps from a single market to a multi-sectoral system. Potential issues for econometric analyses of multivariate, dynamic, and evolving systems are noted. The resulting system is a caricature of a large practical model but illustrates the main relationships of the major sectors including: household (which determine consumption, saving, wealth accumulation, and labour supply); company (which determine investment, labour demand, output, and inventory accumulation); financial (money, bonds, equity, and interest rates); overseas (imports, exports, exchange rates, and capital flows); and government (taxes, expenditure, and debt creation). Methods for analysing stochastic, dynamic macro-econometric systems are discussed.

The treatment in these appendices aims to make the book relatively self-contained and explain the essential background material underpinning the main text in a logical development, but is not intended to be either rigorous or comprehensive. Some knowledge of set theory, of calculus, and of economics is assumed, although a brief treatment of the required aspects of the first is included in the next chapter and some results for the last are described in Chapter A6. The elements of matrix algebra are discussed in the remainder of this chapter.

A1.2 Matrices

Multivariate statistical and econometric theory is usually expressed in terms of matrices. Much of the book can be understood without a detailed knowledge of matrix algebra and the properties of matrices, but it is essential in some places, so this chapter describes a number of widely-used results. Useful references include Gantmacher (1959), Gel'fand (1967), Theil (1971), Rao (1973, Ch.1), Anderson (1984, App. A), Dhrymes (1984) and Magnus and Neudecker (1988).

A matrix is an $m \times n$ array of the form:

$$\begin{pmatrix} a_{1,1} & a_{1,2} & \cdots & a_{1,n-1} & a_{1,n} \\ a_{2,1} & a_{2,2} & \cdots & a_{2,n-1} & a_{2,n} \\ \vdots & \vdots & \ddots & \vdots & \vdots \\ a_{m-1,1} & a_{m-1,2} & \cdots & a_{m-1,n-1} & a_{m-1,n} \\ a_{m,1} & a_{m,2} & \cdots & a_{m,n-1} & a_{m,n} \end{pmatrix}$$

where $a_{i,j}$ denotes the element in the ith row and j^{th} column. Usually, the ',' between the subscripts i and j is omitted unless essential for clarity, so the $(i,j)^{th}$ element is written simply as a_{ij}. A column vector is the special case where $n = 1$, denoted by:

$$\begin{pmatrix} a_1 \\ a_2 \\ \vdots \\ a_{m-1} \\ a_m \end{pmatrix}.$$

Matrices are written in bold-face upper case and vectors in bold-face lower case so that if we denote the first two arrays by $\boldsymbol{A}$ and $\boldsymbol{a}$:

$$\boldsymbol{A} = \{a_{ij}\}_{m,n} = \begin{pmatrix} a_{11} & \cdots & a_{1n} \\ \vdots & \ddots & \vdots \\ a_{m1} & \cdots & a_{mn} \end{pmatrix} \text{ and } \boldsymbol{a} = \{a_i\}_m = \begin{pmatrix} a_1 \\ \vdots \\ a_m \end{pmatrix}. \tag{A1.1}$$

Then (A1.1) also notes the convention that matrices can be shown as $\boldsymbol{A} = \{a_{ij}\}_{m,n}$ where the dimensions of the array are recorded as subscripts to the $\{\cdot\}$. The next section describes the basic algebraic operations on matrices, but to understand the example which concludes this section, we state two results.

First, when two matrices have the same dimensions, they can be added element by element. When $\boldsymbol{A}$ and $\boldsymbol{B}$ are $m \times n$ then $\boldsymbol{C} = \boldsymbol{A} + \boldsymbol{B}$ is the $m \times n$ matrix:

$$\boldsymbol{C} = \begin{pmatrix} a_{11} + b_{11} & \cdots & a_{1n} + b_{1n} \\ \vdots & \ddots & \vdots \\ a_{m1} + b_{m1} & \cdots & a_{mn} + b_{mn} \end{pmatrix}.$$

Symbolically, we write the outcome in terms of the elements as $\{c_{ij}\}_{m,n} = \{a_{ij} + b_{ij}\}_{m,n}$.

Secondly, when $\boldsymbol{A}$ is $m \times n$ and $\boldsymbol{b}$ is an $n \times 1$ vector, the product $\boldsymbol{c} = \boldsymbol{A}\boldsymbol{b}$ is an $m \times 1$ vector obtained by multiplying the column $\boldsymbol{b}$ by the rows of $\boldsymbol{A}$ in turn:

$$\boldsymbol{c} = \boldsymbol{A}\boldsymbol{b} = \begin{pmatrix} a_{11}b_1 + a_{12}b_2 + \cdots + a_{1n}b_n \\ \vdots \\ a_{m1}b_1 + a_{m2}b_2 + \cdots + a_{mn}b_n \end{pmatrix}.$$

Thus, $c_i = \sum_{k=1}^{n} a_{ik}b_k$ where $\sum_{k=1}^{n}$ denotes the sum of the elements. If the a_{ik} were the prices on the ith day of the kth good, and the b_k were fixed quantities of the kth good purchased, then c_i would be the expenditure on the ith day. Consequently, the multiplication of 'row into column' has a natural interpretation in some settings.

Consider a linear two-equation econometric model for consumption (c_t) and income (i_t) where the subscripts t denote the time of observation:

$$\begin{aligned} c_t &= a_{10} + a_{11}c_{t-1} + a_{12}i_{t-1} \\ i_t &= a_{20} + a_{22}i_{t-1}. \end{aligned} \tag{A1.2}$$

Then (A1.2) seeks to describe the evolution of c_t and i_t over time. Consumption this period depends on a fixed amount a_{10} plus consumption and income in the previous period, with weights a_{11} and a_{12}. Income only depends on a fixed amount a_{20} plus its value in the previous period with weight a_{22}. Implicitly, $a_{21} = 0$. The system can be expressed more concisely in matrix form as:

$$\begin{pmatrix} c_t \\ i_t \end{pmatrix} = \begin{pmatrix} a_{10} \\ a_{20} \end{pmatrix} + \begin{pmatrix} a_{11} & a_{12} \\ 0 & a_{22} \end{pmatrix} \begin{pmatrix} c_{t-1} \\ i_{t-1} \end{pmatrix}, \tag{A1.3}$$

or:

$$\boldsymbol{y}_t = \boldsymbol{a} + \boldsymbol{A}\boldsymbol{y}_{t-1}, \tag{A1.4}$$

in which the matrix $\boldsymbol{A}$ is 2×2, and the vectors $\boldsymbol{y}_t$, $\boldsymbol{y}_{t-1}$ (the lagged value of $\boldsymbol{y}_t$), and $\boldsymbol{a}$ are 2×1. When observations on the system in (A1.4) are available over $t = 0, 1, \ldots, T$, we can combine the available data using matrices ($'$ denotes transposition: see §A1.3):

$$\boldsymbol{Y}' = (\boldsymbol{y}_1 \ldots \boldsymbol{y}_T) = \begin{pmatrix} c_1 \ldots c_T \\ i_1 \ldots i_T \end{pmatrix}, \tag{A1.5}$$

so the system becomes:

$$\boldsymbol{Y}' = \boldsymbol{a}\boldsymbol{\iota}' + \boldsymbol{A}\boldsymbol{Y}'_1, \tag{A1.6}$$

in which $\boldsymbol{Y}$ and $\boldsymbol{a}\boldsymbol{\iota}'$ are $T \times 2$, $\boldsymbol{Y}_1$ is the lagged matrix of $\boldsymbol{Y}$ in (A1.5), and $\boldsymbol{\iota}'$ is the $1 \times T$ row vector of ones: $\boldsymbol{\iota}' = (1 \ldots 1)$. Check the result by writing (A1.6) in full.

A1.3 Matrix operations

The following matrix operations occur regularly.

- *Addition*: when $\boldsymbol{A}$ is $m \times n$ and $\boldsymbol{B}$ is $m \times n$:

$$\boldsymbol{A} + \boldsymbol{B} = \{a_{ij} + b_{ij}\}_{m,n} \,.$$

- *Transpose*: when $\boldsymbol{A}$ is $m \times n$:

$$\boldsymbol{A}' = \{a_{ji}\}_{n,m} \,.$$

  Thus, the element in the $(i,j)^{th}$ position is switched to the $(j,i)^{th}$.
- *Symmetric matrix*: when $\boldsymbol{A}$ is $n \times n$, then $\boldsymbol{A}$ is symmetric if:

$$\boldsymbol{A}' = \boldsymbol{A}.$$

- *Multiplication*: when $\boldsymbol{A}$ is $m \times n$ and c is a scalar:

$$c\boldsymbol{A} = \{ca_{ij}\}_{m,n} \,.$$

- *Multiplication*: when $\boldsymbol{A}$ is $m \times n$ and $\boldsymbol{B}$ is $n \times p$:

$$\boldsymbol{A}\boldsymbol{B} = \left\{\sum_{k=1}^{n} a_{ik}b_{kj}\right\}_{m,p} \,.$$

  This generalizes the result noted above for $p = 1$. Further, $\boldsymbol{A}(\boldsymbol{B} + \boldsymbol{C}) = \boldsymbol{A}\boldsymbol{B} + \boldsymbol{A}\boldsymbol{C}$. Finally, writing $\boldsymbol{A}' = (\boldsymbol{a}_1 \ldots \boldsymbol{a}_n)$ (a row of column vectors), then:

$$\boldsymbol{A}'\boldsymbol{A} = \sum_{i=1}^{n} \boldsymbol{a}_i \boldsymbol{a}'_i,$$

  which is the sum of the outer products.

- *Trace*: when $\boldsymbol{A}$ is $n \times n$, the trace of $\boldsymbol{A}$ is the sum of its diagonal elements:

$$\text{tr}\boldsymbol{A} = \sum_{i=1}^{n} a_{ii}.$$

- *Rank*: when $\boldsymbol{A}$ is $m \times n$, the rank of $\boldsymbol{A}$ (denoted rank$(\boldsymbol{A})$) is the number of linearly independent columns (or rows, as row rank always equals column rank) in $\boldsymbol{A}$, where rank$(\boldsymbol{A}) \leq \min(m, n)$. If $\boldsymbol{A}$ is $n \times n$ and of full rank, then rank$(\boldsymbol{A}) = n$. Also:

$$\text{rank}\,(\boldsymbol{AB}) \leq \min\,(\text{rank}\,(\boldsymbol{A})\,, \text{rank}\,(\boldsymbol{B}))\,.$$

- *Determinant*: when $\boldsymbol{A}$ is $n \times n$, the determinant of $\boldsymbol{A}$ is defined by:

$$|\boldsymbol{A}| = \sum (-1)^{t(j_1,\ldots,j_n)} \prod_{i=1}^{n} a_{ij},$$

where the summation is over all permutations $(j_1, \ldots, j_n)$ of the set of integers $(1, \ldots, n)$, and $t(j_1, \ldots, j_n)$ is the number of transpositions required to change $(1, \ldots, n)$ into $(j_1, \ldots, j_n)$. In the 2×2 case, the set $(1, 2)$ can be transposed once into $(2, 1)$, so:

$$|\boldsymbol{A}| = (-1)^0 a_{11} a_{22} + (-1)^1 a_{12} a_{21}.$$

- *Inverse*: when $\boldsymbol{A}$ is $n \times n$ of full rank n, $|\boldsymbol{A}| \neq 0$, and $\boldsymbol{A}$ is said to be non-singular. The inverse of $\boldsymbol{A}$ is denoted by $\boldsymbol{A}^{-1}$, and is the unique $n \times n$ matrix such that:

$$\boldsymbol{A}\boldsymbol{A}^{-1} = \boldsymbol{I}_n,$$

where $\boldsymbol{I}_n$ is the $n \times n$ identity matrix:

$$\boldsymbol{I}_n = \begin{pmatrix} 1 & 0 & \cdots & 0 \\ 0 & 1 & \cdots & 0 \\ \vdots & \vdots & \ddots & \vdots \\ 0 & 0 & \cdots & 1 \end{pmatrix}.$$

This also implies that $\boldsymbol{A}^{-1}\boldsymbol{A} = \boldsymbol{I}_n$. A singular matrix has a determinant of zero and has no inverse.

- *Adjoint matrix*: denoted by Adj$(\boldsymbol{A})$, this is the transpose of the matrix whose $(i, j)^{th}$ element A_{ij} is $(-1)^{i+j}$ times the determinant formed from $\boldsymbol{A}$ after deleting its ith row and j^{th} column. When $|\boldsymbol{A}| \neq 0$:

$$\boldsymbol{A}^{-1} = \frac{\text{Adj}\,(\boldsymbol{A})}{|\boldsymbol{A}|} \quad \text{where Adj}\,(\boldsymbol{A}) = \{A_{ij}\}_{n,n}\,.$$

- *Orthogonal matrix*: when $\boldsymbol{A}$ is $n \times n$, $\boldsymbol{A}$ is orthogonal if

$$\boldsymbol{A}'\boldsymbol{A} = \boldsymbol{I}_n.$$

Also, $\boldsymbol{A}\boldsymbol{A}' = \boldsymbol{I}_n$, and as rank$(\boldsymbol{A})$ must be n, $\boldsymbol{A}' = \boldsymbol{A}^{-1}$.

- *Orthogonal complement*: when $\boldsymbol{A}$ is $m \times n$ with $m > n$ and $\text{rank}(\boldsymbol{A}) = n$, the orthogonal complement $\boldsymbol{A}_\perp$ is the $m \times (m-n)$ matrix such that $\boldsymbol{A}'\boldsymbol{A}_\perp = \mathbf{0}$ with $\text{rank}(\boldsymbol{A}_\perp) = m - n$ and $\text{rank}(\boldsymbol{A} : \boldsymbol{A}_\perp) = m$. Then $\boldsymbol{A}_\perp$ spans the null space of $\boldsymbol{A}$, and $\text{rank}(\boldsymbol{A}_\perp)$ is called the nullity of $\boldsymbol{A}$.
- *Idempotent matrix*: when $\boldsymbol{A}$ is $n \times n$, $\boldsymbol{A}$ is idempotent if:

$$\boldsymbol{A}\boldsymbol{A} = \boldsymbol{A}^2 = \boldsymbol{A}.$$

An example is the identity matrix $\boldsymbol{I}_n$. The rank of an idempotent matrix equals its trace (see below for a proof).
- *Projection matrix*: when $\boldsymbol{X}$ is $m \times n$ with $m > n$, then the $n \times n$ matrix $\boldsymbol{Q}_X = \boldsymbol{I}_n - \boldsymbol{X}(\boldsymbol{X}'\boldsymbol{X})^{-1}\boldsymbol{X}'$ is called the projection matrix. $\boldsymbol{Q}_X$ is symmetric and idempotent:

$$\boldsymbol{Q}_X = \boldsymbol{Q}_X',$$

and as $\boldsymbol{Q}_X\boldsymbol{Q}_X = \boldsymbol{Q}_X^2$:

$$\boldsymbol{Q}_X^2 = \boldsymbol{I} - 2\boldsymbol{X}\left(\boldsymbol{X}'\boldsymbol{X}\right)^{-1}\boldsymbol{X}' + \boldsymbol{X}\left(\boldsymbol{X}'\boldsymbol{X}\right)^{-1}\boldsymbol{X}'\boldsymbol{X}\left(\boldsymbol{X}'\boldsymbol{X}\right)^{-1}\boldsymbol{X}' = \boldsymbol{Q}_X.$$

Then $\text{rank}(\boldsymbol{Q}_X) = \text{tr}(\boldsymbol{Q}_X) = m - n$.
- *Vectorization*: when $\boldsymbol{A}$ is $m \times n$, the $(\cdot)^v$ vectorizing operator stacks its columns in an $mn \times 1$ vector $\boldsymbol{a}$:

$$(\boldsymbol{A})^v = \begin{pmatrix} a_{11} \\ \vdots \\ a_{m1} \\ \vdots \\ a_{1n} \\ \vdots \\ a_{mn} \end{pmatrix} = \boldsymbol{a}.$$

For example, the vectorized form of the $\boldsymbol{A}'$ matrix in (A1.3) is:

$$(\boldsymbol{A}')^v = \begin{pmatrix} a_{11} \\ a_{12} \\ 0 \\ a_{22} \end{pmatrix},$$

which stacks the coefficients of the model by equation. When $\boldsymbol{a}$ is an $n \times 1$ vector, $(\boldsymbol{a})^v = \boldsymbol{a}$.
- *Kronecker product*: When $\boldsymbol{A}$ is $(m \times n)$ and $\boldsymbol{B}$ is $(p \times q)$:

$$\boldsymbol{A} \otimes \boldsymbol{B} = \{b_{ij}\boldsymbol{A}\}_{mp,nq}.$$

Some writers define the opposite order in this product (e.g. Doornik and Hendry, 1994a), leading to awkward re-orderings when vectorizing matrix products. Here, for example when $\boldsymbol{A} = \{a_{ij}\}_{2,2}$ and $\boldsymbol{B} = \{b_{ij}\}_{2,2}$:

$$\boldsymbol{A} \otimes \boldsymbol{B} = \begin{pmatrix} b_{11}\boldsymbol{A} & b_{12}\boldsymbol{A} \\ b_{21}\boldsymbol{A} & b_{22}\boldsymbol{A} \end{pmatrix} = \begin{pmatrix} b_{11}a_{11} & b_{11}a_{12} & b_{12}a_{11} & b_{12}a_{12} \\ b_{11}a_{21} & b_{11}a_{22} & b_{12}a_{21} & b_{12}a_{22} \\ b_{21}a_{11} & b_{21}a_{12} & b_{22}a_{11} & b_{22}a_{12} \\ b_{21}a_{21} & b_{21}a_{22} & b_{22}a_{21} & b_{22}a_{22} \end{pmatrix}.$$

- *Unrestricted elements*: when deriving econometric estimators, to restrict attention to the parameters which are to be estimated and ignore the remaining parameters, we use the operator $(\cdot)^u$. This selects the unrestricted elements of a vector, or crosses out rows and columns of a matrix, reducing the dimensionality. $(\cdot)^{v_u}$ both vectorizes a matrix and selects the unrestricted elements. For the $\boldsymbol{A}$ matrix in (A1.3), when the zero is a restriction, the remaining parameters are:

$$(\boldsymbol{A}')^{v_u} = ((\boldsymbol{A}')^v)^u = ((\boldsymbol{A}')^u)^v = \begin{pmatrix} a_{11} \\ a_{12} \\ a_{22} \end{pmatrix}.$$

- *Diagonal*: when $\boldsymbol{A}$ is $n \times n$, the diagonal matrix dg$\boldsymbol{A}$ is defined by:

$$\mathrm{dg}\boldsymbol{A} = \begin{pmatrix} a_{11} & 0 & \cdots & 0 \\ 0 & a_{22} & \cdots & 0 \\ \vdots & \vdots & \ddots & \vdots \\ 0 & 0 & \cdots & a_{nn} \end{pmatrix} = \mathrm{diag}\,(a_{11}, a_{22}, \ldots, a_{nn}).$$

- *Positive definite*: when $\boldsymbol{A}$ is $n \times n$ and symmetric, $\boldsymbol{A}$ is positive definite if $\boldsymbol{x}'\boldsymbol{A}\boldsymbol{x} > 0$ for all $n \times 1$ vectors $\boldsymbol{x} \neq \boldsymbol{0}$. Also, $\boldsymbol{A}$ is positive semi-definite if $\boldsymbol{x}'\boldsymbol{A}\boldsymbol{x} \geq 0$, and negative definite if $\boldsymbol{x}'\boldsymbol{A}\boldsymbol{x} < 0\ \forall \boldsymbol{x} \neq \boldsymbol{0}$. A symmetric, idempotent matrix $\boldsymbol{A}$ must be positive semi-definite, since letting $\boldsymbol{z} = \boldsymbol{A}'\boldsymbol{x}$, then $\boldsymbol{x}'\boldsymbol{A}\boldsymbol{x} = \boldsymbol{x}'\boldsymbol{A}\boldsymbol{A}'\boldsymbol{x} = \boldsymbol{z}'\boldsymbol{z} \geq 0$.
- *Eigenvalues and eigenvectors*: when $\boldsymbol{A}$ is $n \times n$, the eigenvalues λ_i of $\boldsymbol{A}$ are such that $\boldsymbol{A}\boldsymbol{x} = \lambda_i \boldsymbol{x}$ so are the n roots of the (characteristic) equation:

$$|\boldsymbol{A} - \lambda \boldsymbol{I}_n| = 0.$$

When λ_i is an eigenvalue of $\boldsymbol{A}$, then $\boldsymbol{h}_i \neq \boldsymbol{0}$ is an eigenvector of $\boldsymbol{A}$ if it satisfies:

$$(\boldsymbol{A} - \lambda_i \boldsymbol{I}_n)\, \boldsymbol{h}_i = \boldsymbol{0}. \tag{A1.7}$$

When $\boldsymbol{A}$ is symmetric, positive definite, pre-multiplying (A1.7) by $\boldsymbol{h}_i'$ yields:

$$\boldsymbol{h}_i'\boldsymbol{A}\boldsymbol{h}_i = \lambda_i \boldsymbol{h}_i'\boldsymbol{h}_i > 0,$$

so all its eigenvalues must be real and positive. Collect all the eigenvectors in the matrix $\boldsymbol{H} = (\boldsymbol{h}_1 \ldots \boldsymbol{h}_n)$ and the eigenvalues in $\boldsymbol{\Lambda}$ =diag$(\lambda_1 \ldots \lambda_n)$ then:

$$\boldsymbol{A}\boldsymbol{H} - \boldsymbol{H}\boldsymbol{\Lambda} = \boldsymbol{0},$$

or pre-multiplying by $\boldsymbol{H}^{-1}$:

$$\boldsymbol{H}^{-1}\boldsymbol{A}\boldsymbol{H} = \boldsymbol{\Lambda}.$$

Further, $\boldsymbol{A} = \boldsymbol{H}\boldsymbol{\Lambda}\boldsymbol{H}^{-1}$ so that:

$$\boldsymbol{A}^2 = \left(\boldsymbol{H}\boldsymbol{\Lambda}\boldsymbol{H}^{-1}\right)\left(\boldsymbol{H}\boldsymbol{\Lambda}\boldsymbol{H}^{-1}\right) = \boldsymbol{H}\boldsymbol{\Lambda}^2\boldsymbol{H}^{-1}$$

and the eigenvalues of $\boldsymbol{A}^2$ are $\{\lambda_i^2\}$. When $\boldsymbol{A}$ is non-singular, the eigenvalues of $\boldsymbol{A}^{-1}$ are $\{\lambda_i^{-1}\}$. When $\boldsymbol{A}$ is symmetric, transposition reveals that $\boldsymbol{H}' = \boldsymbol{H}^{-1}$ and hence $\boldsymbol{H}'\boldsymbol{H} = \boldsymbol{I}_n$, so distinct eigenvectors are mutually orthogonal and $\boldsymbol{A} = \boldsymbol{H}\boldsymbol{\Lambda}\boldsymbol{H}'$. In that case, $|\boldsymbol{H}'| = |\boldsymbol{H}|^{-1} = 1$, and when $\boldsymbol{A}$ is positive definite, we can express it as $\boldsymbol{A}^{-1} = \boldsymbol{H}\boldsymbol{\Lambda}^{-1}\boldsymbol{H}' = \boldsymbol{P}\boldsymbol{P}'$ say, where $\boldsymbol{P} = \boldsymbol{H}\boldsymbol{\Delta}$ and $\boldsymbol{\Delta} = \text{diag}(1/\sqrt{\lambda_1} \dots 1/\sqrt{\lambda_n})$. When $\boldsymbol{A}$ is symmetric idempotent, its eigenvalues and those of $\boldsymbol{A}^2$ must be the same, so $\lambda_i = \lambda_i^2$ and the only possible eigenvalues are zero and unity. Then $\text{rank}(\boldsymbol{A}) = \text{rank}(\boldsymbol{H}\boldsymbol{\Lambda}\boldsymbol{H}') = \text{rank}(\boldsymbol{\Lambda}) = \text{tr}(\boldsymbol{\Lambda})$.
Finally, when $\boldsymbol{B}$ is a second symmetric, positive definite $n \times n$ matrix, it can be simultaneously diagonalized by the eigenvector matrix $\boldsymbol{H}$ of $\boldsymbol{A}$ such that:

$$\boldsymbol{H}'\boldsymbol{B}\boldsymbol{H} = \boldsymbol{I}_n.$$

Thus, the eigenvalues of $\boldsymbol{A}$ in the metric of $\boldsymbol{B}$, given by solving $|\boldsymbol{A} - \lambda\boldsymbol{B}| = 0$, are $\boldsymbol{\Lambda}$. These results hold by letting $\boldsymbol{B}^{-1} = \boldsymbol{K}\boldsymbol{K}'$, so that $\boldsymbol{K}'\boldsymbol{B}\boldsymbol{K} = \boldsymbol{I}_n$ and $\boldsymbol{K}'\boldsymbol{A}\boldsymbol{K} = \boldsymbol{A}^* = \boldsymbol{P}\boldsymbol{\Lambda}\boldsymbol{P}'$, say, since $\boldsymbol{A}^*$ is symmetric, positive definite. Then for $\boldsymbol{H} = \boldsymbol{K}\boldsymbol{P}$:

$$\boldsymbol{H}'\boldsymbol{B}\boldsymbol{H} = \boldsymbol{P}'\boldsymbol{K}'\boldsymbol{B}\boldsymbol{K}\boldsymbol{P} = \boldsymbol{P}'\boldsymbol{P} = \boldsymbol{I}_n,$$

and:

$$\boldsymbol{H}'\boldsymbol{A}\boldsymbol{H} = \boldsymbol{P}'\boldsymbol{K}'\boldsymbol{A}\boldsymbol{K}\boldsymbol{P} = \boldsymbol{P}'\boldsymbol{A}^*\boldsymbol{P} = \boldsymbol{\Lambda}.$$

- *Choleski decomposition*: when $\boldsymbol{A}$ is $n \times n$ and symmetric, positive definite, then:

$$\boldsymbol{A} = \boldsymbol{L}\boldsymbol{L}'$$

where $\boldsymbol{L}$ is a unique, lower-triangular matrix with positive diagonal elements:

$$\boldsymbol{L} = \begin{pmatrix} l_{11} & 0 & \cdots & 0 \\ l_{12} & l_{22} & \cdots & 0 \\ \vdots & \vdots & \ddots & \vdots \\ l_{1n} & l_{2n} & \cdots & l_{nn} \end{pmatrix}.$$

- *Singular value decomposition*: here we decompose an $m \times n$ matrix $\boldsymbol{A}$ for $m \geq n$ and $\text{rank}(\boldsymbol{A}) = r > 0$, into:

$$\boldsymbol{A} = \boldsymbol{U}\boldsymbol{W}\boldsymbol{V}'$$

where

$\boldsymbol{U}$ is $m \times r$ with $\boldsymbol{U}'\boldsymbol{U} = \boldsymbol{I}_r$,
$\boldsymbol{W}$ is $r \times r$ diagonal, with non-negative diagonal elements,
$\boldsymbol{V}$ is $n \times r$ with $\boldsymbol{V}'\boldsymbol{V} = \boldsymbol{I}_r$.

This can be used to find the orthogonal complement of $\boldsymbol{A}$. When $\text{rank}(\boldsymbol{A}) = n$, compute the singular value decomposition of the $m \times m$ matrix $\boldsymbol{B} = (\boldsymbol{A} : \mathbf{0})$. The last $m - n$ diagonal elements of $\boldsymbol{W}$ will be zero. Corresponding to that are the last $m - n$ columns of $\boldsymbol{U}$ which form $\boldsymbol{A}_{\perp}$:

$$\boldsymbol{B} = (\boldsymbol{A} : \mathbf{0}) = \boldsymbol{U}\boldsymbol{W}\boldsymbol{V}' = (\boldsymbol{U}_1 : \boldsymbol{U}_2) \begin{pmatrix} \boldsymbol{W}_1 & \mathbf{0} \\ \mathbf{0} & \mathbf{0} \end{pmatrix} \begin{pmatrix} \boldsymbol{V}_1' \\ \boldsymbol{V}_2' \end{pmatrix}.$$

Here $\boldsymbol{U}$, $\boldsymbol{V}$ and $\boldsymbol{W}$ are $m \times m$ matrices; $\boldsymbol{U}_2'\boldsymbol{U}_1 = \mathbf{0}$ of dimension $(m-n) \times n$, so that $\boldsymbol{U}_2'\boldsymbol{A} = \boldsymbol{U}_2'\boldsymbol{U}_1\boldsymbol{W}_1\boldsymbol{V}_1' = \mathbf{0}$, and $\text{rank}(\boldsymbol{A} : \boldsymbol{U}_2) = m$ as $\boldsymbol{U}_2'\boldsymbol{U}_2 = \boldsymbol{I}_{(m-n)}$.

- *Vector function*: when $f(\boldsymbol{x})$ is a scalar function of the $m \times 1$ vector $\boldsymbol{x}$, then it maps from $\mathbb{R}^m \mapsto \mathbb{R}$ where $\mathbb{R}$ denotes the real line (set of all real numbers): an example of such a function is the quadratic form:

$$f(\boldsymbol{x}) = \boldsymbol{x}'\boldsymbol{A}\boldsymbol{x}.$$

An $n \times 1$ vector function $\boldsymbol{f}(\cdot)$ of the $m \times 1$ vector $\boldsymbol{x}$ mapping from $\mathbb{R}^m \mapsto \mathbb{R}^n$ is defined by:

$$\boldsymbol{f}(\boldsymbol{x}) = \begin{pmatrix} f_1(\boldsymbol{x}) \\ \vdots \\ f_n(\boldsymbol{x}) \end{pmatrix}.$$

For example, when $\boldsymbol{A}$ is $n \times m$:

$$\boldsymbol{f}(\boldsymbol{x}) = \boldsymbol{A}\boldsymbol{x}.$$

- *Vector differentiation*: let $f(\cdot) : \mathbb{R}^m \mapsto \mathbb{R}$, then the first derivative of $f(\boldsymbol{x})$ with respect to $\boldsymbol{x}$ is:

$$\frac{\partial f(\boldsymbol{x})}{\partial \boldsymbol{x}} = \begin{pmatrix} \dfrac{\partial f(\boldsymbol{x})}{\partial x_1} \\ \vdots \\ \dfrac{\partial f(\boldsymbol{x})}{\partial x_m} \end{pmatrix},$$

where $\partial f(\boldsymbol{x})/\partial x_i$ is the usual (scalar) derivative. For example, when $\boldsymbol{A}$ is symmetric:

$$\frac{\partial \boldsymbol{x}'\boldsymbol{A}\boldsymbol{x}}{\partial \boldsymbol{x}} = \left\{ \frac{\partial}{\partial x_k} \left(\sum_{i=1}^{m} \sum_{j=1}^{m} a_{ij} x_i x_j \right) \right\} = \left\{ 2 \left(\sum_{j=1}^{m} a_{ij} x_j \right) \right\} = 2\boldsymbol{A}\boldsymbol{x}.$$

The second derivative of $f(\boldsymbol{x})$ with respect to $\boldsymbol{x}$ is the matrix:

$$\frac{\partial^2 f(\boldsymbol{x})}{\partial \boldsymbol{x} \partial \boldsymbol{x}'} = \left\{ \frac{\partial^2 f(\boldsymbol{x})}{\partial x_i \partial x_j} \right\}_{m,m}.$$

For the previous example:

$$\frac{\partial^2 \boldsymbol{x}'\boldsymbol{A}\boldsymbol{x}}{\partial \boldsymbol{x} \partial \boldsymbol{x}'} = 2\frac{\partial \boldsymbol{A}\boldsymbol{x}}{\partial \boldsymbol{x}'} = 2\boldsymbol{A}\frac{\partial \boldsymbol{x}}{\partial \boldsymbol{x}'} = 2\boldsymbol{A}.$$

- *Matrix differentiation*: for $f(\cdot) : \mathbb{R}^{m\times n} \mapsto \mathbb{R}$, we define the first derivative of $f(\boldsymbol{X})$ (a scalar function of a matrix) with respect to $\boldsymbol{X}$ as:

$$\frac{\partial f(\boldsymbol{X})}{\partial \boldsymbol{X}} = \left\{ \frac{\partial f(\boldsymbol{X})}{\partial x_{ij}} \right\}_{m,n}.$$

- *Jacobian matrix*: for a vector function $\boldsymbol{f}(\cdot) : \mathbb{R}^m \mapsto \mathbb{R}^n$, define the $n \times m$ Jacobian matrix $\boldsymbol{J}$:

$$\frac{\partial \boldsymbol{f}(\boldsymbol{x})}{\partial \boldsymbol{x}'} = \begin{pmatrix} \frac{\partial f_1(\boldsymbol{x})}{\partial x_1} & \cdots & \frac{\partial f_1(\boldsymbol{x})}{\partial x_m} \\ \vdots & \ddots & \vdots \\ \frac{\partial f_n(\boldsymbol{x})}{\partial x_1} & \cdots & \frac{\partial f_n(\boldsymbol{x})}{\partial x_m} \end{pmatrix}.$$

The Jacobian is the absolute value of the determinant of $\boldsymbol{J}$ when $m = n$: $||\boldsymbol{J}||$. To compute the Jacobian matrix for the transformation $\boldsymbol{\Psi} = \boldsymbol{F}(\boldsymbol{\Pi}')$ when $\boldsymbol{F}$ is a matrix function, $\boldsymbol{F}(\cdot) : \mathbb{R}^{m\times n} \mapsto \mathbb{R}^{p\times q}$:

$$\boldsymbol{J} = \frac{\partial \boldsymbol{\Psi}^v}{\partial [(\boldsymbol{\Pi}')^v]'},$$

where $\boldsymbol{\Pi}$ is $n \times m$ and $\boldsymbol{\Psi}$ is $p \times q$, so that $\boldsymbol{J}$ is $pq \times mn$.

A1.4 Relations between operations

There are a number of important relationships between the various operations using the notation established in the previous section.

- *Product, determinant, trace and rank*:

$$\begin{aligned}
&(\boldsymbol{AB})' = \boldsymbol{B}'\boldsymbol{A}' \\
&(\boldsymbol{AB})^{-1} = \boldsymbol{B}^{-1}\boldsymbol{A}^{-1} \text{ when } \boldsymbol{A}, \boldsymbol{B} \text{ are non-singular} \\
&(\boldsymbol{A}^{-1})' = (\boldsymbol{A}')^{-1} \\
&|\boldsymbol{AB}| = |\boldsymbol{A}|\,|\boldsymbol{B}| \text{ when } \boldsymbol{A}, \boldsymbol{B} \text{ are } n \times n \\
&|\boldsymbol{A}'| = |\boldsymbol{A}| \\
&|c\boldsymbol{A}| = c^n\,|\boldsymbol{A}| \text{ when } \boldsymbol{A} \text{ is } n \times n \\
&\left|\boldsymbol{A}^{-1}\right| = |\boldsymbol{A}|^{-1} \\
&\text{tr}(\boldsymbol{AB}) = \text{tr}(\boldsymbol{BA}) \\
&\text{tr}(\boldsymbol{A} + \boldsymbol{B}) = \text{tr}\boldsymbol{A} + \text{tr}\boldsymbol{B} \\
&\text{tr}(\boldsymbol{Axx}') = \boldsymbol{x}'\boldsymbol{Ax} \\
&\text{tr}\boldsymbol{A} = \textstyle\sum \lambda_i \text{ when } \boldsymbol{A} \text{ is } n \times n \\
&|\boldsymbol{A}| = \textstyle\prod \lambda_i \text{ when } \boldsymbol{A} \text{ is } n \times n
\end{aligned}$$

- *Kronecker product and vectorization*:

$$(\boldsymbol{A} \otimes \boldsymbol{B})' = \boldsymbol{A}' \otimes \boldsymbol{B}'$$
$$(\boldsymbol{A} \otimes \boldsymbol{B})^{-1} = \boldsymbol{A}^{-1} \otimes \boldsymbol{B}^{-1} \text{ when } \boldsymbol{A}, \boldsymbol{B} \text{ are non-singular}$$
$$|\boldsymbol{A} \otimes \boldsymbol{B}| = |\boldsymbol{A}|^{m} |\boldsymbol{B}|^{n} \text{ when } \boldsymbol{A} \text{ is } (n \times n) \text{ and } \boldsymbol{B} \text{ is } m \times m$$
$$(\boldsymbol{A} \otimes \boldsymbol{B})(\boldsymbol{C} \otimes \boldsymbol{D}) = \boldsymbol{AC} \otimes \boldsymbol{BD}$$
$$c \otimes \boldsymbol{A} = c\boldsymbol{A} = \boldsymbol{A}c = \boldsymbol{A} \otimes c$$
$$\text{tr}(\boldsymbol{A} \otimes \boldsymbol{B}) = \text{tr}\boldsymbol{A}\text{tr}\boldsymbol{B}$$
$$(\boldsymbol{A}^{v})'\boldsymbol{B}^{v} = \text{tr}(\boldsymbol{A}'\boldsymbol{B}) \text{ when } \boldsymbol{A}, \boldsymbol{B} \text{ are both } m \times n$$
$$(\boldsymbol{a}')^{v} = (\boldsymbol{a})^{v} = \boldsymbol{a} \text{ when } \boldsymbol{a} \text{ is } n \times 1$$
$$(\boldsymbol{ABC})^{v} = (\boldsymbol{A} \otimes \boldsymbol{C}')\boldsymbol{B}^{v} \text{ when } \boldsymbol{ABC} \text{ is defined}$$
$$\text{tr}(\boldsymbol{AB}) = ((\boldsymbol{A}')^{v})' \boldsymbol{B}^{v} = (\boldsymbol{A}^{v})' (\boldsymbol{B}')^{v}$$
$$\text{tr}(\boldsymbol{ABCD}) = ((\boldsymbol{D}')^{v})' (\boldsymbol{A} \otimes \boldsymbol{C}')\boldsymbol{B}^{v}$$

- *Differentiation*:

$$\frac{\partial \log |\boldsymbol{A}|}{\partial \boldsymbol{A}} = \boldsymbol{A}'^{-1} \text{ if } \boldsymbol{A} \text{ is asymmetric}$$
$$\frac{\partial \log |\boldsymbol{A}|}{\partial \boldsymbol{A}} = 2\boldsymbol{A}^{-1} - \text{dg}\left(\boldsymbol{A}^{-1}\right) \text{ if } \boldsymbol{A} \text{ is symmetric}$$
$$\frac{\partial \text{tr}(\boldsymbol{BA})}{\partial \boldsymbol{B}} = \boldsymbol{A}' \text{ if } \boldsymbol{B} \text{ is asymmetric}$$
$$\frac{\partial \text{tr}(\boldsymbol{BA})}{\partial \boldsymbol{B}} = \boldsymbol{A} + \boldsymbol{A}' - \text{dg}\boldsymbol{A} \text{ if } \boldsymbol{B} \text{ is symmetric}$$
$$\frac{\partial \boldsymbol{g}(\boldsymbol{f}(\boldsymbol{a}))}{\partial \boldsymbol{a}'} = \frac{\partial \boldsymbol{g}(\boldsymbol{b})}{\partial \boldsymbol{b}'}\frac{\partial \boldsymbol{f}(\boldsymbol{a})}{\partial \boldsymbol{a}'}$$
$$\text{with } \boldsymbol{f}(\cdot)\colon \mathbb{R}^{m} \mapsto \mathbb{R}^{n},\ \boldsymbol{g}(\cdot)\colon \mathbb{R}^{n} \mapsto \mathbb{R}^{p},\ \boldsymbol{b} = \boldsymbol{f}(\boldsymbol{a})$$
$$\frac{\partial (\boldsymbol{ABC})^{v}}{\partial (\boldsymbol{B}^{v})'} = \boldsymbol{A} \otimes \boldsymbol{C}'$$
$$\frac{\partial \left(\boldsymbol{A}^{-1}\right)^{v}}{\partial (\boldsymbol{A}^{v})'} = -\boldsymbol{A}^{-1} \otimes \boldsymbol{A}^{-1\prime}$$

A1.5 Partitioned inverse

Consider the $(n+m) \times (n+m)$ non-singular matrix $\boldsymbol{F}$ defined by:

$$\boldsymbol{F} = \begin{pmatrix} \boldsymbol{A} & \boldsymbol{B} \\ \boldsymbol{C} & \boldsymbol{D} \end{pmatrix}, \tag{A1.8}$$

where $\boldsymbol{A}$ is $n \times n$, $\boldsymbol{B}$ and $\boldsymbol{C}'$ are $n \times m$, and $\boldsymbol{D}$ is $m \times m$. When $\boldsymbol{A}$ and $\boldsymbol{H} = (\boldsymbol{D} - \boldsymbol{C}\boldsymbol{A}^{-1}\boldsymbol{B})$ are non-singular, then:

$$\begin{pmatrix} \boldsymbol{A} & \boldsymbol{B} \\ \boldsymbol{C} & \boldsymbol{D} \end{pmatrix}^{-1} = \begin{pmatrix} \boldsymbol{A}^{-1} + \boldsymbol{A}^{-1}\boldsymbol{B}\boldsymbol{H}^{-1}\boldsymbol{C}\boldsymbol{A}^{-1} & -\boldsymbol{A}^{-1}\boldsymbol{B}\boldsymbol{H}^{-1} \\ -\boldsymbol{H}^{-1}\boldsymbol{C}\boldsymbol{A}^{-1} & \boldsymbol{H}^{-1} \end{pmatrix}, \tag{A1.9}$$

with:

$$|F| = |D - CA^{-1}B|\,|A|.$$

The result in (A1.9) can be checked from the definition of an inverse, namely that F has inverse F^{-1} if $FF^{-1} = I_{(m+n)}$.

Alternatively, when D and $G = (A - BD^{-1}C)$ are non-singular then:

$$\begin{pmatrix} A & B \\ C & D \end{pmatrix}^{-1} = \begin{pmatrix} G^{-1} & -G^{-1}BD^{-1} \\ -D^{-1}CG^{-1} & D^{-1} + D^{-1}CG^{-1}BD^{-1} \end{pmatrix} \tag{A1.10}$$

with:

$$|F| = |A - BD^{-1}C|\,|D|.$$

It follows from comparing the upper left-hand terms in (A1.9) and (A1.10) that:

$$\left(A - BD^{-1}C\right)^{-1} = A^{-1} + A^{-1}B\left(D - CA^{-1}B\right)^{-1}CA^{-1}. \tag{A1.11}$$

When F is symmetric ($A = A'$, $D = D'$, and $C = B'$):

$$\begin{pmatrix} A & B \\ B' & D \end{pmatrix}^{-1} = \begin{pmatrix} \left(A - BD^{-1}B'\right)^{-1} & -\left(A - BD^{-1}B'\right)^{-1}BD^{-1} \\ -\left(D - B'A^{-1}B\right)^{-1}B'A^{-1} & \left(D - B'A^{-1}B\right)^{-1} \end{pmatrix}. \tag{A1.12}$$

A1.6 Polynomial matrices

A polynomial matrix $A(L)$ is an $n \times n$ matrix whose elements $\{a_{ij}(L)\}$ are scalar polynomials of finite order k_{ij} in an argument L:

$$a_{ij}(L) = \sum_{r=0}^{k_{ij}} a_{ij,r}L^r \text{ where } k_{ij} < \infty. \tag{A1.13}$$

Then $A(1)$ is a standard matrix, and (A1.13) generalizes the usual concept in a way that is relevant to dynamic systems. The degree of $A(L)$ is the highest order k of the element polynomials:

$$k = \underset{ij}{\operatorname{argmax}}\{k_{ij}\} < \infty. \tag{A1.14}$$

Letting $A_r = \{a_{ij,r}\}$, from (A1.13) $A(L)$ can be expressed as:

$$A(L) = \sum_{r=0}^{k} A_rL^r = A_0 + A_1L + A_2L^2 + \cdots + A_{k-1}L^{k-1} + A_kL^k. \tag{A1.15}$$

The determinant $|A(L)|$ of a polynomial matrix $A(L)$ is a scalar polynomial. An example of a polynomial matrix is $A(\lambda) = (A - \lambda I_n)$ leading to the characteristic equation:

$$c(L) = |A(\lambda)| = |A - \lambda I_n| = 0, \tag{A1.16}$$

which occurs when solving eigenvalue problems. Every matrix satisfies its own characteristic equation since:

$$c(\boldsymbol{A}) = |\boldsymbol{A}(\boldsymbol{A})| = |\boldsymbol{A} - \boldsymbol{A}\boldsymbol{I}_n| = |\boldsymbol{0}| = 0. \tag{A1.17}$$

If $\boldsymbol{B}$ is a conformable $m \times p$ matrix, the $n \times p$ matrix $\boldsymbol{A}(\boldsymbol{B})$ is defined by:

$$\boldsymbol{A}(\boldsymbol{B}) = \sum_{r=0}^{k} \boldsymbol{A}_r \boldsymbol{B}^r.$$

The roots of $\boldsymbol{A}(L)$ are the roots μ_i of the equation $|\boldsymbol{A}(L)| = 0$; the number and form of these roots is established below. When $|\mu_i| > 1\ \forall i$, $\boldsymbol{A}(L)$ is invertible and $\boldsymbol{C}(L) = [\boldsymbol{A}(L)]^{-1}$ is an infinite-order matrix with $\boldsymbol{C}(1) < \infty$ where:

$$\boldsymbol{C}(1) = \boldsymbol{C}(L)_{\rfloor L=1}$$

since:

$$|\boldsymbol{A}(L)|\,[\boldsymbol{A}(L)]^{-1} = \mathrm{Adj}\,(\boldsymbol{A}(L)). \tag{A1.18}$$

The right-hand side of (A1.18) is a polynomial matrix and $|\boldsymbol{A}(\mu)|$ is non-zero $\forall|\mu| > 1$.

Every polynomial matrix $\boldsymbol{A}(L)$ can be divided on the right by a matrix of the form $(\boldsymbol{B} - L\boldsymbol{I}_n)$ for any conformable matrix $\boldsymbol{B}$ so that:

$$\boldsymbol{A}(L) = \boldsymbol{C}(L)(\boldsymbol{B} - L\boldsymbol{I}_n) + \boldsymbol{D}, \tag{A1.19}$$

where $\boldsymbol{C}(L)$ is of order $k-1$, and $\boldsymbol{D}$ is a constant matrix given by a linear transformation of $\boldsymbol{A}(L)$. Indeed:

$$\begin{aligned}
\boldsymbol{A}(L) &= \boldsymbol{A}_0 + \boldsymbol{A}_1 L + \boldsymbol{A}_2 L^2 + \cdots + \boldsymbol{A}_{k-1} L^{k-1} + \boldsymbol{A}_k L^k \\
&= \boldsymbol{A}_0 + \boldsymbol{A}_1 L + \cdots + \boldsymbol{A}_{k-1} L^{k-1} + \boldsymbol{A}_k \boldsymbol{B} L^{k-1} - \boldsymbol{A}_k \boldsymbol{B} L^{k-1} + L\boldsymbol{A}_k L^{k-1} \\
&= \boldsymbol{A}_0 + \cdots + (\boldsymbol{A}_{k-1} + \boldsymbol{A}_k \boldsymbol{B}) L^{k-1} - \boldsymbol{A}_k (\boldsymbol{B} - L\boldsymbol{I}_n) L^{k-1} \\
&= \boldsymbol{A}_0 + \cdots + (\boldsymbol{A}_{k-2} + (\boldsymbol{A}_{k-1} + \boldsymbol{A}_k \boldsymbol{B}) \boldsymbol{B}) L^{k-2} \\
&\quad - (\boldsymbol{A}_{k-1} + \boldsymbol{A}_k \boldsymbol{B})(\boldsymbol{B} - L\boldsymbol{I}_n) L^{k-2} - \boldsymbol{A}_k (\boldsymbol{B} - L\boldsymbol{I}_n) L^{k-1} \\
&= \ldots \\
&= -\textstyle\sum_{i=0}^{k-1} \left(\sum_{j=i+1}^{k} \boldsymbol{A}_j \boldsymbol{B}^{j-i-1} \right) (\boldsymbol{B} - L\boldsymbol{I}_n) + \sum_{i=0}^{k} \boldsymbol{A}_i \boldsymbol{B}^i
\end{aligned} \tag{A1.20}$$

and hence:

$$\boldsymbol{D} = \sum_{i=0}^{k} \boldsymbol{A}_i \boldsymbol{B}^i = \boldsymbol{A}(\boldsymbol{B}). \tag{A1.21}$$

A similar result holds for left division. When $\boldsymbol{B} = \boldsymbol{I}_n$:

$$\boldsymbol{B} - L\boldsymbol{I}_n = (1 - L)\,\boldsymbol{I}_n = \Delta \boldsymbol{I}_n \quad \text{and} \quad \boldsymbol{D} = \boldsymbol{A}(\boldsymbol{I}_n) = \boldsymbol{A}(1).$$

There is an isomorphic relationship between polynomial matrices and companion matrices which thereby have the same latent roots. This relation simplifies analyses of dynamics and cointegration. Consider a system of n exact linear equations:

$$\mathbf{A}(L)\,\mathbf{x}_t = \mathbf{x}_t + \mathbf{A}_1\mathbf{x}_{t-1} + \mathbf{A}_2\mathbf{x}_{t-2} + \cdots + \mathbf{A}_{k-1}\mathbf{x}_{t-k+1} + \mathbf{A}_k\mathbf{x}_{t-k} = \mathbf{0} \quad \text{(A1.22)}$$

where $\mathbf{A}_0 = \mathbf{I}_n$ is a normalization. The information in (A1.22) can be represented in companion form by defining the following matrices and vectors: let $\mathbf{f}_t' = (\mathbf{x}_t' : \mathbf{x}_{t-1}' : \cdots : \mathbf{x}_{t-k+1}')$, and stack the coefficients in (A1.22) in a conformable $nk \times nk$ matrix:

$$\boldsymbol{\Pi} = \begin{pmatrix} \mathbf{A}_1 & \mathbf{A}_2 & \cdots & \mathbf{A}_{k-1} & \mathbf{A}_k \\ -\mathbf{I}_n & \mathbf{0} & \cdots & \mathbf{0} & \mathbf{0} \\ \mathbf{0} & -\mathbf{I}_n & \cdots & \mathbf{0} & \mathbf{0} \\ \vdots & \vdots & \ddots & \vdots & \vdots \\ \mathbf{0} & \mathbf{0} & \cdots & -\mathbf{I}_n & \mathbf{0} \end{pmatrix}. \quad \text{(A1.23)}$$

By direct multiplication, (A1.22) maps into:

$$\mathbf{f}_t + \boldsymbol{\Pi}\mathbf{f}_{t-1} = \mathbf{0},$$

where the top block delivers (A1.22) augmented by identities of the form $\mathbf{x}_{t-j} - \mathbf{x}_{t-j} \equiv \mathbf{0}$. Thus:

$$\mathbf{A}(L)\,\mathbf{x}_t = \mathbf{0} \text{ implies and is implied by } \mathbf{f}_t + \boldsymbol{\Pi}\mathbf{f}_{t-1} = \mathbf{0}. \quad \text{(A1.24)}$$

The advantage of companion forms is that they are first order $\forall k$, and hence can be analysed using conventional tools. For example, the eigenvalues of $\mathbf{A}(L)$ are given by solving:

$$|\mathbf{A}(L)| = |\boldsymbol{\Pi} - \lambda\mathbf{I}_n| = 0. \quad \text{(A1.25)}$$

It is more convenient to express (A1.25) in terms of the inverses of the eigenvalues, $\mu = -1/\lambda$, and solve:

$$|\mathbf{I}_n + \mu\boldsymbol{\Pi}| = 0 \quad \text{(A1.26)}$$

where from (A1.23) in (A1.26):

$$|\mathbf{I}_n + \mu\boldsymbol{\Pi}| = \begin{vmatrix} \mathbf{I}_n + \mu\mathbf{A}_1 & \mu\mathbf{A}_2 & \cdots & \mu\mathbf{A}_{k-1} & \mu\mathbf{A}_k \\ -\mu\mathbf{I}_n & \mathbf{I}_n & \cdots & \mathbf{0} & \mathbf{0} \\ \mathbf{0} & -\mu\mathbf{I}_n & \cdots & \mathbf{0} & \mathbf{0} \\ \vdots & \vdots & \ddots & \vdots & \vdots \\ \mathbf{0} & \mathbf{0} & \cdots & -\mu\mathbf{I}_n & \mathbf{I}_n \end{vmatrix} = \begin{vmatrix} \mathbf{E} & \mathbf{B} \\ \mathbf{C} & \mathbf{I}_n \end{vmatrix} \quad \text{(A1.27)}$$

when $\mathbf{E}$ is the $n(k-1) \times n(k-1)$ matrix in the top left and $\mathbf{C} = (\mathbf{0}\,\mathbf{0} \cdots \mathbf{0} \; -\mu\mathbf{I}_n)$. Next, use the partitioned inversion theorem above on the bottom block ($\mathbf{I}_n$) in (A1.27), namely:

$$\left|\mathbf{E} - \mathbf{B}\mathbf{I}_n^{-1}\mathbf{C}\right| |\mathbf{I}_n| = |\mathbf{E}| \left|\mathbf{I}_n - \mathbf{C}\mathbf{E}^{-1}\mathbf{B}\right|. \quad \text{(A1.28)}$$

Then, $\boldsymbol{B}\boldsymbol{I}_n^{-1}\boldsymbol{C}$ is zero except for its top-right block which is $-\mu^2\boldsymbol{A}_k$, and $|\boldsymbol{I}_n| = 1$ so that:

$$|\boldsymbol{I}_n + \mu\boldsymbol{\Pi}| = \begin{vmatrix} \boldsymbol{I}_n + \mu\boldsymbol{A}_1 & \mu\boldsymbol{A}_2 & \cdots & \mu\boldsymbol{A}_{k-2} & \mu(\boldsymbol{A}_{k-1} + \mu\boldsymbol{A}_k) \\ -\mu\boldsymbol{I}_n & \boldsymbol{I}_n & \cdots & \mathbf{0} & \mathbf{0} \\ \mathbf{0} & -\mu\boldsymbol{I}_n & \cdots & \mathbf{0} & \mathbf{0} \\ \vdots & \vdots & \ddots & \vdots & \vdots \\ \mathbf{0} & \mathbf{0} & \cdots & -\mu\boldsymbol{I}_n & \boldsymbol{I}_n \end{vmatrix}. \quad \text{(A1.29)}$$

The analysis now repeats on the new $n(k-1) \times n(k-1)$ matrix in the determinant, eventually leading to $|\boldsymbol{A}(\mu)|$ after k steps. Thus:

$$|\boldsymbol{I}_n + \mu\boldsymbol{\Pi}| = |\boldsymbol{A}(\mu)|,$$

and solving either expression equated to zero generates the nk roots ($\boldsymbol{A}$ is $n \times n$ of order k whereas $\boldsymbol{\Pi}$ is $nk \times nk$ of order 1).

A2

Probability and Distributions

The outcomes of a random experiment generate a large number of events. A probability calculus is developed to characterize these events, and to handle the probabilities of joint events and of some events given that others occur. Next, events are mapped to random variables, the outcomes of which are real numbers which cannot be precisely predicted in advance. The stochastic behaviour of random variables is described by their distribution functions and density functions, which are the theoretical counterparts of empirical distributions. This supports the formulation of probability models comprising families of possible distributions, indexed by parameters which determine the characteristics of those distributions. Properties of random variables and their distributions are analysed, including expectations and higher moments, which are often directly related to the distributions' parameters. The normal distribution is considered in detail.

A2.1 Introduction

A2.1.1 Chance

The idea of probability is an old one, deriving from gambling and games of chance. The modern formalization is in part an attempt to explain the outcomes of such games, including accounting for the betting odds established as fair over the centuries from the empirical experience of participants. Chance, randomness, and unpredictability seem pervasive in everyday life, and we assume that this intuitive notion is already understood: for example, the value of next month's balance of payments deficit in the USA, or next year's price of gold, are not known at present, and could take any one of a range of values for a variety of reasons most of which themselves cannot be foreseen (including human and natural disasters, discoveries etc.).

A2.1.2 Empirical distributions and histograms

The first manifestation of randomness is the existence of empirical distributions of outcomes: examples include incomes of individuals in a population, rates of inflation across countries, heights of humans, exam marks of students etc. Histograms are a graphical representation of the proportions of cases which occur in each of a set of intervals (such as the proportions of recorded incomes under \$1,000 per annum, between \$1,001 p.a. and \$2,000 p.a., etc.). These provide useful summaries of distributions, and the four graphs in Fig. A2.1 record the distributions over 1964(1)–1989(2) of quarterly UK money growth (seasonally adjusted), the annual change in constant-price consumers' expenditure, the quarterly change in constant-price unit labour costs, and the central government budget deficit. Vertical axes record the relative frequencies of occurrence, and horizontal axes report the associated standardized values which occurred (scaled to be centred on zero and to have about two-thirds of the values between -1 and $+1$). The four histogram shapes are similar, as are the smoothed shapes approximating them on each graph (see §A3.6 for details of the smoothing algorithm).

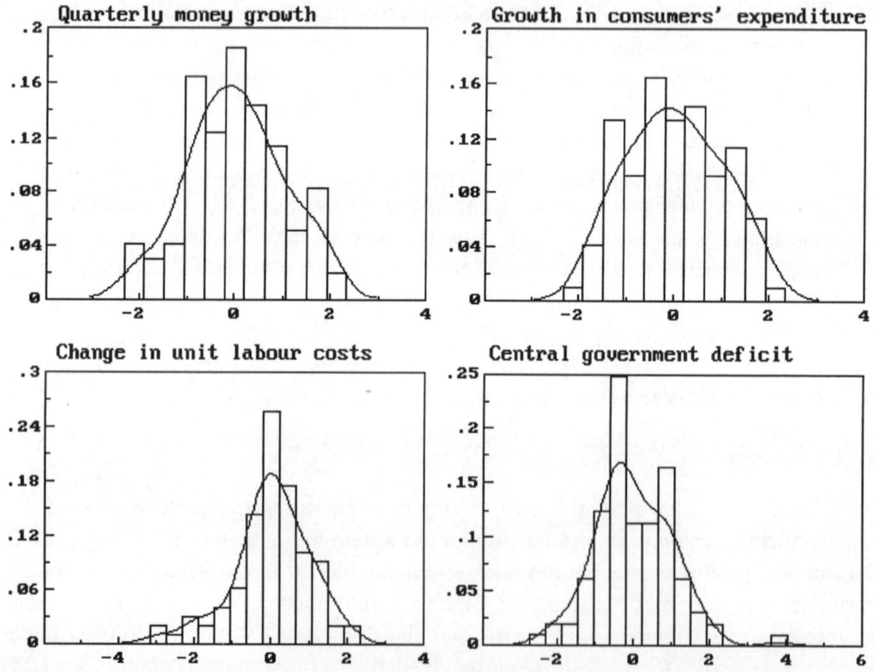

Fig. A2.1 Four empirical histograms with smoothed approximating shapes

Natural questions concern why the histograms have the shapes shown, whether we can explain why particular outcomes fell into their observed intervals, whether the shapes of the distributions remain the same over time, and so on.

A2.2 Events

A2.2.1 Random experiments, sets, and sample spaces

A random experiment is an experiment where more than one outcome is possible, in the sense that replications of the given experiment under apparently identical conditions can produce different outcomes, for unknown reasons. Well-known examples are coin-tossing experiments, rolling dice, and dealing cards. Less obvious examples include marks achieved on a given exam, age at death, income per capita, and share prices.

Let $\Re$ denote a random experiment. An outcome of an experiment is a single result such as a head (H, with T denoting a tail), a four, or an ace of spades, as in the first three illustrative experiments. Prior to their occurrence, such outcomes are random since different outcomes materialize on different trials. Repeatedly tossing a coin tends to yield a string of outcomes of the form $\{H, T, H, H, T, \ldots\}$. Recording whether a share price goes up (U) or not (N) from day to day yields a similar sequence to the string of H and T obtained by tossing a coin.

It is difficult to conceive of an economy as being a random experiment, since replication is impossible, yet it is easy to view economic outcomes as being random: changes in the exchange rate or stock prices from day to day are hard to predict, and yet the shapes of their empirical distributions are similar in different countries. Whatever resources are devoted to studying the economy, we will never precisely predict the outcomes of all economic phenomena. Consequently, we treat economic magnitudes as if they were the outcomes of a gigantic random experiment. Such an argument neither precludes accurate prediction of some aspects of economic behaviour, nor the possibility that with sufficient effort, time, knowledge, and brilliance we might resolve uncertainties about other aspects. Sources of unpredictability include climate, inventions and discoveries, mutations, accidents, and human indecision. The main text considers the concepts and tools needed to study the economic mechanism. Here, we first develop a probability calculus for random experiments that can be repeated, then extend the analysis to random processes which evolve over time, called stochastic processes, after which the approach will be justified for economics.

All possible outcomes of $\Re$ can be collected together in a set of outcomes called the sample space, and denoted by Ω, drawing an analogy between outcomes and points in space, as in the diagrams in Fig. A2.2. Individual outcomes in $\Re$ are called elementary events as they are elements ω of Ω denoted by $\omega \in \Omega$. In the case of share prices, $\Omega = \{U, N\}$, where $\{\cdot\}$ denotes the set of relevant elements. We could imagine finer recordings such as up, same (S), or down (D) leading to $\Omega = \{U,\ S,\ D\}$, or even the actual price changes, so that Ω could be a set of real numbers. An example we often use because of its simple structure, despite being far removed from macro-economics, is the experiment of rolling a six-sided die with faces numbered 1 through 6, although we do not assume for the present that the die is necessarily symmetric and balanced. An outcome of that experiment is any one of the numbers — say 4 — in the sample space $\Omega = \{1, 2, 3, 4, 5, 6\}$.

Any specific outcome induces the occurrence of many events: e.g., the outcome 4 also leads to the events 'a number less than 5', 'an even number', 'a square', and so on. To discuss more complicated features of random experiments than just elementary outcomes, such as getting a prime number when rolling a die, involves investigating collections, or sets, of elementary outcomes denoted by $\mathcal{A}_i$. For example, $\mathcal{A}_1 = \{1, 2, 3, 5\}$ is the set for the face of the die being a prime number and $\mathcal{A}_2 = \{2, 4\}$ is the set for an even number smaller than 5. When the outcome is 2, then $\mathcal{A}_1$ and $\mathcal{A}_2$ both occur, along with many other events including $\{2\}$, which is the set with one element equal to the number 2. The set Ω can now be interpreted as the event 'something happens'. Events in $\mathcal{A}$ are characterized by $\mathcal{A} = \{\omega : \omega \in \Omega \text{ and } \omega \text{ has some property}\}$, also written as $\mathcal{A} = \{\omega \in \Omega : \omega \in \mathcal{A}\}$ so $\mathcal{A}$ is a sub-set of Ω, denoted $\mathcal{A} \subseteq \Omega$, where $\Omega \subseteq \Omega$. A proper subset is denoted by $\subset$ so $\mathcal{A}_1 \subset \Omega$ and $\mathcal{A}_2 \subset \Omega$. The next step involves developing tools for analysing event sets and their connections.

A2.2.2 Complements, unions, and intersections

If we allow that any given event can occur, then we must also allow that event not to occur, which is another event, namely 'not getting the first event'. For example, not tossing H implies we got T, and if $\mathcal{A}_1$ above did not happen on a single roll of the die, then the set 'not-a-prime number' must have happened, namely $\mathcal{A}_3 = \{4, 6\}$, which is called the complement of $\mathcal{A}_1$ and is denoted by $\mathcal{A}_1^c$. The complement of any set $\mathcal{B}$ relative to the sample space Ω is:

$$\mathcal{B}^c = \{\omega \in \Omega : \omega \notin \mathcal{B}\},$$

to be read as 'the set of outcomes ω in Ω but not in $\mathcal{B}$'. Thus, from above, $\mathcal{A}_3 = \mathcal{A}_1^c$. The complement of Ω is:

$$\Omega^c = \emptyset = \{\omega : \omega \notin \Omega\},$$

called the empty set since there are no ω in Ω but not in Ω.

If two events can each occur, then there is an event where either or both might occur. This event is given by the union of the sets: members of either set are members of the union. The union $\cup$ of two sets $\mathcal{A}$ and $\mathcal{B}$ is:

$$\mathcal{A} \cup \mathcal{B} = \{\omega \in \Omega : \omega \in \mathcal{A} \text{ or } \omega \in \mathcal{B}\}.$$

For example, $\mathcal{A}_1 \cup \mathcal{A}_2 = \{1, 2, 3, 4, 5\}$, $\mathcal{B} \cup \mathcal{B}^c = \Omega$, and $\mathcal{B} \cup \mathcal{B} = \mathcal{B}$. The union operator is both commutative and associative since:

$$\mathcal{A} \cup \mathcal{B} = \mathcal{B} \cup \mathcal{A} \text{ and } (\mathcal{A} \cup \mathcal{B}) \cup \mathcal{C} = \mathcal{A} \cup (\mathcal{B} \cup \mathcal{C}).$$

Such theorems are proved by showing that the two sides of the claimed equality define the same set.

Often, we consider a collection of sets $\mathcal{A}_i$, where $i \in \mathsf{N}_+$ and N_+ is a finite set of positive integers, also called the index set. We denote the union of the collection by $\bigcup_i \mathcal{A}_i$. When $\bigcup_i \mathcal{A}_i = \Omega$ the sets are said to be collectively exhaustive. For the three-way record of share price changes, if $\mathcal{D}_1 = \{U, S\}$, $\mathcal{D}_2 = \{S\}$ and $\mathcal{D}_3 = \{D\}$, then:

$$\bigcup_{i=1}^{3} \mathcal{D}_i = \mathcal{D}_1 \cup \mathcal{D}_2 \cup \mathcal{D}_3 = \Omega.$$

To describe a situation where both events can occur, we need the intersection ($\cap$) of the sets, namely the set whose elements are members of both original sets. For two sets $\mathcal{A}$ and $\mathcal{B}$:

$$\mathcal{A} \cap \mathcal{B} = \{\omega \in \Omega : \omega \in \mathcal{A} \text{ and } \omega \in \mathcal{B}\}.$$

As examples, $\mathcal{A}_1 \cap \mathcal{A}_2 = \{2\}$, $\mathcal{B} \cap \mathcal{B}^c = \emptyset$, and $\mathcal{B} \cap \mathcal{B} = \mathcal{B}$. Sets $\mathcal{A}$ and $\mathcal{B}$ which have an empty intersection, so that $\mathcal{A} \cap \mathcal{B} = \emptyset$, are said to be disjoint, and the events are mutually exclusive. The intersection operator is commutative and associative since:

$$\mathcal{A} \cap \mathcal{B} = \mathcal{B} \cap \mathcal{A} \text{ and } (\mathcal{A} \cap \mathcal{B}) \cap \mathcal{C} = \mathcal{A} \cap (\mathcal{B} \cap \mathcal{C}).$$

When a collection of sets $\mathcal{A}_i$, $i \in \mathbb{N}_+$, is disjoint, so that $\mathcal{A}_i \cap \mathcal{A}_j = \emptyset$, and exhaustive, so $\bigcup_i \mathcal{A}_i = \Omega$, then the sets are said to form a partition of Ω. The intersection of a collection of sets is denoted by $\bigcap_i \mathcal{A}_i$.

Union, intersection and complement are related by:

$$(\mathcal{A} \cup \mathcal{B})^c = \mathcal{A}^c \cap \mathcal{B}^c,$$

since both sides of that equality are the set $\{\omega \in \Omega : \omega \notin \mathcal{A} \text{ and } \omega \notin \mathcal{B}\}$. All of the sets generated by ^{c}, $\cap$, and $\cup$ are subsets of Ω, so that $\mathcal{A} \subseteq \Omega$, $\mathcal{A}^c \subseteq \Omega$, etc., and one of these must be a proper subset. Any set $\mathcal{A}$ can be expressed as:

$$\mathcal{A} \equiv (\mathcal{A} \cap \mathcal{B}) \cup (\mathcal{A} \cap \mathcal{B}^c),$$

since the right-hand side is the set:

$$\{\omega \in \Omega : (\omega \in \mathcal{A} \text{ and } \omega \in \mathcal{B}) \text{ or } (\omega \in \mathcal{A} \text{ and } \omega \notin \mathcal{B})\} = \{\omega \in \Omega : \omega \in \mathcal{A}\} \quad \text{(A2.1)}$$

which is the set $\mathcal{A}$. Finally, there are two distributive relations:

$$\mathcal{A} \cap (\mathcal{B} \cup \mathcal{C}) = (\mathcal{A} \cap \mathcal{B}) \cup (\mathcal{A} \cap \mathcal{C}) \text{ and } \mathcal{A} \cup (\mathcal{B} \cap \mathcal{C}) = (\mathcal{A} \cup \mathcal{B}) \cap (\mathcal{A} \cup \mathcal{C}). \quad \text{(A2.2)}$$

The distributive relation establishes the important result that any union of two sets can be decomposed into the union of two disjoint sets: $\mathcal{A} \cap \mathcal{B}^c$ and $\mathcal{B}$ are disjoint sets since

$$(\mathcal{A} \cap \mathcal{B}^c) \cap \mathcal{B} = \mathcal{A} \cap (\mathcal{B}^c \cap \mathcal{B}) = \mathcal{A} \cap \emptyset = \emptyset. \quad \text{(A2.3)}$$

Thus, by defining $\mathcal{C}$ as $\mathcal{A} \cap \mathcal{B}^c$, we can write $\mathcal{A} \cup \mathcal{B}$ as $\mathcal{C} \cup \mathcal{B}$ where $\mathcal{C} \cap \mathcal{B} = \emptyset$. These connections between events will prove useful in calculating probabilities of compound or joint events.

Figure A2.2 illustrates several of the set relationships just discussed: Ω is the set of points forming the large square; $\mathcal{A}$ is the small square; $\mathcal{B}$ is the long rectangle; $\mathcal{A} \cap \mathcal{B}$ is the portion of overlap between $\mathcal{A}$ and $\mathcal{B}$; $\mathcal{B}^c$ is the set of points in Ω and not in $\mathcal{B}$; $(\mathcal{A} \cup \mathcal{B})$ is the area in $\mathcal{A}$ plus that in $\mathcal{B}$ less $\mathcal{A} \cap \mathcal{B}$ which is also $(\mathcal{A} \cap \mathcal{B}^c) \cup \mathcal{B}$, namely points in $\mathcal{A}$ and not in $\mathcal{B}$, plus points in $\mathcal{B}$.

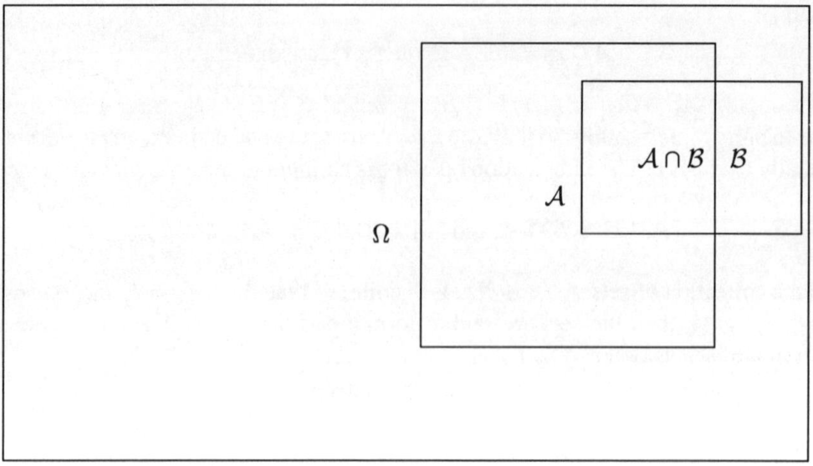

Fig. A2.2 Set relationships

All of these results hold for linking any finite number of sets by repeated application. However, we also want the framework to be capable of handling countable numbers of sets $\mathcal{A}_i$, when $\mathbb{N}_+$ denotes the set of all positive integers, as well as sets of real numbers where the elements are uncountable. The next section sketches the relevant extensions.

A2.2.3 Event space

To be able to discuss all events of interest which might occur within $\mathcal{R}$, we introduce the concept of an event space denoted by $\mathcal{F}$. When all possible events can be enumerated, $\mathcal{F}$ is the set of all subsets $\mathcal{A}_i \subseteq \Omega$, denoted by $\wp(\Omega)$ for the power set. In the illustration of a single roll of the six-sided die, $\mathcal{F}$ comprises all of the $N = 2^6 = 64$ distinct event sets:

$$\emptyset, \{1\}, \{2\}, \ldots, \{6\}, \{1,2\}, \{1,3\}, \ldots, \{5,6\}, \{1,2,3\}, \{1,2,4\}, \ldots, \{4,5,6\}, \ldots, \Omega \tag{A2.4}$$

where $\{1,2,3,4,5,6\} = \Omega$. Any conceivable description of the outcome is allowed, including all examples used above (e.g. $\{5,6\}$ describes an outcome greater than 4). Hence, every possible event will be a member of the event space in this illustration. Note that events $\mathcal{A}$ are elements of $\mathcal{F}$, denoted by $\mathcal{A} \in \mathcal{F}$, as well as subsets $\mathcal{A} \subseteq \Omega$, so here:

$$\mathcal{F} = \{\mathcal{A}_i : \mathcal{A}_i \subseteq \Omega,\ i = 1, \ldots, N\} = \wp(\Omega).$$

When the sample space is uncountable (e.g. a set of real numbers), all possible events cannot be enumerated and the mathematics becomes tricky. The power set $\wp(\Omega)$ turns out to be too large, and the event space $\mathcal{F}$ comprises most but not all of the events $\mathcal{A}_i \subseteq \Omega$, a feat accomplished by restricting the properties of $\mathcal{F}$. Let $\mathcal{F} = \{\mathcal{A}_i : \mathcal{A}_i \subseteq \Omega,\ i \in \mathbb{N}_+\}$, which is similar to the definition for a finite sample space. From what we have already established about events, if $\mathcal{A} \in \mathcal{F}$ and $\mathcal{B} \in \mathcal{F}$, then so are other events derived from these by operations which define events, such as $\mathcal{A} \cup \mathcal{B} \in \mathcal{F}$, $\mathcal{A}^c \in \mathcal{F}$, and $\mathcal{A} \cap \mathcal{B}^c \in \mathcal{F}$ etc. Two universal members of $\mathcal{F}$ are Ω and its complement $\Omega^c = \emptyset$. To allow for continuous as well as discrete outcomes, including cases where too many events occur to sustain enumeration of all possible events, and to develop a mathematically valid treatment of events, $\mathcal{F}$ is required to satisfy three properties:

(a) $\mathcal{F} \neq \emptyset$ (otherwise there is nothing to discuss);
(b) if $\mathcal{A} \in \mathcal{F}$ then $\mathcal{A}^c \in \mathcal{F}$ (so that $\mathcal{F}$ is closed under complements);
(c) if $\mathcal{A}_i \in \mathcal{F}$ for $i \in \mathbb{N}_+$ and $\mathcal{C} = \bigcup_{i=1}^{\infty} \mathcal{A}_i$, then $\mathcal{C} \in \mathcal{F}$.

Requirement (c) is distinctly more complicated than (a) and (b). The set $\mathcal{C}$ is such that all elements in any of the sets $\mathcal{A}_i$ are in the union, which is a countable union with as many members as there are positive integers, and so could be interpreted as 'all possible events'. We require that such an event is also a member of $\mathcal{F}$. Thus, $\mathcal{F}$ must be closed under complements and countable unions, so that such operations on events produce events. A condition like (c) is needed to deal with infinite sample spaces (such as all real numbers), and samples which increase in size without bound as will occur in many econometric derivations. From (b) and (c), taking $\mathcal{B} = \mathcal{A}^c$ proves that $\mathcal{A} \cup \mathcal{A}^c = \Omega \in \mathcal{F}$, so that $\emptyset = \Omega^c \in \mathcal{F}$. We can handle intersections of sets using the earlier relations to prove theorems such as:

$$\text{if } \mathcal{A} \in \mathcal{F} \text{ and } \mathcal{B} \in \mathcal{F} \text{ then } \mathcal{A} \cap \mathcal{B} \in \mathcal{F},$$

since $\mathcal{A} \cap \mathcal{B} = (\mathcal{A}^c \cup \mathcal{B}^c)^c$ with $\mathcal{A}^c \in \mathcal{F}$ and $\mathcal{B}^c \in \mathcal{F}$, so $\mathcal{A}^c \cup \mathcal{B}^c \in \mathcal{F}$, and hence so is its complement; and so on.

The mathematics of the event space is close to that of a field, and because of such a relation to that branch of algebra, the event space $\mathcal{F}$ is often called a sigma field (written as σ-field , although σ here is unconnected with its conventional usage in econometrics for an equation standard error): a good reference is Clarke (1975). We will call $\mathcal{F}$ an event space to stress both its being the set of events, and its dependence on the sample space, leading on to the concept of a probability space below. A simple example of an event space $\mathcal{F}$ when $\mathcal{A} \subset \Omega$ is a member, is given by $\{\emptyset, \mathcal{A}, \mathcal{A}^c, \Omega\}$. It is easy to check that this space satisfies the three axioms, and is the smallest which does so when $\mathcal{A} \in \mathcal{F}$. We could denote such an $\mathcal{F}$ by $\sigma(\mathcal{A})$ to show that it is the σ-field or event space generated by $\mathcal{A}$. For share prices, when $\Omega = \{U, N\}$ and $\mathcal{A} = \{U\}$, then $\mathcal{A}^c = \{N\}$ and $\mathcal{F} = \sigma(\mathcal{A}) = \{\emptyset, \{U\}, \{N\}, \Omega\}$.

Despite appearing somewhat arcane at first sight, event spaces are intimately related to the idea of information, and are a vital component for understanding such diverse notions as probability, rational expectations, and dynamic econometric models, so this section should not be seen as a digression. As an example, let Ω be the sample space of an economy, and consider a sequence of events $\{\mathcal{A}_t, t \in \mathcal{T}\}$, where $\mathcal{A}_{t-1}$ denotes the events up to time $t-1$, with event space $\mathcal{F}_{t-1}$, and $\mathcal{T}$ is the relevant set of time. Because of the close connection between the event space and the event sequence in this context, the former is usually denoted by $\mathcal{F}_{t-1} = \sigma(\mathcal{A}_{t-1})$, and is the smallest event space generated by $\mathcal{A}_{t-1}$. By time t, the event space has grown to $\mathcal{F}_t = \sigma(\mathcal{A}_t)$, since more has happened and consequently $\mathcal{F}_{t-1} \subseteq \mathcal{F}_t$. The σ-field has usually increased and $\mathcal{F}_t$ is more informative than $\mathcal{F}_{t-1}$: if you wanted to predict (say) the exchange rate at time $t+1$, a better prediction can be made using $\mathcal{F}_t$ than $\mathcal{F}_{t-1}$. Admittedly that result is rather obvious, but it is a good start to have the formalization coincide with common sense. See Grimmett and Welsh (1986) and Spanos (1986) for further details about events and event spaces, and Chow and Teicher (1988) for a more advanced treatment of σ-fields .

A2.2.4 Measurability

An analysis of this difficult topic is beyond the scope of the present treatment, but several points can be considered (see McCabe and Tremayne, 1993, for further details). To measure anything requires a metric and well-defined units, such as length in centimetres. A crucial metric for econometrics is probability, and we consider that in the next section. Even prior to measurement, an obvious requirement is that the relevant events are recorded: in the stock price example, $\{D\}$ is not measurable with respect to $\sigma(\{U\})$ since $\mathcal{F} = \{\emptyset, \{U\}, \{N\}, \Omega\}$ only, which does not convey information about $\{D\}$. Conversely, a given event may be measurable with respect to many event spaces: for example, $\{U\}$ is measurable with respect to both $\sigma(\{U\})$ and $\sigma(\{U, D, S\})$. Measurement can take place with differing degrees of crudeness, from a binary scale of 'no/yes' (implemented as $(0, 1)$), through an ordinal scale (as occurs for utility theory in economics, where $a > b$ is a possible judgement, but not by how much), an interval scale (e.g. temperature), up to a ratio scale (such as length). Intermediate scales can be constructed from these (e.g. where differences between outcomes can be ordered). It is essential to know the scale of measurement when analysing data as some operations are not valid on cruder scales. Clearly, finer measurements are easily aggregated to cruder ones, but not vice versa. We briefly return to measurability when considering random variables, and consider data measurement issues in Chapter 12.

A2.3 Probability

The everyday notion of probability is the basis for the axiomatic treatment discussed here. We seek a probability measure that corresponds to our intuitive ideas, but has clearly-defined mathematical properties. To relate probability to relative frequency, we define probability to lie between 0 and 1. From games of chance like dice, it has been observed that the relative frequency of events (e.g. a $\{6\}$ on a single roll of a 'fair' die) is constant (here at a sixth), which is an essential condition for betting odds to be accepted by participants in the game. One natural requirement is that the probability of this event derived from probability theory matches that found by experience over prolonged time periods. Further, relative frequencies of mutually exclusive events are additive; e.g., the relative frequency of a $\{5\}$ or a $\{6\}$ on a roll of a die is a third ($1/6 + 1/6 = 1/3$). Marked deviations from such outcomes during gambling could induce violent results.

A2.3.1 Probability spaces

To model such features, introduce a function $\mathsf{P}(\cdot)$ that relates sets of events $\mathcal{A} \in \mathcal{F}$ to numbers in $[0, 1]$, a closed interval of the real line $\mathbb{R} = (-\infty, \infty)$. Thus, $\mathsf{P}(\cdot)$ maps from $\mathcal{F}$ to $[0, 1]$, denoted by $\mathsf{P}(\cdot) : \mathcal{F} \mapsto [0, 1]$. Then, $\mathsf{P}(\cdot)$ is a probability measure if it satisfies three conditions analogous to the three requirements for an event space also designed to ensure that $0 \leq \mathsf{P}(\cdot) \leq 1$:[1]

(a) $\mathsf{P}(\mathcal{A}) \geq 0$ for all $\mathcal{A} \in \mathcal{F}$ (naturally, given the definition that $\mathsf{P}(\cdot) : \mathcal{F} \mapsto [0, 1]$);
(b) $\mathsf{P}(\Omega) = 1$ (so some event is certain to occur);
(c) if $\mathcal{A}_i \in \mathcal{F}$ for $i \in \mathbb{N}_+$ when $\mathcal{A}_i \cap \mathcal{A}_j = \emptyset$ for $i \neq j$, then for $\mathcal{C} = \bigcup_{i=1}^{\infty} \mathcal{A}_i$:

$$\mathsf{P}(\mathcal{C}) = \mathsf{P}\left(\bigcup_{i=1}^{\infty} \mathcal{A}_i\right) = \sum_{i=1}^{\infty} \mathsf{P}(\mathcal{A}_i). \tag{A2.5}$$

In (c), all $\mathcal{A}_i$ and $\mathcal{A}_j$ are disjoint, so all events are mutually exclusive. Since $\mathcal{C}$ is the countable union of the $\mathcal{A}_i$, from §A2.2.3, $\mathcal{C} \in \mathcal{F}$, and hence $\mathcal{C}$ is an event. Since we want probability to be additive across disjoint events, we require $\mathsf{P}(\mathcal{C})$ to be the sum of the probabilities of the $\mathcal{A}_i$. Thus, probability is defined as an additive measure for disjoint events in a random experiment: the main complication is allowing for countable numbers of events.

Since $\mathcal{C} \in \mathcal{F}$, from (a) and (b), $0 \leq \mathsf{P}(\mathcal{C}) \leq 1$, which places restrictions on the values of the sequence $\mathsf{P}(\mathcal{A}_i)$ to ensure that the sum is convergent. Let $\mathsf{p}_i = \mathsf{P}(\mathcal{A}_i)$ and $\mathsf{p} = \mathsf{P}(\mathcal{C})$, then (c) is the condition that the probability p of the event $\mathcal{C} = \bigcup_{i=1}^{\infty} \mathcal{A}_i$ is:

$$0 \leq \mathsf{p} = \sum_{i=1}^{\infty} \mathsf{p}_i \leq 1.$$

As a necessary condition, the sum must be convergent. When Ω is finite and $\mathcal{F} = \wp(\Omega)$, the axioms capture the intuitive and experimental notions with which we began. Moreover, they allow us to handle infinite sequences of events (e.g. indefinitely tossing a coin).

This formulation has created a triple $(\Omega, \mathcal{F}, \mathsf{P})$ called a probability space, where Ω is the sample space of outcomes, $\mathcal{F}$ is the event space of Ω, and $\mathsf{P}(\cdot)$ is the probability measure for the events in $\mathcal{F}$. The structure of a probability space is rich enough to generate many interesting results, including establishing a close link to what we know empirically about gambling odds from games of chance. In particular, given some base probabilities such as $\mathsf{P}(\mathcal{A})$ and $\mathsf{P}(\mathcal{B})$, we can calculate the probabilities of other events such as

[1] These are known as Kolmogorov's axioms. We do not provide an independent definition of probability, but merely characterize its properties axiomatically to avoid circularity difficulties by defining probability in terms of 'equally likely outcomes', or empirical frequencies.

$\mathcal{A}^c$ and $\mathcal{A} \cap \mathcal{B}$ as follows. First, $\mathcal{A} \in \mathcal{F}$ implies that $\mathcal{A}^c \in \mathcal{F}$, and since $\mathcal{A} \cup \mathcal{A}^c = \Omega$ and $\mathcal{A} \cap \mathcal{A}^c = \emptyset$, then:

$$1 = \mathsf{P}(\Omega) = \mathsf{P}(\mathcal{A} \cup \mathcal{A}^c) = \mathsf{P}(\mathcal{A}) + \mathsf{P}(\mathcal{A}^c), \tag{A2.6}$$

so we deduce that $\mathsf{P}(\mathcal{A}^c) = 1 - \mathsf{P}(\mathcal{A})$. Also, since $\emptyset = \Omega^c$, then:

$$\mathsf{P}(\emptyset) = \mathsf{P}(\Omega^c) = 1 - \mathsf{P}(\Omega) = 0,$$

the impossible event, given (b). However, a set $\mathcal{A}$ can have $\mathsf{P}(\mathcal{A}) = 0$ without being impossible, or $\mathsf{P}(\mathcal{A}) = 1$ without being certain. For example, if $\Omega = \mathbb{R}$, and $\mathcal{A} = \{1\}$, then $\mathsf{P}(\mathcal{A}) = 0$: any single point has a zero probability of being selected in an uncountable set, although some point is certain to be selected. Sets like $\mathcal{A} \neq \emptyset$ such that $\mathsf{P}(\mathcal{A}) = 0$ are said to be of measure zero, but we will not delve deeper into such aspects here (see Dhrymes, 1989, for a more advanced treatment).

Secondly, we note a general result on the distribution of probabilities across a partition of Ω, namely a group of disjoint sets whose union is Ω, such as $\mathcal{B} \cup \mathcal{B}^c$. Then:

$$\mathsf{P}(\mathcal{A}) = \mathsf{P}(\mathcal{A} \cap \Omega) = \mathsf{P}(\mathcal{A} \cap [\mathcal{B} \cup \mathcal{B}^c]) = \mathsf{P}(\mathcal{A} \cap \mathcal{B}) + \mathsf{P}(\mathcal{A} \cap \mathcal{B}^c). \tag{A2.7}$$

Next, since $\mathcal{A} \cup \mathcal{B} = (\mathcal{A} \cap \mathcal{B}^c) \cup \mathcal{B}$, and the last two sets are disjoint:

$$\mathsf{P}(\mathcal{A} \cup \mathcal{B}) = \mathsf{P}(\mathcal{A} \cap \mathcal{B}^c) + \mathsf{P}(\mathcal{B}). \tag{A2.8}$$

Finally, combining the results in (A2.7) and (A2.8) to eliminate $\mathsf{P}(\mathcal{A} \cap \mathcal{B}^c)$ yields:

$$\mathsf{P}(\mathcal{A} \cap \mathcal{B}) = \mathsf{P}(\mathcal{A}) + \mathsf{P}(\mathcal{B}) - \mathsf{P}(\mathcal{A} \cup \mathcal{B}). \tag{A2.9}$$

Thus, the framework can be extended to deal with events which are not disjoint. Heuristically, $\mathsf{P}(\mathcal{A})$ measures the proportion of the space $\mathcal{A} \subseteq \Omega$ occupied by the event set $\mathcal{A} \in \mathcal{F}$. Consistent with this interpretation, when $\mathcal{A} \subseteq \mathcal{B} \subseteq \Omega$, since $\mathcal{B} = \mathcal{A} \cup (\mathcal{A}^c \cap \mathcal{B})$, then $\mathsf{P}(\mathcal{A}) \leq \mathsf{P}(\mathcal{B})$. This interpretation should not be taken to extremes, but may help in understanding $\mathsf{P}(\cdot)$ as shown in the diagrams in Fig. A2.3.

Many important theorems can be established from the axioms but since the purpose of this chapter is to outline the main ideas rather than provide an exhaustive treatment, we conclude this section by stressing that probability is defined over events. As noted above, if Ω is the set of real numbers, any single outcome has a probability of zero although some outcome is certain to occur. Events correspond to intervals rather than points in this example, so many of them have non-zero probabilities. Nevertheless, some care is needed to avoid paradoxes, and we return to this issue in §A2.4. First, we consider a concept of importance to the econometric implementation of probability, concerned with the occurrence of some events given that other events occur.

A2.3.2 Conditional probability

The concept of conditional probability concerns the probability of some event $\mathcal{A}$ occurring given that another event $\mathcal{B}$ occurs, and is denoted by $\mathsf{P}(\mathcal{A}|\mathcal{B})$. An example is the probability of a head on a second toss of a coin given that a tail occurs on the first toss. A more relevant example is the probability of any given individual being unemployed. Let $\mathcal{A}$ denote the event that unemployment occurs, and $\mathcal{B}_j$ the event of j years of full-time education. Let $M(\mathcal{A})$ individuals in a population of N be unemployed, and let $K(\mathcal{B}_j)$ have j years of education. Let $R(\cdot)$ denote the relative frequency of an event, so that $R(\mathcal{A}) = M(\mathcal{A})/N$ and $R(\mathcal{B}_j) = K(\mathcal{B}_j)/N$. We have not established a formal relationship between relative frequency and probability, and will not do so till Chapter A4, but for large enough N, $R(\mathcal{A})$ converges on $\mathsf{P}(\mathcal{A})$ in a sense we can make precise. That prospect guides the formulation of conditional probability. When $J(\mathcal{A} \cap \mathcal{B}_j)$ individuals with j years of education are unemployed, then the event 'both $\mathcal{A}$ and $\mathcal{B}_j$' occurs in the population with relative frequency given by $R(\mathcal{A} \cap \mathcal{B}_j) = J(\mathcal{A} \cap \mathcal{B}_j)/N$. If we want to know the relative frequency of unemployment in the group with j years of education, we calculate $J(\mathcal{A} \cap \mathcal{B}_j)/K(\mathcal{B}_j)$. Dividing numerator and denominator by N, that last ratio is $R(\mathcal{A} \cap \mathcal{B}_j)/R(\mathcal{B}_j)$ which we could denote by $R(\mathcal{A}|\mathcal{B}_j)$.

By choosing to consider events conditional on $\mathcal{B}$, we restrict attention to the smaller probability space associated with $\mathcal{B}$ (instead of that associated with Ω), and so need $\mathsf{P}(\mathcal{B}) > 0$ for a meaningful analysis. The probability that both $\mathcal{A}$ and $\mathcal{B}$ occur is $\mathsf{P}(\mathcal{A} \cap \mathcal{B})$, so that relative to $\mathcal{B}$ occurring, which is $\mathsf{P}(\mathcal{B})$, $\mathcal{A}$ occurs on $\mathsf{P}(\mathcal{A} \cap \mathcal{B})/\mathsf{P}(\mathcal{B})$ occasions. Thus, when $\mathsf{P}(\mathcal{B}) > 0$, we define:

$$\mathsf{P}(\mathcal{A} \mid \mathcal{B}) = \frac{\mathsf{P}(\mathcal{A} \cap \mathcal{B})}{\mathsf{P}(\mathcal{B})}. \tag{A2.10}$$

Since $\mathcal{B} \equiv (\mathcal{B} \cap \mathcal{A}) \cup (\mathcal{B} \cap \mathcal{A}^c)$, and the two sets in that union are disjoint, we have that $\mathsf{P}(\mathcal{B}) \geq \mathsf{P}(\mathcal{A} \cap \mathcal{B})$, and hence $0 \leq \mathsf{P}(\mathcal{A}|\mathcal{B}) \leq 1$. Also, $\mathsf{P}(\mathcal{A}) \equiv \mathsf{P}(\mathcal{A}|\Omega)$.

A simple illustration of conditioning is to consider a sample space of a hat containing the four numbers $\{0, 0, 1, 1\}$ where $\mathsf{P}(\{0\}) = \mathsf{P}(\{1\}) = 1/2$. Draw a number and look at its value; say the outcome is a zero, then the probability from the remaining set $\{0, 1, 1\}$ of the next outcome being $\{1\}$ is two-thirds, so when sampling without replacement, $\mathsf{P}(\{1\}|\{0\}$ on first draw$) = 2/3$. Sampling numbers from the hat without replacement alters the probabilities of later drawings. If we had replaced the number after noting its value, later probabilities would be the same as the initial ones, so conditional and unconditional probabilities would be the same: $\mathsf{P}(\{1\}|\{1\}$ on first draw$) = 1/2$.

Let $\mathsf{P}_B(\mathcal{A}) = \mathsf{P}(\mathcal{A}|\mathcal{B})$, then conditioning has created a new (smaller) probability space $(\Omega, \mathcal{F}, \mathsf{P}_B)$, and we can prove that claim by showing that $\mathsf{P}_B(\cdot)$ is a probability measure on $(\Omega, \mathcal{F})$, namely:

$$\mathsf{P}_B(\mathcal{A}) \geq 0 \text{ for } \mathcal{A} \in \mathcal{F}; \quad \mathsf{P}_B(\Omega) = 1, \tag{A2.11}$$

and:

$$\mathsf{P}_B\left(\bigcup_{i=1}^{\infty} \mathcal{A}_i\right) = \sum_{i=1}^{\infty} \mathsf{P}_B(\mathcal{A}_i) \text{ for disjoint } \mathcal{A}_i \in \mathcal{F}. \tag{A2.12}$$

We have already proved the first claim; the second follows from the fact that $\mathcal{B} \cap \Omega = \mathcal{B}$ and hence $\mathsf{P}_B(\mathcal{A}) = \mathsf{P}(\Omega|\mathcal{B}) = \mathsf{P}(\Omega \cap \mathcal{B})/\mathsf{P}(\mathcal{B}) = \mathsf{P}(\mathcal{B})/\mathsf{P}(\mathcal{B}) = 1$; and the third by an extension of the distributive result (A2.2):

$$\left(\bigcup_{i=1}^{\infty} \mathcal{A}_i\right) \cap \mathcal{B} = \bigcup_{i=1}^{\infty} (\mathcal{A}_i \cap \mathcal{B}), \tag{A2.13}$$

so that:

$$\mathsf{P}_{\mathcal{B}}\left(\bigcup_{i=1}^{\infty} \mathcal{A}_i\right) = \frac{\mathsf{P}\left(\bigcup_{i=1}^{\infty} [\mathcal{A}_i \cap \mathcal{B}]\right)}{\mathsf{P}(\mathcal{B})} = \frac{\sum_{i=1}^{\infty} \mathsf{P}(\mathcal{A}_i \cap \mathcal{B})}{\mathsf{P}(\mathcal{B})} = \sum_{i=1}^{\infty} \mathsf{P}_{\mathcal{B}}(\mathcal{A}_i). \tag{A2.14}$$

In each case, the result is established by applying the definition of conditional probability to return to $\mathsf{P}(\cdot)$ in order to use its properties. As an example, the probability of a prime number on a roll of a die is (for $\mathsf{P}(\{i\}) = 1/6\ \forall i \in \{1, \ldots, 6\}$):

$$\mathsf{P}(\{1,2,3,5\} \mid \{1,2,3,4,5,6\}) = \tfrac{4}{6} = \tfrac{2}{3};$$

however, when we know that the result is a number less than 6, then:

$$\mathsf{P}(\{\omega \in \Omega : \omega \text{ is prime } \mid \omega \leq 5\}) = \mathsf{P}(\{1,2,3,5\} \mid \{1,2,3,4,5\}) = \tfrac{4}{5},$$

so the probability is higher here on the smaller set of events, conditional on the face showing a number less than 6. Since:

$$\mathsf{P}(\{\omega \in \Omega : \omega \leq 5\}) = \tfrac{5}{6},$$

we can recover the joint probability from (A2.10) as:

$$\mathsf{P}(\{\omega \in \Omega : \omega \text{ is prime and } \omega \leq 5\}) = \tfrac{4}{5} \times \tfrac{5}{6} = \tfrac{2}{3},$$

corresponding to the set $\{1, 2, 3, 5\}$.

Finally, when a set of disjoint $\mathcal{B}_i \in \mathcal{F}$ are a partition of Ω, so $\bigcup_i \mathcal{B}_i = \Omega$, then for $\mathcal{A} \in \mathcal{F}$:

$$\mathsf{P}(\mathcal{A}) = \mathsf{P}\left(\mathcal{A} \cap \left(\bigcup_i \mathcal{B}_i\right)\right) = \sum_i \mathsf{P}(\mathcal{A} \cap \mathcal{B}_i) = \sum_i \mathsf{P}(\mathcal{A} \mid \mathcal{B}_i)\, \mathsf{P}(\mathcal{B}_i), \tag{A2.15}$$

where we have used (A2.2) and (A2.10).

Probabilities can be represented in terms of Venn diagrams, and these are especially useful for understanding conditional probabilities. The six diagrams in Fig. A2.3 illustrate various possibilities. The diagrams should be self-explanatory; in the last figure, $\mathcal{A}$ is 50 per cent of Ω and $\mathcal{B}$ is 50 per cent of $\mathcal{A}$. Carefully check that you understand every case. The idea of a probability space is a natural one when its representation is in terms of such diagrams.

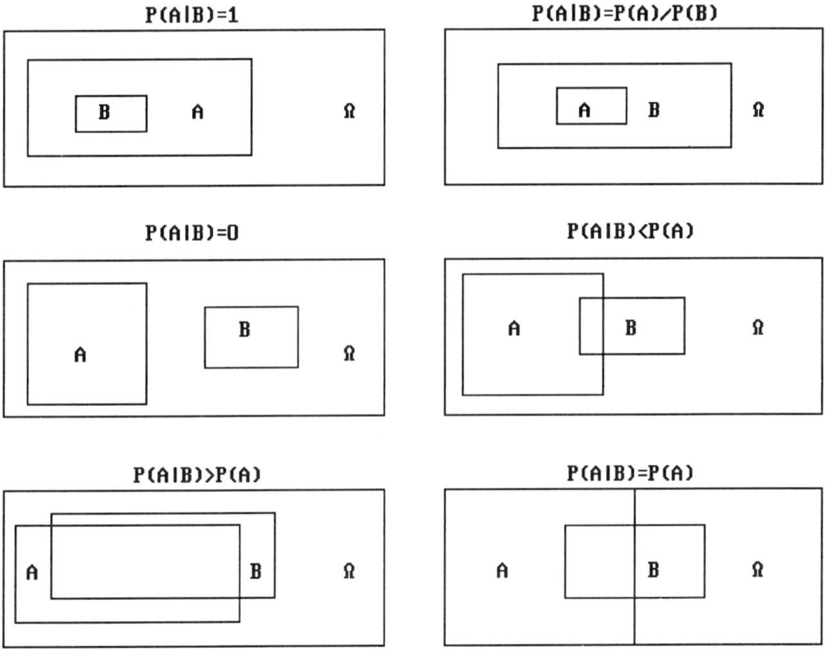

Fig. A2.3 Probability relations

A2.3.3 Stochastic independence

Define the events $\mathcal{A}$ and $\mathcal{B}$ to be stochastically independent if $\mathsf{P}(\mathcal{A}|\mathcal{B}) = \mathsf{P}(\mathcal{A})$, in which case $\mathcal{B}$ is uninformative about $\mathcal{A}$; alternatively, the probability structure of $\mathcal{A}$ is unaltered by $\mathcal{B}$ occurring. From the previous section, an equivalent definition of stochastic independence is $\mathsf{P}(\mathcal{A} \cap \mathcal{B}) = \mathsf{P}(\mathcal{A})\mathsf{P}(\mathcal{B})$. We drop the adjective stochastic, and just refer to independence, unless an ambiguity is likely. Independence is a distinct property from disjointness: when two sets are disjoint, then $\mathcal{A} \cap \mathcal{B} = \emptyset$ (as in Fig. A2.3c) so $\mathsf{P}(\mathcal{A} \cap \mathcal{B}) = 0$, whereas when $\mathsf{P}(\mathcal{A}) \neq 0,\ \mathsf{P}(\mathcal{B}) \neq 0$, and the events are independent, then $\mathsf{P}(\mathcal{A} \cap \mathcal{B}) = \mathsf{P}(\mathcal{A})\mathsf{P}(\mathcal{B}) \neq 0$ (as in Fig. A2.3f).

Extending the conditional sequence to three events $\mathcal{A},\ \mathcal{B}$, and $\mathcal{C}$:

$$\mathsf{P}(\mathcal{A} \cap \mathcal{B} \cap \mathcal{C}) = \mathsf{P}(\mathcal{A} \cap \mathcal{B} \mid \mathcal{C})\,\mathsf{P}(\mathcal{C}) = \mathsf{P}(\mathcal{A} \mid \mathcal{B} \cap \mathcal{C})\,\mathsf{P}(\mathcal{B} \mid \mathcal{C})\,\mathsf{P}(\mathcal{C}) \qquad \text{(A2.16)}$$

(and so on for more events), provided the various conditioning events have non-zero probabilities. Independent events are the special case of the conditional result:[2]

$$\mathsf{P}(\mathcal{A}\cap\mathcal{B}\cap\mathcal{C}) = \mathsf{P}(\mathcal{A})\,\mathsf{P}(\mathcal{B})\,\mathsf{P}(\mathcal{C}). \tag{A2.17}$$

Before exploring independence and conditioning further, note that when $\mathcal{A}$ and $\mathcal{B}$ are independent, then so are $\mathcal{A}^c$ and $\mathcal{B}$, $\mathcal{A}^c$ and $\mathcal{B}^c$ etc. For example, to prove the first, use $\mathsf{P}(\mathcal{B}) = 1 - \mathsf{P}(\mathcal{B}^c)$ and $\mathcal{A} = (\mathcal{A}\cap\mathcal{B})\cup(\mathcal{A}\cap\mathcal{B}^c)$, so that:

$$\begin{aligned}
\mathsf{P}(\mathcal{A}) &= \mathsf{P}(\mathcal{A}\cap\mathcal{B}) + \mathsf{P}(\mathcal{A}\cap\mathcal{B}^c)\\
&= \mathsf{P}(\mathcal{A})\,\mathsf{P}(\mathcal{B}) + \mathsf{P}(\mathcal{A}\mid\mathcal{B}^c)\,\mathsf{P}(\mathcal{B}^c)\\
&= \mathsf{P}(\mathcal{A}) + [\mathsf{P}(\mathcal{A}\mid\mathcal{B}^c) - \mathsf{P}(\mathcal{A})]\,\mathsf{P}(\mathcal{B}^c),
\end{aligned}$$

and hence $\mathsf{P}(\mathcal{A}|\mathcal{B}^c) = \mathsf{P}(\mathcal{A})$ as required.

Let $(\Omega, \mathcal{F}, \mathsf{P})$ be the probability space of an economy. A key area of application in macro-econometrics of conditional probability is when $\mathcal{A}$, $\mathcal{B}$, $\mathcal{C}$ etc. are events in $\mathcal{F}$ at different points of time in which case independence is not a reasonable assumption. Denote these events by $\{\mathcal{A}_t : \mathcal{A}_t \in \mathcal{F},\ t = 1, \ldots, T\}$. Although the events are not independent, we need such probabilities as:

$$\mathsf{P}\left(\bigcap_{t=1}^{T}\mathcal{A}_t\right), \tag{A2.18}$$

which is the probability of the joint event $\{\mathcal{A}_1 \ldots \mathcal{A}_T\}$. From expression (A2.16) applied in a sequence:[3]

$$\begin{aligned}
\mathsf{P}\left(\bigcap_{t=1}^{T}\mathcal{A}_t\right) &= \mathsf{P}\left(\mathcal{A}_T \mid \bigcap_{t=1}^{T-1}\mathcal{A}_t\right)\mathsf{P}\left(\bigcap_{t=1}^{T-1}\mathcal{A}_t\right)\\
&= \mathsf{P}\left(\mathcal{A}_T \mid \bigcap_{t=1}^{T-1}\mathcal{A}_t\right)\mathsf{P}\left(\mathcal{A}_{T-1} \mid \bigcap_{t=1}^{T-2}\mathcal{A}_t\right)\cdots\mathsf{P}(\mathcal{A}_1)\\
&= \prod_{t=1}^{T}\mathsf{P}\left(\mathcal{A}_t \mid \bigcap_{i=1}^{t-1}\mathcal{A}_{t-i}\right).
\end{aligned} \tag{A2.19}$$

This sequential factorization will prove as useful as independence for econometrics, where independence is the special case that:

$$\prod_{t=1}^{T}\mathsf{P}\left(\mathcal{A}_t \mid \bigcap_{i=1}^{t-1}\mathcal{A}_{t-i}\right) = \prod_{t=1}^{T}\mathsf{P}(\mathcal{A}_t). \tag{A2.20}$$

Sequential factorization is as much as we can hope to obtain in a subject as complicated, dynamic, and inter-related as economics, where few events are independent. Moreover,

[2] Pair-wise independence, whereby $\mathsf{P}(\mathcal{A}\cap\mathcal{B}) = \mathsf{P}(\mathcal{A})\mathsf{P}(\mathcal{B})$, $\mathsf{P}(\mathcal{A}\cap\mathcal{C}) = \mathsf{P}(\mathcal{A})\mathsf{P}(\mathcal{C})$, and $\mathsf{P}(\mathcal{B}\cap\mathcal{C}) = \mathsf{P}(\mathcal{B})\mathsf{P}(\mathcal{C})$, is not sufficient for independence, although it is necessary.

[3] When $t = 1$, the last term is $\mathsf{P}(\mathcal{A}_1)$.

it seems sensible to condition on past (and therefore immutable) events to calculate probabilities of present and future events.

In the case of a fixed finite population with N outcomes, where $\Omega = \{\omega_1, \ldots, \omega_N\}$ with $\mathcal{F} = \wp(\Omega)$, when $R(\cdot)$ is the relative frequency, then $(\Omega, \mathcal{F}, R)$ is a probability space, so we could reasonably call $R(\cdot)$ the empirical probability. There are many interpretations of probability extant in the literature (see Leamer, 1987, for a vocabulary) consistent with the axioms above, but we adopt the frequency viewpoint and later confront the two issues of relating empirical to theoretical probability for uncountable sample spaces, and of extending probability to random experiments which cannot be replicated (as in re-running an economy over the inter-war period).

A2.4 Random variables

A2.4.1 Mapping events to numbers

We have formulated probability notions in terms of a probability space $(\Omega, \mathcal{F}, \mathsf{P})$ where probabilities are defined for sets of events such as $\mathsf{P}(\mathcal{A})$ when $\mathcal{A} \in \mathcal{F}$. That is a cumbersome framework for daily use, so we now map from outcomes described in terms of events like 'heads or tails', or 'a face showing a six' to numerical values, such that the probabilities are preserved. The function that achieves this mapping is called a random variable denoted by $X(\cdot) : \Omega \mapsto \mathbb{R}$, which is read as: '$X$ maps from Ω to $\mathbb{R}$' (where $\mathbb{R}$ is the real line, so comprises all possible real, rational, and integer numbers). Thus, a random variable maps from events to real numbers.

A much-cited example is that of letting a head equal 1 and a tail equal 0, so that:

$$\mathsf{P}(\{H\}) = \mathsf{P}(\{X = 1\}) = \tfrac{1}{2},$$

and:

$$\mathsf{P}(\{T\}) = \mathsf{P}(\{X = 0\}) = \tfrac{1}{2}.$$

Here, $\Omega = \{H, T\}$, $\mathcal{F} = \{\emptyset, \{H\}, \{T\}, \Omega\}$, so we only need the subset of $\mathbb{R}$ given by $[0, 1]$. Reporting the outcome as $\{H\}$ or as $\{X = 1\}$ is equally informative, since we can recover the events (i.e. $\{H, T\}$) from knowledge of the random variable's outcome.

Thus, X is a function from the set Ω to $\mathbb{R}$ which preserves probabilities. We use the notation x for a value of that function (which is an outcome in $\mathbb{R}$), so $x = X(\omega)$ is the value of X when the event $\omega \in \Omega$ occurs. The objective of mapping to random variables is to facilitate numerical calculations without losing information about the probabilities of the underlying events. In economics, many interesting events are numerical naturally (e.g. prices and quantities, as when we consider the event that the price of gold exceeds \$400), and the transformation $X(\cdot)$ may seem redundant. However, the sample space is not inherently numerical in all its aspects (e.g. illness may make a trader miss a deal), so it is worth developing the analysis more generally. Since we could assign numerical values to X in many different ways consistent with the domain being Ω and the range $\mathbb{R}$, we next characterize the conditions needed for $X : \Omega \mapsto \mathbb{R}$ to preserve the probability structure.

A2.4.2 Image sets

The mapping X from Ω to $\mathbb{R}$ can be explained as follows. Let $\mathcal{A} \in \mathcal{F}$ be a subset of Ω, with outcome $\omega \in \mathcal{A}$, where the random variable is $X(\omega)$. The claim to be established is that for every X which occurs, there exists an outcome $\omega \in \mathcal{A}$; since events are the basis for assigning probabilities, we must be certain that there are events corresponding to the values of the random variable. To do so, introduce two sets. First, the image set $X(\mathcal{A})$ of $\mathcal{A}$ is the set:

$$\{X(\omega) \in \mathbb{R} : \omega \in \mathcal{A}\} \subseteq \mathbb{R},$$

which is the set of values of $X(\omega)$ for which there are outcomes in $\mathcal{A}$, and is a subset of $\mathbb{R}$. Secondly, for a subset $\mathcal{B} \subseteq \mathbb{R}$, the inverse image of $\mathcal{B}$ under $X(\cdot)$ is the set:

$$\{\omega \in \Omega : X(\omega) \in \mathcal{B}\} \subseteq \Omega,$$

so the inverse image is a subset of the sample space, and is the set of outcomes that lead to the random variable being in $\mathbb{R}$. These sets are inverses in the sense that if the first were $\mathcal{B} = \{X(\omega) \in \mathbb{R} : \omega \in \mathcal{A}\}$, then its inverse would be $\{\omega \in \Omega : X(\omega) \in \mathcal{B}\} = \mathcal{A}$, and conversely. Inverse image sets are elements of the event space $\mathcal{F}$, as well as subsets of Ω. We now construct $X(\omega) \in \mathcal{B}$ corresponding to $\mathcal{A} \in \mathcal{F}$, such that probabilities of events are preserved.

A convenient way to assign numerical values to events which applies to both discrete and continuous spaces, and has an eye on later developments, is to select $\mathcal{B}$ as an ordered set of intervals on the real line. Intervals are sets of the form $\mathcal{B}_z = (-\infty, z]$ for $z \in \mathbb{R}$, where the notation denotes a set open at the lower end but closed (including z) at the upper to ensure that the integers are included exactly once in a partition of $\mathbb{R}$. Thus, $\mathcal{B}_z$ is an example of the subset $\mathcal{B}$ above with $\mathcal{B}_z \subset \mathcal{B}_y$ if $z < y$. Formally:

$$\mathcal{B}_z = \{r \in \mathbb{R} : r \leq z\} \subseteq \mathbb{R},$$

where we have in mind the set $\{x : x = X(\omega) \leq z\}$ so that $X(\omega) \in \mathcal{B}_z$ means that $X(\omega) \leq z$.

To be sure that there exists an $\omega \in \Omega$ for $\mathcal{B}_z = \{x : x = X(\omega) \leq z\}$, we require that the inverse image set of $\mathcal{B}_z$ under $X(\omega)$ is an element of $\mathcal{F}$ (i.e. an event). Since the inverse image set for $\mathcal{B}_z$ is:

$$\{\omega \in \Omega : X(\omega) \in \mathcal{B}_z\},$$

which is the event for which the random variable is less than z, we require that:

$$\{\omega \in \Omega : X(\omega) \in \mathcal{B}_z\} \in \mathcal{F}.$$

In words, the symbols state that there do exist events corresponding to the random variable. If all subsets $\mathcal{B}_z$ have this property, then there are always corresponding events in $\mathcal{F}$.

Thus, $X(\omega)$ is a random variable on $(\Omega, \mathcal{F}, \mathsf{P})$ if, $\forall x \in \mathbb{R}$, its inverse image set for $\mathcal{B}_x$ is an event in $\mathcal{F}$. Initially this description may seem back-to-front, but on reflection it makes sense to define $X(\omega)$ as a random variable if all of its possible values correspond to events, so that whatever number x we pick, the outcome ω which generates $X(\omega) \leq x$ is an element of Ω (see Clarke, 1975).

For the coin-tossing example, X takes only the two values of zero and unity. When $x < 0$:

$$\{\omega \in \Omega : X(\omega) \leq x\} = \emptyset \in \mathcal{F};$$

when $0 \leq x < 1$:

$$\{\omega \in \Omega : X(\omega) \leq x\} = \{T\} \in \mathcal{F};$$

and when $1 \leq x$:

$$\{\omega \in \Omega : X(\omega) \leq x\} = \Omega \in \mathcal{F},$$

so events correspond to the numerical assignment. For the event $\mathcal{A}$ that a car accident occurs at a road junction in any 10 minute interval, we could assign $X = 0$ when no accident occurs ($\mathcal{A}^c$), and $X = 1$ when one or more accidents occur. Then $\mathsf{P}(\mathcal{A}) = \mathsf{P}(\{X = 1\})$. This is a crude representation; a finer measure would use $X = k$ when k accidents occur.

To summarize, when:

$$\{\omega \in \Omega : X(\omega) \leq x\} \in \mathcal{F} \;\; \forall x \in \mathbb{R},$$

then $X(\omega)$ is a well-defined random variable for which $\mathsf{P}(\{\omega \in \Omega : X(\omega) \leq x\})$ can be calculated, because we know that $\mathsf{P}(\mathcal{A})$ can be calculated $\forall \mathcal{A} \in \mathcal{F}$.

A2.4.3 Functions of random variables

What the previous section achieved is a mapping from $(\Omega, \mathcal{F}, \mathsf{P})$ to $(\mathbb{R}, \mathcal{B}, \mathsf{P}_{\mathsf{x}})$ where $\mathcal{B}$ is the event space generated by the sets $\{\mathcal{B}_x\}$ of intervals of the real line $\mathbb{R}$, and P_{x} is the corresponding probability measure ($\mathcal{B}$ is called a Borel field). A function $X(\omega)$ on Ω is said to be measurable if and only if:

$$\{\omega \in \Omega : X(\omega) \leq x\} \in \mathcal{F} \; \forall x \in \mathbb{R},$$

in which case $X(\omega)$ is a random variable.

Economics abounds with random variables including prices, incomes, expenditures, and outputs, all of which take different numerical values at different times and places, and do not seem to be perfectly predictable. The events which generated these random variables are immensely complicated, involving myriads of individual transactions, with decisions dependent on changing information. Thus, the switch to random variables which permits numerical calculations is an essential step for further progress. Indeed, econometrics is primarily concerned with analysing random variables, so we will need to develop appropriate tools to describe, categorize, and analyse their behaviour.

Such tools must allow operations on functions of random variables. When $X(\omega)$ is a random variable, for well-behaved functions $g(\cdot)$, then $g(X)$ is a random variable as well; the class of admissible $g(\cdot)$ includes continuous functions, and hence taking logs or sums of random variables etc. When $g(\cdot)$ is a continuous, monotone, increasing, measurable function of $X(\omega)$ then:

$$\begin{aligned} \mathsf{P}(\{\omega \in \Omega : X(\omega) \leq x\}) &= \mathsf{P}(\{\omega \in \Omega : g(X(\omega)) \leq g(x)\}) \\ &= \mathsf{P}(\{\omega \in \Omega : Y(\omega) \leq y\}), \end{aligned} \tag{A2.21}$$

which is the probability of a well-defined event for the random variable $Y(\omega)=g(X(\omega))$.

To summarize, random variables $X(\omega)$ take numerical values on the real line $\mathbb{R}$ corresponding to events $\omega \in \Omega$. We derived them by creating intervals $\mathcal{B}_x$ of $\mathbb{R}$ of the form $(-\infty, x]$, then considered probabilities such as $\mathsf{P}(\{\omega \in \Omega : X(\omega) \leq x\})$, often written just as $\mathsf{P}(X \leq x)$. The next set of tools involves the study of these probabilities.

A2.5 Distribution and density functions

A2.5.1 Cumulative distribution function

The symbol $\mathsf{F}_{\mathsf{X}}(x)$ is used to denote $\mathsf{P}(\{\omega \in \Omega : X(\omega) \leq x\})$, and is called the cumulative distribution function of X, abbreviated to CDF (the adjective 'cumulative' is redundant and is usually omitted). CDFs have a number of useful properties. For $r \leq s$:

(a) $\mathsf{F}_{\mathsf{X}}(r) \leq \mathsf{F}_{\mathsf{X}}(s)$;
(b) $\mathsf{F}_{\mathsf{X}}(r) \to 0$ as $r \to -\infty$;
(c) $\mathsf{F}_{\mathsf{X}}(r) \to 1$ as $r \to \infty$;
(d) $\mathsf{P}(r < X \leq s) = \mathsf{F}_{\mathsf{X}}(s) - \mathsf{F}_{\mathsf{X}}(r)$;
(e) $\mathsf{F}_{\mathsf{X}}(r + \delta) \to \mathsf{F}_{\mathsf{X}}(r)$ as $\delta \to 0$ for $\delta > 0$.

Thus, $\mathsf{F}_{\mathsf{X}}(\cdot)$ lies between zero and unity inclusive, is monotonically non-decreasing in its argument, and is continuous on the right. Two common standardized CDFs are the uniform distribution on the unit interval:

$$\mathsf{F}_{\mathsf{X}}(x) = x \text{ for } x \in [0, 1], \text{ and } \mathsf{F}_{\mathsf{X}}(x) = 1 \text{ for } x > 1;$$

and the exponential:

$$\mathsf{F}_{\mathsf{X}}(x) = 1 - \exp(-\lambda x) \text{ for } x \in [0, \infty) \text{ and } \lambda > 0,$$

where both CDFs are zero outside the ranges shown. The importance of CDFs is that they record everything about the random variable, as they are just another notation for $\mathsf{P}(\{\omega \in \Omega : X(\omega) \leq x\})$. In the coin-tossing example, $\mathsf{F}_{\mathsf{X}}(0) = ½$ and $\mathsf{F}_{\mathsf{X}}(1) = 1$, with $\mathsf{F}_{\mathsf{X}}(\cdot)$ being zero for $x \leq 0$ and unity for $x \geq 1$, so the CDF is a step function with jumps at $x = 0$ and $x = 1$. Other CDFs will appear below.

A2.5.2 Density function

When X is a discrete random variable, $\mathsf{P}(\{X = x\})$ is well defined, and equals the probability at $X = x$. We call $\mathsf{P}(\{X = x\})$ the probability density at x and denote it by:

$$\mathsf{f}_{\mathsf{X}}(x) = \mathsf{P}(\{X = x\}).$$

A random variable X is continuous if there exists a function $\mathsf{f}_{\mathsf{x}}(x) \geq 0$ such that:

$$\mathsf{F}_{\mathsf{x}}(x) = \int_{-\infty}^{x} \mathsf{f}_{\mathsf{x}}(z)\, \mathrm{d}z \ \ \forall x \in \mathbb{R}. \tag{A2.22}$$

If this is the case, then $\mathsf{f}_{\mathsf{x}}(x)$ is the density function of X and:

$$\int_{-\infty}^{\infty} \mathsf{f}_{\mathsf{x}}(x)\, \mathrm{d}x = 1. \tag{A2.23}$$

From (d), and the definition of a derivative, when $\mathsf{F}_{\mathsf{x}}(\cdot)$ is differentiable:

$$\mathsf{P}(x < X \leq x + \delta_x) = \mathsf{F}_{\mathsf{x}}(x + \delta_x) - \mathsf{F}_{\mathsf{x}}(x) \simeq \mathsf{f}_{\mathsf{x}}(x)\, \delta_x \text{ as } \delta_x \to 0,$$

so

$$\mathsf{f}_{\mathsf{x}}(x) = \frac{\mathrm{d}\mathsf{F}_{\mathsf{x}}(z)}{\mathrm{d}z}\Big\rfloor_{z=x}.$$

When X is continuous, $\mathsf{f}_{\mathsf{x}}(x)$ cannot be interpreted as $\mathsf{P}(\{X = x\})$ which is zero even though the outcome x could happen. We usually write $\mathsf{f}_{\mathsf{x}}(x)$ without the trailing δ_x (except when we need to change random variables) despite the potential logical problems of doing so, taking care not to attach non-zero probability to points rather than to intervals. Although CDFs provide a more general framework than densities, it is often convenient to work with density functions.

A2.5.3 Change of variable

Transformations often occur and induce a change of variable in the density function. Consider the mapping from $x \in \mathcal{X}$ to $y = g(x) \in \mathcal{Y}$, where $g(\cdot)$ is the one–one function $g(\cdot) : \mathcal{X} \mapsto \mathcal{Y}$ with inverse $x = g^{-1}(y) = h(y)$. The one–one requirement is to ensure that events are preserved under the transformation. When X has density $\mathsf{f}_{\mathsf{x}}(x)$, we seek the density $\mathsf{f}_{\mathsf{y}}(y)$ of $Y = g(X)$, tracking the transformation from $\mathcal{X}$ to $\mathcal{Y}$. Assume that $h(\cdot)$ is continuously differentiable and not zero everywhere in $\mathcal{Y}$, with derivative $\mathrm{d}h(y)/\mathrm{d}y$ denoted by $J \neq 0$ and called the Jacobian of the transformation, despite relating to the inverse transformation. Taking the absolute value $|J|$ to ensure a positive density:

$$\mathsf{f}_{\mathsf{y}}(y) = \mathsf{f}_{\mathsf{x}}(x)\,|J| = \mathsf{f}_{\mathsf{h(y)}}(h(y))\,|J|\,. \tag{A2.24}$$

When $g(\cdot)$ is not one–one, a similar analysis can be constructed over separate regions where $g(\cdot)$ is one–one. The result in (A2.24) has many applications as the next section illustrates.

A2.5.4 Normal distribution

We often use the normal or Gaussian density defined by:

$$\mathsf{f}_{\mathsf{x}}(x) = \left(2\pi\sigma_x^2\right)^{-\frac{1}{2}} \exp\left(-\frac{(x - \mu_x)^2}{2\sigma_x^2}\right), \tag{A2.25}$$

where $|\mu_x| < \infty$, and $0 < \sigma_x^2 < \infty$ for $x \in \mathbb{R}$. The normal density function reaches a maximum at $x = \mu_x$, is symmetric about μ_x (which is the mean), and its spread increases with σ_x^2 (the variance: $\sigma_x = \sqrt{\sigma_x^2}$ is the standard deviation). Usually the normal distribution is denoted by $X \sim \mathsf{N}[\mu_x, \sigma_x^2]$, and read as: X is distributed as a normal random variable with mean μ_x and variance σ_x^2.

Let $Y = (X - \mu_x)/\sigma_x$ so that $X = \sigma_x Y + \mu_x$. From (A2.24), this transform alters the density and since the Jacobian is σ_x:

$$\mathsf{f}_\mathsf{y}(y) = \left(2\pi\sigma_x^2\right)^{-\frac{1}{2}} \exp\left(-\tfrac{1}{2}y^2\right)\sigma_x = (2\pi)^{-\frac{1}{2}} \exp\left(-\tfrac{1}{2}y^2\right). \tag{A2.26}$$

This is the standardized form of the density, denoted by $\mathsf{N}[0, 1]$. Note that $\mathsf{f}_\mathsf{x}(x) \geq 0$ since the exponential function is always positive, but we must wait to section A2.8 to prove that the density in (A2.25) integrates to unity.

A2.5.5 Parameters, probability models, and distributions

The new aspect present in the formula $\mathsf{N}[\mu_x, \sigma_x^2]$ is that $\mathsf{f}_\mathsf{x}(x)$ depends on the values taken by some parameters, here denoted by μ_x and σ_x^2, where a parameter is a numerical entity which does not depend on the event space. More generally, parameters are denoted by a vector $\boldsymbol{\theta}$ which may involve many elements stacked in a column. Strictly, therefore, the density should be denoted by $\mathsf{f}_\mathsf{x}(x; \boldsymbol{\theta}_p)$, where $\mathsf{f}_\mathsf{x}(x; \boldsymbol{\theta})$ defines a family of density functions, corresponding to different values of $\boldsymbol{\theta}$, and $\boldsymbol{\theta}_p$ is the population parameter value. The set of admissible values of $\boldsymbol{\theta}$ is called the parameter space, and denoted by Θ so that $\boldsymbol{\theta} \in \Theta$.

A probability model is a completely specified family of distributions denoted by:

$$\left\{\mathsf{f}_\mathsf{x}(x; \boldsymbol{\theta}) \text{ for } \boldsymbol{\theta} \in \Theta\right\}.$$

For example, the normal family in §A2.5.4 is:

$$\left\{\mathsf{N}\left[\mu_x, \sigma_x^2\right] \text{ for } \left(\mu_x, \sigma_x^2\right) \in \mathbb{R} \times \mathbb{R}_+\right\},$$

where $\Theta = \mathbb{R} \times \mathbb{R}_+$ denotes the cross-product of the real line with the positive part of itself, and means that for every value of $\mu_x \in \mathbb{R}$, any value of $\sigma_x^2 \in \mathbb{R}_+$ is admissible. Parameters with this form of parameter space are said to be variation free.

Probability models are one avenue for relating economic analysis to data. In applications, the structure of $\mathsf{f}_\mathsf{x}(\cdot)$ and $\boldsymbol{\theta}$ are suggested by subject-matter theory and accumulated empirical knowledge, but the actual value of $\boldsymbol{\theta}$ is generally unknown and has to be estimated from the data on X. Observations $(x_1 \ldots x_T)$ on X are viewed as a sample realization from $\mathsf{f}_\mathsf{x}(x; \boldsymbol{\theta}_p)$, and the evidence from the $\{x_t\}$ is used to learn about $\boldsymbol{\theta}_p$. The properties of the sampling procedure whereby the data are generated are important in relating data to the parameters of probability models, which is where the factorization result in §A2.2 above is used. When modelling empirical data, it must also be acknowledged that the form of $\mathsf{f}_\mathsf{x}(\cdot)$ is unknown.

To exploit the generality of this approach for economics, we first extend the analysis to allow for several random variables at once, where these may be inter-related, as in a consumption function relating consumers' expenditure to income, and wealth, or a money demand equation relating the money stock to the price level, income, and interest rates. Hence, we now consider joint distribution functions.

A2.6 Joint distributions

A2.6.1 Joint distribution functions

We have already considered joint probabilities, so it is natural to map to the joint distribution of several random variables using their joint CDF. Denote the random variables by X, Y, Z (three will suffice, but any number is feasible), then their joint CDF is:

$$\mathsf{F}_{\mathsf{x,y,z}}(x, y, z) = \mathsf{P}(\{\omega \in \Omega : X(\omega) \leq x; Y(\omega) \leq y; Z(\omega) \leq z\}).$$

For continuous random variables:

$$\mathsf{F}_{\mathsf{x,y,z}}(x, y, z) = \int_{-\infty}^{x} \int_{-\infty}^{y} \int_{-\infty}^{z} \mathsf{f}_{\mathsf{x,y,z}}(u, v, w)\, dudvdw, \quad \text{(A2.27)}$$

for all $(x, y, z) \in \mathbb{R}^3$, where $\mathbb{R}^3$ denotes 3-dimensional real space, and $\mathsf{f}_{\mathsf{x,y,z}}(x, y, z) \geq 0$ is the density function of the vector random variable $(X : Y : Z)$, which satisfies:

$$\int_{-\infty}^{\infty} \int_{-\infty}^{\infty} \int_{-\infty}^{\infty} \mathsf{f}_{\mathsf{x,y,z}}(u, v, w)\, dudvdw = 1. \quad \text{(A2.28)}$$

One of the advantages of the formulation adopted earlier is the ease with which this generalization to many random variables is achieved. We can recover the special case of a single random variable by eliminating the others from the joint distribution, and that is the concern of the next section.

A2.6.2 Marginal distributions

The distribution of any single (or sub-vector) random variable is called its marginal distribution, and is obtained from the joint distribution by eliminating all of the unwanted random variables. The terminology derives from the margins of tables of numbers which sum over other variables, so that in the joint distribution of (say) income and age, each entry in the table is the income of one age group, whereas the marginal totals correspond to the overall income distribution (ignoring age), and the age distribution (ignoring income). For the hypothetical discrete variables of the number of strikes (S, in hundreds per annum) and level of unemployment (U, as a percentage of the labour force), across a hundred countries in a given year, treated as the population of all possible outcomes, consider:

		S				
		$0-2$	$3-5$	$6-9$	>10	$\sum_s$
U	$1-5$	1	5	6	12	24
	$6-10$	5	11	9	8	33
	$11-15$	6	4	12	3	25
	>15	8	7	1	2	18
	$\sum_u$	20	27	28	25	100

The joint distribution is reported in the body of the table, so that the (empirical) probability of a country having 300–500 strikes and an unemployment rate of 6–10 per cent is 0.11, etc. The marginal distribution of unemployment across countries is given in the last column, and the marginal distribution of strikes across countries in the final row, so there is a probability of 0.25 of having less than 200 strikes per annum, etc.

For the trivariate example above, the marginal distribution of X is given by:

$$\begin{aligned} \mathsf{F_x}(x) &= \lim_{y\to\infty,z\to\infty} \mathsf{F_{x,y,z}}(x,y,z) \\ &= \int_{-\infty}^{x}\int_{-\infty}^{\infty}\int_{-\infty}^{\infty} \mathsf{f_{x,y,z}}(u,v,w)\,dudvdw \\ &= \int_{-\infty}^{x} \mathsf{f_x}(u)\,du, \end{aligned} \tag{A2.29}$$

where:

$$\lim_{y\to\infty,z\to\infty} \mathsf{F_{x,y,z}}(x,y,z) = \mathsf{P_{x,y,z}}(X \le x, Y \le \infty, Z \le \infty) = \mathsf{P_x}(X \le x). \tag{A2.30}$$

Similar formulae hold for the marginal distributions of Y and Z. Also, the distribution of the bivariate random variable $(X : Y)$ is the marginal distribution having eliminated Z:

$$\mathsf{F_{x,y}}(x,y) = \mathsf{P}(\{\omega \in \Omega : X(\omega) \le x; Y(\omega) \le y; Z(\omega) \le \infty\}). \tag{A2.31}$$

This notion is important in economics where all random variables are thought to be interconnected, so that the distributions of subsets of random variables should be conceived of as marginalized with respect to all other (eliminated) variables.

We defined independence for events, and now extend that notion to two random variables X and Y:

$$X \text{ and } Y \text{ are independent if } \mathsf{f_{x,y}}(x,y) = \mathsf{f_x}(x)\,\mathsf{f_y}(y). \tag{A2.32}$$

The left-hand side of this expression is the joint density function of X and Y derived from $\mathsf{P_{x,y}}(X \le x, Y \le y)$, and the right-hand side is the product of the two marginal densities. It is useful to have a general notation in which to express statements about groups of random variables, and we use bold-face letters: lower-case for column vectors of numbers, capitals for vectors of random variables (or matrices of numbers, where the context should clarify which sense operates). Using a single capital subscript on $\mathsf{F}(\cdot)$ to represent the vector of n scalar random variables, denoted by $\boldsymbol{X}' = (X_1 \dots X_n)$, the joint distribution and density function are $\mathsf{F_X}(\boldsymbol{x})$ and $\mathsf{f_X}(\boldsymbol{x})$ respectively. When the X_i are independent, then:

$$\mathsf{f_X}(\boldsymbol{x}) = \prod_{i=1}^{n} \mathsf{f_x}(x_i). \qquad \text{(A2.33)}$$

Let $\boldsymbol{X}' = (\boldsymbol{Y}' : \boldsymbol{Z}')$, then the marginal density of $\boldsymbol{Y}$ is:

$$\mathsf{f_Y}(\boldsymbol{y}) = \int_{\mathcal{Z}} \mathsf{f_{Y,Z}}(\boldsymbol{y}, \boldsymbol{v})\, \mathrm{d}\boldsymbol{v},$$

where integration is over the space $\mathcal{Z}$, usually $\mathbb{R}^m$ for m elements in $\boldsymbol{Z}$.

A2.6.3 Conditional distributions

The notion of conditional probability was developed above for events that were not necessarily independent. The table in §A2.6.2 provides an illustration: conditional on having an unemployment rate of greater than 15 per cent , the probability of having a strike rate greater than $1,000$ p.a. is $2/18 = 0.11$, which is less than the unconditional probability for that strike rate of 0.25.

However, to apply conditional arguments to random variables, we must check that all the events are well defined. In the case of a bivariate random variable $(X : Y)$, conditioning X on Y makes sense only if $\mathsf{P}(\{\omega \in \Omega : Y(\omega) \leq y\}) > 0$, since:

$$\begin{gathered}\mathsf{P}(\{\omega \in \Omega : X(\omega) \leq x; Y(\omega) \leq y\}) = \\ \mathsf{P}(\{\omega \in \Omega : X(\omega) \leq x\} \mid \{Y(\omega) \leq y\}) \cdot \mathsf{P}(\{\omega \in \Omega : Y(\omega) \leq y\}).\end{gathered} \qquad \text{(A2.34)}$$

The factorization for random variables in terms of conditional distributions is:

$$\mathsf{F_{x,y}}(x, y) = \mathsf{F_{x|y}}(x \mid y)\, \mathsf{F_y}(y). \qquad \text{(A2.35)}$$

As before, one of the important cases in economics is sequential factorization given the past:

$$\mathsf{F_X}(x_1 \ldots x_n) = \prod_{i=1}^{n} \mathsf{F_x}(x_i \mid x_{i-1} \ldots x_1). \qquad \text{(A2.36)}$$

A similar factorization holds for density functions, with the caveat about its interpretation for events of probability zero. Such difficulties could be avoided by defining conditioning with respect to the σ-field of the random variables, at the cost of more formidable expressions. While that route is preferable from the point of view of rigour, it would take the mathematical level beyond that of the rest of this book, so we will merely footnote when a difficulty arises. For a good treatment relevant to econometrics, see Spanos (1986). In the bivariate case when the relevant densities are well defined:

$$\mathsf{f_{y,z}}(y, z) = \mathsf{f_{y|z}}(y \mid z)\, \mathsf{f_z}(z), \qquad \text{(A2.37)}$$

and hence for $\mathsf{f_z}(z) > 0$:

$$\mathsf{f_{y|z}}(y \mid z) = \frac{\mathsf{f_{y,z}}(y, z)}{\mathsf{f_z}(z)}. \qquad \text{(A2.38)}$$

The notion of a probability model as a parametric family of distributions extends naturally to vector random variables, and we write the general case as:

$$\{\mathsf{f}_{\mathsf{X}}(\boldsymbol{x};\boldsymbol{\theta}),\ \boldsymbol{\theta} \in \boldsymbol{\Theta},\ \boldsymbol{x} \in \mathbb{R}^n\}. \tag{A2.39}$$

An important distributional family in econometrics is the multivariate normal distribution, which is the many-variable generalization of the univariate $\mathsf{N}[\mu_x, \sigma_x^2]$ distribution in §A2.5 above, and so first analyse the bivariate case in §A2.8. However, that section will be easier to understand after studying §A2.7, since one way of relating data to parameters is via expectations. Later, we distinguish between data densities, denoted by $\mathsf{D}(\cdot)$, and estimator or statistic densities and distributions, denoted by $\mathsf{f}(\cdot)$ and $\mathsf{F}(\cdot)$.

A2.7 Expectations

A2.7.1 Expectations, moments, and correlations

Define the expected value of a continuous scalar random variable X with density function $\mathsf{f}_{\mathsf{x}}(x)$ to be:[4]

$$\mathsf{E}[X] = \int_{-\infty}^{\infty} x\mathsf{f}_{\mathsf{x}}(x)\,\mathrm{d}x = \mu_x, \tag{A2.40}$$

which is the first moment of the distribution of X. For many distributions, μ_x is finite, but in other cases the integral does not converge so no moments of the distribution exist, as with the Cauchy distribution defined by $\mathsf{f}_{\mathsf{x}}(x) = [\pi(1+x^2)]^{-1}$ for $x \in \mathbb{R}$.

For any real number a, $\mathsf{E}[a] = a$, whereas for a function $g(X)$ of X:

$$\mathsf{E}[g(X)] = \int_{-\infty}^{\infty} g(x)\,\mathsf{f}_{\mathsf{x}}(x)\,\mathrm{d}x. \tag{A2.41}$$

An important example of such a function, when $|\mu_x| < \infty$, is:

$$\mathsf{V}[X] = \mathsf{E}\left[(X-\mu_x)^2\right] = \int_{-\infty}^{\infty} (x-\mu_x)^2\,\mathsf{f}_{\mathsf{x}}(x)\,\mathrm{d}x = \sigma_x^2 \geq 0, \tag{A2.42}$$

which is the variance or central second moment of X (we refer to moments of X rather than of their distribution as a shorthand). A random variable X whose first two moments exist is often standardized to have $\mu_x = 0$ and $\sigma_x = 1$, but not all distributions have finite variances. When the nth moment exists, so do all lower-order moments.

Expectations are a linear operator: when a and b are real numbers, but X and Y are random variables, then:

$$\mathsf{E}[aX + bY] = a\mathsf{E}[X] + b\mathsf{E}[Y]. \tag{A2.43}$$

[4] Subject to the convergence of the relevant integrals. For discrete random variables, $\mathsf{E}[X] = \sum x\mathsf{P}(x)$.

Thus, provided X takes more than one value:

$$\begin{aligned} \mathsf{E}\left[(X-\mu_x)^2\right] &= \mathsf{E}\left[X^2\right] - 2\mu_x \mathsf{E}\left[X\right] + \mu_x^2 \\ &= \mathsf{E}\left[X^2\right] - \mu_x^2 \geq 0, \end{aligned} \tag{A2.44}$$

so that $\mathsf{E}[X^2] > (\mathsf{E}[X])^2$ when $\sigma_x^2 > 0$.

The covariance $\mathsf{E}[(X-\mu_x)(Y-\mu_y)] = \mathsf{C}[X,Y] = \sigma_{xy}$ between X and Y in their joint distribution is defined to be:

$$\sigma_{xy} = \int_{-\infty}^{\infty}\int_{-\infty}^{\infty} (x-\mu_x)(y-\mu_y)\,\mathsf{f}_{\mathsf{x,y}}(x,y)\,dxdy. \tag{A2.45}$$

The standardized covariance $\sigma_{xy}/\sigma_x\sigma_y = \rho$ is the correlation with the important property that $|\rho| \leq 1$. To prove that last condition, consider the standardized random variables:

$$W = \frac{(X-\mu_x)}{\sigma_x} \text{ and } U = \frac{(Y-\mu_y)}{\sigma_y}. \tag{A2.46}$$

Then $\mathsf{E}[W-U] = \mathsf{E}[W] - \mathsf{E}[U] = 0$, and noting that $\mathsf{E}[WU] = \sigma_{xy}/\sigma_x\sigma_y = \rho$:

$$\mathsf{V}[W-U] = \mathsf{E}\left[(W-U)^2\right] = \mathsf{E}\left[W^2\right] + \mathsf{E}\left[U^2\right] - 2\mathsf{E}\left[WU\right] = 2(1-\rho). \tag{A2.47}$$

Since $\mathsf{V}[\cdot] \geq 0$, then $\rho \leq 1$. Similarly $\mathsf{V}[W+U] = 2(1+\rho) \geq 0$, so $\rho \geq -1$.

Expectations are defined element by element for vector random variables, so for an n-dimensional random vector $\boldsymbol{X}' = (X_1 \ldots X_n)$:

$$\mathsf{E}\left[\boldsymbol{X}'\right] = (\mathsf{E}\left[X_1\right] \ldots \mathsf{E}\left[X_n\right]) = (\mu_1 \ldots \mu_n) = \boldsymbol{\mu}', \tag{A2.48}$$

and:

$$\mathsf{V}\left[\boldsymbol{X}\right] = \mathsf{E}\left[(\boldsymbol{X}-\boldsymbol{\mu})(\boldsymbol{X}-\boldsymbol{\mu})'\right] = \{\mathsf{E}\left[(X_i-\mu_i)(X_j-\mu_j)\right]\} = \boldsymbol{\Sigma}, \tag{A2.49}$$

where $\boldsymbol{\Sigma}$ is the variance (or variance-covariance) matrix of $\boldsymbol{X}$. The notation in (A2.49) entails that $\mathsf{E}[(X_i-\mu_i)(X_j-\mu_j)] \doteq \sigma_{ij}$ denotes the $(i,j)^{th}$ element of $\boldsymbol{\Sigma}$. In the bivariate case:

$$\boldsymbol{\Sigma} = \begin{pmatrix} \sigma_{11} & \sigma_{12} \\ \sigma_{12} & \sigma_{22} \end{pmatrix}, \tag{A2.50}$$

since $\sigma_{12} = \sigma_{21}$ by definition. Thus, $\boldsymbol{\Sigma}$ is symmetric and has a determinant:

$$|\boldsymbol{\Sigma}| = \sigma_{11}\sigma_{22} - \sigma_{12}^2 = \sigma_{11}\sigma_{22}\left(1-\rho^2\right) \geq 0. \tag{A2.51}$$

A2.7.2 Conditional expectations and minimum variance

Consider two random variables (X, Z). The conditional expectation of X given $Z = z$ is defined by:

$$\mathsf{E}\left[X \mid Z = z\right] = \int_{-\infty}^{\infty} v \mathsf{f}_{\mathsf{x}|\mathsf{z}}\left(v \mid z\right) \mathrm{d}v.$$

Thus, terms like $\mathsf{E}[X|Z = z]$ follow from earlier definitions as the expectation of X in the conditional distribution $\mathsf{f}_{\mathsf{x}|\mathsf{z}}(x|z)$. Much of econometric analysis is concerned with conditional expectations and the important case of the normal distribution leads to linear regression, which is the topic of the next section.

When the first two moments of a random variable exist, a powerful minimum variance property of $\mathsf{E}[X] = \mu_x$ can be established as follows. Let $g(X)$ be any function of X such that:

$$\mathsf{E}\left[g\left(X\right)\right] = \eta_x \text{ where } |\eta_x| < \infty,$$

and consider the second moment of X around η_x:

$$\begin{aligned} \mathsf{E}\left[(X - \eta_x)^2\right] &= \mathsf{E}\left[\{(X - \mu_x) - (\eta_x - \mu_x)\}^2\right] \\ &= \mathsf{E}\left[(X - \mu_x)^2\right] - 2\mathsf{E}\left[(X - \mu_x)(\eta_x - \mu_x)\right] + (\eta_x - \mu_x)^2 \\ &\geq \mathsf{E}\left[(X - \mu_x)^2\right]. \end{aligned} \tag{A2.52}$$

The middle term vanishes because $(\eta_x - \mu_x)$ is fixed (non-stochastic) and $\mathsf{E}[X - \mu_x] = 0$, whereas $(\eta_x - \mu_x)^2 \geq 0$. Thus, the dispersion of X around η_x is minimized by the choice $\eta_x = \mu_x$. While unimpressive in the present context, a generalization of this result underlies much of the theory of prediction for conditional means of the form $\mathsf{E}[X|Z = z]$, where z might be a vector of variables, and we wish to predict the outcome of X conditional on having observed Z at a value z.

Another important result is the close link that often exists between moments and parameters of density functions. The normal density exhibits this property vividly since when $X \sim \mathsf{N}[\mu_x, \sigma_x^2]$, then $\mathsf{E}[X] = \mu_x$ and $\mathsf{E}[(X - \mu_x)^2] = \sigma_x^2$. To prove this claim for the mean, consider $Z = (X - \mu_x)/\sigma_x$: we show that $\mathsf{E}[Z] = 0$ and so $\mathsf{E}[X] = \mu_x$. Thus:

$$\mathsf{E}\left[Z\right] = (2\pi)^{-\frac{1}{2}} \int_{-\infty}^{\infty} u e^{-\frac{1}{2}u^2} \mathrm{d}u = (2\pi)^{-\frac{1}{2}} \left[\int_{0}^{\infty} u e^{-\frac{1}{2}u^2} \mathrm{d}u + \int_{-\infty}^{0} u e^{-\frac{1}{2}u^2} \mathrm{d}u\right]. \tag{A2.53}$$

Let $v = u^2/2$, so $\mathrm{d}v = u\mathrm{d}u$, then for the positive half of the integral:

$$\int_{0}^{\infty} u e^{-\frac{1}{2}u^2} \mathrm{d}u = \int_{0}^{\infty} \frac{\mathrm{d}e^{-v}}{\mathrm{d}v} \mathrm{d}v = -\int_{0}^{\infty} e^{-v} \mathrm{d}v = -\left[e^{-v}\right]_{0}^{\infty} = 1. \tag{A2.54}$$

Similarly, the negative half is -1, so $\mathsf{E}[Z] = 0$ as required. The variance is derived in an analogous manner to show $\mathsf{E}[Z^2] = 1$.

A2.7.3 Indicator functions

Next, we relate expectations directly to probabilities as follows. Let $I_{\mathcal{A}}(\omega)$ be the indicator function of the set $\mathcal{A}$ defined by:

$$I_{\mathcal{A}}(\omega) = 1 \text{ if } \omega \in \mathcal{A}; \text{ and } I_{\mathcal{A}}(\omega) = 0 \text{ if } \omega \in \mathcal{A}^c. \qquad \text{(A2.55)}$$

The indicator function is a discrete random variable by construction, and corresponds to the occurrence or otherwise of an event. Let $\mathsf{P}(\mathcal{A}) = \mathsf{P}(\{\omega \in \mathcal{A}\}) = \mathsf{p}$, then:

$$\mathsf{E}[I_{\mathcal{A}}] = \mathsf{p} I_{\mathcal{A}}(\omega \in \mathcal{A}) + (1 - \mathsf{p}) I_{\mathcal{A}}(\omega \notin \mathcal{A}) = \mathsf{p} \qquad \text{(A2.56)}$$

so $\mathsf{P}(\mathcal{A}) = \mathsf{E}[I_{\mathcal{A}}]$. In words, the probability of the event $\mathcal{A}$ occurring is the average value of the indicator function which is unity when $\mathcal{A}$ does occur and zero otherwise. Thus, there is an intimate link between the two concepts of probability and expectation, and neither is more basic than the other (see Whittle, 1970). It can be useful to switch between probability and expectation using indicator functions.

Indicator functions are useful for characterizing independence: when two events $\mathcal{A}$ and $\mathcal{B}$ are independent, then:

$$\mathsf{P}(\mathcal{A} \cap \mathcal{B}) = \mathsf{P}(\mathcal{A}) \mathsf{P}(\mathcal{B}).$$

Let $\mathcal{C}$ denote the event that both $\mathcal{A}$ and $\mathcal{B}$ occur, then, under independence, by direct application of (A2.56):

$$\mathsf{E}[I_{\mathcal{C}}] = \mathsf{E}[I_{\mathcal{A}}] \mathsf{E}[I_{\mathcal{B}}].$$

The converse also holds. Now consider two random variables X and Y: the independence of X and Y implies that:

$$\mathsf{F}_{\mathsf{x,y}}(x, y) = \mathsf{F}_{\mathsf{x}}(x) \mathsf{F}_{\mathsf{y}}(y).$$

Hence:

$$\begin{aligned} \mathsf{E}[XY] &= \int_{-\infty}^{\infty} \int_{-\infty}^{\infty} xy \mathsf{f}_{\mathsf{x,y}}(x, y) \, dx dy \\ &= \int_{-\infty}^{\infty} x \mathsf{f}_{\mathsf{x}}(x) \, dx \int_{-\infty}^{\infty} y \mathsf{f}_{\mathsf{y}}(y) \, dy = \mathsf{E}[X] \mathsf{E}[Y]. \end{aligned} \qquad \text{(A2.57)}$$

It follows that $\mathsf{E}[(X - \mu_x)(Y - \mu_y)] = \sigma_{xy} = 0$, and so the random variables are uncorrelated. However, the converse to this result is false because expectations are only a linear operator: $\mathsf{E}[XY] = \mathsf{E}[X]\mathsf{E}[Y]$ is insufficient to imply that the joint density function factorizes into the product of the marginal densities. The sufficient condition needed is that:

$$\mathsf{E}[g(X) h(Y)] = \mathsf{E}[g(X)] \mathsf{E}[h(Y)] \qquad \text{(A2.58)}$$

for all (measurable) functions $g(\cdot)$ and $h(\cdot)$.

A2.7.4 Chebychev's inequality

Finally, a remarkable property of all possible density functions which have their first two moments finite (namely $\mathsf{E}[X] = \mu_x$ when $|\mu_x| < \infty$ and $\mathsf{E}[(X - \mu_x)^2] = \sigma_x^2 < \infty$), known as Chebychev's inequality, is that:

$$\mathsf{P}\left(|X - \mu_x| \geq k\sigma_x\right) \leq \frac{1}{k^2}. \tag{A2.59}$$

For $k = 1$, this inequality is uninformative, but for $k = 2$, deviations of more than $2\sigma_x$ have a maximum probability of 25 per cent, and more extreme outcomes such as five standard deviations will be exceeded only 4 per cent of the time whatever the distribution. Generally, the inequality is conservative (e.g., for a normal distribution, two standard deviations are exceeded less than 5 per cent of the time), but can be useful in theoretical work, as well as illustrating relationships between expectations and probabilities.

The inequality is proved from the definition of $\sigma_x^2 = \mathsf{E}\left[(X - \mu_x)^2\right]$ by constructing the set $\mathcal{A} = \{x : (x - \mu_x)^2 \geq c\} \subseteq \Omega = \mathbb{R}$:

$$\begin{aligned} \sigma_x^2 &= \int_{-\infty}^{\infty} (x - \mu_x)^2 \, \mathsf{f_x}(x) \, \mathrm{d}x \\ &= \int_{\Omega} (x - \mu_x)^2 \, \mathsf{f_x}(x) \, \mathrm{d}x \\ &\geq \int_{\mathcal{A}} (x - \mu_x)^2 \, \mathsf{f_x}(x) \, \mathrm{d}x \\ &\geq c \int_{\mathcal{A}} \mathsf{f_x}(x) \, \mathrm{d}x = c\mathsf{E}\left[I_{\mathcal{A}}\right] = c\mathsf{P}(\mathcal{A}). \end{aligned} \tag{A2.60}$$

The first inequality follows by discarding a positive part of the positive integral, the second because $(x - \mu_x)^2 \geq c$ in $\mathcal{A}$, and the last step uses the definition of $\mathsf{P}(\cdot)$. Since:

$$\mathsf{P}(\mathcal{A}) = \mathsf{P}\left(\left\{(X - \mu_x)^2 \geq c\right\}\right), \tag{A2.61}$$

letting $c = k^2\sigma_x^2$ in (A2.60), then from (A2.61):

$$\sigma_x^2 \geq k^2\sigma_x^2 \mathsf{P}\left(\left\{(X - \mu_x)^2 \geq k^2\sigma_x^2\right\}\right) \tag{A2.62}$$

or equivalently, $\mathsf{P}(|X - \mu_x| \geq k\sigma_x) \leq 1/k^2$. This inequality is one of a large class used in proofs of limiting distributional results (see Ch.A4).

A2.8 Bivariate normal distribution

A2.8.1 Change of variable

Consider two random variables denoted Y_1 and Y_2. To express these in terms of standardized variables (X_1, X_2) (i.e. with means of zero and standard deviations of unity), let $X_1 = (Y_1 - \mu_{y_1})/\sigma_{y_1}$ and $X_2 = (Y_2 - \mu_{y_2})/\sigma_{y_2}$ so that $Y_1 = \sigma_{y_1}X_1 + \mu_{y_1}$ and $Y_2 = \sigma_{y_2}X_2 + \mu_{y_2}$. This transform involves a multivariate change of variable extending §A2.5.3. The events are preserved by such a transform, and it is usually easy to derive the change in the spaces of the random variables. The Jacobian J of the transformation from $\boldsymbol{y}' = (y_1 : y_2)$ to $\boldsymbol{x}' = (x_1 : x_2)$ is the absolute value of the determinant of the (vector) derivative:

$$J = \|\boldsymbol{J}\| = \left\| \frac{\partial \boldsymbol{x}}{\partial \boldsymbol{y}'} \right\|,$$

and hence:

$$\mathsf{f}_\mathsf{Y}(\boldsymbol{y}) = \mathsf{f}_\mathsf{X}(\boldsymbol{x}) \left\| \frac{\partial \boldsymbol{x}}{\partial \boldsymbol{y}'} \right\|.$$

For the above standardizing transform, when Y_1 and Y_2 are independent:

$$\left(\frac{\partial \boldsymbol{x}}{\partial \boldsymbol{y}'} \right) = \begin{pmatrix} \frac{\partial x_1}{\partial y_1} & \frac{\partial x_1}{\partial y_2} \\ \frac{\partial x_2}{\partial y_1} & \frac{\partial x_2}{\partial y_2} \end{pmatrix} = \begin{pmatrix} \frac{1}{\sigma_{y_1}} & 0 \\ 0 & \frac{1}{\sigma_{y_2}} \end{pmatrix}; \tag{A2.63}$$

since both terms are positive:

$$\left| \frac{\partial \boldsymbol{x}}{\partial \boldsymbol{y}'} \right| = \frac{1}{\sigma_{y_1}\sigma_{y_2}}.$$

More general transforms are derived in a similar way.

A2.8.2 The bivariate normal density

Consider two standardized random variables denoted X and W with a correlation of ρ where $-1 < \rho < 1$, distributed according to a joint normal distribution. The formula for the standardized bivariate normal density $\mathsf{f}_{\mathsf{x,w}}(x, w)$ is:

$$\mathsf{f}_{\mathsf{x,w}}(x, w) = \left(2\pi\sqrt{1-\rho^2}\right)^{-1} \exp\left[-\frac{(x^2 - 2\rho x w + w^2)}{2(1-\rho^2)} \right]. \tag{A2.64}$$

Since $\exp[\cdot]$ has a non-positive argument, its value is positive but less than unity, and hence:

$$\left(2\pi\sqrt{1-\rho^2}\right)^{-1} \geq \mathsf{f}_{\mathsf{x,w}}(x, w) \geq 0. \tag{A2.65}$$

For the bivariate normal distribution $\sigma_{xy} = \rho = 0$ is necessary and sufficient to ensure independence.

Although it is difficult to integrate a univariate normal, it is not too hard to show that:

$$\int_{-\infty}^{\infty} \int_{-\infty}^{\infty} \mathsf{f}_{\mathsf{x,w}}(u, v)\, \mathrm{d}u\mathrm{d}v = 1, \tag{A2.66}$$

so that $\mathsf{f}_{\mathsf{x,w}}(x, w)$ is indeed a density. To illustrate the analysis, consider the case where X and W are independent, so that the joint is the product of the marginals:

$$\int_{-\infty}^{\infty} \int_{-\infty}^{\infty} \mathsf{f}_{\mathsf{x,w}}(u, v)\, \mathrm{d}u\mathrm{d}v = (2\pi)^{-1} \int_{-\infty}^{\infty} \int_{-\infty}^{\infty} e^{-\frac{1}{2}(u^2+v^2)} du dv. \tag{A2.67}$$

Change variables in the integration from (u, v) to (r, θ) where $u = r\sin\theta$ and $v = r\cos\theta$ when $r \in [0, \infty)$ with $\theta \in [0, 2\pi)$ and $u^2 + v^2 = r^2$. Since:

$$J = \left\| \begin{array}{cc} \frac{\partial u}{\partial r} & \frac{\partial u}{\partial \theta} \\ \frac{\partial v}{\partial r} & \frac{\partial v}{\partial \theta} \end{array} \right\| = \left| \begin{array}{cc} \sin\theta & r\cos\theta \\ -\cos\theta & r\sin\theta \end{array} \right| = r,$$

the Jacobian of the transform is r. Thus:

$$\begin{aligned} (2\pi)^{-1} \int_{-\infty}^{\infty} \int_{-\infty}^{\infty} e^{-\frac{1}{2}(u^2+v^2)} \mathrm{d}u\mathrm{d}v &= (2\pi)^{-1} \int_0^{2\pi} \mathrm{d}\theta \int_0^{\infty} re^{-\frac{1}{2}r^2} \mathrm{d}r \\ &= \int_0^{\infty} re^{-\frac{1}{2}r^2} \mathrm{d}r = 1, \end{aligned} \tag{A2.68}$$

using the result for the positive-half mean in (A2.54) (see Feller, 1971).

Linear combinations of jointly normal variables are also normal. The proof is similar in style, based on deriving the distribution of the random variables $(aX + bW : W)$ where $(X : W)$ is bivariate normal and $a \neq 0$.

A2.8.3 Conditional normal

Next, we derive the marginal distribution of W and show that it is still normal, from which we can use the formula in §A2.6 to obtain the conditional distribution of X given W namely $\mathsf{f}_{\mathsf{x}|\mathsf{w}}(x|w)$. By definition, the marginal density of W is:

$$\int_{-\infty}^{\infty} \mathsf{f}_{\mathsf{x},\mathsf{w}}(u, w)\, \mathrm{d}u. \tag{A2.69}$$

Calculating that expression for the standardized bivariate normal yields:

$$\int_{-\infty}^{\infty} \left(2\pi\sqrt{1-\rho^2}\right)^{-1} \exp\left[-\frac{(u^2 - 2\rho uw + w^2)}{2(1-\rho^2)}\right] \mathrm{d}u. \tag{A2.70}$$

The numerator in $[\cdot]$ can be rewritten as $[(u-\rho w)^2 + (1-\rho^2)w^2]$ (a result of independent interest below). Since $\exp(a+b) = \exp(a)\exp(b)$ then $\int_{-\infty}^{\infty} \mathsf{f}_{\mathsf{x},\mathsf{w}}(u, w)\mathrm{d}u$ is:

$$\begin{aligned} &\left(2\pi\sqrt{1-\rho^2}\right)^{-1} \int_{-\infty}^{\infty} \exp\left[-\frac{(u-\rho w)^2}{2(1-\rho^2)}\right] \cdot \exp\left[-\frac{(1-\rho^2)w^2}{2(1-\rho^2)}\right] \mathrm{d}u \\ &= (2\pi)^{-\frac{1}{2}} \exp\left(-\tfrac{1}{2}w^2\right) \int_{-\infty}^{\infty} \left(2\pi\left(1-\rho^2\right)\right)^{-\frac{1}{2}} \cdot \exp\left[-\frac{(u-\rho w)^2}{2(1-\rho^2)}\right] \mathrm{d}u. \end{aligned} \tag{A2.71}$$

The term inside the final integral is the density of a normal random variable with mean ρw and standard deviation $\surd(1-\rho^2)$ and hence the integral is unity. Thus, the marginal distribution of W is the term before the integral, and so is $\mathsf{N}[0, 1]$.

Also, $(X - \rho W)/\sqrt{(1-\rho^2)}$ and W are independent, standardized normal random variables since they have zero means, unit variances, are jointly normal, and have a covariance of:

$$\mathsf{E}\left[\frac{W(X-\rho W)}{\sqrt{1-\rho^2}}\right] = \frac{\mathsf{E}[WX] - \rho\mathsf{E}[W^2]}{\sqrt{1-\rho^2}} = 0, \tag{A2.72}$$

which provides a shortcut to checking the density factorization.

A2.8.4 Regression

Moreover, our efforts are worthwhile because the term inside the final integral in (A2.71) must be the conditional density since:

$$\mathsf{f}_{\mathsf{x,w}}(x,w) = \mathsf{f}_{\mathsf{x|w}}(x \mid w)\,\mathsf{f}_{\mathsf{w}}(w). \tag{A2.73}$$

Thus:

$$(X \mid W = w) \sim \mathsf{N}\left[\rho w, (1-\rho^2)\right].$$

The conditional expectation, $\mathsf{E}[X|W = w] = \rho w$, considered as a function of w, is the regression function, and ρ is the regression coefficient. However, because the random variables are standardized here, ρ is also the correlation coefficient (matching the requirement $|\rho| \leq 1$), but in general the regression coefficient will not be ρ itself. To demonstrate that claim will involve a brief, but generally useful, digression. Note that other conditional moments can be defined in a similar way, so that $\mathsf{V}[X|W = w]$ is the conditional scedastic, or variance, function. For the normal distribution, $\mathsf{V}[X|W = w] = (1-\rho^2)$ does not depend on w, so the conditional variance is said to be homoscedastic.

Reverting to the unstandardized variables, the Jacobian of the transformation from $\boldsymbol{U}'$ to $\boldsymbol{V}'$ is the obverse of (A2.63), so that $\mathsf{f}_{\mathsf{v}}(\boldsymbol{v})$ is:

$$\frac{1}{2\pi\sigma_y\sigma_z\sqrt{1-\rho^2}}\exp\left[-\frac{(y-\mu_y)^2}{2(1-\rho^2)\sigma_y^2} + \frac{\rho(y-\mu_y)(z-\mu_z)}{(1-\rho^2)\sigma_y\sigma_z} - \frac{(z-\mu_z)^2}{2(1-\rho^2)\sigma_z^2}\right].$$

The marginal distribution of Z is $\mathsf{N}[\mu_z, \sigma_z^2]$, and by an equivalent factorization to (A2.71), since $\rho = \sigma_{yz}/\sigma_y\sigma_z$ and $\sigma_y^2[1-\rho^2] = [\sigma_y^2 - (\sigma_{yz})^2/\sigma_z^2]$, then:

$$(Y \mid Z = z) \sim \mathsf{N}\left[(\mu_y - \beta\mu_z) + \beta z, \omega^2\right], \tag{A2.74}$$

where:

$$\beta = \frac{\sigma_{yz}}{\sigma_z^2} \text{ and } \omega^2 = \sigma_y^2 - \frac{(\sigma_{yz})^2}{\sigma_z^2}.$$

We comment on the implications of (A2.74) in the context of multiple regression which follows.

A2.9 Multivariate normal

A2.9.1 Multivariate normal density

Going beyond the bivariate distribution necessitates matrix formulations, but in many respects these simplify the formulae. Denote the k-dimensional multivariate normal density of a random vector $\boldsymbol{V}$ of length k by $\boldsymbol{V} \sim \mathsf{N}_k[\boldsymbol{\mu}, \boldsymbol{\Sigma}]$, where $\mathsf{E}[\boldsymbol{V}] = \boldsymbol{\mu}$ is the vector of means (i.e. for the ith element, $\mathsf{E}[V_i] = \mu_i$) and $\boldsymbol{\Sigma}$ is the variance-covariance matrix of rank k:

$$\mathsf{E}[(\boldsymbol{V} - \boldsymbol{\mu})(\boldsymbol{V} - \boldsymbol{\mu})]' = \boldsymbol{\Sigma},$$

(i.e. for the $(i, j)^{th}$ element, $\mathsf{E}[(V_i - \mu_i)(V_j - \mu_j)] = \sigma_{ij}$), then the multivariate normal density function is:

$$\mathsf{f_v}(\boldsymbol{v}) = \left[(2\pi)^k |\boldsymbol{\Sigma}|\right]^{-\frac{1}{2}} \exp\left[-\tfrac{1}{2}(\boldsymbol{v} - \boldsymbol{\mu})' \boldsymbol{\Sigma}^{-1} (\boldsymbol{v} - \boldsymbol{\mu})\right], \qquad \text{(A2.75)}$$

where $|\boldsymbol{\Sigma}|$ is the determinant of $\boldsymbol{\Sigma}$. When $k = 2$, (A2.75) specializes to the bivariate case.

A2.9.2 Multiple regression

To obtain multiple regression, partition $\boldsymbol{v}$, $\boldsymbol{\mu}$, and $\boldsymbol{\Sigma}$ conformably into:

$$\boldsymbol{v} = \begin{pmatrix} y \\ \boldsymbol{z} \end{pmatrix}, \ \boldsymbol{\mu} = \begin{pmatrix} \mu_y \\ \boldsymbol{\mu}_z \end{pmatrix} \ \text{and} \ \boldsymbol{\Sigma} = \begin{pmatrix} \sigma_{yy} & \boldsymbol{\sigma}_{zy} \\ \boldsymbol{\sigma}_{yz} & \boldsymbol{\Sigma}_{zz} \end{pmatrix} \qquad \text{(A2.76)}$$

where y is a scalar, and the sub-vector $\boldsymbol{z}$ is $(k-1)\times 1$. Thus, $\boldsymbol{\mu}_z$ and $\boldsymbol{\sigma}_{zy}$ are $(k-1)\times 1$, $\boldsymbol{\sigma}_{yz}$ is $1 \times (k-1)$, and $\boldsymbol{\Sigma}_{zz}$ is $(k-1) \times (k-1)$. The conditional distribution of Y given $\boldsymbol{Z} = \boldsymbol{z}$ is derived as in section A2.8, by factorizing the joint distribution. It is common in econometrics to adopt a shorthand where the lower-case letters denote both the outcome and the random variable (when no confusion is likely — but does sometimes ensue) and we will do so henceforth. The marginal distribution of $\boldsymbol{z}$ is a special case of the general formula in (A2.75):

$$\mathsf{f_z}(\boldsymbol{z}) = \left((2\pi)^{(k-1)} |\boldsymbol{\Sigma}_{zz}|\right)^{-\frac{1}{2}} \exp\left(-\tfrac{1}{2}(\boldsymbol{z} - \boldsymbol{\mu}_z)' \boldsymbol{\Sigma}_{zz}^{-1} (\boldsymbol{z} - \boldsymbol{\mu}_z)\right). \qquad \text{(A2.77)}$$

To derive the conditional distribution $\mathsf{f_{y|z}}(y|\boldsymbol{z})$ of y given $\boldsymbol{z}$, express $\mathsf{f_v}(\cdot)$ in the transformed space of $(y|\boldsymbol{Z} = \boldsymbol{z})$ and $\boldsymbol{z}$. From Chapter A1, using partitioned inversion:

$$\boldsymbol{\Sigma}^{-1} = \begin{pmatrix} \sigma_{yy\cdot z}^{-1} & -\sigma_{yy\cdot z}^{-1}\boldsymbol{\sigma}_{yz}\boldsymbol{\Sigma}_{zz}^{-1} \\ -\boldsymbol{\Sigma}_{zz}^{-1}\boldsymbol{\sigma}_{zy}\sigma_{yy\cdot z}^{-1} & \boldsymbol{\Sigma}_{zz}^{-1}\left(\boldsymbol{I}_{(k-1)} + \boldsymbol{\sigma}_{zy}\sigma_{yy\cdot z}^{-1}\boldsymbol{\sigma}_{yz}\boldsymbol{\Sigma}_{zz}^{-1}\right) \end{pmatrix},$$

where $\sigma_{yy\cdot z}=(\sigma_{yy} - \boldsymbol{\sigma}_{yz}\boldsymbol{\Sigma}_{zz}^{-1}\boldsymbol{\sigma}_{zy})$ and:

$$|\boldsymbol{\Sigma}| = |\boldsymbol{\Sigma}_{zz}| \left|\sigma_{yy} - \boldsymbol{\sigma}_{yz}\boldsymbol{\Sigma}_{zz}^{-1}\boldsymbol{\sigma}_{zy}\right| = |\boldsymbol{\Sigma}_{zz}| \left|\sigma_{yy\cdot z}\right|.$$

Letting $\boldsymbol{\beta} = \boldsymbol{\Sigma}_{zz}^{-1}\boldsymbol{\sigma}_{zy}$, then $(\boldsymbol{v} - \boldsymbol{\mu})'\boldsymbol{\Sigma}^{-1}(\boldsymbol{v} - \boldsymbol{\mu})$ can be factorized as:

$$\begin{aligned}&(y - \mu_y)^2 \sigma_{yy\cdot z}^{-1} - 2(\boldsymbol{z} - \boldsymbol{\mu}_z)' \boldsymbol{\beta}\sigma_{yy\cdot z}^{-1}(y - \mu_y) \\ &+ (\boldsymbol{z} - \boldsymbol{\mu}_z)' \boldsymbol{\beta}\sigma_{yy\cdot z}^{-1}\boldsymbol{\beta}'(\boldsymbol{z} - \boldsymbol{\mu}_z) + (\boldsymbol{z} - \boldsymbol{\mu}_z)' \boldsymbol{\Sigma}_{zz}^{-1}(\boldsymbol{z} - \boldsymbol{\mu}_z)\end{aligned} \tag{A2.78}$$

since $(y - \mu_y)\sigma_{yy\cdot z}^{-1}\boldsymbol{\beta}'(\boldsymbol{z} - \boldsymbol{\mu}_z)$ is a scalar and equals its transpose. On rearranging:

$$(\boldsymbol{v} - \boldsymbol{\mu})' \boldsymbol{\Sigma}^{-1}(\boldsymbol{v} - \boldsymbol{\mu}) = (y - \alpha - \boldsymbol{\beta}'\boldsymbol{z})^2 \sigma_{yy\cdot z}^{-1} + (\boldsymbol{z} - \boldsymbol{\mu}_z)' \boldsymbol{\Sigma}_{zz}^{-1}(\boldsymbol{z} - \boldsymbol{\mu}_z),$$

where $\alpha = \mu_y - \boldsymbol{\beta}'\boldsymbol{\mu}_z$. Substituting these results in $\mathsf{f}_{\mathsf{v}}(\cdot)$, then:

$$\mathsf{f}_{\mathsf{y|z}}(y \mid \boldsymbol{z}) = (2\pi\sigma_{yy\cdot z})^{-\frac{1}{2}} \exp\left(-\tfrac{1}{2}(y - \alpha - \boldsymbol{\beta}'\boldsymbol{z})^2 \sigma_{yy\cdot z}^{-1}\right),$$

so:

$$(Y \mid \boldsymbol{Z} = \boldsymbol{z}) \sim \mathsf{N}\left[\alpha + \boldsymbol{\beta}'\boldsymbol{z}, \sigma_{yy\cdot z}\right]. \tag{A2.79}$$

There are three important implications of the result in (A2.79). First, $\mathsf{E}[Y|\boldsymbol{Z} = \boldsymbol{z}]$ is a linear function of $\boldsymbol{z}$; this is dependent on having assumed a normal distribution since many distributions do not have linear regression functions. Secondly, the parameters of that conditional distribution, namely $(\alpha, \boldsymbol{\beta}, \sigma_{yy\cdot z})$ depend on all the moments of the joint distribution of $\boldsymbol{V}$. Finally, since $\boldsymbol{\sigma}_{yz}\boldsymbol{\Sigma}_{zz}^{-1}\boldsymbol{\sigma}_{zy} \geq 0$, the variance $\sigma_{yy\cdot z}$ of the conditional distribution is less than that of the unconditional distribution σ_{yy}.

A2.9.3 Multivariate regression

Multivariate regression, where $\boldsymbol{y}$ is a vector, is similar and involves partitioning $\boldsymbol{v}, \boldsymbol{\mu}$ and $\boldsymbol{\Sigma}$ into:

$$\boldsymbol{v} = \begin{pmatrix} \boldsymbol{y} \\ \boldsymbol{z} \end{pmatrix}, \ \boldsymbol{\mu} = \begin{pmatrix} \boldsymbol{\mu}_y \\ \boldsymbol{\mu}_z \end{pmatrix} \text{ and } \boldsymbol{\Sigma} = \begin{pmatrix} \boldsymbol{\Sigma}_{yy} & \boldsymbol{\Sigma}_{zy} \\ \boldsymbol{\Sigma}_{yz} & \boldsymbol{\Sigma}_{zz} \end{pmatrix}, \tag{A2.80}$$

where the $\boldsymbol{y}$ and $\boldsymbol{z}$ sub-vectors are $n \times 1$ and $m \times 1$ with $n + m = k$. The conditional distribution of $\boldsymbol{Y}$ given $\boldsymbol{Z} = \boldsymbol{z}$ is derived as in §A2.9.2. First, the marginal distribution of $\boldsymbol{z}$ is the same as (A2.77) with m in place of $k - 1$. The conditional distribution $\mathsf{f}_{\mathsf{y|z}}(\boldsymbol{y}|\boldsymbol{z})$ of $\boldsymbol{Y}$ given $\boldsymbol{Z}$ again transforms $\mathsf{f}_{\mathsf{v}}(\cdot)$ using the partitioned inverse:

$$\boldsymbol{\Sigma}^{-1} = \begin{pmatrix} \boldsymbol{\Sigma}_{yy\cdot z}^{-1} & -\boldsymbol{\Sigma}_{yy\cdot z}^{-1}\boldsymbol{\Sigma}_{yz}\boldsymbol{\Sigma}_{zz}^{-1} \\ -\boldsymbol{\Sigma}_{zz}^{-1}\boldsymbol{\Sigma}_{zy}\boldsymbol{\Sigma}_{yy\cdot z}^{-1} & \boldsymbol{\Sigma}_{zz}^{-1}\left(\boldsymbol{I}_m + \boldsymbol{\Sigma}_{zy}\boldsymbol{\Sigma}_{yy\cdot z}^{-1}\boldsymbol{\Sigma}_{yz}\boldsymbol{\Sigma}_{zz}^{-1}\right) \end{pmatrix},$$

where now $\boldsymbol{\Sigma}_{yy\cdot z} = (\boldsymbol{\Sigma}_{yy} - \boldsymbol{\Sigma}_{yz}\boldsymbol{\Sigma}_{zz}^{-1}\boldsymbol{\Sigma}_{zy})$ and:

$$|\boldsymbol{\Sigma}| = |\boldsymbol{\Sigma}_{zz}|\left|\boldsymbol{\Sigma}_{yy} - \boldsymbol{\Sigma}_{yz}\boldsymbol{\Sigma}_{zz}^{-1}\boldsymbol{\Sigma}_{zy}\right| = |\boldsymbol{\Sigma}_{zz}||\boldsymbol{\Sigma}_{yy\cdot z}|.$$

Letting $\boldsymbol{\Pi}_1 = \boldsymbol{\Sigma}_{yz}\boldsymbol{\Sigma}_{zz}^{-1}$, then $(\boldsymbol{v} - \boldsymbol{\mu})'\boldsymbol{\Sigma}^{-1}(\boldsymbol{v} - \boldsymbol{\mu})$ becomes:

$$\begin{aligned}&(\boldsymbol{y} - \boldsymbol{\mu}_y)' \boldsymbol{\Sigma}_{yy\cdot z}^{-1}(\boldsymbol{y} - \boldsymbol{\mu}_y) - 2(\boldsymbol{z} - \boldsymbol{\mu}_z)' \boldsymbol{\Pi}_1'\boldsymbol{\Sigma}_{yy\cdot z}^{-1}(\boldsymbol{y} - \boldsymbol{\mu}_y) \\ &+ (\boldsymbol{z} - \boldsymbol{\mu}_z)' \boldsymbol{\Pi}_1'\boldsymbol{\Sigma}_{yy\cdot z}^{-1}\boldsymbol{\Pi}_1(\boldsymbol{z} - \boldsymbol{\mu}_z) + (\boldsymbol{z} - \boldsymbol{\mu}_z)' \boldsymbol{\Sigma}_{zz}^{-1}(\boldsymbol{z} - \boldsymbol{\mu}_z),\end{aligned}$$

or:

$$(\boldsymbol{y}-\boldsymbol{\pi}_0-\boldsymbol{\Pi}_1\boldsymbol{z})'\,\boldsymbol{\Sigma}_{yy\cdot z}^{-1}\,(\boldsymbol{y}-\boldsymbol{\pi}_0-\boldsymbol{\Pi}_1\boldsymbol{z})+(\boldsymbol{z}-\boldsymbol{\mu}_z)'\,\boldsymbol{\Sigma}_{zz}^{-1}\,(\boldsymbol{z}-\boldsymbol{\mu}_z),$$

where $\boldsymbol{\pi}_0=\boldsymbol{\mu}_y-\boldsymbol{\Pi}_1\boldsymbol{\mu}_z$. Substituting into $\mathsf{f}_{\mathsf{v}}(\cdot)$ yields $\mathsf{f}_{\mathsf{y}|\mathsf{z}}(\boldsymbol{y}|\boldsymbol{z})$ as the direct generalization:

$$\mathsf{f}_{\mathsf{y}|\mathsf{z}}(\boldsymbol{y}\mid\boldsymbol{z})=\left((2\pi)^n\left|\boldsymbol{\Sigma}_{yy\cdot z}\right|\right)^{-\frac{1}{2}}\exp\left[-\tfrac{1}{2}(\boldsymbol{y}-\boldsymbol{\pi}_0-\boldsymbol{\Pi}_1\boldsymbol{z})'\,\boldsymbol{\Sigma}_{yy\cdot z}^{-1}\,(\boldsymbol{y}-\boldsymbol{\pi}_0-\boldsymbol{\Pi}_1\boldsymbol{z})\right]$$

and hence:

$$(\boldsymbol{Y}\mid\boldsymbol{Z}=\boldsymbol{z})\sim\mathsf{N}_n\left[\boldsymbol{\pi}_0+\boldsymbol{\Pi}_1\boldsymbol{z},\,\boldsymbol{\Sigma}_{yy\cdot z}\right]. \tag{A2.81}$$

As noted above, once matrices are used, more general cases follow easily. Here, $\boldsymbol{\Sigma}_{yz}\boldsymbol{\Sigma}_{zz}^{-1}\boldsymbol{\Sigma}_{zy}$ is positive semi-definite, so $\boldsymbol{\Sigma}_{yy\cdot z}$ is 'smaller' than $\boldsymbol{\Sigma}_{yy}$ in that $\boldsymbol{\Sigma}_{yy\cdot z}\preceq\boldsymbol{\Sigma}_{yy}$ where '$\preceq$' denotes an appropriate metric such as the trace or determinant.

A2.9.4 Functions of normal variables: χ^2, t and F distributions

Three important functions of normally distributed random variables are distributed as the χ^2, t, and F distributions. First we define these three distributions then consider generalizations. Let $Z\sim\mathsf{N}[0,1]$, then:

$$Z^2\sim\chi^2(1),$$

where $\chi^2(1)$ is the chi-square distribution with one degree of freedom. For a set of k independent random variables $Z_i\sim\mathsf{IN}[0,1]$:

$$\sum_{i=1}^{k}Z_i^2\sim\chi^2(k), \tag{A2.82}$$

where $\chi^2(k)$ is the χ^2-distribution with k degrees of freedom.

Next, let $X\sim\mathsf{N}[\mu_x,\sigma_x^2]$, and let $\eta(k)$ be a $\chi^2(k)$ distributed independently of X then:

$$\tau=\frac{\sqrt{k}\,(X-\mu_x)}{\sigma_x\sqrt{\eta(k)}}\sim\mathsf{t}(k),$$

where $\mathsf{t}(k)$ is Student's t-distribution with k degrees of freedom.

Thirdly, let $\eta_1(k_1)$ and $\eta_2(k_2)$ be two independent chi-squares of k_1 and k_2 degrees of freedom, then:

$$\phi=\frac{(\eta_1(k_1)/k_1)}{(\eta_2(k_2)/k_2)}\sim F(k_1,k_2),$$

where $F(k_1,k_2)$ is the F-distribution with k_1 and k_2 degrees of freedom. By using these three results: $\mathsf{t}(k)^2\sim F(1,k)$. All of these distributions have been tabulated (in more modern terms, programmed into computer packages), and occur frequently in empirical research, since an underlying normal distribution is often assumed, or is used as an approximation in large samples (see Ch.A4).

Figures A2.4a–d show the shapes based on 10 000 random drawings from: (a) $\chi^2(6)$; (b) $F(6,50)$; (c) $\mathsf{t}(50)$, and (d) $\mathsf{N}[0,1]$. The first two are skewed to the right (i.e. asymmetric) and have to be positive (so are truncated at zero by definition), whereas (c) and (d) are both symmetric, have neither upper nor lower bounds, and have similar bell-like shapes.

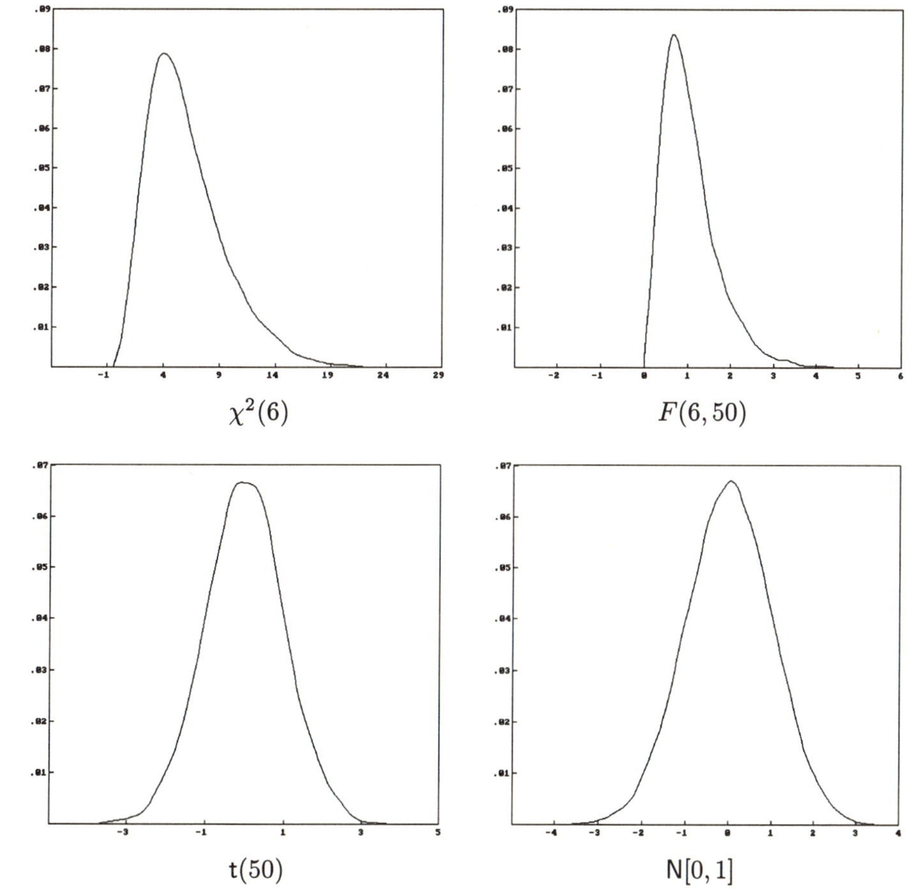

Fig. A2.4 Distributional shapes

In the context of the multivariate normal, let $\boldsymbol{V} \sim \mathsf{N}_k[\boldsymbol{\mu}, \boldsymbol{\Sigma}]$, then:

$$\eta(k) = (\boldsymbol{V} - \boldsymbol{\mu})' \boldsymbol{\Sigma}^{-1} (\boldsymbol{V} - \boldsymbol{\mu}) \sim \chi^2(k). \tag{A2.83}$$

This result follows from the definition of a χ^2 by noting that any positive-definite matrix $\boldsymbol{\Sigma}$ can be written as $\boldsymbol{\Sigma} = \boldsymbol{H}\boldsymbol{H}'$ where $\boldsymbol{H}$ is a non-singular lower-triangular matrix, so that:

$$\boldsymbol{H}^{-1}(\boldsymbol{V} - \boldsymbol{\mu}) = \boldsymbol{\zeta} \sim \mathsf{N}_k[\mathbf{0}, \boldsymbol{I}_k],$$

and hence from (A2.83):

$$\eta(k) = \zeta'\zeta = \sum_{i=1}^{k} \zeta_i^2 \sim \chi^2(k). \tag{A2.84}$$

Partition ζ' into the k_1 and k_2 independent components $(\zeta_1' : \zeta_2')$, each of which is normal, then for $k_1 + k_2 = k$:

$$\eta_1(k_1) = \zeta_1'\zeta_1 \sim \chi^2(k_1) \text{ and } \eta_2(k_2) = \zeta_2'\zeta_2 \sim \chi^2(k_2) \tag{A2.85}$$

are also independent.

A2.10 Exercises

A2.1 A die has six faces with the set of possible outcomes defined by:

$$\mathcal{C} = \{c; c = 1, 2, 3, 4, 5, 6\}.$$

Let $\mathcal{C}_1 = \{c; c = 2, 4, 6\}$ and $\mathcal{C}_2 = \{c; c = 1, 2, 3, 5\}$. When $\mathsf{P}(\{c\}) = 1/6\ \forall c \in \mathcal{C}$:

(a) Calculate $\mathsf{P}(\mathcal{C}_1), \mathsf{P}(\mathcal{C}_2), \mathsf{P}(\mathcal{C}_1 \cup \mathcal{C}_2), \mathsf{P}(\mathcal{C}_1 \cap \mathcal{C}_2)$.

(b) Show that: $\mathsf{P}(\mathcal{C}_1 \cap \mathcal{C}_2) \leq \mathsf{P}(\mathcal{C}_1) \leq \mathsf{P}(\mathcal{C}_1 \cup \mathcal{C}_2) \leq \mathsf{P}(\mathcal{C}_1) + \mathsf{P}(\mathcal{C}_2)$.

A2.2 Let $\mathcal{C} = \{c; 0 < c < \infty\}$ and let $\mathcal{C}_1,\ \mathcal{C}_2 \subset \mathcal{C}$ be given by $\mathcal{C}_1 = \{c; 4 < c < \infty\}$ and $\mathcal{C}_2 = \{c; 2 < c < 8\}$.

(a) For $\mathsf{P}(\mathcal{C}) = \int_{\mathcal{C}} e^{-x} dx$, evaluate $\mathsf{P}(\mathcal{C}_1), \mathsf{P}(\mathcal{C}_1^c), \mathsf{P}(\mathcal{C}_2)$ and $\mathsf{P}(\mathcal{C}_2^c)$.

(b) Evaluate $\mathsf{P}(\mathcal{C}_1 \cap \mathcal{C}_2)$ and $\mathsf{P}(\mathcal{C}_1 \cup \mathcal{C}_2)$.

A2.3 The probability of a head $\{H\}$ is p and a tail $\{T\}$ is $(1-\mathsf{p})$ on independent tosses of a coin. Let $\mathcal{B}$ denote the event that two successive heads are observed earlier than the first occurence of two successive tails.

(a) When $\mathcal{A}$ is the outcome on the first toss, show that:

$$\mathsf{P}(\mathcal{B} \mid \mathcal{A} = \{H\}) = \mathsf{p} + \mathsf{p}[(1-\mathsf{p})\mathsf{p}] + \mathsf{p}[(1-\mathsf{p})\mathsf{p}]^2 + \cdots = \frac{\mathsf{p}}{[1 - \mathsf{p}(1-\mathsf{p})]}.$$

(b) Find a similar expression for $\mathsf{P}(\mathcal{B}|\mathcal{A} = \{T\})$.

(c) Using:

$$\mathsf{P}(\mathcal{B}) = \mathsf{P}(\mathcal{B} \mid \mathcal{A} = \{H\})\,\mathsf{P}(\mathcal{A} = \{H\}) + \mathsf{P}(\mathcal{B} \mid \mathcal{A} = \{T\})\,\mathsf{P}(\mathcal{A} = \{T\})$$

find $\mathsf{P}(\mathcal{B})$. Check your answer by symmetry (two successive tails before two successive heads) when $(1 - \mathsf{p}) = \mathsf{p}$.

A2.4 Consider a random variable X which is uniformly distributed between a and b, when $b > a$, so $X \sim \mathsf{U}[a, b]$ with $\mathsf{f_x}(x) = (b - a)^{-1}$ for $a \leq x \leq b$ and zero elsewhere.

(a) Show that $\mathsf{f_x}(x)$ is a density function, derive the distribution function $\mathsf{F_x}(x) = \int_{-\infty}^{x} \mathsf{f_x}(z)\mathrm{d}z$ and calculate $\mathsf{E}[X] = \int_a^b z\mathsf{f_x}(z)\mathrm{d}z$ and $\mathsf{E}[X^2] = \int_a^b z^2\mathsf{f_x}(z)\mathrm{d}z$. Find $\mathsf{P}(a \leq X \leq \frac{b-a}{2})$.

(b) When X_1, X_2 are two drawings from $\mathsf{U}[0,1]$ and $\bar{X} = (X_1+X_2)/2$, draw $\mathsf{f_x}(\bar{x})$. Find $\mathsf{P}(1/4 \leq \bar{X} < 1/2)$.

(c) When $a = 0$ and $b = 1$, so $X \sim \mathsf{U}[0,1]$, show that its distribution function is given by:

$$\mathsf{F_x}(x) = \begin{cases} 0 & \text{for } x < 0 \\ x & \text{for } 0 \leq x \leq 1 \\ 1 & \text{for } x > 1. \end{cases}$$

Hence show that for $0 < x < 1$, $x = \mathsf{F_x}^{-1}(x)$ as well.

A2.5 For $\lambda > 0$, and $y > 0$, consider the exponential distribution:

$$\mathsf{F_y}(y) = 1 - \exp(-\lambda y),$$

(zero for $y \leq 0$). Show that $\mathsf{F_y}(\cdot)$ satisfies the requirements of a CDF. Also show that an exponentially-distributed random variable Y can be obtained from a uniformly-distributed random variable X by:

$$Y = -\frac{\log(1-X)}{\lambda},$$

when $\lambda \neq 0$ (use the previous question for $\mathsf{F_y}^{-1}(\cdot)$). This result underpins the generation of non-uniform random numbers on a computer, as in PcNaive.

A2.6 The standardized normal distribution is characterized by the density:

$$\mathsf{f_x}(x) = (2\pi)^{-\frac{1}{2}} \exp\left(-\frac{x^2}{2}\right) \quad \text{for } -\infty < x < \infty.$$

Show that $\mathsf{E}(X) = 0$ and $\mathsf{E}[X^2] = 1$. This density is usually shown as $\mathsf{N}[0,1]$ since its mean and variance fully describe it. Calculate some values of the density and plot them.

Let $Y = (\sigma_y X + \mu_y)$ (so $X = (Y - \mu_y)/\sigma_y$), where Y has the density $\mathsf{f_y}(y)$, then by using the result that (for $y = g(x)$ where $x = g^{-1}(y)$):

$$\mathsf{f_y}(y) = \mathsf{f_x}(x)\left|\frac{\partial x}{\partial y}\right|,$$

show that $Y \sim \mathsf{N}[\mu_y, \sigma_y^2]$.

A2.7 For two events $\mathcal{A}$ and $\mathcal{B}$: $\mathsf{P}(\mathcal{A},\mathcal{B}) = \mathsf{P}(\mathcal{A}|\mathcal{B})\mathsf{P}(\mathcal{B})$. This definition applies to CDFs and to joint densities:

$$\mathsf{f_{y,z}}(y,z) = \mathsf{f_{y|z}}(y \mid z)\,\mathsf{f_z}(z),$$

where $\mathsf{f}_{\mathsf{y}|\mathsf{z}}(y|z)$ is the conditional distribution of Y given $Z = z$, so that:

$$\mathsf{f}_{\mathsf{y}|\mathsf{z}}(y \mid z) = \frac{\mathsf{f}_{\mathsf{y},\mathsf{z}}(y, z)}{\mathsf{f}_{\mathsf{z}}(z)},$$

providing that $\mathsf{f}_{\mathsf{z}}(z) > 0$ [where $\mathsf{f}_{\mathsf{z}}(z)$ is the marginal distribution of z]. Apply this reasoning to the bivariate normal distribution to derive: (i) the joint distribution; (ii) one marginal distribution; and (iii) one conditional distribution.

A2.8 Consider a random variable $X > 0$ with an exponential distribution for $\lambda > 0$:

$$\mathsf{F}_{\mathsf{x}}(x; \lambda) = 1 - \exp(-\lambda x),$$

which is zero for $x \leq 0$. Obtain the density function of X, and hence calculate $\mathsf{E}[X]$ and $\mathsf{E}[(X - \mathsf{E}[X])^2]$. (Hint: these are functions of λ.) What is the family of density functions $\mathsf{f}_{\mathsf{x}}(x; \lambda)$ of X? Sketch $\mathsf{f}_{\mathsf{x}}(x; \lambda)$ for $x = 1, 2, 3$ when $\lambda = 1, 2$; do the graphs suggest that data on X might help to determine the value of λ when that parameter is unknown? From what you have already established about $\mathsf{E}[X]$, discuss how you might estimate λ from data on X.

A2.9 Consider the joint distribution function:

$$\mathsf{F}_{\mathsf{x},\mathsf{y}}(x, y; \lambda) = 1 - e^{-\lambda x} - e^{-\lambda y} + e^{-\lambda(x+y)} \text{ for } x, y, \lambda > 0.$$

Show that X and Y are independent and hence derive the marginal distributions of X and Y. What does your result tell you about $\mathsf{E}[XY]$? How might you evaluate from data on X and Y whether (i) each is exponentially distributed; (ii) they are independent?

A2.10 The standardized bivariate normal distribution of two random variables X and Y with a correlation of ρ is characterized by the density ($|\rho| < 1$):

$$\mathsf{f}_{\mathsf{x},\mathsf{y}}(x, y; \rho) = (2\pi)^{-1}\left(1 - \rho^2\right)^{-\frac{1}{2}} \exp\left(-\frac{[x^2 - 2\rho xy + y^2]}{2(1 - \rho^2)}\right),$$

for $-\infty < x, y < \infty$. What are $\mathsf{E}[XY]$ and $\mathsf{E}[Y|X = x]$ (the latter as a function of x and ρ)? Show that X and Y are independent if $\rho = 0$. Derive $\log(\mathsf{f}_{\mathsf{x},\mathsf{y}}(x, y; \rho))$ and differentiate that expression with respect to ρ. Can you solve the result for ρ?

A3

Statistical Theory

This chapter focuses on modelling random processes by specifying an appropriate family of distributions, and estimating the values of their parameters from observed data. Observations are summarized in terms of sample statistics and their sampling distributions. The χ^2, t, and F distributions, which result when the random variables are normally distributed, are considered. Sufficient, and minimal sufficient, statistics are discussed. The likelihood function is used to link parameters and statistics, leading to the method of maximum likelihood estimation (MLE) in which the score, Hessian, and information matrix play a major role. The properties of MLEs are considered, and related to the Cramér–Rao bound for efficient estimation. Alternative estimators of their variances are noted. Hypothesis testing is considered in relation to powerful test procedures. Non-parametric density estimation is described. Finally, the linear regression model is discussed in detail.

A3.1 Sampling distributions

A3.1.1 Statistics

Let $\boldsymbol{X}' = (X_1 \ldots X_T)$ denote a set of T random variables defined with respect to the probability space $(\Omega, \mathcal{F}, \mathsf{P})$. In this section, we take $(X_1 \ldots X_T)$ to be independently sampled from the common data density function $\mathsf{D}_{\mathsf{x}}(x|\boldsymbol{\theta})$ for $\boldsymbol{\theta} \in \Theta \subseteq \mathbb{R}^k$, reserving the notation $\mathsf{F}(\cdot)$ for distributions of functions of the sample $\boldsymbol{X}$. Letting $\boldsymbol{x}' = (x_1 \ldots x_T)$:

$$\mathsf{D}_{\mathsf{X}}(\boldsymbol{x} \mid \boldsymbol{\theta}) = \mathsf{D}_{\mathsf{X}}(x_1 \ldots x_T \mid \boldsymbol{\theta}) = \prod_{t=1}^{T} \mathsf{D}_{\mathsf{x}}(x_t \mid \boldsymbol{\theta}).$$

Chapter A2 discussed sequential factorization when independence is not valid; for the present, independence is simplifying but not essential. The homogeneity assumption, where all random variables in the sample are drawn from the same density, is more restrictive, but is discussed in the main text and weakened in important respects in Chapter A4. One of the simplest examples of this formulation is when $X_t \sim \mathsf{IN}[\mu_x, \sigma_x^2]$ with $|\mu_x| < \infty$, and $0 < \sigma_x^2 < \infty$, so that $\{X_t\}$ constitutes an independent normal sample, $\boldsymbol{\theta}' = (\mu_x, \sigma_x^2)$ and $\Theta \subseteq \mathbb{R} \times \mathbb{R}_+$ where $\times$ denotes the Cartesian product.

A (measurable) function $g(\cdot)$ of one or more of these random variables is a statistic if it does not depend on any unknowns. Thus, $g(X_1 \dots X_T)$ is a statistic if it can be calculated from the random variables without knowing anything about $\mathsf{D_X}(\boldsymbol{x}|\boldsymbol{\theta})$. Since the distribution of $g(\cdot)$ depends on the distribution of the original $\{X_t\}$, the choice of which functions $g(\cdot)$ to calculate depends on conjectures (or knowledge) about the form of $\mathsf{D_X}(\boldsymbol{x}|\boldsymbol{\theta})$, and the objectives of the statistical study. Investigating the properties of alternative choices, and specifying criteria to decide on their 'goodness', are concerns of statistical theory. In this chapter, we assume that the form of $\mathsf{D_X}(\boldsymbol{x}|\boldsymbol{\theta})$ is known but that the population value $\boldsymbol{\theta}_p$ of $\boldsymbol{\theta}$ is unknown.

A3.1.2 Derived distributions

Even when $\mathsf{D_X}(\boldsymbol{x}|\boldsymbol{\theta})$ is known, deriving the distribution of $g(\cdot)$ can be difficult, especially when $g(\cdot)$ depends on $\{X_t\}$ in a complicated way. For scalar random variables and 'well-behaved' functions $g(\cdot)$, such that $g^{-1}(\cdot)$ exists, the mapping from X to $Y = g(X)$ was obtained in Chapter A2 as:

$$\mathsf{D_y}(y) = \mathsf{D_x}(x) \left| \frac{\mathrm{d}x}{\mathrm{d}y} \right| = \mathsf{D_x}(x) \left| \frac{\mathrm{d}g^{-1}}{\mathrm{d}y} \right|. \tag{A3.1}$$

However, in many cases, the distributions of statistics have to be derived directly. Well-known examples of statistics are the sample mean ($\bar{X}$), and sample variance ($\tilde{\sigma}_x^2$, where $\tilde{}$ denotes a statistic interpreted as estimating some parameter: see §A3.1.3) defined by:

$$\bar{X} = T^{-1} \sum_{t=1}^{T} X_t \quad \text{and} \quad \tilde{\sigma}_x^2 = (T-1)^{-1} \sum_{t=1}^{T} \left(X_t - \bar{X}\right)^2. \tag{A3.2}$$

When $X_t \sim \mathsf{IN}[\mu_x, \sigma_x^2]$, the population mean and variance of X_t are $\mathsf{E}[X_t] = \mu_x$ and $\mathsf{V}[X_t] = \sigma_x^2$. The sample mean is a linear function of the $\{X_t\}$, so its properties can be derived from the results in Chapter A2:

$$\mathsf{E}\left[\bar{X}\right] = T^{-1} \sum_{t=1}^{T} \mathsf{E}\left[X_t\right] = \mu_x,$$

and since $\mathsf{E}[(X_t - \mu_x)(X_s - \mu_x)] = 0 \; \forall t \neq s$:

$$\begin{aligned} \mathsf{V}\left[\bar{X}\right] &= \mathsf{E}\left[\left(\bar{X} - \mu_x\right)^2\right] &&= \mathsf{E}\left[\left(T^{-1} \textstyle\sum_{t=1}^{T} \left(X_t - \mu_x\right)\right)^2\right] \\ &= \mathsf{E}\left[T^{-2} \textstyle\sum_{t=1}^{T} \left(X_t - \mu_x\right)^2\right] &&= T^{-1}\sigma_x^2. \end{aligned}$$

Since the $\{X_t\}$ are jointly normal:

$$\bar{X} \sim \mathsf{N}\left[\mu_x, \frac{\sigma_x^2}{T}\right]. \tag{A3.3}$$

Further:

$$T^{-1}\sum_{t=1}^{T}\left(X_t-\bar{X}\right)^2 = T^{-1}\sum_{t=1}^{T}\left[\left(X_t-\mu_x\right)-\left(\bar{X}-\mu_x\right)\right]^2$$
$$= T^{-1}\sum_{t=1}^{T}\left[\left(X_t-\mu_x\right)^2-\left(\bar{X}-\mu_x\right)^2\right], \tag{A3.4}$$

since the cross-product is $(\bar{X}-\mu_x)^2$ by definition of $\bar{X}$. From (A3.3), $\mathsf{E}[(\bar{X}-\mu_x)^2] = T^{-1}\sigma_x^2$, so using (A3.4):

$$\mathsf{E}\left[\tilde{\sigma}_x^2\right] = (T-1)^{-1}\,\mathsf{E}\left[\sum_{t=1}^{T}\left(X_t-\bar{X}\right)^2\right] = (T-1)^{-1}\sum_{t=1}^{T}\left(\sigma_x^2-T^{-1}\sigma_x^2\right) = \sigma_x^2.$$

This result is why many authors divide by $(T-1)$ rather than T to define the sample variance.

Thus, the sample mean has the same population mean as the original random variables, and a variance which is smaller by a factor of T; the sample variance has a mean equal to the population variance. Few cases will prove so simple in econometrics although, in principle, when $\mathsf{D}_\mathsf{x}(x|\boldsymbol{\theta})$ is known we can calculate $\mathsf{P}(X \leq x)$ and $\mathsf{P}(\bar{X} \leq r)$ etc. More generally, letting S denote a statistic, we seek to derive $\mathsf{F}_\mathsf{s}(s;\boldsymbol{\theta})$ from $\mathsf{D}_\mathsf{X}(\boldsymbol{x}|\boldsymbol{\theta})$.

A sample realization $\boldsymbol{x}' = (x_1 \ldots x_T)$ is a set of observations on the random variables $(X_1 \ldots X_T)$. The values of $\boldsymbol{x}$ lie in an observation space $\mathcal{X}$ which is usually a subset of T-dimensional Euclidean space (real numbers). From the realization, we can calculate analogues of the sample statistics such as:[1]

$$\bar{x} = T^{-1}\sum_{t=1}^{T}x_t \text{ and } v^2 = (T-1)^{-1}\sum_{t=1}^{T}\left(x_t-\bar{x}\right)^2. \tag{A3.5}$$

Entities such as $\boldsymbol{x}$, $\bar{x}$, and v^2 are just numbers, to be interpreted in the light of the previously derived distributions of the equivalent functions of the random variables. Imagine drawing N independent samples of size T on $\{X_t\}$, with means $\{\bar{x}_1 \ldots \bar{x}_N\}$ (say, for large N), and calculating their empirical distribution $\mathsf{F}_{\bar{\mathsf{x}}}(\bar{x};\boldsymbol{\theta})$, then this should be a facsimile of $\mathsf{P}(\bar{X} \leq r)$. We will often use this repeated-sampling notion below. We can now compute the probabilities associated with having observed certain realizations of the random variables. For example, when $X_t \sim \mathsf{IN}[1,1]$ and $T = 16$, from (A3.3):

$$\mathsf{P}\left(\left|\bar{X}\right| \geq 1.5\right) \simeq 0.05, \tag{A3.6}$$

so we should be unlikely to observe $|\bar{x}|$ any larger than 1.5.

[1] The divisor of $(T-1)$ for v^2 (called the degrees of freedom) adjusts for subtracting the sample mean. When many parameters have been estimated, as regularly occurs in econometrics, some adjustment for degrees of freedom is essential, but for a defence of T, see Hogg and Craig (1978).

Three difficulties need to be resolved. First, given $\mathsf{D}_\mathsf{X}(\boldsymbol{x}|\boldsymbol{\theta})$, we need methods for deriving the distributions $\mathsf{F}_\mathsf{s}(s;\boldsymbol{\theta})$ of statistics like $S = g(X_1 \dots X_T)$; secondly, we must develop methods for learning about $\boldsymbol{\theta}$ from sample realizations $(x_1 \dots x_T)$; and thirdly, we must choose good methods from those alternative ways, which pre-supposes criteria for judging goodness in this context. The method on which we focus for learning about $\boldsymbol{\theta}$ is that of maximum likelihood, discussed in §A3.3 following a discussion of the likelihood function in §A3.2.

In this chapter, we only consider (jointly) normal independent random variables with identical distributions, in which case, sampling distributions will be functions of normal variates. Several of the functions noted in Chapter A2 are discussed in §A3.1.3, namely χ^2, t, and F distributions. Chapter A4 deals with more general sampling distributions, using large sample approximations. Some important criteria for selecting statistics are described in sections A3.1.4–A3.1.6.

A3.1.3 χ^2, t, and F distributions

A range of useful results can be derived for the distributions of statistics when X_t is normally distributed. We denote the sample mean by $\hat{\mu}_x$ for consistency with later notation, so as shown in (A3.3), $\hat{\mu}_x \sim \mathsf{N}[\mu_x, \sigma_x^2/T]$. To establish that $\tilde{\sigma}_x^2$ is a function of a $\chi^2(T-1)$ distribution, six results are needed.

First, the formula for the distribution of $\chi^2(r)$ is:

$$\mathsf{f}_{\chi^2(r)}[z] = 2^{-(r/2)}\Gamma\left(\frac{r}{2}\right)^{-1} z^{(r/2-1)}e^{-z/2} \quad \text{for } z > 0,$$

where $\Gamma(r) = (r-1)\Gamma(r-1)$ and $\Gamma(1/2) = \sqrt{\pi}$. Next, we have shown that $\mathsf{E}[\tilde{\sigma}_x^2] = \sigma_x^2$. Thirdly, noting that $\mathsf{E}[(\hat{\mu}_x - \mu_x)^3] = 0$ by the symmetry of the normal distribution, and using (A3.4):

$$\begin{aligned}
\mathsf{E}\left[\tilde{\sigma}_x^2\left(\hat{\mu}_x - \mu_x\right)\right] &= (T-1)^{-1}\,\mathsf{E}\sum_{t=1}^{T}\left[\left(X_t - \hat{\mu}_x\right)^2\left(\hat{\mu}_x - \mu_x\right)\right] \\
&= (T-1)^{-1}\sum_{t=1}^{T}\mathsf{E}\left[\left(X_t - \mu_x\right)^2\left(\hat{\mu}_x - \mu_x\right) - \left(\hat{\mu}_x - \mu_x\right)^3\right] \\
&= \left[T\left(T-1\right)\right]^{-1}\sum_{t=1}^{T}\sum_{s=1}^{T}\mathsf{E}\left[\left(X_t - \mu_x\right)^2\left(X_s - \mu_x\right)\right] = 0,
\end{aligned}$$

since when $t = s$, odd moments around the mean vanish and when $t \neq s$, cross-products are zero because the $\{X_t\}$ are independent. Fourthly, to prove that $\hat{\mu}_x$ and $\tilde{\sigma}_x^2$ are independent requires more powerful tools which will not be developed until §A3.7, so we assume the truth of that claim at this stage. Fifthly, from the definition of a χ^2, the transform $(X_t - \mu_x)^2/\sigma_x^2 \sim \chi^2(1)$ and hence:

$$\sum_{t=1}^{T}\frac{\left(X_t - \mu_x\right)^2}{\sigma_x^2} \sim \chi^2\left(T\right). \tag{A3.7}$$

Finally, as $T(\hat{\mu}_x - \mu_x)^2/\sigma_x^2 \sim \chi^2(1)$ from (A3.3):

$$\tilde{\sigma}_x^2 = \frac{1}{(T-1)}\sum_{t=1}^{T}\left[(X_t-\mu_x)^2 - (\hat{\mu}_x-\mu_x)^2\right] = \frac{1}{(T-1)}\sigma_x^2\left[\chi^2(T) - \chi^2(1)\right]. \quad \text{(A3.8)}$$

We have not developed rules for relating χ^2s, but in §A3.7, it will be shown by a more general approach that the term in $[\cdot]$ in (A3.8) is a $\chi^2(T-1)$, so that:

$$\frac{(T-1)\,\tilde{\sigma}_x^2}{\sigma_x^2} \sim \chi^2(T-1). \quad \text{(A3.9)}$$

Consistent with this result, assuming the independence of $(\hat{\mu}_x - \mu_x)$ and $\tilde{\sigma}_x^2$:

$$\frac{T\,(\hat{\mu}_x-\mu_x)^2}{\sigma_x^2} \sim \chi^2(1) \quad \text{and} \quad \frac{(T-1)\,\tilde{\sigma}_x^2}{\sigma_x^2} \sim \chi^2(T-1) \quad \text{(A3.10)}$$

are independently distributed.

Since $\sqrt{T}(\hat{\mu}_x - \mu_x)/\sigma_x \sim \mathsf{N}[0,1]$, using the definitions in §A2.9:

$$\frac{\sqrt{T}\,(\hat{\mu}_x-\mu_x)}{\tilde{\sigma}_x} \sim \mathsf{t}(T-1), \quad \text{(A3.11)}$$

because it is a ratio of a normal variate to the square root of an independent $\chi^2(T-1)$ divided by its degrees of freedom $(T-1)$. The formula for the $\mathsf{t}(r)$ distribution is:

$$\mathsf{f}_{\mathsf{t}(r)}[t] = \frac{\Gamma([r+1]/2)}{\sqrt{\pi r}\,\Gamma(r/2)}\left(1+\frac{t^2}{r}\right)^{-(r+1)/2}.$$

Thus:

$$\frac{T\,(\hat{\mu}_x-\mu_x)^2}{\tilde{\sigma}_x^2} \sim \frac{(T-1)\,\chi^2(1)}{\chi^2(T-1)} = F(1, T-1), \quad \text{(A3.12)}$$

which is the F-distribution (being a ratio of independent χ^2s relative to their degrees of freedom). Since these distributions have been tabulated, comparisons are feasible between the sample value obtained in any given instance, and the anticipated value from the corresponding distribution; this provides a basis for testing hypotheses about unknown parameters, as described in §A3.4 and §A3.5. However, none of the functions in (A3.9)–(A3.12) is a statistic unless the relevant parameter (μ_x or σ_x) is known.

A3.1.4 Sufficiency

A major use of sample statistics is to summarize the information in a sample. Naturally, we need criteria to determine how well they do so, and the single most important criterion is whether the statistics are sufficient for the parameters $\boldsymbol{\theta}$ of the underlying distribution. First, consider an example using the independent sample $(X_1 \ldots X_T)$ on a random variable X from a normal distribution which has the joint density $\mathsf{D}_X(x_1 \ldots x_T|\boldsymbol{\theta})$

where $\boldsymbol{\theta}' = (\mu_x, \sigma_x^2)$:

$$\mathsf{D_X}(\boldsymbol{x} \mid \boldsymbol{\theta}) = \prod_{t=1}^{T} \mathsf{D_x}(x_t \mid \boldsymbol{\theta}) = \left(2\pi\sigma_x^2\right)^{-\frac{T}{2}} \exp\left(-\frac{\sum_{t=1}^{T}(x_t - \mu_x)^2}{2\sigma_x^2}\right). \quad \text{(A3.13)}$$

From (A3.4):

$$\sum_{t=1}^{T}(X_t - \mu_x)^2 = \sum_{t=1}^{T}(X_t - \hat{\mu}_x)^2 + T(\mu_x - \hat{\mu}_x)^2. \quad \text{(A3.14)}$$

Let $\hat{\sigma}_x^2 = (T-1)\tilde{\sigma}_x^2/T$, so the first term is $T\hat{\sigma}_x^2$, then the log density function can be expressed as:

$$\begin{aligned} \log \mathsf{D_X}(\boldsymbol{x} \mid \boldsymbol{\theta}) &= -\tfrac{T}{2}\left[\log(2\pi) + \log\left(\sigma_x^2\right) + \sigma_x^{-2}\left\{\hat{\sigma}_x^2 + (\mu_x - \hat{\mu}_x)^2\right\}\right] \\ &= \log \mathsf{f}_{\hat{\mu}_x, \hat{\sigma}_x^2}\left(\hat{\mu}_x, \hat{\sigma}_x^2 \mid T, \mu_x, \sigma_x^2\right). \end{aligned} \quad \text{(A3.15)}$$

From the first line, the original arguments $(x_1 \ldots x_T)$ no longer appear explicitly, but only as functions of $\hat{\mu}_x$ and $\hat{\sigma}_x^2$ (or $\tilde{\sigma}_x^2$ after correcting by a function of T). Thus, the first two sample moments are sufficient statistics for the entire sample information about (μ_x, σ_x^2) in this distribution. The importance of sufficient statistics is that a considerable reduction of sample information (from T random variables to two statistics) is achieved with no loss of relevant information about the parameters of the distribution. Moreover, the re-organization in (A3.15) links the parameters and the sufficient statistics in a suggestive way.

A general result on sufficient statistics is: $\boldsymbol{Y} = \boldsymbol{g}(\boldsymbol{X})$ is a sufficient statistic for the family $\{\mathsf{D_X}(\boldsymbol{x}|\boldsymbol{\theta}), \boldsymbol{\theta} \in \Theta\}$, if and only if the conditional distribution $\mathsf{D_{X|Y}}(\boldsymbol{x}|\boldsymbol{g}(\boldsymbol{x}) = \boldsymbol{y})$ of $\boldsymbol{X}$ given $\boldsymbol{Y} = \boldsymbol{y}$ is the same for all members of the family (i.e. is independent of $\boldsymbol{\theta}$). In practice, an easier method of identifying sufficient statistics is to use the factorization theorem which states that the density $\mathsf{D_X}(\boldsymbol{x}|\boldsymbol{\theta})$ factorizes in terms of $\boldsymbol{Y} = \boldsymbol{g}(\boldsymbol{X})$ if and only if:

$$\mathsf{D_X}(\boldsymbol{x} \mid \boldsymbol{\theta}) = h(\boldsymbol{x})\,\psi(\boldsymbol{g}(\boldsymbol{x}), \boldsymbol{\theta}). \quad \text{(A3.16)}$$

This expression entails that $h(\boldsymbol{x})$ does not depend on $\boldsymbol{\theta}$, and the only dependence of $\psi(\boldsymbol{g}(\boldsymbol{x}), \boldsymbol{\theta})$ on $\boldsymbol{x}$ is through $\boldsymbol{g}(\boldsymbol{x})$. When $\psi(\cdot)$ in (A3.16) is $\mathsf{f}_{\mathsf{g(x)}}(\cdot)$, then $\boldsymbol{g}(\boldsymbol{X})$ is sufficient for $\boldsymbol{\theta}$.

The whole sample $\boldsymbol{X}$ is clearly sufficient ($h(\boldsymbol{x}) = 1$), so to achieve data summarization, we need to look for minimal-sufficient statistics, where $\boldsymbol{g}(\boldsymbol{X})$ is minimal sufficient if any further reduction loses sufficiency. This is true in (A3.15), where $\psi(\cdot)$ is $\mathsf{f}_{\hat{\mu}_x, \hat{\sigma}_x^2}(\cdot)$ and $h(\boldsymbol{x}) = 1$, so that:

$$\left(\hat{\mu}_x, \hat{\sigma}_x^2\right) \text{ are minimal sufficient for } \left(\mu_x, \sigma_x^2\right). \quad \text{(A3.17)}$$

Thus, there is no loss of information about (μ_x, σ_x^2) in summarizing the sample by the pair $(\hat{\mu}_x, \hat{\sigma}_x^2)$: this would not be true if we were unsure whether the distribution $\mathsf{D_x}(\cdot)$ really was normal.

A3.1.5 Estimation criteria

The link between sufficient statistics and parameters leads to the concept of an estimator. Let X be a random variable on $(\Omega, \mathcal{F}, \mathsf{P})$ with density $\mathsf{D_x}(x|\theta)$, $\theta \in \Theta$. An estimator $\hat{\theta}$ for a parameter θ is any statistic $g(X_1 \dots X_T) : \Omega \mapsto \Theta$. An estimate of θ is given by $g(x_1 \dots x_T)$. Since $g(\cdot)$ could depend on all or only a subset of the sample, some statistics may be better estimators than others, and we need to develop criteria to select between them. Such criteria are bound to be somewhat arbitrary, and depend on the objectives of the analysis. For example, if a sequence of experiments is being conducted to learn about a parameter θ, where each experiment is summarized by an estimate of θ based on a formula $\hat{\theta}$ (say), but we wished to pool or average those estimates, then we might require the estimator to be unbiased, namely:

$$\mathsf{E}\left[\hat{\theta}\right] = \theta \ \ \forall \theta \in \Theta. \tag{A3.18}$$

Unbiasedness has to hold at all points in the parameter space, not just at a single value of θ. The unbiasedness of each estimator ensures that the average of a set of $\{\hat{\theta}_i\}$ will also be unbiased. In other contexts, bias may not be a serious drawback, especially if it vanishes as the sample size increases.

Of course, one might ask why the average of $\{\hat{\theta}_i\}$ is a better estimator than any one $\hat{\theta}_j$ alone, and here the answer is in terms of variance around θ: other things equal, we prefer estimators with smaller variances to those with larger (assuming the second moment exists). Then $\hat{\theta}$ is a relatively more efficient unbiased estimator of θ than $\tilde{\theta}$ if it satisfies:

$$\mathsf{V}\left[\hat{\theta}\right] \leq \mathsf{V}\left[\tilde{\theta}\right] \ \ \text{where } \mathsf{E}\left[\tilde{\theta}\right] = \theta \ \forall \theta \in \Theta. \tag{A3.19}$$

A minimum variance unbiased estimator (MVUE) $\hat{\theta}$ of θ satisfies:

$$\mathsf{V}\left[\hat{\theta}\right] \leq \mathsf{V}\left[\tilde{\theta}\right] \ \forall \tilde{\theta} \ \text{ such that } \mathsf{E}\left[\tilde{\theta}\right] = \theta \ \ \forall \theta \in \Theta. \tag{A3.20}$$

Relatively smaller mean-square error (MSE) estimators are defined by replacing $\mathsf{V}[\hat{\theta}]$ by $\mathsf{E}[(\hat{\theta} - \theta)^2] = \mathsf{MSE}[\hat{\theta}, \theta]$, and similarly for $\tilde{\theta}$ such that:

$$\mathsf{MSE}\left[\hat{\theta}, \theta\right] \leq \mathsf{MSE}\left[\tilde{\theta}, \theta\right] \ \ \forall \theta \in \Theta. \tag{A3.21}$$

Minimum mean-square error (MMSE) estimators are defined in an analogous way.

Relative efficiency seems a reasonable criterion in many circumstances, but such estimators are rare, and almost none exists in time-series econometrics. Moreover, MMSE estimators never exist $\forall \theta \in \Theta$, since a fixed value estimator $\breve{\theta}$ of θ must win when $\breve{\theta}$ equals θ, even though that is only one point in the parameter space, however bad $\breve{\theta}$ may be elsewhere.

It might be thought that more progress should result by seeking the converse, namely excluding dominated methods. In particular, $\tilde{\theta}$ is said to be inadmissible if (A3.21) holds for another estimator $\hat{\theta}$. However, difficulties remain, highlighted by the example of an estimator $\tilde{\theta}$ whose second moment does not exist, so that $\mathsf{MSE}[\tilde{\theta}, \theta]$ is infinite. While inadmissible on the criterion selected, for all practical purposes, $\tilde{\theta}$ could be preferable to $\hat{\theta}$, in that there could be a higher probability of $\tilde{\theta}$ being in any finite neighbourhood of θ_p, denoted $\mathcal{N}[\theta_p]$: i.e., $\mathsf{P}(\tilde{\theta} \in \mathcal{N}[\theta_p]) > \mathsf{P}(\hat{\theta} \in \mathcal{N}[\theta_p])$ (see e.g. Anderson, 1976).

An alternative strategy for finding 'good' estimators is to restrict the class within which we search. The best known example of this is to consider only unbiased linear estimators and find the minimum variance, or best, of these, usually denoted BLUE for best linear unbiased estimator. If linearity is reasonable, BLUE may be worth having and section A3.7 examines an important case: however, a slightly biased linear, or unbiased but slightly non-linear estimator may be greatly preferable in terms of MSE, so the arbitrariness of the criterion is starkly revealed. Again, in time series, BLUEs are rare. A different but related approach will be considered in sections A3.2 and A3.3, based on the likelihood function.

The final approach is to ask of estimators only that they be well behaved in some sense in indefinitely large samples: that approach will be pursued in Chapter A4, and is the basis for the main text. Two large-sample criteria need to be introduced at this stage to facilitate progress and these are briefly described in §A3.1.6.

A3.1.6 Consistency and asymptotic efficiency

An important point about (A3.3) is that as $T \to \infty$, then $\sigma_x^2/T \to 0$ and so $\mathsf{V}[\bar{X}] \to 0$. Such behaviour suggests that as $T \to \infty$, $\bar{X} \to \mu_x$ in a probability sense (formalized in Ch.A4). This is a desirable property of a statistic whereby it converges on the value of the parameter it purports to estimate as the sample size tends to infinity, and is called consistency. Another key property of an estimator is how efficiently a statistic estimates the unknown parameter in large samples. An estimator is defined to be asymptotically efficient if no other estimator has a smaller variance as the sample size tends to infinity, after appropriate normalization to ensure a finite, non-degenerate variance. To study that issue formally requires more tools, and introduces the concept of the likelihood function.

A3.2 Likelihood

The development, from probabilities over events to families of density functions which characterize random variables, assumed that the underlying parameters were known. In empirical research, that will not usually be the case, and we need to switch from deriving probabilities of outcomes given the parameters of the stochastic mechanism, to estimating the parameters given the observed outcomes of the random process.

A3.2.1 Likelihood function

The tool for accomplishing this switch is the likelihood function $\mathsf{L}(\cdot)$ defined in terms of the density function of the sample but exchanging the roles of variables and parameters:

$$\mathsf{D_x}(x \mid \boldsymbol{\theta}) \propto \mathsf{L}(\boldsymbol{\theta} \mid x) \text{ for } \boldsymbol{\theta} \in \Theta. \tag{A3.22}$$

$\mathsf{D}_\mathsf{X}(\boldsymbol{x}|\boldsymbol{\theta})$ maps from $\mathbb{R}^T$ to $\mathbb{R}_+$, whereas $\mathsf{L}(\boldsymbol{\theta}|\boldsymbol{x})$ maps from $\mathbb{R}^k$ to $\mathbb{R}_+$ when $\boldsymbol{\theta}$ is $k \times 1$, so they are linked by a function $\varphi(\boldsymbol{x})$ which does not depend on $\boldsymbol{\theta}$. Any monotonic transformation of $\mathsf{L}(\cdot)$ is also admissible, and this feature will be useful below where we work with the log-likelihood function, and its first derivative. We set $\varphi(\boldsymbol{x})$ to unity so that the integral of the likelihood function is unity:

$$\int_{-\infty}^{\infty} \mathsf{L}\left(\boldsymbol{\theta} \mid x\right) \mathrm{d}x = 1. \tag{A3.23}$$

The density function $\mathsf{D}_\mathsf{x}(x|\boldsymbol{\theta})$ describes the mechanism that generates random variables. For a given value of $\boldsymbol{\theta}$, the outcomes of random variables differ due to random variation, characterized by the form of $\mathsf{D}_\mathsf{x}(\cdot)$: for example, the location, spread, and shape of the distribution of a random sample $(X_1 \ldots X_T)$ is determined by $\mathsf{D}_\mathsf{x}(\cdot)$. However, at different points in the parameter space, the distribution will also differ, and when the impact of distinct values of $\boldsymbol{\theta}$ on $\mathsf{D}_\mathsf{x}(\cdot)$ is sufficiently marked, using the argument in §A3.1.2 we might hope to infer what the value of $\boldsymbol{\theta}$ is, despite the randomness from $\mathsf{D}_\mathsf{x}(\cdot)$.

For example, when $X_t \sim \mathsf{IN}[\mu_x, \sigma_x^2]$, where $\mu_x = 0$, and $\sigma_x = 1$, then $|X| < 2$ will occur roughly 95 per cent of the time, whereas when $\mu_x = 5$ and $\sigma_x = 1$, almost every observed X-value will exceed 2. Thus, the data on X yield information on μ_x and σ_x, and from a sufficiently large sample, we may be able to determine the unknown parameter values precisely.

A3.2.2 Log-likelihood

An important point about CDFs, and so implicitly about densities, is that for suitably continuous and one–one functions $g(\cdot)$, $\mathsf{P}(X \leq g^{-1}(x)) = \mathsf{P}(g(X) \leq x)$, so such transformations do not affect the probability structure. Since $\mathsf{D}_\mathsf{x}(x) \geq 0$ for all x, take the logarithm of $\mathsf{D}_\mathsf{x}(x|\boldsymbol{\theta})$ (as we did above) and hence of $\mathsf{L}(\boldsymbol{\theta}|x)$, which is denoted by $\ell(\boldsymbol{\theta}|x)$:

$$\ell\left(\boldsymbol{\theta} \mid x\right) = \log \mathsf{L}\left(\boldsymbol{\theta} \mid x\right). \tag{A3.24}$$

For an independent sample of T observations on X:

$$\mathsf{D}_\mathsf{X}\left(x_1 \ldots x_T \mid \boldsymbol{\theta}\right) = \prod_{t=1}^{T} \mathsf{D}_\mathsf{x}\left(x_t \mid \boldsymbol{\theta}\right) = \exp\left[\sum_{t=1}^{T} \ell\left(\boldsymbol{\theta} \mid x_t\right)\right]. \tag{A3.25}$$

Thus, after taking logs, the log-likelihood of the sample is the sum of the individual log-likelihoods, and this will prove convenient for later analysis.

A3.2.3 Estimation

The next tool required is how to estimate $\boldsymbol{\theta}$ using the log-likelihood. The principle we adopt is that of maximum likelihood estimation (MLE), namely, locate that value of $\boldsymbol{\theta}$ in the parameter space which produces the highest value of the log-likelihood:

$$\widehat{\boldsymbol{\theta}} = \underset{\boldsymbol{\theta} \in \Theta}{\operatorname{argmax}}\, \ell\left(\boldsymbol{\theta} \mid \boldsymbol{x}\right) = \underset{\boldsymbol{\theta} \in \Theta}{\operatorname{argmax}} \sum_{t=1}^{T} \ell\left(\boldsymbol{\theta} \mid x_t\right), \tag{A3.26}$$

where the second equality holds for independent Xs. It is important to remember the notational conventions. Since we are considering the sample realization $\boldsymbol{X} = \boldsymbol{x}$, then $\ell(\boldsymbol{\theta}|\boldsymbol{x})$ is written with the realization as an argument because of (A3.22), but is construed as a function of the random variable X as in (A3.27) below. Thus, it makes sense to take the expectation of functions of $\ell(\boldsymbol{\theta}|\boldsymbol{x})$ (such as derivatives), or to consider the large-sample distribution of functions of $\ell(\boldsymbol{\theta}|\boldsymbol{x})$, and so on.

The form of any MLE depends on $\mathsf{D}_{\mathsf{X}}(\cdot)$. For the normal distribution, $\boldsymbol{\theta}' = (\mu_x, \sigma_x^2)$ and so:

$$\ell(\boldsymbol{\theta} \mid x_t) = -\tfrac{1}{2}\log(2\pi) - \log(\sigma_x) - \frac{(x_t - \mu_x)^2}{2\sigma_x^2} = \ell_t. \tag{A3.27}$$

Hence from (A3.15):

$$\begin{aligned}\ell(\boldsymbol{\theta} \mid \boldsymbol{x}) &= -\tfrac{T}{2}\log(2\pi) - T\log(\sigma_x) - \tfrac{1}{2\sigma_x^2}\textstyle\sum_{t=1}^{T}(x_t - \mu_x)^2 \\ &= -\tfrac{T}{2}\left[\log(2\pi) + \log(\sigma_x^2) + \tfrac{1}{\sigma_x^2}\left\{\hat{\sigma}_x^2 + (\mu_x - \hat{\mu}_x)^2\right\}\right].\end{aligned} \tag{A3.28}$$

A3.2.4 The score and the Hessian

When the log-likelihood is differentiable, $\ell(\boldsymbol{\theta}|x)$ can be maximized by differentiating with respect to $\boldsymbol{\theta}$ and equating to zero (a necessary condition for a maximum). The first derivative of $\ell(\cdot)$ with respect to $\boldsymbol{\theta}$ is the score, denoted by:

$$\boldsymbol{q}(\boldsymbol{\theta} \mid \boldsymbol{x}) = \frac{\partial \ell(\boldsymbol{\theta}|\boldsymbol{x})}{\partial \boldsymbol{\theta}} = \sum_{t=1}^{T} \frac{\partial \ell_t(\boldsymbol{\theta}|\boldsymbol{x})}{\partial \boldsymbol{\theta}} = \sum_{t=1}^{T} \boldsymbol{q}_t(\boldsymbol{\theta} \mid \boldsymbol{x}), \tag{A3.29}$$

where the second and third equalities hold for independent Xs. Solving for $\hat{\boldsymbol{\theta}}$ such that $\boldsymbol{q}(\hat{\boldsymbol{\theta}}) = \mathbf{0}$ yields the MLE when the second derivative (matrix) is negative (definite). For the normal distribution illustration:

$$\boldsymbol{q}(\boldsymbol{\theta} \mid \boldsymbol{x}) = \begin{pmatrix} q(\mu_x|\boldsymbol{x}) \\ q(\sigma_x^2|\boldsymbol{x}) \end{pmatrix} = \begin{pmatrix} T(\hat{\mu}_x - \mu_x)/\sigma_x^2 \\ -\tfrac{T}{2}\sigma_x^{-2}\left[1 - \left\{\hat{\sigma}_x^2 + (\hat{\mu}_x - \mu_x)^2\right\}/\sigma_x^2\right] \end{pmatrix}. \tag{A3.30}$$

Then $\boldsymbol{q}(\hat{\boldsymbol{\theta}}|\boldsymbol{x}) = \mathbf{0}$ occurs at $\hat{\boldsymbol{\theta}}' = (\hat{\mu}_x, \hat{\sigma}_x^2)$, where these are the sample mean and (unadjusted) sample variance. At the maximum $\hat{\boldsymbol{\theta}}$:

$$\ell(\hat{\boldsymbol{\theta}} \mid x) = -\frac{T}{2}\left(\log(2\pi) + \log(\hat{\sigma}_x^2) + 1\right). \tag{A3.31}$$

The second derivative matrix of $\ell(\boldsymbol{\theta}|\boldsymbol{x})$ with respect to $\boldsymbol{\theta}$ is the Hessian of the likelihood, and evaluated at $\hat{\boldsymbol{\theta}}$ can be shown to be negative definite here. Differentiate $\boldsymbol{q}(\boldsymbol{\theta}|\boldsymbol{x})$ with respect to $\boldsymbol{\theta}$ once more:

$$\boldsymbol{H}(\boldsymbol{\theta} \mid \boldsymbol{x}) = \frac{\partial^2 \ell(\boldsymbol{\theta}|\boldsymbol{x})}{\partial \boldsymbol{\theta}\partial \boldsymbol{\theta}'} = \sum_{t=1}^{T} \frac{\partial^2 \ell_t(\boldsymbol{\theta}|\boldsymbol{x})}{\partial \boldsymbol{\theta}\partial \boldsymbol{\theta}'} = \sum_{t=1}^{T} \boldsymbol{H}_t(\boldsymbol{\theta} \mid \boldsymbol{x}), \tag{A3.32}$$

where the last two equalities hold for independent Xs. Thus, from (A3.30):

$$\boldsymbol{H}(\boldsymbol{\theta} \mid \boldsymbol{x}) = \begin{pmatrix} -T/\sigma_x^2 & -T(\hat{\mu}_x - \mu_x)/\sigma_x^4 \\ -T(\hat{\mu}_x - \mu_x)/\sigma_x^4 & -T\sigma_x^{-6}\{\hat{\sigma}_x^2 + (\hat{\mu}_x - \mu_x)^2\} + \frac{T}{2}\sigma_x^{-4} \end{pmatrix},$$

and when evaluated at $\hat{\boldsymbol{\theta}}$:

$$\boldsymbol{H}\left(\hat{\boldsymbol{\theta}} \mid \boldsymbol{x}\right) = \begin{pmatrix} -T\hat{\sigma}_x^{-2} & 0 \\ 0 & -\frac{T}{2}\hat{\sigma}_x^{-4} \end{pmatrix},$$

which is negative definite.

A3.3 Maximum-likelihood estimation

A natural question is 'why use maximum likelihood'? The justification is that the principle is general, and when the form of the data density is known and the sample size is sufficiently large, MLE usually yields estimators of $\boldsymbol{\theta}$ that are as good as can be obtained. To demonstrate that result will involve yet more tools, so we turn to that task directly.

A3.3.1 Efficiency and the information matrix

Subject to reasonable regularity conditions, maximum likelihood estimators are consistent, and also tend to be efficient in large samples in that no other method dominates MLE. This last claim can be proved to hold in finite samples for the special class of unbiased estimators defined by $\mathsf{E}[\hat{\boldsymbol{\theta}}] = \boldsymbol{\theta}\ \forall \boldsymbol{\theta} \in \Theta$, and this section outlines the proof. To simplify notation, we drop the reference to x in the arguments. Five steps are required in that proof, many of which are of independent interest, but we only consider a scalar case where $\ell(\theta)$ is a quadratic function of θ, and hence $q(\theta)$ is linear in θ. That restriction entails that $H(\theta_p) = H$ is constant, and so higher order derivatives vanish: in large samples, such a condition provides a good approximation (see Ch.A4).

(i) Expand $q(\theta_p)$ around $q(\hat{\theta})$ in a Taylor series:

$$q(\theta_p) = q\left(\hat{\theta}\right) + \frac{\mathrm{d}q(\theta)}{\mathrm{d}\theta}\Big|_{\hat{\theta}}\left(\theta_p - \hat{\theta}\right) + \frac{1}{2}\frac{\mathrm{d}^2 q(\theta)}{\mathrm{d}\theta^2}\Big|_{\hat{\theta}}\left(\theta_p - \hat{\theta}\right)^2. \tag{A3.33}$$

Since $q(\hat{\theta}) = 0$ by definition, and the last term in (A3.33) is zero by the assumption that H is constant:

$$q(\theta_p) = H(\cdot)\left(\theta_p - \hat{\theta}\right), \tag{A3.34}$$

or, noting that $H(\cdot) = H$ is constant, and therefore does not depend on $\hat{\theta}$ or θ_p:

$$\left(\hat{\theta} - \theta_p\right) = -H^{-1}q(\theta_p). \tag{A3.35}$$

Consequently, the estimator $\hat{\theta}$ differs from θ_p by a linear function of $q(\theta_p)$.[2]

[2] This last expression holds more generally but is only an approximation when $H(\theta)$ is not constant, needing iterative solution.

(ii) Next, assuming sufficient regularity the main text proves the important result that $\mathsf{E}[q(\theta_p)] = 0$. Since we solve $q(\hat{\theta}) = 0$ to obtain $\hat{\theta}$, it is important that on average $\mathsf{E}[q(\theta_p)]$ is indeed zero. Taking expectations in (A3.34), for linear score functions $q(\theta_p)$, $\mathsf{E}[\hat{\theta}] = \theta_p$, so the MLE is unbiased under the present assumptions.

(iii) Since $\mathsf{E}[q(\theta_p)] = 0$, the variance of $q(\theta_p)$ is $\mathsf{E}[q(\theta_p)^2] = \mathcal{I}(\theta_p)$ which is the information matrix (although it is a scalar here). The main text proves the result that:

$$\mathsf{E}\left[q(\theta_p)^2\right] = \mathcal{I}(\theta_p) = -\mathsf{E}\left[H(\theta_p)\right],$$

so the information matrix is the negative of the expected value of the Hessian.[3]

(iv) The variance of $\hat{\theta}$ can be obtained using its definition as $\mathsf{E}[(\hat{\theta} - \theta_p)^2]$ and the Taylor-series expansion of $q(\theta_p)$ around $q(\hat{\theta})$. In the linear case with constant H, from (A3.35):

$$\mathsf{E}\left[\left(\hat{\theta} - \theta_p\right)^2\right] = \mathsf{E}\left[H(\theta_p)^{-1}q(\theta_p)^2 H(\theta_p)^{-1}\right] = H^{-1}\mathcal{I}H^{-1} = \mathcal{I}^{-1}, \quad \text{(A3.36)}$$

using (i) and (iii). Thus, $\mathsf{V}[\hat{\theta}]$ is the inverse of the information matrix. This result is of sufficient importance to merit a separate section, which also solves the fifth step.

A3.3.2 Cramér–Rao bound

(v) Let $\tilde{\theta}$ be any other unbiased estimator of θ so that $\mathsf{E}[\tilde{\theta}] = \theta_p$ with variance given by $\mathsf{E}[(\tilde{\theta} - \theta_p)^2] = V$. We show that $V \geq \mathcal{I}^{-1}$ and hence prove that the MLE is the minimum variance unbiased estimator here. First, we state an intermediate result which is rather surprising: $\mathsf{E}[q(\theta_p)\tilde{\theta}] = 1 \; \forall \tilde{\theta}$ such that $\mathsf{E}[\tilde{\theta}] = \theta_p$. In words, all unbiased estimators have a covariance of unity with the score. This uses the results in (ii) and the unbiasedness of $\tilde{\theta}$ for θ_p (again proved in the main text).

Next, the squared correlation between $q(\theta_p)$ and $\tilde{\theta}$ is:

$$\mathsf{r}^2 = \frac{\mathsf{E}\left[\left(q(\theta_p)\tilde{\theta}\right)^2\right]}{V\mathcal{I}} = \frac{1}{V\mathcal{I}}. \quad \text{(A3.37)}$$

Since a squared correlation must be between 0 and 1 (see Ch.A2), $V\mathcal{I} \geq 1$ so that $V \geq \mathcal{I}^{-1}$. This result is called the Cramér–Rao bound, and shows that no unbiased estimator $\tilde{\theta}$ can have a smaller variance than $\mathcal{I}(\theta_p)^{-1}$; since the unbiased MLE had that variance, it is not dominated by any other $\tilde{\theta}$. More generally, the Cramér–Rao bound holds for most MLEs as $T \to \infty$, as proved in Chapter A4.

[3] $\ell(\theta|x)$ is equated to $\mathsf{D}_{\mathsf{X}}(x|\theta)$ in such derivations, even though $\ell(\theta|x)$ is specified by the investigator and $\mathsf{D}_{\mathsf{X}}(x|\theta)$ by nature.

A3.3.3 Properties of the information matrix

So far we have established that $\mathsf{E}[q(\theta_p)^2] = \mathcal{I}(\theta_p) = -\mathsf{E}[H(\theta_p)]$; $\mathsf{V}[\hat{\theta}] = \mathcal{I}(\theta_p)^{-1}$; and $\mathsf{V}[\tilde{\theta}] \geq \mathcal{I}(\theta_p)^{-1}$ for all unbiased estimators $\tilde{\theta}$ of θ. Several other properties merit note, especially the effects of sample size. First, from (A3.29), since $q(\theta_p) = \sum_{t=1}^{T} q_t(\theta_p)$:

$$\begin{aligned} \mathsf{E}\left[q(\theta_p)^2\right] &= \mathsf{E}\left[\left(\sum_{t=1}^{T} q_t(\theta_p)\right)^2\right] \\ &= \mathsf{E}\left[\sum_{s=1}^{T}\sum_{t=1}^{T} q_t(\theta_p)q_s(\theta_p)\right] \\ &= \sum_{s=1}^{T}\sum_{t=1}^{T} \mathsf{E}\left[q_t(\theta_p)q_s(\theta_p)\right]. \end{aligned} \tag{A3.38}$$

Under independence (or a sequential factorization), $\mathsf{E}[q_t(\theta_p)q_s(\theta_p)] = 0$, but otherwise is non-zero (which will pose problems for estimation and inference later: see Ch.10).

Secondly, assuming that $\mathsf{E}[q_t(\theta_p)q_s(\theta_p)] = 0$, (A3.38) becomes:

$$\mathsf{E}\left[q(\theta_p)^2\right] = \sum_{t=1}^{T} \mathsf{E}\left[q_t(\theta_p)^2\right] = \sum_{t=1}^{T} \mathcal{I}_t(\theta_p) = \mathcal{I}_{(T)}(\theta_p). \tag{A3.39}$$

Thus, the information matrix is additive over independent random variables. When the expectation $\mathsf{E}[q_t(\theta_p)^2]$ is constant over t, then $\mathcal{I}_{(T)}(\theta_p) = T\mathcal{I}_0(\theta_p)$, where $\mathcal{I}_0(\theta_p)$ is the information matrix for a single sample point. From the fact that $\mathcal{I}_{(T)}(\theta_p)$ is $T\mathcal{I}_0(\theta_p)$, we see that information increases linearly with sample size in this setting. Conversely, when $\mathcal{I}_t(\theta_p)$ is not constant, inference difficulties may again ensue (see Ch.10).

When $\mathcal{I}_t(\theta_p)$ is constant over t, so $\mathsf{V}[q(\theta_p)] = T\mathcal{I}_0(\theta_p)$, when $q(\theta_p)$ is a linear function of θ_p for a normally-distributed random variable (as in (A3.28) for known σ_x^2):

$$q(\theta_p) \sim \mathsf{N}\left[0, T\mathcal{I}_0(\theta_p)\right] \text{ so that } \sqrt{T}q(\theta_p) \sim \mathsf{N}\left[0, \mathcal{I}_0(\theta_p)\right]. \tag{A3.40}$$

Consequently, using (A3.35), $(\hat{\theta} - \theta_p) = -H^{-1}q(\theta_p)$:

$$\sqrt{T}\left(\hat{\theta} - \theta_p\right) \sim \mathsf{N}\left[0, \mathcal{I}_0(\theta_p)^{-1}\right]. \tag{A3.41}$$

This result is dependent on many strong assumptions which are weakened in Chapter A4, and investigated in Part II of the main text.

Finally, when there is a set of sufficient statistics $\boldsymbol{g}(\boldsymbol{X})$, such that (A3.16) holds, then since $h(\boldsymbol{x})$ does not depend on $\boldsymbol{\theta}$, $\boldsymbol{q}(\boldsymbol{\theta}; \boldsymbol{x})$ is a function of $\boldsymbol{g}(\boldsymbol{x})$, and hence so is $\mathcal{I}(\cdot)$. Thus, the MLE retains all of the available information.

A3.3.4 Estimating the information matrix

Having established the MLE $\hat{\boldsymbol{\theta}}$ of $\boldsymbol{\theta}$, and how to solve for it from $\boldsymbol{q}(\hat{\boldsymbol{\theta}}) = \mathbf{0}$, we now consider how to estimate $\mathsf{V}[\hat{\boldsymbol{\theta}}] = T\mathcal{I}_0(\boldsymbol{\theta}_p)^{-1}$. The first way uses the result that $T\mathcal{I}_0(\boldsymbol{\theta}_p) = -\mathsf{E}[\boldsymbol{H}(\boldsymbol{\theta}_p)]$, which holds more generally than the quadratic log-likelihood considered above. On replacing $\boldsymbol{\theta}_p$ by $\hat{\boldsymbol{\theta}}$:

$$\widehat{\mathsf{V}\left[\hat{\boldsymbol{\theta}}\right]} = -\boldsymbol{H}(\hat{\boldsymbol{\theta}})^{-1}. \tag{A3.42}$$

Since $\hat{\boldsymbol{\theta}}$ converges on $\boldsymbol{\theta}_p$ as $T \to \infty$ due to consistency, and from (A3.41), $\sqrt{T}(\hat{\boldsymbol{\theta}} - \boldsymbol{\theta}_p)$ has a well defined distribution, we might anticipate that $-T[\boldsymbol{H}(\hat{\boldsymbol{\theta}})^{-1}]$ will tend to $\mathcal{I}_0(\boldsymbol{\theta}_p)^{-1}$: Chapter A4 establishes such a result.

Finally, $\boldsymbol{q}(\hat{\boldsymbol{\theta}})\boldsymbol{q}(\hat{\boldsymbol{\theta}})'$ cannot be used as an estimator of $\mathsf{V}[\hat{\boldsymbol{\theta}}]$ since $\boldsymbol{q}(\hat{\boldsymbol{\theta}}) = \mathbf{0}$. However, since $\boldsymbol{q}(\hat{\boldsymbol{\theta}}) = \sum_{t=1}^{T} \boldsymbol{q}_t(\hat{\boldsymbol{\theta}})$, and $\boldsymbol{q}_t(\hat{\boldsymbol{\theta}}) \neq \mathbf{0}\ \forall t$, the estimator:

$$\widehat{\mathsf{V}\left[\hat{\boldsymbol{\theta}}\right]} = \sum_{t=1}^{T} \boldsymbol{q}_t(\hat{\boldsymbol{\theta}})\boldsymbol{q}_t(\hat{\boldsymbol{\theta}})', \tag{A3.43}$$

is feasible. In Part II, we confront the issues which arise when modelling data using such results, since in any realistic application, the form of $\mathsf{D}_{\mathsf{X}}(\boldsymbol{x}|\boldsymbol{\theta})$ is unknown, and the postulated likelihood function may not be proportional to the data density. Many of the above results depend on that identity holding, and important issues arise when it is invalid.

A3.4 Statistical inference and testing

Economists often disagree about how economies function, how agents make their plans, how they form their expectations etc., entailing disagreements about the specifications of relationships between economic variables. Thus, the issue of testing theoretical claims arises. In the framework of probability models and maximum likelihood estimation of parameters with unknown values, tests concern hypotheses about parameter values, such as whether the marginal propensity to spend equals 0.85 say.

A3.4.1 Null and alternative hypotheses

For a scalar parameter $\theta \in \Theta$, let $\Theta_0 \subset \Theta$ be a conjectured interval within which it is anticipated θ will lie when the theory is correct. Such a conjecture constitutes the null hypothesis, and is denoted by H_0: $\theta \in \Theta_0$ (the null may be a single point θ_0 say). The remainder of the parameter space is given by $\Theta_1 \subset \Theta$ where $\Theta_1 \cup \Theta_0 = \Theta$ and $\Theta_1 \cap \Theta_0 = \emptyset$, so Θ_1 is the alternative hypothesis H_1. For example, Θ_0 may be the hypothesis that a parameter value lies in $[0.9, 1.0]$. A test comprises a formal rule for using data evidence to reach a decision as whether to retain or reject H_0, and usually is a statistic with a distribution which is known when H_0 is true, and is different when H_0 is false; the rule must decide when the latter occurs. Because the test has a distribution of possible outcomes when the null is true, there is some probability that any given outcome will have been generated by the null: when that probability is sufficiently small, it is more reasonable to conclude that the null is false than that an unlikely event has arisen, although how small a probability is tolerable depends on the problem, and on any previous evidence accumulated about the hypothesis under test.

A3.4.2 Critical regions, error types, and power

Partition the observation space $\mathcal{X}$ of a random variable $\boldsymbol{X}$ with realization $\boldsymbol{x}$ into two regions, $\mathcal{C}$, called the critical region, and its relative complement, $\mathcal{C}^c = \mathcal{X} - \mathcal{C}$, such that when the outcome of the random variable $\mathbf{X}$ is $\mathbf{x} \in \mathcal{C}$, we reject H_0. To partition $\mathcal{X}$ correctly, we need to know the probability of observing $\mathbf{x} \in \mathcal{C}$, and hence of $\mathbf{x} \notin \mathcal{C}$, when each hypothesis is true. First:

$$\mathsf{P}(\mathbf{X} \in \mathcal{C} \mid \mathsf{H}_0) = \mathsf{P}(\mathbf{X} \in \mathcal{C} \mid \boldsymbol{\theta} \in \Theta_0) \tag{A3.44}$$

is called a Type I error, and is the probability of rejecting H_0 even though it is true, which may depend on the actual value of $\boldsymbol{\theta} \in \Theta_0$. Secondly:

$$\mathsf{P}(\mathbf{X} \in \mathcal{C} \mid \mathsf{H}_1) = \mathsf{P}(\mathbf{X} \in \mathcal{C} \mid \boldsymbol{\theta} \in \Theta_1) \tag{A3.45}$$

is called the power function of the test, and is the probability of rejecting H_0 when it is false. The power must depend on the value of $\boldsymbol{\theta}$ if the test is to be useful. Conversely:

$$1 - \mathsf{P}(\mathbf{X} \in \mathcal{C} \mid \mathsf{H}_1) = \mathsf{P}(\mathbf{X} \notin \mathcal{C} \mid \mathsf{H}_1) \tag{A3.46}$$

is the Type II error, which is the probability of not rejecting H_0 even though it is false. Naturally, we would like tests with zero, or very small, errors of both types, but since $\mathbf{X}$ is random, that is not possible. Consequently, we seek a test which minimizes the costs of incorrect decisions. In empirical research, however, such costs are virtually impossible to calculate, since the uses to which an empirical result will be put cannot be known in advance. Thus, investigators have adopted a conventional strategy of deciding on the Type I error they are willing to accept for the given problem and sample size, then seeking a test with high power against alternatives that might matter in practice. We now formalize that approach.

A3.4.3 Significance level

The first problem concerns how to calculate $\mathsf{P}(\mathbf{X} \in \mathcal{C}|\theta \in \Theta_i)$ for $i = 0, 1$. In practice, it is more convenient to reduce the dimensionality of the problem by considering well-behaved functions (usually statistics) $g(\mathbf{X})$ for which we can compute:

$$\mathsf{P}(g(\mathbf{X}) \geq r), \tag{A3.47}$$

where r is called the critical value. $\mathsf{P}(g(\mathbf{X}) \geq r)$ can be calculated when $g(\mathbf{X})$ has a known distribution, so that $g(\mathbf{X})$ can be used as a test statistic.

For example, when $X_t \sim \mathsf{IN}[\mu_x, \sigma_x^2]$ where σ_x^2 is known, the mean $\hat{\mu}_x$ of T observations is distributed as:

$$\hat{\mu}_x \sim \mathsf{N}\left[\mu_x, \frac{\sigma_x^2}{T}\right],$$

and hence:

$$\eta = \frac{\sqrt{T}(\hat{\mu}_x - \mu_x)}{\sigma_x} \sim \mathsf{N}[0,1].$$

When H_0: $\mu_x = \mu_{x0}$ is true:

$$\eta_0 = \frac{\sqrt{T}(\hat{\mu}_x - \mu_{x0})}{\sigma_x} \sim \mathsf{N}[0,1].$$

As this distribution has no unknowns, $\eta_0 = g(X)$ can be used to test the null once an appropriate critical value r is selected.[4] When H_0 is true, from the normal distribution:

$$\mathsf{P}\left(|\eta_0| > 1.96 \mid \mathsf{H}_0\right) = 0.05 = \alpha, \tag{A3.48}$$

(say) where α is called the significance level, or the size if α does not depend on $\boldsymbol{\theta}$. Given a type I error of α, the power of the test is:

$$\mathsf{P}\left(|\eta_0| > 1.96 \mid \mathsf{H}_1\right) \tag{A3.49}$$

for $\mu_x \neq \mu_{x0}$. Let $\mu_x = \mu_{x1} \neq \mu_{x0}$ then:

$$\eta_0 = \frac{\sqrt{T}\left([\hat{\mu}_x - \mu_{x1}] + [\mu_{x1} - \mu_{x0}]\right)}{\sigma_x} \sim \mathsf{N}\left[\frac{\sqrt{T}\left(\mu_{x1} - \mu_{x0}\right)}{\sigma_x}, 1\right], \tag{A3.50}$$

from which $\mathsf{P}(|\eta_0| > 1.96|\mathsf{H}_1)$ can be calculated for any value of μ_{x1}. For example, when $\mu_{x0} = 0$, $\mu_{x1} = 1$, $T = 100$, and $\sigma_x = 5$, then $\eta_0 \sim \mathsf{N}[2, 1]$, so that $\mathsf{P}(|\eta_0| > 1.96|\mathsf{H}_1) \approx 0.5$. Hence the test would correctly reject H_0 roughly half the time.

A3.5 Powerful tests

A3.5.1 Neyman–Pearson lemma

Obtaining the 'best' test is desirable but difficult. When H_0 and H_1 are simple (so Θ_0 and Θ_1 are both points), the best critical region of size $\alpha = \mathsf{P}(X \in \mathcal{C}|\mathsf{H}_0)$ is $\mathcal{C}$ if:

$$\mathsf{P}\left(X \in \mathcal{C} \mid \mathsf{H}_1\right) \geq \mathsf{P}\left(X \in \mathcal{A} \mid \mathsf{H}_1\right) \tag{A3.51}$$

for all other subsets $\mathcal{A} \subseteq \mathcal{X}$ such that $\mathsf{P}(X \in \mathcal{A}|\mathsf{H}_0) = \alpha$. The main result is the Neyman–Pearson lemma:

if $\Theta = \{\boldsymbol{\theta}; \boldsymbol{\theta} = \boldsymbol{\theta}_0, \boldsymbol{\theta}_1\}$, $r > 0$ is a constant and $\mathcal{C}$ is such that:

$$\frac{\mathsf{L}\left(\boldsymbol{\theta}_0|\boldsymbol{x}\right)}{\mathsf{L}\left(\boldsymbol{\theta}_1|\boldsymbol{x}\right)} \leq r \; \forall \boldsymbol{x} \in \mathcal{C},$$

whereas:

$$\frac{\mathsf{L}\left(\boldsymbol{\theta}_0|\boldsymbol{x}\right)}{\mathsf{L}\left(\boldsymbol{\theta}_1|\boldsymbol{x}\right)} \geq r \; \forall \boldsymbol{x} \notin \mathcal{C},$$

when $\mathsf{P}(X \in \mathcal{C}|\boldsymbol{\theta}_0) = \alpha$, then $\mathcal{C}$ is the best critical region of size α for testing H_0: $\boldsymbol{\theta} = \boldsymbol{\theta}_0$ against H_1: $\boldsymbol{\theta} = \boldsymbol{\theta}_1$ (see e.g. Hogg and Craig, 1978).

This lemma underpins quality-control tests. An important aspect is that the decision depends on the likelihood ratio $\lambda = \mathsf{L}(\boldsymbol{\theta}_0|\boldsymbol{x})/\mathsf{L}(\boldsymbol{\theta}_1|\boldsymbol{x})$. This is consistent with the

[4] For unknown σ_x, $\sqrt{T}(\hat{\mu}_x - \mu_x)/\hat{\sigma}_x \sim \mathsf{t}(T-1)$, as shown in (A3.11). The proof by Student (1908) of this result was a major step in the development of statistics: see e.g., Mood, Graybill and Boes (1978).

earlier emphasis on the likelihood function, which is central to much of statistical inference, and leads on to the widely-used class of tests discussed in §A3.5.2. Two general difficulties prevent fruitful direct applications of the lemma in econometrics. First, few economic hypotheses can be expressed as selecting between two disparate points: that difficulty can be resolved in part for the case of a point hypothesis versus an interval, but no 'obviously-best' test need result. Secondly, it is rare that the exact distributions of test statistics can be obtained in time-series econometrics, so rather than develop the present theme, we conclude this section by noting three closely-related tests which perform well in large samples for composite hypotheses.

A3.5.2 Likelihood-ratio, Wald, and efficient-score tests

Likelihood-ratio tests can be generalized for large samples to composite hypotheses Θ_1 and Θ_0 of dimensions $n+k$ and n. Let $\hat{\boldsymbol{\theta}}$ and $\tilde{\boldsymbol{\theta}}$ denote MLEs in Θ and Θ_0 respectively, where the latter imposes k restrictions on $\boldsymbol{\theta}$. If we are only concerned with the 'distance' between the null hypothesis and the evidence, and unconcerned as to the direction in which any departure occurs, then we can use a generalized likelihood-ratio (LR) test. This uses the log-likelihood difference defined by:

$$2\left[\ell(\hat{\boldsymbol{\theta}} \mid \boldsymbol{x}) - \ell(\tilde{\boldsymbol{\theta}} \mid \boldsymbol{x})\right] \underset{a}{\sim} \chi^2(k) \text{ on } \mathsf{H}_0\colon \boldsymbol{\theta} \in \Theta_0, \qquad \text{(A3.52)}$$

where $\underset{a}{\sim}$ denotes 'asymptotically distributed as' which means 'distributed as $T \to \infty$'. When the null is true, the restrictions imposed on $\boldsymbol{\theta}$ to make it an element of Θ_0 should not greatly lower the log-likelihood, and, correspondingly, the restricted and unrestricted estimates of $\boldsymbol{\theta}$ should be similar. The formula in (A3.52) then entails that imposing k valid restrictions will on average lower $\ell(\cdot)$ by k, that being $\mathsf{E}[\chi^2(k)]$. When the null is false, a larger loss of likelihood will generally ensue, leading to a bigger statistic value in (A3.52) and a higher probability that the observed outcome will exceed the α-point value of a $\chi^2(k)$ distribution. A similar result to (A3.52) holds if the null is a point $\boldsymbol{\theta}_0$, which then replaces the restricted estimator.

Several other test forms are available, of which we have used the Wald (W) type above in deriving the distribution of η_0. Generally, a Wald test only calculates the unrestricted estimator, and uses its large-sample distribution to conduct the test. For example, (A3.41) can be extended directly to a vector distribution, so that:

$$\sqrt{T}\left(\hat{\boldsymbol{\theta}} - \boldsymbol{\theta}_p\right) \underset{a}{\sim} \mathsf{N}\left[\mathbf{0}, \mathcal{I}_0\left(\boldsymbol{\theta}_p\right)^{-1}\right]. \qquad \text{(A3.53)}$$

When the null is the point $\boldsymbol{\theta}_0$, then (A3.53) holds with $\boldsymbol{\theta}_p = \boldsymbol{\theta}_0$, so that from §A2.9.4:

$$T\left(\hat{\boldsymbol{\theta}} - \boldsymbol{\theta}_0\right)' \mathcal{I}_0(\hat{\boldsymbol{\theta}}) \left(\hat{\boldsymbol{\theta}} - \boldsymbol{\theta}_0\right) \underset{a}{\sim} \chi^2(k) \text{ on } \mathsf{H}_0\colon \boldsymbol{\theta} = \boldsymbol{\theta}_0. \qquad \text{(A3.54)}$$

Finally, the efficient-score, or Lagrange-multiplier (LM), test is based on $\boldsymbol{q}(\tilde{\boldsymbol{\theta}})$, which is not identically zero, unlike $\boldsymbol{q}(\hat{\boldsymbol{\theta}})$ (see Ch.13) From an extension of (A3.40):

$$\sqrt{T}\boldsymbol{q}\left(\boldsymbol{\theta}_p\right) \sim \mathsf{N}\left[\mathbf{0}, \mathcal{I}_0\left(\boldsymbol{\theta}_p\right)\right], \qquad \text{(A3.55)}$$

and hence:

$$T\boldsymbol{q}(\boldsymbol{\theta}_0)' \mathcal{I}_0(\boldsymbol{\theta}_0)^{-1} \boldsymbol{q}(\boldsymbol{\theta}_0) \underset{a}{\sim} \chi^2(k) \text{ on } \mathsf{H}_0\colon \boldsymbol{\theta} = \boldsymbol{\theta}_0. \tag{A3.56}$$

Under both null and alternatives close to, but distinct from, H_0, all three test types have the same distribution in large samples from stationary processes, namely $\chi^2(k)$ under H_0, and a non-central chi-square otherwise (see Ch.13). Such χ^2 tests are invariant to the direction in which an hypothesis is false, because they are quadratic functions, and only depend on the distance between the null $\boldsymbol{\theta}_0$ and the population value $\boldsymbol{\theta}_p$. LR, W, and LM tests use different measures of that distance, so although they are all distributed as chi-squares asymptotically, that may provide a more or less good approximation in finite samples.

A3.6 Non-parametric density estimation

Consider a data set $(x_1 \ldots x_T)$ for any variable $\{x_t\}$. Divide the range of $\{x_t\}$, centred at the sample mean of x, into n intervals of length h, where h is usually about $\hat{\sigma}_x/4$ when $\hat{\sigma}_x$ is the sample standard deviation of x. Then the proportion of all $\{x_t\}$ falling into each interval constitutes the histogram. The histogram is a crude representation of the underlying density, and, unless the sample is large, the apparent shape can be altered by the choice of h. In effect, information is lost by treating all observations within an interval as if they were equal, leading to a block-like representation. Let $I_k(x)$ be an indicator function, equal to unity when x falls in the kth interval, and zero otherwise. Denote the kth interval of the histogram by $\mathtt{H}_k$ then:

$$\mathtt{H}_k = T^{-1} \sum_{t=1}^{T} I_k(x_t) \text{ for } k = 1, \ldots, n \tag{A3.57}$$

where:

$$\sum_{k=1}^{n} I_k(x_t) = 1 \ \forall x_t. \tag{A3.58}$$

Assigning a weight of unity to an observation within an interval, and zero outside, makes no use of information about the spread of observations within intervals, and is susceptible to marked changes for small changes in the choice of intervals. Both problems are a reflection of the discrete nature of the weighting system defined by $T^{-1}I_k(\cdot)$ in (A3.57). A natural development is to consider a continuous weighting function, called a kernel, and denoted by $\mathtt{K}(\cdot)$ where:

$$\int_{-\infty}^{\infty} \mathtt{K}(v)\, dv = 1. \tag{A3.59}$$

Denote the actual, but unknown, density of X by $\mathsf{D}_\mathsf{x}(\cdot)$. This is estimated from the sample at an arbitrary value x by:

$$\widehat{\mathsf{D}_\mathsf{x}(x)} = T^{-1} \sum_{t=1}^{T} \mathtt{K}\left(\frac{x - x_t}{w}\right) \tag{A3.60}$$

where w is a window width, or smoothing, parameter. Frequently, the window width is taken as $w = 1.06\hat{\sigma}_x T^{-0.2}$, and the normal density is a widely-used choice for $\mathsf{K}(\cdot)$:

$$\mathsf{K}\left(\frac{x - x_t}{w}\right) = \left(2\pi w^2\right)^{-\frac{1}{2}} \exp\left[-\frac{1}{2}\left(\frac{x - x_t}{w}\right)^2\right]. \tag{A3.61}$$

$\widehat{\mathsf{D}_\mathsf{x}(x)}$ can be calculated at many values of x and the result is a much smoother estimate of $\mathsf{D}_\mathsf{x}(\cdot)$; the analogy with an improved histogram should be clear. An excellent reference on density-function estimation is Silverman (1986). Many of the graphs in the main text report densities estimated in this way: Figs. A2.1 showed some examples.

A3.7 Multiple regression

This section formulates the multiple-regression model in §A3.7.1 and the least-squares estimator of its parameters in §A3.7.2, followed by distributional results in §A3.7.4. Parameter subset estimation is developed in §A3.7.5, and partitioned inversion in §A3.7.6, which is then used in §A3.7.7 to relate regression to inversion. Finally, multiple and partial correlation are discussed in §A3.7.8 and §A3.7.9. The analysis is for a conditional model, but large-sample results for more realistic statistical processes are derived in Chapter A4.

A3.7.1 The multiple-regression model

Since linear models play a major role in econometrics, we begin by investigating the empirical counterpart of regression. The notation adopted for the linear regression model, viewed as the mechanism which generated the observed data, is:

$$y_t = \boldsymbol{\beta}' \boldsymbol{z}_t + u_t \ \text{ with } \ u_t \sim \mathsf{IN}\left[0, \sigma_u^2\right], \tag{A3.62}$$

where $\boldsymbol{\beta} = (\beta_1 \dots \beta_k)' \in \mathbb{R}^k$ is the $k \times 1$ parameter vector of interest, and $\boldsymbol{z}_t = (z_{1t} \dots z_{kt})'$. Then $\boldsymbol{\beta}' \boldsymbol{z}_t = \sum_{i=1}^k \beta_i z_{it}$. One of the elements in $\boldsymbol{z}_t$ is unity with the corresponding parameter being the intercept in (A3.62). We interpret (A3.62) as a regression equation, based on a joint normal distribution for $(y_t : \boldsymbol{z}_t')$ conditional on $\boldsymbol{z}_t$, so that from Chapter A2:

$$\mathsf{E}\left[y_t \mid \boldsymbol{z}_t\right] = \boldsymbol{\beta}' \boldsymbol{z}_t \ \text{ with } \ \mathsf{E}\left[\boldsymbol{z}_t u_t\right] = \mathbf{0}.$$

Hence $\mathsf{E}[(y_t - \boldsymbol{\gamma}' \boldsymbol{z}_t)^2]$ is minimized at σ_u^2 by the choice of $\boldsymbol{\gamma} = \boldsymbol{\beta}$. Chapter 5 considers the conditions necessary to sustain a factorization of a joint density into a conditional model of y_t given $\boldsymbol{z}_t$, and a marginal model for $\boldsymbol{z}_t$ which is then ignored. Chapter 6 considers other feasible interpretations of linear equations like (A3.62) and their implications.

Grouping the observations so that $\boldsymbol{y}' = (y_1 \dots y_T)$ and $\boldsymbol{Z}' = (\boldsymbol{z}_1 \dots \boldsymbol{z}_T)$, which is a $T \times k$ matrix with $\text{rank}(\boldsymbol{Z}) = k$, and $\boldsymbol{u}' = (u_1 \dots u_T)$:

$$\boldsymbol{y} = \boldsymbol{Z}\boldsymbol{\beta} + \boldsymbol{u} \ \text{ with } \ \boldsymbol{u} \sim \mathsf{N}_T\left[\mathbf{0}, \sigma_u^2 \boldsymbol{I}\right]. \tag{A3.63}$$

To simplify the derivations, we impose the stronger requirement that $\mathsf{E}[\boldsymbol{y}|\boldsymbol{Z}] = \boldsymbol{Z\beta}$, and hence $\mathsf{E}[\boldsymbol{Z}'\boldsymbol{u}] = \mathbf{0}$. Although conditioning on $\boldsymbol{Z}$ is too strong to be justifiable in economics, and essentially entails an experimental setting, most of the results hold in large samples under weaker assumptions as seen in Chapter A4. The assumptions about $\boldsymbol{u}$ are almost equally strong, but less objectionable in practice given the discussion in Chapters 1 and 2.

A3.7.2 Ordinary least squares

The algebra of ordinary least-squares (OLS) estimation can now be established in matrix notation. Many of these algebraic results do not depend on the statistical status of $\boldsymbol{Z}$ and hold even when conditioning is invalid. In statistical terms, the OLS estimator will also be the maximum likelihood estimator under the present assumptions (see §A3.3), but the emphasis here is on the properties of OLS. The analysis draws on Chapter A1.

The objective of OLS estimation is to find the value $\widehat{\boldsymbol{\beta}}$ of $\boldsymbol{\beta}$ which minimizes the quadratic function:

$$h(\boldsymbol{\beta}) = (\boldsymbol{y} - \boldsymbol{Z\beta})' (\boldsymbol{y} - \boldsymbol{Z\beta}). \tag{A3.64}$$

Differentiate $h(\boldsymbol{\beta})$ with respect to $\boldsymbol{\beta}$

$$\frac{\partial h(\boldsymbol{\beta})}{\partial \boldsymbol{\beta}} = -2\boldsymbol{Z}' (\boldsymbol{y} - \boldsymbol{Z\beta}),$$

then solving the resulting expression equated to zero yields:

$$\widehat{\boldsymbol{\beta}} = (\boldsymbol{Z}'\boldsymbol{Z})^{-1} \boldsymbol{Z}'\boldsymbol{y}. \tag{A3.65}$$

Alternatively, the sample analogue of $\mathsf{E}[\boldsymbol{Z}'\boldsymbol{u}] = \mathbf{0}$ is $\boldsymbol{Z}'(\boldsymbol{y} - \boldsymbol{Z}\widehat{\boldsymbol{\beta}}) = \mathbf{0}$ which is the same as (A3.65). Since:

$$\frac{\partial^2 h(\boldsymbol{\beta})}{\partial \boldsymbol{\beta} \partial \boldsymbol{\beta}'} = 2\boldsymbol{Z}'\boldsymbol{Z},$$

the value $\widehat{\boldsymbol{\beta}}$ of $\boldsymbol{\beta}$ in (A3.65) minimizes $h(\boldsymbol{\beta})$ in (A3.64).

To determine the properties of $\widehat{\boldsymbol{\beta}}$ as an estimator of $\boldsymbol{\beta}$, substitute for $\boldsymbol{y}$ from (A3.63) to obtain:

$$\widehat{\boldsymbol{\beta}} = \boldsymbol{\beta} + (\boldsymbol{Z}'\boldsymbol{Z})^{-1} \boldsymbol{Z}'\boldsymbol{u}. \tag{A3.66}$$

Taking expectations conditional on $\boldsymbol{Z}$:

$$\mathsf{E}\left[\left(\widehat{\boldsymbol{\beta}} - \boldsymbol{\beta}\right) \mid \boldsymbol{Z}\right] = \mathsf{E}\left[(\boldsymbol{Z}'\boldsymbol{Z})^{-1} \boldsymbol{Z}'\boldsymbol{u} \mid \boldsymbol{Z}\right] = (\boldsymbol{Z}'\boldsymbol{Z})^{-1} \boldsymbol{Z}'\mathsf{E}[\boldsymbol{u}] = \mathbf{0}. \tag{A3.67}$$

Conditioning on $\boldsymbol{Z}$ will be left implicit where that simplifies formulae.

Next, $\mathsf{V}[\widehat{\boldsymbol{\beta}}]$ is given by:

$$\begin{aligned} \mathsf{E}\left[\left(\widehat{\boldsymbol{\beta}} - \boldsymbol{\beta}\right)\left(\widehat{\boldsymbol{\beta}} - \boldsymbol{\beta}\right)' \mid \boldsymbol{Z}\right] &= \mathsf{E}\left[(\boldsymbol{Z}'\boldsymbol{Z})^{-1} \boldsymbol{Z}'\boldsymbol{u}\boldsymbol{u}'\boldsymbol{Z} (\boldsymbol{Z}'\boldsymbol{Z})^{-1} \mid \boldsymbol{Z}\right] \\ &= (\boldsymbol{Z}'\boldsymbol{Z})^{-1} \boldsymbol{Z}'\mathsf{E}[\boldsymbol{u}\boldsymbol{u}'] \boldsymbol{Z} (\boldsymbol{Z}'\boldsymbol{Z})^{-1} \\ &= \sigma_u^2 (\boldsymbol{Z}'\boldsymbol{Z})^{-1}. \end{aligned} \tag{A3.68}$$

Letting $\hat{\boldsymbol{u}} = (\boldsymbol{y} - \boldsymbol{Z}\hat{\boldsymbol{\beta}})$ be the residual vector, σ_u^2 can be estimated by:

$$\hat{\sigma}_u^2 = \frac{\hat{\boldsymbol{u}}'\hat{\boldsymbol{u}}}{T-k}, \tag{A3.69}$$

where $\hat{\boldsymbol{u}}'\hat{\boldsymbol{u}} = RSS$ (an acronym for residual sum of squares). In turn, $\mathsf{V}[\hat{\boldsymbol{\beta}}]$ can be estimated by:

$$\widehat{\mathsf{V}\left[\hat{\boldsymbol{\beta}}\right]} = \hat{\sigma}_u^2 \left(\boldsymbol{Z}'\boldsymbol{Z}\right)^{-1}. \tag{A3.70}$$

From (A3.63)–(A3.68), since $\hat{\boldsymbol{\beta}}$ is a linear function of the normally distributed vector $\boldsymbol{u}$:

$$\hat{\boldsymbol{\beta}} \sim \mathsf{N}_k \left[\boldsymbol{\beta}, \sigma_u^2 \left(\boldsymbol{Z}'\boldsymbol{Z}\right)^{-1}\right]. \tag{A3.71}$$

Consequently, from (A3.71) (see §A2.9.4):

$$\eta_1 = \frac{\left(\hat{\boldsymbol{\beta}} - \boldsymbol{\beta}\right)' \left(\boldsymbol{Z}'\boldsymbol{Z}\right) \left(\hat{\boldsymbol{\beta}} - \boldsymbol{\beta}\right)}{\sigma_u^2} \sim \chi^2(k). \tag{A3.72}$$

Let $\boldsymbol{Q}_Z = \boldsymbol{I}_T - \boldsymbol{Z}(\boldsymbol{Z}'\boldsymbol{Z})^{-1}\boldsymbol{Z}'$ which is a symmetric and idempotent matrix, so that $\boldsymbol{Q}_Z = \boldsymbol{Q}_Z'$, $\boldsymbol{Q}_Z = \boldsymbol{Q}_Z^2$ and $\boldsymbol{Q}_Z(\boldsymbol{I}_T - \boldsymbol{Q}_Z) = \boldsymbol{0}$. From (A3.72) and (A3.65):

$$\begin{aligned} \sigma_u^2 \eta_1 &= \left[\boldsymbol{u}'\boldsymbol{Z}\left(\boldsymbol{Z}'\boldsymbol{Z}\right)^{-1}\right] \left(\boldsymbol{Z}'\boldsymbol{Z}\right) \left[\left(\boldsymbol{Z}'\boldsymbol{Z}\right)^{-1} \boldsymbol{Z}'\boldsymbol{u}\right] \\ &= \boldsymbol{u}'\boldsymbol{Z}\left(\boldsymbol{Z}'\boldsymbol{Z}\right)^{-1} \boldsymbol{Z}'\boldsymbol{u} = \boldsymbol{u}'\left(\boldsymbol{I}_T - \boldsymbol{Q}_Z\right)\boldsymbol{u}. \end{aligned} \tag{A3.73}$$

Further, $\boldsymbol{Q}_Z$ annihilates $\boldsymbol{Z}$ since $\boldsymbol{Q}_Z\boldsymbol{Z} = \boldsymbol{0}$, so that:

$$\boldsymbol{Q}_Z\boldsymbol{y} = \boldsymbol{y} - \boldsymbol{Z}\left(\boldsymbol{Z}'\boldsymbol{Z}\right)^{-1}\boldsymbol{Z}'\boldsymbol{y} = \boldsymbol{y} - \boldsymbol{Z}\hat{\boldsymbol{\beta}} = \hat{\boldsymbol{u}} = \boldsymbol{Q}_Z\boldsymbol{u}, \tag{A3.74}$$

where the last equality follows from pre-multiplying (A3.63) by $\boldsymbol{Q}_Z$. Consequently:

$$RSS = \boldsymbol{y}'\boldsymbol{Q}_Z\boldsymbol{y} = \boldsymbol{u}'\boldsymbol{Q}_Z\boldsymbol{u}. \tag{A3.75}$$

Since $\boldsymbol{Q}_Z$ is real and symmetric, let $\boldsymbol{Q}_Z = \boldsymbol{H}\boldsymbol{\Lambda}\boldsymbol{H}'$ where $\boldsymbol{\Lambda}$ is the diagonal matrix of eigenvalues, and $\boldsymbol{H}$ is the non-singular matrix of eigenvectors with $\boldsymbol{H}'\boldsymbol{H} = \boldsymbol{I}_T$. By idempotency, all the eigenvalues of $\boldsymbol{Q}_Z$ are either zero or unity (see Ch.A1) and $\text{rank}(\boldsymbol{Q}_Z) = \text{tr}(\boldsymbol{Q}_Z)$, so:

$$\text{tr}\left(\boldsymbol{Q}_Z\right) = \text{tr}\left(\boldsymbol{I}_T - \boldsymbol{Z}\left(\boldsymbol{Z}'\boldsymbol{Z}\right)^{-1}\boldsymbol{Z}'\right) = \text{tr}\left(\boldsymbol{I}_T\right) - \text{tr}\left(\left(\boldsymbol{Z}'\boldsymbol{Z}\right)^{-1}\boldsymbol{Z}'\boldsymbol{Z}\right) = T - k.$$

Thus, there are $(T-k)$ unit and k zero eigenvalues, and $\boldsymbol{Q}_Z$ is singular of rank $(T-k)$.

A3.7.3 The Gauss–Markov theorem

We now prove the Gauss–Markov theorem, namely that the OLS estimator $\widehat{\beta}$ is the best linear unbiased estimator (BLUE) conditional on Z (Ch.5 discusses the precise conditions). First, $\widehat{\beta}$ is a linear function of $\{y_t\}$ from (A3.63). Secondly, OLS is unbiased as shown in (A3.67). Thirdly, the variance of $\widehat{\beta}$ is given by (A3.68).

Consider any other linear unbiased estimator defined by:

$$\breve{\beta} = W'y,$$

where:

$$\mathsf{E}\left[\breve{\beta}\right] = \mathsf{E}\left[W'\left(Z\beta + \epsilon\right)\right] = W'Z\beta,$$

so $\mathsf{E}[\breve{\beta}] = \beta$ implies that:

$$W'Z = I_k. \tag{A3.76}$$

In that case:

$$\mathsf{V}\left[\breve{\beta}\right] = \mathsf{E}\left[W'\epsilon\epsilon W\right] = W'\mathsf{E}\left[\epsilon\epsilon\right]W = \sigma_\epsilon^2 W'W.$$

The difference between the two variance matrices is:

$$\mathsf{V}\left[\breve{\beta}\right] - \mathsf{V}\left[\widehat{\beta}\right] = \sigma_\epsilon^2\left(W'W - (Z'Z)^{-1}\right), \tag{A3.77}$$

and we wish to prove that this is always positive semi-definite. By definition, letting $Q_Z = (I_T - Z(Z'Z)^{-1}Z')$:

$$\begin{aligned} W &\equiv Q_Z W + (I_T - Q_Z)W \\ &= Q_Z W + Z(Z'Z)^{-1}Z'W \\ &= Q_Z W + Z(Z'Z)^{-1} \end{aligned} \tag{A3.78}$$

from (A3.76). Substituting (A3.78) in (A3.77):

$$\begin{aligned} \mathsf{V}\left[\breve{\beta}\right] - \mathsf{V}\left[\widehat{\beta}\right] &= \sigma_\epsilon^2\left(W'Q_Z W + (Z'Z)^{-1}Z'Z(Z'Z)^{-1} - (Z'Z)^{-1}\right) \\ &= \sigma_\epsilon^2 W'Q_Z W \succeq 0, \end{aligned}$$

since $W'Q_Z W$ is a matrix idempotent quadratic form, and so is positive semi-definite. Thus, the minimum variance is when $W = Z(Z'Z)^{-1}$ so that $Q_Z W = 0$, which yields $\widehat{\beta}$.

A3.7.4 Distributional results

Since $u \sim \mathsf{N}_T[0, \sigma_u^2 I]$, then $u'u/\sigma_u^2 \sim \chi^2(T)$. However, as Q_Z is singular, we cannot apply the theorems of §A2.9.4 on the distributions of functions of normal variables to $Q_Z u$ or $u'Q_Z u$. An alternative route is nevertheless feasible. Collect all of the unit eigenvalues of Q_Z in the first $(T-k)$ diagonal elements of Λ, with the last k diagonal elements being zeros. Let $\boldsymbol{\nu} = \boldsymbol{H}'\boldsymbol{u} \sim \mathsf{N}_T[\mathbf{0}, \sigma_u^2 \boldsymbol{H}'\boldsymbol{H}] = \mathsf{N}_T[\mathbf{0}, \sigma_u^2 \boldsymbol{I}]$, and consider the quadratic form:

$$\boldsymbol{u}'\boldsymbol{Q}_Z\boldsymbol{u} = \boldsymbol{u}'\boldsymbol{H}\boldsymbol{\Lambda}\boldsymbol{H}'\boldsymbol{u} = \boldsymbol{\nu}'\boldsymbol{\Lambda}\boldsymbol{\nu} = \boldsymbol{\nu}_1'\boldsymbol{\nu}_1, \qquad \text{(A3.79)}$$

where $\boldsymbol{\nu}' = (\boldsymbol{\nu}_1' : \boldsymbol{\nu}_2')$, so that $\boldsymbol{\nu}_1$ and $\boldsymbol{\nu}_2$ correspond to the unit and zero roots respectively in $\boldsymbol{\Lambda}$. Then, $\boldsymbol{\nu}_1$ denotes the first $(T-k)$ elements of $\boldsymbol{\nu}$ corresponding to the unit eigenvalues of $\boldsymbol{Q}_Z$ such that $\boldsymbol{\nu}_1 \sim \mathsf{N}_{T-k}[\mathbf{0}, \sigma_u^2 \boldsymbol{I}]$. Since $\boldsymbol{\nu} \sim \mathsf{N}_T[\mathbf{0}, \sigma_u^2 \boldsymbol{I}]$, $\boldsymbol{\nu}_1$ and $\boldsymbol{\nu}_2$ are distributed independently. Hence:

$$\eta_2 = \frac{\boldsymbol{u}'\boldsymbol{Q}_Z\boldsymbol{u}}{\sigma_u^2} = \frac{\boldsymbol{\nu}_1'\boldsymbol{\nu}_1}{\sigma_u^2} \sim \chi^2(T-k). \qquad \text{(A3.80)}$$

Thus, an idempotent quadratic form in standardized normal variables is distributed as a χ^2 with degrees of freedom equal to the rank of the idempotent matrix. Also:

$$\eta_2 = \frac{(T-k)\,\hat{\sigma}_u^2}{\sigma_u^2} \quad \text{so that} \quad \hat{\sigma}_u^2 \sim \frac{\sigma_u^2 \chi^2(T-k)}{T-k}. \qquad \text{(A3.81)}$$

The properties of $\hat{\sigma}_u^2$ can be calculated from this last result using the χ^2-distribution since $\mathsf{E}[\chi^2(T-k)] = T-k$ and $\mathsf{V}[\chi^2(T-k)] = 2(T-k)$.

Since $(\boldsymbol{I}_T - \boldsymbol{Q}_Z) = \boldsymbol{H}(\boldsymbol{I}_T - \boldsymbol{\Lambda})\boldsymbol{H}'$:

$$\boldsymbol{u}'(\boldsymbol{I}_T - \boldsymbol{Q}_Z)\boldsymbol{u} = \boldsymbol{\nu}'(\boldsymbol{I}_T - \boldsymbol{\Lambda})\boldsymbol{\nu} = \boldsymbol{\nu}_2'\boldsymbol{\nu}_2,$$

so $\eta_1 = \boldsymbol{\nu}_2'\boldsymbol{\nu}_2/\sigma_u^2$. As $\boldsymbol{\nu}_1$ and $\boldsymbol{\nu}_2$ are distributed independently, η_1 and η_2 are also independent, matching their being $\chi^2(k)$ and $\chi^2(T-k)$ respectively. Tests of H_0: $\boldsymbol{\beta} = \mathbf{0}$ (or components thereof) follow from these results using the F-distribution, since $\boldsymbol{y} = \boldsymbol{u}$ when $\boldsymbol{\beta} = \mathbf{0}$, so that on H_0:

$$\boldsymbol{u}'(\boldsymbol{I}_T - \boldsymbol{Q}_Z)\boldsymbol{u} = \boldsymbol{y}'(\boldsymbol{I}_T - \boldsymbol{Q}_Z)\boldsymbol{y} = \hat{\boldsymbol{\beta}}'(\boldsymbol{Z}'\boldsymbol{Z})\hat{\boldsymbol{\beta}}, \qquad \text{(A3.82)}$$

and hence:

$$\eta_\beta = \frac{(T-k)\,\eta_1}{k\eta_2} = \frac{(T-k)\,\boldsymbol{y}'(\boldsymbol{I}_T - \boldsymbol{Q}_Z)\boldsymbol{y}}{k\boldsymbol{y}'\boldsymbol{Q}_Z\boldsymbol{y}} = \frac{(T-k)\,\hat{\boldsymbol{\beta}}'(\boldsymbol{Z}'\boldsymbol{Z})\hat{\boldsymbol{\beta}}}{kRSS} \underset{\mathsf{H}_0}{\sim} F(k, T-k). \qquad \text{(A3.83)}$$

The last expression for η_β is the statistic which is actually computed. If $\boldsymbol{\beta} \neq \mathbf{0}$, then from (A3.71), the numerator of η_β becomes a non-central χ^2 with non-centrality parameter $\boldsymbol{\beta}'\boldsymbol{Z}'\boldsymbol{Z}\boldsymbol{\beta} \geq 0$, whereas the denominator is unchanged. Thus, the statistic η_β will on average lead to values larger than the $F(k, T-k)$ anticipated under the null. We investigate the issue of test power in Chapter 13.

Finally, from (A3.71) each element $\hat{\beta}_i$ of $\hat{\boldsymbol{\beta}}$ is normally distributed with variance given by the ith diagonal element d_{ii} of $\sigma_u^2(\boldsymbol{Z}'\boldsymbol{Z})^{-1}$, and is independent of η_2. Thus:

$$\frac{\left(\hat{\beta}_i - \beta_i\right)}{\hat{\sigma}_u\sqrt{d_{ii}}} \sim \mathsf{t}(T-k), \qquad \text{(A3.84)}$$

where $\mathsf{t}(T-k)$ denotes Student's t-distribution with $(T-k)$ degrees of freedom and:

$$\hat{\sigma}_u \sqrt{d_{ii}} = \mathsf{SE}\left(\hat{\beta}_i\right) \tag{A3.85}$$

is the standard error of $\hat{\beta}_i$. On the hypothesis H_0: $\beta_i = 0$:

$$\tau_i = \frac{\hat{\beta}_i}{\mathsf{SE}\left(\hat{\beta}_i\right)} \underset{\mathsf{H}_0}{\sim} \mathsf{t}\left(T-k\right), \tag{A3.86}$$

which is a computable statistic from sample evidence alone.

We now prove the independence of the sample mean and variance asserted in §A3.1.3. Take the special case $k = 1$, $z_{1t} = 1 \; \forall t$, so $\hat{\beta}_1$ is the sample mean and $\hat{\sigma}_u^2$ is the sample variance. Then $(\hat{\beta}_1 - \beta_1)$ is a linear function of $\boldsymbol{u}$, given by $(\boldsymbol{z}'\boldsymbol{z})^{-1}\boldsymbol{z}'\boldsymbol{u} = \boldsymbol{G}\boldsymbol{u}$. The sample variance is the quadratic function $\boldsymbol{u}'\boldsymbol{Q}_Z\boldsymbol{u}/(T-1)$, where $\boldsymbol{Q}_Z = \boldsymbol{I}_T - \boldsymbol{z}(\boldsymbol{z}'\boldsymbol{z})^{-1}\boldsymbol{z}' = \boldsymbol{Q}_Z'$. Since $\boldsymbol{u}'\boldsymbol{Q}_Z\boldsymbol{u} = \boldsymbol{u}'\boldsymbol{Q}_Z'\boldsymbol{Q}_Z\boldsymbol{u}$ and:

$$\boldsymbol{G}\boldsymbol{Q}_Z = \left(\boldsymbol{z}'\boldsymbol{z}\right)^{-1}\boldsymbol{z}'\left(\boldsymbol{I}_T - \boldsymbol{z}\left(\boldsymbol{z}'\boldsymbol{z}\right)^{-1}\boldsymbol{z}'\right) = \boldsymbol{0},$$

the linear functions $\boldsymbol{G}\boldsymbol{u}$ and $\boldsymbol{Q}_Z\boldsymbol{u}$ depend on different components of $\boldsymbol{u}$, and so are independent. In the above notation, the former depends on $\boldsymbol{\nu}_1$ and the latter on $\boldsymbol{\nu}_2$.

A3.7.5 Subsets of parameters

Consider estimating a subset of k_b parameters $\boldsymbol{\beta}_b$ of $\boldsymbol{\beta}$ where $k_a + k_b = k$. Partition $\boldsymbol{Z} = (\boldsymbol{Z}_a : \boldsymbol{Z}_b)$ and $\boldsymbol{\beta}' = (\boldsymbol{\beta}_a' : \boldsymbol{\beta}_b')$ so that:

$$\boldsymbol{y} = \boldsymbol{Z}_a\boldsymbol{\beta}_a + \boldsymbol{Z}_b\boldsymbol{\beta}_b + \boldsymbol{u}. \tag{A3.87}$$

Let $\boldsymbol{Q}_a = \boldsymbol{I}_T - \boldsymbol{Z}_a(\boldsymbol{Z}_a'\boldsymbol{Z}_a)^{-1}\boldsymbol{Z}_a'$ so that $\boldsymbol{Q}_a\boldsymbol{Z}_a = \boldsymbol{0}$, and:

$$\boldsymbol{Q}_a\boldsymbol{y} = \boldsymbol{Q}_a\boldsymbol{Z}_b\boldsymbol{\beta}_b + \boldsymbol{Q}_a\boldsymbol{u}. \tag{A3.88}$$

Hence:

$$\hat{\boldsymbol{\beta}}_b = \left(\boldsymbol{Z}_b'\boldsymbol{Q}_a\boldsymbol{Z}_b\right)^{-1}\boldsymbol{Z}_b'\boldsymbol{Q}_a\boldsymbol{y}. \tag{A3.89}$$

From (A3.88) and (A3.89):

$$\hat{\boldsymbol{\beta}}_b = \boldsymbol{\beta}_b + \left(\boldsymbol{Z}_b'\boldsymbol{Q}_a\boldsymbol{Z}_b\right)^{-1}\boldsymbol{Z}_b'\boldsymbol{Q}_a\boldsymbol{u}, \tag{A3.90}$$

so that

$$\mathsf{V}\left[\hat{\boldsymbol{\beta}}_b\right] = \sigma_u^2\left(\boldsymbol{Z}_b'\boldsymbol{Q}_a\boldsymbol{Z}_b\right)^{-1}. \tag{A3.91}$$

Thus:

$$\hat{\boldsymbol{\beta}}_b \sim \mathsf{N}_{k_b}\left[\boldsymbol{\beta}_b, \sigma_u^2\left(\boldsymbol{Z}_b'\boldsymbol{Q}_a\boldsymbol{Z}_b\right)^{-1}\right]. \tag{A3.92}$$

Hypothesis tests about β_b follow analogously to the previous section. In particular, from §A3.7.4 and (A3.92):

$$\eta_b = \frac{\left(\hat{\beta}_b - \beta_b\right)' \left(Z_b' Q_a Z_b\right) \left(\hat{\beta}_b - \beta_b\right)}{k_b \hat{\sigma}_u^2} \sim F\left(k_b, T - k\right). \tag{A3.93}$$

When $k_b = 1$, this matches (A3.86) under H_0: $\beta_b = 0$, and when $k_b = k$, (A3.93) reproduces (A3.83) under H_0: $\boldsymbol{\beta} = \mathbf{0}$. A useful case of (A3.93) is when $k_b = (k - 1)$ and $\boldsymbol{Z}_a = \boldsymbol{\iota}$ (the $T \times 1$ vector of ones), so all coefficients other than the intercept are tested.

If, instead of estimating (A3.87), $\boldsymbol{Z}_a$ is omitted from the model in the incorrect belief that $\boldsymbol{\beta}_a = \mathbf{0}$, the equation to be estimated becomes:

$$\boldsymbol{y} = \boldsymbol{Z}_b \boldsymbol{\beta}_b + \boldsymbol{e}. \tag{A3.94}$$

The resulting estimator of $\boldsymbol{\beta}_b$, denoted by $\tilde{\boldsymbol{\beta}}_b = (\boldsymbol{Z}_b' \boldsymbol{Z}_b)^{-1} \boldsymbol{Z}_b' \boldsymbol{y}$, confounds the effects of $\boldsymbol{Z}_a$ and $\boldsymbol{Z}_b$:

$$\begin{aligned} \tilde{\boldsymbol{\beta}}_b &= \left(\boldsymbol{Z}_b' \boldsymbol{Z}_b\right)^{-1} \boldsymbol{Z}_b' \left(\boldsymbol{Z}_a \boldsymbol{\beta}_a + \boldsymbol{Z}_b \boldsymbol{\beta}_b + \boldsymbol{u}\right) \\ &= \boldsymbol{B}_{ba} \boldsymbol{\beta}_a + \boldsymbol{\beta}_b + \left(\boldsymbol{Z}_b' \boldsymbol{Z}_b\right)^{-1} \boldsymbol{Z}_b' \boldsymbol{u}, \end{aligned} \tag{A3.95}$$

where $\boldsymbol{B}_{ba} = (\boldsymbol{Z}_b' \boldsymbol{Z}_b)^{-1} \boldsymbol{Z}_b' \boldsymbol{Z}_a$. Thus:

$$\mathsf{E}\left[\tilde{\boldsymbol{\beta}}_b\right] = \boldsymbol{B}_{ba} \boldsymbol{\beta}_a + \boldsymbol{\beta}_b, \tag{A3.96}$$

which equals $\boldsymbol{\beta}_b$ if and only if $\boldsymbol{B}_{ba} \boldsymbol{\beta}_a = \mathbf{0}$. Moreover, let $\boldsymbol{Q}_b$ have the same form as $\boldsymbol{Q}_a$ but using $\boldsymbol{Z}_b$, then:

$$\widehat{\mathsf{V}\left[\tilde{\boldsymbol{\beta}}_b\right]} = \tilde{\sigma}_u^2 \left(\boldsymbol{Z}_b' \boldsymbol{Z}_b\right)^{-1} \quad \text{where } \tilde{\sigma}_u^2 = \frac{\boldsymbol{y}' \boldsymbol{Q}_b \boldsymbol{y}}{T - k_b} = \frac{\tilde{\boldsymbol{u}}' \tilde{\boldsymbol{u}}}{T - k_b} \tag{A3.97}$$

where $\tilde{\boldsymbol{u}} = \boldsymbol{y} - \boldsymbol{Z}_b \tilde{\boldsymbol{\beta}}_b$ and:

$$\mathsf{E}\left[\tilde{\sigma}_u^2\right] = \sigma_u^2 + \frac{\boldsymbol{\beta}_a' \boldsymbol{Z}_a' \boldsymbol{Q}_b \boldsymbol{Z}_a \boldsymbol{\beta}_a}{T - k_b} \geq \sigma_u^2. \tag{A3.98}$$

The estimated variance matrix in (A3.97) may exceed, or be less than, that given by the relevant sub-matrix of (A3.70), in the sense that the difference could be positive or negative semi-definite.

Conventionally, $\tilde{\boldsymbol{\beta}}_b$ is often interpreted as a biased estimator of $\boldsymbol{\beta}_b$ where the bias is given by $\boldsymbol{B}_{ba} \boldsymbol{\beta}_a$. The sign of an estimated coefficient from (A3.94) can be the same as, or the opposite to, that expected from prior theoretical reasoning, and the latter is sometimes called a 'wrong sign'. In the main text, we interpret the outcome in (A3.96) as delivering a different coefficient than $\boldsymbol{\beta}_b$ given by $\boldsymbol{\gamma}_b = \boldsymbol{B}_{ba} \boldsymbol{\beta}_a + \boldsymbol{\beta}_b$, consonant with the following argument. First:

$$\boldsymbol{Z}_a \equiv \boldsymbol{Q}_b \boldsymbol{Z}_a + \left(\boldsymbol{I}_T - \boldsymbol{Q}_b\right) \boldsymbol{Z}_a = \boldsymbol{Q}_b \boldsymbol{Z}_a + \boldsymbol{Z}_b \boldsymbol{B}_{ba}. \tag{A3.99}$$

Consequently, from (A3.87):

$$\begin{aligned} y &= (Q_b Z_a + Z_b B_{ba}) \beta_a + Z_b \beta_b + u \\ &= Z_b \gamma_b + (u + Q_b Z_a \beta_a) \\ &= Z_b \gamma_b + v, \end{aligned} \tag{A3.100}$$

where $\mathsf{E}[v] = Q_b Z_a \beta_a \neq 0$; but since $Q_b Z_b = 0$:

$$\mathsf{E}[Z_b' v] = \mathsf{E}[Z_b' u] + Z_b' Q_b Z_a \beta_a = 0. \tag{A3.101}$$

Thus, the model is implicitly re-parameterized by omitting Z_a, and OLS is an unbiased estimator of γ_b despite $\mathsf{E}[v] \neq 0$. Under more general assumptions, a related large-sample result holds and is established in Chapter A4.

A3.7.6 Partitioned inversion

The results on estimating subsets of parameters can be obtained by partitioned inversion of $(Z'Z)$. The formulae are provided in Chapter A1 and are also used in §A3.7.7. Consider the matrix $(Z'Z)^{-1}$. Using (A1.12) with $H = (Z_b' Q_a Z_b)$ and $G = (Z_a' Q_b Z_a)$:

$$\begin{pmatrix} Z_a' Z_a & Z_a' Z_b \\ Z_b' Z_a & Z_b' Z_b \end{pmatrix}^{-1} = \begin{pmatrix} (Z_a' Q_b Z_a)^{-1} & -(Z_a' Q_b Z_a)^{-1} B_{ba}' \\ -B_{ab} (Z_b' Q_a Z_b)^{-1} & (Z_b' Q_a Z_b)^{-1} \end{pmatrix} \tag{A3.102}$$

where $B_{ab} = (Z_a' Z_a)^{-1} Z_a' Z_b$. Further, $Z'y$ can be partitioned conformably as:

$$\begin{pmatrix} Z_a' y \\ Z_b' y \end{pmatrix}, \tag{A3.103}$$

and multiplication of (A3.103) by (A3.102) delivers (A3.89) together with corresponding expressions for estimating β_a; the coefficient variance matrix follows from (A3.102).

Using the formulation in (A1.10) where $(Z'Z)^{-1}$ is given by:

$$\begin{pmatrix} (Z_a' Q_b Z_a)^{-1} & -(Z_a' Q_b Z_a)^{-1} B_{ba}' \\ -B_{ba} (Z_a' Q_b Z_a)^{-1} & (Z_b' Z_b)^{-1} + B_{ba} (Z_a' Q_b Z_a)^{-1} B_{ba}', \end{pmatrix} \tag{A3.104}$$

then multiplication of (A3.103) by (A3.104) delivers for the second row:

$$\begin{aligned} \hat{\beta}_b &= -B_{ba} (Z_a' Q_b Z_a)^{-1} Z_a' y + (Z_b' Z_b)^{-1} Z_b' y + B_{ba} (Z_a' Q_b Z_a)^{-1} B_{ba}' Z_b' y \\ &= \tilde{\beta}_b - B_{ba} (Z_a' Q_b Z_a)^{-1} Z_a' \left(I_T - Z_b (Z_b' Z_b)^{-1} Z_b' \right) y \\ &= \tilde{\beta}_b - B_{ba} \hat{\beta}_a, \end{aligned} \tag{A3.105}$$

from which it follows that:

$$\tilde{\beta}_b = \hat{\beta}_b + B_{ba} \hat{\beta}_a. \tag{A3.106}$$

Then (A3.106) is the exact estimation analogue of (A3.96). In words, the simple regression estimate of β_b equals the corresponding multiple regression estimate of β_b plus the auxiliary regression matrix multiplied by the multiple regression estimate of the omitted effect. Consequently, a regression coefficient is interpretable as a partial derivative of y with respect to the relevant z only when all other effects have either been included in the regression or are orthogonal to the variables under study.

A3.7.7 Regression and inversion

Regression estimation (in the sense of OLS) can be reformulated as a single matrix inversion using the partitioned formulae in §A3.7.6. Consider the complete data matrix $\boldsymbol{X} = (\boldsymbol{y} : \boldsymbol{Z})$ so that:

$$\boldsymbol{X}'\boldsymbol{X} = \begin{pmatrix} \boldsymbol{y}'\boldsymbol{y} & \boldsymbol{y}'\boldsymbol{Z} \\ \boldsymbol{Z}'\boldsymbol{y} & \boldsymbol{Z}'\boldsymbol{Z} \end{pmatrix}. \tag{A3.107}$$

From (A1.10), $(\boldsymbol{X}'\boldsymbol{X})^{-1}$ is given by:

$$\begin{pmatrix} \left(\boldsymbol{y}'\boldsymbol{y} - \boldsymbol{y}'\boldsymbol{Z}\left(\boldsymbol{Z}'\boldsymbol{Z}\right)^{-1}\boldsymbol{Z}'\boldsymbol{y}\right)^{-1} & -\boldsymbol{y}'\boldsymbol{Z}\left(\boldsymbol{Z}'\boldsymbol{Z}\right)^{-1}h^{-1} \\ -\left(\boldsymbol{Z}'\boldsymbol{Z}\right)^{-1}\boldsymbol{Z}'\boldsymbol{y}h^{-1} & \left(\boldsymbol{Z}'\boldsymbol{Z}\right)^{-1} + \widehat{\boldsymbol{\beta}}\widehat{\boldsymbol{\beta}}'h^{-1} \end{pmatrix} = h^{-1}\begin{pmatrix} 1 & -\widehat{\boldsymbol{\beta}}' \\ -\widehat{\boldsymbol{\beta}} & \boldsymbol{V} + \widehat{\boldsymbol{\beta}}\widehat{\boldsymbol{\beta}}' \end{pmatrix} \tag{A3.108}$$

where $\boldsymbol{V} = (T-k)\mathsf{V}[\widehat{\boldsymbol{\beta}}]$ and $h = (\boldsymbol{y}'\boldsymbol{y} - \boldsymbol{y}'\boldsymbol{Z}(\boldsymbol{Z}'\boldsymbol{Z})^{-1}\boldsymbol{Z}'\boldsymbol{y}) = RSS$. Thus, merely by inverting $\boldsymbol{X}'\boldsymbol{X}$, we obtain the estimators of σ_u^2 (from $RSS/(T-k)$), of $\boldsymbol{\beta}$, and of its variance. The first column of the inverse delivers $-\widehat{\boldsymbol{\beta}}$ because the first element is normalized at unity. If a different normalization was chosen on the diagonal of $(\boldsymbol{X}'\boldsymbol{X})^{-1}$ than the first (say the ith), then the result would be the corresponding regression of the ith variable on all the others. Implicitly, therefore, by inverting $(\boldsymbol{Z}'\boldsymbol{Z})$, the auxiliary regressions of each component on every remaining component are obtained *en route*, as can be seen from (A3.102).

A3.7.8 Multiple correlation

Let $\widehat{\boldsymbol{y}} = \boldsymbol{Z}\widehat{\boldsymbol{\beta}}$, then $\boldsymbol{y} = \widehat{\boldsymbol{y}} + \widehat{\boldsymbol{u}}$ and $\boldsymbol{Z}'\widehat{\boldsymbol{u}} = \boldsymbol{0}$ since $\boldsymbol{Q}_Z\boldsymbol{Z} = \boldsymbol{0}$. Thus, $\widehat{\boldsymbol{y}}'\widehat{\boldsymbol{u}} = \boldsymbol{0}$, implying that:

$$\boldsymbol{y}'\widehat{\boldsymbol{y}} = \widehat{\boldsymbol{y}}'\widehat{\boldsymbol{y}} \text{ and } \boldsymbol{y}'\boldsymbol{y} = \widehat{\boldsymbol{y}}'\widehat{\boldsymbol{y}} + \widehat{\boldsymbol{u}}'\widehat{\boldsymbol{u}}. \tag{A3.109}$$

It is convenient to have a measure of 'goodness of fit' between $\boldsymbol{y}$ and $\widehat{\boldsymbol{y}} = \boldsymbol{Z}\widehat{\boldsymbol{\beta}}$, and a natural choice is their correlation coefficient. When a constant is present in $\boldsymbol{Z}$ as the vector of ones $\boldsymbol{\iota}$, since $\boldsymbol{Q}_Z\boldsymbol{Z} = \boldsymbol{0}$, then $\boldsymbol{\iota}'\widehat{\boldsymbol{u}} = \boldsymbol{\iota}'\boldsymbol{Q}_Z\widehat{\boldsymbol{u}} = \boldsymbol{0}$ and $T^{-1}\boldsymbol{\iota}'\boldsymbol{y} = T^{-1}\boldsymbol{\iota}'\widehat{\boldsymbol{y}} = \bar{y}$ (the sample mean). Consequently, the squared correlation between $\boldsymbol{y}$ and $\widehat{\boldsymbol{y}}$ is given by:

$$\mathsf{R}^2(\boldsymbol{y}, \widehat{\boldsymbol{y}}) = \frac{\left[(\boldsymbol{y} - \boldsymbol{\iota}\bar{y})'(\widehat{\boldsymbol{y}} - \boldsymbol{\iota}\bar{y})\right]^2}{\left[\left\{(\boldsymbol{y} - \boldsymbol{\iota}\bar{y})'(\boldsymbol{y} - \boldsymbol{\iota}\bar{y})\right\}\left\{(\widehat{\boldsymbol{y}} - \boldsymbol{\iota}\bar{y})'(\widehat{\boldsymbol{y}} - \boldsymbol{\iota}\bar{y})\right\}\right]}.$$

Substituting $(\boldsymbol{y} - \boldsymbol{\iota}\bar{y}) = (\widehat{\boldsymbol{y}} - \boldsymbol{\iota}\bar{y}) + \widehat{\boldsymbol{u}}$ (i.e., taking deviations about means in $\boldsymbol{y} = \widehat{\boldsymbol{y}} + \widehat{\boldsymbol{u}}$), and using the results that $\widehat{\boldsymbol{y}}'\widehat{\boldsymbol{u}} = 0$ and $\boldsymbol{\iota}'\widehat{\boldsymbol{u}} = 0$:

$$\mathsf{R}^2 = \frac{(\widehat{\boldsymbol{y}} - \boldsymbol{\iota}\bar{y})'(\widehat{\boldsymbol{y}} - \boldsymbol{\iota}\bar{y})}{(\boldsymbol{y} - \boldsymbol{\iota}\bar{y})'(\boldsymbol{y} - \boldsymbol{\iota}\bar{y})}, \tag{A3.110}$$

and hence:

$$\left(1-\mathsf{R}^2\right)=\frac{\widehat{\boldsymbol{u}}'\widehat{\boldsymbol{u}}}{\left(\boldsymbol{y}-\iota\bar{y}\right)'\left(\boldsymbol{y}-\iota\bar{y}\right)}.$$

R^2 is the squared multiple correlation between $\boldsymbol{y}$ and $\boldsymbol{z}$. The statistic η_b in (A3.93) for testing the hypothesis that all coefficients other than the intercept are zero can be written as a function of $\mathsf{R}^2/(1-\mathsf{R}^2)$. On H_0: $\boldsymbol{\beta}_b=\mathbf{0}$, since $\widehat{\boldsymbol{y}}=\iota\widehat{\beta}_a+\boldsymbol{Z}_b\widehat{\boldsymbol{\beta}}_b$ and:

$$\widehat{\beta}_a=\bar{y}-\bar{\boldsymbol{z}}_b'\widehat{\boldsymbol{\beta}}_b=\bar{y}-T^{-1}\iota'\boldsymbol{Z}_b\widehat{\boldsymbol{\beta}}_b,$$

then:

$$\widehat{\boldsymbol{y}}=\iota\bar{y}-T^{-1}\iota\iota'\boldsymbol{Z}_b\widehat{\boldsymbol{\beta}}_b+\boldsymbol{Z}_b\widehat{\boldsymbol{\beta}}_b=\iota\bar{y}+\boldsymbol{Q}_a\boldsymbol{Z}_b\widehat{\boldsymbol{\beta}}_b,$$

as $\boldsymbol{Q}_a=(\boldsymbol{I}_T-\iota(\iota'\iota)^{-1}\iota')=(\boldsymbol{I}_T-T^{-1}\iota\iota')$, so that:

$$\eta_b=\frac{(T-k)\,\widehat{\boldsymbol{\beta}}_b'\boldsymbol{Z}_b'\boldsymbol{Q}_a\boldsymbol{Z}_b\widehat{\boldsymbol{\beta}}_b}{(k-1)\,\widehat{\boldsymbol{u}}'\widehat{\boldsymbol{u}}}=\frac{(T-k)\,(\widehat{\boldsymbol{y}}-\iota\bar{y})'\,(\widehat{\boldsymbol{y}}-\iota\bar{y})}{(k-1)\,\widehat{\boldsymbol{u}}'\widehat{\boldsymbol{u}}}=\frac{(T-k)\,\mathsf{R}^2}{(k-1)\,(1-\mathsf{R}^2)}. \tag{A3.111}$$

As $\mathsf{R}^2\rightarrow 1$, highly significant results are bound to occur. Chapter 4 considers a case where $\mathsf{R}^2\rightarrow 1$ even though the variables involved are not related.

A3.7.9 Partial correlation

The notions of partial correlations and partial regression coefficients are fundamental to interpreting econometric evidence. At the level of empirical modelling, equations like (A3.62) are usually formulated on the basis of subject-matter theory, with the implicit assumption that:

$$\frac{\partial y_t}{\partial z_{it}}=\beta_i \text{ for } i=1,..,k. \tag{A3.112}$$

OLS estimates $\widehat{\beta}_i$ are often interpreted as if they have the same properties (see §A3.7.5). When $i=b$, β_b is a scalar so that $\boldsymbol{Z}_b$ is a vector $\boldsymbol{z}_b$, and the marginal distribution of $\widehat{\beta}_b$ is given in (A3.92). Then the partial correlation $\mathsf{r}_{by\cdot a}$ between y and z_b having removed the linear influence of $\boldsymbol{Z}_a$ (assumed to contain ι) is the correlation between $\boldsymbol{Q}_a\boldsymbol{y}$ and $\boldsymbol{Q}_a\boldsymbol{z}_b$:

$$\mathsf{r}_{by\cdot a}=\frac{\boldsymbol{y}'\boldsymbol{Q}_a\boldsymbol{z}_b}{\sqrt{(\boldsymbol{y}'\boldsymbol{Q}_a\boldsymbol{y})\,(\boldsymbol{z}_b'\boldsymbol{Q}_a\boldsymbol{z}_b)}}=\frac{\widehat{\beta}_b\sqrt{\boldsymbol{z}_b'\boldsymbol{Q}_a\boldsymbol{z}_b}}{\sqrt{\boldsymbol{y}'\boldsymbol{Q}_a\boldsymbol{y}}}. \tag{A3.113}$$

Note that $\boldsymbol{Q}_a\boldsymbol{y}$ and $\boldsymbol{Q}_a\boldsymbol{z}_b$ have zero means and that:

$$\mathsf{r}^2_{by\cdot a}=\frac{\widehat{\beta}_b\,(\boldsymbol{z}_b'\boldsymbol{Q}_a\boldsymbol{z}_b)\,\widehat{\beta}_b}{\boldsymbol{y}'\boldsymbol{Q}_a\boldsymbol{y}}. \tag{A3.114}$$

The numerator of $(1-\mathsf{r}^2_{by\cdot a})$ is $\boldsymbol{y}'\boldsymbol{Q}_a\boldsymbol{y}-\widehat{\beta}_b(\boldsymbol{z}_b'\boldsymbol{Q}_a\boldsymbol{z}_b)\widehat{\beta}_b=\boldsymbol{y}'\boldsymbol{Q}^*_Z\boldsymbol{y}$ where:

$$\begin{aligned}\boldsymbol{Q}^*_Z &= \boldsymbol{Q}_a-\boldsymbol{Q}_a\boldsymbol{z}_b\left(\boldsymbol{z}_b'\boldsymbol{Q}_a\boldsymbol{z}_b\right)^{-1}\boldsymbol{z}_b'\boldsymbol{Q}_a \\ &= \boldsymbol{Q}_a\left[\boldsymbol{I}_T-\boldsymbol{Q}_a\boldsymbol{z}_b\left(\boldsymbol{z}_b'\boldsymbol{Q}_a\boldsymbol{z}_b\right)^{-1}\boldsymbol{z}_b'\boldsymbol{Q}_a\right]\boldsymbol{Q}_a.\end{aligned} \tag{A3.115}$$

Applying the formula for partitioned inversion in (A3.102) and noting that the term in $[\cdot]$ annihilates $\boldsymbol{Q}_a \boldsymbol{z}_b$ reveals that $\boldsymbol{Q}_Z^* = \boldsymbol{Q}_Z$. As a check, rearrange the regressors so that $\boldsymbol{Q}_Z^* \boldsymbol{Z} = \boldsymbol{Q}_Z^*(\boldsymbol{Z}_a : \boldsymbol{z}_b) = \boldsymbol{0} = \boldsymbol{Q}_Z \boldsymbol{Z}$. Then, from the earlier formula for τ_i when $i = b$:

$$\tau_b^2 = \frac{(T-k)\,\mathsf{r}_{by\cdot a}^2}{1-\mathsf{r}_{by\cdot a}^2}, \tag{A3.116}$$

In the special case that $k = 2$ and $\boldsymbol{z}_a = \boldsymbol{\iota}$ (A3.111) coincides with (A3.116). Other implications of partial correlations are considered in Chapter 7.

More generally, when $\boldsymbol{Z}_a$ includes $\boldsymbol{\iota}$ and $k_b > 1$, (A3.115) holds in the form:

$$\boldsymbol{Q}_Z = \boldsymbol{Q}_a - \boldsymbol{Q}_a \boldsymbol{Z}_b \left(\boldsymbol{Z}_b' \boldsymbol{Q}_a \boldsymbol{Z}_b\right)^{-1} \boldsymbol{Z}_b' \boldsymbol{Q}_a,$$

so that:

$$\boldsymbol{y}' \boldsymbol{Q}_Z \boldsymbol{y} = \boldsymbol{y}' \boldsymbol{Q}_a \boldsymbol{y} - \boldsymbol{y}' \boldsymbol{Q}_a \boldsymbol{Z}_b \left(\boldsymbol{Z}_b' \boldsymbol{Q}_a \boldsymbol{Z}_b\right)^{-1} \boldsymbol{Z}_b' \boldsymbol{Q}_a \boldsymbol{y} = \boldsymbol{y}' \boldsymbol{Q}_a \boldsymbol{y} - \widehat{\boldsymbol{\beta}}_b' \boldsymbol{Z}_b' \boldsymbol{Q}_a \boldsymbol{Z}_b \widehat{\boldsymbol{\beta}}_b. \tag{A3.117}$$

Substituting (A3.117) in (A3.93):

$$\eta_b = \frac{(T-k)\left[\boldsymbol{y}' \boldsymbol{Q}_a \boldsymbol{y} - \boldsymbol{y}' \boldsymbol{Q} \boldsymbol{y}\right]}{k_b \widehat{\boldsymbol{u}}' \widehat{\boldsymbol{u}}} = \frac{(T-k)\left[\tilde{\boldsymbol{u}}' \tilde{\boldsymbol{u}} - \widehat{\boldsymbol{u}}' \widehat{\boldsymbol{u}}\right]}{k_b \widehat{\boldsymbol{u}}' \widehat{\boldsymbol{u}}} = \frac{(T-k)}{k_b}\left[d\frac{\tilde{\sigma}_u^2}{\hat{\sigma}_u^2} - 1\right] \tag{A3.118}$$

where $d = (T-k_a)/(T-k)$. Thus, when $\hat{\sigma}_u^2 = \tilde{\sigma}_u^2$, $\eta_b = 1$, and $\hat{\sigma}_u^2 > \tilde{\sigma}_u^2$, then $\eta_b < 1$. In words, deleting k_b regressors when the F-test for the significance of their coefficients is less than unity will lower the estimated residual standard error. For $k_b = 1$, deleting a single variable with $\tau_b^2 < 1$ will lower the estimated residual standard error.

A3.7.10 Maximum-likelihood estimation

When $\boldsymbol{u} \sim \mathsf{N}_T[\boldsymbol{0}, \sigma_u^2 \boldsymbol{I}]$, the conditional log-likelihood function is given by:

$$\ell\left(\boldsymbol{\beta}, \sigma_u^2 \mid \boldsymbol{Z}; \boldsymbol{y}\right) = -\frac{T}{2}\log(2\pi) - \frac{T}{2}\log\left(\sigma_u^2\right) - \frac{(\boldsymbol{y}-\boldsymbol{Z}\boldsymbol{\beta})'(\boldsymbol{y}-\boldsymbol{Z}\boldsymbol{\beta})}{2\sigma_u^2},$$

so OLS is the MLE, and from previously established results, $\ell(\boldsymbol{\beta}, \sigma_u^2 | \boldsymbol{Z}; \boldsymbol{y})$ equals:

$$-\frac{T}{2}\log(2\pi) - \frac{T}{2}\log\left(\sigma_u^2\right) - \frac{\left(\widehat{\boldsymbol{\beta}}-\boldsymbol{\beta}\right)' \boldsymbol{Z}'\boldsymbol{Z}\left(\widehat{\boldsymbol{\beta}}-\boldsymbol{\beta}\right)}{2\sigma_u^2} - \frac{\widehat{\boldsymbol{u}}'\widehat{\boldsymbol{u}}}{2\sigma_u^2}. \tag{A3.119}$$

From (A3.119), $(\widehat{\boldsymbol{\beta}}, \hat{\sigma}_u^2)$ are jointly sufficient for $(\boldsymbol{\beta}, \sigma_u^2)$, and by independence, the joint distribution of $\widehat{\boldsymbol{\beta}}$ and $\hat{\sigma}_u^2$ factorizes into the products of their marginals. As a final comment, since $\widehat{\boldsymbol{\beta}} \sim \mathsf{N}_k[\boldsymbol{\beta}, \sigma_u^2(\boldsymbol{Z}'\boldsymbol{Z})^{-1}]$:

$$\log \mathsf{f}_{\widehat{\boldsymbol{\beta}}}\left(\widehat{\boldsymbol{\beta}} \mid \boldsymbol{Z}; \boldsymbol{y}; \sigma_u^2\right) = -\frac{k}{2}\log\left(2\pi\sigma_u^2\right) + \tfrac{1}{2}\log|\boldsymbol{Z}'\boldsymbol{Z}| - \frac{\left(\widehat{\boldsymbol{\beta}}-\boldsymbol{\beta}\right)' \boldsymbol{Z}'\boldsymbol{Z}\left(\widehat{\boldsymbol{\beta}}-\boldsymbol{\beta}\right)}{2\sigma_u^2}$$

so that (A3.119) contains the distribution of $\widehat{\boldsymbol{\beta}}$ as one of its components ($\log|\boldsymbol{Z}'\boldsymbol{Z}|$ is a constant).

A3.8 Exercises

A3.1 A sample of n random variables $\{X_i\}$ is independently distributed as $\mathsf{N}[\mu_x, \sigma_x^2]$. What is $\mathsf{E}[X_i]$ for every i? Let $\bar{X} = n^{-1}\sum_{i=1}^{n} X_i$ where $\sum$ denotes the sum. Show that $\mathsf{E}[\bar{X}] = \mu_x$, and discuss how that finding helps estimate μ_x when it is unknown. Let $v^2 = \sum_{i=1}^{n}(X_i - \bar{X})^2/(n-1)$ be the sample variance of X around its sample mean. Using the result that $\mathsf{E}[X - \mu_x]^2 = \sigma_x^2$, show that $\mathsf{E}[\bar{X} - \mu_x]^2 = \sigma_x^2/n$ and hence that $\bar{X} \sim \mathsf{N}[\mu_x, \sigma_x^2/n]$. Finally, show that $\mathsf{E}[v^2] = \sigma_x^2$ and comment on that result.

A3.2 Prove that the value $\hat{\boldsymbol{\beta}}$ of $\boldsymbol{\beta}$ in (A3.65) minimizes $h(\boldsymbol{\beta})$ in (A3.64).

A3.3 Prove that the estimated variance matrix in (A3.97) may exceed, equal, or be less than that given by the relevant sub-matrix of (A3.70), in the sense that the difference could be positive or negative semi-definite.

A3.4 By applying the formula for partitioned inversion in (A3.102) prove that the matrix:

$$\boldsymbol{Q} = \left[\boldsymbol{I}_T - \boldsymbol{Q}_a\boldsymbol{z}_b\left(\boldsymbol{z}_b'\boldsymbol{Q}_a\boldsymbol{z}_b\right)^{-1}\boldsymbol{z}_b'\boldsymbol{Q}_a\right],$$

in (A3.115) is symmetric, idempotent, and annihilates $\boldsymbol{Q}_a\boldsymbol{z}_b$ when

$$\boldsymbol{Q}_a = \left(\boldsymbol{I}_T - \boldsymbol{Z}_a\left(\boldsymbol{Z}_a'\boldsymbol{Z}_a\right)^{-1}\boldsymbol{Z}_a'\right).$$

Obtain the rank of $\boldsymbol{Q}$. What interpretation can be given to $\boldsymbol{Q}_a\boldsymbol{z}_b$? Prove that $\boldsymbol{Q}_Z^* = \boldsymbol{Q}_a\boldsymbol{Q}\boldsymbol{Q}_a = \boldsymbol{Q}_Z$ when $\boldsymbol{Z} = (\boldsymbol{Z}_a : \boldsymbol{z}_b)$ and $\boldsymbol{Q}_Z = (\boldsymbol{I}_T - \boldsymbol{Z}(\boldsymbol{Z}'\boldsymbol{Z})^{-1}\boldsymbol{Z}')$.

A3.5 When $k_b = 1$, derive conditions on (A3.106) such that $\tilde{\beta}_b$ and $\hat{\beta}_b$ have the same sign (see, e.g., Oksanen, 1987, and Visco, 1988).

A4
Asymptotic Distribution Theory

Even when the correct member of a family of probability distributions is known, deriving the exact distributions of statistics is often difficult. Here we investigate what happens in indefinitely large samples. The analysis commences from measures of orders of magnitude, and concepts of stochastic convergence. Laws of large numbers and central-limit theorems are reviewed for the simplest case of an independent, identically-distributed, scalar random variable. Vector processes are analysed, and two worked examples are presented to illustrate the various steps in practical derivations as well as some of the problems which can ensue. Next, stationary dynamic processes are studied, and instrumental variables estimators are described, followed by mixing and martingale processes. These methods are applied to maximum likelihood estimation. The chapter concludes with a brief look at asymptotic approximations.

A4.1 Introduction

Statistical analysis in econometrics distinguishes between the unknown data-generation process and the econometric model which attempts to represent the salient data features in a simplified form. Models are of necessity incomplete representations of reality, and the issue of their properties is discussed in the main text. The problem considered now is the behaviour of estimators and tests based on models when the data-generation process is only specified in general terms. For pedagogic purposes, the analysis proceeds through simple cases (homogeneous, independent, identically-distributed random variables) to explain the basic ideas, and then introduces complications which arise almost inevitably when analysing economic time series (dependence and heterogeneity, with only low-order moments of the underlying distributions). The present section describes the framework for the analysis, why asymptotic distribution theory is needed and what problems must be confronted, followed in sections A4.2–A4.7 by formal definitions and notation, orders of magnitude, concepts of stochastic convergence, laws of large numbers, and central-limit theorems for IID random variables, generalizations to vector random variables, and two detailed examples. Sections A4.8–A4.11 deal with dependent data series, focusing on dynamic processes under stationarity and ergodicity, and discuss mixing conditions and martingale limit theory. Sections A4.9 and A4.11 discuss instrumental-variables and maximum-likelihood estimation as important applications. Finally, some of the issues involved in asymptotic expansions in simple cases are noted.

In many ways, the use of asymptotic theory, which is a statistical distribution theory for large numbers of observations, is an admission of failure relative to obtaining exact sampling distributions. However, the latter are not only often intractable given present techniques, but can be unenlightening even when obtained due to their complicated forms. Thus, simplifications resulting from assuming large samples of observations can clarify the essential properties of complicated estimators and tests, although one must then examine the usefulness of such asymptotic findings for relevant sample sizes.

As an illustration, consider a random sample of T observations $\boldsymbol{x}' = (x_1 \ldots x_T)$ drawn from an unknown density function $\mathsf{D_X}(\boldsymbol{x}|\theta)$ for $\theta \in \Theta$. The distribution is assumed by an investigator to be $\mathsf{G_X}(\boldsymbol{x};\mu)$ where $\mu \in \mathbb{R}$. A sample statistic $W_T(x_1 \ldots x_T)$ is formed as an estimate of μ. The properties of $W_T(\boldsymbol{X})$ depend on those of $\mathsf{D_X}(\cdot)$, and are characterized by its distribution function $\mathsf{F}_{\mathsf{w}_T}(\cdot)$:

$$\mathsf{F}_{\mathsf{w}_T}(r) = \mathsf{P}(W_T \leq r) \ \forall r \in \mathbb{R}. \tag{A4.1}$$

Often, the CDF is analytically intractable, yet, as T increases, it takes on an increasingly simple form, which can be used as an approximation to (A4.1) when T is sufficiently large. This limiting distribution, denoted by $\mathsf{F_w}(\cdot)$, provides a first-order approximation, and, if that is not sufficiently accurate, higher-order approximations may be developed (see §A4.13 for a more precise statement). The sense of the word 'approximation' must be carefully specified, since $\mathsf{F_w}(\cdot)$ may not be adequate in all desired senses. For example, (A4.1) may be a distribution which possesses no moments, whereas all the moments of $\mathsf{F_w}(\cdot)$ could exist, and this may or may not be an important simplification and/or a serious limitation.

Letting W be a normal random variable with CDF $\mathsf{F_w}(\cdot)$, assume for illustration that:

$$W_T = W + \frac{1}{T^{\alpha}\nu} \quad \text{where } \nu \sim \mathsf{N}[10, 1]. \tag{A4.2}$$

Then $\mathsf{E}[W_T]$ does not exist whereas $\mathsf{E}[W]$ does by assumption. If $\alpha = 10^{10}$ and $T > 10$, then W_T and W coincide for all practical purposes despite the divergence in their moments. Conversely, if $W_T = W + 10^{\alpha}/T$ (for the same α), W_T and W coincide for 'sufficiently large T', but are not remotely alike in practice even when all moments of both exist.

Equation (A4.2) expresses the general nature of one approach to deriving limiting distributions, namely relate W_T to a simpler random variable W whose distribution is known, such that $(W_T - W)$ converges to zero (in a sense to be made precise) as T increases without bound. Many concepts of convergence are possible, and these cannot all be ordered such that type A implies type B implies C etc.; major alternatives are discussed in §A4.3 after noting some notions of the 'size' of the difference between W_T and W in §A4.2.

All of the main results have to be established for vector random variables which may be non-linear functions of the original random variables $\{X_t\}$. Thus, we wish to know how a continuous function $g(W_T)$ behaves as $T \to \infty$. Such behaviour usually relates to both central tendency, for which laws of large numbers apply, and the form of the distribution for large T, for which central-limit theorems are required. For independent sampling, various theorems are reported in sections A4.4 and A4.5, and generalized to vector processes in §A4.6. Section A4.7 then discusses two examples in detail. The level in these sections is introductory, in as much as IID assumptions are usually made.

The later sections are more advanced. Dependent random variables are introduced in §A4.8 for data processes which are stationary and ergodic, then §A4.10 and §A4.11 consider mixing conditions and martingale processes.[1] These have recently been used in econometrics as the basis for establishing limiting distributions, and seem to offer a natural characterization of important features of suitably transformed economic time series, while being sufficiently strong to allow useful limit results to be established. The following comments are intended to motivate the usage of mixing conditions and martingales in deriving asymptotic distributions.[2]

Heuristically, a process is uniformly mixing if knowledge as to its present state is uninformative about its state in the distant future. For economic systems, current knowledge about the state of the system is often informative about nearby future states, but seems relatively uninformative concerning distant states. Thus, the assumption of uniform mixing is not unreasonable for appropriately transformed economic variables. Moreover, with mixing, the system has a long but restricted memory: X_T and X_{T+n} become independent as $n \to \infty$, so that new information about the system continually accrues from larger samples, a condition of importance for the convergence of estimators and the consistency of tests.

More generally, let $\boldsymbol{X}_t$ denote a vector random process with respect to the probability space $(\Omega, \mathcal{F}, \mathsf{P})$. As in Chapter A2, the joint data density $\mathsf{D_X}(\cdot)$ can be sequentially factorized as:

$$\mathsf{D_X}(\boldsymbol{x}_1 \ldots \boldsymbol{x}_T \mid \mathcal{I}_0, \boldsymbol{\theta}) = \prod_{t=1}^{T} \mathsf{D_x}(\boldsymbol{x}_t \mid \mathcal{I}_{t-1}, \boldsymbol{\theta}) \quad \text{for } \boldsymbol{\theta} \in \boldsymbol{\Theta}, \tag{A4.3}$$

where $\mathcal{I}_{t-1}$ denotes previous information (strictly, the σ-field generated by $(\boldsymbol{X}_{t-1}, \ldots)$). By removing the predictable component from the past, the remainder acts like the difference of a martingale, called a martingale difference process as shown in §A4.11.

Finally, since the data are generated by $\mathsf{D_X}(\cdot)$, but a model may be based on $\mathsf{G_X}(\cdot)$, it is natural to consider theorems relating to the behaviour of data moments in large samples (usually the first two moments suffice), and derive the properties of estimators therefrom (see e.g. Hannan, 1970, Ch.4, and Hendry, 1979a). For mixing processes, direct

[1] The extension of asymptotic distribution theory to non-stationary processes with a unit root in their autoregressive representation is treated in Chapter 3, and is the subject of a separate book (see Banerjee, Dolado, Galbraith and Hendry, 1993).

[2] I am grateful to Ian Domowitz and Hal White for first drawing my attention to mixing processes, and freely providing their early work (see Domowitz and White, 1982, and White, 1984) which greatly facilitated the task of writing this chapter, and to Steve Alpern for helpful discussions about the relevant concepts.

derivations are possible (see e.g. White, 1984, and Domowitz and White, 1982). Sections A4.9 to A4.11 provide some illustrations.

It is worth stressing that we use asymptotic theory in order to derive approximate distributions in finite samples, and the validity of such results does not depend on the economic process remaining constant as $T \to \infty$. Thus, even though $\boldsymbol{\theta}$ may change in the next period, this does not affect the accuracy of approximating (A4.1) by $\mathsf{F}_{\mathsf{w}}(\cdot)$, although it does affect the usefulness of the underlying econometric model. Also, no attempt is made in what follows either to produce the most general possible results, or specify the weakest possible assumptions, nor is comprehensive coverage sought. Rather, we aim to provide a basis for results relevant to the class of models discussed in the main text, taking account of subject-matter considerations, but simplifying by stronger than necessary assumptions where this eases the derivations. Useful references to asymptotic distribution theory in the field of econometrics are Davidson (1994), Davidson and MacKinnon (1993), McCabe and Tremayne (1993), Sargan (1988), Schmidt (1976), Spanos (1986), Theil (1971) and White (1984); in statistics, see Cox and Hinkley (1974), Cramér (1946), Rao (1973) and Wilks (1962); and in time-series analysis, see Anderson (1971), Fuller (1976), Hannan (1970) and Harvey (1981a). Formal proofs are not provided for most of the theorems presented below, but may be found in these references.

Finally, as noted earlier, while limiting distributional results both clarify the relationships in large samples between apparently different methods and provide insight into the properties of estimators and tests, nevertheless, the accuracy of such results is dependent on the true value of $\boldsymbol{\theta}$ as well as on T. Thus, for important problems, a check should always be made on the accuracy of the asymptotic approximation for the problem at hand, either by Monte Carlo methods (as in Ch.3) or by higher-order approximations as described in the final section.

A4.2 Orders of magnitude

A4.2.1 Deterministic sequences

Let $\{W_t\}$, $\{X_t\}$, and $\{Y_t\}$ denote sequences of scalar random variables and $\{A_t\}$, $\{B_t\}$, and $\{C_t\}$ denote sequences of non-stochastic real numbers for $t = 1, \ldots, T$, where we allow $T \to \infty$. We first define convergence for a deterministic sequence.

Definition 1. *The sequence $\{A_T\}$ converges to the constant A as $T \to \infty$, if $\forall \delta > 0$, there exists a T_δ, such that $\forall T > T_\delta$, $|A_T - A| < \delta$. We write $\lim_{T\to\infty} A_T = A$, or $A_T \to A$.*

From the definition of continuity, if $g(\cdot)$ is a function continuous at A, and $A_T \to A$, then $g(A_T) \to g(A)$. Next, we define the order of magnitude for a deterministic sequence.

Definition 2. *$\{A_T\}$ is at most of order one, denoted by $\{A_T\} \approx O(1)$, if the sequence is bounded as $T \to \infty$, namely, there exists a constant, finite $M > 0$ such that $|A_T| < M\ \forall T$. Further $\{A_T\} \approx O(T^k)$ if $\{T^{-k}A_T\} \approx O(1)$.*

Definition 3. *$\{B_T\}$ is of smaller order than T^n if $\lim_{T\to\infty} T^{-n}B_T = 0$, denoted by $\{B_T\} \approx o(T^n)$.*

If $\{B_T\} \approx o(T^n)$, then $\{T^{-n}B_T\}$ is bounded as $T \to \infty$, so that $\{B_T\} \approx O(T^n)$, but the converse is not necessarily true: that $\{B_T\} \approx O(T^n)$ need not imply that $\{B_T\} \approx o(T^n)$. Further, from these definitions (denoted by D1, D2 etc.):

Theorem 1. *If $\{A_T\} \approx O(T^k)$ and $\{B_T\} \approx O(T^s)$, then:*

(a) $\{A_T\} \approx o(T^{k+m})\ \forall m > 0$;
(b) $\{A_T \pm B_T\} \approx O(T^r)$ *where* $r = \max(k, s)$;
(c) $\{A_T B_T\} \approx O(T^{k+s})$.

Since $O(T^k) + o(T^k) \approx O(T^k)$, terms in $o(\cdot)$ are negligible for sufficiently large T relative to equivalent terms in $O(\cdot)$ and can be ignored. Thus, from (b) and (c):

$$\{A_T \pm T^{-m}B_T\} \approx O\left(T^k\right) \text{ for } m \geq s - k. \tag{A4.4}$$

A4.2.2 Stochastic sequences

These results on $O(\cdot)$ and $o(\cdot)$ can be applied to standard deviations to provide one characterization of the order of magnitude of a random variable. For example, when $X_t \sim \mathsf{IN}[\mu_x, \sigma_x^2]$, then:

$$\bar{X}_T = T^{-1}\sum_{t=1}^{T} X_t \sim \mathsf{N}\left[\mu_x, \frac{\sigma_x^2}{T}\right] \tag{A4.5}$$

has a standard error $\sigma_x/\sqrt{T}$ of $O(1/\sqrt{T}) \approx o(1)$, and hence $\bar{X}_T$ has a degenerate limiting distribution (i.e. with a zero variance). Nevertheless, at all sample sizes:

$$\frac{\sqrt{T}\left(\bar{X}_T - \mu_x\right)}{\sigma_x} \sim \mathsf{N}\left[0, 1\right], \tag{A4.6}$$

and hence has a standard error of $O(1)$. Thus, $\sqrt{T}$ is the scaling transformation of $(\bar{X}_T - \mu_x)$ required to produce a finite-variance, non-degenerate, limiting distribution. However, not all small-sample distributions have finite variances.

When we consider stochastic sequences, the concept 'bounded' must be replaced by 'bounded in probability':

Definition 4. *$\{W_T\}$ is at most of order unity in probability, denoted by $\{W_T\} \approx O_p(1)$, if $\forall \epsilon > 0$, $\exists$ finite $M_\epsilon > 0$ and $T_\epsilon > 0$ such that $\forall T > T_\epsilon$, $\mathsf{P}(|W_T| > M_\epsilon) < \epsilon$.*

Thus, $\{W_T\} \approx O_p(1)$ if for large enough T, there is a negligibly small probability of the absolute value of its terms exceeding an upper bound, which may depend on the probability ϵ. Correspondingly, $\{W_T\} \approx O_p(T^k)$ if $\{T^{-k}W_T\} \approx O_p(1)$.

Definition 5. *$\{Y_T\} \approx o_p(1)$ if $\forall \epsilon > 0$, $\lim_{T\to\infty} \mathsf{P}(|Y_T| > \epsilon) = 0$.*

Hence $1/T^\alpha \nu$ in (A4.2) is $o_p(1)$ for $\alpha > 0$. Similar results to Theorem 1 apply to $O_p(\cdot)$ and $o_p(\cdot)$. For example, if:

$$X_T = W_T + Y_T \approx O_p(1) + o_p(1), \tag{A4.7}$$

then $\{X_T\} \approx O_p(1)$ and $\{X_T - W_T\} = Y_T \approx o_p(1)$. We can treat $O_p(\cdot)$ and $o_p(\cdot)$ as if they were $O(\cdot)$ and $o(\cdot)$ respectively (see Madansky, 1976).

Theorem 2. *If $f_T(\cdot) \approx O(A_T)$ and $g_T(\cdot) \approx o(B_T)$ imply that $h_T(\cdot) \approx O(C_T)$, then $f_T(W_T) \approx O_p(A_T)$ and $g_T(W_T) \approx o_p(B_T)$ imply that $h_T(W_T) \approx O_p(C_T)$.*
For example, if $\{X_T\}$ and $\{Y_T\}$ are $O_p(T^k)$ and $O_p(T^s)$ respectively, then $\{Y_T X_T\}$ is $O_p(T^{k+s})$.

Finally, we can paraphrase the earlier result on using the order of magnitude of a standard deviation to determine a finite-variance limiting distribution: if $\{W_T\}$ has a variance of $O(1)$, then $\{W_T\} \approx O_p(1)$, although the converse is false. Mann and Wald (1943a) developed most of the results in this section.

A4.3 Stochastic convergence

We now apply the notions of stochastic orders of magnitude to ascertain the relationships between two (or more) random variables. Two random variables could be deemed to converge if:

(a) their distribution functions converge;
(b) their difference is $o_p(1)$;
(c) the variance of their difference exists $\forall T$ and is $o(1)$;
(d) they are equal except on a set of probability zero.

These notions need not coincide, as shown below. Precise definitions for (a)–(d) are:

Definition 6. *W_T tends in distribution to W, denoted by $W_T \overset{D}{\to} W$, if for all continuity points of $\mathsf{F}_{\mathsf{w}}(\cdot)$, $\lim_{T\to\infty} \mathsf{F}_{\mathsf{w}_T}(r) = \mathsf{F}_{\mathsf{w}}(r)$, where $\mathsf{F}_{\mathsf{w}}(r) = \mathsf{P}(W \leq r)$ denotes the CDF of W.*

More generally, if for all continuity points of a CDF $\mathsf{F}_{\mathsf{w}_T}(\cdot)$, $\lim_{T\to\infty} \mathsf{F}_{\mathsf{w}_T}(r) = \mathsf{F}_{\mathsf{w}}(r)$, then $\mathsf{F}_{\mathsf{w}_T}(r)$ converges weakly to $\mathsf{F}_{\mathsf{w}}(r)$ written as $\mathsf{F}_{\mathsf{w}_T}(r) \Rightarrow \mathsf{F}_{\mathsf{w}}(r)$.

Definition 7. *W_T tends in probability to W if $\lim_{T\to\infty} \mathsf{P}(|W_T - W| > \epsilon) = 0 \; \forall \epsilon > 0$, denoted by $W_T \overset{P}{\to} W$. Thus, from D5, $(W_T - W) \approx o_p(1)$.*

Definition 8. *W_T tends in mean square to W, denoted $W_T \overset{MS}{\to} W$, if $\mathsf{E}[W_T]$ and $\mathsf{E}[W_T^2]$ exist $\forall T$ and $\lim_{T\to\infty} \mathsf{E}[(W_T - W)^2] = 0$.*

Definition 9. *W_T tends almost surely to W if $\lim_{T\to\infty} \mathsf{P}(|W_t - W| \leq \epsilon,\ \forall t \geq T) = 1 \; \forall \epsilon > 0$, denoted $W_T \overset{AS}{\to} W$.*

Since CDFs are real numbers, ordinary convergence holds in D6: the more general definition holds without specific reference to an associated random variable, and weak convergence will prove of importance in the main text. In D9, the whole collection of $\{|W_t - W|,\ t \geq T\}$ must have a limiting probability of unity of being less than or equal to ϵ, so that the two random variables must come together except for a set of probability zero. An equivalent definition is:

Definition 10. *$W_T \overset{AS}{\to} W$, if $\mathsf{P}(\lim_{T\to\infty} W_T = W) = 1$.*

Almost sure convergence implies that W_T converges to W for almost every possible realization of the stochastic process. Thus, D9 implies D7. When definition D8 holds, from Chebychev's inequality (see §A2.7):

$$\mathsf{P}\left(|W_T - W| > \epsilon\right) \leq \frac{\mathsf{E}\left[(W_T - W)^2\right]}{\epsilon^2}, \tag{A4.8}$$

so D8 implies D7. However, neither D7 nor D9 imply D8 (since no moments need exist), nor is D8 by itself sufficient to ensure D9. If $(W_T - W) \approx o_p(1)$, the difference between W_T and W is asymptotically negligible, so D7 implies D6. Finally, if W is a constant, D6 implies D7 since the CDF is degenerate and becomes a step function at $W = \kappa$:

$$\mathsf{F}_{\mathsf{W}_T}(r) \Rightarrow \mathsf{F}_{\mathsf{W}}(r) = \mathsf{P}(W \leq r) = \begin{cases} 0 & r < \kappa \\ 1 & r \geq \kappa \end{cases} \tag{A4.9}$$

and hence $\lim_{T\to\infty} \mathsf{P}(|W_T - \kappa| \geq \epsilon) = 0 \; \forall \epsilon > 0$, which is the probability limit, written as:

$$\operatorname*{plim}_{T\to\infty} W_T = \kappa.$$

Summarizing these results in schematic form, where $\Longrightarrow$ denotes implies:

$$\begin{array}{ccc} & D9 & \\ & \Downarrow & \\ D8 \Longrightarrow & D7 & \Longrightarrow D6, \end{array}$$

with none of the converse implications holding, except for D6$\Longrightarrow$D7 if $W = \kappa$: this last condition is sufficient for W_T to be $O_p(1)$, but not necessary, so that if W_T is $O_p(1)$, it does not follow that $\operatorname{plim}_{T\to\infty} W_T$ is a constant. Further, D6 does not imply that the moments of W_T tend in probability to the moments of W unless the random variables have bounded range. Finally, if W_T tends in distribution to W, we say that W_T is asymptotically distributed as W, and denote that expression by $\underset{a}{\sim}$, writing $W_T \underset{a}{\sim} W$. In such a case:

Theorem 3. *If* $\operatorname{plim}_{T\to\infty}(W_T - W) = 0$, $\operatorname{plim}_{T\to\infty} Y_T = c$ *and* $|Y_T - c| \geq |X_T - c|$, *for constants* $a, b, c > 0$, then:

(i) $\lim \mathsf{P}(aW_T + bY_T \leq r) = \mathsf{F}_{\mathsf{w}}([r - bc]/a)$;
(ii) $\lim \mathsf{P}(W_T Y_T \leq r) = \mathsf{F}_{\mathsf{w}}(r/c)$;
(iii) $\operatorname{plim}_{T\to\infty} X_T = c$.

For example, Theorem 3(i) follows because $\mathsf{P}(aW_T + bY_T \leq r) \to \mathsf{P}(aW + bc \leq r) = \mathsf{P}(W \leq (r - bc)/a)$. Generally, we omit the limiting argument when no confusion is likely, writing $\operatorname{plim} X_T = c$.

Next, a useful theorem due to Slutsky, which follows from D7 and the definition of continuity:

Theorem 4. *When* $g(\cdot)$ *is a continuous function independent of* T, *if* $W_T \xrightarrow{P} W$, *then* $g(W_T) \xrightarrow{P} g(W)$; *and if* $W_T \xrightarrow{AS} W$, *then* $g(W_T) \xrightarrow{AS} g(W)$.

Since $\xrightarrow{P}$ implies $\xrightarrow{D}$, if $W = \kappa$, then Slutsky's theorem implies that:

$$\operatorname{plim} g(W_T) = g(\kappa) = g(\operatorname{plim} W_T).$$

Theorem 4 has many important applications. For example, if $W_T \xrightarrow{P} W \sim \mathsf{N}[0,1]$ then since D7$\Longrightarrow$D6, $W_T^2 \underset{a}{\sim} \chi^2(1)$.

A4.4 Laws of large numbers

We next consider the behaviour in large samples of averages of random variables. The behaviour of such averages depends on three factors, namely: the degree of interdependence between successive drawings (in this section we assume independence); the extent of heterogeneity in successive drawings (which is different between the two theorems cited below); and the existence of higher moments of the distributions (which needs to be stronger the greater the heterogeneity or interdependence allowed). Weak and strong laws of large numbers exist and we have the following results ($|\mu_t| < \infty, 0 < \sigma_t^2 < \infty$).

A4.4.1 Weak law of large numbers

We denote the weak law of large numbers by WLLN, and cite two famous results:

Theorem 5(i). *If X_t is* IID *with* $\mathsf{E}[X_t] = \mu$ *where μ is finite, then* $\bar{X}_T \xrightarrow{P} \mu$ *(Khintchine's theorem).*

Theorem 5(ii). *If X_t is* $\mathsf{ID}[\mu_t, \sigma_t^2]$ *with* $\bar{\mu}_T = T^{-1}\sum_{t=1}^{T}\mu_t$, *and* $\lim_{T\to\infty} T^{-2}\sum_{t=1}^{T}\sigma_t^2 = 0$, *then* $(\bar{X}_T - \bar{\mu}_T) \xrightarrow{P} 0$.

Thus, if the X_t are identically distributed with a common finite mean, then plim $\bar{X}_T = \mu$, even if the second moment of X_t does not exist. However, if the distributions are not identical as in Theorem 5(ii), extra conditions are required on the second moments of the $\{X_t\}$, to ensure that they are finite, and the average variance divided by T vanishes. Constant, finite, first two moments are sufficient for 5(ii) to hold, even when X_t is not IID (perhaps because the third moment is not constant).

A4.4.2 Strong law of large numbers

The corresponding strong laws of large numbers (SLLN) are:

Theorem 6(i). *If X_t is* IID, *then* $\mathsf{E}[X_t] = \mu$ *being finite is necessary and sufficient for* $\bar{X}_T \xrightarrow{AS} \mu$.

Theorem 6(ii). *If X_t is* $\mathsf{ID}[\mu_t, \sigma_t^2]$ *and* $\lim_{T\to\infty}\sum_{t=1}^{T} t^{-2}\sigma_t^2 < \infty$, *then* $\bar{X}_T \xrightarrow{AS} \bar{\mu}_T$.

Thus, WLLN(i) actually implies almost-sure convergence without additional conditions, whereas, since $t^{-2} \geq T^{-2}$, the second condition of WLLN(ii) needs strengthening to achieve almost-sure convergence. Distributions like the Cauchy without finite moments do not satisfy the assumptions of either WLLN or SLLN. Consequently, neither law applies and the sample mean does not converge.

For estimators of a constant population parameter μ, we have the following definitions:

Definition 11. *An estimator $\hat{\mu}_T$ is consistent for μ if* $\text{plim}_{T\to\infty}\hat{\mu}_T = \mu$.

Thus, $\bar{X}_T$ is consistent for μ given WLLN(i). Also:

Definition 12. $\hat{\mu}_T$ *is asymptotically unbiased for μ if* $\mathsf{E}[\hat{\mu}_T]$ *is finite* $\forall T$ *and:* $\lim_{T\to\infty}\mathsf{E}[\hat{\mu}_T] = \bar{\mathsf{E}}[\hat{\mu}_T] = \mu$.

Consistency does not imply asymptotic unbiasedness (e.g. $\mathsf{E}[\hat{\mu}_T]$ need not exist), nor conversely (since an unbiased estimator need not have a degenerate limiting distribution). These last two definitions (D11 and D12) highlight one of the main roles for laws of large numbers, namely to allow us to establish the consistency of estimators. In sections A4.10 and A4.11, weaker assumptions will be discussed which still sustain laws like WLLN and SLLN.

A4.5 Central-limit theorems

For consistent estimators, the limiting CDF $\mathsf{F}_{\mathsf{w}}(r)$ is a step function, and, as this has the same limiting distributional form for all consistent estimators, it is uninformative about the rate of convergence. For example, $\bar{X}_T$ and:

$$\tilde{X}_T = \bar{X}_T + \frac{10^{10}}{\log T} \tag{A4.10}$$

both have a plim of μ under WLLN(ii), but the latter is useless for all practical T. To discriminate between estimators and compare their properties, we must rescale the random variables to $O_p(1)$. If $\text{plim}(W_T - W) = 0$, and a random variable of $O_p(1)$ is achieved by multiplying by T^k where $\mathsf{V}[W_T - W] \approx O(T^{-2k}) > 0$, then we can investigate the behaviour of $T^k(W_T - W)$ as $T \to \infty$ and expect to obtain a non-degenerate limiting distribution.[3] This will let us compare distributional forms across alternative estimators or tests.

As with laws of large numbers, the outcome is determined by an interaction between the extent of memory (i.e. interdependence, which is absent here due to assuming independence), heterogeneity (allowed in Theorems 8(i) and (ii)), and the existence of higher moments (finite second moments are assumed in all the theorems, and the $(2+\delta)$ moment by 8(i)). We have three central-limit theorems, inducing asymptotic normality (generalized in §A4.11).

Theorem 7. *If* $X_t \sim \mathsf{IID}[\mu, \sigma^2]$ *with* $|\mu| < \infty$, $0 < \sigma^2 < \infty$, *and* $W_T = \sqrt{T}(\bar{X}_T - \mu)/\sigma$, *then* $W_T \xrightarrow{D} W \sim \mathsf{N}[0,1]$.

This result can also be written as $W_T \underset{a}{\sim} \mathsf{N}[0,1]$.

Theorem 8. *If* $X_t \sim \mathsf{ID}[\mu_t, \sigma_t^2]$ *where* $|\mu_t| < \infty$ and $0 < \sigma_t^2 < \infty\ \forall t$ *with* $S_T^2 = \sum_{t=1}^T \sigma_t^2$, *and either:*

(i) $\beta_t = \mathsf{E}[|X_t - \mu_t|^{2+\delta}] < \infty$ *and* $\lim((\sum_{t=1}^T \beta_t)/S_T^{2+\delta}) = 0$ *for* $\delta > 0$; *or*
(ii) $\lim\ S_T^{-2} \sum_{t=1}^T \mathsf{E}[(X_t - \mu_t)^2 I(|X_t - \mu_t| \geq \epsilon S_T)] = 0\ \forall \epsilon > 0$; *then:*

$$W_T = \sum_{t=1}^T \left[\frac{X_t - \mu_t}{S_T}\right] = \sqrt{T}\left[\frac{\bar{X}_T - \bar{\mu}_T}{S_T/\sqrt{T}}\right] \xrightarrow{D} W \sim \mathsf{N}[0,1]. \tag{A4.11}$$

[3] If $\mathsf{V}[W_T - W]$ exists, otherwise alternative ways of establishing $O_p(1)$ must be found.

The three versions 7–8(ii) of the central-limit theorem (CLT) are referred to as the Lindeberg–Lévy, Lyapunov and Lindeberg–Feller theorems respectively. In each case, the random variable W_T to be studied has been normalized to have a mean of zero and a unit variance.

Theorem 7 makes the strongest assumptions in terms of homogeneity (identical distributions) and moments existing (finite second moment). Whittle (1970) provides an elegant explanation as to why Theorem 7 holds by demonstrating a closure property as follows. Consider a sequence of standardized IID $\{Y_t\}$, each of which has the same distributional form as the limit of W_T with distribution W. Define $Z_T = \sum Y_t/\sqrt{T}$, then Z_T must also converge to the same limiting distribution W. Thus, the characteristic function of Z_T is the Tth power of the characteristic function of the IID variates and yet of the same form. Whittle then shows that $\exp(-\nu^2/2)$ (for argument ν) is the only function with that property, which is the characteristic function of $\mathsf{N}[0, 1]$.

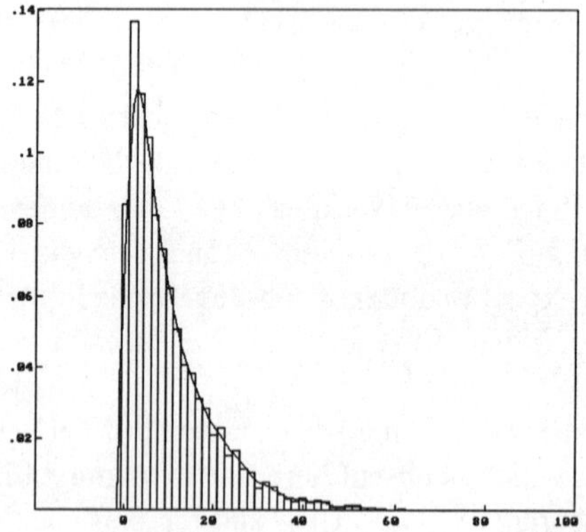

$0.1 \exp(-0.1x)$

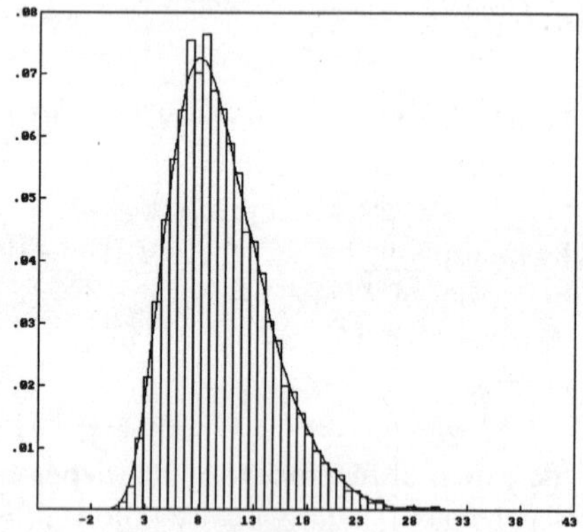

Means from samples of size 5

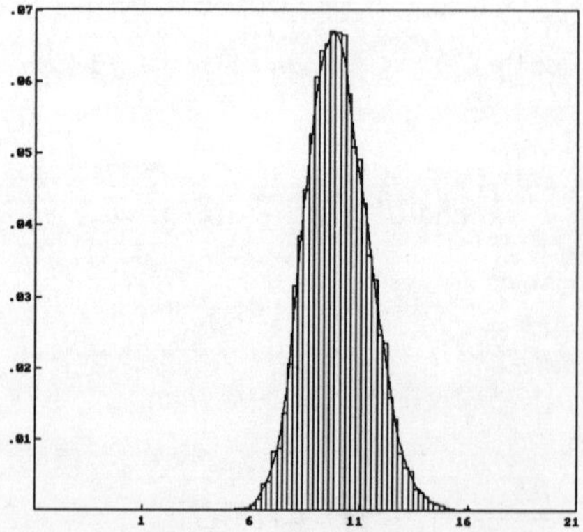

Means from samples of size 50

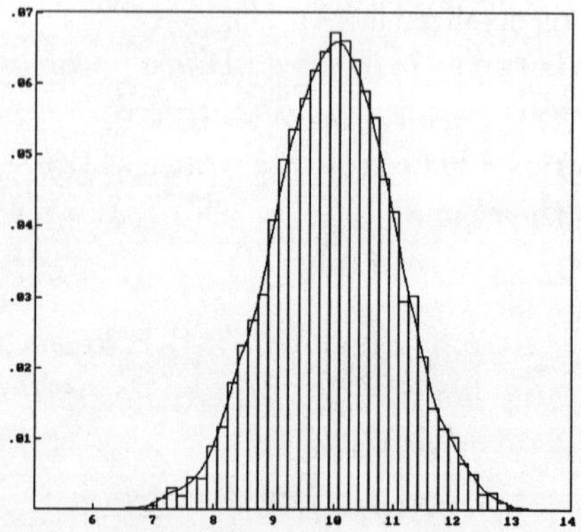

$\mathsf{N}[10, 1]$

Fig. A4.1 Central-limit convergence

As an illustration of the operation of central-limiting effects, Figs. A4.1a–d show the histograms and density functions for 10 000 drawings from the exponential distribution $\lambda \exp(-\lambda x)$ with parameter $\lambda = 0.1$, so the mean and standard deviation are both 10. The first shows the original distribution (which is highly skewed and covers a large range), then the means of samples of size 5 and size 50 therefrom, and finally $\mathsf{N}[10, 1]$ for comparison. The convergence to normality is rapid for this IID setting.

In Theorem 8(i), the identical-distributions assumption is dropped, and instead a finite absolute moment of order $(2+\delta)$ is required for which $\delta = 1$ is sufficient and entails that the third absolute moment exists. If so, then for example, when μ_t, σ_t, and β_t are constant:

$$\frac{\left(\sum_{t=1}^{T} \beta\right)}{S_T^3} = \frac{T\beta}{(T\sigma^2 S_T)} = \frac{\beta\sigma^{-3}}{\sqrt{T}} \to 0, \qquad \text{(A4.12)}$$

which provides sufficient conditions, although these are too strong given Theorem 7.

However, Theorem 8(ii) provides most insight into what features of the DGP are required to sustain central-limiting normality, and thereby needs most explanation. First, if the limit in (ii) is to be zero, a necessary condition is that $S_T^2 \to \infty$ as $T \to \infty$ (so that information continually accrues). Next, since $I(\cdot)$ denotes the indicator function of the argument (see §A2.7), when the event $\{|X_t - \mu_t| \geq \epsilon S_T\}$ occurs, then $I(|X_t - \mu_t| \geq \epsilon S_T)$ is unity, and is zero otherwise, so that:

$$\mathsf{E}\left[I\left(|X_t - \mu_t| \geq \epsilon S_T\right)\right] = \mathsf{P}\left(|X_t - \mu_t| \geq \epsilon S_T\right).$$

Also, $\mathsf{E}[(X_t - \mu_t)^2 I(|X_t - \mu_t| \geq \epsilon S_T)]$ is the expected value of $(X_t - \mu_t)^2$ over the interval where $|X_t - \mu_t| \geq \epsilon S_T$ when $\mathsf{E}[(X_t - \mu_t)^2] = \sigma_t^2$. Since $(X_t - \mu_t)^2 / S_T^2 \geq \epsilon^2$ when $I(|X_t - \mu_t| \geq \epsilon S_T) = 1$, as $T \geq t$, we have:

$$\begin{aligned} S_T^{-2} \sum_{t=1}^{T} \mathsf{E}\left[(X_t - \mu_t)^2 I\left(|X_t - \mu_t| \geq \epsilon S_T\right)\right] &\geq \sum_{t=1}^{T} \mathsf{E}\left[\epsilon^2 I\left(|X_t - \mu_t| \geq \epsilon S_T\right)\right] \\ &\geq \epsilon^2 \sum_{t=1}^{T} \mathsf{P}\left(|X_t - \mu_t| \geq \epsilon S_T\right), \end{aligned}$$

which can tend to zero as $T \to \infty$ only if the largest $\epsilon^2 \mathsf{P}(|X_t - \mu_t| \geq \epsilon S_T)$ goes to zero $\forall \epsilon$. Thus, it is necessary that $\sigma_T^2 / S_T^2 \to 0$ for 8(ii) to hold, and indeed all individual terms must be asymptotically negligible. However, the two conditions $\sigma_T^2 / S_T^2 \to 0$ and $S_T^2 \to \infty$ as $T \to \infty$ are not sufficient, whereas the conditions in Theorem 8 are. Sufficient conditions for Theorem 8 can be found which have intuitive appeal, namely that $\mathsf{E}[|X_t|^{2+\delta}] < K < \infty \; \forall t$ for some $\delta > 0$ and $T^{-1} S_T^{2+\delta} \to \infty$, so that the $|X_t|$ do not grow without bound. Then, no one term dominates, and information accrues sufficiently rapidly for asymptotic normality to hold. The trade-off between the existence of higher moments and increased heterogeneity is apparent from comparing Theorems 7 and 8.

Three generalizations are needed to render central-limit theory applicable to economic data. First, it must apply to vector random variables, and the following section analyses that case. Secondly, it must allow for processes with memory rather than independence, and sections A4.8–A4.11 do so. Finally, integrated processes must be incorporated, and that aspect is analysed in Chapter 3.

A4.6 Vector random variables

While the concepts above carry over directly for elements of vectors, results for vector processes in general follow from the Cramér–Wold device. Let $\{\boldsymbol{W}_T\}$ be a k-dimensional vector process, and $\boldsymbol{W}$ a $k \times 1$ vector random variable, then:

Theorem 9. *$\boldsymbol{W}_T \xrightarrow{D} \boldsymbol{W}$ if and only if $\boldsymbol{\lambda}' \boldsymbol{W}_T \xrightarrow{D} \boldsymbol{\lambda}' \boldsymbol{W}$ for all fixed finite $k \times 1$ vectors $\boldsymbol{\lambda}$.*

For example, if $\boldsymbol{\lambda}' \boldsymbol{W} \sim \mathsf{N}[0, \boldsymbol{\lambda}' \boldsymbol{\Psi} \boldsymbol{\lambda}]$ then $\boldsymbol{W}_T \xrightarrow{D} \mathsf{N}_k[\mathbf{0}, \boldsymbol{\Psi}]$. Moreover, certain stochastic functions of $\boldsymbol{W}_T$ also converge to normality if $\boldsymbol{W}_T$ does (see Cramér, 1946). This important result is referred to below as Cramér's theorem:

Theorem 10. *If $\boldsymbol{W}_T \xrightarrow{D} \boldsymbol{W} \sim \mathsf{N}_k[\boldsymbol{\mu}, \boldsymbol{\Psi}]$ and $\boldsymbol{A}_T$ is $n \times k$ with $\text{plim}_{T\to\infty} \boldsymbol{A}_T = \boldsymbol{A}$, then $\boldsymbol{A}_T \boldsymbol{W}_T \xrightarrow{D} \boldsymbol{A}\boldsymbol{W}$ where $\boldsymbol{A}\boldsymbol{W} \sim \mathsf{N}_n[\boldsymbol{A}\boldsymbol{\mu}, \boldsymbol{A}\boldsymbol{\Psi}\boldsymbol{A}']$.*

The theorem is clearly valid if $\boldsymbol{A}_T = \boldsymbol{A}\ \forall T$; otherwise, use is made of $(\boldsymbol{A}_T - \boldsymbol{A}) \approx o_p(1)$ so that:

$$\boldsymbol{A}_T \boldsymbol{W}_T = \boldsymbol{A}\boldsymbol{W}_T + (\boldsymbol{A}_T - \boldsymbol{A})\, \boldsymbol{W}_T \approx O_p(1) + o_p(1) \tag{A4.13}$$

where the second term is asymptotically negligible.

Next, consider an $n \times 1$ continuously differentiable vector function $\boldsymbol{g}(\boldsymbol{W}_T)$:

Theorem 11. *If $\sqrt{T}(\boldsymbol{W}_T - \boldsymbol{\mu}) \xrightarrow{D} \mathsf{N}_k[\mathbf{0}, \boldsymbol{\Psi}]$ and $\boldsymbol{G}(\boldsymbol{W}) = \partial \boldsymbol{g}/\partial \boldsymbol{w}'$ exists and is continuous in the neighbourhood of $\boldsymbol{\mu}$, then:*

$$\sqrt{T}\left(\boldsymbol{g}(\boldsymbol{W}_T) - \boldsymbol{g}(\boldsymbol{\mu})\right) \xrightarrow{D} \mathsf{N}_n\left[\mathbf{0}, \boldsymbol{G}(\boldsymbol{\mu})\, \boldsymbol{\Psi} \boldsymbol{G}(\boldsymbol{\mu})'\right].$$

To prove this claim, since plim $\boldsymbol{W}_T = \boldsymbol{\mu}$, then plim $\boldsymbol{g}(\boldsymbol{W}_T) = \boldsymbol{g}(\boldsymbol{\mu})$, and by the mean-value theorem:

$$\boldsymbol{g}(\boldsymbol{W}_T) = \boldsymbol{g}(\boldsymbol{\mu}) + \boldsymbol{G}(\boldsymbol{W}_T^*)(\boldsymbol{W}_T - \boldsymbol{\mu}) \tag{A4.14}$$

where $|\boldsymbol{W}_T^* - \boldsymbol{\mu}| \leq |\boldsymbol{W}_T - \boldsymbol{\mu}|$ so that:

$$\sqrt{T}\,[\boldsymbol{g}(\boldsymbol{W}_T) - \boldsymbol{g}(\boldsymbol{\mu})] = \boldsymbol{G}(\boldsymbol{\mu})\sqrt{T}\,(\boldsymbol{W}_T - \boldsymbol{\mu}) + [\boldsymbol{G}(\boldsymbol{W}_T^*) - \boldsymbol{G}(\boldsymbol{\mu})]\,\sqrt{T}\,(\boldsymbol{W}_T - \boldsymbol{\mu}).$$

Since $\boldsymbol{G}(\boldsymbol{W}_T^*) \xrightarrow{D} \boldsymbol{G}(\boldsymbol{\mu})$ (a constant), $\boldsymbol{G}(\boldsymbol{W}_T^*) \xrightarrow{P} \boldsymbol{G}(\boldsymbol{\mu})$, noting that $\text{plim}(\boldsymbol{W}_T - \boldsymbol{\mu}) = \mathbf{0}$ implies $\text{plim}(\boldsymbol{W}_T^* - \boldsymbol{\mu}) = \mathbf{0}$.

The following two examples seek to illustrate applications of the preceding results. In many cases, almost-sure convergence can be established where we focus on convergence in probability below: establishing the stronger result in relevant cases makes an interesting and useful exercise (see White, 1984, for a number of helpful developments).

A4.7 Solved examples

A4.7.1 Example 1: an IID process

Let $\mathsf{E}[y_t|\mathbf{z}_t] = \boldsymbol{\beta}'\mathbf{z}_t$ for $t = 1,\ldots,T$, and $\epsilon_t = (y_t - \mathbf{z}_t'\boldsymbol{\beta}) \sim \mathsf{IID}[0,\sigma_\epsilon^2]$, $0 < \sigma_\epsilon^2 < \infty$, where the $k \times 1$ vector $\mathbf{z}_t \sim \mathsf{IID}_k[\mathbf{0}, \boldsymbol{\Psi}]$ with $\boldsymbol{\Psi}$ finite, positive definite, and $\{\mathbf{z}_t\}$, $\{\epsilon_t\}$ are independent processes. The least-squares estimator of $\boldsymbol{\beta} \in \mathbb{R}^k$ (where $\text{rank}(\mathbf{z}_1 \ldots \mathbf{z}_T) = k$) is:

$$\widehat{\boldsymbol{\beta}} = \left(\sum_{t=1}^{T} \mathbf{z}_t\mathbf{z}_t'\right)^{-1} \sum_{t=1}^{T} \mathbf{z}_t y_t = \boldsymbol{\beta} + \left(T^{-1}\sum_{t=1}^{T} \mathbf{z}_t\mathbf{z}_t'\right)^{-1} \left(T^{-1}\sum_{t=1}^{T} \mathbf{z}_t\epsilon_t\right). \quad \text{(A4.15)}$$

We seek to derive the asymptotic distribution of a suitably normalized function of $\widehat{\boldsymbol{\beta}}$.

First, $\boldsymbol{\nu}_t = \mathbf{z}_t\epsilon_t \sim \mathsf{IID}_k[\mathbf{0}, \sigma_\epsilon^2 \boldsymbol{\Psi}]$, so that:

$$u_t = \boldsymbol{\lambda}'\boldsymbol{\nu}_t \sim \mathsf{IID}\left[0, \sigma_\epsilon^2 \boldsymbol{\lambda}'\boldsymbol{\Psi}\boldsymbol{\lambda}\right] = \mathsf{IID}\left[0, \sigma_u^2\right]. \quad \text{(A4.16)}$$

WLLN(i) applies to $\{u_t\}$, so letting:

$$\bar{\mathbf{b}}_T = T^{-1}\sum_{t=1}^{T} \mathbf{z}_t\epsilon_t,$$

then:

$$\bar{u}_T = \boldsymbol{\lambda}'\bar{\mathbf{b}}_T = \boldsymbol{\lambda}'\left(T^{-1}\sum_{t=1}^{T} \mathbf{z}_t\epsilon_t\right) \xrightarrow{P} 0. \quad \text{(A4.17)}$$

Hence, by the Cramér–Wold device:

$$\bar{\mathbf{b}}_T = T^{-1}\sum_{t=1}^{T} \mathbf{z}_t\epsilon_t \xrightarrow{P} \mathbf{0}. \quad \text{(A4.18)}$$

Next, since $\mathbf{z}_t$ is IID, $\mathbf{z}_t\mathbf{z}_t'$ is IID with $\mathsf{E}[\mathbf{z}_t\mathbf{z}_t'] = \boldsymbol{\Psi}$. Let

$$v_t = \boldsymbol{\lambda}'\mathbf{z}_t\mathbf{z}_t'\boldsymbol{\lambda} \sim \mathsf{IID}\left[\boldsymbol{\lambda}'\boldsymbol{\Psi}\boldsymbol{\lambda}, C\right],$$

so that WLLN(i) applies again and hence:

$$\bar{v}_T = T^{-1}\sum_{t=1}^{T} \boldsymbol{\lambda}'\mathbf{z}_t\mathbf{z}_t'\boldsymbol{\lambda} \xrightarrow{P} \boldsymbol{\lambda}'\boldsymbol{\Psi}\boldsymbol{\lambda}. \quad \text{(A4.19)}$$

Thus, $\text{plim}_{T\to\infty} T^{-1}\sum \mathbf{z}_t\mathbf{z}_t' = \boldsymbol{\Psi}$, and hence $\sum \mathbf{z}_t\mathbf{z}_t' \approx O_p(T)$. By Slutsky's Theorem, since the inverse of a positive definite matrix is a continuous function of its elements:

$$\underset{T\to\infty}{\text{plim}} \left(T^{-1}\sum_{t=1}^{T} \mathbf{z}_t\mathbf{z}_t'\right)^{-1} = \boldsymbol{\Psi}^{-1}.$$

Consequently, again by Slutsky's Theorem from (A4.18):

$$\operatorname*{plim}_{T\to\infty} \hat{\boldsymbol{\beta}} = \boldsymbol{\beta} + \boldsymbol{\Psi}^{-1} \cdot \mathbf{0} = \mathbf{0},$$

and hence $\hat{\boldsymbol{\beta}}$ is consistent for $\boldsymbol{\beta}$. Further, since:

$$\mathsf{V}\left[\sum_{t=1}^{T} \mathbf{z}_t \epsilon_t\right] = \mathsf{E}\left[\sum_{t=1}^{T}\sum_{s=1}^{T} \mathbf{z}_t \epsilon_t \mathbf{z}_s' \epsilon_s\right] = \sum_{t=1}^{T}\sum_{s=1}^{T} \mathsf{E}\left[\boldsymbol{\nu}_t \boldsymbol{\nu}_s'\right] = \sum_{t=1}^{T} \mathsf{E}\left[\boldsymbol{\nu}_t \boldsymbol{\nu}_t'\right] = T\sigma_\epsilon^2 \boldsymbol{\Psi},$$

which is $O(T)$, then $(\sum \mathbf{z}_t \epsilon_t)/\sqrt{T} \approx O_p(1)$. Hence, by central-limit Theorem 7:

$$W_T = \frac{1}{\sqrt{T}}\left(\sum_{t=1}^{T} \boldsymbol{\lambda}' \mathbf{z}_t \epsilon_t\right) = \sqrt{T}\bar{u}_T \xrightarrow{D} \mathsf{N}\left[0, \sigma_\epsilon^2 \boldsymbol{\lambda}' \boldsymbol{\Psi} \boldsymbol{\lambda}\right]. \tag{A4.20}$$

Consequently, by the Cramér–Wold device:

$$\frac{1}{\sqrt{T}} \sum_{t=1}^{T} \mathbf{z}_t \epsilon_t \xrightarrow{D} \mathsf{N}_k\left[\mathbf{0}, \sigma_\epsilon^2 \boldsymbol{\Psi}\right]. \tag{A4.21}$$

Finally, by Cramér's Theorem:

$$\frac{1}{\sqrt{T}}\left(T^{-1}\sum_{t=1}^{T} \mathbf{z}_t \mathbf{z}_t'\right)^{-1}\left(\sum_{t=1}^{T} \mathbf{z}_t \epsilon_t\right) \xrightarrow{D} \mathsf{N}_k\left[\mathbf{0}, \sigma_\epsilon^2 \boldsymbol{\Psi}^{-1}\right],$$

and therefore:

$$\sqrt{T}\left(\hat{\boldsymbol{\beta}} - \boldsymbol{\beta}\right) \xrightarrow{D} \mathsf{N}_k\left[\mathbf{0}, \sigma_\epsilon^2 \boldsymbol{\Psi}^{-1}\right]. \tag{A4.22}$$

This result generalizes the theorem on the (asymptotic) normality of least squares in §A3.7 to stochastic regressors which are independent over time, and independent of the difference $(y_t - \mathbf{z}_t'\boldsymbol{\beta})$.

A4.7.2 Example 2: A trend model

Let $y_t = \beta t^\alpha + \epsilon_t$ where $\epsilon_t \sim \mathsf{IN}[0, \sigma_\epsilon^2]$ and α is a known, fixed constant. Given normality of ϵ_t, the exact distribution of the least-squares estimator of β can be obtained; yet there are problems in obtaining its limiting distribution for some values of α, due to the regressor being a trend. We have:

$$\hat{\beta} - \beta = \left(\sum_{t=1}^{T} t^{2\alpha}\right)^{-1} \sum_{t=1}^{T} t^\alpha \epsilon_t \tag{A4.23}$$

so that:

$$\mathsf{E}\left[\hat{\beta} - \beta\right] = 0 \text{ and } \mathsf{E}\left[\left(\hat{\beta} - \beta\right)^2\right] = \sigma_\epsilon^2 \left(\sum_{t=1}^{T} t^{2\alpha}\right)^{-1}, \tag{A4.24}$$

and:

$$\hat{\beta} \sim \mathsf{N}\left[\beta, \sigma_{\epsilon}^{2}\left(\sum_{t=1}^{T} t^{2\alpha}\right)^{-1}\right]. \tag{A4.25}$$

Five values of α will be considered: $\alpha = 0,\ \pm½$ and ± 1.

(a) If $\alpha = 0$, then $\sqrt{T}(\hat{\beta} - \beta) \sim \mathsf{N}[0, \sigma_{\epsilon}^{2}]$ holds $\forall T$.

(b) If $\alpha = ½$, then $\sum_{t=1}^{T} t^{2\alpha} = \sum_{t=1}^{T} t = T(T+1)/2 \approx O(T^{2})$. Consequently:

$$\underset{T\to\infty}{\text{plim}} \left(\hat{\beta} - \beta\right) = \underset{T\to\infty}{\text{plim}} \sqrt{T}\left(\hat{\beta} - \beta\right) = 0,$$

and the distribution 'collapses' rather rapidly. Nevertheless:

$$T\left(\hat{\beta} - \beta\right) \sim \mathsf{N}\left[0, \frac{2\sigma_{\epsilon}^{2}}{(1 + T^{-1})}\right] \to \mathsf{N}\left[0, 2\sigma_{\epsilon}^{2}\right]. \tag{A4.26}$$

Thus, a higher-order rescaling produces a normal limiting distribution.

(c) $\alpha = -½$ could arise from trending heteroscedasticity when $y_{t}^{*} = \beta + \epsilon_{t}^{*}$ where:

$$\epsilon_{t}^{*} \sim \mathsf{IN}\left[0, \sigma_{\epsilon}^{2} t\right] \text{ and } y_{t} = \frac{y_{t}^{*}}{\sqrt{t}}. \tag{A4.27}$$

Then:

$$\left(\hat{\beta} - \beta\right) = \left(\sum_{t=1}^{T} t^{-1}\right)^{-1}\left[\sum_{t=1}^{T}\left(\frac{\epsilon_{t}}{\sqrt{t}}\right)\right]. \tag{A4.28}$$

Although $\sum t^{-1} \approx O(\log T) \to \infty$, it converges very slowly (see e.g. Binmore, 1983). Thus:

$$(\log T)^{\frac{1}{2}}\left(\hat{\beta} - \beta\right) \sim \mathsf{N}\left[0, \sigma_{\epsilon}^{2}\left(\left(\sum_{t=1}^{T} t^{-1}\right)^{-1} \log T\right)\right] \to \mathsf{N}\left[0, \sigma_{\epsilon}^{2} V\right],$$

where V is a finite constant.

(d) When $\alpha = 1$, a different rescaling is necessary compared with (a)–(c), since now:

$$\sum t^{2} = \tfrac{1}{6}\, T\,(T+1)\,(2T+1) \approx O\left(T^{3}\right) \tag{A4.29}$$

so that:

$$T^{\frac{3}{2}}\left(\hat{\beta} - \beta\right) \sim \mathsf{N}\left[0, \frac{3\sigma_{\epsilon}^{2}}{1 + 1.5T^{-1} + 0.5T^{-2}}\right] \to \mathsf{N}\left[0, 3\sigma_{\epsilon}^{2}\right].$$

(e) Finally, when $\alpha = -1$, $\lim_{T\to\infty}(\sum_{t=1}^{T} t^{-2}) = \pi^{2}/6$ and hence:

$$\left(\hat{\beta} - \beta\right) \xrightarrow{D} \mathsf{N}\left[0, \frac{6\sigma_{\epsilon}^{2}}{\pi^{2}}\right]. \tag{A4.30}$$

Thus, $\hat{\beta}$ is unbiased but inconsistent for β, since the variance does not go to zero as $T \to \infty$. In effect, the error 'swamps' β/t once t becomes large and so additional observations on y are not informative about $\hat{\beta}$, reflected in $\mathsf{V}[\hat{\beta}]$ being non-zero even asymptotically. Thus, the non-singularity of $\text{plim}(f(T)^{-1}\Sigma z_t z_t')$ is an essential condition for consistent regression estimation, for some function $f(T) \to \infty$ as $T \to \infty$.

Combining these two examples and weakening the assumptions, we can extend the limiting normal distribution established in §A3.7 for least-squares estimation conditional on $\boldsymbol{Z}_T^1$ (see e.g. Anderson, 1971):

Theorem 12. *Let* $y_t = \beta' z_t + \epsilon_t$ *where* $\mathsf{E}[y_t|z_t] = \beta' z_t$ *and* $\epsilon_t \sim \mathsf{IID}[0, \sigma_\epsilon^2]$. *Let* $\boldsymbol{A}_T = \sum z_t z_t'$ *and denote its* $(i, j)^{th}$ *element by* $a(T)_{ij}$, *and let* $\boldsymbol{B}_T = \boldsymbol{C}_T^{-1}\boldsymbol{A}_T\boldsymbol{C}_T^{-1}$ *where* $\boldsymbol{C}_T$ *is a diagonal matrix with elements* $\sqrt{a(T)_{ii}}$. *If as* $T \to \infty$*:*

(i) $a(T)_{ii} \to \infty,\ i = 1, \ldots, k$;
(ii) $z_{i,T+1}^2 / a(T)_{ii} \to 0,\ i = 1, \ldots, k$;
(iii) $\boldsymbol{B}_T \to \boldsymbol{B}$ *where* $\boldsymbol{B}$ *is finite positive definite;*

then:

$$\boldsymbol{C}_T\left(\hat{\boldsymbol{\beta}} - \boldsymbol{\beta}\right) \xrightarrow{D} \mathsf{N}_k\left[\boldsymbol{0}, \sigma_\epsilon^2 \boldsymbol{B}^{-1}\right].$$

This theorem covers example 2 for the values of $\alpha \neq -1$ as these cases satisfy its assumptions.

A4.8 Stationary dynamic processes

A4.8.1 Vector autoregressive representations

It is essential to generalize from the assumption of IID observations characterizing the previous derivations to dynamic processes in order to obtain theorems relevant to economic time series. Consider the data-generation process for $t = \ldots -m, \ldots, 1, \ldots, T$:

$$\boldsymbol{x}_t = \sum_{i=1}^{s} \boldsymbol{\pi}_i \boldsymbol{x}_{t-i} + \boldsymbol{\epsilon}_t \text{ where } \boldsymbol{\epsilon}_t \sim \mathsf{IID}_n\left[\boldsymbol{0}, \boldsymbol{\Sigma}\right], \tag{A4.31}$$

which is an sth-order vector autoregression (VAR) in the n variables $\boldsymbol{x}_t$, where $\boldsymbol{\Sigma}$ is an unrestricted $n \times n$ covariance matrix, the initial values $\boldsymbol{x}_{1-s}, \boldsymbol{x}_{2-s}, \ldots, \boldsymbol{x}_0$ are fixed, and s is finite. Bounded deterministic functions could be introduced without altering the form of the results for stationary processes (but would alter the algebra), whereas trends require a generalization of Theorem 12, and even intercepts matter if the process is non-stationary.

Equation (A4.31) can be written as a matrix polynomial in the lag operator L, where $L^k \boldsymbol{x}_t = \boldsymbol{x}_{t-k}$:

$$\boldsymbol{\pi}(L)\boldsymbol{x}_t = \boldsymbol{\epsilon}_t \text{ where } \boldsymbol{\pi}(L) = \boldsymbol{I}_n - \sum_{i=1}^{s} \boldsymbol{\pi}_i L^i, \tag{A4.32}$$

so $\pi(L)$ is a polynomial matrix (see Ch.A1). The roots of the polynomial:

$$\left|\mu^s I_n - \sum_{i=1}^{s} \mu^{s-i} \pi_i\right| = 0 \qquad \text{(A4.33)}$$

determine the statistical properties of $\{x_t\}$ We begin with the case that all ns roots of (A4.33) lie inside the unit circle. Such processes $\{x_t\}$ are called weakly stationary since the first two unconditional moments of $\{x_t\}$ are independent of t: $\mathsf{E}[x_t] = \mathbf{0}\ \forall t$ and $\mathsf{E}[x_t x'_{t+k}]$ is both independent of t for all k, and tends to zero as $k \to \infty$. If:

$$\mathsf{D_X}(x_{t_1}, \ldots, x_{t_k} \mid \theta) = \mathsf{D_X}(x_{t_1+h}, \ldots, x_{t_k+h} \mid \theta)\ \forall h, k, \qquad \text{(A4.34)}$$

so that the joint distribution of all collections $\{x_{t_1}, \ldots, x_{t_k}\}$ is unaltered by 'translation' h-periods along the time axis, then $\{x_t\}$ is strictly stationary. Neither concept implies the other, since strictly stationary processes need not have finite second moments, and weak stationarity is not enough to ensure that the CDF of $\{x_{t_1}, \ldots, x_{t_k}\}$ is constant over time (see Ch.2).

Having allowed data dependency, it is unnecessarily restrictive to retain the assumption that $\{\epsilon_t\}$ is an independent process, which in effect restricts the analysis to dealing only with data-generating processes, and excludes models where the error process is most unlikely to be independent. Instead, ϵ_t can be interpreted as $x_t - \mathsf{E}[x_t|\mathcal{I}_{t-1}]$, where $\mathcal{I}_{t-1}$ denotes the available information, so that $\mathsf{E}[\epsilon_t|\mathcal{I}_{t-1}] = \mathbf{0}$ and so $\{\epsilon_t\}$ is a martingale difference sequence (see Ch.2). A range of powerful limiting results has been established for martingale processes (see Hall and Heyde, 1980, and §A4.11). To ensure that information continuously accrues and no individual observations dominate, conditions are required about the underlying data process which is being modelled, such as mixing conditions as discussed in White (1984) and §A4.10. Spanos (1986) considers martingale central-limit theorems as well as mixing processes.

A4.8.2 Mann and Wald's theorem

When $\{z_t\}$ is a weakly stationary and ergodic n-dimensional vector random process:

$$\operatorname*{plim}_{T\to\infty} T^{-1} \sum_{t=1}^{T} z_t z_t' = M_Z = \mathsf{E}[z_t z_t'] \qquad \text{(A4.35)}$$

where M_Z is finite, positive definite. Then (see Mann and Wald, 1943b):
Theorem 13. *Let* $\nu_t \sim \mathsf{IID}[0, \sigma_\nu^2]$ *with finite moments of all orders. Then if* $\mathsf{E}[z_t \nu_t] = \mathbf{0}\ \forall t$:

$$\frac{1}{\sqrt{T}} \sum_{t=1}^{T} z_t \nu_t \xrightarrow{D} \mathsf{N}_n\left[\mathbf{0}, \sigma_\nu^2 M_Z\right].$$

Mann and Wald's theorem again extends the conditions under which asymptotic normality occurs. If $\nu_t \sim \mathsf{IID}_k[\mathbf{0}, \Sigma]$ is a k-dimensional vector process with finite higher-order moments, their result generalizes. Let $\otimes$ denote the Kronecker product defined in

Chapter A1, and let $(\cdot)^v$ be the vectoring operator which stacks columns of a matrix in a vector then:

$$\frac{1}{\sqrt{T}}\sum_{t=1}^{T}(\boldsymbol{z}_t\boldsymbol{\nu}_t')^v = \frac{1}{\sqrt{T}}\sum_{t=1}^{T}(\boldsymbol{z}_t\otimes \boldsymbol{I}_k)\,\boldsymbol{\nu}_t \xrightarrow{D} \mathsf{N}_{nk}\left[\mathbf{0}, \boldsymbol{M}_Z\otimes\boldsymbol{\Sigma}\right].$$

This theorem is applicable when the model coincides with the stationary DGP, as is assumed in much of econometric theory. An example would be the error ϵ_t in (A4.31) relative to lagged $\boldsymbol{x}$s. We consider the case where the model and DGP differ in §[A3.8.d] and Chapter 11.

A4.8.3 Hannan's theorem

It is convenient to write (A4.31) in companion form as:

$$\boldsymbol{f}_t = \boldsymbol{\Pi}\boldsymbol{f}_{t-1} + \boldsymbol{\eta}_t \;\text{ with }\; \boldsymbol{\eta}_t \sim \mathsf{IID}_{ns}\left[\mathbf{0}, \boldsymbol{\Psi}\right], \tag{A4.36}$$

where:

$$\boldsymbol{f}_t = \begin{pmatrix} \boldsymbol{x}_t \\ \boldsymbol{x}_{t-1} \\ \vdots \\ \boldsymbol{x}_{t-s+1} \end{pmatrix},\; \boldsymbol{\eta}_t = \begin{pmatrix} \boldsymbol{\epsilon}_t \\ \mathbf{0} \\ \vdots \\ \mathbf{0} \end{pmatrix} \;\text{ and }\; \boldsymbol{\Pi} = \begin{pmatrix} \boldsymbol{\pi}_1 & \boldsymbol{\pi}_2 & \cdots & \boldsymbol{\pi}_{s-1} & \boldsymbol{\pi}_s \\ \boldsymbol{I} & \mathbf{0} & \cdots & \mathbf{0} & \mathbf{0} \\ \vdots & \vdots & \ddots & \vdots & \vdots \\ \mathbf{0} & \mathbf{0} & \cdots & \boldsymbol{I} & \mathbf{0} \end{pmatrix}.$$

In (A4.36), $\boldsymbol{\Psi}$ is non-negative definite, but singular for $s > 1$, and the eigenvalues of $\boldsymbol{\Pi}$ are the same as the roots in (A4.31) (see Ch.A1). Let:

$$\boldsymbol{\pi} = \boldsymbol{I}_n - \sum_{i=1}^{s}\boldsymbol{\pi}_i = \boldsymbol{\pi}(1). \tag{A4.37}$$

This is the 'long-run' matrix, and the rank of $\boldsymbol{\pi}$ plays an important role in determining the asymptotic properties of estimators and tests (see Ch.11). Although $\{\boldsymbol{\epsilon}_t\}$ is stationary, the n variables in $\boldsymbol{x}_t$ need not all be stationary, and $r = \text{rank}(\boldsymbol{\pi})$ determines how many levels variables are stationary, and how many are integrated of first order, denoted $\mathsf{I}(1)$, so that Δx_{it} is stationary or $\mathsf{I}(0)$. Three cases can be distinguished:

(i) $r = n$, so all n variables in $\boldsymbol{x}_t$ are $\mathsf{I}(0)$ and hence stationary;
(ii) $r = 0$, so all n variables in $\boldsymbol{x}_t$ are $\mathsf{I}(1)$, but $\Delta\boldsymbol{x}_t$ is stationary; and
(iii) $0 < r < n$, so $(n - r)$ linear combinations of $\Delta\boldsymbol{x}_t$, and r linear combinations of $\boldsymbol{x}_t$, are $\mathsf{I}(0)$.

Case (ii) leads to differencing transformations on all variables, and case (iii) to cointegration; for the present we consider stationary distributions (i).
(i) When $\boldsymbol{\pi}$ has full rank n, since $\mathsf{E}[\boldsymbol{f}_{t-1}\boldsymbol{\epsilon}_s'] = \mathbf{0}\;\forall s \geq t$, the second moments of $\boldsymbol{f}_t$, namely $\boldsymbol{M}_F = \mathsf{E}[\boldsymbol{f}_t\boldsymbol{f}_t']$ and $\boldsymbol{M}_1 = \mathsf{E}[\boldsymbol{f}_t\boldsymbol{f}_{t-1}']$, are given from (A4.36) by:

$$\boldsymbol{M}_F = \boldsymbol{\Pi}\boldsymbol{M}_F\boldsymbol{\Pi}' + \boldsymbol{\Psi} \;\text{ and }\; \boldsymbol{M}_1 = \boldsymbol{\Pi}\boldsymbol{M}_F, \tag{A4.38}$$

so that vectorizing:

$$(\boldsymbol{M}_F)^v = (\boldsymbol{I} - \boldsymbol{\Pi} \otimes \boldsymbol{\Pi})^{-1} \boldsymbol{\Psi}^v. \tag{A4.39}$$

The sample estimators of $\boldsymbol{M}_F$ and $\boldsymbol{M}_1$ are:

$$\hat{\boldsymbol{M}}_F = T^{-1}\boldsymbol{F}'\boldsymbol{F} \text{ and } \hat{\boldsymbol{M}}_1 = T^{-1}\boldsymbol{F}'\boldsymbol{F}_1 \tag{A4.40}$$

where $\boldsymbol{F}' = (\boldsymbol{f}_1\boldsymbol{f}_2 \ldots . \boldsymbol{f}_T)$. From Hannan (1970, Ch.4), under the above assumptions:

Theorem 14. $\sqrt{T}(\hat{\boldsymbol{M}}_F - \boldsymbol{M}_F)^v \xrightarrow{D} \mathsf{N}_{ns}[\boldsymbol{0}, \boldsymbol{C}]$.

When $\boldsymbol{\Pi} = \boldsymbol{P}\boldsymbol{\Lambda}\boldsymbol{P}^{-1}$ and $\boldsymbol{\Lambda}$ has a real diagonal, $\boldsymbol{C}$ is obtained in Hendry (1982) and Maasoumi and Phillips (1982); Govaerts (1986) extends the derivation to complex roots. As before, asymptotic normality results.

We now briefly consider the two cases of the VAR remaining from above, which involve unit roots in some or all of the processes.

(ii) When $\boldsymbol{\pi}(1) = \boldsymbol{0}$ in (A4.31), so that $r = 0$, the system can be transformed to a VAR in the I(0) variables $\Delta\boldsymbol{x}_t$. Then the results of (i) apply to the differenced data. Otherwise, if (A4.31) is estimated in levels, the asymptotic distribution of the least-squares estimator is given in Phillips and Durlauf (1986) who show that conventional statistics do not have the usual limiting normal distributions.

(iii) When $\boldsymbol{x}_t$ is I(1), but $0 < r < n$, then $\boldsymbol{\pi}$ can be factorized as $\boldsymbol{\alpha}\boldsymbol{\beta}'$ where $\boldsymbol{\alpha}$ and $\boldsymbol{\beta}$ are $n \times r$ matrices of rank r. Then $\boldsymbol{\alpha}$ is a matrix of adjustment parameters, and $\boldsymbol{\beta}$ contains r cointegrating vectors, such that the linear combinations $\boldsymbol{\beta}'\boldsymbol{x}_t$ are I(0). Once it is known that there are r cointegrating vectors, it is possible to estimate the parameters of (A4.31) subject to the restriction that $\boldsymbol{\pi} = \boldsymbol{\alpha}\boldsymbol{\beta}'$, with $\boldsymbol{\alpha}$ and $\boldsymbol{\beta}$ of rank r, using a procedure proposed by Johansen (1988). As with (ii), unless the system is transformed to be I(0), which would involve only either $\boldsymbol{\beta}'\boldsymbol{x}_t$ or $\Delta\boldsymbol{x}_t$ variables, then the limiting distributions are not normal. We consider system cointegration in Chapters 8 and 11.

A4.8.4 Limiting distribution of OLS for a linear equation

Since a wide range of econometric estimators are functions of data second moments, and so their distributions asymptotically converge to functions of $\boldsymbol{C}$, Hannan's theorem (Theorem 14) is useful for stationary processes. As an illustration, let $\boldsymbol{x}_t' = (y_t : \boldsymbol{z}_t' : \boldsymbol{w}_t')$ and consider an arbitrary linear econometric equation of the form:

$$\boldsymbol{\phi}'\boldsymbol{f}_t = y_t - \boldsymbol{\gamma}'\boldsymbol{z}_t = e_t \tag{A4.41}$$

where $\boldsymbol{\phi}' = (1 : -\boldsymbol{\gamma}' : \boldsymbol{0}')$ and $\boldsymbol{\gamma}$ is an $m \times 1$ vector defined by:

$$\mathsf{E}[\boldsymbol{z}_t e_t] = \boldsymbol{0}. \tag{A4.42}$$

Then $\boldsymbol{z}_t = \boldsymbol{S}\boldsymbol{f}_t$ where $\boldsymbol{S} = (\boldsymbol{0} : \boldsymbol{I}_m : \boldsymbol{0})$ is a selection matrix. Given the model in (A4.41)+(A4.42), $\boldsymbol{\gamma}$ would be estimated by OLS:

$$\begin{aligned}\hat{\gamma}-\gamma &= \left(\sum_{t=1}^{T} z_t z_t'\right)^{-1} \sum_{t=1}^{T} z_t e_t \\ &= \left(T^{-1}S\sum_{t=1}^{T} f_t f_t' S'\right)^{-1} S\left(T^{-1}\sum_{t=1}^{T} f_t f_t'\right)\phi \\ &= \left(S\hat{M}_F S'\right)^{-1} S\hat{M}_F\phi.\end{aligned} \tag{A4.43}$$

From (A4.42), $SM_F\phi = \mathbf{0}$ and hence:

$$\underset{T\to\infty}{\text{plim}}\ (\hat{\gamma}-\gamma) = (SM_F S')^{-1} SM_F\phi = \mathbf{0}.$$

Neglecting the sampling variability in $(S\hat{M}_F S')$ by Cramér's theorem, so that it is replaced in (A4.43) by $(SM_F S')$:

$$\begin{aligned}\sqrt{T}(\hat{\gamma}-\gamma) &= (SM_F S')^{-1}\sqrt{T}S\left(\hat{M}_F - M_F\right)\phi + O_p\left(1/\sqrt{T}\right) \\ &= (SM_F S')^{-1}(S\otimes\phi')\sqrt{T}\left(\hat{M}_F - M_F\right)^{v} + o_p(1) \\ &= H\sqrt{T}\left(\hat{M}_F - M_F\right)^{v} + o_p(1)\end{aligned} \tag{A4.44}$$

using $(ABC)^v = (A\otimes C')B^v$ where $H = (SM_F S')^{-1}(S\otimes\phi')$. The limiting distribution of $\sqrt{T}(\hat{\gamma}-\gamma)$ now follows from Theorem 14:

$$\sqrt{T}(\hat{\gamma}-\gamma) \xrightarrow{D} \mathsf{N}\left[\mathbf{0}, HCH'\right]. \tag{A4.45}$$

The result in (A4.45) only depends on the distribution of the second moments of the data and is independent of the validity of the postulated model or of any distributional properties of $\{e_t\}$ which an investigator may have claimed. The coefficient γ need not be of any interest, and the fact that $\hat{\gamma}$ is consistent for γ is achieved by constructing γ as the population value of the distribution of $\hat{\gamma}$. The variance matrix HCH' of the limiting distribution of $\hat{\gamma}$ need not bear any relationship to the probability limit $(SM_F S')^{-1}$ of the OLS variance formula. Even though the asymptotic distribution theory delivers a limiting normal distribution for an arbitrary coefficient estimator in a linear stationary process, that is at best cold comfort to an empirical modeller. However, when the model has constant parameters and a homoscedastic, innovation error, so $\{e_t\}$ is well behaved, the OLS variance is consistently estimated by the conventional formula.

Even when the model coincides with the DGP and is stationary, convergence to normality can be relatively slow. In finite samples, OLS estimators in dynamic models are usually biased so convergence to normality requires both that the central tendency of the distribution shifts and its shape changes. Figures A4.2a–d show the histograms and density functions for 10 000 drawings for the OLS estimator $\hat{\rho}_1$ of ρ_1 in $y_t = \rho_0 + \rho_1 y_{t-1} + \epsilon_t$

where $\epsilon_t \sim \mathsf{IN}[0,1]$ when $\rho_0 = 0$, $\rho_1 = 0.8$ at T=10, 25, 50, and 300. When T=10, the distribution is skewed and centred on $\mathsf{E}[\hat{\rho}_1|T = 10] \simeq 0.46$ with $\mathsf{SD}[\hat{\rho}_1|T = 10] \simeq 0.31$; at T=25, the bias has fallen and $\mathsf{E}[\hat{\rho}_1|T = 25] \simeq 0.66$; at T=50, $\mathsf{E}[\hat{\rho}_1|T = 50] \simeq 0.73$; and only by T=300 does $\mathsf{E}[\hat{\rho}_1|T = 300] \simeq 0.79$. An approximation to the bias is given by $\mathsf{E}[(\hat{\rho}_1 - \rho_1)|T] \simeq -(1 + 3\rho_1)/T$ (see §A4.13.3 for the special case when $\rho_0 = 0$). The SD falls somewhat faster than $O(1/\sqrt{T})$. The distribution becomes symmetric slowly, and is noticeably skewed even at T=300; however, derived distributions such as those for t-tests converge more rapidly to normality.

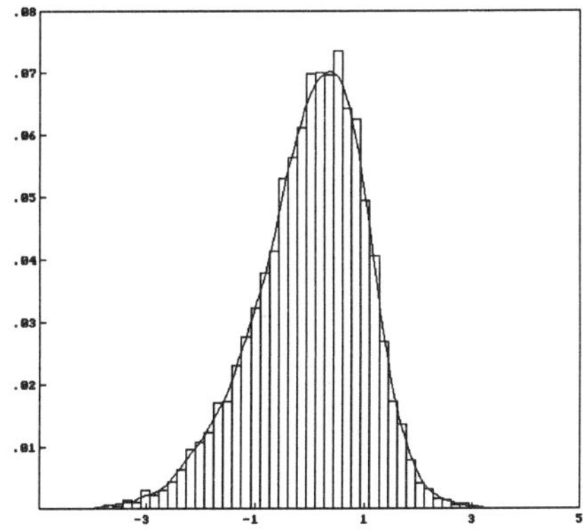

$T = 10$: $\mathsf{E}[\hat{\rho}_1] \simeq 0.46, \mathsf{SD}[\hat{\rho}_1] \simeq 0.31$

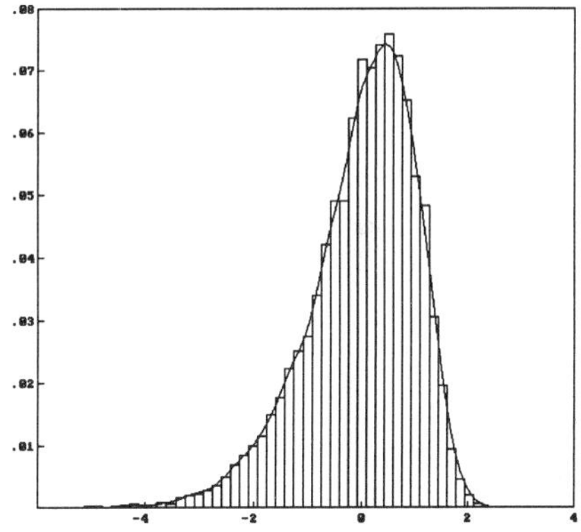

$T = 25$: $\mathsf{E}[\hat{\rho}_1] \simeq 0.66, \mathsf{SD}[\hat{\rho}_1] \simeq 0.17$

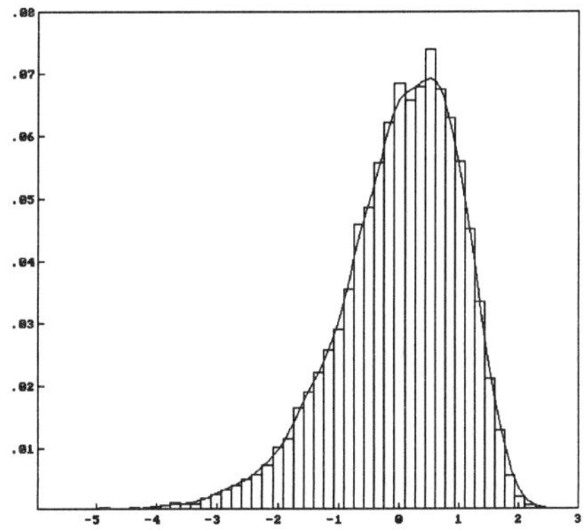

$T = 50$: $\mathsf{E}[\hat{\rho}_1] \simeq 0.73, \mathsf{SD}[\hat{\rho}_1] \simeq 0.11$

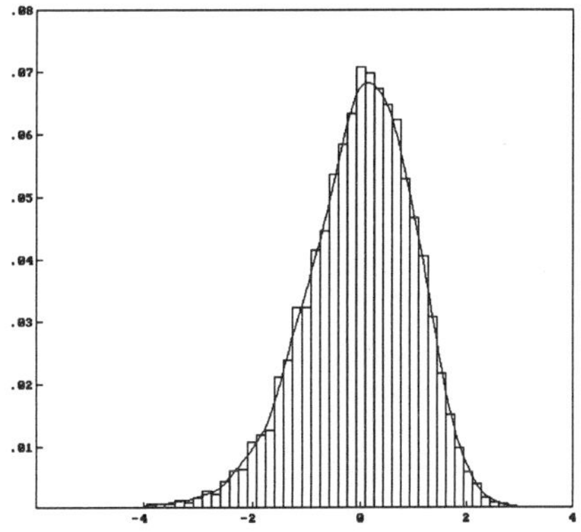

$T = 300$: $\mathsf{E}[\hat{\rho}_1] \simeq 0.79, \mathsf{SD}[\hat{\rho}_1] \simeq 0.04$

Fig. A4.2 Convergence of OLS in a dynamic equation

A4.9 Instrumental variables

The method of instrumental variables is an extension of least squares due to Geary (1943) and Reiersøl (1945); see Sargan (1958). Consider the linear equation:

$$y_t = \boldsymbol{x}_t'\boldsymbol{\beta} + u_t \text{ where } u_t \sim \mathsf{IN}\left[0, \sigma_u^2\right] \tag{A4.46}$$

where $\boldsymbol{\beta}$ is $k \times 1$. However, $\mathsf{E}[y_t|\boldsymbol{x}_t] \neq \boldsymbol{x}_t'\boldsymbol{\beta}$, so that, from (A4.46), $\mathsf{E}[\boldsymbol{x}_t u_t] \neq \mathbf{0}$. Thus, regression will not yield a consistent estimator of $\boldsymbol{\beta}$, as in the case discussed in §A4.8.4. There is assumed to exist a $k \times 1$ vector $\boldsymbol{z}_t$ such that:

$$\mathsf{E}\left[y_t \mid \boldsymbol{z}_t\right] = \boldsymbol{\beta}'\mathsf{E}\left[\boldsymbol{x}_t \mid \boldsymbol{z}_t\right] \text{ or } \mathsf{E}\left[\boldsymbol{z}_t' u_t\right] = \mathbf{0}.$$

The role of $\boldsymbol{z}_t$ is purely instrumental in solving the problem of estimating $\boldsymbol{\beta}$. We develop the algebra of instrumental variables (IV) estimators and their large-sample behaviour when there are k instruments: the case of more than k instruments is considered in Chapter 11. $\boldsymbol{\beta}$ is not estimable if there are fewer than k instruments.

In matrix terms:

$$\boldsymbol{y} = \boldsymbol{X}\boldsymbol{\beta} + \boldsymbol{u} \tag{A4.47}$$

with $\mathsf{E}[\boldsymbol{X}'\boldsymbol{u}] \neq \mathbf{0}$ but $\mathsf{E}[\boldsymbol{Z}'\boldsymbol{u}] = \mathbf{0}$. When (A4.47) holds, consider pre-multiplying by $\boldsymbol{Z}'$:

$$\boldsymbol{Z}'\boldsymbol{y} = \boldsymbol{Z}'\boldsymbol{X}\boldsymbol{\beta} + \boldsymbol{Z}'\boldsymbol{u}.$$

Providing $\operatorname{rank}(T^{-1}\boldsymbol{Z}'\boldsymbol{X}) = k$, and so $\operatorname{rank}(T^{-1}\boldsymbol{Z}'\boldsymbol{Z}) = k$ at all sample sizes, then:[4]

$$\tilde{\boldsymbol{\beta}} = \left(\boldsymbol{Z}'\boldsymbol{X}\right)^{-1}\boldsymbol{Z}'\boldsymbol{y} = \boldsymbol{\beta} + \left(T^{-1}\boldsymbol{Z}'\boldsymbol{X}\right)^{-1}\left(T^{-1}\boldsymbol{Z}'\boldsymbol{u}\right) \tag{A4.48}$$

exists $\forall T$ and is called the instrumental variables estimator. When $(y_t : \boldsymbol{x}_t' : \boldsymbol{z}_t')$ is a stationary vector process, then given the above assumptions, the results in §A4.8 apply and:

$$\operatorname*{plim}_{T\to\infty} \tilde{\boldsymbol{\beta}} = \boldsymbol{\beta} + \operatorname*{plim}_{T\to\infty}\left(T^{-1}\boldsymbol{Z}'\boldsymbol{X}\right)^{-1} \operatorname*{plim}_{T\to\infty}\left(T^{-1}\boldsymbol{Z}'\boldsymbol{u}\right) = \boldsymbol{\beta} \tag{A4.49}$$

from Slutsky's theorem and the law of large numbers. Hence, by Mann and Wald's theorem together with Cramér's theorem :

$$\sqrt{T}\left(\tilde{\boldsymbol{\beta}} - \boldsymbol{\beta}\right) = \left(T^{-1}\boldsymbol{Z}'\boldsymbol{X}\right)^{-1}\left(\frac{1}{\sqrt{T}}\boldsymbol{Z}'\boldsymbol{u}\right) \xrightarrow{D} \mathsf{N}_k\left[\mathbf{0}, \sigma_u^2\boldsymbol{R}\right],$$

where $\boldsymbol{R}$ is defined by:

$$\operatorname*{plim}_{T\to\infty}\left(T^{-1}\boldsymbol{Z}'\boldsymbol{X}\right)^{-1}\left(T^{-1}\boldsymbol{Z}'\boldsymbol{Z}\right)\left(T^{-1}\boldsymbol{X}'\boldsymbol{Z}\right)^{-1} = \operatorname*{plim}_{T\to\infty}\left[T^{-1}\boldsymbol{X}'\boldsymbol{Z}\left(\boldsymbol{Z}'\boldsymbol{Z}\right)^{-1}\boldsymbol{Z}'\boldsymbol{X}\right]^{-1}. \tag{A4.50}$$

[4] The condition $\operatorname{rank}(T^{-1}\boldsymbol{Z}'\boldsymbol{X}) = k$ is sufficient to uniquely identify $\boldsymbol{\beta}$: see White (1984).

The matrix in $[\cdot]$ is a consistent estimator of $\boldsymbol{R}$ by construction. Let:

$$\tilde{\boldsymbol{u}} = \boldsymbol{y} - \boldsymbol{X}\tilde{\boldsymbol{\beta}} \text{ and } \tilde{\sigma}_u^2 = \frac{\tilde{\boldsymbol{u}}'\tilde{\boldsymbol{u}}}{T}.$$

Since plim $\tilde{\boldsymbol{\beta}} = \boldsymbol{\beta}$, then $\tilde{\sigma}_u^2$ is a consistent estimator of σ_u^2, so that $\sigma_u^2 \boldsymbol{R}$ can be consistently estimated from sample evidence. An extension of §A4.8.4 could apply.

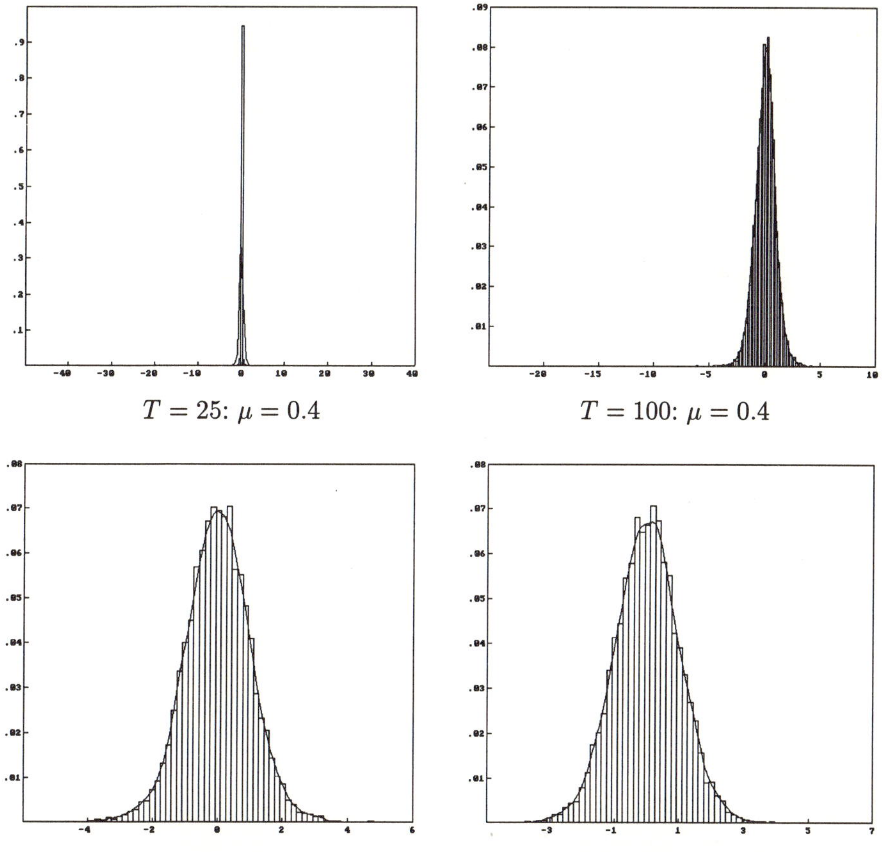

Fig. A4.3 Behaviour of IV estimation in a just-identified equation

In finite samples, other issues arise than merely the rate of convergence to normality. Because $\mathsf{E}[(T^{-1}\boldsymbol{Z}'\boldsymbol{X})^{-1}]$ need not exist, the distribution of $\tilde{\boldsymbol{\beta}}$ need not have any finite-sample moments, so large outliers are possible. The occurrence of these depends on the probability that $(\boldsymbol{Z}'\boldsymbol{X})$ gets close to singularity, as is most easily seen when $k = 1$. Now:

$$\tilde{\beta} = \frac{\boldsymbol{z}'\boldsymbol{y}}{\boldsymbol{z}'\boldsymbol{x}} = \frac{(\boldsymbol{z}'\boldsymbol{z})^{-1}\boldsymbol{z}'\boldsymbol{y}}{(\boldsymbol{z}'\boldsymbol{z})^{-1}\boldsymbol{z}'\boldsymbol{x}} = \frac{\hat{\gamma}}{\hat{\mu}}$$

where $\boldsymbol{x} = \mu \boldsymbol{z} + \boldsymbol{e}$ when $e_t \sim \mathsf{IN}[0, \sigma_e^2]$ so that:

$$y_t = \beta x_t + u_t = \beta \mu z_t + (u_t + \beta e_t) = \gamma z_t + v_t$$

and $\hat{\gamma} \sim \mathsf{N}[\gamma, (\sigma_u^2 + \beta^2 \sigma_e^2)(\boldsymbol{z}'\boldsymbol{z})^{-1}]$ with $\hat{\mu} \sim \mathsf{N}[\mu, \sigma_e^2 (\boldsymbol{z}'\boldsymbol{z})^{-1}]$. Then $\mathsf{P}(|\hat{\mu}| < \delta) \neq 0$ even for small δ so $\mathsf{E}[\hat{\gamma}\hat{\mu}^{-1}]$ does not exist ($\hat{\gamma}\hat{\mu}^{-1}$ is a Cauchy random variable): or, in practice, outliers abound when $\hat{\mu}$ can be close to zero. However, when the non-centrality $c = T\mu^2 m_{zz}/\sigma_e^2$ is large (where $m_{zz} = \mathsf{E}[T^{-1}\boldsymbol{z}'\boldsymbol{z}]$), there is a small probability of $\hat{\mu} \simeq 0$ so well-behaved outcomes result. Figures A4.3a–d show the histograms and density functions for 10 000 drawings for the IV estimator $\tilde{\beta}$ of β in $y_t = \beta x_t + u_t$ where $u_t \sim \mathsf{IN}[0, 1]$ when $\beta = 1.0$ for $\mu = 0.4$ at T=25 and 100 and μ =0.8 at T=50 and 100, where $\sigma_e^2 = 1$ and $m_{zz} = 1$ (so $c = 4$, 16, 32, and 80). The sampling distribution is badly behaved until $c \geq 32$, after which it looks close to normality (although no moments exist).

A4.10 Mixing processes

Mixing conditions restrict the memory of a stochastic process such that the distant future is virtually independent of the present and past. This provides an upper bound on the predictability of future events from present information. The past and future cannot be interchanged in these statements so that the relationship is asymmetric.

A4.10.1 Mixing and ergodicity

By way of analogy, imagine a sample space Ω which is a cup of coffee comprising 90 per cent black coffee and 10 per cent cream carefully placed in a layer at the top which defines the initial state $\boldsymbol{x}_0$ of the system. The whole space is of unit measure $\mu(\Omega) = 1$, fixed throughout, where the measure is the volume. A transformation on Ω is defined by a systematic stir of the liquid in the cup, in which a spoon is moved in a 360° circle; let $\boldsymbol{S}$ denote the transformation and $\boldsymbol{x}_t$ the state of the system at time t so that:

$$\boldsymbol{x}_{t+1} = \boldsymbol{S}\boldsymbol{x}_t = \boldsymbol{S}^2 \boldsymbol{x}_{t-1} \ldots \tag{A4.51}$$

where $\boldsymbol{S}$ is a mixing transformation in a literal sense. The experiment involves stirring the coffee/cream mixture, then drawing tiny samples of liquid from the cup at different points in time. The mixing is uniform if after enough stirs, any measurable set (i.e. volume of coffee drawn from the cup) contains 10% cream. In technical terms, let $\mathcal{A}$ and $\mathcal{B}$ respectively denote the sets of cream and black coffee, and $\mu(\cdot)$ the measure function so that $\mu(\mathcal{A}) = 0.1$, $\mu(\mathcal{B}) = 0.9$. Then $\boldsymbol{S}$ is uniformly mixing if, for any subset $\mathcal{C} \subset \Omega$ with $\mu(\mathcal{C}) > 0$:

$$\mu\left(\boldsymbol{S}^n \left(\mathcal{A} \cap \mathcal{C}\right)\right) \rightarrow \mu\left(\mathcal{A}\right) \mu\left(\mathcal{C}\right) \text{ as } n \rightarrow \infty \tag{A4.52}$$

i.e. if the transformation shifts $\mathcal{A}$ around enough so that the amount of $\mathcal{A}$ ending up in $\mathcal{C}$ equals their relative shares of the whole space (see e.g. Halmos, 1950). For dynamical systems, one can take $\mathcal{A}$ and $\mathcal{C}$ to be subsets of the phase space of the system, and consider such questions as: What is $\mathsf{P}(\boldsymbol{x}_t \in \mathcal{C} | \boldsymbol{x}_0 \in \mathcal{A})$?

An important implication of uniform mixing for stationary processes is the property of ergodicity. Consider a subset $\mathcal{C}$; then $\boldsymbol{S}$ is ergodic if $\boldsymbol{S}\mathcal{C} = \mathcal{C}$ implies that $\mu(\mathcal{C}) = 0$ or 1. In terms of the example, the transformation $\boldsymbol{S}$ is ergodic if the only sets which are invariant under $\boldsymbol{S}$ are the null set $\emptyset$ and the whole space Ω. This property certainly holds for mixing cream into coffee. Consider any $\mathcal{C}$ such that $\boldsymbol{S}\mathcal{C} = \mathcal{C}$, when $\boldsymbol{S}$ is uniform mixing from (A4.52):

$$\mu\left(\boldsymbol{S}^n\left(\mathcal{C}\cap\mathcal{C}\right)\right) \to \mu\left(\mathcal{C}\right)\mu\left(\mathcal{C}\right) = \mu\left(\mathcal{C}\right)^2. \tag{A4.53}$$

But as $\boldsymbol{S}^n\mathcal{C} = \mathcal{C}$ also, then $\mu(\boldsymbol{S}^n(\mathcal{C}\cap\mathcal{C})) = \mu(\mathcal{C}\cap\mathcal{C}) = \mu(\mathcal{C})$ so we have $\mu(\mathcal{C}) = \mu(\mathcal{C})^2$ which implies $\mu(\mathcal{C}) = 0$ or 1. Thus, uniform mixing transformations are ergodic.

The importance of this result derives from what is entailed by the statistical ergodic theorem (see e.g. Walters, 1975), namely, if a strictly stationary stochastic process $\{X_t\}$ is ergodic with finite expectation, then the time average for one realization:

$$\bar{X}_T = T^{-1}\sum_{t=1}^{T} X_t \tag{A4.54}$$

and the expectation $\mathsf{E}[X_t]$ converge when T is sufficiently large. This is an essential condition for conducting inference about $\mathsf{E}[X_t]$ from the time average.

A4.10.2 Uniform mixing and α-mixing processes

Formally, let $\mathcal{F}_m^k$ denote the σ-field generated by $(X_m \ldots X_k)$, $\mathcal{A} \in \mathcal{F}_{-\infty}^t$ and $\mathcal{B} \in \mathcal{F}_{t+\tau}^{\infty}$.

Definition 13. *$\{X_t\}$ is a uniform mixing process if for integer $\tau > 0$, and $\mathsf{P}(\mathcal{A}) > 0$:*

$$|\mathsf{P}\left(\mathcal{B}\mid\mathcal{A}\right) - \mathsf{P}\left(\mathcal{B}\right)| \leq \phi\left(\tau\right) \quad \textit{where} \quad \lim_{\tau\to\infty}\phi\left(\tau\right) = 0 \quad \textit{and} \quad \phi\left(\tau\right) > 0\ \forall\tau.$$

Further, D13 implies that:

$$|\mathsf{P}\left(\mathcal{B}\cap\mathcal{A}\right) - \mathsf{P}\left(\mathcal{B}\right)P\left(\mathcal{A}\right)| = |\mathsf{P}\left(\mathcal{B}\mid\mathcal{A}\right) - \mathsf{P}\left(\mathcal{B}\right)|\,\mathsf{P}\left(\mathcal{A}\right) \leq \phi\left(\tau\right)\mathsf{P}\left(\mathcal{A}\right) = \alpha\left(\tau\right),$$

say, then $\lim_{\tau\to\infty}\alpha(\tau) = 0$ when $\lim_{\tau\to\infty}\phi(\tau) = 0$. This second stronger condition is called α-mixing. In the limit as $\tau \to \infty$, for uniform-mixing processes, events in $\mathcal{F}_{t+\tau}^{\infty}$ are essentially independent of events in $\mathcal{F}_{-\infty}^t$.

For example, if $\{X_t\}$ is an IID process, then D13 is satisfied with $\phi(\tau) = 0$ for $\tau \geq 1$, so $\{\epsilon_t\}$ in (A4.31) is a uniform mixing process. Similarly, an m-dependent process, which is a process where terms more than m-periods apart are independent, as in an mth-order moving average, is mixing with $\phi(\tau) = 0$ for $\tau \geq m+1$. Moreover, if $\boldsymbol{x}_t$ is given by (A4.31), then:

$$\boldsymbol{x}_t = \sum_{j=0}^{\infty} \boldsymbol{R}_j\epsilon_{t-j} \quad \text{where} \quad \sum_{j=0}^{\infty} \|\boldsymbol{R}_j\|^2 < \infty, \tag{A4.55}$$

so that if ϵ_t is IID, then $\{x_t\}$ is mixing. However, the autocorrelations of $\{x_t\}$ need only vanish geometrically, rather than exponentially as with (A4.31), and yet the process remains mixing with sufficient independence to allow useful asymptotic results to be established. Thus, (A4.31) is overly restrictive for the class of admissible data-generation processes.

An important implication of uniform mixing is ergodicity as noted above, so that $\{x_t\}$ in (A4.31) is ergodic when the process is stationary, and:

$$\bar{x}_T = T^{-1}\sum_{t=1}^{T} x_t \overset{AS}{\rightarrow} \mathsf{E}[x_t] = \mathbf{0}. \tag{A4.56}$$

Moreover, if $\{x_t\}$ is ergodic so is $\{x_t x'_{t+s}\}$, so that sample second moments also converge almost surely to their population counterparts. Indeed, if $\{x_t\}$ is uniform mixing (and hence ergodic) so that $\phi(\tau) \to 0$ as $\tau \to \infty$, then any functions of a finite number of $\{x_t\}$ are also uniform mixing (with a new $\phi(\tau)$ which tends to zero as $\tau \to \infty$) so (e.g.) $\{x_t x'_{t+s}\}$ is uniform mixing. More generally (see e.g. White, 1984):

Theorem 15. *When $\{X_t\}$ is mixing with $\phi_x(\tau) \approx O(\tau^{-r})$ where $r > 0$, letting $Y_t = h_t(X_t \ldots X_{t-k})$ for a finite integer $k > 0$ when $h_t(\cdot)$ is a measurable function onto $\mathbb{R}$, then $\{Y_t\}$ is mixing with $\phi_y(\tau) \approx O(\tau^{-r})$.*

Theorem 16. *Further, when $Z_t(\theta) = b_t(Y_t, \theta)$ where $b_t(\cdot)$ is a function measurable in Y onto $\mathbb{R}$ and is continuous on Θ, then $\phi_z(\tau, \theta) \leq \phi_y(\tau)\ \forall \theta \in \Theta$, so $Z_t(\theta)$ is mixing.*

Consequent on this last theorem, quite complicated functions of mixing processes remain mixing.

A4.10.3 Laws of large numbers and central-limit theorems

The above developments allow us to formulate the analogue of a WLLN for mixing processes.

Theorem 17. *If, in addition to the conditions in Theorems 15 and 16, there exist measurable functions $d_t(Z_t)$ so that $|b_t(\cdot)| < d_t(\cdot)\ \forall \theta \in \Theta$, and $m \geq 1$ and $\delta > 0$ such that $\mathsf{E}[|d_t(Z_t)|^{m+\delta}] \leq \Delta < \infty\ \forall t$ with $r > m/(2m-1)$ then:*

$$\left| T^{-1}\sum_{t=1}^{T} \{b_t(Y_t, \theta) - \mathsf{E}[b_t(Y_t, \theta)]\} \right| \overset{AS}{\rightarrow} 0. \tag{A4.57}$$

This theorem provides a uniform weak law of large numbers for mixing processes. The larger is m, then the greater the order of moments assumed to exist, but the weaker the memory restrictions in terms of the value of r. If $\phi(\tau)$ vanishes exponentially, then m can be set arbitrarily close to unity.

Next, we have a central-limit theorem for mixing processes of the form $\{Z_t\}$ subject to the further conditions that:

(a) $\mathsf{E}[Z_t] = 0$ and $\mathsf{E}[|Z_t|^{2m}] \leq \Delta < \infty\ \forall t$ and $m > 1$;
(b) there exists a sequence $\{V_T\}$, $0 < \delta \leq V_T \leq \Delta$, such that for $S_T(j) = T^{-\frac{1}{2}}\sum_{t=1+j}^{T} Z_t$, then $\mathsf{E}[S_T(j)^2 - V_T] \to 0$ uniformly in j where $\{V_T\}$ need not

be constant, but the variability depends only on T and not on the starting point of the sum (i.e. the date). Then:

Theorem 18. *If* $\{Z_t\}$ *satisfies Theorems 15, 16 and 17 and conditions (a) and (b) with* $r > m/(m-1)$*:*

$$V_T^{-\frac{1}{2}} S_T(0) \xrightarrow{D} \mathsf{N}[0,1]. \tag{A4.58}$$

While certain of the required conditions are neither very transparent nor easily verified, the need for continuity, finite moments of an appropriate order, and bounding functions in addition to mixing is unsurprising given the discussion in earlier sections. Conversely, this theorem is general and potentially covers a large class of econometric estimators providing $\{x_t\}$ is mixing, irrespective of any assumptions concerning the correct specification of the model under consideration (see White, 1984). As will be seen in the next section, mixing provides a useful set of sufficient conditions for Crowder's Theorem.

A4.11 Martingale difference sequences

A4.11.1 Constructing martingales

The earlier laws of large numbers and central-limit theorems were framed in terms of independent random variables. For data-generation processes with autonomous innovations, this restriction is not too serious; but, for models defined by their error processes just being an innovation relative to the information used in the study, the assumption of independence is untenable. The necessary statistical apparatus already exists for developing a theory relevant for models, in the form of martingale limit theory (see Hall and Heyde, 1980). This theory includes as special cases many of the limit results discussed in earlier sections, since sums of independent random variables (as deviations about their expectations) are in fact martingales. Indeed, there is an intimate link between martingales, conditional expectations on σ-fields, and least-squares approximations, which is why the associated theory is useful for econometric modelling.

Let $\{X_t\}$ be a sequence of zero-mean random variables on the probability space $\{\Omega, \mathcal{F}, \mathsf{P}\}$, and let $\boldsymbol{X}_{(t-1)} = (X_{t-1}, \ldots, X_{t-n}, \ldots)$ such that:

$$\mathsf{E}\left[X_t \mid \boldsymbol{X}_{(t-1)}\right] = \mathbf{0}. \tag{A4.59}$$

Let $Y_T = \sum_{t=1}^{T} X_t$, then:

$$\mathsf{E}\left[Y_T \mid \boldsymbol{Y}_{(T-1)}\right] = Y_{T-1}, \tag{A4.60}$$

and Y_T is called a martingale.[5] Since $X_T = Y_T - Y_{T-1}$, then $\{X_T\}$ is a martingale-difference sequence (MDS).

[5] More precisely, $\mathsf{E}[Y_t|\mathcal{F}_{t-1}] = Y_{t-1}$ *a.s.* where $\mathcal{F}_{t-1}$ is the σ-field generated by $\boldsymbol{X}_{(t-1)}$.

A salient feature of economic data is their high degree of inter-dependence and temporal dependence. Thus, let $\boldsymbol{X}_t$ denote a vector random process with respect to the probability space $(\Omega, \mathcal{F}, \mathsf{P})$. As in Chapter A2, the joint data density $\mathsf{D}_{\mathsf{X}}(\cdot)$ can be sequentially conditioned as in (A4.3). Then a linear representation of $\boldsymbol{X}_t$, given the past, takes the form:

$$\mathsf{E}\left[\boldsymbol{X}_t \mid \mathcal{I}_{t-1}\right] = \sum_{j=1}^{s} \boldsymbol{\pi}_j \boldsymbol{X}_{t-j}, \tag{A4.61}$$

where $\mathcal{I}_{t-1}$ denotes previous information, $\boldsymbol{\pi}_j$ is the matrix of coefficients whereby each $\boldsymbol{X}_{t-j}$ influences $\boldsymbol{X}_t$, and s is the longest time dependence. In general, therefore, $\{\boldsymbol{X}_t\}$ is not a martingale. However, define:

$$\boldsymbol{\epsilon}_t = \boldsymbol{X}_t - \sum_{j=1}^{s} \boldsymbol{\pi}_j \boldsymbol{X}_{t-j}, \tag{A4.62}$$

then implicitly we have created the model:

$$\boldsymbol{X}_t = \sum_{j=1}^{s} \boldsymbol{\pi}_j \boldsymbol{X}_{t-j} + \boldsymbol{\epsilon}_t, \tag{A4.63}$$

where $\{\boldsymbol{\epsilon}_t\}$ is a process such that, by construction, $\mathsf{E}[\boldsymbol{\epsilon}_t \mid \mathcal{I}_{t-1}] = \mathbf{0}$ and hence:

$$\mathsf{E}\left[\boldsymbol{\epsilon}_t \mid \boldsymbol{E}_{t-1}\right] = \mathbf{0}, \tag{A4.64}$$

where $\boldsymbol{E}_{t-1} = (\boldsymbol{\epsilon}_{t-1} \ldots)$ is a subset of $\mathcal{I}_{t-1}$. The derived process $\{\boldsymbol{\epsilon}_t\}$ in (A4.64) is a vector of martingale-difference sequences. Successive $\boldsymbol{\epsilon}_t$ are not independent in general, but are uncorrelated, and in particular:

$$\mathsf{E}\left[\boldsymbol{\epsilon}_t \mid \boldsymbol{\epsilon}_{t-1}\right] = \mathbf{0}. \tag{A4.65}$$

Let:

$$\boldsymbol{\nu}_T = \sum_{t=1}^{T} \boldsymbol{\epsilon}_t,$$

then:

$$\mathsf{E}\left[\boldsymbol{\nu}_T \mid (\boldsymbol{\nu}_{T-1}, \ldots, \boldsymbol{\nu}_1)\right] = \boldsymbol{\nu}_{T-1}. \tag{A4.66}$$

Hence, $\{\boldsymbol{\nu}_T\}$ is a martingale. This result is intimately related to the famous Wold decomposition theorem (see Wold, 1938) that the purely non-deterministic component of any stationary time series can be represented in terms of an infinite moving average of uncorrelated errors.

A4.11.2 Properties of martingale-difference sequences

If $\{X_t\}$ is an MDS from Y_t whose second moment exists $\forall t$, we can generalize Chebychev's inequality to:

$$\mathsf{P}\left(|Y_j| \leq \delta,\ j = 1, \ldots, T\right) \geq 1 - \frac{\mathsf{E}\left[Y_T^2\right]}{\delta^2}. \tag{A4.67}$$

Also, generalizations of the SLLNs hold, noting that $T^{-1}Y_T = \bar{X}_T$ (see e.g. White, 1984):

(a) if $\sum_{t=1}^{\infty} t^{-(1+r)}\mathsf{E}[|X_t|^{2r}] < \infty$ for $r \in [1,2]$, then $T^{-1}Y_T \overset{AS}{\rightarrow} 0$.
(b) if $\mathsf{E}[|X_t|^{2r}] < B < \infty \ \forall t$ and some $r \in [1,2]$, then $T^{-1}Y_T \overset{AS}{\rightarrow} 0$.

For IID random variables, the condition $r > 1/2$ is necessary and sufficient, so we come close to that requirement despite much weaker dependence assumptions.

Before discussing asymptotic distributions based on MDSs, we need an important additional concept. We met Borel sets in Chapter A2 when we wished to construct random variables from the basic event space, in terms of the sequence of intervals $\mathcal{B}_z = (-\infty, z]$, which are the sets $\{x : -\infty < x \le z,\ z \in \mathbb{R}\}$. Technically, the Borel field $\mathcal{B}$ is the smallest collection of $\mathcal{B}_z,\ z \in \mathbb{R}$ which is closed under complements and countable unions. $\mathsf{P}(\cdot)$ was well defined for such sets, which comprised all the relevant events, and we moved to a new probability space $(\mathbb{R}, \mathcal{B}, \mathsf{P}_{\mathsf{x}})$. If we think of the sample space here as $\mathbb{R}$ repeated indefinitely often (to allow for infinite sequences), then the Borel sets again generate an event space. This approach generalizes to q-dimensional vector random variables $\boldsymbol{X}$, with a probability space which we could write as $(\mathbb{R}^q_\infty, \mathcal{B}, \mathsf{P}_{\mathsf{X}})$. If the basic event space increases over time due to information accrual, so does the Borel field, and we can now exploit that feature. The following two theorems sustain the use of martingale difference sequences for asymptotic distributions of model estimates (see e.g. Whittle, 1970, and White, 1984).

Theorem 19. *Let $\{\mathcal{B}_n\}$ be an increasing sequence of Borel fields $\mathcal{B}_n \subseteq \mathcal{B}_{n+1}$, and Z be a fixed random variable where $Y_n = \mathsf{E}[Z|\mathcal{B}_n]$. Then:*

$$\mathsf{E}[Z \mid \mathcal{B}_n] = \mathsf{E}[(Z \mid \mathcal{B}_{n+1}) \mid \mathcal{B}_n] = \mathsf{E}[Y_{n+1} \mid \mathcal{B}_n],$$

so that $Y_n = \mathsf{E}[Y_{n+1}|\mathcal{B}_n]$. Consequently, $\{Y_n\}$ is a martingale relative to $\mathcal{B}_n$.
Further:

$$\mathsf{E}\left[Y_n^2\right] = \mathsf{E}\left[(\mathsf{E}[Z \mid \mathcal{B}_n])^2\right] \le \mathsf{E}\left[Z^2\right].$$

Indeed, Y_n is the random variable defined on $\mathcal{B}_n$ by minimizing $\mathsf{E}[Z - Y_n]^2$, and so is a conditional expectation, or least-squares approximation, with the property that $Y_n \perp Z - Y_n$ (read as Y_n is orthogonal to $Z - Y_n$). Alternatively:

$$\mathsf{E}\left[Z^2\right] = \mathsf{E}\left[Y_n^2\right] + \mathsf{E}[Z - Y_n]^2 \ge \mathsf{E}\left[Y_n^2\right] \qquad \text{(A4.68)}$$

as required. This result provides a general way to construct an MDS of the form $Y_T - Y_{T-1}$, from an increasing sequence of Borel fields. Next:

Theorem 20. *If $\{Y_T\}$ is a martingale for which $\mathsf{E}[Y_T^2]$ is uniformly bounded, then Y_T converges a.s. to a genuine random variable $Y = \mathsf{E}[Z|\mathcal{B}_\infty]$.*
The key here is that:

$$\mathsf{E}\left[Y_T^2\right] = \sum_{t=1}^{T} \mathsf{E}\left[X_t^2\right] \qquad \text{(A4.69)}$$

by the martingale property, and if $\sum_{t=1}^{\infty} \mathsf{E}[X_t^2]$ is finite due to the uniform bound on $\mathsf{E}[Y_T^2]$, then the SLLN applies. There are many applications of these results of which two immediate ones are that:

(i) if $X_t \sim \mathsf{IID}[\mu, \sigma^2]$, then $T\bar{X}_T$ is a martingale and so by (a), $\bar{X}_T \overset{AS}{\rightarrow} \mu$;
(ii) a sequence of conditional expectations on an increasing sequence of $\mathcal{B}_n$ is a martingale, so the innovations from a congruent model are a martingale difference sequence to which the above theorems apply (see Ch.9).

Finally, we need a central-limit theorem for MDS corresponding to the Lindeberg–Lévy result earlier:
Theorem 21. *If $\{X_t\}$ is an MDS with $\mathsf{E}[X_t^2] = \sigma_t^2$ where $0 < \sigma_t^2 < \infty$, and $W_T = T^{-1}\sum_{t=1}^{T} X_t$, with $S_T^2 = \sum_{t=1}^{T} \sigma_t^2$ when:*

$$\lim S_T^{-2} \left[\sum_{t=1}^{T} \mathsf{E}\left[X_t^2 I\left(|X_t| \geq \epsilon S_t\right)\right] \right] = 0 \; \forall \epsilon > 0,$$

and $\sum_{t=1}^{T} X_t^2/S_T^2 \overset{P}{\rightarrow} 1$, then:

$$\frac{W_T}{S_T} \overset{D}{\rightarrow} \mathsf{N}\left[0, 1\right]. \tag{A4.70}$$

Note the additional requirement that $\sum_{t=1}^{T} X_t^2/S_T^2 \overset{P}{\rightarrow} 1$, which was implied by the Lindeberg-Lévy theorem when the sequences were independent. We now apply Theorem 21 to MLE.

A4.11.3 Applications to maximum-likelihood estimation

We maintain the regularity assumptions made in Chapter A3, assume stationarity and uniform mixing of $\{X_t\}$, but weaken the sampling assumption, using results in Crowder (1976). Mixing ensures that information continually accrues, yet the process is ergodic as shown in §A4.10. Let $\ell_t(\boldsymbol{\theta}) = \ell(\boldsymbol{\theta}; x_t|\mathcal{I}_{t-1})$ denote the log-likelihood function for one observation on the random variable X from the sequential density $\mathsf{D_x}(x|\mathcal{I}_{t-1}, \boldsymbol{\theta})$ for $\boldsymbol{\theta} \in \Theta \subseteq \mathbb{R}^k$ and history $\mathcal{I}_{t-1}$, and let:

$$\bar{\ell}(\boldsymbol{\theta}) = T^{-1} \sum_{t=1}^{T} \ell_t(\boldsymbol{\theta}) \tag{A4.71}$$

where

$$\boldsymbol{q}_t(\boldsymbol{\theta}) = \frac{\partial \ell_t(\cdot)}{\partial \boldsymbol{\theta}} \text{ and } \boldsymbol{H}_t(\boldsymbol{\theta}) = \frac{\partial^2 \ell_t(\cdot)}{\partial \boldsymbol{\theta} \partial \boldsymbol{\theta}'} \tag{A4.72}$$

with:

$$\bar{\boldsymbol{q}}_T(\boldsymbol{\theta}) = T^{-1} \sum_{t=1}^{T} \boldsymbol{q}_t(\boldsymbol{\theta}). \tag{A4.73}$$

Let $\boldsymbol{\theta}_p$ denote the population value of $\boldsymbol{\theta}$. It is assumed that $\mathsf{E}[\boldsymbol{q}_t(\boldsymbol{\theta}_p) \mid \mathcal{I}_{t-1}] = \mathbf{0}$ and:

$$\mathsf{V}\left[\boldsymbol{q}_t\left(\boldsymbol{\theta}_p\right) \mid \mathcal{I}_{t-1}\right] = -\mathsf{E}\left[\boldsymbol{H}_t\left(\boldsymbol{\theta}_p, \boldsymbol{\theta}_p\right) \mid \mathcal{I}_{t-1}\right] \qquad \text{(A4.74)}$$

where the notation $\boldsymbol{H}_t(\boldsymbol{\theta}_p, \boldsymbol{\theta})$ potentially allows different rows to be evaluated at different points in $[\boldsymbol{\theta}_p, \boldsymbol{\theta}]$, and:

$$\bar{\boldsymbol{H}}_T\left(\boldsymbol{\theta}_p, \boldsymbol{\theta}\right) = T^{-1}\sum_{t=1}^{T} \boldsymbol{H}_t\left(\boldsymbol{\theta}_p, \boldsymbol{\theta}\right) = T^{-1}\boldsymbol{H}_{(T)}\left(\boldsymbol{\theta}_p, \boldsymbol{\theta}\right). \qquad \text{(A4.75)}$$

Therefore, $Z_t = \boldsymbol{\lambda}'\boldsymbol{q}_t(\boldsymbol{\theta}_p)$ is an MDS, so that:

$$Z_{(T)} = \sum_{t=1}^{T} Z_t = T\boldsymbol{\lambda}'\bar{\boldsymbol{q}}_T\left(\boldsymbol{\theta}_p\right) = \boldsymbol{\lambda}'\boldsymbol{q}_{(T)}\left(\boldsymbol{\theta}_p\right) \qquad \text{(A4.76)}$$

is a martingale, essentially achieved by sequential factorization of the joint density function. Its (normal) limiting distribution can be derived from the results in Theorem 21 under the present assumptions, via the martingale version of the Lindeberg-Lévy central-limit theorem. Let:

$$\mathsf{V}\left[\bar{\boldsymbol{q}}_T\left(\boldsymbol{\theta}_p\right)\right] = \boldsymbol{B}_T = -\mathsf{E}\left[\boldsymbol{H}_{(T)}\left(\boldsymbol{\theta}_p, \boldsymbol{\theta}_p\right)\right] \qquad \text{(A4.77)}$$

then:

$$\mathsf{E}\left[\boldsymbol{B}_T^{-\frac{1}{2}}\bar{\boldsymbol{q}}_T\left(\boldsymbol{\theta}_p\right)\right] = \mathbf{0} \text{ and } \mathsf{E}\left[\boldsymbol{B}_T^{-\frac{1}{2}}\bar{\boldsymbol{q}}_T\left(\boldsymbol{\theta}_p\right)\bar{\boldsymbol{q}}_T\left(\boldsymbol{\theta}_p\right)'\boldsymbol{B}_T^{-\frac{1}{2}}\right] = \boldsymbol{I}_k. \qquad \text{(A4.78)}$$

Using the Cramér-Wold device for the martingale $Z_{(T)}$:

$$\boldsymbol{B}_T^{-\frac{1}{2}}\bar{\boldsymbol{q}}_T\left(\boldsymbol{\theta}_p\right) \xrightarrow{D} \mathsf{N}_k\left[\mathbf{0}, \boldsymbol{I}\right]. \qquad \text{(A4.79)}$$

Next, we need to relate that distribution to the limiting distribution of the MLE. A first-order Taylor-series expansion around $\boldsymbol{\theta}_p$ is taken to be valid for $\boldsymbol{\theta} \in \mathcal{N}(\boldsymbol{\theta}_p)$, so that asymptotically, the average likelihood function is quadratic in the neighbourhood of $\boldsymbol{\theta}_p$ (a mean-value theorem could be used, given the consistency of the MLE noted below):

$$\bar{\boldsymbol{q}}_T\left(\boldsymbol{\theta}\right) \simeq \bar{\boldsymbol{q}}_T\left(\boldsymbol{\theta}_p\right) + \bar{\boldsymbol{H}}_T\left(\boldsymbol{\theta}_p, \boldsymbol{\theta}\right)\left(\boldsymbol{\theta} - \boldsymbol{\theta}_p\right). \qquad \text{(A4.80)}$$

Assume that the MLE $\hat{\boldsymbol{\theta}}_T$, based on solving the score equation $\bar{\boldsymbol{q}}_T(\hat{\boldsymbol{\theta}}_T) = \mathbf{0}$, is unique. Then:

$$\boldsymbol{B}_T^{-\frac{1}{2}}\bar{\boldsymbol{H}}_T\left(\boldsymbol{\theta}_p, \boldsymbol{\theta}\right) \to \infty \text{ for } \boldsymbol{\theta} \in \mathcal{N}\left(\boldsymbol{\theta}_p\right) \qquad \text{(A4.81)}$$

and

$$\boldsymbol{B}_T^{-1}\bar{\boldsymbol{H}}_T\left(\boldsymbol{\theta}_p, \hat{\boldsymbol{\theta}}_T\right) \xrightarrow{P} -\boldsymbol{I}_k. \qquad \text{(A4.82)}$$

Consequently, from (A4.75) and (A4.81), $\boldsymbol{B}_T^{-1}$ is $O_p(T^{-1})$. From (A4.80):

$$\boldsymbol{B}_T^{-\frac{1}{2}}\bar{\boldsymbol{q}}_T\left(\boldsymbol{\theta}\right) = \boldsymbol{B}_T^{-\frac{1}{2}}\bar{\boldsymbol{q}}_T\left(\boldsymbol{\theta}_p\right) + \boldsymbol{B}_T^{-\frac{1}{2}}\bar{\boldsymbol{H}}_T\left(\boldsymbol{\theta}_p, \boldsymbol{\theta}\right)\left(\boldsymbol{\theta} - \boldsymbol{\theta}_p\right). \qquad \text{(A4.83)}$$

Crowder proves the existence of a divergent sequence $\{C_T\}$ (related to the lower bound of the eigenvalues of $\boldsymbol{H}_{(T)}(\cdot)\boldsymbol{H}_{(T)}(\cdot)'$) such that on scaling (A4.83) by C_T^{-1}, the first two terms converge to zero, whereas the third diverges except at $\boldsymbol{\theta}_p$ (see (A4.81)), which allows him to prove consistency of the MLE (see Ch.11).

Next, from the mean-value expression corresponding to (A4.80), but for the MLE:

$$\hat{\boldsymbol{\theta}}_T - \boldsymbol{\theta}_p = -\left[\bar{\boldsymbol{H}}_T\left(\boldsymbol{\theta}_p, \hat{\boldsymbol{\theta}}_T\right)\right]^{-1} \boldsymbol{B}_T \boldsymbol{B}_T^{-1} \bar{\boldsymbol{q}}_T\left(\boldsymbol{\theta}_p\right) \xrightarrow{P} \boldsymbol{B}_T^{-1} \bar{\boldsymbol{q}}_T\left(\boldsymbol{\theta}_p\right). \qquad \text{(A4.84)}$$

From (A4.84) and (A4.81), scaling by $\sqrt{T}$ in (A4.84) achieves a non-degenerate limiting normal distribution based on (A4.79):

$$\sqrt{T}\left(\hat{\boldsymbol{\theta}}_T - \boldsymbol{\theta}_p\right) \xrightarrow{D} \mathsf{N}_k\left[\mathbf{0}, \boldsymbol{B}_1^{-1}\left(\boldsymbol{\theta}_p\right)\right], \qquad \text{(A4.85)}$$

where $\boldsymbol{B}_1^{-1}(\boldsymbol{\theta}_p)$ denotes the matrix for a single observation, so we rely on ergodicity and stationarity again.

Transient parameters can be allowed for, as can logistic growth in the data series. This provides a general result for maximum-likelihood estimation in stationary, ergodic processes, with considerable initial data dependence and some heterogeneity, extending section A4.7.

A4.12 A solved autoregressive example

Consider the following stationary data generation process for a random variable y_t:

$$y_t = \beta y_{t-1} + e_t \ \text{ where } \ e_t \sim \mathsf{IN}\left[0, 1\right], \qquad \text{(A4.86)}$$

when $|\beta| < 1$ and $y_0 \sim \mathsf{N}[0, (1-\beta^2)^{-1}]$.

(a) Obtain the population moments of the process.
(b) Derive (i) $\mathsf{E}[T^{-1}\sum_{t=2}^{T} y_{t-1}e_t]$; (ii) $\mathsf{E}[T^{-1}\sum_{t=1}^{T} y_t^2]$; (iii) $\mathsf{E}[T^{-1}\sum_{t=2}^{T} y_t y_{t-1}]$; and (iv) $V = \mathsf{V}[T^{-1}\sum_{t=1}^{T} y_t^2]$.
(c) Derive the limiting distribution of the sample mean.
(d) Obtain the limiting distribution of the least-squares estimator of β.

(Adapted from Oxford M.Phil., 1987)

Solution to (a)

When $|\beta| < 1$, the population moments of a first-order autoregressive process are derived as follows. Solve (A4.86) backwards in time as:

$$y_t = y_0 + \sum_{i=0}^{t-1} \beta^i e_{t-i},$$

so that:

$$\mathsf{E}\left[y_t\right] = \mathsf{E}\left[\sum_{i=0}^{t-1} \beta^i e_{t-i}\right] = 0. \qquad \text{(A4.87)}$$

Letting $\mathsf{V}[y_t] = \sigma_y^2 = \mathsf{E}[y_t^2]$:

$$\sigma_y^2 = \mathsf{E}\left[\beta^2 y_{t-1}^2 + 2\beta y_{t-1}e_t + e_t^2\right] = \beta^2\sigma_y^2 + 1 = \frac{1}{(1-\beta^2)}. \tag{A4.88}$$

since $\{y_t\}$ is stationary. Further, since $\mathsf{E}[e_t^4] = 3$, noting only the non-zero terms:

$$\mathsf{E}\left[y_t^4\right] = \beta^4\mathsf{E}\left[y_{t-1}^4\right] + 6\beta^2\mathsf{E}\left[y_{t-1}^2 e_t^2\right] + \mathsf{E}\left[e_t^4\right] = \frac{3+6\beta^2\sigma_y^2}{1-\beta^4}. \tag{A4.89}$$

Finally:

$$\mathsf{C}\left[y_t, y_{t-1}\right] = \mathsf{E}\left[y_t y_{t-1}\right] = \beta\mathsf{E}\left[y_{t-1}^2\right] + \mathsf{E}\left[y_{t-1}e_t\right] = \beta\sigma_y^2. \tag{A4.90}$$

Also $\mathsf{C}[y_t, y_{t-k}] = \beta\mathsf{C}[y_t, y_{t-k+1}]$ as $\mathsf{E}[y_{t-k}e_t] = 0\ \forall k > 0$, so $\mathsf{corr}(y_t, y_{t-k}) = \beta^k$.

Solution to (b)

$$\text{(i) } \mathsf{E}\left[T^{-1}\sum_{t=2}^{T} y_{t-1}e_t\right] = T^{-1}\sum_{t=2}^{T}\mathsf{E}\left[y_{t-1}e_t\right] = 0.$$

$$\text{(ii) } \mathsf{E}\left[T^{-1}\sum_{t=1}^{T} y_t^2\right] = T^{-1}\sum_{t=1}^{T}\mathsf{E}\left[y_t^2\right] = T^{-1}\sum_{t=1}^{T}\frac{1}{1-\beta^2} = \frac{1}{1-\beta^2} = \sigma_y^2.$$

$$\text{(iii) } \mathsf{E}\left[T^{-1}\sum_{t=2}^{T} y_t y_{t-1}\right] = T^{-1}\sum_{t=2}^{T}\mathsf{E}\left[y_t y_{t-1}\right] = T^{-1}\sum_{t=2}^{T}\frac{\beta}{1-\beta^2} \simeq \frac{\beta}{1-\beta^2} = \beta\sigma_y^2.$$

$$\begin{aligned}
\text{(iv) } V &= \mathsf{E}\left[\left(T^{-1}\sum_{t=1}^{T} y_t^2 - \sigma_y^2\right)^2\right] = T^{-2}\sum_{t=1}^{T}\sum_{s=1}^{T}\mathsf{E}\left[y_t^2 y_s^2\right] - \sigma_y^4 \\
&= T^{-2}\sum_{t=1}^{T}\mathsf{E}\left[y_t^4\right] + 2T^{-2}\sum_{t=1}^{T}\sum_{s=1}^{t-1}\mathsf{E}\left[y_t^2 y_s^2\right] - \sigma_y^4 \\
&= 3T^{-1}\sigma_y^4 - \sigma_y^4 + 2T^{-2}\sum_{t=1}^{T}\sum_{s=1}^{t-1}\left(1 + 2\beta^{2(t-s)}\right)\sigma_y^4 \\
&= \sigma_y^4\left(\frac{3}{T} - 1\right) + 2\frac{\sigma_y^4}{T^2}\left(\frac{T(T-1)}{2} + \frac{2\beta^2}{(1-\beta^2)}\left[T - \sum_{t=1}^{T}\beta^{2(t-1)}\right]\right) \\
&= \sigma_y^4\left[3T^{-1} - T^{-1} + 4T^{-1}\beta^2\left(1-\beta^2\right)^{-1}\right] + O\left(T^{-2}\right) \\
&\simeq 2T^{-1}\sigma_y^4\left(1+\beta^2\right)/\left(1-\beta^2\right).
\end{aligned}$$

Thus, even in this simple stationary dynamic process, the derivation of population moments is tedious.

Solution to (c)

Since y_t is stationary, the only difficulty in the derivation of the distribution of the sample mean is that $\{y_t\}$ is not an IID process, although it is ergodic. A general strong law of large numbers and a central-limit theorem are applicable to such processes (see e.g. White, 1984, p42 and p118, and §A4.10 above), so that the sample mean converges almost surely to the population mean of zero, and is normally distributed around zero. However, we will tackle the problem from first principles as follows:

$$\mathsf{E}[\bar{y}] = \mathsf{E}\left[T^{-1}\sum_{t=1}^{T} y_t\right] = T^{-1}\sum_{t=1}^{T}\mathsf{E}[y_t] = 0; \tag{A4.91}$$

and:

$$\begin{aligned} \mathsf{V}[\bar{y}] &= \mathsf{E}\left[\left(T^{-1}\sum_{t=1}^{T} y_t\right)^2\right] \\ &= T^{-2}\sum_{t=1}^{T}\sum_{s=1}^{T}\mathsf{E}[y_t y_s] \\ &= \sigma_y^2 T^{-2}\sum_{t=1}^{T}\sum_{s=1}^{T}\beta^{|t-s|} \\ &= \sigma_y^2 T^{-1}\left(1 + 2\sum_{j=1}^{T}\left(1 - \tfrac{j}{T}\right)\beta^j\right) \\ &\simeq T^{-1}\sigma_y^2\,(1+\beta)\,/\,(1-\beta). \end{aligned} \tag{A4.92}$$

As $T \to \infty$, $\mathsf{V}[\bar{y}] \to 0$ so $\text{plim}_{T\to\infty}\, \bar{y} = 0$. However:

$$\mathsf{V}\left[\sqrt{T}\bar{y}\right] \to \sigma_y^2\frac{(1+\beta)}{(1-\beta)} = \frac{1}{(1-\beta)^2}.$$

Next, $\sqrt{T}\bar{y}$ is a linear function of independent, normally-distributed components $\{e_t\}$, with a finite, non-zero variance in large samples, so that:

$$\sqrt{T}\bar{y} \overset{D}{\to} \mathsf{N}\left[0, \frac{1}{(1-\beta)^2}\right]. \tag{A4.93}$$

Solution to (d)

We can use the results just established to extend the analysis to the distribution of the least-squares estimator of β. Using Slutsky's theorem:

$$\underset{T\to\infty}{\text{plim}}\left(\hat{\beta} - \beta\right) = \frac{\text{plim}_{T\to\infty}\, T^{-1}\sum_{t=2}^{T} y_{t-1}e_t}{\text{plim}_{T\to\infty}\, T^{-1}\sum_{t=2}^{T} y_{t-1}^2} = \frac{0}{\sigma_y^2} = 0. \tag{A4.94}$$

Next, from Mann and Wald:

$$\frac{1}{\sqrt{T}}\sum_{t=2}^{T} y_{t-1}e_t \xrightarrow{D} \mathsf{N}\left[0, \frac{1}{(1-\beta^2)}\right]. \tag{A4.95}$$

Finally, from (A4.95), using Cramér's theorem:

$$\sqrt{T}\left(\hat{\beta}-\beta\right) \xrightarrow{D} \mathsf{N}\left[0, (1-\beta^2)\right]. \tag{A4.96}$$

Derivations in the main text follow this general form.

A4.13 Higher-order approximations

In stationary stochastic processes, when $\hat{\theta}$ is the MLE of θ_p, $\sqrt{T}(\hat{\theta}-\theta_p)$ is $O_p(1)$, so preceding results for $(\hat{\theta}-\theta_p)$ are only accurate to order $O_p(1/\sqrt{T})$, which may be inadequate in some situations. Asymptotic distributions were derived above as approximations to finite-sample behaviour, and it is the latter in which we are really interested: asymptotic normality is of little use if it is a good approximation only for $T > 10^{10}$. We now consider the use of higher-order approximations in developing more accurate results: an excellent discussion is provided by Barndorff-Nielsen and Cox (1989).

A random variable, its moments, density, or distribution are all potential targets for approximation. We consider all four in what follows, but no attempt is made to provide a comprehensive discussion.

A4.13.1 Delta method

Above, when $\hat{\theta}$ depended on a small number of sample moments whose asymptotic distributions could be obtained, the asymptotic distribution of $\sqrt{T}(\hat{\theta}-\theta_p)$ followed from a linear approximation. It seems possible that a better approximation might be obtained using a higher-order polynomial. As an illustration, consider a non-linear function $g(\cdot)$ of a statistic $\hat{\mu} \sim \mathsf{N}[\mu, \sigma^2/T]$ (say). Let $\sqrt{T}(\hat{\mu}-\mu)/\sigma = v \sim \mathsf{N}[0,1]$ then the δ-method sets:

$$\hat{\mu} = \mu + \frac{\sigma v}{\sqrt{T}} = \mu + \delta,$$

where δ is $O_p(T^{-\frac{1}{2}})$ so δ^k is $O_p(T^{-\frac{k}{2}})$: Johnson and Kotz (1970c) call this the method of statistical differentials. Using a linear Taylor series:

$$g(\hat{\mu}) = g(\mu+\delta) = g(\mu) + \delta g'(\mu) + \tfrac{1}{2}\delta^2 g''(\mu) + \cdots \tag{A4.97}$$

when $g'(\cdot) \neq 0$ is the first derivative of $g(\cdot)$ evaluated at μ etc., and the remainder is $O_p(\delta^k) = O_p(T^{-\frac{k}{2}})$ as $T \to \infty$ when the first neglected term is of order k in δ. To first order, the properties of $g(\hat{\mu})$ can be analysed as those of $\{g(\mu) + g'(\mu)\sigma v/\sqrt{T}\}$, providing an increasingly good approximation as $T \to \infty$, although in finite samples,

(A4.97) entails that $\mathsf{E}[g(\hat{\mu})] = g(\mu) = g(\mathsf{E}[\hat{\mu}])$ which may be inaccurate. To second order:

$$\mathsf{E}\left[g\left(\hat{\mu}\right)\right] = g\left(\mathsf{E}\left[\hat{\mu}\right]\right) + \tfrac{1}{2}\mathsf{V}\left[\hat{\mu}\right] g''\left(\mu\right),$$

so the curvature of $g(\cdot)$ determines whether $g(\mu)$ over- or under-estimates $\mathsf{E}[g(\hat{\mu})]$. For example, when $g(\hat{\mu}) = \hat{\mu}^n$:

$$\hat{\mu}^n = (\mu + \delta)^n = \mu^n + n\delta\mu^{n-1} + \tfrac{1}{2}n\left(n-1\right)\delta^2\mu^{n-2} + \cdots + \delta^n,$$

so to first order: $\hat{\mu}^n \simeq \mu^n + n\mu^{n-1}(\hat{\mu} - \mu)$. Consequently:

$$\mathsf{E}\left[\hat{\mu}^n\right] \simeq \mu^n \text{ and } \mathsf{V}\left[\hat{\mu}^n\right] \simeq \mathsf{V}\left[n\mu^{n-1}\left(\hat{\mu} - \mu\right)\right] = n^2\mu^{2(n-1)}\mathsf{V}\left[\hat{\mu}\right] \tag{A4.98}$$

with $\hat{\mu}^n \underset{app}{\sim} \mathsf{N}[\mu^n, n^2\mu^{2(n-1)}\sigma^2/T]$. The variance formula in (A4.98) replicates that for a non-linear estimation function:

$$\mathsf{V}\left[g\left(\hat{\mu}\right)\right] \simeq \frac{\partial g\left(\mu\right)}{\partial \mu}\mathsf{V}\left[\hat{\mu}\right]\frac{\partial g\left(\mu\right)}{\partial \mu}. \tag{A4.99}$$

When $n = 2$, the δ-method of order two is exact, and as $\delta^2 \sim T^{-1}\sigma^2\chi^2(1)$, then $\mathsf{E}[\delta^2] = T^{-1}\sigma^2$, $\mathsf{E}[\delta^3] = 0$, and $\mathsf{E}[\delta^4] = 3\sigma^4/T^2$, so the exact results are (see e.g. Barndorff-Nielsen and Cox, 1989):

$$\mathsf{E}\left[\hat{\mu}^2\right] = \mu^2 + \frac{\sigma^2}{T} \text{ and } \mathsf{E}\left[\left(\hat{\mu}^2 - \mathsf{E}\left[\hat{\mu}^2\right]\right)^2\right] = \frac{4\mu^2\sigma^2}{T} + \frac{2\sigma^4}{T^2}.$$

Thus, the mean and variance in (A4.98) are accurate to $O(T^{-1})$ and $O(T^{-2})$ respectively, but the exact distribution is skewed. Analysing the second-order term in δ can help reveal potential problems, and δ-methods are useful in deriving moments of multi-step forecasts (see e.g. Clements and Hendry, 1995).

A4.13.2 Asymptotic expansions

An asymptotic expansion is a series in inverse powers of T such that, for the appropriately scaled random variable, as $T \to \infty$ only the term in T^0 remains, and this reproduces the known limiting distributional result; for smaller sample sizes, higher powers of T are retained to try and produce a better approximation. An example of an asymptotic expansion to a standardized density $\mathsf{f}(\cdot)$ in terms of the standard normal $\phi(\cdot)$ is:

$$\mathsf{f}(r) \simeq \phi(r)\left(\sum_{i=0}^{k} a_i(r)T^{-\frac{i}{2}}\right) \quad \forall r \in \mathbb{R} \tag{A4.100}$$

where $a_0 = 1\ \forall r$, so $\mathsf{f}(r) \to \phi(r)$ as $T \to \infty$. For fixed T, as $k \to \infty$ the series need not converge, so more terms may yield a worse approximation. Usually a small value of k is used (e.g. $k = 2$), but if $k \neq 0$ is too small (e.g., unity), a poor approximation can again result — for example, $\mathsf{f}(\cdot)$ may not integrate to unity. Indeed, since some of the $\{a_i(r)\}$ may be negative, the approximating density may become negative at large

$|r|$. Nevertheless, this idea underlies the Edgeworth approximation to the distribution function which is often used in econometrics (see e.g. Sargan, 1976, and Rothenberg, 1984).

Let $\Phi(r) = \mathsf{P}(W \leq r)$ denote the CDF of the standardized normal:

$$\Phi(r) = \frac{1}{\sqrt{2\pi}} \int_{-\infty}^{r} \exp\left(-\tfrac{1}{2}x^2\right) \mathrm{d}x. \tag{A4.101}$$

Let:

$$\Phi^{(j)}(r) = \left[\frac{\partial^j \Phi(x)}{\partial x^j}\right]_{x=r} \tag{A4.102}$$

so that

$$\Phi^{(1)}(r) = \frac{1}{\sqrt{2\pi}} \exp\left(-\tfrac{1}{2}r^2\right) = \phi(r) \tag{A4.103}$$

and hence $\Phi^{(2)}(r) = -r\phi(r)$. Consequently, the sequence is:

$$\Phi^{(3)}(r) = \left[r^2 - 1\right]\phi(r),\ \Phi^{(4)}(r) = -\left[r^3 - 3r\right]\phi(r), \tag{A4.104}$$

etc. The $[\cdot]$ terms are Hermite polynomials in r where $\mathsf{h}_2(r) = [r^2 - 1]$ is second order, and so on. The 'reproductive property' of $\phi(r)$ under differentiation in (A4.104) was used when formulating (A4.100), and the resulting presence of the Hermite polynomials was the reason for letting the $\{a_i\}$ depend on r. Matching the means and standard deviations of the original and approximating distributions eliminates terms due to $\Phi^{(1)}(r)$ and $\Phi^{(2)}(r)$.

Let $X_t \sim \mathsf{IID}[\mu_x, \sigma_x^2]$ with $\alpha_j = \mathsf{E}[(X_t - \mu_x)^j]/\sigma_x^j$ assumed finite for $j = 1, \ldots, 5$. Let $W_T = \sqrt{T}(\bar{X}_T - \mu_x)/\sigma_x \overset{D}{\rightarrow} \mathsf{N}[0,1]$, where $\mathsf{f}_{W_T}(r)$ is unknown. The Edgeworth approximations to $\mathsf{f}_{W_T}(r)$ and $\mathsf{F}_{W_T}(r)$ are awkward to derive from first principles but are exemplars of (A4.100) which we simply state as:

$$\begin{aligned} \mathsf{f}_{W_T}(r) &= \phi(r)\left(1 + \sqrt{\tfrac{1}{T}}\left[\tfrac{\alpha_3}{3!}\right]\mathsf{h}_3(r) + \tfrac{1}{T}\left[\left(\tfrac{(\alpha_4-3)}{4!}\right)\mathsf{h}_4(r) + \left(\tfrac{10}{6!}\right)\alpha_3^2\mathsf{h}_6(r)\right]\right) \\ &\quad + R_f(r); \\ \mathsf{F}_{W_T}(r) &= \Phi(r) - \phi(r)\left(\sqrt{\tfrac{1}{T}}\left[\tfrac{\alpha_3}{3!}\right]\mathsf{h}_2(r) + \tfrac{1}{T}\left[\left(\tfrac{(\alpha_4-3)}{4!}\right)\mathsf{h}_3(r) + \left(\tfrac{10}{6!}\right)\alpha_3^2\mathsf{h}_5(r)\right]\right) \\ &\quad + R_F(r), \end{aligned} \tag{A4.105}$$

where $R(r)$ is of $O(T^{-\frac{1}{2}(k+1)})$ when terms up to $O(T^{-\frac{1}{2}k})$ are retained, so here $R(r) = O(T^{-3/2})$ (for good explanations, see Johnson and Kotz, 1970c, and Rothenberg, 1984). The formula for $\mathsf{F}_{W_T}(r)$ is obtained by integrating that for $\mathsf{f}_{W_T}(r)$. Alternatively, $\mathsf{F}_{W_T}(r)$ can be expressed in terms of a non-standard cumulative normal approximation.

The value of (A4.105) here is that it highlights when asymptotic theory will work well. First, (A4.105) reveals that using only $\Phi(r)$ (the asymptotic CDF) for $\mathsf{F}_{W_T}(r)$ has an error of $O(T^{-\frac{1}{2}})$ when $\alpha_3 \neq 0$. Next, when W_T is nearly symmetric $\forall T$, the skewness is small ($\alpha_3 \simeq 0$) so the error in using $\Phi(r)$ is $O(T^{-1})$, and hence the asymptotic approximation is more accurate in such a case. If also the kurtosis is close to that for a normal distribution (i.e. $\alpha_4 \simeq 3$), then $\Phi(r)$ is accurate to $O(T^{-3/2})$, which is hardly surprising as the first four moments then match the normal. Similar considerations apply to the CDF of $\sqrt{T}(\hat{\theta} - \theta_p)/\sqrt{\mathcal{I}(\theta_p)}$. Choosing $\psi = g(\theta)$ to obtain approximate symmetry in $(\hat{\psi} - \psi_p)$ may be worthwhile, but improves the asymptotic approximation only for $\hat{\psi}$, not $\hat{\theta}$.

The accuracy of an Edgeworth approximation is not guaranteed to be good $\forall r$, especially in the tails of the distribution. As the approximating CDF need not even be monotonic, other approximations, such as the related saddlepoint, or tilted Edgeworth, method are often used (see Barndorff-Nielsen and Cox, 1989, and Phillips, 1983).

Asymptotic expansions are also used for moments of statistics and estimators. Here the analysis is more delicate as will be seen shortly. Let:

$$W_T = W + o_p(1) \quad \text{where } W \sim \mathsf{N}[0, V], \tag{A4.106}$$

and assume for fixed k that:

$$\mathsf{E}[W_T] \simeq \sum_{i=0}^{k} \Psi_i T^{-i} \quad \text{where} \lim_{T \to \infty} \mathsf{E}[W_T] = \Psi_0 = \mathsf{E}[W] = 0. \tag{A4.107}$$

The series is asymptotic for $T \to \infty$ and need not converge as $k \to \infty$; rather k is again taken relatively small to produce a better approximation to $\mathsf{E}[W_T]$. For the case considered in §A4.11, a fourth-order expansion of $\bar{q}(\hat{\theta})$ around $\bar{q}(\theta_p)$, where the remainder is neglected on taking expectations, yields to $O(T^{-1})$:

$$\mathsf{E}\left[\hat{\theta} - \theta_p\right] \simeq -\tfrac{1}{2}T^{-1}\mathcal{I}(\theta_p)^{-2}(\kappa_{11} + \kappa_{30}) = \frac{b(\theta_p)}{T}, \tag{A4.108}$$

(say), where $\kappa_{ij} = \mathsf{E}[q(\theta_p)^i Q(\theta_p)^j]$ and $q(\cdot) = T\bar{q}(\cdot)$ etc. (see the addendum §A4.13.4). Thus, direct calculation establishes that the bias in $\hat{\theta}$ (if it exists) is $O(T^{-1})$ (see Cox and Hinkley, 1974).

A4.13.3 Power-series expansions

A third approach uses a power-series expansion of the data second moments around their plims (see Nagar, 1959, and Srinivasan, 1970). The assumption is that the expectation of the approximation provides an approximation to the expectation, and that this is useful in the sense explained above of being an asymptotic expansion. However, the expectation may not exist; or it may exist whereas the expectation of the approximation does not.

Consider the stationary first-order autoregression for $t = 1, \ldots, T$:

$$y_t = \rho y_{t-1} + \epsilon_t \quad \text{where } \epsilon_t \sim \mathsf{IN}\left[0, \sigma_\epsilon^2\right] \tag{A4.109}$$

when $|\rho| < 1$ and $y_0 \sim \mathsf{N}[0, \sigma_\epsilon^2/(1-\rho^2)]$. The least-squares estimator of ρ is:

$$(\hat{\rho} - \rho) = \left(T^{-1}\sum_{t=1}^{T} y_{t-1}^2\right)^{-1}\left(T^{-1}\sum_{t=1}^{T} y_{t-1}\epsilon_t\right) \xrightarrow{P} 0 \tag{A4.110}$$

since $\mathsf{E}[y_{t-1}\epsilon_t] = 0$. Let $\omega = \mathsf{E}[y_{t-1}^2] = \sigma_\epsilon^2/(1-\rho^2)$. To approximate $\mathsf{E}[\hat{\rho} - \rho]$, a power-series expansion is used for $\hat{\omega}^{-1} = (T^{-1}\sum y_{t-1}^2)^{-1}$ as follows. First:

$$\hat{\omega}^{-1} = (\omega + [\hat{\omega} - \omega])^{-1} = \omega^{-1}\left(1 + \omega^{-1}\{\hat{\omega} - \omega\}\right)^{-1} := \omega^{-1}(1+\delta)^{-1}. \tag{A4.111}$$

Now, $\delta = (\omega^{-1}\{\hat{\omega} - \omega\})$ depends on the difference between a convergent sample moment $\hat{\omega}$ and its plim of ω in a stationary process, and so is $O_p(T^{-\frac{1}{2}})$. Thus, a power-series expansion in δ seems reasonable as terms are increasing powers of T^{-1}:

$$(1+\delta)^{-1} = 1 - \delta + \delta^2 - \delta^3 \cdots = 1 - \delta + O_p\left(T^{-1}\right). \tag{A4.112}$$

Further, $T^{-1}\sum_{t=1}^{T} y_{t-1}\epsilon_t$ is also $O_p(T^{-\frac{1}{2}})$ so to $O_p(T^{-1})$:

$$\begin{aligned}(\hat{\rho} - \rho) &= \omega^{-1}(1+\delta)^{-1}\left(T^{-1}\textstyle\sum_{t=1}^{T} y_{t-1}\epsilon_t\right) \\ &\simeq 2\omega^{-1}\left(T^{-1}\textstyle\sum_{t=1}^{T} y_{t-1}\epsilon_t\right) - \omega^{-2}\left(T^{-1}\textstyle\sum_{t=1}^{T} y_{t-1}^2\right)\left(T^{-1}\textstyle\sum_{t=1}^{T} y_{t-1}\epsilon_t\right).\end{aligned} \tag{A4.113}$$

Taking expectations of both sides in (A4.113), the first right-hand term vanishes and the second yields:

$$\mathsf{E}[\hat{\rho} - \rho] \simeq -T^{-2}\omega^{-2}\sum_{t=1}^{T}\sum_{s=1}^{T}\mathsf{E}\left[y_{t-1}^2 y_{s-1}\epsilon_s\right]. \tag{A4.114}$$

Since the variables are jointly normal, the fourth cumulant is zero so the last term in (A4.114) becomes:

$$\mathsf{E}\left[y_{t-1}^2 y_{s-1}\epsilon_s\right] = \mathsf{E}\left[y_{t-1}^2\right]\mathsf{E}\left[y_{s-1}\epsilon_s\right] + 2\mathsf{E}\left[y_{t-1}y_{s-1}\right]\mathsf{E}\left[y_{t-1}\epsilon_s\right]. \tag{A4.115}$$

The first term in (A4.115) is zero $\forall t, s$ and the second is zero except when $t - 1 \geq s$ in which case, as:

$$y_t = \rho^{t-s}y_s + \sum_{j=0}^{t-s-1}\rho^j\epsilon_{t-j},$$

then $\mathsf{E}[y_{t-1}y_{s-1}] = \rho^{t-s}\omega$ and $\mathsf{E}[y_{t-1}\epsilon_s] = \rho^{t-s-1}\sigma_\epsilon^2$. Let $j = t - 1 - s$, so j runs from 0 to $T-2$, then substituting all these results into (A4.114):

$$\mathsf{E}[\hat{\rho} - \rho] \simeq -2T^{-2}\omega^{-1}\sigma_\epsilon^2\sum_{t\geq s+1}^{T}\sum_{s=1}^{T}\rho^{2(t-s)+1} = -2T^{-1}\rho\omega^{-1}\sigma_\epsilon^2\sum_{j=0}^{T-2}\rho^{2j} \simeq -\frac{2\rho}{T},$$

(see Hurwicz, 1950, and Shenton and Johnson, 1965). The last term provides an estimate of the bias to $O(T^{-1})$. Such results are helpful both in interpreting Monte Carlo simulation findings (see Sargan, 1982), and in evaluating empirical evidence.

A4.13.4 Addendum

Let $q(\cdot),\ H(\cdot)$ denote the score and the Hessian for one observation. Expand $\bar{q}(\hat{\theta}) = 0$ around θ_p in an approximation accurate to $o_p(T^{-1})$:[6]

$$\bar{q}(\hat{\theta}) = 0 = \bar{q}(\theta_p) + \bar{H}(\theta_p)\left(\hat{\theta} - \theta_p\right) + \tfrac{1}{2}\bar{B}(\theta_p)\left(\hat{\theta} - \theta_p\right)^2 + O_p\left(T^{-\frac{3}{2}}\right). \quad \text{(A4.116)}$$

Then, neglecting the remainder (which requires that its expectation is small relative to retained terms as $T \to \infty$), we use the following results, all holding for one observation from the data-generation process $\mathsf{D}_\mathsf{x}(x|\theta_p)$ denoted by $\mathsf{D}(x)$ below (so the model and DGP coincide):

$$\int \mathsf{D}(x)\mathrm{d}x = 1, \quad \text{(A4.117)}$$

i.e., $\mathsf{E}[1] = 1$. Further:

$$\frac{\partial}{\partial x}\int \mathsf{D}(x)\mathrm{d}x = 0 = \int \frac{\partial}{\partial x}\mathsf{D}(x)\mathrm{d}x = \int \frac{\partial \log \mathsf{D}(x)}{\partial x}\mathsf{D}(x)\,\mathrm{d}x = \int q(x)\mathsf{D}(x)\mathrm{d}x \quad \text{(A4.118)}$$

which shows that $\mathsf{E}[q(\theta_p)] = 0$. Next:

$$\frac{\partial}{\partial x}\int q(x)\mathsf{D}(x)\,\mathrm{d}x = 0 = \int H(x)\mathsf{D}(x)\mathrm{d}x + \int q(x)^2\mathsf{D}(x)\mathrm{d}x, \quad \text{(A4.119)}$$

and hence $\mathsf{E}[H(\theta_p)] = -\mathcal{I}(\theta_p) = -\mathsf{E}[q(\theta_p)^2]$. Differentiating once more:

$$\frac{\partial^2}{\partial x^2}\int q(x)\mathsf{D}(x)\mathrm{d}x$$

is:

$$\int B(x)\mathsf{D}(x)\mathrm{d}x + \int H(x)q(x)\mathsf{D}(x)\mathrm{d}x + 2\int q(x)H(x)\mathsf{D}(x)\mathrm{d}x + \int q(x)^3\mathsf{D}(x)\mathrm{d}x \quad \text{(A4.120)}$$

which is zero from (A4.119) so that $\mathsf{E}[H(\theta_p)] = -(3\kappa_{11} + \kappa_{30})$ where $\kappa_{ij} = \mathsf{E}[q^iH^j]$.

Taking expectations in (A4.116) and using the definition that for any two random variables X_1 and X_2 with finite first two moments:

$$\mathsf{E}[X_1X_2] = \mathsf{E}[X_1]\,\mathsf{E}[X_2] + \mathsf{C}[X_1, X_2] \quad \text{(A4.121)}$$

and noting (A4.118), then:

$$\mathsf{E}\left[\bar{H}(\theta_p)\left(\hat{\theta} - \theta_p\right)\right] + \tfrac{1}{2}\mathsf{E}\left[\bar{B}(\theta_p)\left(\hat{\theta} - \theta_p\right)^2\right] = 0 \quad \text{(A4.122)}$$

6 This section relies heavily on Cox and Hinkley (1974).

so that applying (A4.121) to both terms in (A4.122), (when the relevant second moments exist):

$$\mathsf{E}\left[\bar{H}\left(\theta_p\right)\right]\mathsf{E}\left[\hat{\theta}-\theta_p\right]+\mathsf{C}\left[\bar{H}\left(\theta_p\right),\left(\hat{\theta}-\theta_p\right)\right]+\tfrac{1}{2}\mathsf{E}\left[\bar{B}\left(\theta_p\right)\right]\mathsf{E}\left[\left(\hat{\theta}-\theta_p\right)^2\right]$$
$$+\tfrac{1}{2}\mathsf{C}\left[\bar{B}\left(\theta_p\right),\left(\hat{\theta}-\theta_p\right)^2\right] \tag{A4.123}$$

is zero. However, from section A4.11:

$$\left(\hat{\theta}-\theta_p\right)=\mathcal{I}\left(\theta_p\right)^{-1}\bar{q}\left(\theta_p\right)+o_p\left(T^{-\frac{1}{2}}\right)\simeq\mathcal{I}\left(\theta_p\right)^{-1}\bar{q}\left(\theta_p\right). \tag{A4.124}$$

This approximation is now used to evaluate both covariance terms in (A4.123) and also:

$$\mathsf{E}\left[\left(\hat{\theta}-\theta_p\right)^2\right]=T^{-1}\mathcal{I}\left(\theta_p\right)^{-1},$$

but is not used for $\mathsf{E}[\hat{\theta}-\theta_p]$ in (A4.123), which is given by (A4.126) below. Thus, substituting from (A4.124) into (A4.123), and using the definitions for κ_{ij} from (A4.120):

$$-\mathcal{I}\left(\theta_p\right)\mathsf{E}\left[\hat{\theta}-\theta_p\right]+T^{-1}\mathcal{I}\left(\theta_p\right)^{-1}\kappa_{11}-\tfrac{1}{2}\left(3\kappa_{11}+\kappa_{30}\right)T^{-1}\mathcal{I}\left(\theta_p\right)^{-1}\simeq 0, \tag{A4.125}$$

since the fourth term in (A4.123) is $o(T^{-1})$ given (A4.124), and so is negligible relative to the second and third terms. Thus, to the accuracy of $O(T^{-1})$:

$$\mathsf{E}\left[\hat{\theta}-\theta_p\right]=-\tfrac{1}{2}T^{-1}\mathcal{I}\left(\theta_p\right)^{-2}\left(\kappa_{11}+\kappa_{30}\right), \tag{A4.126}$$

which is equation (A4.108). The following example illustrates the application of these formulae in a simple setting.

A4.13.4.1 An example

Let $Y_t \sim \mathsf{IN}[\beta,1]$ where $\hat{\beta}=\bar{Y}=T^{-1}\sum_{t=1}^{T}Y_t$ when we want to approximate the bias $\mathsf{E}[\hat{\beta}^2]-\beta^2$ in the MLE of β^2. A direct calculation yields the answer easily here since:

$$\mathsf{E}\left[\left(\hat{\beta}-\beta\right)^2\right]=\mathsf{V}\left[\hat{\beta}\right]=\frac{1}{T}=\mathsf{E}\left[\hat{\beta}^2\right]-2\mathsf{E}\left[\hat{\beta}\right]\beta+\beta^2=\mathsf{E}\left[\hat{\beta}^2\right]-\beta^2 \tag{A4.127}$$

so the bias is exactly T^{-1}. However, to illustrate the techniques involved, let $\gamma=\beta^2$ be the parameter of interest. Then, since $\mathsf{E}[\bar{Y}]=\sqrt{\gamma}$ and:

$$\bar{q}\left(\gamma\right)=-\tfrac{1}{2}\left(1-\frac{\bar{Y}}{\sqrt{\gamma}}\right)\quad\text{which implies }\mathsf{E}\left[\bar{q}\left(\gamma\right)\right]=0; \tag{A4.128}$$

$$\bar{H}\left(\gamma\right)=-\tfrac{1}{4}\frac{\bar{Y}}{\gamma^{3/2}}\quad\text{which implies }\mathsf{E}\left[\bar{H}\left(\gamma\right)\right]=-\frac{1}{4\gamma}; \tag{A4.129}$$

$$\bar{B}(\gamma) = \tfrac{3}{8}\frac{\bar{Y}}{\gamma^{5/2}} \text{ which implies } \mathsf{E}\left[\bar{B}(\gamma)\right] = \frac{3}{8\gamma^2}; \tag{A4.130}$$

$$\mathsf{E}[Hq] = \kappa_{11} = -\frac{1}{8\gamma^2} \text{ since } \mathsf{E}\left[Y_t^2\right] = \beta^2 + 1 = 1 + \gamma; \tag{A4.131}$$

$$\mathsf{E}\left[q^3\right] = \kappa_{30} = 0 \tag{A4.132}$$

so that from (A4.126):

$$\mathsf{E}\left[\hat{\beta}^2 - \beta^2\right] = \mathsf{E}[\hat{\gamma} - \gamma] = -\tfrac{1}{2}T^{-1}(4\gamma)^2\left(-\frac{1}{8\gamma^2}\right) = \frac{1}{T} \tag{A4.133}$$

as required.

A4.14 Exercises

A4.1 A sample $\boldsymbol{X}_T^1 = (\boldsymbol{x}_1 \dots \boldsymbol{x}_T)$ where $\boldsymbol{x}_t = (y_t : z_t)' \sim \mathsf{IN}_2[\mathbf{0}, \boldsymbol{\Omega}]$ is obtained from the process:

$$\begin{pmatrix} y_t \\ z_t \end{pmatrix} \sim \mathsf{IN}_2\left[\begin{pmatrix} 0 \\ 0 \end{pmatrix}, \begin{pmatrix} (\sigma_{11} + 2\gamma\sigma_{12} + \gamma^2\sigma_{22}) & (\sigma_{12} + \gamma\sigma_{22}) \\ (\sigma_{12} + \gamma\sigma_{22}) & \sigma_{22} \end{pmatrix}\right]. \tag{A4.134}$$

(a) Derive: (i) the marginal distribution of z_t; (ii) the marginal distribution of z_t^2; (iii) the conditional distribution of y_t given z_t; (iv) the joint distribution of $\boldsymbol{X}_T^1$; (v) the (joint) marginal distribution of $\boldsymbol{Z}_T^1$. Which parameters of the joint distribution are identified?

(b) An investigator hypothesizes the model:

$$y_t = \beta z_t + u_t \tag{A4.135}$$

where β is a parameter of interest in an economic analysis. Under what conditions is $\mathsf{E}[y_t|z_t] = \beta z_t$? If $\mathsf{E}[y_t|z_t] \neq \beta z_t$, can β nevertheless be estimated from data on $(y_t : z_t)$?

(c) Since $\mathsf{E}[z_t^4] = 3\sigma_{22}^2$, if $m_{22} = T^{-1}\sum_{t=1}^{T} z_t^2$ and $v_t = y_t - \mathsf{E}[y_t|z_t]$, show that:

$$\sqrt{T}(m_{22} - \sigma_{22}) \xrightarrow{D} \mathsf{N}\left[0, 2\sigma_{22}^2\right]$$

and

$$\sum_{t=1}^{T} z_t v_t / \sqrt{T} \xrightarrow{D} \mathsf{N}\left[0, (\sigma_{11}\sigma_{22} - \sigma_{12}^2)\right].$$

Carefully state any theorems and assumptions used. (Hint: what are the distributions of the random variables $\eta_t = z_t^2$ and $\nu_t = z_t v_t$?)

(d) The investigator decides to estimate β using OLS estimation of (A4.135). From the results in (c), or otherwise, derive the limiting distribution of the OLS estimator of β.

(Oxford M.Phil., 1983)

A4.2 An investigator postulates the following economic model:

$$y_t = \beta z_t + u_t \text{ where } \mathsf{E}[z_t u_s] = 0 \; \forall t, s \text{ and } u_t \underset{c}{\sim} \mathsf{IN}\left[0, \sigma_u^2\right] \quad \text{(A4.136)}$$

when $\underset{c}{\sim}$ denotes 'is claimed to be distributed as'.

(a) Derive the least-squares estimator $\tilde{\boldsymbol{\theta}}$ of $\boldsymbol{\theta} = (\beta : \sigma^2)'$ assuming the claims in (A4.136) are valid. Obtain the large-sample distribution of $\sqrt{T}(\tilde{\boldsymbol{\theta}} - \boldsymbol{\theta})$.

(b) Unknown to the investigator, the structure of the data generation process induces:

$$u_t^2 = k z_t^2 + \epsilon_t \text{ where } \epsilon_t \sim \sigma_\epsilon^2 \chi^2(1) \text{ and } k \geq 0. \quad \text{(A4.137)}$$

Obtain the expectation of $\tilde{\boldsymbol{\theta}}$ in the postulated model in (A4.136) when (A4.137) is true. Derive the large sample distribution of $\sqrt{T}(\tilde{\beta} - \beta)$. How could $\mathsf{V}[\tilde{\beta}]$ be consistently estimated?

(c) Suggest a test of the null hypothesis H_0: $k = 0$.

(Oxford M.Phil., 1993)

A4.3 Consider the equation:

$$y_t = \boldsymbol{x}_t'\boldsymbol{\beta} + \epsilon_t \quad \text{(A4.138)}$$

where $\mathsf{E}[\boldsymbol{x}_t \epsilon_t] \neq \mathbf{0}$ when:

$$\boldsymbol{x}_t = \boldsymbol{\pi} \boldsymbol{z}_t + \boldsymbol{v}_t \quad \text{(A4.139)}$$

such that $\mathsf{E}[\boldsymbol{z}_t \epsilon_t] = \mathbf{0}$ and $\mathsf{E}[\boldsymbol{z}_t \boldsymbol{v}_s'] = \mathbf{0} \; \forall t, s$ when $\boldsymbol{x}_t$ and $\boldsymbol{z}_t$ are $k \times 1$ and $n \times 1$ respectively, with $k < n$, and $\text{rank}(\boldsymbol{\pi}) = k$.

(a) Obtain the limiting distribution of the instrumental-variables estimator $\hat{\boldsymbol{\beta}}$ of $\boldsymbol{\beta}$,

(b) Does any loss of (asymptotic) efficiency result when a subset $\boldsymbol{z}_{at}$ of $\boldsymbol{z}_t$ is used as the instruments?

(c) Suggest a test for the validity of the instruments (i.e. a test of the hypothesis that $\mathsf{E}[\boldsymbol{z}_t \epsilon_t] = \mathbf{0}$).

(Oxford M.Phil., 1982)

A4.4 For the model:

$$y_t = \alpha y_{t-1} + u_t \text{ where } |\alpha| < 1$$

when

$$u_t = \rho u_{t-1} + \epsilon_t \text{ with } |\rho| < 1$$

and $\epsilon_t \sim \mathsf{IN}[0, \sigma_\epsilon^2]$, let:

$$\hat{\alpha} = \left(T^{-1} \sum_{t=2}^{T} y_{t-1}^2 \right)^{-1} T^{-1} \sum_{t=2}^{T} y_t y_{t-1} = \hat{m}^{-1} \hat{m}_1,$$

where:

$$m = \operatorname*{plim}_{T \to \infty} T^{-1} \sum_{t=2}^{T} y_{t-1}^2 \text{ and } m_1 = \operatorname*{plim}_{T \to \infty} T^{-1} \sum_{t=2}^{T} y_t y_{t-1}.$$

(a) Prove that:

$$\underset{T\to\infty}{\text{plim}}\ \hat{\alpha} = m^{-1}m_1 = \alpha^* = \frac{\alpha+\rho}{1+\alpha\rho}.$$

(b) When $\rho = 0$, derive the limiting distribution $\sqrt{T}(\hat{\alpha}-\alpha) \underset{a}{\sim} \mathsf{N}[0, V]$, and express V parametrically in $(\alpha, \sigma_\epsilon^2)$.

(c) When $\rho \neq 0$, derive $\sqrt{T}(\hat{\alpha}-\alpha^*) \underset{a}{\sim} \mathsf{N}[0, V^*]$ and express V^* parametrically in $(\alpha, \rho, \sigma_\epsilon^2)$.

(d) Prove that:

$$\boldsymbol{M} = \begin{pmatrix} m & m_1 \\ m_1 & m \end{pmatrix} = \frac{\sigma_u^2}{(1-\alpha\rho)(1-\alpha^2)}\begin{pmatrix} 1+\alpha\rho & \alpha+\rho \\ \alpha+\rho & 1+\alpha\rho \end{pmatrix}.$$

(e) Let

$$\hat{\sigma}_u^2 = (T-1)^{-1}\sum_{t=2}^{T}(y_t - \hat{\alpha}y_{t-1})^2.$$

Prove that $\text{plim}_{T\to\infty}\,\hat{\sigma}_u^2\hat{m}^{-1} = \boldsymbol{\phi}'\boldsymbol{M}\boldsymbol{\phi}/m$ and compare that outcome (the asymptotic standard error) with V^* when $\boldsymbol{\phi}' = (1 : -\alpha^*)$.

Hints

(i) When $\rho \neq 0$ the analysis is awkward but does yield to an indirect approach (see Hendry, 1979a, Maasoumi and Phillips, 1982, and Hendry, 1982). Let:

$$\boldsymbol{f}_t = \begin{pmatrix} y_t \\ y_{t-1} \end{pmatrix} = \begin{pmatrix} \alpha+\rho & -\alpha\rho \\ 1 & 0 \end{pmatrix}\begin{pmatrix} y_{t-1} \\ y_{t-2} \end{pmatrix} + \begin{pmatrix} \epsilon_t \\ 0 \end{pmatrix} = \boldsymbol{D}\boldsymbol{f}_{t-1} + \boldsymbol{w}_t,$$

so that:

$$y_t - \alpha^* y_{t-1} = \boldsymbol{\phi}'\boldsymbol{f}_t = \boldsymbol{\phi}'\boldsymbol{D}\boldsymbol{f}_{t-1} + \boldsymbol{\phi}'\boldsymbol{w}_t = \alpha\rho\left[\frac{(\alpha+\rho)}{1+\alpha\rho}y_{t-1} - y_{t-2}\right] + \epsilon_t = e_t$$

where y_{t-1} is asymptotically uncorrelated with e_t.

(ii) To apply Hannan's theorem, let $\boldsymbol{D} = \boldsymbol{P\Lambda P}^{-1}$ where (for $\alpha \neq \rho$ and $\rho \neq 0$):

$$\boldsymbol{P} = \begin{pmatrix} \alpha & \rho \\ 1 & 1 \end{pmatrix}, \quad \boldsymbol{\Lambda} = \begin{pmatrix} \alpha & 0 \\ 0 & \rho \end{pmatrix}$$

and so:

$$\rho\boldsymbol{\phi}' = \boldsymbol{\zeta}' = -\left[\frac{\rho^2(1-\alpha^2)}{1+\alpha\rho} : \frac{(1-\rho^2)}{1+\alpha\rho}\right].$$

A5
Numerical Optimization Methods

Given a data-set and a model, the log-likelihood function $\ell(\boldsymbol{\theta})$ only depends on $\boldsymbol{\theta}$, so its maximum can be located by numerical optimization. The choice of algorithm matters for computational efficiency and robustness: poor methods may even alter the statistical properties of estimators. Iterative methods are described in general, then scalar optimization is discussed as a basis for line searches. The analysis is illustrated using linear models with autoregressive errors. Four categories of multivariate optimization methods are distinguished: gradient-based procedures; stepwise optimization; conjugate directions; and variable metric methods, where the last is the preferred option in general.

A5.1 Introduction

The approach to estimation and inference described in the main text implicitly assumes that it is feasible to obtain a maximum likelihood estimator (MLE) in all situations of interest.[1] For any fixed set of data and a given model specification, the log-likelihood function $\ell(\cdot)$ depends only on the parameters $\boldsymbol{\theta}$ of the model. Consequently, obtaining the MLE entails locating the value $\widehat{\boldsymbol{\theta}}$ of $\boldsymbol{\theta}$ which maximizes $\ell(\boldsymbol{\theta})$, and this is a numerical, rather than a statistical, problem. Such an issue of computational technique could be considered peripheral to econometrics, but there are two groups of reasons for investigating methods for maximizing non-linear functions.

The first set of reasons concerns numerical efficiency. Optimization algorithms differ dramatically in their speeds of locating $\widehat{\boldsymbol{\theta}}$, and hence in their computational costs. A statistical technique which needed many hours of computer time could not expect routine application if a closely similar statistical method required only a few seconds on the same computer. Moreover, algorithms also have different computer-memory requirements, and certain methods may be too large in their demands for the available computers. Next, some algorithms are more robust than others, that is, are much more likely to obtain $\widehat{\boldsymbol{\theta}}$, and not fail for mysterious reasons in the calculation process. Finally, some approaches are more flexible than others in that they can be readily modified for new

[1] This chapter is best consulted after reading Part I.

problems. While all of these points are in the province of numerical analysis and computing, in order to implement methods, econometricians need to be aware of the problems involved in numerical optimization.

The second group of reasons for studying non-linear optimization algorithms is the intimate connection between the statistical and the numerical aspects of estimation. One cannot fully understand maximum-likelihood estimation without understanding how the maximum of $\ell(\boldsymbol{\theta})$ is obtained in practice. In turn, studying methods of maximizing $\ell(\boldsymbol{\theta})$ yields considerable insight into the statistical properties of $\hat{\boldsymbol{\theta}}$. Some algorithms only calculate an approximation to $\hat{\boldsymbol{\theta}}$, say $\tilde{\boldsymbol{\theta}}$, but when they are well-defined rules which always yield unique values of $\tilde{\boldsymbol{\theta}}$ from given data, then $\tilde{\boldsymbol{\theta}}$ is an estimator of $\boldsymbol{\theta}$ with statistical properties which may be similar to those of $\hat{\boldsymbol{\theta}}$, but may also be very different. Thus, computing the maximum of $\ell(\boldsymbol{\theta})$ only approximately can have statistical implications. The converse of this result, as shown by the estimator-generating equation approach in Chapters 10 and 11, is that different estimators can be reinterpreted as alternative numerical methods for approximating the maximum of $\ell(\boldsymbol{\theta})$, which allows a simplification of existing estimation theory in econometrics. Thus, numerical optimization is not a digression from the main theme of studying dynamic econometric methods, but instead plays an important role.

There is a vast literature on non-linear optimization techniques (see, among many others, Box, Davies and Swann, 1969, Dixon, 1972, Jacoby, Kowalik and Pizzo, 1972, Adby and Dempster, 1974, Fletcher, 1987, Gill, Murray and Wright, 1981, Cramer, 1986, and Thisted, 1988). The presentation aims to relate optimization to estimation, so attention is restricted to techniques which have proved useful in econometrics research (see e.g. Goldfeld and Quandt, 1972, 1976, Hendry, 1976, Sargan and Sylwestrowicz, 1976, Hendry and Srba, 1980, and Quandt, 1983). It does seek to provide a comprehensive description of methods, nor a list of all the difficulties likely to arise when implementing any chosen method. The reader is assumed to have access to a computer with programmed versions of the main algorithms (such as Doornik and Hendry, 1994a), and seeks to understand how these work. The combination of publication lags and rapid improvements in optimization methods, with new techniques often being impressively faster than existing ones, ensures that some of the following discussion is out of date. Nevertheless, since the complexity and scale of estimation problems which can be solved at feasible cost given available computers is dependent on the computational efficiency of the available optimization methods, future developments in applied econometrics will continue to reflect improvements in numerical optimization so the topic merits study.

Section A5.2 overviews the topic of numerical optimization and offers some intuitive explanations; §A5.3 describes the logic of maximizing likelihood functions in the context of an autoregressive error process; §A5.4 considers scalar optimization and direct search algorithms (which play an essential role as the line-search component in vector methods); §A5.5 analyses multivariate optimization focusing on gradient and variable metric (quasi-Newton) methods; and §A5.6 concludes.

A5.2 An overview of numerical optimization

To understand intuitively how to locate the maximum of (say) a likelihood function $\mathsf{L}(\alpha)$, a useful analogy is to consider $\mathsf{L}(\cdot)$ as a one-dimensional hill as in Fig. A5.1. To maximize $\mathsf{L}(\cdot)$, we need to climb to the top of the hill. Start somewhere on the hill, say at α_1, and take a step of length δ. Either the step will go down the hill or up the hill: in computing terms, move some distance δ each way and compute the functions $\mathsf{L}_1 = \mathsf{L}(\alpha_1 - \delta)$ and $\mathsf{L}_2 = \mathsf{L}(\alpha_1 + \delta)$. Depending on $\mathsf{L}_1 \geq \mathsf{L}_2$ or $\mathsf{L}_2 \geq \mathsf{L}_1$, we discover in which direction to continue: e.g. $+\delta$ if $\mathsf{L}_2 \geq \mathsf{L}_1$. Take a second step of 2δ in the appropriate direction, compute $\mathsf{L}(\alpha_1 + \delta + 2\delta)$ and repeat until, from comparison, we go downhill again and hence have overshot the maximum. Take a step back equal to half the last step, and compute the function. We have now bracketed the maximum.

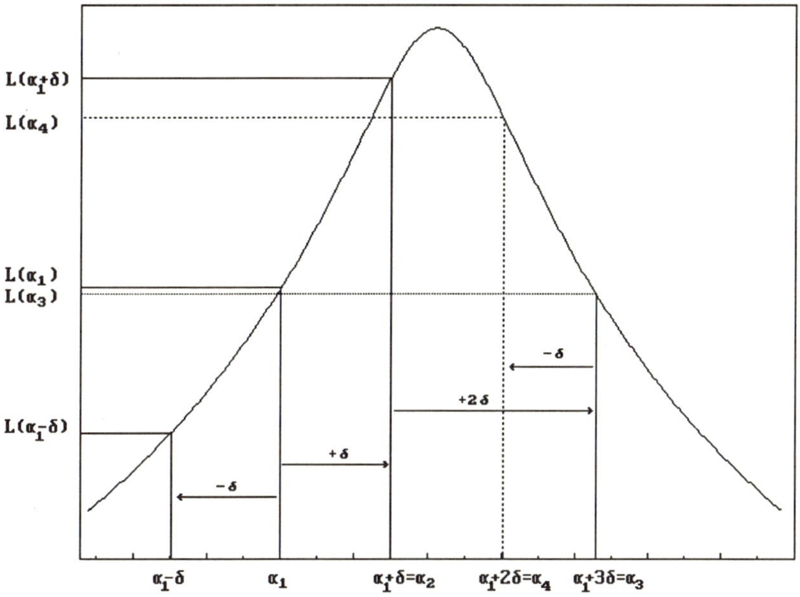

Fig. A5.1 Climbing a one-dimensional hill

Choose the three highest points, which here are $\mathsf{L}(\alpha_1)$, $\mathsf{L}(\alpha_1 + \delta)$,and $\mathsf{L}(\alpha_1 + 2\delta)$. These must occur at equidistant values of α, namely, α_1, α_2, α_4. Now fit a quadratic through them as shown in Fig. A5.2. The maximum of the quadratic $ax^2 + bx + c$ is at $-b/2a$ so can be found immediately. Select this value (α_m) as the approximation to the maximum of the function and recommence from there. This is a simple method for finding the maximum of a univariate non-linear function.

Such an approach extends to climbing a three-dimensional hill, applying exactly the same principles as above, but using two-dimensional iso-likelihood contours to represent a three-dimensional hill as in Fig. A5.3a (the graph is equivalent to an indifference-curve map, where the tangent to the highest indifference curve locates the maximum).

Start from the point α_a^1, and apply the above method to find the maximum point along one line, say parallel to the α_b axis. Next, turn 90° to the previous path at the point α_b^1, and search until the highest point in the α_a direction is reached at α_a^2. Turn 90° again, check for the uphill direction and climb to the peak, then keep iterating the procedure. In this way, we can finally get to the top of the hill.

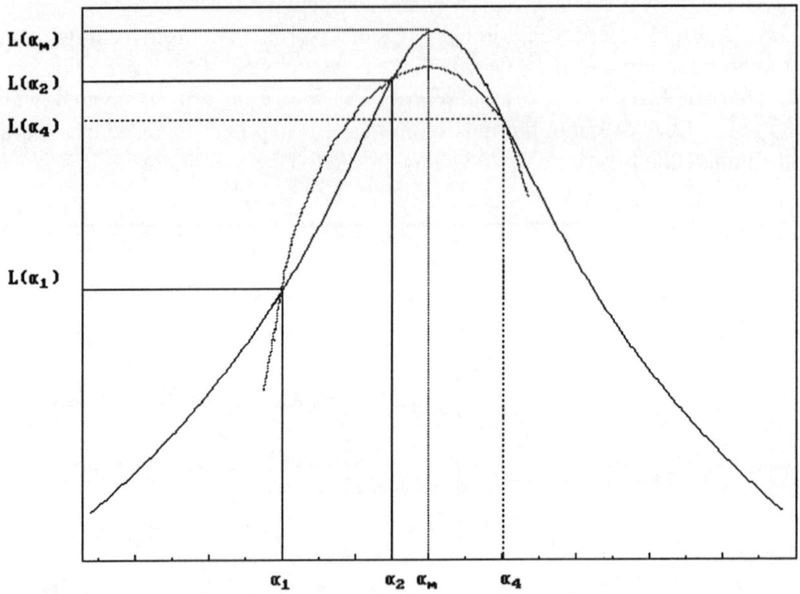

Fig. A5.2 Fitting a quadratic in a line search

Applying this method to more than three dimensions is relatively expensive, since it does not fully utilize the information that accrues while climbing the hill. Fig. A5.3b illustrates a better approach in three dimensions. After changing direction once, and finding the locally highest point for a second time, notice that we could have done better by taking the direction corresponding to the hypotenuse instead of walking along the two sides of the hill. This 'average' direction of the first two directions corresponds to a better path than either alone, and is known as the direction of total progress (marked from α^2 to α^1 on Fig. A5.3b). After following that direction of total progress to its nearest maximum, climb either vertically or horizontally till the next highest (tangent) position is reached. From there, find the second direction of total progress, and use that to climb more rapidly to the top of the hill.

If the hill happens to be circular, then one search along each coordinate axis leads to the maximum as shown in Fig. A5.3c. This method (called conjugate directions) makes use of a Euclidean theorem: the line joining any two parallel tangent points of two concentric ellipses goes through their centre. So if a bivariate likelihood surface is elliptical and we find one tangent of an iso-likelihood ellipse, then a parallel tangent to a higher contour, and follow the direction of total progress joining them, we go straight to the centre (maximum here) of the ellipse as shown in Fig A5.3d. Methods based on this principle have proved reasonably robust and efficient in practice.

A second way of climbing a hill is to exploit information at the starting point about the steepness of the slope: if the gradient is known, it seems worth trying to climb along the direction of steepest ascent (normal to the tangent at that point). In many cases, this method progresses rapidly and beats the previous methods. However, there are a couple of caveats. First, the slope of a hill is not necessarily uniform, and a gradient method might be poor if the slope changes too much. Secondly, the slope might be too flat or even point in the wrong direction in the starting neighbourhood. However, the solution to that problem is to provide better initial values, perhaps using a direct-search algorithm, or a method which does not require iterative solution.

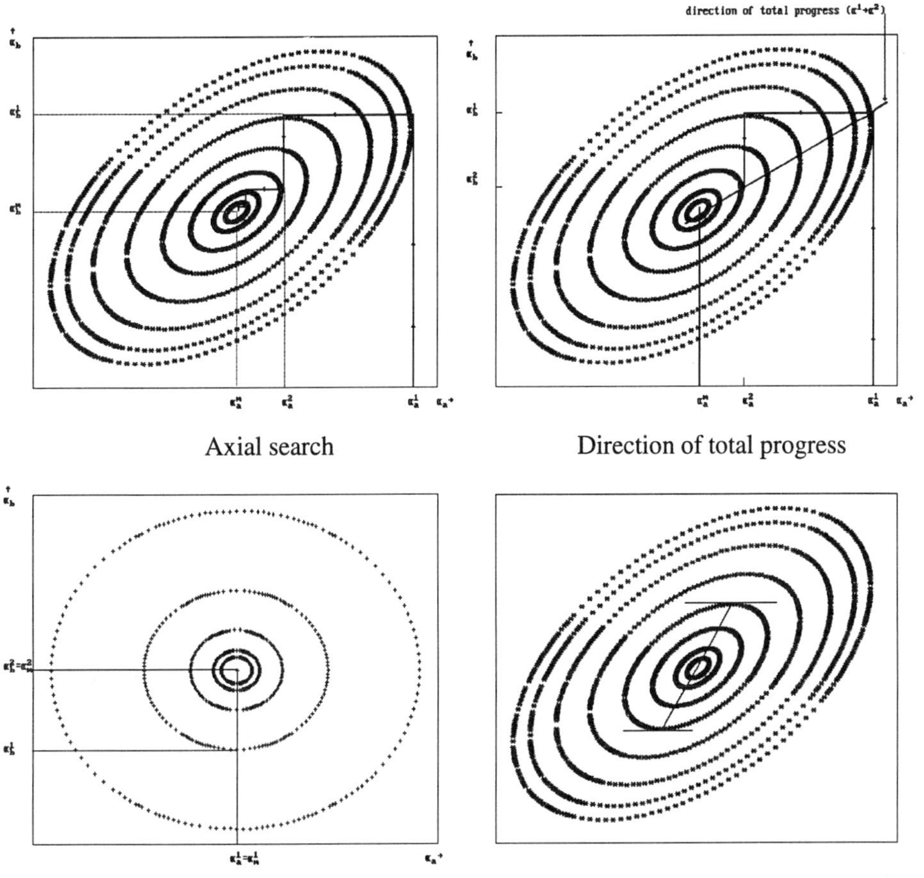

Axial search — Direction of total progress

Climbing a quadratic hill — Parallel tangents to an ellipse

Fig. A5.3 Climbing three-dimensional hills

We will consider iterative approaches in which a sequence of values denoted $\boldsymbol{\theta}_j$ at the jth step is obtained for the argument $\boldsymbol{\theta}$ of a function $\ell(\cdot)$ (often the log-likelihood), corresponding to the non-decreasing sequence of values:

$$\ell(\boldsymbol{\theta}_{j+1}) \geq \ell(\boldsymbol{\theta}_j) \text{ for } j = 1, 2, \ldots, J \leq N \tag{A5.1}$$

given by:

$$\boldsymbol{\theta}_{j+1} = \boldsymbol{g}(\boldsymbol{\theta}_j) \text{ for } j = 1, 2, \ldots, J \leq N \tag{A5.2}$$

where N is a terminal maximum number of steps, from an initial value $\boldsymbol{\theta}_1$. When strict inequality is not imposed on (A5.1), a check is required to avoid cycling between two successive values $\boldsymbol{\theta}_k$ and $\boldsymbol{\theta}_{k+1}$ which have equal function values. A rule for terminating the iteration must be provided. This should be in terms of an upper bound N on the number of iterations J, such that (A5.2) is never performed more than N times, together with a convergence criterion such as $|\ell(\boldsymbol{\theta}_{j+1}) - \ell(\boldsymbol{\theta}_j)| \leq \varepsilon$ or $\boldsymbol{q}(\boldsymbol{\theta}_{j+1}) \simeq \mathbf{0}$, that causes the sequence to stop before N iterations when a value $\boldsymbol{\theta}_k$ has been located, which is deemed sufficiently close to the maximum of $\ell(\cdot)$. In the context of non-linear optimization, $\ell(\cdot)$ is called the criterion function, and different numerical algorithms correspond to different choices of $\boldsymbol{g}(\cdot)$. This brief statement of iterative methods highlights most of the major issues requiring resolution.

First, there is no optimal choice for $\boldsymbol{g}(\cdot)$, since optimization methods differ in their robustness, in the time taken to calculate successive values of $\boldsymbol{\theta}_j$, in the number of iterations required to achieve any accuracy level (which may differ between problems), and in the effort needed to write a computer program to calculate $\boldsymbol{g}(\cdot)$. Moreover, an algorithm which performs excellently for a small number of parameters may be hopeless for a large number. The direct-search methods just discussed only require $\ell(\cdot)$ to be programmed, and are robust, but often require large N. Other methods use gradient information based on the derivatives of $\ell(\cdot)$. It is difficult to evaluate the relative costs of these differences, but reasonable choices are possible for many problems in econometrics.

The next major issue is the choice of initial value $\boldsymbol{\theta}_1$. This plays an important role, since starting close to $\widehat{\boldsymbol{\theta}}$ will not only reduce the number of iterations required to achieve convergence, but will also increase the probability of converging at all: few optimization techniques are guaranteed to converge for general functions from arbitrary starting points. Additionally, it is obviously helpful when possible to select $\boldsymbol{\theta}_1$ which is close to the global optimum $\widehat{\boldsymbol{\theta}}$ to avoid any problems of converging to a second-best local optimum. Because of the statistical context of the problem here, good $\boldsymbol{\theta}_1$ values can be found for many estimation situations. In particular, it may be possible to use as $\boldsymbol{\theta}_1$ another estimator $\widetilde{\boldsymbol{\theta}}$ which does not require iterative methods, but has the same large-sample distribution as the relevant $\widehat{\boldsymbol{\theta}}$: estimation and optimization are two facets of the same problem.

A further issue is that $\ell(\cdot)$ is assumed to be an unconstrained function of $\boldsymbol{\theta}$. Optimization subject to restrictions tends to be even less tractable than the already hard unconstrained problem and we will only consider methods for functions with unrestricted parameters. This is more general than first appearances suggest, since constraints can often be eliminated by appropriate transformations of the parameters. For example, if one sought the maximum of $\ell(\theta)$ subject to $\theta \geq 0$, in a scalar case, then substituting $\theta = \phi^2$ yields a new parameter ϕ which is unrestricted, and ensures that θ is never negative. Thus, $\ell(\cdot)$ can be optimized unrestrictedly with respect to ϕ, and $\hat{\theta}$ is obtained at the end as $\hat{\phi}^2$, since:

$$\underset{\theta \geq 0}{\operatorname{argmax}}\, \ell\left(\theta\right) = \underset{\phi}{\operatorname{argmax}}\, \ell\left(\phi^2\right) = \underset{\phi}{\operatorname{argmax}}\, \ell^*\left(\phi\right), \tag{A5.3}$$

where the transformed function $\ell^*(\phi)$ is just $\ell(\phi^2)$ reinterpreted as a function of ϕ. In particular, if (say) $\ell(\theta) = -\theta + 2\sqrt{\theta}$ then $\ell^*(\phi) = -\phi^2 + 2\phi$. Also, transformations can be used to simplify the function to be maximized. Thus, the use of $\ell(\cdot)$ rather than the original likelihood $\mathsf{L}(\cdot)$ is because the logarithmic transformation is monotonic, so the maxima of $\mathsf{L}(\cdot)$ and $\ell(\cdot)$ occur at the same values of $\boldsymbol{\theta}$, but $\ell(\cdot)$ is a simpler function.

Three small but important points require clarification before detailed discussion of alternative choices of $\boldsymbol{g}(\cdot)$ in (A5.2) is possible. The first relates to the irrelevance of specifying an optimization problem as a maximizing or a minimizing one since:

$$\underset{\boldsymbol{\theta}}{\operatorname{argmax}}\, \ell\left(\boldsymbol{\theta}\right) \equiv \underset{\boldsymbol{\theta}}{\operatorname{argmin}} \left\{-\ell\left(\boldsymbol{\theta}\right)\right\}. \tag{A5.4}$$

Much of the literature, and most extant computer programs for optimization, solves the minimization problem, and for the most part, the following sections will do likewise. The second point concerns the importance of univariate optimization: this has little intrinsic interest, but almost all multi-parameter optimization techniques depend on univariate algorithms at many stages of their iterations. Thus, although few interesting econometric problems involve only one parameter, the following section on one parameter optimization is an essential prerequisite for understanding multivariate methods. Finally, many econometric estimators are explained in an iterative or step-wise way (e.g. three-stage least-squares for simultaneous equations systems, or lagged-residual methods for autocorrelation). Some of these estimators do, but others do not, correspond to some iterative method of optimizing a well-defined function. A central feature of numerical optimization is the use of the criterion function $\ell(\cdot)$ to ensure that successive values of $\boldsymbol{\theta}_j$ yield an increase in $\ell(\cdot)$. Iterative methods that eschew any criterion function, including likelihood, are not considered below. Conversely, strategies which can ensure that every $\boldsymbol{\theta}_j$ guarantees an increase (strictly, non-decrease) in $\ell(\cdot)$ receive prominent consideration.

The following sections discuss methods which operate with no, one, or two derivatives, and so exploit whatever gradient information is available.

A5.3 Maximizing likelihood functions

A first approach to obtaining the MLE $\hat{\boldsymbol{\theta}}$ from $\ell(\boldsymbol{\theta})$ is to consider solving the score equations, assuming the relevant partial derivatives exist:

$$\frac{\partial \ell\left(\boldsymbol{\theta}\right)}{\partial \boldsymbol{\theta}} = \boldsymbol{q}\left(\boldsymbol{\theta}\right) \tag{A5.5}$$

where $\boldsymbol{q}(\widehat{\boldsymbol{\theta}}) = \mathbf{0}$ defines the necessary conditions for a local maximum of $\ell(\boldsymbol{\theta})$ at $\widehat{\boldsymbol{\theta}}$. A sufficient condition is that:

$$\frac{\partial^2 \ell(\boldsymbol{\theta})}{\partial \boldsymbol{\theta} \partial \boldsymbol{\theta}'} = \frac{\partial \boldsymbol{q}(\boldsymbol{\theta})}{\partial \boldsymbol{\theta}'} = \boldsymbol{H}(\boldsymbol{\theta}) \qquad \text{(A5.6)}$$

exists and is negative definite at $\widehat{\boldsymbol{\theta}}$. When $\boldsymbol{q}(\boldsymbol{\theta})$ is a set of equations which can be transformed to be linear in $\boldsymbol{\theta}$, (A5.5) can be solved explicitly for $\widehat{\boldsymbol{\theta}}$. In such a situation, it is easy to implement the estimator without recourse to numerical optimization.

For example, in the multiple-regression model:

$$\boldsymbol{y} = \boldsymbol{Z}\boldsymbol{\beta} + \boldsymbol{u} \ \text{ where } \boldsymbol{u} \sim \mathsf{N}_T\left[\mathbf{0}, \sigma_u^2 \boldsymbol{I}\right] \text{ and } \mathsf{E}\left[\boldsymbol{Z}'\boldsymbol{u}\right] = \mathbf{0}, \qquad \text{(A5.7)}$$

the log-likelihood function, conditional on $\boldsymbol{Z}$ is:

$$\ell(\boldsymbol{\theta} \mid \boldsymbol{Z}) = K_0 - \tfrac{1}{2} T \log \sigma_u^2 - \frac{(\boldsymbol{y} - \boldsymbol{Z}\boldsymbol{\beta})'(\boldsymbol{y} - \boldsymbol{Z}\boldsymbol{\beta})}{2\sigma_u^2}, \qquad \text{(A5.8)}$$

where $\boldsymbol{\theta}' = (\boldsymbol{\beta}' : \sigma^2)$ and K_0 is a constant independent of $\boldsymbol{\theta}$. The equations for $\boldsymbol{q}(\boldsymbol{\theta})$ are:

$$\boldsymbol{q}(\boldsymbol{\theta}) = \frac{1}{\sigma_u^2} \begin{pmatrix} (\boldsymbol{Z}'\boldsymbol{y} - \boldsymbol{Z}'\boldsymbol{Z}\boldsymbol{\beta}) \\ -\frac{1}{2}\left[T - \sigma_u^{-2}(\boldsymbol{y} - \boldsymbol{Z}\boldsymbol{\beta})'(\boldsymbol{y} - \boldsymbol{Z}\boldsymbol{\beta})\right] \end{pmatrix} = \frac{1}{\sigma_u^2} \begin{pmatrix} \boldsymbol{Z}'\boldsymbol{u} \\ -\frac{1}{2}\left(T - \sigma_u^{-2}\boldsymbol{u}'\boldsymbol{u}\right) \end{pmatrix}. \qquad \text{(A5.9)}$$

If rank$(\boldsymbol{Z}) = k$ when there are k parameters in $\boldsymbol{\beta}$, then the equations in (A5.9) yield the well-known unique solutions at $\boldsymbol{q}(\widehat{\boldsymbol{\theta}}) = \mathbf{0}$:

$$\begin{pmatrix} \widehat{\boldsymbol{\beta}} \\ \widehat{\sigma}_u^2 \end{pmatrix} = \begin{pmatrix} (\boldsymbol{Z}'\boldsymbol{Z})^{-1}\boldsymbol{Z}'\boldsymbol{y} \\ T^{-1}\boldsymbol{y}'\boldsymbol{Q}_Z\boldsymbol{y} \end{pmatrix} \qquad \text{(A5.10)}$$

where $\boldsymbol{Q}_Z = (\boldsymbol{I}_T - \boldsymbol{Z}(\boldsymbol{Z}'\boldsymbol{Z})^{-1}\boldsymbol{Z}')$. Finally:

$$\boldsymbol{H}\left(\widehat{\boldsymbol{\theta}}\right) = -\begin{pmatrix} \widehat{\sigma}_u^2(\boldsymbol{Z}'\boldsymbol{Z})^{-1} & \mathbf{0} \\ \mathbf{0}' & T/\left(2\widehat{\sigma}_u^4\right) \end{pmatrix} \qquad \text{(A5.11)}$$

which is negative definite here. In (A5.9), although $\boldsymbol{q}(\boldsymbol{\theta})$ is not linear in $\boldsymbol{\theta}$, an explicit formula for $\widehat{\boldsymbol{\theta}}$ can be obtained from simple manipulation of the two blocks of equations.

Unfortunately, the equations $\boldsymbol{q}(\widehat{\boldsymbol{\theta}}) = \mathbf{0}$ are rarely solved so easily and are often highly non-linear, yielding a problem of locating $\widehat{\boldsymbol{\theta}}$ which is no more tractable than the original aim of maximizing $\ell(\boldsymbol{\theta})$. Thus, we consider the iterative approach to maximization noted above, in which a sequence of values $\boldsymbol{\theta}_j$ of $\boldsymbol{\theta}$ is obtained, corresponding to increasing values of $\ell(\cdot)$ from the recursive formula:

$$\boldsymbol{\theta}_{j+1} = \boldsymbol{g}(\boldsymbol{\theta}_j) \ \text{ for } j = 1, 2, \ldots, J \leq N, \qquad \text{(A5.12)}$$

where the initial value $\boldsymbol{\theta}_1$ has been provided.

Convergence criteria are necessarily arbitrary, being a compromise between premature termination and excessive computation, and hence between an inadequate approximation to $\hat{\boldsymbol{\theta}}$ and failing to stop the iteration when a close approximation to $\hat{\boldsymbol{\theta}}$ has been achieved. Practical criteria are based on the rate of change of the approximation, regarding the process as converged if, for suitably-small pre-assigned positive numbers $\varepsilon_1, \varepsilon_2$ and ε_3 chosen to achieve the desired accuracy, some or all of:

$$|\ell(\boldsymbol{\theta}_{j+1}) - \ell(\boldsymbol{\theta}_j)| < \varepsilon_1, \tag{A5.13}$$

$$|\boldsymbol{q}(\boldsymbol{\theta}_{j+1})| < \varepsilon_2 \boldsymbol{\iota} \tag{A5.14}$$

and:

$$|\boldsymbol{\theta}_{j+1} - \boldsymbol{\theta}_j| < \varepsilon_3 \boldsymbol{\iota} \text{ where } \boldsymbol{\iota}' = (1 \ldots 1) \tag{A5.15}$$

are satisfied. Alternatively, percentage changes in $\ell(\cdot)$ and $\boldsymbol{\theta}$ could be used to avoid scale dependence, and a cautious user may require all of (A5.13)–(A5.15) to be satisfied for several successive iterations. A further test to ensure that an optimum value of $\boldsymbol{\theta}$ has been obtained is to restart an algorithm from a new initial value, iterate to convergence again, and check that similar answers are obtained. This second set may instead reveal that the likelihood has several local optima (as happens in practice) in which case one selects the set with higher likelihood, perhaps also recomputing from further different starting points.

The ease with which parameter transformations can be implemented is a useful feature of a class of algorithms which directly maximize $\ell(\cdot)$ using only information about the value of the function at every $\boldsymbol{\theta}_j$ and do not require values of $\boldsymbol{q}(\boldsymbol{\theta}_j)$ or $\boldsymbol{H}(\boldsymbol{\theta}_j)$. Conversely, other techniques are invariant to changes in the scales of the parameters (called scale invariance) which is also useful, although such methods may not handle non-linear transformations easily since they usually require values of either or both $\boldsymbol{q}(\cdot)$ and $\boldsymbol{H}(\cdot)$. Again, some compromise is in order, but when an algorithm is not scale invariant, then its performance can be radically worsened by an inappropriate scaling of the elements of $\boldsymbol{\theta}$. It would be best to scale, such that equal changes in the elements of $\boldsymbol{\theta}$ caused equal changes in $\ell(\cdot)$, but this is difficult to ensure and may vary during the course of the iteration. A more practical aim is to scale the data, such that every parameter in $\boldsymbol{\theta}_1$ (assuming this constitutes a good initial value) lies between (say) 0.1 and 1.0 in absolute value.

A5.4 Scalar optimization

Two main groups of technique are in general use. The first comprises search methods, of which two examples are considered below, while the second comprises methods for finding roots of $q(\theta) = 0$. To illustrate these various methods, and those analysed in the discussion of multivariate algorithms later, a standard example will be used. It represents a problem of historical interest in estimating econometric models from time-series data, and is one of the simplest estimators to embody most of the features relevant to numerical optimization.

Consider the linear model in (A5.7) with $k = 1$ for $t = 1, \ldots, T$:

$$y_t = z_t \beta + u_t \tag{A5.16}$$

where:

$$u_t = \rho u_{t-1} + \epsilon_t \tag{A5.17}$$

with $|\rho| < 1$ and $\epsilon_t \sim \mathsf{IN}[0, \sigma_\epsilon^2]$. The set $\{z_t\}$ is fixed in repeated samples[2], and the error process $\{u_t\}$ is stationary so that:

$$u_1 \sim \mathsf{N}\left[0, \frac{\sigma_\epsilon^2}{1-\rho^2}\right],$$

and is independent of $(\epsilon_2 \ldots \epsilon_T)$. The probability density of $(u_1 \epsilon_2 \ldots \epsilon_T)$ given $\boldsymbol{\theta}' = (\beta, \rho, \sigma_\epsilon^2)$ is:

$$\mathsf{D}(u_1 \epsilon_2 \ldots \epsilon_T \mid \boldsymbol{\theta}) = \mathsf{D}(u_1 \mid \boldsymbol{\theta}) \prod_{t=2}^{T} \mathsf{D}(\epsilon_t \mid \boldsymbol{\theta}) \tag{A5.18}$$

which yields:

$$\left(1-\rho^2\right)^{\frac{1}{2}} \left(2\pi\sigma_\epsilon^2\right)^{-\frac{T}{2}} \exp\left(-\sum_{t=2}^{T} \frac{\epsilon_t^2}{2\sigma_\epsilon^2}\right) \exp\left(-\frac{u_1^2\left(1-\rho^2\right)}{2\sigma_\epsilon^2}\right). \tag{A5.19}$$

Hence, the log-likelihood function $\ell(\beta, \rho, \sigma_\epsilon^2 | \boldsymbol{y}, \boldsymbol{z})$ for $(\beta, \rho, \sigma_\epsilon^2)$ is:

$$K_0 - \frac{T-1}{2} \log \sigma_\epsilon^2 - \frac{1}{2\sigma_\epsilon^2} \sum_{t=2}^{T} \epsilon_t^2 - \left\{ \frac{u_1^2\left(1-\rho^2\right)}{2\sigma_\epsilon^2} + \tfrac{1}{2} \log\left[\frac{\sigma_\epsilon^2}{1-\rho^2}\right] \right\} \tag{A5.20}$$

where:

$$\epsilon_t = u_t - \rho u_{t-1} = (y_t - \rho y_{t-1}) - (z_t - \rho z_{t-1})\,\beta,$$

and:

$$u_1 = (y_1 - z_1 \beta)\,.$$

For expository purposes, and for simplicity of calculation in practice, it is convenient to neglect the term $\{\cdot\}$ in (A5.20) as $O_p(T^{-1})$ relative to the terms retained when $|\rho|$ is well below unity. This is equivalent to dropping the first observation and using the transformed model:

$$\boldsymbol{y}^+ = \boldsymbol{z}^+ \beta + \boldsymbol{\epsilon} \tag{A5.21}$$

where $y_t^+ = y_t - \rho y_{t-1}$ with $\boldsymbol{y}^+ = (y_2^+ \ldots y_T^+)'$ and so $\boldsymbol{y}^+ = (\boldsymbol{y} - \rho \boldsymbol{y}_1)$ when $\boldsymbol{y}_1$ denotes $\boldsymbol{y}$ lagged one period. Hence:

$$\boldsymbol{\epsilon} = \boldsymbol{u} - \rho \boldsymbol{u}_1 = (\boldsymbol{y} - \rho \boldsymbol{y}_1) - (\boldsymbol{z} - \rho \boldsymbol{z}_1)\,\beta = \boldsymbol{y}^+ - \boldsymbol{z}^+ \beta.$$

[2] More precise, $\{z_t\}$ is assumed to be strongly exogenous for $(\beta,\ \rho,\ \sigma_\epsilon^2)$: see Ch.5.

The resulting approximate log-likelihood function $\ell_0(\cdot)$ can be concentrated with respect to σ_ϵ^2 using:

$$\frac{\partial \ell_0}{\partial \sigma_\epsilon^2} = -\frac{T-1}{2\sigma_\epsilon^2} + \frac{\epsilon'\epsilon}{2\sigma_\epsilon^4}, \tag{A5.22}$$

and setting this to zero yields the conditional optimum:

$$\left(\sigma_\epsilon^2\right)_c = \frac{\epsilon'\epsilon}{(T-1)} \tag{A5.23}$$

leading to the partially optimized function:

$$\ell_1\left(\beta, \rho \mid \left(\sigma_\epsilon^2\right)_c; \boldsymbol{y}^+, \boldsymbol{z}^+\right) = K_1 - \frac{T-1}{2} \log\left\{\left(\boldsymbol{y}^+ - \boldsymbol{z}^+\beta\right)'\left(\boldsymbol{y}^+ - \boldsymbol{z}^+\beta\right)\right\}. \tag{A5.24}$$

Maximizing ℓ_1 can be achieved by minimizing the sum of squares in $\{\cdot\}$ in (A5.24). Moreover, the problem can be reduced to a one-parameter optimization by concentrating $\ell_1(\cdot)$ with respect to β using:

$$\frac{\partial \ell_1}{\partial \beta} = \frac{\partial \ell_0}{\partial \beta}\rfloor_{(\sigma_\epsilon^2)_c} = \left(\sigma_\epsilon^2\right)_c^{-1}\left[\boldsymbol{z}^{+\prime}\left(\boldsymbol{y}^+ - \boldsymbol{z}^+\beta\right)\right]. \tag{A5.25}$$

This is zero at the optimum so that:

$$\beta_c = \left(\boldsymbol{z}^{+\prime}\boldsymbol{z}^+\right)^{-1}\boldsymbol{z}^{+\prime}\boldsymbol{y}^+, \tag{A5.26}$$

which is OLS applied to the transformed model, inducing the further optimized function:

$$\ell_2\left(\rho \mid \beta_c, \left(\sigma_\epsilon^2\right)_c; \boldsymbol{y}^+, \boldsymbol{z}^+\right) = K_2 - \frac{T-1}{2}\log\left(\boldsymbol{y}^{*\prime}\boldsymbol{y}^*\right), \tag{A5.27}$$

where $\boldsymbol{y}^* = \boldsymbol{Q}^+\boldsymbol{y}^+$ and $\boldsymbol{Q}^+ = \boldsymbol{I}_T - \boldsymbol{z}^+(\boldsymbol{z}^{+\prime}\boldsymbol{z}^+)^{-1}\boldsymbol{z}^{+\prime}$. Thus, $\boldsymbol{y}^*$ is the vector of residuals from regressing $\boldsymbol{y}^+$ on $\boldsymbol{z}^+$, and the optimization problem becomes that of finding:

$$\underset{\rho}{\operatorname{argmin}}\left(\boldsymbol{y}^{*\prime}\boldsymbol{y}^*\right) = \underset{\rho}{\operatorname{argmin}}\, f(\rho) \tag{A5.28}$$

where $\boldsymbol{y}^{*\prime}\boldsymbol{y}^*$ is a non-linear function of ρ, and does not depend on any other parameter:

$$\boldsymbol{y}^{*\prime}\boldsymbol{y}^* = (\boldsymbol{y}-\rho\boldsymbol{y}_1)'\left(\boldsymbol{I}_T - (\boldsymbol{z}-\rho\boldsymbol{z}_1)\left[(\boldsymbol{z}-\rho\boldsymbol{z}_1)'(\boldsymbol{z}-\rho\boldsymbol{z}_1)\right]^{-1}(\boldsymbol{z}-\rho\boldsymbol{z}_1)'\right)(\boldsymbol{y}-\rho\boldsymbol{y}_1).$$

The minimizing value of ρ in (A5.28) is $\hat{\rho}$, the MLE of ρ, from which $\hat{\beta}$ can be calculated using (A5.26), and $\hat{\sigma}_\epsilon^2$ using (A5.23).

A5.4.1 Search methods

Perhaps the most obvious approach to locating $\hat{\rho}$ is grid tabulation, in which $f(\rho)$ in (A5.28) is calculated at each of an equally-spaced set of values of ρ in the open interval

$(-1, 1)$, choosing the $\hat{\rho}$ corresponding to the smallest observed value of $f(\rho)$. For example, one might select the 20 points $\rho = (-0.95, -0.85, \ldots, 0.95)$. Then for the cost of 20 function evaluations (and a graph), the minimum can be located within ± 0.1. If required, the process could be repeated using a finer grid with steps of 0.01 over the new interval of length 0.2, and so on. In econometrics, this approach is sometimes referred to as the Hildreth–Lu technique following Hildreth and Lu (1960). Figure A5.4 shows the graph of a CLF grid for an autocorrelation problem which is manifestly badly behaved. The grid is calculated at 1000 points to demonstrate the potential problem of multiple optima, here, with a boundary point as the second optimum.

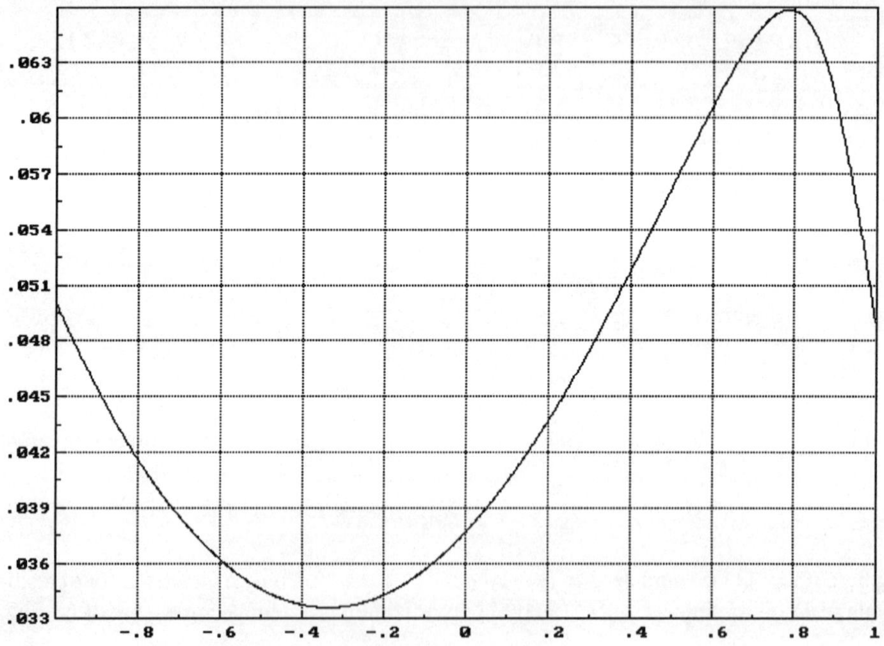

Fig. A5.4 Autoregressive error function grid

The main advantages of grid search are its certainty of convergence, provided there is a minimum to $f(\rho)$ with $|\rho| < 1$, and its ability to reveal multiple optima to $\ell(\cdot)$, assuming these are not sharp spikes. Thus, if the initial grid is sufficiently fine, there is a high probability of locating the global optimum. The process involves a substantial amount of computation if the required precision is four or five significant digits and does not generalize sensibly to multivariate problems. Nevertheless, for estimating autocorrelation, a grid search by steps of 0.1 is a good starting point from which to commence a more sophisticated approach.

When the range of possible parameter values has no obvious a priori bounds, an alternative approach is required, so we consider a second univariate method which can locate a minimum using only function values (i.e., without using derivatives of $f(\cdot)$). The general idea is to approximate the function $f(\rho)$ around some value ρ_0 by another function $h(\rho)$ which has a known minimum at ρ^*, say, and use ρ^* as the next approximation to the minimum of $f(\cdot)$. The procedure can be repeated in the neighbourhood of ρ^* and so on. For example a quadratic approximation can be obtained using a second-order Taylor-series expansion of $f(p)$ around an arbitrary value ρ_0:

$$\begin{aligned} f(\rho) &= f(\rho_0) + q(\rho_0)(\rho - \rho_0) + \tfrac{1}{2}H(\rho_0)(\rho - \rho_0)^2 + r \\ &\simeq d_0 + d_1\rho + d_2\rho^2 \\ &= h(\rho), \end{aligned} \tag{A5.29}$$

where the remainder r depends on $(\rho - \rho_0)^3$, and so becomes negligible as $(\rho - \rho_0)$ tends to zero. From (A5.29):

$$\begin{aligned} d_0 &= f(\rho_0) - q(\rho_0)\rho_0 + \tfrac{1}{2}H(\rho_0)\rho_0^2; \\ d_1 &= q(\rho_0) - H(\rho_0)\rho_0; \\ d_2 &= \tfrac{1}{2}H(\rho_0). \end{aligned} \tag{A5.30}$$

The minimum of $h(\rho)$ occurs at:

$$\frac{\partial h(\rho)}{\partial \rho} = 0 \text{ given by the point } \rho^* = -\frac{d_1}{2d_2}, \tag{A5.31}$$

which yields the next approximation to the minimum of $f(\cdot)$, assuming $d_2 > 0$.

At first sight, it seems that the calculation of ρ^* involves the formulae for the derivatives $q(\cdot)$ and $H(\cdot)$. However, it is straightforward to formulate an iterative algorithm based only on function values, using the result that a unique quadratic passes through three distinct points. For simplicity, assume that $f(\cdot)$ is unimodal and has been evaluated at three equally-spaced points, denoted $\rho_1 < \rho_2 < \rho_3$, with the minimum lying in the interval $[\rho_1, \rho_3]$. The approximating function $h(\cdot)$ is selected to coincide with $f(\cdot)$ at the three values of ρ:

$$h(\rho_i) = f(\rho_i) = f_i \text{ for } i = 1, 2, 3, \tag{A5.32}$$

where the f_i are known. However, $h(\rho)$ in (A5.29) can be rewritten as:

$$h(\rho) = a_0 + a_1(\rho - \rho_1) + a_2(\rho - \rho_1)(\rho - \rho_2) \tag{A5.33}$$

where:

$$\begin{aligned} a_0 &= d_0 + d_1\rho_1 + d_2\rho_1^2; & & d_0 = a_0 - a_1\rho_1 + a_2\rho_1\rho_2; \\ a_1 &= d_1 + d_2(\rho_1 + \rho_2); & \text{and so} \quad & d_1 = a_1 - a_2(\rho_1 + \rho_2); \\ a_2 &= d_2 & & d_2 = a_2. \end{aligned}$$

We now evaluate $h(\rho)$ in (A5.33) at $\{\rho_i\}$ to obtain:

$$h(\rho_1) = a_0 = f_1; \tag{A5.34}$$

$$h(\rho_2) = a_0 + a_1(\rho_2 - \rho_1) = f_2 \tag{A5.35}$$

implying that $a_1 = (f_2 - f_1)/(\rho_2 - \rho_1)$; and:

$$\begin{aligned} h_3 &= a_0 + a_1(\rho_3 - \rho_1) + a_2(\rho_3 - \rho_1)(\rho_3 - \rho_2) \\ &= f_1 + 2a_1(\rho_2 - \rho_1) + 2a_2(\rho_2 - \rho_1)^2 \\ &= f_3, \end{aligned} \tag{A5.36}$$

since $(\rho_3 - \rho_1) = 2(\rho_2 - \rho_1)$ and $(\rho_3 - \rho_2) = (\rho_2 - \rho_1)$ because ρ_1, ρ_2, ρ_3 are equally spaced. Thus:

$$a_2 = \frac{(f_3 - 2f_2 + f_1)}{2(\rho_2 - \rho_1)^2}.$$

Consequently, the a_i only depend on known values of f_i and ρ_i. Solving back for the ds in terms of a_i, f_i and ρ_i, and using the result in (A5.31) that $\rho^* = -d_1/2d_2$ yields:

$$\rho^* = \tfrac{1}{2}(\rho_1 + \rho_2) + \frac{(\rho_2 - \rho_1)(f_2 - f_1)}{(f_3 - 2f_2 + f_1)}, \tag{A5.37}$$

when $(f_3 - 2f_2 + f_1) \neq 0$, so the appropriate optimum can be calculated immediately the three pairs (f_i, ρ_i) are known. Since $a_2 = d_2 = H(\cdot)/2$, we have incidentally derived a formula for numerically calculating the second derivative of $f(\rho)$ at the central point ρ_2.

The main practical difficulty with the above idea is to fulfil the condition that the minimum lies in the interval $[\rho_1, \rho_3]$ with mid-point ρ_2. One solution which has been applied successfully is the method of Davies, Swann and Campey (see Box *et al.*, 1969). The function is first evaluated at the initial point ρ_0, and a pre-assigned increment $\nabla\rho$ (the step-length) is added to ρ_0 to yield ρ_a, then $f(\rho_a)$ is calculated. If $f(\rho_a) \leq f(\rho_0)$ then the step is doubled to ρ_b, then $f(\rho_b)$ is calculated, and so on until an increase in $f(\cdot)$ is obtained at ρ_c. The procedure has then bracketed the minimum. This is the minimization equivalent of the situation portrayed in Fig. A5.1. If $f(\rho_a) > f(\rho_0)$, $\nabla\rho$ is subtracted from ρ_0, the function is re-evaluated, and if this produces a decrease then the preceding method is followed. If both adding and subtracting $\nabla\rho$ leads to an increase, then the minimum is immediately bracketed.

If either of the first two possibilities materializes, then, although the minimum lies in the interval $[\rho_a, \rho_c]$, the points ρ_a, ρ_b, ρ_c are not equally spaced. However, because the step-length was doubled at every stage, computing $f(\cdot)$ at the mid-point ρ_d of the interval $[\rho_b, \rho_c]$ yields four equally spaced points $(\rho_a, \rho_b, \rho_d, \rho_c)$ (corresponding to $(\alpha_1, \alpha_1 + \delta, \alpha_1 + 2\delta, \alpha_1 + 3\delta)$ in Fig. A5.1a). To ensure that $(f_3 - 2f_2 + f_1)$ in (A5.37) is positive, (so that $d_2 > 0$ occurs), the central point must correspond to the smallest function value $f(\rho_d)$, which together with the adjacent function values $f(\rho_b)$ and $f(\rho_c)$, completes the trio for use as f_1, f_2, f_3 in (A5.37). To achieve a higher degree of accuracy, the process can recommence from ρ^*, using a smaller step length. If $f(\rho^*)$ is the smallest function value obtained, then, by taking as two of the three points ρ^* and the nearest other value of ρ already used, a new approximation to the minimum can be computed for the cost of one additional function evaluation.

There are alternative algorithms based on similar procedures (e.g. using cubic approximating functions, or different ways of choosing the three function values in expression (A5.37)), including methods which do not depend on bracketing the minimum. These are referred to collectively as line-search methods when used to locate minima in one dimension of a higher-dimensional space. Their basic feature is the use of function values alone to determine a direction of progress (i.e. whether to increase or decrease the parameter to reduce $f(\cdot)$) but more efficiently than simply comparing function values as occurred with grid search.

It should be obvious from the above discussion how important a good initial value can be, and for the estimation of autocorrelation in an equation like (A5.16), instead of using the optimum point from a grid search, ρ_1 could be the residual autocorrelation from OLS estimation of β:

$$\rho_1 = \sum_{t=2}^{T} \tilde{u}_t \tilde{u}_{t-1} / \sum_{t=2}^{T} \tilde{u}_{t-1}^2 \tag{A5.38}$$

where $\tilde{u}_t = y_t - \hat{\beta} z_t$, and:

$$\hat{\beta} = \sum_{t=1}^{T} z_t y_t / \sum_{t=1}^{T} z_t^2.$$

A more precise statement about the numerical properties of ρ_1 is given below.

A5.4.2 Gradient methods

Since $\hat{\theta}$ is the particular value of θ such that $q(\hat{\theta}) = 0$, it is worth investigating methods which iteratively approximate the unknown root of (A5.5) even when, unlike (A5.9), no explicit formula for $\hat{\theta}$ can be obtained. Figure A5.5a illustrates a plot of a score $q(\mu)$ against the parameter μ, for an arbitrary function $\ell(\mu)$, with the desired root ($\hat{\mu}$) being the point of intersection of $q(\mu)$ with the μ-axis which corresponds to $\hat{\mu}$ if $H(\hat{\mu}) < 0$ when maximizing.

Consider an iteration commencing at μ_1, where $q(\mu)$ is approximated by its tangent at μ_1, using:

$$q(\mu) \simeq e_0 + e_1 (\mu - \mu_1). \tag{A5.39}$$

Since the objective is to solve $q(\mu) = 0$, it seems reasonable to equate the right-hand side of (A5.39) to zero to obtain the next approximation, denoted μ_2:

$$\mu_2 = \mu_1 - e_0 / e_1. \tag{A5.40}$$

In terms of the graph, μ_2 is the point at which the tangent to $q(\mu)$ at μ_1 intersects the μ-axis; obviously, the process can be repeated from μ_2. Moreover, since the expansion in (A5.39) is a first-order Taylor-series:

$$q(\mu) \simeq q(\mu_1) + H(\mu_1)(\mu - \mu_1) = 0, \tag{A5.41}$$

written as a general iterative rule:

$$\mu_{i+1} = \mu_i - H(\mu_i)^{-1} q(\mu_i). \tag{A5.42}$$

The gradient, $q(\mu_i)$ determines the direction in which the next step is to be taken, and $H(\mu_i)^{-1}$ modifies the size of the step (referred to as determining the metric). The algorithm in (A5.42) is commonly known as the Newton–Raphson technique, or sometimes as Newton's method, and a standard convergence criterion is $|q(\mu_i)| < \varepsilon_2$.

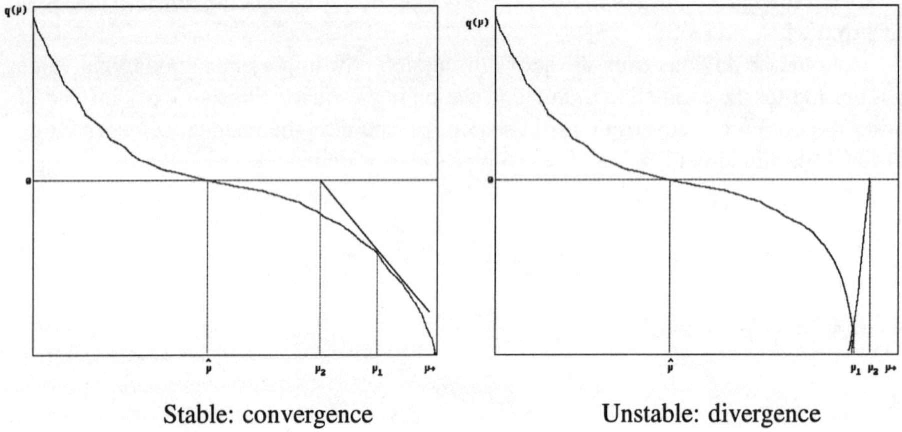

Fig. A5.5 Gradient optimization

The advantages of the Newton–Raphson method are its generality, since (A5.42) could equally well hold for a vector of parameters, and its speed of convergence from a sufficiently good initial value (it is said to be second-order convergent in that an error of $O(\varepsilon)$ at the ith iteration becomes $O(\varepsilon^2)$ at the $(i+1)^{th}$; see, e.g., McCalla, 1967). Unfortunately, there are drawbacks: if the initial value is not sufficiently good, the method may diverge, as would occur from μ_1 in Fig. A5.5b, where $H(\mu_1) > 0$. Also, implementing (A5.42) requires analytic formulae for the first two derivatives of $\ell(\cdot)$, which may be labour intensive.

The divergence problem can be partly circumvented by generalizing (A5.42) using $\ell(\cdot)$ as the criterion to check that successive approximations yield higher likelihoods as follows. Rewrite (A5.42) for a parameter θ in the general form:

$$\theta^*_{i+1} = \lambda_i \theta_{i+1} + (1-\lambda_i)\theta_i = \theta_i - \lambda_i H(\theta_i)^{-1} q(\theta_i) = \theta_i - \lambda_i \theta^c_i \tag{A5.43}$$

where, as before:

$$\theta_{i+1} = \theta_i - H(\theta_i)^{-1} q(\theta_i) = \theta_i - \theta^c_i,$$

when $\theta^c_i = H(\theta_i)^{-1} q(\theta_i)$. Thus, λ_i introduces a scaling factor that was implicitly equal to unity in (A5.42), which can be chosen to ensure that $\ell(\theta^*_{i+1}) \geq \ell(\theta_i)$ by optimizing

$\ell(\theta_i - \lambda_i\theta_i^c)$ with respect to λ_i. Since θ_i and θ_i^c are fixed numbers, $\ell(\theta_i - \lambda_i\theta_i^c)$ is a function of λ_i only, and so:

$$\underset{\lambda_i}{\operatorname{argmax}}\, \ell\left(\theta_i - \lambda_i\theta_i^c\right) \tag{A5.44}$$

can be determined by a line-search procedure. This would be pointless when θ_i is a scalar, since a line search could have found $\max_\theta \ell(\theta)$ directly (without needing the calculation of $H(\cdot)$ and $q(\cdot)$), but the idea is important in multi-parameter problems.

For estimating ρ in the econometric model defined by (A5.16) and (A5.17), the formulae for $q(\cdot)$ and $H(\cdot)$ have an interesting structure. When minimizing $(\boldsymbol{y}^{*\prime}\boldsymbol{y}^*)$ in (A5.28), since $\boldsymbol{Q}^+\boldsymbol{z}^+ = \boldsymbol{0}$:

$$\boldsymbol{y}^* = \boldsymbol{Q}^+\boldsymbol{y}^+ = \boldsymbol{Q}^+\left(\boldsymbol{z}^+\beta + \boldsymbol{\epsilon}\right) = \boldsymbol{Q}^+\boldsymbol{\epsilon} = \boldsymbol{Q}^+\boldsymbol{u} - \rho\boldsymbol{Q}^+\boldsymbol{u}_1 \tag{A5.45}$$

where $\boldsymbol{u} = \boldsymbol{y} - \boldsymbol{z}\beta$, and $\boldsymbol{u}_1$ is the vector $\boldsymbol{u}$ lagged one period. Thus:

$$\boldsymbol{y}^{*\prime}\boldsymbol{y}^* = \boldsymbol{u}'\boldsymbol{Q}^+\boldsymbol{u} - 2\rho\boldsymbol{u}'\boldsymbol{Q}^+\boldsymbol{u}_1 + \rho^2\boldsymbol{u}_1'\boldsymbol{Q}^+\boldsymbol{u}_1 = f(\rho). \tag{A5.46}$$

Under the present assumptions, $\mathsf{E}[\boldsymbol{u}\boldsymbol{z}'] = \mathsf{E}[\boldsymbol{u}\boldsymbol{z}^{+\prime}] = \mathsf{E}[\boldsymbol{u}_1\boldsymbol{z}'] = \boldsymbol{0}$. Consequently, terms like $\boldsymbol{z}'\boldsymbol{u}$ etc., can be neglected when differentiating (A5.46) with respect to ρ if they arise from the dependence of $\boldsymbol{Q}^+$ on ρ. Letting $\tilde{\boldsymbol{u}} = \boldsymbol{Q}^+\boldsymbol{u}$, and using the fact that $\boldsymbol{Q}^+$ is idempotent:

$$q(\rho) = \frac{\partial f(\rho)}{\partial \rho} = -2\tilde{\boldsymbol{u}}'\tilde{\boldsymbol{u}}_1 + 2\rho\tilde{\boldsymbol{u}}_1'\tilde{\boldsymbol{u}}_1, \tag{A5.47}$$

and:

$$H(\rho) = 2\tilde{\boldsymbol{u}}_1'\tilde{\boldsymbol{u}}_1, \tag{A5.48}$$

so that:

$$\rho^c = \left(\tilde{\boldsymbol{u}}_1'\tilde{\boldsymbol{u}}_1\right)^{-1}\tilde{\boldsymbol{u}}_1'\tilde{\boldsymbol{u}}. \tag{A5.49}$$

From an initial value ρ_1, $\boldsymbol{z}^+, \boldsymbol{y}^+, \tilde{\boldsymbol{u}}$, and $\tilde{\boldsymbol{u}}_1$ can be calculated; and for $\lambda = 1$, formula (A5.43) yields:

$$\rho_2^* = \left(\tilde{\boldsymbol{u}}_1'\tilde{\boldsymbol{u}}_1\right)^{-1}\tilde{\boldsymbol{u}}_1'\tilde{\boldsymbol{u}}, \tag{A5.50}$$

so that the next value of ρ_i is obtained by regressing $\tilde{\boldsymbol{u}}$ on $\tilde{\boldsymbol{u}}_1$ where $\tilde{\boldsymbol{u}} = (\boldsymbol{y} - \boldsymbol{z}\tilde{\beta})$, with $\tilde{\beta} = (\boldsymbol{z}^{+\prime}\boldsymbol{z})^{-1}\boldsymbol{z}^{+\prime}\boldsymbol{y}^+$ as seems intuitively reasonable. The same expression results on equating $q(\rho)$ to zero in (A5.47), since $f(\rho)$ is being treated as a quadratic in ρ. When $\rho_1 = 0$, $\tilde{\beta}$ is the OLS estimator, and $\tilde{\boldsymbol{u}} = \boldsymbol{Q}_Z\boldsymbol{y}$, so ρ_1 is the residual autocorrelation in (A5.38) (approximately equal to $(1 - DW/2)$ where DW is the Durbin–Watson statistic). The statistical implications of this finding (and several related results) are discussed below.

A5.5 Multivariate optimization

A5.5.1 Gradient methods

The generality of the iterative formula in (A5.42) makes Newton–Raphson a convenient device for introducing multivariate optimization, when $\ell(\cdot)$ depends on a vector of m parameters $\boldsymbol{\theta}$. As earlier, the MLE $\hat{\boldsymbol{\theta}}$ satisfies $\ell(\hat{\boldsymbol{\theta}}) \geq \ell(\tilde{\boldsymbol{\theta}})$ for all $\tilde{\boldsymbol{\theta}}$, a necessary condition being that $q(\hat{\theta}) = \mathbf{0}$, and a sufficient condition being that $H(\hat{\theta})$ is also negative definite. From an arbitrary value θ_i, $q(\cdot)$ can be approximated by a first-order Taylor-series expansion:

$$q(\theta) \simeq q(\theta_i) + H(\theta_i)(\theta - \theta_i) = \mathbf{0}, \tag{A5.51}$$

yielding the next approximation to $\hat{\theta}$:

$$\theta_{i+1} = \theta_i - H(\theta_i)^{-1} q(\theta_i) = \theta_i - \theta_i^c. \tag{A5.52}$$

Thus, a restatement of the iterative rule in (A5.43) is:

$$\theta_{i+1} = \theta_i - \lambda_i \theta_i^c, \tag{A5.53}$$

where λ_i is a scalar chosen by the line search to maximize $\ell(\theta_i - \lambda_i \theta_i^c)$ for fixed θ_i, θ_i^c. In (A5.53), θ_i^c determines the search direction, and λ_i fixes a step-length common to all m parameters, so that θ_i^c must be measured in an appropriate metric, as is ensured by weighting $q(\cdot)$ by $H(\cdot)^{-1}$. It will become apparent below that (A5.53) provides a sufficiently-general framework to describe almost all iterative optimization procedures.

The numerical optimization involved in the estimation of the model in (A5.16) and (A5.17) is most easily understood by considering the two-dimensional likelihood space of (β, ρ) in terms of iso-likelihood contours of $\ell_1(\beta, \rho|\sigma^2; y, z)$. Since $\ell_1(\cdot)$ is proportional to $f(\beta, \rho) = (y^+ - z^+\beta)'(y^+ - z^+\beta)$, then the contour for a fixed value of $\ell_1(\cdot)$ is defined by all combinations of (β, ρ) that yield a constant value of $f(\beta, \rho)$. Figure A5.3 illustrates the case where z has been scaled to yield $|\beta| < 1$: the arrow denotes decreasing values of $f(\cdot)$ on an arbitrary scale, and the optimum occurs at $(\hat{\beta}, \hat{\rho})$, where $f(\cdot)$ is minimized. Since:

$$\epsilon = y^+ - z^+\beta = u - \rho u_1, \tag{A5.54}$$

the first two derivatives of $f(\cdot)$ with respect to (β, ρ) are:

$$q(\theta) = \begin{pmatrix} \frac{\partial f(\beta,\rho)}{\partial \beta} \\ \frac{\partial f(\beta,\rho)}{\partial \rho} \end{pmatrix} = -2 \begin{pmatrix} z^{+\prime}\epsilon \\ u_1'\epsilon \end{pmatrix} = -2\, W'\epsilon \tag{A5.55}$$

where $W = (z^+ : u_1)$, and:

$$H(\theta) = 2 \begin{pmatrix} z^{+\prime}z^+ & z^{+\prime}u_1 \\ u_1'z^+ & u_1'u_1 \end{pmatrix} = 2\, W'W. \tag{A5.56}$$

The term $(z_1'\epsilon)$ has been dropped from the second-derivative matrix as being negligible.

The similarities of (A5.55) to, and its differences from, the usual least-squares estimation equations in (A5.9) are worth noting. In common, both select the estimator value by an orthogonality condition between the predetermined variables and the white-noise errors. Thus, selecting the equations relating to β from (A5.9) and (A5.10), which is equivalent to minimizing $[(y - Z\beta)'(y - Z\beta)]$, yields:

$$q(\cdot) = -2Z'(y - Z\beta) \quad \text{and} \quad H(\cdot) = 2Z'Z \tag{A5.57}$$

where $\boldsymbol{H}(\cdot)$ is constant and positive definite provided rank$(\boldsymbol{Z}) = k$. Consider solving (A5.57) by Newton–Raphson from an arbitrary initial value β_1:

$$\beta_2 = \beta_1 - (\boldsymbol{Z}'\boldsymbol{Z})^{-1}(\boldsymbol{Z}'\boldsymbol{y} - \boldsymbol{Z}'\boldsymbol{Z}\boldsymbol{\beta}_1) = \hat{\boldsymbol{\beta}}, \tag{A5.58}$$

which is the OLS estimator for all choices of β_1. This occurs because the function to be minimized is quadratic and hence Newton–Raphson converges to the optimum in one iteration. The argument does not apply to the autocorrelation problem since $f(\beta, \rho)$ is not quadratic in (β, ρ), and $\boldsymbol{H}(\boldsymbol{\theta})$ varies with the value of $\boldsymbol{\theta}$ used in computing both $\boldsymbol{z}^+$ (which depends on ρ) and $\boldsymbol{u}_1$ (which depends on β). Nevertheless, (A5.52) provides a reasonable algorithm for this problem. Explicitly:

$$\begin{pmatrix} \beta_{i+1} \\ \rho_{i+1} \end{pmatrix} = \begin{pmatrix} \beta_i \\ \rho_i \end{pmatrix} + \begin{pmatrix} \boldsymbol{z}^{+\prime}\boldsymbol{z}^+ & \boldsymbol{z}^{+\prime}\boldsymbol{u}_1 \\ \boldsymbol{u}_1'\boldsymbol{z}^+ & \boldsymbol{u}_1'\boldsymbol{u}_1 \end{pmatrix}^{-1} \begin{pmatrix} \boldsymbol{z}^{+\prime}\boldsymbol{\epsilon} \\ \boldsymbol{u}_1'\boldsymbol{\epsilon} \end{pmatrix}_{\rfloor(\beta_i,\rho_i)}. \tag{A5.59}$$

By partitioned inversion, the inverse of $(\boldsymbol{W}'\boldsymbol{W})$ in (A5.59) is:

$$\begin{pmatrix} (\boldsymbol{z}^{+\prime}\boldsymbol{Q}_1\boldsymbol{z}^+)^{-1} & -(\boldsymbol{z}^{+\prime}\boldsymbol{Q}_1\boldsymbol{z}^+)^{-1}\boldsymbol{z}^{+\prime}\boldsymbol{u}_1(\boldsymbol{u}_1'\boldsymbol{u}_1)^{-1} \\ -(\boldsymbol{u}_1'\boldsymbol{Q}^+\boldsymbol{u}_1)^{-1}\boldsymbol{u}_1'\boldsymbol{z}^+(\boldsymbol{z}^{+\prime}\boldsymbol{z}^+)^{-1} & (\boldsymbol{u}_1'\boldsymbol{Q}^+\boldsymbol{u}_1)^{-1} \end{pmatrix}$$

where $\boldsymbol{Q}_1 = \boldsymbol{I}_T - \boldsymbol{u}_1(\boldsymbol{u}_1'\boldsymbol{u}_1)^{-1}\boldsymbol{u}_1'$. Hence using (A5.54) and rearranging:

$$\begin{pmatrix} \beta_{i+1} \\ \rho_{i+1} \end{pmatrix} = \begin{pmatrix} (\boldsymbol{z}^{+\prime}\boldsymbol{Q}_1\boldsymbol{z}^+)^{-1}\boldsymbol{z}^{+\prime}\boldsymbol{Q}_1\boldsymbol{y}^+ \\ (\boldsymbol{u}_1'\boldsymbol{Q}^+\boldsymbol{u}_1)^{-1}\boldsymbol{u}_1'\boldsymbol{Q}^+\boldsymbol{u} \end{pmatrix}_{\rfloor(\beta_i,\rho_i)}. \tag{A5.60}$$

Interpreting equation (A5.60) reveals that β_{i+1} is obtained by regressing $\boldsymbol{y}^+$ on $\boldsymbol{z}^+$ and $\boldsymbol{u}_1$, whereas ρ_{i+1} is obtained by regressing $\boldsymbol{u}$ on $\boldsymbol{u}_1$ and $\boldsymbol{z}^+$, both steps being based on values of $\boldsymbol{y}^+$, $\boldsymbol{z}^+$, $\boldsymbol{u}$ and $\boldsymbol{u}_1$ calculated using (β_i, ρ_i). Such an iterative algorithm is intuitively reasonable. Consider the equation $\boldsymbol{y}^+ = \boldsymbol{z}^+\beta + \epsilon$ evaluated at an arbitrary value of (β_i, ρ_i):

$$(\boldsymbol{y} - \rho_i\boldsymbol{y}_1) = (\boldsymbol{z} - \rho_i\boldsymbol{z}_1)\beta + \boldsymbol{u}_{1(i)}(\rho - \rho_i) + [\epsilon - \boldsymbol{z}_1(\rho - \rho_i)(\beta - \beta_i)] \tag{A5.61}$$

where $\boldsymbol{u}_{1(i)} = (\boldsymbol{y}_1 - \boldsymbol{z}_1\beta_i)$. Letting $\boldsymbol{y}^+_{(i)} = \boldsymbol{y} - \rho_i\boldsymbol{y}_1$ etc.:

$$\boldsymbol{y}^+_{(i)} = \boldsymbol{z}^+_{(i)}\beta + \boldsymbol{u}_{1(i)} \nabla \rho + \epsilon^{\diamond} \tag{A5.62}$$

where $\epsilon^{\diamond}$ differs from ϵ by a term which is of second order of smallness relative to the terms retained, since $(\rho - \rho_i)(\beta - \beta_i)$ is no larger than $O_p(T^{-1})$ from consistent initial values (β_i, ρ_i). Pre-multiplying (A5.62) by $\boldsymbol{Q}_1$ removes the term $\boldsymbol{u}_{1(i)}\nabla\rho$, and applying least squares yields the formula for β_{i+1} in (A5.60). A corresponding analysis can be applied to derive the equation for ρ_{i+1} in (A5.60), which is also the result obtained in (A5.50) for scalar optimization with respect to ρ. In the algorithm in §A5.4, β_{i+1} and ρ_{i+1} are sequentially calculated, whereas in (A5.60) they are calculated simultaneously.

Initial values (β_1, ρ_1) can be obtained in many ways of which OLS estimates are the most obvious. If the point $\beta_1 = \rho_1 = 0$ is chosen, the equations in (A5.59) become:

$$\begin{pmatrix} \beta_2 \\ \rho_2 \end{pmatrix} = \begin{pmatrix} \boldsymbol{z}'\boldsymbol{z} & \boldsymbol{z}'\boldsymbol{y}_1 \\ \boldsymbol{y}_1'\boldsymbol{z} & \boldsymbol{y}_1'\boldsymbol{y}_1 \end{pmatrix}^{-1} \begin{pmatrix} \boldsymbol{z}'\boldsymbol{y} \\ \boldsymbol{y}_1'\boldsymbol{y} \end{pmatrix}, \tag{A5.63}$$

so that (β_2, ρ_2) are equal to the estimates obtained by regressing $\boldsymbol{y}$ on $\boldsymbol{z}$ and $\boldsymbol{y}_1$. Alternatively, the best values from a grid tabulation over $|\rho| < 1$ could be chosen.

The second-derivative matrix used in (A5.56) is not $\partial \boldsymbol{q}(\boldsymbol{\theta})/\partial \boldsymbol{\theta}'$, and hence the algorithm in (A5.59) is a modified rather than a full Newton–Raphson. Similar modifications (i.e., neglecting terms of small order of importance) are used frequently, either to simplify formulae, or in an attempt to ensure that $\boldsymbol{H}(\cdot)$ is positive definite for all relevant values of $\boldsymbol{\theta}$; dropping $\boldsymbol{z}_1'\boldsymbol{\epsilon}$ from (A5.56) helps achieve both aims. However, a different interpretation is possible as follows. First, $f(\cdot) = \boldsymbol{\epsilon}'\boldsymbol{\epsilon}$ is a sum of squares which depends non-linearly on $\boldsymbol{\theta}$, the vector (β, ρ). Since the transformed equation is:

$$\boldsymbol{\epsilon} = \boldsymbol{y}^+ - \boldsymbol{z}^+\beta = \boldsymbol{y} - \beta\boldsymbol{z} - \rho\boldsymbol{y}_1 + \rho\beta\boldsymbol{z}_1',$$

letting $\boldsymbol{\phi}' = (1 : -\beta : -\rho : \rho\beta)$ and $\boldsymbol{F} = (\boldsymbol{y} : \boldsymbol{z} : \boldsymbol{y}_1 : \boldsymbol{z}_1)$, then $\boldsymbol{\epsilon} = \boldsymbol{F}\boldsymbol{\phi}$. Therefore, $f(\cdot) = \boldsymbol{\phi}'\boldsymbol{F}'\boldsymbol{F}\boldsymbol{\phi}$ and:

$$\boldsymbol{q}(\cdot) = \frac{\partial f}{\partial \boldsymbol{\theta}} = 2\frac{\partial \boldsymbol{\phi}'}{\partial \boldsymbol{\theta}}\boldsymbol{F}'\boldsymbol{F}\boldsymbol{\phi} = -2\boldsymbol{J}'\boldsymbol{F}'\boldsymbol{\epsilon}, \tag{A5.64}$$

where $\boldsymbol{J}$ is the Jacobian matrix of the transform $\boldsymbol{\phi} = \boldsymbol{\phi}(\boldsymbol{\theta})$, such that:

$$\boldsymbol{J}' = \begin{pmatrix} 0 & 1 & 0 & -\rho \\ 0 & 0 & 1 & -\beta \end{pmatrix}. \tag{A5.65}$$

Then (A5.64) yields the same solution as (A5.55). This Gauss–Newton algorithm takes the form:

$$\boldsymbol{\theta}_{i+1} = \boldsymbol{\theta}_i - \lambda_i \left(\boldsymbol{J}'\boldsymbol{F}'\boldsymbol{F}\boldsymbol{J}\right)^{-1} \boldsymbol{J}'\boldsymbol{F}'\boldsymbol{\epsilon}_{|\boldsymbol{\theta}_i}. \tag{A5.66}$$

Manipulation shows that (A5.66) is identical to (A5.60) when applied to the estimation of error autocorrelation since $\boldsymbol{J}'\boldsymbol{F}^{+\prime} = (\boldsymbol{z}^+ : \boldsymbol{u}_1)' = \boldsymbol{W}'$.

Another modification of Newton–Raphson also used in statistics is the method of scoring, where in (A5.52), $\boldsymbol{H}(\boldsymbol{\theta})$ is replaced by the matrix $\boldsymbol{H}^*(\cdot) = \mathsf{E}[\boldsymbol{H}(\cdot)]$ or sometimes $T \operatorname{plim}_{T\to\infty} T^{-1}\boldsymbol{H}(\cdot)$. The use of the expected value or plim can effect a considerable simplification in the formulae to be programmed. For example, when $\mathsf{E}[\boldsymbol{z}^{+\prime}\boldsymbol{u}_1] = 0$, $\mathsf{E}[\boldsymbol{W}'\boldsymbol{W}]$ in (A5.56) is:

$$\boldsymbol{H}^*(\boldsymbol{\theta}) = \mathsf{E}[\boldsymbol{W}'\boldsymbol{W}] = \begin{pmatrix} \boldsymbol{z}^{+\prime}\boldsymbol{z}^+ & 0 \\ 0 & \dfrac{(T-1)\sigma_\epsilon^2}{1-\rho^2} \end{pmatrix}, \tag{A5.67}$$

which is a diagonal matrix, and reveals that $\hat{\beta}$ and $\hat{\rho}$ are independently distributed. The resulting scoring algorithm is:

$$\begin{pmatrix} \beta_{i+1} \\ \rho_{i+1} \end{pmatrix} = \begin{pmatrix} \beta_i \\ \rho_i \end{pmatrix} - \begin{pmatrix} \left(\boldsymbol{z}^{+\prime}\boldsymbol{z}^{+}\right)^{-1} \boldsymbol{z}^{+\prime}\boldsymbol{\epsilon} \\ \dfrac{1-\rho^2}{(T-1)\,\sigma_\epsilon^2}\boldsymbol{u}_1^{\prime}\boldsymbol{\epsilon} \end{pmatrix}_{\rfloor(\beta_i,\rho_i)} . \tag{A5.68}$$

This result leads to a useful control variate in Monte Carlo methods (see Ch.3).

Berndt, Hall, Hall and Hausman (1974) suggested using a Gauss–Newton approach even when $\ell(\cdot)$ is not a sum of squares of non-linear functions. Rewrite (A5.66) in the form:

$$\boldsymbol{\theta}_{i+1} = \boldsymbol{\theta}_i - \lambda_i \boldsymbol{H}^0\left(\boldsymbol{\theta}_i\right)^{-1} \boldsymbol{q}\left(\boldsymbol{\theta}_i\right) \tag{A5.69}$$

using $\boldsymbol{H}^0(\cdot)$ determined by:

$$\boldsymbol{H}^0\left(\boldsymbol{\theta}_i\right) = \sum_{t=2}^{T} \boldsymbol{q}_t\left(\boldsymbol{\theta}_i\right) \boldsymbol{q}_t\left(\boldsymbol{\theta}_i\right)^{\prime} \tag{A5.70}$$

where in (A5.64), $\boldsymbol{q}(\cdot) = \sum_{t=2}^{T} \boldsymbol{q}_t(\cdot) = \sum_{t=2}^{T} \boldsymbol{J}^{\prime}\boldsymbol{f}_t\epsilon_t$, and hence:

$$\boldsymbol{q}_t\left(\cdot\right) = -2\begin{pmatrix} z_t^{+}\epsilon_t \\ u_{t-1}\epsilon_t \end{pmatrix}. \tag{A5.71}$$

This technique has the advantage that only the first derivatives need to be calculated, yet the resulting $\boldsymbol{H}(\cdot)$ is positive definite so long as $(\boldsymbol{q}_2(\cdot)\ldots\boldsymbol{q}_T(\cdot))$ has full column rank.

Nevertheless, most of the algorithms in this section ((A5.60), (A5.66), and (A5.69) but not (A5.68)) can fail for some combinations of data sequences $\{z_t\}$ and initial values (β_1, ρ_1) because of a singular $\boldsymbol{H}(\cdot)$ matrix. If such an outcome occurs, several pragmatic solutions are possible, including replacing the singular matrix $\boldsymbol{H}(\cdot)$ by the unit matrix $\boldsymbol{I}_k$ (known as the method of steepest descent, since the step is in the direction of the gradient vector $\boldsymbol{q}(\cdot)$, and so is useful only if $\boldsymbol{\theta}$ is sensibly scaled), or using $\boldsymbol{H}_\mu(\cdot) = (\boldsymbol{H}(\cdot) + \mu\boldsymbol{I}_k)$ where $\mu > 0$ is chosen to ensure that $\boldsymbol{H}_\mu(\cdot)$ is positive definite (this is known as quadratic hill climbing — see Goldfeld and Quandt, 1972). The matrix $\boldsymbol{H}_\mu(\cdot)$ varies between $\boldsymbol{H}(\cdot)$ (Newton–Raphson) and $\boldsymbol{I}_k$ (steepest descent) as μ increases from zero; a similar idea could be applied to $\boldsymbol{H}^0(\cdot)$.

A5.5.2 Step-wise optimization

Apart from the method of scoring, none of the multivariate algorithms described so far has explicitly incorporated any special features arising from the statistical context of optimization, although some of the iterative rules derived above had statistical interpretations. The equation $\boldsymbol{q}(\boldsymbol{\theta}) = \boldsymbol{0}$ is discussed in Chapter 10 as an estimator-generating rule, and hence it is natural to attempt to solve the equations in (A5.55) directly. Using (A5.54), $\boldsymbol{q}(\boldsymbol{\theta}) = \boldsymbol{0}$ in (A5.55) yields:

$$\begin{pmatrix} \boldsymbol{z}^{+\prime}\left(\boldsymbol{y}^{+} - \boldsymbol{z}^{+}\beta\right) \\ \boldsymbol{u}_1^{\prime}\left(\boldsymbol{u} - \rho\boldsymbol{u}_1\right) \end{pmatrix} = \boldsymbol{0};$$

or:

$$\begin{pmatrix} \beta_{i+1} \\ \rho_{i+1} \end{pmatrix} = \begin{pmatrix} (z^{+\prime}z^{+})^{-1}\, z^{+\prime}y^{+} \\ (u_1^{\prime}u_1)^{-1}\, u_1^{\prime}u \end{pmatrix}_{\rfloor(\beta_i,\rho_i)} . \tag{A5.72}$$

This sequential (step-wise) optimization method is known in econometrics as the Cochrane–Orcutt procedure after Cochrane and Orcutt (1949) (but see Gilbert, 1989). Initial values of zero for β_1 and ρ_1 are frequently used. Figure A5.3 illustrated the successive steps of (A5.72) from the origin; note that (A5.68) and (A5.72) yield the same algorithm for the econometric model presently being considered, although this is not true in general.

When $\rho_1 = 0$, $\beta_2 = (z'z)^{-1}z'y$ is the OLS estimator, so $u_{(2)} = y - z\beta_2$ are the OLS residuals, and $\rho_2 = (u_{1(2)}^{\prime}u_{1(2)})^{-1}u_{1(2)}^{\prime}u_{(2)}$ is the residual-autocorrelation coefficient. When z_t is strictly exogenous, (β_2, ρ_2) are consistent for (β, ρ). Consequently, β_3 is (approximately) the generalized least-squares estimator based on ρ_2, and so is asymptotically efficient. Each step involves OLS estimation (either regressing y^+ on z^+ or u on u_1), and hence produces a decrease in $f(\cdot)$; Sargan (1964) has shown that the algorithm converges with probability unity, and, for strictly-exogenous regressors, the convergence tends to be rapid, with β_2 and the MLE having closely similar values since both are independent of the MLE of ρ. Figure A5.3c illustrated such a case.

In terms of numerical optimization, every step of (A5.72) involves two axial searches since the successive values of (β_i, ρ_i) are given by tangency conditions between lines parallel to either the β or ρ axes and the lowest attainable contour $f(\cdot) = c$ (for constant c). When the contours $f(\cdot) = c$ are not roughly circular (or vertical ellipses), axial search looks rather unimpressive as suggested by Fig. A5.3a for a situation with elongated ellipses which are not parallel to either axis but describe a ridge of $\ell(\cdot)$. A large number of iterations could be required to achieve convergence. Such a situation implies that β_2 and ρ_2 are not independent: when the contour f_2 defines a likelihood-based 95 per cent confidence region, the unconditional 95 per cent confidence interval for ρ_2 is from ρ_a to ρ_b, whereas, given $\beta = \beta_2$, the corresponding conditional interval is from ρ_c to ρ_d. Consequently, Fig. A5.3c is the likely graph only when z_t is strictly exogenous.

A special feature of the estimation problem exploited in the step-wise method is that $f(\cdot)$ is bi-quadratic in (β, ρ), and hence $q(\cdot)$ is bilinear; holding ρ (β) fixed, the first (second) row of $q(\cdot) = \mathbf{0}$ is linear in β (ρ). Thus, for the estimation of (A5.16) and (A5.17), every step of the axial search can be done without involving such sub-iterations as line searches, and the step-wise technique would cease to be appealing if each step required many function values. Moreover, the calculations involved in (A5.72) are simple to program and can be executed efficiently by computer. It seems worth investigating whether there are cases when Fig. A5.3a is the more likely description and if so, whether the step-wise approach can be improved for such problems.

First, when the regression equation (A5.16) is itself dynamic, that is, y_{t-1} occurs as a regressor, then taking $z_t = y_{t-1}$ as a simple example:

$$\begin{aligned} \mathsf{E}\left[z^{+\prime}u_1\right] &= (T-1)\,\mathsf{E}\left[y_{t-1}u_{t-1} - \rho y_{t-2}u_{t-1}\right] \\ &= (1-\rho^2)\,(T-1)\,\mathsf{E}\left[y_t u_t\right] \neq 0. \end{aligned} \tag{A5.73}$$

Consequently, $\mathsf{E}[\boldsymbol{H}(\cdot)]$ is not diagonal and so (β_2, ρ_2) are not independent. Since:

$$\mathsf{V}\left[\widehat{\theta}\right] \simeq -\boldsymbol{H}\left(\widehat{\theta}\right)^{-1},$$

from (A5.59) when $z_t = y_{t-1}$, $\boldsymbol{z}^+ = \boldsymbol{y}_1^+$ then:

$$\mathsf{C}\left[\beta_2, \rho_2\right] = -\left(\boldsymbol{y}_1^{+\prime} \boldsymbol{Q}_1 \boldsymbol{y}_1^+\right)^{-1} \boldsymbol{y}_1^{+\prime} \boldsymbol{u}_1 \left(\boldsymbol{u}_1^{\prime} \boldsymbol{u}_1\right)^{-1} \neq 0. \tag{A5.74}$$

Most econometric models of time-series data are dynamic, so the Fig. A5.3a situation is a common occurrence.

The second issue is to choose other initial values than $(0, 0)$; for example, the grid-tabulation method could be used first to obtain (β^*, ρ^*) say, and the iterative rule (A5.72) commenced from there. For a first-order autoregressive error, the combination of grid tabulation followed by step-wise optimization provides some protection against multiple optima and sloping ellipses, and has proved fast and reliable in practice.

However, a third idea for accelerating the progress of (A5.72) is to generalize the rule in (A5.72) to allow a variable step length as in (A5.53). Thus, let the values given for $(\beta_{i+1}, \rho_{i+1})$ by (A5.72) be denoted β_i^{c} and ρ_i^{c}, and consider using:

$$\begin{pmatrix} \beta_{i+1} \\ \rho_{i+1} \end{pmatrix} = \begin{pmatrix} \beta_i \\ \rho_i \end{pmatrix} - \lambda_i \begin{pmatrix} \beta_i^{\mathrm{c}} \\ \rho_i^{\mathrm{c}} \end{pmatrix}. \tag{A5.75}$$

Figure A5.3b illustrated the first few steps commencing from the initial values $(\beta_1, 0)$ corresponding to $\boldsymbol{a} = (\alpha_{\mathrm{a}}^1, \alpha_{\mathrm{b}}^0)$. Apply (A5.72) in the order of first locating $\tilde{\rho} = \rho_1^{\mathrm{c}}$ (at α_{b}^1), using this to generate β_2^{c} (the point $(\alpha_{\mathrm{a}}^2, \alpha_{\mathrm{b}}^1)$) and then move to ρ_1^{c} at $\boldsymbol{b} = (\alpha_{\mathrm{a}}^2, \alpha_{\mathrm{b}}^2)$. The direction of total progress of the algorithm is given by the line joining the two points $\boldsymbol{a}$ and $\boldsymbol{b}$, which is the vector difference (in general notation):

$$\begin{pmatrix} \beta_2^{\mathrm{c}} \\ \rho_2^{\mathrm{c}} \end{pmatrix} - \begin{pmatrix} \beta_1 \\ 0 \end{pmatrix} = \boldsymbol{\theta}_1^{\mathrm{c}} - \boldsymbol{\theta}_1. \tag{A5.76}$$

Since this shows the directions in which the parameter values are changing after one complete iteration (i.e. β is decreasing and ρ is increasing), it is a good direction to investigate (as is obvious from the two-dimensional diagram). The minimum along the line can be found by the univariate search:

$$\underset{\lambda_1}{\operatorname{argmin}}\, f\left(\boldsymbol{\theta}_1 - \lambda_1 \boldsymbol{\theta}_1^{\mathrm{c}}\right), \tag{A5.77}$$

which yields a point close to (β_m, ρ_m) (in Fig. A5.3b, at α_{a}^m). By using the values of $f(\cdot)$ at $\boldsymbol{a}$ and $\boldsymbol{b}$, the minimum of (A5.77) can be determined closely enough at the cost of one or two function evaluations.

A5.5.3 Conjugate directions

There are many problems where neither $\boldsymbol{H}(\cdot)$ nor $\boldsymbol{q}(\cdot)$ can be derived mathematically without inordinate labour input, and so it is of value to investigate routines which can optimize general non-linear functions using information based on function values alone, (i.e., without requiring analytical first or second derivatives). Axial search in every one-dimensional subspace is possible, but not at all efficient if the search directions are unrelated to the elongation of the contours of $f(\cdot)$. A more practical idea is to try and incorporate the information derived from directions of total progress to form more appropriate coordinate axes, which are then retained for later searches. For example, in Fig. A5.3b, when the iteration recommences from $\boldsymbol{c} = (\beta_3, \rho_3)$, the search directions most worth exploring are the ρ-axis and the direction $\boldsymbol{ab}$, where the latter replaces the β-axis. Searching in these directions yields another point (say) $\boldsymbol{d} = (\beta_4, \rho_4)$ as the next approximation to the optimum. Now the line $\boldsymbol{cd}$ provides a new direction of total progress, and a further axis for later searches (in place of the ρ-axis).

The m-dimensional structure of the above ideas is best understood in an algebraic approach, which also overcomes the heuristic nature of the previous geometrical exposition. Consider a case where $f(\cdot)$ is a quadratic in $\boldsymbol{\theta}$ defined by:

$$f(\boldsymbol{\theta}) = k_0 + \boldsymbol{\kappa}'\boldsymbol{\theta} + \boldsymbol{\theta}'\boldsymbol{H}\boldsymbol{\theta} \tag{A5.78}$$

where $\boldsymbol{\kappa}$ and $\boldsymbol{H}$ are constants independent of $\boldsymbol{\theta}$, and $\boldsymbol{H}$ is positive definite. Then the $m \times 1$ vectors $\boldsymbol{h}^{(i)}$ and $\boldsymbol{h}^{(j)}$ are defined to be conjugate with respect to $\boldsymbol{H}$ if:

$$\boldsymbol{h}^{(i)\prime}\boldsymbol{H}\boldsymbol{h}^{(j)} = 0 \ (i \neq j)\,. \tag{A5.79}$$

In effect, conjugacy generalizes the concept of orthogonality. Now let $(\boldsymbol{h}^{(1)} \ldots \boldsymbol{h}^{(m)})$ be a set of m directions, mutually conjugate with respect to $\boldsymbol{H}$, and hence linearly independent, so that (A5.79) holds for $i, j = 1, \ldots, m$. Since the $\boldsymbol{h}^{(j)}$ span the space of all m-dimensional vectors, any point in that space can be written as a linear function of the $\boldsymbol{h}^{(j)}$. Thus, given any initial value $\boldsymbol{\theta}_1$, the value $\boldsymbol{\theta}^*$ which minimizes $f(\cdot)$ can be written as:

$$\boldsymbol{\theta}^* = \boldsymbol{\theta}_1 + \sum_{j=1}^{m} \gamma_j \boldsymbol{h}^{(j)}. \tag{A5.80}$$

Since $\boldsymbol{\theta}^*$ is given by minimizing $f(\boldsymbol{\theta})$ over $\boldsymbol{\theta}$, the γ_j are given by:

$$\underset{\gamma_1 \cdots \gamma_m}{\operatorname{argmin}} f\left(\boldsymbol{\theta}_1 + \sum_{j=1}^{m} \gamma_j \boldsymbol{h}^{(j)}\right), \tag{A5.81}$$

where, from (A5.78):

$$\begin{aligned} f(\cdot) &= k_0 + \boldsymbol{\kappa}'\left(\boldsymbol{\theta}_1 + \sum_{j=1}^{m} \gamma_j \boldsymbol{h}^{(j)}\right) + \left(\boldsymbol{\theta}_1 + \sum_{j=1}^{m} \gamma_j \boldsymbol{h}^{(j)}\right)' \boldsymbol{H}\left(\boldsymbol{\theta}_1 + \sum_{j=1}^{m} \gamma_j \boldsymbol{h}^{(j)}\right) \\ &= f(\boldsymbol{\theta}_1) + \sum_{j=1}^{m} \left[\gamma_j \left(\boldsymbol{\kappa}'\boldsymbol{h}^{(j)} + 2\boldsymbol{\theta}_1'\boldsymbol{H}\boldsymbol{h}^{(j)}\right) + \gamma_j^2 \boldsymbol{h}^{(j)\prime}\boldsymbol{H}\boldsymbol{h}^{(j)}\right], \end{aligned} \tag{A5.82}$$

since all cross-products of the form (A5.79) vanish. Consequently, $f(\cdot)$ can be minimized separately with respect to each γ_j, and so, searching once along each direction $\boldsymbol{h}^{(j)}$ to locate the minimizing value of γ_j in that direction, yields the global optimum $\boldsymbol{\theta}^*$. In summary, the quadratic function (A5.78) can be minimized in exactly m steps, each of which is a simple line search, when a set of m mutually conjugate directions is available. Looking back, this analysis helps explain why the axial-search method worked well for circular contours, since the Euclidean coordinates are nearly conjugate in such a case. The crucial step in developing a practical procedure is that the directions of total progress $(\boldsymbol{\theta}_i^c - \boldsymbol{\theta}_i)$ can be used to create a set of conjugate directions.

Specifically, the procedure due to Powell (1964) commences from $\boldsymbol{\theta}_1$ and searches along each coordinate axis in turn to locate $\boldsymbol{\theta}_1^c$ (the univariate searches utilize a variant of the quadratic approximation method described in §A5.4 above). The first new search direction is given by $\nabla\boldsymbol{\theta}_1 := (\boldsymbol{\theta}_1^c - \boldsymbol{\theta}_1)$, and the minimum at $\boldsymbol{\theta}_2$ in this direction is found by searching along the line joining $\boldsymbol{\theta}_1^c$ to $\boldsymbol{\theta}_1$:

$$\boldsymbol{\theta}_2 = \boldsymbol{\theta}_1 + \lambda^* \nabla \boldsymbol{\theta}_1 \text{ where } \lambda^* = \underset{\lambda}{\operatorname{argmin}} f\left[\boldsymbol{\theta}_1 + \lambda\left(\boldsymbol{\theta}_1^c - \boldsymbol{\theta}_1\right)\right] \tag{A5.83}$$

again solved by the quadratic approximation method. For $m = 2$, the situation is identical to the steps taken to locate (β_2, ρ_2). Then $\boldsymbol{\theta}_2$ becomes the new approximation to the optimum, the search directions are altered from $(\boldsymbol{h}^{(1)} \ldots \boldsymbol{h}^{(m)})$ to $(\boldsymbol{h}^{(2)} \ldots \boldsymbol{h}^{(m)} \nabla \boldsymbol{\theta}_1)$ and the process is repeated. For the quadratic defined in (A5.78), $\nabla\boldsymbol{\theta}_1$ is conjugate to the remaining axes, a point most easily seen by reconsidering the two-dimensional case show in Fig. A5.3b. Let $\boldsymbol{h}^{(1)}$ denote the ρ-axis and $\boldsymbol{h}^{(2)}$ the β-axis with $\boldsymbol{\theta}_1 = (\beta : 0)'$ and $\boldsymbol{\theta}_1^c = (\beta_1^c : \rho_1^c)'$, then both $\boldsymbol{\theta}_1$ and $\boldsymbol{\theta}_1^c$ are minima of $f(\cdot)$ in the direction $h^{(2)}$, but correspond to different values of ρ. By definition:

$$f(\boldsymbol{\theta}_1) = \min_{\lambda} f\left(\boldsymbol{\theta}_1 + \lambda \boldsymbol{h}^{(2)}\right), \tag{A5.84}$$

and this must occur at $\lambda = 0$ so that:

$$\frac{\partial f\left(\boldsymbol{\theta} + \lambda \boldsymbol{h}^{(2)}\right)}{\partial \boldsymbol{\theta}} = \mathbf{0} \text{ at } \lambda = 0. \tag{A5.85}$$

Similar reasoning applies to $\boldsymbol{\theta}_1^c$. When the function $f(\cdot)$ is the quadratic (A5.78) (for $m = 2$), from (A5.82) the partial derivative (A5.85) is:

$$2\lambda \boldsymbol{h}^{(2)\prime} \boldsymbol{H} \boldsymbol{h}^{(2)} + \boldsymbol{h}^{(2)\prime}\left(\boldsymbol{\kappa} + 2\boldsymbol{H}\boldsymbol{\theta}_1\right), \tag{A5.86}$$

which vanishes for $\lambda = 0$. Similarly for $\boldsymbol{\theta}_1^c$:

$$2\lambda \boldsymbol{h}^{(2)\prime} \boldsymbol{H} \boldsymbol{h}^{(2)} + \boldsymbol{h}^{(2)\prime}\left(\boldsymbol{\kappa} + 2\boldsymbol{H}\boldsymbol{\theta}_1^c\right) = 0 \text{ at } \lambda = 0, \tag{A5.87}$$

so that subtracting (A5.86) from (A5.87) yields the required conjugacy condition:

$$\boldsymbol{h}^{(2)\prime} \boldsymbol{H}\left(\boldsymbol{\theta}_1^c - \boldsymbol{\theta}_1\right) = 0. \tag{A5.88}$$

The principle here is general, since only the diagram necessarily relates to the two-dimensional case; for a quadratic, the difference between two minima in any given direction is conjugate to that direction (see Fig. A5.3d). At the nth stage when n mutually conjugate directions have been located, the initial value of the $(n+1)^{st}$ iteration is a minimum with respect to these directions. But so is the final value of that iteration, and hence the new direction is conjugate to the existing directions; by an inductive extension, after m iterations all of the search directions are mutually conjugate. Since the minimum can be located by one search in each conjugate direction, $\boldsymbol{\theta}^*$ can be found for (A5.78) in m iterations.

There are two important qualifications, however. First, most log-likelihood functions are not quadratic, and the above analysis provides a rigorous justification of the algorithm only for the quadratic case. In practice this issue is not too serious since many log-likelihood functions can be approximated adequately by a quadratic in the neighbourhood of their optimum. Moreover, the rate of progress of Powell's algorithm is often impressive even from poor initial values for non-quadratic functions, and it has proved robust in a wide range of applications. In Fig. A5.3b, note that progress would be as rapid commencing from $\mathbf{0}$ as from $\boldsymbol{\theta}_1$. The second qualification is that the conjugate directions may become nearly linearly dependent if a direction in which little progress has been made is discarded, so that almost no component in that direction is retained for later searches. Powell's algorithm contains a modification to guard against this possibility, and so ensure that every new direction contains an appreciable component of the one discarded (for precise details, see Powell, 1964 , and Dixon, 1972; also, Zangwill, 1969, has proposed an alternative, but closely related, method for creating and selecting linearly-independent search directions). Although such a modification implies that the routine need not converge in m iterations for a quadratic (in m parameters), Powell's method still seems to be one of the more reliable of the algorithms which use only function values. Additionally, the avoidance of derivatives imparts an important element of flexibility in moving from one set of parameters $\boldsymbol{\theta}$ to any function ϕ of these where $\phi = \phi(\boldsymbol{\theta})$: a similar advantage applies to a variant of the Gill–Murray–Pitfield algorithm described below.

A5.5.4 Variable metric or quasi-Newton methods

The Newton–Raphson form of the general expression (A5.53) (namely, $\boldsymbol{\theta}_{i+1} = \boldsymbol{\theta}_i - \lambda_i \boldsymbol{\theta}_i^c$) computed the search direction $\boldsymbol{\theta}_i^c$ by weighting the gradient vector $\boldsymbol{q}(\cdot)$ using as a metric the inverse of $\boldsymbol{H}(\cdot)$. It was noted that $\boldsymbol{H}(\boldsymbol{\theta}_i)$ may not be positive definite for non-optimal $\boldsymbol{\theta}_i$ even if $\boldsymbol{H}(\hat{\boldsymbol{\theta}})$ is, in which case $\boldsymbol{\theta}_i^c$ may be a poor search direction. Moreover, for large m, $\boldsymbol{H}(\cdot)$ is expensive to invert, although the same value of $\boldsymbol{H}(\cdot)$ could be used for several successive iterations with different $\boldsymbol{q}(\cdot)$.

A substantial variation of this idea, which avoids inversion, is to replace $\boldsymbol{H}(\boldsymbol{\theta}_i)^{-1}$ by another positive-definite matrix $\boldsymbol{K}_i$, the structure of which evolves during the course of the iteration. Thus in place of (A5.52) consider:

$$\boldsymbol{\theta}_i^c = \boldsymbol{K}_i \boldsymbol{q}(\boldsymbol{\theta}_i) \quad \text{for } i = 1, 2, \ldots \tag{A5.89}$$

with:

$$\boldsymbol{\theta}_{i+1} = \boldsymbol{\theta}_i - \lambda_i \boldsymbol{\theta}_i^c, \tag{A5.90}$$

as before, where the value of λ_i is chosen by (A5.77), and where $\boldsymbol{K}_i$ is constructed using the general recursive formula:

$$\boldsymbol{K}_{i+1} = \boldsymbol{K}_i + \boldsymbol{D}_i. \tag{A5.91}$$

There are many rules defining a sequence of $\boldsymbol{D}_i$ such that every $\boldsymbol{K}_i$ is positive definite, and for the quadratic in (A5.78), $\boldsymbol{K}_{m+1} = \boldsymbol{H}^{-1}$. Let $\boldsymbol{d}_i = \boldsymbol{\theta}_{i+1} - \boldsymbol{\theta}_i$ and $\boldsymbol{p}_i = \boldsymbol{q}(\boldsymbol{\theta}_{i+1}) - \boldsymbol{q}(\boldsymbol{\theta}_i)$, then the Davidon–Fletcher–Powell (DFP) approach uses:

$$\boldsymbol{D}_i = \frac{\boldsymbol{d}_i \boldsymbol{d}_i'}{\boldsymbol{d}_i' \boldsymbol{p}_i} - \frac{\boldsymbol{K}_i \boldsymbol{p}_i \boldsymbol{p}_i' \boldsymbol{K}_i}{\boldsymbol{p}_i' \boldsymbol{K}_i \boldsymbol{p}_i} \tag{A5.92}$$

which is an updating matrix of rank two, whereas Broyden's rank-one algorithm uses:

$$\boldsymbol{D}_i = \frac{(\boldsymbol{d}_i - \boldsymbol{K}_i \boldsymbol{p}_i)(\boldsymbol{d}_i - \boldsymbol{K}_i \boldsymbol{p}_i)'}{(\boldsymbol{d}_i - \boldsymbol{K}_i \boldsymbol{p}_i)' \boldsymbol{p}_i}. \tag{A5.93}$$

In both cases, only the first derivatives $\boldsymbol{q}(\cdot)$ need to be calculated, and these will often be known for commonly-used estimators since $\boldsymbol{q}(\boldsymbol{\theta}) = \mathbf{0}$ defines the estimator-generating equation (see Ch.10); alternatively, a difference approximation to $\boldsymbol{q}(\cdot)$ can be based on function values alone, as discussed below.

The properties of the DFP algorithm can be understood most easily by considering its application to minimizing the quadratic $f(\boldsymbol{\theta}) = h_0 + \boldsymbol{\kappa}'\boldsymbol{\theta} + \boldsymbol{\theta}'\boldsymbol{H}\boldsymbol{\theta}/2$ with $\boldsymbol{q}(\boldsymbol{\theta}) = \boldsymbol{\kappa} + \boldsymbol{H}\boldsymbol{\theta}$. First:

$$\boldsymbol{p}_i = \boldsymbol{q}(\boldsymbol{\theta}_{i+1}) - \boldsymbol{q}(\boldsymbol{\theta}_i) = \boldsymbol{H}\boldsymbol{\theta}_{i+1} - \boldsymbol{H}\boldsymbol{\theta}_i = \boldsymbol{H}\boldsymbol{d}_i. \tag{A5.94}$$

Moreover, the set $(\boldsymbol{d}_1 \ldots \boldsymbol{d}_m)$ are mutually conjugate $(\boldsymbol{d}_i'\boldsymbol{H}\boldsymbol{d}_j = 0$ for $i \neq j)$ as in the method of conjugate directions. Then, post-multiplying $\boldsymbol{D}_i$ in (A5.92) by $\boldsymbol{p}_i$ yields:

$$\boldsymbol{D}_i \boldsymbol{p}_i = \boldsymbol{d}_i - \boldsymbol{K}_i \boldsymbol{p}_i$$

so that from (A5.91):

$$\boldsymbol{K}_{i+1} \boldsymbol{p}_i = \boldsymbol{d}_i. \tag{A5.95}$$

The mutual conjugacy of the $\boldsymbol{d}_i$, together with $\boldsymbol{p}_i = \boldsymbol{H}\boldsymbol{d}_i$ from (A5.94), implies that $\boldsymbol{d}_j'\boldsymbol{p}_i = 0$ $(i \neq j)$. Hence $\boldsymbol{p}_j'\boldsymbol{K}_{i+1}\boldsymbol{p}_i = 0$ $\forall i < j$ from (A5.95), leading to $\boldsymbol{D}_j \boldsymbol{p}_i = \mathbf{0}$ $\forall i < j$ from (A5.92). Thus:

$$\boldsymbol{K}_j \boldsymbol{p}_i = \boldsymbol{d}_i \text{ for } i = 1, \ldots, j-1.$$

When $j = m + 1$, using (A5.94):

$$\boldsymbol{K}_{m+1} \boldsymbol{H} (\boldsymbol{d}_1 \ldots \boldsymbol{d}_m) = (\boldsymbol{d}_1 \ldots \boldsymbol{d}_m) \quad \text{or} \quad \boldsymbol{K}_{m+1} \boldsymbol{H} = \boldsymbol{I}_m,$$

so that $K_{m+1} = H^{-1}$ as required.

If $K_1 = I_m$, the first step is that of steepest descent (so appropriate scaling is important), and as the iteration proceeds, K_i tends to the inverse of $H(\cdot)$ (assuming that $\ell(\cdot)$ can be approximated by a quadratic), so the metric becomes more appropriate. If an initial positive-definite estimate of $H(\cdot)^{-1}$ is available, this could be used for K_1 and should improve the speed of convergence. It has been found, however, that $q_i' K_i q_i$ is monotonically decreasing, and to avoid successively smaller values of $K_i q_i$, the procedure may have to be restarted occasionally at a new K_1.

A variant has been proposed by Gill, Murray, and Pitfield (denoted GMP) which current evidence suggests is more efficient than DFP. Instead of approximating $H(\cdot)^{-1}$ iteratively, the GMP form solves for θ_1^c from:

$$A_i \theta_i^c = q(\theta_i), \tag{A5.96}$$

where $A_i = B_i \Lambda_i B_i'$ with Λ_i diagonal and B_i lower triangular with unit values on its diagonal. Thus, θ_1^c can be obtained by first solving for u_i from $B_i u_i = q_i$, then solving for θ_1^c from $B_i' \theta_1^c = \Lambda_i^{-1} u_i$, where both sets of equations involve relatively simple recursive formulae. The matrix A_i can be updated by rules like (A5.91) combined with variants of (A5.92) or (A5.93), designed to ensure that A_{i+1} is positive definite and θ_{i+1} is obtained as in (A5.90) (although GMP use a cubic approximation for the line searches).

The last technique we consider is a quasi-Newton method that approximates the inverse Hessian, $H(\theta)^{-1}$ according to the Broyden–Fletcher–Goldfarb–Shanno (BFGS) update (see Gill *et al.*, 1981). Either analytic or numerical first derivatives, $q(\theta)$ can be used. Select K_i as an approximation to $H(\cdot)^{-1}$ to satisfy the quasi-Newton condition $K_{i+1} p_i = d_i$, and possess the properties of hereditary symmetry (K_{i+1} is symmetric if K_i is), hereditary positive definiteness, and super-linear convergence. Then the BFGS updating formula is:

$$K_{i+1} = K_i + \left(1 + \frac{p_i' K_i p_i}{p_i' d_i}\right) \frac{d_i d_i'}{p_i' d_i} - \frac{d_i p_i' K_i + K_i p_i d_i'}{p_i' d_i}. \tag{A5.97}$$

There is a close correspondence between the logic underlying recursive least squares (updating of the inverse second-moment matrix as the sample size increases as in Ch.3) and the BFGS method for sequential updating of the inverse Hessian by rank-two updates as the number of iterations increases. When the analytic formula for $q(\theta)$ is available, the variable-metric approach appears to be an efficient algorithm for non-linear optimization of general functions $\ell(\theta)$, especially if there are no special features to be exploited. BFGS seems a reliable choice in that group.

Even if analytic first derivative cannot be obtained, versions of variable-metric algorithms using numerical approximations to $q(\cdot)$, based on function values alone, seem to outperform the Powell algorithm in many situations, while providing an equal degree of flexibility in the choice of parameters in $\ell(\cdot)$. The numerical derivatives are calculated using:

$$\frac{[\ell(\theta + \mu\iota) - \ell(\theta - \delta\mu\iota)]}{(1+\delta)\mu} \simeq \frac{\partial \ell(\cdot)}{\partial(\iota'\theta)} \tag{A5.98}$$

where ι is now a unit vector (e.g. $(10\ldots0)$ for the first element of $\boldsymbol{\theta}$), μ is a suitably chosen step-length, and δ is either zero or unity depending on the accuracy required at the given stage of the iteration. Thus, μ represents a compromise between round-off error (cancellation of leading digits when subtracting nearly equal numbers and then dividing by a very small number), and truncation error (ignoring terms of higher order than μ in the approximation). It is worth noting that numerical values of second derivatives $\partial^2\ell(\cdot)/\partial(\iota_1'\boldsymbol{\theta})\partial(\iota_2'\boldsymbol{\theta})$ can be computed in a corresponding way using:

$$\frac{[\ell(\boldsymbol{\theta}+\boldsymbol{\mu}_1+\boldsymbol{\mu}_2)+\ell(\boldsymbol{\theta}-\boldsymbol{\mu}_1-\boldsymbol{\mu}_2)-\ell(\boldsymbol{\theta}-\boldsymbol{\mu}_1+\boldsymbol{\mu}_2)-\ell(\boldsymbol{\theta}+\boldsymbol{\mu}_1-\boldsymbol{\mu}_2)]}{4\mu_1\mu_2} \tag{A5.99}$$

where $\boldsymbol{\mu}_i = \mu_i\iota_i$ $(i = 1, 2)$, and ι_1 or ι_2 are zero except for unity in the ith or j^{th} position: compare the scalar equivalent following (A5.36) above. When computed from the MLE $\hat{\boldsymbol{\theta}}$, (A5.99) yields a reasonably good approximation to $\boldsymbol{H}(\hat{\boldsymbol{\theta}})$ for use in calculating the variance matrix of $\hat{\boldsymbol{\theta}}$.

A5.6 Conclusion

The main optimization algorithms discussed above were categorized according to type such as step-wise, modified Newton–Raphson, conjugate directions, and variable metric. This organization was dictated by the aim of highlighting the inter-relationships between the numerical and the statistical aspects of optimizing likelihood functions. For practical purposes, a more useful categorization is according to which order of derivative can be obtained analytically and programmed without excessive labour input. Thus the three main cases are when the following are available (for general functions):

(a) $\ell(\boldsymbol{\theta})$ only;
(b) $\ell(\cdot)$ and $\boldsymbol{q}(\boldsymbol{\theta})$; and
(c) $\ell(\cdot)$, $\boldsymbol{q}(\cdot)$, and $\boldsymbol{H}(\boldsymbol{\theta})$.

(a) *No derivatives*
When only function values are available, the choice is between a conjugate-directions method and a variable-metric method using finite differences. The former method has proved reliable for a range of econometric estimation problems, but present experience suggests that BFGS is generally faster and also rarely fails to converge. (see Hendry, Neale and Srba, 1988).

(b) *Analytic first derivatives*
If the analytic score equation is available, that variant of BFGS seems a good choice, as in PcFiml 8 (see Doornik and Hendry, 1994a), usually being considerably faster than either algorithm in (a).

(c) *Analytic first and second derivatives*
When analytic second derivatives have been programmed, a modified Newton–Raphson algorithm seems most efficient.

Even such general guidelines as those offered above need to be qualified if a good choice of algorithm is to be made for a specific problem. Thus, account should be taken of the relative costs of calculating $\ell(\cdot)$, $\boldsymbol{q}(\cdot)$, and $\boldsymbol{H}(\cdot)$; of inverting $\boldsymbol{H}(\cdot)$; of the flexibility of the resulting computer program; of any special features of the estimator such as those which make the step-wise method efficient in some cases; or of the function, such as when $\ell(\cdot)$ is a sum of squares of non-linear functions; and so on. No method has proved best for all problems — nor is such an algorithm likely to be produced; however, those techniques noted under (a)–(c) seem to operate with a high degree of success in practice. The present state of the science (art?) of numerical optimization, and the computational speeds of modern computers, are such that large estimation problems can be solved quickly and cheaply. Many estimators which were once described as 'computationally burdensome' or complex are now as easy to use as OLS: for example, PcFiml computes full-information maximum likelihood estimates recursively. Thus, the complexity of the appropriate estimator is no longer a binding constraint, although it remains easy to invent large, highly non-linear problems which would be prohibitively expensive to solve.

A5.7 Exercises

A5.1 Discuss the application of alternative non-linear numerical optimization techniques for computing the maximum likelihood estimator $\tilde{\boldsymbol{\theta}}$ of $\boldsymbol{\theta}$ in the model:

$$y_t = f_1\left(\boldsymbol{z}_t, \boldsymbol{\theta}\right) + f_2\left(\boldsymbol{z}_t, \boldsymbol{g}\left(\boldsymbol{\theta}\right)\right) + \epsilon_t, \tag{A5.100}$$

where $\epsilon_t \sim \mathsf{IN}[0, \sigma_\epsilon^2]$ and $\mathsf{E}[\boldsymbol{z}_t \epsilon_t] = \mathbf{0}$ when $\boldsymbol{g}(\boldsymbol{\theta})$ is a non-linear vector function of the $k \times 1$ vector $\boldsymbol{\theta}$, and $f_1(\cdot)$ and $f_2(\cdot)$ are non-linear scalar functions of the $n \times 1$ vector $\boldsymbol{z}_t$ and $\boldsymbol{\theta}$ for $n > k$; $\boldsymbol{g}(\cdot)$, $f_1(\cdot)$, and $f_2(\cdot)$ could differ substantially in specification between problems.

(a) Explain the main steps in the algorithm or algorithms you propose.

(b) Derive the score and Hessian.

(c) Describe how to compute approximate variances for $\tilde{\boldsymbol{\theta}}$.

(d) Explain how to test the following hypotheses:

(i) H_1: $\boldsymbol{g}(\boldsymbol{\theta}) = \mathbf{0}$;
(ii) H_2: $\boldsymbol{\theta} = \mathbf{0}$;
(iii) H_3: $\boldsymbol{h}(\boldsymbol{\theta}) = \mathbf{0}$;

where $\boldsymbol{h}(\boldsymbol{\theta})$ is a differentiable vector function of $\boldsymbol{\theta}$, with full-rank Jacobian matrix.

(Oxford M.Phil., 1984)

A6

Macro-Econometric Models

The main ingredients of macro-econometric systems are described, including the most important equations and variables, and the sectors and markets they describe. The resulting system is a caricature of a large practical model, but illustrates the main relationships of the major sectors including: household (consumption, saving, wealth accumulation, and labour supply); company (investment, labour demand, output, and inventory accumulation); financial (money, bonds, and interest rates); overseas (imports, exports, exchange rates, and capital flows); and government (taxes, expenditure, and bond creation). An artificial-data example illustrates the analysis.

A6.1 Introduction

An economic system has millions of separate but interdependent agents, producing, consuming, and transacting thousands of commodities and services every day. Economic activity consists in taking the existing state of nature (land; raw materials; physical capital such as buildings, roads, machinery, and vehicles; stocks of intermediate and finished commodities; and human inputs with their myriad skills, abilities, and knowledge) and operating on it by a flow of inputs, namely the services of the items in parentheses, to produce a new flow of intermediate and final goods and services. These are then consumed, invested, stored and traded, although some outputs have negative value (pollution and waste) and others are non-renewable. Economies comprise various sectors (household, firm, government, foreign) and many markets (for goods and services, money, financial assets, labour, housing, foreign exchange). Some agents may buy in one market and sell in another, or may operate across all sectors and markets, both buying and selling (as a consumer and a producer; a supplier of goods and a purchaser of labour services; a lender to a bank but a borrower from a mortgage company, etc.). Consequently, economies are high-dimensional objects which tend to evolve over time, are inherently dynamic and innovative, and exhibit considerable inter-temporal variation.

The objective of a macro-econometric model is to explain the empirical behaviour of the economic system including its growth, cyclical, seasonal, and erratic patterns, changing rates of inflation, levels of output and unemployment, and so on. Empirical macro models are systems of inter-linked equations estimated from time-series data using econometric techniques. The basic formulation of a macro model has one set of magnitudes (called endogenous variables as their behaviour is modelled within the system) determined by functions of lagged values of variables in the system and variables determined outside the system (e.g. policy or world variables). A system needs as many independent, consistent equations as there are endogenous variables in order to determine outcomes uniquely within the model. The equations must capture the regularities inherent in human economic behaviour if the predictions from the model are to be of use and mirror reality. Unknowns in the model must be estimated accurately and precisely. We are not concerned in this chapter with how that is done or whether it could be done better: the main text deals with such issues. Instead, this chapter concerns the structure of macro models, their general rationale, their major building blocks and equations, how they are analysed, and to what ends they are applied. In debates about the behaviour of an economy, empirically estimated macro-econometric systems help in:

(a) forecasting future outcomes;
(b) economic theory evaluation; and
(c) economic policy analyses.

For example, in the UK, HM Treasury's macro-econometric model plays a major role in (a) and (c), though less so in (b). We now consider their ingredients.

A6.2 The skeletal structure of macro models

The type of macro-econometric model of interest here describes an economy as a whole: the overall price level, total unemployment, aggregate expenditure by consumers, total investment by firms, average hours worked, national tax revenue, the balance of payments deficit or surplus, the rate of interest, the stock of money issued, the size of the government budget, and so on. Even the smallest economy-wide model will be large, a remark which applies to the skeletal structure presented here. When many disaggregate variables are also modelled, very large systems result (300–1000 or more equations).[1]

A6.2.1 Modelled variables

Each variable to be explained in the system, like investment in physical capital (denoted I), is affected by a number of factors. For example, investment is usually influenced by the cost of borrowing (R) to finance the investment, the amount of existing spare capacity (dependent on the capital stock K and the demand for output Q), the cost of capital equipment (P_K) relative to labour input (often taken as the wage W, perhaps adjusted for related labour costs), profits, and tax rates thereon, etc. Note the distinction between a stock (a cumulative magnitude measured at a point in time such as wealth, physical capital or the money stock), and a flow (an integral of a rate between two time periods such as income): a lake and a river are obvious analogies. Every modelled variable is

[1] Nevertheless, such systems can be run on a personal computer: for example, it is possible to design and analyse economic policies on the PC version of the Oxford Economic Forecasting (OEF) model.

subject to a cognitive theoretical analysis based on available insights and empirical evidence, then described by an equation involving the resulting determinants:

$$I = f\left(R, K, \frac{P_K}{W}, Q, \ldots\right) \quad \text{where} \quad f(\cdot) \text{ denotes a function.} \tag{A6.1}$$

These equations are then fitted to data to get quantitative estimates of the effects of R, Q etc. on I. In turn, another equation in the system may explain the determination of Q and so on. Such equations are multivariate and the system is multi-equation.

A6.2.2 Time lags

Events in the economy are contingent on the existing state and take time to happen. An investment decision by a firm may take several years to plan, acquire legal consent and finance; orders for equipment may take months to be fulfilled; buildings take around a year to construct, etc. The lags between determinants changing and outcomes materializing make the system dynamic. Lags persist even when agents are modelled as attempting to anticipate what the future will bring forth (we ignore perfect foresight as unrealistic in a world where discovery and invention are a crucial input to living standards). Extreme assumptions in models of economies can lead to instant adjustment, almost complete inertia, or random changes; rather than assuming such features, the main text allows data evidence to determine the dynamics. In this chapter, we represent dynamics by a lag of one period, without being explicit as to the length of that period.

For simplicity, we take (A6.1) to be linear as a proportion of the capital stock (the scale variable). Such a choice is based on dimensionality arguments and the nature of stock–flow connections, namely that the relevant scale for judging the size of an investment is as a proportion of the existing stock of capital. A possible formulation for quarterly data is a relationship like:

$$\Delta\left(\frac{I_t}{K_{t-1}}\right) = \alpha_0 + \alpha_1 \Delta R_{t-1} + \alpha_2 \Delta q_t + \alpha_3 \left(\frac{I_{t-1}}{K_{t-2}}\right) + \cdots \tag{A6.2}$$

where $\Delta x_t = x_t - x_{t-1}$ is the one quarter change, lower-case letters denote logs, and $\Delta(I/K)$ is the proportional change in K. Usually, economists anticipate that $\alpha_1 < 0$ (increased borrowing cost lowers the incentive to invest), $\alpha_2 > 0$ (the accelerator effect as a change in output alters investment), and $\alpha_3 < 0$ (to ensure a convergent dynamic outcome for I/K). For simplicity, we have not provided a complete list of possible determinants: the specification in terms of levels and changes is discussed below.

When I_t is measured as gross investment, made up of replacement, or maintenance, investment to offset 'wear and tear' and depreciation (I_t^r), plus net investment (I_t^n), which augments the capital stock, then:

$$I_t \equiv I_t^n + I_t^r,$$

($\equiv$ denotes an identity, where the two sides must be identically equal). By definition, the capital stock evolves according to :

$$K_t \equiv K_{t-1} + I_t^n, \tag{A6.3}$$

adding two dynamic equations, relating to the change in, and the level of, the capital stock respectively. Often $I_t^r = \delta K_{t-1}$ is taken as a convenient approximation to replacement investment, where δ is an assumed constant rate of depreciation, inducing the approximate capital stock equation:

$$K_t = (1 - \delta) K_{t-1} + I_t.$$

Nothing ensures that any of the coefficients in these equations are constants in reality (a topic of the main text), and generalizations to allow (say) δ to vary with economic conditions are easily imagined. Note how the number of equations grows as different aspects of each variable need to be modelled; this difficulty (the curse of dimensionality) will get worse as we model the determinants of I_t in turn.

A6.2.3 Error terms

All empirical macro models are stochastic and allow for error components or 'shocks' such as:

$$\epsilon_t \sim \mathsf{IN}\left[0, \sigma_\epsilon^2\right], \qquad \text{(A6.4)}$$

so that ϵ_t has a well-defined error distribution, here using an independent, normal distribution with mean zero and constant variance σ_ϵ^2. The error represents unanticipated factors in the economy, errors of measurement in the data, omitted variables, incorrect choice of $f(\cdot)$ etc. Consequently, behavioural equations are specified as:

$$\Delta\left(\frac{I_t}{K_{t-1}}\right) = \alpha_0 + \alpha_1 \Delta R_{t-1} + \alpha_2 \Delta q_t + \alpha_3 \left(\frac{I_{t-1}}{K_{t-2}}\right) + \cdots + \epsilon_t. \qquad \text{(A6.5)}$$

A6.2.4 Time aggregation

A major practical difficulty is the measure of a time interval, especially if the macro-model is to be related to a dynamic economic theory. Few dynamic stochastic systems are invariant to the frequency of the data observations. One limiting case is continuous-time decisions; an alternative is to examine the consequences when the observation frequency differs from the decision frequency, and we briefly do so here. Let decisions on a variable X_t be made by economic agents at intervals denoted 1,2,3,..., whereas observations are at m, $2m$, $3m$ etc. For end-of-period stocks, the observations are X_m, $X_{2m}, X_{3m}, \ldots$, so in effect we just sample less often. For flows, we must cumulate X_t over m of the original intervals, and denoting the new flow by X_t^*, then:

$$X_{jm}^* = \sum_{i=(j-1)m+1}^{jm} X_i.$$

Responses through time, such as measured lagged adjustment, may be distorted by such aggregation over time. Modellers rely on governmental agencies for most of their data, and in OECD countries, tend to use quarterly observations (sometimes supplemented by monthly, and, less often, annual data).

A6.2.5 Interdependence

Economic behaviour is highly interdependent: when I_t is higher than an economy can sustain (e.g. when the industries producing investment goods are at full capacity), then R_t might increase in response to the pressure of demand for finance, so we must allow for such connections. Likewise, what is investment for the car industry (a new factory) is output for the building industry, wages for workers, demand for bricks for the brick industry, and, eventually, more demand for cars (from the building contractors). The best analogy (once suggested by Terence Gorman) is a water-bed: shake it anywhere and it shakes everywhere eventually. The usefulness of a model depends on its ability to capture the salient links.

A6.2.6 Size

Economies are huge with up to 200 million consumers in OECD countries, and more than one billion in China. There is a vast number of commodities and services: ships, apples, telephone calls, haircuts, bus rides, education etc., and each of us consumes many thousands of such things per annum. Thus, the total number of transactions is simply beyond our ability to monitor. We must aggregate and look only at, say, total expenditure on durable goods by households as one variable, or total tax revenue. The sheer size and complexity of the macro economy preclude accurate or comprehensive modelling.

A6.2.7 The economy as a system

The economic system is not like any one of its components. My expenditure reduces my bank balance, but it is someone else's income and their bank balance goes up. We must anticipate some surprises when we piece together the whole structure. Equally, in a decentralized economic system, coordination failures are possible, namely different groups of agents may make plans which are incompatible or mutually inconsistent (this was a central concern of Keynes, 1936). In particular, outcomes must reconcile these disparate plans, and so something must adjust to equate desires with realizations. In micro-economic theory, prices are generally assumed to fulfil such a role, but at the aggregate level, quantities may adjust first (see e.g. Hahn, 1988).

A further system characteristic is that even if every equation is linear by itself, the system cannot be. There are quantities (Q: kilos of apples), prices (P: £1 per kilo) and values (V: apple sales of £25 million per annum), but $V := P \cdot Q$ where the symbol $:=$ denotes 'is defined to be equal to'. For economic magnitudes which are inherently positive, logarithms provide a useful transform which linearizes products: $v := p + q$. Unfortunately, other aspects then go wrong. For example, total income Y is the sum $\sum_{i=1}^{n} Y_i$ of each individual's income Y_i, but $\log Y \neq \sum \log Y_i$. More generally, linear identities do not hold and have no convenient log-linear approximations. Even so, in practice, estimated econometric systems seem quite close to linearity, so to help us understand macro models, we take them to be linear initially.

A6.3 The national income accounts

Finally, the measurement system at the national level is a human invention, based on national income accounts originally designed to be a consistent and operational system for guiding government policy. This system of national accounts is based on the fundamental identity:

$$E \equiv Y \equiv Q. \tag{A6.6}$$

What is earned (Y denotes income) is spent (E is expenditure) in exchanged for output (Q), all in nominal or value terms. Several important issues arise.

A6.3.1 Commodity flows

Commodities flow round an economic system in the opposite direction to money. Money comes out of your pocket into a theatre till and in exchange you see the play and consume the actors' services: money goes to the bookstore and the books to you. Thus, two flows must be modelled: a monetary one and a physical one, flowing in opposite directions. Moreover, these flows must be mutually consistent.

A6.3.2 Aggregating economic transactions

£1 from you and £1 from me add to £2; but what is a tractor plus a house? Or an apple plus a haircut? To make sense of the physical side and keep it consistent with the monetary one, we exploit the definition $E := P \cdot Q$. First add up values (nominal expenditures) across all items (N of them, say) to calculate total nominal expenditure $E = \sum_{i=1}^{N} E_i$. Every individual item has a price, and from these we can develop an average price, or price index, of the form:

$$P = \sum_{j=1}^{N} \omega_j P_j \text{ where } \sum_{i=1}^{N} \omega_i = 1,$$

where the index is weighted by the relative importance of the commodity in total expenditure. A natural choice for ω_i is the value share $= E_i/E$ which automatically ensures that $\sum_{i=1}^{N} \omega_i = 1$. Finally, treat P as the price of E, and divide total nominal expenditure by the price index to calculate the average real quantity as $Q := E/P$.

A6.3.3 Reconciling nominal and real magnitudes

If the national accounts are to hold in both nominal and real terms, approximations must be made. Say $E \equiv C + I$ where only consumers spend (C) and firms invest (I), so the economy is a closed one with no government. Adding over the different commodities, the equations $C = \sum C_j$ and $I = \sum I_j$ hold in nominal terms. The price indices $P^{(c)}$ and $P^{(i)}$ are:

$$P^{(c)} = \sum_{j=1}^{N} \omega_j^{(c)} P_j^{(c)} \text{ and } P^{(i)} = \sum_{j=1}^{N} \omega_j^{(i)} P_j^{(i)}$$

where the indices are weighted by the value shares of their own commodity groups. From these price indices, we can construct measures of constant-price, or real, expenditure in each group (temporarily using lower-case letters for real-value magnitudes) by $c := C/P^{(c)}$ and $i := I/P^{(i)}$, from which $e \equiv c + i$ could be constructed as real total expenditure. Usually, value shares differ, so that the weights $\{\omega_j^{(c)}\}$ and $\{\omega_j^{(i)}\}$ are different between C and I. Aggregate across all commodity expenditures to define the corresponding overall price index:

$$P^{(e)} = \sum_{j=1}^{N} \omega_j^{(e)} P_j^{(e)}. \tag{A6.7}$$

Generally, $P^{(e)} \neq P^{(c)}$ and $P^{(e)} \neq P^{(i)}$, so that now $E/P^{(e)} \neq e$, whereas equality is needed for a consistent set of national accounts.

To resolve this difficulty, construct a new entity called an implicit deflator. Let $e \equiv c + i$ be total real expenditure defined as the sum of component real expenditures, then define $P_{(e)} := E/e$ as the implicit deflator of E needed to ensure that both $e \equiv c + i$ and $E \equiv C + I$ hold simultaneously. Note that $P^{(e)} \neq P_{(e)}$ now, so care is needed in choosing price indices. In practice, we construct disaggregate price indices to compute disaggregate real magnitudes, but rather than use aggregated price indices like $P^{(e)}$ in (A6.7), we reconcile aggregates by defining implicit-price indices $P_{(e)}$ which ensure that identities hold in both nominal and real terms. Over time, major departures can occur between price indices due to changes in the composition of the 'basket' of commodities and services on which the $\{\omega_j\}$ are based. This issue is considered in Chapter 12.

A6.4 The components of macro models

A6.4.1 Kinds of variables

Not all variables in a macroeconomic system are modelled, since only endogenous variables are explained within the model. Those variables that are not modelled are sometimes called exogenous, but that name can be misleading as it connotes that the variable is in fact determined outside the economic system under study, a property that is not automatically endowed on a variable merely by choosing not to model it: either non-modelled, or extraneous, are preferable names. Also, there are lagged values of both kinds of variable, sometimes called predetermined to denote that their values are already fixed: again this is a potentially misleading name, so we generally just call them lagged.

A second important distinction is between latent and realized variables. The former include plans and expectations formulated in advance of actions (e.g. supply and demand, planned output, expected inflation etc.), whereas the latter are their actual outcomes (with the possibility that the measured outcomes may differ from the realized values). Economists distinguish between *ex ante* (before the event) and *ex post* (after the event). *Ex ante* it is not known who will win a competition; *ex post* it is obvious. *Ex ante* you may plan to carry out certain actions (e.g. buy a kilo of apples); *ex post* you may or may not have done so (e.g. if the price were 10p. per kilo, you may buy two kilos and make an apple pie; or if £2 per kilo, you may buy oranges instead). Plans and expectations are *ex ante* constructs, outcomes are *ex post*.

A6.4.2 Kinds of equations

Just as there are several kinds of variables, there are several kinds of equations. The most important of these are:

(a) behavioural equations, such as (A6.2), which seek to represent the behaviour of economic agents;
(b) identity, or exact, equations like (A6.3), which hold by accounting convention, without error terms;
(c) technical equations which are given by the technology of the society;
(d) equilibrium equations (denoted by $\overset{e}{=}$) which define the conditions for an equilibrium to occur;[2]
(e) stock–flow equations such as $\Delta K_t \equiv I_t^n$;
(f) adjustment equations showing how temporary disequilibria are removed;
(g) expectational equations relating expectations formation to available information;
(h) observability equations relating latent variables to observed outcomes.

Although the chapter seeks to explain macro-econometric models, we first discuss the issues in the context of a single market. Denote by ^{p} a plan made *ex ante* about a variable which the relevant agent controls; ^{e} an expectation formed on the basis of available information (denoted $\mathcal{I}_{t-1}$) about an uncontrolled variable which enters the plan, where the conditional expectations operator is denoted by $\mathsf{E}[\cdot \mid \cdot]$; ^{o} an outcome; Q^d quantity demanded; Q^s quantity supplied; Q the quantity transacted; and P the price at which it is transacted.[3] Since Q^d and Q^s are planned magnitudes, an additional superscript ^{p} is redundant; alternatively, a different Q^p is needed for suppliers and demanders. Similarly, Q is the outcome by assumption and so ^{o} is not needed (what any of these magnitudes is measured to be in reality is yet another matter, dependent on the accuracy and comprehensiveness of the measurement process). Let Y_t be national income and K_{t-1} the relevant national capital stock from which Q_t is produced or is producible, where both Y_t and K_{t-1} are given and non-modelled. Consider the following simple market model:

behavioural:

$$Q_t^d = f_1\left(Y_t^e, P_t^e, \epsilon_{1t}\right) \text{ and } Q_t^s = f_2\left(K_{t-1}, P_t^e, \epsilon_{2t}\right); \qquad \text{(A6.8)}$$

equilibrium:

$$Q_t^d \overset{e}{=} Q_t^s; \qquad \text{(A6.9)}$$

[2] It would introduce a long digression to define equilibrium precisely. That concept might mean: (a) a state with no inherent tendency to change; (b) a situation in which a market clears; (c) a stationary point of a dynamic process; or (d) a state in which no rational agent will change their strategy given the strategies of other agents. These notions can coincide, but often differ. Generally, we use the first as the meaning of equilibrium, refering to the second as market clearing.

[3] Subsets of transactions could be made at different prices, but that is a different problem from the issues on which we focus here.

observability:

$$Q_t = \xi\left(Q_t^d, Q_t^s\right); \tag{A6.10}$$

adjustment:

$$P_t = P_{t-1} + \phi\left(Q_t^d - Q_t^s\right) + \epsilon_{3t}; \tag{A6.11}$$

expectations formation:

$$P_t^e = \mathsf{E}\left[P_t \mid \mathcal{I}_{t-1}\right] \text{ and } Y_t^e = \mathsf{E}\left[Y_t \mid \mathcal{I}_{t-1}\right]. \tag{A6.12}$$

In (A6.8), demand is assumed to depend on expected incomes and prices (formulated in (A6.12) as conditional expectations given an information set $\mathcal{I}_{t-1}$), and supply depends on capacity and profitability (proxied by expected prices). Equilibrium occurs when supply equals demand, and (A6.11) induces price changes otherwise. What is observed depends on the specification of the mapping $\xi(Q_t^d, Q_t^s)$. The $\{\epsilon_{it}\}$ are assumed to be independent of each other, of the arguments in the $f_i(\cdot)$, and of $\mathcal{I}_{t-1}$. The roles of these various constructs and equations will appear as we proceed.

A6.4.3 Behavioural equations

The investment equation in (A6.2) was intended to be behavioural (describing how investors behave), with I_t endogenous, R, P_K/W, and Q non-modelled, and K_{t-1} lagged. It is unlikely that any of the non-modelled variables could be legitimately treated as exogenous in this context. Behavioural equations characterize the plans on which agents base their actions, and make a weak-rationality assumption: agents are assumed to plan such that they will achieve their plans on average. There seems little point in making plans that are not expected to be achieved; nevertheless, the assumption has important empirical implications. When the plan at time t is y_t^p, the outcome is y_t, and the deviation of the outcome from the plan is $\nu_t = y_t - y_t^p$. Thus, the assumption entails:

$$\mathsf{E}\left[y_t \mid y_t^p\right] = y_t^p \text{ so that } \mathsf{E}\left[\nu_t \mid y_t^p\right] = 0.$$

Consequently, no information used in formulating the plan can explain the deviation from the plan. If the plan used past values of the outcomes, then the deviations cannot be serially correlated.

A6.4.4 Identity equations

$E \equiv Y$ is an identity, fixed by national income accounting conventions. It is important to be clear about the role of identities, as these only hold *ex post*, not *ex ante*. By definition $E \equiv Y$ *ex post*; but *ex ante*, spenders may not plan to spend all of their income, perhaps planning net saving. If consumers planned to save more than firms planned to invest, firms would not sell all the output they had produced, inventories would accumulate and so firms would cut back production and lay off workers, perhaps causing incomes to fall. This process continues till plans match, even though by definition $E \equiv Y$ throughout. The identity is usually achieved by defining inventory accumulation as part of expenditure, even when it is not desired by firms. Identities must hold and cannot cause anything. A failure to be clear on this point has induced some confused analyses in economics. For example, consider the simplest 'Keynesian' model:

$$C_t = \beta Y_t + \epsilon_{1t} \text{ where } I_t = \phi R_t + \epsilon_{2t} \text{ and } Y_t \equiv C_t + I_t,$$

where consumption is explained as a function of income, investment by the interest rate, and R_t is non-modelled. In such a model, income appears to be generated by adding up expenditure (rather than produced by work!). The identity has been substituted out by $Y_t \equiv E_t \equiv C_t + I_t$ and so is an allocation equation, stating that income can only be either consumed or invested ($\equiv$ saved), which has no causal connotations. Here, the errors $\{\epsilon_{it}\}$ are independent of R_t and each other, but cannot be independent of Y_t since, by substitution, the identity entails:

$$Y_t = \frac{\phi R_t + \epsilon_{1t} + \epsilon_{2t}}{(1-\beta)}.$$

Consequently, $\mathsf{E}[I_t|R_t] = \phi R_t$, but $\mathsf{E}[C_t|Y_t] \neq \beta Y_t$. This issue is discussed in more detail in Chapter 11.

A6.4.5 Technical equations

A production function is sometimes claimed to be a technical equation. An example is $Q = h(K, \ell, L, N, E_g, \epsilon_{2t})$ where K and ℓ denote services from capital and land, and L, N, and E_g denote input flows of (quality-adjusted) labour, intermediate goods, and energy (including natural resources). This form uses gross-input measures, but often valued-added measures are adopted so only K and L appear explicitly. In practice, the choice of technology from within existing techniques is influenced by economic considerations. Thus, a production function is technical only to the extent that the techniques must exist, and that firms use efficient modes of production within the available set; the rest is economics. At the aggregate level, a production function is one of the less clear concepts; although inputs are manifestly needed for, and hence are related to, output, a unique mapping is a bold assumption. One resolution is to set $Q^* = h(K, L, \cdots)$ where Q^* is optimum output, then introduce a production plan that seeks to minimize the deviations of planned output from the optimum, given the behaviour of inventories; finally, map plans for output, inputs and inventories onto outcomes as in §A6.4.3 (see e.g. Holt, Modigliani, Muth and Simon, 1960).

A6.4.6 Equilibrium conditions

'Supply equals demand' is an equilibrium condition of a market-clearing kind. This should be denoted by $Q^s \stackrel{e}{=} Q^d$ (read as 'supply equals demand in equilibrium') to clarify that equality need not hold, but when it does hold, then an equilibrium occurs in the sense defined. A macro model needs to embody the forces which bring about equilibrium, and should not obtain outcomes (such as clearing) by assertion. For example, $\Delta K_t \stackrel{e}{=} 0$ is a static-equilibrium condition (of the 'no change' variety) but the forces which drive the system towards such an outcome need to be specified as well as the form of the resulting equilibrium. Corresponding dynamic or steady-state solutions take the form $\Delta K_t/K_{t-1} \stackrel{e}{=} g$ for a (constant) growth rate g. In such a scenario, $I_t \stackrel{e}{=} (g+\delta)K_{t-1}$, which is also a steady-state solution of (A6.2) above.

A temporary equilibrium may be achieved between flows (such as net investment becoming a non-zero constant) which by their nature induce a stock to alter, and hence destroy the previous equilibrium. The simple Keynesian model above implicitly made $E \stackrel{e}{=} Y$ an equilibrium condition, achieved by an unspecified adjustment process. Here, equilibria are hypothetical states defined by a position (path) of no (constant) change; they need not hold, and their not holding can cause a great deal to happen. A difficult issue relates to the choice of variables which adjust to achieve an equilibrium. Possible contenders include domestic prices and output; inventories; imports; unemployment; interest rates; financial assets; and government deficits. In the later analysis, we introduce a different, but related, notion of equilibrium based on the concepts of equilibrium correction and cointegration.

A6.4.7 Stock–flow equations

Inventories I_{vt} occur when either the good produced or the inputs to its production process are durable. In the former case, when output Q_t^s does not equal sales transacted Q_t^d, inventories adjust according to $I_{vt} \equiv I_{vt-1} + Q_t^s - Q_t^d$. Sometimes, implicit changes in stocks due to differences in flows are not modelled (e.g. wealth in response to savings or capital revaluations), which can generate misleading implications from models.

A6.4.8 Adjustment equations

Equation (A6.11) is a typical *ad hoc* adjustment process which implies that P_t alters so long as $Q_t^d \neq Q_t^s$, and is the mechanism whereby the postulated equilibrium in §A6.4.6 is achieved. However, other adjustment processes may hold in reality. There is little economic theory of market-adjustment processes, since in the absence of an auctioneer, no specific agent has the objective of minimizing the costs of market adjustment. At best, an arbitrageur may operate to exploit price differentials. Even when identifiable agents are involved (firms, for example), classical economic theory finds it difficult to account for their appearing empirically to be quantity rather than price adjusters in response to demand changes, so what is called a non-Walrasian approach seems needed (see Benassy, 1986). Thus, in reality, most macro models contain large numbers of adjustment equations obtained by their proprietors as the best empirical descriptions.

A6.4.9 Expectations formation

The postulated expectations equations seek to model how the agents form their expectations using the information set $\mathcal{I}_{t-1}$. For the moment, the same information is assumed to be used by both suppliers and demanders (which will not usually be true), and for prices and incomes (again, different information will generally be relevant for different variables). No problem arises in a theory model from making $\mathcal{I}_{t-1}$ the union of all non-redundant information, but this poses severe problems in empirical econometrics where data are scarce. It is a strong assumption to treat statistical operators like $\mathsf{E}[\cdot \mid \mathcal{I}_{t-1}]$

as corresponding to latent constructs such as Y^e, and entails that agents process information using knowledge of the economic mechanism (or a valid representation thereof). Whether or not the result is an accurate expectation depends on the contents of $\mathcal{I}_{t-1}$; and whether or not it is sensible to form expectations with complete information depends on the costs of collecting and processing relevant information (including discovering the data-generation process) versus the benefits resulting from the improvement in the accuracy of the expectation. In practice, it is doubtful if the contents of $\mathcal{I}_t$ are exogenously determined (see Feige and Pearce, 1976, and Ch.6).

A6.4.10 Observation equations

The conflation of observation equations with causal links has also clouded economic analysis. Many models of the mapping $\xi(\cdot,\cdot)$ from plans and expectations to outcomes are possible, and three distinct cases of the former are noted in §A6.5.2. It is sometimes assumed that $Q_t^d = Q_t^s = Q_t$, which mixes *ex ante* with *ex post*, as well as equilibrium conditions with observational equations. Demand and supply equations *per se* do not determine P and Q (there are two equations for four unknowns); the assertion of clearing really determines the outcome, but hardly constitutes an explanation. Dynamics should be specified explicitly, allowing convergence to the equilibrium to be investigated (see Samuelson, 1947). The model for Q_t^s here mixes behavioural and technical aspects by conflating planned supply with the output producible from the production process. In some models, planned supply is assumed to depend on expected future prices, and is equated to actual output by clearing, so commodities arrive out of thin air.

A6.5 A simultaneous system of equations

This simplest economic model of a market has raised many issues about how prices are determined. Economists have sought to solve some of these by formulating economic systems as sets of simultaneous equations. If we ignore the distinction between the expected variables and their outcomes, and take linear approximations to $f_1(\cdot)$, $f_2(\cdot)$, and $\phi(\cdot)$, then the exemplar system becomes:

$$\begin{aligned} Q_t^d &= \alpha_0 + \alpha_1 Y_t + \alpha_2 P_t + \epsilon_{1t} & & \alpha_1 > 0,\ \alpha_2 < 0 \\ Q_t^s &= \beta_0 + \beta_1 K_{t-1} + \beta_2 P_t + \epsilon_{2t} & \text{where} \quad & \beta_1 > 0,\ \beta_2 > 0 \\ P_t &= P_{t-1} + \phi\left(Q_t^d - Q_t^s\right) + \epsilon_{3t} & & \phi > 0 \\ Q_t &= \xi\left(Q_t^d, Q_t^s, P_t\right). & & \end{aligned} \qquad \text{(A6.13)}$$

The final equation has been generalized to allow the outcome to depend on the price. The assumptions about the $\{\epsilon_{it}\}$ are as before.

A6.5.1 Price dynamics

Solve for P_t from the first three equations:

$$P_t = P_{t-1} + \phi\left\{(\alpha_0 - \beta_0) + \alpha_1 Y_t - \beta_1 K_{t-1}\right\} + \phi\left(\alpha_2 - \beta_2\right) P_t + \phi\left(\epsilon_{1t} - \epsilon_{2t}\right) + \epsilon_{3t} \qquad \text{(A6.14)}$$

where $\{\cdot\}$ denotes the non-modelled component. The solved price equation is:

$$P_t = \mu\left[P_{t-1} + \{\cdot\}\right] + \nu_t \quad \text{where} \quad \mu = \left[1 - \phi\left(\alpha_2 - \beta_2\right)\right]^{-1} \tag{A6.15}$$

and $\nu_t = \mu[\phi(\epsilon_{1t} - \epsilon_{2t}) + \epsilon_{3t}]$ when $\phi(\alpha_2 - \beta_2) \neq 1$. Since $\phi(\alpha_2 - \beta_2) < 0$, then $0 < \mu < 1$, so (A6.15) is a stable difference equation. Let Y and K settle at Y^* and K^* respectively, and take expected values so the errors vanish, then (A6.14) has the static equilibrium solution $P_t = P_{t-1} = P^*$ yielding:

$$P^* = \frac{\left[(\alpha_0 - \beta_0) + \alpha_1 Y^* - \beta_1 K^*\right]}{(\beta_2 - \alpha_2)}. \tag{A6.16}$$

Define P_t^* corresponding to using the actual values Y_t and K_{t-1} in (A6.16):

$$P_t^* = \frac{\left[(\alpha_0 - \beta_0) + \alpha_1 Y_t - \beta_1 K_{t-1}\right]}{(\beta_2 - \alpha_2)},$$

then substituting for P_t^* in (A6.15):

$$(P_t - P_t^*) = \mu\left(P_{t-1} - P_t^*\right) + \nu_t \quad \text{or} \quad \Delta P_t = (\mu - 1)\left(P_{t-1} - P_t^*\right) + \nu_t. \tag{A6.17}$$

Thus, prices rise (fall) when P_{t-1} is less than (exceeds) P_t^*, and (A6.17) is an example of an equilibrium-correction mechanism, in that disequilibrium prices are corrected towards the equilibrium. While the price-adjustment equation is *ad hoc* and not wholly reasonable, it does at least allow us to explain how the market achieves equilibrium prices. Stability need not occur if P_t^e is used in place of P_t, since demand may rise today if prices are expected to be higher in the future, though demand will fall if prices actually are higher.

A6.5.2 Simultaneity

A 'chicken and egg' problem arises from modelling the system as $Q_t^d = f_1(P_t, \epsilon_{1t})$, $Q_t^s = f_2(P_t, \epsilon_{2t})$, and $\Delta P_t = \phi(Q_t^d - Q_t^s) + \epsilon_{3t}$. This is resolved by solving the system simultaneously for P_t, Q_t^d, and Q_t^s. It is no surprise that P_t^* is also the price that equates Q_t^d to Q_t^s. Conversely, when $P_t^* \neq P_t$, then $Q_t^d \neq Q_t^s$, in which case, how does Q_t relate to Q_t^d and Q_t^s, and what happens to discrepancies between demand and supply? At first sight, the level of Q_t seems irrelevant in determining P_t, but it is hidden in $\{\cdot\}$ which determines the levels of Q_t^d and Q_t^s. There are three main ways of relating Q_t to Q_t^d and Q_t^s.

A6.5.2.1 Clearing: $Q_t = Q_t^d = Q_t^s$

When ϕ is essentially infinite, re-normalizing the third equation in (A6.13) yields:

$$\left(Q_t^d - Q_t^s\right) = \phi^{-1}\left(\Delta P_t - \epsilon_{3t}\right) = 0;$$

in words, prices adjust so rapidly that the market is always cleared (e.g. the market for stocks and shares). Then the quantity transacted is precisely what was demanded and supplied. In such a case, $\mu = 0$ in (A6.17) so $P_t = P_t^*$.

A6.5.2.2 Short-side: $Q_t = \min(Q_t^d, Q_t^s)$

Whichever of Q_t^d and Q_t^s is smaller is assumed to dominate the outcome. Rationing, or min-condition, markets have been proposed for a number of situations (see Quandt, 1988, for econometric analyses). However, they pose technical and conceptual difficulties, and are not fully plausible. One must agree that more cannot be bought than exists, but it is less obvious that more cannot be sold than is demanded. For example, assume that you wish to sell your two camels, and I want to buy one. Certainly no more than two can change hands; but 0, 1, or 2 might. I may be desperate to cross a desert and buy both because you refuse to sell only one; or again I might be indifferent to buying 0 or 1, you insist on both, so none is exchanged. Although the weaker condition $Q_t \leq Min(Q_t^d, Q_t^s)$ seems to follow from physical constraints, that may not be so for all definitions of latent constructs like Q_t^d and Q_t^s. When physical inventories I_{vt} can be held, and planned magnitudes depend on expectations of future prices and possible excesses or shortages, then the observed outcome could exceed both plans.

A6.5.2.3 One side lags

An example is the following system:

$$\begin{aligned} P_t &= \beta_0 + \beta_1 C_{ot} + \beta_2 P_{t-1} + \beta_3 \left(Q_{t-1} - Q_{t-1}^d\right) + \epsilon_{2t} \\ Q_t^d &= \alpha_0 + \alpha_1 Y_t + \alpha_2 P_t + \epsilon_{1t} \\ \Delta I_{vt} &= Q_t - Q_t^d \end{aligned}$$

where C_{ot} denotes costs. By distinguishing output, Q_t, from sales, $S_t = Q_t^d$, the third equation shows inventories adjusting according to the difference between production and sales. In effect, the supply side sets the price, and demand determines the volume. Many macro models use this type of formulation, assuming an imperfectly competitive environment in which firms set prices and consumers determine quantities given the prices, but prices respond to excess demand. A physically productive sector is still needed but chronic shortages are ignored ($I_{vt} \geq 0$ is not imposed, so negative inventories correspond to orders).

Such a model introduces the issue of which agents 'accept' any disequilibrium ($Q_t^d - Q_t^s$), sometimes called the residual, or buffer, problem. In practice, economies have many buffers for disequilibrium pressures, and which buffer responds depends on what other disequilibria operate. In the simplest models (clearing markets), prices are the buffer, and are assumed to adjust to clear markets. At the next level, as in the preceding example, inventories adjust, but in some models many variables such as net imports, the government deficit, and monetary variables like bank balances may adjust as well.

A6.6 Sectors and markets

We now pull together the various ingredients to formulate an embryonic macro model. The model assume that firms set prices and sell as much as they can at those prices, households determine quantities given prices, and these are the only sectors. More general models would include government, financial, and overseas sectors, and these are introduced below. There is one malleable good with a price of P_t, also used as the price unit (numeraire), and all other variables are in constant price or real terms. Households supply labour services (L_t^s) depending on the past profit rate (π_{t-1}) and wage earnings (at a rate w_t) to spend (C_t) or invest (I_t); they earn dividends (Π_t) from past investments (K_{t-1}). Firms organize production, demanding labour and capital as inputs to a production process, distributing all profits, and holding stocks (I_{vt}) of finished goods. The only markets are labour and goods, so financial and foreign exchange markets are ignored. Implicitly, all agents have objective functions which they seek to optimize subject to their constraints, available information, and endowments, but since it is difficult to formalize that approach realistically, we use it as a guide rather than as a straitjacket. Thus, agents are assumed to make simplified contingent plans given extrapolative forecasting rules for the next period. The resulting equations have been formulated for tractability rather than realism: in particular, the simple choices of arguments of functions and the lags in (A6.18)–(A6.27) help make the system solvable, although problems remain as will be seen. Further, we have omitted the stochastic component from the behavioural equations for simplicity.

A6.6.1 Households

Four equations determine the behaviour of the household sector, namely their supply of labour, consumption demand, saving (identically equal to investment here), and wages:

labour supply:

$$L_t^s = \psi\left(w_t, \pi_{t-1}, N_t\right); \; w_t \equiv \frac{W_t}{L_t}; \; \pi_t \equiv \frac{\Pi_t}{K_t}; \; Y_{dt} \equiv W_t + \Pi_t; \qquad \text{(A6.18)}$$

consumption demand:

$$C_t^d = f\left(Y_{dt-1}, \pi_t\right); \; C_t = C_t^d; \qquad \text{(A6.19)}$$

investment supply:

$$\Delta K_t \equiv Y_{dt} - C_t; \; K_t \equiv (1-\delta)\, K_{t-1} + I_t; \qquad \text{(A6.20)}$$

wage determination:

$$w_t = \theta\left(\frac{Q}{L}\right)_{t-1} - \lambda U_t; \; U_t \equiv L_t^s - L_t^d; \qquad \text{(A6.21)}$$

identities:

$$E_t \equiv C_t + I_t + I_{vt} - I_{vt-1}; \; Q_t \equiv Y_t; \; Y_t \equiv E_t.$$

Labour supply depends on the relative return to work as against investment given population (N_t), although in practice many other factors matter including benefits, demographic structure, educational attainments, etc. The first two identities define wage rates as the total-wage bill divided by employment, and the profit rate as total profits divided by the capital stock (so the price of capital is implicitly set at unity). Disposable income is equal to wages plus dividends (taxes are introduced below). Next, consumption demand is made to depend on past disposable income and the profit rate (reflecting savings decisions). Consumers obtain what they demand (i.e. are unrationed in this system). Wealth, demography, inflation, and expectations are often included in consumption equations: the literature on this equation alone is vast. Because disposable income can only be consumed or invested, and $C_t = C_t^d$ then $\Delta K_t = Y_{dt} - C_t$. The capital stock is the accumulation of gross investment less depreciation (assumed to be δK_{t-1}). Households own all of the capital stock, which is leased to firms, to be paid for at the end of the period out of net profits at the real rate π_t and returned intact, so δK_{t-1} represents firms' maintenance costs. Finally, wages depend on a proportion of the average product (a proxy for the marginal product) attenuated by unemployment, so disequilibria in the labour market induce deviations in the real wage from its share of (average) productivity in (A6.21). This equation is tantamount to $\Delta w_t = \lambda(L_t^s - L_t^d)$, and is the wage equivalent of the third equation in (A6.13). As usual, many other factors influence actual wage bargains (see Layard, Nickell and Jackman, 1991). The identities define total expenditure as the sum of its components ($I_{vt} - I_{vt-1}$ is inventory accumulation), and confirm the national-accounts convention that aggregate output, income, and expenditure are identical (what is earned is spent and produced).

A6.6.2 Firms

Firms produce output from labour and capital given the production technology, plan sales and inventories, set prices, and demand labour and capital services:

production function:

$$Q_t = h\left(L_t, K_t\right); \tag{A6.22}$$

production plan:

$$Q_t^s = (1+g)\,Q_{t-1} + I_{vt}^d - I_{vt-1}; \tag{A6.23}$$

inventory:

$$I_{vt}^d = \rho Q_t^s; \tag{A6.24}$$

pricing:

$$P_t = 1;\ \Pi_t \equiv Q_t - W_t - \delta K_{t-1}; \tag{A6.25}$$

labour demand:

$$L_t^d = \ell\left(Q_t^s, w_t\right);\ L_t = L_t^d; \tag{A6.26}$$

capital demand:

$$K_t^d = k\left(\pi_t, Q_t^s\right); CU_t = K_t^d - K_t. \tag{A6.27}$$

The production function determines the optimum output level as a function of input flows, where L_t is employed-person hours. Q_t^s is the planned supply of output (anticipated sales), set by the adjustment rule in (A6.23), formulated jointly with planned inventories which are intended to be a proportion ρ of sales (since the model is non-stochastic, the variance of sales is not defined). *Ex post*, deviations between planned and actual expenditures change inventories, which affect future output plans. Prices are simply normalized at unity for the present. Profits are the residual from revenue after paying wages and maintenance. Labour and capital are demanded as factor inputs in the light of production plans given their relative costs, and unemployment and capacity utilization (U_t and CU_t respectively) are the differences between their demands and supplies. Firms pay wages to employees, are assumed to have the right to manage, and there are no physical constraints on L_t^s (e.g. population), so L_t must be interpreted as L_t^d, as is made explicit in (A6.26). The capital and labour hired generate production given $h(\cdot)$, so (A6.22), (A6.26) and (A6.27) cannot be independently formulated.

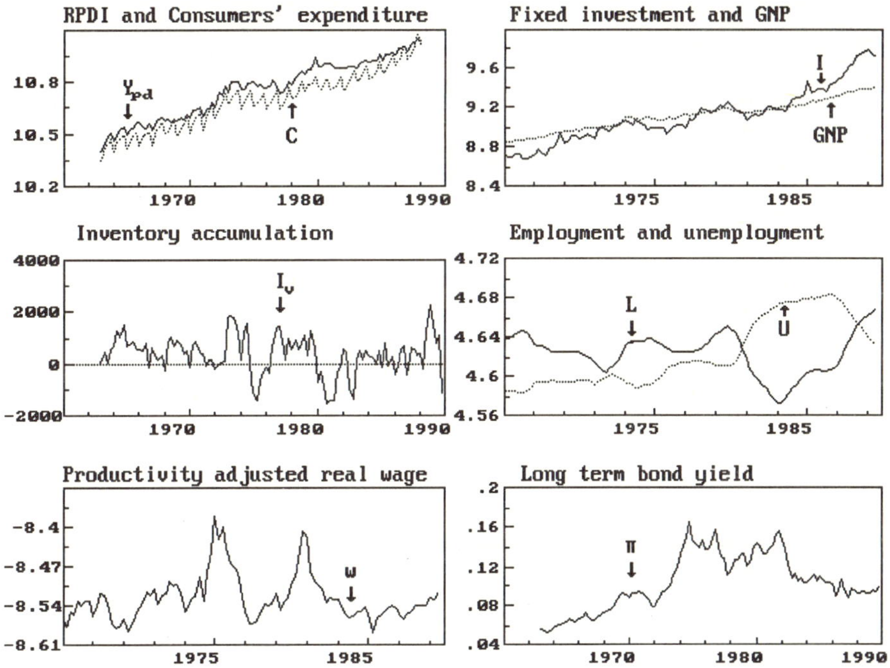

Fig. A6.1 UK quarterly macroeconomic time series

To illustrate the analysis, Fig. A6.1 shows some quarterly time-series graphs for the UK: real personal disposable income and consumption; real domestic fixed capital formation and real gross national product (GNP); stock accumulation; employment and unemployment; productivity-adjusted real wages; and the long-term bond yield (a proxy for π). The variables are scaled as necessary to highlight salient features; the first four expenditure series are in logs. The growth in the expenditure and output series is obvious, as is the relative variation in consumption compared to income, and investment to GNP. Unemployment has moved in the opposite direction to employment, and has fluctuated considerably over the period shown, as has the productivity-adjusted real wage.

Returning to the model, non-negativity constraints are ignored, so that negative values of I_t, U_t, and I_{vt} are interpreted as scrapping, overtime, and unfilled orders. All savings are automatically invested, but unused capacity is possible; inflation is precluded by definition at this stage. The focus of the model is on the consequences of distinguishing planned and realized magnitudes in a simple framework: for example, if L_t^d and L_t^s were just written as L_t, then U_t would be zero by construction. Similar remarks apply to capacity utilization. Many features of the model can be generalized (e.g. by including additional arguments in various functions); however, other features are restrictive and potentially misleading (no savings or wealth, no inflation, no technical progress, no stochastic components, etc.), and we comment on these below. For a related analysis, see Nickell (1990).

Already there are twenty-two equations in twenty-two endogenous variables, with: initial values:

$$Q_{t-1},\ Y_{t-1},\ K_{t-1},\ I_{vt-1},\ L_{t-1},\ Y_{dt-1},\ \pi_{t-1};$$

plans:

$$C_t^d,\ L_t^d,\ I_{vt}^d,\ K_t^d,\ Q_t^s,\ L_t^s; \tag{A6.28}$$

outcomes:

$$Y_t,\ Q_t,\ E_t,\ Y_{dt},\ W_t,\ \Pi_t,\ C_t,\ I_t,\ K_t,\ I_{vt},\ L_t,\ U_t,\ CU_t,\ w_t,\ \pi_t,\ P_t. \tag{A6.29}$$

Anticipated sales and stock building are predetermined, and hence so is planned expenditure. There is a simultaneous block determining consumption, investment, capital, the profit rate, and net profits; employment, labour supply, unemployment, the wage rate, and hence the wage bill; output and income; and the remaining components. Consumers' plans are always realized; net investment $(I_t - \delta K_{t-1})$ augments next period's capital stock; the deviation of actual from planned inventories influences future output and employment. Plans of households and firms need not be equal, and prices do not adjust immediately to remove such disequilibria, although wages gradually respond. The system is said to have a block-recursive structure with a simultaneous sub-block.

A6.6.3 Static-equilibrium solutions

Since this economy is a dynamic non-linear simultaneous system, it is difficult to prove that a solution exists at all points in time for every endogenous variable, and that any equilibrium solution so derived is stable. The system could have several types of equilibria including:

(a) static, which could occur when differenced variables such as $\Delta K_t, \Delta I_{vt}$ etc. are zero, requiring that $g = 0$;
(b) dynamic, or steady-state growth, when $\Delta K_t = gK_{t-1}$ etc. (constant growth for real variables).

In (a), time ceases to matter, and all plans are realized: e.g., $Q^s \overset{e}{=} Q$, $K_t \overset{e}{=} K_{t-1}$, $CU \overset{e}{=} 0$, and so on. To analyse the system by hand, consider the static state, linearizing all the functions ($f(\cdot)$, $\phi(\cdot)$, $h(\cdot)$ etc.), setting all changes to zero and all plans to realizations: this equilibrium state is simultaneous, not block-recursive. Assume that the adjustment equations induce a stable equilibrium, and interpret θ as the wage share (W/Q) with a positive autonomous capital stock. To ensure no net investment (which would violate a static equilibrium when $g = 0$), $C \stackrel{e}{=} Y_d$, $I \stackrel{e}{=} \delta K$, and $I_v \stackrel{e}{=} \rho Q$ (plans and outcomes coincide with $Q^s \stackrel{e}{=} Q$). Eliminating these, yields the static equilibrium for a given population:

$$L = \psi_1 w + \psi_3 N \tag{A6.30}$$

$$Q = h_1 L + h_2 K \tag{A6.31}$$

$$L = 1 - \ell_1 w + \ell_2 Q \tag{A6.32}$$

$$K = 1 + k_1 \pi + k_2 Q \tag{A6.33}$$

$$\Pi \equiv Q - W - \delta K \tag{A6.34}$$

$$W \equiv wL; \; \pi \equiv \Pi/K. \tag{A6.35}$$

There are eight equations in eight variables, so the system is exactly determined. All parameters are positive. Set $\psi_2 = 0$ for simplicity, and $\ell_0 = 1$ and $k_0 = 4$, where the units of labour are ten millions, and real values are in £100 billions, corresponding roughly to an economy the size of the UK. Substituting for L in (A6.32) from (A6.30):

$$w = \frac{[1 + \ell_2 Q - \psi_3 N]}{(\psi_1 + \ell_1)} = (\omega_0 + \omega_2 N) + \omega_1 Q = \omega_0^* + \omega_1 Q \tag{A6.36}$$

where * denotes dependence on N. From (A6.36), using (A6.31) and (A6.33):

$$Q = h_1 \psi_1 [\omega_0^* + \omega_2 Q] + h_2 [1 + k_1 \pi + k_2 Q] = \tau_0^* + \tau_1 \pi, \tag{A6.37}$$

when $(1 - h_1 \psi_1 \omega_1 - h_2 k_2) \neq 0$. From (A6.36) and (A6.37):

$$w = \omega_0^* + \omega_1 (\tau_0^* + \tau_1 \pi) = \iota_0^* + \iota_1 \pi \tag{A6.38}$$

so:

$$L = 1 - \ell_1 (\iota_0^* + \iota_1 \pi) + \ell_2 (\tau_0^* + \tau_1 \pi) = l_0^* + l_1 \pi.$$

But from the identities in (A6.34) and (A6.35):

$$\begin{aligned} Q &\equiv \Pi + W + \delta K = (\pi + \delta) K + wL \\ &= (\pi + \delta)(1 + k_1 \pi + k_2 [\tau_0^* + \tau_1 \pi]) + \psi_1 (\iota_0^* + \iota_1 \pi)(l_0^* + l_1 \pi) \\ &= \gamma_0^* + \gamma_1^* \pi + \gamma_2 \pi^2, \end{aligned} \tag{A6.39}$$

where γ_0^* and γ_1^* depend on N. Thus, using (A6.37):

$$(\gamma_0^* - \tau_0^*) + (\gamma_1^* - \tau_1) \pi + \gamma_2 \pi^2 = 0. \tag{A6.40}$$

The economy has two possible equilibrium solutions, corresponding to the roots of the quadratic in π. The addendum describes the solution for $\delta = 0.05$, $h_1 = 0.5$, $h_2 = 0.4$, $k_1 = 5$, $k_2 = 0.8$, $\psi_1 = 1.2$, $\psi_3 = 0.7$, $N = 5$, $\ell_1 = 3.8$, and $\ell_2 = 1.5$. This yields a positive real root of $\pi = 0.03$ (i.e. 3 per cent p.a.). Given π, then $I = 0.31$ (i.e. £31 billion), $K = 6.2$, $Q = 2.58 = Y = E$, $C = 2.27 = Y_d$, $L = 4.4$, $w = 0.475$ (= £4*750 p.a.), $\Pi = 0.18$, $W = 2.09$, and $I_v = 2.6\rho$. Thus, 88 per cent of the population choose to work (which is too high unless weighted by experience), and they earn 81 per cent of national income. Different parameter values may allow no solution.

Distinguishing between $L_t^d = L_t$ and L_t^s introduces U_t, and, with the wage adjustment equation, this extended system produces a determinate solution, allowing unemployment due to inconsistencies in plans. In the actual economy, if firms rather than households make investment decisions, then planned-savings flows $S_{vt}^d = Y_{dt} - C_t^d$ and assets $A_t \equiv A_{t-1} + S_{vt}$ must be introduced, allowing a potential inconsistency between planned saving S_{vt}^d and planned investment I_t^d, even though their realized values are equal *ex post* ($S_{vt} \equiv I_t$), and they are equal in equilibrium ($S_{vt} \stackrel{e}{=} I_t$). When wealth can be held in liquid form, we require a financial sector, and a mechanism for determining interest rates, in which case inflation must be modelled, as well as capital gains from asset revaluations. We do so below.

A6.6.4 Dynamic adjustment

The next issue is whether or not the dynamics in (A6.18)–(A6.27) ensure a convergent adjustment to the equilibrium. If the demand for labour (A6.26) is obtained by equating the marginal product of labour to the real wage, and there are constant returns to scale with a log-linear (value-added) production function (so $h(\cdot)$ is Cobb-Douglas), then $Q/L = w/h_1$ where $h_1 = \partial h(\cdot)/\partial L$. Convergence will occur in (A6.21) if $\theta \leq h_1$, even when there is no unemployment. A fall in unemployment will raise the real wage, and so lower the demand for, and increase the supply of, labour, moving the system back towards equilibrium. A one-off increase in planned consumption will raise actual consumption, and since firms do not respond within the period, output will not alter, inducing an unplanned fall in inventories. Profits and wages etc. are unaffected. Firms then plan to increase output in the next period to re-stock (from (A6.23)+(A6.24)), and will increase their demand for labour and hence the real wage. The out-turn depends on the relative responsiveness of (A6.18), (A6.21), and (A6.26) to output and real-wage factors. Meantime, consumption will have returned to its equilibrium, leading to excess inventories, so the system will oscillate: a coefficient of less than unity on ΔI_{vt}^d in (A6.23) would smooth adjustment. When the model is dynamic it must be solved sequentially through time, given its initial conditions.

The dynamic steady-state analysis is similar in principle, but more difficult in practice, and is left as an exercise: find the solution where the system grows at a constant rate $g > 0$. Naturally, you should check that a constant-growth solution is possible for (A6.18)–(A6.27), and a log-linear representation is usually required for this to be sensible. The point of this exercise is its implication for the care needed when formulating, solving, and interpreting the solutions of computerized models.

A6.7 Additional aspects of the first model

A6.7.1 Financial markets

An important omitted market from the model in the previous section is finance, concerning the determination of outstanding stocks of narrow and broad money; bank loans; bills, bonds, and equity; and loans and deposits of other financial intermediaries, together with their interest rates, dividends etc. Keeping to the schematic formulation in (A6.18)–(A6.24), and leaving most lag effects implicit, we could formulate this sector as:

demand for money:

$$M_t^d = \zeta\left(P_t, Y_{t-1}, R_{nt}\right); \quad M_t \equiv M_t^d; \; R_{nt} \equiv R_t - R_{ct}; \tag{A6.41}$$

commercial interest rate:

$$R_{ct} = \Lambda\left(R_t, \frac{E_t}{M_{t-1}}\right); \tag{A6.42}$$

central bank interest rate:

$$R_t = r\left(\Delta P_{t-1}, Y_{t-1}, \left[\frac{M}{P}\right]_{t-1}\right). \tag{A6.43}$$

Money is demanded as an asset to finance future purchases, so the demand for money to hold responds to transactions needs (measured by P_t and Y_{t-1}) and the opportunity cost of being liquid (R_{nt}) rather than investing in a Treasury Bill (say). In an economy like the UK, money mainly comprises the liabilities of the banking sector. As cash is available on demand to banks, (A6.41) assumes that commercial banks accept all deposits offered ($M_t \equiv M_t^d$) at their rate of interest R_{ct}. Legally required bank-liquidity ratios do not vitiate this approach so long as the central bank stands ready to rediscount bills at its announced rate of interest. The commercial interest rate is set in relation to the central monetary authority's rediscount rate R_t, and the demand for loans, proxied by total expenditure in relation to deposits. In turn, R_t is determined by a feedback control rule depending on inflation, output, and real money.

A6.7.2 Government sector

The government raises taxes on income, on capital, on expenditure, and on employment (denoted T_t, in aggregate real terms). The revenue raised is spent (G_t, also real) on employment, goods and services for public consumption and public investment, transfer payments (netted out here), and interest on the debt D_t (nominal), being the integral of past deficits/surpluses, denoted D_f. Any surplus or deficit is met by borrowing from the private sector via bills and bonds (central bank loans are omitted). We do not distinguish the maturity composition of government debt, all of which is issued at a single, market-determined, nominal interest rate R_{lt}.

government expenditure:

$$G_t = \eta\left(U_t, L_t, R_{lt} D_t\right); \; \left(\frac{D_f}{P}\right)_t \equiv G_t - T_t; \; P_{dt} = \frac{1}{R_{lt}}; \tag{A6.44}$$

government revenue:

$$T_t = \tau(Y_t, E_t, L_t, K_t);\ D_t^s \equiv \left(\frac{P_{dt-1}}{P_{dt}}\right) D_{t-1} + \left(\frac{D_{ft}}{P_{dt}}\right); \tag{A6.45}$$

government debt:

$$D_t^d = d(R_{lt}, R_t, Y_t, K_t);\ D_t \equiv D_t^s;\ D_t^d \stackrel{e}{=} D_t^s. \tag{A6.46}$$

Since all of the debt issued must be held, the market clears by essentially instantaneous adjustment of the bond rate R_{lt}, which is the inverse of the bond price P_{dt}. Debt accumulates past debt (interest payments are part of G_t) plus the deficit, but the market value of the debt is affected by changes in its price, which may induce changes in future plans. Expectations of capital gains or losses are ignored, and (A6.46) should include (e.g.) R_{lt+1}^e. Inflation (a change in aggregate prices), affects real taxes and expenditure since these are rarely indexed, but is again ignored. The earlier identity for expenditure should now include D_{ft} as an additional term. Disposable income also needs redefining to include transfers less direct taxes. The need to finance the debt forces a connection between R_t and R_{lt}.

A6.7.3 Foreign sector

Next, we introduce the foreign sector. This involves flows of real imports and exports of goods and services, I_m and X, with prices P_m (in dollars, as a shorthand for foreign currencies) and P_x (in £) respectively. Such flows are dependent on world trade J and world prices P_w (in \$). The nominal balance of trade deficit or surplus (in £) alters the nominal stock of net foreign assets F (in \$), depending on the exchange rate e_r (in terms of £/\$) and foreign interest rates R_{ft}:

exports:

$$X_t^d = \chi\left(J_t, \frac{P_{xt}}{[e_{rt}P_{wt}]}\right);\ B_t \equiv P_{xt}X_t - e_{rt}P_{mt}I_{mt};\ X_t^d = X_t; \tag{A6.47}$$

imports:

$$I_{mt}^d = \imath\left(E_t, \frac{[e_{rt}P_{mt}]}{P_t}\right);\ F_t \equiv (1 + R_{ft-1})F_{t-1} + \frac{B_t}{e_{rt}};\ I_{mt}^d = I_{mt}; \tag{A6.48}$$

export prices:

$$P_{xt} = \aleph\left(w_t, P_t, \left(\frac{Q}{L}\right)_t\right); \tag{A6.49}$$

import prices:

$$P_{mt} = \mu(P_{wt}, C_{owt}); \tag{A6.50}$$

exchange rates:

$$\Delta e_{rt} = \zeta\left(R_t - R_{ft}, \left[\frac{e_r P_w}{P}\right]_{t-1}\right). \tag{A6.51}$$

The assumption is that the observed volume of exports is determined by world demand and relative prices, and equals foreign demand; this is dubious since domestic demand can pre-empt exports. Imports are determined by domestic expenditure and relative prices. Exporters are assumed to modify their profit margins in the light of domestic costs per unit output, and not to be merely price takers in world markets; similarly for importers (proxied by world production costs, C_{owt}). Balance of trade surpluses depend on many forces and alter foreign assets, together with 'invisibles' which are treated here as earnings on existing assets. The key variable to explain is e_{rt}, and the equation offered assumes that the major short-run determinants are capital flows due to interest-rate differentials and, implicitly, anticipated capital gains, with a long-run feedback from competitiveness, ensuring eventual purchasing-power parity (i.e. allowing for transport costs, identical goods sell for the same price everywhere due to competition). However, no claim is made that (A6.51) would allow changes in e_{rt} to be predicted *ex ante* more accurately than transactions costs would offset. The identity for total domestic expenditure should now include B_t as a further additional term.

A6.7.4 Completing equations

To complete the cognitive scheme formulated so far, we let firms own capital by borrowing from the household sector via new issues of equity Q_{et} (in nominal terms) on which they pay dividends D_{et}, and which has a market price P_{et}. Households save S_{vt} out of their income, accumulating wealth A_t. We will not disaggregate into durables, housing and other goods, even though these variables play an important role in linking real and financial sectors in most empirical systems:

dividends:

$$D_{et} = d\left(\Pi_t\right);\ Q^s_{et} = Q^d_{et};\ Q_{et} \equiv Q_{et-1} + \Delta Q_{et}; \tag{A6.52}$$

demand for equity:

$$Q^d_{et} = q\left(D_{et}, R_{lt}, A_t, \Delta P_t\right);\ Q_{et} \equiv Q^d_{et}; \tag{A6.53}$$

new issues of equity:

$$\Delta Q_{et} = v\left(\Delta K^d_t, \pi_{t-1}, P_{et}, P_t\right);\ P_{et} = \frac{P_t D_{et}}{R_{lt} Q_{et}}; \tag{A6.54}$$

savings:

$$S^d_{vt} \equiv Y_{pdt} - f\left(Y_{pdt}\right);\ A_t \equiv \left(\frac{P_{t-1}}{P_t}\right) A_{t-1} + S_{vt};\ S_{vt} = S^d_{vt}; \tag{A6.55}$$

domestic prices:

$$\frac{P_t}{e_{rt} P_{mt}} = \Upsilon\left(w_t, \left(\frac{Q}{L}\right)_t, \left(\frac{E^d_t}{Q^s_t}\right)\right). \tag{A6.56}$$

Dividends are paid out of profits, and the stock market instantaneously adjusts in this model. The demand for equity depends on its own rate of return, relative returns, wealth, and inflation. New issues are undertaken to finance investment, and they augment the stock of equity. Equity prices are determined by market clearing to equate returns to the long-term interest rate (capital gains are ignored as before). Savings are unspent real personal disposable income (Y_{pdt}), and augment wealth subject to revaluations due to inflation (relative asset-price changes also matter greatly in practice). The domestic price level P_t is determined relative to foreign prices in domestic currency units by real wages relative to productivity (i.e. real net unit-labour costs: we have not introduced a symbol for nominal wages which are $P_t w_t$), and excess demand which affects the profit mark-up.

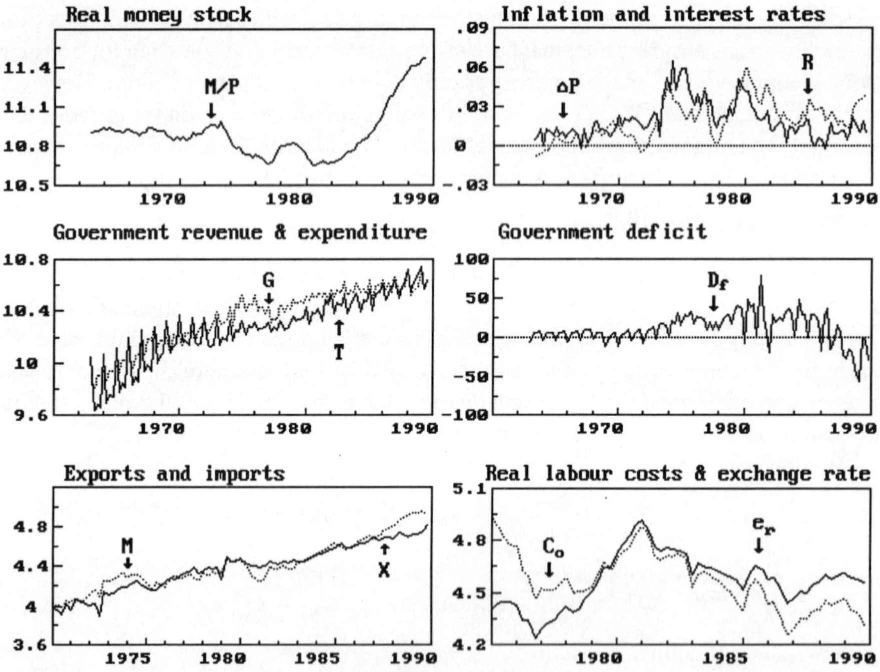

Fig. A6.2 Further UK quarterly macroeconomic time series

Figure A6.2 shows some of the additional time series: real money (M1 measure); quarterly inflation and the 3-month interest rate (local authority); real government revenue and expenditure; the nominal government deficit; real exports and imports; real unit-labour costs and the real average exchange rate. Graphs have been scaled to match units. Real money grew very rapidly in the mid-1980s; inflation was relatively above interest rates in the 1970s and below in the 1980s; revenue is more volatile (and seasonal) than expenditure, inducing considerable changes in the deficit; exports grew in line with imports over most of the period, but fell well behind at the end, matching the rise in consumption relative to income seen in Fig. A6.1; and both real unit-labour costs and the real exchange rate have fluctuated relative to each other (determining competitiveness), but not trended strongly.

A6.7.5 Revised National Income identities

The following are the definitions extended to allow for the additional sectors:

GNP:

$$E_t \equiv C_t + I_t + \Delta I_{vt} + B_t + \frac{D_{ft}}{P_t};$$

total final expenditure:

$$TFE_t \equiv C_t + I_t + \Delta I_{vt} + X_t + G_t; \tag{A6.57}$$

real personal income:

$$Y_t \equiv W_t + D_{et} + \frac{[Y_{ft} + Y_{rt}]}{P_t}; \; Y_{rt} \equiv R_{lt-1} D_{t-1}; \; Y_{ft} \equiv R_{ft-1} F_{t-1};$$

disposable income:

$$Y_{pdt} \equiv (1 - \tau_y) Y_t;$$

wealth:

$$A_t \equiv \frac{(M_t + P_{et} Q_{et} + P_{dt} D_t + e_{rt} F_t)}{P_t}.$$

By omitting the housing sector, rents do not appear in income nor house values in wealth. $(\Pi_t - D_{et})$ are retained earnings of firms. Factor-cost adjustment and stock appreciation terms are also missing. τ_y is the average direct-tax rate. Wealth can be allocated to money, equity, bonds (government debt), or foreign assets, and there are real effects on wealth if relative asset prices change.

This extended system will serve as our macro model; we now consider one possible direction of disaggregation, then formulate a framework for analysing macro models.

A6.8 Industrial disaggregation

This can be done in many ways, such as into manufacturing and non-manufacturing; durables, non-durables, and services; etc. One direction that does not lead to too great an increase in complexity (but does greatly increase size and information requirements), is to add an input–output matrix with appropriate industrial decomposition (e.g. agriculture, extraction, construction, metals, engineering, chemicals, and so on). There are assumed to be m industries, each producing a single but different commodity. Let $\mathbf{q}_t$ be the $m \times 1$ vector of gross outputs of each industry, where q_{it} is the dependent variable of the ith industry's production function (so m production functions, labour-demand equations, investment functions, etc. are needed). Such outputs go in part to final users (i.e. consumption, investment, exports, and government), denoted by the $m \times 1$ vector $\mathbf{f}_t$, with elements f_{it} which record the amount of the output of industry i going to final use (in real-value terms). We allocate intermediate uses of output (going as inputs to other industries) by an $m \times m$ matrix $\boldsymbol{A}$ such that $a_{ij}q_{jt}$ is the amount of industry i's output going as input to industry j, with $a_{ii} = 0\ \forall i$. Then the gross output is allocated by:

$$q_{it} = \sum_{j=1}^{m} a_{ij}q_{jt} + f_{it}. \tag{A6.58}$$

The assumption of constant a_{ij} over time is unrealistic, but (A6.58) highlights the principles involved in allocating intermediate inputs. In matrix terms, the system in (A6.58) is:

$$\boldsymbol{q}_t = \boldsymbol{A}\boldsymbol{q}_t + \boldsymbol{f}_t \text{ so that } \boldsymbol{q}_t = (\boldsymbol{I}_m - \boldsymbol{A})^{-1}\boldsymbol{f}_t \tag{A6.59}$$

where $\boldsymbol{I}_m$ is an $m \times m$ unit matrix. Because of intermediate users, industries need a greater gross than final output to satisfy end-users' demands. By transposing the earlier allocation, we see that the model assumes that the ith industry takes an amount $a_{ji}q_{it}$ as inputs from the jth.

The same system can be used to interrelate output prices. Let p_{it} be the price per unit of output of industry i and $\boldsymbol{p}_t$ the vector of m prices, then the total receipts of the ith industry are $p_{it}q_{it}$, which equates to the costs of the intermediate inputs purchased plus primary inputs (capital, labour, and entrepreneurship etc.) where their per-unit costs are denoted by c_{it}. Thus:

$$p_{it}q_{it} = \sum_{j=1}^{m} p_{jt}\left(a_{ji}q_{it}\right) + c_{it}q_{it}, \tag{A6.60}$$

so that:

$$p_{it} = \sum_{j=1}^{m} p_{jt}a_{ji} + c_{it}, \tag{A6.61}$$

or in matrix terms (where $'$ denotes transposition):

$$\boldsymbol{p}_t = \boldsymbol{A}'\boldsymbol{p}_t + \boldsymbol{c}_t \text{ leading to } \boldsymbol{p}_t = (\boldsymbol{I}_m - \boldsymbol{A}')^{-1}\boldsymbol{c}_t. \tag{A6.62}$$

This model allows us to investigate the impact of a change in the costs of a basic input on the prices per unit of the gross output of each industry.

Unfortunately, we cannot expect $\boldsymbol{A}$ to remain constant for long, and while there are methods of updating it between industrial censuses (see Bacharach, 1970), this approach seems be most useful as a conceptual framework for 'seeing inside' an important aspect of the macro-system.

A6.9 A general framework

Reconsider the simplest supply–demand model with market clearing, where (P,Q) are endogenous:[4]

$$\begin{aligned} Q_t &= \alpha_0 + \alpha_1 Y_t + \alpha_2 P_t + \epsilon_{1t} \\ P_t &= \beta_0 + \beta_1 K_{t-1} + \beta_2 P_{t-1} + \epsilon_{2t}. \end{aligned}$$

We can write this two-equation system as:

$$\begin{aligned} &\begin{pmatrix} 1 & -\alpha_2 \\ 0 & 1 \end{pmatrix} \begin{pmatrix} Q_t \\ P_t \end{pmatrix} + \begin{pmatrix} 0 & 0 \\ 0 & \beta_2 \end{pmatrix} \begin{pmatrix} Q_{t-1} \\ P_{t-1} \end{pmatrix} = \\ &\begin{pmatrix} \alpha_0 & \alpha_1 & 0 \\ \beta_0 & 0 & 0 \end{pmatrix} \begin{pmatrix} 1 \\ Y_t \\ K_t \end{pmatrix} + \begin{pmatrix} 0 & 0 & 0 \\ 0 & 0 & \beta_1 \end{pmatrix} \begin{pmatrix} 1 \\ Y_{t-1} \\ K_{t-1} \end{pmatrix} + \begin{pmatrix} \epsilon_{1t} \\ \epsilon_{2t} \end{pmatrix}. \end{aligned} \quad \text{(A6.63)}$$

Using a more general notation for systems, let $\boldsymbol{y}_t$ be the vector of k endogenous variables, and $\boldsymbol{z}_t$ the vector of n non-modelled variables, possibly with lags of up to r and s periods respectively, although we only consider one lag here. Let $\boldsymbol{B}_0$ be the $k \times k$ matrix of coefficients of all the endogenous variables, $\boldsymbol{B}_1$ the coefficient matrix of the one-lagged endogenous variables, $\boldsymbol{C}_0$ the $k \times n$ matrix of the current-dated non-modelled variables, and $\boldsymbol{C}_1$ their lag-coefficient matrix. Then the system in (A6.63) can be expressed as:

$$\boldsymbol{B}_0 \boldsymbol{y}_t + \boldsymbol{B}_1 \boldsymbol{y}_{t-1} = \boldsymbol{C}_0 \boldsymbol{z}_t + \boldsymbol{C}_1 \boldsymbol{z}_{t-1} + \boldsymbol{\epsilon}_t,$$

where we assume $\boldsymbol{\epsilon}_t \sim \mathsf{IN}_k[\mathbf{0}, \boldsymbol{\Sigma}]$, so $\{\boldsymbol{\epsilon}_t\}$ is an independent, normal random variable with mean zero and covariance matrix $\boldsymbol{\Sigma}$, taken to be independent of $\{\boldsymbol{z}_t\}$. This is called the structural form when it claims to model the decision equations of the relevant agents. The reduced, or solved, form solves for $\boldsymbol{y}_t$ as a function of the givens (the parameters, non-modelled variables, and lagged variables). A necessary condition is that $\boldsymbol{B}_0$ is non-singular, in which case, the solution is:

$$\begin{aligned} \boldsymbol{y}_t &= \boldsymbol{B}_0^{-1} \boldsymbol{C}_0 \boldsymbol{z}_t + \boldsymbol{B}_0^{-1} \boldsymbol{C}_1 \boldsymbol{z}_{t-1} - \boldsymbol{B}_0^{-1} \boldsymbol{B}_1 \boldsymbol{y}_{t-1} + \boldsymbol{B}_0^{-1} \boldsymbol{\epsilon}_t \\ &= \boldsymbol{\Gamma}_0 \boldsymbol{z}_t + \boldsymbol{\Gamma}_1 \boldsymbol{z}_{t-1} + \boldsymbol{\Phi}_1 \boldsymbol{y}_{t-1} + \boldsymbol{\nu}_t. \end{aligned} \quad \text{(A6.64)}$$

Given data up to and including time $t-1$ on $(\boldsymbol{y} : \boldsymbol{z})$, together with $\boldsymbol{z}_t$ and $(\boldsymbol{\Gamma}_0, \boldsymbol{\Gamma}_1, \boldsymbol{\Phi}_1)$, the next value of $\boldsymbol{y}_t$ is generated by (A6.64).

In the supply–demand example, $\boldsymbol{y}_t = (Q_t : P_t)'$ and $\boldsymbol{z}_t = (1 : Y_t : K_t)'$:

$$\boldsymbol{B}_0^{-1} = \begin{pmatrix} 1 & \alpha_2 \\ 0 & 1 \end{pmatrix},$$

[4] This formulation is unconventional to simplify the algebra: usually the second equation would determine Q_t not P_t, but nothing substantive is altered by the normalization adopted.

so that (A6.64) is:

$$\begin{pmatrix} Q_t \\ P_t \end{pmatrix} = \begin{pmatrix} 0 & \alpha_2\beta_2 \\ 0 & \beta_2 \end{pmatrix} \begin{pmatrix} Q_{t-1} \\ P_{t-1} \end{pmatrix} + \begin{pmatrix} \alpha_0 + \alpha_2\beta_0 & \alpha_1 & 0 \\ \beta_0 & 0 & 0 \end{pmatrix} \begin{pmatrix} 1 \\ Y_t \\ K_t \end{pmatrix}$$
$$+ \begin{pmatrix} 0 & 0 & \alpha_2\beta_1 \\ 0 & 0 & \beta_1 \end{pmatrix} \begin{pmatrix} 1 \\ Y_{t-1} \\ K_{t-1} \end{pmatrix} + \begin{pmatrix} 1 & \alpha_2 \\ 0 & 1 \end{pmatrix} \begin{pmatrix} \epsilon_{1t} \\ \epsilon_{2t} \end{pmatrix}.$$

In a static equilibrium when all change has ceased and the errors take their expected values of zero, $Q_t = Q_{t-1} = Q^*$ and $P_t = P_{t-1} = P^*$ etc., so that we can solve for the equilibrium relations:

$$\begin{pmatrix} 1 & -\alpha_2\beta_2 \\ 0 & 1-\beta_2 \end{pmatrix} \begin{pmatrix} Q^* \\ P^* \end{pmatrix} = \begin{pmatrix} \alpha_0 + \alpha_2\beta_0 & \alpha_1 & \alpha_2\beta_1 \\ \beta_0 & 0 & \beta_1 \end{pmatrix} \begin{pmatrix} 1 \\ Y^* \\ K^* \end{pmatrix}. \tag{A6.65}$$

Thus, when $|\beta_2| < 1$:

$$\begin{pmatrix} Q^* \\ P^* \end{pmatrix} = \frac{1}{1-\beta_2} \begin{pmatrix} 1-\beta_2 & \alpha_2\beta_2 \\ 0 & 1 \end{pmatrix} \begin{pmatrix} \alpha_0 + \alpha_2\beta_0 & \alpha_1 & \alpha_2\beta_1 \\ \beta_0 & 0 & \beta_1 \end{pmatrix} \begin{pmatrix} 1 \\ Y^* \\ K^* \end{pmatrix}$$
$$= \frac{1}{1-\beta_2} \begin{pmatrix} \alpha_0(1-\beta_0\beta_2) + \alpha_2\beta_0 & (1-\beta_2)\alpha_1 & \alpha_2\beta_1 \\ \beta_0 & 0 & \beta_1 \end{pmatrix} \begin{pmatrix} 1 \\ Y^* \\ K^* \end{pmatrix}. \tag{A6.66}$$

From these two representations, the immediate, delayed, and total effects on either price or quantity of any changes in their determinants can be obtained. For example, the effects of a change in income tax on output or price can be analysed.

In the general formulation, $\mathbf{y}_t = \mathbf{y}^*$ and $\mathbf{z}_t = \mathbf{z}^*$:

$$\mathbf{y}^* = (\boldsymbol{\Gamma}_0 + \boldsymbol{\Gamma}_1)\,\mathbf{z}^* + \boldsymbol{\Phi}_1\mathbf{y}^* = (\mathbf{I}_k - \boldsymbol{\Phi}_1)^{-1}(\boldsymbol{\Gamma}_0 + \boldsymbol{\Gamma}_1)\,\mathbf{z}^* \text{ or } \mathbf{y}^* = \boldsymbol{\Psi}\mathbf{z}^*,$$

when $(\mathbf{I}_k - \boldsymbol{\Phi}_1)$ is non-singular. When $\{\mathbf{z}_t\}$ has a well-defined mean, and $\boldsymbol{\Phi}_1^t \to \mathbf{0}$ as $t \to \infty$, then such an outcome is a possible solution. The second condition ensures that the effects of past shocks die out (rather than cumulate explosively or persist indefinitely), whereas the first condition is technically convenient for econometric estimation, although in practice, economic time series are often evolutionary. Economic growth is usually attributed to such factors as technical progress, knowledge accumulation, population growth etc. These factors are affected by economic variables in the long run, but it is rare to close a macro-economic system so that all relevant aspects are endogenized. However, $\boldsymbol{\Phi}_1^t \to \mathbf{0}$ is reasonable only if growth is explained by $\mathbf{z}_t$, which requires that $\Delta z_{it} = g_i$ is also reasonable and that sufficient elements of $\boldsymbol{\Gamma}_0$ and $\boldsymbol{\Gamma}_1$ are non-zero.

A few comments are needed on this issue even though a full treatment is reserved for the main text. Consider a system like (A6.64) but for one variable only, denoted x_t, with one $z_t = t$ (a trend) and an error term $\{\nu_t\}$:

$$x_t = d_0 + d_1 x_{t-1} + d_2 t + \nu_t. \tag{A6.67}$$

For simplicity, $\{\nu_t\}$ is taken to be a normal random variable with zero mean and constant variance σ_ν^2, where successive 'nus' are independent. The values of d_0, d_1, and d_2 determine the properties of $\{x_t\}$ and different sequences of $\{x_t\}$ result as follows.

A6.9.1 Stable process

When $|d_1| < 1$ and $d_2 = 0$, then $\{x_t\}$ fluctuates around a mean of $d_0/(1 - d_1)$ with a variance of $\sigma_\nu^2/(1-d_1^2)$, and the correlation between successive xs is determined by d_1.

A6.9.2 Trending process

When $d_1 = 0$ and $d_2 \neq 0$, then x_t is a trend process. When $d_2 > 0$, the variance around the trend would become negligible relative to the mean unless x_t was the logarithm of the original variable. The conventional measure of variance for x (around the mean) tends to infinity. When $|d_1| < 1$, the behaviour of x_t remains similar to $d_1 = 0$, and is referred to as 'trend stationary'. However, it is hard to see why d_2 should be constant empirically.

A6.9.3 Difference stable process

When $d_1 = 1$ and $d_2 = 0$, then x_t is a random walk (with drift if $d_0 \neq 0$):

$$x_t = d_0 + x_{t-1} + \nu_t \text{ which implies that } \Delta x_t = d_0 + \nu_t,$$

where $\Delta x_t = x_t - x_{t-1}$. First consider $d_0 = 0$, so that Δx_t is just ν_t. Expressing x_t as a function of past $\{\nu_{t-j}\}$:

$$x_t = x_0 + \sum_{i=1}^{t} \nu_i. \tag{A6.68}$$

Past shocks do not die out, and so persist for ever. If $d_0 \neq 0$, then x_t also has a constant drift, since in place of (A6.68):

$$x_t = x_0 + d_0 t + \sum_{i=1}^{t} \nu_i. \tag{A6.69}$$

This class is called 'difference stationary' since the first difference is a well-behaved process. The variance of x_t increases linearly over time, and x_t 'wanders' everywhere eventually. Over millennia, (A6.69) seems an unlikely description of economic variables, many of which have bounds, and most of which need not have constant variance 'inputs'. It is also unclear what might keep d_0 constant, although (A6.69) is a good first approximation to some economic time series (e.g. asset prices).

A6.9.4 Quadratic trend process

When $d_1 = 1$ and $d_2 \neq 0$, there is a quadratic trend in x_t since there will be a trend in Δx_t; such a 'model' could be no more than a local approximation.

A6.9.5 Integrated process

The preceding two processes are non-stationary and are the focus of much current research. The behaviour of estimation methods and statistical tests is affected by whether $\{y_t : z_t\}$ is non-stationary. Since x_t in (A6.68) cumulates, or integrates, past shocks, but does so only once, it is said to be integrated of order one and usually denoted I(1). When x_t is I(1), then Δx_t is I(0), so first differencing removes the integrator. Processes potentially could be I(d), and need Δ^d to remove all of their integrators; equally, their degree of integration is not an inherent characteristic and could change over time (e.g. prices in hyper-inflations).

Not only is statistical inference affected by the degree of integration, the 'balance' of (A6.64) must be re-evaluated. Combinations of orders of integration for ys and zs need not be mutually consistent with the assertion that $\{\nu_t\}$ is I(0). When $\{y_t\}$ is I(1) (say), its linear combination with $\{\boldsymbol{\Gamma}_0 z_t + \boldsymbol{\Gamma}_1 z_{t-1} + \boldsymbol{\Phi}_1 y_{t-1}\}$ is being assumed I(0). One way of that happening is when $\boldsymbol{\Phi}_1 = \mathbf{I}_k$ and $\boldsymbol{\Gamma}_1 = -\boldsymbol{\Gamma}_0$, so that (A6.68) really holds in differences:

$$\Delta y_t = \boldsymbol{\Gamma}_0 \Delta z_t + \nu_t. \tag{A6.70}$$

Now all terms are I(0) when the original data are I(1), and no issue of balance arises.

A6.9.6 Cointegrated process

In (A6.70), the growth of economic variables is independent of their historical levels and of any past disequilibria, which seems counter-factual. Another possibility is when linear combinations of I(1) variables become I(0), and this is called cointegration (see Engle and Granger, 1987). A simple example is when C_t and Y_t are I(1) but saving is I(0) so that $C_t - Y_t$ is I(0), and hence consumption and income are cointegrated (this is not empirically reasonable, merely illustrative). The cointegrating relationships are those that hold in the long run: despite levels of variables changing without bound, combinations of variables move together. Generally, when $\boldsymbol{y}, \boldsymbol{z}$ are I(1) and cointegrated, the static solution above characterizes the cointegrating equations so that $\{y_t - \boldsymbol{\Psi} \boldsymbol{z}_t\}$ must be I(0). Such a system has the form:

$$\Delta y_t = \boldsymbol{\Gamma}_0 \Delta z_t + (\boldsymbol{\Phi}_1 - \mathbf{I}_k)(y_{t-1} - \boldsymbol{\Psi} \boldsymbol{z}_{t-1}) + \nu_t, \tag{A6.71}$$

where every term is I(0) even though the levels are I(1). Past disequilibria influence present growth, and if $\boldsymbol{\Phi}_1$ has the requisite properties (i.e. is stable), the system is continually driven towards the dynamic equilibrium $\boldsymbol{y}^* = \boldsymbol{\Psi} \boldsymbol{z}^*$. Terms of the form $(y_{t-1} - \boldsymbol{\Psi} \boldsymbol{z}_{t-1})$ are called system equilibrium-correction mechanisms and can be solved 'statically' for the cointegrating equations or dynamically for growth paths.

A6.10 Forecasting

Returning to the general notation, consider a 1-step forecast $\hat{y}_{T+1}$ for y_{T+1} when the parameter values and future $\{z_{T+j}\}$ are known:

$$\hat{y}_{T+1} = \boldsymbol{\Gamma}_0 z_{T+1} + \boldsymbol{\Gamma}_1 z_T + \boldsymbol{\Phi}_1 y_T. \tag{A6.72}$$

The forecast error is:

$$\hat{\nu}_{T+1} = y_{T+1} - \hat{y}_{T+1} = \nu_T \tag{A6.73}$$

and hence coincides with the shock to the system. The forecast uncertainty is determined by the variance matrix of $\{\nu_t\}$. When parameters are estimated, an additional variance term is added.

In an operational environment, the future values of the z_t will be unknown and will have to be forecast as well (e.g. world trade, oil prices). Denote parameter estimates and forecasts by $\hat{}$. Then to forecast up to a horizon of h steps ahead, iteratively use:

$$\hat{y}_{T+j} = \hat{\boldsymbol{\Gamma}}_0 \hat{z}_{T+j} + \hat{\boldsymbol{\Gamma}}_1 \hat{z}_{T+j-1} + \hat{\boldsymbol{\Phi}}_1 \hat{y}_{T+j-1} \quad \text{for } j = 1, \ldots, h, \tag{A6.74}$$

commencing from the end-of-sample values of the data. When forecasting more than 1-period ahead, outside the historical sample, the errors on (A6.74) will cumulate. Their sum will converge when $\hat{\boldsymbol{\Phi}}_1$ is stable, but otherwise the errors will cumulate indefinitely, so the forecast errors will have a trending variance as shown next.

A6.10.1 Forecast standard errors

Model outcomes and residuals are statistics, subject to sampling fluctuations, so $y_{T+1} - \hat{y}_{T+1}$ and $\{y_{T+j} - \hat{y}_{T+j}\}$ have standard errors. For example, when parameters and zs are known:

$$\hat{\nu}_{T+j} = y_{T+j} - \hat{y}_{T+j} = \sum_{i=0}^{j-1} \boldsymbol{\Phi}_1^i v_{T+j-i}. \tag{A6.75}$$

Since forecasts from a correctly-specified linear model are essentially unbiased, when the errors are independent over time, the forecast error variance from (A6.75) is given by:

$$\mathsf{V}\left[\hat{\nu}_{T+j}\right] = \mathsf{E}\left[\sum_{i=0}^{j-1}\sum_{k=0}^{j-1} \boldsymbol{\Phi}_1^i \nu_{T+j-i}\nu'_{T+j-k}\boldsymbol{\Phi}_1^{k\prime}\right] = \sum_{i=0}^{j-1} \boldsymbol{\Phi}_1^i \boldsymbol{\Sigma} \boldsymbol{\Phi}_1^{i\prime}. \tag{A6.76}$$

Thus, forecast standard errors increase with the horizon ahead. If all the latent roots of $\boldsymbol{\Phi}_1$ lie inside the unit circle, the expression in (A6.76) will converge to the unconditional variance of y_t given current and past z_t. Otherwise, it will diverge. For a more detailed treatment, see Clements and Hendry (1995).

A6.10.2 Model evaluation

Because of their size and non-linearity, large-scale macro-econometric models are rarely evaluated using formal econometric tests. In part, their size precludes direct application of conventional test statistics, although many modellers do rigorously test single equations or small blocks as components of systems. In practice, systems as units have generally been evaluated using *ad hoc* procedures. Methods for testing small systems are discussed in the main text.

A6.11 An example

To allow an omniscient overview, consider the PcGive data-set: the data-generation process is explained in its book. There are four variables, C, Y, ΔP, and Q and the system is closed except for an exogenous oil shock in 1973(4). These four variables are modelled by the one-lag linear dynamic system:

$$y_t = \boldsymbol{\Pi} y_{t-1} + \nu_t,$$

after having removed the means of the variables. While all four variables are in fact I(0), some test statistics suggest that y_t is I(1).[5]

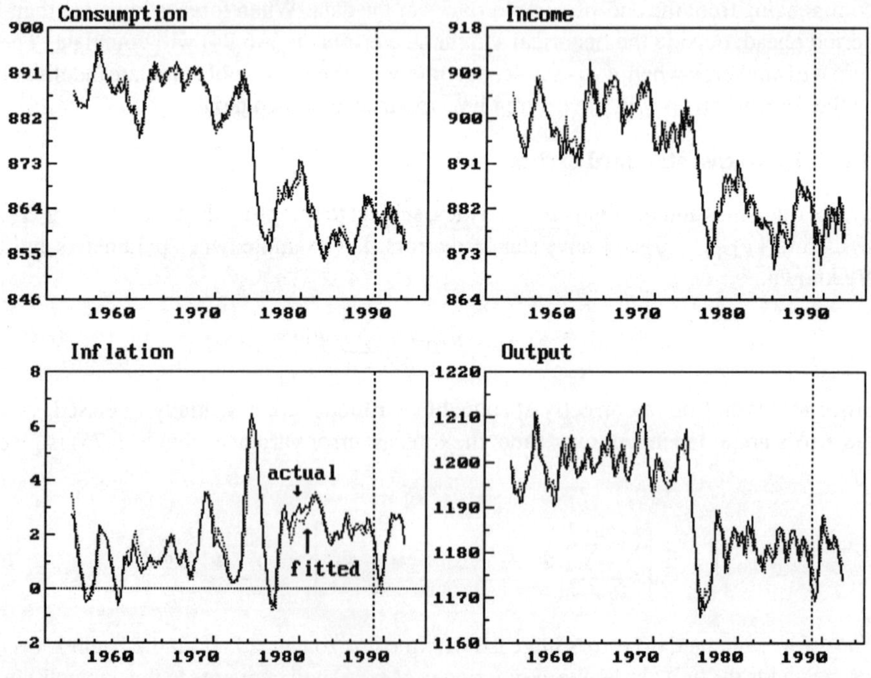

Fig. A6.3 Time series and fits for C, Y, ΔP, and Q

Figure A6.3 shows the time-series graphs over the historical sample period 1953(1)–1992(3) together with fitted values from multiple regression, and 1-step forecasts for the last fifteen observations. The forecast-period start is shown by the vertical dotted line. The track looks good to the eye, and the forecasts are near the outcomes, but here the model is almost the same as the mechanism which generated the data.

The $\boldsymbol{\Pi}$ matrix is 4×4 and equals:

[5] An exception to this statement is the Johansen (1988) procedure described in Ch.11.

Π Matrix

	C_{t-1}	Y_{t-1}	ΔP_{t-1}	Q_{t-1}
C_t	0.84	0.11	– 1.22	0.03
SE	(0.05)	(0.06)	(0.16)	(0.03)
Y_t	0.03	0.75	0.53	0.18
SE	(0.08)	(0.09)	(0.26)	(0.05)
ΔP_t	– 0.03	– 0.01	0.91	0.06
SE	(0.01)	(0.01)	(0.04)	(0.01)
Q_t	0.16	– 0.11	– 1.07	0.84
SE	(0.09)	(0.09)	(0.27)	(0.05)

where the standard error of each coefficient is shown in parentheses. Many of the estimated coefficients are significantly different from zero, and most have signs and magnitudes that make sense (e.g. the effect of income on consumption is positive, whereas inflation has a negative effect; output positively affects income and inflation, but inflation reduces output, etc.).

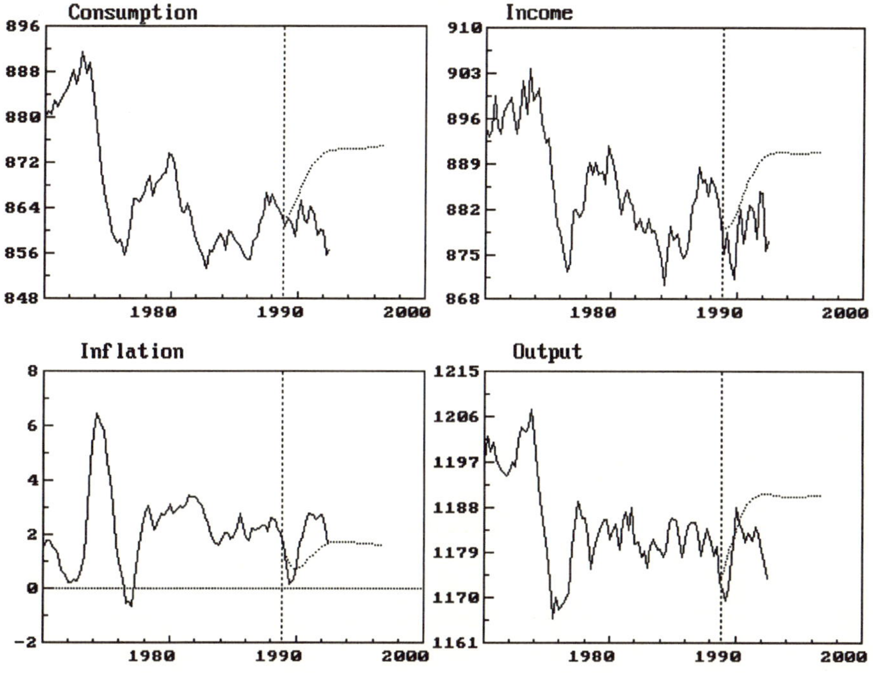

Fig. A6.4 Dynamic forecast of C, Y, ΔP, and Q

The standard deviations, denoted by $\hat{\sigma}_{ii}$ and reported as a percentage of the ith variable, and the inter-correlations between the ν_{it} over the sample (shown on the diagonal and off-diagonal respectively), are:

Residual correlations

	$\hat{\sigma}$	C_t	Y_t	ΔP_t	Q_t
C_t	1.80	1	–	–	–
Y_t	2.86	0.78	1	–	–
ΔP_t	0.40	−0.14	0.03	1	–
Q_t	3.00	0.20	0.27	0.02	1

Figure A6.4 shows the dynamic forecasts over 1989(1)–1996(4) together with a sub-sample of the data. These are calculated assuming zero shocks, so the projections look very 'certain', although the departures from the out-turns shown reveal that any confidence in them is misplaced. However, the picture looks very different when uncertainty measures (shown as 95 per cent error bars around the forecast) are added to the graph as in Fig. A6.5: not only does the uncertainty increase rapidly, it swamps the variation in the average forecast, and by the mid-1990s almost every previous value would be included in the forecast range except the 'oil-crisis' period.

The model can be split into a domestic-economy block (C, Y) and a world economy (ΔP, Q), in which the second block is recursively determined relative to the first. This allows multipliers to be calculated, showing the impact, interim, and long-run effects of changes in (ΔP, Q) on (C, Y), reformulated for convenience to have ΔC, ΔY as dependent variables. The impact multipliers are (with estimated standard errors in parentheses):

Impact multipliers

	ΔP_t	ΔP_{t-1}	Q_t	Q_{t-1}	C_{t-1}	Y_{t-1}
ΔC_t	– 0.66	– 0.49	0.13	– 0.03	– 0.20	0.11
SE	(0.37)	(0.38)	(0.05)	(0.06)	(0.05)	(0.05)
ΔY_t	0.12	– 0.37	0.26	– 0.04	– 0.02	– 0.22
SE	(0.59)	(0.60)	(0.08)	(0.09)	(0.08)	(0.09)

The long-run multipliers are given by:

Long-run multipliers

	ΔP	Q
C	– 6.3	0.98
SE	(2.0)	(0.16)
Y	– 0.81	0.91
SE	(0.13)	(1.62)

Thus, C and Y are almost proportional to output in the long run, and vary negatively with inflation (as does $C - Y$ due to the larger effect of ΔP on C than on Y). All of these results were produced using PcFiml 8 (see Doornik and Hendry, 1994a).

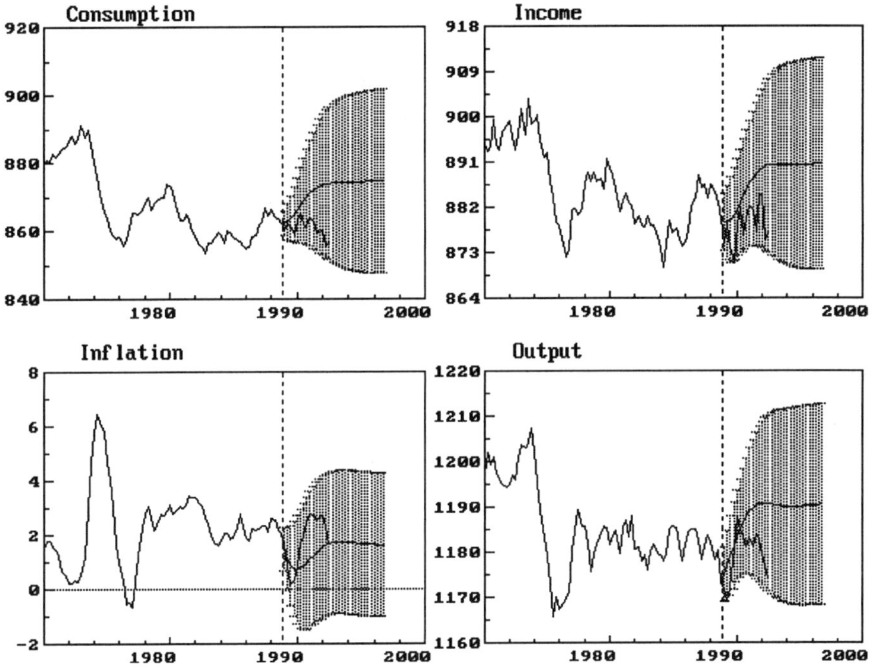

Fig. A6.5 Dynamic forecast of C, Y, ΔP, and Q with error bars

Chapter 8 considers the analysis of non-stationary dynamic systems in more detail, and Chapter 11 discusses the associated theory of estimation.

A6.12 Addendum: static-model solution

Using the parameter values noted in the text, the key equations are:

$$L = 1.2w + 2.5. \tag{A6.77}$$

$$Q = 0.5L + 0.4K. \tag{A6.78}$$

$$L = 1 - 3.8w + 1.5Q. \tag{A6.79}$$

$$K = 4 + 5\pi + 0.8Q. \tag{A6.80}$$

$$W \equiv wL;\ \pi \equiv \Pi/K. \tag{A6.81}$$

$$\Pi \equiv Q - W - 0.05K. \tag{A6.82}$$

From (A6.36):

$$w = -0.30 + 0.30Q. \tag{A6.83}$$

From (A6.37):

$$Q = 2.462 + 4\pi, \tag{A6.84}$$

so:

$$w = -0.30 + 0.30\,(2.462 + 4\pi) = 0.44 + 1.2\pi, \tag{A6.85}$$

and:

$$K = 4 + 5\pi + 0.8\,(2.462 + 4\pi) = 5.97 + 8.2\pi,$$

with:

$$L = 1 - 3.8\,(0.44 + 1.2\pi) + 1.5\,(2.462 + 4\pi) = 4.365 + 1.44\pi.$$

Hence from (A6.39):

$$Q = 2.2185 + 12.252\pi + 9.928\pi^2, \tag{A6.86}$$

and so (A6.40) yields:

$$-\,0.2435 + 8.252\pi + 9.928\pi^2 = 0. \tag{A6.87}$$

Thus, the only positive root is $(-0.831 + \sqrt{0.789})/2$ or $\pi = 0.029$. The other values follow by back-substitution.

A6.13 Macro-model notation

A_t	household wealth (real)
B_t	balance of trade deficit or surplus (nominal)
C_t	aggregate consumers' expenditure (real)
C_{ot}	costs of production (nominal)
C_{owt}	world costs of production (nominal)
CU_t	capacity utilization
D_t	government debt (market value)
D_{ft}	government deficit/surplus (nominal)
D_{et}	dividend payments (nominal)
E_t	aggregate expenditure (real)
e_{rt}	exchange rate (in terms of £/$)
E	expectations operator
F_t	stock of net foreign assets (in foreign currency, nominal)
f_t	total demand by final users (real)
G_t	total government expenditure (real)
I_t	aggregate investment (real)
I_{vt}	stocks or inventories (real)
I_{mt}	imports of goods and services (real)
$\mathcal{I}_{t-1}$	available information
J_t	world trade (real)
K_t	capital stock (real)
L_t	employment
L_t^d	labour demand
L_t^s	labour supply
M_t	money stock (liabilities of the banking sector) (nominal)
N_t	population
P_t	aggregate price level
P_{et}	market price of equity
P_{mt}	price of imports (in foreign currency)
P_{wt}	world prices (in foreign currency)
P_{xt}	price of exports (in domestic currency)
Q_{et}	market value of equity (real)
Q_t^d	quantity demanded in a market (real)
Q_t^s	quantity supplied in a market (real)
Q_t	quantity transacted and total output (real)
R_t	monetary authority's rediscount rate
R_{ct}	commercial bank rate of interest
R_{ft}	foreign interest rate
R_{lt}	interest rate on government debt
R_{nt}	net interest rate ($R_t - R_{ct}$)
S_{vt}	household saving (real)
T_t	aggregate taxes (real)
T_{ct}	taxes on capital (nominal)
T_{et}	taxes on expenditure (nominal)
T_{lt}	taxes on employment (nominal)
TFE	total final expenditure (real)
U_t	unemployment
V_t	value (nominal)
w_t	wage rate
W_t	wage bill
X_t	exports of goods and services (real)
Y_t	national income (real)
Y_{pdt}	personal disposable income (real)
Y_{ft}	income from foreign assets ($R_{ft-1}F_{t-1}$)
Y_{mt}	income from monetary assets ($R_{nt-1}M_{t-1}$)
Y_{rt}	income from government debt ($R_{lt-1}D_{t-1}$)
π_t	profit rate
Π_t	profits (real)
$\Pi_t - D_{et}$	retained earnings (real)
τ_y	income tax rate
δ	rate of depreciation
Δ	first difference operator

References

Abadir, K. M. (1994). The joint density of two functionals of a Brownian motion, Discussion paper 94-03, University of Exeter.

Adby, P. R. and Dempster, M. A. H. (1974). *Introduction to Optimization Methods.* London: Chapman and Hall.

Aigner, D. J. (1984). The welfare econometrics of peak-load pricing for electricity, *Journal of Econometrics*, **26**, 84–83.

Aigner, D. J., Hsiao, C., Kapteyn, A. and Wansbeek, T. (1984). Latent variables models in econometrics, in Griliches and Intriligator (1984), Ch. 23.

Aitchison, J. and Silvey, S. D. (1960). Maximum likelihood estimation and associated tests of significance, *Journal of the Royal Statistical Society B*, **22**, 154–171.

Akerlof, G. A. (1973). The demand for money: A general equilibrium inventory-theoretic approach, *Review of Economic Studies*, **40**, 115–130.

Akerlof, G. A. (1979). Irving Fisher on his head: The consequences of constant target-threshold monitoring of money holdings, *Quarterly Journal of Economics*, **93**, 169–188.

Aldrich, J. (1989). Autonomy, *Oxford Economic Papers*, **41**, 15–34.

Anderson, G. J. and Hendry, D. F. (1984). An econometric model of United Kingdom building societies, *Oxford Bulletin of Economics and Statistics*, **46**, 185–210.

Anderson, T. W. (1958). *An Introduction to Multivariate Statistical Analysis.* New York: John Wiley & Sons.

Anderson, T. W. (1971). *The Statistical Analysis of Time Series.* New York: John Wiley & Sons.

Anderson, T. W. (1976). Estimation of linear functional relationships: Approximate distributions and connections with simultaneous equations in econometrics, *Journal of the Royal Statistical Society B*, **38**, 1–36.

Anderson, T. W. (1984). *An Introduction to Multivariate Statistical Analysis* 2nd edition. New York: John Wiley & Sons.

Anderson, T. W. and Rubin, H. (1949). Estimation of the parameters of a single equation in a complete system of stochastic equations, *Annals of Mathematical Statistics*, **20**, 46–63.

Ando, A. and Shell, K. (1975). Demand for money in a general portfolio model in the presence of an asset that dominates money, In Fromm, G. and Klein, L. R. (eds.), *The Brooking Model: Perspective and Recent Developments*, pp. 560–583. New York: North Holland.

Andrews, D. W. K. (1989). An empirical process central limit theorem for dependent non-identically distributed random variables, Cowles Foundation discussion paper 907, Yale University.

Artis, M. J., Bladen-Hovell, R. C., Osborn, D. R., Smith, J. P. and Zhang, W. (1993). Turning point prediction in the UK: Preliminary results using CSO leading indicators, Presented to the Royal Economic Society Conference, York.

Baba, Y., Hendry, D. F. and Starr, R. M. (1992). The demand for M1 in the U.S.A., 1960–1988, *Review of Economic Studies*, **59**, 25–61.

Bacharach, M. (1970). *Biproportional Matrices and Input-Output Change*. Cambridge: Cambridge University Press.

Backhouse, R. E. (1992). The significance of replication in econometrics, Discussion paper 92–23, Birmingham University.

Banerjee, A., Dolado, J. J., Galbraith, J. W. and Hendry, D. F. (1993). *Co-integration, Error Correction and the Econometric Analysis of Non-Stationary Data*. Oxford: Oxford University Press.

Banerjee, A., Dolado, J. J., Hendry, D. F. and Smith, G. W. (1986). Exploring equilibrium relationships in econometrics through static models: Some Monte Carlo evidence, *Oxford Bulletin of Economics and Statistics*, **48**, 253–277.

Banerjee, A. and Hendry, D. F. (1992). Testing integration and cointegration: An overview, *Oxford Bulletin of Economics and Statistics*, **54**, 225–255.

Bårdsen, G. (1989). The estimation of long run coefficients from error correction models, *Oxford Bulletin of Economics and Statistics*, **50**.

Bårdsen, G. and Fisher, P. G. (1993). The importance of being structured, Discussion paper, Norwegian School of Economics, Bergen.

Barndorff-Nielsen, O. E. (1978). *Information and Exponential Families in Statistical Theory.* Chichester: John Wiley.

Barndorff-Nielsen, O. E. and Cox, D. R. (1989). *Asymptotic Techniques for use in Statistics*. London: Chapman and Hall.

Barnett, W. A. (1980). Economic monetary aggregates: An application of index number and aggregation theory, *Journal of Econometrics*, **14**, 11–48.

Barro, R. J. (1987). *Macroeconomics* 2nd edition. New York: John Wiley.

Bartelsman, E. and Cleveland, W. P. (1993). Joint seasonal adjustment of economic time series, Mimeo, Board of Governors of the Federal Reserve System, Washington, DC.

Basmann, R. L. (1957). A generalized classical method of linear estimation of coefficients in a structural equation, *Econometrica*, **25**, 77–83.

Baumol, W. J. (1952). The transactions demand for cash: An inventory theoretic approach, *Quarterly Journal of Economics*, **66**, 545–556.

Beaulieu, J. J. and Miron, J. A. (1993). Seasonal unit roots in aggregate U.S. data, *Journal of Econometrics*, **55**, 305–328.

Benassy, J.-P. (1986). *Macroeconomics: An Introduction to the Non-Walrasian Approach.* New York: Academic Press.

Bernal, J. D. (1971). *Science in History*, Vols. 1–4. Cambridge, MA: MIT Press.

Berndt, E. K., Hall, B. H., Hall, R. E. and Hausman, J. A. (1974). Estimation and inference in nonlinear structural models, *Annals of Economic and Social Measurement*, **3**, 653–665.

Berndt, E. K. and Savin, N. E. (1977). Conflict among criteria for testing hypotheses in the multivariate linear regression model, *Econometrica*, **45**, 1263–1278.

Bewley, T. F. (ed.)(1987). *Advances in Econometrics*. Cambridge: Cambridge University Press.

Bhargava, A. (1986). On the theory of testing for unit roots in observed time series, *Review of Economic Studies*, **53**, 369–384.

Bhargava, A. (1989). Testing covariance restrictions in systems of simultaneous equations with vector autoregressive errors, *International Economic Review*, **30**, 357–372.

Binmore, K. G. (1983). *Calculus.* Cambridge: Cambridge University Press.

Birchenhall, C. R., Bladen-Hovell, R. C., Chui, A. P. L., Osborn, D. R. and Smith, J. P. (1989). A seasonal model of consumption, *Economic Journal*, **99**, 837–843.

Blalock, H. M. J. (1961). *Causal Inferences in Nonexperimental Research.* Chapel Hill: University of North Carolina Press.

Blanchard, O. and Quah, D. (1989). The dynamic effects of aggregate demand and supply disturbances, *American Economic Review*, **79**, 655–673.

Blaug, M. (1980). *The Methodology of Economics.* Cambridge: Cambridge University Press.

Boland, L. A. (1982). *Foundations of Economic Method.* London: Allen and Unwin.

Boland, L. A. (1989). *The Methodology of Economic Model Building.* London: Routledge.

Bollerslev, T., Chou, R. S. and Kroner, K. F. (1992). ARCH modelling in finance – A review of the theory and empirical evidence, *Journal of Econometrics*, **52**, 5–59.

Boswijk, H. P. (1992). *Cointegration, Identification and Exogeneity*, Vol. no. 37 of *Tinbergen Institute Research Series.* Amsterdam: Thesis Publishers.

Box, G. E. P. and Jenkins, G. M. (1976). *Time Series Analysis, Forecasting and Control.* San Francisco: Holden-Day.

Box, G. E. P. and Pierce, D. A. (1970). Distribution of residual autocorrelations in autoregressive-integrated moving average time series models, *Journal of the American Statistical Association*, **65**, 1509–1526.

Box, M. J., Davies, D. and Swann, W. H. (1969). *Non-Linear Optimization Techniques.* ICI Monograph no. 5. Edinburgh: Oliver and Boyd.

Breusch, T. S. (1986). Hypothesis testing in unidentified models, *Review of Economic Studies*, **53**, 635–651.

Breusch, T. S. (1990). Simplified extreme bounds, in Granger (1990), pp. 72–81.

Breusch, T. S. and Pagan, A. R. (1980). The Lagrange multiplier test and its applications to model specification in econometrics, *Review of Economic Studies*, **47**, 239–253.

Brown, R. L., Durbin, J. and Evans, J. M. (1975). Techniques for testing the constancy of regression relationships over time (with discussion), *Journal of the Royal Statistical Society B*, **37**, 149–192.

Brundy, J. M. and Jorgenson, D. W. (1971). Efficient estimation of simultaneous equations by instrumental variables, *Review of Economics and Statistics*, **53**, 207–224.

Burridge, P. and Wallis, K. F. (1984). Unobserved-components models for seasonal adjustment filters, *Journal of Business and Economic Statistics*, **2**, 350–359.

Cagan, R. (1956). The monetary dynamics of hyperinflation, in Friedman (1956), pp. 25–117.

Caldwell, B. (1982). *Beyond Positivism: Economic Methodology in the Twentieth Century.* London: George Allen and Unwin.

Calzolari, G. (1981). A note on the variance of ex post forecasts in econometric models, *Econometrica*, **49**, 1593–1596.

Campbell, J. Y. and Mankiw, N. G. (1991). The response of consumption to income. A cross-country investigation, *European Economic Review*, **35**, 723–767.

Campos, J. and Ericsson, N. R. (1988). Econometric modeling of consumers' expenditure in Venezuela, International Finance discussion paper 325, Federal Reserve Board of Governors, Washington, DC.

Campos, J., Ericsson, N. R. and Hendry, D. F. (1993). Cointegration tests in the presence of structural breaks, *Journal of Econometrics*. Forthcoming.

Canova, F., Finn, M. and Pagan, A. R. (1992). Evaluating a real business cycle model, Discussion paper, Australian National University.

Cartwright, N. (1983). *How the Laws of Physics Lie*. Oxford: Clarendon Press.

Cartwright, N. (1989). *Nature's Capacities and their Measurement*. Oxford: Clarendon Press.

Chalmers, A. F. (1982). *What is this Thing Called Science?* Milton Keynes: Open University Press.

Chan, N. H. and Wei, C. Z. (1988). Limiting distributions of least squares estimates of unstable autoregressive processes, *Annals of Statistics*, **16**, 367–401.

Charemza, W. and Kiraly, J. (1986). A simple test for conditional super exogeneity, Mimeo, University of Birmingham.

Chong, Y. Y. and Hendry, D. F. (1986). Econometric evaluation of linear macro-economic models, *Review of Economic Studies*, **53**, 671–690. Reprinted in Granger (1990).

Chow, G. C. (1960). Tests of equality between sets of coefficients in two linear regressions, *Econometrica*, **28**, 591–605.

Chow, G. C. and Corsi, P. (eds.)(1982). *Evaluating the Reliability of Macro-Economic Models*. New York: John Wiley.

Chow, Y. S. and Teicher, H. (1988). *Probability Theory*. New York: Springer-Verlag.

Christ, C. F. (1966). *Econometric Models and Methods*. New York: John Wiley.

Clarke, L. E. (1975). *Random Variables*. London: Longmans Group.

Clements, M. P. and Hendry, D. F. (1993). On the limitations of comparing mean squared forecast errors, *Journal of Forecasting*, **12**, 617–637. With discussion.

Clements, M. P. and Hendry, D. F. (1994). Towards a theory of economic forecasting, in Hargreaves (1994), pp. 1–50.

Clements, M. P. and Hendry, D. F. (1995). *Economic Forecasting*. Cambridge: Cambridge University Press.

Clements, M. P. and Mizon, G. E. (1991). Empirical analysis of macroeconomic time series: VAR and structural models, *European Economic Review*, **35**, 887–932.

Cleveland, W. P. and Tiao, G. C. (1976). Decomposition of seasonal time series: A model for the census X–11 program, *Journal of the American Statistical Association*, **71**, 581–587.

Clower, R. (1967). A reconsideration of the microfoundations of monetary theory, *Western Economic Journal* (now *Economic Inquiry)*, **6**, 1–8.

Cochrane, D. and Orcutt, G. H. (1949). Application of least squares regression to relationships containing auto-correlated error terms, *Journal of the American Statistical Association*, **44**, 32–61.

Coen, P. G., Gomme, E. D. and Kendall, M. G. (1969). Lagged relationships in economic forecasting, *Journal of the Royal Statistical Society A*, **132**, 133–163.

Coghlan, R. T. (1978). A transactions demand for money, *Bank of England Quarterly Bulletin*, **18**, 48–60.

Cook, S. and Hendry, D. F. (1993). The theory of reduction in econometrics, *Poznań Studies in the Philosophy of the Sciences and the Humanities*, **38**, 71–100.

Cooper, R. L. (1972). The predictive performance of quarterly econometric models of the United States, In Hickman, B. G. (ed.), *Econometric Models of Cyclical Behaviour*, No. 36 in National Bureau of Economic Research Studies in Income and Wealth, pp. 813–947. New York: Columbia University Press.

Courakis, A. S. (1978). Serial correlation and a Bank of England study of the demand for money: An exercise in measurement without theory, *Economic Journal*, **88**, 537–548.

Cox, D. R. (1961). Tests of separate families of hypotheses, In *Proceedings of the Fourth Berkeley Symposium on Mathematical Statistics and Probability*, Vol. 1, pp. 105–123 Berkeley: University of California Press.

Cox, D. R. (1962). Further results on tests of separate families of hypotheses, *Journal of the Royal Statistical Society B*, **24**, 406–424.

Cox, D. R. and Hinkley, D. V. (1974). *Theoretical Statistics*: Chapman and Hall.

Cramér, H. (1946). *Mathematical Methods of Statistics*. Princeton: Princeton University Press.

Cramer, J. S. (1986). *Econometric Applications of Maximum Likelihood Methods*. Cambridge: Cambridge University Press.

Cross, R. (1982). The Duhem-Quine thesis, Lakatos and the appraisal of theories in macroeconomics, *Economic Journal*, **92**, 320–340.

Crowder, M. J. (1976). Maximum likelihood estimation for dependent observations, *Journal of the Royal Statistical Society B*, **38**, 45–53.

Cuthbertson, K. (1988). The demand for M1: A forward looking buffer stock model, *Oxford Economic Papers*, **40**, 110–131.

Davidson, J. E. H. (1994). *Stochastic Limit Theory*. Oxford: Oxford University Press.

Davidson, J. E. H. and Hall, S. (1991). Cointegration in recursive systems, *Economic Journal*, **101**, 239–251.

Davidson, J. E. H. and Hendry, D. F. (1981). Interpreting econometric evidence: Consumers' expenditure in the UK, *European Economic Review*, **16**, 177–192. Reprinted in Hendry (1993a).

Davidson, J. E. H., Hendry, D. F., Srba, F. and Yeo, S. (1978). Econometric modelling of the aggregate time-series relationship between consumers' expenditure and income in the United Kingdom, *Economic Journal*, **88**, 661–692. Reprinted in Hendry (1993a).

Davidson, R. and MacKinnon, J. G. (1981). Several tests for model specification in the presence of alternative hypotheses, *Econometrica*, **49**, 781–793.

Davidson, R. and MacKinnon, J. G. (1993). *Estimation and Inference in Econometrics*. Oxford: Oxford University Press.

Davies, G. (1979). The effects of government policy on the rise in unemployment, Discussion paper 95/16, Centre for Labour Economics, London School of Economics.

Deaton, A. S. (1992). *Understanding Consumption*. Oxford: Oxford University Press.

Desai, M. J. (1981). *Testing Monetarism*. London: Francis Pinter.

Desai, M. J. and Low, W. (1987). Financial innovations: Measuring the opportunity for product innovations, In De Cecco, M. (ed.), *Changing Money: Financial Innovations in Developed Countries*. Oxford: Basil Blackwell.

Dhrymes, P. J. (1984). *Mathematics for Econometrics* 2nd edition. New York: Springer-Verlag.

Dhrymes, P. J. (1989). *Topics in Advanced Econometrics*. New York: Springer-Verlag.

Dickey, D. A. and Fuller, W. A. (1979). Distribution of the estimators for autoregressive time series with a unit root, *Journal of the American Statistical Association*, **74**, 427–431.

Dickey, D. A. and Fuller, W. A. (1981). Likelihood ratio statistics for autoregressive time series with a unit root, *Econometrica*, **49**, 1057–1072.

Dickey, D. A., Hasza, D. P. and Fuller, W. A. (1984). Testing for unit roots in seasonal time series, *Journal of the American Statistical Association*, **79**, 355–367.

Diebold, F. X. and Rudebusch, G. D. (1991). Forecasting output with the composite leading index: An ex ante analysis, *Journal of the American Statistical Association*, **86**, 603–610.

Diewert, W. E. (1988). *The Early History of Price Index Research*. Cambridge, MA: NBER.

Dijkstra, T. (1992). Pyrrho's lemma, Mimeo, Namur University.

Ding, Z., Granger, C. W. J. and Engle, R. F. (1993). A long memory property of stock market returns and a new model, *Journal of Empirical Finance*, **1**, 83–106.

Dixon, L. W. C. (1972). *Nonlinear Optimization*. London: English Universities Press.

Doan, T., Litterman, R. and Sims, C. A. (1984). Forecasting and conditional projection using realistic prior distributions, *Econometric Reviews*, **3**, 1–100.

Dolado, J. J. (1992). A note on weak exogeneity in VAR cointegrated systems, *Economic Letters*, **38**, 139–143.

Domowitz, I. and White, H. (1982). Mis-specified models with dependent observations, *Journal of Econometrics*, **20**, 35–58.

Doornik, J. A. and Hansen, H. (1994). A practical test for univariate and multivariate normality, Discussion paper, Nuffield College.

Doornik, J. A. and Hendry, D. F. (1994a). *PcFiml 8: An Interactive Program for Modelling Econometric Systems*. London: International Thomson Publishing.

Doornik, J. A. and Hendry, D. F. (1994b). *PcGive 8: An Interactive Econometric Modelling System*. London: International Thomson Publishing, and Belmont, CA: Duxbury Press.

Drake, S. (1980). *Galileo*. Oxford: Oxford University Press.

Duffie, D. and Singleton, K. J. (1989). Simulated moments estimation of Markov models of asset prices, Mimeo, Stanford University.

Durbin, J. (1954). Errors in variables, *Review of the Institute of International Statistics*, **22**, 23–54.

Durbin, J. (1960). Estimation of parameters in time-series regression models, *Journal of the Royal Statistical Society B*, **22**, 139–153.

Durbin, J. (1963). Maximum likelihood estimation of the parameters of a system of simultaneous regression equations, Paper presented to the Copenhagen meeting of the Econometric Society. Published in *Econometric Theory* (1988), **4**, pp. 159–170.

Durbin, J. (1970). Testing for serial correlation in least squares regression when some of the regressors are lagged dependent variables, *Econometrica*, **38**, 410–421.

Durbin, J. (1988). Maximum likelihood estimation of the parameters of a system of simultaneous regression equations, *Econometric Theory*, **4**, 159–170. Paper presented to the Copenhagen Meeting of the Econometric Society, 1963.

Durbin, J. and Watson, G. S. (1950). Testing for serial correlation in least squares regression I, *Biometrika*, **37**, 409–428.

Durbin, J. and Watson, G. S. (1951). Testing for serial correlation in least squares regression II, *Biometrika*, **38**, 159–178.

Durlauf, S. N. and Phillips, P. C. B. (1986). Trends versus random walks in time series analysis, Cowles Foundation discussion paper 788, Yale University.

Edison, H. J., Marquez, J. R. and Tryon, R. W. (1987). The structure and properties of the Federal Reserve Board multicountry model, *Economic Modelling*, **4**, 115–315.

Eicker, F. (1967). Limit theorems for regressions with unequal and dependent errors, In *Proceedings of the Fifth Berkeley Symposium on Mathematical Statistics and Probability*, Vol. 1, pp. 59–82 Berkeley: University of California.

Eisner, R. and Strotz, R. H. (1963). *Determinants of Business Investment.* Englewood Cliffs, NJ: Prentice-Hall.

Emerson, R. A. and Hendry, D. F. (1994). An evaluation of forecasting using leading indicators, Mimeo, Nuffield College, Oxford.

Engle, R. F. (1982a). Autoregressive conditional heteroscedasticity, with estimates of the variance of United Kingdom inflations, *Econometrica*, **50**, 987–1007.

Engle, R. F. (1982b). A general approach to Lagrange multiplier model diagnostics, *Annals of Applied Econometrics*, **20**, 83–104.

Engle, R. F. (1984). Wald, likelihood ratio, and Lagrange multiplier tests in econometrics, in Griliches and Intriligator (1984), Ch. 13.

Engle, R. F. and Bollerslev, T. (1987). Modelling the persistence of conditional variances, *Econometric Reviews*, **5**, 1–50.

Engle, R. F. and Granger, C. W. J. (1987). Cointegration and error correction: Representation, estimation and testing, *Econometrica*, **55**, 251–276.

Engle, R. F. and Granger, C. W. J. (eds.)(1991). *Long-Run Economic Relationships.* Oxford: Oxford University Press.

Engle, R. F. and Hendry, D. F. (1993). Testing super exogeneity and invariance in regression models, *Journal of Econometrics*, **56**, 119–139.

Engle, R. F., Hendry, D. F. and Richard, J.-F. (1983). Exogeneity, *Econometrica*, **51**, 277–304. Reprinted in Hendry (1993a).

Engle, R. F., Hendry, D. F. and Trumbull, D. (1985). Small sample properties of ARCH estimators and tests, *Canadian Journal of Economics*, **43**, 66–93.

Engle, R. F. and Yoo, B. S. (1987). Forecasting and testing in co-integrated systems, *Journal of Econometrics*, **35**, 143–159.

Ericsson, N. R. (1983). Asymptotic properties of instrumental variables statistics for testing non-nested hypotheses, *Review of Economic Studies*, **50**, 287–303.

Ericsson, N. R. (1992a). Cointegration, exogeneity and policy analysis: An overview, *Journal of Policy Modeling*, **14**, 251–280.

Ericsson, N. R. (1992b). Parameter constancy, mean square forecast errors, and measuring forecast performance: An exposition, extensions, and illustration, *Journal of Policy Modeling*, **14**, 465–495.

Ericsson, N. R. (1993a). Comment on 'On the limitations of comparing mean squared forecast errors', by M.P. Clements and D.F. Hendry, *Journal of Forecasting*, **12**, 617–637.

Ericsson, N. R. (1993b). The fragility of sensitivity analysis: An encompassing perspective, mimeo, Federal Reserve Board.

Ericsson, N. R., Campos, J. and Tran, H.-A. (1990). PC-GIVE and David Hendry's econometric methodology, *Revista De Econometria*, **10**, 7–117.

Ericsson, N. R. and Hendry, D. F. (1989). Encompassing and rational expectations: How sequential corroboration can imply refutation, Discussion paper 354, Board of Governors of the Federal Reserve System.

Ericsson, N. R., Hendry, D. F. and Tran, H.-A. (1994). Cointegration, seasonality, encompassing and the demand for money in the United Kingdom, in Hargreaves (1994), pp. 179–224.

Ericsson, N. R. and Irons, J. S. (1994). The Lucas critique in practice: Theory without measurement, In Hoover, K. D. (ed.), *Macroeconometrics: Developments, Tensions and Prospects*. Dordrecht: Kluwer Academic Press. Forthcoming.

Ermini, L. and Hendry, D. F. (1991). Log income versus linear income: An application of the encompassing principle, Mimeo, University of Hawaii at Manoa.

Fair, R. C. (1984). *Specification, Estimation, and Analysis of Macroeconometric Models*. Cambridge, MA: Harvard University Press.

Favero, C. (1989). Testing for super exogeneity: The case of the term structure of interest rates, Discussion paper 67, Institute of Economics and Statistics, Oxford.

Favero, C. and Hendry, D. F. (1992). Testing the Lucas critique: A review, *Econometric Reviews*, **11**, 265–306.

Feige, E. L. and Pearce, D. K. (1976). Economically rational expectations, *Journal of Political Economy*, **84**, 499–522.

Feller, W. (1971). *An Introduction to Probability Theory and its Applications*, Vol. 1. Chichester: John Wiley.

Feyerabend, P. (1975). *Against Method: Outline of an Anarchistic Theory of Knowledge*. London: New Left Books.

Fisher, F. M. (1965). Dynamic structure and estimation in economy-wide econometric models, In Duesenberry, J. S., Klein, L. R., Fromm, G. and Kuh, E. (eds.), *Brookings Quarterly Econometric Model of the United States*. Amsterdam: North-Holland Publishing Company.

Fisher, F. M. (1966). *The Identification Problem in Econometrics*. New York: McGraw Hill.

Fisher, R. A. (1922a). The goodness of fit of regression formulae, and the distribution of regression coefficients, *Journal of the Royal Statistical Society*, **85**, 597–612.

Fisher, R. A. (1922b). On the mathematical foundations of theoretical statistics, *Philosophical Transactions of the Royal Society, A*, **222**, 309–368.

Flemming, J. S. (1973). The consumption function when capital markets are imperfect: The permanent income hypothesis reconsidered, *Oxford Economic Papers*, **25**, 160–172.

Flemming, J. S. (1976). *Inflation*. Oxford: Oxford University Press.

Fletcher, R. (1987). *Practical Methods of Optimization* 2nd edition. New York: John Wiley & Sons.

Florens, J.-P., Hendry, D. F. and Richard, J.-F. (1994). Encompassing and specificity, Discussion paper cahier 91c, GREMAQ, University of Toulouse.

Florens, J.-P., Mouchart, M. and Rolin, J.-M. (1990). *Elements of Bayesian Statistics*. New York: Marcel Dekker.

Friedman, M. (1953). *Essays in Positive Economics*. Chicago: University of Chicago Press.

Friedman, M. (ed.)(1956). *Studies in the Quantity Theory of Money.* Chicago: University of Chicago Press.

Friedman, M. (1957). *A Theory of the Consumption Function.* Princeton: Princeton University Press.

Friedman, M. and Schwartz, A. J. (1982). *Monetary Trends in the United States and the United Kingdom: Their Relation to Income, Prices, and Interest Rates, 1867–1975.* Chicago: University of Chicago Press.

Frisch, R. (1933). Editorial, *Econometrica*, **1**, 1–4.

Frisch, R. (1934). *Statistical Confluence Analysis by means of Complete Regression Systems*: University Institute of Economics, Oslo.

Frisch, R. (1938). Statistical versus theoretical relations in economic macrodynamics, Mimeograph dated 17 July 1938, League of Nations Memorandum. Reproduced by University of Oslo in 1948 with Tinbergen's comments. Contained in Memorandum 'Autonomy of Economic Relations', 6 November 1948, Oslo, Universitets Økonomiske Institutt.

Frisch, R. and Waugh, F. V. (1933). Partial time regression as compared with individual trends, *Econometrica*, **1**, 221–223.

Fuller, W. A. (1976). *Introduction to Statistical Time Series.* New York: John Wiley & Sons.

Galbraith, J. W. (1987). Modelling the formation of expectations, Oxford D.Phil. thesis, University of Oxford.

Gale, D. (1982). *Money: In Equilibrium.* Cambridge: Cambridge University Press.

Gale, D. (1983). *Money: In Disequilibrium.* Cambridge: Cambridge University Press.

Gantmacher, F. R. (1959). *The Theory of Matrices*, Vols. 1–2. Boston: Chelsea Publishing.

Geary, R. C. (1943). Relations between statistics: the general and the sampling problem when the samples are large, In *Proceedings of the Royal Irish Academy (Section A)*, Vol. 49, pp. 177–196.

Gel'fand, I. M. (1967). *Lectures on Linear Algebra.* New York: Interscience.

Geman, S. and Geman, D. (1984). Stochastic relaxation, Gibbs distributions and the Bayesian restoration of images, *IEEE Transactions on Pattern Analysis and Machine Intelligence*, **6**, 721–741.

Geweke, J. B. (1988). Acceleration methods for Monte Carlo integration in Bayesian inference, In *Proceedings of the 20th Symposium on the Interface: Computing Science and Statistics.*

Ghysels, E., Lee, H. S. and Noh, J. (1991). Testing for unit roots in seasonal time series: Some theoretical extensions and a Monte Carlo investigation, Mimeo 89–55, Department of Economics, University of Montréal.

Ghysels, E. and Perron, P. (1993). The effect of seasonal adjustment filters on tests for a unit root, *Journal of Econometrics*, **55**, 57–98.

Gilbert, C. L. (1986). Professor Hendry's methodology, *Oxford Bulletin of Economics and Statistics*, **48**, 283–307. Reprinted in Granger (1990).

Gilbert, C. L. (1989). LSE and the British approach to time-series econometrics, *Oxford Review of Economic Policy*, **41**, 108–128.

Gill, P. E., Murray, W. and Wright, M. H. (1981). *Practical Optimization.* New York: Academic Press.

Godfrey, L. G. (1978). Testing for higher order serial correlation in regression equations when the regressors include lagged dependent variables, *Econometrica*, **46**, 1303–1313.

Godfrey, L. G. (1988). *Misspecification Tests in Econometrics*. Cambridge: Cambridge University Press.

Goldberger, A. S. (1964). *Econometric Theory*. New York: John Wiley.

Goldfeld, S. M. (1973). The demand for money revisited, *Brookings Papers in Economic Activity*, **3**, 577–646.

Goldfeld, S. M. (1976). The case of the missing money, *Brookings Papers on Economic Activity*, **6**, 683–730.

Goldfeld, S. M. and Quandt, R. E. (1972). *Non-linear Methods in Econometrics*. Amsterdam: North-Holland.

Goldfeld, S. M. and Quandt, R. E. (eds.)(1976). *Studies in Nonlinear Estimation*. Cambridge, MA: Bollinger Publishing Company.

Goldfeld, S. M. and Sichel, D. E. (1990). The demand for money, In Friedman, B. M. and Hahn, F. H. (eds.), *Handbook of Monetary Economics*, Vol. 1, pp. 299–356. Amsterdam: North-Holland.

Gonzalo, J. (1989). Comparison of five alternative methods of estimating long run equilibrium relationships, Discussion paper 89–55, University of California at San Diego.

Goodhart, C. A. E. (1978). Problems of monetary management: the UK experience, In Courakis, A. S. (ed.), *Inflation, Depression and Economic Policy in the West: Lessons from the 1970s*. Oxford: Basil Blackwell.

Gordon, R. J. (1984). The short-run demand for money: A reconsideration, *Journal of Money, Credit, and Banking*, **16**, 403–434.

Gould, S. J. (1989). *Wonderful Life*. London: Penguin.

Gourieroux, C. and Monfort, A. (1991). Testing non-nested hypotheses, Mimeo, INSEE.

Gourieroux, C. and Monfort, A. (1992). Testing, encompassing and simulating dynamic econometric models, Mimeo, INSEE.

Gourieroux, C., Monfort, A. and Trognon, A. (1984). Pseudo-maximum likelihood methods: Theory, *Econometrica*, **52**, 681–700.

Govaerts, B. (1986). Application of the encompassing principle to linear dynamic models, Ph.D. dissertation, Universite Catholique de Louvain.

Govaerts, B., Hendry, D. F. and Richard, J.-F. (1993). Encompassing in stationary linear dynamic models, *Journal of Econometrics*, **63**, 245–270.

Granger, C. W. J. (1969). Investigating causal relations by econometric models and cross-spectral methods, *Econometrica*, **37**, 424–438.

Granger, C. W. J. (1978). Seasonality: Causation, interpretation, and implications, in Zellner (1978).

Granger, C. W. J. (1986). Developments in the study of cointegrated economic variables, *Oxford Bulletin of Economics and Statistics*, **48**, 213–228.

Granger, C. W. J. (ed.)(1990). *Modelling Economic Series*. Oxford: Clarendon Press.

Granger, C. W. J. and Lee, T.-H. (1991). Multicointegration, in Engle and Granger (1991), pp. 179–190.

Granger, C. W. J. and Newbold, P. (1974). Spurious regressions in econometrics, *Journal of Econometrics*, **2**, 111–120.

Gregory, A. W. and Veale, M. R. (1985). Formulating Wald tests of non-linear restrictions, *Econometrica*, **53**, 1465–1468.

Grether, D. M. and Nerlove, M. (1970). Some properties of 'optimal' seasonal adjustment, *Econometrica*, **38**, 682–703.

Griliches, Z. and Intriligator, M. D. (eds.)(1983). *Handbook of Econometrics*, Vol. 1. Amsterdam: North-Holland.

Griliches, Z. and Intriligator, M. D. (eds.)(1984). *Handbook of Econometrics*, Vols. 2–3. Amsterdam: North-Holland.

Grimmett, G. R. and Stirzaker, D. R. (1982). *Probability and Random Processes*. Oxford: Oxford University Press.

Grimmett, G. R. and Welsh, D. (1986). *Probability: An Introduction*. Oxford: Oxford University Press.

Haavelmo, T. (1943). The statistical implications of a system of simultaneous equations, *Econometrica*, **11**, 1–12.

Haavelmo, T. (1944). The probability approach in econometrics, *Econometrica*, **12**, 1–118. Supplement.

Hacche, G. (1974). The demand for money in the United Kingdom: Experience since 1971, *Bank of England Quarterly Bulletin*, **14**, 284–305.

Hahn, F. (1988). On monetary theory, *Economic Journal*, **98**, 957–973.

Hajivassiliou, V. A. (1989). Macroeconomic shocks in an aggregate disequilibrium model, Mimeo, Yale University.

Hajivassiliou, V. A. and McFadden, D. L. (1989). The method of simulated scores for the estimation of LDV models with an application to the problem of external debt crisis, Mimeo, Yale University.

Hall, P. and Heyde, C. C. (1980). *Martingale Limit Theory and its Applications*. London: Academic Press.

Hall, R. E. (1978). Stochastic implications of the life cycle-permanent income hypothesis: Evidence, *Journal of Political Economy*, **86**, 971–987.

Hall, S. and Sola, M. (1993). Structural breaks and GARCH modelling, Mimeo, London Business School.

Hall, S. G., Henry, S. G. B. and Wilcox, J. B. (1990). The long-run determination of UK monetary aggregates, In Henry, S. G. B. and Patterson, K. D. (eds.), *Economic Modelling at the Bank of England*. London: Chapman and Hall.

Halmos, P. R. (1950). *Lectures on Ergodic Theory*. New York: Chelsea Publishing Co.

Hannan, E. J. (1970). *Multiple Time Series*. John Wiley: New York.

Hannan, E. J. and Deistler, M. (1988). *The Statistical Theory of Linear Systems*. John Wiley & Sons: New York.

Hansen, B. E. (1992a). Testing for parameter instability in linear models, *Journal of Policy Modeling*, **14**, 517–533.

Hansen, B. E. (1992b). Tests for parameter instability in regressions with I(1) processes, *Journal of Business and Economic Statistics*, **10**, 321–335.

Hansen, H. and Johansen, S. (1992). Recursive estimation in cointegrated VAR-models, Discussion paper, Institute of Mathematical Statistics, University of Copenhagen.

Hansen, L. P. (1982). Large sample properties of generalized method of moments estimators, *Econometrica*, **50**, 1027–1054.

Hargreaves, C. (ed.)(1994). *Non-stationary Time-series Analyses and Cointegration.* Oxford: Oxford University Press.

Harré, R. (1981). *Great Scientific Experiments.* Oxford: Oxford University Press.

Harré, R. (1985). *The Philosophies of Science.* Oxford: Oxford University Press.

Harvey, A. C. (1981a). *The Econometric Analysis of Time Series.* Deddington: Philip Allan.

Harvey, A. C. (1981b). *Time Series Models.* London: Philip Allan.

Harvey, A. C. (1990). *The Econometric Analysis of Time Series* 2nd edition. Hemel Hempstead: Philip Allan.

Harvey, A. C. and Scott, A. (1993). Seasonality in dynamic regression models, Unpublished paper, London School of Economics.

Harvey, A. C. and Shephard, N. (1993). Estimation and testing of stochastic variance models, Discussion paper, Nuffield College.

Hausman, D. M. (1984). *The Philosophy of Economics.* Cambridge: Cambridge University Press.

Hausman, J. A. (1975). An instrumental variable approach to full-information estimators for linear and non-linear econometric models, *Econometrica*, **43**, 727–753.

Hausman, J. A. (1978). Specification tests in econometrics, *Econometrica*, **46**, 1251–1271.

Hausman, J. A. and Wise, D. A. (1985). *Social Experimentation.* Chicago: Chicago University Press.

Healey, J., Mann, C., Clews, R. and Hoggarth, G. (1990). Monetary aggregates in a changing environment: A statistical discussion paper, Bank of england discussion paper 47, London.

Heckman, J. J. (1981). Statistical models for discrete panel data, in Manski and McFadden (1981), Ch. 3.

Heckman, J. J. and McCurdy, T. F. (1980). A life cycle model of female labor supply, *Review of Economic Studies*, **47**, 47–74.

Hempel, C. G. (1965). *Aspects of Scientific Explanation.* New York: Free Press.

Hempel, C. G. (1966). *Philosophy of Natural Science.* Englewood Cliffs, NJ: Prentice-Hall.

Henderson, J. M. and Quandt, R. E. (1971). *Microeconomic Theory: A Mathematical Approach* 2nd edition. New York: McGraw-Hill.

Hendry, D. F. (1971). Maximum likelihood estimation of systems of simultaneous regression equations with errors generated by a vector autoregressive process, *International Economic Review*, **12**, 257–272. Correction in **15**, p.260.

Hendry, D. F. (1975). The consequences of mis-specification of dynamic structure, autocorrelation and simultaneity in a simple model with an application to the demand for imports, In Renton, G. A. (ed.), *Modelling the Economy*, Ch. 11. London: Heinemann Educational Books.

Hendry, D. F. (1976). The structure of simultaneous equations estimators, *Journal of Econometrics*, **4**, 51–88. Reprinted in Hendry (1993a).

Hendry, D. F. (1977). On the time series approach to econometric model building, In Sims, C. A. (ed.), *New Methods in Business Cycle Research*, pp. 183–202. Minneapolis: Federal Reserve Bank of Minneapolis. Reprinted in Hendry (1993a).

Hendry, D. F. (1979a). The behaviour of inconsistent instrumental variables estimators in dynamic systems with autocorrelated errors, *Journal of Econometrics*, **9**, 295–314.

Hendry, D. F. (1979b). Predictive failure and econometric modelling in macro-economics: The transactions demand for money, In Ormerod, P. (ed.), *Economic Modelling*, pp. 217–242. London: Heinemann. Reprinted in Hendry (1993a).

Hendry, D. F. (1980). Econometrics: Alchemy or science?, *Economica*, **47**, 387–406. Reprinted in Hendry D. F. (1993), *Econometrics: Alchemy or Science?* Oxford: Blackwell Publishers.

Hendry, D. F. (1982). A reply to Professors Maasoumi and Phillips, *Journal of Econometrics*, **19**, 203–213.

Hendry, D. F. (1983a). Comment, *Econometric Reviews*, **2**, 111–114.

Hendry, D. F. (1983b). Econometric modelling: The consumption function in retrospect, *Scottish Journal of Political Economy*, **30**, 193–220. Reprinted in Hendry (1993a).

Hendry, D. F. (1984a). Econometric modelling of house prices in the United Kingdom, in Hendry and Wallis (1984), pp. 135–172.

Hendry, D. F. (1984b). Monte Carlo experimentation in econometrics, in Griliches and Intriligator (1984), Ch. 16.

Hendry, D. F. (1985). Monetary economic myth and econometric reality, *Oxford Review of Economic Policy*, **1**, 72–84. Reprinted in Hendry (1993a).

Hendry, D. F. (1986a). Empirical modelling in dynamic econometrics: The new-construction sector, *Applied Mathematics and Computation*, **21**, 1–36.

Hendry, D. F. (1986b). An excursion into conditional variance land, *Econometric Reviews*, **5**, 63–69. (Comment).

Hendry, D. F. (1987). Econometric methodology: A personal perspective, in Bewley (1987), Ch. 10.

Hendry, D. F. (1988). The encompassing implications of feedback versus feedforward mechanisms in econometrics, *Oxford Economic Papers*, **40**, 132–149.

Hendry, D. F. (1993a). *Econometrics: Alchemy or Science?* Oxford: Blackwell Publishers.

Hendry, D. F. (1993b). The roles of economic theory and econometrics in time-series economics, Invited address, European Econometric Society, Stockholm.

Hendry, D. F. (1994a). HUS revisited, *Oxford Review of Economic Policy*, **10**, 86–106.

Hendry, D. F. (1994b). On the interactions of unit roots and exogeneity, *Econometric Reviews*. Forthcoming.

Hendry, D. F. (1994c). Topologies of linear dynamic systems and models, *Jornal of Statistical Inference and Planning*. Forthcoming.

Hendry, D. F. and Anderson, G. J. (1977). Testing dynamic specification in small simultaneous systems: An application to a model of building society behaviour in the United Kingdom, In Intriligator, M. D. (ed.), *Frontiers in Quantitative Economics*, Vol. 3, pp. 361–383. Amsterdam: North Holland Publishing Company. Reprinted in Hendry (1993a).

Hendry, D. F. and Clements, M. P. (1992). On a theory of intercept corrections in macro-economic forecasting, In Holly, S. (ed.), *Money, Inflation and Employment*, pp. 160–182. Aldershot: Edward Elgar. Essays in Honour of James Ball.

Hendry, D. F. and Doornik, J. A. (1994). Modelling linear dynamic econometric systems, *Scottish Journal of Political Economy*, **41**, 1–33.

Hendry, D. F. and Ericsson, N. R. (1991a). An econometric analysis of UK money demand in monetary trends in the United States and the United Kingdom by Milton Friedman and Anna J. Schwartz, *American Economic Review*, **81**, 8–38.

Hendry, D. F. and Ericsson, N. R. (1991b). Modeling the demand for narrow money in the United Kingdom and the United States, *European Economic Review*, **35**, 833–886.

Hendry, D. F., Leamer, E. E. and Poirier, D. J. (1990). A conversation on econometric methodology, *Econometric Theory*, **6**, 171–261.

Hendry, D. F. and Mizon, G. E. (1978). Serial correlation as a convenient simplification, not a nuisance: A comment on a study of the demand for money by the Bank of England, *Economic Journal*, **88**, 549–563. Reprinted in Hendry (1993a).

Hendry, D. F. and Mizon, G. E. (1990). Procrustean econometrics: or the stretching and squeezing of data,. pp. 121–136. Reprinted in Granger (1990).

Hendry, D. F. and Mizon, G. E. (1993). Evaluating dynamic econometric models by encompassing the VAR, In Phillips, P. C. B. (ed.), *Models, Methods and Applications of Econometrics*, pp. 272–300. Oxford: Basil Blackwell.

Hendry, D. F. and Morgan, M. S. (1989). A re-analysis of confluence analysis, *Oxford Economic Papers*, **41**, 35–52.

Hendry, D. F. and Morgan, M. S. (1995). *The Foundations of Econometric Analysis*. Cambridge.

Hendry, D. F., Muellbauer, J. N. J. and Murphy, T. A. (1990). The econometrics of DHSY, In Hey, J. D. and Winch, D. (eds.), *A Century of Economics*, pp. 298–334. Oxford: Basil Blackwell.

Hendry, D. F. and Neale, A. J. (1987). Monte Carlo experimentation using PC-NAIVE, In Fomby, T. and Rhodes, G. F. (eds.), *Advances in Econometrics*, Vol. 6, pp. 91–125. Greenwich, Connecticut: Jai Press Inc.

Hendry, D. F. and Neale, A. J. (1991). A Monte Carlo study of the effects of structural breaks on tests for unit roots, In Hackl, P. and Westlund, A. H. (eds.), *Economic Structural Change, Analysis and Forecasting*, pp. 95–119. Berlin: Springer-Verlag.

Hendry, D. F., Neale, A. J. and Ericsson, N. R. (1991). *PC-NAIVE, An Interactive Program for Monte Carlo Experimentation in Econometrics. Version 6.0.* Oxford: Institute of Economics and Statistics, University of Oxford.

Hendry, D. F., Neale, A. J. and Srba, F. (1988). Econometric analysis of small linear systems using PC-FIML, *Journal of Econometrics*, **38**, 203–226.

Hendry, D. F., Pagan, A. R. and Sargan, J. D. (1984). Dynamic specification, in Griliches and Intriligator (1984), Ch. 18. Reprinted in Hendry (1993a).

Hendry, D. F. and Richard, J.-F. (1982). On the formulation of empirical models in dynamic econometrics, *Journal of Econometrics*, **20**, 3–33. Reprinted in Granger (1990) and in Hendry (1993a).

Hendry, D. F. and Richard, J.-F. (1983). The econometric analysis of economic time series (with discussion), *International Statistical Review*, **51**, 111–163. Reprinted in Hendry (1993a).

Hendry, D. F. and Richard, J.-F. (1989). Recent developments in the theory of encompassing, In Cornet, B. and Tulkens, H. (eds.), *Contributions to Operations Research and Econometrics. The XXth Anniversary of CORE*, pp. 393–440. Cambridge, MA: MIT Press.

Hendry, D. F. and Richard, J.-F. (1991). Likelihood evaluation for dynamic latent variables models, In Amman, H. M., Belsley, D. A. and Pau, L. F. (eds.), *Computational Economics and Econometrics*, Ch. 1. Dordrecht: Kluwer.

Hendry, D. F. and Srba, F. (1977). The properties of autoregressive instrumental variables estimators in dynamic systems, *Econometrica*, **45**, 969–990.

Hendry, D. F. and Srba, F. (1980). AUTOREG: A computer program library for dynamic econometric models with autoregressive errors, *Journal of Econometrics*, **12**, 85–102. Reprinted in Hendry (1993a).

Hendry, D. F. and Starr, R. M. (1993). The demand for M1 in the USA: A reply to James M. Boughton, *Economic Journal*, **103**, 1158–1169.

Hendry, D. F. and Trivedi, P. K. (1972). Maximum likelihood estimation of difference equations with moving-average errors: A simulation study, *Review of Economic Studies*, **32**, 117–145.

Hendry, D. F. and von Ungern-Sternberg, T. (1981). Liquidity and inflation effects on consumers' expenditure, In Deaton, A. S. (ed.), *Essays in the Theory and Measurement of Consumers' Behaviour*, pp. 237–261. Cambridge: Cambridge University Press. Reprinted in Hendry (1993a).

Hendry, D. F. and Wallis, K. F. (eds.)(1984). *Econometrics and Quantitative Economics*. Oxford: Basil Blackwell.

Herschel, J. (1830). *A Preliminary Discourse on The Study of Natural Philosophy*. London: Longman, Rees, Browne, Green and John Taylor.

Hicks, J. R. (1979). *Causality in Economics*. Oxford: Basil Blackwell.

Hildreth, C. and Lu, J. Y. (1960). Demand relations with autocorrelated disturbances, Technical bulletin 276, Agricultural Experimental Station, Michigan State University.

Hogg, R. V. and Craig, A. T. (1978). *Introduction to Mathematical Statistics*. London: Collier Macmillan.

Holt, C., Modigliani, F., Muth, J. F. and Simon, H. (1960). *Planning Production, Inventories and Work Force*. Englewood Cliffs: Prentice-Hall.

Hood, W. C. and Koopmans, T. C. (eds.)(1953). *Studies in Econometric Method*. No. 14 in Cowles Commission Monograph. New York: John Wiley.

Hooker, P. H. (1901). Correlation of the marriage rate with trade, *Journal of the Royal Statistical Society*, **64**, 485–492.

Hoover, K. D. (1990). The logic of causal inference: Econometrics and the conditional analysis of causation, *Economics and Philosophy*, **6**, 207–234.

Hurwicz, L. (1950). Least squares bias in time series, in Koopmans (1950a), Ch. 15.

Hurwicz, L. (1962). On the structural form of interdependent systems, In Nagel, E. and others. (eds.), *Logic, Methodology and the Philosophy of Science*. Palo Alto: Stanford University Press.

Hylleberg, S. (1986). *Seasonality in Regression*. Orlando, Florida: Academic Press.

Hylleberg, S. (ed.)(1992). *Modelling Seasonality*: Oxford University Press.

Hylleberg, S., Engle, R. F., Granger, C. W. J. and Yoo, B. S. (1990). Seasonal integration and cointegration, *Journal of Econometrics*, **44**, 215–238.

Jacoby, S. L. S., Kowalik, J. S. and Pizzo, J. T. (1972). *Iterative Methods for Nonlinear Optimization Problems*. New Jersey: Prentice-Hall Inc.

Jarque, C. M. and Bera, A. K. (1980). Efficient tests for normality, homoscedasticity and serial independence of regression residuals, *Economics Letters*, **6**, 255–259.

Jevons, W. S. (1884). *Investigations in Currency and Finance*. London: Macmillan.

Johansen, S. (1988). Statistical analysis of cointegration vectors, *Journal of Economic Dynamics and Control*, **12**, 231–254.

Johansen, S. (1992a). Cointegration in partial systems and the efficiency of single-equation analysis, *Journal of Econometrics*, **52**, 389–402.

Johansen, S. (1992b). A representation of vector autoregressive processes integrated of order 2, *Econometric Theory*, **8**, 188–202.

Johansen, S. (1992c). Testing weak exogeneity and the order of cointegration in UK money demand, *Journal of Policy Modeling*, **14**, 313–334.

Johansen, S. (1993). Identifying restrictions of linear equations, Discussion paper, Institute of Mathematical Statistics, University of Copenhagen.

Johansen, S. (1995). *Likelihood based Inference on Cointegration in the Vector Autoregressive Model.* Forthcoming.

Johansen, S. and Juselius, K. (1990). Maximum likelihood estimation and inference on cointegration – With application to the demand for money, *Oxford Bulletin of Economics and Statistics*, **52**, 169–210.

Johnson, N. L. and Kotz, S. (1970a). *Continuous Univariate Distributions – 1.* New York: John Wiley.

Johnson, N. L. and Kotz, S. (1970b). *Continuous Univariate Distributions – 2.* New York: John Wiley.

Johnson, N. L. and Kotz, S. (1970c). *Distributions in Statistics.* New York: John Wiley.

Johnston, J. (1963). *Econometric Methods* 1st edition. New York: McGraw-Hill.

Johnston, J. (1972). *Econometric Methods* 2nd edition. New York: McGraw-Hill.

Jorgenson, D. W. (1966). Rational distributed lag functions, *Econometrica*, **34**, 135–149.

Judd, J. and Scadding, J. (1982). The search for a stable money demand function: A survey of the post-1973 literature, *Journal of Economic Literature*, **20**, 993–1023.

Judge, G. G., Griffiths, W. E., Hill, R. C., Lütkepohl, H. and Lee, T.-C. (1985). *The Theory and Practice of Econometrics* 2nd edition. New York: John Wiley.

Juselius, K. (1993). VAR modelling and Haavelmo's probability approach to econometrics, Discussion paper 9305, University of Copenhagen.

Kakwani, N. C. (1967). The unbiasedness of Zellner's seemingly unrelated regression equations estimator, *Journal of the American Statistical Association*, **62**, 141–142.

Kendall, M. G. and Stuart, A. (1977). *Advanced Theory of Statistics.* London: Charles Griffin and Co.

Kennan, J. (1979). The estimation of partial adjustment models with rational expectations, *Econometrica*, **47**, 1441–1455.

Kenny, P. B. and Durbin, J. (1982). Local trend estimation and seasonal adjustment of economic and social time series, *Journal of the Royal Statistical Society A*, **145**, 1–41 (with discussion).

Keynes, J. M. (1936). *The General Theory of Employment, Interest and Money.* London: Macmillan.

Keynes, J. M. (1939). Professor Tinbergen's method, *Economic Journal*, **44**, 558–568.

Keynes, J. N. (1891). *The Scope and Method of Political Economy.* New York: Kelley and Millman.

Kim, K. and Pagan, A. R. (1993). The econometric analysis of calibrated macroeconomic models, Discussion paper, Australian National University.

Kiviet, J. F. (1985). Model selection test procedures in a single linear equation of a dynamic simultaneous system and their defects in small samples, *Journal of Econometrics*, **28**, 327–362.

Kiviet, J. F. and Phillips, G. D. A. (1992). Exact similar tests for unit roots and cointegration, *Oxford Bulletin of Economics and Statistics*, **54**, 349–367.

Klein, L. R. (1969). Estimation of interdependent systems in macro-econometrics, *Econometrica*, **37**, 171–192.

Kmenta, J. and Ramsey, J. B. (1981). *Large-Scale Macro-Econometric Models*. Amsterdam: North Holland Publishing Company.

Kohn, A. (1987). *False Prophets*. Oxford: Basil Blackwell.

Koopmans, T. C. (1937). *Linear Regression Analysis of Economic Time Series*. Haarlem: Netherlands Economic Institute.

Koopmans, T. C. (1947). Measurement without theory, *Review of Economics and Statistics*, **29**, 161–179.

Koopmans, T. C. (ed.)(1950a). *Statistical Inference in Dynamic Economic Models*. No. 10 in Cowles Commission Monograph. New York: John Wiley.

Koopmans, T. C. (1950b). When is an equation system complete for statistical purposes?, in *Statistical Inference in Dynamic Economic Models* (1950a), Ch. 17.

Kremers, J. J. M., Ericsson, N. R. and Dolado, J. J. (1992). The power of cointegration tests, *Oxford Bulletin of Economics and Statistics*, **54**, 325–348.

Kuhn, T. (1962). *The Structure of Scientific Revolutions*. Chicago: University of Chicago Press.

Kuznets, S. (1946). *National Income. A Summary of Findings*. New York: National Bureau of Economic Research.

Kydland, F. E. and Prescott, E. C. (1991). The econometrics of the general equilibrium approach to business cycles, *Scandanavian Journal of Economics*, **93**, 161–178.

Laffont, J. J. and Monfort, A. (1979). Disequilibrium econometrics in dynamic models, *Journal of Econometrics*, **11**, 353–361.

Lahiri, K. and Moore, G. H. (eds.)(1991). *Leading economic indicators: New approaches and forecasting records*. Cambridge: Cambridge University Press.

Laidler, D. E. W. (1984). The 'buffer stock' notion in monetary economics, *Economic Journal*, **94**, 17–34. Supplement.

Laidler, D. E. W. (1985). *The Demand for Money: Theories, Evidence, and Problems*. New York: Harper and Row.

Lakatos, I. (1974). Falsification and the methodology of scientific research programmes, In Lakatos, I. and Musgrave, A. (eds.), *Criticism and the Growth of Knowledge*, pp. 91–196. Cambridge: Cambridge University Press.

Layard, R., Nickell, S. J. and Jackman, R. (1991). *Unemployment Macroeconomic Performance and the Labour Market*: Oxford University Press.

Leamer, E. E. (1978). *Specification Searches. Ad-Hoc Inference with Non-Experimental Data*. New York: John Wiley.

Leamer, E. E. (1983). Let's take the con out of econometrics, *American Economic Review*, **73**, 31–43. Reprinted in Granger (1990).

Leamer, E. E. (1987). Econometric metaphors, in Bewley (1987), pp. 1–28.

Lee, H. S. and Siklos, P. L. (1991). Seasonality in time series: Money-income causality in U.S. data revisited, Mimeo, Department of Economics, Tulane University, New Orleans, Louisiana.

Lee, H. S. and Siklos, P. L. (1993). The influence of seasonal adjustment on the Canadian consumption function 1947–1991, *Canadian Journal of Economics*, **26**, 575–589.

Lehfeldt, R. A. (1914). The elasticity of the demand for wheat, *Economic Journal*, **24**, 212–217.

Lerman, S. and Manski, C. (1981). On the use of simulated frequencies to approximate choice probabilities, in Manski and McFadden (1981).

Little, I. M. D. (1962). Higgledy piggledy growth, *Bulletin of the Oxford University Institute of Statistics*, **24**, 387–412.

Liu, T. C. (1960). Underidentification, structural estimation, and forecasting, *Econometrica*, **28**, 855–865.

Losee, J. (1980). *A Historical Introduction to the Philosophy of Science*. Oxford: Oxford University Press.

Lovell, M. C. (1963). Seasonal adjustment of economic time series and multiple regression analysis, *Journal of the American Statistical Association*, **58**, 993–1010.

Lubrano, M., Pierse, R. G. and Richard, J.-F. (1986). Stability of a UK money demand equation: A Bayesian approach to testing exogeneity, *Review of Economic Studies*, **53**, 603–634.

Lucas, R. E. (1976). Econometric policy evaluation: A critique, In Brunner, K. and Meltzer, A. (eds.), *The Phillips Curve and Labor Markets*, Vol. 1 of *Carnegie-Rochester Conferences on Public Policy*, pp. 19–46. Amsterdam: North-Holland Publishing Company.

Lütkepohl, H. (1991). *Introduction to Multiple Time Series Analysis*. New York: Springer-Verlag.

Maasoumi, E. and Phillips, P. C. B. (1982). On the behaviour of inconsistent instrumental variables estimators, *Journal of Econometrics*, **19**, 183–201.

MacKinnon, J. G. (1991). Critical values for cointegration tests, in Engle and Granger (1991), pp. 267–276.

Madansky, A. (1976). *Foundations of Econometrics*. Amsterdam: North-Holland.

Maddala, G. S. (1984). Disequilibrium, self-selection and switching models, in Griliches and Intriligator (1984), Ch. 28.

Magnus, J. R. and Neudecker, H. (1988). *Matrix Differential Calculus with Applications in Statistics and Econometrics*. New York: John Wiley & Sons.

Malinvaud, E. (1966). *Statistical Methods of Econometrics*. Amsterdam: North-Holland.

Mann, H. and Wald, A. (1943a). On stochastic limit and order relationships, *Annals of Mathematical Statistics*, **14**, 217–226.

Mann, H. and Wald, A. (1943b). On the statistical treatment of linear stochastic difference equations, *Econometrica*, **11**, 173–220.

Manski, C. and McFadden, D. (eds.)(1981). *Structural Analysis of Discrete Data with Econometric Applications*. Cambridge, MA: MIT Press.

Maravall, A. (1993). Stochastic linear trends: Models and estimators, *Journal of Econometrics*, **56**, 5–37.

Maravall, A. and Pierce, D. A. (1987). A prototypical seasonal adjustment model, *Journal of Time Series Analysis*, **8**, 177–193.

Marks, R. W. (ed.)(1967). *Great Ideas in Modern Science.* New York: Bantam Books.

Marschak, J. (1953). Economic measurements for policy and prediction, in Hood and Koopmans (1953).

Mason, S. F. (1962). *A History of the Sciences, (2nd ed. 1977).* New York: Collier Books.

Mayo, D. (1981). Testing statistical testing, In Pitt, J. C. (ed.), *Philosophy in Economics*, pp. 175–230: D. Reidel Publishing Co. Reprinted as pp. 45–73 in Caldwell B. J. (1993), *The Philosophy and Methodology of Economics*, Vol. 2, Aldershot: Edward Elgar.

McAleer, M., Pagan, A. R. and Volker, P. A. (1985). What will take the con out of econometrics?, *American Economic Review*, **95**, 293–301. Reprinted in Granger (1990).

McCabe, B. and Tremayne, A. R. (1993). *Elements of Modern Asymptotic Theory with Statistical Applications.* Manchester: Manchester University Press.

McCalla, T. R. (1967). *Introduction to Numerical Methods and FORTRAN Programming.* New York: Wiley.

McCallum, B. T. (1976). Rational expectations and the natural rate hypothesis: Some consistent estimates, *Econometrica*, **44**, 43–52.

McCloskey, D. (1983). The rhetoric of economics, *Journal of Economic Literature*, **21**, 481–517.

McFadden, D. L. (1989). A method of simulated moments for estimation of discrete response models without numerical integration, *Econometrica*, **57**, 995–1026.

Medawar, P. (1969). *Induction and Intuition in Scientific Thought.* London: Methuen.

Messadié, G. (1991). *Great Scientific Discoveries.* Edinburgh: Chambers.

Milbourne, R. (1983). Optimal money holding under uncertainty, *International Economic Review*, **24**, 685–698.

Mill, J. S. (1865). *A System of Logic: Ratiocinative and Inductive.* London: Longmans, Green.

Miller, M. H. and Orr, D. (1966). A model of the demand for money by firms, *Quarterly Journal of Economics*, **80**, 735–759.

Mirowski, P. (1988). *More Heat than Light: Economics as Social Physics.* Cambridge: Cambridge University Press.

Mizon, G. E. (1977a). Inferential procedures in nonlinear models: An application in a UK industrial cross section study of factor substitution and returns to scale, *Econometrica*, **45**, 1221–1242.

Mizon, G. E. (1977b). Model selection procedures, In Artis, M. J. and Nobay, A. R. (eds.), *Studies in Modern Economic Analysis*, Ch. 4. Oxford: Basil Blackwell.

Mizon, G. E. (1984). The encompassing approach in econometrics, in Hendry and Wallis (1984), pp. 135–172.

Mizon, G. E. (1993a). Empirical analysis of time series: Illustrations with simulated data, In de Zeeuw, A. (ed.), *Advanced Lectures in Quantitative Economics*, Vol. II, pp. 184–205. New York.: Academic Press.

Mizon, G. E. (1993b). A simple message to autocorrelation correctors: Don't, Discussion paper, European University Institute, Florence.

Mizon, G. E. and Hendry, D. F. (1980). An empirical application and Monte Carlo analysis of tests of dynamic specification, *Review of Economic Studies*, **49**, 21–45. Reprinted in Hendry (1993a).

Mizon, G. E. and Richard, J.-F. (1986). The encompassing principle and its application to non-nested hypothesis tests, *Econometrica*, **54**, 657–678.

Molinas, C. (1986). A note on spurious regressions with integrated moving average errors, *Oxford Bulletin of Economics and Statistics*, **48**, 279–282.

Monfort, A. and Rabemananjara, R. (1990). From a VAR model to a structural model, with an application to the wage-price spiral, *Journal of Applied Econometrics*, **5**, 203–227.

Mood, A. M., Graybill, F. and Boes, D. (1978). *Introduction to the Theory of Statistics*. New York: McGraw-Hill.

Moore, H. L. (1925). A moving equilibrium of demand and supply, *Quarterly Journal of Economics*, **39**, 359–371.

Morgan, M. S. (1987). Statistics without probability and Haavelmo's revolution in econometrics, In Krüger, L., Gigerenzer, G. and Morgan, M. S. (eds.), *The Probabilistic Revolution*, Vol. 2: MIT Press.

Morgan, M. S. (1989). *The History of Econometric Ideas*. Cambridge: Cambridge University Press.

Morgenstern, O. (1950). *On the Accuracy of Economic Observations*. Princeton: University Press.

Mosbaek, E. J. and Wold, H. O. A. (1970). *Interdependent Systems*. Amsterdam: North-Holland Publishing Company.

Muellbauer, J. N. J. (1979). Are employment decisions based on rational expectations?, Unpublished paper, Birkbeck College.

Muth, J. F. (1961). Rational expectations and the theory of price movements, *Econometrica*, **29**, 315–335.

Nagar, A. L. (1959). The bias and moment matrix of the general k-class estimators of the parameters in simultaneous equations, *Econometrica*, **27**, 575–595.

Nagel, E. (1961). *The Structure of Science*. New York: Harcourt Brace.

Neftci, S. N. (1979). Lead-lag relations, exogeneity and prediction of economic time series, *Econometrica*, **47**, 101–113.

Neftci, S. N. (1994). Optimal prediction of cyclical downturns, *Journal of Economic Dynamics and Control*, **4**, 225–241.

Nelson, C. R. (1972). The prediction performance of the FRB-MIT-PENN model of the U.S. economy, *American Economic Review*, **62**, 902–917.

Nelson, C. R. and Plosser, C. I. (1982). Trends and random walks in macroeconomic time series: some evidence and implications, *Journal of Monetary Economics*, **10**, 139–162.

Nerlove, M. (1964). Spectral analysis of seasonal adjustment procedures, *Econometrica*, **32**, 241–286.

Neyman, J. and Pearson, E. S. (1928). On the use and interpretation of certain test criteria for purposes of statistical inference, *Biometrika*, **20A, 175–240**, 263–294.

Nicholls, D. F. and Pagan, A. R. (1983). Heteroscedasticity in models with lagged dependent variables, *Econometrica*, **51**, 1233–1242.

Nickell, S. J. (1985). Error correction, partial adjustment and all that: An expository note, *Oxford Bulletin of Economics and Statistics*, **47**, 119–130.

Nickell, S. J. (1990). Inflation and the UK labour market, *Oxford Review of Economic Policy*, **6**, 26–35.

Nowak, E. (1991). Discovering hidden cointegration, Discussion paper, University of Munich.

Oksanen, E. H. (1987). On sign changes upon deletion of a variable in linear-regression analysis, *Oxford Bulletin of Economics and Statistics*, **49**, 227–229.

Osborn, D. R. (1988). Seasonality and habit persistence in a life cycle model of consumption, *Journal of Applied Econometrics*, **3**, 255–266.

Osborn, D. R. (1993). Moving average detrending of integrated processes, Mimeo, Manchester University.

Osterwald-Lenum, M. (1992). A note with quantiles of the asymptotic distribution of the ML cointegration rank test statistics, *Oxford Bulletin of Economics and Statistics*, **54**, 461–472.

Pagan, A. R. (1981). Reflections on Australian macro modelling, Unpublished paper, Australian National University.

Pagan, A. R. (1984a). Econometric issues in the analysis of regressions with generated regressors, *International Economic Review*, **25**, 221–247.

Pagan, A. R. (1984b). Model evaluation by variable addition, in Hendry and Wallis (1984), pp. 103–135.

Pagan, A. R. (1985). Time series behaviour and dynamic specification, *Oxford Bulletin of Economics and Statistics*, **47**, 199–211.

Pagan, A. R. (1987). Three econometric methodologies: A critical appraisal, *Journal of Economic Surveys*, **1**, 3–24. Reprinted in Granger (1990).

Pagan, A. R. (1989). On the role of simulation in the statistical evaluation of econometric models, *Journal of Econometrics*, **40**, 125–139.

Pakes, A. (1986). Patents as options: Some estimates of the value of holding european patent stocks, *Econometrica*, **54**, 755–774.

Pakes, A. and Pollard, D. (1989). Simulation and the asymptotics of optimization estimation, *Econometrica*, **57**, 1027–1058.

Palm, F. I. and Zellner, A. (1980). Large sample estimation and testing procedures for dynamic equation systems, *Journal of Econometrics*, **12**, 251–284.

Park, J. Y. and Phillips, P. C. B. (1988). Statistical inference in regressions with integrated processes. part 1, *Econometric Theory*, **4**, 468–497.

Park, J. Y. and Phillips, P. C. B. (1989). Statistical inference in regressions with integrated processes. part 2, *Econometric Theory*, **5**, 95–131.

Pearl, J. (1993). On the statistical interpretation of structural equations, Technical report r-200, Cognitive Systems Lab., UCLA.

Perron, P. (1989). The great crash, the oil price shock and the unit root hypothesis, *Econometrica*, **57**, 1361–1401.

Persons, W. M. (1924). *The Problem of Business Forecasting*. No. 6 in Pollak Foundation for Economic Research Publications. London: Pitman.

Pesaran, M. H. (1974). On the general problem of model selection, *Review of Economic Studies*, **41**, 153–171.

Pesaran, M. H. (1987). Global and partial non-nested hypotheses and asymptotic local power, *Econometric Theory*, **3**, 69–90.

Pesaran, M. H. and Deaton, A. S. (1978). Testing non-nested non-linear regression models, *Econometrica*, **46**, 677–694.

Phillips, A. W. (1954). Stabilization policy in a closed economy, *Economic Journal*, **64**, 290–333.

Phillips, A. W. (1957). Stabilization policy and the time form of lagged response, *Economic Journal*, **67**, 265–277.

Phillips, P. C. B. (1983). Exact small sample theory in the simultaneous equations model, in Griliches and Intriligator (1983), Ch. 8.

Phillips, P. C. B. (1986). Understanding spurious regressions in econometrics, *Journal of Econometrics*, **33**, 311–340.

Phillips, P. C. B. (1987a). Time series regression with a unit root, *Econometrica*, **55**, 277–301.

Phillips, P. C. B. (1987b). Towards a unified asymptotic theory for autoregression, *Biometrika*, **74**, 535–547.

Phillips, P. C. B. (1988a). Error correction and long run equilibrium in continuous time, Cowles Foundation discussion paper 882, Yale University.

Phillips, P. C. B. (1988b). Regression theory for near-integrated time series, *Econometrica*, **56**, 1021–1043.

Phillips, P. C. B. (1991). Optimal inference in cointegrated systems, *Econometrica*, **59**, 283–306.

Phillips, P. C. B. and Durlauf, S. N. (1986). Multiple time series regression with integrated processes, *Review of Economic Studies*, **53**, 473–495.

Phillips, P. C. B. and Loretan, M. (1991). Estimating long-run economic equilibria, *Review of Economic Studies*, **58**, 407–436.

Phillips, P. C. B. and Perron, P. (1988). Testing for a unit root in time series regression, *Biometrika*, **75**, 335–346.

Poincaré, H. (1905). *Science and Hypothesis*. New York: Science Press.

Popper, K. R. (1959). *The Logic of Scientific Discovery*. New York: Basic Books.

Popper, K. R. (1963). *Conjectures and Refutations*. New York: Basic Books.

Powell, M. J. D. (1964). An efficient method of finding the minimum of a function of several variables without calculating derivatives, *Computer Journal*, **7**, 155–162.

Prothero, D. L. and Wallis, K. F. (1976). Modelling macro-economic time series' (with discussion), *Journal of the Royal Statistical Society A*, **139**, 468–500.

Qin, D. (1993). *The Formation of Econometrics: A Historical Perspective*. Oxford: Clarendon Press.

Quah, D. (1993). A comment on Hendry D. F. (1993). *the roles of economic theory and econometrics in time-series economics*. Invited address, European Econometric Society, Stockholm, mimeo, London School of Economics.

Quandt, R. E. (1982). Econometric disequilibrium models, *Econometric Reviews*, **1**, 1–96 (with comments).

Quandt, R. E. (1983). Computational methods and problems, in Griliches and Intriligator (1983), Ch. 12.

Quandt, R. E. (1988). *The Econometrics of Disequilibrium*. New York: Basil Blackwell.

Quandt, R. E. (1989). Bibliography of quantity rationing and disequilibrium models, Discussion paper, Princeton University, Department of Economics.

Quenouille, M. H. (1957). *The Analysis of Multiple Time Series*. London: Griffin.

Ramsey, J. B. (1969). Tests for specification errors in classical linear least squares regression analysis, *Journal of the Royal Statistical Society B*, **31**, 350–371.

Rao, C. R. (1952). *Advanced Statistical Methods in Biometric Research.* New York: John Wiley.

Rao, C. R. (1973). *Linear Statistical Inference and its Applications* 2nd edition. New York: John Wiley & Sons.

Reiersøl, O. (1945). Confluence analysis by means of instrumental sets of variables, *Arkiv for Matematik Astronomi och Fysik*, **32**, 1–19.

Reimers, H.-E. (1992). Comparisons of tests for multivariate cointegration, *Statistical Papers*, **33**, 335–359.

Richard, J.-F. (1980). Models with several regimes and changes in exogeneity, *Review of Economic Studies*, **47**, 1–20.

Richard, J.-F. (1984). Classical and Bayesian inference in incomplete simultaneous equation models, in Hendry and Wallis (1984).

Ripley, B. D. (1987). *Stochastic Simulation.* New York: John Wiley & Sons.

Robbins, L. (1932). *An Essay on the Nature and Significance of Economic Science.* London: Macmillan.

Rose, A. K. (1984). An alternative approach to the American demand for money, *Journal of Money, Credit, and Banking*, **17**, 439–455.

Roth, A. E. (1988). Laboratory experimentation in economics: A methodological overview, *Economic Journal*, **98**, 974–1031.

Rothenberg, T. J. (1984). Approximating the distributions of econometric estimators and test statistics, in Griliches and Intriligator (1984), Ch. 15.

Rothenberg, T. J. and Leenders, C. T. (1964). Efficient estimation of simultaneous equations systems, *Econometrica*, **32**, 57–76.

Said, S. E. and Dickey, D. A. (1984). Testing for unit roots in autoregressive-moving average models of unknown order, *Biometrika*, **71**, 599–607.

Salkever, D. S. (1976). The use of dummy variables to compute predictions, prediction errrors and confidence intervals, *Journal of Econometrics*, **4**, 393–397.

Salmon, M. (1982). Error correction mechanisms, *Economic Journal*, **92**, 615–629.

Salmon, M. (1988). Error correction models, cointegration and the internal model principle, *Journal of Economic Dynamics and Control*, **12**, 523–549.

Samuelson, P. A. (1947). *Foundations of Economic Analysis.* Harvard: Harvard University Press.

Sargan, J. D. (1958). The estimation of economic relationships using instrumental variables, *Econometrica*, **26**, 393–415.

Sargan, J. D. (1959). The estimation of relationships with autocorrelated residuals by the use of instrumental variables, *Journal of the Royal Statistical Society B*, **21**, 91–105. Reprinted as pp. 87–104 in Sargan J. D. (1988), *Contributions to Econometrics*, Vol. 1, Cambridge: Cambridge University Press.

Sargan, J. D. (1964). Wages and prices in the United Kingdom: A study in econometric methodology (with discussion), In Hart, P. E., Mills, G. and Whitaker, J. K. (eds.), *Econometric Analysis for National Economic Planning*, Vol. 16 of *Colston Papers*, pp. 25–63. London: Butterworth Co. Reprinted as pp. 275–314 in Hendry and Wallis (1984), and as pp. 124–169 in Sargan J. D. (1988), *Contributions to Econometrics*, Vol. 1, Cambridge: Cambridge University Press.

Sargan, J. D. (1975). Asymptotic theory and large models, *International Economic Review*, **16**, 75–91.

Sargan, J. D. (1976). Econometric estimators and the Edgeworth expansion, *Econometrica*, **44**, 421–448. Reprinted with errata and other corrections as pp. 98–132 in Sargan J. D. (1988), *Contributions to Econometrics*, Vol. 2, Cambridge: Cambridge University Press.

Sargan, J. D. (1980a). The consumer price equation in the post-war British economy. An exercise in equation specification testing, *Review of Economic Studies*, **47**, 113–135.

Sargan, J. D. (1980b). Some tests of dynamic specification for a single equation, *Econometrica*, **48**, 879–897. Reprinted as pp. 191–212 in Sargan J. D. (1988), *Contributions to Econometrics*, Vol. 1, Cambridge: Cambridge University Press.

Sargan, J. D. (1982). On Monte Carlo estimates of moments that are infinite, In Basmann, R. L. and Rhodes, G. F. (eds.), *Advances in Econometrics: A Research Annual*, Vol. 1, pp. 267–299. Greenwich, Connecticut: Jai Press Inc.

Sargan, J. D. (1988). *Lectures on Advanced Econometric Theory*. Oxford: Basil Blackwell.

Sargan, J. D. and Bhargava, A. (1983). Testing residuals from least squares regression for being generated by the Gaussian random walk, *Econometrica*, **51**, 153–174.

Sargan, J. D. and Sylwestrowicz, J. D. (1976). COMFAC: Algorithm for Wald tests of common factors in lag polynomials, Users' manual, London School of Economics.

Savin, N. E. (1984). Multiple hypothesis testing, in Griliches and Intriligator (1984), Ch. 14.

Schmidt, P. (1976). *Econometrics*. New York: Marcel Dekker.

Schumpeter, J. (1933). The common sense of econometrics, *Econometrica*, **1**, 5–12.

Schwert, G. W. (1989). Tests for unit roots: A Monte Carlo investigation, *Journal of Business and Economic Statistics*, **7**, 147–159.

Shenton, L. R. and Johnson, W. L. (1965). Moments of a serial correlation coefficient, *Journal of the Royal Statistical Society B*, **27**, 308–320.

Silverman, B. W. (1986). *Density Estimation for Statistics and Data Analysis*. London: Chapman and Hall.

Silvey, S. D. (1970). *Statistical Inference*. Harmondsworth: Penguin.

Simon, H. A. (1953). Causal ordering and identifiability, in Hood and Koopmans (1953), Ch. 3.

Simpson, T. D. and Porter, R. (1980). Some issues involving the definition and interpretation of monetary aggregates, Controling monetary aggregates III, Federal Reserve Bank of Boston.

Sims, C. A. (1972). Money, income and causality, *American Economic Review*, **62**, 540–552.

Sims, C. A. (1974). Seasonality in regression, *Journal of the American Statistical Association*, **69**, 618–626.

Sims, C. A. (1980). Macroeconomics and reality, *Econometrica*, **48**, 1–48. Reprinted in Granger (1990).

Sims, C. A., Stock, J. H. and Watson, M. W. (1990). Inference in linear time series models with some unit roots, *Econometrica*, **58**, 113–144.

Slutsky, E. (1937). The summation of random causes as the source of cyclic processes, *Econometrica*, **5**, 105–146. (Translation from the Russian version of 1927.).

Smith, G. W. (1986). A dynamic baumol-tobin model of money demand, *Review of Economic Studies*, **53**, 465–469.

Smith, R. J. (1993). Consistent tests for the encompassing hypothesis, Discussion paper, Economics Department, Universtity of Cambridge.

Smith, R. J. and Weale, M. R. (1992). Measurement error and model specification, Discussion paper, Economics Department, Universtity of Cambridge.

Smith, R. P. (1991). Spurious structural stability, *Manchester School*, **59**, 419–423.

Smith, V. L. (1982). Microeconomic systems as an experimental science, *American Economic Review*, **72**, 923–955.

Spanos, A. (1986). *Statistical Foundations of Econometric Modelling*. Cambridge: Cambridge University Press.

Spanos, A. (1989a). Early empirical findings on the consumption, stylized facts or fiction: A retrospective view, *Oxford Economic Papers*, **41**, 150–169.

Spanos, A. (1989b). On re-reading Haavelmo: A retrospective view of econometric modeling, *Econometric Theory*, **5**, 405–429.

Spanos, A. (1990). Towards a unifying methodological framework for econometric modelling, in Granger (1990), pp. 335–364.

Spanos, A. (1994). On modelling heteroscedasticity: the student's t and elliptical linear regression models, *Econometric Theory*, **10**, 286–315.

Srinivasan, T. (1970). Approximations to finite sample moments of estimators whose exact sampling distributions are unknown, *Econometrica*, **38**, 533–541.

Stock, J. H. (1987). Asymptotic properties of least squares estimators of cointegrating vectors, *Econometrica*, **55**, 1035–1056.

Stock, J. H. and Watson, M. W. (1989). New indexes of coincident and leading economic indicators, *NBER Macro-Economic Annual*, 351–409.

Stock, J. H. and Watson, M. W. (1992). A procedure for predicting recessions with leading indicators: Econometric issues and recent experience, Working paper 4014, NBER.

Stone, J. R. N. (1966). Spending and saving in relation to income and wealth, *L'industria*, **4**, 471–499.

Stone, J. R. N. (1973). Personal spending and saving in postwar Britain, In Bos, H. C., Linneman, H. and de Wolff, P. (eds.), *Economic Structure and Development (essays in honour of Jan Tinbergen)*. Amsterdam: North-Holland Publishing Company.

Student (1908). On the probable error of the mean, *Biometrika*, **6**, 1–25.

Suits, D. B. (1955). An econometric model of the watermelon market, *American Journal of Agricultural Economics* (formerly the *Journal of Farm Economics*), **2**, 237–251.

Summers, L. H. (1991). The scientific illusion in empirical macroeconomics, *Scandanavian Journal of Economics*, **93**, 129–148.

Teräsvirta, T. (1970). *Stepwise Regression and Economic Forecasting*. No. 31 in Economic Studies Monograph. Helsinki: Finnish Economic Association.

Theil, H. (1961). *Economic Forecasts and Policy* 2nd edition. Amsterdam: North-Holland Publishing Company.

Theil, H. (1971). *Principles of Econometrics*. London: John Wiley.

Thisted, R. A. (1988). *Elements of Statistical Computing. Numerical Computation*. New York: Chapman and Hall.

Tinbergen, J. (1930). Determination and interpretation of supply curves: An example [Bestimmung und Deutung von Angebotskurven: ein Beispiel], *Zeitschrift fur Nationalökonomie*, **1**, 779–679. Reprinted in Hendry and Morgan (1995).

Tinbergen, J. (1933). The notions of horizon and expectancy in dynamic economics, *Econometrica*, **1**, 247–264. Reprinted in Hendry and Morgan (1995).

Tintner, G. (1944). An application of the variate difference method to multiple regression, *Econometrica*, **12**, 97–113.

Tobin, J. (1956). The interest-elasticity of the transaction demand for cash, *Review of Economics and Statistics*.

Tobin, J. (1958). Liquidity preference as behavior toward risk, *Review of Economic Studies*, **25**, 65–86.

Trivedi, P. K. (1975). Time series analysis versus structural models: A case study of Canadian manufacturing behavior, *International Economic Review*, **16**, 587–608.

Trundle, J. M. (1982). The demand for M1 in the UK, Mimeo, Bank of England, London.

Urbain, J.-P. (1992). On weak exogeneity in error correction models, *Oxford Bulletin of Economics and Statistics*, **54**, 187–207.

Vining, R. (1949). Methodological issues in quantitative economics, *Review of Economics and Statistics*, **31**, 77–86.

Visco, I. (1988). Again on sign changes upon deletion of a variable from a linear regression, *Oxford Bulletin of Economics and Statistics*, **50**, 225–227.

von Mises, L. (1978). *The Ultimate Foundation of Economic Science*. Kansas City: Sheed, Andrews and McMeel.

Wald, A. (1949). Note on the consistency of the maximum likelihood estimate, *Annals of Mathematical Statistics*, **20**, 595–601.

Wallis, K. F. (1971). Wages, prices and incomes policies: Some comments, *Economica*, **38**, 304–310.

Wallis, K. F. (1974). Seasonal adjustment and relations between variables, *Journal of the American Statistical Association*, **69**, 18–31.

Wallis, K. F. (1978). Seasonal adjustment and multiple time series analysis, in Zellner (1978).

Wallis, K. F. (1980). Econometric implications of the rational expectations hypothesis, *Econometrica*, **48**, 49–73.

Wallis, K. F. (1982). Seasonal adjustment and revision of current data: Linear filters for the X–11 method, *Journal of the Royal Statistical Society A*, **145**, 74–85.

Wallis, K. F. (1983). Models for X–11 and X–11 forecast procedures for preliminary and revised seasonal adjustments, In Zellner, A. (ed.), *Applied Time Series Analysis of Economic Data*. Washington, DC: Bureau of the Census.

Wallis, K. F. (1993). Henderson detrending, symmetric or asymmetric, reduces I(4) series to stationarity, Discussion paper, Department of Economics, University of Warwick, England.

Walsh, C. (1984). Interest rate volatility and monetary policy, *Journal of Money, Credit, and Banking*, **16**, 133–150.

Walters, P. (1975). *Ergodic Theory*: Springer-Verlag.

White, H. (1980a). A heteroskedastic-consistent covariance matrix estimator and a direct test for heteroskedasticity, *Econometrica*, **48**, 817–838.

White, H. (1980b). Non-linear regression on cross-section data, *Econometrica*, **48**, 721–746.

White, H. (1980c). Using least squares to approximate unknown regression functions, *International Economic Review*, **21**, 149–170.

White, H. (1984). *Asymptotic Theory for Econometricians.* London: Academic Press.

White, H. (1990). A consistent model selection, in Granger (1990), pp. 369–383.

Whittle, P. (1970). *Probability.* Harmondsworth: Penguin Library of University Mathematics.

Wilks, S. S. (1962). *Mathematical Statistics.* New York: Wiley.

Wise, J. (1955). The autocorrelation function and the spectral density function, *Biometrika*, **42**, 151–159.

Wold, H. O. A. (1938). *A Study in The Analysis of Stationary Time Series.* Stockholm: Almqvist and Wicksell.

Wold, H. O. A. (1959). Ends and means in econometric model building, In Grenander, U. (ed.), *Probability and Statistics.* New York: John Wiley.

Wold, H. O. A. (1969). Econometrics as pioneering in non-experimental model building, *Econometrica*, **37**, 369–381.

Wold, H. O. A. and Juréen, L. (1953). *Demand Analysis: A Study in Econometrics* 2nd edition. New York: John Wiley.

Wu, D. (1973). Alternative tests of independence between stochastic regressors and disturbances, *Econometrica*, **41**, 733–750.

Yule, G. U. (1926). Why do we sometimes get nonsense-correlations between time-series? A study in sampling and the nature of time series (with discussion), *Journal of the Royal Statistical Society*, **89**, 1–64.

Yule, G. U. (1927). On a method of investigating periodicities in disturbed series, with special reference to Wolfer's sunspot numbers, *Philosophical Transactions of the Royal Society, A*, **226**, 267–298.

Zangwill, W. I. (1969). *Nonlinear Programming: A Unified Approach.* Prentice Hall: Englewood Cliff, NJ.

Zellner, A. (ed.)(1978). *Seasonal Analysis of Economic Time Series.* Washington, DC: Bureau of the Census.

Zellner, A. (1979). Causality and econometrics, In Brunner, K. and Meltzer, A. (eds.), *The Phillips Curve and Labor Markets*, pp. 9–54. Amsterdam: North-Holland Publishing Company.

Zellner, A. and Palm, F. I. (1974). Time series analysis and simultaneous equation models, *Journal of Econometrics*, **2**, 17–54.

Zellner, A. and Theil, H. (1962). Three-stage least-squares: Simultaneous estimation of simultaneous equations, *Econometrica*, **30**, 54–78.

Common Acronyms

2SLS	two-stage least squares
3SLS	three-stage least squares
ADF	augmented Dickey–Fuller
ADL	autoregressive-distributed lag model
AR	autoregressive process
ARCH	autoregressive conditional heteroscedasticity
ARMA	autoregressive-moving average
ASE	asymptotic standard error
BFGS	Broyden–Fletcher–Goldfarb–Shanno
BLUE	best linear unbiased estimator
CLF	concentrated likelihood function
CLT	central limit theorem
CDF	cumulative distribution function
COMFAC	common factor
CUSUM	cumulative sum of squares
DFP	Davidon–Fletcher–Powell
DGP	data-generation process
DHSY	Davidson, Hendry, Srba and Yeo (1978)
DW	Durbin–Watson statistic
ECM	equilibrium-correction mechanism or model
EGE	estimator-generating equation
ESE	estimated standard error
EVM	errors-in-variables model
FIML	full-information maximum likelihood
FIVE	full-information instrumental variables
GARCH	generalized ARCH
GLS	generalized least squares
GMM	generalized method of moments
GMP	Gill–Murray–Pitfield
GNC	Granger non-causality
GNP	gross national product
GUM	general unrestricted model
HCSE	heteroscedastic-consistent standard errors
HET	Hausman encompassing test
IID	independent, identically distributed
IV	instrumental variables
LIML	limited-information maximum likelihood
LIVE	limited-information instrumental variables
LM	Lagrange-multiplier test
LR	likelihood-ratio test
MA	moving-average process
MCSD	Monte Carlo standard deviation
MCSE	Monte Carlo standard error
MDS	martingale difference sequence
MIP	mean-innovation process
MLE	maximum-likelihood estimator
MLS	multivariate least squares
MSE	mean-square error
MMSE	minimum mean-square error
MVUE	minimum-variance unbiased estimator
OLS	ordinary least squares
PI/LCH	permanent income/life-cycle hypothesis
PVAR	parsimonious VAR
RLS	recursive least squares
RSS	residual sum of squares
SC	Schwarz criterion
SE	coefficient standard error
SEM	simultaneous equations model
SET	simplification encompassing test
SGM	statistical generating mechanism
SLLN	strong law of large numbers
URF	unrestricted reduced form
VAD	vector ADL model
VAR	vector autoregressive representation
VECM	vector ECM
W	Wald test
WET	Wald encompassing test
WLLN	weak law of large numbers
WLS	weighted least squares

Glossary

$\alpha(L)$	polynomial in the lag operator L
$\boldsymbol{\beta}$	$k \times 1$ parameter vector $(\beta_1 \dots \beta_k)'$
$\boldsymbol{\gamma}'$	$1 \times n$ (row) vector of parameters $(\gamma_1 \dots \gamma_n)$
$\Delta_n x_t$	n-period time difference of x_t, $x_t - x_{t-n}$
$\Delta^d z_t$	d^{th}-order time difference of z_t
ϵ_t	stochastic error (usually white noise)
λ	likelihood ratio $\mathsf{L}(\theta_0; \boldsymbol{x})/\mathsf{L}(\theta_1; \boldsymbol{x})$
λ_i	i^{th} eigenvalue
$\boldsymbol{\Lambda}$	diagonal matrix of eigenvalues
μ	mean lag
$\boldsymbol{\mu}$	parameter of interest
$\mu(\cdot)$	measure function
ν_t	unpredictable, or innovation, error
$\boldsymbol{\theta} \in \Theta$	parameter vector $(\theta_1 \dots \theta_n)'$, an element in a parameter space Θ
$\boldsymbol{\theta}_p$	population parameter vector
π	ratio of circumference to diameter in a circle
$\boldsymbol{\pi}$	individual-variable reduced-form matrix
$\prod$	product over implicit range
$\prod_{t=1}^{T}$	product over range shown
$\boldsymbol{\Pi}$	system reduced-form matrix
σ_u^2	variance of $\{u_t\}$
σ	standard deviation or standard error
$\sigma(\boldsymbol{X}_{t-1})$	sigma field generated by $\boldsymbol{X}_{t-1}$
$\sum$	summation over implicit range (text)
$\sum_{t=1}^{T}$	summation over range shown
$\boldsymbol{\Sigma}$	error variance matrix with elements $\{\sigma_{ij}\}$

$\phi(\cdot)$	density function of the standardized normal distribution
$\Phi(\cdot)$	CDF of the standardized normal
$\Psi_1 \times \Psi_2$	product of two spaces defined by $\Psi = \{(\psi_1, \psi_2) : \psi_1 \in \Psi_1$ and $\psi_2 \in \Psi_2\}$
$\chi^2(n)$	chi-square distribution with n degrees of freedom
$\chi^2(n, \psi^2)$	$\chi^2(n)$ with non-centrality ψ^2
Ω	sample space of a random experiment
$\boldsymbol{\Omega}$	error variance matrix with elements (ω_{ij})
$(\Omega, \mathcal{F}, \mathsf{P})$	probability space over events
$(\mathbb{R}, \mathcal{B}, \mathsf{P}_X)$	probability space for the random variable X
∇	change in numerical optimization
$\{\cdot\}$	stochastic process or sequence
$[x]$	greatest integer less than x
$\emptyset$	empty set
$\forall t$	for all admissible values of t
$\in$	element of a set
$\notin$	not an element of the relevant set
$\bigcap_{i=1}^{n}$	intersection for range shown
$\cap$	intersection
$\bigcup_{i=1}^{n}$	union for range shown
$\cup$	union
$\subset$	strict subset of
$\subseteq$	subset of
$\subseteq$	nested (models)
$\times$	product of two spaces or numbers

$\otimes$	Kronecker product $\boldsymbol{A} \otimes \boldsymbol{B} = (b_{ij}\boldsymbol{A})$ $((m \cdot n) \times (r \cdot s)$ yielding an $mr \cdot ns$ matrix)
$\perp$	orthogonal in that $x \perp z$ implies $\mathsf{E}[xz] = 0$
$(\cdot)^v$	vectoring operator, stacks columns of a matrix in a vector
$(\cdot)^u$	selection operator of elements from a vector or matrix
$(\cdot)^{vu}$	joint selection and vectoring operator
$\lvert \cdot \rvert$	absolute value
$\lvert \boldsymbol{A} \rvert$	determinant of a matrix (depending on context)
$\lVert \cdot \rVert$	norm of a matrix
$'$	transpose of a matrix
$\int$	integral
$\int_0^1$	integral over range shown
$\Omega \mapsto \Theta$	maps Ω onto Θ
$:=$	defined by
$\stackrel{e}{=}$	equal in equilibrium
$\simeq$	approximately equal to
$\doteq$	isomorphic (models)
$\approx$	equivalent (models)
$\approx$	equivalent order of magnitude or order in probability
$\succ$	variance dominance
$\succeq$	matrix difference is negative semi-definite
$\preceq$	matrix difference is positive semi-definite
$\rightarrow$	tends to
$\Rightarrow$	weak convergence in probability measure
$\Longrightarrow$	implies
$\Leftrightarrow$	one-to-one mapping
$\sim$	is distributed as
$\underset{a}{\sim}$	is asymptotically distributed as
$\underset{app}{\sim}$	is approximately distributed as
$\underset{c}{\sim}$	claimed distribution
$\underset{e}{\sim}$	an estimated distribution
$\underset{\mathsf{H}_0}{\sim}$	is distributed on H_0 as
$\hat{}$	an estimator (usually MLE)
$\tilde{}$	an estimator
$\bar{}$	sample mean
$\rfloor_{\boldsymbol{\theta}}$	evaluated at $\boldsymbol{\theta}$
$(-\infty, z]$	half-open interval, defined by the set $\{x : -\infty < x \leq z,\ z \in \mathbb{R}\}$
$\operatorname{argmax}_{\boldsymbol{\theta} \in \Theta} f(\boldsymbol{\theta})$	value of $\boldsymbol{\theta} \in \Theta$ which yields the highest value of $f(\boldsymbol{\theta})$
$\mathcal{A}, \mathcal{B}, \mathcal{C}$	sets which are subsets of Ω
$\mathsf{AD}(\cdot)$	ADL model
$\mathsf{AV}[\cdot]$	variance of the limiting distribution
$\mathcal{C}^c$	complement of $\mathcal{C}$ with respect to Ω
$\mathcal{C}^{\phi_2}$	class of interventions for changes in ϕ_2
$\mathsf{corr}(y, z)$	correlation of y with z
$\mathsf{C}[y, z]$	covariance of y with z
$dg(\boldsymbol{\Omega})$	the diagonal of $\boldsymbol{\Omega}$, namely $\operatorname{diag}(\omega_{11} \ldots \omega_{nn})$
$\mathsf{D}_{\mathsf{X}}(\boldsymbol{X}; \boldsymbol{\theta})$	joint density or distribution function of $\boldsymbol{X}$ with parameter $\boldsymbol{\theta} \in \Theta$
$\mathsf{D}_{\mathsf{x}}(\boldsymbol{x}_t; \boldsymbol{\theta})$	distribution of $\boldsymbol{x}_t$ with parameter $\boldsymbol{\theta}$
$\mathsf{D}_{\mathsf{y}\mid\mathsf{z}}(y_t \mid z_t, \cdot)$	conditional distribution of y_t given z_t
$\mathsf{D}_{\mathsf{x}}(\boldsymbol{x}_t \mid \mathcal{I}_{t-1}, \cdot)$	sequential distribution of $\boldsymbol{x}_t$ given $\mathcal{I}_{t-1}$
$\mathsf{E}[Y]$	expectation of the random variable Y
$\mathsf{E}[y_t \mid \boldsymbol{z}_t]$	conditional expectation of the random variable y_t given $\boldsymbol{z}_t$
$\mathsf{E}_Z(\mathsf{E}[Y \mid Z])$	expected value over Z of the conditional expectation of Y given Z
$\mathsf{E}_{\text{model}}[z_t \mid \text{model of } z_t]$	expected value of z_t given the model
$\mathbb{E}[\cdot]$	expectation with respect to the random variables in a Monte Carlo

$E[\cdot]$ asserted expectation

$\mathcal{E}$ encompasses

$\mathcal{E}_p$ parsimoniously encompasses

$\mathcal{E}^c$ does not encompass

$\mathcal{F}$ event space or σ-field associated with Ω

$\mathcal{F}_m^k$ event space generated by $(X_m \ldots X_k)$

$\mathcal{F}_{t-1}$ the event space up till time $t-1$

$\mathsf{f}_\mathsf{r}(r)$ density function of R

$\mathsf{f}_\mathsf{w}(w;\boldsymbol{\theta})$ density function of a statistic (or random variable) W

$\mathsf{f}_{\mathsf{w}|\mathsf{z}}(w|z)$ conditional density of W given $Z=z$

$\mathsf{F}_\mathsf{w}(w)$ distribution function of statistic (or random variable) W

$F(n,m)$ F-distribution with $n,\ m$ degrees of freedom

H_0 null hypothesis

H_1 alternative hypothesis

H_m maintained hypothesis

$\mathtt{H}$ histogram

$\boldsymbol{H}(\boldsymbol{\theta})$ Hessian, or second derivative of the log-likelihood function

$\boldsymbol{H}_t(\boldsymbol{\theta})$ Hessian for one observation

$\boldsymbol{I}_k$ unit matrix of dimension k

$\mathsf{I}(d)$ integrated of order d

$I(\cdot)$ the indicator function

$I_{\mathcal{A}}$ the indicator function for a set $\mathcal{A}$

$\mathcal{I}(\boldsymbol{\theta}_p)$ information matrix (variance of the score) evaluated at $\boldsymbol{\theta}_p$

$\mathcal{I}_{t-1}$ previous information

$\mathsf{IID}[\mu,\sigma_\epsilon^2]$ independent, identically distributed with mean μ and variance σ_ϵ^2

$\mathsf{ID}[\mu_t,\sigma_t^2]$ independently distributed with mean μ_t and variance σ_t^2

$\mathsf{IN}[\mu,\sigma^2]$ independent normal distribution with mean μ and variance σ^2

$\mathsf{IN}_\mathsf{k}[\boldsymbol{\mu},\boldsymbol{\Sigma}]$ k-dimensional multivariate independent normal distribution with mean $\boldsymbol{\mu}$ and variance matrix $\boldsymbol{\Sigma}$

$\mathtt{K}(\cdot)$ kernel in non-parametric density estimation

L lag operator $L^k x_t = x_{t-k}$

$\mathsf{L}(\cdot)$ likelihood function

$\ell(\boldsymbol{\theta}|\boldsymbol{x})$ log-likelihood function for the random variable $\boldsymbol{X}$

$\ell(\boldsymbol{\theta}|\boldsymbol{x}_t;\mathcal{I}_{t-1})$ sequential log-likelihood function for one observation on the random variable $\boldsymbol{X}$

$\bar{\ell}_p(\boldsymbol{\theta}_p)$ population standardized log-likelihood

$\ell_t(\boldsymbol{\theta})$ shorthand log-likelihood function for one observation

$\lim_{T\to\infty}$ limit as T tends to infinity

$\mathsf{LN}(\theta,\tau^2)$ log-normal distribution

log natural logarithm

$\max_{\boldsymbol{\theta}\in\Theta} f(\boldsymbol{\theta})$ highest value of a function $f(\cdot)$ with respect to its argument $\boldsymbol{\theta}$

m median lag

M empirical model

M number of Monte Carlo replications

$\boldsymbol{M}_X$ second-moment matrix of $\boldsymbol{X}$

N cross-section sample size

$\mathsf{N}[0,1]$ normal density function with zero mean and unit variance

$\mathcal{N}(\theta)$ neighbourhood of θ

$\mathbb{N}$ the set of integers $\{0,\pm1,\pm2,\ldots\}$

$O(1)$ at most of order one

$o(1)$ of smaller order than unity

$O_p(1)$ at most of order unity in probability

$o_p(1)$ of smaller order than unity in probability

p probability, or test-rejection probability

$\mathsf{P}(Z\le r)$ probability that a random variable Z is less than or equal to r

$\mathsf{P}(\mathcal{B}\|\mathcal{A})$	conditional probability of $\mathcal{B}$ given $\mathcal{A}$
P_t^e	expected price formed for period t from $\mathcal{I}_{t-1}$
$\text{plim}_{T\to\infty} Z_T$	probability limit of the random variable Z_T
$\mathcal{P}(\cdot)$	power function for a test statistic
$\wp(\cdot)$	power set
$\boldsymbol{q}(\boldsymbol{\theta})$	score, or first derivative of the log-likelihood function
$\boldsymbol{q}_t(\boldsymbol{\theta})$	score for one observation
$\boldsymbol{Q}_X$	idempotent matrix which annihilates $\boldsymbol{X}$: $\boldsymbol{Q}_X = \boldsymbol{I} - \boldsymbol{X}(\boldsymbol{X}'\boldsymbol{X})^{-1}\boldsymbol{X}'$
$\text{rank}(\boldsymbol{A})$	rank of $\boldsymbol{A}$
$\mathsf{r}_{by\cdot a}$	partial correlation between $\boldsymbol{y}$ and $\boldsymbol{x}_b$ having removed the effect of $\boldsymbol{X}_a$
R^2	the squared multiple correlation
$\mathbb{R}$	the real line
$\mathbb{R}^k$	k-dimensional real space
$\mathbb{R}_+$	positive part of the real line
$\Re$	random experiment
s^2	sample variance
$\mathsf{t}(n)$	Student's t-distribution with n degrees of freedom
T	number of observations in a sample
$\text{tr}(\boldsymbol{A})$	trace of $\boldsymbol{A}$ (sum of the diagonal elements)
$\mathcal{T}$	the time sequence $\{\dots,-2,-1,0,1,2,\dots\}$
$\mathsf{U}(a,b)$	uniformly distributed between a and b
$V[\bar{x}]$	sample variance of $\bar{x}$
$\mathsf{V}[\boldsymbol{x}]$	variance (matrix) of X
$\mathcal{V}[\cdot]$	variance in a Monte Carlo
$W(j)$	continuous Wiener process for $j \in [0,1]$
$\bar{x}$	sample mean
$\boldsymbol{x}_t$	vector random variable (or realization thereof) $(x_{1t}\dots x_{kt})'$
$\boldsymbol{X}'$	set of T random variables $(X_1\dots X_T)$ $(1\times T)$
$\boldsymbol{X}$	sample observation matrix $(T\times k)$ $(\boldsymbol{x}_1\dots\boldsymbol{x}_k)$
$\boldsymbol{X}_{t-1}^1$	$(\boldsymbol{x}_1\dots\boldsymbol{x}_{t-1})$
$\boldsymbol{X}_{t-1}$	$(\boldsymbol{X}_0,\boldsymbol{x}_1,\dots,\boldsymbol{x}_{t-2},\boldsymbol{x}_{t-1}) = (\boldsymbol{X}_0,\boldsymbol{X}_{t-1}^1)$
$\{X_t(\omega)\}$	discrete-time stochastic process
$\mathcal{X}$	the observation space of a sample $\boldsymbol{X}$
y_t^p	planned value of y_t
z_t^e	expected value of z_t
$Y_T \overset{AS}{\to} Y$	Y_T tends almost surely to Y
$Y_T \overset{D}{\to} Y$	Y_T tends in distribution to Y
$Y_T \overset{MS}{\to} Y$	Y_T tends in mean square to Y
$Y_T \overset{P}{\to} Y$	Y_T tends in probability to Y

Author Index

Subject Index